**William H. Newman**
Director, Strategy Research Center
Graduate School of Business
Columbia University

**James P. Logan**
Professor of Management and Policy
College of Business and Public Administration
The University of Arizona

**W. Harvey Hegarty**
Professor of Administrative Studies
Associate Dean—-Professional Programs
Graduate School of Business
Indiana University

# TRATEGY

## A MULTI-LEVEL, INTEGRATIVE APPROACH

GH80JA
PUBLISHED BY
**SOUTH-WESTERN PUBLISHING CO.**
CINCINNATI    WEST CHICAGO, IL    CARROLLTON, TX    LIVERMORE, CA

ISBN: 0-538-80097-6

Library of Congress Catalog Card Number: 87-63392

2  3  4  5  6  7  8  Ki  3  2  1  0  9

*Printed in the United States of America*

# PREFACE

The study of business strategy is at a crossroads. We have useful models for deciding what a company's strategy should be, and these analytical techniques are being refined and extended almost daily. But the results of planning often fail to live up to expectations. The parts do not fall into place as predicted. Consequently, more attention to the execution phase of strategy is needed.

At universities, there is a related narrowing in scope of the capstone business policy course. In our zeal to communicate research findings, we often crowd out the broad integrating role that a capstone course is expected to fill.

Two ways to make the strategy course more potent for both students and managers are featured in this book. One is giving much more attention to the concerns and capabilities of the operating departments within a company. This is a crucial component of what we call *multi-level strategy*. Second, and tied to better multi-level linkages, is *integrating* diverse strategic targets into workable programs that will generate strong commitment among operating personnel.

## Multi-Level Strategy

Strategy differs at the business-unit, department, and corporate levels, and yet it should be linked adroitly.

Most discussion of business strategy centers around business-units—single-line companies or self-sufficient divisions of a diversified corporation. This is the best level for conceiving a challenging competitive mission. Because of the pivotal role of business-units, Part 1 of this book centers on designing business-unit strategy.

However, business-unit strategy alone is ineffective. Strategy is executed by operating departments, and experience shows that unless these departments actively support the business-unit strategy, competitors or other outsiders will win the day. Obtaining such active support, however, is more complicated than is typically assumed in strategy literature.

Each department interacts with its own distinctive environment and has its own culture, history, commitments, and aspirations. These forces are so powerful that departmental concerns must be melded with business-unit opportunities in shaping and executing the business-unit strategy. The lack of such melding accounts for many difficulties. Ways to link departmental programs with business-unit strategy *and* with each other are explored in Part 2.

In large corporations, business-units must also be closely linked to overall resources, portfolio choices, and opportunities for synergies. Here, again, a two-way dependency between levels should be tailored. Each business-unit must develop a strategy that realistically deals with its distinct environment while at the same time fitting into the corporate strategy of its parent. These linkages between corporate and business-unit strategies are considered in Part 3.

A basic theme of this book, then, is that strategy will be effective only if the distinct concerns of multiple levels—corporation, business-unit, and department—are ministered to and yet integrated into the master plan. A framework is developed that will help students overcome past neglect of the linkages between business-unit strategy and department strategic programs.

## Integrated Strategic Action

Integration is a more elusive concept than multi-level strategy. In contrast to Eastern cultures, where wholeness and harmony are stressed, we Westerners tend to take a *scientific* approach to problems. We typically confront a problem by breaking it into parts and subparts, and then control (or statistically allow for) exogenous variables while each part is being studied. This scientific approach has great power (witness "scientific management" and the "behavioral sciences") but it provides limited help in putting the parts of a complex situation together into an integrated program.

In practice, managers are confronted with whole situations. Prospective managers—your students—should learn to take heed of multiple pressures. Strategy specifically seeks to anticipate all sorts of influences in a company environment and devise a fully coordinated response to opportunities and threats. This process calls for integration fully as much as for analysis. Moreover, future actions need to be integrated to past actions; the sequence and timing are significant—especially in dynamic industries. Thus integration is a second theme running through this book.

The very nature of integration calls for a succession of unique combinations. Consequently, we cannot dispose of the subject in a separate chapter or two. Instead, it is an ever-present dimension. Managers, and students aspiring to be managers, should consider the following questions repeatedly:

1. How well do various actions involved in a strategic move *fit* together? Are the actions at least compatible, that is, one move does not undermine another? And preferably, are the actions synergistic, that is, the performance of one action makes other moves easier or more effective?

2. How can strategic moves and their external and internal impacts be kept in *balance*? Are they in reasonable proportion in terms of marketing, production and other functions, and stability versus change? And is the timing of moves coordinated with that of other moves and with the urgency of action?

Because strategy serves as an overriding guide throughout an organization, integrated strategic thinking is especially critical, both in the study of this book and in real life.

## Role of Multi-Level, Integrative Strategy in Business School Curricula

The two themes of multi-level strategy and integration have a symbiotic relationship with business school curricula.

The main historical reason why most business school curricula include a business policy or strategy course as a "capstone" requirement is to integrate the more specialized courses. Sometimes the rationale also includes "to see a company as a whole" or "to understand how a student's major field contributes to the overall performance of a company," but integration has been the primary reason.[1]

In recent years a dedicated group of scholars has converted business policy into a respected field of scholarly research. Company strategy (also popular in management circles) is the major focus, although other facets of overall management are included. Separate academic journals are flourishing, and the growing body of literature is impressive.

We cheer this development, participate in it, and eagerly use the output. Nevertheless, we have to admit that courses devoted to developing this new field often slide over the primary holistic objectives of the capstone business policy course just referred to. The tendency is to just assume that functional integration will occur rather than to address the task explicitly.

The multi-level approach to strategy overcomes this deficiency. It also has related strengths that fit with the capstone role of business policy courses:

1. By stressing horizontal linkages with other departments as an essential feature of strategic programs, the multi-level model deals directly with the sort of integration that curriculum planners expect from business policy courses.

2. By also stressing the vertical linkages between department programs and business-unit strategy, it provides students majoring in functional fields a better appreciation of how their specialties contribute to—and are constrained by—the company mission. Since virtually all students start working in a single department, being able to see the "big picture" gives meaning to their jobs and helps to build commitment.

Please note that we do not stress multi-level strategy and integration just as pedagogical devices. These features are also dimensions of strategic management that are crucial to successful implementation. Fortunately, study of multi-level

---

[1]See the influential study by R. A. Gordon and J. E. Howell, *Higher Education for Business*. New York: Columbia University Press, 1959, pp. 207–209; 269; also the recent A.A.C.S.B. sponsored study by L. M. Porter and L. E. McKibbin, *Management Education and Development*. New York: McGraw-Hill Book Company, 1988, pp. 307 and 322.

strategy and integration—inherently and at the same time—serves the objectives of a capstone course in a business school curriculum and strengthens the strategic management concept.

## Teaching an Exciting Strategy Course

Giving students a firm grasp of strategy concepts is a challenging adventure. We find a mixture of *both* text and cases useful—text to clarify and expedite the learning of conceptual models and diagnostic approaches, and cases to relate such frameworks to real-life situations. Both text and cases are especially helpful in communicating ideas about multi-level strategy and integration. Our allocation of time between text and cases depends upon the background and the experience of students in each particular class.

### Use of Text for Conceptual Frameworks

The text in this book provides frameworks, or models, for thinking about issues and enough examples for students to see the frameworks as realistic, useful tools. The frameworks (e.g., the multi-level strategy, the four-part business-unit strategy, and the three critical linkages of strategy programs) help managers and potential managers bring order and significance to a great jumble of facts. They are what James O. McKinsey called "a way of thinking" that sharpens and expedites analysis.

Throughout the text we have intentionally minimized the use of technical jargon that specialists in narrow fields find convenient. Since our aim is to help build bridges across boundaries, we try to make basic ideas and examples understandable to individuals who are not specialists in the subject involved.

The frameworks in the text, then, provide an approach or structure for comprehending a complex and dynamic management process. Like most approaches to complex phenomena, however, they typically have to be adapted when applied to a concrete situation. And for training in adaptation we turn to cases.

### Use of Cases for Vicarious Experience in Adaptation and Integration

The forty-six cases, as well as the mini-cases in the chapter questions, make up about half of this book. They have been selected to build skill in *applying frameworks* and in *integrating* such actions into the total organization. Because the cases present real situations calling for managerial action, there are no artificial boundaries on what factors are relevant. Rather, students are expected to identify and confront interrelated issues that were not recognized when the problem first arose.

1. Each *End-of-Chapter Case* involves one or more of the issues discussed in that chapter, but it also has impacts on other parts of the company that a student must include in an optimum resolution.

2. The twelve *Integrating Cases* typically involve issues from several preceding chapters *and* probably require adjustments in still other domains.

3. The longer *Comprehensive Cases* at the end of the book range over the whole territory. For these, students have to decide what is important now and then devise a course of action that has both fit and balance.

Although we think of cases primarily as stimulating instruments to give students drill in integrating, this array does more. The cases have been carefully selected to fit various facets of the multi-level strategy approach; thus, the entire framework—or any part of it—can be illustrated via cases. This set of cases systematically strengthens and enlivens the concepts in the text.

A majority of the cases are newly published here. They deal with strategy issues in a wide range of industries—service as well as manufacturing, both small and large companies, several international settings, highly successful firms, and others on the brink of bankruptcy. Moreover, the questions at the end of each chapter usually include one or more mini-cases. From this array a professor can devote as much or as little time to cases as the local situation warrants.

## Tie to Research Project on Multi-Level Strategy

The source of ideas for any book-length publication are typically numerous and often blurred. This book reflects contributions from many people. Special acknowledgment should be made to two sources.

The Strategy Research Center at Columbia University has in process a study of multi-level strategy with particular emphasis on the role of departments within business-units. Many bridges to related literature remain to be explored, followed by field-testing of central hypotheses. Nevertheless, the central issues are quite clear, and Chapter 6 is based on a working paper related to them. A wide group of strategy professors made comments on this paper, and Chapter 6 incorporates many of their ideas.

The advisors who have already contributed to this research project include the following: S. C. Abraham, Pepperdine University; E. Albert, Indiana University; M. Anshen, Columbia University; W. P. Anthony, Florida State University; R. M. Atherton, Northeastern University; M. M. Besso, M & T Chemicals; H. W. Bloch, University of Missouri; J. J. Boddewyn, City College of New York; J. L. Bower, Harvard University; E. H. Bowman, University of Pennsylvania; W. R. Boulton, University of Georgia; P. D. Brewer, Eastern Kentucky University; G. B. Buntzman, Western Kentucky University; A. D. Carey, Bloomsbury University (PA); H. K. Christensen, Northwestern University; R. A. Comerford, University of Rhode Island; R. D. Ellsworth, Claremont Graduate School; G. E. Fryxell, University of Tennessee; L. Geddes, Pfizer, Inc.; P. Geib, Moorhead State University (MN); S. Greenfield, Salisbury State College (MD); D. W. Griesinger, Claremont Graduate School; D. C. Hambrick, Columbia University; F. C. Haas, Virginia

Commonwealth University; K. R. Harrigan, Columbia University; J. A. Hill, University of Nebraska; M. A. Hitt, Texas A & M University; R. C. Hoffman, College of William & Mary; R. G. Hunt, University of Buffalo; L. R. Jauch, Northeast Louisiana University; M. Kassner, University of North Dakota; M. Lawless, University of Colorado; M. Leontiades, Rutgers University; J. A. Maciariello, Claremont Graduate School; G. C. Mackenzie, IBM; J. P. McCray, University of Texas; R. McGlashan, University of Houston; P. H. Mounts, University of Wisconsin; R. D. Nale, University of South Carolina; H. S. Napier, University of Arkansas; J. O'Shaughnessy, Columbia University; B. Oviatt, Oklahoma State University; R. A. Pitts, Gettysburg College; J. C. Reichenbach, PPG Industries; P. S. Ring, University of Minnesota; B. M. Smackey, Lehigh University; C. E. Summer, University of Washington; G. R. Ungson, Netherlands School of Business; K. H. Vesper, University of Calgary; and C. E. Weber, University of Wisconsin.

## Sequel to *Strategy, Policy, and Central Management*

The antecedents of this book date back more than fifty years, when James O. McKinsey founded his now famous management consulting firm. McKinsey pioneered in studying the overall management of a company, and for this purpose he developed a "general survey outline." That outline dealt with industry outlook, company position in the industry, desirable changes in policy (and strategy), corresponding adjustments in organization and key personnel, and reallocation of resources. The outline was fleshed out by Newman for McKinsey's use in a Marshall Field & Company executive training program in 1937. Following McKinsey's untimely death, that document became the framework for *Business Policy and Management*, which appeared in 1940—the first textbook published in the field of business policy.

Many changes and refinements were made in following editions of the book, as implied by the evolved title of the ninth edition, *Strategy, Policy, and Central Management*. However, the basic approach to positioning a company in a dynamic environment has stood the test of time.

This volume is a sequel. It shifts the primary orientation from a single-line company to multi-level strategy. This broadening of viewpoint, in turn, has required rewriting of many chapters or parts of chapters. Nevertheless, the legacy is large. Although not a sentence of the original McKinsey manuscript can be found in the present book and a great deal of sophistication has been added, McKinsey's focus on a total integrated organization adapting to a swiftly changing environment is a continuing perspective.

## Support Material

*Resources for Strategic Analysis*, by Professors Dan Baugher and Andrew Varanelli, Jr., of Pace University, is a uniquely helpful workbook that strengthens this textbook. Although it is a separate publication that can be used in many connections, Baugher's and Varanelli's willingness to summarize important concepts for students and link their computer analysis to the cases in *Strategy* adds a welcome dimension to our book.

Instructors looking for quantitative, computer-based support for their courses in strategy need go no further than the workbook. It provides specific software to support *Strategy* including quantitative tools and Lotus 1-2-3® templates. It also provides students with guidance in the use and application of this software to cases in *Strategy*. Four additional major cases, with computer support, are included in the workbook for instructors who need more case material. Support for the instructor is provided in a detailed Instructor's Resource Manual.

Of course, students will also benefit significantly from using the workbook. As seasoned instructors, Baugher and Varanelli know what students need, and they have provided it. They have developed detailed outlines of each chapter in *Strategy* as well as cogent instructions on how to analyze strategic situations using quantitative tools. As a result, students who use the workbook will find it of considerable support to them in their efforts to grasp the conceptual issues and diagnostic approaches contained in *Strategy*.

We appreciate this form of coordinated effort, as will users of the two books. Together, the text and the workbook provide diverse instructional material in abundance.

A printed Test Bank also now accompanies *Strategy*. Faculty members who use objective questions in their examinations will find the Test Bank of 1,000 multiple-choice and true-false questions created by Baugher and Varanelli to be of considerable assistance. This Test Bank provides good coverage of material contained in *Strategy* and links well with the material contained in the workbook. The Test Bank can also be obtained in a computerized version, called MicroSWAT II, for those who prefer this method of test construction.

## Other Acknowledgments

Several people have kindly permitted us to use cases that they wrote. The new Comprehensive Cases include: "Tulip City Ambulance Company," by J. Kim De Dee of the University of Wisconsin and Richard C. Johnson of the University of Arkansas; "Citicorp–British National Life Assurance," by John M. Gwin, Per V. Jenster, and William K. Carter, all of the University of Virginia; "Briggs and Stratton vs. Honda," by Richard C. Hoffman of the College of William & Mary; and "Movie Village," by Steven Tax and Walter S. Good of the University of Manitoba.

Other cases, located in the body of the text, include: "Rodo Cattle Company," by Keith Davis of Arizona State University; "The Farm Management System," by John Fellows and Walter S. Good of the University of Manitoba; "World-Class Factory of Today," by Thomas C. Jones of Booz·Allen & Hamilton, Inc.; "G. Heileman Brewing Company," by Beth Sorg and Milton Leontiades of Rutgers University; "GAIN Software" and "Family Service of Gotham," by E. Kirby Warren of Columbia University; and "The New Manager, Tian, Li-geng," by Yu Kai-cheng of Dalian Institute of Technology, China. We are most grateful for this help from so many locations

No book of this size sees the light of day without a lot of assistance from diverse sources. We especially want to thank Camilla Koch for creating and coordinating a single manuscript from dispersed authors.

*William H. Newman*
*James P. Logan*
*W. Harvey Hegarty*

# CONTENTS

# LIST OF CASES

**Case Title**

# INTRODUCTION

## Strategy

# CHAPTER 1

## Strategy: Unified Guidance of a Whole Enterprise

# INTRODUCTION

Western nations, and especially the United States, rely on thousands of independent enterprises to convert resources into desired goods and services. Moreover, these enterprises provide most of the initiative for improving and adapting this flow of goods and services to *new* wants. Consequently, successful management of such enterprises is vital to many people and, in fact, to the survival of our pluralistic society.

Not all companies succeed. Some leaders of past eras, such as International Harvester and the Pennsylvania Railroad, barely survive, while upstarts such as Apple Computers and Hospital Corporation of America take center stage—at least for a short time. The rise or fall of small firms is even more uncertain and challenging.

This book explores "strategy"—the primary tool that managers now use to guide companies in their turbulent existence. In addition to describing what strategy is, we are concerned with putting it into action. Effective application of the strategic approach is neither simple nor mechanistic. For managers, converting an inspired strategic idea into integrated action throughout a company is the most difficult part of their job.

The present chapter is a preview. It includes a definition of business strategy, a brief description of the strategic management process, and a sketch of the way strategy permeates and influences the various levels of an organization. It is a roadmap for the reader, a way of knowing what lies ahead and how the parts are interconnected. Also, the nature and use of the 45 cases interspersed throughout the book are explained.

## The Concept of Business Strategy

"Strategy" has become a fashionable word. People loosely speak of a strategy for preparing for an examination, a strategy for losing weight, and so on. We want to use the term in a sharper sense as it applies to managing a business. To clarify our meaning, we will define strategy in three ways: its role, its characteristics, and its elements.

2

## Role of Strategy

A business strategy sets forth the mission of a company. It reflects the choice of the key services that the organization will perform, and the primary basis for distinctiveness in creating and delivering such services. Because the mission is the overriding aim of the company, the strategy serves as a guide to managers in deciding what to do and what not to do, and it is the rallying theme for coordinating diverse activities. Here are two well-known examples.

For years the Maytag company concentrated on making only home laundry equipment—washing machines and dryers. It did not deal with other electric appliances as most of its competitors did. To be distinctive, Maytag stressed quality and durability. It sold only through well-trained local dealers who handled only Maytag equipment and took pride in providing dependable repair service. Prices were higher than those of competitors, but a group of loyal customers believed that the better quality and service were worth the differential.

Major competitors like G.E. and Whirlpool had a wider range of products, relied on diversified dealers, often had cut-rate promotions, and aggressively sought large orders from big apartment buildings. They won in terms of volume, but Maytag maintained a 16 percent market share and consistently had the highest net profit margin in the industry.

Maytag's strategy was clear about the niche the company sought in the market and about the necessary actions its departments had to take to be the leader in that niche. But competitive conditions change. So, abandoning its long-standing successful strategy, Maytag recently merged with Magic Chef to form a full-line appliance corporation, and its marketing organization is being modified accordingly. The central concept of its business—its strategy—is now being adapted to a more mature and competitive environment.

A company's strategy may revolve around service rather than products. The 7-Eleven division of the Southland Corporation has built an $8 billion volume of sales (within the lifetime of the founder) on the basis of convenience. Long hours—often 24 per day—locations near to customers, products that customers may want without preplanning, self-service, and fast checkout—these are the pedestrian features of over 8,000 small stores that add up to convenience. New products or services are added only if they fit the criteria of convenience and self-service. Among such additions have been gasoline, videotapes, and automatic teller machines for local banks.

7-Eleven stores illustrate the need for a company strategy to fit environmental changes. The increase in two-wage-earner families, for instance, has made convenience more important than the lowest price to many of 7-Eleven's customers, and the company has benefited by fitting into this trend.

The preceding examples suggest three functions that a company strategy should perform:

1. The strategy summarizes the way a company elects to *relate to its environment*. In what particular niche does the company wish to fit, and

how does it expect to excel in that niche? In other words, what contributions will it make, relative to competitors, that earn society's support?[1] And since the environment keeps changing, this adjustment to opportunity and threats is a never-ending task.

2.   Then, looking inward, how can the company conduct its activities so as to perform effectively the role just identified in (1)? Here, the strategy is concerned with basic choices of technology, organization structure, type of employees, mobilization of resources, and related issues. 7-Eleven stores, for example, have an *internal operating design* that supports and complements the company's external mission. Company strategy stipulates at least the distinctive characteristics of this operating design.

3.   Strategy helps to build *integrated action*. It insists on a good fit between the mission in (1) and the operating design just noted in (2); it sets priorities as either or both of these features are modified; it deals with sequences and timing of major moves; and it provides some interim targets for pacing and controlling new activities.

The role of strategy, as we shall see more fully in later chapters, is to provide basic direction for the business—especially with respect to dynamic changes in the relevant environment.

## Characteristics of Strategy

A second way to define business strategy is in terms of its primary characteristics. This set of ideas places some limits on the sweeping task just sketched as the role of strategy. Both to keep business strategy within realistic limits of managers' time and patience, and to focus attention on key issues, strategy formulation is highly selective. Indeed, deciding on which issues are sufficiently crucial to be included in a statement of strategy is in itself a critical choice.

Stating what strategy *is not* helps to remove unnecessary confusion:[2]

1.   Strategy is *not* a response to short-term fluctuations in operations or the environment, nor is it the response to the frequent short-term reports on, for example, sales, labor turnover, weekly output, or competitors' prices that every manager receives. Instead, strategy deals with the predetermined direction toward which these quick responses are pointed. It is concerned with the longer-term course that the ship is steering, not with the waves.

---

[1] The broad social responsibility of a company is treated explicitly in Chapter 25.

[2] The following list appears in B. Yavitz and W.H. Newman, *Strategy in Action* (New York: The Free Press, 1982), pp. 4, 5. Reprinted with permission of the publisher.

2.  Strategy is *not* a set of numbers merely projected out three to five years; it is not an extrapolation exercise based on this year's balance sheet and profit-and-loss statement. Rather, the emphasis in strategy is on the quality and texture of the business. New services, the focus of research, market position, foreign sources of materials, government sharing of high risks—these are the kinds of issues that are molded into a verbal statement of where and how the company hopes to move. General Electric and several other companies, for instance, insist that the qualitative strategic plan be a separate document from the subsequently prepared financial projections.

3.  Strategy is *not* a rationalization of what we did last year or of what appears in next year's budget. With a bit of imagination and artful wording, a statement that looks like a strategy can be written around almost any set of activities of a going concern. An actual strategy, in contrast, is a longer-term plan that sets the direction and tone of the shorter-range plans. Unless the strategy provides underlying guidance, its preparation is mere window dressing.

4.  Strategy is *not* a statement of pious intentions or optimistic wishes. Merely envisioning a future world and selecting an attractive position in that world is not a strategic plan. Instead, a strategy must be feasible in terms of resources that will be mobilized, and it must identify ways by which at least some form of superiority over competitors is to be achieved.

5.  Strategy is *not* a cluster of ideas in the minds of a few select leaders of the company—ideas labeled *strategy* if and when they are voiced because they come from key individuals. Rather, the concepts are disseminated and understood by all managers to at least the middle levels of the organization and perhaps below. Unless there is such widespread understanding, coupled with acceptance and preferably commitment, not much progress toward strategic goals will occur.

This list of "is not's" sets some helpful boundaries on the meaning of company strategy. By weeding out what may mistakenly be called strategy, we can focus on the potential power of the main concept. Of course, considering the contrary of the "is not's" generates a set of positive characteristics—namely, that strategy focuses on basic longer-term direction, is primarily qualitative, provides guidance for preparation of short-term plans, is realistic and action oriented, and is understood throughout the top and middle levels of the organization.

## Elements of Action-Oriented Strategy

We can go one step further in defining business strategy. The role of strategy in managing a business and the preceding characteristics of a strategy tell us the nature of strategy but do not specify what subjects a strategy should cover. For reasons that will be explained in Chapter 5, the strategy of a company should have the four parts shown in Figure 1–1.

1.  *Domain sought.* What sort of business does the company want to be in? Typically, this can be stated in terms of the products or services that the company will sell to a particular group of customers. To select such a domain involves choosing an attractive industry and one or more related niches within that industry in which to operate.

2.  *Differential advantages in serving the domain.* How will the company make itself more attractive than rivals who also are active in the domain? For instance, the basis of superiority may be access to raw materials, better personnel, new technology, low costs and prices, or unusual service. Identifying an attractive domain is not enough; what reason does the company have to presume that it will be successful there?

3.  *Strategic thrusts necessary and their approximate timing.* To move from its present position to where it wants to be, as envisioned in parts (1) and (2), the typical company will have to take a series of actions. Wishing isn't enough, and competitors are also on the move. So selection of

**FIGURE 1–1.**
**FOUR ESSENTIAL PARTS OF A BUSINESS-UNIT STRATEGY**

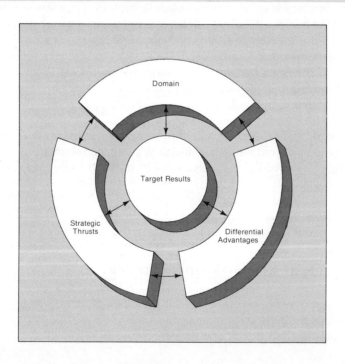

major thrusts, their sequence, and when to launch them is a necessary third part of the strategy.

4.  *Target results expected.* To get stockholders, bankers, materials suppliers, employees, and other resource suppliers to support the company in the strategic action sketched in the preceding parts, the expected results have to be at least acceptable. Unless the results win the continuing cooperation of all these parties, the strategy will have to be revised.

Throughout this book, when we speak of a "company strategy," it is this four-part, action-oriented concept that is meant. Of course, for managers of a company the critical questions are just what will be the specific content of each part, and much of our discussion will deal with these questions. Also, some companies may wish to add other elements. But for most situations, these four parts capture the essential aspects of a company's strategy.

Other books on strategy often deal with only one or two of these four parts. For instance, finance books focus on return on investment (ROI) and related target results, and marketing books stress picking the best domain and competitive actions to secure sales growth. But while these are necessary features of a company strategy, they are incomplete. An effective strategy for a general manager conveys both the selected mission—the domain and differential advantage—and also the major ways to get there—the thrusts and targets. Without all four parts, a strategy is difficult to carry out.

## Multi-Level Strategy

For strategic management to be useful in diverse kinds of companies and in various stages in the life of a single company, at least three levels of management must be recognized. (See Figure 1–2.) The content and nature of strategy are different at each of these levels, yet they are interrelated. So a recurring theme running through this book is dealing with this powerful management tool of strategy from a multi-level viewpoint.

## Business-Unit Strategy

The simplest way to think about business strategy is its application to a "single-line company." That is what we have done in the preceding discussion, and it is the focus of Part 1 of the text. A single-line company may be large or small, but in neither case is it complicated in its scope of activities.

A single-line company sells a closely related group of products or services to a recognized class of customers. Usually it creates all its services or products with the same technology. For instance, as long as Maytag sold only domestic laundry equipment directly to users, we could say that it was a single-line company. On the other hand, retail florists are in a different line of business from wholesale flo-

**FIGURE 1–2.**
**MULTI-LEVEL STRATEGY**

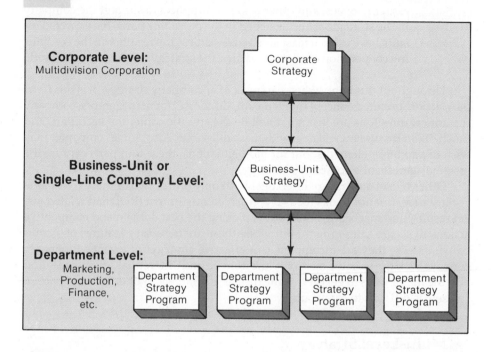

rists because they sell to different sorts of customers with distinct buying requirements and because the techniques of retailing fresh-cut flowers differ radically
from the technology of growing them.

As single-line companies grow or see other opportunities, they often enter a
new line of business. Or they merge with another company just for financial reasons. Then, if size permits, the company creates a separate division for the added
line. Often, the new division has its own group of services or products which it
sells to its own class of customers and is fairly self-sufficient with its own production facilities. In many respects, it operates like a single-line company, except that
it is one of several divisions in a larger corporation. Common practice is to treat
these semiautonomous, self-contained divisions as *business-units*, each with its
own four-part strategy.

The use of strategic management in business-units is quite similar to its use in
a single-line company. So, to simplify our discussion, we treat them together.
Most of the time when we speak of a business-unit, it may be either an independent single-line company or a semiautonomous, self-sufficient division within a
corporation. "Company" normally refers to the same kind of unit, except where
the legal name of a diversified corporation happens to retain the word—as in
"General Electric Company."

An important feature of a business-unit or company is the need for coordinating the marketing, engineering, production, finance, and other functional activities at that level. This is where general managers try to make sure that each department helps the other and, more specifically, that all are working together to support the business-unit strategy.

The formulation of a business-unit strategy is the grist of Part I.

## Department Programs to Execute Strategy

No general manager of a business-unit or president of a single-line company can carry out a strategy single handed. Instead, strategy is implemented (or perhaps undermined) in the operating subdivisions of the business-unit. Designing strategy is a futile exercise unless the players follow the signals called by the "quarterback." So Part 2 of this book explores the vertical linkage between the general management level of a business-unit and the operating subunits, all of which we call departments.

In fact, the role of departments in strategy formulation and execution is much more extensive and complicated that just carrying out instructions, as is explained in Chapter 6 and illustrated throughout Part 2. That is,

1. The departments are typically major contributors to the formulation and revision of business-unit strategy. Because of their firsthand, intimate knowledge of their segment of the company's activities and of their rivals' behavior in that part of the environment, departments are the primary source of data and forecasts that influence strategy decisions. Their views are probably biased, but are better grounded than many of the other inputs into strategy planning.

2. The departments have agendas of their own, reflecting their training—in marketing, finance, production, etc.—and their interactions with outside suppliers, rivals, government bodies, and the like. Any new strategy must somehow be reconciled with this existing momentum and potential strength.

3. Departments are interdependent. There is a lot of give and take, and maybe even push and shove. A change in one plan affects the total system. So when a strategy change is made or even contemplated, it is the departments themselves that must work out new patterns of cooperation.

4. Theoretically, in a business hierarchy orders will be executed (if possible). However, when working with a lot of future uncertainties, as is typical of strategic action, a subordinate can be dedicated to the new strategy, acquiesce to it, or even subvert it. This means that the strategy process must be conducted in a way that builds the motivation of each department to bring about change.

If we are really concerned, then, with how managers can choose workable strategy and get it executed, we have to give close attention to including department people as key members of the team. That is the viewpoint in Part 2.

Because departments cannot be given the range of independent action that business-units enjoy, we call their strategic plans a *department strategy program*. The addition of the term "program" definitely suggests that each department emerges from the strategy planning process with a set of action assignments.

## Corporate Strategy

A business-unit, as we are using the term, focuses on a particular type of business, say group life insurance or video cassette recorders. Each such business has its own markets, technology, competitors, and other distinctive features. Therefore, strategy and department strategy programs must be fitted to that business as just outlined.

A diversified corporation, however, faces a different set of issues. It has a family of business-units. It must decide which of these businesses to expand and which to contract. Capital and other scarce resources must be allocated to the various businesses. Mergers or divestments may be arranged. Perhaps ways can be found for one of its business-units to help another. And, the inputs which the corporation will provide to give its businesses a differential advantage over their competitors should be strengthened. These issues will be explored in Part 3.

This is a third level of strategy issues, and to help the reader distinguish strategy related to multidivision problems from those of business-units and departments, we call this top tier *corporate strategy.*

Note that the company or business-unit continues to be the primary building block for managerial planning. The strength of any diversified corporation rests predominantly on its separate businesses. They are the sources of growth, earnings, stability, etc. And each of these business-units gains strength through its own strategy and departmental programs. For this reason, it is wise first to develop a strategy and program for each business-unit which will enable that business to adapt best to its opportunities and threats. Then a combined corporate strategy for all the businesses can be devised as a superstructure.

This is the way Southland Corporation operates. In addition to its primary business in 7-Eleven stores, Southland owns some dairies, a snack-food manufacturing division, a half-interest in Citgo Petroleum, and a chain of auto-parts stores. Each of these business-units has its own strategy suited to its own opportunities, and the overriding corporate strategy is to help each operating division prosper in its own domain.

The development of strategy at all three levels can be a significant source of strength. Experience shows, however, that these vertical relationships between levels are too often a source of confusion and slippage. We will look frequently throughout the book for ways to minimize the frictions and maximize the benefits of such relationships.

## Strategy Formulation and Execution

The concept of business strategy and its application to multi-levels of a corporation are two major themes that we will be discussing. A third important consideration is the *process* that managers use to go from timely forecasts of the world ahead through to strategic action. What needs to happen between noting a challenging opportunity, like an automated office, and actual results, such as having payroll checks in the mail that were prompted by a production schedule?

## Future-Oriented Steps

Somehow, four broad steps have to be taken (see Figure 1–3):

1.  *Analyze the outlook to search for opportunities and threats.* Many factors impinge on the future development of any enterprise. Some cities grow while others decay. New ways to control insect pests may render chemical plants obsolete, and new social mores may do the same to college dormitories. Inflation distorts cost structures, cable TV changes shopping habits, war in the Middle East creates new shortages of petroleum supply—the list of opportunities and problems could go on and on.

    A practical way to bring some kind of order out of this array of environmental changes is to concentrate on an industry. This industry

**FIGURE 1–3.**
**PROCESS OF STRATEGY FORMULATION AND EXECUTION**

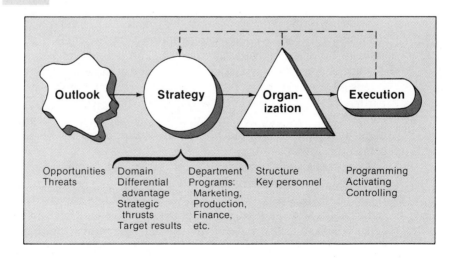

may be one the company is already in, or one that it is thinking about entering. The aim of these industry analyses is to predict growth, profitability, and especially the key factors for future success.

Turning to the specific company, its strengths and limitations relative to its competitors should be carefully assessed. Then, by matching the company strengths with key factors for success in the industry, the outlook for the company can be predicted. For even sharper analysis, the way key actors in the environment are likely to respond to company moves can be predicted. This sequence of analysis is elaborated in Chapters 2, 3, and 4.

A similar analysis can be made for individual departments and for diversified corporations, as will be discussed in Parts 2 and 3. The aim is to anticipate opportunities and threats so that the corporation, business-unit, or department can take advantage of dynamic changes rather than being hurt by them.

2. *Design the strategy and programs.* Armed with a forecast of the world ahead, managers can shift to active, positive thinking: "What are we going to do about it?" "What should be the mission of our unique enterprise?" "What steps do we have to take to fulfill that goal?"

Obviously, picking the right mission is crucial. But it is also difficult. To be most useful, the strategy and strategy programs should cover the four parts sketched earlier in the chapter and in Figure 1–1.

A critical judgment in designing strategy is what to accept as unchangeable. Every company possesses (or can attract) only limited resources, and it has to be careful that the goals it sets are achievable. In addition to sensing a future opportunity, management must realistically assess the cost of grasping the opportunity in terms of people, outside help, and money, as well as evaluating the responses of rivals. It must then decide whether "that is something we can do," as is discussed in Chapter 5.

Business-unit and corporate strategy concentrate on basic directions, major thrusts, and overriding priorities. The full implication of a strategy, however, is clarified by thinking through the more detailed department programs that guide the execution of the strategy. Such an extension is valuable partly because working through necessary department actions is an excellent way to check the practicality of a basic concept, but especially to make sure that the intent of the strategy is correctly integrated into the work of the various departments of the company.

3. *Build an organization to support the strategy.* Strategy programs are carried out by an organization. Unless this organization is well designed for its tasks, the plans, however sound, may lead to mediocre results. In fact, if the strategy relies on, say, pioneering in a new field, an ineffective organization that failed in such leadership could bring disaster.

The way in which activities are combined into sections and departments will affect the choice of problems to receive first attention, the speed of coordination, and the cost of performing the service. Decentralization is well suited to a strategy stressing local service, but it encounters difficulty with computerized production scheduling. A strategic decision to expand internationally alters the optimum power and location of staff units. Product diversification usually modifies the range of decisions that can be made wisely in the senior corporate office. As these examples indicate, management must appraise the company organization in terms of where tasks critical to the success of its strategy can be performed most effectively.

Even more sensitive than the organization structure are the people who fill the key positions. Both a capability to do the work and a commitment to the task are needed. People not only carry out the plans; they originate the ideas and make revisions as work progresses and unexpected external events arise. Because strategy often requires a shift from previous practice, the willingness of key persons to enthusiastically push in new directions is especially important.

Titles vary from company to company. So we will use the term "manager" broadly to include all the individuals, from chief executive through department heads, who get work done primarily through other people. To avoid repetition of the term, occasionally we will refer to high-level managers as executives or central managers. We will use the term "general manager" to denote a manager who coordinates several departments. Usually, however, the status issue will be avoided by using "manager" as the general term.

Organization issues are explored in Part 4 of the text.

4. *Guide the execution.* With strategy, programs, and organization decided, the stage is set. Actual achievement, however, awaits the action. Central management necessarily relies heavily on junior managers for the immediate supervision of operations. But senior executives can never fully divest themselves of leadership in the execution phase of purposeful endeavor. As explained in Part 5, this phase includes specific programming of nonrepetitive work, communicating and motivating, and exercising control over the rate and the quality of performance.

Substantial amounts of time are necessary for this make-happen effort. Many people, inside the company and out, have to be contacted personally, and unexpected difficulties inevitably call for on-the-spot adjustments. But during the process the managers are accumulating both information and a subjective feel for the actual performance of company services that are immensely valuable in planning subsequent cycles of activity.

Having set out the preceding steps, we should note that the strategic management process is much more scrambled in practice. Firmly established organization, for instance, may make a proposed strategy easy (or difficult) to put into action; in that case the organization influences the choice of strategy. Such a "reverse flow" is suggested by the dashed lines at the top of Figure 1–3.

Also, a neatly integrated package of strategy, organization, and execution does not usually stay neat. The environment changes. Even a company's own success creates the need for revision. Consequently, the broad process described must be repeated and repeated again, with ideas for the different steps popping up in random order.

An approach such as that sketched here and developed throughout the book is basically a framework for thinking about strategic management issues. It helps managers organize their ideas. By drawing attention to *a limited (comprehensible) number of basic issues in a systematic arrangement,* and by flagging potential opportunities, the framework expedites analysis and assists in forming a synthesis of action to be taken. It is a *way* to structure ideas, not a procedure.

## The Strategy Process at Multiple Levels

The linking of future opportunities to today's actions is a mental process that managers can apply at each of the three organization levels flagged in Figure 1–2: the corporate, business-unit, and department levels. Of course the subjects will vary, but the process of tying current activities to predicted external conditions pays off at all levels.

Corporate managers, for instance, are concerned with comparing different industries as investments, and with ways to transfer corporate strengths from one industry to another. Their scope is broad, and, being less involved with daily affairs, they are unfettered in the options they weigh. Nevertheless, their problems of organization and execution are very real: the corporate strategy will wither unless able managers are placed in the proper positions and they follow through on planned changes. All steps in the strategic reasoning process should be covered.

Business-unit managers, on the other hand, must forecast much more sharply the developments and competition in their particular industries. They deal with differential advantages which often are finely tuned advantages. Also, designing organizations and controls that reinforce a selected strategy is a continuing process of adjustment to an evolving setting. Here again, the total range of the strategic process is needed.

Department heads are even more constrained in preparing their strategy programs. However, as we shall explain in Chapter 6, department managers are the main bridge between their company and particular segments of the environment, such as financial markets or governmental regulations. They need to forecast changes in those segments and, either within their departments or as a feature of the business-unit strategy, seize opportunities to expand or contract. Moreover, the organization and execution of strategy programs within each department is where front-line action takes place. A strategy perspective here needs a forward-looking, external-internal mixture similar to that which invigorates upper levels of management.

The challenging complication is that vertical integration between levels should take place *simultaneously* with the process of strategy formulation and execution at each level, as indicated in Figure 1–4. A great deal of cross-checking is necessary—up, down, and across. Decentralization provides some relief, but if combined strength is to come from unified action, managers must be skilled in securing progress in a whole network of social relationships.

This task of achieving both change and integration will arise over and over as we move through the book. To reduce the total length of the discussion, considerations of organization and execution are combined for all three levels; the conceptual framework, however, is as shown in Figure 1–4.

### Strategic Management

This brief examination of issues covered in this book may be misleading. In our desire to indicate the array of factors that business managers should be sensitive to, the list gets long. Even the condensed matrix in Figure 1–4 of the multiple organization levels and the steps in the strategic management process creates a lot

**FIGURE 1-4.**
**INTERRELATIONS OF THE STRATEGY MANAGEMENT PROCESS
AND MULTIPLE LEVELS OF STRATEGY ACTION**

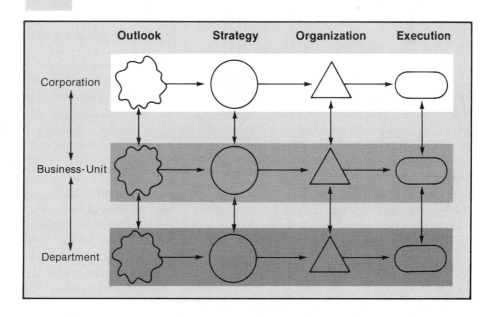

of boxes, and if the breakdown of each heading were added, we could quickly move beyond the number of things a human mind is capable of thinking about simultaneously. Fortunately, in actual situations we can set aside some factors as unimportant in the particular problem facing us, and other considerations can be dealt with sequentially rather than all at once.

Nevertheless, the danger of too much analysis and not enough synthesis is ever present. The strategic management process tries to avoid this trap by stressing selectivity.

First, judgment is used in *selecting critical issues and influences.* Indeed, this narrowing, this separating of dominant forces from less important ones, is almost the essence of wise strategic choices. So while the range of possible factors is staggering, most strategy choices are rather simple propositions. For instance, the 7-Eleven stores' highly successful emphasis on convenience seems elementary. We use the more elaborate frameworks to help distill out such crucial judgments.

Second, effective strategic action comes from *consistent and persistent execution* of the basic choices noted in the preceding paragraph. Part of the reason we explore multiple levels of strategy is to build consistent, integrated effort. The linking of opportunity, strategy, organization, and execution all together is another dimension of consistency. The slang expression is "getting our act together." In addition, managers need faith and commitment to a strategy so that their efforts persist long enough to build skills and reputations.

So, as we study the many cases distributed throughout this book, structured thinking and careful analysis will be necessary. But they are not enough: judgment and integration are also essential. Holistic thinking is a vital feature of strategic management.

## Strategy and Professional Development

Future managers will need skill in strategic management. Whatever it may be called, the timely adjustment of each business firm to its turbulent environment will become increasingly crucial and difficult. External pressures are mounting, payout periods are shrinking, communication technology is speeding up competitive action, more industries are becoming global, and sound institutions are making change more costly.

Consequently, the development of professional managers will include, even more than it already does, concerted efforts to strengthen each person's strategic management capabilities. Skill in directing stable operations will not be enough. Tomorrow's managers, especially those dealing with general, overall problems, will have to be adroit in deciding what changes to make and in getting those changes carried out. Studying the strategic management process can help individuals significantly in building these kinds of skills. That is what this book is about.

## SUMMARY

We have just had a preview of the concepts that will be developed throughout the book. This quick glimpse of what to expect helps the reader—the future manager—to place the separate chapters into a comprehensive model of strategic management, a model that stresses the following elements:

1. *Strategy, a vital management tool.* Strategy can be, and in many companies is, the major instrument that senior managers use to shape the future course of their business. Its role is threefold: to identify how the company will cope with its ever-changing and tough environment, to prescribe initiatives and other actions that the company will take to win its desired position in that turbulent setting, and to articulate a dominant mission that will be the focus around which diverse company activities can be integrated.

   Neither a long-run budget nor a set of pious intentions, a strategy is a largely qualitative, longer term plan that is both realistic and action oriented. A well-developed strategy for a company spells out four elements: the domain of its operations, the sources of differential advantages, strategic thrusts, and target results.

2. *Multi-level strategy.* The foregoing concept of business strategy cannot come to life in the minds of a few central planners. Instead, strategy must become a tool that key managers normally use to adapt their activities to future opportunities. To achieve this status, it is useful to approach strategy from three organization levels: the corporation level, the business-unit level, and the department level. Each tier faces its own set of issues, but these must be resolved so that vertical coordination is present. Without such a multi-level approach, strategy at any one level is likely to wither because of lack of support from the other levels. So multi-level strategy is an important theme in the structure of this book.

3. *Process of strategic management.* Broadly stated, the process that managers follow to bridge the gulf between an intriguing strategic idea and a set of actions that bring that idea to fruition moves from a predicted outlook for the industry to a four-part strategy, on to organization, and finally to execution. This process gives strategy a down-to-earth, operational quality. For strategy to fulfill the role sketched for it here, it has to be pursued through the action phase.

## Guide to the Rest of the Book

### Flow of Ideas

The scope of this book, then, explores how the strategy concept can be applied to multiple levels of an enterprise, each using the strategy process framework.

Part 1 starts with a formulation of business-unit strategy. Business-units are the starting point because they are at the level where overall business management is most critical and where priorities in confronting competitive forces must be set.

Part 2 moves downward to strategy programs for departments. Here, the connection of marketing, production, human resources, and finance to the business-unit strategy, as well as their linkages to each other, is explored.

Next, Part 3 discusses the upper level of formulating corporate strategy. The grist here deals with portfolios, mergers, acquisitions, joint ventures, and corporate inputs to the operating divisions.

Part 4 addresses the design of organization structures that aid in the execution of strategy, along with the crucial task of finding and developing managers well suited to such structures. The baffling question of what sort of a board of directors should be the capstone of the organization is also considered here.

Part 5 highlights the make-happen phases of strategy execution. Programming, activating, and controlling must all be related closely with the strategy if actual behavior is to support the future direction of strategy planning.

The closing Part 6 reviews the general framework of the book from two different perspectives: the management of multinational corporations and the social responsibility of business managers.

### Use of Cases

In this introduction, we have focused on concepts and the exposition portion of the text. By page count, this is only half the story; the other half consists largely of cases. For students who expect to make their professional careers as managers or by working with managers, cases are a very important supplement to concepts, especially in a complex, intangible area such as strategic management.

The cases, which follow chapters, parts, and the entire text, present a wide array of situations. Each calls for managerial decisions, and that provides opportunities for students to practice being managers. Much more important, however, is the use of cases to test one's understanding of concepts, to discover unexpected relationships, and to sense the subtleties of applying conclusions to real situations. This use is a widespread technique for *professional* development.

The cases come from actual situations. Where practical, we use actual names of companies and people. However, often managerial problems involve confidential information or inferences affecting personal privacy. Rather than omit these features of real life, we prefer to switch names and use other camouflage where necessary. Respecting the wishes of our case sources in this way need not alter the richness of issues posed by a case.

Cases serve another purpose as well. We have divided a complex, interrelated phenomenon—strategic management—into parts, levels, and steps. This is necessary because no one can talk about a complex whole all at once. Nevertheless, the division into parts is somewhat artificial: real situations don't have such neat boundaries. Through cases we can restore some of the wholeness. While the cases in this book have been selected and located in such manner as to illustrate at least some of the issues discussed in the preceding text, all of them raise additional issues. The fit is rarely neat, because actual cases have many facets. And that multi-dimensional characteristic is a great benefit. It helps persons studying the cases to put the pieces back together into an organic whole. Such integrating skill is of high value to professional managers.

We believe that you can learn from both the concepts and cases which lie on the pages ahead.

## Questions for Class Discussion

1. Can—or perhaps better, should—a nonprofit organization attempt to develop a long-term strategy when it must seek funding on an annual basis? (Assume that the organization has little in the way of endowments or long-term financial commitments.)

2. Use the four parts of a business-unit strategy suggested in this chapter to outline a career plan that you are seriously considering.

3. Sales solicitation in the consumer's home is undergoing considerable change. The once renowned "Fuller Brush Man" has disappeared. Smooth-talking magazine subscription salespersons who are "working my way through college" have become scarce. And the Avon Lady who sells cosmetics to housewives is generating fewer sales (in the United States) for the Avon Corporation. Consider the Avon situation. Do you think that a high dependence on personal sales in the home is only a problem for the marketing manager? Or is this a strategy issue for the manager of the U.S. cosmetics business? (Avon has several other divisions.) Is it a strategy issue that should go before the corporate board of directors? Who is in the best position to take action?

4. Suppose that your cousin is considering starting a fast-food national chain that features ethnic food—maybe Japanese food or Mongolian food. She asks for

your advice. Use the "strategic management process" described in this chapter to *list the main issues* that your cousin should consider.

5.  A large petroleum corporation owns a pipeline system that connects two of its refineries to (a) terminals that receive crude oil from ocean tankers, (b) a big crude oil production field in the Gulf of Mexico, and (c) other pipelines which transport crude oil from Texas and Oklahoma. In addition to moving crude oil to the corporation's refinery, the pipeline system acts as a common carrier for crude oil going to refineries of other corporations.

    There are three distinct levels of management concerned with the "strategy" of this pipeline system. One is a senior vice president responsible for all aspects of crude supply to the corporation's refineries. A second level is the manager of the pipeline system who has "profit and loss" responsibility for the system. (As a common carrier, the pipeline system is paid posted fees for the movement of any crude oil.) A third level is the operations manager of the pipelines, who is responsible for dependable deliveries and the costs of operating the pipelines.

    Suppose that you have the task of coordinating the strategy for this pipeline system. Do you think that you would have any difficulty securing agreement to a four-part strategy by all three levels?

6.  A well-known private university is internationally famous for its outstanding science division, which consists of several different departments such as physics, chemistry, astronomy, and the like. One of these outstanding departments, biochemistry, is a pioneer in studies of DNA and other studies that relate to changing reproduction codes. Scientists in the department are also investigating monoclonal cells. (See the catalog of your university or college for complete course descriptions for biochemistry. At one state university the catalog states, "Biochemistry is the study of molecules and molecular principles in biology, medicine, health sciences and agricultural sciences . . . Research areas include electron and X-ray crystallography, electron tomography, protein structure and function, bioenergetics, genetic engineering, gene regulation and expression, membrane and cell surface biochemistry, hormone biochemistry, insect biochemistry, etc. . . .")

    Because the subjects under investigation have potential application to treating human diseases, there is strong pressure from some alumni and pharmaceutical companies for the addition of a pharmacology professor to the biochemistry department of the private university. (Look again at your catalog—especially of the college of medicine or pharmacy—for a description of pharmacology. The same catalog as before states that "Pharmacology is the science concerned with all aspects of the action of drugs on living systems. Its primary aim is the development and evaluation of drugs for the treatment of human disease. The scope ranges from the intermolecular reactions of drugs with the chemical constituents of cells to the effects of chemicals in our environment on entire populations . . . Pharmacology is a broad discipline involving the investigation of the actions of chemicals upon living material at all levels of organization. Pharmacologic knowledge is applied to the understanding of the basic mechanisms of drug action, the diagnosis, prevention, cure or relief of the symptoms of disease and the promotion of optimal health.")

(a) Compare this state university structure to the multi-level strategy structure described in this chapter. (b) Do you think the views of the various levels of administration in the state university will differ about the kind of research that should be conducted? (c) Would you endorse the proposed addition of a pharmacology professor to the biochemistry department in the private university?

7. Springfield Press started as a printing service subsidiary of the Springfield *Courier*, a county-seat weekly newspaper that for years has been the only source of city and county news. With the death of the owner-editor, the *Courier* has been sold to a company that publishes several regional and county newspapers. That leaves Springfield Press in the hands of the editor's two children, Robert and Robin.

To a large extent, the activities of Springfield Press reflect the efforts of Robert and Robin to stay in the family business yet avoid the autocratic direction of their father. Robert runs the printing of the newspaper. Robin has focused on outside work not related to the newspaper and has substantially expanded the job-shop printing activities. These now include a variety of photo-offset and Xerox work for business firms and government offices as well as the usual wedding invitations, notices, and the like. In recent years, Springfield Press has been the leading printer in the area, and this printing work has earned a lot more profit than the *Courier*. It is not clear how long the new owner of the *Courier* will continue to have the paper printed by Springfield Press.

There never has been a clear statement about the aims and scope of activities of Springfield Press, and the present situation is ambiguous. Do you recommend that Robert and Robin prepare a strategy for the Press? If so, describe what such a strategy should cover, and explain the benefits of preparing such a statement.

8. While contemplating several acquisitions, the management of Heublein, Inc., the producer of Smirnoff vodka, A-1 steak sauce, Grey-Poupon mustard, Escoffier sauces, and other foods and beverages, stated that it had three long-range goals: (1) to make Smirnoff the number one brand of liquor in the world; (2) to continue a sales growth of 10 percent a year through internal growth and acquisitions; and (3) to keep Heublein's return on equity above 15 percent. In the course of operations, several additional goals became evident: (4) new products or companies acquired must have enough of a financial potential so as not to dilute the present equity; (5) new products must have a sufficient gross margin so that Heublein's expense-to-sales ratios for distribution, advertising, and promotion can be maintained; (6) new products must fit existing channels of distribution and marketing techniques; and (7) all products must be consumer goods, like liquor and toothpaste. Success in the consumer goods business depends upon good products which lead to repeat purchases, distribution which makes the product easy and convenient to get, and advertising which tells a convincing story. Ergo, goal number (8): Heublein's management must be able to improve the operations of an acquired company.

Evaluate this set of goals of a successful company in light of (a) the role of strategy, (b) what a strategy is not, and (c) the four elements of a strategy as explained on pages 6 and 7.

# CASE
## 1  GAIN Software[3]

GAIN Software was founded three years ago by Gerald Mandel, Alice Barber, Ignacio de Santos, and Norma Zimmer. During their senior year in college, the four worked on the idea of forming a business based on developing and selling computer software specifically oriented to the needs of small retail businesses. Typically, these establishments deal with service bureaus or companies which handle their payroll, billings, accounts payable, and other standard services. Few grow large enough to afford to do their own computer or data processing work internally.

"We felt," said Gerry [Gerald Mandel], "that with the development of the P.C. [personal computer] and breakthroughs in telecommunications, we could offer something to even small retailers that they couldn't buy anywhere else. We developed software to help them with their purchasing, inventory control, pricing, and promotions. Our software isn't designed to handle big, basic operations like payroll, billing, etc. It is supposed to give small-to-medium-sized retail stores a means of making better decisions on what to buy in what quantity, where, and for what terms. Then it helps them with inventory control, pricing, and special promotions."

"Using very basic hardware, owners or managers of such businesses can have daily—in some cases, hourly—access to information they need to make key decisions," said Norma Zimmer. "At reasonable prices, we can hook them up to regional data sources and through low cost telecommunications give them access to information and sources that only large stores or chains could tap into before."

"We tested our ideas," Ignacio de Santos said, "as a project in a new ventures course and created a business plan. We wrote some of our own software—Alice is a real genius in that area—and then designed systems using readily available equipment for several small stores. We offered to *give* them the software and our services in selecting equipment and show them how to use it if they paid for the

[3]William H. Newman, E. Kirby Warren, and Andrew R. McGill, *The Process of Management: Strategy, Action, Results*, 6th ed., ©1987, pp. 303–307. Reprinted by permission of Prentice-Hall, Inc., Englewood Cliffs, New Jersey.

equipment and paid telephone access charges, and so on. We did three stores for under $8,000 each and all three are convinced they got their money back in months."

After graduation, Gerald, Ignacio, and Norma created a partnership and launched their venture. Alice Barber decided to accept a very attractive offer from a large company, but agreed to let them use software she had written and to develop new software for the company.

"We agreed to pay her," said Gerry, "a relatively small sum for every package she puts together and to pay her a royalty for every system we sell that incorporates it. Alice is still our biggest software developer, but we have three or four others who we can contract with if she is too busy."

The three partners have done very well since graduation. While the first year was difficult, they believe they now have a winning formula and team.

"For the last two years," Norma said, "we have each earned six-figure salaries and bonuses. While we have been putting in incredible hours, we are making more money than we ever dreamed of at this stage. In addition, we have paid off our original loans and have money in the bank. We have access to a sizable line of credit if we choose to expand; I know we could attract equity money."

Expansion—how and how fast—has created the first serious disagreement among the three partners. Each has a quite different view on how to capitalize further on their current success. The plans are outlined as follows.

## Gerry's Plan

"I want us to keep doing what we are doing now. We have thousands of good-sized communities and cities to target. What we have been doing is picking one and spending a few days to a week researching it. We get data on retail establishments, analyze it, and select a small target group of three to six businesses. Then we really study these businesses and design in rough form systems for them. We all work on these systems jointly. When we are ready, we each take one or two stores and go in for the sale. We often haven't even been in the store before and the owners are amazed at what we know about their businesses.

"We can usually tell them not only the key characteristics of their business and their key numbers, but the names of their grandchildren and pets as well. We show them brochures and testimonials and then demonstrate what we can offer them. Sometimes we cart in our own hardware and rent a hotel suite for a week or two. Sometimes we rent space and equipment from a local service bureau, and in large cities sometimes we set up our own office when we plan to stay a month or more. Norma says we are like a traveling vaudeville team. We do our magic and move on.

"Every time, if we have done our homework, we sell 75%–100% of our initial target group. We 'low ball' the cost and really custom-tailor the product for them. With them as our base, we then blitz the rest of the town. The companies we sell initially become our strongest support team, as long as we stay away from their major competitors.

"We do much more standard packages and charge full price as we move through town. When we have covered the biggest and best stores, we head for home, pick our next target, and start our research and plans again.

"Except for demonstration equipment, we have no real investment. We sell our software, we design the systems, and we order equipment if asked to do so. When it arrives, we move back into the community and set it up and either teach them to use it or hire local people—believe it or not, often high school or college kids—to teach them to use it.

"We have an answering service and a twelve-hour-a-day 'hot line' to handle any questions or problems that crop up. Finally, we *charge* them a small fee to receive our 'newsletter' and our special reports on new equipment and software. We now have a big enough customer base to use the newsletter and reports to set up a good mail order operation, if we could find someone to run it for us.

"My plan is to keep right on doing what we are doing. We travel to some neat places, work real hard for a while, and make lots of money and then pull back. We could work six cities or sixty in a year. We could take a couple of weeks off for each month of high pressure work and still make big money, or we could pile through six months and then spend a month visiting Katmandu. Later, if we want, we could add one, two, three new partners; teach them a piece at a time until we know we can trust them and grow slowly without risk.

"What I love about what we do now is that *we* are in charge. No big capital tie-up, no bureaucracy. We decide where we work, how hard we work, and how much we make. We get along fine so why spoil a good thing?"

## Norma's Plan

"I find a lot of what Gerry says appealing," said Norma, "but his approach has a number of flaws. While I'm not nuts about trying to keep up this pace, I can handle it. What I can't handle is the realization that we may be giving up millions. We have a winning formula but we must leverage our time and capitalize on it. Secondly, if we don't build a bigger, stronger organization *fast,* we may not only lose opportunities but the whole program. A few 'copycats' have already tried to imitate our approach and are using it with some success. They haven't hit us head-on in the same town, and probably won't for a while, but this thing may pyramid and we may have fifty 'carbon copies' to deal with in the near future.

"One of our imitators will do what I want to do and will become a large, well organized regional or national organization. Maybe even worse is if one of them decides to take their version of our formula to an existing large company and sells them the idea. That's what Ignacio wants us to do before someone else has the same idea.

"My plan is to get big as fast as possible. We must set up an organization—not a big one, but one that can do what we do now on a regional or even national basis. We can hire specialists in software, hardware, and telecommunication to design systems. Then through either our own sales group or by franchising, we can sell, install, and maintain the systems.

"With a larger organization, we can look for better prices and/or commissions from the equipment companies and we can really organize and exploit our potential mail order system as well. *What* we do isn't that complex. Unless we get bigger and stronger so that we can offer better service at lower prices, we will lose what we now have.

"I want us to borrow what we can, incorporate, and sell up to 40% of our stock to either a venture capitalist or to the public. I am sure we can raise enough money to operate not only on a larger scale, but a lot more professionally and not have to kill ourselves in the process.

"Unfortunately, I am having trouble convincing either Gerry or Ignacio that this is not just the best approach, but the only way to *survive*. At least I have Gerry convinced that we need to change our name. GAIN was corny enough when we were in college but now with Alice no longer active, we should drop the 'A' and I can't see us as GIN Software. Right now we aren't so well known that a name change would hurt us, but if we grow we need to have a name that fits.

"I like 'Strategic Information Systems' or 'SIS.' We have to make sure it isn't taken, but Gerry is willing to check it out. Ignacio feels it doesn't matter so why waste the money on name research. He wants to 'cash in his chips' and look for another game.

"Frankly, I think he is just worn out. We have been working very hard for the last couple of years. I want us all to just take a month off, rest up, and then spend the next several months getting the money, designing our structure, building systems, and hiring people."

## Ignacio's Plan

"Norma may be right," mused Ignacio. "Maybe I will feel different after a month off but I doubt it. While we are all exhausted, I don't think I will feel any different after a vacation. Even if I do, I don't think Gerry will go along. I don't mind working for a big company but I don't want to be a manager! I don't mind working very hard but don't want responsibility for other people's lives. I manage myself quite well but not others. I am impatient with people who aren't as quick or as willing to sacrifice as I am. I hate having to criticize them or even depend on them.

"If we followed Norma's plan, I would want no part of management. Just give me a territory, some support people, supervised by others, and turn me loose; not in this 'gypsy' approach we now take but in a given geographic area. Then let me work it in a steady way. With salary, commissions, and equity I can make enough money not to need even a big title.

"Gerry isn't like that; he doesn't want any part of a big organization even if it was his own. He hates bureaucracy. He loves to freewheel and work on his own but I don't think he would be happy doing what I described for myself. I don't want to manage but I can be managed. Gerry would have to be the top manager to rise above the bureaucracy, and I don't think he would be a good executive."

"My recommendation is that we sell out and sell out fast while we have something to sell. Sooner than later a big computer or telecommunications company is going to either buy out one of our imitators or set up their own operation. Once they realize just how much there is to make, they will go for it."

"I believe we should spend our month off studying possible buyers. Then we should show them our books—not our 'tricks' but our books. If we get a good lawyer or 'finder' to help us, I'll bet we could get a big chunk of money up front and either royalties or stock."

"I would be willing to work for the big company to help them get started and Norma might, if she had no choice, do the same. In fact, she might parlay this into a big executive job with the acquiring company running this operation for them."

"Gerry might help during the transition but if he wants out, that's o.k. There should be enough money for him to start up something new on his own. Who knows—maybe I'll join him."

"Out of respect for Norma, both Gerry and I have agreed to take a month away from the business and relax. Then we will get together and try to resolve this."

## Questions

1. GAIN Software is a very small company or business-unit; it has neither departments nor a large corporate organization. Nevertheless, the concept of strategy can help its three owner-workers decide how to proceed. (a) Explain briefly how the three functions of strategy listed in this chapter can be applied to GAIN Software. (b) Illustrate briefly how each element of the four-part strategy shown in Figure 1–1 can be applied to GAIN Software.

2. Suppose that you are a friend of Gerry, Norma, and Ignacio's. What strategy do you recommend that they adopt? (If you feel that you must say, "it depends on . . .," then list the determining variables and explain how you would try to resolve them so as to arrive at a strategy.)

# PART 1

## Designing Business-Unit Strategy in Turbulent Times

# CHAPTER 2

## Forecasting Attractiveness
## of an Industry

Strategic planning for a single-line company starts with a vision of a product or service that a lot of people would like to have and that the company might provide. If the company is intrigued with that opportunity, it needs to make a careful analysis of just how practical the proposal really is.

A key part of such a strategic analysis is a forecast of the attractiveness of the industry as a future domain for a lot of intensive effort. Several other aspects will also need to be studied, such as the company's relative strengths, but the nature of the industry is a good place to begin.

## Change: Source of Opportunity and Threats

Two students in Lincoln, Nebraska think that they might earn their university expenses by running a small shop that rents video cassettes. Personally, they like to select the movies they watch on their TV set, but that doesn't prove much about the longer run attractiveness of the industry as a place to earn a living.

Investigation reveals that video cassette recorders (VCRs) are already in more than a third of homes having TV sets. Although a major appeal of VCRs is the ability to tape a broadcast and replay it later at a more convenient time, renting tapes turns out to be even more popular. Renting tapes gives the viewer a much wider choice of what to watch and freedom from commercial advertisements. To be sure, several legal questions about copyrights, royalties, and the like are still lurking in the background, and users may rebel at high fees for pedestrian shows. Nevertheless, VCR watching continues to be upbeat. Also, the industry is easy to enter—indeed, so easy that competing shops, perhaps with a better inventory, are a major threat.

Much more specific and local information should be assembled about running a video cassette shop. However, the two entrepreneurs have concluded that, among the opportunities open to them, renting video cassettes has a near-term industry outlook that is favorable.

## Turbulence, Not Fast Growth, Is the Typical Outlook

The near-term outlook for VCR cassettes is relatively simple to predict. Forecasting in most other industries gets more complex, however, with uncertainty clouding the picture. Maturity, slow growth, and even decline are descriptions often used for the total U.S. economy. However, such terms cover up the sharp changes occurring within many industries. And for specific companies, the outlook is far from stable. Turbulence is high, and new strategy is needed just to stay even. Among the unsettling forces at work are the following:

- *Obsolescence in the smokestack industries.* Many American steel mills, at the forefront of technology for decades, are now obsolete. Their high costs invite imports of cheaper products from abroad. Capacity is thus being reduced, and employment is dropping. The situation is further complicated by high wage rates, even by American standards, and by new pollution control requirements, which demand substantial investment without increasing output or lowering costs.

  The plight of the automobile industry has been compared to the dominance and then decline of the dinosaurs. For over 50 years, automobile production and related activities were a major force in the country's growth. Management techniques of the big auto companies were held up as models for others to follow. But with OPEC's success in skyrocketing petroleum prices, imports of small foreign cars captured a significant and growing share of the total market. The German Volkswagen, followed by several Japanese lines and then even Korean and Yugoslavian models, demonstrated that United States quality standards were lax and prices were high.

  Part of the weakness has been product design. Japanese automobile engineers were somehow able to achieve quality *and* low cost.

  To overcome such obsolescence, basic industries in the United States are redesigning products, technology, plants, customer services, and management practices. In addition, companies dealing with the major players must make corresponding adjustments in their activities.

- *Deregulation.* Even in our "free enterprise" system, for years the federal and state governments have regulated competition in several service industries—finance, transportation, electric power, telephones, and the like. During the 1980s this trend was reversed. For example, airlines were given much more freedom to decide where they would fly and what they would charge. As a consequence, the entire industry is in a process of restructuring, with expansions, failures, and mergers being reported almost weekly.

  Banking is undergoing similar convulsions. Service boundaries are breaking down, brokerage firms and insurance companies are adding banking activities, and banks are invading the former turf of brokers and insurance agents. State and national demarcations are disappearing, making room for nationwide financial service networks. To cite other examples, the breakup of AT&T and deregulation of interstate trucking have revolutionized the patterns of competition in those industries. Of course, each such change creates threats and opportunities for specific companies.

- *New sources of competition.* Traditional industry boundaries are breaking down. For example, tobacco companies are going into beverages and the Singer Company has deserted sewing machines for defense products. So it is not always clear who should be regarded as a potential competitor.

  Indeed, international competition is growing. Improvements in satellite communication and air transportation make possible worldwide trade in an increasing number of products. Grapes from Chile and fashion-designed clothing from Hong Kong are now common in the shops of, say, Omaha, Nebraska. Consumers benefit, but domestic producers and their employees are likely to suffer.

  The shoe industry illustrates the problem many U.S. managers are facing. Although Americans purchase one billion pairs of shoes each year, there are now only half as many manufacturing plants operating in the United States as there were 15 years ago, and employment has shrunk even more. Imports from Italy and Far Eastern countries are rapidly increasing their share of the market. Imports can underprice domestic producers, and with modern methods of communication and transportation desired styles can be delivered from abroad almost as fast as from local plants.

- *United States as a debtor nation.* For 40 years following World War II, the United States was the richest nation in the world. Our loans and capital exports aided Yankee expansion abroad. Recently, however, the country has had huge and continuing trade deficits, deficits that have been financed by loans from Japan, Middle Eastern countries, and Europe. As a result, the United States is now a net debtor nation, with its external debt mounting every year. This decline in financial muscle will make large foreign projects somewhat more difficult for U.S. firms. On the other hand, active foreign management of businesses located here is likely to increase.

- *Environmental protection.* Advocacy groups promoting environmental protection have been especially effective in the United States. Automobile exhausts, endangered species, toxic wastes, and the like must be controlled. But what constraints are appropriate is not always clear. For instance, reducing acid rain may affect the location and technology of industrial plants in much of the midwest.

  Atomic energy is a tender subject—and an emotional one. Fed by the arguments concerning atomic weapons, the safety of atomic energy plants has become a subject of great public concern in the United States, especially after a nuclear power plant accident in the Soviet Union in 1986. As safety requirements have escalated and been made retroactive, the costs of building and operating an atomic energy plant in the United States have more than quadrupled. Very large sums are involved, and several public utility companies will probably go bankrupt before the financial dust settles.

- *Demographic shifts.* Industry attractiveness may be influenced by the number of people in various demographic categories. For instance, as the proportion of persons over 65 years old increases, the demand for diapers and toys "matures" while the demand for second careers and retirement communities rises. Even more striking is the increase in women in the work force. Women have accounted for 60 percent of all new job holders in the post-World War II period. In a shift from the prewar era, most of these working women were married and often had small children at home. This rise in two-career families is associated with more packaged foods, more dining out, the ability to buy more expensive homes, and other consumption patterns.

- *New technology.* Shifts in technology are upsetting some industries and creating new ones. Computers, of course, have become the classic example. Probably, the new uses that will have the most influence on business operations still lie in the future. For example, banks may maintain a whole set of books for depositors, pay their bills, and provide subtotals for use on annual income tax returns. And these changes may contribute to a rearrangement of financial institutions. Medical diagnosis, traffic control, and chemical analysis may experience similar dramatic changes. The postal clerk sorting mail may eventually be as obsolete as a telegraph operator sending messages over the wireless.

    Potentially more dramatic than electronic advances are the technological advances in biology. By tinkering with the DNA structure of a reproductive cell, new living forms can be created. One hopeful prospect is the transfer of genetic information among species of plants, enabling the design of hardy plants that have high protein contents. Such plants could substantially improve the world food supply, especially for countries where the present diet is deficient in protein.

    A related technique is *cloning,* i.e., producing identical copies. Thus, a prizewinning bull or cow might be duplicated over and over again. This process, coupled with the use of surrogate mothers, could quickly change animal husbandry throughout the world.

## Need for an Organizing Framework

The preceding brief review of sources of turbulence highlights a quandary: to which changes should managers give close attention? The total environment is too diverse and complex to comprehend. Some device is needed (a) to help select those forces that are most likely to affect a particular company, and (b) to provide a cognitive framework for combining forecasts about those forces into statements of opportunities and threats which can serve as a basis for company strategy.

Focusing on one industry at a time is a powerful simplifying device. Here, the term "industry" means a set of companies that provide closely related products and/or services to a common group of customers. Typically, companies in an industry will rely, directly or indirectly, on similar technologies to produce the said products and/or services.[1]

An industry focus helps anyone concerned with company strategy to decide which environmental changes are relevant, and also how those changes are likely to affect the company. For strategic planning purposes, predictions of future changes are fully as important as knowledge of past changes. In turbulent times, an assessment of several different industries, or varying scopes of a core industry, may be useful. In all these variations the industry concept can serve as the organizing framework for masses of data. It helps a person develop an integrated picture of the setting in which the company will operate.

Such an industry focus can be built around three perspectives: (1) the demand for products and/or services of the industry, (2) the supply of products and/or services by the industry, and (3) the competitive structure of the industry. A fuller outline of this framework is given in Figure 2–1 and is described in the next sec-

**FIGURE 2–1.**
**INTEGRATED FRAMEWORK FOR ANALYZING AN INDUSTRY**

**ATTRACTIVENESS OF AN INDUSTRY**

    A.  Demand for products and/or services of the industry
        1. Long-run growth or decline
        2. Stability of demand for products and services
        3. Stage in "product life cycle"
    B.  Supply of products and/or services of the industry
        1. Capacity of the industry
        2. Availability of needed resources
        3. Volatility of technology
        4. Social constraints
        5. Government support and regulation
    C.  Competitive structure of the industry
        1. Barriers to mobility
        2. Relative bargaining power
        3. Severity of competition
    D.  Conclusions
        1. Prospects for volume and profits
        2. Key factors for success in the industry

---

[1]To emphasize that an industry or a company may sell either products or services, we often will say "products or services." However, strategy issues for a service company are sufficiently similar to those for a product company that we may just use "products" for both tangible and intangible outputs.

tion. Not all subheadings may be important for a particular industry, and others may be added; nevertheless, the underlying approach applies to large and small, profit and not-for-profit, and new and old industries.

## Demand for Products or Services of the Industry

### Long-Run Growth or Decline

The end uses of an industry's products provide a key to future demand. For instance, if the familiar flashlight battery were used only for flashlights, the demand would be stable and mature. Actually, small dry cells are used in portable radios, cassettes, action toys, emergency lights, and a variety of gadgets. Thus, the resulting high growth rate depends on a rising popularity of the portable entertainment devices.

Dry cells illustrate two other aspects of demand that may be significant. First, dry batteries have a *derived demand*. They are used only in association with some other product, and it is the popularity of these other products that leads to the demand for dry batteries. Manufacturers can do little to influence total industry sales; instead, their sales efforts focus on increasing their share of the market.

Second, the *focus of research and development efforts* is not on new devices that will increase the demand for batteries. Of course, the manufacturers are glad to provide data to the designers of toys and radios, but these end products involve such different considerations that the battery manufacturers feel they have little to contribute. Instead, research by battery manufacturers is directed toward reduction of cost and improvement of quality.

After the possible uses of a product or a service of an industry have been explored, it is often desirable to classify potential customers by type and area. Thus, the customers for automobile insurance may be grouped as private and commercial, and they may be further divided among regions. Then, any major changes affecting these customers can be related easily to the industry in question.

### Stability of Demand for Products

Demand for a product or a service may be steady and predictable, or it may be volatile and uncertain. The following factors give an insight into stability.

#### Substitutes

The desire for the utility of or satisfaction rendered by a product may be reasonably stable, yet the demand for the product itself may be quite unstable because of increased or decreased use of substitutes that render this same satisfaction. Ball-point and felt-tip pens have reduced the demand for pencils. Atomic energy could replace crude oil. In each case the issue is not so much a decline in the demand for the service as the substitution of one product for another.

### Durability of Products

Durable products have wide fluctuations in demand. Once constructed, houses, airports, and washing machines render services over a period of time, and consequently the demand for such products is more active during *periods of original construction* than during periods when existing facilities are merely being replaced. Also, the replacement of durable goods can often be postponed for a substantial period of time. For these reasons, the demand for durable products tends to fluctuate over wider ranges than does the demand for such things as food, clothing, travel, and entertainment, which must be replenished to render additional services. Speculation may play a part in fluctuations of demand for almost any product; however, the more durable the product, the more lasting the maladjustment that may result from the unwarranted speculation.

### Necessity Versus Luxury

Necessities, such as food and medical care, will enjoy a more stable demand than products such as swimming pools and foreign travel that are generally purchased only when people have funds over and above what is necessary for the first class of goods. However, attitudes toward services do switch. For example, air-conditioning and long-distance telephoning have moved from luxury to necessity for many users. Interactive cable TV may someday become a "necessity."

## Stage in Product Life Cycle

Many products and services pass through a life cycle, as shown in Figure 2–2. Although the phases vary widely in length, experience with an array of products—from penicillin to automatic pinsetters in bowling alleys—does show that the concept is a useful analytical tool. Clearly, when electric refrigerators are already in 90 percent of homes, growth prospects are much lower than for microwave ovens; refrigerators have reached the maturity phase. A shift from maturity to decline typically occurs when a substitute product or service appears on the scene—witness what happened to the small-town newspaper.

In addition to being a way of predicting demand, the life-cycle concept bears directly on key factors for success. In the growth phase, a company can take risks with overcapacity and even with quality in an effort to establish a market position; profit margins will permit production inefficiencies. By contrast, in the maturity phase, efficient use of plants and close attention to production costs become much more important.

Every future shift in technology, social behavior, politics, and economic forces will increase or decrease the demand picture for at least some industries. Both small and large firms will feel the impact. Anticipating those impacts that will affect us is a crucial part of effective management.

**FIGURE 2-2.**
**CLASSICAL PRODUCT LIFE CYCLE**

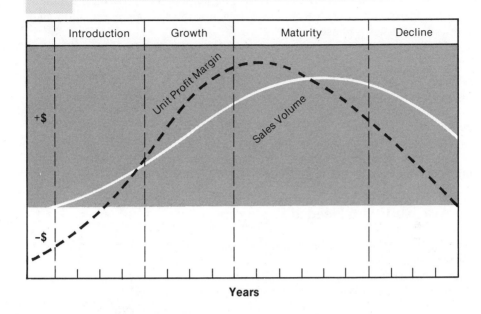

## Supply of Products or Services

The outlook for profitable operations in an industry depends not only on the demand, but also on the available supply and the cost of bringing such products or services to the market.

### Capacity of the Industry

In a dynamic business system, some industries are likely to have excess capacity while others have inadequate capacity. At one stage, sulfa was the wonder antibiotic drug and pharmaceutical producers expanded greatly to meet the urgent demand. Then penicillin and Aureomycin came along, and the sulfa producers found themselves with a large capacity that could not be used. In the finance field, stockbrokers have been plagued with excess capacity when interest in stock speculation declines. In addition to such drops in demand, excess capacity may result from overexpansion. Sometimes a field of business such as personal computers or resort hotels looks so attractive that too many firms enter it.

Inadequate capacity is common in any expanding industry. If a new service like retirement villages meets with wide public acceptance, the original facilities may not be able to fill the demand. When the capacity of an industry is scarcely adequate to meet the demand, most companies will enjoy profitable operations.

Products will find a ready market, prices will be firm, and a high level of operation will permit spreading overhead costs over many units.

In contrast, excess capacity will have a depressing influence on the outlook for an industry, for it may lead to low prices, low rates of operation, and a high proportion of sales expense.

The seriousness of excess capacity depends, in part, upon how large depreciation, interest, and other expenses connected with the facilities are in relation to total costs. If, as in the chemical fertilizer industry, these overhead charges are a high percentage of total expenses, individual companies may cut prices to low levels in an attempt to secure volume and at least some contribution above out-of-pocket expenses toward the fixed burden. On the other hand, if the bulk of expense goes for materials and labor, the excess capacity will have much less effect on supply and price because the relation between out-of-pocket costs and prices will be the controlling influence—whether the plant is busy or not.

## Availability of Needed Resources

The sheer existence of an adequate supply of raw materials may be a factor in the outlook of a few industries, notably those depending upon a natural resource such as timber, crude oil, iron ore, or other minerals. In most cases, however, the problem is the price at which the materials can be obtained.

Future material costs depend on world demand, on new sources of supply—often from developing nations—and/or on production technology, as in the dramatic drop in the cost of computer chips. The number of suppliers is also important: with only a few available, they are more likely to exact high prices and stipulate terms of delivery. And if those few form an alliance, as the OPEC countries did, their bargaining position is further enhanced.

The seriousness of rising costs will depend upon the industry's (or company's) ability to pass such an increase on to its customers in the form of higher prices. Some industries, such as health services, can maintain their margins, whereas industries which face substitutes may be unable to raise their prices. Several pay-TV programs, for example, probably cannot raise their prices to protect their profit margins—although the evidence here is not yet clear.

The supply of labor may pose issues similar to those concerning materials. In a given region, skilled labor may be so scarce that expansion will be very difficult. Or, the costs of labor and of output restrictions may contribute to noncompetitive costs—as has been the case in the U.S. shoe industry.

While materials and labor are more likely to be critical in an industry forecast, the availability of each needed resource should be assessed.

## Volatility of Technology

Industries vary in the frequency with which new products are introduced and the frequency of changes in processing technology. For example, technology jumps quickly in the pharmaceutical, space, and urban-renewal industries.

When confronted with such volatile technology, managers must give close attention to research and development (R & D). They must be prepared to move promptly when either their own efforts or their competitors' create important innovations. The frequency of change means that market positions are insecure; consequently, caution in making capital investments is required. Success depends, in part, on being agile.

## Social Constraints

Companies must act in a socially acceptable manner or face all sorts of delays and penalties. Having the facilities, resources, and technology to supply a desired service or product is not enough. In addition, all the activities of a company are expected to meet various social norms.

The catch is that these norms are not clearly defined. They keep changing, and various segments of society have quite different views on what is acceptable. Moreover, some industries, such as manipulative biology, are under more pressures that others.

Vague though the standards may be, the outlook for an industry should include the constraints with which that industry is—or will be—expected to operate. For example, the norms may relate to:

- pollution of the air, water, ground, etc.
- environmental protection—e.g., strip mining
- equal opportunity in employment and steady jobs
- dealing with people who are unpopular with strong pressure groups—communists, South Africans, Israelis, R.O.T.C., those involved in abortion clinics, etc.
- integrity, honesty, "questionable payments," and the like

The potential seriousness of social constraints is indicated by the prolonged delay they have imposed on the creation of a positive energy program for the country.

## Government Support and Regulation

Even the most ardent advocates of "American individualism" will admit that the forces of demand and supply should not be given free sway in the contemporary business world. Both restraints and assistance are likely to be asserted by government bodies.

Forecasting the nature of restraints is difficult. In the Reagan era, for instance, control over several drugs was increased and AT&T was broken up; at the same time airlines and truckers were given much more freedom for individual action. So, in this arena, specific national and state predictions are necessary.

Also, governments often provide *special advantages* to particular industries. For example, our merchant marine is heavily subsidized, many other industries are protected from foreign competition by tariffs, and agricultural products have been granted large subsidies. In order to qualify for such special advantages, it is often necessary for the industry to conform to stipulations and regulations of the government. This is particularly true in the agricultural industries, where the whole program of subsidies is associated with a plan for controlled production and marketing.

Such government action is frankly and deliberately designed to modify the underlying forces of demand and supply. It is part of the composite picture of the outlook for any industry.

## Competitive Structure of the Industry

The theme of the preceding two sections is that all sorts of external variables can be related to an industry by noting their impact on either demand or supply. Having summarized the combined influences on these two central (intervening) variables, we have a distilled view of the attractiveness of the industry.

But the picture is not quite that simple. There is significant variation in the way the demand and supply forces reach equilibrium. Sometimes the relationship among competing companies in an industry is "statesmanlike," and at other times it is "dog-eat-dog." And the nature of this rivalry has a marked effect on competitive pressures and profits.

Professor Michael E. Porter has developed a model that helps to predict the nature of competition in an industry.[2] His basic framework is shown in Figure 2–3. As with demand and supply, this framework can be used to summarize and relate an array of external forces. Three key concepts are especially important: barriers to mobility, relative bargaining power, and severity of competition.

## Barriers to Mobility

The competitive structure in an industry is determined at least in part by the ease of entry into and exit from the industry. This concept gives us a tool for forecasting how competition is likely to develop in the said industry.

### Barriers to Entry

The basic idea is that, especially in a growing industry, the more difficult it is for new competitors to enter, the more stable and profitable the industry is likely to be. Consider, for example, women's apparel. Almost anyone with a knowledge of dressmaking and enough capital to buy materials and rent sewing machines can enter the industry. The result is very sharp price competition, style piracy, widely fluctuating inventories, and frequent failure.

---

[2]*Competitive Strategy: Techniques for Analyzing Industries and Competitors* (New York: The Free Press, 1980). See especially Chapters 1, 7, and 12.

**FIGURE 2–3.**
**PORTER'S INDUSTRY COMPETITION MODEL**

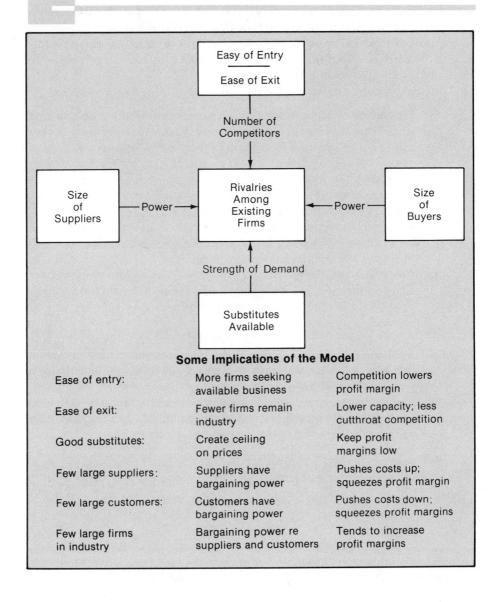

Some Implications of the Model

| Ease of entry: | More firms seeking available business | Competition lowers profit margin |
| Ease of exit: | Fewer firms remain industry | Lower capacity; less cutthroat competition |
| Good substitutes: | Create ceiling on prices | Keep profit margins low |
| Few large suppliers: | Suppliers have bargaining power | Pushes costs up; squeezes profit margin |
| Few large customers: | Customers have bargaining power | Pushes costs down; squeezes profit margins |
| Few large firms in industry | Bargaining power re suppliers and customers | Tends to increase profit margins |

A less obvious example of ease of entry has prevailed in the passenger airline business. Planes are readily available for rent, maintenance and repair can be sub-contracted to shops of the major operators, experienced pilots are looking for work, and airport counter space can be rented. So very little capital is needed to organize charter flights, and—with government deregulation—firms such as

New York Air can grasp significant shares of selected markets with their low-price, low-cost service.

In contrast, other industries are very difficult to enter. Kodak, for instance, has such an established reputation for high-quality film combined with an effective widespread distribution network that new suppliers of film face almost insurmountable barriers. (Note that film developing and printing is much easier to enter and is subject to volatile price competition.)

Potential barriers to entry include the following:

1. Economies of scale. When large volume significantly cuts per-unit costs, entry may be discouraged because years of losses would be necessary before any new firm could expect to achieve such a volume of sales. These economies of scale may exist in marketing or other functions as well as production.

2. Product differentiation. A distinctive product or service—including brand identification—makes entry difficult.

3. Large capital requirements. The high cost of building a new hospital, for example, is one of the factors that restrains newcomers from entering into a locality that has existing facilities.

4. Customers' switching costs. If customers of an existing company have a large investment in training employees to use and maintain products or services of that company, switching to a new supplier will be resisted.

5. Access to distribution channels. Loyal dealers and retailers can be a distinct advantage to existing firms; newcomers may have to rely on less experienced distributors or embark on finding and training a whole new set of distributors.

6. Superior technology. Firms already in an industry may have patented processes or expertise based on long experience. Unless the newcomer can somehow overcome this cost advantage, its profit margin will be squeezed.

7. Favorable access to raw materials or favorable location. In the fast-food industry, for example, new entrants may have difficulty finding good locations not already occupied by older companies. DeBeers Company may have preempted most of the supply of gem-quality diamonds.

When a combination of such factors discourages new firms from entering an industry, the competitive pressures are stabilized; there is less chance that some aggressive newcomer will rock the boat.

### Barriers to Exit

The situation differs if industry demand is falling rather than growing. Here the mobility issue is how fast competitors will leave. If available supply shrinks as fast as industry volume drops, then normal competition is likely to continue. However, when industry capacity substantially exceeds demand, cutthroat competition is apt to emerge. Therefore, in declining industries we need to predict barriers to exit.

Among the reasons why companies may be loath to cut capacity or withdraw from an industry entirely are these:

1.  Durable and specialized assets. Manufacturers of cement, for example, hold heavy investments in mills that have no alternative use. Consequently, the manufacturers are under severe pressure to continue producing cement at whatever price may be had.
2.  High costs of exit. Termination pay for employees or warranty obligations on products may be so large that shutting down costs more than fighting for the remaining business.
3.  Impact on related operations. A faltering product may be continued as a service to customers who buy other, more profitable products from the same supplier. Or, a vertically integrated firm may stay in a declining market because this volume helps to keep its raw material plant busy.
4.  Managers' emotional commitment. Like loyalty to a losing team, managers who have spent years perfecting a product or service may refuse to give up. Professors of Greek keep on offering courses in Greek syntax.
5.  Social pressures. The closing of a business throws people out of work, may disrupt a town, and may provoke government sanctions. For instance, railroads are often not permitted to abandon service to declining communities.

Several alternative strategies are available for what Harrigan calls "playing an end game."[3] Nevertheless, high barriers to exit are likely to create very volatile competition in declining industries.

## Relative Bargaining Power

In addition to barriers to entry and exit, the future competitive structure of an industry will be partly shaped by the relative power of key players—an issue that we will examine in Chapter 4. Generally, when a single firm dominates an industry, it sets a continuing stable pattern. But when several strong aggressive companies clash, all sorts of actions and responses should be anticipated.

---

[3]See K. R. Harrigan, *Strategies for Declining Businesses* (Lexington, MA: D.C. Heath and Company, 1980).

Not only competition among suppliers is involved. If only a few customers buy most of the output—as automobile manufacturers do for purchased parts—they can drive very tough bargains on specifications, delivery, and prices. Similarly, if one or two suppliers of critical services or raw materials have relatively strong bargaining power, they may be able to influence where and how competition takes place. For instance, when du Pont first introduced nylon yarn, it influenced the quality of products made of nylon and the consumer services.

## Severity of Competition

The various factors in Porter's model—the ease of entry and exit, the power of various players, and the availability of substitutes—all affect the keenness of competition. The probable aggressiveness and unwillingness to compromise of each player are suggested in the terse listing in the lower part of Figure 2–3. Pricing behavior is the result noted. (In practice, the competition may take the form of free service or better quality for the same price.)

The severity of competition in a specific industry, however, will result from a *combination* of these several forces. For instance, the difficulty of exit *coupled with* large and powerful customers in the virgin copper industry led to high volatility in prices.

In sum, competitive behavior can be predicted with considerable accuracy. Indeed, it is such an important element in the likely profitability of an industry that it should be weighed along with demand and supply when we assess the attractiveness of that industry.

## Industry Outlook: A Set of Planning Premises

## Capsule Conclusions Regarding Growth and Profit

For strategic planning, a highly condensed statement regarding the outlook of an industry is very useful. The analysis of demand, supply, and competition just outlined provides an array of vital data, but having assembled that, what is the conclusion? How does it all add up?

Two conclusions, among others, are always useful. One is a prediction of the future volume of activity in the industry, in units of output and dollars of revenue. The second is the likely profitability of the companies in the industry expressed both as a ratio to gross revenue and a ratio to total assets required. These conclusions about the growth or decline of the industry will affect business-unit strategy in numerous ways, determining, at least in part, the intensity of efforts to increase market share, expansion or contraction of production capacity, investment in personal development and research, and the like.

The volume and profit outlook for the industry is also a major consideration in corporate portfolio strategy, to be discussed in Part 3. Indeed, in that arena, interest in these two variables may crowd out other significant considerations.

## Key Factors for Success

Predictions about the particular sorts of resources or company capabilities which will be necessary for outstanding company success are also needed. The focus here is on *how* to be a leader in the industry. Attention shifts from probable net results—the growth and profitability forecasts just noted—to ways companies can rise above the average.

Recognizing key factors for success leads directly to strategy design. A choice of activities to be emphasized, i.e., where to build strength, can create (or destroy) a company's differential advantage. For example, in the pharmaceutical industry a succession of new products is essential; in baseball and universities, selection of players is one of the key factors. So the industry analysis should include a lot of probing into the dynamic forces that will shape future developments.

## Redefining "The Industry"

Thinking in terms of an *industry* is a device for drawing conclusions about a very complex environment—conclusions that will help managers design company strategy. However, a hazard in this way of thinking is how we define an industry.

A generation ago, Professor Theodore Levitt became famous for insisting that railroad companies got into trouble because they thought in terms of railroading instead of the broader function of transportation. To cite another classic case, when O.M. Scott & Sons started thinking of being in the lawn-care industry instead of the grass-seed industry, a whole new strategy opened up.

Sometimes thinking small is more useful than thinking big. For instance, the two students mentioned at the beginning of this chapter undoubtedly would have defined their industry as renting or selling video cassettes in Lincoln, Nebraska (and the framework of Figure 2–1 can be applied to an industry of that scope). Perhaps, however, they should expand the concept to a music-supply store, not just a cassette shop; but to structure their analysis around the U.S. entertainment industry would not be very effective.

The scope of an "industry" can vary in terms of (a) products or services included, (b) the geographical area and/or type of customers considered, or (c) the extent of vertical integration and technologies embraced. For strategic planning for a specific company, several definitions should be tried, with an industry analysis of each based on the framework of Figure 2–1. The resulting industry outlooks and key factors for success will usually vary in attractiveness. By itself, this information will suggest an advantageous strategic posture for the company to adopt. Of course, a final choice of the industry that a company considers itself to be in will also depend on its strengths relative to competitors and the values of its dominant executives—the subject of Chapter 3.

## Finding "Propitious Niches"

A by-product of careful industry analysis is helpful in locating attractive segments within the industry. No industry, however defined, is uniform in all respects. There will be a particular set of customers or source of supply which differs from the general pattern. And at least for one or two companies, that niche is more attractive than the industry as a whole.

In the book publishing industry, for example, medical books for doctors is a special niche. This segment is unaffected by best-seller lists, cheap paperbacks, discount chain stores, and royalty advances to famous people. In fast-food restaurants there is a niche for outlets that feature Mexican dishes.

A niche may be attractive because it is growing faster than the industry as a whole, or because the demand may be more stable—as is true of repair parts compared with original equipment for automobiles. In some niches the profit margins are wider, perhaps because those niches are shielded from competition from large firms.

Often, small firms are profitable because they serve a special niche. Larger companies may operate in several distinct niches, as does a Texas printing firm which focuses on multicolor mail-order catalogs and annual financial reports.

Finding propitious niches which a company is capable of serving effectively calls for a sensitive understanding of competition in the larger industry. And if a company hopes to maintain a dominant position in such a segment, it must recognize and carefully adjust its operations to the unique services desired in the niche.

## SUMMARY

Strategy for a single-line company, or business-unit, is the focus in the first part of this book. Subsequently, other tiers in the multi-level approach, viz., the departmental tier and the corporate tier, will also be explored.

A logical point of entry into company strategy is to describe a practical way for company managers to size up the complex external environment in which they will operate. This chapter proposes that the industry concept be the device for identifying relevant external forces and translating them into predictions which can be used easily and directly in formulating company strategy. Thus, the industry outlook becomes a major building block.

A framework for thinking through an industry outlook has been described. Demand, supply, and competitive practices are the chief operative concepts. From an analysis of these, a manager can move to forecasts of industry volume, profitability, and key factors for company success. Through this general approach, a manager can translate an array of external changes into planning premises to be used in strategy design.

In practice, considerable judgment and skill are needed to use the approach described. Two schemes for elaboration were briefly noted. One is to try out different definitions of the scope of the industry. Variations in the resulting outlooks may then throw light on what strategy is desirable. The second elaboration is to look for special niches within the industry which may provide better opportunities for particular companies than those prevailing in the industry generally.

Using industry analysis as a background, Chapter 3 looks at a company's relative strengths and weaknesses in attempting to deal with the opportunities and threats that have been identified.

## Questions for Class Discussion

1. One of Xerox's major competitors in office duplicating machines has thought for most of its life that it was in the office section of the duplicating machine industry. Like Xerox, its machines use a photocopying (not printing) process. Recently the company announced that in the future it will be in the "office systems" industry. What do you think is implied by this announced change in industry scope? How will the factors to be considered in predicting industry demand, supply, and competitive conditions be affected by the change in industry scope? On the basis of what you already know, do you believe the outlook is more attractive in the office systems industry than in the office duplicating machine industry?

2. Following several years of record sales and profits, Ford Motor Company had amassed, by 1988, about $10 billion in cash and marketable securities. The company announced that it would concentrate on three possible areas for acquisitions: defense and aerospace, financial services, and electronics. (a) What opportunities for sales and profits do these three areas hold for Ford? (b) Analyze the ease of entry and exit into each, the power relationships between Ford and its suppliers or buyers, and the availability of substitutes in accordance with the scheme shown in Figure 2–3. (c) Ford might also buy back some of the approximately 250 million shares of its common stock which are outstanding. This action might stabilize or increase the price of Ford shares, thus making the company's stock more attractive to those who

would otherwise wish to invest in the automobile and truck industry. What do you recommend in regard to choosing between acquisitions and the purchase of common stock?

3. Use the framework outlined in Figure 2–1 to prepare an outlook for the students contemplating purchasing the video cassette rental shop mentioned at the beginning of the chapter. Pay attention especially to (a) identifying the environmental forces that they should consider and (b) the way the forces that you select fit into the framework.

4. For years the restaurant industry has attracted small entrepreneurs; it is an arena where entry and exit have been relatively rapid. How do you think the growth of fast-food chains has affected restaurant competition in the locality in which you live? Use concepts from this chapter to prepare an outlook for the restaurant industry in your locality.

5. Select an industry in which you are considering taking a job. Develop an outlook for that industry using the framework outlined in this chapter. Do you still want to work in that industry?

6. Harley Davidson motorcycles are made for a distinctive niche in the U.S. motorcycle industry. They are among the most highly powered and heaviest motorcycles available in the world and are often called "hogs." Also, they are expensive, costing $4,000 to $10,000 each, a price that is up to 50 percent higher than competing Japanese models. How do you explain Harley Davidson's ability to survive in this niche? What are the critical factors for success in the niche?

7. (a) Compare what you consider to be the key success factors in the following industries: aerospace, auto repair, cigarettes, coal mining, cosmetics, electric utilities, ski resorts, and women's dresses. (b) In which industry would you prefer to build your career?

8. (a) Assume that the president of a mobile home manufacturing company asks you, "What are the half-dozen key factors in the environment that I should watch in order to anticipate the growth or decline in our industry?" Give your answer. (b) Do the same for eggs.

9. Choose a company in your city, county, or state which has a turbulent environment that is caused by one or more of the seven causal factors discussed on pages 29–31. Which of these factors most explains the turbulence in your chosen firm's environment? Is the strength or influence of that variable likely to change in the near future?

10. In 12 months Americans purchased a record $102 billion in the stocks of foreign companies, but that was dwarfed by the $278 billion foreigners invested in U.S. stock, also a record, said a report issued by the Securities Exchange Commission (S.E.C.) in 1987. In this major study, the S.E.C. told Congress that investments across international boundaries have soared since 1980. As

an example, the total amount of international bonds was $38 billion in 1980 and $254 billion in 1986. Of this total, $44 billion were borrowed through issues of bonds by U.S. investors. Do these events and facts provide evidence that the United States is a debtor nation? Are other factors also at work?

11. In a recent publication the World Future Society forecast that "By the year 2000, the average car will be mostly plastic and will last an average of 22 years." What elements of "turbulence" might bring this about in the auto industry? Are there any "mostly plastic" cars now being made? Do you put much stock in this forecast?

# CASE
## 2 Goodyear Tires

What does a world champion do when the tough task of maintaining its laurels loses allure? Diversify! That was the decision Goodyear Tire & Rubber Company made a few years ago. Goodyear took major steps into the aerospace, motor wheels, sun-belt real estate, and energy industries, including building a $1 billion pipeline from California to Texas.

### Retreat from Diversification

Finding attractive diversification targets is rarely easy, especially when the starting base is as large as Goodyear's worldwide tire and rubber operations— over $7 billion in sales a year. And Goodyear's timing was unfortunate. For instance, the pipeline and related crude oil and gas activities would have been in high demand a decade earlier, but the reversal from a world shortage to a surplus of crude oil turned these investments into a long-term speculation.

Also unfortunately timed was an unfriendly company takeover attempt by Sir James Goldsmith. Goldsmith's aim, if he won control, was to "restructure" Goodyear, selling off the recently acquired nonrubber operations and disposing of unprofitable parts of the tire business. This attack caused the existing management of Goodyear to make an abrupt change in strategy: existing management, rather than Goldsmith, would do the restructuring.

Consequently, Goodyear paid Goldsmith the equivalent of $52.50 per share for his 10.5 percent stake in the company's common stock—a total of $659 million which included a $90 million profit for Goldsmith. In addition, Goodyear bought back stock from other stockholders at $50 per share. These two buy-back moves reduced Goodyear's outstanding stock by 48 percent! And the company took on a staggering $2.3 billion debt to finance the purchases.

Now the company is in the process of selling its diversification assets in an attempt to repay this debt. Over $1 billion has come from the former aerospace, wheel, and real estate operations. The rest is slated to come from the energy investments, if and when the pipeline is sold.

These moves put Goodyear almost completely back in the tire and rubber business. The future of the company now depends largely upon what it is able to do in the tire industry. In 1986 Goodyear tire sales were $6.63 billion, or 85 percent of its revenues. Two-thirds of this "tires and related transportation products" business is in the United States. Therefore, the outlook for tires in the United States must be the primary base for Goodyear's future strategy.

Accordingly, the focus of this case is on analyzing the future prospects for the tire industry in the United States. On the following pages we review recent developments in the tire business as background for your personal assessment of the future prospects for this industry.

## Wheels Requiring Tires

The demand for tires depends, of course, on the number of rubber-borne vehicles in use. Both new vehicles and existing vehicles needing replacement tires are involved. Table 2–1 shows the total number of, and the growth in, motor vehicles registered in the United States. Table 2–2 gives the number of new cars sold in recent years.

**TABLE 2–1**
**MOTOR VEHICLE REGISTRATIONS IN THE U.S. (millions at year end)**

|  | Passenger Cars | Buses | Trucks Number | Trucks Percent of Total | Total |
|---|---|---|---|---|---|
| 1985 | 130 | 0.6 | 39 | (23.1) | 170 |
| 1984 | 128 | 0.6 | 38 | (22.9) | 166 |
| 1983 | 127 | 0.6 | 37 | (22.3) | 164 |
| 1982 | 124 | 0.6 | 35 | (22.1) | 160 |
| 1981 | 123 | 0.5 | 34 | (21.7) | 158 |
| 1980 | 122 | 0.5 | 34 | (21.6) | 156 |
| 1979 | 120 | 0.5 | 33 | (21.6) | 154 |
| 1978 | 117 | 0.5 | 32 | (21.3) | 149 |
| 1977 | 114 | 0.5 | 30 | (20.6) | 144 |
| 1976 | 110 | 0.5 | 28 | (20.0) | 139 |

**TABLE 2–2**
**RETAIL SALES OF NEW CARS IN THE U.S. (millions)**

|      | U.S. Cars | Imported Cars | Total |
|------|-----------|---------------|-------|
| 1986 | 8.2       | 3.2           | 11.4  |
| 1985 | 8.2       | 2.8           | 11.0  |
| 1984 | 8.0       | 2.4           | 10.4  |
| 1983 | 6.8       | 2.4           | 9.2   |
| 1982 | 5.8       | 2.2           | 8.0   |
| 1981 | 6.2       | 2.3           | 8.5   |
| 1980 | 6.6       | 2.4           | 9.0   |
| 1979 | 8.3       | 2.3           | 10.6  |
| 1978 | 9.3       | 2.0           | 11.3  |
| 1977 | 9.1       | 2.1           | 11.2  |

Imports of new cars, recently about 28 percent of new car sales, are relevant to tire demand because they are almost always equipped with tires manufactured outside the United States. Over 80 percent of the car imports come from Japan, and restrictions on increases in this number have been negotiated. (The present maximum is 2.3 million cars per year.) However, new foreign imports—notably Korean Hyundais and Yugoslavian Yugos— will swell the flow. Other potential sources of imports into the United States are indicated in Table 2–3.

The decline in the value of the U.S. dollar relative to the local currency in exporting countries reduces the attractiveness of our market to foreign producers. And improvements in U.S. productivity tend to hold back automobile imports. So you might conclude that imports will taper off.

## More Ride per Tire

Tires are lasting longer, and this reduces the demand for replacements. Factors contributing to longer tire life include the lighter weight of cars, less high-speed driving, and especially improvements in tire construction.

In the 1970s Michelin Tire Company, a French manufacturer, started aggressive promotion of its radial ply (steel-belted) tires in the United States, where the company soon built a plant. The construction of Michelin radial ply tires gave the tires significantly longer life than the then-common bias ply tires, and U.S. producers have been struggling ever since to convert their production equipment to this new design.

By 1985, virtually all new cars and trucks were equipped with radial ply tires. Replacement tires are rapidly moving in the same direction, even though radial plies sell at roughly a 50 percent premium over the older type of bias ply tires. The

**TABLE 2-3**
**WORLD VEHICLE PRODUCTION, 1986 (in millions)**

|  | Cars | Trucks | Total |
|---|---|---|---|
| United States | 7.8 | 3.5 | 11.4 |
| Canada | 1.1 | 0.8 | 1.9 |
| Total North America | 8.9 | 4.3 | 13.2 |
| Brazil | 0.8 | 0.2 | 1.0 |
| Other Latin America | 0.3 | 0.2 | 0.5 |
| Total Central & South America | 1.1 | 0.4 | 1.5 |
| USSR* | 1.4 | 0.8 | 2.2 |
| Other Eastern Europe* | 0.9 | 0.2 | 1.1 |
| Total Eastern Europe | 2.3 | 1.0 | 3.3 |
| France | 2.8 | 0.4 | 3.2 |
| Italy | 1.6 | 0.2 | 1.8 |
| Spain | 1.3 | 0.2 | 1.5 |
| United Kingdom | 1.0 | 0.2 | 1.2 |
| West Germany | 4.3 | 0.3 | 4.6 |
| Other Western Europe | 0.5 | 0.2 | 0.7 |
| Total Western Europe | 11.5 | 1.5 | 13.0 |
| Japan | 7.8 | 4.5 | 12.3 |
| Other Far East | 0.9 | 0.2 | 1.1 |
| Total Asia | 8.7 | 4.7 | 13.4 |
| World Total | 32.5 | 11.9 | 44.4 |

*1985.

following table illustrates the growth in radial ply replacement tires from 1981 to 1985:

|  | Radial Ply Tire Share of Replacement Sales |
|---|---|
| 1985 | 85% |
| 1984 | 80 |
| 1983 | 70 |
| 1982 | 64 |
| 1981 | 59 |

The addition of radial ply production capacity left a large overcapacity of bias ply facilities, and the tire companies have been slowly closing down such plants.

Other product design features have also affected tire demand. The small and much cheaper spare tire has cut the value of tires on new cars, and an all-season tread has reduced the interest in an extra set of snow tires. Indeed, tires with all-season treads increased from 17 percent of production in 1982 to 32 percent in 1985. Further improvements in tire construction may be expected from time to time. In fact, Goodyear estimates that more complete use of radial ply tires and other technical advances may further reduce the demand for replacement tires by eight percent during the last half of the 1980s.

## Who Buys How Many Tires

Recent trends in the sale of tires in the United States are shown in Tables 2–4 and 2–5. Replacement tires are especially important to the tire manufacturers, because the prices and profit margins on these are significantly higher than prices and profits on sales to automobile manufacturers for new cars. The size of the automobile companies gives them so much bargaining power that they pay only about half of the retail price. Whether the tire producers recover their costs on such sales depends upon how they allocate overhead. While replacement tire sales account for about 74 percent of domestic passenger car unit sales, the dollar amount is closer to 85 percent of the income from this type of tire.

Replacement tires reach the vehicle owner through a variety of channels. The volume is divided roughly as follows:

| | |
|---|---|
| Independent tire dealers | 55% |
| Department and chain stores | 20 |
| Company-owned stores | 10 |
| Service stations | 10 |
| Auto dealers and others | 5 |
| | 100% |

**TABLE 2–4**
**SHIPMENTS OF TIRES IN THE UNITED STATES (millions)**

| | Passenger Cars | Trucks & Buses | Tractors & Implements | Total |
|---|---|---|---|---|
| 1986 | 203 | 41 | N.A. | 246 |
| 1985 | 201 | 41 | 3 | 245 |
| 1984 | 202 | 41 | 4 | 246 |
| 1983 | 182 | 37 | 3 | 222 |
| 1982 | 167 | 34 | 3 | 204 |
| 1981 | 165 | 36 | 4 | 205 |
| 1980 | 146 | 31 | 4 | 181 |
| 1979 | 174 | 40 | 5 | 219 |
| 1978 | 193 | 43 | 5 | 241 |
| 1977 | 190 | 37 | 5 | 232 |
| 1976 | 177 | 33 | 3 | 214 |

**TABLE 2-5**
**TIRE SHIPMENTS, BY USE, 1985 (millions of units)**

|  | Passenger Cars | Trucks & Buses | Tractors & Implements | Total |
|---|---|---|---|---|
| Original equipment | 54.8 | 7.7 | 0.6 | 63.1 |
| Replacement | 141.5 | 32.1 | 2.4 | 175.9 |
| Total* | 200.9 | 41.1 | 3.2 | 245.2 |

*Totals include exports.

The department and chain store channel includes chains such as Sears Roebuck, Montgomery Ward, Atlas, K-Mart, Western Auto Supply, and Pep Boys. It's a very competitive market.

## The Eager Giants

A great deal of restructuring is occurring among the suppliers of tires in the United States. One important overall change is the recent reduction in total capacity. Twenty-six plants have been closed permanently in the last decade, and obsolete machinery has been removed from many of the remaining plants—especially in the shift to radial ply equipment already noted. The net effect is shown in Table 2–6. Currently, capacity is not much above what can be sold.

A related change has been the reduction in the number of independent tire producers. Many smaller firms have shut down or been absorbed by their larger competitors. Now only eight companies (including two European branches, viz., Michelin and Dunlop) make 95 percent of the tires produced in the United States, as indicated in Table 2–7.

Even this number of competitors is misleading because all but Goodyear serve only part of the market. Firestone, once a strong second in the industry, now

**TABLE 2-6**
**U.S. TIRE INDUSTRY CAPACITY (thousands of units daily)**

|  | Auto | Truck | Farm |
|---|---|---|---|
| 1985 | 653 | 144 | 18 |
| 1980 | 717 | 170 | 23 |
| 1975 | 848 | 149 | 23 |
| 1970 | 734 | 105 | 22 |
| 1965 | 576 | 75 | 20 |
| 1960 | 453 | 67 | 17 |

**TABLE 2–7**
**MARKET SHARES OF TIRE PRODUCTION IN THE UNITED STATES, 1986**

| | |
|---|---|
| Goodyear | 30% |
| Goodrich & Uniroyal | 21 |
| Firestone | 13 |
| Gencorp | 10 |
| Armstrong | 6 |
| Cooper | 6 |
| Michelin | 5 |
| Dunlop | 5 |
| Other | 4 |
| | 100% |

focuses on passenger cars and light trucks. Goodrich pulled out of the original equipment market, while Uniroyal concentrated on it. (The recent merging of the tire activities of these two corporations does recreate a second broad-line competitor.) General Tire (now Gencorp) appears to be withdrawing entirely, as does Dunlop. Cooper Tire survives in a closely defined niche, offering only replacement tires through independent dealers. To some extent, foreign companies are taking over where U.S. firms are leaving off, so the production capacity is not removed. Nevertheless, the trend toward fewer global products persists.

The purchase of a former Firestone truck tire plant in Nashville, Tennessee, by Bridgestone, the leading Japanese tire producer, signals a new player seeking a global position. Bridgestone already makes half of Japan's tires and is seeking to maintain its fast growth rate by expansion abroad. In the United States it has grabbed 10 percent of the truck tire business, but to date it is not a strong force in car tires.

A major change in the supply of tires for the U.S. replacement market is the rise in imports. Tires from Japan, Korea, Brazil, and other countries have cut the need for domestic production sharply, as the following data show:

| | *Imports' Share of Car* *Replacement Market* |
|---|---|
| 1985 | 23.2% |
| 1984 | 20.8 |
| 1983 | 17.0 |
| 1982 | 12.8 |
| 1975 | 7.6 |

Indeed, without imports, U.S. producers lack the capacity to fill domestic needs.

In spite of the reduction in capacity and in the number of suppliers, competition in the United States remains intense. A few companies succeed for a time in marketing a premium tire, but basically, tires have become a homogenous product and price differentials are very difficult to maintain.

## Narrow Margins

Several trends are squeezing the operating profits of U.S. tire companies. On the income side, prices appear to be sagging, as indicated by the following index numbers:

| | *Producer Price Index for Tires, January* | | |
|---|---|---|---|
| | 1987 | 1986 | 1985 |
| Radials, auto (1974=100) | 158.5 | 161.0 | 162.0 |
| Truck (1967=100) | 234.3 | 239.9 | 246.5 |

Meanwhile, hourly labor costs in the tire division of the rubber products industry are rising, as shown in Table 2–8.

The price of crude oil also affects tire costs. About 10 gallons are used to make an average-size radial ply tire, for synthetic rubber, carbon black, energy, etc. The future of crude oil prices is, of course, uncertain. Natural rubber, which is used for about half the rubber content of a tire, has recently been in adequate supply with prices firming. So labor and raw materials are moving upward in cost, while prices are softening.

The only way tire producers have lived with this squeeze is by improving productivity. Goodyear especially has sought increases in productivity. During the last decade, the company invested about $1.2 billion in automation—in addition to its $2 billion invested for conversion to radial ply facilities. Several outside financial analysts have questioned such a large investment in a declining industry; Goodyear's *operating* profit in tires and related transportation products compared to assets involved in that activity was 14.3 percent in 1984, 10.6 percent in 1985, and 6.3 percent in 1986. As a result of these outlays, however, Goodyear is now considered the most efficient U.S. producer, with a productivity per man-hour on a par with Japanese competitors. Incidentally, the president of the rubber workers' union supports this effort to increase productivity, but is being sharply criticized by some of his peers.

Several of Goodyear's U.S. competitors appear to be diversifying out of the tire business instead of making such a large investment in productivity. Their present return on tire-making assets typically is no better than Goodyear's.

**TABLE 2-8**
**HOURLY EARNINGS IN TIRE DIVISION OF RUBBER PRODUCTS INDUSTRY**

| | | | |
|---|---|---|---|
| 1985 | $13.21 | 1980 | $9.74 |
| 1984 | 12.94 | 1979 | 8.59 |
| 1983 | 12.35 | 1978 | 7.28 |
| 1982 | 11.66 | 1977 | 7.23 |
| 1981 | 11.05 | 1976 | 6.24 |

## Questions

1. Using the model for industry analysis presented in this chapter, prepare a forecast of the volume and profits in the U.S. tire industry during the 1990s.
2. What will be the critical factors for success in this segment of the total rubber industry?
3. What strategy do you recommend that Goodyear pursue with respect to tires?

# CHAPTER 3

## Assessing a Company's Competitive Strengths

Success comes from matching opportunity with capability. The industry analyses discussed in the preceding chapter may flag an array of such opportunities (as well as threats). The next part of the puzzle, then, is to examine the particular strengths and weaknesses of a company to grasp these opportunities.

For instance, Reed Shoe Company correctly forecast that low-cost production of its distinctive jogging shoes would be a key factor in maintaining its precarious position in this growing segment of the shoe business. Unfortunately, no one in the company had international business experience, and Reed lacked the capital to support foreign expansion. Thus, study of the company's supply position relative to competitors such as Nike signaled that the time to sell out had arrived.

### Framework for Company Analysis

As in the study of an industry, numerous facts about a company can be obtained. To help give meaning to these facts, and to aid in relating company data to industry data, the following framework is useful:

#### Position of Company in Its Industry

A. Market position of the company
  1. Relation of company sales to total industry and to leading competitors
  2. Relative appeal of company products and services
  3. Strength of the company in major markets
B. Supply position of the company
  1. Comparative access to resources
  2. Unique productivity advantages
  3. R & D strength
C. Special competitive considerations
  1. Relative financial strength
  2. Community and government relations
  3. Ability and values of company managers
D. Conclusions
  Comparative strengths and weaknesses of the company in terms of key success factors identified in analysis of industry outlook

Several refinements are important when using this framework. First, the significance of each heading in a specific situation depends on the technology and basis of competition in the industry and on the strategy pursued by the company. Thus, R & D capability is crucial in the fast-evolving personal computer field, but unimportant to a Paris restaurant. Similarly, access to low-cost raw materials (bauxite) is vital for a company producing virgin aluminum, but unimportant to firms producing secondary (recycled) aluminum. Although the weights for each topic may differ greatly, the underlying model does help to diagnose most company strengths and weaknesses.

Second, for strategic planning, we are particularly concerned about a company's strength *relative to its competitors*. Occasionally in a new venture there may be doubt whether the company can operate at all—perhaps the local farmers will refuse to pool their land in a cooperative. Usually, however, the issue is whether the company can perform as well or better than its competitors.

Finally, we must define carefully just who a relevant competitor is. We compete to obtain capital, for example, with quite different firms than we do to obtain customers for our goods and services. Likewise, a hospital's competitors for patients to fill up its beds are a different set than its competitors for nursing staff; there will be some—but not complete—overlap, and a hospital's relative standings in the two markets may differ considerably.

The relevant competition will also depend on a company's strategy, i.e., on what it wants to do. The local fuel dealer in Oshkosh cares little about who sells fuel in Madison, but if it becomes a wholesaler, then competitors in both cities are likely to be the same. Moreover, potential competition must be weighed. New firms may enter the business, substitute products may reduce customers, and separate industries may bid away resources. So when we weigh relative strengths and weaknesses, we should consider all the principal rivals for the resources and patronage that we would like to have.

With these qualifications in mind, the main headings and subheadings of the preceding framework can be a significant aid in putting facts about a company into a meaningful structure.

## Market Position of the Company

The survival of each enterprise depends, along with other essentials, upon providing goods or services that people want. Therefore, a critical part of the basis for company strategy is knowing how well, relative to competitors, those needs are being fulfilled.

## Relation of Company Sales to Total Industry and to Leading Competitors

The ups and downs of a total industry often obscure how well a specific company is being managed. A revealing way to screen out such external influences is to watch the company's sales as a percentage of those of the total industry and to observe the company's major competitors.

A dramatic example of loss of industry position is Univac, the computer subsidiary of Sperry Rand Corporation. Although its forebear was the leading pioneer in digital computers, Univac failed to capture the lion's share of the market. Here was a company very technically oriented. It was good at product development, but slow in exploiting commercially sound products. Its competitors, notably IBM, were more sensitive to customer needs and had stronger marketing organizations. As soon as the key to success embraced the market as well as the laboratory, Univac slipped.

Typically, a company's share of its target market is closely related to its profitability. The Strategic Planning Institute has found that for a wide range of businesses, higher market share is linked to higher profits. (See Figure 3–1.) This

**FIGURE 3–1.**
**RELATION OF MARKET SHARE TO PROFITABILITY**

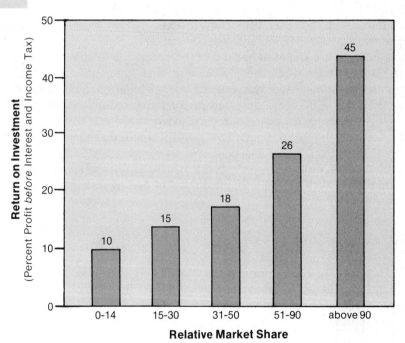

**Relative Market Share**
(Percentage of Company Sales to its Three Largest Competitors)

*Source:* Strategic Planning Institute.
This chart and later ones are based on confidential data covering the experience of over 1,200 highly diversified business-units. In its PIMS Program, the Institute makes very sophisticated statistical analyses of over 50 variables affecting profits and cash flow. Only a few of the simple relationships are shown on these charts, but the inferences are consistent with the more elaborate findings.

relationship probably reflects economies based on greater experience, economies of scale, and relative bargaining power. Clearly, the "little guy" must find a distinctive niche in order to prosper.

The capabilities of a company's competitors compared to that of the company is so important that relative market share should be studied company by company as well as by percentage of the total industry. Hospitals, banks, and even churches or professional athletic teams can use the market share concept. Measurement may be more difficult and profit may not be the goal, but the tie to viability is much the same.

## Relative Appeal of Company Products and Services

The market position of a company is strongly influenced by the quality and the distinctiveness of its products and services. The TV set that has unique engineering features, the motel that serves good food, the hospital equipment that is dependable and durable, or the airline with a good on-time record is the product that will improve the company's position in the market. The important characteristics from the *user's point of view* should be determined and the company's products appraised in terms of these characteristics. In this process it is necessary to distinguish between various price ranges, because the controlling characteristics may not be the same for, say, low-priced shoes as compared to high-priced shoes.

Sometimes the past success of a company is attributable to a single product, whereas future success in the industry must be built upon an *ability to develop new products*. For example, the Mead Johnson Company has enjoyed very large sales of its prepared baby cereal Pablum, but possible substitutes and changes in ideas regarding child feeding made this single product an inadequate base for maintenance of a leading position in the industry. The company, fully recognizing the danger, developed a wide line of baby foods and then hit upon another winner—Metrecal.

The importance of a full line of products depends on both customer buying habits and the appeal the company elects to stress. When buying men's shirts—or skis, for that matter—the customer expects to find a full range of sizes and would like an array of colors in each size. In contrast, the manager of a mutual fund or theater production may focus on providing the best single product that appeals to a particular segment of the market. In the medical field there is debate about whether doctors and clinics should be generalists or specialists.

## Strength of the Company in Major Markets

A company's position in its industry is also affected by its reputation in major markets. For instance, some motels cater to commercial travelers and business conferences, while competitors carefully nurture the tourist trade. Supplementary services and sales promotion help to focus on their target markets.

Often the reputation of a firm varies by area as well as by type of customer. This is illustrated by different brands of coffee. Many local brands are known in only one metropolitan area or perhaps one region; even the nationally advertised brands experience substantial differences in consumer acceptance in different sections of the country. In the same way, a particular manufacturer of farm machinery may have a strong *dealer organization* in the corn-belt states but have weak dealers and acceptance in the cotton states.

Reputation is an intangible thing including, in addition to being known, a prominence for giving service, for offering a good buy in terms of product and price, and for fair dealings. Many companies have a niche in the industry where they are outstanding. Harley Davidson motorcycles are an example, as indicated in Figure 3–2. For purposes of forecasting, the problem is to identify those areas or types of trade from which a company will obtain its business and then consider the prospects for such groups on the basis of the outlook for the general industry.

## Unique Strengths of Small Businesses

In the discussion of market position and other issues, most of our examples are large companies. This is normal practice because such companies are quickly recognized by readers and the behavior of such companies is often generally known. Nevertheless, most of the concepts described also apply to medium- and small-sized firms.

**FIGURE 3–2.**
**MARKET SHARES IN LARGE-SIZE MOTORCYCLE INDUSTRY**

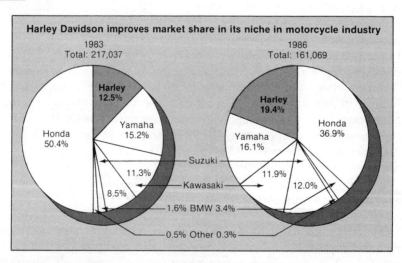

*Source:*  R. L. Polk, Detroit.

The market position of small firms is a good example. If the little firm plays a "me too" game and tries to do the same things as much bigger companies, the little one is sure to get bruised and may not survive. However, if the little firm can carve out a special niche with a distinct product or a distinct set of customers, then we have a big frog in a little puddle. And the evidence indicates that such distinctive performance pays off, even in small puddles.

The key is, first, to find a distinctive product or service, not offered by bigger firms, which a relatively small group of customers wants strongly enough to buy separately and probably to pay a somewhat higher price. An alternative is to focus on the needs of a particular group of customers who want custom-tailored service that is not available from large companies. Then, second, the small firm must concentrate on delivering the distinctive product or service within the bounds acceptable to the selected market segment.

Examples of successful small businesses are all around us. In products, for instance, the leading manufacturer of horseshoe nails enjoys a much wider profit margin than do big producers of building nails. Similarly, for years Crown Cork & Seal Company has focused on aerosol and beverage cans only; for these products, its engineering and delivery services are outstanding. And Crown Cork has been consistently more profitable than larger, more diversified container manufacturers.

In services, many localities are favored with a restaurant that continues to be crowded because it serves exceptionally good food. Among magazines, the leading special-interest publications have moved far ahead of the general-readership magazines (except for Number 1, *Reader's Digest*). And the Mayo Clinic attracts patients to Rochester, Minnesota, from all over the nation because of its outstanding diagnostic service.

So mere size is not the critical dimension; when analyzing market position, we learn more from observing whether a firm is at or near the top of a separable market segment.

## Supply Position of the Company

The position of a firm in its industry depends upon its ability to deal with supply factors as well as with demand or market factors. Its relative supply position influences the extent and the direction of company expansion and may be the key to survival itself.

## Comparative Access to Resources

### Materials

Ready and inexpensive access to materials is a major asset for companies using bulky products. The newsprint mills of Canada, for instance, now have a controlling advantage over their former competitors in Wisconsin, Michigan, and the New England states because the virgin timber in the latter areas has been cut off and logs—or pulp—must be transported long distances to the mills. In fact, most of the remaining mills in these areas have turned to specialty paper products to counteract the disadvantage of their location.

With improvements in air and specialized water transportation, the potential supply of many materials is becoming global. So a wary eye must be kept on future foreign sources when assessing a company's access to materials. For instance, copper, ball bearings, and computer chips may come from the East or the West. Even fresh-cut roses from Columbia, South America, can now be landed in Manhattan or Los Angeles at a lower cost than similar roses shipped from nearby greenhouses.

### Labor in the United States

Location with respect to labor is sometimes a definite advantage or disadvantage to a company. Minimum-wage legislation and union activity have greatly reduced geographic differentials in wage rates within the United States, so "cheap labor" is now obtainable only in foreign countries. Occasionally a company located in a rural area is at a disadvantage if expansion requires that skilled workers must be induced to move from the cities.

### Foreign Labor

Increasingly throughout the world, low-wage countries are seeking ways to provide employment for their rising populations. Clothing, electronic products such as radios and calculators, and many sorts of toys are examples of goods that are likely to come from halfway around the world.

Foreign wage rates alone are often misleading. A better measure is labor cost per unit, which takes into account labor efficiency, fringe benefits, and the like. Even low labor cost may be offset by poor quality or unreliable delivery, and tariff barriers, import quotas, and foreign exchange problems may also play a role in a company's situation. Nevertheless, in many industries—from shoes to autos—a company's ability to use foreign labor is a serious factor in costs relative to competitors.

### Proximity to Customers

In some industries, location close to markets is crucial. This is obvious for retail stores, for which buyer traffic may mean the difference between success and failure. Similarly, printing firms that wish to serve advertising agencies must locate nearby so as to provide the necessary speed in service. For heavy products like cement, shipping expense becomes a significant factor.

Industry analysis should indicate the significance or insignificance of a favorable location with respect to materials, labor, or markets. Of course, most services, in contrast to physical goods, are delivered directly from producers to users, so these have low inventory and shipping costs.

### Vertical Integration

Favorable access to resources and customers may arise from ownership or contractual ties as well as from physical location. A primary advantage sought in the vertical integration of ore mines and steel plants, and of oil wells, refineries, and filling stations, is an assured supply. In times of inflation, favorable costs also arise from vertical ties. Of course, in dynamic industries vertical ties can become an oppressive burden. So when analyzing the supply position of a company, its long-term commitments both "upstream" and "downstream" should be compared with those of its major competitors.

## Unique Productivity Advantages

Experience is a great teacher. The second time we perform a task it is easier than the first, the third time easier than the second, and so on. In fact, experience is so important for complex activities, that cost estimates and output schedules in the aircraft and space industries are adjusted for the number of times a particular product has been produced and The Boston Consulting Group has developed a whole theory of competitive behavior on the concept.

According to the *experience-curve* theory, the company with the most cumulative experience (a result of high market position) should have the lowest production costs. Personal learning plus opportunities to specialize and automate should lead to higher productivity. In practice, newcomers may catch up, especially when product designs are changed or new processing technology becomes available. A critical question is whether companies have made maximum use of the opportunities to lower cost that the experience curve provides.

In fact, some firms develop poor work habits instead of good ones, and these become entrenched in *work rules and social structure*. Then, becoming relatively efficient is an almost insurmountable task, as current difficulties in some steel plants, insurance offices, stockbrokerage houses, and hospitals clearly reveal. In contrast, a few firms have a strong tradition—like the Japanese—of persistently looking for ways to increase productivity.

A further consideration is that a company's facilities may become outmoded. The prime issue is whether the plant can make products suited to the trends in demand. To take an example from a service industry, high-ceilinged hotel rooms without air-conditioning no longer serve the lodging market satisfactorily. Bowling alleys as a form of entertainment are in a similar fix.

Often such *outmoded facilities* are doubly disadvantageous, because other companies are also likely to have excess equipment for the declining products;

therefore, profit margins tend to be narrow, especially in contrast to margins on the expanding products that may be in short supply.

*Flexibility* of equipment is often a factor in operating costs. For example, large jet planes such as the Boeing 747 are efficient for transatlantic and cross-continental flights, but they are expensive and hard to handle on short runs where traffic is lighter. Smaller, flexible planes cost more to operate per passenger mile than a 747 when the latter is fully loaded on a long flight, but they have decided advantages in fulfilling other needs. Again, the crucial point is having equipment suited to the market the company wants to serve.

## R & D Strength

If industry analysis indicates that research and development is a key success factor, then any company staking its future in that domain must have access to current technology. The need is well recognized in pharmaceuticals and electronics, but also is vital in some areas of agriculture, communications, energy, office equipment, and space, to name just a few examples.

Small companies cannot afford broad-ranging, basic research. However, even a tiny technically oriented firm may be a pioneer in a very specific application. Also, licensing is common practice in some industries, in which case an ability to qualify as a licensee is crucial.

As with access to resources and productivity, a company must assess its R &D strengths relative to competitors as a basis for its strategy.

## Special Competitive Considerations

In addition to market and supply factors, three further considerations throw light on the ability of an enterprise to grasp new opportunities, namely, financial strength, community and government relations, and the ability and values of company executives.

## Relative Financial Strength

Adequate capital is one of the necessary means of putting the plans of the business administrator into action. A company may enjoy a distinctive product, an unusually low cost, or some other advantage over its competitors; but virtually every type of expansion requires additional capital for inventory and accounts receivable if not also for fixed assets. Moreover, if a firm is to maintain its position, it must have sufficient financial strength to withstand depressions and aggressive drives by competitors for choice markets. Competition may force a company to expand the variety of products offered for sale, to establish district warehouses and local sales organizations, or to buy new equipment. All of these require capital.

The simplest way for a company to meet these capital requirements is from its own cash balances, which may be larger than necessary for day-to-day operations. Most concerns, however, do not carry large amounts of idle cash (or nonoperating assets readily convertible into cash, such as government securities), so financial strength is primarily a question of ability to borrow new capital or to secure it from stockholders. Ability to raise new capital will reflect not only past and probable future earnings, but also the existing debt structure and fixed charges of the company. So the entire financial structure of the company should be examined, particularly if there are likely to be major readjustments in industry operations.

## Community and Government Relations

Governments are formally required to treat everyone alike. Nevertheless, over time one company may have antagonized governmental officials while another firm has carefully developed good rapport. Also, representatives of a company may have learned governmental procedures and the particular issues which are sensitive. Friendships help, but even more significant is identification with a cause that is cherished by a block of voters (along the lines considered in the next chapter). The overall effect is that companies differ in their ability to work with governments.

Community relations are even more intangible. For a variety of reasons, a company may (or may not) be regarded as a "good citizen." Then, when special police protection, a zoning variance, or perhaps prompt resolution of a complaint is needed, opposition does not automatically arise. Most of the time, for most companies, good community and government relations lead simply to a permissive situation, but in crisis situations the very right to continue operating may be at stake.

## Ability and Values of Company Managers

The most important single factor influencing the position of a company in its industry is the ability of its executives. The executives of a business turn potential sales into actual sales, keep costs in line, and face the endless stream of new and unanticipated problems. Consider two well-publicized examples. In the early 1980s the "tough" conservative approach of the CEO of International Harvester brought the company to the brink of bankruptcy. During the same period, an aggressive, confident CEO of the Chrysler Corporation narrowly saved the number three U.S. auto producer from bankruptcy.

The qualities desired for executives are numerous and vary to some extent for different types of companies; for example, the manager of a specialty shop needs a sense of style, whereas the head of a hospital must have the ability to supervise a diverse collection of professional employees. Outstanding research capability or a willingness to take risks might be the key to success.

A related issue is whether entrenched executives are so committed to the existing company strategy that they will be unable to change. This sort of commitment clearly restricts the strategic options that can realistically be considered. Executives of competitors may likewise have strong commitments that shape their range of possible actions.

No single executive should be expected to have all the talents required, but within the management group there should be vision, creativeness, supervisory ability, human understanding, diligence, and other qualities essential to the planning, direction, and control of the enterprise. In fact, partly due to age and the personal motivations of people in central management posts, the capacities of company managements differ sharply.

In predicting the future of a business, it is also necessary to consider the extent to which success is dependent on a few individuals and the provision that has been made for a succession of capable leadership. This is crucial in the outlook for a small "one-person company."

## Company Capability to Adapt Strategically

### Readiness to Change

The framework just described helps to identify a company's strengths and weaknesses relative to its competitors. First, the market position of the company, then its comparative strengths as a supplier, and finally its power as a competitor should be carefully assessed. These are vital answers to the question, Where do we now stand?

Knowing "where we are at" aids in planning for the future. We can build on our strengths, and we can circumvent or buttress our weaknesses. Note, however, that the analysis of strengths and weaknesses is intended to be a snapshot—a picture as of a moment in time. Because of this balance-sheet character, it is inherently static. Our subsequent planning, then, tends to focus on moving from one fixed position to another fixed position. Such neat, clear-cut planning is basic to progress on many fronts.

Frequently, however, strategic change is more messy than making well-timed moves from position A to position B sounds. Uncertainty abounds—about how the external world will change, about our ability to execute plans, about countermoves by competitors for customers and resources. Much of the change is incremental—small steps to test the water, or delaying actions until forecasts become more reliable. And to deal with these less clear-cut situations, our analysis of company strengths and weaknesses needs to be supplemented.

Two supplements to the basic study of existing strengths and weaknesses are especially valuable: (1) strategic positioning, which is described in the next few pages, and (2) key actor analysis, which is the subject of the next chapter. By adding these two perspectives, a company can significantly increase its capability to deal with irrepressible changes.

## Strategic Positioning

Strategic positioning deals with acquiring at an early date a tangible or intangible asset which will later place the company in an advantageous position. A very simple example is buying extra land around an office or plant so that expansion at some indefinite future time will be relatively easy.

Developing intangible assets may be a significant form of strategic positioning. A small industrial-scale company, for instance, employed an electrical engineer several years before anyone knew just how his skills might be applied. Actually, it was a fortuitous move, because having such an engineer already familiar with company products enabled the company to move into electronic controls and weighing systems ahead of competitors.

Another example is U.S. firms establishing business relations with mainland Chinese enterprises. Sometimes the potential short-run trade is attractive, but more often the aim is to build a relationship that could be the foundation of large future transactions if and when foreign exchange and other factors become more favorable.

Three kinds of strategic positioning warrant attention.

### Defensive Positioning

The aim here is to avoid being squeezed by a powerful supplier, customer, or competitor. Petroleum companies, for example, may acquire leases on crude oil properties in their own country, primarily as protection against exorbitant demands such as OPEC imposed in the 1970s. Amax Aluminum retained leases on large Australian bauxite deposits partly as a protection against the large firms that were currently supplying its reduction plants. Similarly, one reason some companies do not utilize all their ability to borrow capital is to save some borrowing capacity for a "rainy day."

### Prepared Opportunism

This is a posture of preparedness—being ready to act if and when conditions are right, as in the China trade example cited above. Many banks and other financial institutions made moves of this sort in the early 1980s. Large New York banks established ties with banks in the midwest and far west. When legislation permitting national banking is passed, these ties may be converted into national networks. Insurance companies bought real estate brokerage firms, and so on. While some of these affiliations were converted into combined activities immediately, uncertainty about the future structure of the industry was so great that most affiliations simply remained as a readiness to act.

### Preemptive Positioning

I. C. MacMillan has defined this strategy as a move by a company "ahead of its adversaries which allows the company to secure an advantageous position from which it is difficult to be dislodged."[1] The folklore example is the rancher who buys up land that probably will be a necessary access to the primary water supply. Then, as more cattle are brought into the outlying regions, the rancher has an asset which must be included in development plans.

A modern parallel is the current scramble for cable TV franchises and for preferred network channels. At present, it is unclear whether an increase in available channels or other changes in technology will undermine the national networks. Also, the use of cable TV connections for interactive programs is uncertain. Nevertheless, several large companies are investing heavily to preempt positions in this form of mass communication.

The current value of any of these forms of positioning—defensive, prepared opportunism, or preemption—is difficult to place on a financial balance sheet. They are a type of "contingency" investment which defies the conventional ROI (return on investment) justification. And yet they might be vital to the future of the company.

We conclude that strategic positioning should be included in the assessment of the strengths and weaknesses of a company. Although many positioning moves may turn out to be of little value, for the execution of a particular strategy a few of these early actions may be crucial. Since other companies will be jockeying for position, we need to know, in addition to our current demand and supply position, how well poised we are relative to competitors to strike off in new directions.

## SUMMARY

Wise strategy calls for an adroit mating of opportunities and threats in an industry with the strengths and weaknesses of a particular company. We have focused here on the second part of this coupling, with an emphasis on strengths compared with other firms which might want the same customers or the same resources.

A useful framework for this company evaluation is given by the following questions: (1) How strong is our market position? Are we big or small in the total picture? Are our products distinctive? Do we have unusual strength with particular customers or in special localities? (2) Do we have advantages in supplying the

---

[1] I. C. MacMillan, "Preemptive Strategies" (Working paper, Strategy Research Center, Graduate School of Business, Columbia University, 1983.)

market? For instance, favorable location and access to materials? Is our productivity high and our cost low? Does our R & D strength enable us to pioneer in new products or new technology? (3) Are we a strong competitor—due to unusual financial strength, favorable government relations, or exceptionally well-qualified and dedicated executives?

Answers to these questions will provide basic information about the kind of strategy that is likely to succeed. However, to provide a stronger future orientation, and to suggest strengths and weaknesses in striking out in new directions, the company's readiness to make new moves should also be assessed. In this connection, three kinds of strategic positioning are important: defensive possibilities, prepared opportunism, and preemptive moves.

A further input to strategy formulation is predicting how key actors in the industry will respond to a company's initiatives. That is the subject of the next chapter.

## Questions for Class Discussion

1. "It's the deal of a lifetime," said Jack Welch, chairman of the Board and chief executive officer of the General Electric Company (G.E.), when he completed the swap of his firm's consumer electronics business for the medical technology business and $800 million in cash from the French electronics giant, Thomson S.A. The consumer electronics business that G.E. traded consisted of television receiver manufacturing and selling operation, which was a year-old amalgamation of RCA's and G.E.'s television businesses and which had contributed $3.5 billion in sales and almost nothing in profits to G.E.'s profit-and-loss statement for that year.

   The purchase by G.E. of the RCA Corporation for about $6.3 billion dollars, the largest acquisition in U.S. history by a firm that was not an oil company, had resulted in a merger of the RCA and G.E. television receiver and RCA color television picture tube businesses, had given G.E. about a 27 percent share of the U.S. market, and had then made G.E. into the market leader. This conformed nicely to G.E.'s policy, as emphasized often by Mr. Welch, that G.E. products had to be first or second in sales volume in their industries. Any smaller share made the product a prime candidate for divestiture. (See Figure 3–1.) G.E.'s three largest competitors and their approximate U.S. market share at the time were Zenith (17 percent), Phillips N.V. (6 percent), and Sony (6 percent).

   Security analysts said at the time of the merger that G.E. would continue to market consumer electronics products like TV sets and video cassette recorders because the valuable G.E. brand recognition would benefit more profitable consumer lines such as light bulbs and major appliances.

Despite the slightly better than break-even performance of the combined G.E. and RCA lines, Mr. Welch had promised to allow the consumer electronics division a three-year period to turn the business around. A similar turnaround effort for the major appliance division, headquartered in Louisville, Kentucky, had paid off handsomely. Major appliances are now a major money producer for G.E. Strenuous cost-cutting, product development, and marketing efforts were under way when Welch suddenly sold the consumer electronics division to Thomson S.A., in exchange for cash and Thomson's medical equipment business.

Before the deal, G.E. had been the world leader in the medical equipment business, with worldwide sales of $1.6 billion. The Thomson swap added yearly sales of $770 million to this. G.E. added the cash to its existing $3 billion war chest. After the deal, Thomson vaulted into second place in the worldwide consumer electronics industry with sales of about $7.8 billion as compared to the revenues of about $8.9 billion of Phillips N.V. of the Netherlands and about $6.9 billion of Japan's Matsushita Electric Industrial Company.

(a) Did television sets marketed under the RCA and G.E. trademarks seem to you a strength of the General Electric Company? (b) Did the separation into G.E.'s low end and RCA's high end of the industry provide niches for success of the combined venture? (c) Has the French firm, Thomson S.A., added to its strength in the consumer electronics industry? (d) What is happening now in U.S. sales of consumer electronics?

2. Select a company in which you would like to get a permanent job, and prepare a statement of the company's competitive position using the framework described in this chapter. Of course, your statement cannot be complete, but for the thin spots indicate where you believe missing data are very important and where missing data are not significant to the major picture.

3. Company analysis outlined in this chapter focused on profit-making enterprises. To test the applicability of the same approach to non-profit enterprises, use the outline to analyze the outlook for your university or college.

4. At one stage in its history, Franklin National Bank was the largest and fastest growing commercial bank on Long Island (a part of New York state on which Brooklyn and the John F. Kennedy Airport are located). Filled with confidence, the bank then moved to the center of the midtown financial district of New York City and announced that it planned to join the ranks of the large multinational banks located in the city. In other words, Franklin National Bank changed from being a big frog in a small pond to a smallish frog in a big pond. (a) What, if anything, did this shift in location and strategy do to Franklin National Bank's relative competitive strength? Give examples. (b) What did the shift do to Franklin National Bank's outlook for growth and profits? (c) Why do you think Franklin National Bank made the shift?

5. Suppose that you have decided to open a new car wash in your city. Your alternatives in regard to production methods range from a hand operation with only hoses, brushes, and rags as equipment to a fully automatic tunnel that can be run by an individual who collects money as the cars enter. (a) Would you invest in the capital-intensive process or the labor-intensive process? (b) Does your answer to (a) imply a general view that new operations in your city in any line of business should be as capital intensive (or labor intensive) as technology will permit? (c) What other competitive strengths do you believe will be crucial to the success of your new venture?

6 Suppose that your aunt has been president of Early Learning Associates for several years. (Early Learning Associates is a prestigious distributor of equipment and materials to kindergartens, nursery schools, and day-care centers. Through its professional selection of products and its 15 field representatives, each with 200 key school accounts, Early Learning stresses the educational benefits of its products. Competing jobbers typically are mere order takers and quite willing to supply items that merely entertain children.) Your aunt agrees with industry experts that (a) government support for day-care centers and Head Start programs will diminish during the next five years, but (b) the number of families with preschool children and both parents working (or single-parent homes with that parent working) will increase.

   How might Early Learning Associates position itself in anticipation of these trends? What are its chief options? Which do you recommend?

7. As of the time this book goes to press, a cure for AIDS (acquired immune deficiency syndrome) has not been found and the probability that many more people will be affected by the disease is high. Suppose that you are advising the CEO of a prominent hospital in your state about the strategy the hospital should follow in preparing to deal with AIDS. The CEO asks you, "How should we position ourselves now to be in a strong position when the epidemic expands?" Give your reply. (Note: This hospital, like many others, is experiencing a reduction in its occupancy rate, i.e., patient days per month. Excess bed capacity is common throughout the state.)

8. (a) Using the framework presented in this chapter, describe the position and relative strengths and weaknesses of an independent (nonchain) restaurant which you frequently patronize. (b) How do you explain this restaurant's ability to survive in face of competition from McDonald's? (c) Will McDonald's and other chains eventually take over the restaurant business?

9. Select two automobile dealerships with which you are familiar that carry different lines of cars from each other. Use as much of the framework of this chapter as you believe is relevant to describe the competitive practice of each dealership. (You may have to resort to indirect sources of data—for example, number of salespeople as an indication of sales volume, or interviews with one-time customers. Go bravely ahead. The purpose of this exercise is not exactness; rather, it is to show how the various points raised in this chapter can be used to assess the competitive position of a specific firm.)

10. Have you heard of Hush Puppies shoes? What about Reebok? Hush Puppies are manufactured and sold by Wolverine World Wide, Inc., and, years ago, created the casual-shoe market. Reebok International Ltd. has run away with the casual-shoe market recently. Its sales in the U.S. jumped from $13 million in 1983 to about $1 billion in 1987. Reebok is hurdling sales barriers by purchasing the Rockport Co., which sold $100 million worth of walking shoes in 1986, and John A. Frye Shoe Co., the bootmaker. Some say that Reebok's Achilles' heel is performance. Its reputation was made in soft leather shoes, but these, when used for rigorous turning, stopping, and twisting, may well fall apart. But Reebok is also expanding into the sales of sportswear and into non-U.S. markets, which recently have been 5 percent of its revenues.

Contrast this with Hush Puppies, the 30-year-old brand that now accounts for less than a third of the revenues of Wolverine World Wide, but is still the company's largest-selling and best-known brand. In 1987 and 1988, Wolverine is preparing its biggest marketing and selling effort in years in an attempt to move the brand away from having an image of being a shoe that would be bought by someone like my grandmother or maiden aunt.

(a) Do Hush Puppies have a particular strength that could be built upon? (b) Given what you know of the casual-shoe market, what can Wolverine World Wide do in its marketing effort to prove that it has put its best foot forward in styling, manufacturing, and marketing? Can its pet brand both fetch younger customers and take a bite out of imports?

## CASE

### 3 G. Heileman Brewing Company[2]

In the bitter beer wars of the past decade, the G. Heileman Brewing Company should not have had a prayer. Tiny beermakers of its kind were supposed to be guzzled up by the brewing giants who were blitzing the marketplace. But a Heileman ad campaign asserts that their beer comes from "God's Country"—and whether or not Wisconsin deserves that billing, the brewer clearly has something special on its side. Instead of giving up the ghost, Heileman has faced off against the majors, engineering a number of acquisitions that have made it the fastest growing firm in the industry.

---

[2]This case was prepared by Beth Sorg under the supervision of Milton Leontiades at Rutgers University.

Tucked away in La Crosse, Wisconsin, the company has been quietly edging into the big leagues of the American brewing industry. By selectively buying struggling brands at bargain-basement prices, by building a huge and faithful network of wholesalers, and by carefully developing regional marketing campaigns to support its extensive array of products, the company has gone in just 23 years from $18 million to $1.3 billion in sales as of 1983. In the process, it has risen from number 31 among the nation's brewers to number 4.

Along the way, it has not sacrificed financial stability. Most of the company's acquisitions have been small enough to come out of earnings, not borrowings, and Heileman's profit margins have not suffered. Of the largest public corporations in the United States, Heileman's total return of 31.3 percent to investors for the 10 years ending December 31, 1982, ranked as the seventh best performance among the nation's top 500 companies. Additionally, *Forbes Magazine*'s "36th Annual Report on American Industry" rated Heileman's performance number one in every five-year performance category as compared to both brewing and beverage industry participants (see Tables 3–1 and 3–2). The company has consistently been rated number one in both profitability and growth vis-à-vis its competitors within the brewing industry. Competitors have been steadily decreasing, however. In 1968 there were 163 breweries; by 1983 the number had shrunk to 89.

## Management

Founded in 1853 by German immigrant Gottlieb Heileman, the brewery bubbled along for more than a century on its founder's motto: "We don't aim to make the most beer, only the best." But things have changed somewhat since Russell Cleary, the company's chief executive officer, took over. In the industry, Cleary was seen as an outsider, and everything about Heileman seemed to invite disaster. Several of its breweries were old enough to be museums of used equipment. It had an unwieldly patchwork of wholesalers, few being exclusive, and it offered customers a bewildering array of labels. Against a competitor's three or four brands, Heileman, the original market segmenter, might be represented in one area with as many as seven. In the days before Miller's success made market segmentation orthodox, the collective wisdom insisted that you could have any beer you want provided it was lager. Yet Heileman risked confusing customers with miscellaneous malt liquors and many different labels in one market.

But Cleary had a strategy that turned Heileman's apparent disadvantages into advantages. The additional markets protected it against being squeezed out by the nationals' advertising blitzes. Cleary masterminded increasingly larger acquisitions, and the company grew enough to receive the discounts on bulk purchases of grain, aluminum, and glass usually reserved for national brewers.

A company that gives .22-caliber working-replica Thompson submachine guns as sales awards instead of plaques, Heileman has pursued an aggressive tone over the past 13 years set by Messrs. Cleary and Pedace, the brewer's vice president for marketing. Among other strengths, Pedace cites Heileman's lack of bu-

**TABLE 3-1.**
**YARDSTICKS OF MANAGEMENT PERFORMANCE: THE BEVERAGE INDUSTRY**

| Company | Profitability | | | | | | | Growth | | | |
|---|---|---|---|---|---|---|---|---|---|---|---|
| | Return on Equity | | | Return on Total Capital | | | Net Profit Margin | Sales | | Earnings Per Share | |
| | 5-Yr. Avg. | 5-Yr. Rank | Latest 12 mos. | 5-Yr. Avg. | 5-Yr. Rank | Latest 12 mos. | | 5-Yr. Avg. | 5-Yr. Rank | 5-Yr. Avg. | 5-Yr. Rank |
| G. Heileman Brewing | 31.7% | 1 | 28.7% | 21.9% | 1 | 14.5% | 5.1% | 29.2% | 1 | 29.4% | 1 |
| General Cinema | 29.2 | 2 | 54.3 | 15.8 | 5 | 22.0 | 10.1 | 14.2 | 8 | 24.6 | 4 |
| Allegheny Beverage | 29.0 | 3 | 35.3 | 14.0 | 6 | 10.2 | 2.1 | 27.5 | 3 | 23.9 | 5 |
| MEI | 28.5 | 4 | 27.1 | 17.2 | 4 | 15.4 | 6.3 | 27.8 | 2 | 27.5 | 2 |
| Phillip Morris[1] | 23.7 | 5 | 23.7 | 13.1 | 8 | 12.4 | 6.8 | 18.6 | 5 | 18.2 | 8 |
| Brown-Forman Dist. | 22.9 | 6 | 21.6 | 17.8 | 3 | 18.5 | 10.3 | 15.0 | 7 | 25.6 | 3 |
| Coca-Cola | 22.2 | 7 | 19.9 | 20.2 | 2 | 16.4 | 8.2 | 12.8 | 9 | 9.9 | 9 |
| Anheuser-Busch Cos. | 20.0 | 8 | 18.7 | 11.7 | 9 | 11.2 | 5.9 | 18.7 | 4 | 21.7 | 6 |
| Pepsi Co. | 18.3 | 9 | 14.7 | 13.2 | 7 | 10.4 | 3.2 | 17.3 | 6 | 8.7 | 10 |
| Wometco Enterprises | 15.7 | 10 | 14.3 | 10.6 | 10 | 8.9 | 3.4 | 16.0 | 11 | 10.9 | 11 |
| Royal Crown Cos. | 14.3 | 11 | 14.1 | 10.6 | 10 | 10.7 | 3.4 | 8.6 | 11 | 4.6 | 11 |
| Seagram | 13.5 | 12 | 8.7 | 10.0 | 11 | 7.3 | 9.6 | 4.1 | 13 | 21.6 | 7 |
| National Distillers | 9.8 | 13 | 4.4 | 8.1 | 13 | 4.5 | 2.3 | 6.3 | 12 | -2.4 | 13 |
| Adolph Coors | 9.0 | 14 | 10.8 | 8.2 | 12 | 9.6 | 8.0 | 10.2 | 10 | 0.9 | 12 |
| Pabst | — | NR[2] | — | — | NR[2] | — | — | — | — | — | NR[2] |

[1]Classified as a tobacco company.
[2]Not ranked.

Source: *Forbes*, January 2, 1984.

**TABLE 3–2.**
**MARKET SHARES BY MAJOR BREWERS (millions of barrels)**

|                  | 1978 | 1979 | 1980 | 1981 | 1982 | 1983E |
|------------------|------|------|------|------|------|-------|
| Anheuser-Busch   |      |      |      |      |      |       |
| (bbls)           | 41.6 | 46.2 | 50.2 | 54.5 | 59.1 | 60.5  |
| (%)              | 25.3 | 27.1 | 28.4 | 30.4 | 33.0 | 33.5  |
| Miller           |      |      |      |      |      |       |
| (bbls)           | 31.3 | 35.8 | 37.2 | 40.3 | 39.3 | 37.7  |
| (%)              | 19.0 | 21.0 | 21.1 | 22.5 | 22.0 | 20.9  |
| Stroh[a]         |      |      |      |      |      |       |
| (bbls)           | 29.8 | 26.4 | 24.8 | 23.4 | 22.9 | 24.2  |
| (%)              | 18.1 | 15.5 | 14.1 | 13.1 | 12.8 | 13.4  |
| Heileman[b]      |      |      |      |      |      |       |
| (bbls)           | 10.5 | 11.3 | 13.3 | 14.0 | 14.5 | 17.5  |
| (%)              | 6.4  | 6.6  | 7.5  | 7.8  | 8.1  | 9.7   |
| Coors            |      |      |      |      |      |       |
| (bbls)           | 12.6 | 12.9 | 13.8 | 13.3 | 11.9 | 13.6  |
| (%)              | 7.7  | 7.6  | 7.8  | 7.4  | 6.6  | 7.5   |
| Other            |      |      |      |      |      |       |
| (bbls)           | 38.8 | 38.1 | 37.2 | 33.7 | 31.3 | 27.0  |
| (%)              | 23.6 | 22.3 | 21.1 | 18.8 | 17.5 | 15.0  |

[a]Schaeffer, Schlitz, and Stroh (now merged) are combined for all years.
[b]Includes Carling National for all periods except first three months of 1979.

*Source:* Lehman Brothers Kuhn Loeb Research, as reprinted in *Beverage Industry,* January 1984.

reaucracy as a factor in its success. He says, "We have the ability to move quickly, from the management perspective. Cleary can make immediate decisions if necessary, and he is always available for consultation. I can get answers to an emergency within two minutes."

Some observers call Cleary and Pedace the best tactical team in the business for responding to short-term opportunity, yet note that there is no depth of management at headquarters. Pedace acknowledges that the company is lean on management people, but not to the point where it hurts Heileman.

There are three division managers who are responsible for sales and merchandising of all the brands in each of Heileman's three geographical divisions. The East and West divisions can handle about 500 wholesalers and the Central division about twice as many.

Division managers report to John Pedace, who explains, "A multiregional marketer has to be flexible and act quickly. The geographic concept accomplishes this more effectively than the national one-brand-per-manager concept." Both Cleary and Pedace note that the three divisions are always subject to subdivision or additions, should market conditions warrant.

## Merger History and Strategy

During the late sixties, Heileman acquired Wiedemann of Kentucky and the popular Milwaukee brand, Blatz. By the end of the seventies, the company had bought four more brewing companies (Jacob Schmidt, Sterling, Carling National, and Rainier) and was clearly attempting to go national. Acquisitions during the eighties include Lone Star Brewing (San Antonio, Texas) and the Blitz-Weinhard Company (Portland, Oregon).[3]

Acquisitions have been the springboard for Heileman's well-managed sales growth, which averaged 29.2 percent over the last five years. Cleary calculates that buying breweries with modern facilities, rather than building from scratch, has allowed the company to expand production and distribution at a cost of about $4 a barrel instead of $50. What's more, each acquisition has given Heileman a new base from which to make and sell its beers, all the while broadening its product line with no development costs. Heileman now sells more than 30 products, ranging from super-premium brands like Special Export to popular regional brews like Schmidt's and Blatz. The firm refuses to tinker with an already successful beer; instead, it employs management resources and aggressive price-cutting to parlay homegrown identity into wider sales. "Locally there's a lot of pride in a beer," says Cleary, "and we try not to change that."

The key to Heileman's competitiveness is the low cost of its growth. Major acquisitions since 1967 have given it added capacity at bargain prices. Heileman doesn't hesitate to close a newly acquired brewery that is unprofitable and produce the brand at one of its other plants, thereby capitalizing on both brand loyalty and the impressive economies of scale. From the closed plants, Heileman strips usable equipment to outfit its other breweries. The company also buys surplus equipment from breweries being liquidated, often at fire-sale prices. Aided by $52.7 million in capital expenditures between 1970 and 1979 to modernize the plants, each Heileman production worker can now turn out 6,000 barrels a year (Busch workers produce 7,000 each). And labor costs are lower in the small towns where Heileman operates. In 1984, the estimated typical plant age of Heileman's breweries was four years, in contrast to seven years for those of Anheuser-Busch. (A completely modernized plant in the original building is considered new.)

## Production and Distribution Network

With the completion of the Pabst acquisition, Heileman is now positioned to competitively service all of the U.S. beer markets without freight disadvantage.

---

[3]In 1981, Heileman was unsuccessful in acquiring Schlitz, principally because of opposition posed by the Justice Department.

Until recently, Heileman was restricted in its expansion efforts because it lacked substantial capacity across the country. Now, however, eleven breweries are situated in strategic shipping points to penetrate virtually the whole country—except for the Northeast, where the company is light of capacity.

No one brewery produces all Heileman brands. Rather, each plant brews those brands that are popular to its area. With its expansive network of breweries, especially those recently acquired, the company has positioned itself to execute major expansion efforts in the South, where its beer sales are only 2 percent of the regional total. By brewing its beer in Georgia instead of such distant cities as Baltimore or Evanston, and by shipping it at high costs to the South, Heileman will be able to cut costs, if necessary, to increase market share. This also applies to the company's expansion into the West, another market being eyed by this aggressive brewer.

Each acquisition has brought Heileman a new group of wholesalers with additional marketing territory and clout. These recruits have provided new outlets for the company's established labels, while the old dealers got to sell the new brands in their territories.

Managing the largest force of wholesalers in the business (2,400 distributors) creates headaches that national brewers with fewer brands and more exclusive distributorships don't have to be bothered with. Heileman has bothered because its brands often don't generate enough sales volume for exclusive distribution. For instance, even in Minneapolis and St. Paul, it deals with three sets of competing wholesalers, each handling one brand. "This isn't the routine textbook method of selling beer," admits Cleary. "But we've fine-tuned the arrangement so that each brand receives more attention this way."

According to Pedace, the vice president for marketing, the company's relationship to wholesalers is its key to success. He says, "We've gotten bigger, but we keep our contact personal and on a partnership level. It's not big business thinking, but it works for Heileman."

## Product Line

Heileman's has the most extensive product line in the industry. Its principal brands are Old Style, Blatz, Rainier, Schmidt, Wiedemann, Black Label, Red/White/and Blue, Lone Star, Colt .45, and Mickey's Malt Liquor, which, together with super-premium Special Export and Henry Weinhard's, account for 80 percent of total company beer sales.

Heileman's product line is heavily weighted (about 40 percent of production) to popular-priced brews. This is the segment of the beer industry where price competition is the most intense. The national rollout of Miller's Meister Brau, for example, will heat up the competition in Heileman's backyard, the Midwest, where it has 19 percent of the market, and down south where Heileman is in the midst of a major expansion. To protect its market share, Heileman is going to have to keep the ad/promotional dollars flowing, while holding the line on price hikes.

Old Style, the company's closest thing to a national premium brand, accounts for about 39 percent of its beer volume. However, "It's a myth that you have to have one national brand," says Cleary. "Our regional concept has proven that." But some wholesalers in the South believe that Heileman will have to introduce a strong brand such as Old Style to build a major presence. Selling lesser-known regional brands isn't very popular with wholesalers, since the only way to sell them is to price them low, and that gives wholesalers low margins.

## Advertising and Promotion

A penny-pinching determination to stretch its dollar extends to Heileman's advertising. The company spends mostly on expensive single-city TV advertising and substantially less than what Anheuser-Busch spends. Heileman promotes only its top labels and varies the campaigns little year by year. Its ads celebrate the beer, not the consumer, thereby avoiding the high costs of hiring celebrity spokesmen. Recent comparative industry TV expenditures appear in Table 3.

The commercials reflect Heileman's country shrewdness. They either pitch into the national audience with comparative advertising and taste tests—techniques long deplored as underhanded in the tradition-bound beer business—or build brand mystique by romanticizing a brand's regionalism. The company promotes its Old Style beer with the slogan, "Brewed in God's Country." But all the fuss about its "kraeusening," the traditional lengthy European way of making beer, also digs slyly at competitors' shortcut manufacturing methods.

Heileman uses the pinpoint ad approach and stresses quality. The company treats each market differently, with a lineup of brands and a pricing policy specifically fashioned for it. But its promotion funds are limited. This constraint has forced Heileman to expand brands gradually, state by state, and may pose a serious problem if the company goes head to head with the industry's big spenders, Anheuser-Busch and Miller.

## Financial Condition

During the forthcoming year, Heileman intends to launch the most aggressive and comprehensive expansion program in its history, with emphasis on the Southeast and Southwest. Also, the company expects to repay the remaining $45 million of the $120 million borrowed to finance the acquisition of the Pabst/ Olympia brewing capacity.

The financial condition of Heileman is indicated in Tables 3–4, 3–5, and 3–6.

**TABLE 3-3.**
**FIRST-HALF TV AD EXPENDITURES AMONG BREWERS**

| | '82 Network TV ($000) | '83 Network TV ($000) | '82 Spot TV ($000) | '83 Spot TV ($000) | '82 Total TV ($000) | '83 Total TV ($000) | Total %Change from '82 |
|---|---|---|---|---|---|---|---|
| Anheuser-Busch | 43,824.3 | 49,314.5 | 19,608.7 | 20,565.5 | 63,433.0 | 69,880.0 | + 10% |
| Miller | 26,827.1 | 40,924.6 | 13,185.1 | 12,214.9 | 40,012.2 | 53,139.5 | + 32% |
| Stroh Brewery | 3,200.0 | 16,701.4 | 10,593.5 | 6,107.5 | 13,793.5 | 22,808.9 | + 66% |
| G. Heileman | 6,085.0 | 8,776.4 | 8,581.0 | 10,408.9 | 14,666.0 | 19,185.3 | + 31% |
| Coors | 3,286.1 | 2,478.8 | 5,855.7 | 8,727.3 | 9,141.8 | 11,206.1 | + 23% |
| Pabst | 873.8 | 6,789.8 | 4,327.9 | 3,992.4 | 5,201.7 | 10,791.2 | +107% |
| Christian Schmidt | — | 692.4 | 775.2 | 2,065.8 | 775.2 | 2,758.2 | +256% |
| Senessee | — | — | 2,817.8 | 2,725.0 | 2,817.8 | 2,725.0 | – 3% |

*Source:* Television Bureau of Advertising, New York, NY, from analysis of *Broadcast Advertisers Reports; Beverage World,* December 1983, p. 45.

**TABLE 3–4.**
**CONSOLIDATED STATEMENTS OF INCOME (For the Years Ended December 31, 1983, 1982, and 1981) (in thousands, except earnings per share)**

|  | 1983 | 1982 | 1981 |
|---|---|---|---|
| SALES | $1,325,632 | $1,000,567 | $931,940 |
| Less excise taxes | 174,667 | 129,726 | 124,899 |
|  | $1,150,965 | $ 870,841 | $807,041 |
| COSTS AND EXPENSES: |  |  |  |
| Cost of goods sold | $ 822,100 | $ 624,169 | $590,061 |
| Marketing, general and administrative | 220,599 | 163,768 | 140,872 |
| Income from operations | $ 108,266 | $ 82,904 | $ 76,108 |
| OTHER INCOME (EXPENSES): |  |  |  |
| Investment income | 4,350 | 8,355 | 5,811 |
| Interest expense | (9,821) | (4,219) | (2,819) |
| Other net | 3,540 | 1,266 | (529) |
| Income before income taxes | $ 106,335 | $ 88,306 | $ 78,571 |
| PROVISION FOR INCOME TAXES | 49,366 | 42,652 | 38,341 |
| NET INCOME | $ 56,969 | $ 45,654 | $ 40,230 |
| EARNINGS PER SHARE | $ 2.15 | $ 1.73 | $ 1.53 |

*Source: 1983 Annual Report.*

## Questions

1. What are Heileman's competitive advantages?
2. What are the major threats in the brewing industry environment?
3. Why has Heileman been successful by employing strategies that other industry exports say spell doom?
4. Can Heileman possibly repay the incurred debt and retain its expansion strategy?
5. Some companies have diversified out of the brewing industry, trying to capture other markets using name recognition and market savvy. Would you suggest this for Heileman? Why or why not?

**TABLE 3–5.**
**CONSOLIDATED BALANCE SHEETS**
**(For the Years Ended December 31, 1983 and 1982) (in thousands)**

|  | *1983* | *1982* |
|---|---|---|
| **ASSETS** | | |
| **CURRENT ASSETS:** | | |
| Cash and temporary investments | $ 21,258 | $ 30,264 |
| Receivables | 37,603 | 48,343 |
| Inventories | 112,947 | 98,064 |
| Prepaid expenses | 6,514 | 4,988 |
| TOTAL CURRENT ASSETS | $178,322 | $181,659 |
| **PROPERTIES, at cost:** | | |
| Land and buildings | $119,538 | $114,037 |
| Machinery and equipment | 298,796 | 278,276 |
| Accumulated depreciation | (93,485) | (84,878) |
| TOTAL PLANT AND EQUIPMENT | $324,849 | $307,435 |
| Returnable containers | 15,402 | 16,832 |
| TOTAL PROPERTIES | $340,251 | $324,267 |
| OTHER ASSETS | 11,728 | 12,731 |
|  | $530,301 | $518,657 |
| **LIABILITIES** | | |
| **CURRENT LIABILITIES:** | | |
| Current maturities of long-term debt | $ 2,631 | $ 4,004 |
| Accounts payable | 84,125 | 57,049 |
| Accrued expenses | 39,298 | 47,577 |
| Reserve for income taxes | 11,307 | 5,926 |
| TOTAL CURRENT LIABILITIES | $137,361 | $114,556 |
| **LONG-TERM DEBT,** | | |
| less current maturities | 95,719 | 170,530 |
| **DEFERRED CREDITS:** | | |
| Income taxes | 50,605 | 31,587 |
| Pension obligations | 7,301 | 7,911 |
| **SHAREHOLDERS' INVESTMENT:** | | |
| Common stock, $1 par, 28,000,000 shares authorized, 26,837,052 and 13,368,286 shares issued in 1983 and 1982, respectively | $ 26,837 | $ 13,368 |
| Paid-in surplus | 368 | 423 |
| Reinvested earnings | 213,631 | 180,913 |
| Treasury shares, at cost, 291,243 and 129,895 shares at December 31, 1983 and 1982, respectively | (1,521) | (631) |
| TOTAL SHAREHOLDERS' INVESTMENT | $239,315 | $194,073 |
| TOTAL LIABILITIES & EQUITY | $530,301 | $518,657 |

*Source: 1983 Annual Report.*

**TABLE 3-6.**
**CONSOLIDATED STATEMENTS OF CHANGES IN FINANCIAL POSITION**
**(For the Years Ended December 31, 1983, 1982, and 1981) (in thousands)**

|  | 1983 | 1982 | 1981 |
|---|---|---|---|
| WORKING CAPITAL PROVIDED BY: |  |  |  |
| Operations— |  |  |  |
| Net Income | $ 56,969 | $ 45,654 | $40,230 |
| Depreciation and amortization | 23,494 | 18,716 | 13,158 |
| Income tax deferrals and benefits | 20,104 | 15,913 | 16,172 |
| Working capital provided from operations | $100,567 | $ 80,283 | $69,560 |
| Increase in long-term debt | 1,589 | 120,744 | 10,758 |
| Stock options exercised | 209 | 74 | 811 |
| TOTAL WORKING CAPITAL PROVIDED | $102,365 | $201,101 | $ 81,129 |
| WORKING CAPITAL USED FOR: |  |  |  |
| Reduction of long-term debt | $ 77,792 | $ 4,009 | $ 2,639 |
| Plant & equip. additions, net | 33,757 | 21,528 | 37,493 |
| Payment of cash dividends | 11,936 | 10,584 | 9,164 |
| Additions to returnable containers | 2,276 | 3,819 | 2,325 |
| Acquisitions | 2,746 | 158,220 | 975 |
| TOTAL WORKING CAPITAL USED | $128,507 | $198,160 | $52,596 |
| (Decrease) increase in working capital | $(26,142) | $ 2,941 | $28,533 |
| CHANGES IN WORKING CAPITAL: |  |  |  |
| Increase (decrease) in current assets— |  |  |  |
| Cash & temporary investments | $ (9,006) | $ (15,596) | $13,469 |
| Receivables | (10,740) | 25,341 | 650 |
| Inventories | 14,883 | 30,189 | (2,534) |
| Prepaid expenses | 1,526 | 84 | 263 |
|  | $ (3,337) | $ 40,018 | $11,848 |
| Decrease (increase) in current liabilities— |  |  |  |
| Current maturities of long-term debt | $ 1,373 | $ (1,276) | $ (1,084) |
| Accounts payable | (27,076) | (12,392) | 16,499 |
| Accrued expenses | 8,279 | (20,600) | (3,558) |
| Reserve for income taxes | (5,381) | (2,809) | 4,828 |
|  | $ (22,805) | $ (37,077) | $16,685 |
| (DECREASE) INCREASE IN WORKING CAPITAL | $ (26,142) | $ 2,941 | $28,533 |

*Source: 1983 Annual Report.*

# CHAPTER 4

# Predicting Interplay Among Competitors and Other Key Actors

In the preceding two chapters, we treated external dynamics as unresponsive forces to which a firm should adjust. A lot of change and uncertainty might prevail, but the presumption was that our actions would not alter the environment. This chapter adds another dimension, looking at the way key people are likely to respond to fresh actions which we or other persons initiate. To at least a limited degree, each of us tries to reshape our world. So we need to predict responses and counterresponses to initiatives we or our peers thrust into the system. The wisdom of any strategic move depends in part on the resistance and retaliation or the cooperation which that move is likely to evoke.

After explaining the way a variety of organizations, or "stake-holders," become involved in strategic moves, the chapter deals with two issues: How can we predict the likely response of such key actors to our strategic moves? And, in light of those predicted responses, what kind of alignments among key actors should we try to establish?

## Who Pushes Whom

### Passive Environment

Our pioneer heritage creates a bias about strategy. In the traditional Western scenario, the physical obstacles were great, but customers liked the new services provided, employees welcomed new and better jobs, and supporting organizations such as railroads cooperated. Despite a few hostile Indians in the background and occasional feuds between the cattle-ranchers and settlers, the environment was basically friendly and benevolent. Our task in that setting would have been to provide the vision, mobilize resources, and share in the hard systematic work of turning opportunity into achievement.

Note that in this view a series of well-planned moves would have overcome the obstacles, and the response of the people affected was preset. Occasionally such a relatively simple situation exists, but most strategy today runs into other people's strategies and must deal with their countermoves.

## Hostile Environment

In a "hostile" environment, several key groups will resist the moves called for in our strategy. In fact, they probably will be aggressively pursuing their own objectives, which may include our fitting into *their* plans. How much direct conflict arises will depend, of course, on the strategy we elect. Perhaps some arrangement can be found which will be at least acceptable to two or more groups. But negotiations will be necessary, and in that process our strategy may have to be modified. Everyone is pushing; our aim in this game is to position ourselves so that we are not pushed way off course—or, if we are lucky and smart, we occasionally get pulled along toward our goal by others' efforts (like riding the surf).

The scramble for production of wide-body, medium-range jet airplanes at the beginning of the 1980s illustrates this kind of process. Airbus Industries, a joint French-German venture, was several years ahead in the market with its 240-seat model. Boeing countered with a proposed new line of planes (B757, B767) focused on a similar market segment. The physical characteristics of both the Airbus and Boeing lines were sharply competitive: lower fuel consumption, less noise, wide body, a medium range, and around 200-passenger size. But much more than plane design was involved in making sales in the important international market. Foreign airlines need the financial backing of their local governments, and that backing could be secured only by recognizing other concerns of the respective governments. To help deal with local employment and nationalism, Boeing negotiated subcontracts for components in Italy and Japan, and for Rolls-Royce engines in England. Airbus, via the French government, courted Spain with support for entry into the Common Market and India with broad trade benefits. Clearly the groups vitally concerned extended beyond the plane producers and airline customers, and an array of interlocking strategies on issues far removed from plane production were involved.

Lease financing of computers is a simpler example of a hostile environment, as we are using the term. For several years financial firms thought lease financing was a splendid investment. The firm with capital to invest located a company that had just made a large purchase of computers. The financial firm bought the computers from the user and leased them back again. In this arrangement the user in effect borrowed capital at favorable terms and usually obtained tax benefits; the lessor found an attractive investment. Soon, however, more people became involved. Smaller manufacturers of computers and peripheral equipment relied on (and often had formal agreements with) leasing firms to help make sales. But these manufacturers also relied on local service companies to maintain their equipment, and this service was vital to keep the equipment running and the lease viable. Then, users occasionally went bankrupt or their needs changed, so part of the equipment had to be resold; this often brought in a fifth party. The business was complicated by rapid technological change, and by a practice of manufacturers such as Digital Equipment Corporation to lower prices on older models.

Consequently, to be successful in lease financing of computers, a financial firm has to develop formal or informal understandings with equipment manufacturers, service companies, technical consultants, and resale agents, in addition to its direct "customers," the equipment users. Each of these "actors" has a particular environment and a particular strategy, and the terms on which cooperation will be continued have to be negotiated.

In both of these examples, wide-bodied jets and computer leasing, strategy goes beyond selecting an attractive domain. Key parts of the environment are busily pushing their own objectives, and our strategy must be linked to theirs. Directly or indirectly, we try to manipulate this environment. In the process our strategy may be modified, especially because the various actions and reactions of other actors are hard to predict.

In a "hostile" environment, strategy must be adroit and adaptive.

## Range of Options

Relationships with key actors vary widely. We may elect to fight with a competitor head-on, as Avis does with Hertz. Or the competition may be mixed with cooperation, even to the point where competition is publicly denied, as is the usual relation among universities and among hospitals.

Sometimes a desired result is so expensive or so risky that no one firm wants to seek it alone. So a joint venture focused on a particular outcome is created. The pipeline bringing crude oil from the north slope of Alaska is such a venture. Similarly, the sale of Conrail common stock was underwritten by a group of investment banks which compete on many other fronts.

In many other relationships mutual dependence is pervasive and continuing. Professional football and the TV networks, for instance, have a durable marriage; clearly, the football teams could not operate in their present manner without the broadcast income. Automobile manufacturers and their dealer organizations are likewise dependent on each other.

Coalitions and alliances may be multifaceted. For example, a company in the specialized business of insuring real estate titles is valuable to—and also dependent on the goodwill of—mortgage lenders, surveyors, real estate brokers, and, in some areas, local lawyers who make the title search. In this arena, exchange of favors and mutual trust is vital to success. Similarly, in the growing field of solid-waste disposal, strategy must recognize the interaction between equipment manufacturers (and their maintenance organizations), trash collectors, environmental control agencies, bond underwriters, and users of the output, such as steam for utility generators.

Society is increasingly complex and interdependent in terms of technology, trade, regulation, and geographic scope. External alignments must fit these trends and change with them. And as just illustrated, there are a variety of choices in the way the relationships will be structured.

## Analysis of Key Actors

The success and, indeed, survival of every business depends upon either obtaining the support or neutralizing the attacks of key actors in its environment. We live in a highly interdependent world. And to steer a course through this everchanging structure, we need a keen insight into the behavior of those actors who affect our fate.

## Who Must Be Considered?

Several different types of organization may have a strong impact on the success of a strategic move, as is shown in Figure 4–1. Too often strategic planners become so concerned with the response of one or two powerful players, that they overlook others whose cooperation is also essential. Each type warrants at least consideration.

*Resource suppliers and customers* interact directly with the business. Included are employees, material suppliers, bankers, stockholders, governmental agencies, and other community groups. Because all these contributors are more or less dependent on the company, they are often called *stakeholders.* An exchange relationship typically exists—a trading of inducements for inputs; so for actors in these groups, we are concerned with both what we give up and what we get in return.

Of course, as indicated in Figure 4–2, each stakeholder will have its own array of suppliers and customers. We are only one part of the network. The stakeholder

**FIGURE 4-1.**
**PARTICIPANTS IN STRATEGIC INTERACTIONS**

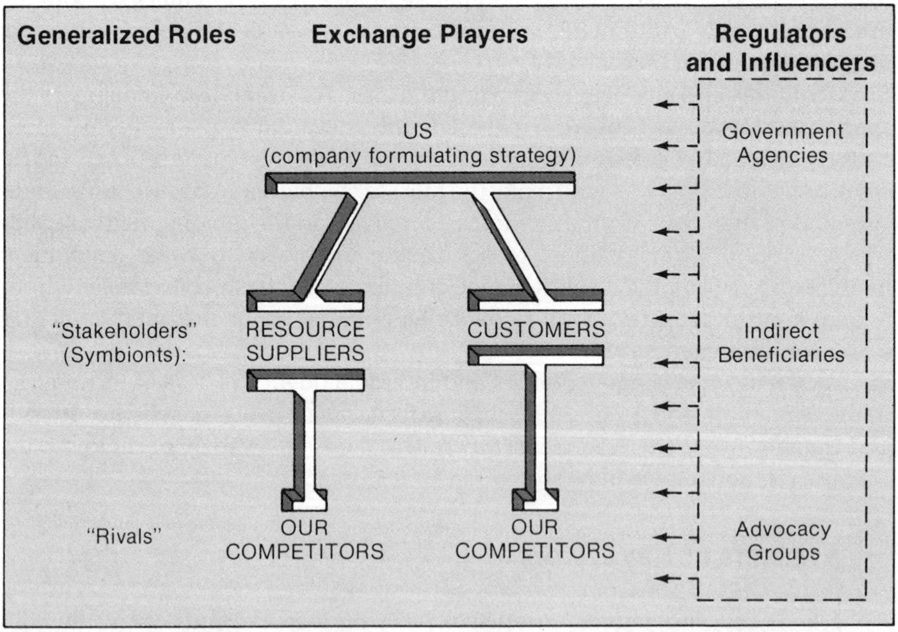

| Generalized Roles | Exchange Players | Regulators and Influencers |
|---|---|---|
| | US (company formulating strategy) | Government Agencies |
| "Stakeholders" (Symbionts): | RESOURCE SUPPLIERS / CUSTOMERS | Indirect Beneficiaries |
| "Rivals" | OUR COMPETITORS / OUR COMPETITORS | Advocacy Groups |

**FIGURE 4–2.**
**STAKEHOLDER ANALYSIS**

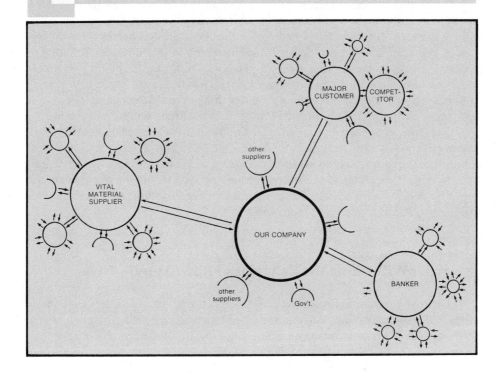

is trading on many fronts, just as we are doing. Consequently, to anticipate the response to our inducements, we should understand the stakeholder's relationships with its other resource suppliers and customers.

*Competitors* are also important—competitors for *resources* and competitors for *customers*. But note that, unlike our relations with stakeholders, we rarely deal directly with competitors. Rather, we focus on wooing stakeholders. We try to offer inducements that will be more attractive than those offered by our rival(s) by (1) improving our package and/or (2) undercutting what our rival offers. Since our rival is playing the same game, it is important to predict how the rival will respond to our efforts to attract a continuing, growing flow of orders or resources. The rival might upset our best laid plans.

*Government regulators* and *interest group representatives* are a third set of potential key actors. Virtually all industries—food, drugs, banking, agriculture, health care, horse racing; the list could go on endlessly—are now regulated in some respects. To open a metal refinery in New Jersey now requires approval of 17 different agencies. Not infrequently, the constraints apply to past as well as future actions. Of course, assistance may also be provided; unprecedented moves, especially, are apt to need government endorsement.

In addition, pressure groups may want a company to withdraw from South Africa, or not want a utility company to open an atomic energy plant. For a manager, such groups often seem to be unreasoning as well as unreasonable. Skill is needed to know when and how to deal with them.

As a practical matter, only *key* actors in the above groups warrant close analysis. A key actor is a stakeholder or competitor who in relation to us has a lot of *power*—a customer who buys over 25 percent of our output, the only available supplier of fuel for our plant, a competitor who has the capability of hiring away our engineering staff, or a regulatory agency that approves the quality of our new products. Sometimes likely future entrants into the arena will be key actors.

For most purposes we can treat an entire company—a supplier, a customer, or a competitor—as a single key actor. As in the legal concept of a corporation, we assume that the company is an independent being with a mind of its own. Occasionally in critical situations we go a step further and look inside the company at the specific persons who are key actors within that organization. But normally, it is company actions that are our main concern.

## What Will Guide the Behavior of Key Actors?

Because we want to predict what key actors are likely to do if left alone, how they will respond to our initiatives, and often how we can modify their behavior, it behooves us to know what makes them tick. How do they normally behave, and what might cause them to change?

### Goals, Values, and Beliefs

Each key actor is motivated by a set of goals or aspirations with respect to such characteristics as its size, type of business, place in the industry, status, profitability, and the like. Efforts to achieve these goals will be conditioned by its willingness to take risks, its loyalty to friends, the importance it attaches to service to the nation, and a variety of other values. Also, beliefs about the way the monetary system works, the future of communism, new technology, the reliability of first-line workers, and many other matters guide and restrain decisions of that actor. Because these goals, values, and beliefs influence strongly what the actor will do, we should learn all we can about this mind set.

### Patterns of Behavior

Like any of us, a key actor operates in a specific socioeconomic system and has a going enterprise with its particular resources and established relationships with external groups. (We should know what these are.) Inevitably there will be *patterns of behavior*—normal responses to normal pressures. This established flow gives us a base for predicting future behavior. To understand it, we should do our best to look at the world as the key actor sees it.

### Capability Profile

Just as we appraise our own relative strengths and weaknesses in estimating our own outlook, so too should we size up the strengths and weaknesses of each key actor. Such a "capability profile" of our competitors is especially valuable. It will tell us what is *possible* for the key actor to do and where its limitations lie.

### Future Pressures

For these actors, what *new pressures and opportunities* (e.g., shifts in their markets, cost changes, new technology) are likely to arise, and how are the actors likely to react? In particular, what will be absorbing most of their attention? What internal or external resource limitations will they confront? What commitments which restrict their options are they likely to make? What are their chief risks? What could upset their plans?

Experience indicates that a surprising amount of information about any organization operating in the public sphere can be assembled by systematic observation. Speeches, press releases, published data, announced plans, positions taken on controversial issues give a broad picture when regularly pulled together and analyzed. And many kinds of alignments with key actors provide personal contacts which are an additional source of data. More subtle is assessing the personalities of important executives and the values they cherish. But even here, insights can be picked up both directly and indirectly.

Such a key actor assessment serves several purposes. (1) The predicted behavior indicates what the actor is likely to try to impose on other actors—including us. (2) From the assessment, events or actions which will appeal to the actor can be surmised, as can weaknesses and vulnerabilities. These conclusions can be very useful in negotiating a desired alignment with that actor. (3) More specifically, the likely reaction of the actor to particular strategic moves that we might initiate can be predicted.

## What Is the Relative Power of Key Actors?

In addition to evaluating which key actors should be considered in a specific setting and how they are likely to behave, a manager must assess how much power each actor wields. In the present context, power is the ability of key actors to modify the conduct of others and, on the other hand, their ability to prevent someone else from modifying their conduct. Obviously, relative power will affect which actor can pursue a strategy with the least concession to others.

In relationships between business organizations, power is based largely on an *ability to restrict the flow of desired inputs on attractive terms.* Thus, if OPEC can withhold needed crude oil it has a lot of power over petroleum refineries, and if a bank can call in necessary loans it has power over the borrower. To simplify the discussion, we will consider a large customer withholding an order or a governmental agency withholding approval as other examples of restriction of a desired input.

When we start analyzing power relationships, we soon see that there are degrees of power, costs of exercising power, and all sorts of countervailing powers. For example, the degree of power I have over you depends on the number of good *alternative* sources you can turn to for the input I am providing. The fewer and less attractive the alternatives you have, the greater is my power. So one consideration in designing strategy is its effect on the number of alternatives which will remain open to you and to me. For instance, you may be a large and prestigious customer, but I will hesitate to sell you a third of my output if there are few ways to replace this volume in the event you threaten to withdraw.

Of course, the other side of the coin is that I have power over you, if *you* lack alternative sources of supply. Or, if through the help of my friends, the teamsters, I can delay your use of alternative sources, the impact is similar. Coalitions gain strength when, directly or indirectly, their membership can narrow the number of options various actors have.

The kind of power we are discussing is *potential*; only rarely is it actually exercised. In fact, most people are reluctant to use their power for several reasons: the person being pressured may call up countervailing power and will start to develop new alternatives (coal or solar energy, for instance, as alternatives to crude oil); or future friendship and trust will be lost; or a reputation for harsh dealings may spoil relationships with other suppliers. On the other hand, total reluctance to use power can undercut the influence of a person, who will soon be regarded as a "paper tiger." Consequently, in assessing power we have to consider willingness to use it as well as capability.

In summary, the analytical approach just outlined gives a basis for setting up external alignments. First, key actors are identified—the external organizations or individuals whose continuing cooperation is vital to our strategic moves. Second, for each key actor, an assessment is made of his or her motivations, strengths and weaknesses, probable future behavior, and likely response to our actions. And third, the relative power of each key actor to pursue a particular course is estimated. This analysis provides insights about the present and probable future behavior of the human forces in our environment, the dynamic elements from which a realistic interaction strategy must be forged.

## Choice of Alignments

As when a nation designs its international strategy, a look first at the simpler one-to-one relationships shows the varying colored pieces that must be fitted into the overall mosaic.

## One-to-One Relationships with Stakeholders

A business-unit's relations with its diverse resource suppliers and customers are sure to take different forms. In fact, they range from close cooperation to sharp conflict. The matrix shown in Figure 4–3 suggests a way to deal with this array.

**FIGURE 4–3.**
**AN APPROACH TO ONE-TO-ONE RELATIONSHIPS (with a key supplier or customer)**

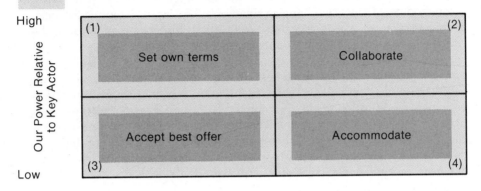

Note: The matrix is not intended to show the entire array of options for dealing with competitors. When to fight, stall, ignore, or defend is a study in itself, However, the kind of key actor analysis already recommended does provide essential information for competitive strategy and tactics.

### When Cooperation Is Likely To Pay Off

On one axis of the matrix, we show the benefits to us of cooperating with a specific key actor. Our interests may be highly interdependent, as between Pratt & Whitney and Boeing in designing engines for the new wide-bodied jets; or, at the other extreme, the interest may be too small to warrant more than routine treatment.

The other axis reflects relative power—our ability to impose our will on the other actor compared with that actor's capacity to make us conform to his or her will. Availability of alternatives and backup resources are the usual sources of such power. Sears, Roebuck and a small South Carolina manufacturer of dungarees are a classical example of the range on this scale.

The descriptions in the quadrants merely suggest the kind of relationship with a key supplier or customer that we can readily achieve under the different conditions. Of course, each actor will view the situation from a unique perspective and may prefer a course of action different from ours. So some negotiation and testing of power may be necessary.

When the benefits of working together predominate (the right-hand side of the matrix), cooperative alignments are called for. The more dynamic and uncertain the environment, the more attractive will be joint efforts with financiers, equipment suppliers, customers, regulatory agencies, and so on. The electronics and computer industries grew rapidly partly because collaboration has been the prevailing relationship between suppliers and users. In contrast, there is little agreement on joint action for dealings with terrorists.

Relative power obviously affects the kind of joint action it is wise to seek. Two comparatively strong actors—for instance, Texas Instruments and GM—approaching computerization of automobiles can work as roughly equal partners. However, if one firm is weak relative to the other, it will probably have to accommodate—fit into the changing situation as best it can, accepting the dictates of the stronger actor as constraints while trying to develop some capabilities which will be attractive to the dominant partner.

While these two considerations, relative power and the potential benefits of cooperation, provide insight into desirable one-to-one alignments, other factors deserve careful attention as well. For example, are the stakes high or low? If low, perhaps a modification of the traditional relationship does not warrant the expense. Also, legislation may prohibit certain kinds of joint effort. Or, past experience with either fighting or collaborating may set the stage for future alignments. Because all such factors are likely to vary from actor to actor, the optimum path to pursue in each relationship calls for particular attention.

### Use of Supplier Analysis

A specific case will illustrate how the type of analysis just outlined clearly shaped the strategy of one company, Ethicon Sutures, at a critical stage in its development. Ethicon manufactures surgical sutures for stitching-up operations ranging from delicate eye repair to leg amputations. For years, surgeons threaded sutures through the eye of the needle used. (The needles, of course, vary greatly in size and shape.) Then a new kind of needle was invented that could be crimped at the factory onto the end of a piece of suture. This arrangement saved the trouble of threading the needle, but much more important, it reduced the hole that was pierced to draw the suture through the tissue.

Ethicon adopted a strategy of featuring the new needle-suture combination, each encased in a sterile container. But it ran into difficulty obtaining needles. Its primary needle supplier dealt chiefly in textile needles; surgical needles were merely a sideline. So when Ethicon asked this supplier to devise a technology to make the new type of needle, the supplier expressed reluctance and insisted on large volumes of each size and shape. Moreover, to increase volume, the supplier reserved the right to sell needles to other suture companies. A second supplier, also focusing on textile needles, was even less interested; and a third, much smaller manufacturer lacked capital to tool up and also lacked the quality control so important for the surgical market.

In terms of the matrix, the primary supplier had substantial power over Ethicon but did not see much benefit in close collaboration, so its relations with Ethicon fell into the first quadrant. Ethicon was in a weak bargaining position, yet the outcome of negotiations was vital to its new strategy. Further analysis of the R & D activity of the primary supplier indicated that this company intended to move away from the needle business. So Ethicon predicted that long-run prospects were poor for getting the relationship into quadrant 4, let alone quadrant 2.

Consequently, Ethicon decided it could not risk staying so dependent on an uninterested supplier. It first explored a joint venture with the smaller company to make one or two sizes of the new needle, but soon worked out an arrangement to acquire a stockholder position in the company. That enabled Ethicon to establish a collaborative relation with the company—quadrant 2. Several years were needed to develop the capability of this company to make the various kinds of needles with the necessary quality. And, as Ethicon cut back on purchases of traditional needles, its old suppliers became even less interested in maintaining prompt delivery and quality. All this slowed Ethicon's growth and delayed pushing its new product across the total market. But in the end Ethicon escaped from its dependent and therefore weak position.

## Degrees of Collaboration

Economic theory and much of the business literature is preoccupied with competition. We are conditioned to think in terms of zero-sum games. A broader view of society, however, highlights the mechanisms by which people cooperate. The miracle of modern civilization is the way specialized outputs are combined, traded, and combined again to generate sophisticated services and goods. So when we talk of collaboration as one form of external alignment, we are dealing with a fundamental phenomenon.

Collaboration between key actors varies in degree.

1.  *Informal mutual aid* is the most common. You help me as a neighborly act; later I probably return the favor. Sociologist Peter Blau observes that this sort of cooperation permeates social relations; it differs from economic exchanges in the unspecified nature of the return help, and it requires a high amount of trust that mutually supportive actions will be continued.[1] This is the foundation of good will with employees, suppliers, customers, bankers, and a host of other points in the environment.

2.  *Formal agreements* covering the scope and nature of cooperation become necessary when advance commitments are large and when many individuals must have a consistent understanding about the relationship.

3.  *Joint ventures* break out a particular area for intense collaborative activity and provide for a pooling of knowledge and resources related to that activity. The joint venture may be a temporary consortium for a large project, such as the construction of a dam, or it may be a corporation with indefinite life.

---

[1]See Peter M. Blau, *Exchange and Power in Social Life* (New York: John Wiley & Sons, 1964).

4. *Mergers* carry collaboration to the extreme, where separate identity is sacrificed for the benefits of central direction of the combined activities.[2]

Many other variations are possible. Nevertheless, these four degrees of collaboration clearly indicate the profound impact that external alignments can have on the process of strategy formulation.

Collaboration implies some sharing of decision making. For instance, when Aloha Airlines decides to collaborate with hotels along the Kona coast of Hawaii to promote tourism, each of the organizations will have to adjust prices, schedules, and the like in order to present a coordinated package. And under accommodation, the adjustment of initial plans is likely to be even greater. In other words, strategic planning involves a dynamic give-and-take in which more than our own interests must be considered.

Of course, managers of a business-unit may choose to limit the extent of collaboration. Crown Cork & Seal, for instance, as a point of strategy, rarely installs can-making equipment in customers' plants—as do its leading competitors—because it wishes to retain greater flexibility. This successful company builds strong informal ties to its suppliers and customers, but minimizes formal agreements.

The alignment with each key actor is a separate, unique relationship. The approach to shaping these relations outlined thus far stresses a one-to-one analysis because each key actor is important to us and each presents a distinct set of factors and opportunities. Nevertheless, a *collective view* of all of a company's external alignments is also desirable.

A company develops a reputation for aggressiveness, for fair dealings, for consistency, and the like, so the way one actor is treated raises expectations in other dealings. For example, in its early history, Sears, Roebuck & Co. had a reputation for squeezing its suppliers once they became highly dependent on Sears's purchase orders. Later, Sears adopted a strategy assuring its efficient suppliers that they could earn reasonable profits; to carry out this strategy, close collaboration in product design and production scheduling is often undertaken. Not every one of Sears's thousands of suppliers agrees with the application, but the policy is clear: it does not use its power for short-run benefits, but rather for building a reputation as an attractive customer.

It is entirely possible to be ruthless in some spheres and cooperative in others—say, purchasing and labor relations, respectively—but some public rationalization of such behavior is desirable in order to create an aura of reliability, and even integrity.

---

[2] An economist, Oliver E. Williamson, has argued in *Markets and Hierarchies* (New York: The Free Press, 1975) that merged operations are more effective than competitive markets for handling exchange when mutual trust is vital. Mutual trust is necessary, he says, when uncertainty is high and key actors are few (two features of a hostile environment we listed at the opening of this chapter).

The combined set of alignments must also be weighed in terms of the total demands on resources. Few business-units have the personnel and capital to support several aggressive fights at the same time. In fact, even simultaneously maintaining close collaboration in several different areas may create severe problems of internal coordination. So, while the very essence of strategy deals with change, it is often advisable to ration or stagger the volatility.

## Coalitions

The careful analysis of each key actor recommended early in this chapter provides the underlying data base upon which the various relationships are built. That same bank of data may suggest desirable alliances or coalitions. A coalition is an agreement among at least three actors on joint action; often some of the actors have only indirect relationships with each other.

### Circumstances Leading to Coalitions

Often a business-unit discovers that by itself it cannot bring about the changes it desires. It lacks the necessary power. To reach its objectives, it rallies allies. In practice, this use of allies in coalitions is much more common than generally realized.

Quite diverse organizations may form a coalition around a common cause. For example, the "gun lobby" which opposes restrictions on private ownership and use of guns is supported by strange bedfellows: hunters, people who want guns to protect their homes, criminals, and firms with a commercial interest in the sale of guns and ammunition. Acting separately, they would have limited impact on Congress, but their united strength has been remarkably potent.

In the gun lobby example, each participant has a direct concern about the outcome. A variation is found in the support of tariff barriers. Here, trading of support is common—I'll support your protection if you'll support mine. Such mutual helping of friends is found in all sorts of business situations, from the sale of consulting services to "professional courtesy" among doctors. We are not suggesting that participants in such coalitions are cavalier about giving their support, although some may be; considerable effort may be devoted to deserving the support. Rather, the point is that coalitions are necessary to achieve the desired impact.

As already noted, the allies may embrace people who are only indirectly involved. Thus, in the finance company example cited at the beginning of this chapter, equipment manufacturers, service agencies, and resale brokers are all included in the coalition. All are required to make the purchase and lease-back practice a viable business, and each actor has to adopt a strategy regarding the coalitions to be joined.

Basically, when coalitions are formed, one or more business-units recognize that they cannot passively wait until the people with whom they have direct dealings are all set to act. Instead, they actively sponsor a whole chain of events by several different agencies. Consider a grain dealer wishing to sell feed to catfish raisers. Taking a cue from the way frying chickens are now raised and marketed by the millions, the grain dealer has to interest farmers in mass production of catfish in artificial lakes. This is appealing because catfish are very efficient converters of grain feed into meat. But to market the output, local "factories" are necessary to clean, cut, package, and freeze the meat. Refrigerated trucks must take the frozen fish to wholesale distribution points. And a marketing company has to sell the product either to "fish and chips" and other restaurants or to a slowly emerging retail-store market. These are the main actors, although the cooperation of zoologists, government inspectors, and others is also essential.

The way such a new industry is developed and the successful entrepreneurs establish themselves is through a coalition. Perhaps one enterprise will undertake two or more steps, but complete vertical integration is unlikely. So someone has to appreciate what conditions are necessary to attract collaborators into each step, and then induce related actors to adjust their activities in a way that will create these conditions. The leading and profitable firms in this new business will be those who have mastered the art of forming and guiding coalitions.

### Coalition in the Health Field

Coalitions may be vital in all sorts of settings. For example, an old hospital located in the downtown section of a typical city faced a dismal outlook. Its leading doctors and full-paying patients were moving to the suburbs, a proud history carried with it outmoded facilities, and Medicaid patients could not provide or attract resources for rebuilding. The bold new strategy was to become a teaching hospital focusing on specialties; this would attract a high-quality staff, and full-paying patients would be sent for special treatment on referral from suburban hospitals. However, a wide array of allies was needed. The state medical authorities had to bow to local political pressure for a teaching hospital in that part of the state. The Veterans Administration had to locate one of its new health centers on an adjacent site, providing an additional volume of use of the specialty capabilities. The city had to clear land for new buildings and help finance a closed (safe) parking garage. The trustees had to raise additional funds for upgrading the plant. And the hospital complex had to be a significant part of a broad plan for revitalizing the downtown section of the city.

Throughout several years of planning and development, the critical job of the hospital administrators was to keep all the contributing elements in back of the plan. This proved to be predominantly a political task. Alternative suggestions were made frequently, usually with sponsorship from competing locations. To meet these challenges, some modifications in the original strategy were negotiated. A continuing promotional effort has been necessary to sustain commitment to the venture at national, state, and local levels. Withdrawal of support at any one of these levels would probably kill the plan.

Coalitions may be necessary for survival, as the preceding examples indicate. We suggest that they be approached as elaborations of the simpler direct alignments every enterprise must cultivate. A coalition network is indeed more complicated since more actors are involved and inducements to cooperate may come from third parties, but the analysis of the motivations and options of each key actor is still the starting point.

## SUMMARY

Predicting the behavior of key actors is an important supplement to judgment about the industry and company outlook recommended in the previous chapters. The broader forecasts about the setting in which company action will take place are indeed essential; but those forecasts pass over the more specific help or hindrance which can be expected from other people who are also active in that same setting. A forecast of likely moves of at least the key actors should be added to our total assessment.

Especially useful is a prediction of the responses and counterresponses of key actors to our own initiatives. The business environment is not inert and passive. Instead, many firms are each pushing their own programs, and these firms may welcome or oppose what we try to do. The ensuing negotiations may then modify previous drives. A whole array of alignments with stakeholders and competitors will be developed. Obviously, we should try to anticipate how this dynamic give-and-take process will work out.

Such a careful analysis of our competitors, our major suppliers, and our major customers will provide valuable input into the decision making of central management. It probably will influence the design of strategy and the choice of policy.

An approach for predicting the responses of key actors has been outlined in this chapter. First comes careful analysis—leading to capability profiles—of key actors: *who* must be considered, *what* motivates each one, what is the *relative power* of each. Then, with this background, the likely alignments are predicted. Among the possible arrangements which should be considered are (1) simple one-to-one relationships, (2) varying degrees of collaboration where joint action appears feasible, and (3) coalitions.

The next chapter will discuss how these forecasts, along with those from Chapters 2 and 3, are used to design a strategy for a business-unit. Design of the more focused strategic programs for functional departments also utilizes key actor analyses. (See Part 2.) Note again that strategy formulation does not follow a simple sequence. Instead, it is iterative. Forecasts suggest possible strategies, analysis of these strategies calls for further forecasts, these new forecasts point to other alternatives, and so on. This recycling is especially true of key actor analysis, because we are specifically concerned with the way competitors and stakeholders are likely to respond to various strategic moves that we are contemplating. The recommended approach continues to be useful throughout. But the first application rarely will provide all the estimates which will eventually be needed.

## Questions for Class Discussion

1. Over 8,000 7-Eleven stores in 41 states constitute the largest chain of convenience stores in the United States. Most stores are open 24 hours a day, selling
   fast-turnover groceries, drugs, and related items. Many of the stores also sell
   fast foods and/or self-service gasoline. Because the stores are open, lighted,
   and attended round the clock, customers drop in often.

   Large California banks are starting to install automatic teller machines in
   7-Eleven stores. (a) Why do you think these banks want to use 7-Eleven stores
   for this purpose? (b) What sort of relationship would you predict between one
   of these banks and the 7-Eleven company? Why?

2. To practice key actor analysis, select a student organization that you know
   well (co-op laundry, mid-city tutoring, artist concert series, radio station, or
   the like). Who are the key actors within and outside the organizations who
   primarily determine its continuing success? For three of these key actors, use
   the outline suggested in the chapter to determine the main factors that will influence their future behavior. What power does each of the three have?

3. Who are the major stakeholders in your college? Do the interests of these
   stakeholders coincide? Do they conflict? Is it possible for the college administration to devise a strategy that will satisfy all the major stakeholders?

4. Executives of All-Gene Genetics, Inc., a rapidly growing maker of machinery
   for gene splicing and cloning, felt fortunate when they were able to persuade
   one of the five major investment banking companies to lead a syndicate and
   sell a new offering of All-Gene's common stock at a price of $28 per share,
   yielding $50 million to the company and $7.5 million to the investment bankers. The sale of the stock took place several years ago at the height of a new-
   issue, high-technology stock boom and after All-Gene Genetics had shown
   two years of increasingly profitable operations. Following the offering, however, the price of the stock was at first stable and then dropped steadily to $15
   per share in the over-the-counter market. All-Gene Genetics had hoped that
   the well-known and highly regarded investment banking firm would alert
   potential investors to its advanced biotechnology products. But the firm's
   biotechnology analyst did not produce a single research report for investors.
   Visits by All-Gene executives to the prestigious New York-based investment
   firm revealed that the two young dealmakers who had managed the first offering had moved on to other tasks and then to other companies. The partner
   in charge of the technology group did promise to look into All-Gene's situation to see whether more than two of the members of its syndicate would be
   willing to make a market for All-Gene's stock. Nothing much came of this,
   however. Now All-Gene wants to sell some bonds to raise $10 million. Com-
   pany management has recommended to the directors that they hire a differ-

ent, but still prestigious New York investment banking firm to help All-Gene market its bonds. The first partner approached has suggested that All-Gene talk with a much smaller, regional investment banking firm that specializes in high-technology companies. The directors, however, still would like to utilize a firm with high status in investment banking. (a) What interest groups are involved in this series of transactions? Develop a diagram like that of Figure 4–2. (b) In which cell of Figure 4–3 do you think that All-Gene Genetics, Inc., fits?

5. (a) Where would you place each of the following on the matrix appearing in this chapter? (Assume that you are the first actor named in each pair.) (1) a Chevrolet dealer in relation to the Chevrolet Division of GM; (2) your school cafeteria in relation to you; (3) the Springfield Hospital in relation to the union which is the certified bargaining agent for nurses in the hospital; (4) Exxon and the prime contractor building a supertanker for you. (b) In accordance with the descriptive words in the quadrant selected in each situation, suggest what you think the relationship would be?

6. Key actor analyses have been recommended in this chapter covering goals, values, and beliefs; patterns of behavior; capability profiles; and future pressures. The focus has been on studying other organizations in the environment. Do you recommend that the management of a company make a similar analysis of itself? Explain your answer.

7. Builders and operators of nuclear power plants are frequently confronted by protest groups. The larger groups usually include local people together with other individuals who travel long distances to join in the protest. Work at a number of plants has been at least slowed down as a result of such protests, and changes in plans have been made. Because of the high investment in a nuclear power plant, the cost of these delays and changes involves millions of dollars.

   Apply the key actor analysis framework recommended in this chapter to the protest groups identified. What, if anything, can management learn from this study that might be useful in its dealings with other advocacy groups? (This question does *not* deal with the merits of the specific claims made by the protesters. Instead, the issue is how management should diagnose and treat advocacy groups which are concerned with some other cause.)

8. In the Ethicon example described in the chapter, the company needed specially designed sterile containers as well as special needles. The containers were to be molded plastic tubes, which could be produced by quite a few firms. What degree of collaboration should Ethicon seek in obtaining these containers?

9. A prominent analyst observes, "Coalition members do not join the coalition without bringing with them their demands, and the support of these members could easily be given to alternative coalitions. . . . Each member will,

therefore, make a set of demands on the coalition to commit itself to certain goals. . . . However, it is often impossible for the coalition to satisfy *all* the demands of *all* its members. . . . A potential member will join only if he feels that the policy commitments of the coalition will promote his own goals, and he will stay only as long as he expects the coalition to be successful."[3] Use the hospital example appearing near the end of this chapter to illustrate these points.

10. Suppose that you wish to establish a "Teen Canteen" in your home community (a place for senior high school students to meet in the late afternoons and evenings to buy snacks and dance). Describe the *alliance* that would have to be established to make the project viable.

11. Colombia in northern South America is located on the equator. Much of the country is very mountainous, and Bogota, the capital, is located in a large fertile valley 9,000 feet above sea level. Because this valley and others are so high, they have steady year-round temperatures that range from cool to temperate. (The coasts, on the other hand, are hot.) Moreover, there is ample rainfall. This climate is uniquely favorable to raising roses, carnations, and other cut flowers. Once packed in chilled containers, these flowers can be shipped by cargo plane to U.S. and European markets. Indeed, over 30,000 people work in the Colombian cut-flower industry.

     Using as a guide the brief description on page 96 of the coalition necessary for catfish raising, describe the coalitions that you think would be suited to the Colombian cut-flower industry.

12. At one point in its struggle to survive in the steel industry in the United States, the largest firm in the industry, U.S. Steel Corporation, won major concessions from the United Steel Workers Union, viz., reduced wage rates and more flexible work rules in a 41-month contract (a contract of unusual length). The company's position was that the concessions were necessary to preserve jobs. U.S. Steel also lobbied extensively and strenuously with the U.S. Tariff Commission and the White House, seeking administrative action (and higher duties) against foreign steel that was, said the company, heavily subsidized by the foreign governments.

     Subsequently, U.S. Steel announced that it was seeking an agreement with the government-owned British Steel Corp. whereby British Steel would invest $100 million in U.S. Steel's Fairless works near Trenton, New Jersey, and would also supply semifinished steel ingots and slabs to the U.S. firm for further processing. This would allow U.S. Steel to close its outmoded and costly open-hearth furnaces that turned blast-furnace iron into steel and thus cut its costs by 10 percent. British Steel could then keep open a Scottish plant

---

[3]I. C. MacMillan, *Strategy Formulation: Political Concepts* (St. Paul: West Publishing Company, 1978).

which employed 4,000 workers and which had been mentioned as one that the British government might close to halt British Steel's large losses. British Steel had earlier been cited as one of the more heavily subsidized foreign producers.

Predict the reactions to the proposed agreement of the following actors in U.S. Steel's network: U.S. Steel's management, the USW leaders, the White House, the U.S. Tariff Commission, the British Ministries of Labour and Industry, members of the British parliament of the party not then in power, and purchasing agents of large steel users in the United States.

13. Facing full-page ads in *The Wall Street Journal* showed Mr. Lee Iacocca standing next to a military version of the famous Jeep automobile with a big smile, a hopeful expression, and crossed arms while the facing-page ad stated, "An American legend has come home again. Jeep, and the people of AMC, are now part of Chrysler. That's good for us. Good for you. And good for America." (a) Has the addition of the Jeep line—Wrangler, Cherokee, Wagoneer, and Comanche, which will be built in a very modern Canadian plant— strengthened Chrysler in the international automobile industry? (b) With what network of stakeholders will Chrysler have to interact? With which group will Chrysler have the least difficulty? The most?

# CASE
## 4 PACCAR Truck Leasing

A Seattle banker comments, "Although we are a long way from Detroit, our local customer, PACCAR, is one of the few companies in the automobile and truck industry to have uninterrupted profits over the last ten years. Now the top managers are thinking of moving into a related activity, full-service leasing, and that is a very different ball game. I just hope some of the giants don't knock them for a loop."

The present position of PACCAR as well as its new frontier are described in the following paragraphs.

### PACCAR's Present Niche

PACCAR, Inc., has been adept at keeping pace with changes in the transportation industry. As overland freight shifted from railroads to trucks, PACCAR made a corresponding change. Originally a freight car and lumbering equipment manufacturer, PACCAR's primary business now is building heavy-duty trucks. Currently, well over 80 percent of its $1.2 billion sales and its $32 million net income comes from the manufacture and sale of Class 8 diesel trucks (gross weight of 33,000 pounds and over).

Another striking feature of PACCAR in this troubled industry is its strong financial position, as shown in Table 4–1. The parent company has virtually no long-term debt, and its current ratio is 2.6. Net income did fall sharply during the recent depression, but it was the dwindling freight car volume that showed the steepest decline.

PACCAR makes only the Class 8 trucks, using the trade names of Peterbilt and Kenworth. These trucks sell for $50,000 to $80,000 each. They are made to customer specifications, including such features as CB radios, air-conditioning, bunks for sleeping, and an array of controls over the engine and the brakes.

Actually, PACCAR manufactures (in six regional plants) only the tractor part of a tractor-trailer rig; trailers are sold separately by other companies. Customers include all sorts of manufacturing companies, big and small, which ship their products all over the country.

Most of PACCAR's competitors in the Class 8 field also make smaller trucks. International Harvester, clearly the largest producer, makes many kinds of trucks, construction equipment, and all sorts of agricultural equipment. A former "blue chip" company, International Harvester got into a severe financial crisis following a long strike and is in a selective retrenchment program. Mack Truck, which competes with PACCAR's combined output of Peterbilt and Kenworth trucks for second place in the Class 8 field (each has about one-sixth of the total), also makes middleweight trucks. Mack Truck has a checkered financial history and is now controlled by a foreign conglomerate.

The half-dozen remaining producers, below the top three, have their main base in other fields and moved into Class 8 as an extension from these operations. For example, Ford, GM, and Mercedes (a worldwide truck supplier outside the U.S.) only offer more standardized trucks than the three leaders.

**TABLE 4–1.**
**SELECTED FINANCIAL DATA FOR PACCAR, INC. (in millions except per-share data)**

|                                    | 1982    | 1978    | 1973   |
|------------------------------------|---------|---------|--------|
| Sales                              | $1,230  | $1,552  | $766   |
| Net income                         | 32      | 87      | 42     |
| Total assets                       | 807*    | 613     | —      |
| Long-term debt                     | 13      | 21      | 18     |
| Stockholders' equity               | 584     | 393     | 203    |
| Net income per share common stock  | 4.16    | 9.56    | 5.20   |

*Over 40 percent of these assets are invested in or loaned to PACCAR financing affiliates.

PACCAR's survival and success in its selected niche largely reflects three related strengths:

1. *Built-in product quality.* Engineering specifications and care in production create a truck that on the average is more trouble free and lasts longer than competing products. And such performance is important where dependable delivery is vital to the user. There is a cost to achieve this quality, so PACCAR trucks are priced at a premium over competitors'.

2. *Reputation among drivers as "the Cadillac" of the industry.* Long-haul truck drivers are a breed apart—self-reliant, independent, proud, clannish, dependable. They are the modern Knights of the Road. Most of the time they work without supervision, and they must cope reliably with a variety of situations. As a result, they feel that they deserve the best, and they take pride in driving a Cadillac.

3. *A strong distribution and service network.* PACCAR has 250 independent dealers who both sell and offer full maintenance and repair service.[4] This network is crucial in keeping Peterbilt and Kenworth trucks in top operating condition and in making emergency repairs rapidly.

In addition, PACCAR does have a subsidiary company that helps customers finance their purchases. This affiliate benefits from the strong financial standing of its parent and in turn extends credit in about one-third of the truck sales.

## The Impact of Truck Leasing

However, the world does not stand still. The recession of the early 1980s cut sales of the entire truck manufacturing industry to 56 percent of its 1978 total. Deregulation of commercial carriers led to rate cutting and lower income in their ranks. High interest rates discouraged purchase of all capital goods, including trucks. Consequently, new alignments and new ways to improve efficiency are being sought throughout the transportation sector.

One development is a sharp rise in the full-service leasing, instead of buying, of trucks by companies that want to transport their products. Estimates indicate that by 1983 a third of Class 8 trucks sold were on full-service lease to actual users; this figure was expected to increase to 48 percent by 1987, and one prediction foresaw 80 percent by 1992.

Under a typical full-service lease, a separate company owns the truck and maintains it in good running condition. The user pays rent on a monthly and mileage basis. The situation is similar to renting a passenger car at an airport, except that large truck rentals often extend from three to five years. *Full-service* leasing

---

[4]Basically, the relationship of a dealer to PACCAR is like that of an automobile agency to its supplier of cars—for example, a Ford agency to the Ford Motor Company.

also includes a variety of other services which simplify life for the traffic manager at the user company. Such services may include logistics studies; full insurance; multistate vehicle licensing; multistate tax reporting; a fuel program; preventive maintenance; emergency repair; substitute vehicles; extra trucks for peak needs; parking, storage, and washing; and driver recruiting and testing. Recently the Interstate Commerce Commission removed one more restraint: now it is permissible for a leasing company to provide the driver as well. This involves the delicate tasks of supervising and motivating those Knights of the Road.

Note that full-service leasing differs from merely financing a purchase. Under full service, the leasing company carries the risks and takes over special administrative burdens—tasks that few users are well suited to perform. Instead, the user avoids a diverting chore and can concentrate on its main line of business. Other attractions may include tax benefits, avoiding a capital appropriation hassle, balance sheet effects, and improved productivity through the use of the expertise and scale economies of the leasing firm. The user is buying an array of services, not just borrowing money to pay for the initial cost of the truck.

PACCAR has to decide how far it wants to get into this leasing business. Major competitors already exist. The largest truck leasing firm, in all sizes of trucks, including Class 8's, is Ryder, a firm with 600 locations that has an annual revenue of $2 billion. Hertz-Penske also is active in heavy-duty truck leasing (an operation completely separate from Hertz auto rentals).

A sharp constraint on entry into heavy-duty truck leasing is the need for a far-flung servicing network. Many of the automobile leasing firms can take care of light trucks—a field where Japanese competition is expected to increase; but they lack the capability to handle large trucks. Firms such as Saunders, Gelco, and Rollins support their heavy-duty truck leasing through contracts with a network of independent repair shops. And a couple of associations of independent leasing companies have reciprocal servicing agreements. However, such arrangements are difficult to maintain on a nationwide basis, especially when the leasing companies undertake to maintain all kinds of trucks.

How and why should PACCAR get into the leasing business? For over eighty years, PACCAR has been a manufacturer of large transportation vehicles, not an operator of transportation fleets. A senior marketing executive answers:

"We should go into leasing for defensive reasons and to grasp an opportunity. If we don't, as the leasing companies become stronger they will take over our close relationships with users. Our chances to give distinctive services would be replaced by sharp price competition for just truck orders from the leasing companies. Then, with our premium prices, we would rapidly lose volume. Many of our dealers would lose the truck sales they need to survive, and our service organization would disintegrate.

"Instead, we can treat our existing dealer and service organization as an asset. We can put those dealers who wish into the leasing business. They are competent business people and know their customers well. Of course, we will have to create a central staff of experts who can provide all sorts of technical assistance to the dealers—contract forms, insurance leads, logistic studies, personnel training, etc. The setup for truck maintenance and repair is already in place.

"Our experience shows that a large number of users in our niche are willing to pay for quality, and quality will be even more important in full-service leasing. Also, good drivers like our trucks.

"Leasing through the dealers is something we must do and can do well."

A financial executive of PACCAR is more skeptical. He points out:

"There are a lot of risks in leasing. Both working capital and equipment costs are laid out first. Then you have to do everything right to keep the rental payments flowing back in. Not all our dealers are willing and able to take that sizable risk. A large dealer would have millions outstanding, you realize.

"You would be taking on a major education task—converting dealers and their salespeople to a new kind of business. When they stub their toes, we would have an obligation to help bail them out. And if very many stub their toes, there goes our reputation for quality service.

"And one other angle bothers me: the more we compete with the leasing companies, the less likely they are to buy our trucks. We would be boxing ourselves out of what you predict will be the largest part of the market. Just last week one of our plant managers asked me what we were doing to *improve* our chances of shipping to the large leasing companies."

## Questions

1. List the key actors in this situation. For a representative sample of the actors you list, prepare a "key actor analysis" as proposed in this chapter.
2. To what extent, if any, should PACCAR enter into truck leasing?

# CHAPTER 5

## Forming Four-Part Business-Unit Strategy

For a short period a company may simply drift along just doing what is customary. Or if the competition is tough, it may react to each new crisis as seems best at the moment. Only if it is lucky and has a lot of resources will such passive or "fire-fighting" behavior enable the enterprise to survive very long in today's turbulent environment. The constructive alternative is to be *proactive* instead of *reactive*. This requires company managers to energetically forestall trouble and seize new opportunities. They must provide positive, future-oriented direction to company activities. An essential part of such proactive behavior is the development of a *master strategy* for the business-unit as a whole.

The three preceding chapters on industry outlook, company strengths, and interactive behavior of key actors outline the array of forces that should be considered in designing master strategy. Essentially, they set the stage. The next step is for the central managers of the business-unit to decide how their company can best adapt to the anticipated opportunities and threats. As noted in Chapter 1, a business-unit strategy normally should indicate the following items:

1. *Domain sought.* What products or intangible services will the business-unit sell to what group of customers?

2. *Differential advantage in serving that domain.* On what basis—e.g., access to raw materials, better personnel, new technology, or low costs and prices—will the business-unit seek an advantage over competitors in providing its products or services?

3. *Strategic thrusts necessary and their approximate timing.* For the business-unit to move from its present position to where it wants to be—as laid out in items 1 and 2—which moves will be made early and which can be deferred?

4. *Target results expected.* What financial and other criteria will the business-unit use to measure its success, and what levels of achievement are expected?[1]

Too often, statements of strategy deal with only a single dimension. A new market or a desired financial return on investment, for instance, may be labeled as

---

[1]By listing targets as the fourth element, rather than the first, we place emphasis on the operational content of strategy. The more abstract goals, such as growth, usually serve better as criteria for acceptability than as guides for action. In practice, possible strategies are debated back and forth so often that no clear priority exists between target results and mission.

"our company strategy." Such a goal may indeed be part of the strategy, but its narrowness robs that strategy of a needed balanced operational quality. A company strategy should be a well-conceived, practical commitment. To achieve this realistic quality, all four of the elements just listed should be carefully considered. The resulting strategy will then be an *integrated*, forward-looking plan. This integration is depicted in Figure 5–1.

Although strategy has many dimensions to consider—the domain sought, differential advantage, strategic thrusts, and target results—it need not be detailed and comprehensive. Rather, strategy should concentrate on *key* factors necessary for success and on *major* moves to be taken by the particular company at the current stage in its development. The selectivity of key points, and by implication the designation of other points as supportive, gives strategy much of its value as a planning device.

Full elaboration of plans is a necessary sequel to selecting company strategy, as we shall see in Parts 2 and 3. The role of company strategy, however, is primarily to identify missions and to set forth major ways of achieving distinctiveness— our focus in this chapter.

## Domain Sought

## Product/Market Scope

The starting point in clarifying the mission of almost any enterprise is to define the services it will provide. It may design and manufacture a broad range of

**FIGURE 5–1.**
**FOUR ESSENTIAL PARTS OF BUSINESS-UNIT STRATEGY**

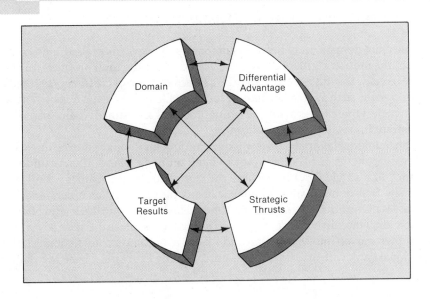

physical products, or it may merely sell advice. But to continue to exist, it must provide some package of services for which some segment in society is prepared to pay. For example, after carefully examining the anticipated growth in the use of computers for billing retail customers, two enterprising IBM salespeople set up their own firm that (1) leases time on a central computer and (2) assists medium-sized stores in adapting their records and procedures to make use of this service. Note that this young firm has a sharp definition of the kind of computer work it will undertake and the kind of customers it seeks. This definition is a vital element in its strategy.

## Attractive Industries

Most business-units have their resources and strengths so deeply committed to an industry that they have only limited choice in this matter. Nevertheless, a careful analysis of that industry outlook, as suggested in Chapter 2, provides an essential basis for deciding whether to harness a favorable underlying trend or to seek unusual segments in a mature or declining situation. For example, most companies dealing with mobile homes are trying to increase their industry position. In contrast, the senior managers of the former Illinois Central Railroad are seeking ways to get rid of their railroad operations. (In recent years, less than 20 percent of I. C. Industries' operating profits came from railroading.)

A redefinition of one's industry sometimes suggests an attractive domain. A typical example is an overbuilt hospital that redefined its industry as health care. This expanded domain included preventive medicine and out-patient clinics, activities which substantially increased the hospital's income. A glass-bottle firm has significantly shifted the nature of its business by thinking in terms of containers.

## Finding a Niche Suited to Company Strengths

The chief domain issue for most companies, however, is picking a propitious niche in the industry. The niche may be a segment of the total products (or services) offered by the industry, or it may be a selected group of customers defined by a characteristic such as size, income, or location. Obviously, each business tries to select a niche where the growth and profit prospects are attractive, and also where it has strengths relative to competitors.

The Franklin National Bank switched the domain it sought during its exciting history. Starting as just a small country bank on Long Island, it grew under the guidance of a single CEO to become the thirteenth largest bank in the United States. Its first domain was commercial banking serving consumers and local businesses in the limited area of Long Island. Having become the leading bank in this domain, Franklin National expanded its goals (as soon as the state law permitted). It then moved into Manhattan and sought to become a truly national and international bank with an array of services matching Citibank, Chase Manhattan, and the other giants. This enlarged domain drastically altered the character of the bank, with results which we explore in the next sections.

Small firms, such as the new venture described in Figure 5–2, often try to find a niche where their particular skills will give them a foothold in a much larger industry.

Even a basic product, such as coal, raises strategy questions. The Island Creek Coal Company, to cite a specific case, has large deposits of coal especially suited for the production of steel. Clearly, the company should serve these metallurgical customers. But the recent growth in coal demand is in generating electricity. Island Creek is handicapped in serving this large market because its coal must be dug in high-cost underground mines and because electric utilities are unwilling to pay a

**FIGURE 5–2.**
**CONDENSED EXAMPLE OF FOUR-PART STRATEGY**

### SWIFT & PEACOCK, FINANCIAL COUNSELORS

*Domain*:

Complete financial services for individuals (insurance, investments, real estate, income tax returns, cash flow, wills & trusts, etc.)

Niche: individuals with sudden high income, very busy, no finance background—e.g., professional athletes and rock stars

*Differential Advantage*:

Coordinated, personalized, complete service (accountant, stockbroker, lawyer, banker—all in one)

"Your agent helps you earn what you're worth; Swift & Peacock helps you keep it."

*Strategic Thrusts*:

Credible organization—front office, financial backing, references

Resource contacts—investments, lawyer, banking, others

Client information system—records, computer programs, reports

Marketing program

*Target Results*:

Ready to operate in three months

Five new clients under contract every month for two years

Break even at end of first year

Double selling partners each year

*Note*:    Swift, a professional football star who was recently injured and retired, will do selling on basis of his contacts. Peacock, Swift's teammate at UCLA, sold insurance for three years and has just completed his MBA in accounting/finance; he will "produce" the services.

premium for the high quality of Island Creek coal. So Island Creek must decide whether to (1) concentrate only on metallurgical customers who will pay a premium, (2) sell its high-quality coal to utilities at low prices, (3) try to capture some of the utility business by buying strip mines and learning a new technology, or (4) hold onto its reserves until techniques for converting coal into gas and gasoline become practical.

Clear identification of a desired domain enables a business to concentrate on the particular activities necessary to serve that domain well. Especially important is anticipating changes in demand, supply, and regulation in the domain and preparing in advance to meet these new requirements. A secondary benefit of a well-defined domain is that it provides a guide for what *not* to do. Activities which are irrelevant to serving the domain can be pushed aside.

The desired domain does not remain static. The nature of markets and competition in those markets frequently change. Products mature. A business may achieve a dominant position in one niche and have to look elsewhere for growth. But until a change is decided upon, the selected domain provides positive direction to other business-unit planning.

## Multiple Niches

The strategic advantages of picking a niche very carefully do not necessarily imply that a company should confine its activities to a single niche. As a firm grows, it frequently spots an additional service it can provide effectively. Thus, an auditing firm may also do consulting on management information systems.

Such expansion is desirable because it secures synergistic benefits. *Synergy* arises when two actions performed jointly produce a greater result than they would if performed independently. A simple example is building a restaurant with a motel; the restaurant makes the motel a more convenient place to stop, and the motel contributes business to the restaurant; the total business is larger than it would be if the two units were located five miles apart. Often this is called the "2 + 2 = 5" effect.

Because synergy is often involved in considering multiple niches, a framework for thinking about it is desirable. The *expansion matrix* depicted in Figure 5–3 suggests that growth arising from finding new customers for present products leads in quite different directions from adding different products for existing customers. Thus, the producer of Eveready flashlight batteries took virtually the same product from the United States to many developing countries and expanded its use from flashlights to portable radios and toys. In contrast, Head Ski Company went from skis to skiwear and then to tennis rackets and summer sport clothing—all to the same (or a closely related) group of customers.

As a firm moves further away from its present customers and/or its present products, the prospects for synergistic benefits diminish. At the extreme (lower right corner), if new customers are to require completely different products, synergy almost disappears; the firm is thus involved in unrelated "conglomerate" expansion.

**FIGURE 5–3.**
**EXPANSION MATRIX**

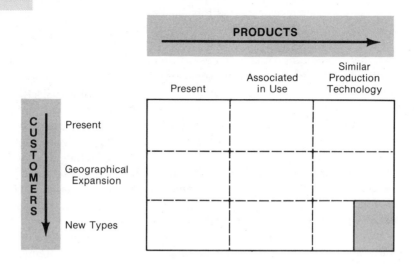

Naturally, a firm will seek combinations of niches that supplement or rein-force each other in a synergistic way. Managers should be aware, however, that negative synergy can occur; perhaps "2 + 2 = 3." A women's dress shop almost went bankrupt because of this problem. The shop had a long and successful re-cord of serving middle-aged and older women. Its inventory and sales personnel matched that niche well. Then the shop decided to cater also to young women. It purchased the latest styles of clothing and featured them in window displays. Also, several much younger salespersons were added to the staff. The net effect of trying to serve both niches was to annoy the former customers and fail to attract younger women because of the store's reputation for being conservative if not stodgy. Sales dropped and unsold inventory skyrocketed. The synergy was negative.

If a business-unit elects to serve two or more niches, it is highly desirable to analyze and plan for each separately. In this way, the benefits that come from con-centrated attention will not be lost. When and if the volume of work in a single niche can support its own organization, and if economies of scale permit separate marketing and production activities, the creation of an additional business-unit may be wise. The desirability of having two or more separate but related business-units is discussed in Chapter 15 as a portfolio issue.

Early writers on business strategy gave almost exclusive attention to this task of finding attractive niches suited to company strengths and to building a large market share in each niche. Indeed, selection of the domain is crucial to success. Experience with strategic management, however, shows clearly that being well situated in an attractive market is not enough. Business-unit strategy should in-clude three additional elements.

## Differential Advantage in Serving Selected Domain

The second essential pillar in a company strategy is identifying one or more bases in which superiority over competitors will be sought. If our particular enterprise is to continue to attract customers and resources, we must perform at least some parts of the total industry task with distinction. New product design, quick deliveries, low production costs, better personnel policies, fewer fights with environmentalists—these examples only suggest the many possibilities.

Franklin National Bank, to return to that example, differentiated itself during its Long Island growth phase by (1) promptly opening branches in expanding residential areas, and (2) offering unusual services first. (Its "firsts" included parking for customers, drive-in windows, evening hours, prompt FHA home mortgage loans, and the like.) However, when the bank moved to Manhattan, it found itself in a "me too" situation, running hard to catch up with the services offered by established competitors. Consequently, the primary differential advantage it found itself forced to adopt was the granting of higher-risk loans. And this latter practice led directly to Franklin National's collapse.

A company may seek a differential advantage in *any* of its external relations or in its internal resource conversion technology. The strategic requirement is to become—somehow, in at least a few respects—a favorable supplier in the selected domain. Several commonly used ways of getting at least some comparative advantage are highlighted in the following paragraphs.

## Products and Services Tailored for Selected Niches

Having selected a niche which is growing fast or is being inadequately served by competing suppliers, a company may adjust its products and services to suit the particular needs of customers in that niche. Familiar examples are radio stations which focus on sophisticated listeners by programming classical music or on Hispanic listeners by offering Spanish-language programs. Such stations then have a differential advantage for advertisers who want to reach those particular audiences.

Pioneer Life, a medium-sized insurance company, revamped a large part of its operations for a similar purpose. Pioneer could not compete successfully with large insurance companies for most *group* business (group life, insured pension plans, group health and disability, and the like). However, the large companies were giving little attention to clients with fewer than 200 employees. Such small clients usually lacked an insurance specialist on their own staff, and they were often confused by government tax and reporting requirements and by union requests for insurance as a fringe benefit. So Pioneer decided to cater to this niche.

To build a differential advantage in serving the smaller clients, Pioneer (1) selected and trained agents (salespersons) to advise small companies on *all* aspects of employee insurance; (2) prepared an array of standard options suited to small companies from which an insurance plan for a specific client could be quickly assembled; (3) wrote computer programs which store employment and vital statistics on company employees and quickly calculate costs of various kinds of insurance; (4) designed a monthly (or quarterly) report form for the client showing the contributions and status of insurance coverage on each employee; and (5) reorganized internally so that group insurance became a self-contained business-unit within Pioneer. Of course, this kind of service is expensive on a per-employee basis, but Pioneer is now able to relieve smaller clients of almost all of their headaches in this technical area of employee insurance.

## High Volume, Low Cost

A very different approach to differential advantage is to seek high volume, which, it is hoped, will result in low cost per unit. The low cost, in turn, will enable the company to set a lower selling price—or spend more on promotion and service—than its competitors can afford.

The classic concept of high volume leading to low cost has been popularized by the Boston Consulting Group. B.C.G. talks of large market share, which gives a company higher volume than its competitors, and of the "experience curve," which explains why costs can be expected to drop as a result of that higher volume. More specifically, the argument is that a company (like a person) learns from experience; each time the cumulative output doubles, cost per unit should drop, say, 30 percent. Indeed, experience in production of aircraft and electronic components, two well-known examples, conforms with the theory.

Fortunately, for small firms and newcomers the B.C.G. theory is subject to a variety of qualifications. For instance, with a new product or a new production technology, a company may start with as much "experience" as its more prominent competitors. Nevertheless, the central point remains: using some relevant concept of volume, a company can seek a differential advantage by playing the high-volume, low-cost game.

## Distinctive Research and Development

In some industries, such as pharmaceuticals and electronics, strong company research and development is regarded as the touchstone for success. Especially for firms that hope to serve new technical markets, an imaginative engineering department is vital. Two college professors who set up a firm to design and install equipment to control air pollution of chemical processing plants considered their research program as a key element in the firm's basic strategy.

But what is good for one firm is not necessarily wise for another. For instance, a leading British cement company relies on very good customer service, not on distinctive products, to win business from competitors. Hence, it spends no money on product research; rather, its engineering is focused on reducing operating costs. In contrast, many advertising agencies rely heavily on their ability to create unusual campaigns. For them, as for fashion dress manufacturers, creative design is the main way they try to differentiate themselves from competitors.

## Favorable Strength in Resources

A company may gain an advantage in serving a particular niche by having greater strength in key resources, such as scarce raw materials, unusual people, or cash for investment. For strategic planning, an ability to acquire the resource quickly is almost the same as having it in hand. Of course, to provide a differential advantage, the resource must be vital in serving the niche and it must not be readily available to competitors. Thus, in times of inflation, having timberlands can be a comparative advantage to a paper company. Whether owning a tomato farm similarly places a catsup plant in a superior position depends upon the availability and price of tomatoes for competitors.

Access to capital creates a distinct advantage in some circumstances. For instance, large sums of risk capital must be available for any firm engaged in exploring the ocean floor. Small equipment companies have difficulties expanding into niches where end products are leased rather than sold. Even urban renewal firms have discovered that one requirement for growth is equity capital. Again, the underlying question is, "Do we have, or can we get, the financing needed, and in this respect, will we be at any advantage or disadvantage relative to others serving the same need?"

In service operations, personnel is *the* critical resource. For this reason, one of the leading management consulting firms insists that staff members devote 10 percent of their working time to training and development, even though billable work for clients is available. The aim is to have the best staff in the profession fully informed on the latest developments. A secondary benefit is that this training appeals to the professional pride of the individuals, and that aids morale and recruiting. Of course, any enterprise can benefit or suffer from the relative capability of its management and technical team. Realistic strategic planning should always take this resource into account.

## Choice of Emphasis

Many potential sources of differential advantages exist. The preceding examples only suggest the possibilities. As a practical matter, any single company becomes ineffective if it tries to excel on all fronts. Instead, a key feature of strategy is selection of a few ways in which the company seeks to distinguish itself.

A few examples will highlight this feature of strategy. IBM has always stressed customer service, customer orientation in product design, and liberal treatment of its employees. Humble Oil rose to prominence because it gave high priority to acquiring an advantageous crude oil supply. Merck and Boeing stressed building better mousetraps—ethical pharmaceuticals and aircraft, respectively. Conglomerates derive their differential advantage predominantly by the way they raise capital.

Each company singles out perhaps one, but more likely a few, areas having synergistic ties. In these areas it tries to develop a relationship with the resources that is more favorable than that of its competitors. Typically, it establishes a new symbiotic relationship between a key group of resources and the internal technology of the company. If the company is wise (or lucky), it selects relationships for emphasis which will become especially important strengths in the future competition within its industry. The distinction in managing competitively superior activities versus "satisficed" activities is explored further in Part 2.

In the numerous external relationships not selected as a source of differential advantage, a company "satisfices"; that is, it merely seeks to be acceptable but not to excel. Often a company is too small to attempt any more than following general industry practice; its location, history, the personal preferences of key executives, or the existing resource base may not provide a good springboard; or management may deliberately decide that effort applied in other directions will be more rewarding. These secondary relationships cannot be neglected; they must be adequately maintained, like Herzberg's hygiene factors. Moreover, the secondary relationships should be designed so that they support or at least are compatible with the primary features of the selected strategy. For instance, one small pharmaceutical firm is preparing to be a (or the) leader in all aspects of treating AIDS.

Of course, over time a company may shift its choice of areas in which it seeks differential advantage. Critical factors for success change, the company changes, and new opportunities for distinctiveness emerge. Adapting to these opportunities by adjusting the emphasis placed on sources of distinction is a crucial aspect of successful strategy.

Unless a business-unit can devise a strategy which couples obtainable differential advantage with an attractive domain, the domain is likely to be captured by a competitor.

## Strategic Thrusts

Normally a gap exists between the present position of a business-unit and the domain and differential advantages it seeks. Obstacles to closing that gap will vary in magnitude and over time, and the business-unit will have limited personnel, capital, existing external relationships, and other resources to use in dealing with these obstacles. Consequently, a third basic strategic consideration is deciding what major thrusts to make and how fast to press for changes. Besides identifying what these major thrusts should be, this element of strategy also involves steering a course between too-much-too-soon and too-little-too-late.

## Major Steps to Be Taken

A few years ago, Crown Cork & Seal Company faced a threat to its strong position in high-pressure cans. The aluminum companies began producing a two-piece aluminum can. This new can had a differential advantage over the conventional three-piece steel can that Crown Cork, American, Continental, and National can companies were making. It was lighter in weight, it had less possibility of leaky seams, it avoided the remote chance of producing lead poisoning from lead on the seams, and it had printing on the can that looked slightly better. Crown Cork did not want to switch to the aluminum can, because it would then find itself buying raw material (roughly half the cost) from companies which would also be its competitors for the end product. A possible alternative was a two-piece steel can.

So a new thrust, vital to maintaining Crown Cork's position in the can business, was forged: the development of a low-cost technology to manufacture a two-piece steel can. This involved high-speed drawing of a thin steel sheet into the sides and bottom of the can, a task previously believed impractical. A complicating factor was that Crown Cork's low-overhead policy meant that it normally spent very little on manufacturing-process R & D. So a joint engineering venture with steel companies, which also had a substantial stake in the outcome, was launched. Five years later a technology that involved both steel making and can making emerged, and the two-piece steel can became a viable competitor of the two-piece aluminum can.

A second issue then arose. How fast should Crown Cork convert to manufacturing two-piece steel cans? A large investment in machinery was involved, the technology could change, excess three-piece capacity would create price pressure in the total market, and the environmental agitation against nonreturnable containers could swing demand back to glass bottles. In spite of these drawbacks, Crown Cork decided to beat its competitors in building two-piece steel can lines. As a result of this second thrust, the company already has over half of the installed capacity for making the new steel cans.

Clearly, these two moves have been crucial points of Crown Cork's strategy. They illustrate what we have called "thrusts" and what some other people term "initiatives" or "key programs." A strategic thrust is a vital, positive undertaking which moves a company toward its differential advantage in its desired domain.

Failure to include thrusts in a strategic plan may leave the selected objectives floating; it is probably the major "missing link" in moving strategy from ideas to action. This was a contributing weakness in Franklin National Bank's move into Manhattan. In addition to taking risky loans, Franklin National failed to tool up to do the broader business it said it wanted. There was no thrust focused on developing and/or acquiring a pool of talented personnel necessary for the new tasks. And there was only slow recognition of the need to modify the informal centralized organization which had suited Long Island. The necessary shift to a complex, sophisticated organization needed by a major bank of world stature posed so many difficulties that it should have been set up as an explicit thrust. By contrast, when Citibank adopted its strategy to go after more business from "world corporations," it recognized the organizational and personnel hurdles and established thrusts to overcome them.

## Timing of Thrusts

The sequence and timing of thrusts may be tricky. Some actions obviously must precede others, for example, land acquisition before plant construction. But often a strategic choice can be made. When British Petroleum moved into the U.S. market, the company deferred heavy commitment in marketing until a source of U.S. crude was in sight. To have started marketing alone, relying completely on local purchases of finished products, would have exposed the company to very high risks. Note also that building or acquiring refining capacity came even later; clearly, refining capacity was not regarded as a critical factor and it could be manipulated later without paying high penalties.

A different sequence is being followed by a manufacturer of fiberglass boats. A low selling price is a key feature of the marketing strategy, and in order to achieve costs permitting this low price, a large modern plant is necessary. Starting up such a plant is clearly a strategic thrust. However, the company's current sales are not large enough to keep an optimum-sized plant busy. Nevertheless, the management decided to build the plant in order to be in a strong competitive position. While market demand is being built up, the company has taken on several subcontracts at break-even prices and is even selling some boat hulls to another boat builder to help cover overhead costs of the plant. Here is an instance of moving first into large-scale production facilities, hoping that demand will catch up.

Even after a sequence has been selected, the manager has to decide how fast to move. It is quite possible to be too early. A leading East Coast department store, for example, correctly predicted a major shift of population to the suburbs, and it became a leader in establishing suburban branches. However, at the time it selected branch locations, few of the large modern shopping centers with their vast parking spaces were in existence. Consequently, the store established branches in locations that are now being passed by. The irony of the situation is that the management of this store had more foresight than several of its competitors, yet because it moved too soon, it is now at a relative disadvantage in suburban operations.

In these examples, and in most other timing decisions, the likely response of other key actors to company moves is a significant consideration. As noted in Chapter 4, the possibility of gaining cooperation or of provoking countermoves depends upon the involvement of the other actors at the time we initiate our moves.

Although difficult to do wisely, the timing of thrusts does provide a desirable "flexibility" in the execution of strategy. Delaying or even shifting the sequence of major moves permits postponing heavy commitments. This introduces a degree of flexibility without a total change in strategy with each shift in the wind.

In dealing with thrusts, even more than with differential advantages, a business-unit should be highly *selective*. Highlighting the critical moves, in contrast to all sorts of minor maneuvers, is a significant part of the guidance strategy provides.

## Target the Results Expected

The three elements of company strategy just described deal primarily with what to do, when to do it, and, by implication, what not to do. They are guides to more detailed planning and action which are to follow. But this emphasis leaves out one important dimension of strategy: if these things are done (and the environment is largely as predicted), what results are expected?

A small manufacturer of testing instruments for metallurgical industries, for instance, adopted a strategy of major commitment to research in the use of lasers. Translated into targets or anticipated results, this research commitment meant aiming for (1) a breakthrough in testing equipment in two to five years, (2) a reputation as a technical leader in the field within three years, and (3) reaching a break-even point in company profit and loss during the next three to five years. Note how much clearer the strategy is when we state *both* the means (laser research) and the ends (the three targets).

There are several reasons why strategy should include some statement of anticipated results. First, the people who must endorse the strategy, especially those who contribute resources, will be able to reasonably hold back until they get some feel for what the situation is likely to be as a consequence of all this activity. Also, the individuals designing the strategy will have their personal objectives and values, and they, too, will be concerned about how results are expected to match these criteria. And by no means least important, target results set the stage for shorter run goals and controls which are essential ingredients of effective implementation.

How does the senior manager who is responsible for the selection of strategy decide, "O.K., that's it"? Fundamentally, the process involves (1) selecting the criteria for judging the strategy, (2) translating and stating the expected results of the strategy in terms of these criteria, and (3) deciding whether the expected results (the targets) meet acceptable minimum levels of achievement and are better than expected results of alternative targets.

## Criteria to Be Considered

The following criteria are often used to evaluate a strategy:

1. Return on investment (usually this is profit related to financial investment, but it might be the return on any critically scarce resources)
2. Risk of losing investment in scarce resources
3. Company growth (in absolute terms or as a percentage of the market)
4. Contribution to social welfare (in one or more dimensions)
5. Stability and security of employment and earnings (of all employees and/or of executives)
6. Prestige of the company and of company representatives
7. Future control (or influence) over company decisions

Different individuals naturally stress one or two of the above criteria—finance people the return on investment, research people the company prestige, marketing people the company growth, and so forth—and occasionally they may wish to add other criteria such as cash flow or international balance of payments. Fortunately, doing well on one criterion does not necessarily detract from all of the others. A specific strategy has not one, but a whole set of results, and the only practical way to judge a strategy is to consider several criteria simultaneously. To expedite the evaluation process, three or four of these various criteria should be singled out as dominant in the specific situation.

## Expressing Strategy in Terms of Criteria

Meaningful strategies must be conceived in *operational* terms, such as products to sell, markets to reach, materials to acquire, research to perform, and the like. However, such actions take on value only as they contribute to desired results. And the pertinent results are defined by the criteria just discussed.

So to relate a strategy to the selected criteria, a conversion or translation is needed. For instance, the actions contemplated in a strategy have to be expressed in anticipated costs and revenues, which give us an estimated profit. Similarly, the proposed actions have to be restated in terms of human resources to estimate their effect on stability of employment (if that is one of the key criteria). And likewise for other criteria.

These restatements of anticipated results become the targets at which the strategy is aimed. But since the success of any strategy is never certain, these targets will be surrounded by many "ifs" and "maybes." Often they should be expressed as a range, not a single point, with subjective probabilities attached. Nevertheless, tentative though the estimates may be, this is the basis on which a strategy will be evaluated.

## Are Targets Acceptable?

Now, with criteria selected and the anticipated results of strategy expressed in terms of these criteria, the manager is in a position to say, "Let's go" or "That's not good enough." Rarely is there a choice among several strategies, each of which is quite attractive. Instead, the pressing question is whether any proposed plan is acceptable at all. The reason for this scarcity of attractive choices is that all of us have *high aspirations,* at least for one or two criteria. Thirty percent profits, no real risk, worldwide prestige, half of industry sales—any and all of these may be part of our dreams. The blunt facts are that few of these dreams will be realized by any strategy we can conceive. So we have to decide what *level of achievement* will be acceptable for each of our criteria.

This picking of acceptable levels is complicated by differences in values held by key executives. For instance, Strategy A may promise a 30 percent return on capital, but with a 15 percent chance of complete loss and a sure transfer of ownership; whereas Strategy B promises only a 15 percent return of capital, but with small risk of total loss and little danger of change in control of the company. Many quantitative techniques exist for computing optimal combinations. Reality, however, indicates that personal perceptions and values strongly affect the decision. The chair of the board—say, a wealthy person and a large stockholder—may prefer Strategy A; while the president, who came up from the ranks and owns little stock, may prefer Strategy B. Or, if the chairperson likes the prestige of the position and the president thinks the chairperson is too conservative, the preferences may be reversed.

It is difficult to generalize about whose values will predominate. Generally, the most active and aggressive senior executives will establish the pattern, *provided* that their objectives meet at least the minimum acceptable requirement of each interest group whose withdrawal of support could paralyze the company. In the language of Chapter 1, the "output" of the strategy must enable the company to fulfill at least the minimum needs of resource contributors. Thus, while there is no simple resolution of how high targets should be, we obviously should not evade the translation of operational plans into key targets (or vice versa).

A strategy expressed in terms of targets alone is little more than wishful thinking. On the other hand, an operational strategy that is not translated into targets is primarily an article of faith. A well-developed strategy has *both* an operational plan and targets.

## SUMMARY

Company strategy deals with the basic ways a business-unit seeks to take optimum advantage of its environment. As we saw in Chapter 2, changes in technology, politics, social structure, and economics create opportunities as well as problems. To bring these environmental factors into sharper focus, we urged that they be woven into industry analyses. Such industry studies identify growth and profit prospects, and also the key factors necessary for future participation in the growth. Still more pointed is analysis of company strengths and weaknesses outlined in Chapter 3, and a matching of these against the key success factors for each industry. The final narrowing, proposed in Chapter 4, calls for an analysis of key actors and their likely responses to our moves.

Armed with this background, central management selects its strategy. The strategy indicates (1) the *domain* to be sought, (2) our *differential advantages* in serving that domain, (3) *strategic thrusts* necessary to move from our present position to the desired one, and (4) *target results* to be achieved. These elements interact and should reinforce each other.

Of course, the master plan evolves. As the environment changes, some uncertainties become realities and new uncertainties arise. And the company strategy may be shifted to take advantage of the new situation. Competitors are also responding to the same environment, and their actions may open up—or require—adjusted action. Meanwhile the company itself moves forward and/or runs into snags, so it has new internal information and modified strengths and weaknesses. Inevitably the strategy needs reassessment.

Nevertheless, at any point in time, and hopefully for a long enough span to translate plans into action, the main elements of strategy remain stable. With this overriding guidance, central management moves to elaboration and implementation of the scheme (as we do in the next parts of the book).

Small companies benefit from well-conceived strategies fully as much as large ones. Their strengths and options differ, but their flexibility and growth rate can be greater.

# Questions for Class Discussion

1. The Hudson School in Hoboken, New Jersey, is a nonprofit, interracial private school for gifted children in grades 5 through 8. It was established 10 years ago because the local public schools are weak, especially in regard to bright pupils. From the start, Hudson School has operated on a shoestring. The city lets the school use an old library building, and charitable foundations make annual grants for scholarships for children whose parents cannot afford the $3,000 per year tuition. Most teaching is done by part-timers who will take low pay because they are interested in the project; their qualifications in terms of degrees, experience, and commitment far exceed those of teaching staffs in most school systems, but scheduling classwork is difficult with so many people coming and going.

   Enrollment has now reached 100 students, and if growth is to continue a firmer base is needed. The most pressing problems are that the building is being used to its capacity, annual grants from foundations make three-to-five-year planning difficult, a larger nucleus of full-time professional staff is needed to coordinate the innovative teaching of the part-timers, and pressure to admit more (very bright) students from outside Hoboken is rising. The board of directors of this successful small business would like to maintain the momentum, but on what fronts, in what sequence, and how fast is unclear.

   List and defend the strategic thrusts that you recommend for the Hudson School.

2.  H.J. Heinz Company has achieved considerable success recently (a return of
    23.3 percent on shareholder's equity after taxes, a five-year average growth
    rate of sales of 4.1 percent—just equal to the average rate of inflation—and a
    five-year growth rate of 13.4 percent of net income) while trying to reach two
    goals: (1) added convenience of its food products—pickles, Ore-Ida potatoes,
    Weight Watchers products, and ketchup, among others; and (2) becoming the
    low-cost producer in each line of its products. (a) Use each of the boxes in Fig-
    ure 5–3 to identify possible alternative ways of the company's expanding.
    (b) Do the same for a medical clinic consisting of five doctors concentrating on
    pediatrics.

3.  A large stockholder in Neptune Pharmaceuticals says, "Fundamentally, our
    strategic objective should be to maximize the return on investment in the long
    run." Is this a useful way for managers to state their strategic target?

4.  One company's statement of objectives calls for "a decent return to stock-
    holders, an example to the community of corporate citizenship, payment of
    better than a living wage and stability of employment for all employees, hon-
    orable treatment of suppliers, and the willingness to undertake business risks
    to provide an example of dynamic management." How can the concept of
    "strategy" as outlined in this chapter help sharpen the meaning and the focus
    of such a statement?

5.  Wilda Winters is a well-known landscape architect in the San Francisco Bay
    area. She is often employed by building architects to plan the layout and
    planting around commercial buildings and "Silicon Valley" plants, especially
    on irregular terrain. These contacts lead to her obtaining private jobs for
    homeowners, mostly long-range plans that integrate gradual growth with
    seasonal beauty. Also, she has two small annual retainers with community
    governments.

    Winters is discussing the formation of a corporation with B.P. Green As-
    sociates, landscape contractors who primarily have annual contracts for full
    responsibility for maintenance of the grounds surrounding large business es-
    tablishments. Green Associates also seeks grading and planting jobs around
    new construction, which frequently include installing sprinklers and
    drains.

    The rationale back of the Winters/Green proposal is (a) more steady in-
    come for Winters, and (b) entry into "big time" landscaping for Green, hope-
    fully replacing some of the routine lawn mowing the company currently
    performs.

    Suppose that you are a partner in B.P. Green Associates. (You do the fi-
    nancial and accounting work, a job that is paying your way through school.)
    Do you recommend going ahead with the new corporation? Are there any
    strategy issues that you want resolved first?

6.  Steiger Tractors, Inc., has dominated its particular niche in the farm tractor in-
    dustry. Steiger tractors not only have four-wheel drive; they are "articulated"

in the middle so that all four wheels stay on the ground, even in rough terrain. And they are at the top of farm tractors' power range, with models varying from 200 to 450 horsepower. Moreover, the 267-gallon fuel tank and lighting system allow 20 hours of uninterrupted running time. These features enable farmers of large tracts to work in wet fields and otherwise act fast when planting and harvesting should be done. But the tractors cost a lot of money: $50,000 to $90,000 when fully equipped.

Steiger tractors are sold as an extra line by local dealers whose main business is with J.I. Case, Massey Ferguson, or other major suppliers of farm equipment. This works reasonably well when farmers are prospering and equipment sales are brisk. But when farm profits are low, Steiger's niche does not have enough volume to support the small, feisty North Dakota producer.

Steiger's problem, then, is how to stay alive in a single volatile niche. Its alternatives include, but are not limited to, merging production in some other company's plant to cut overhead, adding special equipment used with its tractors, making two-wheel drive tractors (thereby competing with major producers), seeking subcontracts for assembling heavy machinery, slashing cash outlays, and waiting for the farm equipment industry to become prosperous again.

What course do you recommend that Steiger Tractors, Inc., take?

7. Under the leadership of Mr. Richard J. Ferris, the former United Airlines Corporation bought Hertz Car Rentals from RCA Corporation and added Hertz to other purchases of the Hilton International Company and Westin Hotel Company chains. Mr. Ferris's goal for a travel supermarket strategy was to seek synergy among the airline, car rental, and hotel groups while changing the combined companies' name to Allegis Corporation. The acquisitions took two years to complete, but the new name lasted for only four months. The board of directors fired Mr. Ferris and planned to sell off the four units. Three active bidders immediately showed up for the two hotel groups and the airline, while the Hertz operation was rumored to be on the block for $800 million. Use Mr. Ferris's actions to illustrate each of the four elements in company strategy discussed in this chapter. (The aim of this question is to evince the meaning of strategy, so make assumptions if you need to.)

Two British investors have offered to buy the Hilton International Co. for slightly more than Allegis paid for it, but the price of $1 billion is so high that there is considerable skepticism about anyone's ability to earn a profit or a return on this investment. One source was quoted as saying, "That's more than any U.S. company would ever pay for it based on its earnings." How would this change in ownership affect the strategy you would recommend for the hotels?

8. Continuing education (education of people already employed in business for 5 to 25 years) will become much more important during the next decade. Two reasons are (a) a decline in the college-age pool of potential students, and (b) rapid technological changes which will make obsolescent much of what

we are learning today. Assuming that this forecast is correct, what changes, if any, in its present strategy should your school make?

9. "After Slow Start, Gene Machines Approach a Period of Fast Growth and Steady Profits." So read the headline, and Leon Wood, president of Applied Biotechnologies, thought he agreed. His machines make DNA, the basic raw material of the genetic code and the essential raw material in the growing business of genetic engineering. Applied Biotechnologies machines sell for about $80,000 each and allow users to turn out 10 strands of DNA (deoxyribonucleic acid) each week, 10 times the rate of manual production. The gene machine is a chemical robot. Housed inside a suitcase-sized metal cabinet containing a maze of computer-controlled valves and bottles holding the chemical ingredients of DNA, it pumps the chemicals in a programmed sequence onto a glass column, where the strand of DNA "grows." Having a machine is like having an earth-mover to build a dam. The manual method was like using a shovel.

   Applied Biotechnologies has worked its cash flow up to a point that successfully covers its heavy debt and interest payments, and it expects to show a profit soon. With five other competitors in the gene-machine game, Leon Wood expects to have a significant market share and steady profits in competition with the three independent manufacturers (subsidized by venture capital companies) and the two subsidiaries of large pharmaceutical firms. His problem is to decide whether or not to try to make and sell the chemicals used in the DNA machine. "Shall we imitate Gillette?" he asks. Doing so would put him in a different game—competing with chemical companies like Merck and du Pont and also searching out new resource suppliers. "We would have the same customers, but different suppliers of raw materials and of money. Perhaps our sales force would need to be different also. We know how to build the machine, but we don't know, as yet, how to make the chemicals."

   What is your evaluation of a strategy for Applied Biotechnologies that would mean a somewhat varied domain and an uncertain differential advantage?

10. In the middle and late 1980s, Exxon Corporation and Royal Dutch/Shell Group appeared to be carrying on a long-continued rivalry for first place in the worldwide oil business and for future dominance of the petroleum industry. Exxon had reigned for decades as the world's undisputed leader in corporate size. But in 1986 Shell took over first place.

   Mr. Lawrence G. Rawls, Exxon's chairman of the board, said, "Revenues don't count with me. What counts is net income after taxes." Mr. Peter E. Holmes, the head of the British side of Royal Dutch/Shell, said, "It would be very nice to be number one (in profitability), [but] that is not our prime objective." Both companies are betting on an eventual resurgence in the oil business. Both cut employment after 1982, Exxon from 182,000 to 102,000 persons and Shell from 165,000 to 138,000. In 1987 Exxon's capital and exploration budget amounted to $6.5 billion, while Shell's outlays were $7.2 billion. In total sales, Shell in 1986 vaulted over Chevron, Texaco, and Exxon to be the nation's leading gasoline marketer. Exxon and Shell are reputed to attract different types of people—the Texas wildcatter against the Oxford types who consider Shell as the next best thing to going into the foreign office. Both Exxon and Shell share the "problem" of investing enormous cash flows. Bankers estimate that Exxon's "free cash"—total cash received less dividend payouts and capital expenses—will amount to $1.5 to $1.6 billion a year until 1990. Shell will accumulate "free cash" totaling $4.7 billion from 1987 to 1990. Like other American corporations, Exxon is under pressure from stockholders and Wall Street for quarterly earnings performance, even as it plans for the next 20 years. Shell is headquartered in London and Amsterdam and has a different philosophy about business. Mr. Holmes says, "I don't lose any sleep over one quarter." Since 1983, Exxon has spent more than $7 billion buying back its own shares. Exxon officials say that this helps raise the price of the stock and is a way to acquire oil reserves—its own—at a bargain price of $3 per barrel. Over the past three years, Exxon has acquired $2.1 billion of oil properties while Royal Dutch/Shell has spent $11 to $12 billion on acquisitions. One Shell official said that the group was disappointed when Exxon urged scaling back their joint venture in the Kittiwake North Sea oil field after oil prices plunged in 1986. The companies had been committed to spending $1.5 billion each, but at Exxon's urging, said the official, development spending was reduced to between $350 million and $400 million each. "We were surprised at Exxon. We didn't think that it was one of the companies that had to worry." But Mr. Rawls called the Kittiwake a "modest" field and says Exxon has had bigger differences with its partners over more significant projects.

Do Exxon and Shell seem to you to have different objectives and strategies? Much different or about the same? Explain.

(Data and information for this question came from *The Wall Street Journal*, July 8, 1987.)

11. Mr. Michael Bozic, an executive from Sears, Roebuck & Co.'s Canadian operations, was appointed chairman and chief executive officer of Sears's merchandising group in late 1986. Among the problems he faced were the company's sales growth rate of 2 percent versus the industry average of 5 percent; a decline in profits of about 0.8 percent for the year; an expense ratio to sales of more than 30 percent, contrasted with a ratio of less than 20 percent for some fast-growing competitors such as Wal-Mart Stores, Inc.; a general belief that the future in retailing is to be either a mass merchant with low prices or a specialty store with higher priced goods, and not a general-merchandising retailer such as Sears; an inability to improve Sears's appeal to women (the company has trouble selling such high-margin items as apparel for teenagers and career women); and diversification attempts such as Business Systems Centers—a network of computer retailers—and neighborhood

hardware and paint stores which have stalled and contributed little to net profits.

Sears's objective has been to use its name and retail customer base to build a national financial services network: Allstate Insurance, Coldwell Banker Real Estate, Dean Witter stocks and bonds, and the Discover credit card. Sears's executives see the retailing base as the link between the younger, product-oriented customer of today and tomorrow's older, more affluent consumer with an appetite for services and investments. In 1985 the merchandise group, with a profit of $766 million, contributed about 60 percent of the company's overall profit, and the group's revenue of $26.6 billion was about two-thirds of the total.

Mr. Bozic did well in Canada by accelerating an aggressive cost-cutting campaign which helped to double the operating profit (to Canadian $76 million) during his 2½-year term as president of merchandising and by stressing apparel by carrying such brand names as Arrow shirts and Robert Stock men's wear.

(a) In your opinion, why is Sears losing market share in the U.S. although it is still the world's biggest retailer? What have K-mart Corp., J.C. Penney, and Montgomery Ward & Co. done recently?

(b) What is Sears's differential advantage?

(c) What do you see as Sears's future domain?

(d) What targets should Sears strive for?

## CASE
### 5 Sun Microsystems, Inc.

Four 27-year-old graduate students founded Sun Microsystems five years ago. Sales of the company last year topped $500 million, with net income rising to $36 million. Having no obvious protection against competition, Sun's young managers must decide where to go from here.

### Industry Setting

As the company name proclaims, Sun Microsystems sells small computer systems, often called work stations. Familiar examples of computer systems include the ticket reservation scheme now used by airlines and the use of computers by supermarkets at their checkout counters. The systems made by Sun differ from these examples in size: they are small in the sense that typically they are run by a single person, but they are capable of doing very complex calculations.

The industry that makes these amazing devices is new, unclearly structured, and turbulent. Nevertheless, deciding how to fit into the tangle is crucial for a young firm like Sun. Broadly speaking, many companies in the industry make only *components*, while other companies combine these components into *systems*. And blurring that distinction, the larger corporations are often vertically integrated, making some of the components that go into their systems.

The components of an electronic computer system include (1) the physical parts which go into the machine that we see and feel, commonly called *the* computer; these are the chips, keyboard, display, cabinet, etc. (2) the software, which consists of sets of standard instructions, or "programs," that tell the computer how to proceed; since users may want their computer to do many different things, a bewildering array of programs has been written. And (3) "peripheral" equipment, which does additional tasks directly related to the data that go into or comes out of a computer. Peripherals include printers, graphic displays, storage devices, transmitters, and the like. Perhaps communication devices such as telephone lines, fiber optics cabling, or satellite transmission should also be included, because getting information from one place to another is an essential feature of a computer system.

Fitting components—parts, programs, and peripherals—into an effective computer system is not easy. A few users of computer systems may understand the characteristics of various components, or the task they want done may be so simple that they (or their consultant) can design their own system. Most users, however, want a package that does a complete task—just as you want an automobile that is ready to drive. Building a good system calls for knowledge about the capability and capacity of each part, or perhaps modifying that part so that it suits the specific needs of a customer. Even more troublesome is finding parts that can be connected together. The available software may not match the physical capabilities of a given computer, or the printer may have been designed for a different sort of output signals.

These compatibility problems are partly a result of the way companies that make computer systems compete with each other. In the United States especially, competition takes the form of doing something different than competitors— offering users a system that is faster, or prints out specifications at 30 plants around the world simultaneously, or has some other unusual feature. Each product differentiation is featured. Moreover, each company would like to deny competitors the ability to match its unusual feature, at least for a period of time. Such a barrier to entry prevents price competition and encourages the user to come back to the same supplier for additional equipment.

Indeed, all large system suppliers, and most component suppliers, devote large R & D efforts to differentiating their products. (See Table 5–1.) They seek state-of-the-art features and try to predict what competitors are developing. Of course, this effort accelerates the technological change, adding to the normal uncertainty of a new industry like computers. In practice, it is difficult for any one

**TABLE 5–1.**
**LARGE COMPUTER SYSTEMS MANUFACTURERS**
**1986, in millions of dollars except last column**

|  | Operating Revenue | Net Income | R & D Expense | Ratio R & D to Operating Revenue |
|---|---|---|---|---|
| Amdahl Corp. | 966 | 59 | 119 | 12.3% |
| Computervision Corp. | 495 | 6 | 47 | 9.4 |
| Control Data Corp. | 3,347 | 269 | 405 | 12.1 |
| Cray Research, Inc. | 597 | 125 | 88 | 14.7 |
| Data General Corporation | 1,286 | 6 | 145 | 11.3 |
| Digital Equipment Corp. | 7,590 | 617 | 814 | 10.7 |
| Hewlett-Packard Corp. | 7,102 | 516 | 824 | 11.6 |
| Intergraph Corporation | 606 | 70 | 58 | 9.5 |
| IBM | 51,256 | 4,789 | 5,221 | 10.2 |
| NCR Corp. | 4,881 | 337 | 321 | 6.6 |
| Prime Computer | 860 | 47 | 92 | 10.7 |
| Unisys Corp. | 7,432 | 43 | 441 | 5.9 |
| Wang Laboratories | 2,642 | 51 | 187 | 6.9 |
| Sun Microsystems, Inc.* | 538 | 36 | 70 | 13.0 |

*Sun Microsystems data are for fiscal year ending June 30, 1987.

company to maintain product superiority for long. Within a couple of years competitors learn how to match the design or technique, or they come out with a design that bypasses the previous leader. The manufacturers of computer chips and peripherals, who are playing a similar game, make their new products available to several systems companies, and this adds to the volatility.

Not all companies, however, rely so heavily on new product development for competitive differential advantage. The large Japanese parts suppliers, for instance, have won very strong positions in world markets, including the United States, by focusing on low cost and high quality. For computer chips, especially, their research centers on production technology. Furthermore, they persist in developing state-of-the-art production by making incremental improvements over a period of years (whereas U.S. producers often abandon a line and seek a new product when their comparative costs are high). Thus, as product designs stabilize, the Japanese firms become the dominant parts suppliers. Meanwhile, U.S. producers probably find themselves with excess capacity, and if they elect to continue producing what is no longer a unique part, they will have to match the efficient Japanese firms' prices and quality.

As a result of frequent technological advances, who is doing what in the industry changes from year to year.

During the mid-1980s the computer industry experienced a sharp slowdown. A large number of computers were sold, but the rate of increase did not match the previous pattern. For instance, all but one of the companies listed in Table 5–1 had an increase in sales volume in 1986 compared with 1985, but because of competitive pressures, almost half of them had a decline in their net income. The smaller, start-up firms had mixed experience during this period. As has always happened, some survived and some failed, but in the mid-1980s the proportion that failed was much higher than in the 1970s. A blanket of disbelief, even gloom, spread over Silicon Valley.

Sun Microsystems, Inc., entered the computer industry during this slowdown period. But luckily the demand for work stations was on the rise, especially compared to that for large mainframe computers. So in Sun's domain, the outlook for sales volume was good. The prospects for profit, however, depended on careful selection of niches and on developing differential advantages that would not require long periods of expensive development.

## Sun's Selected Niches

Sun's entry into this turmoil in 1982 was guided by four young men who were entranced by computers. The company was brought together by Vinod Khosla, a Stanford MBA candidate who was impressed by a system design of a shy electrical engineering student, Andreas Bachtolsheim. Khosla also recruited his roommate, Scott McNealy, and a frustrated graduate student at the University of California at Berkeley, Bill Joy, who is a software artist. All four were 27 years old and neophytes in the computer industry. But they shared a concept for a high-powered work station, a concept that defies much of the widespread industry practice described in the opening section of this case.

A work station is a localized computer system with its own computer, software, and peripherals that can serve the immediate needs of a professional employee. Although such a station may get data from or send data to a central information center, basically it is a stand-alone system. Sun's work stations are portable, desk-top machines, but they contain a lot of up-to-date chips which make them very powerful (like a mainframe computer of only a few years ago). Another feature of Sun's original and present work stations is the use of the UNIX operating system, an off-the-shelf set of programs for controlling the computer's basic functions. The choice of UNIX illustrates Sun's dominant aim to use standard, readily available hardware and software whenever possible, an aim in direct contrast with the typical U.S. company effort to differentiate its products.

Sun selected a niche for its first work stations: the engineering, scientific, and technical markets. Professionals in these areas quickly recognized the advantages of Sun's powerful, simple, standard systems for resolving some of their complex problems. And the relatively low price made it feasible for a customer to establish a whole series of work stations instead of trying to tie into a large centralized mainframe computer. This means that customers buy not just one, but dozens of Sun's work stations. And buy they did: Sun's revenue curve shows shipments more than doubling each year for the five years that the company has been in existence. (See Table 5–2.)

The scientific and engineering niche has been a good launching pad for Sun (as it was for Digital Computer Corporation 25 years earlier). And now the company is branching out to the government market—one federal intelligence agency just placed a $200 million order—and tentatively into the financial analyst arena.

Competitors are active in each of these and other likely niches. Actually, Apollo Computer Co. started selling work stations a year and a half before Sun, and it has reached a $400 million volume with the more conventional differentiated product approach. Digital Equipment Corporation, the second largest computer company in the U.S., considers microcomputers an important part of its domain, and it is sure to respond vigorously. Fully as threatening are smaller firms which, like Sun, have the flexibility of a fresh start. As will be noted in the next section, Sun lacks proprietary products and software that might serve as barriers to entry for such firms.

## Differential Advantages of Sun

Sun appeals to users of work stations by doing several key activities differently than its competitors.

1. Its products are *compatible* with a wide range of other computers and systems. Instead of seeking ways to make its product different, as most U.S. competitors do, Sun has designed its equipment and software so that a Sun work station

**TABLE 5-2.**
**SUN MICROSYSTEMS, INC., OPERATING DATA**
**in millions of dollars, except unit and share figures for fiscal years ending June 30**

|  | 1987 | 1986 | 1985 | 1984 | 1983 |
|---|---|---|---|---|---|
| Net revenue | 538 | 210 | 115 | 39 | 9 |
| Cost and expenses: | | | | | |
| Cost of sales | 273 | 102 | 62 | 21 | 4 |
| R&D expense | 70 | 31 | 15 | 5 | 2 |
| Selling & administrative expense | 127 | 57 | 24 | 9 | 2 |
| Total | 469 | 190 | 101 | 35 | 8 |
| Operating income before income tax | 69 | 20 | 14 | 4 | 1 |
| Net income after tax | 36 | 11 | 9 | 3 | 1 |
| Net income per share (dollars) | 1.11 | 0.42 | 0.36 | 0.13 | 0.04 |
| Units shipped | 24,600 | 9,900 | 5,900 | 2,200 | 500 |
| Revenue per unit (dollars) | 21,900 | 21,200 | 19,500 | 17,700 | 17,300 |

*Balance Sheet: June 30, 1987*

| | | | |
|---|---|---|---|
| Current assets | 397 | Current liabilities | 155 |
| Net property | 100 | Long-term debt | 128 |
| Other assets | 27 | Stockholders' equity | 241 |
| Total assets | 524 | Total debt & equity | 524 |

can easily be connected to other computer systems that a customer may have or acquire and so that all sorts of peripheral equipment can be connected to it.

This compatibility overcomes customers' hesitation to buy a special-purpose local system that adds to isolation rather than fitting into coordinated capability. Likewise, compatibility with peripherals means that all sorts of variations in functions that particular users want (laser printers, mass storage, etc.) can readily be provided. Instead of trying to lock a customer into a Sun family of products, Sun's aim is to link into the perceived strengths of other companies' products.

2. Sun buys standard, well-known components; it does not try to manufacture them in-house. This practice makes Sun systems more acceptable, for instance, to government agencies, because the components are already recognized as being reliable and future replacement or repair will be easier due to the widespread use of a standard item.

Indeed, when Sun wanted a particular kind of microprocessor chips that was not available on the merchant market (a simplified RISC chip for "reduced instruction set computing"), it contracted for several chip manufacturers to make them and urged the manufacturers to sell them to other computer system companies. Sun wants these RISC chips to be not a proprietary item of Sun's, but a standard product in the industry.

3. A corollary of using standard components is that their cost is normally low. Competition in the industry, already described, drives the prices of standard items down. Moreover, by using standard items, Sun avoids R & D expenses related to their design and manufacturing technology. As a result, Sun's costs of goods are as low or lower than competitors' costs, and its selling prices are correspondingly low. With its production operations being primarily the assembly of purchased parts, Sun was able to turn over half a billion dollars worth of products with only 3,750 employees.

Sun's strategy to feature simple, powerful systems that have broad compatibility, standard components, and low price clearly appeals to many users, as shown by a sales growth rate far faster than the computer industry generally, and also faster than Apollo Computers or Digital Equipment Corporation, Sun's close competitors. However, a major disadvantage of the strategy is that it can be easily copied by existing and new competitors. The openness of the system and the use of widely available components remove typical barriers to entry.

As a defense against such newcomers, Sun hopes to keep a jump ahead in designing systems that incorporate recently available components. In fact, during its five-year life Sun has introduced four generations of work stations, each doubling the power of its predecessor for roughly the same price. Carol Bartz, the 38-year-old vice president who manages Sun's government business, says, "We wouldn't hesitate to bring out a new product at a price and performance level that absolutely destroyed an existing line. Why should we wait for competition to do it?"[2]

Of course, this puts a high premium on agility in systems design, purchasing, and assembly. To assist the engineers in this process, Sun's marketing director keeps detailed two-year forecasts of what each major competitor and component supplier is likely to offer. However, if the frequency of technological change in computers slows down, as is likely, then keeping a jump ahead of imitators provides less protection. Or, if an important development is available only to one or two competitors and does not find its way into the merchant market as a standard design, then Sun would be constrained in its jumping.

## Strategic Thrusts

The importance to Sun of moving promptly affects its strategic thrusts. Having found a profitable niche, Sun needed to exploit it rapidly before competitors moved in. Sun's hectic growth was a necessity, not merely an option.

---

[2]*Fortune*, August 17, 1987, p. 90.

Fortunately for Sun, the computer industry had a slowdown at the same time Sun was expanding. This meant that many experienced managers and engineers were looking for jobs when Sun needed them. Other resources also were in plentiful supply. Even with these available resources, managing the fast growth of Sun has been a remarkable achievement; nevertheless, the timing was favorable.[3]

Where to place major efforts remains an issue. Scientific and technical research work stations were the first targets; many local professionals were able to use the large computer power that Sun systems provided. A second thrust has been military and other government agencies concerned with technical issues. How and when to approach commercial operations is not so clear. Meanwhile, Sun has pushed into both Europe and Japan, with Europe accounting for 25 percent of total sales in 1987 (mostly shipped from the U.S.).

Two considerations affect the choice of thrusts: where the highest short-run profits can be earned, and forestalling competitors. In the latter regard, by making the sort of business that Sun engages in unattractive in their home markets, the company hopes that foreign competitors will be less likely to invade the niches that Sun is already in.

## Target Results

Sun's CEO, Scott McNealy, makes speeches about becoming a broad-based general-purpose computing company and changing the fundamentals of the computer industry, but such objectives are too vague to serve as strategic targets. Even financial results like those shown in Table 5–2 provide inadequate managerial direction.

More useful are operating targets. For the R & D group, these state the performance characteristics desired in a new system design and the dates when such a design will be turned over to production managers. For marketing, sales quotas for customer groups and geographic regions are set, along with goals for market positions and gross margins. For production (including purchasing), delivery schedules and quantities available for sales commitments are vital in this rapidly expanding company, along with cost targets.

In other words, to keep the total company in balance, Sun's strategy has to be converted into quite specific goals for each division. These goals are often adjusted, but at any point in time each division knows what other parts of the company are expecting of it. The subtleties come in guessing what future changes in goals will be like and getting ready for them, an activity at which Sun thus far has been unusually adept.

---

[3]McNealy has been CEO during the largest expansion. Khosla retired with his wealth at age 30, as he said he would do.

## Questions

1. Where will Sun Microsystems, Inc., be vulnerable during its next five years?
2. What changes, if any, do you recommend in Sun Microsystems's present four-part strategy?

# PART 2

## Shaping Department Programs to Execute Strategy

# Department Programs: Channeling Functional Excellence into Integrated Strategic Action

Business-unit strategy provides the dominant, overall guidance for a "company"—a single-line firm or a self-contained operating division of a large corporation. Such strategy is a vital instrument for focusing management's attention on future opportunities.

Business-unit strategy, however, is only an expression of intentions, until people in the operating departments of the company carry it out. The departments are where goods and services are produced, customers' orders are obtained, new products are designed, employees are trained, etc. So a bridge between business-unit strategy and department operations is crucial. In other words, the multi-level approach to strategy must be extended downward to the department level, as indicated in Figure 6–1.

The extension of business-unit strategy into department activities is the subject of Part 2 of the text. First, in this chapter we will present a general framework for building the bridge. Then, in the following chapters we will look at key issues faced by the primary functional departments: marketing, R & D, production, purchasing, human resources, and finance. Here the aim is to see how resolution of department-related issues can be tied into business-unit strategy. Of course, not all of the possible linkages can be considered, but Chapters 7 through 14 flag typical interconnections. And in the process of this examination, the basic framework presented in the present chapter will be frequently called on.

## Why the Department Level Warrants More Attention

Most of the current writing about business strategy deals with either corporate strategy or business-unit strategy. To a surprising extent, an assumption has been made that departments within a business-unit meekly conform to whatever role is assigned to them. In fact, such conformity often does not take place.

### Need for Closer Links

Each department in a company faces its own set of problems and has developed distinctive traditions. Indeed, in many ways it marches to its own drummer. So when a change in business-unit strategy is announced, departments do not au-

**FIGURE 6-1.**
**MULTI-LEVEL STRATEGY**

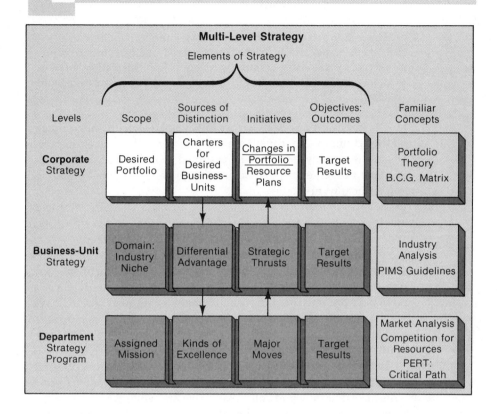

tomatically revise their actions. Instead, the fitting together of the new strategy with behavior within a department calls for considerable managerial skill.

Serious efforts to fuse department programs with strategic moves at the business level are important for several reasons:

1. *Execution of strategy is frequently held back or distorted at the department level.* For instance, RCA was ahead of most competitors in adopting a strategy for intensive effort to design and sell video recordings for home use. However, its research department was so wedded to disks (reflecting long experience with phonograph records), that attention to videotapes was sidetracked. Consequently, competing companies introduced the more versatile VCRs before RCA's research department could design a practical video disk. The RCA business-unit strategy was pointed in the right direction, but department execution was shortsighted and sluggish.

Indeed, middle-level managers have their own agendas. For example, Guth and MacMillan report the following on the behavior of several hundred such managers:

> . . . The data and analysis of this study provide strong, if indirect, evidence that middle managers who believe that their self-interest is being compromised cannot only redirect a strategy, delay its implementation or reduce the quality of its implementation, but can also even totally sabotage the strategy.[1]

The implication is clear: a close linkage between business strategy and the actions of department managers is vital. Congruence of objectives at the two levels cannot be assumed or mandated. Instead, the reasons for divergence must be appreciated and reshaped if planned strategic actions are to take place.

2. *The business-unit strategy itself may be unrealistic.* Unwise choices of strategy are often made because inadequate attention has been given to the distinct needs and capabilities of various departments. A supplier of automobile parts, for instance, almost went bankrupt because the strategic planners assumed that the production department could double its output within a few months. Sales boomed, but deliveries and quality became so erratic that the major customer canceled its orders. Here, a very competent supervisor could not personally direct so rapid an expansion, and he was unable to design and train the larger organization that was needed.

Too often strategy planners at the business-unit level presume, without realistic advice from people at the operating level, that departments are separately and collectively able and willing to do whatever the strategy calls for. In fact, the degrees of freedom for a department are often constrained, especially within necessary time and cost frames. For instance, sales leadership in a particular market niche or a research breakthrough cannot be decreed—or even bought—overnight. And it is at the department level that the amount of stretch and risk in particular competitive arenas are probably best known.

3. *A single industry outlook is unlikely to fit all departments.* The usual process of preparing a business strategy (including that recommended in Part 1) builds upon the outlook of a single industry, with the industry typically defined in terms of products or services to be sold. Thus, the focus may be on the home video industry or on the automobile production industry.

In reality, however, the key departments of any business-unit deal with several different "industries." The finance department, the

---

[1]"Strategy Implementation vs. Middle Management Self-Interest," *Strategic Management Journal* 7 (July 1986): 313.

human resource department, and the management information department, for instance, do most of their business in markets which have boundaries and competitive situations that differ sharply from those in the selling market. In other words, if you are treasurer of a company, the people you see and problems you confront are very different from those of the sales manager.

The outlook in these diverse industries should be taken into account when specific strategy is being developed. A practical approach for doing so is to link the department viewpoints more closely to the business-unit strategy.

## Department Entanglements: The Triple Linkage

Recognizing that gaps often exist between business-level strategy and department actions is a good start. But to remove such gaps, managers need a much fuller grasp of what is involved. What is required is an approach or model that helps identify the necessary conditions, inputs, and relationships of a department which will lead to desired strategic action.

One revealing approach is to analyze three critical links between a department and its close neighbors (see Figure 6–2):

**FIGURE 6–2.**
**THREE CRITICAL LINKAGES OF STRATEGY PROGRAMS FOR** *EACH*
**DEPARTMENT**

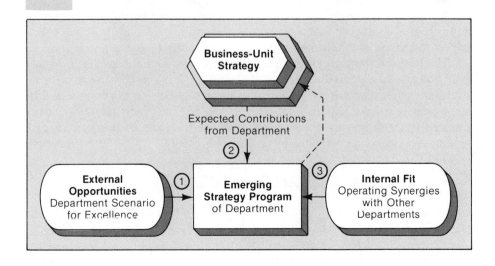

1.  The department manager (together with his or her associates) must deal with a slice of the world *outside* of its business-unit. Whatever the function of the department—finance, advertising, technological research, human resources, transportation, purchasing, etc.—there will be a special set of suppliers, rivals, regulators, consultants, and other people who affect what the department can do. The department itself must decide how best to cope with this distinct relevant environment.

2.  The department also has a set of internal horizontal relationships with other departments within its business-unit. For instance, the research department of Sterling Drug Co. works with the engineering department on new processes, provides technical data to the sales promotion department, relies on the finance and human resources departments for inputs, and so on. Each department has to negotiate interactions with other departments which will keep the total system running.

3.  In addition, each department has a role to play in its business-unit's strategic moves. It takes some part in formulating the business strategy, and it has assigned tasks in the execution of that strategy. As we shall see, this *vertical* linkage is more sensitive than often assumed.

The art of strategy programming at the department level lies in maintaining good linkages in all three directions *simultaneously*. Often pressures conflict. Grasping an external opportunity, for example, may upset internal commitments or divert resources from a strategic thrust. Meanwhile, other departments will be pressing the focal department to adapt to their opportunities.

These three linkages have such a strong impact on department strategy, that we will look at each separately. To simplify this scrutiny, we will focus on functional departments in established businesses. (The linkage problems of departments based on, say, geography or customers pose similar issues.) The presumption is that each department already has an assigned role, but that this role is subject to change as the strategy of the business changes.

The term "strategy program," as used here, refers to the steps that a department will take to support the business-unit strategy; it covers activities and/or results. Like other discussions of strategic management, not everything a department does is considered strategic. Rather, strategy programs deal with *major* changes in established operations and with new efforts that are necessary to provide agreed-upon support to the business-unit strategy.

## Scenario for an Excellent External Linkage

Of the three sorts of linkages—external, horizontal, and vertical—external relationships persistently draw departments in diverse directions. Functional departments are created to be experts in a particular type of work—finance, marketing, personnel, engineering, public relations, and the like. Each department concentrates on its specialty and is expected to seek excellence in its output. It keeps abreast of the latest advances in its area and acts for the company in that arena.

So to understand what makes a department "tick," we should know how the management of that department believes it can achieve excellence. That is, if given a free rein, what would the department do to become (remain) outstanding? What is its scenario for excellence?

Scenarios for excellence will differ sharply among departments due to the wide variations in the kind of work they do, their competitive setting, and the opportunities they have for innovative action. Some scenarios will be compatible with the current business-unit strategy, while others will clash with it. In order to get a better understanding of the fit between department programs and business-unit strategies, we need an appreciation of the forces leading to a department's preferred scenario. In fact, the viewpoint that a department takes is strongly influenced by three things: its distinctive external environment, its history, and its culture. Let us consider each of these in turn.

## Distinctive Environment of Each Department

As already noted, every department of a company operates in its own "industry": it has competitors, opportunities, relative strengths, a reputation, etc., which are distinct from similar attributes that other departments have in their respective industries. For instance, the purchasing department of a restaurant—like the exploration department of a petroleum firm—must know local markets, establish personal relationships with specific suppliers, anticipate actions of competitors, consider possible technological or legislative changes, and deal with a host of similar factors. The department manager is expected to devise ways in which the department can adjust to its industry so that it will win an outstanding position relative to competitors in that market.

Again, the advertising department of Pepsi Cola or of your local department store provides the liaison between the central business and the world of advertising—ad agencies, media, brand names, rankings, and the like. And this is a very different "ball game" than, say, finance in terms of concepts, issues, institutions, and competitive practices.

Each functional department naturally has a provincial view of the world. Thus, normally a marketing manager is engrossed in marketing affairs, and any external information he or she receives is likely to be market oriented because most of the marketing manager's business contacts will be with marketing people. Moreover, past success probably reflects skillful dealing with marketing problems. Consequently, the marketing department's scenario for an excellent external linkage will be based heavily on that provincial insight.

Managers of other functional departments will take a similar provincial viewpoint, and for similar reasons. Their daily problems, past experience, external contacts, rewards, and probably formal training as well as their assigned responsibilities all create a predominant concern with issues relating to their respective functions.

The total environment of a company is too far-flung and diffuse for any one department to comprehend it all. Instead, functional specialists pay attention to different parts or aspects of that environment. Having perceived different things and attached different values to what they perceived, it is only natural for a functional specialist to recommend a different strategy from that of other departments. This selective perception is indicated in Figure 6–3.

## Department History: What's Past Is Prelude

Each of us builds on our personal experiences. Thus, if you have found a personal computer helpful, you are likely to recommend one to a friend. And, almost

**FIGURE 6–3.**
**DEPARTMENT LINKAGES TO RELEVANT ENVIRONMENTS**

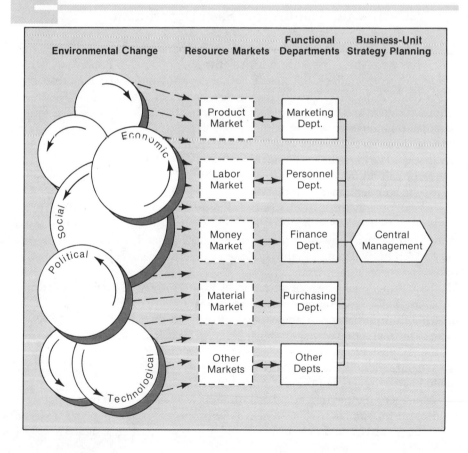

always, the form of government that U.S. diplomats recommend to developing countries includes an elected legislature and a separate executive branch.

Similarly, proposals for, and responses to, new business-unit strategies will vary from department to department partly because of the department histories. Every department in any successful company will have a lot of procedures and traditions that have worked well in the past. When faced with a new problem, the department naturally turns first to a familiar pattern. Thus, for years IBM sold its software and hardware bundled together.

Using established practices to deal with new problems is quite understandable. A lot of social momentum exists. Relationships are settled, behavior can be predicted, values are already embedded in procedures; so "why reinvent the wheel?"

Strong commitment may also be present. For instance, when a human resources department has worked hard on a promotion-from-within policy, any proposals from that department are likely to assume that newly created jobs will be filled by persons already employed by the company. In a similar vein, for a long time the engineering department of Baldwin Locomotive Company was so committed to steam rather than diesel power, that all its suggestions for strategic programs were built around steam locomotives. This sort of commitment may be more emotional than rational.

Such habits, attitudes, and values change slowly. Department scenarios for achieving excellence will deviate from them only to a small degree. Even if one department sees an advantage in a frame-breaking change, the other departments are likely to resist.

## Impact of Local Cultures Within Departments

A further reason why the scenarios for external excellence of a department may differ from the general management's view about what the department should do arises from contrasts in local cultures. A culture sets values and ways of looking at the world. These local values will affect both the content and daring of a department's proposed strategic programs.

For example, a research department in general actively seeks new insights and promotes change. Its planning horizon is at least several years ahead, and uncertainty is normal or even welcome. By contrast, a typical production department prefers stable, predictable activities. The time focus is on getting this year's or this month's output completed according to standards, and uncertainty is unwelcome or at least minimized.[2]

---

[2]The concept of different orientations of departments is developed in P. R. Lawrence and J. W. Lorsch, *Organization and Environment: Managing Differentiation and Integration* (Boston: Harvard Graduate School of Business Administration, 1967).

A department takes some if its values from the outside groups with which it works. For example, a finance department thinks in terms of conventional profit and loss, short-run cash flow, and balance sheets partly because these are strong values of banks and other external financial institutions. It is not surprising, then, that scenarios for excellence proposed by finance departments are usually stated in bland accounting terms.

Similarly, the values of an advertising department center on customers' feelings and perceptions partly because such intangibles are very important in the world of advertising agencies and TV programming. With this cultural background, the scenarios for excellence coming from a typical advertising department will stress quite different issues than a program of, say, a finance department.

## Summary

Each department, insofar as it has freedom to design its strategy program, will seek excellence according to its particular ideology or point of view. This distinctive viewpoint will be strongly influenced by (1) the relevant environment of the department, (2) the department's history and commitments, and (3) the local cultural values. Failure of business-unit managers to recognize the diversity and strength of these department viewpoints can lead to impractical strategy. A department naturally feels much more loyalty to its own scenario than to a more remote central strategy, and, these provincial loyalties are diverse by design.

Learning about department scenarios serves two important purposes. First, in strategy formulation, obtaining proposals and assessments from heterogeneous departments is healthy: the viability of a selected strategy is crucially dependent upon inputs from sources close to the several scenes of action. Second, a department's motivation to carry out an official program depends to a large degree on how closely the official program agrees with the department's scenario for excellence. After a department's proposed scenario has been tailored to suit the business-unit strategy, as it almost always will be, some of the enthusiasm for strategic planning will have been sacrificed. However, knowing about, and preferably having an empathetic appreciation for, the program which a department most prefers is a great aid in finding ways to rekindle that enthusiasm.

## Finding Good Internal Fits Among Departments

A department's scenario for excellence, although provincial, is important because the department knows more and cares more than anyone else about the content of its program. However, that external linkage is only a start. Such a proposed program must fit internally with programs of related departments and with the overall business strategy.

## Dimensions of Internal Fit

By a "fit," we mean (a) that the proposed program is *compatible* with the activities of related departments, i.e., it does not undermine the results of those activities or make them much more difficult. In fact, (b) a good fit is *synergistic:* the proposed program would make the activities of another department easier and/or improve their outcomes. Moreover, (c) a scenario that fits would be of an acceptable *size*, neither so large that it overwhelms and soaks up resources needed by the related department, nor so small that it would be only a nuisance. And (d) the *timing* of interdependent activities should be synchronized; for instance, people should be hired and trained as soon as, but not much before, they are needed.[3]

## Negotiating Adaptations

While it is preparing its scenario for strategic excellence, a department should approach other departments that will be significantly affected and try to negotiate with each a "fit" in the sense just defined. Note what occurs in such a process: the initiating department, having devised a way to respond to opportunities or threats in its particular segment of the external environment, acts as an intermediary, seeking to get other departments to support the proposed linkage insofar as these departments are affected by it.[4]

A simple example of this kind of negotiation occurred recently in a fast-food chain. The marketing department made studies that indicated that sales of existing outlets could be increased by adding (and advertising) several breakfast items to the menu, viz., eggs, hot cereal, and French toast. The estimated additional income earned on the existing investment looked good. So the marketing department asked the human resource department about recruiting more people for the morning hours. This proposal did not coincide with the human resource department's current drive to recruit more attractive high school part-time help, but it did not hurt, so it was compatible with that drive. The human resource department accordingly welcomed the possibility of better utilizing the morning shift.

The engineering department, on the other hand, was only lukewarm about providing additional equipment that would be necessary—"just one more inconvenient thing, although it can be done." But a major objection was raised by the quality assurance department (a separate department in the company). Quality assurance contended that standards to ensure a uniformly high quality of individual orders for fried or scrambled eggs are hard to set and even harder to enforce. And if the quality of new items that were advertised fluctuated, the entire reputa-

---

[3]See B. Yavitz and W. H. Newman, *Strategy in Action* (New York: The Free Press, 1982), Chapter 13.

[4]In this respect, departments perform roles analogous to the "gatekeepers" described by D. L. Gladstein and D. Caldwell in *Beyond the Boundary: Managing External Relationships in New Product Teams,* Cambridge: Sloan School of Management, MIT, Working Paper #1805-86 (1986).

tion of the chain might suffer. "At six-thirty in the morning our employees are not very alert," the department said. The proposal has gone back to engineering for mechanical devices that will ensure good quality at any time of the day.

As this example suggests, any proposal is likely to require several modifications before an acceptable internal fit is achieved. Meanwhile, however, the external opportunity may be slipping away.[5]

## ▨ Concurrent Negotiations

Of course, in an aggressive company several strategic proposals are being tested for fit at the same time: other departments have plans of their own and are also pushing for internal adjustments.

The impact of new technology on just the retail division (transactions with individuals) of a commercial bank illustrates the diverse proposals that may be circulating at the same time. First, the marketing department of this bank is promoting the "friendly banker" concept, which is intended to build a base for a full line of financial services—stockbrokerage, insurance, credit cards, etc. To serve and hold this customer base, the marketing vice president wants a carefully designed network of branches in "yuppie" neighborhoods. Instant recall on local computer screens of complete on-line records of each customer's accounts are part of this plan.

But the bank's information processing department, with its bevy of computer experts, wants to position the bank so as to be able to take part in a "checkless society." As a start, the bank would pay customers' bills and accept charges directly from stores, making immediate entries in customers' accounts. Note that this proposal is compatible with the "friendly banker" concept, but would not need the same branch network.

Meanwhile, two other units in the division are pushing services that the bank has had for several years: automatic teller machines and credit cards. The technical aims here are improvements in security and better ways to handle overdrafts.

To serve the foregoing present and proposed activities, the human resource department has a special program for recruiting and training computer personnel. But turnover is high and the specific skills desired keep changing, so the department is trying to get some predictability in computer activities. On the other hand, the cashier, who watches over operating expenses, believes that the bank already has too much money tied up in computers, software, and automatic teller machines.

---

[5]Incidentally, synergy—which sometimes is an alleged benefit of a proposed strategy—depends primarily on achieving an internal fit of the sort discussed in this section. The frequent difficulties in actually achieving synergy often reflect an unwillingness (or inability) of departments to find ways to fit their scenarios together.

As is plain, finding an acceptable internal fit for department strategy programs in this setting will be difficult, although not impossible. In negotiating internal fits, a lot of modifications and slowing down is normal, and political deals for mutual support may be made.

For instance, in this same example, the information processing department might agree to confine its work on a checkless system to software that keeps customer accounting adaptable to such a development. And in exchange, the marketing vice president would agree to experiment with a more versatile system of customer records. Such a plan would suit the cashier because cash outlays during the trial period would be much lower than called for by the original proposal of the marketing department.

Note that negotiating internal fits is as much a political process as a financially rational one. To secure agreement on internal linkages, bold actions tend to be minimized and short-run outcomes valued much higher than long-run positions. However, negotiated agreements do have the great benefit that work can proceed in a coordinated manner. And, of course, not all agreed-upon fits involve any serious compromise.

## Need for Oversight

Some modifications of the business-unit strategy may occur during the internal fitting process. While many mutual adjustments involve only small sacrifices, a few may undermine progress on major thrusts or lead off in an unwanted direction. For instance, the overeagerness of E. F. Hutton's branches to earn interest on the float in clearing checks, and Polaroid's South African distributor's surreptitiously selling film to the South African police, were both examples of lower level operating units engaging in activities contrary to top company strategy. Consequently, some oversight on agreements between departments is wise if not absolutely necessary.

As a rule, too little, rather than too much, voluntary give-and-take is more common when negotiating internal fits. For reasons noted earlier, departments are often reluctant to modify their scenario for excellence. Only arbitration by general management forces major concessions.

## Maintaining Business-Wide Direction of Departments

A departmental viewpoint has been stressed in the preceding discussion—a department's linkages with its external environment and its linkages with other departments within the business. Such an emphasis brings strategy programming much closer to actual operations. However, the third major linkage—the tie between a department program and business-wide strategy—is also crucial. To deal with this linkage, the general management of the business and the department management will need to interact on four sorts of issues.

# Design of Business-Unit Strategy

Typically, department managers participate, at least to some extent, in shaping the strategy of their business-unit. When linkages are good, information flows upward at several steps in the strategic process. Ideally,

1.  During the strategy formulation period, department management tells the business-unit executives about its scenario for excellence—new developments, opportunities, threats, and what the department would like to do for its own development and to aid the business.
2.  When one or more tentative business-unit strategies are being weighed and refined, each major department checks and reports back on the feasibility of the role that it would be assigned. Also, if necessary, a second plea for the department's preferred strategic program can be made at this stage, and attention can be called to the risks and opportunity costs of proposed business-unit strategies.
3.  During execution of the selected business-unit strategy, the department reports its progress and problems in fulfilling its particular role— the results to date and the quality, timeliness, and costs of obtaining those results. Any synchronization with other departments is also noted.
4.  Then, as both the business and its competitive environment evolve, the department participates in progressive adjustments of the business-unit strategy, repeating steps 1 through 3.

In actuality, the bridging between department scenarios and business-unit strategy is rarely built this smoothly. The open communication may break down for several reasons. First, the central executives may not really listen. Often they are preoccupied with a grand design and, as a consequence, lack empathy for department views and brush off suggestions as biased and narrow-minded; they simply assume that the departments can and will fall into line.

More basic is a second hurdle. Inevitably, a business-unit strategy favors some departments more than others. A business-unit strategy cannot be all things to all people. Instead, it selects niches and seeks a few differential advantages. This means that the contributions of a few departments will be stressed or optimized, while other departments will have facilitating assignments where "satisficing" will be adequate, as indicated in Figure 6–4. So a lot of scenarios for excellence will be scuttled by the central executives. A department may be placed in only a supporting or in merely a protecting role. For a department in the last group in Figure 6–4, the candid communication assumed in the four steps listed previously may increase its vulnerability.

A third obstacle is that departments play bargaining games. As will be noted shortly, departments have turf to protect, budget allocations to secure, incentive standards to negotiate, and personal reputations to build. And in most companies these matters are not promptly adjusted to each change in strategy. Thus, the can-

FIGURE 6–4.
**POSSIBLE ROLES FOR DEPARTMENTS IN BUSINESS-UNIT STRATEGIC MANAGEMENT.**
*(Prescribed inputs of each department to execution of strategy will be much more specific.)*

| ALTERNATIVE ROLES OF DEPARTMENTS IN BUSINESS-UNIT STRATEGY | | | |
|---|---|---|---|
| *Department Characteristics* | *Strategic Potency* | *Strong Support* | *Adequate Protection* |
| Desired standing of our department relative to similar departments of competitors | Ahead of all rivals | Among top 15% | Typical of protective stance |
| Department initiative expected | Proactive | Reactive to systematic scanning | Reactive |
| Degree of improvement sought | Innovations that keep rivals running just to keep up | Be among the leaders | Keep up with the pack |
| Participation in business-unit strategy decisions | Frequent, in depth | Agree on updated targets; then decentralize to department | Infrequent review, but have warnings of trouble |
| Willingness of companies to invest in department improvements | Invest to keep state-of-the-art skills | Use rather low R.O.I. hurdle rates | Do only what is necessary |
| Department slogan | "Crucial clout" | "Powerful collaborations" | "Keep company out of trouble" |

dor that is desirable for strategic management can be a handicap in pursuing other department objectives: all the cards would then be face up on the table.

So the flow of information from departments, together with their passive, docile attitude about emerging business strategies, which are both often assumed in discussions of strategy formulation, may not occur. The hurdles suggest what needs to take place to open up the interchange: central executives must demonstrate a sympathetic understanding of the department scenarios and the forces they represent and try to accommodate them; reasons for the selective emphasis in a chosen strategy must be explained and, if possible, "sold"; and the related structural elements must be adjusted to reinforce, rather than detract from, the strategy.

Such promotion of frank communication about opportunities, costs, and reasons for strategy choices can help to bind together department managers and business-unit executives. The aim, of course, is to win at least some voluntary department support for "the big picture."

## Arbitration of Department Fits

A second way of shaping the linkage between departments and their managers arises—in addition to verbal coaxing—when the central management arbitrates disputes among the departments. This brings us back to internal fits.

While give-and-take among departments resolves many problems of fitting department strategy programs together, disagreements are common. The proposed programs for department excellence often clash, and their proponents are loathe to cut back for another department whose goals and culture are so different.

In this case, central managers must arbitrate. They decide which programs get priority and which must adapt to that focus. Maybe stable employment will be given preference over plant consolidation, or maybe new product leadership will be given priority over market volume. Such arbitration draws senior managers into quite specific operations issues. Occasionally, the senior managers may even veto a compromise program agreement because it does not go all out for a preferred strategic thrust. It is in this support or constraint of department programs that business strategy gets more sharply defined.

If a clear business-unit strategy exists and is expected to continue, this will reduce the need for program arbitration; the department managers already know which activities are to be stressed and will trim their requests of other departments accordingly. On the other hand, if a business-unit strategy is ambiguous, its real meaning emerges in the arbitration awards among the proposed department programs. The importance of protecting market position, for instance, will become clear by the support (or lack of support) for this objective given to the marketing department.

## Allocation of Scarce Resources

Proposed department programs are also aligned with business-unit strategy in the resource allocation process. If money (or skilled personnel) is scarce, as it almost always is, the department programs which are not closely linked to business-unit strategy may not be funded.

Because financial budgeting often has a set of norms not directly tied to strategy, the budget allocations themselves do not clarify strategy programs. Frequently, the measurements and criteria that a finance department adopts from its specialized environment (discounted cash flows, hurdle rates, tax quirks, etc.) dominate the budget, leaving long-run strategy and opportunity costs on the sidelines. Indeed, a department management may be penalized in budget reports, in money grants, and perhaps in bonuses, for doing what the business strategy calls for. And money talks.

In one *Fortune 500* company, for instance, the president often talks about "a strategy for the future" and "finding new uses for our talents." However, the annual bonuses are based strictly on "beating the departmental budget," and promotions usually go to those managers who "run a tight ship." The net result at the department level is that strategy moves which may be risky or which call for expenses that will not yield returns promptly receive only lukewarm support.

If the linkage between business-unit strategy and department action is to be close, the general managers of the business will probably have to override the conventional internal financing process. For instance, an outlay to put a department in a favorable long-run competitive position will get funded even though it does not meet the usual hurdle rate of return. An even better arrangement is to make explicit allocations to departments for strategy development.[6]

## Motivation to Execute Department Strategy Programs

Along with participation, arbitration of disputes, and resource allocation, motivation is the fourth critical element in the general management–department linkage. The decisions that general management makes about department scenarios for excellence, dominance in internal fits, and allotments of money, skilled personnel and other scarce resources have psychological impact: they can either enthuse or demoralize a department. Moreover, in these decisions, general management can encourage supportive political behavior and discourage sabotage. Much of this political activity occurs at the department level.

Formal power may be in the hands of general management, but personal commitment of the doers has to be won. Since commitment is closely aligned with the department's culture, the way departments are fitted into the business culture is an emotional as well as a rational matter.

In sum, the vertical linkage between departments and the general management of the business are more sensitive than is often assumed in discussions of strategy management. Departments are not, nor should they be, meek and compliant, merely providing data and working out budgets for central executives. Instead, their proposals should be based on current opportunities and threats in a set of real worlds. Each department's arena is an action site where the "enacted"

[6]See B. Yavitz and W. H. Newman, *Strategy in Action* (New York: The Free Press, 1982), Chapter 11; J. C. Camillus and J. H. Grant, "Operational Planning: The Integration of Programming and Budgeting," *Academy of Management Review,* July 1980; P. J. Stonich, "How to Use Strategic Funds Programming," *The Journal of Business Strategy,* Fall 1980.

strategy of a business emerges; approval or disapproval of a proposal shapes competitive conduct.

Power is always present. Resource allocation and arbitration of internal fits enforce boundaries on what departments can do, and these decisions may undermine the commitment of people on the firing line. Thus, strategy formulation at this interface is more than an intellectual exercise.

## Conclusion

Multi-level strategy helps managers to convert bold insights into practical operating programs. The insights that shape corporate and business-unit strategies provide challenging direction and stirring missions, two objectives that are especially important in today's world. But not much will happen in a company until those upper level strategies are closely linked to strategy programs at the department level.

The present chapter opened our analysis of these department strategy programs. It presented a framework for or approach to designing such programs realistically. The resulting integration of forward thinking at several organization levels adds potency to the entire strategic planning process; but the process is by no means simple.

## Getting the Whole Act Together

### Strategy Program for a Department

The harnessing of a department into a strategic team, as outlined in this chapter, uses a triple-linkage model. All three links—exterior, horizontal, and vertical—must be recognized and reconciled. Without all of them, the contributions of any department will be seriously weakened.

We call the emerging reconciliation of these three viewpoints the *department strategy program*. It is the plan of action the department should follow until it is revised. An ideal department strategy program (1) fulfills an assigned role in the business-unit strategy, (2) builds long-run strength relative to competitors in the department's functional area, (3) fits in with strategic programs of other departments, and (4) keeps the costs of achieving all three linkages low relative to the value of its inputs to the business.

Building a consensus about such a strategy program takes time. There are numerous elements, as the foregoing discussion has indicated. In an established business, however, building the program is an on-going process. There will be an existing business-unit strategy that provides a first cut on priorities. Then, on each of the three dimensions, preliminary cross-checks should be normal and reiteration of proposed changes should be customary. Also, updating should be expected as key events occur.

### A Mosaic of All Department Strategic Programs

Since the strategy program of each department involves designing internal fits and reaching a mutual understanding with the overall management of the business, our model implies a grand, total integration. Even in a stable business, this sort of complete coordination can never be fully attained because too many dynamic elements are present. For instance, the following sources of tension are especially prickly.

The optimum time for making changes will vary from department to department. The various relevant external environments (finance, labor, sales, procurements, etc.) have their own separate dynamics in which opportunities and threats will call for action at different and irregular dates. Also, departments have their own internal ups and downs regarding personnel shifts, new technology, and other transitions. So internal fits don't necessarily stay fitted.

A different sort of complexity arises out of the variation among departments in degrees of decentralization. For instance, a vice president of finance may be the person who proposes financing changes while a branch manager in Timbuktu wants to cut prices to meet local competition. Thus, a department's status and physical location affect the way it responds to external change.

Actually, all this diversity of pressures arising concurrently in separate departments makes the basic triple-linkage model even more useful. A familiar, sound approach to building strategic programs in a department helps a manager cut through the complexity. With such an approach to external, horizontal, and vertical linkages, a department can be a better participant in multi-level strategic management.

## A Closer Look at Basic Departments

The triple-linkage approach is a generalized framework. To assure that the resulting strategic programs embrace all vital operations of the business-unit, managers (and students) should apply this approach to each key department.

Obviously, in this text we cannot discuss the innumerable departments found in all sorts of enterprises. Instead, we will focus on basic functional departments that are necessary in some form or other to any productive organization. Every productive organization assembles and converts resources into services and goods wanted by customers. Consequently, there will be functions involving at least marketing, production, purchasing, human resources, and finance. It is departments dealing with these basic areas that are covered in Chapters 7 through 14.

This closer look at basic functional departments will (a) provide a richer and deeper overview of strategic management than is obtained from studying only the business-unit and corporate levels; (b) identify typical issues that call for attention in virtually all comprehensive strategic efforts; and (c) illustrate the thinking necessary for a department to develop a triple linkage with its environment, related departments, and the overall strategy of its business-unit.

## Questions for Class Discussion

1. The new sales manager of the Western Texas and Eastern New Mexico division of Lance Drugs, Inc., arrived in Lubbock with strict instructions from the marketing vice president of this drug manufacturing and wholesaling company to "bring West Texas wholesaling up to date, halt the downward drift of its market share, install our new promotional and merchandising methods, and revamp the sales representatives' territories to nationalize sales expenses and revenues." On his first day on the job, the division manager called him in and said, "We have many old-timers here who have literally created their own territories and who sell in the old ways they know best to their long-term customers— retail pharmacies, drugstores, and hospitals. A couple of territories are probably too large, and we may have one or two that are too small. Whatever you do about these, I don't want the morale of the sales force harmed in any way. Selling is hard enough work without having some New York ideas loaded on us here in the west."

   Can the instructions to the new sales manager be explained by the elements in Figures 6–1, 6–2, and 6–3? What might the new sales manager do?

2. It was mentioned in the text that departments within a company interact with different industries. For an electric utility company (use the one serving your college community or your home community), illustrate this separate industry concept for the finance department, the purchasing department, and the customer service (marketing) department. If the pressures from these three viewpoints diverge, how can a reconciliation be obtained?

3. In each of the TV networks, preparing news broadcasts is assigned to a separate department. Suppose that you are asked to develop a "scenario for excellence" for the news department of you favorite network. (a) What would be the main features of your scenario? (b) What problems, if any, would you expect to find in fitting your scenario in with the interests of other departments? (c) Explain how top management's arbitration of any such clashes will affect the network's strategy.

4. Why do functional departments want to pursue their own scenarios for excellence? Why not permit each department to do so? What role does business-unit strategy play in deciding which scenarios for excellence to support?

5. P. J. Russo, president of Consolidated Industries, says, "In our corporation we believe strongly in extending active participation in strategy formulation down to at least department heads. Because we are so diversified, we must draw on the judgments of lower level managers for data about their industry." See (1) through (4) on page 148 for the kind of participation Russo has in mind. Then

(a) make a list of reasons why Russo may not get the full and candid inputs that are needed for wise strategy formulation. (b) Are these reasons so persuasive that you believe Russo should not bother with department participation in strategy formulation?

6. When Kawasaki Motorcycle Company established its midwest assembly plant, the finance manager soon sought to adopt a "just-in-time" inventory strategy. By having parts arrive at the plant only a few hours before they would be used on the assembly line, the investment in inventory could be kept very low. Problems of fit with other departments immediately arose, however. Adjustments were necessary in (a) production scheduling, which was tied to marketing, (b) the selection of vendors, (c) the location and rigidity of quality control, (d) the period covered by purchase orders and the prices paid, and (e) the design of parts in relation to necessary production processes. Explain how all these activities were involved in creating viable internal and external linkages. What does your answer imply about the practicality of "just-in-time" procurement in the upholstered furniture industry? In a college bookstore?

7. Because of demographic shifts which are causing a nationwide drop in high school graduates, a prominent private university in New England anticipates a significant decline in its undergraduate enrollment. The dean of the business school of the university wants to offset that drop in undergraduate business students by expanding non-degree programs for experienced managers and staff specialists. Indeed, the dean has spoken of the "new strategy" in several public addresses. However, these statements have caused mixed reactions among faculty members of the school, so the dean recently asked the chairpersons of each department (economics, accounting, marketing, management, finance, and international business) to submit a report on how the department could contribute to carrying out the new strategy.

   (a) What differences in reaction to the strategy of expanding non-degree programs would you anticipate from the three administrative levels of the university, i.e., the university itself, the business school, and the departments? (b) What differences, if any, would you anticipate from each of the various departments? Why? (c) Is it important for the dean to get each department to prepare its strategic program? If so, how should the dean get the departments to produce strategic programs that work toward the best interests of the school?

8.    (a) Suppose that you are in an important job in the advertising department of a pharmaceutical company (or another department that suits your career goals); it's a good job that you feel lucky to have. The company is about to launch its first pesticide that utilizes scientists' decisions about the alteration of DNA codes in its production. The product is a state-of-the-art, but controversial, development. You personally feel strongly that this product should not be marketed because of the uncertain and potentially dangerous side effects; other people in your department feel the same way. What could you do to discourage the company's strategic thrust into DNA products?

(b) Now switch roles and put yourself in the position of the head of the pesticide division. Also, adopt the view that the DNA strategy is very desirable. You are aware of foot-dragging in the advertising department (or the other department you chose in answering (a)). What can you do to gain support for the DNA strategy?

9. The academic vice president of a third-rate university trying hard to be second-rate has been heard to complain that faculty members of the business school seem to have little loyalty to the institution and little concern over how the university has been governed. "They don't volunteer to run for the faculty senate. If elected, they try to avoid serving on university-wide committees such as the University Writing Committee or the Undergraduate Curriculum Oversight Committee. They do, however, appeal for funds to attend meetings, to hire research assistants, and to use telephones and computers to search for data well beyond the university's capacity to supply the money. Department heads ask for additional funds for copying and reproducing, while the library is besieged for additional journal subscriptions. They also resist teaching large undergraduate courses while trying to add new senior-level or graduate seminars." When asked to comment, the dean of the school of business said, "To increase the university's standing and prestige, we need better facilities, more graduate students, research publications that have an impact on faculty members elsewhere and on research scientists around the world, and alumni support for major programs. We emphasize hiring faculty for our two strongest departments (marketing and finance) who are known for their research work by their peers or who have shown great potential for research publications during their doctoral studies at other universities. We emphasize contributions to their fields of study."

Explain the external and vertical linkages (Figures 6–1 and 6–2) of the finance and marketing departments that contribute to the behavior of the faculty members.

# CASE
## 6 Wardwell Vinyl Coatings, Inc. (R-2)

"I think that there are four strategic issues we face about which you will want to make up your own mind. The first is the product-market mix. Do we have a tenable domain—a particular part of the market—to work in? The second is our differential advantage. Harleton Rowe thinks that we can do some things better than our competitors—especially the big things. But my cousin is not so sure and wants to change how we operate. We need to understand these first two issues very clearly. The third strategic issue includes the returns we make and the risks we run. How do we look from the standpoint of return on equity and return on sales? Does our financial position seem sound, or are we running a big risk? Financially, where will we be years from now? Are we in a position to borrow a healthy amount of money? How much? The fourth issue is the one the Board hired you to make a recommendation about: do we have programs in place that will keep the company moving in the way we want it to go, and is the organization in such a shape that I can step aside as president and turn over the operating responsibilities?

"I'll take you around to introduce you to our people so that you can start your investigation."

In this manner, Beckley Wardwell, president of Wardwell Vinyl Coatings, Inc., helped me get started on the project for which the directors of this firm had engaged the consulting firm in which I am one of many senior investigators.* We work internationally on the problems and projects of many organizations. One matter that I have learned to be careful about and needed to pursue in this company was to find out just how the organization was tied together. A functioning organization is more than just the sum of its parts, and I needed to see how the parts were put together. Or in other words, I had to see how integration of the specialized activities was brought about.

In a short time, I developed the information that follows.

## Nature of Company

Wardwell Vinyl Coatings, Inc., of Charleston, West Virginia, designs and makes vinyl-coated fabrics for the automobile, luggage, shoe, and furniture industries. Wardwell's fabrics cover interior panels of some of Ford and Cadillac's more expensive models, and they grace Knoll Associates' line of Saarinen-designed chairs.

Wardwell Vinyl Coatings is directed by Beckley Wardwell, the president, who started in the firm as a salesperson on house accounts. Even though his duties in the organization have since changed, Beckley has continued to sell to some customers; in fact, at present he still does all the sales work with the two largest customers, whose purchases are now $2,950,000 annually. Under Beckley Wardwell's supervision, the company's sales have grown and profits are at such an all-time high that he is thinking about a political career. With some satisfaction, he contemplates reducing his operating responsibilities, changing his position to chair of the board of directors, and beginning an effort toward a higher post in the state legislature. Occasionally Mr. Wardwell muses, "If Winthrop, Nelson, and Jay Rockefeller can be state governors, why not a Wardwell?"

---

*The questions at the end of this case put *you* in the position of this senior investigator.

The family-owned firm has competed successfully for years in the fabric coating industry with subsidiaries of B. F. Goodrich and the other major rubber companies, with divisions of General Motors and Ford Motor Company, with departments of E. I. du Pont de Nemours, Monsanto, Eastman Kodak, and Dow Chemical Company, and with a host of smaller competitors.

Within the past month, the firm has received a proposal from a European company that provides a chance to broaden and diversify Wardwell's product lines.

## Marketing

Harleton Rowe, the sales manager, came to Charleston four years ago after a 15-year career as salesperson and product manager with eight garment manufacturers and textile producers. His first move was to add a person who specialized in sales to the furniture industry. Earlier, Wardwell Vinyl Coatings, Inc., had sold only through manufacturer's representatives, whose total compensation was an eight percent commission.

Half of the manufacturer's representatives have now been replaced by six company salespeople who specialize by industry. They are guaranteed an annual draw of $30,000 and are then paid by commission at an increasing rate when their sales exceed $1,000,000 to a maximum rate of eight percent.

Beckley Wardwell approved the changes in sales representatives and their compensation as being consonant with his belief in putting great trust in his senior managers and in allowing them all the responsibility they are willing to take. Harleton Rowe had come highly recommended by some old family friends of the Wardwells who were associated with the J. P. Stevens Company.

Mr. Rowe commented that he attempted to give some direction to the selling effort. "In the past, for the most part, we took any order that came along. We did well because of the quality of our products. I don't reject orders that come in, of course, but I believe that it is also possible to define certain industry groups that will naturally want to buy what a small firm like this can best sell—fast delivery, a short order cycle, design help, and a quality product. It did not take any particular marketing skill to figure this out; just look at those customers whose buying characteristics and decision-making fitted our demonstrated skills.

"I did this on my own. Beckley Wardwell does not question what you are doing and lets you alone so long as you keep him informed. On any scheduling problems with new orders I talk directly with him. Leon Torbit, the plant manager, listens to Beckley but runs around the factory so much that I have found it difficult to reach him, let alone work out a decision with him."

Products of the vinyl resin coated fabric industry are upholstery for vehicles; coverings for luggage; engine and equipment covers; baby carriages; casings for typewriters; yard goods sold by mail-order houses and department stores; shoe materials; furniture upholstery materials; shower curtains; wall coverings; surgical tape; ribbons; and other applications. Major producers in the industry include rubber and chemical companies that specialize in organic and polymer chemistry and a large number of smaller producers who purchase their resin in bulk from a major supplier and concentrate their efforts on the production process of coating fabrics at the lowest possible cost.

Buyers want their color, finish, and durability needs met carefully. Successful selling also depends on preconsultation with designers about the various fabrics needed in the customer's line. Frequently a Wardwell salesperson works for several days, at various intervals, with a customer's designer. A supplier is also expected to furnish samples rapidly—even samples of new materials—when new items are being considered for a customer's line.

Automobile manufacturers and the consumer divisions of the rubber companies, which do not necessarily buy from producing divisions of the same firm, generally place large orders. Furniture, shoe, and luggage manufacturers tend to place small orders, but to repeat them frequently if sales of the item for which the coated fabric is used catch on. A customer's pressure for a low price is related to the number of yards of coated fabric bought and to the ultimate price line at which the product—be it baby carriages or washable wall covering—is offered to the great consuming public.

Harleton Rowe said that Wardwell succeeds by marketing a high-quality product to a large number of customers who desire fast and accurate service. Individual orders are often small, but they are repeated 8 to 10 times a year.

## Manufacturing

Wardwell coats the cloth it purchases from textile producers with a resinous liquid. The mixtures can be sprayed on, as is common practice in the industry, but Wardwell uses a calendering process to control the amount of liquid applied, its spread rate, and its penetration.

Fabric is bleached, stretched, and then run between calenders (large steel rollers) to dry it and smooth it before coating. Vinyl resin, in combination with color pigments and solvents, is applied on the coating machine as the cloth is pulled through to a drying oven at the end of the coater. Coated cloth is later finished by stamping or by rolling it on embossing machines to impart a grain, a raised surface (such as pigskin texture), or any other finish desired. Until recently, each of these three processes—bleaching and smoothing, coating, and then finishing—has been done in batches on separate pieces of equipment.

Coating is the crucial production department. The resin ingredients are prepared and applied under closely controlled conditions, and the tensile strength of the resin has to be related closely to the speed of the coating machines. Both the temperature and the concentration of chemicals have to be held within exact tolerances. Stains left by the rollers or rips in the fabric cause spoilage losses or reduce fabric quality. Close attention by the plant workers to the fabric belt as it is calendered and rolled is required for a satisfactory product.

The process is dangerous to unskilled or careless employees. The machinery is heavy and runs at high speeds. Chemical odors are strong and cannot all be removed from the building even by the best of ventilating and solvent extraction processes. While the equipment is kept in the best repair, the rest of the plant is old and facilities are rundown.

Worker turnover is high. Experienced workers can be hired from the glass factory or the chemical plants near the city. When absolutely necessary, new workers are taken on from the large pool of migrants from the hill country and are trained at some cost in lost productivity or rapid turnover.

Last year a Teamster's Union local was voted in to replace an AFL craft union. After one month, the company settled a strike for higher wages for 85 percent of the union's demand.

Leon Torbit, the plant manager, rose through the ranks. He knows the process and the equipment, and he demands careful attention to plant activities by his supervisors, who spend most of their time closely overseeing production runs to minimize spoilage and waste. Leon Torbit also spends at least half of his time touring the plant, checking on the status of individual orders, and questioning various machine operators. He knows most of the two hundred plant employees by sight, but few by name. Hiring, firing, and discipline are entirely the responsibility of the various supervisors, subject to negotiation with union stewards on some disciplinary matters.

## Chemical Research and Development

Chemical research and development is directed by John Minton, who earned an advanced degree in organic chemistry years ago and has since followed the old tradition of experimentation. He has six assistants with university training in chemistry, but they basically "engineer" his suggestions. Professional conflicts arise occasionally because John diverges in some instances from currently accepted laboratory and analysis techniques, but his methods are often quite ingenious. Chemical research at Wardwell is really "mixing and brewing" and relies but little on modern quantitative polymer theory. John Minton firmly believes in using "art" and experience in his formulations. However, if manufacturing difficulties arise, he will modify his processes, and he constantly checks the application of his new product ideas to make sure they work out in the plant.

The present vinyl resin resulted from "rational" trial and error that converged on the successful mixture. Knowing the desired properties of the finished compound and the characteristics of the component chemicals, John Minton exhausted many combinations of reactants, allowing for fine differences among different brands of the same product. The result is Wardwell's vinyl resin, which has advantages over its competitor's products. The coating is less likely to crack, has better tensile strength, absorbs dye more easily, and can be applied at lower temperatures. It is a quality product demanded for more expensive applications, yet its production cost is not much higher than that of common vinyls.

John Minton has also adapted other processes to vinyl manufacturing. For example, the dyeing process used at Wardwell came from an industrial magazine article about coloring fabrics in the garment industry.

John has over 30 years of experience in working with vinyl, and finding a replacement for him will be difficult; nevertheless, he plans to retire within the next year. "I'll be 70 years old soon, and threescore and 10 is enough for anyone." Any replacement director would probably be accustomed to using more sophisticated equipment, and new methods might be incompatible with the methods used by the existing staff of technical people, who would then have to be retrained. The greatest incompatibility to a modern researcher would be the responsibility for watching after the production process; any new person might be surprised at the autonomy given to perform the development activities.

## Engineering

Process development—the improvement of equipment used in manufacturing—is carried on by Spencer Wardwell, the president's cousin and a mechanical engineer trained at California Institute of Technology. Spencer joined the company to carry out some recommendations made by his consulting firm. He devotes his time to machine design, to some outside consulting work, and to a complete factory redesign now in process. The goal of this change is a factory that will produce fewer defects while utilizing much less labor.

On Spencer's recommendation, a wall was knocked out and the factory floor space was extended by about a third. The result was a longer, more efficient linear series of rollers that made each run easier to mount, process, and finish. This improvement was beneficial since Wardwell depends on a manufacturing process that has little downtime and that can handle orders in a very short time. Increases in roller speed have reduced the crucial turnaround time, but on the very oldest equipment they have also led to increased defects as tension overcomes the fabric's tensile strength. Workers cannot follow the process at very high speeds. Even at lower rates a marred roller that leaves a mark with each revolution is difficult to detect. Now a pilot model of a new coating machine is under test to prove out its design characteristics of a 50 percent reduction in labor hours and a 10 percent increase in fabric output. Discretionary settings have been reduced substantially, mechanical handling has been substituted for manual, and tension-controlling devices have been added to reduce tearing.

Engineers seldom stay with the company more than three years. As one said, "I learned a great deal from Spencer about both mechanical engineering and consulting and put up with him to get this knowledge. In a weak moment he once told me that company policy was to kick the worker when he didn't produce and to reward him as little as possible when he did. Of course, that was only Spencer's idea of it. I don't know how Torbit carries out company policy."

Spencer Wardwell said, "We have efficient competitors. Although their manufacturing cost is, as a percent of sales, about the same as ours, their average length of run is 48,000 yards, while ours is more like 12,000. The number of items they carry in inventory is one-fourth our number. But dollar totals are about the same. If we used their methods, we could drop our manufacturing cost to 55 percent of sales. Then we could really afford to drop our prices somewhat, undercut them, and shoot up the volume. This would give us a hefty return on the new equipment we need.

"For a near-term investment of $12,000,000 over two and one-half years, I calculate that we can cut our labor force by 30 percent and thus reduce our labor cost by $1,400,000 annually. After that, another investment of $3,000,000 per year for five years will eventually allow us to cut our labor force to 50 percent of what it is now and save another $800,000 per year. This is investment in machinery only—the only kind we really need.

"We need to do this because the Teamsters are now really at our throats. The last contract we signed jumped wage costs 25 percent over two years. They are surely going to ask for more next time. The only way to fight them is to get them out of the plant.

"Our policy should be to triple the length of each run, cut the setup and changeover time by two-thirds, reduce the number of employees, and pay them enough so that they won't quit to work at Union Carbide. Just give me seven years and twenty-five million dollars."

## General Management

Beckley Wardwell believes in getting expert outside advice. One consulting firm recommended the recent plant expansion. Another firm recommended increased coordination among the managerial group and attempts at cooperation through dinner meetings and general discussion. Dinners were held for awhile and then discontinued when Spencer Wardwell had to be out of town. Meetings led by Leon Torbit for the plant supervisors were discontinued when the bleaching, coating, and finishing supervisors argued at length over technical matters.

Beckley Wardwell spends 20 percent of his time with two customers and, at times, assists individual salespersons with difficult relationships with other customers or accompanies them on visits to celebrate unusually large orders. But the balance of his work is mainly on financial matters. He analyzes cash balances and cash flows each day with the treasurer. He looks at actual and predicted budget comparisons for previous and succeeding months. He, the treasurer, and the purchasing agent check the investment in inventory each month, both in total dollars and by reviewing summary tally sheets prepared from the detailed records.

With the purchasing agent, Roy Ascoli, Beckley Wardwell reviews individual purchase orders amounting to more than $2,000 and analyzes alternative sources of supply for new items. Beckley Wardwell says, "Clay Weston, the treasurer, and Ascoli are perfectly competent executives. They can perform all the duties asked of them, and they do careful work. I spend time with them to keep myself informed. I need the data to press for increased revenues and decreased costs. In my view, a chief executive's major role is to establish the rate of return on investment and the rate of sales growth that he wants and then push continuously for these. Secondly, I need it to keep the family happy.

"Spencer Wardwell is the only family member in the firm. I was lucky to attract him away from his full-time consulting business with the help of a special stock option arrangement. No one member or one branch of the family has controlling stock interest, but they all have a personal interest. One or two of them are in the investment business and are convinced they know as much about coated fabrics as anyone else. A few of the others I would call professional Monday morning quarterbacks; this is not something I have told them directly.

"While a few nephews, cousins, uncles, and aunts have asked for jobs here, I have refused to hire them—except for Spencer. I can't see that they would be any more competent than the people we already have, and none of them seems to want to start in the coating room.

"Judge our managerial methods by our results. Sales are now $45,000,000 a year, whereas they were $9,000,000 ten years ago. Our manufacturing cost is 65 percent of sales—4 percentage points lower than ten years ago. We now spend 7 percent rather than 9 percent of sales on our total marketing effort. Research and engineering cost us 9 percent of sales. That compares well with any of the big chemical companies. After taxes, we net out 9 percent of sales, which is even better than General Motors. A dividend payout ratio of 60 percent takes better than adequate care of the three branches of the family.

"Look at our balance sheet (Table 6–1), and I think you will have to agree that I can begin to satisfy all those impulses I have had toward politics in recent years. I'll give up my sales work and that will free up a lot of time. Harleton Rowe can handle all our marketing effort. School board membership, chairman of local welfare organizations, and two terms in the state legislature have not been enough. I've traveled this state—and the country—widely over the past two decades, and have gotten to know a fair number of people. I think I can contribute politically."

**TABLE 6–1.**
**WARDWELL VINYL COATINGS, INC. CURRENT BALANCE SHEET (In Thousands of Dollars)**

| | | | |
|---|---|---|---|
| Cash | $ 4,800 | Accounts Payable | $ 2,500 |
| Receivables, Net | 7,500 | Accruals | 2,000 |
| Inventory | 7,200 | Long-Term Debt* | 2,000 |
| Marketable Securities | 4,000 | Common Stock and Retained Earnings | 27,500 |
| Plant and Equipment, Net | 10,500 | | |
| Total Assets | $34,000 | Total Liabilities & Equity | $34,000 |

*Debt due in equal amounts over a five-year period; Current amount carried as an accrued item.

## New Opportunity

A month ago Harleton Rowe learned that a European manufacturer was looking for U.S. firms to produce and sell a poromeric leather that the European manufacturer has developed and introduced successfully in some regions of the
European Common Market. Beckley Wardwell, in his characteristic manner, encouraged Harleton Rowe to "follow up on any idea that looks promising."

The following information has been assembled by Harleton Rowe, and now
he feels ready to report back to Beckley Wardwell.

The European manufacturer is seeking two U.S. licensees for its product. To
date, the artificial leather has been used primarily for shoe uppers and to a lesser
extent for lightweight shoe innersoles. It can be given the appearance of any kind
of leather, is more durable than ordinary leather, and has some of the same
"breathing" characteristics of leather.

Poromeric leather (of which du Pont's Corfam was the first sold on any scale
in the U.S.) is not an animal product, but a synthetic leather made by coating a
nonwoven substrate with either a polyurethane or vinyl finish. In the case of Corfam, the substrate had three layers, including one of a woven polyester. When
sales did not reach the expected volume, du Pont sold its process and remaining
inventory to a Polish company.

The proposal by the Common Market firm is that each licensee should manufacture the substrate (one layer of nonwoven material) and coat it with polyurethane in its own plants and then sell the product primarily to shoe manufacturers,
using a specialized sales force. The European company wants the U.S. affiliate to
carry out the entire process for both quality control and process security reasons.

The European developer seeks two U.S. licensees because a tariff of $.12 per
pound plus 15 percent ad valorem effectively rules out exports to the U.S. from
Western European and Eastern European manufacturers. European technology is
widely thought to be two to three years ahead of U.S. technology in its development stage. The European firm expects to continue its development work and
would keep the U.S. licensees fully advised of any process and product advances
as a part of the licensing agreement. The license fee would average about 1 percent
of net sales.

Current U.S. efforts to manufacture an acceptable leather substitute have
failed on the three desirable properties of the substrate (strength, absorbability,
breathability). The European firm claims that it has exported one million square
yards of its substrate to U.S. coating firms and has had acceptance from them.
Preliminary checks by Harleton Rowe with three of his present competitors (the
coating firms) have substantiated this claim.

Several market studies by the European manufacturer indicate the information shown in Table 6–2.

The market study was carried out using an assumed U.S. price of $23.50 per
square yard as contrasted with the shoe upper leather price of $47.50 per square
yard.

**TABLE 6–2.**
**U.S. SALES AND POTENTIAL SALES OF LEATHER AND LEATHER SUBSTITUTES FOR SHOE UPPERS AND INNERSOLES (Millions of Square Yards)**

| Product | Current year | 5 years hence | 10 years hence |
|---|---|---|---|
| Leather shoe uppers | 75 | 58 | 35 |
| Nonleather shoe uppers | 5 | 20 | 35 |
| Leather shoe innersoles | 75 | n.a. | n.a. |
| Nonleather shoe innersoles | 1 | 15 | 20 |

Harleton Rowe is enthusiastic about seeking a license. His arguments are that (1) the firm would have an early entry into a rapidly expanding market and thus could capture a major market share; (2) the proposed selling price makes the synthetic leather highly competitive; (3) neither du Pont nor Monsanto Chemical is now interested in the product (du Pont's plant for making Corfam had been built to produce 100 million square yards annually, but its total sales in two years were only 35 million square yards); and (4) the proposed product would have only two layers, and thus would tend to stretch and adapt itself to the wearer's foot, whereas Corfam did not.

In a short conversation Rowe had with Spencer Wardwell about the proposal, Spencer Wardwell said, "It's not worth serious attention. I'm having enough difficulty getting money for the new plant, so why bother with something in addition? We don't have the extra $20,000,000 for the initial poromeric leather investment."

Clay Weston said, "Well, we can probably finance the investment by borrowing since, based on preliminary figures, it promises a rate of return close to what we are now earning. But what is the risk? What will the competition be? Will sales of our present products be affected? If sales turn out to be half the amount predicted, will the fixed overhead bankrupt the rest of the company, since the pattern of costs of this venture will be about average for the industry?"

## Questions

Suppose that you are the senior investigator making the study of Wardwell Vinyl Coatings, Inc.

1. How do you explain the differences in opinion on what the company should do that are held by Harleton Rowe, John Minton, Spencer Wardwell, Leon Torbit, and Clay Weston?

2. How would you answer Beckley Wardwell with respect to the four issues that he raises in the first paragraph of the case?
3. What strategy do you recommend that the company adopt? Include in your answer (but do not limit yourself to) recommendations on the poromeric leather license and on Spencer Wardwell's proposed new plant. Also, cover the strategic thrusts that should be started within the next six months.

# CHAPTER 7

## Strategy Programs in Marketing: Product Line and Customers

The first encounter that a university graduate has with business strategy will almost always occur in a department. Strategy is often initiated, and certainly is elaborated, at this operating level. So a closer look at the issues which are typically involved in the department/business-unit interchange will help in understanding the total strategic management process.

Because of time and space limitations, only the basic functional departments will be discussed in our examination. Marketing is a convenient place to begin (Chapters 7 and 8); such a start emphasizes the need for every enduring organization to offer some combination of goods and services that customers really prefer. Then the production of the goods and services to be sold must be confronted (Chapters 9 and 10). This in turn raises issues of mobilizing resources—people, materials, and capital (Chapters 11 through 14).

All of the preceding functions are interrelated, and it is impossible to make wise decisions for one function without considering the other functions. Also, many companies will have additional, more specialized functions. Nevertheless, the sequence consisting of marketing, production, and mobilization of resources provides a logical approach to overall company activities (and is often used by management consulting firms).

## Marketing Issues Linked into Business-Unit Strategy

A marketing department serves as a company's primary interface with its customers. It finds customers, identifies their needs, woos them, and serves them. Moreover, marketing managers are expected to foresee shifts in demand and in competition, and to help central managers chart new marketing strategies. To perform this role, a marketing department must give particular attention to the following issues:

1. Lines of products and services offered to customers.
2. Types and locations of customers preferred by the company.
3. Prices to be charged.
4. Marketing mix of sales appeals to be stressed and sales promotion efforts.

The first of these are discussed in this chapter, the last two in the next.

Following the model outlined in Chapter 6, options for external linkages are highlighted first. Then horizontal linkages with other departments and vertical linkages with business-unit strategy are noted. In each section the aim is neither a detailed checklist nor a comprehensive treatment—laborious tasks far beyond the limits of a few chapters. Instead, concepts and illustrations are presented of typical strategic thrusts or policies which can be combined into department strategy programs. These examples indicate how ideas that students have already studied in functional courses can be incorporated into the strategy perspective.

## Designing Product and Service Lines

For more than a century Levi Strauss & Company made sturdy dungarees for rough outdoor labor such as gold mining—a single kind of product for a modest sort of customer. Then fortune smiled: Levi's became fashionable for the beatnik set, a symbol of protest against conventional behavior. Sales boomed to a completely different customer group.

Levi Strauss & Company might have stuck to its century-tested product line, treating the fashion demand as a temporary bit of good luck. Not so, however. The marketing opportunity was seized, and now a variety of trendy outdoor clothes for men carry the prestigious Levi label. Moreover, women have been squeezed into tight-fitting Levi's and provide a new set of customers. Style is a critical factor in expanding sales. Indeed, subtle changes in styles have replaced the former emphasis on the same long-wearing quality generation after generation.

Four product-line issues are illustrated in the Levi Strauss transformation: the domain to be served, the breadth of the line, product differentiation, and the frequency of design change. These issues arise in almost all marketing programs, and the way they are handled has a significant effect on both marketing and business-unit strategy.

In the next few pages, then, our viewpoint will be that of a marketing department—the department in the company which is predominantly concerned with strong relationships with customers. A marketing department will not be indifferent to other company problems, but the issues that it encounters day after day and the measures of its excellence will be related mostly to building durable, warm ties to an ever-increasing number of attractive customers.

This focus on external relationships with customers—and through them with ultimate consumers, competitors, and the whole market structure—does not imply that customer preferences are the only factors to be considered; other considerations are examined at the end of the chapter also. The immediate aim, however, is to get a sense of the pressing questions that goad most marketing managers.

## Domain to Be Served

A major hurdle in the Levi Strauss growth was shifting the thinking of marketing managers from working clothes to fashion clothes—from construction and forestry laborers to upbeat college students as customers. There was a basic question about what target market should be served.

The Holiday Inns face a similar issue. In addition to comfortable lodging for traveling business people, should the marketing department seek conferences, and if so, of what size? Should it try to enter the growing but competitive casino hotel business or tie into vacation resorts? Can one organization serve several price/quality segments of the market, or should it carefully cultivate a national reputation for a single predictable level of service?

The issue of an attractive domain has already been discussed in Part 1 from a company viewpoint. The marketing department, however, is especially concerned with it. Marketing managers will seek boundaries of the domain, or domains, that will provide fertile fields for marketing activities.

## Breadth of Product/Service Line

For each strategic niche, the marketing department must decide what variety of products and services will be offered to its customers. This is a recurring and often controversial issue as markets change, competition grows, and new technology becomes available.

### Cost of Diversity

Customers are continually asking for products that are smaller, stronger, of another voltage, or otherwise different from what is offered, and sales representatives will contend that sales volume could be increased materially if they had a larger variety of products to sell.

One manufacturer of soaps yielded to this pressure. Whenever the sales manager noted that competitors were offering a new soap or that a number of customers had requested a soap that differed in color, shape, fragrance, or composition, a new product meeting these specifications would be introduced. Examination of sales records showed that sales of most of these new products were satisfactory for several months but would gradually dwindle. Apparently, the initial sales were largely due to the enthusiasm of the sales representatives for a new product and a willingness on the part of the retailers to try an original stock to see how the product would sell. After this original distribution, however, most new products were discovered to have no unique appeal. This particular company, therefore, had a large number of products for which the sales volume was inadequate to justify the cost of manufacturing, warehousing, and selling. Only by careful study was the marketing department able to reduce the number of items carried to comparatively few products that really had significant differences. It then concentrated its attention on selling these products rather than dissipating its effort on unnecessary additions to its line.

One way to deal with this recurring controversy is to fix a limit on the number of items. Then any proposal for a new item must be accompanied by a recommendation to drop an existing one. While exceptions may be necessary, this plan has the advantage of forcing attention to pruning items along with justifying the new item.

### Need for Complete Line

Sometimes the customer wants to buy a variety of products or services from the same source. For example, each of us expects the druggist to be able to fill within a few hours any prescription our doctor may write. The druggist, in turn, expects the same kind of complete line service from drug wholesalers. Since a single slow delivery is likely to result in a long-time loss in patronage, a complete line is very important.

In contrast, a marketing department may seek a distinction as a specialist. The sales representatives of Crown Cork & Seal, for instance, are experts in canning carbonated beverages. An even more extreme example is a firm that specializes in putting out fires at oil and gas wells. By focusing on a narrow line, costs can be reduced, and if the product is sold in *large enough units* to warrant separate action by customers, the lack of a complete line may be no serious handicap. A narrow line policy relies on specialization to achieve a competitive advantage in pricing, unique service, or concentrated attention. One way to look at the product line is suggested by Figure 7–1.

### Ways of Customizing Products

A middle position may be feasible. Perhaps some variety can be offered without too much added expense. Common practice with automobiles or refrigerators, for instance, is to have a standard product in two or three sizes, with other options to choose from, such as color and accessories. The number of variations is strictly limited, and the optional items are available only by paying a premium. While inventory and production scheduling are complicated by this practice, it does give the customer some choice.

## Product Differentiation

Maintaining a variety of products is one way to seek differential advantage. A related and perhaps less costly possibility is to offer "better" products—that is, better in the eyes of a desired set of customers.

### What Is Quality?

Quality cannot be defined exactly. The purchaser of garden tools may define quality in terms of *durability,* while the buyer of a fashionable dress may be more interested in richness of *appearance.* For medical products, quality usually refers to *purity:* customers will pay a premium for a product they feel confident is pure. *Dependability* is crucial in the space industry. So if a marketing department believes that distinctiveness can be obtained on the basis of product quality, it must decide

**FIGURE 7–1.**
**PROFITABILITY OF NARROW VS. WIDE PRODUCT LINES IN VARIOUS STAGES OF PRODUCT LIFE CYCLE (A narrow product line tends to give low profits in early or middle stages of the cycle)**

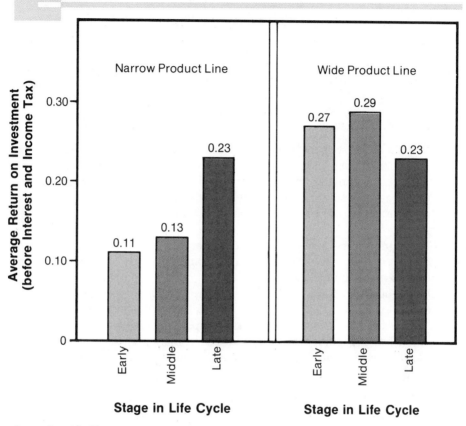

*Source:* Strategic Planning Institute.

which particular characteristics it will stress. Here, desired market segmentation often is the key.

### Consumer Recognition of Product Differences

In deciding on the kind of distinctiveness to emphasize, the marketing department must consider not only the desires of its customers but also the customers' ability to appreciate variations in quality. Even purchasers of stereos are limited in their ability to detect differences in tone quality. The department must therefore determine (1) what characteristics of its product its customers feel are important;

(2) the extent to which its customers can appreciate the differences in such features and how much they are willing to pay for the extra quality; and (3) whether the cost of producing extra features is more or less than customers are willing to pay for them.

## Frequency of Design Change

Related to the question of how product distinction is to be achieved is the troublesome issue of how frequently changes in design should be made.

### Pressures to Change

The most recent style may be so important to consumers that frequent design changes are inevitable. Today, even staple products are styled according to the current mode. Kitchenware and bathtubs, which still render the same service they did 30 years ago, are streamlined and styled to the modern taste. Bath towels and sheets come in all colors of the rainbow, and even steam hammers are streamlined.

Change may be necessary for more technical reasons. New developments are occurring every year in color television, microfilming, and solid-state controls of machines, to mention only a sample.

The pressures of style or technology are strong by themselves. Competitors' actions, however, may make the need to change irresistible. When a clearly preferred product is offered by a competitor, a company must respond in some manner, usually by redesigning its own products. The marketing department should anticipate how strong this competitive pressure will be.

### Frequency of Change

Several alternative ways of reconciling the pressures with the costs of redesign of products are available to managers. Annual models are often used for consumer goods. Another tack, more common in industrial goods, is a policy of "product leadership." Here the firm wants to be first on the market with improvements, and new designs are introduced as rapidly as new technology is developed. But as one urban planner observed, "You don't tear down your house every time a new heat pump is invented." A common practice of marketing departments is to rely on advertising of minor changes which are portrayed as the latest developments.

## Product-Line Policy of a Service Company

Issues regarding product lines are easier to grasp when we use physical products as examples. However, most service enterprises face comparable problems. For example, a similar set of questions confronts advertising agencies, hospitals, and management consultants. What characteristics of quality are significant, and can the consumer recognize the differences? How frequently should programs change? Clearly, these issues are fundamental in developing a viable, continuing relationship between a firm and the people who use its products or services.

## Types and Location of Customers

In conceiving of a scenario for excellence, marketing managers must include guidelines for selecting customers. Of course, customer choice—like product-line policy—will be broadly defined by the selection of a domain. Nevertheless, further elaboration is necessary.

Three kinds of issues arise again and again: What body of ultimate consumers does the company wish to serve? What channel of distribution will be most effective in reaching these consumers? And what limits on size or other characteristics should be placed on customers with whom the company deals directly? Because of its knowledge of the total market structure and the actions of competitors, the marketing department is the primary source of answers to these questions.

## Consumer Sought

### Distinction Between Customers and Consumers

Confusion sometimes arises because of a failure to distinguish between customers and consumers. The term *consumer* means one who *uses* a product (or service) for personal satisfaction or benefit; or in the case of industrial materials, one who so *changes* the form of the product as to alter its identity. A *customer*, on the other hand, is anyone who *buys* the goods or services. A customer may be a consumer, or a dealer who will resell the product to someone else.

### Types of Consumers

Various kinds of consumers want services of a very different nature. For example, the restaurant catering to business executives offers a different service from the campus kitchen seeking the trade of students. In one instance, the marketing department of a patent medicine company found, as a result of studying its market, that a major group of its consumers were people who spoke only foreign languages. Such groups were located primarily in large industrial centers and could be reached only by foreign language newspapers and foreign language radio broadcasts.

When a manufacturer of electric-powered hand tools decided to tap the do-it-yourself market in addition to its established market with the professional building trades, it failed to recognize the difference in needs of the two types of customers. The amateurs required more foolproof machines and elementary instruction sheets. After two years of losses, the manufacturer returned to its policy of focusing only on the professional market.

The relation of the marketing arm of a company to consumers of its products is normally continuous over a period of years. Reputations are established, and expectations—so vital to careful planning—are built up. Consequently, marketing departments naturally resist moving in and out of a market from week to week. Instead, well-established and relatively stable policies regarding consumers to be served are followed.

### Location of Consumers

The large mail-order houses such as Sears, Roebuck and Montgomery Ward built their businesses with rural consumers—people who had difficulty getting to cities to shop. But conditions have changed. Now there are fewer farmers, and they drive automobiles. One adjustment to this shift has been an impressive expansion of retail stores operated by these companies. Also, the merchandise offered has been adapted to appeal to the nonfarm customer, and telephone ordering is replacing the mailed order. But, vital to the marketing department's planning of what will be offered is a clear concept of where the potential buyers live.

Full utilization of an existing strength may influence a marketing department's choice of customers. Most common is adoption of *national distribution* because national advertising of the company—already necessary for part of the market—is reaching consumers in all areas. In these cases, sales promotion considered to be desirable dictates the market scope, rather than consumer policy determining what promotion is feasible. A somewhat similar situation arises when a company invests heavily to acquire technical expertise for a specific problem and then feels impelled to serve all people having this problem regardless of where they are located.

Competitive tactics may also influence policy regarding the location of desired consumers. For instance, Company A may immediately follow Company B into a new area because A does not want B to acquire a possible source of strength that might be extended to other markets. On the other hand, if a pattern of normal territories has evolved, Company X may not move into Company Y's home market for fear that Y will reciprocate. Such intangible considerations may result in a marketing department's pushing its territorial limits no further than the point where incremental selling and delivery costs match incremental revenue.

### Consumers of a "Small Business"

Over the years small businesses have typically catered to local consumers. Dramatic improvements in transportation and communication, however, have undercut the local butcher, baker, and candlestick maker. National concerns now reach even the remotest consumers, and consumers drive many miles to shop. Local semimonopolies are fast disappearing. Consequently, most small businesses now are seeking more distinction in their products and services, while expanding the geographical location of their potential consumers.

## Channels of Distribution

By a *channel of distribution* we mean the *steps* by which products are *distributed* from the one who first converts them into usable form to the consumer. Many enterprises, of course, render services rather than manufacture products—for example, airlines, banks, public accountants, and all sorts of retail stores. Because of their nature, such services are almost always sold directly to consumers. But for manufacturers, the selection of the proper channels of distribution is a very real issue.

Changes in buying habits, transport, communications, and market locations have modified methods of distribution greatly during recent years. The whole field is in a state of flux, and few marketing departments are justified in assuming that their traditional channels are necessarily the most effective ways of reaching the consumer they prefer. The farsighted choice of the right channel of distribution sometimes becomes a major differential advantage.

### Through Jobbers

Utilizing jobbers or wholesalers was long regarded as the orthodox method of distribution. Jobbers assemble products from many manufacturers, store them, and sell them to retailers. In so doing, they also assume risks of price change, damage, or obsolescence, extend credit to retailers, and sort and ship products according to retailer needs.

Today, retailers are larger and many manufacturers have set up distribution systems which deal directly with them. Nevertheless, there are auto supply jobbers who serve repair shops, plumbing supply houses that serve plumbers, and similar specialty jobbers for a particular trade or industry. A baffling issue for marketers of widely consumed goods is the extent to which to use such distributors; they add at least 20 percent to the selling price of the products.

### Directly to Retailers

Distribution by the manufacturing firm directly to retailers has some distinct advantages. By using its own sales representatives to call on retailers, the manufacturer may secure more aggressive selling efforts. By contrast, a jobber's general-line salespeople sell a wide variety of products and cannot concentrate their efforts upon the sale of one particular product. Marketing departments also feel that direct sales to retailers gives them more control over pricing, supply, etc. Dealing with retailers may also enable a sales representative to ascertain better the consumers' desires, since the retailer has firsthand contact at the final point of sale.

The plan of selling directly to retailers, however, may lead to excessive costs if it is used unwisely. If the manufacturing firm eliminates the jobber entirely, it may incur unbearable costs because many retailers buy in such small quantities that the expense of selling and servicing them may exceed the gross profits on the goods they purchase.

Companies that manufacture a variety of products may set up their own *sales branches*. These branches perform in many respects as does a jobber, except that they sell only products of the parent company.

### Directly to Consumers

Direct sale to consumers is usually preferred when the salesperson needs a high degree of technical training to sell the product and when technical services must be provided after the product is sold. This type of plan is often used to sell large computers and group insurance.

Use of *exclusive dealers*, adopted by automobile manufacturers and many oil companies, combines many advantages of direct sales to consumers while retaining the initiative of local businesspeople. The dealers "run their own business," but to retain a franchise the dealer must join in company sales programs and conform to service standards set by the marketing department.

### Through Brokers or Agents

A broker usually performs only one major function of distribution—selling. As contrasted with the jobber, the broker usually sells only one type of product, or at most a few closely related products. Marketing managers of small canneries, for example, typically use brokers because they do not have sufficient output to justify a full-time sales force. Anyone who has publicly announced an intention to buy a house knows that brokers are also used in the real estate field. Here, again, it is difficult for buyers and sellers to get together without the aid of someone who is in close contact with the market.

### Selecting a Channel of Distribution

One flexible approach to resolving the channel-of-distribution issue is to view it as a problem of organizing the total distribution system. More specifically, this approach involves:

1. Listing all actions necessary between the producer and the consumer: promotion, actual selling, transportation, financing, warehousing, repackaging, risk-taking, installation and repair service, and the like.
2. Grouping these activities into jobs that can be effectively and efficiently performed by separate firms. These firms may be banks or warehouse workers who also do other things, or they may be firms exclusively involved in this particular channel. The crucial matter here is to conceive of jobs (packages of activities) that are the most effective combinations.
3. Defining relationships between the jobs that will assure cooperation and the necessary flow of information. Also to be defined is how each firm involved is to be compensated for its efforts. And necessary, minimum controls to be exercised by various members over other members must be worked out.

4.  Developing specifications for the firms that are to fill each job on the basis of the organization design (the *policy* adopted by the designer).
5.  Then moving on to execution of the plan by recruiting people to take the specified jobs (some negotiation may arise here since independent firms will be participants), educating people on how the plan is to work, supervising the day-to-day operations, and exercising necessary controls.

One of the significant aspects of the approach outlined is that the channel-of-distribution problem is not viewed as a choice between a few predetermined alternatives. Instead, each marketing department can work out a design regarding the best way to get its products to the consumers it has selected. Also implied is the idea that tasks assigned to participants are apt to need modification as economic and competitive conditions change.

A strong, well-designed distribution system may spell the difference between the success and failure of the entire enterprise.

## Size of Customer Market

Customers that a marketing department would otherwise like to deal with directly may buy in quantities either too small or too large for it to do so. The department should know how much it costs to serve each type of customer and the amount the customers must buy if their business is to yield a profit to the company. One manufacturing concern, for example, was selling to 8,000 retail accounts. An analysis of these accounts revealed that 55 percent of the total number purchased only 5 percent of its entire sales volume and that none of these 55 percent purchased more than $200 worth of merchandise a year. A newly appointed marketing manager decided to eliminate all such accounts, except a few with high potential for growth; as a consequence, the number of customers was reduced to 4,000. This enabled the department to reduce its sales staff from 82 to 43 and to make a number of other substantial reductions in selling costs.

On the other hand, a customer may purchase too much merchandise! If a concern is dependent on one or two customers for most of its business, its market position is vulnerable because loss of patronage of one such important buyer will disrupt the entire organization. As noted in Chapter 2, those few customers exercise too much relative power.

Companies in the aerospace industry often depend upon one or two large government contracts for the bulk of their business. Cancellation of or failure to win renewal of such a contract can then spell disaster for the firm. Advertising agencies may develop a similar overdependency on one or two large accounts; then, when an account is "dropped," the agency has to lay off most of its talented employees and may close entirely. Consequently, companies may have a policy that says no more than 20 percent of their business will be done with one customer.

## Crucial Horizontal and Vertical Linkages

The marketing department of a company will have preferences on how the product-line and customer issues just discussed should be fitted into a strategy program for marketing. These and related issues could be resolved in a "scenario for excellence," that is, a program which the marketing department believes would enable it to achieve excellence.

But, as noted in Chapter 6, marketing actions have an impact on other departments, and they support (or undercut) business-unit strategy. Consequently, the preferred scenario must be tailored to "fit" with the plans of related departments, and the tailored program must also be compatible with the strategy for the overall operation.

Such tailoring, or linking, is necessarily quite specific for each situation. Nevertheless, we can identify the places where crucial linkages often arise. These are spots where the fit should at least be checked; also, they illustrate the kind of dovetailing that should be sought wherever interdependence is high—which is especially the case in designing product lines.

## Relating Product-Line Changes to Operations in Other Departments

A change in the products that a company sells often affects almost every department. Some typical links are as follows:

### Engineering

- New products call for new design specifications. In preparing these, the engineering department must weigh quality in performance, feasibility of production, production costs, and the time required to bring the product to the market.

### Production

- The production department considers such questions as, Will different machinery be needed? Is worker safety affected? What new production methods will be required? and How will quality be controlled? In addition, aside from changes in the production process, the length of production runs may affect scheduling and costs profoundly.

### Purchasing

- The availability and cost of any different or additional materials or parts is a purchasing department concern. New suppliers may be needed, and the use of patented items may have to be negotiated.

### Human Resources

- If the changes in products or associated production processes are large, the number of workers needed, as well as their skills, may change. If so, the human resource department will be involved with transfer, training, and perhaps dismissals or recruitment of personnel.

### Finance

- All of the preceding departmental adjustments will involve extra expense for the transition and perhaps capital investment. Thus, the finance department will probably be asked for special allocations; and most finance departments have a relentless habit of insisting on justifications in terms of return on investment or cash flow.

### Control and Administration

- Pervasive change, like that often stirred up by new product lines, upsets the prevailing measurement and control system. So the controller's department should adjust its standards accordingly. Possibly some reorganization will be involved as well.

Clearly, the marketing department will have to do a lot of negotiating to win support from other departments for a scenario that involves a major change in the product line.

Of course, if the company deals in services instead of physical products, the production/purchasing changes will involve more paperwork (e.g., in insurance) or greater emphasis on human resources (e.g., with hospitals), or the like. The impact of a product-line change, however, will be no less pervasive.

## Relating Customer Changes to Operations in Other Departments

Although a shift in types of customers sought is usually less upsetting to activities outside the marketing department than a change in product lines, some kinds of customer changes do have many ramifications. For example, a change in channels of distribution, say, from the use of jobbers to direct sale to retailers, or a switch from technically sophisticated computer customers who provide their own servicing and software to naive, nontechnical customers, as Digital Equipment Company did, involves a lot more than the marketing department. At least the following departments will be affected:

### Engineering

- When the use of a product changes, usually the specifications regarding whether and how it is producible, its controls, its ease of repair, and the like must be adjusted. Often the engineering department will have to write an instruction manual that is quite different from the previous one.

## Production

- Customers vary in when and where they want delivery, and in the size of individual orders. So when the production department serves a different type of customer, it may be faced with a new seasonal variation in production and a new size of run. These in turn may affect the size, location, and versatility of an optimum plant or branch office.

## Human Resources

- The number of people needed in the selling force of a company, as well as the skills of those individuals, will be directly affected by the kind of customer the company serves. Consider, for instance, Bell Labs versus a vacation tour company, both of which use computers. And with the change in skills and volume of sales, the human resource department will have to shift the base pay of its personnel and the design of the incentives they require.

## Distribution

- Getting products to the consumer in good condition involves all sorts of packaging. As customers change, the transportation department finds itself involved in much more than hauling. In fact, the whole logistics of distribution may need to be redesigned.

## Finance

- Shifting customers changes the credit activities of a finance department. The kinds of risks undertaken and opportunities to earn income on unpaid balances differ greatly by size of customer.

## Control and Administration

- As with product changes, when the roles of various departments are modified to fit new customer types, the controller's department should revise its control system.

Although the foregoing list is primarily suggestive, it does flag many places where a marketing proposal to switch types of customers will require significant changes in other departments. Here again, a strategic move calls for integrated effort.

## Tying Product-Line and Customer Changes in Business-Unit Strategy

In addition to tying the marketing department to its external environment and fitting marketing moves in with operations of other departments, the mating of the marketing department's preferred strategy with the business-unit strategy must be considered.

Fortunately, in the areas of product lines and customers, the give-and-take between the marketing department and managers of the business-unit is likely to be frequent. These two areas are always vital considerations in forming the business-unit strategy. The question of domain—the first element in the four-part strategy—boils down to what products and services will the company sell to what customers? The central managers are inescapably concerned with this question. Typically, they will seek all the help they can get from the marketing department because it is the company's major contact with customers and with competitors for those customers.

This means that the department normally participates actively in formulating business-unit strategy. It is not isolated and forgotten. And with that relationship established, the marketing department is well positioned to recommend changes in strategy. Of course, the department managers may not be completely candid with their bosses if they anticipate that a recommendation will receive a cool reception or if they wish not to upset a friendly alliance with other departments which oppose the recommendation. Nevertheless, the opportunities for the marketing department to take an active part in shaping business-unit strategy are inherently good.

The advice that the marketing department gives may not be accepted. Most departments prefer to continue to do what they are already doing. They have worked hard to build friendly relations with existing customers, their personnel are trained to promote the existing product line, and their internal social structure is predictable. Consequently, the marketing department is likely to propose and defend only incremental changes rather than major shifts in products or customers, even when top management believes the latter are needed.

Also, the marketing department typically will recommend increasing the volume of sales, because that is the way marketing success is usually measured and bonuses are earned. And to obtain this increase, the normal proposal will be heavier use of variables that the marketing department can manipulate, such as more advertising, more customer service, lower prices, and the like.

Perhaps incremental changes and more volume are indeed wise strategy for the business-unit. But not always. The marketing proposals usually serve the marketing department's interests and often lack synergistic balance for the overall company. In other words, they may be short-sighted.

Thus, in regard to changes in product lines and customers, the vertical linkage between the marketing department and central management is likely to be frequent and influential. However, the advice from the marketing department probably will be "provincial." Central managers still have to balance marketing considerations against the interests of other departments, and they have to sense the need for major shifts in direction.

Besides product-line and customer issues, the marketing department must deal with pricing and an appropriate mix of sales promotion efforts. We turn to these issues in the next chapter.

## Questions for Class Discussion

1. In its high-quality cookie line, Pepperidge Farm has a wide variety of cookies. By contrast, in its bottled soft-drink line, Coca Cola for years focused on one basic flavor. (Recently variations for "diet," "no caffeine," and "new" Coca Cola have been marketed; but these all center on the basic flavor.) How do you explain this difference in variety between Pepperidge Farm cookies and bottled Coca Cola? Do you think the Coca Cola Company could increase its sales, and hence it profits, by increasing the number of flavors sold under its brand name.

2. McCracken & Daughters is a well-established regional public accounting firm. It has a professional staff of about 80 CPAs and offices in several cities. To date, the firm has done primarily auditing and tax work for mid-sized companies. A new assistant to the managing partner recommends that the firm add management consulting to its line of services. She says, "We already know a lot about our clients and are aware of the management problems they face. This provides a natural market in which to start. In the longer run, there is no reason why we have to confine our consulting work to auditing clients." (a) Do you agree that management consulting is a normal and attractive way for McCracken & Daughters to expand? (b) If the firm decides to go into management consulting, what internal adjustments would it need to make in addition to plans for promoting the new service?

3. The 7-Eleven stores have moved into the retailing of gasoline in a big way. The move from groceries and related items to self-service gasoline has added about $1.5 billion to the sales of the 7,400-unit chain. How do you explain the success of this unconventional addition to the 7-Eleven product line?

4. Einstein University's strengths and its attractiveness as regards outside funding were primarily in the various sciences, medicine, and engineering, and in some selected departments of its other colleges, including information systems in the College of Business. The president, academic vice president, and

other administrators had been chemists, physicists, biochemists, botanists, and astronomers. The management department recently lost its production and operations management major when this subject was transferred by the dean of the college to the information systems department.

For recruiting, the management department had two vacant positions to fill. A recommendation by one member of the department's recruiting committee who was about to retire that it hire, with the dean's approval, a specialist in the management of research and development work and in the diffusion of innovations drew only blank stares and not one comment from the other committee members. They eventually decided to make offers to a specialist in organization behavior and another in organization theory—the "micro" and "macro" views of organizations according to the committee.

After conferring with the academic vice president, the dean of the college announced that the specialist in the management of research and development was to be hired and that the committee could fill the other vacancy with either one of its two choices. The department head wondered if any of the other eighteen department members would be interested in and supportive of the R & D man and how his subject and interests would fit into and match with the teaching and research interests of the professors of business law, organization behavior, organization theory, personnel management, health services, and business policy and strategy.

Explain the events in this situation in terms of the vertical linkages of the product line—the various majors—of the management department; the horizontal linkages with outside groups such as the American Society for Training and Development, the Operations Research Society of America, and many others; and the linkages with other departments in the university, such as the sociology, economics, psychology, and urban planning departments, and the law school with which the management department shared joint professorships and joint or identical courses.

5. For years, T.V. Black & Associates has made parts for automobile brake systems. Recently it has concentrated on a single critical part, made in various sizes and specifications in conformity with designs of the auto manufacturers. About half of the output has gone to the replacement market, and the company has a policy of selling no more than 20 percent of its annual output to a single customer. During the recession of the early 1980s, sales for original equipment dropped sharply and all three of the U.S. auto manufacturers insisted on a price freeze. Nevertheless, T.V. Black & Associates continued to take some orders at below-cost prices in order to remain on the "approved vendor" lists. Recently Ford has circulated a general statement about its "preferred vendor lists." Ford wants vendors who (a) adopt quality assurance practices that Ford believes will ensure virtually no defects, and (b) are prepared to cooperate with a "just-in-time" delivery scheduling (which has been so successful for the Japanese). Ford has invited T.V. Black & Associates to qualify as a preferred vendor, indicating that large orders will be placed with

firms on the preferred list. Mr. Black says, "With our present plant management we can easily qualify as a preferred supplier, and Ford might place orders equal to 50 percent of our capacity if we were competitive on price. Running at capacity, we surely would make money." Do you recommend that the company go after the Ford business?

6. A producer of room air conditioners for use in homes is having difficulty obtaining adequate distribution. Use the approach outlined on page 176 to build a model of the total distribution system of the industry. Then select places in that system where you believe a company with only 12 percent of the total market could develop some comparative advantage. Assume that the products of all competitors have about the same characteristics and quality.

7. In a speech to a group of financial analysts, the president and chief executive officer of Campbell Soup Company said:

> We are trying to organize this company to give it some flavor and some vitality for the 1980s. . . . [Our objective] came from looking at what the good, top-notch food companies have done in the last couple of years and from deciding whether we can play in this game up there with the best. We don't want to be down in the middle stream where we appeared to be. . . . Let's look back at the heritage of this company and see where we take this. . . . I tried to dredge out . . . what the quality of this company was. . . . The first thing . . . is that this is a company that wants to make quality products. We are not in the schlock business. We are also interested in a product line that has value added. We are not in the commodity business. . . .
>
> [Nonfood activities] do not play a role at Campbell Soup. In the immediate five-year plan they do not. But over the long term we've said that we are in a business that is designed to give healthy well-being to people. It is conceivable that we could be involved in bicycles, for instance.

(a) What is wrong with the commodity business—the tomato soup business, for example? Toward what food products should Campbell Soup move?
(b) Should Campbell Soup make and sell bicycles? Explain.

8. In addition to gasoline and oil, possibilities for the product line of a filling station include batteries, tires, antifreeze, oil filters, fan belts, windshield wipers, mufflers, brake linings, tire chains, soft drinks, cigarettes, souvenirs, candy, and an array of repair services ranging from motor tune-ups, front-end repairs, body work, and transmission replacement to greasing and car washing. (a) If you owned and operated a filling station, how would you decide on your product line? (b) If you were the manager of a major oil company's nationwide chain of filling stations, what policy would you establish regarding filling station product lines? What would you insist on? Forbid? Leave up to the local operator?

9.  (a) As briefly described in this chapter, Levi Strauss & Company expanded its target customer group from only men who do rough outdoor work to teenagers and young adults who are mainly interested in Levi's as a style of

clothing as well. What departments within Levi Strauss & Company, in addition to marketing, do you think were significantly affected by this expansion of the customer base? Explain the interconnections. Do you think that the affected departments welcomed the change? Why?

(b) More recently, Levi Strauss & Company has added clothing for women to its line. Again, what departments within the company do you think were affected by the expanded customer base? Do you think that the affected departments welcomed the change? Explain your answers.

10. With sales volume steady and costs rising constantly, Brown Food Brokers, Inc., felt the pinch of declining profits. Its principals (manufacturers) were demanding more and more service in the way of promotions, store displays, stocking of retailers, inventory counting, and other selling aids which required increased contact with the retail food chains, buying groups, and wholesalers who were Brown's as well as the manufacturers' customers. Sales could be increased by adding more principals and by hiring more salespeople, but this might well lead to a profitless prosperity. Along came a local manufacturer of crackers, biscuits, and cookies who offered to sell out his company to Brown's. As president, J.P. Brown, a third-generation Brown, thought little of the baker's selling efforts and believed that his firm could cut the selling expense in half. Then another opportunity—private labeling using the Brown name—came around. A California producer of jams, jellies, marmalades, and preserves (the second highest selling product group for Brown's) offered a quality product at a price substantially below that of existing brands. The manufacturer might well finance Brown's inventory.

As alternatives to increasing the productivity of a food broker—a service firm—what do you think about buying out the bakery-goods manufacturer or taking on the private-label line?

## CASE
### 7 The Farm Management System*

The management of Homestead Computers was considering the future of its primary proprietary product, the Farm Management System (FMS). Their early hopes for rapid market penetration had not been realized through their current corporate strategy. Management was also very concerned about the way in which

*Prepared by John Fallows under the direction of Walter S. Good, University of Manitoba.

they were approaching the market in regard to this product. In addition, they were aware that they had to consider the strengths, weaknesses, and positioning of the company as a whole in reaching a decision regarding how to proceed with the FMS.

## The Microcomputer Software Industry

The commercial introduction of microcomputers in 1976 sparked a revolution in the field of information processing. A proliferation of hardware created tremendous opportunities for the creation and sale of integrated systems and applications software, programs that enable microcomputers to perform particular jobs. Perhaps surprisingly, the demand for software for the new micros was not met by the established (mainframe computer) software producers. Thus, a new industry was born, largely spawned in the basements of numerous creative entrepreneurs.

## Homestead Computer Services, Ltd.

Since its creation three years ago, Homestead has followed a strategy of trying to carve out specialized target markets for itself. The firm has concentrated on combining its expertise in microcomputers with applications within selected industries. Homestead was an outgrowth of Westburn Development Consultants, an agricultural consulting firm with a number of years of experience in the grain industry and related fields, such as transportation and information systems.

One of Homestead's target industries was agriculture. The company enjoyed excellent success in the area of custom software development, with its major achievement being the development and installation of a computer-assisted trading system for the Winnipeg Commodity Exchange. This led to a contract to develop a similar system for the London International Financial Futures Exchange. At the same time, the company also developed a number of proprietary products including an Elevator Information System and the Farm Management System.

Homestead employed 15 people, most of whom had expertise in fields such as business administration, computer science, engineering, electronics, agricultural economics, and science. Sales were approaching one million dollars annually, with the Westburn division providing a steady $250,000. The company was seeking sales growth of 50 percent each year and expected this growth to come mainly from the sale of customized and proprietary information systems. The financial condition of the company was good, with a debt-to-equity ratio of 0.3, a current ratio of 1.2, and a return on sales exceeding 10 percent.

## The Farm Management System

Homestead's primary growth was expected to come through the sale of its proprietary Farm Management System. Sales revenue forecasts for the FMS were based on the sale of 300 to 400 such systems each year for the next three years. However, early results were disappointing.

## Product Description

The software for the FMS is a double-entry accounting system for nine product centers. It has a comprehensive inventory control system, fixed asset recording, and labor use and manpower planning. Simulation modules for cash flow and product planning in special fields such as feedlot management are also part of the package. The hardware features a Vector Graphics microcomputer with 56K RAM, dual floppy disks with 1.26M storage, and a Centronics dot matrix printer. While the system was normally sold on a turnkey basis, it was also available on a software-only basis. Homestead enjoyed OEM status with Vector Graphics, and with this status it was able to buy the hardware as an "original equipment manufacturer" for a very low price per computer. Homestead then packaged its software into the Vector Graphics machine and sold a final product consisting of a "system" of both hardware and software. The software was configured to run on any microcomputer which used the CP/M operating system. This included a broad range of equipment using an Intel 8080-type CPU. However, it did *not* include other eight-bit CPUs, such as the Motorola 6500 types common to Apple and Commodore computers, and the 16-bit CPU machines, such as the IBM PC.

FMS was customized to the specific needs of farmers and, therefore, enjoyed an advantage over generic accounting software packages available from other firms. It performed more functions than either the generic systems or those of other competitors that were also targeted toward the farm market. Furthermore, the accounting system operated on a cash as well as an accrual basis, the former approach being more meaningful to the farmer. The hardware was well built and reliable; the system operated on a stand-alone basis and could prepare reports at any time. This was a distinct advantage, providing much faster turnaround than competitors who offered a centralized "mail-in" accounting system (where delays of 10 to 14 days could occur). It was also superior to the time-shared remote computing systems, since telecommunications charges could be expensive. (Also, because many farms were served by party-line telephone systems, the telephone companies would not allow computers to tie up these phone lines.) Farm Management System competitors include other stand-alone, microcomputer-based systems; on-line, remote access mainframe systems; batch mail-in systems; accounting consulting services; manual accounting systems; and the "old shoe box."

## Pricing

In many respects, the decision as to the price to charge for computer software was quite arbitrary. Regardless of the method used to allocate development costs, such outlays were "sunk" costs. The variable cost of production was, at most, a few dollars per unit. The sale of software to commercial microcomputer users was still quite new, and little was known about the price elasticity of demand. The general approach taken with most software products was competitive pricing, although some price-level positioning was starting to appear. General-purpose business packages sold at $500 to $700 retail, while specialized agricultural software was somewhat more expensive.

Homestead positioned itself with a premium price for a superior system ($12,500 in Canada, $8,000 in the U.S.). American selling prices were lower for two reasons. First, the hardware was cheaper since the company didn't have to pay duty on the equipment (Vector Graphics was an American manufacturer) and there was a favorable exchange rate differential. Second, Homestead provided less support in the U.S. On software sales, the dealer discount ranged from 25 percent to 30 percent in Canada and up to 50 percent in the U.S. On the sale of a turn-key system in Canada, the contribution received by Homestead was about $5,500, of which $2,500 came from software. Competitive specialized agricultural software sold in the range of $500 to $1,300.

## ▪ Product Market

In general, Homestead felt that the FMS was most appropriate for larger farms (i.e., with gross sales exceeding $100,000) operated by younger owners (i.e., between 20 and 50 years of age). The target market was 6,000 Canadian and 45,000 U.S. farms. Aside from the increasing availability of lower cost computing hardware, Homestead saw three factors which contributed to the potential of the FMS. First, farmers were continuing to place more emphasis on high productivity and increased profitability as a key to their long-term survival. Farming was becoming more of a business, and farmers were starting to perceive themselves as professional managers. Second, with higher costs and better education, modern farmers were less tied to traditional ways of doing things and were more receptive to innovation. Third, the small rural communities were becoming less cohesive, and farmers were prepared to look farther afield for their supplies and capital equipment. The younger, better educated farmer and the larger, progressive farmer were likely to be the "principal innovators" who would try the FMS first. (See Tables 7–1 and 7–2.) In general, the "opinion leaders" were those who would try the FMS second. They were fairly progressive farmers likely with more than average-sized farms who would be willing to experiment with an innovation, but not as the initial users. This type of adoption process tended to indicate that Homestead would have to be prepared to devote a number of years to market penetration, with substantial sales increases coming probably only after the "opinion leaders" passed judgment on the acceptability of the product. There was a real danger, however, that a company like Homestead could devote a lot of money and effort to introducing the product (perhaps profitably, perhaps not), with other firms reaping the benefits after the market was established.

**TABLE 7-1.**
**AGE OF FARMERS IN THE U.S.**

| Age of Farmer | 1,000 Farmers | | |
|---|---|---|---|
| | *1974* | *1978* | *1982* |
| Under 25 years | 52 | 66 | 62 |
| 25–34 years | 240 | 285 | 294 |
| 35–44 years | 400 | 433 | 443 |
| 45–54 years | 577 | 549 | 505 |
| 55–64 years | 589 | 552 | 536 |
| 65 and older | 421 | 370 | 400 |
| TOTAL | 2,279 | 2,250 | 2,240 |

## Product Distribution

Homestead's distribution objective was to have broad geographic coverage which was not too expensive to manage. Their initial coverage included western Canada, southern Ontario, and the north central United States. The original distributorship agreement established by Homestead specified that each distributor must sell 25 systems in the first six months and 100 in the first year. Ten distributors were established, including three in the U.S. These were mainly computer businesses specializing in the sale of hardware and software. In Canada, first-year sales were only 24 units, with Alberta and Saskatchewan each accounting for one-third of these. In the U.S., three units were sold out of Dayton, Ohio; five units out of Fargo, North Dakota; and one unit out of Great Falls, Montana. Within Manitoba and Saskatchewan, Homestead marketed the system on a turnkey basis only. Outside this area, the company supplied its dealers with software only, and users were free to select whatever compatible hardware on which they wished to run the programs.

**TABLE 7-2.**
**NUMBER OF FARMS IN U.S., BY SIZE**

| Size of farm, acres harvested | 1,000 Farms | | | | | |
|---|---|---|---|---|---|---|
| | *1959* | *1964* | *1969* | *1974* | *1978* | *1982* |
| 1–49 | 1,675 | 1,375 | 1,078 | 872 | 847 | 829 |
| 50–99 | 564 | 462 | 372 | 316 | 292 | 256 |
| 100–199 | 537 | 455 | 364 | 316 | 297 | 262 |
| 200–499 | 352 | 329 | 311 | 318 | 319 | 293 |
| 500–999 | 60 | 64 | 74 | 100 | 109 | 119 |
| 1,000 or more | 14 | 15 | 20 | 33 | 40 | 49 |
| TOTAL | 3,202 | 2,700 | 2,219 | 1,958 | 1,904 | 1,808 |

Due to its highly specialized nature and newness, the product required extensive demonstration and personal selling; distribution was very important.

## Product Promotion

Homestead took the position that the product and its distribution must be well established before a major promotion effort was undertaken. One promotion technique used was demonstration of the FMS at agricultural trade shows. Another was a small technical booklet which explained and outlined the various features of the system. A third technique was the generation of publicity in newspapers and specialized agricultural publications such as *Country Guide*.

## Problems and Opportunities

Personal computer use was growing at between 50 and 100 percent a year, and this trend was expected to continue into the near future. In addition, personal computer users stimulated an even greater growth in the software market. The question was, How could a company like Homestead best address the opportunities presented by this tremendous growth?

In the past, Homestead had concentrated on turnkey sales combining both hardware and software, and the results were disappointing. A major problem appeared to be the use of the Vector Graphics computer. The brand had a small following in the United States, but was largely unknown in Canada. Indeed, given current trends, the very survival of the manufacturer over the next five years was uncertain. Apple, Tandy (Radio Shack), and Commodore emerged as household names, and industry observers speculated that these major firms would dominate the market. IBM had also entered the market with its PC, a move which early indications suggested would be very successful. Homestead's turnkey approach resulted in some consumer resistance due to the hardware's being an "unknown brand." Perhaps the system should be redesigned around another computer, such as the Apple or IBM PC, or both, if Homestead was to continue selling on a turnkey basis. However, it is not clear, given the present level of sales, that Homestead could achieve OEM status with these other manufacturers.

Another alternative available to the company was to sell the software only. This would require modifying the software to run on other operating systems, especially that used by the IBM PC. The sale of software only would result in a lower per-unit contribution margin than a turnkey sale, but this difference could be offset by greater volume. Preliminary industry surveys of pioneering farm computer users indicated market domination by the best known "brand" names—Apple, IBM, and Radio Shack. These machines had been successful due to heavy advertising, widespread availability and support, and low cost. Neither Radio Shack nor Apple offered substantial support for the CP/M operating system. Industry experts expected the IBM PC to dominate the market within two years.

Homestead also had to revitalize its distribution strategy. Its alternatives included (a) continued emphasis on developing a system of many small distributors, (b) an emphasis on developing a number of larger distributors, and (c) the development of a direct sales force. In addition, if it used distributors, it had to consider what type of firms they should be. Yet another idea under consideration was to get out of downstream distribution altogether and license the product to an established software distributor.

Parallel with these considerations, Homestead was also facing some critical decisions regarding possible areas for new product development. First, the company already had several computer programs at various stages of development which could extend the FMS. These included programs in the following areas:

1. Marketing information, including buying and selling, trends, and options
2. Livestock breeding
3. Tax preparation
4. Leasing versus purchasing analysis

Some of these applications were already available to farmers on time-shared systems, but not on a stand-alone basis.

The second area under consideration was the development of business software for firms operating in other segments of the agribusiness sector. Homestead thought there might be an opportunity for synergy with the FMS by providing software products for businesses in other industries which served the farming community.

## Question

Do you recommend that Homestead Computers seek to increase its sales (a) by changing the product package now called the Farm Management System, and/or (b) by changing its marketing policies for the Farm Management System, and/or (c) by adding another product line closely related to its differential strengths? Justify your answer by describing the programs that you have in mind.

# CHAPTER 8

## Strategy Programs in Marketing: Pricing and Marketing Mix

Decisions about product-line and customer issues, discussed in Chapter 7, refine the strategic domain of a company, helping to clarify its *mission*. For marketing, defining the mission is just a start. The work of most people in a marketing department is concerned with getting there. They are involved with inducing customers to place orders—large orders again and again. Broadly speaking, two kinds of issues arise in this operating phase of marketing: *pricing* and the design of a *marketing mix*, i.e., the selection of sales appeals and sales promotion suited to the target group of customers.

As in Chapter 7, we will first take the marketing department viewpoint, reviewing the way marketing managers typically see pricing and marketing mix problems. This discussion will highlight several major relationships of a company with its customers and will provide a feeling for the sorts of issues that the marketing department faces day after day. Naturally, the marketing department will have strong opinions about the way these matters should be handled; its preferred department strategy program will reflect these opinions. Following this examination of the marketing view of pricing and marketing mix, we will note the horizontal linkages that the marketing department must establish with other departments and the vertical linkages between marketing and the business-unit strategy.

## Pricing: Keystone in Relations with Customers

### Pricing as a Competitive Weapon

One way to think of pricing is as a competitive weapon. By setting our prices higher, the same, or lower than competitors' prices, we are establishing a basic relation to the competitive market. We signal to both customers and competitors how we intend to play the game. In this respect, pricing is one part of the total marketing mix that we will use to attract customers.

#### Position Relative to Competitors' Prices

The extent to which a company can wisely establish its prices either higher or lower than those charged by competitors depends on the kind of products it is selling. Highly standardized products such as cotton or gold have such a competitive market that continuing differentials are not practical. At the other extreme, consulting services or art objects are so unique that only the most general comparisons with competitors are possible.

In between are the vast majority of products, which are somewhat distinctive in their characteristics or services provided with them. For these the customer does perceive some difference, and there is an open question whether my products are worth more than yours. For instance, is an IBM computer with its reputation for quality and known availability of repair service worth 20 percent more than a physically similar computer offered by a new competitor?

When significant product or service differentiation is achieved, the marketing department must decide whether (a) a higher price than that of competitive products will be charged, or (b) a comparable price will be set and the superior quality or service will be used as a means of building sales volume, or (c) a high price will be used initially to "skim the cream off the market" and then the price will be cut to competitive levels. The choice of one of these alternative policies depends, in part, upon how long the product or service distinctiveness can be maintained and how much premium consumers are willing to pay for the superior quality.

### Marketing Benefits Sought from Pricing

If pricing is thought of as a marketing tool, then the marketing objectives being sought via pricing should be clear. Here are some of the possibilities:

- *Increased volume of orders from present customers* is a common aim. For this purpose, prices somewhat below competitors' is an obvious option, especially for smaller companies trying to increase their share of the total market. Manufacturers of room air conditioners, for instance, often use relatively low prices with this aim. A serious drawback is that customers often assume that a lower price means lower quality.
- *Attracting new customers* is another frequent goal. Typically, since the target group is only a part of the total market, special prices for that group are devised. A low introductory price—commonly used by publishers of magazines—or even free samples may be a way to get new customers acquainted with the product.
- *Maintaining an attractive position* is a normal view for well-established firms. In these situations, keeping prices on a par with competitors' is the usual policy. "Don't rock the boat" is the goal.
- *Maximizing short-run cash flow* is another possibility, but not a popular one among marketing executives. Here, prices are kept high even though doing so results in losing some customers to competitors. When there is reason to believe that future demand for the product will fall regardless of pricing, and good alternative uses for cash are available, short-run return takes priority.

Pricing should give support to the broad strategy being pursued by the company. This requires that the linkage between marketing goals and pricing practice be clearly understood.

## Pricing in Relation to Costs

In addition to seeking marketing benefits, a second basic approach to pricing policy is relating prices to costs. Experts differ on what costs to consider, but no one argues that costs can be ignored.

### Selling at a Normal Profit Above Cost

A policy to set prices at cost plus a normal profit is much more common than economic textbooks imply. It suits three kinds of situations especially well. (1) For unique services—a consultation with a doctor or the repair of furniture, for instance—there can be no market price, and the benefit received by the customer is hard to measure. So a "professional" relationship is established in which the fee is based on time spent. (2) Public utilities, other monopolies, and diverse nonprofit enterprises basically aim to set prices that cover costs and enough margin to attract capital needed. (3) Other marketing departments may choose to subordinate price as a sales appeal and, if competition will permit, simply charge what both buyer and seller feel is a "fair" price, which typically is cost plus a normal profit.

### Selling Below Cost

A number of conditions may lead a company to establish prices below the total cost of a product. Every firm has certain expenses such as interest, rent, and executive salaries that must be paid regardless of the volume of sales. Other costs, such as those for materials and direct labor, vary with the volume of activity. These latter costs are *out-of-pocket expenses*, and theoretically any sale above such incremental costs will make some contribution to overhead and profit. Especially when a marketing department is trying to gain market position, selling at incremental costs is appealing.

Strong feeling exists in many industries against selling goods at a price below the total cost. Doing so may "spoil the market," they say. Competitors may follow suit, and soon all business will have to be taken at the low price. Moreover, once the price has infiltrated the market, it will be difficult to return it to the current level. In other words, pricing followed at one time may materially affect the price structure for subsequent sales.

Still another reason why retail stores occasionally sell below cost is to attract customers to the store. In such cases one or more standard products are sold at a loss, and it is hoped the loss will be more than offset by the profit on the sale of other merchandise to the customer while in the store or on subsequent visits. In many states there is agitation to prohibit the use of *loss leaders*, but from a strictly business point of view it is difficult to see any valid distinction between incurring a loss on certain types of merchandise and spending money for other forms of advertising. (Misrepresenting the reasons for selling below cost or selling below cost for the purpose of eliminating competition are already contrary to federal law.)

A company may sell some minor item at a price below the total cost just to render a service to its regular customers. Such a practice is distinct from using loss leaders in that it is done as an accommodation and is not featured.

## Effect of Prices on Volume, Costs, and Profits

In most companies the cost per unit of a product varies with the volume sold. A partially filled airliner (or classroom), for example, may handle a substantial increase in passengers (or students) with little change in total operating cost. In the production of many metal products, the cost of making dies and setting up machinery for production is often half of the total expense of producing a normal volume. This fixed expense will remain the same whether the volume is cut in half or doubled. Thus, there will be a substantial variation in the *average cost per unit*.

Note that the foregoing tendency holds true only when the production capacity of facilities is not fully used. If a motel, for instance, had to build an addition and increase its staff in order to handle additional customers, its profit on each customer might not increase at all.

There are, of course, many companies in which the fixed expenses are comparatively small, and consequently the unit costs do not change greatly with the changes in volume. For example, the expenses of a commission merchant dealing in fruits and vegetables consist largely of material costs. Similarly, contractors building homes have low fixed expense. Nevertheless, for most companies, the effect of price levels on volume and via volume on average unit costs should be weighed when establishing pricing policy.

### Estimating Profits for Different Price Levels

When per-unit cost varies with volume, the manager should estimate the quantity of output that can be sold at different prices; the effect of a change in volume on the cost of goods produced as well as on the cost of selling; and the combined effect of changes in the price, the volume, and the cost on total net profits.

The way these factors can affect profits is illustrated in Figure 8–1. The estimates for the dress manufacturer show a rising volume with reductions in prices. However, costs do not drop as fast as prices, and when the increase in volume slackens the total profits start to decline. The paper mill, with its high fixed costs, benefits sharply from increases in volume. But when competitors also seek to expand and a price war results, price cuts fail to yield much additional volume. Even worse, in a depression further price cuts fail to maintain volume and profits plunge.

### Factors Affecting Response of Volume to Changes in Price

As Figure 8–1 shows, the total profit secured at each price depends upon the volume of sales as well as the average cost per unit. Clearly, the marketing department must estimate as best it can not only the effect of volume on the total cost, but also the volume of sales that will be secured at different prices. In practice, the response of volume to price changes depends upon many factors, including the following.

The effect of a price change on competitors will depend significantly on the *size of the company quoting low prices*. Price changes by a large and dominant firm

**FIGURE 8-1.**
**ECONOMIC PRICING VARIABLES: PRICE ELASTICITY, FIXED COSTS,
FAIRLY STABLE VARIABLE COSTS PER UNIT, VOLATILE OPERATING
PROFIT**

### EFFECT OF PRICE ON VOLUME, COST, AND PROFIT

*(A) Model of Small Dress Manufacturer*

| (1) Price | (2) Number of Units Sold | (3) Total Cost per Unit[a] | (4) Profit per Unit | (5) Total Profit (2) × (4) |
|---|---|---|---|---|
| $60 | 800 | $42.00 | $18.00 | $14,400 |
| 54 | 1,200 | 34.50 | 19.50 | 23,400 |
| 48 | 2,000 | 33.00 | 15.00 | 30,000 |
| 42 | 2,500 | 32.40 | 9.60 | 24,000 |
| 36 | 3,000 | 31.80 | 4.20 | 12,600 |

[a]Fixed costs of company are low, about $8,000.

*(B) Model of a Paper Mill*

| (1) Price | (2) Number of Tons Sold | (3) Total Cost per Ton[a] | (4) Profit per Ton | (5) Total Profit (2) × (4) |
|---|---|---|---|---|
| $100 | 500 | $276 | $−176 | $−88,000 |
| 94 | 2,000 | 95 | − 1 | − 2,000 |
| 90 | 3,000 | 75 | + 15 | +45,000 |
| 80[b] | 3,200 | 77 | + 3 | + 9,600 |
| 74[c] | 2,500 | 82 | − 8 | −20,000 |

[a]Fixed costs of mill are high - about $120,000.
[b]Price war; mad scramble for volume.
[c]Depression.

in an industry are very likely to affect the prices of the entire industry. Thus, in the farm machinery industry, a recognized *price leader* must anticipate that its price changes will be copied by most, though not all, of its competitors. On the other hand, a small company may be able to quote prices lower than those of the large competitors because its total sales volume is not important enough to the large company to warrant an adjustment of its entire price schedule. In the steel industry, for example, several small concerns have been able to increase their business by shading the prices quoted by the leading companies.

If there are two or three price leaders (oligopolistic competition), any one of them typically will raise its price only when it predicts that major competitors will follow. Such predictions are based on rising labor and material cost throughout the industry and on guesses about the competitors' desire to increase their volume—to fill up plant capacity and/or gain market position—even at the sacrifice of profit.

Another factor in the response of volume to price changes is the *elasticity of the demand*. The use of synthetic fibers has expanded greatly as its real price has declined. On the other hand, a doctor would not greatly increase the volume of his business if he were to make a 25 percent reduction in his charges, nor would an electric company sell much more current for household use if it were to make a similar reduction in its rates.

*The behavior of the price of one product* may affect the response of volume to price changes in another product. Packing companies have observed that if the price of pork rises while the price of beef remains constant, there will be a significant decrease in the consumption of pork. Should beef prices rise at the same time pork prices are increased, there will be a much smaller drop in the volume of pork consumed.

Professional buyers for industrial concerns as well as retail stores *adjust the volume of their purchases to anticipated prices* as well as to changes that have actually occurred. Thus, if a company reduces its price and the buyer anticipates that this is just the beginning of a series of price reductions, the buyer may actually diminish the volume rather than increase it. Contrarily, if an increase in price is interpreted as a sign of future scarcity of goods, the buyer may place large orders so as to be assured of an adequate supply at the current market price. This is one of the reasons for temporary spurts in business activities during periods of business prosperity and a sharp contraction in activity when a decline in prices is anticipated.

Clearly, pricing is not an exact science. Responses of competitors to our changes must be anticipated (as recommended in Chapter 4). Then the impact of our new prices and those of competitors on purchases by customers should be estimated. Next, the effect of the estimated volume on our costs is predicted. Finally, the combined impact of the new prices, costs, and volumes on profit should be estimated. And this calculation is only a start because, as already suggested, much pricing is aimed at longer term market position when still another combination of price, cost, and volume will be relevant.

### Composite Policies

Often marketing departments use both competitors' prices and their own costs in formulating their general pricing policy. A local manufacturer of electrical fixtures who uses price as a sales appeal, for example, follows a policy of (a) establishing prices that are 10 percent below the prices of a well-known competitor, except that (b) this differential is narrowed to avoid selling below "cost" (total manufacturing costs at estimated sales volume), and (c) sales below "cost" are made only temporarily to close out an item or to combat a "price leader" of a competitor. In contrast, a company producing high-quality, shortwave intercommunication systems relies on technical service and quality to attract customers. This firm normally quotes prices on the basis of total engineering, manufacturing, and selling costs (with a liberal allowance for overhead) plus 15 percent. However, downward adjustments are made when it is known that the normal price is more than 20 percent above either of two reputable competitors.

## Different Prices for Different Customers

### One-price Policy

Every marketing department must decide whether its products will be sold at the same price to all customers. In the United States the so-called one-price policy has wide acceptance, particularly in retail transactions. Retail stores typically have a set price marked on the merchandise, and every customer coming into the store must pay this set price.

The horse-trading days in the United States, however, are by no means over. New automobile prices are not rigidly fixed, and the secondhand market and trade-in values retain many opportunities for deception and bargaining. Large customers, however, have greater bargaining power. Here, the marketing department has to guess whether the customer will actually shift to a competitor if special concessions are not granted, and also guess how other customers will react to any such concessions that might be granted.

### Discounts from Established Prices

Many marketing departments wish to have the benefits of a one-price policy, but they find it desirable to have different prices for different types of customers. This is often accomplished by maintaining a list price and then granting discounts to certain classes of customers.

The need for *trade discounts* is generally recognized, but there is much debate as to how large such discounts should be and who is entitled to them. Clearly, a company's discount practice will have a marked effect on its success in winning patronage from different types of customers and, hence, should be coordinated with customer policies.

*Quantity discounts* are commonly offered to anyone who purchases in large volume. These customers may be so important to a company that there is a temptation to give them very high discounts. Under the Robinson-Patman Act and related legislation, however, quantity discounts are limited to actual savings in producing and selling the larger orders.

There are, of course, other forms of discounts, such as cash discounts and advertising allowances, that are not intended to be price reductions. In actual practice, however, they are sometimes so large and are granted in such a way that their effect is a price reduction in a somewhat disguised form.

In addition, a company may offer price concessions in an effort to build up volume during slack periods. A 10 percent discount for early orders of Christmas cards is not uncommon; and electric utility companies offer special "off-peak" rates. When a well-recognized policy has been set up, such discounts can be granted without upsetting the basic price structure.

## Fitting Pricing into a Marketing Strategy Program

The marketing department is the front-line operator of company pricing. Because it learns daily how customers respond to various prices, often negotiates changes in prices, knows best what competitors are charging, and finds its total selling task made easier or more difficult as a result of the prices quoted, the marketing department typically has strong opinions about how prices should be set.

To summarize what has been so far presented, first, pricing is viewed as a competitive weapon. The relation of our company's prices to those of competitors should be established, at least tentatively, to achieve selected marketing benefits. Second, this viewpoint should be tempered by the relation between our costs and prices. In practice, especially during inflation, these cost considerations may dominate pricing policy. Third, a consolidated picture of the effect of price on volume, costs, and prices is required. Both short-run and long-run estimates are needed, and in particular, the long-run view should be matched with broad company strategy. Fourth, the underlying pricing policy which comes out of the preceding analysis must be tailored to a variety of specific situations. Important here will be a discount structure and regional differentials which adjust prices to various types of customers.

As is plain, pricing is closely connected with many aspects of managing a firm. Its most intimate connection, however, is with various elements of the marketing mix to which we now turn.

## Marketing Mix Program

### Strategy and the Consumer

The strategy of a company identifies the domain it seeks—its industry and preferred market niche(s). And perhaps, though not necessarily, the selected differential advantage will further define the way the company will deal with customers. Then, product and customer policy expand and specify the marketing efforts. Essential as all this planning is, however, it is not enough.

The analysis and planning of a marketing department should also take a consumer viewpoint. Marketing managers should envisage all the actions necessary to complete the full transformation of company products (or services) into consumer satisfactions.

Rarely does a consumer merely buy a physical product. Instead, the consumer purchases a *package* that fulfills some "need," that provides a psychological pride of ownership and/or consumption, that involves a minimum of anxiety about breakdown or damage, that is considered a "good buy at the price," that can be acquired without great financial upset, that will be delivered when wanted, and so forth. An essential part of a marketing plan, then, is to conceive of a practical package of satisfactions that will appeal to a significant number of consumers.

Normally, providing each of these consumer satisfactions involves a cost. The cost may be a direct expense incurred by the producing company, or it may be a fee or margin charged by a distributor. Keeping these costs within acceptable bounds is, of course, an inherent aspect of designing a viable package of satisfactions.

### Marketing Mix

In addition to seeking a winning combination of consumer satisfactions, marketing managers must consider how to communicate with the consumer to present an offer. An array of alternative forms of advertising is available for this purpose, and the role of sales representatives and agents in this total distribution process has to be defined.

But advertising and sales staffs involve costs, as do the satisfactions discussed in the previous section. Inevitably, a choice must be made. How much of each—consumer services, higher quality, convenient packages, lower price, advertising, or personal solicitation—should be offered? This allocation among such competing uses for the distribution dollar is called the *marketing mix*.

Finding a marketing mix suited to consumers in a specific product or market niche can be addressed in terms of three broad issues:

1. A lean, low-cost approach versus a full-service approach
2. The sales appeals to be emphasized
3. Sales promotion activities that will support the selected appeals

## Lean, Low-Cost Approach Versus Full-Service Approach

An overriding policy affecting the entire design of a marketing mix deals with the total effort and expense to be devoted to embellishing the product or service package offered to consumers. Should we focus on selling an austere, stripped-down product at a low cost, or should we strive for more complete consumer satisfaction of some important need?

Digital Equipment Company, for instance, commenced business with the lean, low-cost approach. It sold simple, low-cost minicomputers to research laboratories with no accompanying software and no organized repair service. The assumption was that a lot of technically trained customers wanted bare-bones equipment which they could afford and that they already understood how to use and to repair such computers. In contrast, IBM has always provided its customers with user-oriented technical assistance, and it has a service organization that maintains and repairs its computers. The price is high, but if that is an obstacle, IBM will lease the equipment so that the customer pays as the equipment is being used. Digital Equipment Company was not strong enough to challenge IBM on IBM's terms, but it was highly successful in appealing to an untapped market on the basis of low cost and low service.[1]

The forerunners of today's supermarkets had a similar beginning. They sold only case lots of canned goods piled in old warehouses located along railroad tracks. There was no credit, no returns, and the customer carried the boxes out to his or her car. This was during the Great Depression, when low prices attracted a lot of customers in spite of the very limited service. Today, farm auctions operate in a similar manner, and the "I can get it wholesale" markets for clothing are not much different.

Of course, the bargain-basement approach need not mean that no service whatsoever will be provided. However, it does imply that in production, as well as in marketing, expenses will be minimized. As in East Coast commuter airlines, parsimony is a way of life—at least for a while.

Such a low-expense policy sharply restricts marketing mix options. The catch is that not enough customers may be willing to accept such spartan service for very long. Experience shows that in almost every business that starts out with very low prices, a shift occurs to more service. Running very lean is not a steady state, at least in the U.S. The tough question then becomes how much of which services to add.

## Sales Appeals to Be Emphasized

Important among the possible sales appeals that a marketing department may choose to emphasize (sooner or later) in its marketing mix are:

1. Associated services
2. Quality
3. Style and packaging
4. Company reputation
5. Pricing

Except for style and packaging, these appeals can be related to services just as well as to physical goods. Also, they can be used in both small companies and large ones.

### Associated Services

In designing and promoting services, the marketing department can significantly shape the concept of a product in the customer's mind.

---

[1]After its early success, Digital Equipment Company modified its original policy so as to serve other market niches; however, its reputation was founded on a unique marketing approach in the industry at that time.

**Personal Assistance**    A recurring question is how much personal assistance to the customer should be a part of the total sales package. For example, a driver who pulls up to a gas pump in Honolulu will find someone checking tire pressure, washing the windows, filling the radiator, and inspecting the battery while the gasoline is being pumped. In contrast, at a New York City "full service" station the driver has to ask to have the windshield washed, and checking tire pressure is clearly a do-it-yourself operation.

A shift is occurring as well in personal service in the hotel field. Motels grew up with a minimum of personal service in contrast to the traditional hotels with doormen, bellhops, and room maids. But as motels are becoming more luxurious, they are adding more personal assistance; meanwhile, the large downtown hotels will permit guests to carry their own bags and to find their own rooms. With changing attitudes about personal assistance, matching services to a particular desired clientele calls for sharp perception.

**Maintenance and Repair**    One of the pillars of IBM's marketing success is its maintenance service policy. Most of its machines are covered by a contract under which IBM provides regular maintenance service and is available for prompt repair work in the event of a breakdown. Other manufacturers have a less elaborate service organization and often merely maintain a stock of repair parts for all equipment sold during, say, the past 20 years.

Policies on customer service and on channels of distribution are closely related. The further removed manufacturers are from the consumers of their product, the more difficult is control of consumer service. Marketing managers who elect to stress service often find it necessary to maintain their own branches; some television and stereo manufacturers even establish exclusive distributorships in order to ensure the quality of repair service available to consumers.

**Installment Credit and Leasing**    The day is gone when installment credit was available only on durable goods. Now financing may be arranged on almost any large purchase. However, the ease of obtaining credit and the terms on which it is granted vary. Part of the marketing mix, then, is the extent to which marketing gets into the financing business.

Equipment leasing is a service provided by some manufacturers. Dental equipment, postal meters, and even transponders on a satellite are all available under lease. Many of these lease arrangements are similar to installment credit, calling for periodic payments during the period when the product is being used and giving the customer an option to buy the equipment at the end of the lease. The major difference between leasing and buying is that the leasing customer may return the equipment when it is only partially used. For customers with limited financial resources or fluctuating needs, such leases can be quite attractive.

**Prompt Availability**    This is a valuable dimension for both products and services. An employer with a potential strike wants consulting advice promptly—not next week. Similarly, a loan from the bank or a delivery of fuel oil has much greater sales value if customers know they can depend on the services being available when needed.

Small local companies can often gain significant advantage by providing this prompt delivery. They can reach the scene of action quickly, they are already familiar with local conditions, and their small size permits considerable flexibility. If larger firms choose to stress availability, they have to set up local representatives or branches and then give the local units both the incentive and the authority to meet unusual customer requirements.

Considerable opportunity for creative variation is available in customer services that a marketing department elects to stress, as these examples show. Some of these services may be so important to customers that they are regarded as part of the product itself. Since they are intimately tied up with the product in the mind of the customer, it is important that their use be integrated with product, customer, and other marketing practices.

### Quality as a Sales Appeal

Quality higher than the prevailing level can be used as part of the marketing mix.

Extra quality involves extra effort and cost. Strawberry jam made with only pure sugar and no corn syrup has added raw material cost; hand-rubbed furniture has extra labor cost. The question for the marketing manager is, Does distinctive quality hold strong appeal for the particular customers we are trying to reach?

One limitation to using quality as a sales appeal is that consumers may be unable to detect the differences advertised and may be skeptical about the claims made. So, to clinch the appeal, some companies *guarantee* their products. For instance, one automobile manufacturer extended its guarantee from one year to five years. The move attracted so much attention that competitors were forced to follow. In the meantime, the first company added to its reputation for producing dependable products.

Professional ethics prevent doctors or lawyers from guaranteeing the results of their services. Nevertheless, quality is especially significant in intangible services, so a professional person's reputation for quality work becomes very important.

### Emphasis on Style and Packaging

"Pick the right style" is merely a wish, not a policy. However, the degree of emphasis on style in the total selling effort may be a significant marketing choice. A French restaurant, for instance, may go to great lengths to create a Louis XIV decor and atmosphere. A few men's shoe manufacturers stress the latest style, at the sacrifice of durability. Producers of household items—from hand tools to garbage cans—need some guidance on how much to add to design and production expense to have currently popular styles and colors.

Packaging is one means of giving a product stylish appearance, and it may play an even more important role in the marketing mix. Packaging can affect the product service itself, as in the use of aerosol cans for paint. If a product is to be sold through self-service stores, the size, sturdiness, and shelf appeal of the package are critical to the product's success. So, while packaging may add significantly to the unit cost, the right kind of package can be an integral part of providing distinctive service for a group of consumers.

### Place of a Company's Reputation in Marketing Mix

Banks, insurance companies, and other financial institutions must guard their reputations jealously because this is a major factor in the business they secure. Likewise, a well-regarded brand name is so important in the sale of large kitchen appliances that an unknown company has a hard time breaking into the market. The Whirlpool Corporation, to cite a specific case, for years made appliances for Sears, Roebuck & Company but was unknown to the general public; lacking a reputation with consumers and dealers, it entered into a long-term agreement to use the highly regarded RCA label. Several years later, after the Whirlpool reputation had become established, the association with RCA was dropped.

Even the highly competitive bidding process of the federal government makes allowance for company reputation. A low bid may be rejected if the bidder lacks a demonstrated ability to perform. And for high-technology contracts, as in the aerospace industry, reputation is often the deciding factor.

Good reputations are not bought on Madison Avenue. They arise primarily from a sustained willingness to devote extra effort to assure dependability and use of the latest state of the art, to avoid exaggerated claims, and to adjust such errors as do occur in a prompt and liberal fashion.

### Pricing

As noted earlier price may (or may not) be featured as a sales appeal. "We will not be underpriced" is a claim of some auto dealers, for instance. Alternatively, a "fair price" may be part of a building contractor's reputation. These examples clearly illustrate that in the total package of consumer satisfactions, price is a part of the marketing mix.

In general, no marketing department can stress all the sales appeals we have discussed. Some are incompatible with each other (for example, low price versus high quality and service), others are inappropriate, and all involve some expense. In thinking through what combination of appeals makes sense for a particular company, marketing managers should recognize both the differences in the attractiveness of various appeals to the groups they seek as customers and the compatibility, and perhaps synergistic effect, of a particular appeal with the company's master strategy.

## Sales Promotion That Will Support the Selected Appeals

A third major ingredient of the marketing mix is sales promotion: our selected sales appeals, and even a low-price image if that is to be part of our scheme, have to be communicated to our target customers. The marketing department can do this with various kinds of advertising and personal solicitation.

### Advertising

We are bombarded by advertising. No matter whether we walk, drive a car, ride a bus, watch television, read a newspaper or magazine, or open our mail, we are brought face to face with advertising. This creates a difficult situation for marketing management, for it must determine what advertising on behalf of the company will justify its cost amid the bewildering array of advertisements by other companies. Two major questions are, What purposes is the advertising to be used for, and What media will be employed to accomplish these purposes.

**Purpose of Advertising**    Among the major options are the following:

- Bringing customers to the place where the goods are sold
- Persuading customers to ask for a specific product
- Assisting a sales representative in making sales when calling on customers
- Producing direct sales via mail or telephone
- Building institutional goodwill

In a specific marketing program, the role(s) assigned to advertising will depend on (1) the channel of distribution the company has selected, (2) the buying habits of the target customers for the company's kind of product, and (3) the way the company wants those customers to perceive its product. Also, the choice will be influenced by whether and by how much the company outmaneuvers competitors' advertising.

**Choice of Advertising Media**    Closely related to a definition of the purpose of advertising is the selection of media to be used. Possibilities include the following:

- Television
- Radio
- Magazines
- Newspapers
- Trade papers
- Direct mail

The list is not intended to be complete. Other types of sales promotion that might be classified as advertising are as well displays, dealer helps, and sampling.

The selection among these media involves a delicate choice between economy and effectiveness in reaching objectives. For example, an airline wished to build goodwill among a large number of people and also develop immediate traffic on its planes. For the latter purpose, it confined expenditures to short TV commercials, direct mail to executives known to be frequent travelers along its routes, and circulars to passengers on its planes. However, to develop institutional goodwill, it used magazine ads and general newspaper publicity as the chief media.

For small companies with limited budgets, media choice is strongly influenced by what competitors are doing; the marketing department must jockey to find imaginative ways of attracting attention within the budget limitations.

## Personal Solicitation

Although sales representatives have a role in most selling transactions, the extent and purpose of personal solicitation vary greatly.

**Differences in the Use of Sales Representatives**     Most management consulting firms operate on a professional basis and, like doctors, limit their advertising to a few dignified announcements. Such a firm secures its business largely through personal contacts by partners and supervisors, and rarely by salespeople employed just for this type of work.

In contrast, insurance is typically sold by individuals who devote their whole effort to selling.

The selling of ethical pharmaceuticals illustrates another arrangement. When they write a prescription, physicians choose what drugs will be purchased. Consequently, drug manufacturers send "detail reps" to call on physicians and explain the virtues of products made by their particular firm. Since the actual purchase is made by the patient at a drugstore, the detail rep stops into the local drugstores just to be sure products are in stock.

A representative selling industrial equipment, say printing presses, not only knows more about various kinds of equipment than the printing company usually does, but also is an expert in the entire technology. Such a person should be qualified as an expert technical advisor. This is in sharp contrast to a ticket-seller at a theater box office.

**An Analytical Approach**     In deciding what role sales representatives should play—and thinking about other parts of the marketing mix as well—the marketing manager should ask four questions:

1.  Who consumes the product or alters it so that its identity is lost?
2.  Who makes the final decision as to the products that such a consumer buys?
3.  What factors influence those who make final decisions?
4.  How is it possible to influence those factors by varying the marketing mix?

## Need for Synergy

In marketing, no single factor makes a sale. Nor can the several factors—price, other sales appeals, and various forms of sales promotion—be considered separately. Instead, each part should complement the other in a synergistic way. Thus, technical bulletins and engineer-trained salespeople or well-styled products and magazine advertising should reinforce each other. Likewise, sales promotion and other policy should be synergistic. In IBM's repair service, leasing machines, capital financing, and high-wage policy, for instance, each service gives added impact to the other.

The final marketing mix selected need not be complicated if a relatively simple combination fits the basic mission of the company. Here are three examples:

1.  Handy & Harman, a leading processor of silver, makes bimetals, brazing compounds, and a variety of other fabricated silver products for industrial uses. To reach the industrial users, it stresses (a) closely controlled quality, (b) engineering advice to customers by sales representatives, backed up by technical bulletins, (c) sales representatives who understand the problems of their respective industries, and (d) a company reputation built up over 100 years. A relatively high amount of money is spent on the first two appeals. In contrast, advertising expenditure is very low (occasional ads in trade journals and Christmas greetings), price is simply kept "in line" with competition, and no thought is given to style.

2.  A prominent correspondence school offers courses in computers, programming, mathematics, and a wide variety of semitechnical subjects. It concentrates heavily on advertising in trade and do-it-yourself magazines and by direct mail. A low price is featured—low, that is, in relation to potential earnings resulting from a course. Also, considerable effort goes into "product design" so that courses are up to date and easily grasped by the students. The school has no sales representatives, quality of performance is not stressed, and the reputation of the institution is not a major appeal.

3.  The Paper Wrapper Company prints and finishes wrappers for bread, candy, and other food products. It obtains business primarily on the basis of low price, willingness to accept short runs, and personal friendships of sales representatives. It does no advertising, provides no technical advice, and gives no special emphasis to style, reputation, or quality.

Each of these companies has a marketing mix carefully designed to fit its master strategy. The mixes differ sharply, but this is a reflection of very different jobs to be done. In each example, the marketing approach builds on company strengths and avoids efforts that would create internal strain with other activities of the company.

## Crucial Horizontal and Vertical Linkages

The array of issues that a marketing department faces in setting prices and designing a marketing mix cannot be resolved by the marketing department alone. Other departments in the company will have to create many of the services that are combined into the total package which the marketing people offer to customers. Also, choices of prices depend on expected achievements in several other departments. Therefore, in building its strategy program, the marketing department has to obtain a variety of horizontal concurrences.

## Relating the Proposed Pricing and Marketing Mix to Operations in Other Departments

The primary horizontal linkages that need to be negotiated are suggested in the following list. Of course, the specific pricing and marketing mix issues faced in particular companies, and their unique organization structures, vary a great deal, so the list merely identifies relationships that are *likely* to warrant thoughtful attention.

### Production

- The costs of producing the company's products or services are a vital element in setting prices; and the production department is probably the best informed about the present level and future behavior of these costs.
- Also, the production department is directly concerned with the problems and costs of creating a *variety of products and options* that might be offered to customers.
- Product *quality* will be created in the production department, so any plans for future changes in quality must be negotiated with this department.
- *Delivery service*, even from branch locations, has to be coordinated with the schedules and flow of output from production operations.

### Procurement

- Except in retail and other trading operations, the tie between the marketing and procurement departments is indirect, via production. Nevertheless, the *timing, price, and quality of incoming materials* often dominate what the production department can do. So marketing is well advised to synchronize its plans with those who manage the inflow of materials, subassemblies, and services.

### Consumer Maintenance and Repair Service

- The consumer maintenance and repair activity may be in the marketing, production or engineering department. Wherever located, its cooperation is important to any marketing department that features *after-sale service*.

### Finance

- The stress that the marketing department puts on *long-run market development* will require the support of the finance department because short-run profits and cash flow will be lowered.
- The finance department will also be actively concerned about *building sales volume* by pricing at a narrow profit margin. Profits may then be

lower; certainly, requirements for working capital and even fixed capital will rise.

- If the marketing mix calls for heavy use of *installment finance or leasing,* the finance department will have to obtain more working capital and may administer the entire credit program.

### Research & Development

- The marketing department may want state-of-the-art products to maintain a reputation for technical leadership and to *sidestep cutthroat price competition.* For this, a joint effort with the R & D department is crucial.
- Process R & D is one way to *lower production costs,* an important activity if Japanese firms are active competitors in the market.
- In consumer goods, *styling and packaging* are important to marketing. Here, the R & D department may be crucial to high achievement.

### Human Resources

- In addition to helping to contain labor cost increases, the human resource department plays an important role in *preparing employees for change,* in both marketing and related departments.

### Controller's Department

- Especially in small firms where managers have many duties, they may *lack sophistication in calculating* incremental costs, long-term cash flows, and other estimates needed in pricing and designing a good marketing mix. Perceptive assistance from the "numbers people" may be just the tonic needed.

In view of all these interdependencies, a marketing department obviously must build numerous horizontal linkages if its strategy program is to have the support it will need when placed in operation. Although usually stated for a company making a physical product, almost all of the preceding linkages apply to companies marketing only services. Except for the absence of inventory—and some changes in terminology—insurance companies, consulting firms, hospitals, and other service organizations need similar joint efforts in their pricing and marketing mix.

## Tying Pricing and Marketing Mix with Business-Unit Strategy

The product-line and customer issues faced by a marketing department are very closely tied to the "domain" part of business-unit strategy, as mentioned at the end of Chapter 7. Although the distinction is not sharp, pricing and marketing mix issues relate more to the "differential advantage" part of business-unit strategy. In this chapter we have been more concerned with finding a set of actions that will attract customers to us and away from competitors. A company gets a competitive advantage by serving customers' wants better.

To a certain extent, the marketing department itself creates the services that the company elects to offer. However, most of the services—quality products, low cost, dependable delivery, new style and designs, convenient financing, etc.—are created wholly or partly by other departments. The marketing department assembles the services, packages them in an appealing bundle, and sells the package. But in the final analysis, the effort is joint.

Because so much of what the customer recognizes and receives has been created jointly, there are many opportunities for disagreement. The marketing department empathizes with the customer and may ask for services or prices that the originating departments cannot or do not wish to provide. (The bases for such positions of other departments will be reviewed in the chapters that follow.) At this point, central management and its business-unit strategy enter the picture to guide and arbitrate.

To a greater or lesser degree, differential advantage provides the guidelines to resolve clashes among departments. Often, however, central management arbitrates. Its decisions become the "common law" interpretation of the strategy. And, assuming that central management's decisions are consistent, its allocations of resources further interpret how differential advantage will be sought. In this process, the marketing department's view of what the prices and marketing mix should be usually gets reshaped a bit.

Note that these emerging clarifications of what the strategy means with respect to pricing and marketing mix are not "written on stone"; rather, they are revised as conditions change. New competition, an R & D breakthrough, a cash squeeze, or the like may shift priorities. But considerable stability is desirable, so that internal coordination can proceed smoothly and so that customers know what to expect.

Often gaps will exist between decisions regarding what the company wants to do with respect to product lines, customers, pricing, and marketing mix and actual behavior and results. The strategy and its refinements are plans for the future which the prevailing status may not match up to. These gaps call for strategic thrusts, the third element in a four-part strategy. So the respective departments are told to lay out a series of steps to bring their operations into line with the current strategy.

The marketing department's "strategic program" consists of the policies and steps which emerge from the process just described. The process starts with a scenario of what the marketing department would like to do about such issues as product line, customers, pricing, and marketing mix. This scenario is then trimmed and adjusted on the basis of negotiations with other departments about horizontal linkages. Further revisions occur in review and by arbitration of central management. Then the gaps between this final plan and current reality are recognized, and steps are laid out to close them.

## Questions for Class Discussion

1. "...Mr. O'Guinn says, 'I buy a Mercedes not because it is a fine piece of German engineering but because I value it as a symbol of my success.'" (*The Wall Street Journal*, July 30, 1987.) The Mercedes-Benz company consistently advertises the performance of its cars, the care with which they are built, and the engineering that goes into their design. Is Mr. O'Guinn buying a Mercedes for the wrong reason? Are there other automobiles being built in the United States, Japan, England, France, West Germany, Italy, and Korea to be symbols of success? What pricing and marketing mix do you propose for the manufacturers and distributors of these cars in the United States and/or in any other country with which you are familiar?

2. How do you explain the wide range of prices charged by airlines for an almost identical service—transporting someone from location X to location Y? Are marketing managers thinking of price as the major marketing tool? Is there a better way of pricing?

3. When Japanese cameras were first sold in the United States, their price was well below the price of most other cameras then available. But times have changed, as has the reputation of the Japanese cameras, along with their features and options. Also, primarily due to changes in foreign exchange rates, the production cost of a Japanese-made camera in the United States is now about the same as the cost to produce a U.S.-made camera. On the basis of your familiarity with competitive factors in the camera industry, what marketing mix do you recommend that, say, Minolta adopt for the near-term future?

4. Two of your friends like outdoor work and have decided to set up a landscape gardening business. They hope to get regular customers for whom they will mow the lawn weekly, trim shrubbery, fertilize, etc. Their location will be in an upper middle class suburban area north of Cincinnati, focused within a five-mile radius to reduce travel time. They have enough capital for the necessary equipment. "You've studied business," they say. "How should we market our services? Will advertising pay?" What marketing mix do you recommend?

5. Contrast the marketing mix policy that you would recommend for two companies that make men's shirts but differ in their strategy regarding the domain they seek. Company C-P sells only high-quality shirts under the brand name of "Arrow." Company E-Z sells much less expensive shirts under any brand name that a wholesale distributor likes.

6. (a) During a period of general inflation, many companies own buildings and equipment that cost a lot less than their current replacement costs. In pricing its products, should such a company therefore use actual costs, replacement

costs, or neither in thinking about its cost-to-price ratio? (b) How would you answer the question if replacement costs of equipment and inventory were below actual costs?

7. An analytical approach to sales promotion and the marketing mix has been outlined on page 206. Apply this outline to the development of a program for (a) a chocolate pudding mix, (b) folding fishing rods for backpackers and others to carry, (c) sightseeing tours in San Diego, California, and (d) an office building skyscraper to be named for an insurance company that will use one-half of the total space and plans to lease the rest.

8. The Medical Center Hospital has unexpectedly filled 98 percent of its available beds at a time when the usual bed-fill rate is 75 percent. Other hospitals in the city report bed-fill rates ranging from 80 to 90 percent. And all medical facilities in the city must plan for an influx of winter visitors beginning in one month which usually increases demand for hospital bed places by 20 to 25 percentage points. Although Medicare and the private insurance companies have standard daily rates and length-of-stay standards, the hospitals are free to set their own rates so that the patient pays whatever the insurance companies and Medicare will not cover. Medical Center has at least two options. (1) It can set up a *triage system* which judges the relative severity of a patient's problem and, on the basis of this, may refuse to allow physicians to admit their patients. Ordinarily, a physician schedules a hospital admission to suit his or her and the patient's convenience. (2) It can raise room rates well above the standard rates and admit patients on the basis of what they can pay. Like two other hospitals in the city, Medical Center is run for profit.

   Which pricing method do you recommend to the hospital, rationing at current prices in an attempt to respond to public concern about rising medical expenses or using a price set by market forces to open up bed spaces and admit sick patients?

9. The *Guinness Book of World Records* has accepted Barnes and Noble, a New York City retailer of books, as the biggest bookstore anywhere. This world record was achieved by the lure of low prices in a store with shopping carts, checkout counters, and cavernous salesrooms like those of an off-the-rack discount house. Tables are loaded high with books and signs saying "Books for a Buck." The *Random House Encyclopedia* is discounted about 30 percent, J.K. Lasser's *Your Income Tax* sells at 13 percent off the newsstand price, the fifteen best-sellers (both fiction and nonfiction) go for 35 percent less than the prices on their covers, and the latest paperbacks are knocked down 20 percent each from their newsstand prices. The president of Barnes and Noble has a theory that any book can be sold if it is priced right and that overall the store will be profitable. This theory is general enough to include treatises on agriculture in prehistoric times and tomes on biliary-duct surgery. About 4,000 customers per day go through the checkout counters, averaging out to 4.5 volumes per person. By contrast, most large bookstores are satisfied with traffic of 25,000 to 30,000

customers per month, and some of them are discounting best-sellers from 10 to 15 percent in order to bring in customers.

The president of Bantam Books, a big paperback publisher, said that he expects Barnes and Noble to inspire imitators in many cities. Has this happened in your city? Is price discounting a way to stop the erosion of sales volume being felt by U.S. publishers? Publishers claim that the rise in the list prices of books has not exceeded the rise in the nation's consumer price index, but they are nonetheless selling fewer books and facing sales resistance. Are bookstores on or near your campus discounting best-sellers? Textbooks? Reference books? What marketing benefits might Barnes and Noble, be trying to gain by discounting list prices so heavily?

# CASE
## 8 "QuiknEasy" Sauce*

Six weeks ago Eileen Reilly was hired as product manager of "QuiknEasy" sauce, one of the products of the Convenience Food Division of Radford Foods Company. A new Division management has undertaken to bring profitability of the Division up to the company average, and Reilly's appointment is one of the moves made for that purpose.

### Reilly's Challenge

Sales and profits of "QuiknEasy" sauce have been slipping for several years, and last year only $155,000 operating profit was earned on $12.3 million sales. This led to the "resignation" of Reilly's predecessor.

The position was an attractive challenge for Reilly. The salary and potential bonus are good for a person only nine years out of college and five years beyond her MBA. And she can use her experience in an advertising agency (two years) and, more recently, in another food company where she progressed—rather slowly, she felt—to an associate brand manager. Her new boss, John Silver, said:

"This is a turnaround opportunity. Find what's wrong and fix it, and you can move on here to a much bigger product manager job. I don't want to fool you, however, you've got two years. If you strike out, that's when you'll be gone. My

*Adapted from a longer case on Radford Foods Company written by Professor Melvin Anshen, Graduate School of Business, Columbia University.

head's on the chopping block, too—for the whole Division—and I intend to make good things happen. If I can help you, let me know, but basically this is your job."

The organization of the Convenience Food Division has just been restructured. Under the new setup Reilly has primary profit responsibility for her product line. She has direct control over pricing, advertising, and sales promotion. Actual selling is done by the corporate market department; however, if Reilly wants extra sales or promotion programs, she can request them and "pay" the additional cost from her budget. Moreover, Reilly can "buy" services from the Division's market research staff or the product develpment staff to the extent that she decides is wise. Production of all convenience foods is done by a centralized manufacturing department; products are transferred to product managers at full cost, including a planned manufacturing "profit."

In her new job Reilly is assisted by two key people: Peter Selowitz, transferred from the divisional marketing staff in the earlier organization setup, now responsible, under Reilly's direction, for market analysis, pricing, and liaison with the corporate marketing group; and Carl Wilks, transferred from the divisional advertising department, now responsible, under Reilly's direction, for advertising and promotion.

## Reilly's Inheritance

"QuiknEasy" sauce, available in beef, chicken, and "Italian-style" flavors, is a dry sauce mix. A user pours the contents of the package of dry ingredients into a cup of boiling water and stirs the mixture for one minute. "QuiknEasy" sauce competes directly with two national brands and several regional brands of similar mixes, as well as grocery chains' private brands. Canned sauces requiring only heating are viewed as indirect competitors.

The downward trend of sales and profits was attributed by divisional management to a variety of causes: increasing popularity of frozen dinners complete with their own sauces, preference of some consumers for prepared sauces requiring no mixing or stirring, intense competition from national and regional dry sauce mixes, and unaggressive and unimaginative marketing administration by the former "QuiknEasy" product manager.

The existing annual budget for "QuiknEasy" sauces was put together by Reilly's immediate boss, Silver, after the former product manager was discharged. He explains:

"It was our judgment that 'QuiknEasy' has been suffering in sales and profits because it has been overpriced and underadvertised relative to competition. So we reduced the selling price the equivalent of two cents a package and increased advertising 15 percent over last year. Reflecting the results of these two actions, we projected a sales increase of 15 percent and a better bottom line than last year. [See first column in Table 8–1.] The results show some improvement, but not as much as we budgeted. Right now the line is just breaking even.

"You can interpret these results in several different ways. One conclusion might be that the price cut and the increased advertising have only begun to make

**TABLE 8-1.**
**"QUIKNEASY" BUDGETS**
**EXISTING BUDGET AND REILLY'S PROJECTIONS FOR SELF-FINANCING NEW PRODUCTS (in thousands)**

| | Existing Present-Year Budget[a] | Present Year Revised[b] | Self-Financing New Products | | | | | |
| --- | --- | --- | --- | --- | --- | --- | --- | --- |
| | | | 1st Year | | 2nd Year | | 3rd Year | |
| | | | Staple Line | Gourmet Line[c] | Staple Line | Gourmet Line[d] | Staple Line | Gourmet Line |
| Sales | 9,500 | 12,750 | 11,250 | 500 | 9,000 | 2,500 | 7,500 | 6,000 |
| Costs of Goods Sold | | 8,670 | 7,650 | 400 | 6,300 | 1,750 | 5,250 | 3,600 |
| Gross Margin | 4,600 | 4,080 | 3,600 | 100 | 2,700 | 750 | 2,250 | 2,400 |
| Selling Expense | 1,100 | 1,000 | 900 | 250 | 800 | 400 | 600 | 600 |
| Advertising and Promotion Expense | 2,700 | 900 | 250 | 250 | 250 | 750 | 200 | 1,500 |
| Product Development Expense | — | 200 | — | 100 | — | — | — | — |
| Administrative Expense | 350 | 350 | 250 | 100 | 250 | 200 | 150 | 300 |
| Operating Profit | 450 | 1,630 | 2,200 | (600) | 1,400 | (600) | 1,300 | — |

[a]Prepared by Silver.
[b]Reflects cash-cow strategy for "QuiknEasy" and investment in development of new gourmet line.
[c]Reflects intensive test marketing.
[d]Assumes favorable consumer acceptance of gourmet line and regional rollout campaign.

an impact on consumer perceptions and therefore on sales. Resulting decision: maintain the twin price and advertising strategy and watch what happens through, say, the spring months.

"Another conclusion might be that the price cut is too small—only two cents on a package of mix that usually sells at retail for about twenty-nine cents. Possible decision: cut the price further, another two cents or more. Maybe also put additional advertising pressure behind the line—say, to an annual rate of more than $3 million. Of course, we'd have to get a really big lift in sales to come out with a better bottom line under these conditions of shrinking gross margin percentage and higher advertising dollars. A critical issue here is the extent to which economies of scale in production will bring down the cost-of-goods-sold percentage as sales rise. My guess is that we ought to get a 1 percent savings for each 10 percent increase in sales, exclusive of price changes.

"Third conclusion: the line is mature; it won't respond much to either price-cutting or advertising. Possible decision: cut the advertising way back and enjoy a big fat bottom line for a few years while sales slowly slump. You might speculate that if we stopped all advertising as soon as we could cancel space and time contracts, sales for the balance of this year might not decline more than about 10 percent. That would suddenly make 'QuiknEasy' the most profitable brand in the Division by a huge margin. Then let sales and market share drift on down while we invest part of the profit in new product development or an acquisition.

"Of course, there are other options. Maybe when we concluded that we had an overpriced package of mix we were wrong. What if we put the price up? Could we retain something like the present sales volume with a fatter gross margin? If we could do that and also cut the advertising way down, there'd be a simply beautiful bottom line  At least for a while. Come back and see me when you've got a proposal."

## Reilly's Quandry

Since arriving at Radford Foods Company, Reilly has immersed herself in marketing studies of "QuiknEasy" drawn from the files and updated informally in conversations with knowledgeable staff personnel from the corporate market research group. She also talked with Pete Selowitz and Carl Wilks about their views of the brand's position and prospects. Further, she visited buyers in three major grocery chains to solicit their ideas, and she talked to the "QuiknEasy" account executive at the brand's advertising agency. From these and other sources, she has concluded the following:

1.   The total national market for dry sauce mixes last year was valued at about $150 million at producers' prices. The market was growing about 5 percent annually, with sales heavily concentrated in the 10 largest metropolitan market areas. "QuiknEasy" had about a 10 percent share nationally, slipping in market share from above 15 percent

five years ago. "QuiknEasy's" major competitor had sales of $7.5 million last year.

2.  No single cause for the steady decline of market share and dollar sales could be isolated in the research findings. Nor was there any indication of strong consumer attitudes for or against the brand. Most purchasers and users of dry sauce mixes viewed the product class as a convenience item—easy to use when dinner had to be prepared in a hurry, although inferior in flavor to "homemade" sauces. They had much the same attitude toward canned sauces. The big buying motivation was saving time in preparing meals. Among competing brands of dry mixes, there were no strongly marked preferences for one brand against another. A common reply to a question probing for perceived distinctions among dry mix brands was, "They're all alike. They taste about the same and they sell for about the same price." Merchandisers in supermarket chains viewed dry sauce mixes as a product they had to stock because a small but significant share of their customers bought them regularly. But the annual sales volume and dollar gross margin per shelf-foot generated by sauce mixes were too low to get store operators excited about the product or disposed to give it prominent display space. The typical large supermarket carried two brands, of which one was often its own "private" brand. Smaller stores typically stocked only one brand.

Peter Selowitz argues that the two-cent price reduction now in effect is not likely to induce any sales increase beyond the relatively small gain already experienced. A deeper price cut would, he believes, draw more purchasers from competing brands temporarily; the shift would compel competitors to reduce their prices to protect their market share. Lower prices for all brands would not, in his judgment, materially enlarge the total market for dry sauce mixes because price is a less important consideration than convenience in their purchase. This conclusion leads him to recommend an increase in price several cents above the level prior to the experimental two-cent cut. "We could raise the gross margin per package without significantly hurting unit sales."

Carl Wilks argues that increased advertising expenditure above the level already budgeted would have two favorable effects: (1) it would induce some customer brand-shifting from competing mixes; (2) it would increase the total market for dry mixes, with much of the increase coming to "QuiknEasy." He favors increasing the advertising budget by at least 20 percent, with all the increment invested in the 10 major metropolitan markets.

As Eileen Reilly ponders these findings, opinions, and proposals, she has become increasingly disturbed by the thought that she is in a personal "no-win" situation. The rational decision at the divisional level might well be the present strategy of treating "QuiknEasy" as a cash cow with the mission of generating profits to invest in other divisional products with attractive sales and profit potential. But if she follows such a course, what would it do to her career? In three years

"QuiknEasy" sales might decrease by 25 percent or more. She would be managing a very profitable business headed for extinction.

## Reilly's Bright Idea

While turning this problem over in her mind, a new option occurred to Reilly. "QuiknEasy" and competing dry mixes were all offered in varieties of staple sauces and advertised as convenience or timesaving products. What if dry mixes could be formulated for gourmet-type sauces, such as hollandaise, béarnaise, mornay, and béchamel? Here, the issue of fast, convenient preparation would be of small significance compared with the fact that many (possibly most) individuals responsible for daily food preparation are relatively unskilled in preparing such sauces. A supporting consideration might be the widely publicized growing interest in gourmet cooking and its "fit" with emerging life-styles. Many of these nonstaple sauces are difficult to prepare, requiring careful combination of ingredients and close attention in cooking. Would a dry-mix line of gourmet sauces, under "QuiknEasy" or another brand name, be a way to convert a minimum-growth, low-profit situation into a high-growth, high-profit situation?

Intrigued by the notion, she took the idea to the Division's product development staff. After some study and experimentation, the staff's director reported that it is feasible to formulate such a line of sauces. She estimates that developing and testing dry mixes for three gourmet sauce varieties would involve at least six months of work and a cost of about $200,000, which Reilly would have to fund from her budget. The end product, the product development staff believes, would be a convenience version of a "homemade" gourmet concoction, not equal in flavor, taste, and texture to the creation of a skilled amateur chef, but of good quality and as easy to prepare as the present varieties of staple sauces. The costlier ingredients would necessitate a selling price at least double the current "QuiknEasy" price. The product development staff offered no judgment about possible consumer reactions to such a line of sauces.

The potential gains and risks suggested by the gourmet sauce notion added to, rather than simplified, Reilly's problems. One strategic possibility would be to combine a recommendation to treat the existing three sauce types as "cash cows" with a recommendation to assign their enriched bottom line to finance the development and then, if successful, the marketing of a gourmet sauce line. The substantial advertising costs required to launch such a new product would certainly absorb much of the operating profits created by sharply curtailing advertising support for the staple product line, leaving little for the rest of the Division. If she should propose such a venture, get an approval up the line, and then have it fail in the market, she could envision no outcome for herself but discharge and a "loser" reputation to take into the job market.

Reilly is aware that (1) most new food products fail in the market, and (2) new food products that meet with favorable consumer acceptance usually lose money for at least three years while distribution is being rolled out nationally and heavy advertising and promotional support is committed to persuading consumers to make the initial purchase. Thus, assurance from the product development staff that the formulation of a dry-mix line of gourmet sauces would be technically feasible was only the first step in a risky sequence of events. Test marketing would have to be undertaken, with the possibility that consumers would reject the product. Then, even if successful in test markets, the line would have to be introduced in major markets with very strong initial advertising and promotional support.

To quantify the possibilities, Reilly projected the present budget for three years as shown in Table 8–1. This projection assumes (1) a decision to convert the existing staple sauce line to cash-cow status at once, (2) investment in formulating the gourmet line, (3) steady decline of sales for the staple line with drastically curtailed advertising support, (4) test marketing of the gourmet line next year, (5) favorable consumer reception for the gourmet line in test markets, (6) subsequent rollout of the gourmet line with strong advertising and promotional support, and (7) a break-even result for the gourmet line in its third year with the likelihood of substantial profits in future years. She anticipates that the success of the gourmet line would bring one or more competitive offerings into the market.

Considering the list of assumptions that have to be fulfilled to make the venture a success, Reilly wonders whether her best personal strategy might not be to abandon the gourmet option, recommend converting "QuiknEasy" into a cash cow serving other divisional investment opportunities, and immediately start looking for a new job.

## Questions

1. As an outside consultant, what would you recommend that Radford Foods Company do with its "QuiknEasy" line of sauces?
2. If you were in Eileen Reilly's position, what would you propose?

# INTEGRATING CASES

## Strategy and Marketing

# HYGEIA INTERNATIONAL

Expansion in Nigeria is the issue. Henry Livingstone, vice president of the Africa/Middle East Region of Hygeia International, has just received a proposal from his Nigerian managing director for a major move into poultry production. This would extend Hygeia's profitable agricultural activities even more in that West African country.

## Corporate Base

Hygeia International is a pseudonym for one of the 10 leading pharmaceutical companies of the world. Based in the United States, Hygeia also has laboratories and plants in many countries. Over a third of its net income is earned outside the U.S., and, because of growing federal regulation, Hygeia looks abroad for a rising percentage of its future income.

Like other large pharmaceutical firms, Hygeia has converted drugs designed for humans to use in farm animals. This opens up a large market with relatively low R & D expense. In addition to veterinary products for the control and treatment of disease, Hygeia produces a variety of feed supplements. Currently, about 15 percent of Hygeia's total sales of over a billion dollars come from "agricultural" activities!

Hygeia's agricultural business includes active participation in mass production of poultry. Today, frying chickens are raised in 100,000-chick batches. Thanks to genetic selection, scientific feeding, and a strictly controlled environment, friers can be ready for market in 10 weeks. Egg production is similarly engineered. Significantly, these mass production methods provide one of the most efficient conversions of cereal grains into protein known on earth.

Of course, two essential features of such operations are drugs for disease control and feed supplements. Hygeia makes both (as do several competitors). Moreover, to keep in contact with the latest developments, Hygeia has a subsidiary focusing on development of new genetic strains in chickens—for faster growth, a larger proportion of white meat, more eggs, resistance to disease, or other desired characteristics. In the U.S., Hygeia itself does not produce chickens or eggs commercially or sell chicks for this purpose, but it does have experts familiar with the entire technology.

As part of its international expansion, Hygeia has helped promote modern poultry technology in Europe, Latin America, and now Nigeria.

## Potential Market

A British colony until 1960, Nigeria is growing dramatically. It is by far the leading black African country economically. Its large population of over 90 million (growing 2.7 percent per year) coupled with massive foreign exchange from its crude oil exports ($15 billion in 1980) provide a base for all sorts of expansion.

At the time of independence, Nigeria was a relatively poor developing country with only modest agricultural exports. Probably 90 percent of its population relied on the small village economy, almost unchanged for centuries. Political independence provided the drive, and oil the financial means, to modernize. Even now the average annual per capita income of about $500 is unevenly distributed, with many village people being very poor.

National plans call for universal education and the improvement of hospitals, roads and airports, electric plants, radio and TV, and industry. Lagos, the capital, already has a population of over a million and so many automobiles that new bridges and a fine elevated highway cannot handle the traffic.

Such a rapid transition naturally creates strains. Politically, the most important task is to unite three major tribal groups: the Hausa-Fulani in the north, Ibo in the east, and Yoruba in the west. They speak many different languages (English is the common language) and traditionally are suspicious of each other. A serious civil war occurred from 1967 to 1969 when Biafra tried unsuccessfully to secede. The constitution provides for democratic government, but a series of military coalitions has been necessary to maintain national unity.

Although significant European influence in Nigeria is only about a century old along the southern coast, the Moslem religion and associated ideas have been present in the northern, more arid, regions since the twelfth century. (Kano, for example, was a city-state when Europe was still in the Dark Ages.) Nevertheless, society continues to center around the simple village economy with strong emphasis on loyalty to the extended family. Today over three-quarters of the population relies on localized agriculture. The great movement now occurring is from the village to the city, with all the social and economic adjustments tied to such a shift.

The total population growth, and especially the movement to the cities, has created problems of food supplies. Nigeria has much fertile land, but sugar and cereals are being imported. The village society is unsuited to large-scale agricultural technology, and marketing channels are poorly developed. Particularly serious is the shortage of protein foods. The production of peanuts is rising slowly, but the amount of meat going into markets is stable at best.

Therefore, one facet of the national plan is to increase agricultural output. A system of agricultural agents to advise farmers is being established, some research on products and technology is under way, and loans to farmers are available on favorable terms. A major bottleneck in this effort is trained human resources. The number of experts capable of dealing with local farmers is very limited, and farmers with the knowledge, skill, and capital needed for modern agriculture are scarce. As usual, pricing presents a dilemma. High prices, which will stimulate farm output, also lead to high food prices for the city dweller, who is already caught in inflation. Nigeria, like the U.S., has basically a free price system, but resorts to some political control of items that are important in the worker's cost of living.

In this situation, government officials would like to increase substantially the supply of eggs and chickens. And if this can be done without raising the real (adjusted for inflation) prices, that is even more attractive. A relatively small technical staff in the Ministry of Agriculture is working on poultry, and low-interest loans are available to farmers who wish to install modern poultry-raising equipment. A few demonstration farms are in operation, and their results show the advantages of mass production methods. However, the response to date has been limited. The concept of producing eggs or chickens in large quantities is new, and few farmers have a technical background in scientific feeding, disease control, and mechanical equipment.

## Product/Customer Issue for Hygeia

Hygeia International is already well established in Nigeria. It has built a "dosage" plant where several hundred different (imported) pharmaceutical products are put into pills, capsules, bottles, and other forms suited to local use. These pharmaceuticals are sold to hospitals, clinics, and drugstores in much the same way as ethical drugs are sold in the U.S.

The sale of Hygeia products is helped by the local company's full cooperation with the "indigenization program," which requires the employment of Nigerians for virtually all positions. Also, to comply with recent laws, 40 percent of the shares of the local company have been sold to Nigerians. A substantial amount of training and technical advice continues to be provided for a fee by Hygeia offices in Europe and in the U.S.; Hygeia's policy is to cooperate as fully as it can in the development of medical services in Nigeria.

In the agricultural area Hygeia follows a similar practice. It imports and sells unique medicines and feed supplements, and it is active in technical development. Working closely with government and trade association officials, Hygeia helped set up demonstration sites for poultry colony housing and displays on lighting, ventilation, and feeding routines. It trains farmers on disease control and forecasts epidemics or disease frequency. Also, it has helped establish reliable regional feed mills. As a result of the total cooperative program, the number of egg-laying hens has increased to perhaps 3 million.

As with human products, Hygeia uses a wide range of services to build a market for its veterinary and feed products. However, the company does not now operate its own egg-laying colonies or meat colonies. Nor does Hygeia maintain colonies of "parents"—pedigree chickens which produce the millions of first-line workers. In the U.S., parent colonies are usually operated by separate companies closely linked to genetic development; then fertile eggs or chicks are sold to companies in the meat or egg business. The question now facing Hygeia is whether to integrate forward in Nigeria—that is, actually to produce eggs or meat (sold as live chickens or dressed meat) or to stop with fertile eggs or chicks sold to farmers.

## Proposal from Nigeria

Mr. Livingstone received the following letter from Mr. E.P. Murtala of the Hygeia Nigerian branch.

> Dear Mr. Livingstone:
>
> This letter outlines a proposed expansion of the agricultural division of our company. Estimates show that this would be a very profitable venture, and it would help meet the food needs of our growing population.
>
> The basic plan is to become a large-scale producer of eggs and of chickens to be sold for meat. The reasons supporting this move are as follows:
>
> 1. We already have the necessary technical staff who are fully acquainted with adapting the latest technology to local conditions.
> 2. There is high potential demand for protein foods, especially eggs, which are less perishable than fresh meat. Considering only our urban population of 15 million people, Nigeria now markets only about 36 eggs per person per year compared with 335 in the United States.
> 3. Government support is available. Much of the plant cost can be financed with low-interest loans, and other cooperation can be expected.
> 4. Our success will attract others into the poultry business. Some of the people we train will leave and start their own operations. This activity, in addition to our own, will increase the demand for veterinary products and feed supplements.
> 5. Facilities for egg production can be shifted to birds for meat as marketing channels for live and/or frozen birds develop.
> 6. During inflation there is some risk that price controls on eggs might squeeze the profit margins. However, if eggs become a stable part of urban dwellers' diets, we doubt that the government will permit sharp reduction in egg production. Therefore, the increased demand for veterinary and feed products will continue.
> 7. To attract and retain good local managers, we plan a series of joint ventures, with the local manager sharing in the ownership and profits. Each will be a separate corporation. Tentatively, we are

thinking of ten ventures located in the environs of the following cities: Lagos (3), Ibadan (2), Benin (2), Kaduna, Kano, and Makurdi. Three will be parent-stock farms—one each in Lagos, Ibadan, and Benin; the others will be commercial egg farms.

8. The financial projection prepared by R. Akobo, our agricultural manager, and checked by M. Suleman, our financial manager, is attached [see Table 1.] You do not have to send us cash; we can simply withhold capital as it becomes needed from remittances due on shipments made to us.

### TABLE 1.
### FINANCIAL SUMMARY
**(Based on detailed estimates—amounts in thousands of dollars)**

| | Parent Stock Farm (day-old chicks) | Commercial Egg Farm (eggs for food) |
|---|---|---|
| Land | 40 | 25 |
| Buildings & Equipment | 960 | 440 |
| Development Expenses | 100 | 60 |
| Total fixed investment | 1,100 | 525 |
| Working Capital | 500 | 175 |
| Total investment | 1,600 | 700 |
| Sales[a] | 2,300 | 850 |
| Direct Expenses | 870 | 685 |
| Administration, Sales, etc. | 150 | 45 |
| Operating profit | 1,020 | 120 |
| Income taxes @ 50%[b] | 510 | 60 |
| Net Profit | 510 | 60 |
| Government and Bank Financing | 1,000 | 450 |
| Equity | 600 | 250 |
| Total investment | 1,600 | 700 |
| Return on Equity before Taxes/yr[c] | 170% | 48% |
| Return on Equity after Taxes/yr | 85% | 24% |

[a]Sales figures, but not expenses, reduced 20% to allow for contingencies.
[b]Actually, most Nigerian taxes will be rebated during first four years.
[c]Figures converted from naira to dollars at rate of 1N = $1.50.
Inflation will increase all estimates, but the proportions should remain the same.

Estimates are for full-scale operations. It will take two to three years to reach this level. Estimates show both cash and net income break-even by end of first year and, with tax rebate, full recovery of equity early in third year.

I hope you will Telex your approval of this proposal in the near future so we can start negotiations with government officials and possible venture managers. I feel confident that local stockholders will approve the expansion.

Sincerely yours,


E. P. Murtala, President
Nigerian Hygeia, Ltd.

When Mr. Livingstone received Mr. Murtala's letter, he immediately asked Hygeia's treasurer and the corporate vice president for agriculture for their comments on the proposal. The treasurer noted that "the estimated return is well over the 30 percent hurdle rate used for domestic investment. Also, with Nigeria's favorable foreign exchange position, the danger of exchange rate losses is not high. So the main question relates to political risks—revolution, confiscation, controls on repatriation of profits, arbitrary actions to promote diplomatic ends (e.g., South Africa), etc. And you are in the best position to assess these risks."

The agriculture vice president replied, in part, "My chief concern is whether Hygeia should enter into agricultural production. In the U.S., Europe, and most other locations we confine our activities to *helping others* (local people who know local problems) improve their output. That posture keeps us out of a lot of trouble. In particular, we must be sure that what we do in poultry does not upset sales of livestock veterinary and feed products, or more important, sales of products for humans. My preference is to enter production only when that is the only feasible way to start the use of our regular line of products, and to pull out as soon as local operators are ready to carry on. So I urge you to think of the Nigerian proposal only as a sales promotion device. You can decide whether there are better ways to promote sales."

## Question

Assume that you are a personal assistant to Mr. Livingstone and that he has asked you to study the total Nigerian situation and recommend what he should do regarding Mr. Murtala's proposal. What do you tell Mr. Livingstone?


# ALPHA PYRO GLASS, INC. (APG)

Peter Donald, marketing vice president, is attempting to decide into which product lines his firm, Alpha Pyro Glass, Inc. (better known as APG), should put its total marketing effort and what will be the most effective three-year marketing program for those product lines. APG had once been a manufacturer of special glass products, but now, as a wholly owned subsidiary of a major petroleum company, it concentrates entirely on making and selling fiberglass panels which are used to shade patios, as siding for vehicles, and for other applications.

In its new status as part of a diversified corporation, APG has an opportunity—indeed is under pressure—to refocus its marketing efforts on market segments where it can become one of the leaders. Mr. Donald is well aware, however, that this effort must be selective. There are limits on his own time and energy, and in addition, the supervising executives of the parent company have in effect placed the following constraints on APG: (1) APG should not lose position or market share for its present products; (2) marketing expenditures should not increase by more than one-half of one percent of sales (an increase of about $120,000 per year); and (3) the new program should not call for major capital expenditures on plant and equipment.

Instructions from APG's president are that investment has to be minimized because executives of the parent firm place major emphasis on the division's return on investment. High returns on investment meet with great approval from the central executives. Mr. Donald is, of course, very interested in increasing sales volume as measured by square feet of panels sold, in the price per square foot of the panels, and in market share for individual product lines.

APG competes directly with seven other companies. Three of them are independent, middle-sized companies, and the others are subsidiaries of major chemical, petroleum, or construction companies. The eight competitors, however, do not have identical interests or positions in the various markets to which they sell.

## ▦ The Product and How It Is Made

APG manufactures its fiberglass-reinforced plastic (FRP) panels by impregnating a fiberglass mat with a polyester resin and then forming and curing the panel with pressure and heat to make a strong, lightweight building material. The panels can vary by weight per square foot, by profile (flat or corrugated, for instance), by width, by length, and by color. Colors are a part of the resin used in making the panels and so are uniform throughout the panel, not just a surface coating.

FRP panels are a useful substitute for other building materials when strength, lightness in weight, durability, and transmission of light are desirable features. FRP panels are generally resistant to most corrosive atmospheres commonly encountered in coastal, industrial, and commercial areas. They can be used safely in the presence of salt air, hydrocarbons, alcohols, peroxides, carbonates, and diluted halogens, as well as many acids and alkalies. With a proper composition of the resin, FRP panels can be made resistant to fire.

To make a finished panel, the APG factory feeds a glass mat (which it purchases from one of several large suppliers who compete strongly with one another in price, product, and service) onto a conveyor belt. This belt may have a textured surface—dimpled or pebbled or with long ridges or with various geometric shapes such as that of a brick wall. With heat and pressure, the textured or shaped surface is eventually imparted onto the resin-filled glass mat.

With further curing by heat and pressure, a gel coat can be added onto one side of the FRP panel. This gel coat adds resistance to scratches, to chemicals, to ultraviolet light, and to dents. The process for adding the gel coat has been carefully and most thoroughly developed by APG. Its cost of making and applying the gel coat has been lowered considerably by the experience of the processing department. The production manager says that APG has dropped to a low point on the learning curve for the gel coat process and that his people have learned to overcome readily the many hazards of the process.

A gel-coated FRP panel is clearly superior in use to noncoated panels and is a higher quality product for most customers of APG.

APG also has a product superiority advantage for some flat or uncoated panels through its use of a high-quality resin, through imaginative product development for new uses of FRP panels, and through careful tailoring of its products to the needs of customers.

Several competitors of APG have a cost advantage for their products which results from their use of longer mats, vacuum deaeration equipment, and longer ovens. This equipment allows them to process their FRP panels continuously, whereas APG uses a batch system. The resulting cost advantage is about 20 percent of manufactured cost, or 13 percent of the selling price. The advantage shows up only when long runs of standard panels are made or when similar products which cause little change or setup time are run.

A few (perhaps two) competitors have recently widened their conveyor systems. This will soon give them a marked product advantage in wide sheets for trailers, large trucks, and other uses.

## Product Lines

APG competes in a wide variety of markets and has the constant issue of deciding to enter, stay in, or drop out of various markets. Four markets—recreational vehicle siding, liner panels, greenhouses, and traffic-control signs—have been identified as having relatively high growth, substantial unit volume (square feet), desirability of FRP panels for the application, and ease of entry for APG.

**Recreational Vehicle (RV) Siding**    The size of this industry is estimated at 40 to 50 million square feet of siding annually for trailers, motor homes, and campers. Currently, about 50 percent of this is aluminum and Harrison Plastics has another 30 percent. APG has a 10 percent share, and two other firms share the balance of the market. FRP panels are growing in market share because gel-coated panels are markedly superior to aluminum in resisting dents and scratches, have a weight advantage, and are easier to handle in the factory.

Large RV manufacturers (Winnebago, Fleetwood, Champion, and Open Road) dominate the market and are notorious for playing one supplier off against another to gain a product or cost advantage.

This market has a very marked cyclical pattern, but it has recovered strongly from the recession of the early 1980s, and it promises growth of 11 percent or more per year for several years to come.

APG has a product-quality advantage. To use this effectively to gain market share, the company will have to increase selling expense by about $100,000 per year to put more personal selling effort into national accounts. The panels sell for about $.55 per square foot.

**Liner Panels**      FRP panels are sold in this market for new construction and remodeling in food-processing equipment, cold storage plants, restaurant kitchens, slaughterhouses, pigpens, and building facades. Resistance to chemicals and to fire, smoke, and temperature attack is important. Total demand is about 50 million square feet of FRP panels supplied in a standard width of 4 feet as well as in custom widths varying from 32 to 100 inches.

To enter this market, APG will need to develop an advertising campaign for about $35,000 per year, train its district salespeople in the particular needs of this part of the construction industry, set up a prospecting program for its salespeople, offer discounts to customers to persuade them to switch, and probably devise an incentive bonus for the sales representatives. A substantial amount of Peter Donald's time and effort will be required.

Five important competitors are all involved in this market. Two of them sell to the commercial division of Masonite, the largest customer for liner panels. Masonite currently uses the FRP panels as laminates for its building sheets. Berg Glass-Like dominates this market, but the four other major competitors are struggling to increase market share, so pricing is competitive. Thinner gauge liner panels for laminating are increasing by 10 to 15 percent per year in usage and offer an opportunity for wider sales margins than do standard panels.

Overall prices average about $.47 per square foot with Wold Panels, Inc., probably obtaining an average of $.52 for its wider, smoke-resistant sheets.

**Commercial Greenhouse Glazing**      Greenhouses use clear and translucent FRP panels because they offer superior light transmission in the visible part of the spectrum, inhibit the transmission of harmful ultraviolet light, carry a guarantee of a 10- to 15-year life, and have much less heat gain and loss than does glass. FRP panels sell for about $.40 per square foot in this market.

The industry uses about 110 million square feet of glazing each year, of which about 20 percent is FRP glazing. Substitute products are tempered glass, a single film of polyethylene, and a double film of polyethylene. Imported glass is cheap ($.20/square foot), breaks easily, allows heat buildup, and is difficult to erect, but it has excellent weathering and consistent light transmission. Single polyethylene film is cheaper yet, lasts two years, and is easy to install, but it has poor solar energy transmission and thermal qualities. Double polyethylene costs slightly less than glass, is easy to install, conserves energy, and lasts two to five years, but it has poor light transmission and thus reduced crop yields.

Harrison Plastics and Navin Fibre-Glass (a subsidiary of a major chemical company) have the largest market share in FRP glazing—about 50 percent and 25 percent, respectively. APG, Berg Glass-Like, and two other firms share the balance of the market. APG's share is about 12 percent. Its panels are acknowledged to be of high quality and sell especially well to florists in the Southeast.

APG can probably increase its market share substantially by adding a "surfactant" (surface tension reducer) to the inside of its panels so that water droplets cannot cling and will run off rapidly. APG has the process—by a license—to apply a surfactant, but minor chemical and engineering adjustments will have to be made. An advertising campaign to promote the surfactant will probably cost about $20,000 per year.

Growers will have to be found throughout the country who require high light transmission for maximum crop turnover and who measure return on their investment over a period of 10 years.

**Traffic Control Sign Panels**    Strong, long-term expansion is predicted for this market, as sign specifications are issued for FRP by the 27 states which do not as yet have such specifications and in which sales, as a result, cannot yet be made. Custom, flat signs are used, both illuminated and not.

APG's sales representatives have to date identified the purchasing contacts and secured specifications in 18 states. The firm has prepared specification data sheets for each of these states and has received purchase source approval by the work of its district salespeople. Samples for testing and an approved vendor listing will be necessary in all other states.

Traffic control sign potential is estimated to be about 240 million square feet per year for the entire country.

APG currently sells FRP panels to fabricators of some industrial and commercial signs and advertises in several trade magazines to a minimal extent. Its volume of about a million square feet per year at $.40 per square foot gives it a market share of less than 1 percent of all plastic signs and of about 20 percent of FRP signs. For traffic control purposes, the product will have to be doubled in thickness and increased in its bonding and temperature-control characteristics. This will require a substantial investment in additional plant facilities.

FRP panels for traffic control signs will sell for about $1.80 per square foot. At present, Mr. Donald is pessimistic about this market, although he sees its great potential.

**Other Products**    APG sells in several other markets. The buyers include manufacturers of garage doors, solar energy devices, and metal buildings and a group of building material distributors, home centers, chain stores, and independent retailers that operate in the do-it-yourself market.

APG has supplied these markets for many years. Some of them are declining, and most do not promise much growth. A summary of the characteristics of these markets is given in Table 1.

**TABLE 1.**
**OTHER MARKETS FOR APG'S PRODUCTS**

| Products and Buyers | Average Volume | Product Forecasts | Competitors | Market Share(%) | Pricing Norms | APG Advantage Over Competition |
|---|---|---|---|---|---|---|
| 1. Manufacturers of garage doors for commercial, industrial, and residential buildings. Many buyers. | 15 million square feet of FRP panels per year. | Volume trend down for the past eight years. Position lost to wood doors and insulated metal doors. | Harrison Plastics<br>Navin Fibre-Glass<br>Wolf Glass-Fibre<br>APG<br>Berg Glass-Like | 47<br>16<br>12<br>20<br>5 | $.35 per square foot and stable | None |
| 2. Perimeter and skylight panels to admit light to metal buildings. Ten major manufacturers of such buildings. | 93 million square feet of paneling: 28% glass; 21% FRP panels; 51% transparent plastics (acrylic or polycarbonate sheets). | Fast growing—twice the rate of all industrial and commercial construction. | Resistex<br>Wholey<br>Fiber-Lite<br>Navin Fibre-Glass<br>Harrison Plastics<br>APG | 28<br>35<br>22<br><br>15<br>0 | $.45 to $1.00 per square foot | None. APG made a major effort three years ago to penetrate this market and lost out because of competitors' contacts, ownership, and price competition. |
| 3. Solar energy panels to cover flat plate collectors at low to medium temperatures. Many buyers. | 28 million square feet of FRP panels. | Volume declining as federal and state subsidies and tax credits are discontinued. Tied to building cycle to some extent. | APG<br>Wold Panels, Inc.<br>Navin Fibre-Glass<br>Berg Glass-Like | 45<br>50<br>3<br>2 | $.60 per square foot | Gel coating is resistant to ultraviolet light. Customer contacts. |

| Products and Buyers | Average Volume | Product Forecasts | Competitors | Market Share(%) | Pricing Norms | APG Advantage Over Competition |
|---|---|---|---|---|---|---|
| | | Tempered glass is a favored substitute. Very optimistic forecasts for the very long run. | | | | |
| 4. Distributors and retail chains who sell FRP panels for new construction and remodeling of commercial, industrial, and residential buildings. Hundreds of buyers who buy in small quantities. | 174 million square feet of FRP panels. | Stable sales volume. Prices declining slightly. | Harrison Plastics<br>Navin Fibre-Glass<br>APG<br>Wolf Glass-Fibre<br>Wholey<br>Fiber-Lite | 18<br><br>22<br>10<br><br>25<br>25 | $.40 per square foot for 50% of the volume.<br>$.18 per square foot for the balance | Higher quality panels. Positioned solidly in a limited niche. Can get higher penetration with heavy promotion and merchandising aid to the distributors. |
| 5. Fire- and corrosion-resistant panels sold directly to original equipment manufacturers (OEMs) of cooling towers, chemical processing plants, sewage systems, and silos. Special resins used. | 15 million square feet of FRP panels. | Stable or declining slightly. | Resistex<br>APG<br>Wholey Fiber-Lite<br>Berg Glass-Like<br>Harrison Plastics<br>Navin Fibre-Glass | 55<br>30<br>n.a.<br><br>n.a.<br>2<br><br>n.a. | $1.10 per square foot and increasing | Lighter weight than other materials (stainless steel, redwood, porcelain, galvanized metal, and aluminum). Better resins than other FRP panel makers. |

## Competitors

*Harrison Plastics* dominates the FRP panel industry in its sales to greenhouse makers, to builders of recreational vehicles, and to several other market segments. The firm sells panels of above-average quality and design, is innovative in product development, has an effective marketing organization, charges high prices, and operates a high-cost plant. Its sales of liner panels are a small part of this market in which it does custom business only and provides slow delivery.

*Navin Fibre-Glass, Inc.,* has a high market share of sales to greenhouses. In this segment its name is well known, and the company provides a high-quality panel. The company sells below-average quality panels in the liner and RV siding market segments, in which it competes mainly on the basis of price. For the liner panel market, the firm has recently developed some well-received new products.

*Wholey Fiber-Lite Co.* is a small producer of liner panels, but is well accepted in the sign market, in which it has a 70 percent market share. It offers high-quality panels for signs at a competitive price which is below the price of comparable acrylic sheets. The company sells nationwide. Its products for other markets are of inconsistent quality, and pricing is on the low end.

*Berg Glass-Like, Inc.,* is very strong in the liner panel market, in which it has the newest line, provides good service at low prices, and offers fast delivery. The firm sells fiberglass panels for laminating to Masonite Corporation—the largest panel manufacturer in the country. Berg is the third largest producer of greenhouse panels, having fair acceptance in the low-price end of this market. Its sign panels are of low quality, and Berg charges the lowest prices for direct sales to O.E.M. accounts. Its sign panels have an eight percent share of the market.

*Wold Panels, Inc.,* is a principal competitor in the RV siding market and in the market for solar panels. Its gel-coated panels are of very high quality. Wold is also the dominant producer of liner panels, with a 55 percent market share based on its long, wide, and heavy panels sold at the highest prices with fast delivery.

*Resistex Corporation* is a special resin producer which concentrates on two market segments: metal buildings and corrosion-resistant panels. The firm has a limited sales force and does not seek sales outside of these two market segments. It has very good product acceptance and a well-known name and has cut prices sharply in the past to maintain its market position.

*Wolf Glass-Fibre Products, Inc.,* has solid positions in sales of garage door panels and in sales to national plastics distributors and retail chains. Its principal advantage appears to be personal relationships with the buyers. It does have a well-known brand name, good product acceptance, and a wide line of less expensive panels.

Mr. Donald recognizes that he has the time and ability to supervise no more than two efforts to enter new market segments or to expand his company's position markedly in an existing segment. Any combination of two would probably use up all the additional funds that he can expend on marketing, and perhaps more.

## Question

On what products and on what market segments do you recommend that APG concentrate to increase sales revenues and sales volume?

# CHAPTER 9

## Strategy Programs in Research and Development

Creating goods and services is just as indispensable as distributing them, and business-unit strategy must embrace both. In fact, it is often an imaginative combination of producing and marketing that gives a company unique strength. Creating goods and services will be discussed in both this and the next chapter.

### Role of Research and Development

Some firms quite wisely do virtually no research and development (R & D). Others rely on their R & D for survival. Between these two extremes are many variations and purposes.

Because R & D has no fixed role, general managers in a business-unit call the first shot; they establish the R & D department, if there is to be one, and assign a broad mission. Once established, however, R & D departments have a tendency to chart their own course. A research project may take years from start to finish, so short-term control is difficult. Typically, the work is performed in a separate location, and the specialized training and interests of research personnel may take years to develop and be hard to redirect. This semiindependence means that effective linkages between the central strategy and the actual R & D effort are not easy to sustain. Yet guidance is sorely needed.

As in the chapters on marketing, we will first review the basic issues faced by an R & D department and the likely preferences of the department if left alone. Then we will note how R & D thrusts should be linked to the work of other departments. Finally, we will examine how such constrained activity can be linked into the overall business-unit strategy.

### Scope

Broadly speaking, R & D deals with numerous activities from basic research to placing a product on the market and utilizing a new process. Here, we are primarily concerned with *innovation*—the effective application of a new idea. Innovations occur in all kinds of human activity, but we will focus on technological changes in products and processes.

Clearly, an R & D manager is concerned with more than just *invention*, i.e., conceiving a new and useful idea. Invention is an essential part of the total process, but it is only a part. R & D departments may engage in activities that lead to inventions; but if they do, they must also devote a great deal of effort to converting the invention into a practical application.

## Stages

When planning for R & D, a recognition of the stages involved in innovation is helpful. The normal stages of technological innovation are as follows:

1.  Basic research—the scientific investigation of a physical phenomenon without any defined use that might be made of the resulting knowledge.
2.  Applied research—studies designed to identify specific potential applications of general knowledge.
3.  Development—testing and elaborating a potential application into a model or a set of specifications that demonstrates the physical practicality of a new process or product.
4.  Pilot plant or prototype testing—testing the economic as well as the physical feasibility of actually using a model or specifications emerging from the development stage.
5.  Manufacturing, tooling, and debugging—designing and assembling new manufacturing equipment, and then testing and modifying it until full-scale operations at acceptable efficiencies are possible.
6.  Marketing start-up—overcoming any new technical problems of physical distribution and customer use.

Table 9–1 presents an outline of these six stages of technological innovation with respect to output, predictability of results, and types of personnel involved.

In practice, the separation of these six stages of technological innovation is fuzzy. Problems encountered at any one stage may require backtracking to a previous stage. For instance, a difficulty uncovered in a pilot plant may signal the need for further development or even an applied research effort. Similarly, good management practice requires forward bridging. Thus, basic research shades into applied research, and applied research shades into development. Especially important in private R & D work is a frequent checking of market potentials and market requirements during all of the stages except basic research.

In laying out programs for R & D work, it is important to recognize that research expenses are normally very much smaller than development expenses for a successful project. Statistics on this point are far from precise, but Figure 9–1 indicates the range in three important industries.

The reasons for the high expense in the later stages are not hard to find. Many work hours are required to design and test each of the subparts of a new product or process. Moreover, as the work progresses, it must be done on a larger and larger scale, requiring greater inputs of materials and machinery. In some in-

**TABLE 9–1.**
**NORMAL STAGES OF TECHNOLOGICAL INNOVATION**

| Stages | Output | Ability to Predict Results | Kinds of People Involved |
|---|---|---|---|
| 1. Basic research | Knowledge | None | Idealists and dreamers—young, professionally oriented |
| 2. Applied research | Directed knowledge, leading to identified applications* | Little | May be prickly personalities |
| 3. Development | Product or process model—operational feasibility | Some | |
| 4. Pilot plant | Cost knowledge— economic feasibility | | Engineers— organization oriented |
| 5. Manufacturing, tooling, and debugging | Total operating system, specifications, and process costs | High probability | Persons with efficiency and effectiveness as values |
| 6. Marketing start-up | Product acceptance | | |

*Many inventions by individual tinkerers arise without benefit of knowledge from basic research; all major inventions sparking the Industrial Revolution were of this sort.

stances, such as the current work on monoclonal antibodies in the pharmaceutical industry, entirely new processes for acquiring raw material in the quantity and the quality desired have to be invented. The identification and recording of all the specifications in an experimental model is time consuming. Clearly, any R & D department that engages in applied research must be prepared to invest substantially larger additional amounts if it is to reap full benefit from its research efforts.

## Progress by Increments

A single dramatic invention such as Carlson's Xerography or Land's Polaroid camera catches our attention when we think about innovation. However, it is a mistake to assume that the success of all R & D work depends upon major discoveries. Much more common is a succession of small improvements, one built upon another, that in total add up to a major change. The development of mobile homes

**FIGURE 9-1.**
**COST DISTRIBUTION OF SUCCESSFUL INNOVATIONS IN CHEMICAL, ELECTRONIC, AND MACHINERY INDUSTRIES**

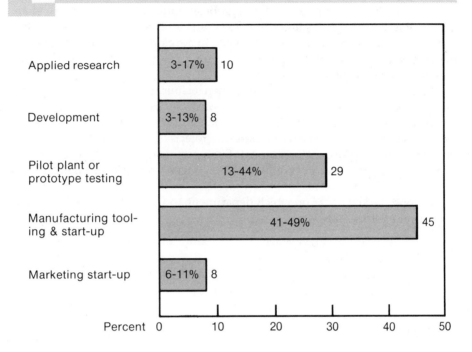

*Source:* Edwin Mansfield *et al., The Production and Application of New Industrial Technology* (New York: W.W. Norton & Co., Inc., 1977), p. 71. Lengths of bars show mean percentages of sample cases; numbers within bars show the range.

and self-service stores are examples of innovations that occurred in this incremental fashion.

The incremental process permits several different companies to participate in an innovation. Frequently one firm builds on the advances of another, and it is possible to enter the game late and still be successful. Of course, a basic invention protected by a patent is of great competitive value, but a great majority of R & D work is not of this character. Most R & D departments advance a step at a time, and R & D success is measured by who is stepping fastest.

## Risk Entailed

Both uncertainty and expense permeate the design of all R & D programs. Of course, business expenditures in R & D of about $50 billion per year (one-half of which comes from government contracts) produce a stream of new products and processes, but the output of a single company laboratory is by no means sure. For example, laser theory was discovered and published by Charles Towne early in the 1950s. Many different laboratories started applied research with this new concept, but 20 years later only a few significant industrial applications had appeared. R & D managers estimate that less than 20 percent of the ideas that look good enough to move from applied research to development actually end up in a marketable product (or applied process), and only a part of these are commercially successful. Uncertainty in R & D is real.

Moreover, R & D work is expensive. When technical assistants and other laboratory expenses are added to salary, a scientist or a senior engineer may cost a company from $100,000 to $175,000 a year. Of course the cost of routine engineering is lower, but so is the useful output. Projects that call for a team approach quickly entail a significant investment. Such cost, coupled with uncertainty of outcome, puts pressure on business-unit managers to think through carefully how R & D should be used.

Among the key issues on which department and overall management views may differ are the following:

1. Targets for improvement
2. Depth of the research effort
3. Offensive versus defensive R & D
4. Getting R & D done by outsiders

## Targets for Improvement

R & D activities tend to wander. Researchers and engineers must be given considerable freedom to organize their own work, and each person prefers to move in directions that are intellectually exciting to that individual. No department can afford such a diffused effort on a large scale, although occasionally a department does permit its researchers to devote, say, 20 percent of their time to anything that intrigues them. Instead, guideposts or targets are needed to focus the effort. These should be at least compatible with company strategy.

## Product Versus Process Focus

A recurring management question is how the R & D effort will be divided between developing new and improved products and seeking improvements in production processes. The key to a policy on this matter lies in the *industry analysis*, which we have urged as a prerequisite to drawing up company strategy. In a mature industry where low cost is necessary to meet price competition, for instance, the R & D effort on processes may be crucial. On the other hand, newly designed products may be the primary success factor in another industry, so here R & D should focus on products.

A large chemical company used this simple but fundamental approach to sharply alter its targets. For years, this company had focused on tonnage production of carbon compounds. It was an efficient producer and maintained a steady position in its segment of a growing industry. Good process R & D was an important contributor to this achievement. Then the oil companies entered the chemical industry on a large scale. In terms of tonnage and low cost, the oil companies had some relative advantages: ready access to low-cost carbon inputs in the form of oil and gas and a large cash flow available for the huge investments needed for new plants. Analysis of these developments led the independent chemical company to conclude that maintaining its position in the tonnage business would probably yield a declining return on its invested capital. Prospects were brighter for complex products that produced special effects and carried greater added value. Consequently, a new strategy was adopted of gradually phasing out the heavy petrol chemicals and replacing this business with new complex products. To implement this strategy, the R & D department's activities were sharply altered. New products became the dominant theme, whereas process research was confined to modifications of existing plants.

Adoption of the change just cited was no easy matter. For years the company had prided itself on being an aggressive, successful competitor. The personal careers of several of the key executives were based on this success. To them, the target change was like forfeiting a football game in midseason. Of course, the firm would continue to be a major factor in the segment of the industry these individuals knew so well, probably beyond the date of their retirement, but they were well aware that the change in the R & D objectives would probably shape the character of the company in the future.

Many U.S. companies in basic industries—such as automobiles, machine tools, and even electronics—are now worried about their future ability to meet foreign price competition. This concern has spurred greater interest in process R & D.

## Existing Lines Versus New Lines

A decision to support product research still leaves open the question of what type of product to concentrate on. For example, the R & D department of one jet engine manufacturing company sticks to its existing products. It believes that the future market in this line alone is very large and that technological improvements from company R & D will be the key determinant of who gets the lion's share.

In contrast, Minnesota Mining and Manufacturing Company, makers of Scotch tape, photographic material, and a variety of other products, has achieved considerable success with R & D focused on new lines. The company has a clear policy about the kinds of products on which money is to be spent. The emphasis is to be on products that are (1) new, (2) patentable, and (3) consumable (heavy repeat business). Here again, the R & D policy is a direct extension of the expansion strategy that this particular company has selected.

One dimension of a product line sometimes debated is the amount of forward integration. For instance, should a transistor manufacturer do research on products using transistors? In its fiber division, the Du Pont company has stayed away from end products such as hosiery, shirts, and rugs. The R & D people must know enough about the subsequent processing and final consumption of its fibers to build desirable characteristics into its products, but that is as far as its R & D people are expected to go. Incidentally, when there is no clear breaking point, Du Pont researchers do extend their studies all the way to the consumer level, as in paints. Nevertheless, for years the department's basic policy was to stick to chemical manufacturing. This forward limit has had a significant effect upon the character of Du Pont research and the innovations it has produced.

## Process Improvements That Count

In process R & D, as with product R & D, a careful choice of research programs is needed. One approach is to deal only with those aspects of production where significant savings are possible. Thus, a farm equipment manufacturer turned down a proposal from its engineering department to develop a new way of heat-treating a special type of steel. Even if the project had been as successful as hoped, it would have cut total manufacturing costs only by a fraction of one percent. The company preferred to concentrate its limited resources where the potential payback was greater.

The number of units affected by a process change is also critical. In a large copper company, for instance, substantial effort was devoted to finding ways to improve the recovery of copper from its ore-crushing process by just a small percentage. Since millions of tons went through this process, even a small improvement in recovery could be significant. Unfortunately, a special study showed that the R & D department of this company was proceeding with equal zeal on the recovery of other metals that were produced in minor amounts as by-products of the copper operation. The study resulted in a sharper definition of what kind of process improvements to seek.

Managers of R & D usually argue for some degree of freedom, especially in the research stages. Many new discoveries have come through serendipity—finding one thing when looking for another. Penicillin and X-rays are examples. However, an interest in bright ideas that may be unrelated to the purposes of the project at hand does not diminish the value of policy about where to put the major effort. With such policy, most of the output will be directly usable by the company. Additional insights are welcome by-products, but they should be treated as by-products.

## Depth of Research Effort

Identification of a promising research area still leaves R & D managers with a question of depth of effort. For example, does a research interest in vertical takeoff planes mean that the department will undertake theoretical research in aerial dynamics or the structural properties of lightweight metal? Where on the continuum from a search for new knowledge to practical specifications for a marketable product should an R & D department focus its efforts?

## Basic Research Versus Applied Research

No company research department proposes to study whatever intrigues its scientists. Even basic research will be in areas related to the company's strategic mission—biochemistry for pharmaceutical companies, geology for oil companies, and the like. The issue is whether (1) simply to investigate a phenomenon without any specific idea of how the new knowledge acquired will be used (basic research), or (2) to pick a potential application of knowledge—human need—and try to devise ways of meeting this need (applied research). The distinction is like studying the geography of Central Africa just to learn more about it or to identify attractive sites for hydroelectric power plants.

### Exceptional Companies in Basic Research

A few companies have had outstanding success with their policy of doing basic research. A notable example is the work at Bell Telephone Laboratories on semiconductors. Because of a possible connection with solid-state amplifiers, Bell Labs set up a semiconductor basic research group of physicists, chemists, and metallurgists in 1946. In the process of their investigation, they discovered the transistor in 1948, and by 1951 they had develped the theoretical knowledge on which transistors with all their manifold applications are based. In passing, note that the initial effort took over 5 years of basic research by a whole group of scientists and that 10 to 15 years elapsed before the transistor was in widespread commercial application.

The Du Pont discovery of nylon is another classic example where basic research paid off. Here, the research was on polymerization, and by accident one of the researchers discovered that the fiber formed by pulling a stirring rod out of an experimental batch had unusual flexibility and strength. This led to a change in the direction of the research; but after two years of intensive work, the results were so discouraging that the entire project was almost abandoned. It took seven years after the initial discovery before nylon could be produced on a commercial basis. Just when this undertaking moved from "basic research" to "applied research" is hard to define. But it is clear that the basic research provided the situation in which the initial discovery was possible.

Occasional commercial success growing out of basic research, however, does not mean that all R & D departments interested in new products and processes should embark on basic research. In fact, experience in most companies indicates that the costs and the difficulties of basic research make it an unwise investment of company funds. Even large research-minded companies like Xerox and Monsanto have recently redirected their R & D efforts to applied, market-oriented projects.

### Criteria for Basic Research

If a company is going to support basic research by its R & D department, it should (1) be prepared to take the risk of incurring long periods of research without discovering ideas that have commercial value; (2) have a "payout" period threshold that permits a long time between investment and return (over 25 years elapsed between Fleming's discovery of penicillin and its large-scale production); and (3) possess enough capital to exploit discoveries when and if they are made—often millions of dollars are needed after the discovery to bring it into commercial use.

In addition to these criteria, which are essentially financial, a fourth operating consideration is usually necessary to justify basic research: the company should be sufficiently large in the industry where the discovery is applied to take full advantage of the new concept. This means that the company should have an existing position that will permit it to obtain synergistic benefits when the new product or process is introduced. Of course, a company can license or sell its patents to other companies, or it might enter a new industry in an effort to exploit a discovery it had made; but the return from such use of a new idea is much smaller than enhancing an existing market position or production capability.

Government financing of research can mitigate these rather severe criteria. In the aerospace industry and some other industries, government financing does permit a lot of *applied* research and development. To a much smaller extent, this same approach can be utilized for basic research. (Typically, however, government funds for this purpose go to universities or other nonprofit research institutes.) Of course, government financing means that the company will not have exclusive use of the knowledge obtained, but direct access to scientists familiar with the latest developments might be advantageous to the company.

## Applied Research Versus Development

If basic research looks nebulous to a company, maybe it should also back away from applied research. Instead of spending time and money in finding how to accomplish a desired end, perhaps effort could better be concentrated on developing economical methods of utilizing ideas that are already known to work.

The considerations in making this choice are similar to those just listed for basic research, but the risks here are fewer and the payout periods somewhat shorter. The main advantage of sticking to "development" is assurance that results will reinforce existing activity. Thus, the outcome can be directed toward strategic objectives (new products or production economy) rather than the less predictable outcomes of applied research, which at least occasionally go off on tangents.

One category of applied research has a different twist. An R & D department may develop a store of background knowledge about a phenomenon it often confronts. Then, as specific problems are faced, the research findings expedite solutions. For instance, the design engineers in a relatively small company making automatic materials-handling systems frequently needed to know how different materials (flour, paint, pigment, fertilizer, and cement) flowed; any tendency to lump, dust, or bridge required special design modifications. A research project on all factors affecting the way materials in general flow created a bank of information that enabled the engineers to give company customers distinctive advice on materials handling. The desirability of such applied research depends, of course, on the kind of service a company seeks to provide. One oil company may study the behavior of lubricants in Arctic temperatures, whereas an oil company selling only to Midwest customers would not bother. For the research scientist, this may seem like a narrow distinction.

## Offensive Versus Defensive R & D

The amount of research on a given subject depends, in part, on the R & D department's emphasis on being a leader or a follower.

### First with the Best

If company strategy endorses a strong leadership position in any industry where technological change is a significant factor, an aggressive R & D program is essential. Money, time, and executive effort must be devoted toward this end.

Maxwell House Coffee, the largest division of General Foods Corporation, illustrates the price of such leadership. Having won a preeminent position in the U.S. coffee market by pioneering instant coffee, the division might have concentrated on maximizing short-run profits. Instead, the basic strategy was to retain this strong position over the long run, and this required product leadership. Consequently, Maxwell House retained a large research effort on ways to improve its product—notably, to capture the aroma of freshly ground coffee. The freeze-dry method of making instant coffee was finally perfected in the laboratory, and, despite the company's existing market leadership, additional millions of dollars were spent on tooling up and introducing this new type of coffee to the consumer. Incidentally, Nestlé developed a freeze-dried coffee about the same time, and if Maxwell House had not engaged in "offensive R & D" during the preceding 10 years, Nestlé probably would have captured a large piece of the Maxwell House business.

The fact that a company encourages its R & D department to undertake offensive R & D does not, of course, guarantee a dominant position such as Maxwell House gained. RCA, for instance, spent millions of dollars pioneering in video disk technology. It did launch a product in this rapid growth market, but other companies entered with a more versatile system, so the market has always been shared with half a dozen other leading manufacturers. (The RCA researchers clung too long to a technology that was familiar to them.) Also, even a successful R & D effort, to be effective, must be combined with good production and marketing for the investment to pay off. We noted in Chapter 3 that Univac did very well with its offensive program in computer research, but then failed to capitalize on its initial technological advantage.

## Running a Close Second

The price of being first is high. Many firms, especially those which are not giants in their industries, adopt an R & D policy that they hope will enable them to defend themselves against advances made by competitors. The approach has two phases. First, a systematic scanning of the research efforts and results of others is maintained in all fields that could seriously upset present competitive strengths. Such surveillance requires a few people of fine technical perception, but does not require large outlays of money for laboratory and staff. Second, the R & D department needs unusual competence to perform development work; its engineers must be able to move rapidly and be ingenious in devising methods of accomplishing results someone else has demonstrated as possible. The aim is to match competitors' offerings before the delay seriously upsets market positions.

Such a defensive policy has advantages. The most obvious is avoiding long, unproductive expenses for applied research and perhaps basic research. In addition, typically a new product does not work well in all its early applications; these initial problems create customer dissatisfaction, delays, and perhaps makeshift remedies. For instance, despite all the testing, a really new model of an automobile usually develops a series of weak points that require tedious trips back to the shop and perhaps a "recall." If a second-runner can avoid these difficulties, it may rightfully claim that it has the more dependable product. So, for that very large part of innovation that is developed by a series of modifications rather than a dramatic "breakthrough," a defensive R & D policy may not be a serious handicap.

Patents do create difficulties for the department using a defensive R & D policy. Basic patents are the serious ones, because they may cut off an entire new area; for example, Hall's patent on electrolytic reduction of aluminum prevented new entry into the basic aluminum business until the patent expired. Patents for modifications or refinements are less troublesome because often the same effect can be achieved in a slightly different way. In some industries, such as pharmaceuticals and automobiles, cross-licensing of the use of patents is fairly common. Nevertheless, the possibility of a patent block is one of the hazards that must be weighed in considering the defensive approach.

## A Varied Attack

The R & D program does not have to be the same for all product lines. A medium-sized pharmaceutical company, for example, concluded that it could afford applied research only in two fields—tranquilizers and anesthetics. In seven other areas it adopted a defensive policy of follow-the-leader, and for two older product lines it simply continued production of established items with existing facilities, doing no R & D.

In practice, this mixture of defensive and offensive R & D created some internal misunderstandings. The need to select a limited area for concentrated research was understood, although not everyone agreed on the selections made. Confusion sometimes arose when high priority was given to intensive development effort on one of the follow-the-leader lines to catch up with competition: "Why don't they make up their minds whether to stay in that business or not? For six months, all hell breaks loose and then we lapse into our 'do-nothing' policy." The idea that the company was playing *both* an offensive and a defensive game was hard to accept by people who found themselves shifted suddenly from one project to another. But to the R & D managers who wanted to get maximum return from a limited R & D budget, the mixed policy made sense.

## Getting R & D Done by Outsiders

R & D does not have to be done "in house." As with other inputs desired by a company, the R & D results may be acquired from outsiders. This is the familiar "make or buy" issue.

An R & D department may consider the use of outsiders for several reasons. Much R & D work requires a minimum-sized effort to be effective; the minimum "critical mass" usually consists of at least two or three scientists, some laboratory technicians, physical facilities, a flow of information and raw materials, travel money, and overhead services. Also, while an improvement in a product or process may be desired by an industry, the potential use by a single company may be too small to justify the cost of the necessary R & D. Or a company may have a more attractive use for its funds; a quicker cash flow return will then be preferred, particularly by a company in a tight capital position. For any of these reasons, a company may hesitate to back a proposal with its own R & D effort, yet strongly desire the result.

## Buying R & D Effort

Like preparing advertising copy, making a computer analysis, or running a training course, R & D effort can be purchased outside the company.

### Tapping the Expertise of Others

In many fields, good independent research laboratories have been established to do special research for people who lack their own facilities. The Battelle Institute, for instance, did development work on Carlson's Xerox invention. (The patent was subsequently sold to what is now Xerox Corporation.) The staffs of these institutes often include a wider array of specialists than many R & D departments can retain on their permanent staff. Especially when a company only occasionally needs a particular type of R & D work, temporary access to such experts may be of great help.

Universities are a second major place to buy research effort. Occasionally a contract is made with the university itself, but more often individual faculty members are employed to work on projects in their special field of expertise. Pharmaceutical companies, for instance, frequently support the private research work of professors in the biochemistry field. The development of one of the oral contraceptives, to cite a specific instance, was done by university professors on sponsored research projects. Normally when university facilities are used, the results of the research must be made public; the sponsor gains by having the task done and being among the first to know about the results.

### Joint Ventures in R & D

If a project will be of value to several companies or perhaps an entire industry, several companies may join in financing the study. Currently, several studies on the control of pollution are being handled in this fashion. Also, leading U.S. computer firms have set up a joint venture to develop a new generation of chips before the Japanese again grasp the lead. Incidentally, the common practice in the oil industry of several companies sharing the cost of an exploratory well is a variation of this general policy of joint ventures in research. In all these instances, the research cost to a single company is lowered and frequently the quality of research is improved; the disadvantage—which may not be serious—is that the results of the research must be shared.

## Relying on Others to Do Desired R & D

A firm's outlay for R & D can be even further reduced without sacrificing all of the benefits from such effort. This policy need not be passive; the R & D department can actively encourage and assist work in particular directions.

### Pay a License or Royalty Fee

In industries where cross-licensing is an established practice, a company can make known in advance its willingness to enter into such agreements. This knowledge, combined with similar assurances from other firms, may encourage a member of the industry or an outsider to conduct research in desired areas. A medium-sized oil company, for instance, concluded that the research it could afford in refining technology was too small to keep it abreast of its competitors. Instead, it publicly announced its willingness to pay substantial royalties for improved technology developed by others. After two decades of experience, the management feels that it has been at no serious technical disadvantage to competitors and that royalty payments, while high, total considerably less than R & D efforts would have cost to achieve similar results. Obviously, the feasibility of this policy rests upon a prediction that licenses will be available.

### Seek Foreign Licenses or Patents

Technical expertise is a significant item in international trade. U.S. companies receive from foreign countries over $1 billion annually in payment for their technical expertise, patent royalties, and the like. The flow of knowledge into the U.S. is only about a fifth of this size, but it does reflect a potential source of technical ideas.

Often a foreign company lacks the desire or the capital to enter the U.S. market, and it may welcome an opportunity to get some additional return on its technical knowledge and designs. The U.S. company will probably have to take some initiative in working out the agreement, and it must be prepared to do considerable engineering work to adapt the foreign concepts to local conditions (just as is necessary in the reverse flow). Nevertheless, our debt to foreigners for important contributions to products ranging from helicopters to ballpoint pens indicates the potential of this approach.

### Encourage Equipment or Materials Suppliers

In a number of industries, the suppliers rather than the fabricators themselves provide most of the innovation. This is clearly true of the textile industry, where most R & D activity has been carried on by producers of manufactured fibers and by equipment manufacturers.

An R & D department can encourage such external developments. For equipment, the most common practice is to place an order for an experimental model or to agree to pay a rather high price for the first two or three units of a product that meet certain performance specifications. Vast sums are spent by the U.S. government in this fashion, and most of the high-speed railroad equipment has been developed on this basis. The amount of premium a company must pay for newly designed equipment naturally depends upon the size of the market the manufacturer anticipates if the equipment works well. Incidentally, from the equipment manufacturer's viewpoint, it is getting a customer to help underwrite its R & D expense.

### Promote Government Research

The U.S. government spends over $50 billion a year to finance R & D work. Most of this goes to defense and space projects, but the remaining amount is still very large. The pressure for the use of these funds is tremendous, and the allocation is based primarily on potential contribution to public welfare. However, since many companies wish to pioneer in the same directions that the government is promoting, the possibility of having government finance expensive research exists. Improved means to control injurious insects, better urban transportation, use of plankton from the ocean, and less expensive hospital services are merely illustrations of the diversity of government interest in R & D work. A company can actively encourage the government to sponsor research that may make technical contributions of interest to the company.

In conclusion, enough alternatives to in-house research have been mentioned to indicate that a company need not abandon all interest in R & D if it cannot do the work itself. Most of the possibilities for getting others to do desired research involve sharing the results. Nevertheless, when the magnitude or the duration of the necessary effort is beyond the resources of a single company, initiative in getting others to help share the load may bear fruit. Finally, a mixed policy is again possible; a company can do its own R & D in some fields and work with outsiders in others.

## Crucial Horizontal and Vertical Linkages

Managing an R & D department is far from simple. In addition to the technical task of managing R & D projects, more general issues about the scope and direction of research activities have to be resolved by someone. Product versus process targets for improvement, the depth of analysis, offensive or defensive studies, in-house work or outside development—these are recurring issues which we have reviewed to provide a feeling for the strategy problems in managing R & D.

To a surprising extent, the R & D department provides the expert judgment and advice on such matters. The development of technology tends to be a world to itself, with its own "lingo," professional associations, information networks, and even mental processes. Few managers in a business-unit outside the R & D department (and perhaps engineering) have the background needed to forecast what innovations are likely to occur. So the key people in the R & D department provide the main interface with the world of science and technology.

Such reliance on company experts is not unique. Each company has experts on finance, law, accounting, and other subjects, and they, too, predict and advise in their respective fields. But in R & D the technical mystique is especially strong. Consequently, managers within the R & D department exercise a lot of influence in resolving the range of issues just raised, but are often confronted with dogmatic, ill-informed decisions made by their peers.

This uniqueness creates a special need for R & D managers to build links of understanding with their peers—with other department heads and with general managers. For R & D, the triple linkage shown in Figure 6–2 ties together quite diverse ways of viewing the world.

## Relating R & D to the Operations of Other Departments

The output of an R & D department—product designs, production methods, and the like—becomes valuable primarily when it is used by the production department to make better, less expensive products, and when those products help the marketing department serve customers. The bright ideas and tested specifications have to be used. So the links between these departments should be close.

Also, the R & D department needs to understand the availability of resources, especially those that are financial, that it can draw upon.

More specifically, the important horizontal linkages of an R & D department typically include the following:

### Marketing

- Agreement on the kinds of *new products* that probably will appeal to customers in the company's selected niches.
- Agreement on *new features* and options for present products that will give the company a competitive advantage in serving its customers.
- Agreement on *priorities* to be given to the preceding new products and new features which reflect marketing competitive needs, company production capabilities, and the cost, timing, and probability of R & D success in creating such products and features.
- Agreement on the importance of the *exclusive use* of R & D ideas versus sharing their use with other companies.
- Providing forecasts of important *technological developments* in the industry and specific forecasts of technological moves by key competitors that will give them superior products or lower costs.
- Adjusting *product designs* to fit the needs of new types of customers (new market niches), for instance, repairability by unsophisticated users or meeting foreign countries' building codes.

### Production

- Designing *priority products and options* which can be produced relatively easily within quality and cost specifications.
- Designing improved *production processes* that will yield timely, quality output at lower costs than competitors'.
- Assisting in modifying product designs and production processes so that *shorter runs and faster changeovers* will permit flexible production scheduling.

### Purchasing

- Preparing materials and parts *specifications* that will help suppliers fit into a just-in-time purchasing system.
- Developing products and parts that will be feasible for several suppliers to meet, so that *company dependence on a single source is decreased.* This includes ways to bypass patents held by one supplier.
- *Forecasting* changes in suppliers' *technology* that will affect the availability of materials or parts; also, forecasting company changes in its technology, packaging, etc., that will affect make-or-buy decisions and the desirability of long-term supply contracts.

### Human Resources

- Incorporating provisions for *employee safety* (and potential company liability) into production processes.
- Arranging for unusual recruiting, training, and incentive practices that may be necessary to *attract outstanding "scientists."*

### Finance

- Developing *criteria for research projects* that will be financed— especially risky research and research that will have only long-run results.
- Agreeing on a total *annual department budget* that will finance the research and development endorsed by the marketing and production departments.
- Assessing the effect of a high percentage of debt financing on the willingness of the finance department to support high-risk or *delayed payout* research projects.

### Controls

- Relying on *steering controls*, instead of accounting reports, to periodically reassess major R & D programs.

It is very unlikely that negotiations among the departments will produce agreement on all the points listed. Marketing, production, and finance probably will not be in agreement among themselves, and the R & D department can do no more than try to mediate their differences. In addition, the R & D department will have strong opinions of its own, based on its perception of the competitive environment and on its internal capabilities and preferences. Nevertheless, these departments should try to reach agreement where they can and identify points of disagreement. The alternative of expecting business-unit managers (or their staffs) to plan all the interrelationships and to communicate the numerous details is unworkable. At best, under that scheme the communications would be blurred and opportunities for voluntary give-and-take would be lost. Instead, *both* lower level negotiations between departments *and* business-unit level guidance and arbitration will be needed.

## Tying R & D Efforts to Business-Unit Strategy

The importance of R & D in a business-unit strategy can range from "strategic potency" for a pharmaceutical firm to "adequate protection" for a television network. As pointed out in Figure 6–4, the basis on which a company seeks distinction will determine how vital its R & D department will be.

For instance, in the ethical drug division of The Upjohn Company, the development of new drugs is the key to long-run survival. The strategy of the business-unit prescribes the illnesses that the researchers are to study. The general manager of the unit participates actively with the senior scientists in layout paths for research. These guidelines are then sharpened and supported in financial allocations for projects and equipment. If a conflict of opinion arises over, say, the licensing of a company patent or the use of outside research laboratories, central management will clarify company policy. Perhaps most important, central management helps to generate a sense of mission throughout the company about the pioneering service the business aims to provide.

In this example, the "strategic potency" of R & D work is so great and the involvement of central management so frequent, that R & D activity has very limited opportunity to stray from business-unit strategy. The linkage is tight.

By contrast, in a large New York hotel R & D scarcely exists. There is only one person, in the engineering department, who is charged with keeping abreast of unusual new equipment for security, offices, laundries, etc. When something new appears—introduced by outside suppliers or competitors, not by the hotel's own research—the general manager gets a memo. Otherwise, the general manager gives no attention to this activity. Success of the hotel depends primarily on service and promotion, not R & D. There are only occasional ties between monitoring and business-unit strategy; "adequate protection" is good enough.

## R & D in Small Companies

Some small firms make R & D their primary business. For example, Advanced Genetic Sciences, Inc., experiments with genetic changes in plants, looking for ways to increase farm productivity. One controversial project involves genetically altered bacteria that live on leaves of plants; when these bacteria are present, the risk of frost damage is reduced. Because the company is small and has limited capital, the managers are intimately involved in all research and testing. Strategy and major research plans are the same thing.

A majority of small companies, however, lack the risk capital and talent to do much R & D. Instead, they rely on being able to buy or license new ideas that they need. For them, a defensive policy is alertness to new developments in their industry coupled with a willingness to adapt rapidly. Here, again, "adequate protection" is good enough.

In each of the examples just cited, the company picked its domain, usually a niche in a larger industry, and then selected a differential advantage—a way to excel in its niche. These elements of strategy make R & D more, or less, crucial. And once that cruciality has been recognized, the role of R & D in the total company operations can be fitted into a management design of either "strategic potency," "strong support," or "adequate protection," as the case may be.

## Questions for Class Discussion

1. Large companies have been reasonably successful in R & D work that is related to their existing type of business. By contrast, many large companies have not succeeded in sponsoring "new ventures" within the company in fields unlike their own industry. In fact, small independent start-up companies seem to be better able to innovate. How do you explain this poor record of *internal* new ventures (sometimes called "intrapreneurship")?

2. More people in the United States are engaged in service industries than in "production" industries (manufacturing, mining, and agriculture). (a) Do you believe that as many opportunities exist for innovation in services as in "production"? Give illustrations. (b) What does your answer imply regarding the nature and the directions of R & D work in service industries?

3. Four key R & D issues have been discussed in this chapter (see the list on page 238). Do similar policy issues arise with respect to *marketing* research done by a company?

4. (a) Do you think McDonald's, i.e., the fast-food chain, should have an R & D department? (b) If so, should the department focus on (1) products or processes? (2) defensive or offensive research? and (3) basic or applied research? (c) Where would your recommended department fit in the "strategic policy," "strong support," and "adequate protection" classification scheme? (d) What lateral relationships between the R & D department and other departments would be especially important?

5. The Strategic Planning Institute finds in its analysis of the experience of over 1,500 business-units that high R & D spending hurts profitability when the business has a relatively low market share. More specifically, the return on investment (before interest and income taxes) for firms with a high R & D-to-sales ratio is 30 percent if the firm has a high market share; but it drops to 4 percent for firms with a low market share. This drop in return on investment which is associated with market share is much less severe for firms which have a low R & D-to-sales return: 27 percent for high-market-share firms and 17 percent for low-market-share firms. (a) What do you think is the explanation for this impact of R & D spending? (b) What are the implications for R & D policy?

6. A "hot potato" at the United Nations is the transfer of technological know-how. Developing countries criticize advanced countries for holding back technological secrets through patent control and other ways: "The advanced countries make profits from our raw materials, and they sell us manufactured products which we could make ourselves if permitted to." (Claims similar to those of the American colonies against England 200 years ago.) On the other hand, organized labor in advanced countries charges that big business is "ex-

porting jobs" when production processing is transferred to developing countries—to save on transportation, use less expensive labor, or comply with local country regulations. From a company viewpoint, under what circumstances should it permit and train people in less developed countries to use the fruits of its R & D activities? How should the company be compensated?

7. Assume that the U.S. Congress passes two laws encouraging the use of generic drugs (that is, drugs described by technical names that are available to any manufacturer, in contrast to drugs with copyrighted names that are available only to one company). One law requires the holders of a product or process patent to cross-license other drug companies to use the patent for a reasonable fee; the other law prohibits any U.S. agency from paying directly or through reimbursement (e.g., Medicare) an amount above the prevailing generic drug price. The first law encourages the manufacture of generic drugs, and the second law encourages the sale of generic drugs. Now, if you managed a large pharmaceutical company that for years had had a large R & D effort leading to the sale of patented products under copyrighted names, what changes in R & D policy would you make because of the new laws?

8. A U.S. manufacturer of small turbine and jet engines was falling back in the race to sell engines designed for executive and commuter aircraft. Company executives believed that the firm had high-quality engines, but was losing out to the Garrett Corporation because its sales force, its service facilities, its ability to sell on extended credit, and its supply of parts were limited since it did not have the financial strength to fund these needs. The firm sold some engines to Cessna and Beech aircraft companies, one British manufacturer, and a German-French consortium, but prospects abroad were not good in the future, even in Europe. The company has been approached by one of the huge Japanese manufacturing and financial conglomerates with an offer to buy its unissued stock. The offer will give the Japanese firm ownership of 35 percent of the U.S. company's common stock and will provide all the capital needed for continued engine development work as well as manufacturing and marketing requirements. The Japanese also insist that the U.S. firm license its patents and know-how to a newly formed Japanese company at a royalty rate of 2 percent of the costs of goods manufacturerd. But the Japanese refuse to engage in a joint venture to make engines in Japan, even though they foresee (as does the U.S. company) the rapid development of a Japanese aerospace industry. The U.S. firm prefers to manufacture and ship goods because that is where it creates the value added. But it estimates that the probability of exporting engines to Japan will be very small because import restrictions will prevent such sales. (a) Does the proposal have any advantage for the U.S. firm? Any drawbacks? State what they are. (b) Will the proposal contribute to technological development in the U.S. and Japan? (c) What stages of the processes of technological innovation are involved in the proposed arrangement? (d) As an executive of the U.S. firm, what is your attitude toward the proposal?

9. Consider the companies that dig coal out of the ground and ship it to electric utility companies, steel mills, and other industrial firms. Should these coal-mining companies spend money on the research and development of coal as a source of energy and as a source of carbon-based chemicals? They do not now and have never done so.

The prospects are that coal will become a more and more important source of energy in the United States over the next hundred years. Presently the federal government, through the Bureau of Mines, does some development work on finding ways to mine and burn "clean coal." The problems of air pollution, acid rain, stream pollution, underground explosions, and other accidents are said by the coal-mining companies to be problems of public utility companies and the federal and state governments. Many of the managers of the 3,000 companies which are operating mines in the United States believe that their firms are engaged in a fiercely competitive struggle for customers and sales.

Do you think that there is a role for expenditures on research and development by the coal miners? Should coal companies spend 4 percent of sales on R & D, as do chemical companies? Or 8 percent, like ethical drug companies? Or 0.8 percent, like oil producers? Or 1.8 percent, like metalmining companies? Or 1.2 percent, like forest-product companies? Or 0.5 percent, like steel companies?

10. If you were the CEO of American Airlines, would you have an R & D department? If so, what activities would you expect it to perform with respect to (a) products or processes, (b) basic or applied research, (c) offensive or defensive R & D, and (d) getting research done by outsiders?

11. In terms of having a policy of either strategic potency, strong support, or adequate protection (see Figure 6–4), where would you expect to find the R & D department of (1) a chain of convenience stores like 7-Eleven? (2) a computer software company? (3) a farm equipment manufacturer such as John Deere Company? (4) a large commercial bank such as Bank of America?

# CASE

## 9 Bio Engineering Co.*

Bio Engineering Co. is the child of an exciting new technology—the redesigning of living cells—and the irrepressible vision of a chemical engineer, Hoke Saunders. Following an impressive start and a public issue of common stock, Bio

---

*Names in this case are pseudonyms.

Engineering Co. is currently short of cash. One consequence of this cash squeeze is that outlays for R & D must be scaled back—a difficult task because research is key to the company's future. This case focuses on where the cuts should be made.

For about 15 years Bio Engineering Co. has been a part of the rapidly growing fields of genetic engineering and biotechnology. The company develops machinery and supplies chemicals used in the research laboratories of universities, the National Institutes of Health, other government agencies, and the major pharmaceutical firms of the world. Early in its existence it designed and sold the first machine to make parts of DNA molecules. This piece of machinery is now part of the permanent collection of the Smithsonian Institution in Washington, D.C. Following the success of its "gene machine," the company has developed other machines to produce the fundamental particles of human cells and the long chains of amino acids known as peptides and proteins.

With the market expanding from research laboratories to pilot plants and then to full-scale production of drugs and pharmaceuticals, the company is attempting to adapt its products and manufacturing skills to make and sell large-scale machinery in addition to the machines needed in research laboratories. This requires extensive research and development work by Bio Engineering Co., as well as the reorientation of the entire firm to seek new market niches and groups of customers that will allow Bio Engineering Co. to survive in this rapidly growing field of microbiology.

## The New Era in Molecular Biology

To appreciate the challenge facing Bio Engineering Co., it is necessary to become familiar with the dramatic discoveries recently made in molecular biology.

Living cells, including cells of the human body, are miniature factories containing several parts and various processes of action. One of the most prominent parts is a *gene*, which is a tiny particle within the nucleus of a cell. Genes determine the characteristics that living things inherit from their parents, for example, the shape of a leaf and the sex, height, and hair color of a child. There are thousands of genes in every cell. They are made up principally of *deoxyribonucleic acid* (DNA). Scientists have identified the structure of DNA molecules (the famous double helix) and are now trying to locate each gene and determine its properties by experimenting with the DNA molecule. (See Figure 9-2).

The structures of cells surrounding a nucleus are built mainly of proteins. Some of the proteins, called *enzymes*, speed up chemical reactions throughout the body. They assist in digesting food, producing energy, and building other proteins. A single mammaliaic cell may contain hundreds of enzymes. Hormones are also proteins, as are the antibodies that protect against disease and fight disease germs.

Thus scientists are very curious about proteins, their structure and their function. Proteins are made up of tiny units called *amino acids*, and these amino acids

**FIGURE 9-2.**
**LAYMAN'S VIEW OF THE MAKE-UP OF A LIVING CELL.**

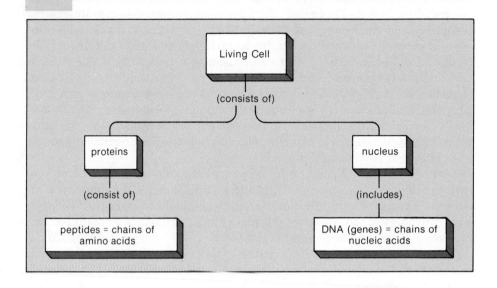

can be joined in long chains to form proteins. DNA contains the blueprints for all of the proteins made in a cell. These instructions designate the order in which the amino acids will be linked together in a line to form proteins.

The intermediate stage between amino acids and proteins is known as a *peptide chain*, or *peptides*. Some peptide chains contain only a few amino acids. G. D. Searle's sweetener, *Nutrasweet*, or *aspartame*, is one of these; it is made up of only two amino acids linked together. Longer peptide chains may contain as many as 100 amino acid links. The number of different peptides—and, thus, different proteins—is practically unlimited. The kinds of proteins actually produced are determined by the DNA in the cell's nucleus.

Bio Engineering Co. enters this emerging scientific field primarily by supplying materials and equipment to the microbiologists who are experimenting with living cells.

The potential applications of biochemistry are awe-inspiring. Relatively near-term applications in agriculture include new strains of plants and animals and various forms of herbicides and insecticides, which can sharply increase the food supply of the world. New vaccines and other pharmaceuticals may be able to combat viruses, cancer, and hereditary diseases. The possibilities are far-reaching.

To date, however, very few commercially feasible products have been marketed. The industry is still limited to research efforts in universities, government supported laboratories, pharmaceutical firms, chemical companies, and the like.

Many small "high tech" businesses have sprung up to serve this research effort. So even though the industry is new and dynamic it is also quite competitive. Companies are seeking niches that will grow rapidly and where they can be distinctive.

Bio Engineering Co. has placed most of its research efforts in four closely related segments that Dr. Saunders believes can be made self-supporting promptly.

### (1) Chemicals Used in Research and Development

Early in the company's life, Dr. Saunders learned that two small firms which supplied specialized chemicals to biological researchers were going out of business. Dr. Saunders seized the opportunity to become a source of hard-to-find materials, and purchased the inventories of both firms. He reasoned that this activity would have two benefits: It would put Bio Engineering Co. in touch with the very people who would be potential customers for other products and services of the company. Fully as important, the resale of this inventory would provide an incoming cash flow that would help support the company while it was developing its own products.

This move makes the company a source of over 250 very specialized compounds including enzyme substrates, amino acid derivatives, and reagents for DNA or peptide synthesis. Of course, for research purposes these chemical compounds are used in small quantities, so the inventory is lasting a long time.

An extension of this material supply activity is for Bio Engineering Co. to sell peptides and DNA fragments that it manufactures on its own equipment. As will be explained in the next few pages, Bio Engineering Co. sells equipment to laboratories so that they can formulate compounds on the spot. However, not all laboratories do have such equipment, and Bio Engineering fills orders for the exact peptide that a laboratory wants. Actually, the volume of this sort of business is not large because researchers who run a whole series of experiments typically buy their own equipment.

Bio Engineering Co. anticipates a related need. After a promising product has been developed in a research laboratory, it has to be tested on a much larger scale. Also, the production technology has to shift from the laboratory bench to a factory-like operation. For this enlarged activity, Bio Engineering Co.'s customers may hesitate to invest in plant and equipment until pilot tests are completed. So, Bio Engineering Co. is thinking of building a facility that can produce various kinds of peptides and DNA particles in much larger volumes. Then the company could take contracts to supply large orders of a particular specification. To prepare for such business, Bio Engineering Co. will have to devote substantial effort developing larger scale, versatile production equipment for its own use.

### (2) Peptide Synthesizing Machines

Bio Engineering Co.'s principal product line to date is equipment that makes peptides. These machines literally construct peptides by chaining together selected amino acids in a specified sequence. The basic process involves the use of small metering equipment, pumps, valves, mixers, filters, and an array of reagents to link molecules of acids together in particular configuration.

Making peptides is a time-consuming and exacting chemical process which diverts the energy of researchers who are primarily interested in experimenting with biological events. So the purpose of peptide synthesizing machines is to carefully control and speed up this chemical process. Such discipline is achieved by assigning supervision to a computer!

The more sophisticated synthesizers (which cost about $80,000 each) have a built-in computer and a convenient storage deck for materials. By inserting a software disk into the computer, and then tapping keys for the desired sequence in the peptide chain an operator can let the machine do the rest of the work. There is also a display panel showing the stage of the process, and if desired a printer can be added to record what took place for each batch.

Bio Engineering Co. is one of three or four companies that make such machines. Competition is keen. With changes occurring frequently in computer technology and in synthesizing technology, all competitors update their equipment every couple of years. Researchers (customers) can get along with quite basic equipment, but like any temperamental professional they much prefer to have the latest model.

Clearly Bio Engineering Co. has to devote some R & D effort to keeping its synthesizers up-to-date. Nevertheless, there is the familiar question of whether to try to be a leader or follower in this race.

### (3) DNA Synthesizers

Bio Engineering Co. also makes machines that create DNA fragments. Such fragments can be used by biologists to reengineer the genetic codes contained in a living cell; and as noted above these DNA codes determine what peptides and proteins the cell will produce. Note that Bio Engineering Co. itself does not do the reengineering in a living cell; rather, it only makes DNA fragments which can be inserted by biologists to modify a cell's "program" in some respect.

DNA fragments used in the reengineering of micro-organisms can be chemically synthesized by the same process as Bio Engineering Co. (and its direct competitors) employs to produce peptides. Consequently, a DNA synthesizer is quite similar to the peptide synthesizer described above. The same technology is built into the machines. And at present the same sort of researchers are potential customers for the machines.

The long-run market for DNA synthesizers, however, differs from that of peptide synthesizers. If, as now seems likely, a reengineered DNA code becomes hereditary, then the modified organism will reproduce itself. Thus, there would be little need for large-scale production such as may be necessary for peptides.

Nevertheless, the likely future effort that will be devoted to reengineering DNA codes is enormous. Undoubtedly the technology will evolve rapidly, and these changes will call for new generations of equipment. Bio Engineering Co. has to decide how extensively it will participate—perhaps pioneer—in these developments, recognizing that two of its competitors are divisions of larger corporations that have much greater financial resources.

### (4) The Butler Peptide

Two years ago Dr. Saunders met Dr. Drayton Butler at a professional meeting and found out that Dr. Butler holds a patent on an exciting peptide. Laboratory tests indicate that this peptide will stop internal bleeding of such ailments as ulcers and tumors.

Recognizing that a pharmaceutical product incorporating this peptide would probably have a large market, Dr. Saunders invited Dr. Butler to join Bio Engineering Co. where he could continue with development work. Extensive tests on mice are needed to assure the effectiveness of the Butler peptide and to look for possible side effects. If the results of these tests are favorable, arrangements will be made with a panel of physicians to test the Butler peptide on humans. The findings from these two sets of tests can then be presented to the FDA (Food and Drug Administration) for permission to place the new product on the market.

Since Bio Engineering Co. is not set up to market pharmaceuticals worldwide, Dr. Saunders plans to license one or more large pharmaceutical firms to make and sell the product as soon as FDA approval is obtained. The Butler peptide project is Bio Engineering Co.'s first strategic thrust into forward integration in the molecular biology industry. As usual, Dr. Saunders is very enthusiastic about this move, and he arranged for the venture capitalist who is backing Bio Engineering Co. to advance $100,000 a month for the animal testing stage.

## Financial Situation

As is common for new ventures emphasizing research and development, Bio Engineering Co. has been operating with a deficit each year throughout its history. During the early years capital was provided by a venture capitalist in New York City. Two years ago when the stockmarket was rising and new ventures were popular, a public sale of common stock added over $8 million of new capital.

Unfortunately, this infusion of capital is disappearing at a rapid rate, as shown in Tables 9–2 and 9–3 on pages 260 and 261. The board of directors is so alarmed that it is insisting that expenditures be sharply curtailed. Among other moves, the directors are asking that outlays for research and development be cut back this year to between $.5 million and $.6 million.

**TABLE 9–1.**
**BIO ENGINEERING CO. FINANCIAL DATA (in thousands)**
**(except per share losses)**

|  | Last year | 2 years ago | 3 years ago | 4 years ago |
|---|---|---|---|---|
| *Profit and Loss* | | | | |
| Net sales | $2,146 | $ 2,664 | $ 2,208 | $ 1,903 |
| Cost of sales | 2,195 | 1,729 | 1,518 | 1,349 |
| Gross profit (loss) | (49) | 935 | 690 | 554 |
| Operating expenses: | | | | |
| Selling, administrative | | | | |
| and general | 2,524 | 1,864 | 1,492 | 1,932 |
| Research and development | 797 | 583 | 377 | 38 |
| Other expenses | 208 | 146 | 162 | 137 |
| Total operating expenses | 3,529 | 2,593 | 2,031 | 2,107 |
| Operating (loss) | (3,578) | (1,658) | (1,341) | (1,553) |
| Non-operating income or | | | | |
| (expenses) | 204 | 244 | (115) | (847) |
| Net (loss) | $(3,374) | $(1,414) | $(1,456) | $(2,400) |
| *Balance Sheet Data* | | | | |
| Current assets | $ 4,228 | $ 7,786 | $ 2,502 | $ 2,448 |
| Current liabilities | 564 | 685 | 844 | 918 |
| Working capital | 3,664 | 7,101 | 1,658 | 1,530 |
| Total assets | 6,467 | 10,031 | 4,937 | 4,866 |
| Long-term debt | 892 | 941 | 1,092 | 7,958 |
| Total liabilities | 1,456 | 1,626 | 1,936 | 8,876 |
| Stockholder equity | | | | |
| (deficit) | 5,011 | 8,405 | 3,001 | (4,010) |
| Shares outstanding | 3,209 | 3,200[a] | 1,800[b] | 1,200 |
| (Loss) per share | $(1.05) | $ (.44) | $ (.81) | $(2.00) |

[a]Two years ago the company sold 1.4 million shares of common stock to the public for a net receipt of $8.3 million.

[b]Three years ago the company converted outstanding loans and preferred stock valued at $8.8 million into 0.6 million shares of common stock.

Bio Engineering Co. is located in an "industrial park" in the southeastern United States and has about 60 employees.

**TABLE 9–2.**
**BIO ENGINEERING CO. FINANCIAL DATA BY CLASS OF PRODUCTS**
**(in thousands)**

|  | Instruments | Biochemicals | Corporate | Total |
|---|---|---|---|---|
| *Last year* | | | | |
| Sales | $   892 | $  1,250 | $   ---- | $  2,146 |
| Operating income (loss) | 263 | (312) | (3,529) | (3,578) |
| Identifiable assets | 672 | 1,100 | 4,695 | 6,467 |
| Depreciation expense | 29 | 155 | 95 | 279 |
| Capital expenditures | 86 | 133 | 54 | 273 |
| *Two years ago* | | | | |
| Sales | 1,712 | 952 | ---- | 2,664 |
| Operating income (loss) | 833 | 702 | (2,593) | (1,658) |
| Identifiable assets | 616 | 2,456 | 6,959 | 10,031 |
| Depreciation expense | 26 | 133 | 113 | 272 |
| Capital expenditures | 6 | 126 | 85 | 217 |

Write-downs of obsolete inventory were charged against operating income as follows: last year $300 against instruments, and $650 against biochemicals; two years ago $65 against instruments and $155 against biochemicals.

## Question

What strategy program do you recommend for research and development in Bio Engineering Co. for the next two or three years?

# CHAPTER 10

## Strategy Programs in Production

Somehow, someplace, the goods and services that a company sells must be obtained. Basically, this involves a *process of converting* labor, materials, etc., into the particular combination of qualities that a selected group of customers wants. The production department shapes and manages most of that vital conversion process.

In most businesses, the production department is the big boy on the block. Indeed, in manufacturing and in many service industries such as airlines, insurance, and education, the "production" department has more employees and more physical facilities than any other department. So the effectiveness of the production department is crucial to company success because it both controls the output of the conversion process and uses up a large portion of the company's inputs (the labor, material, etc.).

The strategy program of a production department is complex, integrating a diverse set of considerations. To simplify the discussion, we will deal primarily with manufacturing (the conversion of physical products). However, a comparable set of problems arises in the creation of intangible services. Banks, brokerage houses, consulting firms, and retail stores, for instance, face issues of capacity, technology, and make-or-buy that are just as vital as production problems in a factory. With relatively minor adjustments, the points raised can be applied to intangible as well as tangible "production."

Note also that the creation of *new* products and processes has already been considered in the previous chapter, but the strategy problems facing purchasing and production are so intertwined that Chapters 10 and 11 are best studied as a single unit.

Like other departments, production departments have their own scenarios for excellence. Among the issues of concern to production managers which also have profound effects on the destiny of virtually every firm are (1) the search for a differential advantage, (2) make-or-buy decisions, i.e., vertical integration, (3) choice of technology, and (4) capacity for growth. In addition to these issues, discussed in this chapter, the logistics of supply for both production and purchasing will be considered in the next.

### Creating a Differential Advantage

While the basic function of a production department is clear, viz., to manage the conversion process, the goals sought need to be much sharper. Just what do the production people wish to achieve?

Improvement is urgent. Major inroads of foreign imports into U.S. markets in automobiles, shoes, television, steel, and other products which U.S. producers previously dominated, along with staggering trade deficits, show that domestic companies are slipping in their relative production capabilities.

For strategy purposes, production departments have to find a way to secure a *differential advantage*. This search for differential advantage can be illustrated by two contrasting strategies: low cost, high volume; and variety plus timeliness.

## Low Cost, High Volume

For years the foremost approach to production in the United States was mass production. The country rose as an industrial power largely on its ability to produce large quantities at low cost.

### Economies of Scale

Producing large volumes of the same product creates opportunities to lower the cost per unit in several ways. Special-purpose machinery becomes practical when volume is high. Detailed industrial engineering studies (motion studies, direct flow layouts, standardized parts and communication, and the like) are warranted. Often the cost of equipment rises more slowly than its capacity, as is evident in oil refineries, ocean tankers, or a movie theater. And quantity discounts on purchases of materials may be available. Experience has shown that limits on "bigger is better" do exist, and many companies operate below the volume they are in fact capable of attaining.

### Low Cost, Mass Markets

Economies of scale can be utilized if a company can reach a large number of consumers who want a standardized product. The classic U.S. formula is to lower the price while advertising the product, so as to move production into the low-cost range. Henry Ford set the pattern with a low-priced automobile. Today we have all sorts of home appliances, prepared foods, and numerous other products that are commonplace because the high-volume, low-cost production approach has succeeded.

### Learning Curve

Further support for selecting a high-volume, low-cost approach to production comes from the learning curve concept. Evidence from aircraft production that the cost of producing each plane drops sharply as the assembly crew learns how to deal with a new set of specifications has been duplicated in many other settings. As the total number of units produced rises, costs per unit usually decline.

The Boston Consulting Group (BCG) linked this observation with the importance of a large market share. Since the company with the largest market share for a particular product will in general have the largest cumulative experience in producing that product, its costs will be lower than those of competitors (assuming that it takes full advantage of its experience).

### Competition from Foreign Imports

During the last 10 or 15 years, the cost benefits arising from a large volume have been inadequate to protect U.S. producers from foreign competition. Low labor costs combined with modern equipment have enabled foreign producers, mostly in developing countries, to undercut the prices of U.S. companies. In many lines this pressure has become so strong that U.S. firms are establishing branch plants or contracting with companies in these low-cost countries.

Japan poses an even stronger challenge. Japanese firms have learned to produce automobiles, cameras, electronic equipment, and other sophisticated products with more dependable quality than comparable domestic producers. Furthermore, their coordinated and persistent efforts to improve productivity often give them a differential advantage in processing costs. Significantly, the Japanese have found that insistence on high quality at all stages of production actually reduces processing costs, so the quality product is also a relatively low-cost product.

As a result of this increasing attack on the large-volume, low-cost markets— not to mention the often stodgy performances by U.S. producers—the large-volume, low-cost approach to production is out of fashion in many industries. In fact, the stronger and more vigorous U.S. companies are taking rigorous steps to get their costs down to competitive levels. In many areas the United States has rich human and natural resources, so it is too early to write off domestic mass production. Nevertheless, the presumption that a production department can secure a differential advantage via large-volume, low-cost output must now be carefully examined.

## Variety Plus Timeliness

A quite different way for a production department to create a differential advantage is to use computers and related equipment to make production much more responsive to variations in product demand. Computer enthusiasts describe a factory of the future that can adjust to individual customer preferences very quickly.

### Variety Within Limits

A plant making electric transformers or dresses, to cite two well-publicized examples, can be built to turn out varied products rather than long runs of a single product. Two kinds of devices are required to obtain this variety: automation and computer controls. The machines automatically feed in raw material; cut, shape, or otherwise process it; and pass it along to the next machine. Moreover, the particular dimensions, color, or finish can be varied easily to "customize" each item if so desired. On the automated machine, the setup time for a different size or color is much faster than if it were done manually, and once set the output is predictable and dependable.

The automated machine is instructed by a computer which is programmed to respond to the specifications on each customer's order. Because the per-unit cost of short production runs is not much higher than that of long production runs, inventories of finished goods can be kept low. Indeed, inventories of slow-moving repair parts may be eliminated and a part made quickly when ordered.

Keep in mind, however, that the variety produced in this factory of the future relates to variations of standard features: an automated dress plant is incapable of quickly switching to overcoats.

### Time Cycles

As mentioned, fast response time is an important feature of the factory of the future. Customers get their customized product quickly. This becomes possible because of (1) rapid and precise communication of the customers' wants (as shown by what is selling in retail shops or by specifications stipulated by a customer) from the field to the plant, (2) processing of this data by computers to develop production schedules, (3) prompt production because of the capability of handling short runs, and (4) preprinted shipping instructions prepared simultaneously with production and scheduling. Of course, such fast response assumes that the entire system is well understood and stable.

Proponents of a production process that stresses variety and timeliness say that the markets for many products are becoming fragmented—that mass consumption of standardized products is being replaced by a diversity of tastes and specialized niches. Consequently, production capability of the sort just described will be a strong differential advantage. The crucial question, however, is not whether customers would like variety, but how much premium they are willing to pay for it. Markets vary, and scattered evidence now available suggests that middle income customers will often pay a small premium—up to, say, 25 percent—but not a large one. So the challenge is to achieve variety and promptness at a cost that is not too far removed from the cost of large-volume production.

## Other Possibilities for Differential Advantage

Large volume, low cost and variety plus timeliness via the factory of the future are only two of the options that a production department might pursue. There are many variations in between, as Figure 10–1 indicates. For instance, a common practice in housing and in machine tools is to standardize parts or "modules" and restrict variety to combinations of these mass-produced modules. Perhaps some of the modules will be purchased from an outside supplier who achieves low cost by serving several producers of the completed product. Or, a large multinational corporation may have a focused plant in one country that produces just part of a total line for sale in many markets.

In exploring different ways to create a differential advantage in production, three basic issues are almost always present: whether to make or buy the component, what technology to rely on, and what capacity is most appropriate to suit an-

**FIGURE 10-1.**
**MATCHING PRODUCTION TECHNOLOGY WITH PRODUCT CHARACTERISTICS**

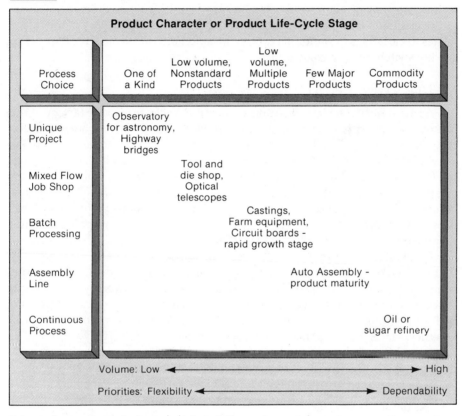

ticipated growth and change. A brief discussion of these issues will provide a better understanding of a production manager's approach to business strategy.

## Make or Buy: Vertical Integration

Should we manufacture what we sell, or should we buy it? If we manufacture, should we just assemble purchased parts or should we make the parts? Should we make or buy raw materials for the parts? Should we produce the supplies needed to make the raw materials? These are questions of vertical integration. Every firm faces them, and for many firms a sound answer is the key to long-run success.

## Vertical Integration in the Aircraft Industry

The problem of whether to make or buy products is well illustrated in the aircraft industry. Clearly, Boeing will design and assemble its planes. Just as clearly, it will buy engines and navigation equipment from suppliers who specialize in those products. In between is a whole array of landing gear, subassemblies, galleys, and other equipment which Boeing could manufacture itself but typically does not. In fact, to simplify its production tasks and to draw on the most advanced ideas of suppliers, 70 percent of Boeing's material costs is likely to be outside purchases.

The Air Force, to move back one step, buys all its planes. However, the Air Force does have its own designers and testing capabilities, so it plays a more active role in overall design than, say, Boeing does in engine design. In this way, the Air Force promotes competition among suppliers and retains a high degree of flexibility in what and when it will buy.

## Combining Publishing, Printing, and Papermaking

The sharp differences in vertical integration in the publishing field throw more light on the issue. Most book publishers do not print or bind their products themselves. Their printing needs fluctuate in volume; one week they may have six printers working for them and the next week none at all. Also, being free to get printing done anywhere gives them greater flexibility in the design of their books. On the other hand, contract printing is expensive. The former president of the company publishing this book, for example, often said as he passed the plant that did most of his printing, "My business made the owner of that company wealthy. But I have enough worries already."

In contrast to book publishing, larger newspapers always do their own composing and printing. Probably this saves them money. The dominant consideration, however, is the need for very close coordination—literally down to a few minutes—between writing copy, setting it in type, proofreading, headlining, laying out the page, and printing. And when a hot story breaks, much of the work may be redone in an hour or two. Such fast coordination can best be supervised by a single management.

Also, newspapers own paper mills and timberlands. The big papers and the chains have a large, fairly steady need of a single product. Production economies are a natural result. To be sure, these same economies might be obtained by an independent supplier under a long-term contract, but some risk would remain for both the newsprint producer and the newspaper. So at least those papers that predict a long-term rise in newsprint prices and that have capital for investment try to reduce supply risks by integrating clear back to the forest.

## To Farm or Not to Farm

Still unsettled is the extent to which frozen food companies should raise their own vegetables and fruits. Several orange juice firms, for instance, raise most of the oranges that they use. Most firms, however, rely on local independent farmers. Farmers tilling their own land conform to the centuries-old cultural pattern;

and reliance on independent growers presumes that the resourceful, close supervision of farmers over their crops will be more effective than hired management. But the frozen food packers must be assured of a supply of quality produce suitable for freezing. So they sign annual contracts with farmers well in advance of planting, provide selected seed, and offer advice. We see here, not vertical integration in the usual sense, but an arrangement with supply sources that accomplishes several of its benefits.

For poultry, however, the advent of "factories" which often process a million birds a season has led to substantial vertical integration, including genetic design, chick production, scientific feeding, and automated processing. Only the actual rearing of the birds is contracted out.

## Key Factors in Vertical Integration

The examples just discussed show that a variety of factors may influence a decision on when to integrate. Among the many possible considerations, the following are likely to be key ones.

### Possible Benefits Resulting from Coordination

If a company manufactures the products or the materials it needs, promptness of delivery and adjustment to emergencies may be easier to achieve. When the parts have to fit together into a complex balance, engineering may be more easily coordinated. Also, unusual quality requirements may be easier to meet. A production department knowing its own needs and being assured of continued use of equipment may develop more specialized machinery than is feasible for an outside supplier. Also, the company avoids the selling expenses of an outside vendor.

### Lower Supply Risks

If there is reason to doubt that raw materials will be readily available, then a production department may want its own sources as a means of protection. For example, virtually all the basic metal processors mine their own ore, and the leading oil companies want a controlled supply of at least part of their crude oil requirements.

### Barriers to Mobility

Company mobility within the supplying industry affects the attractiveness of entering it, as we saw in Chapter 2. If the industry is easy to enter, its products should be readily available (or new suppliers could be encouraged); then, the incentive for a consuming company to integrate into that industry would be low. Contrarily, high entry barriers and a few dominant suppliers in an industry might create conditions where the consuming company would try to get out from under the power of those suppliers by supplying itself.

Exit barriers would become important if a department wished to abandon its integration—for example, Time, Inc., selling off its paper mills. High exit barriers would tend to delay such a switch, whereas low exit barriers would make withdrawal easy. Obviously, the ease or difficulty of exit affects the potential inflexibility associated with vertical integration.

### Flexibility

Vertical integration tends to limit flexibility in product design. Heavy investment in plant or raw material sources hampers the shift to completely new designs or materials, whereas the organization that buys its requirements is not so concerned with making a large investment obsolete.

In the short run, too, the nonintegrated firm may cut down its purchases or shift to another supplier, whereas the integrated firm must recognize the effect of such action on unabsorbed overhead. To guard against such a stultifying effect, General Motors has a long-standing policy that none of its divisions is required to buy from another division if the profit or the long-run development of the first division would suffer from doing so.

### Volume Required for Economic Production

Many small companies simply cannot consider backward integration because the volume of their requirements for any one part or material is too small to keep an efficient plant busy. Also, the requirements may be so irregular that a plant (like a college football stadium) would be kept busy only part of a year. Occasionally a company builds a plant larger than needed for its own use and then sells the balance of the output to other users. Such an arrangement, however, diverts both financial resources and managerial attention from the major activity of the firm.

### Financial Status of the Company

Many firms have only enough capital to operate their principal line of business and may not be in a position to acquire new capital even under favorable conditions. This precludes substantial investments in manufacturing facilities for the production of parts or raw materials. On the other hand, financially strong companies may undertake vertical expansion because their suppliers are financially weak. In such circumstances, the added financial strength may permit substantial improvements in the manufacturing operation.

### Capacity of Management to Supervise Additional Activities

In a great many instances, a decision to produce products that formerly were purchased means that the executives of the company are undertaking activities of a distinctly different nature from those with which they are familiar. While they can employ an executive from that industry, central management cannot escape giving some attention to the new undertaking and bearing responsibility for making final decisions regarding it. Sometimes central management becomes so absorbed in directing the new activity that it fails to give adequate guidance to the older part of the business where it has demonstrated competence.

### General Conclusion

Make-or-buy decisions affect the underlying character of a company. The bulk of the firm's financial assets and other resources either may be entirely committed to production or, at the other extreme, may be minimized as much as possible. In addition to the net balance of the factors just listed, this choice depends on an assessment of key factors for success in the industry, as discussed in Chapter 2. It is a fundamental strategy choice.

In practice, the choice is not a single decision; rather, it is a whole cluster. There is a question of *breadth*—what range of activities will be done in-house; of *depth*—how far back in the chain of production will in-house production go; of *degree*—what percentage of total needs will be covered; and of *form*—how will goods and services acquired outside be managed: wholly owned, as a joint venture, as a long-term contract, as open market purchases, or by some other arrangement.

Answers to these questions will, of course, define the scope of further issues regarding production, such as the technology to be used and overall capacity, considered in the rest of this chapter, and the scope of purchasing, considered in the next chapter.

## Choice of Technology

In the production of many products, the manager has no choice regarding the process to be used. For instance, a company that manufactures wallboard, using sugar cane fiber as its primary raw material, need be in no quandary about the process to be employed in removing the small quantity of sugar remaining in the cane after it passes through a sugar mill. The only commercially practical method is fermentation. By allowing the sugar to ferment, it can be almost completely removed and the remaining fibers are then in a light and workable state.

Not all manufacturers can solve their production process problems as readily as the wallboard company, however. For instance, a company that makes steel must decide upon the extent to which it will use electric furnaces, open-hearth furnaces, or oxygen inverters. Stemming from such basic decisions will come a whole array of plans for equipment, personnel, methods, and organization.

Technology is not confined to physical processes. Universities, engineering firms, and mental hospitals, to mention only a sample, face similar choices. A management consulting firm, for instance, either can design standard solutions (real-time inventory control, sales compensation plans, budget procedures, and the like) and adapt them to each client, or it can make a fresh analysis of each situation with no preconceived ideas about the solution. The choice here does not involve a large investment in facilities, but it does affect personnel, organization, sales appeals, and other facets of the business.

A recurring issue of "production technology" in a business school revolves around the use of cases versus lecture and discussion. And in elementary education the busing of white children to black neighborhoods and vice versa is even more controversial. These examples suggest that when output and processes become more human and less physical, the choice of technology has a lot of subjective value overtones.

A technology may be new and dramatic, as the splicing of DNA instructions in a living cell, but a manager's choice of a conversion technology should be based upon the specific circumstances that a company faces. From a strategy viewpoint, the technology should (a) give the company an advantage in its selected domain, (b) match the availability of necessary resources, and (c) position the company to move into new opportunities.

## Technological Advantage Within a Selected Domain

Overnight mail delivery was only a dream for Federal Express until the technology of flying numerous planes in and out of a single airport (Memphis) each night was perfected. It is a technology uniquely suited to the selected domain.

When U.S. auto firms finally realized that motorists really wanted dependable quality, they faced a technological challenge to come as close to "zero defects" as do the Japanese producers. This requires process changes all along the line, as Figure 10-2, based on a list compiled by Professor Martin Starr, indicates. Developing a dependable quality advantage relative to competitors calls for a whole series of interrelated steps. Fortunately, insisting on "zero defects" from start to finish also reduces costs due to less scrap, lower in-process inventory, better machine utilization, less reworking, and better morale.

**FIGURE 10-2.**
**SECURING A TECHNOLOGICAL ADVANTAGE FROM QUALITY PRODUCTION**

---

**WAYS TO ACHIEVE DEPENDABLE QUALITY OF MANUFACTURED PRODUCTS**

Design parts for quality and for ease in producing that quality

Insist that purchased and produced parts have zero defects

Use automated in-process inspection, with statistical quality control over variation in output

Produce quality items in the first place rather than inspect out defectives

Build multifunctional awareness of the quality program

Encourage worker participation in suggestions for quality improvement

A selected domain may be so price competitive that any company staying in that business must seek a cost advantage by large-volume mass production. Thus, in the mid-eighties, when General Electric Company decided to continue producing large electric appliances (refrigerators, freezers, washing machines, dishwashers, ranges, and the like), a qualification on the decision was that a design and production technology could be developed which would make General Electric the low-cost producer in each niche. In fact, General Electric has spent over a billion dollars redesigning these appliances and retooling its plants to gain this differential advantage. For most of the appliances, General Electric is among the largest three producers, so it does have a volume of production that can benefit from high automation and other features of a factory of the future.

Incidentally, General Electric decided to sell its *small* electric appliance business primarily because it did not foresee a relative technological advantage in producing small appliances. Rather, these are more easily imported, so the competition would have been with foreign as well as domestic suppliers.

Obtaining a technological advantage from a high volume of production is not easy, as the General Electric example just cited suggests. The findings of the Strategic Management Institute in this regard are shown in Figure 10–3. This experience of over 1,500 business-units indicates that high investment does not necessarily lead to profits. Further analysis of these data by the Strategic Planning Institute suggests that mechanization usually does lower costs, as expected, but that the associated high fixed overhead creates such strong pressure to obtain volume that the savings are passed on to consumers in the form of lower prices. The competitive pressure to lower prices and obtain volume is especially severe for firms having low market share.

A related consideration affecting the selection of a technology to secure a competitive advantage is the business' location in its product life cycle (see Figure 2–2). During the introduction and growth stages, producing a product that works and meeting rising demand usually are more important than achieving low cost. Consequently, a flexible technology is desirable. During maturity, low costs become critical. Finally, when a business is on the decline, a large investment in an improved technology, such as a factory of the future, may be imprudent because most companies wish to be in a position to withdraw from the industry without heavy write-offs on abandoned capital assets.

## Technology Matched to Resource Strengths

The wise choice of technology depends not only on competitive conditions in the product market; the availability of company resources to serve particular technologies may also be important. Perhaps the company has better access to raw materials than do competitors, or it might be able to get low-cost labor. Or, the company may lack some resource, so it searches for a technology that calls for a minimum quantity of that resource.

**FIGURE 10–3.**
**RELATION OF DEGREE OF MECHANIZATION TO RETURN ON**
**INVESTMENT OF TYPICAL COMPANY**
**(Bars on chart within each degree of mechanization show, in addition, the**
**influence of company's market share)**

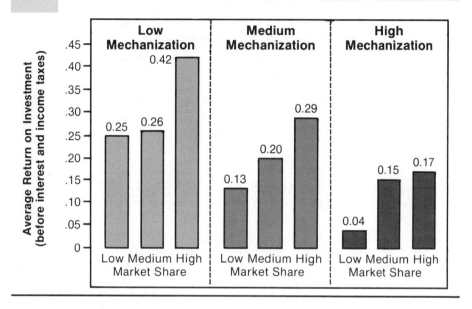

*Source:* Strategic Planning Institute.

A leading midwest bank, for example, wished to sharply expand its network of personal depositors; it was looking forward to interstate expansion as soon as the laws would permit it. One technology for attracting such "retail" customers is widespread automatic teller machines (ATMs), which, in effect, give 24-hour service. However, ATMs are expensive, and a network on the scale that the bank was contemplating would involve a large investment. Unfortunately, this bank—along with several other leading banks—had recently suffered large losses on loans to Latin American countries and was being pressed by regulatory authorities to build up its capital resources. The net result was that the bank dropped consideration of the ATMs, at least until it was in better financial condition. Meanwhile, it is exploring other technologies that are less capital intensive.

The resource position of a small producer of end tables and coffee tables had quite a different impact. The sales of this firm are large enough to support considerably more mechanization than is currently being used, especially in finishing operations. Among the potential benefits would be faster production of rush orders and a corresponding reduction in finished goods inventory. But one of the main strengths of the firm is its access to a plentiful supply of labor. It is located close to the Mexican border, and there is a continuing flow of immigrants—legal or otherwise—seeking work. Managers in the firm are skilled in training and utilizing such labor. Mechanizing production would just reduce the use that is made of this particular strength. So, since neither the workers nor the managers would have a differential advantage in running a mechanized plant, the company intends to stay with its present technology.

Resource strengths take time to develop, time often measured in years. New machinery can be purchased, but someone has to learn to use it, and more tedious is the adjustment of other operations to take full advantage of the new capability. Japan took a full generation to build its capacity for quality production. And part of the strength of the Japanese is a habit to keep on looking for further sources of improvement. Much of their gain has come through a succession of small incremental adjustments. Because resource strengths usually grow slowly, companies cannot shift in and out of a technology very often.

## Technology That Positions a Company to Grasp New Opportunities

A third type of consideration in selecting a production technology is that, at least ideally, the technology should build skills that will give the company a lead in meeting new challenges—opportunities that are uncertain and can be seen only dimly now. If knowing how to deal with the People's Republic of China, or experience with a computerized management information system, is going to be a differential advantage in dealing with some opportunity 5 or 10 years hence, then department managers may select a present technology that builds such strength.

One company that makes parts for computers, for instance, has to meet exacting dimension tolerances for miniature equipment. Critical features in the technology are the stamping dies. To make these dies, the company has invested in state-of-the-art CAD (computer aided design)/CAM (computer aided manufacture) equipment. This CAD/CAM equipment is more elaborate than is necessary for current die-making. However, the company predicts that the trend toward miniaturization will continue, and a capability of making dies and hence parts with very fine tolerances will probably be in high demand in the future. Just what these parts will be is unknown now, but it is assumed that the specialized die-making skill will be a differential advantage.

Such strategic positioning can take various forms. A company that provides replacement parts for automobiles has gone to considerable expense to build a national network of plants and distribution centers. The national coverage is unusual for its kind of product and involves an expensive inventory control and production scheduling system. A significant part of the justification for the national setup is that its existence may become a distinct asset in providing other replacement parts in the future.

## Capacity for Growth

Too little or too much capacity is a recurring issue for a production manager. Company sales rise or fall, plants become obsolete relative to competitors', and new strategic thrusts make unexpected demands for a different product mix. The world of production just does not stay still!

Having the correct production capacity is important. Too little will stifle growth; an excess may bankrupt the company. As already noted, a large part of company assets is often tied up in production facilities, and the carrying costs are large. Also, efficient capacity takes time to develop, but once in place, it tends to persist with limited flexibility. Consequently, decisions should anticipate long-run requirements with considerable accuracy.

The following typical capacity issues illustrate how business-unit strategy can be aided, hurt, and, in general, shaped by output capability.

## Peak Versus Normal Load

Cyclical, seasonal, daily, and even hourly fluctuations in volume of business raise a question of providing capacity to meet peak demands versus normal or average demand. Electric utilities invest millions of dollars so that consumers can receive current with the flip of a switch anytime, including during summer peak loads when air conditioners are running full blast at four o'clock on a hot afternoon.

Most companies let customers bear part of the peak burden, as is obvious when we try to ride a public bus at rush hours or find a hotel room in New Orleans during Mardi Gras. The trade-off is between delay and inconvenience to some percentage of the customers and the cost of providing the increment of capacity to meet the peak.

Other means of meeting peaks in demand will, of course, be considered also:

1. Manufacturers of standard, durable products may produce stock during slack periods. This arrangement is explored in the next chapter.
2. Overtime work may be feasible for operations not already run 24 hours a day.
3. Obsolete or high-cost equipment may be maintained on a standby basis and placed in service just during the peak.
4. Some of the work may be subcontracted, although this is often difficult because potential subcontractors are likely to be busy during the same peak period.
5. Off-peak discounts, "mail early" campaigns, and other measures may be used to induce customers to avoid peak periods. These devices involve extra expense and may be more or less satisfactory to customers.

## Minimum Economic Size

For some operations, there is a minimum size that is economically, and perhaps technologically, feasible. Drilling an offshore oil well in the North Sea, for example, can be done only in multimillion dollar bites. Similarly, a cable television franchise must have thousands of subscribers to break even. And a wind tunnel to test airplane shapes is a very expensive design instrument, and it cannot be cut in half.

Such characteristics place lower limits on the size of production units. And, as noted in Figure 2–3, these minimum size features become barriers to entry into particular businesses.

In some industries, production managers may be able to sidestep these technological requirements for large-scale operations. If a practical option to make or buy exists, the manager may buy only part of the output of an economical unit from a specialized supplier. Or a joint venture may be formed (see Chapter 17), as is becoming increasingly common in mining operations.

After these minimum economic size limits have been met, the production manager has to decide how much more capacity to develop.

## "Backward Taper" of Capacity

Vertically integrated companies may deliberately follow a plan of "backward taper" of capacity. Such firms normally perform final operations on all their finished products, but they manufacture only parts of their material requirements. Thus, a tire manufacturer may have its own textile mill in the south to weave tire fabric. This mill will probably have the capacity to supply only the minimum needs of the tire manufacturer. Additional fabric for peak requirements will be purchased from outside concerns. Such an arrangement has the obvious advantage of keeping the units in the earlier stages of production operating near their productive capacity. The feasibility of this policy depends on the presence of potential suppliers who are willing to supply fluctuating amounts of material.

## Provision for Future Demand

Because of the long lead time necessary to develop productive capacity, companies normally try to anticipate their growth and build for these future needs. Of course, business-unit strategy is the guiding premise in deciding how much and what kind of capacity will be needed in the future. Nevertheless, uncertainty surrounds all strategy, and considerable judgment is involved in deciding the pace of expansion.

Expansion can be too slow, as several U.S. telephone companies discovered. It takes four to six years for a telephone company to acquire central exchange equipment, build transmission lines, train people, and do the myriad of other things necessary for a major expansion in known services—let alone new types of services. In both New York City and Los Angeles, growth in demand was underestimated and the capacity was unavailable when subscribers wanted it. This caused serious waiting for new phones, an overload on existing facilities, a rise in poor connections and related trouble, along with strong resentment among users. Such a situation was especially disappointing to the telephone companies, which for years had gone to great lengths to provide good service. If the customers had had an alternative supplier, the existing companies would undoubtedly have permanently lost a significant part of their patronage.

Overexpansion can also be devastating. Worldwide, the petroleum industry has so much capacity that new crude oil drilling is less than 20 percent of what it was a decade earlier. The paper industry, to cite another example, is going through one of its recurring periods of overexpansion when prices and profits are too low to justify even maintaining present capacity. The exuberance of the computer industry during the mid-eighties carried its capacity far beyond sustainable levels, with a resulting downturn that caused widespread unemployment in Silicon Valley and similar locations. Many individual companies in these industries were so overexpanded that they could not survive the downturn.

Overexpansion by a company may reflect simply a misjudgment about future demand. In other situations, managers may be dubious about sustained rapid growth but go ahead with capacity expansion in order to protect their market position. The gravity concerning overcapacity is not only the extra expense of unused facilities: as mentioned earlier, pressure to use the facilities to recover even a small part of the fixed costs drives both prices and profits down. And, as Professor Michael Porter observes, the more durable the facilities, the longer the overcapacity pressure persists.

Capacity for growth, then, is a risky and high-stake game. Nonetheless, if a business-unit strategy calls for growth, it is a game that neither the business-unit manager nor the production manager can avoid.

## Modernizing Facilities

A related issue that haunts production managers is whether to modernize old facilities. The U.S. steel industry is an example of a condition that is prevalent in our traditional manufacturing. If technological improvements have been made by competitors, then the existing physical capacity of a company may be costly to operate. And this condition makes the company especially vulnerable to declines in market prices.

The obsolescence problem is often compounded by two related factors. The traditional industries tend to be saddled with work rules and wage rates, usually backed by union power, that slow down efforts to modernize the production processes. In addition, current financial practices put so much emphasis on short-run profits and cash flows that financing replacements is difficult. The combined effect is that the old facilities are marginal at best. And while they continue to be operated, they add to the overcapacity pressure.

The major companies in the steel industry are painfully and reluctantly reducing their capacities. Only the "minimills," which rely on reprocessing scrap, are adding capacity in the United States. By contrast, the three U.S. automobile companies are making heroic efforts to modernize their facilities and management practices so that they can compete effectively with foreign sources.

## Using Production to Gain Differential Advantage

The preceding discussion indicates that the role of production in business-unit strategy varies widely. In some circumstances, however, production may be dominant. Because this possibility is often overlooked, we summarize in this section several key ingredients to casting production in a leading role.

The first requirement is a strong belief by general managers and production managers that the company's industry will reward superiority in production capability. Such a conviction comes from (a) a prediction about attractive future technological developments, (b) a recognition of the potential benefits of integrating marketing and engineering decisions with production strategy, and (c) a willingness to undertake long-range programs to acquire capabilities in advance of needs. This attitude contrasts with a feeling that it is better to keep production flexible and reactive to market changes, and that investments should be made only when a fast payback is assured.

The required commitment is evident in the strategies of firms such as Emerson Electric, H.J. Heinz Company, Beaird-Poulan (a manufacturer of chain saws), Lincoln Electric Company, and Chapparal Steel, each of which places primary emphasis on the production-based differential advantage of low cost. Other firms seek a balance of excellence in all their functions, with production having an equal place in establishing a firm's competitive strategy.

If this basic belief in the potential of production exists, then a strategic program including the following three elements should be designed:

1. A production technology that fits the selected domain of the business-unit must be selected.
2. This technology must be refined so that the company's production process creates particular selling benefits attached to the product.
3. Other operating systems must be aligned with the production process so as to reinforce the aims of item 2. Included here are the reward system, the information system, and the planning and control system.

## The Domain-Technology Fit

A company servicing two niches in the copper wire business illustrates the importance of a proper fit of technology with the characteristics of its market. For wire used in communication cable for telephone systems or computer networks, this company uses a batch process. Customer orders vary by thickness, by coating, and by alloy. To provide different combinations of these specifications, drawing, coating, and reeling are performed in different places, with batches of wire moving to machines that can be adjusted for each other.

Magnet wire, in contrast, is a standard commodity used by many customers who make their own motors. It can be manufactured in a continuous process on equipment that operates day after day on the same specifications. So for this item, the company has a separate plant—a "focused factory" with a limited, concise set of products, technology, volume, and markets. Because of this narrow focus, the magnet wire plant has much less overhead than the batch plant and substantially lower costs. Each plant is adapted to its niche.

Of course, both of these plants which are in mature industries differ sharply from plants making optical fiber for telephone cables. Optical fiber (a fine glass thread that transmits laser beams) is in the growth stage of its life cycle, and plants making it are still adjusting to very rapid increase in capacity.

## Refining Technology to Secure Selling Benefits

Within any technology there are many choices which emphasize particular output and cost characteristics. If production is to play a dominant role in business-unit strategy, these special characteristics must be carefully matched with the sales appeals that the target market wants (see Chapter 8).

Crown Cork & Seal Company, for instance, concentrates on selling metal cans to beer and carbonated beverage producers. Here, just-in-time delivery to the bottling plants is vital (only a small supply of the bulky containers can be stored), yet failure to have quality containers will shut down the entire operation. So Crown Cork has adjusted the capacity and location of its production facilities and focused internal operations to assure its customers of can deliveries just when they are needed.

In the space equipment industry, to cite a very different technology, precision and dependability are crucial—as is attested to by sending people into outer space. So a source of differential advantage here is precision on a very small number of products. Or, to turn to the performing arts, polish is a vital characteristic for the production of *Carmen* by the Metropolitan Opera Company.

These important interrelations that must be developed in a superior production process are suggested in Figure 10–4.

## Aligning Production Support Systems

A third requisite for making production a primary source of differential advantage is to tie in the company support systems. The incentives, the measurements, the human resources, and other internal operating systems should all

**FIGURE 10-4.**
**ADAPTING A PRODUCTION PROCESS FOR DIFFERENTIAL**
**ADVANTAGE**

| How Do Products Win Orders in the Marketplace? | Production Process Design | Production Support Systems |
|---|---|---|
| • Price<br><br>• Quality of performance<br><br>• Delivery<br>  speed<br>  reliability<br><br>• Extent of the product line<br><br>• Design leadership<br>  convenience<br>  practicality<br>  ease of repair<br>  attractiveness<br><br>• After-sales service<br><br>• Technical liaison and consultation | • Choice of technology (ies)<br><br>• Cost, quality, speed, and flexibility refinements within the process<br><br>• Design of inventory and logistics system for<br>  materials<br>  in-process inventory<br>  finished goods | • Resource inputs<br><br>• Planning and control<br><br>• Quality control<br><br>• Rewards and incentives<br><br>• Measurements<br>  output<br>  efficiency<br><br>• Organization of work<br>  tasks<br>  interrelationships |

reinforce the selected characteristics of the production process singled out in item 2 in the list on page 2 78. We will consider these support systems in Chapters 13, 14, 19, 21, and 23.

Building a strong, integrated production system takes time. The physical setup, and even more, the social structure, often require years to perfect. Unlike an advertising campaign or a new bond issue, superiority in production requires a persistent commitment for a long period of time. Moreover, the task is never quite finished. As the Japanese are demonstrating, a long series of incremental improvements will probably yield greater results than a conspicuous campaign for only a short period. Long-term belief in and commitment to production are necessary to assure the sustained effort. Fortunately, the inertia that has to be overcome makes it difficult for competitors to catch up once a company has developed a capacity.

## Crucial Horizontal and Vertical Links

In this chapter we have focused on four basic issues that face a production manager: *creating a differential advantage* for the company, *deciding what to make* and what to buy, *choosing a technology* well suited to convert resources into products and services desired by the company's selected domain, and *determining the production capacity* of the department's operations. To reduce the length of the discussion, we have centered on manufacturing businesses, presupposing that production in service and many other types of business will encounter comparable issues.

Resolution of these four basic issues has a powerful impact on the viability of business-unit strategy. Of course, there are numerous other problems facing a production manager and a multitude of technical options which the operating people must consider. But for our purposes of exploring the interplay between business-unit strategy and department strategy programs, a focus on a limited number of basic issues highlights the viewpoints of the two organization levels.

## Sensitive Links Between Production and Other Operating Departments

The production department occupies a distinctive position within a business-unit. Unlike most of the other functional departments, it devotes little of its energies to direct relationships with an outside stakeholder group. It does not have to build continuing cooperative arrangements in a particular market. Instead, the other departments maintain these outside boundaries, and in so doing they enable the production department to concentrate on the core process of converting resources into desired outputs.

Although this internal character of production simplifies life in some respects, it increases the importance of the horizontal links between production and other departments. These all depend upon production, while at the same time production must adjust to their diverse needs. In effect, the horizontal linkages come to a vortex in the production department.

The following links illustrate important horizontal relationships of a production department to other departments in a typical manufacturing firm:

### Marketing

- Providing products and services which match the sales appeals that the marketing department wishes to use, including a *variety* of products, the *speed* of their delivery, and a *cost* which permits competitive pricing.
- Meeting customer expectations regarding *quality*, especially the currently popular "zero defects" and durability.
- Providing *new products* and styles, preferably in advance of competitors, so that the company will receive the benefits of being a market leader.
- Adapting products and services to the particular and changing "needs" of selected *market niches*.

## R & D

- Agreeing on *product designs* and specifications which provide for *ease of production* in addition to being attractive to customers.
- Agreeing on *new production processes* and technologies which will create the output the marketing department promotes with resources available from the purchasing, human resources, and finance departments while also utilizing existing production know-how and management systems.
- Providing *flexibility* to deal with new opportunities and threats promptly, preferably in advance of competitors.

## Purchasing

- Agreeing on make-or-buy decisions, including plans for "backward taper" of capacity and outside coverage of peak demands.
- Participating in logistical planning for inventories.
- Providing materials and parts of dependable quality just in time to meet production plans.

## Human Resources

- Finding ways to accommodate *"enlightened" personnel practices* such as training of minorities, seniority procedures, and other working conditions that aid in attracting a competent work force.
- Developing ways to motivate production managers and other employees to support new strategy programs. This may involve job design and managerial training as well as direct incentives.
- Building consistent, constructive approaches to union relations which will facilitate carrying out strategy changes.

## Finance

- Obtaining investment funds for new facilities for producing the changing products and services needed by the marketing department (perhaps even a factory of the future).
- Financing vertical integration arising out of decisions to make rather than buy parts, materials, or services.
- Financing the modernization of plant, equipment, and practices so as to remain competitive.
- Investing in capacity to meet anticipated future demand.

In negotiating agreements on the wide array of horizontal relationships illustrated in this list, a production manager almost always encounters misfits: the conditions desired by one department are incompatible with the expectations of another department. Perhaps the departments themselves can reach a compromise, but many of the issues involve refinements of business-unit strategy. So the general manager joins in their resolution.

## Linking Production Strategy Programs with Business-Unit Strategy

The head of a production department should be an active participant in formulating business-unit strategy. There is no escape: the feasibility of any marketing program depends on whether the production department can produce the goods and services to be sold to customers. Likewise, a flow of resources and ideas from R & D, purchasing, human resources, and finance will be useful, to a large extent, because they fit the production needs. And it is business-unit strategy—the overriding plan—that provides the central guidelines and rationale for fitting all these activities into unified action.

Companies that overlook this essential role of production often get into trouble. For example, an assumption that the production department can and will produce whatever the company markets recently led to the collapse of several computer companies. Similarly, just a few years ago, stockbrokerage firms were in severe trouble because their "back offices" could not process all the transactions made at the exchanges. Also, the woes of the U.S. smokestack industries are partly due to their past neglect of production efficiency. And it took major inroads of foreign products into U.S. markets to shake the nation out of its complacency.

While the need for active participation is clear, how much dominance production should have in strategy formulation is debatable. Strategic potency, as defined in Figure 6–4, calls for proactive moves which keep competitors running just to keep up, and especially in production such initiative involves substantial investment in state-of-the-art skills. Investing in a computerized factory of the future or in production capacity well ahead of demand are examples. Not many companies are prepared to take such risks.

Instead, the more typical role of a production department is "strong support" for carefully selected strategic thrusts. Here, the department aims to be among the leaders in its niche, reacting promptly to systematic scanning of technological developments. It must have a progressive strategy program, but it is cautious about getting far ahead of the parade. The recent program at Chrysler Motors is a good example. In six years Chrysler cut production man-hours per vehicle from 175 to 102, and it is now the lowest cost producer in the U.S. industry. This was achieved, not by a novel innovation, but by tripling inventory turnover, reducing work stoppages, cutting deficits 42 percent, assigning jobs more flexibly, and adding robots—all difficult but well-recognized techniques. At Chrysler, production is a major contributor to company strategy, but it is not setting the long-run course.

Incidentally, although a production department does not directly encounter competitors in a product, labor, or financial market, its effectiveness *is* compared to its counterparts in other companies. The rivalry and search for differential advantages are definitely present. So when a general manager has to arbitrate priorities among departments (and interpret strategy in doing so), production can also argue its case on the basis of its contribution to competitive distinctiveness. The linkage between production programs and business-unit strategy is aired in such debates, which occur frequently because of the many horizontal relationships of the production department.

## Questions for Class Discussion

1. Integrated petroleum companies have to decide (a) whether they will buy the crude oil they need for their refineries or produce it in their own wells, and (b) if they elect to produce at least some, should the amount be all of their requirements or only a part. On the basis of your impressions of the Mideast oil crisis, U.S. dependency on imported oil, and related phenomena, what answer do you recommend that such a company make to both of these questions?

2. Does a trend toward increasing freedom of trade among nations add to or detract from the attractiveness of vertical integration? Illustrate in terms of a company dealing in (a) shoes, (b) lumber and building materials, and (c) loans to commercial and industrial companies.

3. Midwest State University rarely has the capacity of its facilities in balance. One year it increases its dormitories so that it can admit more students. A couple of years later inadequate classroom space is the basis for a plea to the state legislature for new classroom buildings. When these are in place, the laboratories, library, and even the gym are too small for first-class education. Is this bad planning? Should expansion take place by, say, biannual increments to all types of facilities? Is the concept of tapered capacity applicable to a university?

4. Recently a former RCA plant making TV picture tubes was sold to a large French electronics corporation, along with all other RCA and G.E. TV receiver business. That transaction leaves only Zenith as a U.S.-based and -owned manufacturer of TV receiving sets and tubes. The production and sale of TV receiving equipment has become a highly competitive commodity-like business, with most of the volume now provided by several Japanese corporations.

   Leading firms are seeking technological improvements that will give them a differential advantage and enlarge the replacement market. Two promising developments are (a) a much thinner picture tube which will permit a much smaller front-to-back size of receiving sets, and (b) a revision of the dot system that gives the usual image so that a much sharper picture will be seen, especially on the outer edges.

Assume for this question that Zenith's R & D laboratories have just per-fected a technology that would enable Zenith to produce receiving sets with both of these new features. Zenith's marketing vice president recommends that the company rapidly convert virtually all of its production so that it can use the new technology. Do you think that this is a wise strategic move?

5. Many localities in the United States have more hospital beds than are being used. Two causes of this excess capacity, among many, are a change in medical practice (technology) of getting patients back on their feet sooner, and a change in the formulas used by Medicare and other "third-party payers" to reimburse hospitals for patient care (a fixed amount per type of ailment instead of per diem amounts). So the average time that a patient stays in a hospital has been shortened. In addition, preventive medicine and outpatient clinics reduce the number of patients admitted to hospitals.

Hospitals are responding to the drop in overall demand for their services in a variety of ways. Reducing expenses to match the drop in income (a "businessman's" approach) is proving to be difficult because of high fixed costs, rising wage rates, and a more expensive product mix. Downsizing is also difficult. An alternative approach for individual hospitals is to increase market share. More friendly and fancier service is being tried. More direct is signing contracts with HMO's (health maintenance organizations) which have agree-ments with their members to provide virtually all health care needed. But HMO's bargain with hospitals for quantity discounts.

Still another approach is to acquire state-of-the-art medical equipment and related facilities and technical staff, and thereby "trade up" in the services provided. This entails an *expansion* in modernized capacity. Such an invest-ment is expensive (as prospective donors know), and the prices for using this service reflect the higher costs.

(a) Select any hospital that you know about, and recommend how it should deal with the overcapacity in the hospital industry.

(b) Compare the strategy that you have chosen in answering (a) to the strategy that you would recommend for the U.S. steel industry, which also has overcapacity.

6. Among the possible ways to improve the ratio of actual operation to theoretical maximum capacity are not accepting peak business, manufacturing to stock, and buying goods or otherwise using the idle capacity of another company in the same industry. To what extent can these three ways of reducing capacity be used by (a) a legitimate theater in which plays are presented by both a resident company and traveling companies, (b) a hotel near a major convention center, (c) a cement-block plant, and (d) a bank?

7.    (a) According to the president of the Campbell Soup Company, the firm contracts for its vegetables by giving a farmer the plants and fertilizer and then setting a price in advance of his "farming act." This is as true in Taiwan and Is-rael as in the United States. The farmer then performs "the farming act, not the gambling act."

(b) The president also said that the company should keep and expand its restaurant chains because they will keep the company alive. "Restaurants react to consumers tomorrow morning. If you feed them a bad dinner tonight, they don't come back tomorrow. If you give them a bad can of soup, you find out about it nine months later." He also explained that a high-priced consulting firm and the vice president responsible for retailing operations both recommended that Campbell divest itself of restaurants because they are and had been money losers.

Vertical integration appears to be beneficial one way, but not the other. Explain.

8. To improve the quality of one of its three production processes—teaching—a university's academic vice president established the Center for Teaching Development and hired a well-known professor in the field of teacher education to run the Center. Three programs were immediately established: workshops required once of all teaching assistants, individual consultation with faculty members who ask for help, and a multiple-choice questionnaire process used to help teachers design useful examinations and to provide grades. The technology designed and set up by the Center provided a way for departments to make out examinations and then a way to read, mark, score, and report results for each student as well as print out a frequency distribution of grades, grade summaries by class (senior, junior, etc.) and by instructor, and statistical tests of the validity and reliability of individual questions. One of the standard questionnaires called for student evaluation of their teachers.

The examination, grading, and evaluating processes were used heavily by some departments and not by others. To expand the facilities and the workshops, the director asked for additional funds from the academic vice president and, ultimately, from the legislature of the state. No money was forthcoming. However, some articles written by the director sparked interest from other universities. The director then sold the services of his Center and obtained the money for expansion that way. Data could be sent over AT&T's facilities or by a satellite network that linked the universities directly.

An important piece of the equipment broke down, could not be replaced readily, and shut down, for six months, that part of the Center's work which could not be done manually.

As the Center was about to resume complete operation, the academic vice president assigned the director, despite his opposition, to full-time service in the College of Education. A very popular professor of politics was appointed to half-time duty to be the new director of the Center. His popularity was strongest among the students and with city and county politicians and political groups, so that he could be expected to spend the rest of his time on the third production process of the university—service to local communities and to citizens of the state.

The academic vice president provided enough money to keep one-half of the expanded staff of the Center at work and said that the excellent teaching of the professor of politics could obviously be transferred to teaching assistants and other professors. Two departments of the university, psychology and statistics, complained to the academic vice president about the loss of services valuable to them and the unfortunate effects on their teaching, grading, evaluation, and research efforts. One psychologist said, "He undoubtedly is the most popular professor, but that doesn't mean that he can help others to be effective. He may well not understand what he is doing or why it works."

What do you advise the academic vice president to say and do?

# CASE
## 10 World-Class Factory of Today

*This case deals with a whole group of manufacturing plants observed by Thomas C. Jones, a vice president of Booz-Allen & Hamilton Inc., worldwide management consultants. In the following article\* Mr. Jones argues that most old, large-production facilities in the United States can be brought up to world-class standards by determined management action, without any large investment in automated equipment. While reading the article, think about whether you agree with Mr. Jones's propositions.*

Most mature industrial firms today—particularly in the United States—face the problem of operating at least one large manufacturing facility that is uncompetitive or rapidly becoming so. Many have more than one facility in this category. Regardless of the industry—automotive, steel, durable goods, machinery—uncompetitive plants share certain characteristics. Almost without exception, they are large, multiproduct plants encumbered with higher than average wage rates. They also face mounting competition from "world class" facilities in Japan and, increasingly, in North America.

Dramatic improvement in manufacturing performance is critical to the success and survival of companies still burdened with "factories of the past," but few can afford to invest millions in a factory of the future. Fortunately, there is hope for U.S. industrials that need to achieve dramatic gains in manufacturing performance and don't want to mortgage their future. Despite the uncompetitive operating costs and liabilities hampering many U.S. manufacturers, many enjoy formidable potential advantages in the form of long-term customer relationships,

---

skilled work forces, and usable, upgradable plants and equipment. Combining these inherent advantages with world-class manufacturing techniques could make U.S. industry competitive—now.

To contrast this short-term drive toward competitiveness with longer term "factory of the future" planning, we have used the term "the world-class factory of today" throughout this article. Unglamorous as this phrase is, we believe it emphasizes the benefits to be derived from applying existing "best practices" to today's competitive manufacturing challenge.

## The Dilemma: Yesterday's Operations Versus Today's Competitive Environment

The characteristics of uncompetitive facilities are easy to pinpoint. Typically, these plants produce a plethora of products with little in common from a manufacturing perspective; they are large, with 2,000 to 10,000 employees; and they are unionized, with higher-than-average area wages, excessive job classifications, and inefficient work practices.

Another characteristic these plants have in common is their growth pattern. Over the years, they have expanded on a space- and land-available basis. Spurred by a misguided quest for scale economies, their growth has usually been justified on the basis of flawed analysis. The arguments for individual investment decisions inevitably include: "We already have the space available." "Product X won't be profitable, but it will absorb overhead costs and fill capacity." "The necessary engineering and maintenance skills are in place, so why not expand here?" "We can produce the new product here with less capital."

Such "creeping incrementalism" has driven material handling and inventory costs skyward but added nothing to product value. Just as important, and contrary to popular assumptions, many of these uncompetitive plants have not been starved for capital. Some, in fact, have seen investment in automation in recent years.

Objective analysis of the real competitive position of prototypical large, mature operations quickly reveals some of the underlying problems that make them extremely vulnerable competitively.

> *Poor work practices.* Generally, we find direct workers in these plants working six hours a shift at best; for indirect workers, productive time is usually under five hours. Work pace is mediocre and job classifications excessive. Incentive systems are usually out of control and/or "capped."
>
> *Poor maintenance practices.* Typically, these include high levels of equipment downtime, low use of skilled trades, and inadequate preventive maintenance systems.
>
> *Ineffective materials management.* This results in obsolete systems, excessive inventories at all levels, and poor schedule performance.

*High material handling costs.* When plants grow incrementally without a strategic plan, the inevitable results are poor facility layout and ineffective use of automated equipment.

*Excessive quality costs.* Costs for appraisal, prevention, scrap, rework, and warranty claims account for 10 percent or more of manufacturing value added.

*Too many salaried employees.* Virtually without exception, large U.S. industrials suffer from too many management layers, duplication of tasks and functions, and excessive controls. Excesses of 25 to 35 percent are usually found.

Obviously, not all of these problems exist at all facilities. In our experience, however, a thorough diagnostic review of almost any major North American facility more than 15 years old inevitably uncovers excessive value-added costs in the 25- to 40-percent range.

These plants represent a potentially substantial threat to shareholder equity and even enterprise survival: They are characterized by heavy sunk investments, uncompetitive operating costs, and high exit costs (unfunded separation, pension, health and medical benefits). There are frightening parallels, in fact, between firms with substantial investments in these facilities and the American steel industry in the 1970s. If renewal on a massive scale does not occur, many more manufacturers may play out the steel-industry scenario: profit losses, inability to close inefficient plants, and eventually, bankruptcy. In short, on a competitive basis, these plants are sitting ducks.

## The Imminent Threat: North American World-Class Producers

The major threat facing these "sitting duck" facilities is not offshore Japanese plants, but new world-class facilities in North America. Employing essentially the same techniques they use in their domestic plants, the Japanese are beginning to introduce world-class manufacturing capabilities, with considerable success, into lower labor-cost markets in the United States.

Until recently, world-class plants on the North American continent were primarily restricted to green-field electronics operations. The successful launching of Japanese automotive assembly operations in the United States, however, has stimulated the entrance of some 35 new foreign-owned component producers into the U.S. market—a number that is likely to exceed 200 in the next few years.

The successes these manufacturers experience will probably not be limited to automotive components for long: Domestic appliances and many industrial products will soon be targets. In the very near future, no mature manufacturing-intensive business with uncompetitive facilities will be safe.

The concept of the world-class facility as defined by the Japanese is frequently misunderstood and its impact almost always underestimated by North

American and European manufacturers. The basic principles seem almost too simple; managers who received their manufacturing education and early job experience more than fifteen or twenty years ago may experience a bit of déjà vu.

Typically, world-class operations are driven by hardside attributes such as design for manufacture, balanced capacity and material flows, and engineered minimum setups/changeover times. They also include the key softside concepts of quality at the source, preventive maintenance, and employee involvement.

*These techniques, when knitted into an integrated system, unite to change the basic economics of manufacturing.* In our view, they account for a substantial portion—often from 25 to 30 percent—of the cost advantages of Japanese, Korean, and other overseas manufacturers. According to our competitive analysis, these cost advantages cannot be attributed to such factors as proprietary manufacturing processes, economies of scale, wage factor costs, etc. Exhibit 1, for example, illustrates typical cost disparities in key areas when similar Japanese and American automotive press shops are compared.

## Countering the Threat: The Optimum World-Class Factory of Today

As stated earlier, struggling manufacturers cannot afford to invest millions in "factories of the future"—yet substantial improvement is critical to success and survival. Given this situation, a clear-cut, near-term imperative emerges: Management must restructure existing operations into the optimum world-class factory of today—a facility that will generate significant short-term benefits and provide a basis for future long-term competitive advantage. The means for creating such world-class factories lie in the successful integration of today's best practices in production, engineering, sourcing, and quality control.

**EXHIBIT 1**
**TYPICAL COST DISPARITY**
**AUTOMOTIVE PRESS SHOPS**

|  | Japan | United States |
|---|---|---|
| *Number of Presses* | 20 | 30 |
| Relative output level | 100% | 80% |
| Scrap rate | 1% | 7% |
| Setup time | 15 minutes | 6 hours |
| Typical uptime | 80%–85% | 50%–60% |
| Relative investment | 100% | 119% |
| Relative fixed costs | 100% | 171% |

Source: BA&H Analysis

With this objective in mind, top management can take the first step to survival and competitive health, which is to develop a clear vision of the facility's optimum performance potential—one that recognizes real-world constraints such as plant age, work force skill and training, and the amount of investment capital available.

This vision of the world-class factory of today must define the facility's evolution, taking full advantage of the tools of world-class manufacturing, both hardside and softside. Success in using these techniques changes the economics of manufacturing by attacking the major source of uncertainties within the manufacturing environment. Tactics include tightening variances, shortening feedback control loops, and reducing production time (Exhibit 2).

The vision of an improved, optimum-performance facility must also focus on a number of key operations issues: What degree of facility focus is appropriate? What technology/capacity investments are necessary? What existing excess capacity should be rationalized? How much can handling and inventory costs be reduced by straightening flow lines? How can design for manufacture be improved? Can changeover times be reduced/eliminated? What is the best approach to raise quality levels? Which troubled operations/products should be fixed? Which should be abandoned? What level of vertical integration is required? How should scarce resources be allocated? What tactical program investments are required?

## Barriers to Implementation

A number of barriers to the implementation of world-class manufacturing techniques must be addressed. These usually fall into three broad categories: organization and culture, management and labor, and the manufacturing/marketing interface.

Organizational and cultural barriers have evolved over many years as excess overhead, superfluous management layers, outdated policies and practices, and hidden costs were embedded in the manufacturing structure. In particular, most companies lack sufficiently high-caliber manufacturing resources to make the leap to world-class production levels. They have neither the people nor the equipment to reach manufacturing objectives such as zero downtime, zero defects, and advanced product features. Furthermore, they have organization structure-based transactions and reporting relationships, and their responsibility centers have a financial perspective, rather than a production orientation. Entrenched management incentives that encourage a short-term focus and risk aversion are another cultural inhibitor.

Barriers created by union and nonunion hourly work forces make improvement particularly difficult for industrial companies that have historically operated as two-class (blue-collar and white-collar) societies. This adversarial relationship is at the root of many impediments to world-class manufacturing, including poor hourly work practices, contractual limits on labor reduction, and arcane work rules. In this two-tier society, management is frequently unresponsive to problems and insufficiently involved in manufacturing operations.

292

**EXHIBIT 2
KEYS TO WORLD-CLASS MANUFACTURING**

| | | Hardside | | | Softside | | |
|---|---|---|---|---|---|---|---|
| Source of Uncertainty | Form | Design for Manufacture | Balanced Capacity/ Material Flow | Engineered Minimum Setups | Quality at the Source | Employee Involvement | Preventive Maintenance |
| Demand | Mix | Reduces complexity | | Increases flexibility | | | |
| | Volume | | | | | | |
| Process | Downtime | Matches product and process | Provides PM time | Reduces planned downtime | | Performs minor maintenance | Minimizes unplanned downtime |
| | Quality | Improves quality levels | Provides PM times | | Controls critical process parameters Short feedback loop for quick correction | Provides early detection | Maintains process capability |
| Operator | Quality | Simplifies operator tasks | | | Improved by SQC/SPC activity | Improved operator responsibility | |
| | Throughput time | | Shortens correction loop | | Short feedback loop for quick correction | Improved operator has a stake | |
| Vendor | Quality | Improved through early involvement | | | Leads to vendor certification | | |
| | Delivery | Reduces complexity | | | Develops close working relationship | | |

Finally, ineffective interaction between manufacturing and marketing poses a formidable barrier to change. Since manufacturing and marketing functions have been separated for so long and usually have entirely different perspectives (internally focused versus externally focused), the two functions often have an antagonistic relationship and tend to view each other as problems. Design complexity over the long term and schedule instability over the short term make manufacturing unresponsive to marketing, and make marketing's forecasts inaccurate for manufacturing. In a world-class operation, dramatically reduced product-introduction cycles, just-in-time production, and increased changeover flexibility can provide the basis for much higher levels of responsiveness by manufacturing—and for better interaction with the marketing function.

## Keys to Successful Implementation

Experience has demonstrated that a number of actions are critical to long-term success at the implementation stage:

> *Focus limited resources in high-leverage areas.* World-class manufacturing techniques should be matched to stages of the product life cycle and adopted before capital is expended. Management should focus resources on product design for emerging offerings, on developing world-class factories for start-up products, and on "fixes" to existing products in the growth stage—and expend resources on mature products only with care.
>
> *Consider product-oriented decentralization.* To ensure high levels of flexibility, manufacturing organizations will need to be decentralized and restructured into smaller, more focused, product-oriented production areas. These stand-alone operations should include full production capabilities, maintenance, quality control, manufacturing engineering, and possibly, product engineering resources.
>
> *Concentrate heavily on "softside" aspects to obtain on-the-job experience.* Softside systems, which include quality, maintenance, and employee involvement programs, can make substantial contributions to the effectiveness of existing products and processes. Overcoming softside embedded deficiencies in systems requires extraordinary effort; dollars alone will not solve the problem.
>
> *Stick with proven processes.* Automation is not a panacea and unproven product/process technology can result in poor or missed start-ups. The automation solution must be carefully matched to business needs. Management should not automate for automation's sake; rather, the task is to define clearly the manufacturing strategy and process technology required for the product early in the development cycle. This allows integration of external and internal manufacturing skills into the product design.

*Focus, motivate, and monitor the organization to meet the primary objective:* achieving world-class manufacturing status. The importance of involving all staff at all levels, and communicating to them the overriding objectives of world-class manufacturing and their part in achieving them cannot be overstated. For too long, employees have been segmented into rigid, artificially defined groups that focused on such intermediate goals as throughput and short-term profits. This approach must be changed. What's more, motivation and involvement must be external as well as internal, and suppliers and customers must be part of the improvement process if the goal of world-class manufacturing is to be achieved.

## Question

In your opinion, how realistic are Mr. Jones's proposals for turning large, old plants into world-class facilities?

# CHAPTER 11

## Strategy Programs in Procurement

Regardless of how a company resolves its make-or-buy problems, some sort of goods must be purchased. The manufacturer must buy raw materials and parts, the retailer must buy finished goods, and even the professional firm must buy office supplies. Consequently, issues of dependence on outsiders, choice of specific suppliers, and the logistics of supply have to be confronted.

### Degrees of Dependence on Suppliers

A fundamental shift is occurring in the way companies, and especially purchasing executives, view their suppliers. There always has been, and still is, a wide variation in the amount of reliance placed on specific outside providers of essential materials. Today, the drift is clearly toward selecting suppliers more carefully and expecting more help from them.

In the past, purchasing managers commonly considered their suppliers as mere vendors of products. A company simply bought what it needed from the vendor who offered the best deal. While the relationships were friendly on the surface, it was presumed that suppliers would ask higher prices and give less service when the material being exchanged was scarce. And contrariwise, the purchasing agent was expected to press for concessions when the supply was ample. Where future orders were likely, the amount of pressure either side would exert was tempered a bit, but the underlying view usually was, "This is a win-or-lose bargaining situation, and the person with power uses that power to his advantage."

### The "World-Class Supplier" Concept

An alternative viewpoint, which is part of the current movement to raise U.S. productivity, is that the purchaser and seller are really partners in the creation of an attractive product. By working together, the partners can find ways to cut costs or to improve products and services. Of course, the question of how to divide the net benefits of the cooperation has to be resolved, but the emphasis is on improving the output rather than bargaining over a division of the gain.

The U.S. automobile companies, taking their cue from successful Japanese practice, are pushing this "world-class supplier" approach. Benefits arise from at least three sources. *Dependable quality* is one key feature. Suppliers are required to provide parts with "zero defects" to the auto assembly plant. By having parts that create no problems, the assembly plants save on reworking defective autos, reduce scrap, keep assembly lines running as scheduled, and meet delivery promises, as noted in the previous chapter. Moreover, the finished product is a more reliable machine, thus cutting the consumer's annoyance and repair expenses.

With this approach, in regard to purchased parts, the burden of creating quality is pushed back onto the supplier. Fortunately, Japanese experience indicates, and U.S. companies are finding, that producing parts with zero defects can lead to economy in the supplier plants also. By making parts right in the first place, and culling out deviations promptly, the savings from an orderly production flow often offset the entire extra expense in tooling, training, and care that is necessary to achieve zero defects.

A second feature of the world-class supplier approach is *"just-in-time"* deliveries to the assembly plants. According to this concept, parts suppliers make deliveries of just the right number and size of items needed for the sort of autos being assembled within the next day or two. This virtually eliminates holding an inventory of parts, in turn eliminating rehandling, storage facilities and record keeping, and accidental damage, as well as investment costs. Obviously, the assembly plant becomes considerably dependent on deliveries arriving as planned; one typical safeguard is that suppliers must keep on hand a minimum of at least two weeks' supply of finished goods.

Here again, the supplier is performing tasks normally done by the assembly plant. What happens in just-in-time deliveries is that the burden of maintaining inventories and absorbing the irregularities of assembly line needs for particular parts is pushed back to the supplier. Unlike the quality requirement, however, suppliers do not generate savings from taking over this inventory function. Of course, the assembly plants send suppliers their assembly schedules several weeks in advance, which helps the suppliers to plan their work, and automated changes in setups (see Chapter 10) make variety less troublesome. Nevertheless, just-in-time deliveries help the buyer and burden the supplier.

Suppliers that can consistently maintain quality and meet delivery schedules are often called world-class suppliers. The auto companies watch the performance of their suppliers closely, put them into classes, and encourage and help suppliers to attain the world-class designation.

A third important feature of a cooperative relationship between purchasing managers and suppliers lies in *designing the work*. World-class suppliers can become consultants to the engineering staffs of their customers. Thus, when a new product is being designed, the supplier can advise the auto engineers about modifications that would simplify production or make achievement of quality easier. Similarly, when delivery of products is being explored, plans can be made for special trays or other forms of packaging that will facilitate the movement of the part to the worker on the assembly line.

By exchanging ideas before product designs or processing plans are frozen, changes in one place that will help in another can be weighed. Perhaps the supplier should do something early in the assembly process. Or maybe designs can be modified so that a standardized part can be used in more places. Ease of repair by the consumer can be a consideration, even by the producer of a part. Broadly, the possibilities of integration are opened up because more people are thinking about the whole process instead of focusing only on doing small pieces more cheaply.

A reduction in the number of suppliers is also a feature of the cooperative scheme. For example, Chrysler Motors has already cut the number of its materials and parts suppliers 10 percent from 2,700 in 1985, and expects to reach 1,500 by 1991. Obviously, firms which qualify as world class will do a larger volume of business on the average.

## Unresolved Drawbacks

Of course, drawbacks exist to such closer relations between suppliers and customers. For example, how far should a company commit itself to world-class suppliers along the pattern just described? Clearly, the purchaser is increasing its dependence on other organizations over which it has less control. For instance, a labor slowdown in a supplier's plant could shut down an assembly line. The feasibility of keeping several world-class suppliers tooled up for each part is doubtful. So if use of the scheme becomes more widespread, especially by smaller business-units, some sort of monitoring by the purchaser of conditions in the supply operation will probably have to be devised.

On the other side, how will world-class suppliers be paid for their additional functions? They now spend money and effort to qualify as world class with virtually no assurance that the auto companies will pay them more. Indeed, the president of Chrysler Motors recently told his suppliers to cut prices $2\frac{1}{2}$ percent, gratuitously suggesting as well that they reduce their costs, including those of the materials they buy, by 5 percent and retain only half of that.[1] This sort of talk sounds like Chrysler wants world-class service while continuing to squeeze suppliers as much as its power will allow.

High dependence and close cooperation does work under some circumstances. For example, for years Sears Roebuck & Co. has relied almost entirely on Whirlpool Corporation as a supplier of its laundry appliances. The two corporations have cooperated closely on designing products and on many other decisions. In this instance, however, the purchaser—Sears—owns a large block of Whirlpool's stock, receives detailed monthly costs and profit figures, and keeps an observer in the plant watching for potential delivery problems. Prices are negotiated, with a mutual understanding that Whirlpool will be allowed to earn a "reasonable" profit on the business that it does with Sears.

In the auto industry, and in other industries where something like the world-class supplier concept is being developed, an equity ownership is not expected by

---

[1] See *Fortune*, June 22, 1987, p. 44.

either the purchasing managers or the supplier's managers. Good faith and fairness have not yet taken concrete form. Consequently, in most companies purchasing follows a more traditional pattern. The typical issues in this sort of relationship are summarized next in terms of types and number of suppliers selected.

## Choice of Suppliers

## Types of Suppliers

The type of suppliers selected by a company will depend on the company's requirements in regard to quality, service, reciprocity, and price.

### Importance Attached to Quality

Selection of suppliers by a company will be influenced, in part, by the quality of the products that it wishes. Thus a publishing house, desiring all its books to be made of a high-quality material, buys only from mills that make paper of dependable quality. Although paper is purchased according to detailed specifications, every paper mill has some difficulty controlling quality. The publishing house therefore prefers to pay somewhat higher prices to those mills that have a reputation for exercising care in maintaining the quality of their products.

Even a product that is highly standardized and that has a recognized market price may be purchased from one supplier rather than another in order to secure certain intangible qualities. Operators of textile mills, for instance, point out that considerable variation occurs in the way raw cotton of identical staple and grade will work up in cloth. Consequently, when a textile mill discovers that cotton coming from one region through a given broker is more easily handled on its equipment, that mill will try to concentrate its future purchases on cotton coming from that particular region.

### Service of Suppliers

Suppliers may be selected because of the service they render their customers. For example, companies manufacturing computers, duplicators, and other types of office equipment often give their customers a great deal of aid in designing office forms and in establishing new systems. Most of these companies also maintain an extensive repair service; if a machine should break down, it can be quickly repaired without serious interruption in the work of the office using the equipment.

The importance of such service became striking in Brazil when that market was flooded with relatively inexpensive office equipment of German manufacture. The machines had entered Brazil under a barter agreement in which Brazil exchanged coffee and other raw materials for a specified quantity of machinery from Germany. Inadequate provision had been made for servicing the German machines, however. Consequently, when one of these machines broke down, it was both expensive and time consuming to get it back into working order. As a result, many office managers were turning to more expensive American machines because of the repair service maintained by the American manufacturers.

Under some conditions, promptness of delivery is a controlling factor in the selection of suppliers. This has been one of the primary reasons why small steel companies have been able to secure business in their local territories that otherwise might have gone to the big steel companies. With standardized products and uniform prices prevailing in the industry, such special services as delivery often become controlling influences. The large companies have recently given more recognition to this factor and have spent substantial funds in an effort to expedite the handling of customers' orders.

### Reciprocity

Under special circumstances suppliers are selected on the basis of reciprocity. Thus, commercial banks are likely to favor their big depositors when they buy outside services. Sometimes the reciprocity may be a three-cornered deal. For instance, a Great Lakes steamship company decided to place a large order for motors with a particular manufacturer as a favor to a pig-iron producer. The pig-iron producer shipped large quantities of ore and could therefore demand favors from the steamship company in exchange for a contract to transport ore. To complete the circle, the pig-iron producer used its controls over the order for motors in selling pig-iron to the motor manufacturer. Hence, each of the three concerns selected vendors with an eye to the indirect effect such selection would have on sales.

Formal reciprocity agreements have been challenged legally as a restraint of trade, but this aspect is very cloudy. Much more common is the objection of "professional" purchasing agents. In fact, a policy on reciprocity is often necessary to keep peace between the purchasing department and the sales department.

### Role of Price

Thus far, no mention has been made of price in connection with selection of suppliers. Prices for many products are uniform, and for other products the differences are not of sufficient importance to offset such factors as quality and special service. It should be clear, however, that price is an ever-present consideration, and if for some reason one supplier charges higher prices than another, the former is automatically eliminated unless there is some special reason for dealing with that particular supplier. As already noted, the significance of differences in prices depends partly upon the emphasis that the company buying the material gives to price in reselling the material and also upon the importance of that particular product to the total cost of the company.

### Gifts and Friendship

Especially when large purchases are to be made, gifts and lavish entertainment may be offered to the person who selects the supplier. In its gross form this is clearly bribery. But the line is hard to draw; for instance, is a free lunch unacceptable? While not so strict as government on rules regarding favors, most companies do have a clear-cut policy forbidding the acceptance of any significant gifts from suppliers.

More subtle is the question of friendship. Business relationships naturally lead to numerous contacts and mutual dependencies. Friendship often grows out of such contacts, and cooperation between friends typically flows in both directions. The principle that we assume should guide business relations between friends is clear enough: cooperate to the hilt as long as the interests of the two companies are compatible (and such action is legal), but when interests conflict always give one's own company uncompromising priority. While this norm is usually observed in the United States, a purchasing manager cannot presume that it will be followed, for example, in the Middle East or Far East.

## Summary Regarding Selection of Suppliers

In selecting suppliers, a company is responding to the *sales appeal* of the numerous companies desiring to sell merchandise of the type used by the company. The points of view of the two companies, however, are essentially different because the purchasing company is concerned only with its own specific problems and has no interest in the sales activities of the supplier unless these activities are of some value to it. The purchasing company also has several issues to consider that lie outside the scope of the seller's activities, such as the number of suppliers. The more important factors that should be considered in selecting a supplier are indicated in Table 11-1.

## Number of Suppliers

The number of suppliers of at least the essential products purchased by a firm should receive careful attention. The entire operations of the firm can be jeopardized if this issue is not wisely handled.

### Allocating Buying to Secure the Supplier's Services

A school supply jobber followed the practice for a number of years of buying from as many different manufacturers as possible so that the firm name might be widely known. The company later became involved in financial difficulties and regretted its use of a large number of suppliers. The purchases it made from any one manufacturer were not important enough to that manufacturer to justify granting special credit terms, and each supplier sought to collect its bills promptly. Had this firm concentrated its purchases to a greater extent, it might have induced its suppliers to be more lenient in making collections during the period of financial stress.

**TABLE 11–1.**
**FACTORS INFLUENCING SUPPLIER SELECTION**

| Capacity and Willingness of Supplier to Meet Company Needs | General Characteristics of Desirable Suppliers | Factors Limiting the Choice |
|---|---|---|
| Quality of Product:<br>  Specifications<br>  Dependability | Size of supplier:<br>  Interest in our<br>    business<br>  Financial stability | Reciprocity<br><br>Time and expense of<br>  locating and dealing with<br>  new suppliers |
| Services offered:<br>  Delivery<br>  Technical aid<br>  Repair<br>  Credit terms<br>  Guarantees<br>  Adjustments | Geographic location:<br>  Support of "local"<br>    industry<br>  Dispersion of risks<br><br>Manufacturer *vs.* jobber | Habit and conservatism:<br>  potential "headaches"<br>  in new relationship<br><br>Friendship and loyalty |
| Price:<br>  Competitive level<br>  Inclination to squeeze<br>  Protection on changes | Maintenance of<br>  alternative sources:<br>    Divide equally<br>    One main source,<br>    others minor | Willingness of<br>  departments to try new<br>  suppliers |

## Advantages and Dangers of Concentration

A few companies that buy large quantities of merchandise concentrate their purchases to such an extent that they buy the entire output of the supplier. By doing so, they are able to secure favorable prices because the manufacturer is relieved of all selling cost and is able to concentrate its production operations on just those commodities desired by its one customer. However, a danger in this practice is that the manufacturer may fail to make delivery because of labor troubles, lack of capital, fire, or some other catastrophe, thus leaving the company deprived of its supply of products at a time when they are sorely needed.

Also, relative power—as discussed in Chapter 4—is involved. If there is a single supplier of a vital part or material, that supplier may have a lot of power. A threat, either implied or explicit, to shut off the flow of a needed resource can force the buyer to pay a high price or to accept irregular delivery. The potency of such a threat depends, of course, on the availability of alternative sources of supply.

A large mail-order house that was buying the entire output of a refrigerator plant guarded against these dangers to some degree by having its own representative at the plant who watched accounting records and was familiar with the plant's operations. Such a representative could warn the mail-order house of any impending difficulties. Another large firm followed the policy of buying no more than 25 percent of its requirements of any one product from the same manufacturer. If for any reason something happened to one of these sources of supply, the company would be able to continue to get at least 75 percent of its requirements from its other suppliers. When buying abroad, use of several sources gives protection against political interruptions—as petroleum companies using Middle East crude oil well know.

Many firms seek to gain the advantages of both concentration of purchases and multiple suppliers. They find that buying most of their needs of a particular material from one source is desirable: the quality, price, delivery service, or some other factor makes concentration clearly the best arrangement. So they give 70 to 80 percent of their business to one supplier. The remaining part of the business is divided among several other suppliers. In this manner, business relations are established, specification problems are met and resolved, and the way is prepared for much larger purchases at a later date. Placing these small orders with several suppliers is probably more expensive than buying all required materials from the chief source, but it serves two important purposes: (1) If a strike, fire, or other catastrophe hits the main supplier, the firm can shift to other suppliers much more quickly than it could if no relationship had been established; and (2) the main supplier is "kept on its toes" because the buyer is in close touch with the market and in a position to shift to other suppliers if the price, quality, or service from the main source does not continue to be the best.

### Buying Distress Merchandise

Some retail stores appeal to their customers primarily on the basis of price, and in order to make a profit they continually seek to buy merchandise at "distress" prices. These stores usually offer to pay cash for merchandise, and they are not particularly concerned about being able to secure additional products from the same company. Such stores will deal with any supplier who has merchandise to offer for sale at a reasonable price, and they are continually "shopping around" for more favorable terms. Although such a policy appears to be good for companies operating on a purely price or cut-rate basis, most concerns have learned by experience that it is preferable to build a continuing relationship with suppliers. Such a relationship will not be disrupted by either party because of apparent temporary advantages that may be obtained from time to time under special conditions.

### Factors Determining Number of Suppliers

It is often necessary to balance the advantages of better service and quantity discounts that can be secured by concentrating business with a few suppliers against the disadvantages of possible failure of supply and the passing up of occasional bargain merchandise. The problem often resolves itself into the following questions:

1. Can a limited number of suppliers supply the variety of products required?
2. How much special service and price concession will result from concentration?
3. How important is such service to the purchaser?
4. Is the company too dependent upon any one company for products, parts, or services?

## Logistics of Supply

Even with production facilities in place and suppliers selected, *timing* the flow of goods and services remains a tricky, intriguing issue. Getting the right goods to the right place at the right time is a masterpiece of coordination. We shall discuss this exercise in orchestration in terms of normal coordination of production, purchasing, and sales; integrated, computerized systems; and adjustments to stabilize production and for fluctuating prices. Note that the discussion relates to both production and purchasing. Also, we are concerned here not with specific programs—a topic examined in Chapter 21—but with underlying processes that must be established before programs can be built.

## Normal Coordination of Production, Purchasing, and Sales

### Procurement "to Order" or for Stock

Coordination of procurement with sales is accomplished in some industries by buying or making goods only if the customer's order is already received. For instance, for heavy machinery as well as custom-designed houses, the purchase of raw materials and supplies is not undertaken and production is not started until a firm order is actually received. On the other hand, companies such as producers of radio and television broadcasting equipment make finished products only "on order." But in fact, they produce many parts and even subassemblies for stock; then, when an order is received, only the final assembly operation has to be done according to customer specification.

While making to order reduces inventory risks and gives customers just what they want, it also has serious drawbacks. For example, delivery is inevitably slow and costs tend to be high because mass production techniques cannot be fully utilized.

### Minimum Inventory

If stock is to be carried, a company must establish some general guide to assist the purchasing and production departments in determining how much inventory to have on hand at any one time. Let us look first at the more mechanistic aspects of the problem—ordering points, sizes of production runs, and purchasing quantities—and then note two main reasons for further adjustments, namely, stabilization and speculation on price changes.

How low should inventories be permitted to go before they are reordered? Each retail store in a modern grocery chain, for instance, is expected to maintain a minimum supply of all items regularly sold. Since the store gets frequent deliveries of additional merchandise, the minimum may be only a week's supply. In contrast, because of slow turnover, the minimum inventory carried by many independent furniture stores is equal to a full year's sales.

A company manufacturing rugs carried finished merchandise only at the beginning of each selling season and gave no assurance to its customers that it would carry an inventory throughout the year. On the other hand, it wished to have a minimum stock of raw materials so as to avoid possible delay in production operations. Here the policy was to carry approximately three months' supply of yarn and other raw materials.

A general rule is that the stock level at which replacements will be ordered should approximately equal the sales or use of that merchandise during the period required for replenishment. Since the sale or the use of stock on hand will continue during the period of replenishment, it is customary to add a reasonable margin of safety to any such reordering point as a protection against contingencies. The size of the safety margin will depend upon the likelihood of delays in getting replacements and the seriousness of the delay to production operations or customer service. These considerations lead many firms to carry a minimum inventory much higher than a strict interpretation of the replenishment rule requires.

### Size of Product Run or Purchase Order

When reordering is necessary, how much should be reordered? The primary considerations, in addition to the rate of consumption, are the setup costs versus the inventory carrying costs.

Setup costs cover any special tooling such as dies or artwork for the specific order, assembling necessary materials, preparing the machinery to run, and paperwork involved in instructions, scheduling, record keeping, and the like. These are one-time costs for an order. Once started, the additional per-unit costs are assumed to be constant regardless of the size of the order. Obviously, as production runs get longer, the setup costs can be spread over more units, and the total average cost will fall.

Offsetting this dropping of average production cost is the expense of carrying inventory that has been produced prior to the time of shipment. Inventory carrying costs cover storage expenses, interest on the capital tied up in inventory, and possible spoilage or obsolescence while the stock is being held. Basically, a production run is extended until the inventory carrying costs exceed the savings arising from spreading the setup costs over more units.

The factory of the future sketched in the preceding chapter anticipates that setup costs can be sharply reduced by computers and automation. Where this is achieved, the cost of long production runs will also decrease, leading to shorter production runs and a lower inventory of finished goods.

The most economical size of purchase orders can be calculated in much the same way as for production runs. Here, the setup costs include both the purchaser's expense of handling a separate order and any premium the seller charges for a small order versus a larger one. These costs must be balanced against the costs of carrying a larger inventory arising from buying large quantities.

For both production runs and purchase orders, the normal practice is to compute, for each item in the inventory, the level at which a new order will be placed and the size of the order.

## Integrated, Computerized Systems

Even the preceding brief summary of coordinating the rate of production and purchasing with sales indicates the variety of factors that need to be considered. These include all of the following:

- Real-time inventory level
- Sale or use rate, per day or week
- Delivery period after order is placed
- Safety margin for interrupted delivery
- Ordering point, based on foregoing data

- Setup costs
- Inventory carrying costs
- Costs of spoilage or obsolescence, including uncertainty in sales
- Size of order or run, based on foregoing data

Since these factors vary for each item in the inventory, and since many firms carry thousands of different items when sizes and colors are recognized, the number of computations is formidable. Computers, however, are well suited to performing this kind of task. Formulas and amounts for various factors can be stored in the computer memory, and ordering points can then be calculated and stored. When the inventory drops to this level, the need for and size of a new order can be calculated in a flash.

Valuable as such calculations are, they are only a beginning. An integrated system can be tied to actual sales, and/or it can be extended into sending out purchase orders or preparing preliminary production schedules. More specifically, the memory utilized by the system can monitor actual sales or production and translate these into inventory withdrawals; recompute the estimated rate of future withdrawals; prepare actual purchase orders, including the suppliers' names if they have been selected in advance; accept revised delivery periods or safety margins; provide input for the scheduling of production; and provide finance personnel with estimates of inventory and accounts payable. Such an integrated system would tie together marketing, production, purchasing, and finance at least with respect to logistics.

A few of the grocery chain stores are approaching this kind of integrated system. The checkout registers in the stores not only add up what a customer owes; they simultaneously deduct each purchase from the store's inventory of that item. Then, when the inventory falls below the store's ordering point, a request for replenishment is recorded at the warehouse and shipment to the store is made in a day or two. At the warehouse a similar process is repeated, except that the replenishment decision becomes a purchase order ready for mailing to the supplier of that item. The computer also monitors receipts at the warehouse against orders so that potential shortages are flagged. Consequently, when the customer carries a bag of groceries out of the store, the printer in a warehouse a hundred miles away may already be spewing out a purchase order to the supplier of one or more items in the bag!

This sort of system assures that merchandise will be on the shelf for customer selection. Also, by speeding up the entire procedure, it can reduce the inventory at the warehouse and the stores. But, like the seat reservation system of airlines, it had better be right or the entire flow can get fouled up.

Few companies are prepared for a fully integrated logistics system. There are too many estimates along the line that have yet to be reduced to the mechanistic formulas that computers demand. And there are several variables—like stabilizing employment and anticipating price changes, which we consider next—that managers should balance in light of competition and other environmental changes. The current challenge for each company is to devise a workable system that both purchasing and production managers understand well. These managers can then allow the system to do the standardized work, but intervene whenever their judgment indicates that a standard assumption in the program should be modified.

Two recurring issues which complicate any logistics system are the stabilization of production and adjustments for inflation.

## Stabilization of Production

The business of every company fluctuates by seasons and by cycles. For example, a firm manufacturing electric blankets may find that it sells two-thirds of its products in the last half of each calendar year, and a company manufacturing gloves may find that it sells 45 percent of its products in the last three months of the year. Even articles in daily use, such as cosmetics, have a seasonal fluctuation.

### Production for Stock

Faced with such a seasonal fluctuation, a company may decide to synchronize procurement with its sales volume so that it will not carry inventory in excess of its sales needs at any time. Most women's shoe manufacturers, for instance, do not attempt to produce very far ahead of the season in which they will sell their shoes. Style changes may make shoes produced in advance of a season unsalable or salable only at a reduced price. But, unfortunately, seasonal production means unstable employment.

Other firms produce at approximately a level rate throughout the year. This means that during the seasons of slack sales they accumulate an inventory to satisfy demand during the peak periods. One of the leading manufacturers of skis follows this policy to avoid having an idle plant during part of the year and to keep a group of efficient workers employed the entire year.

Theoretically, a similar policy of production stabilization could be applied to cyclical fluctuations. But few companies have the financial strength to do more than stretch out a product for a few months while looking for a prompt recovery in sales. (The massive stabilization programs undertaken by the federal government for agricultural products involve resources far greater than any company possesses.)

Any company that considers producing during slack periods for sales in later boom times must reckon with obsolescence, deterioration, storage costs, and financing. Fully as important is the ability to forecast the durations and amplitudes of downswings and upswings. Even seasonal drops are difficult to interpret during the downswing because a manager usually cannot tell *at the time* how much of the change is random, trend-related, or seasonal. So an important aspect of a policy to stabilize production is how long production will be maintained above sales—or how large an inventory will be built up—in the face of below-normal sales.

### Other Ways of Dealing with Fluctuations

Production in excess of demand during slack seasons is not the only way companies have sought to adjust to fluctuations in sales volume. Making products that have complementary seasonal fluctuations is one possibility. The combination of motorcycles and snowmobiles is illustrative.

Subcontracting at times of peak demand has been used by some companies in place of a temporary expansion in their own work force. This is not always practical, however, since subcontractors are likely to be busy just at the times when the prime contractor has a peak load.

The automobile industry changed the date for bringing out new annual models from the spring to the fall in an effort to level out seasonal fluctuations. A large number of people prefer to buy new cars in the spring of the year. When the new models were brought out at this time, there was a double incentive to buy during the months of March through June. By changing the time of introducing the new models to the fall, the companies shifted some volume from spring to fall.

These methods, like almost all stabilization devices available to private enterprise, apply best to seasonal fluctuations and have only limited application to cyclical changes.

## Adjustment During Inflationary Periods

Many companies adjust their purchasing and production schedules in anticipation of changes in prices of raw materials and finished products. In this way, these companies hope to secure additional profits. This practice is so hazardous—and yet in inflationary periods so necessary—that the elements involved should be separately evaluated.

### Total Inventory Position

Exposure to inventory price risks involves commitments as well as physical goods in the warehouse. Firm orders to purchase entail just as much price risk as goods in-house. On the other hand, firm orders from customers with fixed prices are an offset against goods on hand. The amount of exposure is the net total of these commitments and goods on hand. In fact, a company making products such as aircraft, which are ordered several years in advance, may have a negative inventory exposure. So when a purchasing manager undertakes to deal with price risk, the focus should be on net exposure.

### Case against Speculation

There are three main reasons why merchandising, manufacturing, and non-profit enterprises should not vary the size of their inventory in an attempt to buy low and sell high. First, doing so detracts from the primary function of the enterprise, and most managements have all they can do to accomplish their primary mission. Second, every enterprise is exposed to a wide variety of risks that cannot be avoided; it is desirable to try to minimize these risks rather than add others. Third, if someone within the company thinks he has exceptional price forecasting ability that person should resign and concentrate all of his or her talent on speculation. Perhaps this person can join a trading firm where speculation is part of the mission.

This injunction against speculation is generally accepted. But it applies to the more extreme situations, and it leaves unresolved a lot of inventory variation that most managers insist is not speculation. These remaining price risks arise directly from performing the regular business. The question is how to deal with them prudently.

### Assuring Uninterrupted Operations

The availability of goods often fluctuates with price. At times of rising prices, demand is brisk and it may take twice as long to get delivery as is necessary when business is dull. Consequently, purchasing agents who are responsible for having an adequate supply of inventory on hand may buy ahead in boom times just to make sure that they get goods on time. On the downswing, prompt deliveries are easier to get and the purchasing agents may safely cut back their inventory.

Thus, in times of material shortages—and these are likely to occur during a period of general inflation—a company quite properly protects itself by building inventory. However, there are practical limits because some inventory may become obsolete due to changes in style or engineering specifications or may deteriorate, as do many food products and sensitive chemicals. Also, storage and other carrying costs may be quite high. These factors place an upper limit on the physical supply it is practical to hold. But within this limit, inventory accumulation is desirable if it is needed to assure uninterrupted operation.

This kind of inventory buildup is not really an anticipation of price changes. The underlying reasons for expansion and contraction are so entwined with price fluctuations, however, that they are difficult to separate. The motive is availability of supply, but an accompanying side effect is exposure to inventory price fluctuation.

### Known Risks of Not Buying

Interwoven with the problems of having inventory when it is needed are adjustments to "known" price changes. Sometimes suppliers announce price increases in advance of an effective date. Clearly, when this occurs, a company should buy its future requirements as far ahead as it is practical to store goods.

More common are situations where the odds are, say, 80 percent that prices will rise in the near future. For instance, the supply may be known to be tight, a labor contract providing higher wages has just been signed, prices of competing products have already gone up, or the world price may have firmed. And there is practical certainty that the price will not fall in the near future. Under these conditions, a firm is assuming greater inventory price risks from not buying than from buying.

### Limits on Exposure

Inventory buildup for the two reasons just discussed—assurance of uninterrupted operations and reduction of "known" risks—should be subjected to one other influence. A company's total risk posture may place constraints on the amount of inventory risk assumed. Overall business uncertainties usually set a time span beyond which it is dangerous for a company to cover its specific needs. Just as we consumers don't buy an oil filter replacement that our car is likely to need two years hence, there are limits on how far ahead a company has full confidence in its detailed projections. In turbulent periods the possibilities of an international monetary crisis, war, overthrow of the government, drastic government intervention, or comparable events may make firm commitments beyond six months unwise. Under more favorable conditions management may feel reasonably confident about the shape of events for a year or more ahead. Regardless, then, of specific expectations about a particular material or part, management often sets a general horizon beyond which commitments should not go.

Likewise, as we shall see in Chapter 13, the scarcity of capital may require a company to set some limits on the total sums tied up in inventory.

## Summary

A strong case can be made against out-and-out speculation on inventories—except for a trading company organized for such a purpose. Nevertheless, especially in periods of inflation, adjustment of inventories in anticipation of external shortages and price shifts may be prudent. An approach to this troublesome issue is to focus on the inventory necessary to assure uninterrupted operations, within the practical limits of holding such an inventory. In addition, inventory may be built up when the price outlook makes the risk of not doing so quite high. Here, again, the inventory is confined to future operating needs. Finally, the accumulations for either of the preceding reasons should be restricted by a general commitment horizon and financial allocation set by central management.

# Triple Linkage of the Purchasing Department

## Transitions in External Links

The discussion in this chapter shows that the typical purchasing department plays a varied and changing role as the interface between its company and an array of suppliers. The current trend toward closer and more dependent relationships with a select group of "world-class" suppliers is in direct contrast to the predominant practice in the past of more aloof shopping for bargains among a larger number of suppliers. How widespread this sort of relationship will become is not yet clear, but in several industries it is seen as an important way to meet foreign competition from the Far East.

Whatever the external relationship, purchasing managers always have to choose suppliers that provide the sorts of services most needed by the company. A sensitive issue here is the wisdom of narrowing down to a single source for some necessary part or material. This balancing of better service versus more risk can significantly affect the strategy of a company.

The logistics of supply—getting the right product in the right place at the right time—at first glance offers a paradise for computer buffs. The challenge here is to avoid getting trapped in mechanistic solutions to recurring problems that should receive sensitive judgments about risks and side effects. Again, the current practice is in transition: we are experimenting with and learning how to use our new tools.

As might be expected, individual purchasing managers often have strong opinions about the foregoing issues. Their scenarios for excellence will often call for a sharp break with past practices.

## Adjusting Links with Other Departments

As purchasing managers wrestle with these and the many associated problems of external relationships, they must also deal with the other two linkages in the triple-linkage model—horizontal links with other departments and vertical links with business-unit managers who are concerned with overall strategy.

Important linkages of the purchasing department with other departments include the following.

### Marketing

- Obtaining *forecasts of sales* in a form that can be translated into purchase requirements.
- Providing, for retailers and distributors, products of a type, quality, cost, and availability that *fit selected market niches.*
- Adjusting sources to major opportunities for *reciprocity.*

### R & D

- Obtaining forecasts of *shifts in technology* that would affect the future need for, and availability of, key materials or parts.
- Looking for ways to bypass *patents* that restrict the sources of key products.
- Promoting *cooperation of R & D with world-class suppliers* in search for production economies.

### Production

- Agreeing on *make-or-buy decisions.*
- Assuring that purchased parts and materials meet the *quality standards* needed for efficient production, preferably "zero defects."
- Arranging for *just-in-time deliveries* that facilitate production.

### Human Resources

- Recognizing the human resource implications of decisions to buy rather than make, including the *loss of U.S. jobs* when production is shifted to foreign sources.
- Arranging supplementary purchasing so that company *employment* may be *stabilized.*

### Finance

- Reducing *inventories* through using world-class suppliers and sophisticated logistics of supply.
- Fitting inventory adjustments to *anticipated price changes* to the risk profile of the company.
- Arranging foreign exchange and capital requirements for using *foreign sources* of parts and materials.

Because purchasing has so many diverse links with other departments in a company, the strategy program of a purchasing department is likely to reflect the interests of other departments fully as much as its own scenario for excellence in purchasing.

## Fitting Purchasing Activities into Business-Unit Strategy

For many years most purchasing departments have served in a support capacity to strategy moves initiated by general managers or by other departments. Purchasing is a necessary activity, and it must be done well. However, new thrusts have originated more often in marketing, R & D, or production. Exceptions to this supporting role have occurred mostly in worldwide searches for raw materials and, of course, in retail and wholesale trading companies where a distinctive supply may be the heart of the business.

Where the strategy lead has arisen outside of purchasing, the purchasing department has usually been notable for its ability to adapt. Support rather than conflict, which, when it occurs perhaps calls for mediation by the general manager, is the common pattern.

Currently, purchasing is becoming more important in strategic action. Increasing reliance by a company on a relatively few world-class suppliers may raise that company's productivity and product quality significantly. Also, computerized logistics—which are quite compatible with factory-of-the-future concepts—will help some companies become more competitive. These are exciting developments. To date, however, U.S. companies are running hard to catch up with Japanese firms. The new techniques may give companies in some industries a competitive advantage over firms that do not use them, but in global competition over purchasing, skills are not yet distinctive.

The tide is turning toward closer cooperation with suppliers and greater mutual dependence. These, in turn, may lead to more joint ventures or alliances, especially with foreign sources. U.S. traditions of rugged individualism along with antitrust laws that nourish arms-length competition on all fronts provide a weak background for this cooperative push. Consequently, we have much to learn.

In the near term, then, purchasing can continue to be a strong supporter of strategic change, but only in a few companies will it provide strategic potency.

## Questions for Class Discussion

1. The Xerox Corporation reduced the number of its suppliers from 5,000 in 1981 to 300 in 1987. What benefits and what disadvantages do you think Xerox experienced from this shift?

2. Do you think that the factory of the future and world-class suppliers are compatible? Would a company with a factory of the future be likely to buy from world-class suppliers? Explain.

3. Among the ways companies have sought to reduce their costs are by (a) buying parts abroad in low-wage countries such as Mexico or Taiwan, either from local firms or from joint ventures, and (b) concentrating their purchases on world-class suppliers. Do you think it would be wise to try to combine these two approaches—that is, buy from world-class suppliers in low-wage countries?

4. Which of the factors listed in Table 11–1 do you think should carry the most weight in the selection of suppliers by (a) a men's clothing store, (b) a franchised steak house, (c) the buying agent at the headquarters of Hospital Corporation of America, which owns and manages scores of small and medium-sized hospitals throughout the United States, (d) a computer store, and (e) your city government's buying agent for desks, files, typing paper, and pens?

5. Most discussions of stabilization of production, including that in this chapter, accept fluctuations in sales and consider ways of adjusting production to those fluctuations. An alternative approach is to set the production volume to a stabilized level and consider ways to adjusting sales to production. This approach (widely used in Japan and in Chile and Zambia in the copper mines) enables companies to provide stable employment and helps maintain the gross national product. Would such a practice be socially desirable in the United States? What would companies have to do to operate in this manner?

6. An integrated, computerized system for grocery chain stores is described on page 306. Do you think that such a system is suitable for other retail stores, including department store chains such as Federated Department Stores or Bullock's? For furniture stores? For jewelry stores like Tiffany's in New York?

7. Approaches to the adjustment of inventories during inflationary periods are explained on pages 308–310. When two solid indicators of a general inflation are announced by the chairman of the Federal Reserve System (a second drop of one-half of one percent in the rediscount rate for money-center banks, and a factory operating rate of over 85 percent when average rates in good times are 81 to 82 percent), what should a buyer of coal for a public utility company do? The proprietor of a ladies' dress wear specialty shop? The purchasing agent for Alpha Pyro Glass, Inc., whose main purchase is fiberglass matting bought from any one of four suppliers and purchased ordinarily on the basis of the lowest bid price?

8. (a) At what point should company policy bar the acceptance of gifts and entertainment from suppliers: lunch at a local restaurant, a golf game at an exclusive club, a three-day technical seminar at a comfortable inn, a Christmas

calendar, a bottle of Scotch, an electronic watch, theater tickets, a mink coat, an opportunity to invest in Florida real estate, assistance in getting one's son a seat on a booked-up plane flight, employment for Uncle Ben, $10,000 to a pet charity, a $50 bet at favorable odds, or you name it? (b) Should the company policy be the same with respect to company bankers? union leaders? advertising agents? customers?

9. Michigan Fabricators is a small firm that is trying hard to win world-class supplier status from its major customer, Ford Motor Company, for its engine parts. It has been successful to the point that it is one of two suppliers for that particular part.

A month ago, the Ford purchasing agent phoned to say that the other supplier had a serious breakdown, and he asked Michigan Fabricators to step up its deliveries 50 percent for two weeks with the understanding that the company will be reimbursed for overtime and any other extra expenses. Michigan Fabricators, grateful for this vote of confidence, ran nine hours a day on Mondays through Fridays and eight hours on two Saturdays and Sundays to produce the extra volume.

Four days later the purchasing agent phoned again, mad as a hornet. After briefly thanking the president for willingness to help in an emergency, he turned loose about quality. On a final check, one engine proved faulty because of a defective part from Michigan Fabricators. That led to rechecking every engine produced the preceding week, those on the line, and all parts waiting for installation. Three more defective parts were found. "If we get one more defective part from you, you are through as a supplier to Ford. I don't care what the reason is. And that's final."

After much scurrying, the president was sure that the defective parts were made on one Sunday. That day only part of the work force agreed to come to work, so people were reassigned jobs on the basis of seniority provisions in the union contract. The result of this shifting was that several workers, including a tester, were on jobs that they had not done before.

The president immediately called a meeting of all plant supervisors and the workers who had been reassigned jobs on that Sunday. After briefly reviewing the facts, which by then almost everyone was aware of, the president said, "From here on out, no one is to do work for which he or she has not been carefully trained. If that happens again, the manager who approved the reassignment, the immediate supervisor, and the worker will be fired immediately. And that holds regardless of what the seniority rules say." Nobody doubted that the president meant exactly what he said.

That afternoon the union steward came to the president's office to point out that the union contract said that any deviations from the seniority procedures should be negotiated by the union steward and a company officer. The president replied, "John, on this issue there is nothing to negotiate. That's the way it has to be."

(a) Do you think that the purchasing agent acted wisely? Do you think that the president acted wisely?

(b) What will probably be the longer run effect of this incident?

10. In several Far Eastern countries, the local culture calls for sending substantial gifts to individuals (often part-owners) who place large orders with a company. These are regarded as expressions of friendship and tokens of appreciation. What should be the policy of a U.S. company with a branch in such countries (a) if it is buying goods or services? (b) if it is selling goods or services?

11. Thomas Products Company regularly buys a special alloy of rolled steel coils used for one-half of its products from one major integrated steel company. Other steel producers rarely make this alloy. The sales representative visits once each quarter to take an order which is shipped to Thomas Products three months later. Just before one of the regular visits, the treasurer and president of this small specialty producer said to the buyer, "We have four months' inventory on hand, and it looks as if business is going to slow down. Try to cut your next order in half."

The buyer then told the sales representative that he was able to order only half the usual amount of steel. The representative replied that he could understand the buyer's problem, but that Thomas's regular order was just large enough to warrant a separate position of its own in the steel-making and rolling sequence for the mill during the next quarter. Cutting the purchase order in half would take it out of sequence and would mean that it would have to be combined in parts with other mill runs that had differing program positions. Shipments to Thomas would be anywhere from four to eight months later. The salesperson's advice was to stay with the customary order. What should the buyer do?

12. Robert Stempel, a new president at General Motors Corporation, has announced a change in GM's make-or-buy strategy. In 1987 GM made roughly 70 percent of each car it sold, compared with about 50 percent at Ford and 30 percent at Chrysler. Partly as a result, GM was the high-cost producer, and GM's earnings per share of common stock had been falling while Ford's and Chrysler's were rising or steady. Mr. Stempel's predecessor had successfully stressed quality of production: "With that task largely accomplished, my main aim is to improve productivity in manufacturing. We will stop producing components that are overabundant or involve low technology."

(a) As GM increases its outside purchases in its program to reduce costs, do you think it will face any difficulty in attracting world-class suppliers of the sort described in this chapter?

(b) Do you recommend that GM seek foreign suppliers for the parts it will no longer manufacture itself?

# CASE
## 11 Olsen Products

Holger Olsen has a clear goal of becoming a world-class supplier of parts for the steering mechanism of automobiles. He was manager of a plant making such parts when the corporation that owned the plant decided to withdraw from the auto parts industry. When it looked like the plant would be closed down, Olsen and some relatives bought the business.

During the past three years Olsen Products has been quite successful in developing good relations with Ford and especially Chrysler as a dependable supplier of two similar parts. Through diligence and uncompromising insistence, Holger Olsen has achieved a zero-defects record on quality. Also, by ingenious use of special fixtures and some automation, he has trimmed production costs.

Contributing to this improvement in results has been a willingness of the work force to try out incremental changes. The older workers had expected to lose their jobs when the plant closed, and now they view Olsen as the person who saved their jobs. Olsen, a hands-on manager, has repeatedly stressed that the only way a small plant can survive in this industry is to produce top-quality products at competitive costs. Almost everyone in the company and the local union accepts this proposition, and all are cooperating to achieve it. A scarcity of good, stable jobs in the vicinity reinforces the attitude.

If Olsen Products maintains its quality one more year, it will be treated as a prime supplier by Chrysler, and perhaps by Ford. That designation means that Olsen Products will be advised in advance of any design changes which may affect its products and will have an opportunity to work with the automobile company engineers on final specifications. The presumption is that two or three companies in this top group will get almost all of the orders—provided, of course, that their prices are "right."

So the company has been turned around, and next year Holger Olsen expects to increase the company's share of the total business in its very narrow niche. With that, and a good year for sales of automobiles, Olsen Products will probably see for the first time a 20 percent return on its equity. The longer term future, however, is not so clear. The automobile companies say that suppliers should find ways to increase their productivity at least 3 percent per year and consequently *reduce* prices 3 percent annually. Holger Olsen doesn't see how he can do this. He says, "In addition to the fact that productivity gains do not cover materials, which probably will rise in price 3 to 5 percent each year, we are already running lean on overhead and have searched for ways to make the plant efficient. Because of our history, there is no fat to cut out.

"My guess," continues Olsen, "is that we will obtain orders at a fair price on newly designed products. For the first year the auto company buyers will stick to suppliers who have been thinking about the changed specifications and can be relied on. After that, the buyers will be under pressure to get lower prices and they will start shopping around. And in years when auto sales are down, they will say 'The whole family has to share this burden,' which means that regular suppliers should cut their prices even though we, too, are being hurt by the drop in volume. Consequently, we must look for ways to cut costs on established products."

Competitors most likely to give Olsen Products serious price competition are foreign firms located in low-labor-cost countries such as Mexico, Taiwan, and Korea. If some way can be found to combine the low costs in these countries with the quality and delivery standards of companies like Olsen Products, that supplier probably could survive the impending squeeze. Holger Olsen is considering two possibilities.

One alternative is to subcontract the production of established designs to a Mexican company located in the Mexico City area. This arrangement really means that Olsen would purchase the finished products from the Mexican company. The company currently makes a variety of metal products for export, so it is already tooled up to fill Olsen's needs. Nevertheless, it would expect to get, and would try to follow, careful instructions from Olsen; i.e., it would use Olsen's know-how. Also, Olsen could place inspectors in the plant to ensure that such instructions were being followed and to perform its own quality checks.

The Mexican-made parts would be shipped to Olsen's Ohio plant, perhaps reinspected there, and held in inventory for just-in-time delivery to the automobile assembly plants. Estimated savings after tariff, trucking, and inventory carrying costs would be about 20 percent below production costs at the main plant. Of course, most of the work would be outside of Olsen's control: if output were behind schedule or defects were discovered, Olsen could return the shipments, but this would not fulfill obligations to the auto companies.

A second alternative is to enter into a "joint venture" with a processing firm just south of the Texas-Mexico border. In this arrangement, which is typical of other joint ventures that the processing firm has, the Mexican partner provides a building with electric power and water, unskilled labor, and first-line supervision. Olsen Products then supplies the materials, machinery, training, inspection, and general supervision such as scheduling. In effect, the Mexican firm provides unspecialized resources—space and labor—which Olsen Products would then manage much like its main plant. One minor variation is that finished products would be placed in a rented warehouse just on the U.S. side of the border and trucked from there directly to the auto assembly plants. Because of Olsen Products' close supervision of the plant, and the supply of raw materials, no further inspection in the United States would be made.

Under this arrangement, savings arise primarily in labor costs. (Wage rates are low; most of the men come to this border town without their families and live in spartan, low-cost housing.) The capital investment for Olsen Products to start up would be about $500,000 for machinery and inventory. Preliminary estimates show a total cost of products delivered to customers at about 12 percent below costs at the Ohio plant. Note also that this would be an inexpensive way for Olsen Products to expand its plant capacity. If additional sales could be secured at current prices and the products were made by the joint venture, Olsen Products would recover its incremental investment in the joint venture in two years.

If Olsen Products expects to use either of the above sources, it should start with small lots so that the supplying organization and headquarters staff can learn to work together and a nucleus of workers can be trained. A start-up period of perhaps a year would be needed before a full volume of work could be expected.

Holger Olsen has raised these possibilities of cost savings with his main customers. Their responses indicated the following. (1) Olsen Products would be fully responsible for the quality and timing of delivery regardless of where the products were made. Its standing as a prime supplier depends on *all* of its business. (2) Because of their dependence on incoming parts, the auto companies would investigate the Mexican source so as to be satisfied with Olsen Products' close guidance and the capability of the outside source. (3) The auto companies would give preference to other prime suppliers which produced in their own domestic plants if those suppliers met Olsen Products' prices.

The present employees of Olsen Products and their union know about the possibility that the company might have some products made in Mexico. They seem willing to accept this move only if the main plant is kept busy, that is, only if there is no reduction in the number of jobs. Nevertheless, they do recognize that labor-intensive operations must either be mechanized or farmed out. Either approach would reduce the number of such jobs, but other (higher paying) jobs would be expected as substitutions.

## Question

To what extent, if any, and from which source, should Olsen Products obtain products from Mexico?

# CHAPTER 12

## Strategy Programs in Human Resources

Every activity a company undertakes requires human resources—people who are qualified and motivated to perform specific tasks. Without the right people, nothing happens.

These people come from what economists call the labor market. And a human resource (personnel) department is the primary representative of its company in that market. Its role is to maintain a continuing flow of just the right kind of employees to design and execute the company strategy.

Arranging the supply of human resources is a never-ending and sensitive task for several reasons:

1. *Company needs for human resources change.* This entire book, for example, deals with ways that companies can adjust to a changing, competitive environment.
2. *The supply of human resources changes.* Not only do individuals enter and leave the market, but they also change radically in their skills, needs, and attitudes during their lifetimes.
3. In spite of these demand and supply changes, *people seek stability and dependability* in their jobs. They may move on, but they would like the jobs to remain predictable and secure.
4. *Expectations overlap.* The way an employee is treated creates hopes or fears in many other people. Also, equity, and preferably equal treatment, is sought.

These factors often constrain the strategic action that a company can take.

An additional array of problems that bear on the effective use of labor involves organization design, motivation, and leadership style. These are largely internal matters, and we will deal with them briefly in Parts 4 and 5. A large body of literature on "organizational behavior" is available regarding various aspects of internal relationships. Our focus here is on the company's boundary looking outward—on mobilizing human talent suited to the specific strategy that a company hopes to pursue.

The human resources department performs an unusual role in most companies. Typically, it operates as a *service* throughout the organization, responding to needs but not initiating basic changes. And in the external labor market it *represents* the company more as an agent than as a doer like a branch manager. In fact, on many human resource matters the department actually decides what the company position will be, but these choices are usually presented as an agent speaking for his or her principal.

In the first sections of this chapter we briefly describe "company" practices related to human resources, but the reader should be aware that virtually all the actions described will have been shaped primarily by the human resources department. Because of its importance, management personnel is discussed separately in Chapter 20.

## Selecting and Developing Personnel

Each person has distinct abilities. Each job has particular duties. One must fit the other. For convenience, we often talk of labor in general, but within that broad resource highly individualistic matches with jobs are essential.

## Skills Matched to Strategic Requirements

### Are Suitable People Available?

A large labor pool is only a start. During the Great Depression, for instance, millions of people were looking for work. However, it was a very unusual group of refugees from Nazi Germany who had the exceptional intellectual skills and training which enabled them to become the founding nucleus of the New York School for Social Research, an unusual graduate school in New York City. Or, to note another example in education, the Nigerian government has plans to build a full-fledged medical school in the northern city of Kano. But there are not yet enough trained medical professors available to make more than a small start. In each example, suitable personnel became a key to the execution of strategy.

### Finding Pools of Talent

A company may have to move to find qualified workers at competitive wages. For example, the scarcity of laboratory personnel in the U.S. has forced several pharmaceutical firms to shift parts of their research work to Europe. Similarly, the movement of textile firms to Korea and Taiwan reflects a search for cheap, though dexterous, labor. And publishers have located part-time editorial staff in middle-class suburbs.

This searching for more favorable sources of labor is similar to marketing executives looking for attractive niches for products. The aim is to establish a strong position before competition becomes tough.

### Adjusting to a Changing Labor Market

Of course, sometimes it is practical to modify company operations to fit available labor. For example, for years a drug wholesale company followed a policy of hiring high-school graduates to staff its large warehousing operations. These people stacked, marked, and kept track of the thousands of different items involved;

assembled orders for prompt delivery to retail druggists, priced the orders, and computed the bills; kept track of back orders; and helped maintain records needed for buying new stocks. High-school graduates had the accuracy and the dependability required, and at the same time they did not find the highly standarized operations offensive. The more energetic employees became supervisors, sales representatives, buyers, and sometimes branch managers.

The company now finds that most of the more able and energetic high-school graduates go to college. Efforts to use men and women who want a full-time job while working their way through college have shown unsatisfactory results because many of these people become bored with their routine work. So a new fit between the changed labor supply and the company's "production" strategy clearly was called for.

A modification in the *structure of jobs* was the first move. Instead of assuming that everyone would have a basic competence to perform a variety of tasks, the work has been more sharply graded in terms of reading, writing, and arithmetic skills. This permits relaxation of the high-school graduation requirement. High-school dropouts when hired are given intensive training on limited tasks. Turnover is high during the early months of employment, but out of the group come a significant number who can do the simpler tasks well and quite a few who quickly move on to the more skilled jobs.

In addition, provision has been made for hiring a few college graduates and moving them rather quickly through various operations with the expectation that they will qualify for buying, selling, or supervisory jobs. Thus, the company's entire mode of production had to be changed to overcome a human resource problem.

The revised practice has some disadvantages. It is more difficult to move people from task to task to meet peak requirements. More significant, the feeling that everyone starts out on an equal basis and progresses to more difficult positions on the basis of demonstrated merit is lost. Even though it is now possible to move up through the hierarchy, and some people do, new employees enter the company at different levels. This generates an undercurrent that some people, because they are lucky enough to get more education, continue to receive favored treatment.

### How Much Provision for Growth?

Communications Systems, Inc., is a growth company centered around some patented devices that transmit and receive multiple electronic messages. These devices are particularly well suited to handle communications between branch offices and a centralized computer. The company founder and president, however, regards the equipment merely as the base from which all communications systems can grow. Among the possibilities already worked on are logistic systems for the Air Force, a nationwide bidding system for commodity exchanges, and complete integrated data processing systems for business firms.

With these possibilities in mind, the firm expanded rapidly. Its stated personnel policy was "to attract the best brains in the country." The glamour of the company's objectives enabled it to hire both theoretical and applied experts in systems design, communications equipment, and computer technology, and in the activities to which the systems might be applied.

The match between the mission conceived for the company and the kinds of people employed was excellent. But serious difficulty developed in terms of the rate of growth. Communications Systems was employed to make a variety of pilot studies, but full-scale applications proved to be complex and costly. Concepts such as national bidding on commodities require legal and institutional changes that probably are decades away. The result was that many members of the high-powered staff became frustrated. The high morale in the early stages turned to internal criticism and disappointment with lack of personal advancement. Since many of the people employed were indeed very capable, they began taking other jobs. Turnover accelerated. Hiring mistakes during the initial expansion became conspicuous because these individuals were less able to find other jobs and so tended to stay with Communications Systems. The company is still in business, but it now has a poor name rather than a good name in its particular labor market.

On the other hand, it *is* possible to have too many bright MBAs on staff. An excess inventory of talented human resources is both hard and expensive to keep in storage.

## Constraints on Selection

In addition to policy guides regarding the types, sources, and numbers of employees it intends to attract, each company—through its human resources department—must decide how it will cope with "thou shalt not" laws.

Hiring, promotion, and discharge of employees are surrounded by increasing government regulation. Equal opportunity for blacks has been extended to other minority groups. Women likewise are guaranteed explicit rights. Discrimination on the basis of age and compulsory retirement ages have been outlawed. And the list is increasing.

In each of these areas there are past injustices to be corrected and worthy social goals to be achieved. The perplexing challenge for managers is that the new laws and the regulations supporting them are inconsistent, and no consensus exists on how rapidly the "equal opportunity" norms are to be evident in various occupations and levels of organization. Preferential treatment must be given to blacks, women, and other underrepresented segments of society; but such preferential treatment may involve reverse discrimination against other individual workers. Or to cite another example, jobs retained by elderly white males block the promotions of younger women or blacks.

Broadly speaking, companies can respond to these and similar issues in one of three ways (as indicated in a key to the alternative department roles shown in Figure 6–4 on page 149). *Minimum compliance* just to stay within the law is a short-run option. Meanwhile, several of the inconsistencies and uncertainties may be resolved. Conscientiously carrying out the *underlying intent* of the laws is the second alternative. Here a company seeks to move with changing social norms. It recognizes that changes are appropriate and tries to be a good "citizen." *Pioneering* is a third possibility. This involves being a leader in social reform, perhaps to the extent that favorable ties to particular segments of the labor market will become a "differential advantage."

## Reliance on Internal Development

Interwoven with decisions on who and where to hire are questions about "promotion from within." One source of specialized talent is to "raise your own." This is like the make option in make-or-buy policy regarding materials.

Companies vary in the degree that they expect to fill better jobs and managerial positions by promotion. General Motors, like the wholesale drug company referred to earlier in this chapter, relies almost entirely on internal sources. Such a policy, of course, requires a company to do a lot of training if people are to be fully prepared for new assignments. And in fact, General Motors has the equivalent of a college, the General Motors Institute, for this purpose. Training on the job and horizontal transfers are even more important. A major hurdle in such internal development of personnel is the lack of opportunity for injecting new ideas, especially when a company's external environment is turbulent.

The primary factors in choosing between "raising your own" versus "hiring seasoned workers" include, first, the probable length of employment. Industries such as construction or the theater, which work on relatively short projects, typically assemble the talent needed for immediate purposes and leave the task of training to the individual worker and to other institutions. Staffing of government contracts in the space and defense industries largely falls into this category. Of course, any company that undertakes to enter a difficult industry on a large scale lacks time to do very much training. Second, the existence of well-established skills or professions affects the need for in-company training. Thus, printers, doctors, and welders are usually hired as experienced individuals. By comparison, if the work of a particular company is primarily unique, internal training is necessary to assure the skills required.

Companies that are technological leaders in their field are always faced with a problem of training people who then go to work for competitors. A substantial number of engineers and sales representatives in the computer industry, for instance, have been trained at IBM expense. If a company's strategy is to be a leader, it should anticipate not only the cost of overcoming the pitfalls of a new product or process, but also a personnel development cost. Moreover, the company will probably have to be a leader in compensation and supplemental benefits in order to keep its turnover low.

## Designing a Realistic Compensation Package

Recruiting and developing personnel, as we just saw, focuses on the inflow of a vital resource to the company. The other side of the coin is an outflow of compensation that will retain this talent.

An attractive job includes a whole set of factors: the work itself, future opportunities, security, status, hours and working conditions, and fringe benefits, as well as monetary compensation. The ability of a company to provide most of these attractions depends especially on two conditions we have already stressed. (1) An economically strong business is crucial. No personnel policy or government regulation can be a substitute. Security, growth opportunities, status, and many other benefits are possible only when a company has a sound strategy that is well executed. (2) People must be well matched to the jobs they hold. Individuals vary and jobs vary. Unless a good fit is achieved, the employment situation will be unstable and probably unsatisfactory.

Assuming that these preconditions are met, there will still remain important issues about both direct compensation and supplemental benefits. As with the selection of personnel, the compensation package may be barely adequate, or at the other extreme it may be a source of strategic potency.

## Level of Pay

### Relation to Prevailing Rates

Many firms simply decide that they will pay "going rates" for each occupation or level of job. Such a policy seeks to neutralize pay as a competitive factor. Employees will have to be attracted and motivated in some other way.

Paying above the market is an alternative that has popular appeal. Here a firm seeks to get the "cream of the crop," to give customers distinctive service, or perhaps to reduce turnover. Of course, if too many companies are prepared to pay above the average, the policy loses its distinctiveness (and the actual average being paid keeps moving up). Moreover, unless the company's technology gives it low labor expenses relative to the total, or unless it has some offsetting cost advantage, a high wage policy cuts into the company's ability to attract other kinds of resources.

Few firms admit that they consistently try to pay less than market average, but it is an option which suits some situations. A small, remote firm drawing from a local labor pool is a convenient place to work; commuting time and expense are low. Or the enterprise may offer offsetting attractions, such as prestige (working for the leading bank in town) or service opportunities (hospitals). Also, if a company does not need high skills, its wage rates may look low when in fact it is paying reasonably well for what it needs.

### Internal Alignment

Workers—from janitor to president—are also sensitive to how their pay compares with their fellow workers. Because internal alignment is such an emotional issue, most companies have an explicit method for setting differentials in pay within the organization. The usual technique involves job evaluation to place jobs into standard pay grades and establishing a fixed relationship between grades.

A serious drawback to such schemes for internal alignment is the inevitable inflexibility in recognizing outstanding performances of specific individuals. Attention to equity—equity that can be proven objectively in this age of government regulation and union surveillance—tends to stifle recognition of individual merit. So in setting a policy of maintaining fair internal alignment, each company must also consider how it will reward its stars.

As with similar issues, central management should attempt to find a compensation policy that gives positive support to company strategy. Just the opposite effect is all too common. The combination of trying to keep pay scales in line with external rates, make some but not catastrophic adjustments for inflation, maintain acceptable internal alignment yet reward outstanding performance, observe government regulations regarding discrimination, maintain maximum permissible increases, and keep those fast-track MBAs happy becomes so complicated that compensation can be a hindrance rather than a help in pushing for selected goals.

## Supplemental Benefits

In today's labor market every company must offer supplemental benefits that are at least in line with general business practice. These benefits typically provide for (1) paid vacations and holidays; (2) protection against risks of illness, unemployment, premature death, and old age; and (3) social and recreational activities. Incidentally, the cost of these benefits plus the company share of social security taxes often exceeds 25 percent of an employee's base pay.

The basic question is whether merely to follow general practice as it develops or to take the lead in one or more of the various areas noted previously.

### Sharing the Costs of Pioneering

The company that pioneers in liberal pensions, early retirement, or a guaranteed annual wage may find itself at a competitive disadvantage because of high costs.

One possibility is to have the employee share the cost of a new benefit. This has been done for medical insurance, pensions, and even recreational activities. In addition to cutting cost, an advantage of this arrangement is that most of us prize those things for which we have made some sacrifice. Thus, employees may appreciate major medical insurance more if they contribute to its cost.

### Employee Expectations

Not so long ago all regular employees expected to work at least half a day on Saturday. Now, an employee who doesn't get a two-day weekend feels abused. The attitudes toward other supplemental benefits follow this same pattern. Consequently, if a company expects to generate strong employee enthusiasm because of its supplemental benefits, it must be prepared to keep adding new ones.

Also, what interests an employee shifts over time. The automobile and television have radically changed the social structure and the recreational patterns at the place of employment. Suburban living segments a person's life, and added purchasing power permits diversified and dispersed recreation. Living patterns diminish the feasibility of mutual family assistance, while government aid reduces the tradition of self-dependence. Because of such changes as these, a supplemental benefit that was heralded a generation ago may generate little excitement today. Consequently, leadership must be sensitive and imaginative.

### Showing Genuine Concern

Mayo found in his famous Hawthorne studies that the employee's belief that the company was concerned about him or her as an individual was more important than the particular actions the company took. This insight suggests that supplemental benefits cannot be passed out with the assumption that the employees will be grateful. A policy of pioneering in this area must be accompanied by other demonstrations of genuine concern about the employee as an individual. Organization, personnel development, and supervision—discussed elsewhere in this book—are all part of the picture. In the proper combinations they give synergistic effects.

### Coordinating Supplemental Benefits with Operations

For reasons just outlined, central management must carefully analyze the particular operations of its company when deciding which supplemental benefits to stress. Generally speaking, companies that want to hold their employees over long periods and have low turnover will probably find their employees more responsive to supplemental benefits. In contrast, companies that use many part-time employees or have wide fluctuations in employment, as in the space industry, are more likely to find their employees saying, "Put it in the pay envelope." Location in or outside a big city will also affect the social and recreational activities that are attractive to employees.

Thus, supplementary benefits do not stand alone. They are feasible and powerful only when they accentuate some other characteristic of company operations.

## Industrial Relations

For managers and employees to work together to accomplish the objectives of an enterprise, they must agree on wages, hours, and other conditions of employment. For many years these agreements were made primarily between managers and individual employees. Even today, about three-fourths of the employees in the United States bargain individually with their employers. However, negotiations with powerful labor unions often receive wide publicity, and agreements reached with such unions set the pattern for many of the individual agreements.

Some people contend that the existence of a union makes the objective consideration of human resource policy futile. The assumption is that if management is not entirely free to make final decisions on such matters, the alternative is an irrational patchwork of agreements based on the bargaining surrounding each issue. Such a view is both unrealistic and unproductive. The manager designs products in terms of what customers will buy, sets prices on the basis of competition and within the limits permitted by law, and buys materials and borrows money under terms negotiated with the supplier. The views and strength of the union will, of course, influence the personnel policy finally established, just as the operating situations influence other policies. But the fact that the decisions are not made by the manager alone does not remove the desirability of a workable, integrated plan of action. The need for unemotional, careful analysis remains unchanged.

The chief broad issues that often have an impact on strategy concerning relations with unions are the character of the union relations, the scope of bargaining, and whether or not there is recourse to outside agencies. We shall consider each of these in turn.

## Character of Union Relations

A key aspect of all union relations is the underlying approach of a company to its relations with the union. The following examples illustrate the wide choice of approaches that are available.

### Belligerent Policy toward Unions

Companies engaged in interstate commerce are required by federal law to bargain with unions that represent a majority of their employees. Similar state laws require collective bargaining by most local businesses. Nevertheless, some employers balk at union activities whenever possible and do anything in their power to weaken the union.

Such an attitude usually stems from a conviction that unions are antisocial. It may be supported by experiences with corrupt union officials, or communist-led unions, or unions that fail to live up to their contracts. Whatever the causes, there is strong dislike and mistrust of the union by the company executives. They try to conduct themselves so as to discredit the union in the eyes of the employees. They hope that sooner or later the employees will repudiate the union and it will no longer have to be recognized as the bargaining agent.

Obviously, such a militant policy keeps the union stirred up; it will probably continue to use defiant tactics in its organizing efforts. At best there will be only an armed truce between the two factions.

### The Horse-trading Approach

Another view accepts the union as being inevitable but anticipates that relations will be conducted along horse-trading lines. The union is assumed to be unreliable and conniving; consequently, negotiations are conducted in an air of suspicion and sharp bargains are quite in order. In keeping with this approach, deals are made that resolve immediate difficulties but that violate sound principles of human relations. As one advocate of this policy said, "It is just a question whether you can outsmart the other guy."

### Follow the Leader

Often smaller companies try to establish an understanding with the union that the company will grant any wage increase or fringe benefits that have been agreed to by the leading companies of the industry or in the local market. These firms feel that they are too small and weak to stand up against the union. The most they hope for is to be no worse off than their large competitors.

This is undoubtedly a practical policy in some circumstances. It does, of course, have the weaknesses of any policy of appeasement. Naturally, the union is going to ask for, and probably get, the most favorable clauses that are granted by any of the leading companies. Having won these points, the union leaders may ask for even more, particularly if they face political problems within their ranks and feel they must win further concessions to strengthen their own position. Moreover, one important way a small company competes with a large one is by making special adaptations to the local situation. The follow-the-leader policy sacrifices this potential strength insofar as industrial relations are concerned.

### Straight Business Relationship

When both company executives and union leaders take a mature view of their relations, a company may approach union negotiations as a straight business proposition. This can occur only after union recognition has been accepted and the bitterness so often associated with such activities has passed into the background. There is mutual confidence, respect, and trust, just as there should be between the company and its major suppliers of raw materials.

This sort of business relationship does not mean that there will be no disagreements. The company may take a firm, even tough, position on certain matters; but the positions it takes are based on long-run business considerations, and there is a strong undercurrent of sound human relations.

Company executives must recognize that union leaders hold elected offices and that at times they must press grievances simply in response to pressure from some of their constituents. Under the straight business policy, this does not create a strong emotional reaction but is regarded simply as a normal part of the relationship. This type of relationship is often found in industries that have been organized for several years by a union which itself is stable and follows a bread-and-butter philosophy.

### Union-Management Cooperation

Still another tack is to regard the union as an ally in improving the efficiency of the business. One of the best examples of union-management cooperation is the agreement developed over a generation ago between Hart, Schaffner & Marx and the union representing its factory employees. The union recognized that the company was in a highly competitive industry; consequently, it helped make improvements in labor productivity. On the other hand, the company acceded to demands for higher wages and better hours.

From the start, there was emphasis on settling disputes by arbitration. The arbitrators have been highly respected individuals who always insist that questions regarding interpretation of an agreement be examined objectively. Even more important than wise administration of fixed agreements, however, are the methods developed to deal with technological and economic changes in new agreements. The actual operation of the plan has required a great deal of patience. Nevertheless, there is substantial evidence that employer and employees alike have benefited by the spirit of cooperation and toleration created by working together under such circumstances.

Union-management cooperation has taken different forms in the steel industry and in other places where it has been tried. In some cases a sharp distinction has been made between cooperative activities at the plant and bargaining over a new contract. In other instances, as in some agreements in the hosiery and ladies' garment industries, plans for improving productivity have become part and parcel of the basic contracts.

The foregoing illustrations range from a belligerent policy to union-management cooperation. The choice among these or other variations will have an impact on a company's ability to change strategy quickly. Modifications of products or technology, for instance, often can be executed only after union acceptance of associated job and wage changes.

An unusual development in union-management relations is management's resort to bankruptcy as a way of abrogating its former union agreement. For example, when Continental Airlines got into serious financial difficulties in 1983, its management said that continuing operations would be possible only if employees accepted large pay cuts and larger workloads. The union disagreed. So, for this and other reasons, Continental went into voluntary bankruptcy. This move opened the way for a fresh start in union-management relations. Note, however, that Continental management immediately faced a new choice of union relations policy within the range just discussed. The fresh start did not remove the issue of such relations.

## Scope of Bargaining

Recognition of a union does not, of course, indicate what activities are to be covered in the union-management relationship. By tradition and law, questions of wages, hours, and physical working conditions are normal subjects of collective bargaining. More recently, employee pensions and similar benefits have been added to this standard list. Most companies would also agree that job assignments, the use of seniority or other factors in selecting employees for layoffs or promotions, and other supervisory activities were legitimate subjects for discussion, although they might firmly oppose any written agreement as to how these matters were to be handled. As soon as discussions extend beyond these traditional subjects, questions arise as to whether the union is interfering with "management prerogatives."

Employees clearly have a real stake in the stability of their company. Their income and their economic future are strongly influenced by the prosperity of the firm for which they work. If the union function is to protect the workers' interests, is it not reasonable, then, that the union should participate in decisions regarding pricing, new customers, product lines, and similar matters?

This line of reasoning led unions in postwar Germany to insist on memberships on boards of directors and other means of codetermination. With a few exceptions, American unions have shied away from such arrangements. Union leaders have recognized that if they participated in such decisions, they would share responsibility for them. By staying away from such matters, they avoid managerial responsibility and continue to be in a position to criticize (a significant weapon in union politics).

While neither union nor management leaders want unions to become involved in the entire managerial process, it is likely that an increasing number of topics will fall within the orbit of union-management relations. Unions can be helpful on such matters as absenteeism, productivity, and installation of new processes. They are concerned about changes in plant locations and mechanization.

A flexible arrangement is to restrict the formal collective bargaining process to conditions of employment, and to work out other matters of mutual interest in a much more informal manner.

## Recourse to Outside Agencies

Union-management relations are not confined to an individual company and the unions representing its employees. Other parties may also enter the picture.

### Impartial Arbitration

Most union contracts provide for arbitration of disputes over the interpretation and application of the contract. Typically, a dispute follows a grievance procedure moving up from the worker and the first-line supervisor through several administrative levels. If the matter cannot be settled by management and union representatives, an impartial arbitrator is called in to make a decision that becomes binding on all parties concerned.

Some such provision is necessary if strikes are to be avoided during the period of the contract. Where a single impartial arbitrator has been used over a period of years, a sort of "common law" develops. Once this common law becomes accepted, many potential disputes are settled without reaching the arbitrator.

### Group Bargaining

The negotiation of a new labor contract is quite a different matter than its interpretation. The distinction is like that between the legislative and the judicial branches of the government. Usually the company itself works out the new agreement with its employees. To an increasing extent, however, employers are joining together in groups to negotiate new contracts with labor unions. Roughly a tenth of all contracts in effect are negotiated through employer groups, and these cover approximately a fourth of all workers under union agreements.

Industry-wide bargaining has been used in a few occupations, such as coal mining and air traffic control. More often, group bargaining covers employers in a city or a region. A company might want to join such a group for several reasons. The executives in small firms lack the time typically consumed in negotiations. In many instances they are not as skilled in the process as the professional union representatives with whom they must deal. Even the larger companies that have full-time industrial relations staffs may join an employer group in an effort to increase their bargaining strength. Moreover, the union has less opportunity to play one company against the other, pushing for different concessions with the several companies and then requesting everyone to agree to the most favorable concessions any competitor made.

On the other hand, such group bargaining makes it much more difficult to adapt the agreements to the particular situation of a given company. Thus, a company that is trying to develop an unusual strategic thrust in the area involved in the group bargaining may have to pursue independent bargaining.

### Government Mediation and Arbitration

When a company and a union cannot agree upon a new contract, and a strike threatens or actually begins, it is possible to call for the assistance of a government *mediator*. This person explores the dispute and tries to find some basis on which the two sides may agree. The company will determine in part when a mediator should be called in and how effective the mediator is likely to be. Some companies believe that this type of mediation is very helpful, while others resent the intrusion of an outsider.

If the impending strike is of sufficient importance to the public interest, the company may face other forms of outside assistance. Public utilities and basic industries are subject to fact-finding boards and impartial commissions of various kinds, depending upon the state or federal laws under which they fall. In this country we have not yet adopted *compulsory arbitration*, in which parties to such a disagreement have to submit the dispute to an arbitrator whose decision is binding. But government seizure and other forms of pressure bring us quite close to that point.

Settling union disputes, then, is not a private affair. As the range of bargaining options just described suggests, the company, its employees, its customers and suppliers, and the general public all have much at stake. For strategic reasons, the company may want a large degree of freedom, but on the human resource front such freedom has to be won.

## Crucial Horizontal and Vertical Linkages

If a company's strategy is to be carried out, human resources suited to that strategy must be available on a continuing basis. As we have seen, involved in obtaining such a flow are selecting and developing a work force that fits specific company needs, designing rewards that will attract and motivate such a work force, and building relations with labor unions that will provide strategic flexibility.

Because a lot of emotion is inevitably mixed into these human arrangements, human resource managers normally have a strongly preferred scenario of the way company relations with the labor market should be structured. Following that scenario, however, can have detrimental effects on other activities in the company. The net impact on strategy execution is hard to both predict and manage.

## Close Ties of Human Resources with Other Departments

Being concerned with supplying resources for other managers to use naturally forces the human resource department into close, continuing contact with almost all other divisions of the company. Departments needing a large number of employees and those needing scarce specialists will be especially concerned about the people they get.

The linking task arises because of the differences in viewpoints. User departments are concerned with achieving output—output with special characteristics. The human resource department, on the other hand, has to deal in the labor market, with all its peculiarities that we have so far discussed. Devising a good, workable fit between the labor market characteristics and the operational needs of a department may require give-and-take on both sides. Moreover, if employees are likely to move from one department to another, compatibility of personnel practices in the several departments becomes necessary.

A sample of the way human resource practices may affect the programs of other departments is summarized in the following list.

### Marketing

- Granting higher wages and fringe benefits often raises company costs relative to competitors; this is an important factor in competitive pricing.

- Agreements with workers about job structures may cut the marketing department's flexibility in making changes in product design. Union-management cooperation agreements also may slow down changes in product design and services.
- Equitable internal alignment of pay and other features of company-wide compensation systems are often hard to reconcile with sales incentive schemes.
- Employee training, especially of present employees for internal promotions, may not fit the marketing department's goals of timing and adequacy.
- Strikes and other slowdowns play havoc with a company's dependability as a just-in-time supplier to a large customer.

## R & D

- Standard company personnel practices become obstacles to designing special deals to attract and retain scientists and other scarce researchers.

## Production

- Increasing minority employment requires time for training and slows down production changes intended to increase productivity and product flexibility.
- Recognition of seniority and other claims to traditional jobs reduces production managers' abilities to reassign workers to fit new technology and new product designs.
- Providing safe work, health protection, flexible hours, and similar improvements in attractiveness of jobs complicate the tasks of production managers, often with no offsetting increase in productivity.

## Purchasing

- Job protection, especially when backed by union participation in decisions, constrains purchasing decisions on make-or-buy and on use of foreign suppliers.

## Finance

- Granting long-term obligations on pensions may create fixed charges that interfere with a company's ability to raise capital through bonds. Pension obligations, especially when provision for past service is not fully funded, can be a factor in mergers.
- Strikes or work stoppages may upset the timing of a new issue of company securities. If union relations are on a "horse-trading" basis, unions may press for concessions when new financing is being arranged.

- High wages and fringe benefits may narrow profit margins and cash flows to a level where the availability and cost of new capital are adversely affected. For instance, credit lines may be trimmed, interest charges may go up, and additional stock may be able to be sold only at low prices.

### Controlling

- Stable employment commitments and practices may make labor largely a fixed rather than variable cost. This upsets the customary ways of estimating costs of products and other accounting cost controls.

Fewer of the horizontal impacts of human resource moves on other departments are resolved by direct negotiation between the departments than occurs for the cross impacts discussed in preceding chapters. The main reason for this is timing: except for strikes and slowdowns, the typical employee response to human resource department moves is welcome acceptance—working for the company has become a bit more attractive. And with better harmony, the day-to-day activities of other departments are not upset. Also, the serious negative consequences, such as high costs or more rigidity, are delayed. Unfortunately, they accumulate to become burdensome at a later date.

Yet another problem is that uncertainty exists about how serious these potential negative consequences will be. Perhaps the internal structure will absorb them; possibly, employees will be more adaptable and energetic. If competitors are making similar moves—raising wages and pensions by comparable amounts—then the relative positions may remain about the same, at least until new competitors appear from outside the industry and/or country. Consequently, other departments are less inclined to challenge many human resource moves at the time they are made. Instead, serious doubts are likely to be passed on up to the general managers of the business-unit.

## Linking Human Resource Programs to Business-Unit Strategy

In contrast to, say, an R & D strategy program, where the business-unit strategy might make research a major competitive weapon, or in some other strategy program, where it might relegate research to a watchdog function, the human resource role is unlikely to be at either extreme.

Only occasionally is the human resource program designed to be a major competitive weapon. The few companies that have tried to make the way they handle personnel so outstanding that it becomes a major source of strategic potency, like IBM, Lincoln Electric, and several consulting firms, have achieved substantial differential advantages through the way they select and motivate their work force. But such superiority is difficult, often expensive, and unusual.

At the other extreme, few companies dare to merely get by with minor attention to human resources. Only if work is simplified and routinized, and an ample supply of eager workers is available—as is the situation in some developing countries—can a company safely make human resource activities a minor feature in its strategic management.

Instead, for the great majority of companies, the human resources department must provide "strong support" to strategic management. In terms of the model developed in Chapter 6, this means that the human resource department should be a leader (in the top 15 percent) among comparable departments in other companies in the strategic niche; that the department should systematically scan changes in its labor markets and respond quickly; and that adjustments in personnel practice should be made to support the strategic moves of the operating departments in the company. In general, the role of the human relations department should be powerful collaboration.

In practice, there is a weakness in the "strong support" that many human resource departments provide: they support only the existing company strategy, not a new strategy. Quite appropriately, the department has over several years cultivated relationships with various segments of its labor market. A set of policies and procedures has been infused throughout the company that are designed to assure equity and to comply with numerous laws on fair employment, collective bargaining, and the like. Moreover, fringe benefits in the form of pensions, vacations, medical plans, etc., have kept the company among the leaders in non-work-related compensation. Looking back, the human resource department has probably helped the company to be a "good employer." But in the process, it has fostered rigidities and committed costs which seriously interfere with changes in company strategy. The current difficulties of the U.S. steel and automobile companies in meeting world competition are caused, in part, by former human relations practices. They have become symbolic of human resource troubles faced in all sorts of industries (including education).

The task ahead is linking human resource systems to *new* company strategy, to building ways to accommodate change. In terms of the central theme of this book, more attention should be given to preparing for the future—to positioning companies to meet global competition and to structuring commitments so that change is a built-in expectation. Because jobs and social structures are so important to individuals, this modernizing of the programs of human resource departments will be one of the most difficult dimensions of effective strategic management.

Two observations on how to go about this lofty task will help keep this chapter placed in the overall framework of the text. First, leadership styles and behavioral approaches like "organization development" may very well *complement but not serve as a substitute* for the greater flexibility in human resource practices that are needed. The interrelationships between a company and its labor markets simply cannot be bypassed. Second, a practical place to begin revising human resource practices is building "strong support" for some specific new company strategy. This can be concrete and useful in the near term. However, such an adjustment should be regarded as only a step in learning how to be more flexible and how to adapt to the inevitable future changes in strategy.

## Questions for Class Discussion

1. Assume that your father is a successful clothing manufacturer in the Los Angeles area. He presumes that you will enter the company when you finish college, and he asks you what he should do about the recent changes in available workers. Starting in 1987, employers are legally responsible for making sure that none of their employees are illegal immigrants. Prior to this change in U.S. law, companies located close to the Mexican border (including your father's) commonly employed persons who might have slipped past immigration controls; such workers were in ample supply and could be hired at minimum wage rates. Currently, it is unclear (a) how much wage rates will increase because of the reduction in the size of the labor pool and increased union activity; (b) how many employers will continue to use illegal immigrants at very low pay, which will be possible because of the great difficulty in enforcing the new law; and (c) how much of the industry's production will move across the border, where very low rates are entirely legal. What is your advice to your father?

2. To assure quality and just-in-time delivery, U.S. automobile manufacturers are reducing the number of firms from which they buy parts and are relying on just one to three excellent suppliers for each part. If a labor union in one of these suppliers' plants goes on strike, not only that plant but also automobile assembly lines may come to a halt. Thus, the change in the automobile company's buying practice increases the bargaining power of unions in the parts plant. In view of this "environment," what sort of a union relations strategy do you recommend for automobile parts companies?

3. For the following positions, do you recommend a hiring policy giving preference to women, giving preference to men, or based solely on objective measurements? (a) taxicab driver; (b) hospital dietitian; (c) coal mine superintendent; (d) office secretary; (e) army officer.

4. For two generations Springfield Hardware Store gave personalized service to its customers. Salespeople had a wealth of knowledge about using tools and hardware products, and they gave friendly advice to do-it-yourself customers as well as to professionals. The pay and year-end bonus for the salespeople reflected this expertise to some extent. But competition has become increasingly tough for Springfield Hardware, and the third generation of owners has

finally sold the store to a chain which operates on a self-service basis. The primary task of the few employees in the expanded store area is to keep the shelves stocked with prepackaged merchandise. Do you recommend that the new owner retain the former Springfield Hardware sales personnel? If so, will retraining be desirable? How should the compensation of these people compare with their former pay? with that of newly hired workers?

5. In selecting an employer after you graduate, will you give preference to a firm that has a strong policy of promotion from within? Explain your answer.

6. Starting salaries for outstanding MBAs (and law-school graduates) paid by investment banks and large management consulting companies have become dazzlingly high—probably double the average pay of experienced supervisors and middle managers at all levels in business generally. These prize salaries tend to increase the starting pay expected by most of the newly minted MBAs each year. Among the consequences are MBA salaries that are out of internal alignment of pay within companies; slower pay increases for MBAs; and for some companies, withdrawal from the MBA market. What policy for employing and paying MBAs do you recommend for (a) your local telephone company? (b) a corner drugstore or other small business? (c) a hospital?

7. Fired employees in more than two-thirds of the states have won cases against employers for wrongful discharge when company manuals, like that of Y Corporation, made benign statements such as "We accept our responsibility to provide you with good working conditions, good wages, good benefits, fair treatment, and the personal respect which is rightfully yours," or when oral promises were made to allow employees to resume old jobs after promotions or transfers that did not work out. In view of these lawsuits, the legal department of Y Corporation proposes to add to the personnel manual, "This manual is not a contract of employment, and we retain the right to alter this manual at any time. This policy does not in any way affect our right to terminate an employee for any reason at any time." In your opinion, will a statement like that proposed by the department affect recruiting in any way? Will it affect other personnel functions?

8. Long-range forecasts by the U.S. Department of Labor show a steady decline in the United States of new workers through 1995 and a period of labor scarcity that could last until the turn of the century. Labor surpluses of the late 1970s and early 1980s have already turned into labor scarcities in some cities and regions. The problem is compounded by a widening mismatch between the skills workers have and the skills employers need. Many jobs in fast-growing service industries require at least a high school education. But high school dropouts and graduates who are barely able to read make up about 1,200,000 of the potential new employees every year. According to the Hudson Institute's Workforce 2000 report, women and minorities will be the largest groups of the new entrants into the work force. Both groups tend to support unions more than do other labor categories, according to various ex-

perts in the field. So unions are working hard to reverse their long decline in membership and in prestige. Explain what human resource departments can do to grapple with these changes and, in light of the changes, to help carry out a company's strategy.

9. Should unions, as representatives of employees, have more, or less, participation in company discussions regarding expansion, product lines, mechanization, location, and vertical integration than representatives of (a) customers, (b) major suppliers of materials, (c) government, (d) bondholders, and (e) stockholders?

10. A three-year international survey commissioned by the Public Agenda Foundation revealed that many American jobholders are giving less than their maximum effort. Only 22 percent of the workers interviewed said that they were performing to their full capacity, while 44 percent said they do not put a great deal of effort into their jobs over and above the minimum requirement. Has the great American work ethic disappeared? No, report the researchers. People still say their jobs mean more to them than just a paycheck and that doing a good job is important to their self-respect. But pay is a different matter. About 50 percent of the work force believes there is no relationship between how well they do a job and how much they are paid. The work place does not reward or recognize people who put in extra effort, the researchers said. (a) What kind of reward systems might overcome this effect? (b) Can management do anything at all to increase worker productivity? (c) Does company strategy have any influence on worker productivity? Should it?

# CASE
## 12 Jennings & Lowe

As a step toward reducing the cost of legal services, Jennings & Lowe is experimenting with the use of "legal assistants." Neither the managing partners nor the legal assistants themselves are satisfied with the results to date.

### Need for Restraints on Legal Costs

In the United States, total outlays for legal fees have increased dramatically—almost as fast as medical costs—during the last decade. Much of this increase reflects a social trend toward suing somebody whenever a loss is suffered. The widening net of governmental regulation adds further to the burden.

In addition to more suits and more reports, the cost per hour (or per case) for a lawyer's time has jumped. This rising "cost per unit" is closely correlated with higher salaries paid to lawyers, especially by the large law firms, and to the higher overhead of these firms (rent in new buildings, price for word processors, and the like).

The widespread professional practice of law firms is to charge each client a fee based on the hours devoted to work for that client. Each member of the firm has a "billing rate," and the fee normally is hours worked multiplied by the appropriate billing rate, plus direct expenses such as travel. So when law firms must pay high salaries to attract the cream of the crop from leading law schools and to retain outstanding individuals on their staff, the billing rates for these individuals are increased, and this in turn leads to higher fees charged to clients.

Jennings & Lowe, one of the largest and most prestigious law firms in Chicago, is concerned about the impact of this rise in the cost of legal services. Although Jennings & Lowe benefits from higher income in the short run, the managing partners are keenly aware that many of their clients are considering ways to hold their legal expenses in check. Greater use of an in-house legal staff, instead of an outside firm, is only one of the various moves that clients are weighing. Moreover, the managing partners feel that they have a professional obligation to keep their fees no higher than necessary to provide first-class legal counsel.

## The Legal Assistant Concept

In 1970 the American Bar Association endorsed, amid much dissent, the use of paraprofessionals. This new stratum of workers, often called "legal assistants" or "assistant attorneys," perform routine and standardized legal activities under the direction of a professional lawyer (a person who has completed law school, passed state bar examinations, and otherwise qualified for a license). Legal assistants can do such work as index and file documents, summarize testimony, prepare wills and tax returns, and prepare copyright and trademark applications. Many of these activities have increased in volume as government regulations have become more complex, and they can consume a lot of the time of fully trained (and high-priced) professionals.

The basic concept is that persons with at least two and preferably four years of college education will take an intensive three- to six-month course specially designed for paralegals. Such a course gives students extensive exposure to legal terminology and methods and then requires a concentration in one field of law: probate-estates, tax, labor litigation, insurance, criminal law, corporate law, trademark and patents, or the like. A few special schools have built a reputation for giving such training. However, state certification standards and examinations have not yet been established, and consequently ambiguity exists about who is entitled to perform paralegal work.

The use of legal assistants can provide some relief on the pressure to lower legal costs. Salaries for legal assistants are only 40 percent or less of salaries for newly minted, lowly lawyers who are brought into law firms as "junior associates." The hourly billing rates to clients is also much lower, typically half of the rate for junior associates. (The ratio of billing rate to salary is larger for beginning personnel than for senior personnel because more of the latter's time is devoted to training and supervising the less experienced persons.)

At first, the new profession of legal assistant mostly attracted single women with bachelor degrees in liberal arts who were having difficulty finding socially acceptable jobs. Others included those who were thinking of or could not get into law school and felt that being a legal assistant was the next best job. More recently, junior colleges have introduced paralegal programs and there has been an influx of 20-year-olds. This influx has tended to lower both the salaries and status of legal assistants. In general, the role and position of legal assistants has not yet stabilized; for example, how legal assistants might compare with trained nurses or other paramedics is far from clear.

## Legal Assistants at Jennings & Lowe

The managing partners at Jennings & Lowe have to decide how the concept of legal assistants can best be fitted into their activities. Indeed, Jennings & Lowe is sufficiently influential in the Midwest to help shape developments in the entire profession.

Founded in 1880, Jennings & Lowe has a long history of successful practice. Its partners over the years have included a presidential candidate, a United Nations Ambassador, an Atomic Energy Commissioner, and an ex-president of the American Bar Association. It has represented many top corporations, railroads, and public utilities, and through its unofficial lobbying it has written many pieces of federal legislation.

The firm now consists of about 250 attorneys, half of whom are junior or senior partners. In addition, there is a staff of 150 secretaries and 75 other supporting personnel. The firm occupies five floors of a very modern office building. It is clearly a prestigious place to work.

Because of Jennings & Lowe's age, size, and traditions, internal relationships tend to be formal and stuffy. The hierarchy among managing partners, senior partners, junior partners, senior associates, and junior associates is well recognized, and orderly procedures are carefully observed.

Officially, management of the firm is exercised through a series of committees of partners. However, the partners are deeply involved in client problems, and daily administration of the supporting staff is performed by an office manager who reports directly to the chairman of the executive committee (which is composed of 17 managing partners).

Recent growth of Jennings & Lowe has created minor strains. Several of the newly hired associates are known to take their suit jackets off while in the office! In an effort to hold rising overhead in check, limits on salaries of the supporting staff have been set, with the result that Jennings & Lowe pay is only average for the city and well below that paid by other top law firms. Turnover of the supporting staff is high.

Five years ago the executive committee decided that Jennings & Lowe should try using legal assistants. The firm now has 30 (27 women and 3 men; see Table 12–1 for the amount of education, length of service, salary, and other information about each legal assistant). They were hired by the office manager, but are assigned to work under lawyers who deal with their respective specialties. These legal assistants are kept busy, and most of the associates—who are the ones who give them most of their assignments—find their help quite satisfactory. The chief drawback is that the newly hired legal assistants require quite a bit of supervision—"and then they quit." The average employment span of legal assistants who have come and gone is under three years.

## Reasons for Turnover

In exit interviews with legal assistants who have left Jennings & Lowe, low pay is mentioned as a reason in ninety percent of the cases. However, other sources of dissatisfaction loom large.

"It's a dead-end job. Without a law degree, there is simply no chance I can ever do much more than I'm already doing."

"I feel like a flunky. The lawyers are very secretive, especially the older ones. They don't tell us what a case is all about or what they wish to prove. That's supposed to be part of 'Jennings & Lowe tradition.' They talk about being assigned to a team, but we aren't treated that way. How can you be part of a team if you don't even know what play has been called?"

"At the office we live in 'no man's land.' We are not accepted as professionals because we don't have a law degree. On the other hand, many of the secretaries resent the fact that we are supposed to be different from ordinary staff and that our time is billed to clients in the same way as a full-fledged lawyer's. Actually, the experienced secretaries make more money than we do, but we're younger and they act like they wish we'd blow away."

"The office manager is a Scrooge. Like the lawyers, our pay is reviewed on employment anniversaries. But they set a maximum percentage on our increases and don't include us in annual bonuses that the lawyers get. As paraprofessionals, we aren't paid for overtime work. The lawyers I worked for—who are great—asked Scrooge to give me a raise, but he said he had to follow firm policy."

"I'm tired of being exploited. I take home only a small fraction of what Jennings & Lowe collects for my services."

A recent incident stirred up the legal assistants. An across-the-board five percent "inflation adjustment" pay increase was announced for all supporting staff. The wording of the announcement could be interpreted to include the legal assistants, but a few hours later a notice was distributed to legal assistants saying that any adjustments in their salaries—like that of the lawyers—would be considered at the time of anniversary reviews. Several legal assistants decided to organize a

**TABLE 12-1.**
**LEGAL ASSISTANTS AT JENNINGS & LOWE**

| Specialty | Age | Education | Prior Experience | Starting Salary | Years at J & L | Current Salary | Billing Rate/hr. |
|---|---|---|---|---|---|---|---|
| **Docket** | | | | | | | |
| Coordinator | 31 | High School | Salesman | $12,000 | 5 | $20,700 | $45 |
| 1 | 26 | B.S. History* | — | 11,200 | 4 | 15,300 | 37 |
| 2 | 25 | B.S. Business† | — | 12,600 | 3 | 16,500 | 33 |
| 3 | 25 | B.S. Business‡ | — | 12,700 | 2 | 16,000 | 33 |
| 4 | 22 | High School* | Legal Secretary | 12,700 | -½ | 12,700 | 30 |
| **Probate** | | | | | | | |
| Coordinator | 47 | 2 yrs. College | Banking | 8,000 | 14 | 25,500 | 52 |
| 1 | 42 | B.S. Home Econ. | Banking | 12,000 | 5 | 20,700 | 45 |
| 2 | 26 | B.S. English* | Accounting | 12,000 | 2½ | 15,200 | 37 |
| 3 | 27 | B.S. Philosophy* | Accounting | 11,700 | 2 | 14,100 | 33 |
| 4 | 25 | B.S. Psychology* | — | 11,200 | 2 | 13,800 | 33 |
| 5 | 51 | High School | Banking | 13,800 | 1 | 15,000 | 37 |
| **Litigation** | | | | | | | |
| Coordinator | 37 | B.S. Pol. Sci.* | Paralegal | 18,000 | 1 | 19,500 | 40 |
| 1 | 25 | B.S. Psychology* | — | 12,300 | 3 | 14,700 | 37 |
| 2 | 24 | B.S. Sociology | Congressional Aide | 12,700 | 3 | 15,000 | 37 |
| 3 | 24 | B.S. Psychology | — | 12,400 | 2½ | 14,100 | 33 |
| 4 | 23 | B.S. Rhetoric* | — | 12,000 | 1½ | 13,600 | 33 |
| 5 | 24 | B.S. French* | — | 12,300 | 1½ | 13,500 | 33 |
| 6 | 25 | B.S. History | — | 12,700 | 1½ | 13,600 | 33 |
| 7 | 25 | B.S. Psychology* | Real Estate | 13,500 | 1½ | 15,700 | 30 |
| 8 | 21 | High School* | — | 12,300 | 1¼ | 13,500 | 30 |
| 9 | 23 | B.S. Art History | — | 12,900 | 1 | 13,900 | 30 |
| 10 | 20 | High School* | — | 12,300 | 1 | 13,800 | 30 |

## TABLE 12-1.
## LEGAL ASSISTANTS AT JENNINGS & LOWE (continued)

| Specialty | Age | Education | Prior Experience | Starting Salary | Years at J & L | Current Salary | Billing Rate/hr. |
|---|---|---|---|---|---|---|---|
| Litigation Coordinator | | | | | | | |
| 11 | 20 | High School* | — | 12,700 | -½ | 12,700 | 30 |
| 12 | 19 | High School* | — | 12,700 | -½ | 12,700 | 30 |
| Real Estate | | | | | | | |
| 1 | 23 | B.S. Sociology* | — | 12,700 | 1 | 14,400 | 40 |
| 2 | 22 | B.S. History* | — | 13,000 | 1 | 13,900 | 37 |
| Environmental Law | | | | | | | |
| 1 | 28 | B.S. Chemistry* | E.P.A. | 13,000 | 3¾ | 18,000 | 50 |
| Corporate | | | | | | | |
| 1 | 27 | B.S. Teaching* | — | 12,000 | 3¾ | 15,700 | 45 |
| 2 | 23 | B.S. Psychology* | — | 12,700 | 1 | 14,100 | 37 |
| Marketing | | | | | | | |
| 1 | 25 | B.S. Advertising* | Advertising | 13,000 | 2½ | 14,700 | 37 |
| 2 | 22 | B.S. Marketing | Advertising | 13,500 | 1½ | 14,200 | 30 |

*Also has certificate from paralegal school.
†Also has 2 years of law school.
‡Also has 1 year of law school.

meeting of paraprofessionals, and this was called off only when the office manager issued a further clarifying notice to the legal assistants stating that they would receive at least a five percent raise at their anniversary date.

## Management Viewpoint

For the older partners who have been skeptical from the beginning about the use of legal assistants, the high turnover is regarded as evidence that the paraprofessional concept does not fit into a high-class legal firm.

The office manager disagrees. "Paraprofessionals make sense. Using them saves money for our clients. The quality of work does not suffer. We make a normal profit. The legal assistants have a nice job in excellent surroundings. Everybody gains.

"Of course there will be turnover. Most of them are not ready to settle down. 'Relationships,' not lifetime commitments, are fashionable these days, and the legal assistant has a relationship with the firm for a few years and then moves on to something else. Oh, there will be a few who are content with the low level of responsibility and will stay on, but the legal assistant position is not a career for most of the people we hire for that spot.

"Remember that a law firm is built around its legal staff. We devote a great deal of effort recruiting young lawyers; *they* will be the future of the firm. We select carefully, pay well, and hope they will stay for a long, long time. That's where we put our money—not on paralegals.

"It's not difficult to replace the legal assistants, given a little time. Most who leave their first job go into some other kind of work, so we depend on the schools for replacements. As we learn to use them, I think we should increase the number substantially."

## Questions

1. Do you think the use of paralegals, as the practice is described in this case, is desirable from the social point of view? Would your answer be the same for the use of paraprofessionals in the medical field?
2. Should Jennings & Lowe change its "production technology" and/or its services for clients so that legal assistants can be used more effectively?

# INTEGRATING CASES

## Strategy and Creating Goods and Services

### Northwest Airlines' Hubs

Senior management at Northwest Airlines has a clear strategy for developing a strong, defensible position in the U.S. airlines industry: build a route system based on "hubs."

The hub-and-spokes concept is well known: schedule incoming flights from many cities to arrive at the hub at about the same time, say 1:00 P.M.; then schedule outgoing flights to leave at about 2:00 P.M. Such a schedule gives passengers many possible connections, not only to large cities but also to and from medium or small cities. For example, jet travel from Grand Rapids, Michigan, to Lincoln, Nebraska, via Minneapolis is a simple matter—at least on the schedules. And for this convenience travelers will probably pay full fares.

Probably more important for a specific airline is retaining the ongoing passengers on its line. By providing convenient connections at the hub, a passenger picked up in a small city is likely to take a continuing flight on a plane of the same line. Thus, the spokes become feeders for other flights.

Deregulation of the airlines, giving them much freer choice of the routes they would fly and the prices they would charge, aided the development of hubs. At first, deregulation encouraged the start-up of a lot of new carriers, often providing flights between cities that previously had been poorly served with only prop planes. The upsurge of People Airline is a well-known example. But severe price competition soon developed, and a wave of failures, acquisitions, and mergers followed. This shakedown has enabled companies like Northwest to build their hub structures quite rapidly.

Several modifications in flight patterns are emerging. The number of nonstop and one-stop flights between city A and city B is diminishing. Instead, passengers are routed through the hubs, where they must change planes to a connecting flight. This increases the optional destinations available to passengers and often the number of flights per day, but it also raises the frequency of changing planes.

More striking is a rise in the concentration of flights in and out of a hub airport by a single airline or two airlines. This concentration arises partly because the larger airlines have acquired smaller carriers that used to serve their hub cities. Also, once an airline has several flights at a hub, an additional spoke to a different city is a further attraction to existing inbound travelers, and the new inbound travelers find an array of possible connections. The degree of the resulting concentrations at several hub airports is shown in Table 1.

A striking feature of the list of hub airports in the table is that Northwest appears to be the dominant carrier in three of the 11 locations, and in each of these three airports Northwest is very strongly entrenched. None of the three—Detroit, Memphis, and Minneapolis—was a major interconnection point prior to Northwest's decision to make it a hub.

The shift in concentration which has taken place since deregulation is reflected in the relative position of airlines serving the Minneapolis/St. Paul airport. As Table 2 indicates, Northwest dominates at this airport.

Northwest's strategy in using hubs as a source of differential advantage has contributed to its recent growth. During the decade 1977 to 1986, its passenger miles more than doubled and its operating revenue more than tripled (see Table 3).

There is another side to Northwest's hub development: the company's ability to create the services that the strategy calls for. As the manager of ramp services at Minneapolis says, "We sometimes face a logistics nightmare." Planes arrive each day in three peaks—in the morning, around noon, and in the early evening—as is necessary to take full advantage of the hub concept. And these peaks strain capacity.

### TABLE 1.
### AIRLINE SHARE OF FLIGHTS AT HUB AIRPORTS

| Airport | Dominant Airline Share | | Second-Ranking Airline Share | |
|---|---|---|---|---|
| Atlanta Hartsfield Int'l. | Delta | 52.5% | Eastern | 42.2% |
| Chicago O'Hare Int'l. | United | 49.2 | American | 27.2 |
| Dallas/Fort Worth | American | 63.4 | Delta | 23.7 |
| Denver Stapleton | United | 44.3 | Continental | 40.9 |
| Detroit Metropolitan | Northwest | 64.9 | American | 5.9 |
| Houston Intercontinental | Continental | 71.5 | Eastern | 5.7 |
| Memphis Int'l. | Northwest | 86.6 | Delta | 7.1 |
| Miami Int'l. | Eastern | 48.5 | Pan Am | 16.6 |
| Minneapolis/St. Paul Int'l. | Northwest | 81.6 | United | 3.5 |
| Pittsburgh Int'l. | US Air | 82.8 | Eastern | 4.1 |
| St. Louis-Lambert Int'l. | TWA | 82.3 | American | 2.4 |

In a typical day at Minneapolis in 1987, Northwest has 229 flights carrying about 15,000 passengers.[1]

---

[1]Following the acquisition of Republic Airlines in the fall of 1987, Northwest had 262 daily flights through Detroit and 208 daily flights through Memphis.

**TABLE 2.**
**SHIFT IN SHARE OF FLIGHTS AT MINNEAPOLIS/ST. PAUL**
**INTERNATIONAL AIRPORT SINCE DEREGULATION**

| 1979 | | 1987 | |
|---|---|---|---|
| Northwest | 40.1% | Northwest | 81.6% |
| Western | 14.5 | United | 3.5 |
| Republic | 10.8 | American | 3.2 |
| Eastern | 3.8 | Continental | 3.1 |
| Ozark | 3.4 | Others | 8.6 |
| Others | 27.4 | | |
| | 100.0% | | 100.0% |

**TABLE 3.**
**OPERATING DATA: NORTHWEST AIRLINES AND U.S. INDUSTRY, 1977–1986**

| | 1986* | 1985 | 1983 | 1981 | 1979 | 1977 |
|---|---|---|---|---|---|---|
| *Northwest Airlines* (U.S. and foreign) | | | | | | |
| Operating revenues ($ millions) | | | | | | |
| Passenger | 2,920 | 2,154 | 1,812 | 1,522 | 1,067 | 861 |
| Freight | 407 | 328 | 289 | 222 | 160 | 121 |
| Total (includes mail & charter) | 3,589 | 2,655 | 2,196 | 1,854 | 1,311 | 1,046 |
| Operating income ($ millions) | 167 | 77 | 69 | 12 | 55 | 104 |
| Net earnings ($ millions) | 77 | 73 | 50 | 10 | 72 | 93 |
| Revenue plane miles (millions) | 247 | 159 | 133 | 120 | 116 | 111 |
| Available seat miles (billions) | 48.4 | 37.1 | 29.5 | 24.8 | 24.1 | 23.0 |
| Revenue passenger miles (billions) | 28.8 | 22.3 | 17.7 | 14.3 | 13.3 | 11.1 |
| Load factor (%) | 59.5 | 60.1 | 60.0 | 57.4 | 55.3 | 48.3 |
| Revenue passengers carried (millions) | 23.2 | 14.5 | 12.7 | 11.1 | 11.6 | 10.3 |
| *Scheduled Operations of Major Domestic Airlines* | | | | | | |
| Revenue plane miles (billions) | 2.5 | 2.3 | 2.0 | 1.9 | 1.9 | 1.8 |
| Revenue passenger miles (billions) | 243 | 223 | 191 | 172 | 181 | 141 |
| Revenue passengers carried (millions) | 290 | 268 | 223 | 205 | 211 | 172 |

*1986 figures for Northwest Airlines include Republic Airlines for the last three months, reflecting the acquisition of Republic by Northwest.

During some periods, planes arrive at the same gate every 25 minutes. To transfer baggage, clean up the cabin, refuel, and reload passengers in that interval requires that everything be done without a hitch. Any delay upsets many other operations, because other gates are fully scheduled as well at peak periods. Holding planes on the runway thus has a domino effect.

Just transferring checked luggage is sensitive. Northwest has installed a $2.5 million system in Minneapolis that can sort 3,600 bags an hour by using bar codes on the tags. But a conveyor breakdown in such a system calls for manual handling at the rate of one bag per second!

The ticket agents—the front-line interface with travelers—face the greatest strain in peak periods. In addition to doing their work accurately while under the pressures of time, they have to be pleasant to impatient travelers who may have stood in line for 30 minutes and are worried about missing their plane. With the frequent changes in special fares and in schedules, there are plenty of opportunities for misunderstandings at the ticket counter.

Of course, the pressure escalates when there is a delay. For instance, if a plane from Des Moines, Iowa, is late due to mechanical trouble, should all connecting flights be held up to help the travelers on the late plane? Or in bad weather, which does happen in Minneapolis, the entire tightly knitted system comes apart; passengers may be stranded, and thousands of reroutings have to be made. Even when there is a later flight, transferring passengers to it often results in overbooking, and then a few people have to be coaxed or bribed to give up their seats. This, in turn, creates another cause for delayed departure.

That Northwest is getting a reputation for poor service is not surprising under these conditions. This feeling of annoyance is compounded in those locations where Northwest is the only carrier offering jet service. In such cities fares are unlikely to be discounted, and the traveler has no good alternative. One analyst of the airline industry estimates that Northwest has increased its fare at the Minneapolis hub 30 percent in the last three years. "These highwaymen are charging us more for poorer service" is a common complaint.

Indeed, the deterioration of airline service generally is so pronounced that several bills are pending in Congress which would mandate stiff penalties for poor service. One House measure calls for an airline to be fined $10,000 for a canceled flight (except for safety reasons); it would also force carriers to hand out free tickets if baggage arrives more than two hours after the flight lands.

A transportation economist, Professor Ernest W. Williams, Jr., comments, "The hub-and-spoke route structure appeals to the individual airline because it keeps the passengers on that line and, thus, increases revenues. But for the industry as a whole it is uneconomic. It significantly increases the number of landings and takeoffs to provide the same number of passenger miles of service. As a consequence, passenger service suffers for three reasons. First, changing planes involves delay even when all goes well. Second, the chances of missed connections and lost luggage are greatly increased. Third, costs go up because of the extra landing, and to offset this rise the airlines are overbooking flights, having fewer substitute planes in case of breakdowns, and failing to match the size of their ground crews with the peaks created by hub routing and scheduling. It is true that the airlines will develop ways to ameliorate the peak problems, but the uncertainties of weather make tight control impossible and the cost of extra landings can't be removed by a computer!"

Although some experts and some Northwest employees believe that the hub approach has been pushed to the limit, Northwest and virtually all major carriers seem to be trying to expand the use of the concept.

## Question

Currently at Northwest Airlines the overall strategy to push growth via the hub-and-spoke route structure has outrun the company's capability to provide good service. What changes, if any, do you recommend in either the strategy or the service supply program to bring the two into better balance?

# Dover Apparel Company

"The apparel industry is a critical source of jobs in the United States—over a million of them," explains an industry representative. "Traditionally poor immigrants, today many garment workers are women and minorities. They are on the border line; for most of them, if they lose their jobs, unemployment and welfare are their only alternatives.

"In fact, the industry has already lost about 200,000 jobs—from a peak of 1,400,000 in 1973—because of foreign imports, and the trend will continue unless steps are taken to stop it. Apparel imports mean more unemployment. The country can't stand more unemployment. So from an economic as well as humanitarian view, imports should be reduced."

The issue expressed in this quotation is only one of the factors Dover Apparel Company must weigh in deciding whether to go abroad for expanded production capacity.

## Need for Expansion

Dover Apparel Company is a successful producer of children's clothing, especially girls' dresses. Under the leadership of Irving Perlman, son of the founder, Dover has become a recognized leader in higher quality girls' dresses and related outer garments. Its Princess line is regularly carried by better stores throughout the country, its styling is good, and stores have learned to depend on consistently high-quality products and reliable deliveries. In a volatile industry, this kind of dependability is a basis for repeat business.

Dover's reputation is no accident. Twenty-five years ago, Irving Perlman (now 58) convinced his father to shift emphasis from women's to girls' dresses, and they were fortunate in hiring a very good designer. Irving then switched his attention to production. Hoping to get a relative cost advantage, Dover opened a new plant close to Atlanta, Georgia. And as the relative sales of girls' dresses grew, the Georgia plant was expanded. Production in New York City was stopped completely by Dover in the early seventies.

Actually, the expected low southern labor costs were not obtained. To ward off unionization, Dover kept its wage rates and benefits almost equal to those in New York City. And to maintain quality and assure delivery, Dover employed technical staff and bought new equipment. Within the last few years the company went even further into "modernization." It has invested over $1 million in recently devised electronic pattern-making equipment and electronic cutting equipment. This equipment greatly speeds up the making of patterns for various sizes of a basic design: it speeds up and probably improves the laying out of the patterns on stacks of cloth so as to reduce waste, and the actual cutting is also faster and more precise. Only large and financially sound manufacturers can afford such equipment.

In addition, Dover has fully computerized its production scheduling and inventory control. While adding to overhead, this computer setup aids in stabilizing the sewing operations and is especially valuable in helping the company meet its delivery promises.

As a result of these and related moves, Dover is on the leading edge of production technology. But its costs are not low. Assuming good volume, it can match New York City costs for comparable quality. However, other southern shops which keep overhead and labor costs low can produce for 5 percent less.

Last year, profits were just over 2 percent of sales. On $51 million sales, net profits were $1.1 million. The condensed balance sheet at year end is shown in Table 1.

A third-generation Perlman, Joseph (age 32), is being groomed for management, and he is spearheading an expansion. Dover does not now sell knit slacks, knit skirts, shorts, or sportswear. Joe has convinced his father that this is a natural

**TABLE 1.**
**BALANCE SHEET, DOVER APPAREL CO.**
**(in thousands)**

| | | | |
|---|---|---|---|
| Cash | $1,350 | Accounts payable | $6,040 |
| Accounts receivable | 6,580 | Other current liabilities | 1,100 |
| Inventories | 7,260 | Long-term debt | 3,040 |
| Fixed assets (net) | 3,090 | Equity | 8,100 |
| Total assets | $18,280 | Total liabilities and equity | $18,280 |

expansion of the present line. Although such products are often sold at low, highly competitive prices, the Perlmans believe that well-styled, color-coordinated numbers could be a good complement to their Princess line—and might even be capable of being extended to boys' wear. Even when treated as a supplement to the Princess line, knitwear sales could add 10 to 20 percent to total sales. And the potential knitwear market is much larger than the niche Dover now services.

The main difficulty with this expansion is production costs. Typical children's knit clothing does not have clear quality differentiation, and production is simpler than for dresses. So low-cost products provide keen competition. Foreign competition is especially severe: more than one-third of children's knitwear clothing is imported, chiefly from Korea, Taiwan, and Hong Kong. Although Dover hopes to sell its knitwear at premium prices (because of styling and company reputation for quality), a wide margin above prevailing prices could severely limit the volume of sales. Success of the new line requires, among other things, production costs which are no higher than costs which other dependable suppliers will have in the future.

## Options for Sources

Joe Perlman has explored alternative locations for the production of the proposed knitwear products. He summarizes his present thinking as follows.

### 1. U.S. Production

"Wherever we go, we want to take advantage of our modern pattern-making equipment and our computerized production scheduling and inventory control. We're ahead of our competitors and must reap the benefit of the investment we have made. There is ample capacity in these operations.

"On the other hand, we are short of space in sewing. Besides, sewing knit goods takes different machines and somewhat different skills. So we do not plan to sew the new products in the present plant.

"The simplest arrangement, especially when the volume is still small, is to subcontract sewing of all knitwear and do everything else in the present plant. Or, if we found the right subcontractor, he or she could also finish and pack. We have subcontracted girls' coats with good results, and there are even more shops looking for knit goods contracts.

"An alternative is to set up a separate knit goods plant of our own. It's just a question of where to send the cut pieces for sewing and finishing.

"The obvious trouble with either subcontracting in the U.S. or opening our own shop here is high labor costs. Labor rates in developing countries are a fifth to a tenth of what we pay. In the U.S., labor is about 30 percent of total costs, so foreign producers have a 25 percent overall f.o.b. cost advantage. Of course, there is freight, tariff, and time to consider. Nevertheless, for as long as we can see, smart foreign competitors will be able to sell in U.S. markets with lower costs than we will have if we manufacture domestically."

### 2. Latin American Production

"How about subcontracting in Latin America instead of in the U.S.? Incidentally, we have reluctantly dropped Puerto Rico from consideration because their cost advantage is narrowing. If we go into a non-English speaking country, we might as well go where the labor differential probably will continue to be substantial.

"The political climate in most Central and South American countries is not attractive for new investment. Governments are unstable, inflation is causing unrest, socialism if not communism is becoming common, and Yankee business is a popular target for nationalistic politicians. I think Colombia has one of the least troublesome situations right now, and that country seems interested in more textile business.

"We have been advised that using a local subcontractor in Colombia would involve much less political risk than setting up our own subsidiary. But that raises other problems. The prospective subcontractors we have contacted so far do not have a long record of dependable, quality work. And if the one we selected got into difficulties, we would be in a poor position to step in to help. We hesitate to be so dependent for a supply of products which we are just launching into the market."

### 3. Far Eastern Production

"Of course, most apparel imports come from the Far East. Japan is no longer competitive; its labor rates have risen so that it is importing products like knitwear much as the U.S. is doing. And the costs in Hong Kong—long an apparel center—are beginning to rise. Taiwan and Korea are now the major sources of low-cost products imported into this country. In the U.S., we can't come even close to their costs.

"Frankly, I'm leery of both Taiwan and Korea on political grounds. Both countries need strong U.S. support to prevent a communist takeover. As we build closer ties with China, our commitment to these buffer states could diminish.

"There is an interesting alternative. Sri Lanka (formerly Ceylon) has unused capacity and is highly interested in establishing new foreign markets. This island, about the size of West Virginia, lies to the southeast of India. Known for centuries as a source of tea, spices, gems, and rubber, industrialization has passed it by. Its 16 million population has a very low average income, and because much food is imported, the country often has an unfavorable balance of trade.

"A study by the World Bank recommended establishing a textile industry, and the Bank advanced funds for training and for equipment. Apparel cut and sewn in Sri Lanka soon flooded the European markets. However, at just this time an 'orderly marketing agreement' was negotiated (under GATT auspices) which set quotas for textile imports into Western Europe. These quotas are based on historical trade and sharply restricted permissible imports from newcomers like Sri Lanka. As a result, textile plants which started with high hopes and grew rapidly for two or three years now are closed or cut way back.

"Dover Apparel Company could easily form a joint venture with a Sri Lanka mill. I know of two enterprises eager to join with us, and the government is encouraging such a scheme. We could lease existing plants and equipment (though additional machines would be needed for our specific requirements) and have low taxes. Probably $200,000 is all we would have to invest in the joint venture.

"Air freight makes production in a country on the opposite side of the world possible. Only three or four days, either way, are necessary for transportation. We might cut cloth here in the U.S. and ship pieces out for sewing—as mentioned for Colombia. The import duty on such work applies only to the value added abroad. More likely, however, we would purchase fabric on the world market (possibly in the U.S.) and have it both cut and sewn in Sri Lanka. They have facilities for cutting and would use the patterns we supply.

"Wages of three dollars a day look attractive to many Sri Lanka workers. In fact, that additional cash income can raise an entire family out of poverty. However, a direct comparison with U.S. rates of four dollars an hour is not warranted because of differences in the social structure and in productivity. Most Sri Lankans are Buddhists, and I understand they have even more holidays than we do! Nevertheless, at present exchange rates, preliminary estimates do indicate that after paying freight and import duties garments made in Sri Lanka would cost us 15 to 20 percent less than comparable products made entirely in the U.S. Estimates for sewing in Colombia show a 10 percent saving.

"The government of Sri Lanka, formed with a new constitution in 1972, is still developing its traditions and institutions. However, the country was ruled by Great Britain from 1796 to 1948, when it became a self-governing dominion of the Commonwealth. English is commonly spoken, and it should be as easy for Yankees to do business there as in India.

"Incidentally, the U.S. government has negotiated some bilateral 'orderly marketing agreements' for textiles with Korea, Taiwan, and Hong Kong—like those restricting imports into Europe. However, Sri Lanka has been such a minor source of textile imports into the U.S. that there is currently no prospect of quota restrictions between these two countries."

## Other Views

Dover's production vice president is skeptical about foreign production. "I have to admit that I can't get costs down to match foreign competition. But I'm afraid we are heading for trouble. We have to work hard to keep on schedule with good quality right here in our own plant. How can Joe or anyone else do that thousands of miles away?

"Even more serious is what may happen to our labor relations. Our workers aren't dumb. They know that importing means fewer jobs here in the U.S. When Dover starts importing even knit garments, some workers will start thinking that their jobs might come next. And that's the kind of issue which labor organizers can exploit—no matter how much we deny it. I'm sure we could learn to live with the ILGWU, but we would have had a rough time installing our new pattern-making and cutting equipment if each move had to be negotiated with a union. We have good relations now. Is it wise to rock the boat?"

Irving Perlman is more venturesome. "When I came into the business my father gave me a chance to try something new. And it succeeded. Now I've told Joe that he should develop a way that we can live with foreign competition. He will have to make whatever plan we adopt work—even if that means spending months abroad every year. We now have many more dollars at stake than I did, but it is much the same. Now, as then, the company might be ruined, or it can position itself to be strong for the next couple of decades."

## Questions

1. What is Dover Apparel Company's social responsibility in this situation?
2. Assuming that Dover does add knitwear to its line, what procurement strategy should it follow? If you wish, consider variations or additions to the alternatives presented.
3. On the basis of the information that you have and your answers to the preceding questions, do you recommend that Dover add knitwear to its line?

# CHAPTER 13

## Strategy Programs in Finance:
## Allocating Capital

### Influence of Financial History

Capital, like personnel, is an essential resource for every enterprise. Equipment must be obtained, materials purchased, employees paid, and sales and administrative expenses met—all before any goods are available for sale. Then a month or more may elapse before customers pay for purchases. Even a law firm selling only services will incur payroll expenses and have accounts receivable. Capital fills the gap between the time outlays are made and revenues flow back in.

In formulating strategy regarding uses and sources of capital, *cash flows* require primary attention. Capital already invested in fixed assets or debts already incurred become active when they affect the inflow or outflow of cash. Occasionally direct exchanges are made of, say, company stock for land, but these are exceptional shortcuts. The most pressing problems relate to (1) getting capital in the form of cash and (2) allocating cash (liquid capital) to the most propitious uses.[1]

The outside sources of this cash—banks, stockmarkets, insurance companies, etc.—are a specialized "industry" or market. They have their own traditions, regulations, and standards. It is with this specialized industry that the finance department of a company must deal. Indeed, the concepts and language used in the industry usually dominate the culture of finance people within companies. And this creates problems!

Recurring issues that arise in applying concepts of the financial industry to companies are that (1) the financial standards used for allocating capital to specific operating activities within the company often conflict with strategic programs desired by marketing, production, R & D, and other departments; (2) the financial conditions within a company that must be present to obtain more capital from the financial markets often give minor weight to important strategic missions and thrusts; and (3) the measures of success carried over from the financial

---

[1]Remember that accounting profit or loss does not refer to cash. A profitable company may be short of cash when expanding sales call for additional inventory and accounts receivable; likewise, it is quite possible for a losing company to liquidate assets (turn them into cash) at a faster rate than losses occur and thereby increase its cash position. Of course, profits should sooner or later generate cash; the question for financial management is when this cash will be available and whether the flow is large enough to meet cash requirements.

markets to company and department performance often fail to emphasize target results flagged in business-unit strategy and department strategy programs.

Because outside capital must be obtained by a growing company from the financial markets, and because financial concepts are based on a vast pool of experience, every general manager should understand the influence of financial thinking on company operations. Accordingly, this chapter focuses on allocation of capital, and the next deals with the sources of capital. Since together, the two deal with a single department—finance—only a single review of vertical linkages is presented. The impact of financial *measurements* is a different issue and is considered in Chapters 20 and 23.

## Relation of Strategy to Allocation of Capital

In a sense, financial policy concerning the use of capital does not stipulate the *specific* uses of capital; these are determined by other management decisions. Plans for sales—such as products to be sold, sales appeals to be stressed, plans for production and purchasing, decisions to "make" rather than "buy," heavy use of automation, and other comparable plans—dictate the uses of capital. Nevertheless, capital plays an essential supporting, facilitating role.

Strategy lays out the positive direction a company will take. Executives throughout the company then create plans for carrying out their respective parts of the strategy. And from these plans come specific requests for capital and other resources. Specific allocations of capital can be made only after the creative planning process has generated alternative proposals.

In a well-managed company, however, planning is not done in isolated bits. Instead, tentative ideas are passed back and forth among departments, alternatives are suggested, rough estimates are provided, and objections are raised while the plans are still being formed. A vital part of this give-and-take process is checking on the availability of capital and other resources that each alternative would need. And as we have already seen, often a resource—people, plant capacity, vendors' cooperation, or capital—can be provided only if certain conditions are met. Bargaining and trade-offs occur, and eventually specific requests for capital emerge out of this discussion.

Before putting such plans into action, however, most companies insist that the plans pass through a financial screening. Requests for fixed assets go through a capital expenditure approval process, while current expenditures go through a financial budgeting process. It is here that criteria that originate in the financial industry may be rigorously applied. And because these standards are quantitative and high, this financial screening often usurps attention; it, instead of strategy, is likely to become the primary hurdle that department planners design their proposals to clear.

Not every company goes through all the steps of the screening process, but their points of view are quite consistent.

## Regulating Investment in Fixed Assets

## General Restrictions

In every active enterprise, from landscape gardening to generating electricity, all sorts of proposals are made for additions to facilities. Managers concerned with a particular operation naturally think of new equipment that would enable them to do their job better or at lower operating expense. Long-term development programs are also proposed. One way to regulate such proposals is to subject them to a series of tests or screens, as indicated in Figure 13–1.

### Consistency with Long-Range Plans

Company strategy often stipulates the markets to be sought or the production technology to be used. Such aspects of strategy can be translated into more specific policy guides.

A paper company with a mill in the northern United States, for example, became concerned about the increasing costs of its pulpwood. Careful study showed that on many of the types of paper it was making, southern mills using southern pine enjoyed a cost advantage. While shifting to specialty papers was a possibility, the company concluded that the best strategy was to move closer to the large sources of raw material. Consequently, a policy of making no major investment in fixed assets in its northern mill was adopted. Only the purchase of miscellaneous equipment necessary to operate existing machines would be permitted, and installation of new machines or substantial expenditures on the existing building would be postponed at least until the outlook for a northern mill improved.

Another firm announced a similar policy because the probable shift in demand for its product would make its present plant somewhat obsolete. If new processes had to be adopted, then the firm wanted to move into a new building in a suburban location. In the meantime, it chose to keep itself in a flexible position and made only essential investments in fixed assets.

### "Hurdle" Rate of Return

The policy just illustrated stipulates a type of fixed asset to be avoided or encouraged. A different kind of investment guide is a minimum rate of return that must be anticipated if capital is to be assigned to a proposal. For example, the policy might be that any new investment in fixed assets must earn at least 15 percent annually on the initial investment after provision for depreciation and taxes. Then, a proposal to buy a computer costing $50,000 that was expected to result in an average net saving of $6,000 per year during its life would be rejected because the 12 percent return falls below the acceptable minimum.

For such a standard to be useful, the method of calculating the rate of return should be defined. Depreciation, taxes, interest, net investment, and several other

**FIGURE 13–1.**
**FINANCIAL SCREENING OF CAPITAL EXPENDITURE PROPOSALS**

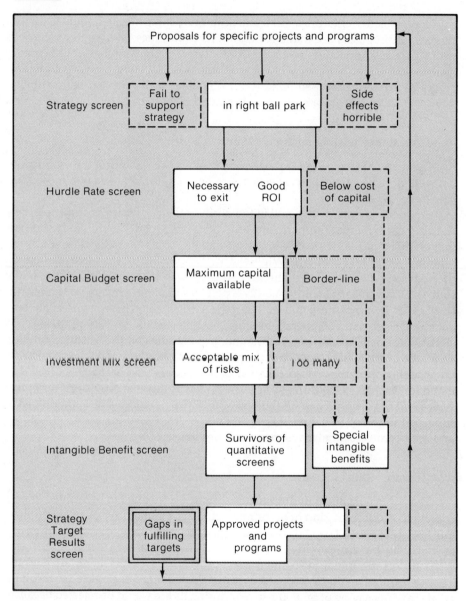

items can be treated in different ways. So, to avoid ambiguity, the standard should indicate the formula that was assumed when the minimum was set.[2]

Theoretically, the minimum permissible rate of return should be the average cost of capital to the company (a weighted average of the company's long-term borrowing rate and the price-to-earnings ratio of the company's common stock). In practice, a desire for expansion, willingness to sell more stock, funds already available, judgment about future risks, and similar considerations affect management's choice of the minimum rate. Since most managers who propose new investment in fixed assets tend to be optimistic in predicting the benefit of the action, financial managers of many companies counter by setting the "hurdle" rate higher than the theoretical minimum.

### Risk Classifications

Many investments are so risky that they should have an expected return higher than the basic hurdle rate. Uncertainty surrounds every investment: the activity made possible by the investment may not work as predicted; workers may not like the change, or they may even sabotage it; materials and energy inputs may cost more than expected or be unavailable; customers' tastes may shift; competitors may react vigorously; and pollution controls may be more severe than predicted. Since one investment often is subject to many more such uncertainties than another investment, we cannot compare them without making an adjustment for differences in risk.

One way to deal with differences in risk is to place proposals into classifications reflecting the odds for success. Table 13–1 illustrates simple classifications.

Either a company can set a minimum acceptable return for each risk class, or the predicted result of an investment can be multiplied by the appropriate discount factor to obtain an "expected return." If the classification and the discount factor are accurate, the "expected returns" for all investments have been adjusted for risk and can be compared with one another.

In theory, discounting for risk can be greatly elaborated. A whole array of possible outcomes with probabilities for each can be projected. Successive contin-

**TABLE 13–1.**
**RISK CLASSIFICATIONS**

| Risk class | Extra Discount Factor for Risk | Representative Investment |
|---|---|---|
| High risk | 0.2 or more | Exploratory oil well |
| Medium risk | 0.5 | R & D on disposable oil can |
| Low risk | 0.8 | Expansion of frozen food display cases |
| Minimum risk | 1.0 | Replacement of 40-year-old elevators |

[2]For most situations, the estimated rate of return in a typical year or average year is as precise as the underlying data warrant. However, for proposals involving long time periods in which the cash outflows and inflows will occur at sharply different and irregular dates, the estimated rate of return should be made by the discounted cash flow method.

gencies can be recognized in a "decision-tree" computation. Risk discounts can be combined with time (interest) discounts. Rarely in practice do the underlying data warrant actual computations of this sort, but the concepts may help clarify the degree of risk involved. More significant and subtle is the absorption of risk by people making various estimates. Central managers should know how much allowance for risk their subordinates have already made in the figures submitted before they do their own classifying or discounting.

The simplest way to use risk classifications is to establish a hurdle rate for investments in each class—say, 15 percent for minimum-risk investments and 30 percent for medium-risk investments. The "expected return" computations give synthetic figures which are best suited to capital budgeting.

## Capital Budgeting

Frequently, a company has many more possible investments in fixed assets than it can prudently finance. The issue then becomes which projects to endorse and which to reject. *Capital budgeting* is a method for making this selection.

First, all major proposals for additions to fixed assets are described and analyzed, and predictions are made of the amount of the investment and the resulting benefits of each proposal. Obviously, this analysis and prediction must be carefully done because the soundness of all subsequent steps can be no better than the data fed into the process. The whole task will be simplified by promptly screening out all proposals that are not consistent with marketing, production, purchasing, and personnel programs and with the general investment policy just discussed.

Next, the predicted investment and results of each proposal should be expressed in dollars insofar as possible. The figures that are pertinent are *additional outlays* the company will make if the project is undertaken and *additional receipts* (or reduced expenditures) that will result from the project. (If outlays are widely separated in time from receipts, they can be made comparable by reducing each to its "present value.") Intangibles should also be recognized, both costs and benefits—for example, the flexibility or strategic advantage of entering a new market. These intangibles must be listed because the budgeting process deals only with dollar figures and time; it tends to deemphasize intangibles and strategic considerations.[3]

---

[3]Theoretically, the dollar estimates can include contributions to strategic moves or detractions from them. In practice, however, these broader effects are difficult to estimate (and may not be fully understood by people making the specific proposal), so they are normally treated as intangibles.

The scope of each proposal determines which intangible factors should be weighed. If the proposal deals only with, say, replacing autos used by sales representatives, we disregard many intangibles because all alternatives assume the same people doing the same work. However, if closing a branch or dropping a product line is at issue, then many questions about employee morale, competitors' reactions, and the like must be included.

Note that the rate of return based on incremental results and incremental investment differs from the overall average. For instance, assuming we stay in business, the incremental value of a telephone vs. no telephone will be very high. One of the major reasons for prior screening of capital proposals against strategy criteria, suggested earlier, is to clarify the assumptions and to narrow the factors to be weighed for a particular proposal.

Then, proposals should be ranked, with those showing the highest rate of return to outlay at the top and those with the lowest return at the bottom.

Finally, management can proceed down the ranked projects until (1) the capital available is exhausted, assuming overriding reasons exist for keeping the total within a fixed amount, or (2) the rate of return falls below the minimum acceptable rate. Before projects below the cutoff point are rejected, intangible benefits should be appraised to decide whether the added advantages are important enough to move a project up into the acceptable list. Similarly, intangible costs of projects above the cutoff point should be assessed with an eye for projects that might be dropped.

## Investment Mix

Every firm makes some high-risk investments and some low-risk investments. The proportions, however, among the high-, medium-, and low-risk commitments can vary a lot. Just as the "marketing mix" (see Chapter 8) used by a company should be adapted to its strategy, so also should the "investment mix." A company that makes only high-risk investments would be too unstable, while all minimum risk forces liquidation. A healthy arrangement is some mixture, just as a healthy human diet provides a mixture of nutrients and energy.

### Risk Profile of a Small Firm

Alain Ribout, the owner-manager of a successful motel in the Laurentian mountain region of Canada, faces several attractive propositions: enlarge and improve his present kitchen and parking facilities, add a large wing to his present building, build a new motel 30 miles away at the site of a proposed new ski lift, and invest in a new ski lift. Both the uncertainty and the potential rate of return rise in the order in which the four alternatives are listed.

Selection of any one investment will affect Ribout's interest in making other investments. For instance, commitments to both the new motel and the ski lift, Ribout feels, would be risking too much on the success of one development. Likewise, if he embarks on a new wing expansion, he hesitates to also start a second motel. But he does want to share in the growth of the area. So to keep his overall risk exposure in balance, Ribout is now inclined to make two moves: (1) ensure continuation of his present success by improving the kitchen and parking facilities, and (2) take a high risk by investing in the ski lift.

A Missouri farmer, to cite another case, is being encouraged by a poultry processor to double his capacity to raise broilers from chicks. This would involve a $100,000 investment in highly mechanized facilities, which could be recovered in four or five years *if* the demand for broilers continues to grow. The farmer actually spends most of his time raising corn, but with present equipment this is not profitable. A shift to large-scale mechanized methods for raising corn would require changing fences and fields and buying new equipment worth $85,000. An alternative is to use fields for grazing beef cattle and to take a job that will provide cash income for current expenses. Since the family can easily muster the small additional labor to care for the expanded broiler activity, the farmer could handle both the broiler and the new corn venture. But he hesitates to take both risks at once. He prefers a choice between (1) the new corn operation plus present broiler activity or (2) expanded broiler activity plus cattle grazing and cash income from an outside job.

A mixture of high-risk and low-risk investments with an eye on dependable cash flow is needed in both of these examples. Since a choice of any one alternative modifies the attractiveness of the others, a view of the total mix is desirable.

The concept of investment mix has application beyond the particular examples for small and large firms just cited. Single-product firms face questions of acquiring sources of raw material or mechanization: an art museum must select the kinds of art and the kinds of services it will provide, and even universities venture forth in some directions and hold back in others. The investment policy on such matters is midway between broad strategic directions and specific projects. It identifies, for all persons involved, areas where investments will be encouraged and other areas where investments will rarely be made. Clearly, the investment mix approach is less mechanistic and more sophisticated than capital budgeting.

An additional risk arises from investment intensity. Data on many businesses analyzed by the Strategic Planning Institute show clearly that heavy investment in mechanization and in inventory and accounts receivable tend to reduce profitability. More capital tied up per dollar of sales increases the risk of low profits. (See Figure 13–2.) The risk is especially great for companies with low market shares.

### Summary

Procedures guiding the investment of capital in fixed assets take several forms. First, we may set up general restrictions that screen out many proposals. Ideally, these restrictions state the kind of activity that will, or will not, be supported, based on company strategy. Also, hurdle rates of return, perhaps refined for different risk classifications, narrow the projects that receive serious consideration. Then, to select among remaining proposals, we can either employ capital budgeting or seek a balanced mixture of high- and low-risk ventures.

The preceding description has indicated where strategy considerations can be introduced into the screening process. In practice, this is difficult to do effectively. Most of the financial inputs are quantitative and often have some accounting figures (perhaps estimates) to back them up. By contrast, the strategy inputs are likely to be "soft" data. Since the hard quantitative data tend to carry more weight in final choices than the soft data, the influence of financial criteria is exaggerated.

**FIGURE 13–2.**
**AN INVESTMENT RELATIVE TO SALES RISES, PROFITABILITY DECLINES**

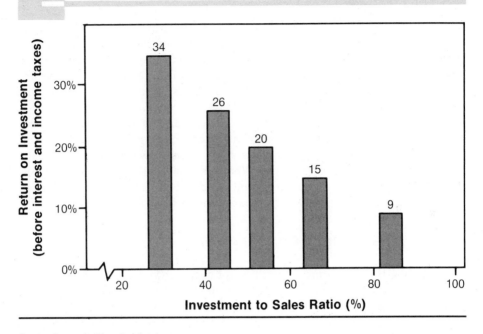

*Source:* Strategic Planning Institute.
"Investment" is fixed assets at book value plus working capital. The sharp drop in profitability is largely due to two very different reasons: (a) arithmetic—investment intensity enlarges the denominator of ROI; (b) intensity of competition—high investments and fixed costs cause anxiety to obtain sales.

See also D.C. Hambrick and I.C. MacMillan, "Asset Parsimony—Managing Assets to Manage Profits," *Sloan Management Review,* Winter 1984.

## Leasing Versus Purchase of Fixed Assets

Analysis of investment proposals may reveal more attractive opportunities than can be absorbed by a company's normal financial structure. When this occurs, long-term leasing instead of buying the fixed assets should be considered.

Of course, reasons other than financing may make leasing attractive. The outlook may be so uncertain that owning your own building is imprudent, or prospects of rapid expansion and relocation may suggest flexibility in asset commitments. However, in the present discussion we are concerned with leasing as a way of reducing the need for tying up capital in fixed assets. Here is the way it works. An investor, perhaps an estate or an insurance company, with funds for long-term investment buys a building or equipment we want to use and at the same time leases it to us for a long period. The rental payments are high enough to cover real estate taxes, depreciation, and repairs, as well as interest on the capital tied up. Note that these are all expenses we would have to pay if we owned the building.

If the asset to be leased has to be constructed to our own peculiar requirements, we may actually build and equip the structure and then *sell and lease back*. Also, we may have the option to buy the asset when the lease expires, 10 or 20 years hence, at a depreciated value. Both of these provisions make leasing even more like owning. The investor, in turn, is in much the same position as a mortgage holder, because the investor relies on our contract for interest and the return of the investment. (In some circumstances, the investor may be able to postpone paying income tax.)

A few companies have a *policy* to lease rather than buy certain types of assets. For example, oil companies and retail chain stores may regularly use such an arrangement for their many retail outlets. Most firms, however, resort to leasing only occasionally for some large asset. Whatever the frequency, the operating cost and the tax implications should be carefully studied because a long-term lease obligation is just as binding as mortgage or debenture bond obligations.

## Policy Restraints on Current Assets

Like long-term investments, the flow of capital into current assets can be a troublesome issue. The marketing department may want liberal credit terms for customers and lots of inventory to assure prompt delivery. The manufacturing department may want to build up inventory so as to stabilize production and to have long production runs. But such a practice ties up capital. The finance department will point out that low accounts receivable and inventories relative to sales will increase the return on assets. Here, again, financial standards are used to help run a tight ship.

## Operating Needs for Inventory

The size and the composition of inventory should be determined primarily by operating needs. As explained in Chapter 11, the following factors should be considered: the minimum inventory necessary for uninterrupted operations, economical sizes of purchase orders and of production runs, production for inventory to stabilize employment, advance purchases to get seasonal discounts, and anticipation of price changes and shortages of supply. Inventory policy blending all these considerations is one of the main issues in wise procurement. Financial limitations are a different and additional constraint.

## Budgetary Limits on Inventory

Inventory absorbs capital. The cash spent for finished goods, work in process, and raw materials is not available for other uses as long as these stocks remain on hand. Consequently, financial policy dealing with the allocation of capital to competing uses frequently places an overall limit on the size of inventories.

A common way to limit inventory is to budget the total size month by month. Each time the budget is revised, the use of capital for inventory is weighed against other needs. This establishes a mechanism for seeking the optimum use of capital throughout the company. Of course, since inventory serves as a buffer between purchasing, production, and sales, the actual inventory may deviate from the budgeted amount, but the guide to desired inventory levels is clear.

Budgetary control of inventories is particularly well suited to companies that have wide seasonal fluctuations. In the automobile industry, for example, cutting back of production and disposing of inventory of one model while scheduling start-up on production of next year's model is a tactical problem of considerable significance. Similarly, the buildup and disposition of Christmas merchandise and agricultural supplies calls for short-run adjustments.

## Policy on Inventory Turnover

A second way to limit inventory is in terms of turnover ratios. Thus, a retail shop may aim for an inventory in relation to sales of 25 percent, or four turns per year. The turnover standard creates pressure to dispose of slow-moving, obsolete stock; accumulation of such stock is likely to lead to future losses. Moreover, high inventory relative to sales increases the company's exposure to price fluctuations. And, since inventory turnover is frequently used by outside credit analysts, a company's credit standing can be improved by fast inventory turnover in relation to industry averages.

For internal administration, separate turnover ratios for raw materials and for finished goods, perhaps broken down by type of product, are more useful than a total composite figure. Often the turnover will be stated in terms of months of supply to avoid arguments about values to be used. A primary purpose of this kind of standard is to induce inventory managers to decide what kind of stock is worth holding and to clean out past mistakes.

Note that as inventory policy becomes more specific, it shifts from a general financial guide to an operating control. This fuzzy dividing line between finance and operations is characteristic of many financial issues and, unless adroitly handled, becomes a source of jurisdictional dispute.

## Investment in Accounts Receivable

The finance department's concern with accounts receivable is similar to its concern with inventory. First, the company's credit policy should aid the execution of strategy. This means that liberality in granting credit to customers and in making collections should be consistent with stress placed on credit as a sales appeal. Defining the function (service) that credit is to perform is essential. Second, budgetary limits may then be set for the total capital allocated to accounts receivable. These limits will arise from the capital-allocating process and will reflect a balancing of alternative uses of capital. Third, turnover ratios can be set to check the soundness of accounts and to avoid further losses from an accumulation of uncollectible accounts. As with inventory, even more detailed constraints, such as "aging" the accounts receivable (that is, listing those 30 days overdue, 60 days overdue, etc.), move from general financial limitations into operations. The basic task of financial management in the area of accounts receivable, then, is to set policy regarding (1) the purpose of extending credit, (2) allocation of capital among competing uses, and (3) maintenance of the quality of the asset.

A special issue is the *use of outside financial institutions*—banks, credit companies, and private lenders—to provide customer credit. Outside firms will be glad to extend installment credit because this is profitable business by itself. For help in carrying regular commercial accounts receivable, the company must pay a fee, the size of which depends on who makes the credit investigation, who collects the accounts when due, and who bears the risk of bad accounts. The basic question that financial management must resolve is whether to reduce capital needs for accounts receivable by turning to outside firms. The answer hinges on two factors: (1) How important to the company is close customer contact and integration of credit with other services provided to the customer? (2) How does the cost of outside service (the fee paid or the installment profit foregone) compare with income that can be earned by using the capital saved for other purposes?

With current assets, then, as with fixed assets, the question of how much to invest arises again and again. Arithmetic won't provide the answer because the estimates of benefits from the investment come from user departments while the estimates of cost come from the finance department, whose viewpoint and culture are shaped by a different outside industry.

## Calculation of Profits

Allocating capital among fixed and current assets is part of a broader task of guiding the flow of capital in, around, and out of the company. Theoretically, at least from a financial viewpoint, maximizing profit will be the key to resolving such problems. Unfortunately, "the bottom line" is not as fixed as it may appear in the annual report of a company.

Management has significant discretion in how profit is calculated. Income taxes, reputation in the financial community and hence ability to raise new capital, and perhaps executive bonuses—all are affected by this calculation. Three main areas where differences of opinion may arise are accounting reserves, capitalization of disbursements, and inventory valuation.

## Accounting Reserves

The extent to which accounting reserves are set up may affect company profits significantly. The issue is what expenses to anticipate in accounting reserves and what decline in asset value to show in such reserves.

Expenses that involve an immediate outlay of cash or those for which there is written evidence, such as a bill from a vendor of raw materials, are easily recognized. On the other hand, expenses that require no immediate outlay of cash but that must be met eventually are subject to greater error or manipulation. Depreciation of equipment and buildings, provision for uncollectible accounts, and anticipated expenses such as unassessed taxes or contingent losses are examples of this latter type. For instance, one spring morning Citibank announced that it was increasing its bad debt reserve by three billion dollars! Often the amount of the expense is not known accurately, and opinion may differ as to how much should be charged against the operations of a particular year.

The customary way of handling such items is to make a reasonable estimate of the amount to be charged against operations each year, and then to include this figure along with other expenses as a deduction from gross income in the calculation of net profit. At the same time, a so-called "reserve" is set up on the accounting books in anticipation of the time when the cash payment or the discarding of assets will take place. It should be remembered that this reserve is not a special cash fund put aside to meet an anticipated cash payment. Such an account does, however, perform an important function in preventing the overstatement of profits.

A conservative policy is to create large reserves, even though this cuts stated earnings. Conversely, a company wanting to show immediate profits may build accounting reserves slowly. For example, a hospital may depreciate equipment that will not wear out with 20 years of continuous use at a rate of 10 percent a year because improved methods of operation will probably make this equipment obsolete in 10 years' time. In contrast, a large resort hotel depreciated its equipment at an average rate that would have taken 50 years to cover the original cost, even though this hotel catered to upper income customers who expected up-to-date service and modern equipment.

## Capitalization of Disbursements

A similar issue arises in the treatment of product development expenses and improvements of fixed assets. Here the cash has been paid out, but the question is whether to treat the disbursement as an expense in the current year, and thereby reduce profits, or to *capitalize* it.

The treatment of patents illustrates the problem. If a company buys a patent, it clearly has an asset the cost of which should be charged as an expense, not all at once, but year by year during the life of the patent. But when a patent comes out of the company's research laboratory, the situation is not so clear. How much research cost should be attached to that patent, treated as an asset, and written off year by year? The more cost that is capitalized as an asset, the higher the profits will be in the current year.

Likewise, when a wooden floor in the plant is replaced with a concrete one, should the cost be treated as a repair expense or should at least part of the outlay be shown as an asset? Disbursements for intangibles like training or advertising a new product are regularly treated as expenses, but what of the cost of an elaborate demonstration model which, while built for a World's Fair, will be used for several additional years?

## Inventory Valuation

Still another fuzzy area in the computation of profits is valuing inventory. Judgment has to be exercised in deciding what is obsolete, what is damaged beyond its point of usefulness, and what is missing an essential bearing. Value depends on future demand as well as on the physical condition of the inventory; but the future need in the company for repair parts, and the demand by customers, often are uncertain. Someone has to say that a specific item is still a good asset or that it should be written off (or down). Here, again, the higher the value attached to inventory carried as an asset, the higher will be the current profit.

Inflation adds further questions to inventory valuation. If inflation causes a specific item to rise in value while it is held in inventory, the company can sell that item at attractive nominal profit. But the cost of replacing the item has also risen; so much or all of the nominal profit is used up just getting the physical inventory back to the starting size. Real profits have been overstated in such a situation. One way to reduce such a misleading statement of profits is to compute cost on a LIFO (last-in-first-out) basis. Here the price of the most recently purchased item (during inflation this will be the highest priced item) is used to compute profits; the remaining inventory is valued at the earlier and lower profits. Thus, the use of LIFO helps to cut down overstating of profits during inflation, but inventory will probably be undervalued in terms of current price levels.

Many companies now use LIFO and then report in a footnote on their balance sheets how much their inventories are undervalued in terms of the current prices.

## Issues in Profit Determination

Limitations surround the size of reserves, the capitalization of costs, and the valuation of inventories. The public accounting profession has devoted much effort to establishing "acceptable practice" in these and related areas. Federal tax regulations of what may be treated as an expense on income tax returns (and hence not be taxed) are comprehensive and complex. Securities and Exchange Commission stipulations stress full disclosure in annual financial reports. Nevertheless, a substantial latitude for management action in these areas remains.

Central management does not, of course, deal with the numerous specific entries involved in the computation of profit. Instead, it should set general policy indicating the degree of conservatism to be followed throughout the company. When room for judgment is present, should it be resolved in favor of low values of assets, large reserves, and, to the extent that these entries are acceptable to the Internal Revenue Service, low taxes? Or will the policy be to show as high a profit as is legitimate within the area of judgment?

A related issue is *when* guides for profit computation should be changed. If a given method for computing profits is followed consistently year after year, the effect of the method chosen tends to balance out. Profits postponed from last year show up this year and largely offset this year's potential profits that have been deferred until next year. However, if a conservative policy is followed one year and then a liberal policy the next, the effect on the results reported for any one year can be much greater. Consequently, many prudently run companies stress *consistency* fully as much as the particular valuation methods employed. Other companies have a policy to postpone and *minimize income taxes* in any legitimate way, including judgmental aspects of determining profits if such should be propitious.

The way profits are calculated has some effect on capital allocation. A "conservative" practice—i.e., recognizing uncertain expenses early and postponing income until it is virtually in the bank—makes investments that are close to the cutoff level look bad. Thus, risk-taking is discouraged. Indeed, there is clear evidence that Japanese companies regularly make long-run investments in product and market developments which would not pass U.S. financial standards.

The other side of the argument is that conservative standards protect the unwary investor.[4] Also, a dependable, steadily growing, stable enterprise will have some advantages in raising new capital, as is discussed in the next chapter.

From a strategy viewpoint, flexibility in the way profits are calculated is preferable, especially for internal decision-making purposes—provided that the basis of the calculation is made known to the user of the resulting figures.

## Sensitive Links Between Capital Allocation and Operating Departments

Allocating long-run (fixed) and short-run capital naturally is of concern to every department of a company: everybody needs cash. However, this flow is especially sensitive in some areas, either because of the large amounts that will be tied up for a long period or because of debatable valuation of the asset. These are the points where a clash between the financial viewpoint and the operating viewpoint is most likely to occur. Here, negotiations over strategic moves may have a high impact.

Differences between the finance department and operating departments come to the surface early because finance usually has simple yes-*or*-no screening controls. Proposed projects that need capital allocation may not proceed without an "o.k." from finance. And in many companies the critieria that finance people

---

[4] A single standard for establishing reserves, which is preferred by the Internal Revenue Service, can be carried too far—especially in a mature industry facing obsolescence of its fixed assets. The U.S. steel industry, for instance, wrote off its old mills too slowly. Thus, it paid taxes and dividends based on unreal profits, when it should have recognized the obsolescence, cut its profits thereby, and used the cash inflow to modernize its plant and equipment.

use for such screening are standards carried over from the financial industry, like those described on the preceding pages.

Subjects on which conflicting opinions are likely to arise include the following:

## Marketing

- Liberal credit for customers may be a sales appeal stressed by the marketing department, but finance sees the resulting accounts receivable as risky, low-return assets.
- Finished goods inventories that are built up to permit prompt deliveries to customers, including just-in-time parts customers, run into similar objections. High inventories reduce turnover and expose the company to risks of obsolescence.
- Control over channels of distribution and company-owned wholesale and retail outlets often requires very large investments in facilities, inventories, and accounts receivable. Viewed separately, the ROI may be low according to finance department standards, but marketing sees the distribution network as a vital way to hold market position.
- Developing new markets—new niches or foreign countries, for instance—usually involves cash for product promotion and other cash outlays that will not produce a positive cash flow for several years, and maybe not at all. For finance, such expansion thrusts may look like dubious investments.

## R & D

- Early stages of research and experimental development always involve a long-run investment, and often high risk. Neat accounting ROI estimates, if prepared at all, are just guesses. Such programs and projects fail to fit the usual financial screening mechanism.
- Capitalizing patents and other research findings help the short-run ROI, but doing so creates doubt about the actual future earning power of stated assets. In financial circles, showing such assets may undercut the credibility of the entire balance sheet.

## Production

- Automation of production calls for large investment in fixed assets. Labor savings are typically used to justify these outlays. But if the move merely matches competitors' actions, an increase in cash flow may not materialize. Finance then asks, How is the interest cost of the invested capital to be covered?
- Inventory can be used as a buffer between stabilized production and fluctuating shipments. But finance people view such inventory as expensive and risky to hold. The offsetting benefits to production and to steady employment for workers are hard to quantify.

- The flexibility to produce a variety of new designs quickly often calls for different equipment and an associated scheduling system, all of which require long-term capital investment. Marketing benefits, but the accounting records may show neither increased total output nor lower costs. Finance people have a hard time finding an ROI on such an investment.

### Purchasing

- Decisions to make rather than buy materials, parts, or services result in substantial investment in production facilities and increase risks of obsolescence. A choice may be made largely to get an assured supply of items of the right quality without revealing technical know-how to competitors. But these are "soft" benefits that carry low weight in financial calculations.
- Foreign sourcing often calls for a loan or investment in the foreign supplier. Such an investment is risky and hard to recover in dollars. Consequently, it faces rough treatment in the financial review.

### Human Resources

- Most human resource outlays are treated as current expenses which can get by an annual budget review. The more serious costs are long-run commitments for pensions and the like. These continuing reductions in operating profits may complicate the finance department's ability to raise new capital.

At several places throughout this chapter, friction between the financial department and operating departments has been noted. This friction arises even though everyone is presumably supporting the same business-unit strategy. *Why does this occur, and what can be done to overcome it?* (Of course, if the business-unit strategy is vague or nonexistent, then we should expect friction as the departments jockey to promote their own scenarios for excellence. But trouble arises even when there is agreement on the strategy.)

First, note that for managers within the business-unit, the finance department is a supplier of an important resource—but only that; it doesn't make anything or sell anything. Like any provider of resources, it has an enabling role, not an active role. In terms of the strategic role categories identified in Chapter 6, finance is a strong supporter rather than a provider of "strategy potency."[5] If all finance people recognized this relation to strategy, life would be simpler.

Second, all sorts of resource suppliers often insist that certain conditions be met before they will provide their resource. Thus, the financial market has a whole battery of such conditions which surround a loan or new stock issue, and

---

[5]Finance also has a role in measuring results which is discussed in Chapter 20.

some of these stipulations have to be transferred to internal allocations of capital. For instance, a hurdle rate—the minimum acceptable return on investment—used internally to screen proposed projects is very much like earnings ratios used in the external financial market. Another example is a ratio measuring the typical age of accounts receivable. Because of their training and association with people in the external financial market, members of an internal finance department tend to emphasize these sorts of conditions when making allocations. Financial ratios rather than strategy is the currency they prefer to use.

Third, most of the guidelines that financial people use are expressed in numbers, often ratios. These "hard" data usually come from (1) accounting records and estimates which follow the conventions established for reports to people outside the company, and (2) publicly quoted prices and related figures arising in financial markets. This data base gives scant recognition to intangibles such as employee morale, new product ideas, strategic positioning, and the like. Consequently, the financial standards discussed in the preceding paragraph likewise give scant attention to intangibles. Theoretically, intangibles can be added into financial data, but in practice the hard data receive most of the attention. This bias toward hard data means that many elements in strategic action are inadequately represented. And this distortion adds to the conflict between a financial viewpoint and an operating viewpoint on strategy issues. When central management arbitrates such conflicts, it is, in part, correcting for the said distortion.

In sum, much of the difficulty in linking a finance view of capital allocation with business-unit strategy arises, not from disagreement with the strategy, but from the inherent nature of finance tools. Because these tools are oriented toward the financial market, they give too little weight to the intangibles which are so important in strategy. Consequently, central management has to arbitrate the inevitable conflicts that arise between the finance department and operating departments which are each pushing their ideas of what the strategy calls for.

Over time, this succession of arbitration decisions should create a "common-law" understanding in a company about the way to fit finance into an integrated strategy effort. Possible points for such an integration are outlined in the allocation procedure mentioned early in this chapter. Further ideas about vertical integration are discussed at the end of the next chapter.

## Questions for Class Discussion

1. Two faculty wives, Maxine and Madge, own and run the M and M Travel Service, which is located close to the campus. They have a steady clientele of faculty

and students, primarily for air travel. Net income for the owners is about $50,000 per year. Except for normal accounts payable, M and M Travel has no debt; however, the local bank would be glad to lend the firm up to $20,000 at 12 percent interest. Yesterday, the computer that connects M and M Travel to the airlines reservation system broke down beyond repair. A replacement could be rented, but Maxine is set against that and believes that buying one for $4,000 would be smarter. Madge thinks that they should buy two, for convenience when they both are in the office and also to have a back-up if one breaks down. They guess that the new machines will be obsolete in five years. (a) What would be the return on investment for the first computer? (b) For a second computer? (c) How many computers do you recommend that they buy?

(d) Several clients have suggested that M and M Travel open an office in the center of the city, which would be more convenient for these clients. Maxine and Madge estimate that the total start-up costs would be $25,000; they could train someone to run the office, since neither of them wants to spend more time in the business. They think that with their contacts, the office would quickly earn enough to cover interest and depreciation; and maybe a new office would open up a whole new market for tourist travel. Besides, it would get them out of the rut they are now in. Do you recommend opening this office?

2. In recent years the U.S. foreign trade balance has had deficits of billions of dollars. Our position relative to Japan is especially weak. This shows deficiencies in the American economy and brings about calls for protectionism in the U.S. Congress. If these events continue, our domestic economy will suffer.

One reason that the U.S. competitive position is weak is the use of financial hurdle rates by U.S. companies on long-run investments. When the current cost of capital is combined with the discounted cash flow concept to establish a hurdle rate, most investments that would show no net return for 10 or 15 years and others which are uncertain get ruled out. In contrast, Japanese companies have "patient money": they are willing to make such long-run investments to develop technologies, people, products, and markets.

What do you recommend that U.S. companies do to overcome this "patient money" handicap?

3. Bill Norris, the new treasurer of the Norris Paper Company and nephew of the chairperson of the board, hoped to quickly put to work the theories and ideas he had learned from studying corporate finance at his university. An inventory turn of four times and 30 days outstanding for accounts receivable were goals that he was convinced were both useful and desirable. When he pushed the credit manager to tighten up on terms and the purchasing manager to cut back purchases, he was surprised to find that they resisted firmly. A complaint to his uncle only drew the response that his Chicago-based wholesaler and distributor of coarse and fine papers and folding boxes had done well for years with 60 to 90 days outstanding receivables and an inventory turn that, at times,

dropped below two. "But," said Bill to his sales manager cousin, "if we cut receivables outstanding to 30 days and increase the inventory turn, we will have enough assets to support a sales increase of at least 20 percent. Don't you want that?" "No," said the cousin, "sales are hard enough to make against my competition without requiring that the bankers, grocers, and stationery stores pay cash. If you want to get cash out of receivables, sell them to Atlantic Factors. We have done this before. They will buy 80 percent of the receivables right away." (a) As Bill Norris, what is your response? (b) What are suitable goals for and constraints over investment in receivables and inventory?

4. Assume that Alain Ribout sold his motel to an aggressive, financial strong motel chain and that he is now a district manager for that company. (a) How should he decide which of the investment alternatives listed on page 361 he should recommend to his new employer? (b) If you think he should recommend more investment than he would have made as owner, do you conclude that big firms do and should take more risks than small firms?

5. One pharmaceutical company uses the following approach to decide the difficult question of how to allocate money for R & D. (a) Set a maximum total annual outlay based on a tolerable percentage of company gross profits or gross sales, i.e., a maximum that competition will permit. (b) Set a minimum total annual outlay equal to the amount that leading competing companies are spending on R & D. (c) Prepare a list of all proposed R & D projects, and rank these projects by "expected rate of profit," that is, the estimated costs and revenues of each project adjusted for uncertainty and time. (d) Prepare a *cumulative* total of the annual outlays for these ranked projects. Assume that all high-profit projects costing less than the minimum set in (b) will be carried out, and then focus on those projects, the annual costs of which fall above the minimum outlay and below the maximum outlay. (e) Tentatively select 40 to 60 percent of these mid-ranking projects, leaving a margin for cost overruns and unanticipated opportunities. (f) Refine this selection to achieve reasonable stability and continuity in R & D activities and to match the company's capability to absorb new products.

How does this approach differ from the capital allocation procedure described in the present chapter? Which procedure do you think is best, and why?

6. For 20 years the Beta Gamma Retailing Co. has paid a dividend to its shareholders amounting to 60 percent of after-taxes earnings. A vocal minority of shareholders has said over the years it prefers to receive its earnings in the form of cash dividends rather than capital gains. The belief of these individuals is that high dividend payouts are important for high market values. But the treasurer of Beta Gamma Retailing has seen three studies during the past year in various academic financial journals that conclude that the stock market as a whole shows a strong preference for capital gains. In these studies the measure

of correlation ($R^2 = 0.80$) is much higher than is the correlation of high dividend yields and high stock prices ($R^2 = 0.30$). So the treasurer wonders if he should try to persuade the directors of the company that, given the present tax laws, Beta Gamma Retailing should either cut the dividend payout in half or reduce it to nothing. The company has several investment opportunities that will widen its market coverage and reduce its business risk, even though they are borderline when their possible returns are compared with his best guess as to the company's cost of capital.

7. As students in corporate finance courses learn, the discounted cash flow method is widely regarded as the sophisticated way to compute the rate of return on a proposed investment. It takes into account all cash outflows and all cash inflows. Not considered, however, are the longer-run consequences of *not* making the investment, such as losing market position or missing a chance to hire an outstanding manager. How do you suggest incorporating such items into the cash flow calculations? Does your answer to this question suggest to you a way to add other intangible strategic considerations into the calculation?

8. Pruitt Materials Co., successor firm to Asbestos Brake Linings, Inc., has been advised by legal counsel to establish a $200 million reserve to cover potential costs and possible judgments against the firm that will result from pending and potential lawsuits by persons exposed in the past to its asbestos. Manville Corporation has put itself into voluntary bankruptcy to protect against such suits, but the directors of Pruitt Materials do not wish to follow the Manville example. The reserve can be established in two ways: by charging one-half of the total amount against the retained earnings accounts this year and charging the other half against retained earnings over five successive years; or by not paying dividends for as long as is necessary to set up the reserve. A third possible course of action is not to establish a reserve; instead, Pruitt Materials would simply wait until the lawsuits begin to be settled and then make payments as required by the courts at unspecified future times. Previous policy has been to pay out 20 percent of each year's earnings as a cash dividend. The present net worth of the company includes three accounts: common stock valued at $25,000,000; additional paid-in capital at $75,000,000; and retained earnings at $100,000,000. This year's net profit is expected to be $20,000,000 after taxes.

   An immediate $100 million charge against retained earnings will mean that no dividends can be paid this year and that expenditures for research and development work will have to be reduced so that the cash can be turned to paying off long-term debt more rapidly. The company's present long-term debt-to-equity ratio of 0.5/1 means, in effect, that no more borrowing can take place and the loan covenant restricts the company's use of cash. What action do you recommend that Pruitt Materials Co. take with respect to the recommended $200 million reserve?

# CASE
## 13 Mott & Company

Mott & Company operates a rapidly growing chain of general merchandise stores. The founder, R.R. Mott, had a flair for unusual sales promotions. He often bought a large lot of, say, sweaters or dolls, at close-out prices and then retailed them at cost amid great fanfare. Or, on Veterans Day, he'd have a band playing outside of his store. There was always something creating a stir at Mott stores, which carried a variety of medium- to low-price merchandise.

The company rode the wave of new shopping centers, seeking locations having a lot of buyer traffic looking for a fresh and stimulating experience in its shopping. By 1975 the Mott chain had 64 stores and earned a 5 percent operating profit on sales of $81 million.

These traditions were continued following R.R. Mott's death in 1974, but the razzle-dazzle has been hard to maintain as the number of stores has increased and as newly appointed store managers were expected to run a tight operation and simultaneously be creative in sales promotion. So the new management of Mott & Company has added some different twists to company strategy. Important in this respect is the use of credit—both extending credit to retail customers and using credit to finance company expansion.

The new strategy emphasizes three thrusts. (1) Maintain growth by opening new stores. Between 1974 and 1987, the number of stores in the chain has increased from 64 to 119. (2) Increase profit margins by encouraging customers to finance their purchases through a company-operated time-payment plan. The margin between the cost of capital and time payment financing charges net of expenses has been 3 percent per annum. (3) Finance the expansion by leasing store properties rather than buying them and by using long-term and short-term debt to improve the leverage of the equity. The cumulative results of these thrusts are reflected in the comparative balance sheets in Table 13–2.

Finding attractive locations and opening new stores is a primary responsibility of regional managers, whose annual bonus is based substantially on increasing the number of stores and thus the sales volume. The managers are assisted in this effort by a central real estate office. On the average, each new store absorbs about $1 million of capital, mostly for inventory and accounts receivable.

The extension of credit to retail customers is under the direct supervision of each store manager, who has a credit manager to handle the paperwork. Guidelines for this activity are provided by the treasurer. In the old days credit was extended only for purchase of large items. Now, customers are urged to open a charge account which can be used for any item in the store. A maximum balance of an individual account is tied to household income, and accounts are considered active if some repayment has been made within 90 days. In the past year credit

**TABLE 13–2.**
**COMPARATIVE BALANCE SHEET, 1987 AND 1975 (in millions of dollars)**

| Assets | 1987 | 1975 | Liabilities and Net Worth | 1987 | 1975 |
|---|---|---|---|---|---|
| Cash and equivalent | 5 | 4 | Accounts payable | 8 | 4 |
| Accounts receivable (net) | 60 | 1 | Notes & bank loans | 45 | — |
| Merchandise | 45 | 14 | Accrued items & deferred income | 16 | 2 |
| Total current assets | 110 | 19 | Total current liabilities | 69 | 6 |
| Land, buildings, & equipment | 15 | 13 | Long-term debt | 20 | 2 |
| Less: reserve for depreciation* | 5 | 5 | Total debt | 89 | 8 |
| Net property | 10 | 8 | Stock and retained | | |
| Other assets | 5 | 1 | earnings | 36 | 20 |
| Total assets | 125 | 28 | Total debt and net worth | 125 | 28 |

*Depreciation charge in 1987 = $1.4 million.

sales in all stores were about $45 million on 290,000 accounts, and outstanding installment receivables were $60 million at the end of the fiscal year.

"Our campaign to increase consumer credit is working well," says Mott's treasurer. "The availability of credit makes selling easier, and store managers are recognizing that selling on credit is a way to earn an extra profit. Providing credit, of course, encourages store managers to stock higher priced inventory, and one result is that the merchandise inventory per store has gone up. It will take time for the new store managers to learn how to keep that kind of merchandise turning over."

Regarding investment in fixed assets, the real estate manager says, "In spite of the inflation of commercial land prices and building costs, we have actually reduced Mott's capital tied up in real estate on a per-store basis. We do this by leasing instead of buying when the deal is right. The regional managers ferret out good locations, often in developments still on the drawing boards, and then we sit down with the owner—or maybe a third party—and work out a deal. A minimum rent plus a small percentage of sales above our break-even volume is the typical arrangement. The lessor makes maybe 10 percent on the investment and stands to gain if land prices in the specific location go up."

Store managers are rarely involved in acquiring real estate. As one young manager remarked, "I just accept the facilities provided to me. My bonus is based on sales volume and bottom-line results, so I like to see customers carrying merchandise out the door. Of course, at the end of each year the accountants may create some ugly surprises with their write-offs, and I've wised up to keeping accounts receivable current and ways to avoid inventory write-downs." Another store manager says, "Each month we get a 'financial analysis' from headquarters. It has so many ratios about things I already know that I don't pay much attention to it. There are a few key figures such as "open to buy," which is a seasonal authorization to order new merchandise based on budgeted cost of goods sold less inventory on hand, and an uncommitted advertising budget that I must watch. My main job, though, is people—customers and employees—and the ratios don't help me psych them out."

Mott & Company's overall operating results are highlighted in Table 13–3. While the growth in volume is attractive, the profits have not yet come up to Mott executives' expectations.

**TABLE 13–3.**
**COMPARATIVE INCOME ACCOUNTS, YEARS ENDING JAN. 31, 1987, 1986, 1975 (in millions of dollars)**

|  | 1987 | 1986 | 1975 |
|---|---|---|---|
| Sales | 185 | 164 | 81 |
| Cost of sales | 128 | 113 | 57 |
| Gross income | 57 | 51 | 24 |
| Selling and administrative expenses | 50 | 43 | 20 |
| Operating profit | 7 | 8 | 4 |
| Other income* | 1 | 1 | |
| Less: Interest paid | 4 | 2 | 0 |
| Profit before income tax | 4 | 7 | 4 |
| Income tax | 2 | 3 | 2 |
| Net profit | 2 | 4 | 2 |

*Mostly interest earned.

## Question

Make an evaluation of Mott & Company's allocation of capital during the period covered by the case. What changes, if any, do you recommend for the immediate future?

# CHAPTER 14

## Strategy Programs in Finance:
## Sources of Capital

The strategic management of sources of capital is primarily concerned about four things:

1. Having enough capital already in the company or readily available to permit flexibility in strategic action and growth.
2. Matching the sources of capital that a company uses to its strengths—strengths reflected in the assets shown on the balance sheet and in cash flows from operations.
3. Keeping the costs of capital low, including recognizing that costs include not only interest and dividends, but also constraints imposed by lenders and risks of forced curtailment during hard times.
4. Permitting the present stockholders to maintain control of the company so that strategic programs will not be suddenly interrupted.

In a typical company these aims are sought by using a mix of sources of capital: stockholders, short- and long-term lenders, internal cash flow, etc. The particular mix that a specific company uses, called its *financial structure*, depends to a large degree on its strategy. Accordingly, to develop a general understanding of the issues involved in establishing a good financial structure, we will first review the instruments and sources that a company can use, and then examine the characteristics of a company's total financial structure.

The massive billion dollar financial duels that are reported in the headlines almost always relate to conglomerate companies which will be discussed later in Part 3, especially in Chapter 16 on mergers and acquisitions.

## Instruments Used to Obtain Capital

### Owners

The primary source of new capital for established companies—even very small ones—is the cash generated from operations. Much of this cash is simply plowed back to meet new needs.

#### Retained Earnings

Theoretically, the owners of a business get the net earnings. In fact, however, owners of corporations listed on the New York Stock Exchange receive dividends of about 25 percent of the net earnings! The other 75 percent is retained, i.e., involuntarily reinvested by the owners. This practice avoids the payment of income taxes by stockholders and presumably increases the value of the stockholders' shares. For corporate management, retaining earnings has the great advantage of being able to obtain new capital without the expenses and uncertainty of going back to outside financial markets.[1]

A dramatic example of this occurred in Japan during its boom in the early 1970s, as Table 14–1 indicates. The companies with high market share and correspondingly high earnings were able to finance almost three-fourths of their rapid growth from retained earnings and reserves. During the period, they actually reduced their debt-to-equity ratio. In contrast, the less profitable companies could not finance their somewhat more modest growth from earnings and had to rely heavily on increased debt. Their debt-to-equity ratio increased sharply, leaving them vulnerable to a downturn in business.

### Stock

The amount of additional direct contributions from owners will depend upon the legal form of organization and the particular rights granted to each class of

---

**TABLE 14–1.**
**RELATIVE IMPORTANCE OF VARIOUS SOURCES OF GROWTH CAPITAL IN LEADING JAPANESE COMPANIES\***

|  | High-Market-Share Companies | Low-Market-Share Companies |
|---|---|---|
| Retained Earnings | 60% | 18% |
| Reserves | 14 | 9 |
| Equity | 3 | 2 |
| Debt | 23 | 71 |
| Total | 100% | 100% |
| Annual sales growth | 17.2% | 11.2% |
| Annual return on equity | 14.4% | 9.3% |

*Source:* Boston Consulting Group.

\*Data cover the growth period 1970–1975 for two prominent companies in each of 13 industries, one company with high market share and one with low market share.

---

[1]Part of the internal cash flow comes from depreciation—a bookkeeping reduction in the value of plant and equipment. Since depreciation is an "expense" but involves no cash outlay, companies that are breaking even have some cash to reinvest somewhere. Sooner or later, however, cash from such depreciation charges will be needed just to maintain existing capacity. Only in companies with very high fixed assets does cash from depreciation contribute much to strategic needs.

owner. In a sole proprietorship the amount of capital is limited by the personal resources of the proprietor. Partnerships expand the potential resources, but the instability of partnerships limits their usefulness. So, as soon as the capital needs of an enterprise exceed the wealth of one or two persons, a corporation usually is created. Then, raising ownership capital becomes a matter of selling stock.

**Common Stock**    A share of common stock is simply a small percentage of the ownership of a company. So when we raise capital by selling stock, we are trading a bit of ownership for cash. If 100,000 shares are outstanding, each share represents 1/100,000 of the owner's claim on profits, and on assets if the corporation is liquidated. When additional shares are sold, profits have to be divided into more pieces, which the original shareholders will not like unless the total earnings increase faster than the number of shares, giving them a smaller portion of what they hope will be a bigger pie. The new stockholders pay in capital primarily for the right to a piece of this bigger pie, usually expressed as "earnings per share."

If the common stock is *split* (several new shares are issued to holders of each old share), the earnings per share go down. The individual shareholders retain their percentage claim on the total, however, since they now own more shares.

**Preferred Stock**    Some investors are willing to buy stock having a limit on the dividend they will receive if they also get assurance that special effort will be made to pay such dividends. More specifically, if a company issues $7 preferred stock, a $7 dividend must be paid on each share before any dividend can be paid on common stock. In addition, preferred stock dividends are usually cumulative. Thus, if no dividends are paid on the preferred stock just mentioned for two years, $14 for back dividends and $7 for current dividends would have to be paid on each share of preferred stock in the third year before any dividend could be declared on common stock. Less significantly, a preferred stock typically has prior claim on, say, $100 of assets if liquidation should occur.

Normally, after the dividend has been paid on preferred stock, all remaining dividends are divided among common stockholders. In exceptional situations the preferred stock *can* be made "participating," which means that both the preferred stock and the common stock will share in dividends after a stipulated amount has been paid on each type of security. Participating preferred stock may be issued, for example, to some stockholders who are reluctant to approve an expansion program; they get preferred treatment if any dividends are paid at all, and if the expansion proves successful they also share in the profits from growth.

**Frequent Use of Stock to Raise Capital**    The sale of additional stock is often used to raise money for expansion. To attract particular types of investors, the rights of an issue may be specially tailored. Different issues of preferred stock will have priority in rank and often will vary in the amount of the preferred dividend, voting rights will vary, occasionally preferred stock will be convertible into common stock, and so forth. A package of preferred and common stock may be sold as a unit. Sometimes *warrants* entitling the bearer to purchase common stock at a stated price are included with a share of preferred or common stock, thus giving the holder of the warrant an opportunity to benefit from a price rise. Or, to ensure that a new issue of common stock will be sold, present stockholders may be given *rights* to buy stock at slightly less than the prevailing market price. These special provisions, however, do not modify the basic transaction of securing additional capital through the sale of additional shares of ownership.

## Long-Term Creditors

In addition to coming from investments by owners, capital may be secured by borrowing it from long-term or short-term creditors. Let us look first at reasons why a company may seek funds through long-term borrowing.

### Trading on the Equity

The advantages and disadvantages of obtaining capital from long-term creditors are illustrated in the situation currently facing the Red River Power Company. This local electric company, with assets of about $40 million, wished to finance an expansion program that would cost $9 million. The new expansion might have been financed by the sale of additional stock. The present common stockholders, however, did not wish to use this source of capital because (1) high income taxes make earning of net profits more difficult than earning money to pay bond interest, and (2) all profits would have to be shared with the new stockholders.

Interest on borrowed capital is an expense deducted from income *before* income tax is computed. Profits available for stockholders are net income *after* income tax has been paid. Consequently, a corporation in the 40 percent income tax bracket has to earn almost $2 for each dollar available to stockholders. On the other hand, if capital is borrowed, less earnings are needed to pay for the use of capital because the tax collector has not taken a toll.

The effect of these factors on the Red River Power Company can be seen by comparing the disposition of operating profits (before paying bond interest) under bond versus that under stock financing. The Red River Company already had outstanding $14,000,000 of 9¾ percent bonds, $9,000,000 of 10 percent preferred stock, and $9,000,000 of common stock. It was estimated that an average annual operating profit of $5,500,000 would be earned when the expansion was completed. The effects of borrowing the necessary $9,000,000 at 9¾ percent as compared to selling stock at par are shown in Table 14–2.

The present stockholders would profit by borrowing because a larger rate of return would be earned on capital than would be required for interest. If for some reason, however, the operating profit of the company should fall to $4,600,000 or $3,700,000, the earnings on common stock would have been altered as illustrated in Table 14–3.

Thus, by borrowing, the common stockholders increase their possibilities for profits but also incur a greater risk of loss. Such use of bonds for raising capital is referred to as *trading on the equity*.

**TABLE 14-2.**
**BOND VS. STOCK FINANCING OF RED RIVER POWER COMPANY**

|  | Borrowing $9,000,000 at 9¾% | Selling $9,000,000 of Common Stock |
|---|---|---|
| Estimated annual operating profit | $5,500,000 | $5,500,000 |
| Less bond interest | 2,242,500 | 1,365,000 |
| Net profit before income tax | 3,257,500 | 4,135,000 |
| Income tax @ 40% | 1,303,000 | 1,654,000 |
| Net profit | 1,954,500 | 2,481,000 |
| Less preferred stock dividends | 900,000 | 900,000 |
| Available for common stockholders | $1,054,500 | $1,581,000 |
| Rate of return on par value of common stock outstanding | 11.7% | 8.8% |

**TABLE 14-3.**
**RATE OF RETURN ON COMMON STOCK OUTSTANDING**

| Annual Operating Profit | Borrowing $9,000,000 at 9¾% | Selling $9,000,000 of Common Stock |
|---|---|---|
| $5,500,000 | 11.7% | 8.8% |
| 4,600,000 | 5.7 | 5.5 |
| 3,700,000 | −0.3 | 2.8 |

### Instruments for Long-Term Borrowing

Trading on the equity may be accomplished through the use of any of the following instruments:

**Mortgages**    To attract long-term capital, a mortgage on real estate or other assets may be given as security. If the interest and the principal of the loan are not paid on schedule, the lender may force the sale of the mortgaged property and use the proceeds to repay the debt. If the proceeds do not cover the entire debt, the borrower is still liable for the remaining balance.

**Bonds**    To borrow large amounts, the total can be divided into a series of identical bonds that can be sold to as many lenders as necessary to secure the sum desired. The bonds may be *secured* by a mortgage or other pledged asset, or they may be *debentures* that rely only on the financial strength of the borrower. Typically, a borrower who issues bonds must continue to meet stipulated requirements such as maintaining minimum working capital, having no senior debt, and paying conservative dividends. Also, most bonds either call for *serial* repayment year by year or have a *sinking fund* in which money to repay the debt is accumulated. Bonds usually are *callable* by the borrower if the borrower is willing to pay a premium. These provisions are stated in the *bond indenture* and are administered by a trustee.

**Long-term Notes**     Increasingly, large sums can be borrowed from a single financial institution like a life insurance company or a trust company. Here, dividing the loan into bonds is unnecessary. Instead, 10-, 15-, or 20-year promissory notes are used. There is, however, an agreement similar to a bond indenture stipulating various protective measures and the repayment schedule. Such *private placements* avoid underwriting costs. Their use depends largely on the total to be borrowed and the comparative interest expense.

In addition, as with preferred stock, numerous variations can be used to tailor long-term securities to attract particular groups of lenders. In addition to the interest rate, maturity date, and protective features mentioned above, some loans are *convertible* into common stock. If the stock price rises above the specified conversion rate, the lender has the option to switch to an equity security at a low cost. Thus, convertible bonds give the investor the security of fixed debts plus the possibility of benefiting from a rise in stock prices. Another variation is to issue warrants along with bonds. In tight money markets, offering a security that appeals to special classes of lenders can reduce interest expense significantly.

Anyone who lends money for a long term is concerned about the continuing ability of the borrower to meet obligations. Hence, new companies lacking a record of demonstrated ability and companies in risky industries may be unable to borrow for long terms. In contrast, loans will be easier to obtain by an established firm that over the previous 10 years has earned at least twice the interest on proposed new debt and in no year has failed to at least equal the fixed payments. Although future earnings are what really matter, past earnings are often used to decide a company's credit worthiness.

## Short-Term Creditors

The sources discussed thus far provide capital for a long period. Short-term creditors, however, are better adapted to supply funds for seasonal requirements or other temporary needs. The most common short-term creditors are commercial banks and vendors of merchandise.

### Commercial Banks

The most desirable way to borrow from a commercial bank is to establish a *credit line*. Under this arrangement, the company anticipates its needs for temporary cash and works out an understanding with the bank, prior to the time the cash is required, that credit up to a certain maximum will be available. This gives the bank ample time to make its customary credit investigation, and it also enables the company to plan on the bank as a temporary source of capital. The bank wants to feel confident that the company will pay off the loan within a year; consequently, it checks the character of the people running the company, the nature of its existing assets, the use to be made of the money borrowed, the obligations already incurred, and the earning record of the company. The bank is also interested in the company's budget of monthly cash receipts and disbursements during the coming year. The aim of the bank is to avoid embarrassing bad debt problems by not making dubious loans in the first place.

For some types of business, a commercial bank makes loans that are secured by collateral. For example, an investment house pledges stocks and bonds as security for its bank loans, and a dealer in commodities backs up its loans by means of warehouse receipts or bills of lading. When such security is provided, the preliminary investigation by the bank is less rigorous.

Commercial banks also make some mortgage loans and buy marketable bonds, but these are not primary services they render to business firms.

### Merchandise Creditors

Companies normally purchase products and services "on account"; that is, they make payment 30 to 60 days after the products are shipped. With a continuing flow of purchases, some bills will always be unpaid. In effect, the vendors are supplying part of the capital needed to carry on operations. If a company is slow in paying its bills, it may have accounts payable equal to two months of its purchases.

Extensive use of such trade credit is usually unwise. Vendors often offer substantial discounts for prompt payment of bills, which means that this is an expensive source of capital. Furthermore, a company with a reputation for slow payment will not receive favorable treatment from vendors when there is a shortage of merchandise or when closeouts are being offered at low prices.

Buying on trade credit is but a counterpart of the use of capital to finance accounts receivable from customers.

### Other Short-Term Credit

Selling on the installment plan clearly increases a company's need for working capital. As noted in the preceding chapter, special arrangements can be made with finance companies either to take over or to lend money on such accounts receivable.

Postponing payment of taxes, installment payments on machinery, loans against inventory placed in a bonded warehouse, and even advance payments by customers can be resorted to in periods of stringency. Few companies, however, care to have a continuing policy of obtaining short-term capital from such sources.

With this summary view of possible sources of capital in mind, we can now turn to the issue of how to combine their use in a sound financial structure.

## Financial Structure

## Meaning of Financial Structure

The various sources of capital used by a company make up its financial structure. In establishing policy for obtaining capital, the overall general structure must be considered because the relative importance of one source will affect the desirability of others.

The size of the company, the nature of its assets, the amount and the stability of its earnings, and the condition existing in the financial market at the time the capital is raised—all these have an influence on the sources of capital used by the company. From time to time, changes will be made, either because capital can be secured more advantageously from another source or because some lender decides to withdraw its capital. Expansion or contraction of the total amount of capital used also will affect the relative importance of the sources.

At any given time the right-hand side of the balance sheet of a company will reflect its financial structure. So, to review the policy followed by three different companies, we will examine briefly their condensed balance sheets.

## Financial Structure of Schultz Electronic Controls, Inc.

The balance sheet of Schultz Electronic Controls, Inc., shown in Table 14–4, is typical of many comparatively small manufacturing companies.

Almost three-fourths of the total capital of $2,685,000 was supplied by owners of the company. The par value of preferred and common stock is $1,600,000, and earnings retained in the business have increased the stockholders' investment by another third of a million dollars. Limited use of long-term notes is shown.

**TABLE 14–4.**
**SCHULTZ ELECTRONIC CONTROLS, INC.**
**BALANCE SHEET DECEMBER 31, 19—**

| *Assets* | | *Liabilities and Stockholders' Equity* | |
|---|---|---|---|
| Cash | $ 140,000 | Accounts payable | $ 117,000 |
| Accounts receivable (net) | 410,000 | Accrued liabilities | 84,000 |
| Finished inventory | 196,000 | Long-term serial notes | 550,000 |
| Materials and in-process | | Preferred stock, 11% | 600,000 |
| inventory | 439,000 | Common stock | 1,000,000 |
| Fixed assets (net after | | Earnings retained in | |
| depreciation | 1,500,000 | business | 334,000 |
| | | Total liabilities and | |
| Total Assets | $2,685,000 | stockholders' equity | $2,685,000 |

These notes are only about one-third of the depreciated value of fixed assets and thus appear to be protected by an ample margin of assets. The serial feature provides for a regular reduction in the amount of the long-term debt.

The short-term debt of the company at the time this balance sheet was prepared was comparatively small, the accounts payable to trade creditors being only a fraction of the total assets and actually less than the cash on hand. The company did, however, have a bank line and normally used bank credit to finance a seasonal peak in inventories and receivables from March through August.

## Financial Structure of the Red River Power Company

The sources of capital used by the Red River Power Company reflect the difference in the nature of the operations of an electric utility company compared with a manufacturing company like Schultz Electronic Controls, Inc. The balance sheet in Table 14–5 shows the financial condition of Red River Power Company after its expansion program was completed.

Perhaps the most striking feature of the financial structure of this company is the large bond issue that represents almost 50 percent of the total assets. The company could obtain such a large bond issue at favorable rates because of the stable earning records of utility companies and also because of the large amount of fixed assets that the company could pledge under a mortgage issue. The company has also issued both common and preferred stock. Earnings retained in the business instead of being paid out as dividends amount to about 27 percent of its total proprietorship.

Inasmuch as there is no such thing as inventories of finished goods in a utility company, and accounts receivable can be collected from customers promptly, the assets of this company are virtually all in the form of fixed assets. The company has used bank loans to finance temporarily the expansion of its facilities.

**TABLE 14–5.**
**RED RIVER POWER COMPANY**
**BALANCE SHEET DECEMBER 31, 19—**

| *Assets* | | | *Liabilities and Stockholders' Equity* | |
|---|---|---|---|---|
| Cash . . . . . . . . . . . . . . . . . . . .$ | | 600,000 | Accounts payable . . . . . . . . . .$ | 600,000 |
| Other current assets . . . . . . . . | | 400,000 | Accrued taxes, etc. . . . . . . . . . | 200,000 |
| Fixed Assets . . . . $55,100,000 | | | Mortgage bonds, 9¾% . . . . . | 23,000,000 |
| Less allowance | | | Preferred stock, 12% . . . . . . . | 9,000,000 |
| for depreciation | 7,600,000 | 47,500,000 | Common stock . . . . . . . . . . . | 9,000,000 |
| | | | Retained earnings . . . . . . . . . | 6,700,000 |
| | | | Total liabilities and stock- | |
| Total assets . . . . . . . . . . . . . . $48,500,000 | | | holders' equity . . . . . . . . . $48,500,000 | |

## Financial Structure of The Long-Shot Printing Company

The balance sheet of a company financed on the proverbial shoestring offers an interesting contrast to those already considered. The financial condition of The Long-Shot Printing Company at the end of its first year of operation is shown in Table 14–6.

The owners of this company have actually contributed less than 22 percent of the total capital and are relying heavily on both long-term and short-term creditors. Machinery, which is the principal fixed asset of the company, was purchased on time payments, and the vendor, in order to protect its claim, still holds a first mortgage on the machinery amounting to almost two-thirds of its book value. It is doubtful, however, whether even the book value could be realized if it became necessary to sell the machinery at a forced sale. Credit from material suppliers has been used to a point where it exceeds the value of the inventory actually on hand. This means that the vendors are financing not only the entire inventory of the company, but other assets as well.

Fortunately, the notes payable are due to an affiliate company that will probably not force their collection at maturity but will accept new short-term promissory notes in exchange for the old ones. Nevertheless, the current ratio is approximately 1 to 1, and any shrinkage in the value of current assets would probably cause immediate financial complications. The company has no bank loan and has been unsuccessful in securing a line of bank credit that it may use in an emergency. It is doubtful that new capital can be attracted to correct the existing weak cash position, with the possible exception that the company might offer a new investor the speculative possibility of sharing in future profits if they are earned. Under such a plan, however, the present management would probably be required to give up part of its control over affairs of the company.

**TABLE 14–6.**
**THE LONG-SHOT PRINTING COMPANY**
**BALANCE SHEET DECEMBER 31, 19—**

| *Assets* | | *Liabilities and Stockholders' Equity* | |
|---|---:|---|---:|
| Cash | $ 5,200 | Trade accounts payable | $ 61,600 |
| Accounts receivable—net | 28,400 | Notes payable | 18,000 |
| Inventories | 52,500 | Accrued liabilities | 7,600 |
| Total current assets | $ 86,100 | Total current liabilities | $ 87,200 |
| Deferred charges | 3,000 | Mortgage on equipment | 72,500 |
| Machinery and other fixed | | Common stock | 40,000 |
| assets—net | 115,300 | Retained earnings | 40,000 |
| | | Total liabilities and stock- | |
| Total assets | $204,400 | holders' equity | $204,400 |

In this situation the company must adopt a strategy of improving short-term earnings with existing assets—a very different strategy from that of Red River Power Company, where the physical expansion financed by debt with a fixed interest cost was the strategic direction to higher earnings per share. In fact, The Long-Shot Printing Company decided to operate on a three-shift basis, cutting its prices close to incremental cost if necessary to keep the plant busy.

The close interrelation between the overall strategy and financial structure of a business is evident in all three of these examples.

## Selecting Sources of Capital

### Industry Patterns

Typical financial structures of other companies in its industry will give management a lead on what the financial community will accept as satisfactory. More often than not, however, wide variations in assets, in earnings, and in existing capital structures, in addition to the differences in management, make reliance upon typical industry patterns both unsatisfactory and even dangerous. The structure adopted should suit both a particular company and the conditions existing at the time plans for the financial structure are made. Important factors to consider appear on page 379.

### Availability of Capital for Strategy Moves

Strategy looks to the future. Moves made today are intended to place the company in a different spot than it currently occupies and to confront new opportunities. But these plans are unlikely to turn out just as predicted. Consequently, an important feature of a company's financial structure is reserve strength and flexibility to change that structure so as to provide the capital that will actually be needed.

This means that a company should try to avoid so much debt that it can barely meet fixed interest charges. Likewise, if possible, its stock should be attractive to new investors at a high price-to-earnings ratio. Surprisingly, these rather obvious strengths are being sacrificed in today's setting by many companies. Staggering debt may be accepted to avoid a hostile takeover, and financial theorists and eager investment bankers bemoan the existence of unused borrowing capacity. For example, to avoid a takeover, United Airline's parent has incurred so much debt that the airline will have serious trouble replacing its fleet with up-to-date aircraft.

Keeping a reserve of financial strength may not be easy for companies that elect a risky strategy. Thus, a small firm that is trying to invent new herbicides by manipulating DNA codes is using all the capital it can muster just on development work; it is gambling that a successful product will bring forth new investors. The risk is high, because several of its potential competitors are large pharmaceutical companies which have kept a conservative financial structure that will permit them to raise more capital if they need it.

## Matching Capital Sources to the Way Capital Is Used

Funds to finance seasonal peaks or other temporary needs can probably best be obtained from short-term creditors, such as commercial banks. This is a comparatively inexpensive way of raising capital and permits an immediate reduction in the total amount owed after the peak requirements are over. On the other hand, capital for fixed assets or for circulating assets that will be permanently retained in the business calls for a different solution. Because the company cannot expect to have cash to return to the lender for several years, owners or long-term creditors present a more logical source for such funds.

The use of capital will also affect the ability of the company to offer the lender some special security for its loan. As an effective guarantee that a loan will be repaid, a company may pledge as security one or more of the following assets: inventories that can be readily sold on the market, machinery that is standard in design and that can be easily moved from one plant to another, buildings located and designed so that they are suitable for use by other companies, and marketable securities. If valuable collateral can be given to the lender, borrowing will be much easier. If the funds are to be used for purposes that cannot be made to yield cash readily, raising capital from owners is indicated.

## Keeping the Costs of Capital Low

To ascertain the cost of capital, consideration should be given to the original cost of obtaining it and also to the compensation to be paid for its use. In sole proprietorships and partnerships, capital is usually secured by negotiations between the owners and those with whom they are intimately acquainted. Other concerns or persons not acquainted with the owners are unlikely to provide capital to such organizations. Therefore, the cost of procuring such capital, if it can be obtained at all, will usually be nominal.

### Underwriting and Registration

In the case of a corporation, securing capital by issuing bonds or selling stock to the public often involves a considerable expenditure. Frequently these securities are sold through an investment banker, who is equipped to reach prospective purchasers of securities, and in most instances substantial commissions must be paid to the investment bankers for these services. Also, complicated legal requirements must be complied with before such securities can be sold. Federal legislation requires the registration of all widely distributed securities with the Securities and Exchange Commission, and the expense involved in preparing the detailed statements required for registration is quite large. In fact, the minimum cost of registration is so large that it makes public offering of less than $2,000,000 of securities uneconomical.

Private placement of bonds and long-term notes also entails legal and accounting fees and perhaps a fee to a consultant who helps arrange the loan, but the total expense of procuring capital in this manner is normally less than half the expense of a public sale.

### Use of Rights

Some companies are able to sell securities directly to present stockholders. This applies particularly to the sale of additional stock similar to that already outstanding. The charters of many corporations require that when additional stock is sold, it must first be offered to the present stockholders; and if the new stock is offered for sale at a price somewhat lower than the current market price, the present stockholders will probably exercise their right to buy the new issue. When this procedure is possible, the cost of securing additional capital may be reduced substantially. If, however, there is any doubt about stockholders exercising all of their rights, it may be necessary to employ an investment banker to underwrite the issue, in which case many of the expenses incident to an initial public sale of securities must be incurred.

### Adjusting Sources to Prevailing Interest Rates

The compensation, or interest, that must be paid for the use of capital not only varies according to the use to be made of the capital, but also is often affected materially by the state of the financial market. Interest rates reflect the anticipated level of inflation during the period of a loan and also the efforts of the Federal Reserve Board to control inflation. During the early 1980s, for instance, these pressures drove interest rates to unprecedented levels. The resulting changes in corporate financing costs in recent years are shown in Figure 14–1.

When interest rates are high, a company may choose short-term obligations, with the provision that these can be paid off from the proceeds of long-term bonds that will be sold at a later date when interest rates are lower. The success of such a plan depends, of course, upon the accuracy with which movement in interest rates is forecast. There is always the danger that the interest rate on the long-term obligation will be even higher when the short-term notes mature, or other changes may occur that will make it difficult for the company to sell its long-term obligations as planned. Income taxes play such an important part in corporate profits that the timing of changes in capital structure may be based on an attempt to get the most favorable tax status.

### Return Paid on New Stock

When common stock is sold to obtain additional capital, the company does not agree to pay a specific amount of interest for the use of the new capital. Nevertheless, the new stockholders will share in any dividends paid, which will reduce the amount of dividends available for former stockholders. This sharing of dividends is a cost of capital so far as the former stockholders are concerned.

Many companies prefer to secure capital from the sale of stock, even though it is anticipated that the earnings necessary to support this stock will exceed the in-

**FIGURE 14-1.**
**CHANGES IN CORPORATE FINANCING COSTS**

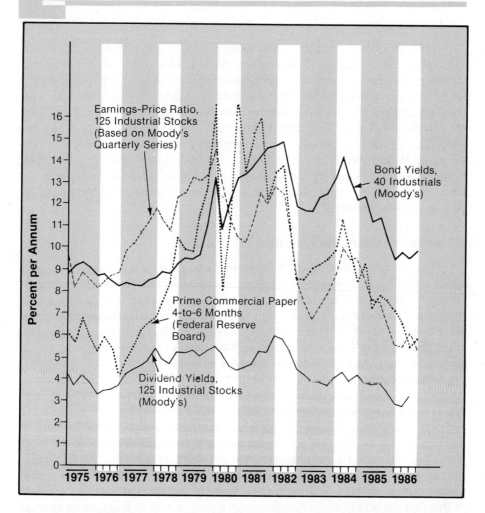

terest that would have to be paid on the bonds. Their willingness to pay this larger cost lies in the fact that dividends do not have to be paid when there is not a sufficient amount of earnings or cash to justify their declaration. Conversely, interest on bonds must be paid regardless of the amount of earnings and cash on hand. If this interest is not paid on time, the stockholders run the risk of losing control of their company and perhaps their investment in it.

We have assumed that capital can be secured from any source at any time provided the compensation offered for its use is high enough. As a practical matter, however, the sale of bonds or stock becomes so difficult in some phases of the business cycle that new capital is virtually unobtainable from these sources.

## Retaining Control of the Company

Keeping control of their company through owning a large part of the common stock is often a high priority for central managers. Many of them have worked for years and staked their careers on guiding the company on a cherished mission. They don't want to step aside and let someone else call the plays before the game is won. Also, they may be fearful of losing their jobs.

For smaller and medium-size companies, this matter of control may affect the use of common stock to raise capital. Alternative sources such as preferred stock, which has fewer votes, or debt that distorts the debt-to-equity ratio may be used. Indeed, sometimes the desire to retain control is so strong that a different strategy which requires less capital will be adopted.

Rarely can all four factors just described be fully satisfied. Low costs may be sacrificed to retain flexibility; mortgage bonds may be avoided if their issue puts the company's "crown jewel" in jeopardy; and so forth. The emerging financial structure is almost inevitably a compromise.

## Crucial Horizontal and Vertical Linkages

### Infrequent Horizontal Strains

Unlike most of the department issues discussed in Part 2, obtaining capital does not involve frequent interaction with other departments. Instead, the issues focus on relationships with outsiders. The primary task is building external relationships and making commitments that will provide a combined pool of capital adequate for today's and tomorrow's needs. Of course, the internal allocation of that capital is a ticklish task, as we saw in the previous chapter, but that is a different matter than financial structure.

There *is* a link between the sorts of assets that grow out of the allocations and the backing that the company can offer for secured loans—mortgages on buildings or liens on accounts receivable, for instance. When cash is scarce, the departments that want assets which can be pledged (or leased) may support their requests with an argument that the assets could be partly self-financing. Such an argument does, indeed, inject the operating department into the debate on sources of capital. However, this kind of issue is usually resolved in terms of a long-run policy and is not a source of recurring friction in day-to-day operations.

## Close Ties Between Capital Sources and Business-Unit Strategy

For those fortunate companies in which available cash is plentiful relative to internal needs, the financial structure is not a major strategy issue. The various sources of capital can be arranged in a way that suits financial considerations without much effect on company strategy. Or, stated another way, the strategy can be designed on the assumption that the necessary capital will be available.

But most growing companies are not in such a favorable situation. Which actions can be undertaken, and when, may be highly dependent on the availability of capital. Since most strategy moves do use capital, the sequence of strategic thrusts and perhaps the feasibility of the entire strategy depend on finding enough capital. To embark on a program with uncertain financial support increases the risk of failure markedly.

Consequently, in these common situations sources of capital should be an integral part of the business-unit strategy. Indeed, a firm's ability to finance is a significant consideration in deciding each particular strategic move. As a result, the financial officer is necessarily an active participant in strategy formulation and in revisions of strategy over a period of time. When cash is short, he or she becomes a member of the top group that weighs the strategic balance for the company between risks and opportunities.

## Nature of the Finance Department's Contribution to Strategy

Thus far, we have pictured the finance department as being locked into using figures based on public accounting traditions and relying on standards reflecting conservative traditions normally prevailing in financial markets. In this role, the department has a useful watchdog function. Company actions are assessed in terms of guidelines distilled from years of experience had by banks and other money lenders. These guidelines are based on safe conduct—on ways to keep out of financial trouble; and all managers benefit from knowing how they measure up to this prudent standard.

The chief drawback of this sort of financial viewpoint, however, is its timidity—its failure to recognize that in today's turbulent world taking well-chosen risks is necessary just to stay even. Strategic action is necessary to keep a company healthy. Because the safe financial standards are not geared to include strategic thrusts and strategy targets, a general manager has to step in and arbitrate between conventional financial opinion and bolder strategy action. Thus, the general manager benefits from the advice but bears the heavy burden of deciding when and how to disregard it.

Happily, not all finance managers are of this conservative ilk. A few take seriously the challenge of maximizing stockholders' wealth in the long run. This alternative view includes (1) recognizing sins of omission—for instance, failing to cultivate public understanding or failing to develop a corps of competent young managers; (2) thinking in terms of opportunities missed and stacking these against those which were at least considered; (3) seeking a mixture of risks, i.e., accepting some because of their high potential while carefully avoiding others; and (4) placing "patient money" where slow growth is the best form of entry.

With values such as these, a finance manager can become a strong ally, and perhaps even a leader, in developing company strategy. The conservative standards should knowingly be transgressed when the potential long-run benefit justifies exposure to unusual financial risk: bold moves and risk-taking become a rational part of the game.

The capital structure of a company can then be designed to match its strategy. The debt-to-equity ratio can be tailored to fit the degree of risk, and bond interest obligations can be matched to steady flows of cash. If the company strategy aims for growth, as most such strategies do, sources of a corresponding influx of cash should be nurtured. This means that the heedless saddling of a company with debt, as is a currently fashionable way to finance takeovers, has to be avoided. Many companies today have exhausted their margins for future borrowing or issuing preferred stock, so they will be unable to grasp new strategic opportunities and may become insolvent during periods of stormy weather.

The aggressive finance manager, in contrast to the watchdog type, will knowingly endorse some risks while at the same time maintaining a financial structure that is suited to grow with company success. And under such guidance, the linking of the finance department program with company strategy will be straightforward.

## Conclusion: Fusing Department Strategy Programs with Business-Unit Strategy

Two broad conclusions stand out in the last eight chapters dealing with the role of departments in strategic management: (1) the triple linkage model reveals sharply the complex of forces that shape a department's response to strategy planning at the business-unit level, and (2) strategy is a necessary, vital device in achieving effective integration of departments' actions.

All three linkages must be well honed for a department to make its best contribution to overall company achievements: (1) Close, perceptive relationships with the department's slice of the outside environment enable the company to know about and perhaps grasp opportunities that only functional specialists can turn to good use. (2) Fitting and coordinating the department's moves with the programs of other departments is essential if the *net* impact is to be constructive. And (3) merging a department's ambitions with the needs of the overall strategy program make possible a focused, united effort. The art lies in keeping all three of these linkages strong *simultaneously*.

Unless the distinctive viewpoints of the various departments are recognized and their potential inputs are harnessed, even a brilliant business-unit strategy will not be fully effective. We have seen how this is so for the primary functional departments which are present in most business-units and single-line companies. A variation in the functional split-up—perhaps having a separate department for advertising, engineering, or distribution, or having departments based on geographic regions—would not alter that conclusion. Whatever the departmental arrangement best suited to a company, strategy programs (based on the triple linkage) in each of those departments is a necessary underpinning for the execution of a business-unit strategy.

The second clear conclusion is that a four-point strategy of the business-unit is needed to fuse the efforts of its departments into an effective, united program. Such a strategy provides not only a common direction; it is also the rationale for priorities among departments when conflicts arise, and it paces the strategic thrusts of the departments into a coordinated campaign.

A refined business-unit strategy encourages initiative at the department level. By understanding and "buying into" the strategy, department managers can take over most of the planning for strategy execution. The strategy, with both its general goals and more specific targets, provides guidance for future-oriented action and a symbol for rallying joint enthusiasm.

## Questions for Class Discussion

1.  Many companies that finance their own installment payment sales establish a separate and distinct subsidiary that extends this credit to their customers and then collects the payments. General Motors Acceptance Corporation, for instance, is one of the largest such companies. These finance subsidiaries rely much more heavily on borrowing rather than issuing stock to obtain their capital than do their parents. (a) How do you explain this sort of separation of accounts receivable from other assets, and the fact that the subsidiary has a very high debt-to-equity ratio? (b) What relation, if any, does this practice have to the parent company's strategy to sell its products "on installment"?

2.  Use the four factors listed at the beginning of this chapter to evaluate your personal "financial structure." That is, have you refrained from borrowing to retain strategic flexibility? matched your sources of capital to the type of assets you have? kept your cost of capital low? obtained your capital so as to avoid unbearable control by your "banker"?

3.  The Abdu brothers own two-thirds of the common stock of Lakeside Real Estate Company. The company is expanding and needs more capital. Instead of investing in additional common stock, the Abdu brothers have made a five-year renewable loan to the company. The interest rate is 12 percent per year. However, both interest and repayment of principal are *subordinated* to any other current liabilities and mortgage loans that Lakeside Real Estate Company may make; that is, these other obligations must be met before any payments

are made on the Abdu loan. Why do you think that the Abdu brothers made a loan to Lakeside instead of investing in more common stock? Consider the viewpoints of the company, the Abdu brothers as individuals, and persons doing business with Lakeside.

4. Many shifts are taking place in the financial services industry: commercial banks are selling insurance and stocks, insurance companies are in the brokerage business, stockbrokers are offering checking accounts, etc. What effect, if any, do you think this reshuffling will have on the "financial structure" of business firms? (For this question, focus on customers of financial service firms, not on the firms themselves.) For instance, will the reshuffling affect the financial structures of firms like Schultz Electronic Controls, Red River Power, or Long-Shot Printing (see pages 386–388)?

5. Look up the current interest rates on bank loans and on high-grade bonds and the dividend yields on utility stocks. On the basis of this information and your forecast for the future, how do you recommend that Red River Power Company raise the $4,000,000 which it needs for transmission lines to tie into a multistate power grid? Assume that the transmission line must be built to maintain service, and that estimates show a 12 percent return on the investment after income taxes. Also assume that the existing financial structure of the company is as shown in Table 14–5 and that it can obtain funds at currently prevailing rates.

6. "Pollution controls are killing us," says Gerald Cox, the owner of a small iron foundry. Sales have been dropping, and a new government requirement for a $40,000 exhaust control would add expense but no income. Joe and Dawn Sandusky, a husband-and-wife team, have a growing precision alloy casting business and need a larger building. Cox's building is very well suited to their requirements, so Cox proposes to sell out to the Sanduskys. Cox wants $120,000 for his entire business—plant, equipment, accounts receivable, and inventory. The Sanduskys can scrape up only $20,000 cash; they already have $30,000 in their business. An insurance company is willing to buy the plant for $85,000 and lease it to the Sanduskys. If the Sanduskys gradually liquidate the iron casting inventory and receivables, they might realize $65,000; a quick sale of these assets would yield only $15,000. But they would have to install the exhaust control if they continue to run the iron foundry. Cox recommends that the Sanduskys continue both businesses and indicates that he will accept one-fifth of the stock in such a venture in place of $35,000 of his sales price. The supplier of the exhaust control equipment will take 25 percent down and a five-year installment mortgage note for the balance. What do you recommend the Sanduskys do?

7. For Schultz Electronic Controls, Inc. (p. 386), calculate the quick ratio (also known as the "acid test"), the current ratio, and inventories as a percent of current equity. Do the same for The Long-Shot Printing Company (p. 388). For the

Red River Power Company (p. 387), calculate the current ratio and the ratio of long-term debt to stockholders' equity.

Then compare the companies' ratios to these standards:

What does your comparison tell you about the financial position of each of the three companies? Which financial managers sleep well?

8. Fast-growing High Temp, Inc., which makes boilers, is doing good business worldwide in the energy equipment and chemical processing plants field. Stockholders will be asked at the next meeting to authorize a four-for-one stock split and a tripling of the number of common shares from 10 million to 30 million. Current earnings are $27 million, or $2.99 per share outstanding, and the company has no preferred stock. A split is estimated by some to increase the number of registered shareholders by 24 percent. Additional shareholders are expected to buy the stock because its new market price will be about 25 percent of the former price. The directors of the company doubled the total amount of dividends paid over the past year to a 60 percent payout ratio. High Temp has heavily publicized its order backlog of $1.7 billion and its recent increases in market share. Can you explain why the directors have approved and put through these undertakings? Will all this make the company less attractive for a possible takeover?

9. Specialty Chemicals, Inc., has been growing rapidly and now needs more and more capital because both inventories and accounts receivable are rising at the same rate as sales. But the owners can put no more equity into the business, since their personal financing has been strained to the hilt. Moreover, their friends at the First National Bank will not lend any more money because the funds are needed for working capital and not for fixed assets. And the long-term bond market has been shut off because very high interest rates—especially after the inflation rate is taken out—mean an excessive strain on company earnings and cash when the sinking fund provisions are considered.

The owners of Specialty Chemicals like to believe that sales will grow forever because the firm sells to only one-third of the North American market and not to the rest of the world. Some financial service companies will make loans secured by inventory up to 80 percent of the LIFO value at an interest rate that is five percentage points above the prime rate. Should the owners slow the growth of the company until profits provide the working capital that is needed, which means no more than a five percent growth rate per year for the next five years? Or should they borrow from a financial service company and continue the 25 percent per year increase in sales? (Assume the following: (1) For every dollar of increased sales, current assets have to increase by one dollar. (2) The current ratio must stay at 2/1, so trade creditors cannot furnish more than half of the funds needed for any increase in current assets. (3) Net profits after tax are a very respectable five percent of sales.)

# CASE
## 14 Cleaning Chemicals, Inc.

William "Bill" Herbert, president, once again contemplated last year's sales and net profits as he thought about future financing for his company and the three possible ways of providing capital for his family-owned firm.

"I'm feeling desperate. We're up against it once again. We've reached the limit of our ability to finance both plant expansion and increased inventories so that we can make the sales that I know are out there. The small recession that hit our industry last year hurt us badly. Now, what should we do—stay as we are, take on a major stockholder and move to Dallas, or borrow more money to expand in Salt Lake City?"

Bill Herbert's company, Cleaning Chemicals, Inc., processed, mixed, and packaged various chemicals, soaps, detergents, and surfactants for sale to janitorial supply, plant and office cleaning, and the maintenance supply industries. It dealt only with large institutions (hospitals, real estate management companies, industrial plants, and large office buildings) and with state, local, and federal governments. To these customers it sold cleaners, cleaning equipment, algicides, acrylic sealers, degreasing chemicals, insecticides, shampoos, liquid and powdered soaps, disinfectants, stain removers, soap dispensers, gasket removers, lubricants, steam cleaners, deodorants, liquid bacteria, rust removers, and many other products in 55-gallon drums and barrels or by the truckload.

The company, with plants in Oakland, California, and Salt Lake City (and headquarters in Salt Lake), marketed its products along the Pacific Coast and in the area west of Omaha and north of Oklahoma City. While in competition with hundreds of other large and small companies, Cleaning Chemicals has grown rapidly and profitably during the past 10 years. (See Tables 14–7 and 14–8.) Bill Herbert envisions extending operations across the United States, following expansion into the Middle West, Texas, and the South. His vision of expansion, however, has been limited by recent financial realities.

"Although our plants perform simple operations, such as diluting, mixing, and packaging chemicals that we buy in bulk, our specialized equipment and low labor costs allow us to sell a good product at a relatively low price and thus provide effectiveness, satisfaction, and value to our customers. Last year we had to reduce prices and increase our sales effort in order to keep volume up, the plants filled with orders, and the employees busy. But that is behind us now, and I am looking forward to further growth. We are operating the plants six days per week for 50 weeks out of the year. Working this close to absolute capacity makes cost control difficult. I think that it would be highly desirable to get a larger plant and somehow reduce shipping costs so that we can sell in the Midwest. Chicago is a great market.

**TABLE 14–7.**
**INCOME STATEMENTS (in thousands)**

| Account | Last Year | Previous Year | Previous Year | Previous Year | Previous Year |
|---|---|---|---|---|---|
| Sales | $6,010 | $5,500 | $4,510 | $3,700 | $3,101 |
| Cost of Goods Sold | 4,400* | 3,570 | 2,760 | 2,230 | 1,860 |
| Gross Margin | 1,610 | 1,930 | 1,750 | 1,470 | 1,241 |
| Selling and Promotional Expense | 920 | 660 | 560 | 505 | 430 |
| General and Administrative Expense | 690 | 568 | 484 | 435 | 360 |
| Taxes | -0- | 312 | 330 | 250 | 210 |
| Profit After Taxes | $ -0- | $ 390 | $ 376 | $ 280 | $ 241 |

*Depreciation expense, included in the cost of goods sold, was $100,000.

**TABLE 14–8.**
**BALANCE SHEET (in thousands)**

| Assets | | Liabilities | |
|---|---|---|---|
| Cash | $ 102 | Notes payable | $ 300 |
| Accounts receivable | 912 | Current portion of | |
| Inventories | 876 | debt due | 100 |
| Prepaid expense | 10 | Accounts payable | 600 |
| | | Accrued expenses | 200 |
| Total current assets | $1,900 | Total current liabilities | $1,200 |
| Equipment | | Long-term debt* | 1,000 |
| (net of depreciation | | Common stock† | 250 |
| reserve) | 1,510 | Retained earnings | 960 |
| Total assets | $3,410 | Total liabilities & net worth | $3,410 |

*14 percent senior notes.

†1,000,000 shares authorized; 250,000 shares outstanding. Two hundred thousand shares were owned by Bill Herbert and his wife. Executives and supervisors owned the rest—acquired through a stock bonus plan.

"After we looked around at various cities for a new plant and headquarters location, we were approached by the city of Dallas and an investor from there with a promise of a leased plant close to highways and to the Dallas-Fort Worth International Airport. The city would provide whatever space we needed for now and for the next 10 years on favorable lease terms, and the investor would provide capital by buying stock in our company.

"The deal we finally worked out was that we would issue an additional 200,000 shares of common stock which the investor would purchase for $1,200,000. This would provide funds to pay off most of our long-term debt, increase cash by $100,000 to improve our current ratio, and provide $300,000 to pay for the move and for expanded equipment needs for the 20 percent increase in sales which I expect will come along when we have the added capacity and the new region for sales of our products.

"After we settle in at Dallas, the balance sheet should look much better and it should provide plenty of debt capacity for further borrowing as sales volume goes up.

"If you look at last year's figures, we need 57 cents in assets to support each dollar of sales. But our working capital was excessively low. Whether we stay here or move, we should improve our net working capital (current assets minus current liabilities) to about $900,000, so we'll need another $200,000 in assets. This will run up our total assets-to-sales ratio to about 0.60, or 60 cents for each dollar of sales (3,160 ÷ 6,010).

"When the word got out that we were planning to move both the Salt Lake plant and our headquarters, some local people swung into action. The mayor and a county supervisor called on us, and the president of a local bank came to see me with an offer. The banker and the mayor both promised us space in a plant that we could lease on favorable terms and that would allow us to expand physical volume by about 50 percent. The banker was not particularly happy with our balance sheet, but she proposed that we combine the notes payable and the long-term debt into another loan which her bank would make at a reduction in interest of two percentage points and with a 15-year term. The total loan would amount to $1,500,000 so that we could acquire enough equipment to let sales grow. Repayment would be in equal amounts each year over the term. The bank would require that we pay no dividends for five years and that the current ratio be kept to a minimum of 1.7 to 1. It also wants accounts receivable and inventories reduced by $100,000 each, since the banker believes that collections were a bit slow (about 55 days outstanding) and that the inventory turnover of five times per year should be increased to about six times.

"We can, in fact, stay where we are and continue with our present level of production and unit sales. My wife wants to do this. If we follow this idea, sales will probably go up about 5 percent in dollar volume because we will be able to raise our prices since economic conditions are improving. We can stay in the present plant and not incur the costs of moving. With more experience in producing at close to capacity, we can probably drop our cost of goods sold back toward the percentage of sales that we used to enjoy. And perhaps all this will get us back to a net return on sales after taxes of four percent. That's not a bad figure, since it is about the average for all U.S. industrial companies, but it is certainly a smaller rate of return on sales than we were accustomed to earning in the past.

"Life would be a lot easier if we didn't move. And we would be solidly established in the West. Selling expenses would not increase more than five percent, and we could hold general and administrative costs to about what they are. Yes, I think I can see a four percent return on sales. Our interest costs went way up with the increase in debt we took on last year, but that will be a little less next year."

## Question

What course of action do you recommend to Mr. Herbert?

# INTEGRATING CASES

## Strategy and Finance

# C. D. Ecker's Approach to Growth

The three top managers of Passmore & Company are debating whether to accept an offer from C.D. Ecker Company to purchase assets of their family company. This offer has forced the three brothers—sons of the company's founder—to face squarely what they should do about future growth.

### Passmore & Company

Passmore & Company makes printing presses, mostly small-size, web-feed letterpresses.[1] The company has been in business for 70 years and enjoys a good reputation in its particular niche. The founder was a restless experimenter, with both successes and failures. When control passed to the three sons, they chose to focus on a few successful designs and have kept the company on a conservative track ever since.

The company has a relatively large group of engineers who keep updating the press designs with new features. For instance, it has been a leader in adding electronic controls to improve pressure, register alignment, and other quality characteristics. However, this segment of the printing industry is mature, and Passmore sales, when adjusted for inflation, have shown only slow growth during the last 10 years.

This conservative approach is reflected in company financing. As shown on the balance sheet in Table 1, there is no long-term debt. Instead, Passmore & Company has credit lines with two commercial banks and pays off all its notes at each bank sometime during each year (though not all at the same time). Since the com-

---

[1]A letterpress is the oldest and most versatile method of printing. In its various sizes and designs, the technology can be used for commercial printing, books, newspapers, and magazines, as well as packaging. Basically, the raised surfaces of metal type or plates are first inked by rollers, and then paper is pressed on these inked surfaces.

In a sheet-fed press, separate sheets of paper are fed (usually automatically) onto the inked surface for each pass. In a web-feed press, impressions are made onto a roll of paper (the web) as it passes through the press. There are many further variations adapted to the end product desired.

Screen printing relies on ink passing through a fine screen. By blocking up the screen in the appropriate areas, ink goes through only for the image desired. Screen printing permits the use of kinds of ink that cannot be used on other sorts of presses.

**TABLE 1.**
**PASSMORE & COMPANY (in thousands)**

| Assets | | Liabilities and Net Worth | |
|---|---|---|---|
| Cash | $ 601 | Bank notes payable | $ 2,500 |
| Accounts receivable | 2,675 | Accounts payable | 756 |
| Deferred charges | 134 | Accrued items | 1,100 |
| Inventories | 5,028 | Deferred income tax | 638 |
| Total current assets | 8,438 | Total liabilities | 4,994 |
| Investments | 248 | Preferred stock (6%) | 668 |
| Land and buildings (net) | 2,946 | Common stock ($100 par) | 2,087 |
| Machinery & equipment (net) | 1,816 | Retained earnings | 5,699 |
| | | Total liabilities & | |
| Total assets | $13,448 | stockholders' equity | $13,448 |

*PROFIT AND LOSS FOR LAST YEAR (in thousands)*

| | |
|---|---|
| Sales | $17,472 |
| Cost of sales: | |
|    Materials | 5,657 |
|    Direct labor | 1,996 |
|    Factory overhead | 3,965 |
| Gross profit | 5,884 |
| Selling expenses | 1,982 |
| General & administrative expenses | 1,987 |
| Retirement plan | 647 |
| Operating profit | 1,268 |
| Income taxes | 507 |
| Net profit | $ 761 |

Annual depreciation is about $340,000. Dividends on preferred and common stock are $210,000 per year.

---

pany was firmly established many years ago, it has relied entirely on retained earnings to increase its equity. The three brothers own 70 percent of the common stock, the remaining 30 percent being held in small lots primarily by family relations or former employees. The 6 percent preferred stock is held by a charitable trust created by the founder and administered by the brothers.

The 9 percent return on equity is adequate but not impressive. Actually, though, the profitability is better than appears on the surface. Each of the three brothers draws the same good salary. Dan, 63, holds the title of chairman and looks after financial matters; Sam, 60, is president and concentrates on sales; Joe, 52, the youngest brother, heads up production. Even more significant than salary is the liberal retirement plan which holds down company income taxes and post-pones personal income taxes. Also, to some extent the current outlays for engineering are used to assure a stable flow of income in the future.

Some parts of the printing industry are going through major technological change. The photo-offset segment, for instance, has many new competitors challenging Xerox's once dominant position with faster ways to spew out multiple copies of all sorts of documents. And new communication techniques facilitate reproduction thousands of miles away. For printing presses, however, the change has been slower. And Passmore & Company has elected not to stray into the greener fields outside its normal domain. The brothers are comfortable where they are, and none has distinctive capabilities better suited to other segments of the communication revolution.

## C.D. Ecker Company

The C.D. Ecker Company, like Passmore & Company, is in the printing machinery business. There are two divisions, Ecker Screen Presses and Springdale Letter Press. The original C.D. Ecker Company manufactures rotary screen presses used to print specialty items such as drapery fabrics, shower curtains, and some advertising display products—a narrow niche in the printing business where unusual color effects are desired.

The Ecker Company was acquired seven years ago by Ruben Altman, an executive in a large textile-converting corporation. Altman had urged his employer to buy the company as a vertical integration move, and when this proposal did not work out he personally bought the company and placed his 26-year-old son, Solomon (Sol), in charge. Three years later Ruben Altman died suddenly, leaving ownership of C.D. Ecker Company to Sol Altman and his mother.

Sol Altman has been quite successful in maintaining Ecker Company's position in its narrow market. He has won the support of the technical experts in the company and has encouraged their efforts to modernize the press designs while leaving the manufacturing plant itself much as he found it. But growth prospects for rotary screen presses are quite limited, so Sol has been searching for ways to expand—ways that do not require much capital since almost all his assets are already tied up in the company.

A major opportunity to expand was Springdale Printing Machinery, Inc., which for many years has been a prominent producer of sheet-fed letterpresses. Located in rural New England, Springdale has an integrated plant including a foundry and machine shops. For at least 20 years Springdale had been living on its past record, and finally the estates of its former owners decided to sell out. Potential buyers were few. (For example, at lunch one day the Passmore brothers, who had heard that Springdale could be purchased, agreed with Sam's comment, "Let's not get into that. The whole organization needs rebuilding. It's as sleepy as the town where it is located.") But this lack of interest created an opportunity for Sol.

C.D. Ecker Company acquired all the stock of Springdale Printing Machinery, Inc., in exchange for $11,500,000 of notes and stock—a senior note of $6,000,000 secured by a mortgage on the Springdale plant and equipment, a series of subordinated notes for $3,000,000, and $2,500,000 of C.D. Ecker Company's second noncumulative preferred stock. The combined effect of this acquisition on C.D. Ecker Company is reflected in the consolidated balance sheet and profit-and-loss summary presented in Table 2.

Sol has already made some economies in the Springdale operation (reflected in the profit-and-loss statement) and expects to make more. The resulting cash

**TABLE 2.**
**C.D. ECKER COMPANY**
**CONSOLIDATED BALANCE SHEET (in thousands)**

| *Assets* | | *Liabilities and Equity* | |
|---|---|---|---|
| Cash | $ 217 | Accounts payable | $ 2,431 |
| Accounts receivable | 4,383 | Notes payable | 5,300 |
| Inventories | 8,422 | Accrued items | 1,645 |
| Other current assets | 366 | | |
| Total current assets | 13,388 | Total current liabilities | 9,374 |
| Land and buildings (net) | 5,461 | Mortgage loan on Springdale plant & equipment | 6,000 |
| Machinery & equipment (net) | 8,729 | Long-term subordinated | |
| Other assets | 431 | notes | 3,000 |
| Total fixed assets | 14,621 | Total liabilities | 18,374 |
| | | Preferred stock (10%) | 1,000 |
| | | Second noncumulative preferred stock (10%) | 2,500 |
| | | Common stock ($10 par) | 3,250 |
| | | Retained earnings | 2,885 |
| | | Total equity | 9,635 |
| | | Total liabilities & | |
| Total assets | $28,009 | equity | $28,009 |

*CONSOLIDATED PROFIT-AND-LOSS STATMENT (in thousands)*

| | |
|---|---|
| Sales | $31,400 |
| Cost of goods sold | 21,300 |
| Gross profit | 10,100 |
| Selling expenses | 3,200 |
| General & administrative expenses | 4,300 |
| | 7,500 |
| Operating profit | 2,600 |
| Income tax | 700 |
| Net profit | $ 1,900 |

flow from combined operations, Sol expects, will enable him to pay off his long-term debt within four or five years.

The acquisition of the Springdale company more than doubled the volume of business of C.D. Ecker Company and puts Ecker into a segment of the industry that has little overlap with its screen printing customers. Sol has, indeed, opened up new horizons—and taken on new problems: Springdale needs revamped products, computerized systems, revitalized personnel, and more aggressive leadership.

As a step toward improving the product line, Sol is seeking another company with a strong engineering staff. Toward this end, he would like to acquire Passmore & Company and probably merge the operations of Springdale and Passmore. Such a merger would create a relatively large player in the letterpress part of the industry, a player which produced both web-fed and sheet-fed presses. There would be potential savings (or increased effectiveness at the same cost) in marketing, administration, and perhaps engineering and production. The first task, however, would focus on adding electronic controls to Springdale presses.

Preliminary feelers indicated that the Passmore brothers would be willing to at least talk about such a merger. The first hurdle, of course, is that Ecker has no cash to invest in the deal. In fact, it has a lot of long-term debt and its accounts receivable are pledged to secure its bank loan. To explore possible ways that the acquisition might be financed, Passmore's two outside directors met with executives of C.D. Ecker Company to find out what sort of a financial deal could be worked out. At the end of a two-day negotiation, Ecker was prepared to make the offer outlined in Table 3.

**TABLE 3.**
**PROPOSED ECKER PURCHASE OF PASSMORE ASSETS (in thousands)**

| *Ecker to purchase:* | | *Ecker to pay:* | |
|---|---|---|---|
| Accounts receivable | $2,675 | Assume Passmore liabilities: | |
| Deferred assets | 134 | Bank notes payable | $2,500 |
| Inventories | 5,028 | Accounts payable | 756 |
| | | Accrued items | 1,100 |
| | 7,837 | | 4,356 |
| Machinery & equipment | 1,816 | Give Passmore 9% serial notes, | |
| Passmore trade name and | | 1/10 maturing at the end of each | |
| "going concern" strengths | -0- | of the next 10 years | 5,297 |
| Total | $9,653 | Total | $9,653 |

Ecker to put Dan Passmore on its board of directors, and employ Sam and Joe for at least five years at their present salaries.

Ecker to rent land and buildings for 15 years at $300,000 per year, plus taxes and upkeep.

Ecker to give Passmore & Company an option to buy 80,000 shares of Ecker common stock at $30 per share.

At the close of the negotiations Sol Altman commented, "This is a good deal. Passmore will convert their assets into cash and have the privilege of buying 20 percent of the combined company at today's value. We gain strength, and the added income from Passmore's business will pay off the serial notes before they are due."

When reporting back to the Passmore brothers, the directors noted, "The building rent alone would support almost a 50 percent increase in dividends. In addition, we would have income from the cash and investments which the company retains and from the serial notes. What's more, Uncle Sam collects no capital gains tax at this time. Eventually, we can sell the land and buildings at a profit because they are already undervalued on the balance sheet." Sam Passmore observed, "We sure would be betting on Sol Altman's ability to run the combined companies. If he trips up, we probably would find ourselves running a merger of Passmore and Springdale—a possibility that we gladly passed up a couple of years ago!"

## Question

As a friend of the Passmore brothers, do you recommend acceptance of the proposal from C.D. Ecker Company?

# Powdered Metals, Inc.

"During our first eight years we had to take large risks," said Mr. Hubler, president of Powdered Metals, Inc. "Bankruptcy was always a threat, but we had no choice. We simply proceeded on faith that our small company would master the art of making high-precision parts out of powdered metals, and then the leading companies of the nation would be glad to do business with us. Now we have mastered the art, at least to some extent, and we are doing business with the Xeroxes and the IBMs. But the risk problem has become tougher because we now have choices. We can use our profits to pay off debts and remove the threat of bankruptcy, or we can seize the opportunity we worked so hard to create and help push powdered metal parts into every sophisticated machine that's made, or we can decide to do something in between."

## Product-Market Target

The company makes an array of specially shaped gears, bearings, and other machine parts. Instead of starting with the usual casting or forging process, the new metallurgy injects a finely powdered form of iron, steel, or other alloy into a mold and packs the powder together under high pressure. The "raw" part is then placed in a furnace where high temperature unites the fine particles into a solid form.

It is the combination of (1) high-pressure molding in very precise molds with (2) heat treatment ("sintering") that makes the company's products distinctive. The molding process enables the company to make oddly shaped parts that are difficult or impossible to produce by ordinary machining. And the sintering process imparts strength and hardness matching or exceeding those same qualities of conventionally formed metal parts. Moreover, the process significantly reduces unit costs, virtually eliminates waste and scrap, and can be used for rapid mass production.

Actually, the technique of producing metal parts by compacting powders has been in use for many years. Early applications were limited to small, relatively crude parts not subjected to heavy bearing or shock loads. The process gained acceptance by providing lower costs than were available through conventional machining or forging methods and by providing unique compositions not readily obtained through conventional melt-alloying methods.

As powder-compacting techniques were refined and improved, the competitive advantage broadened dramatically. It is common practice today for engineers to design components specifically for production by the powdered metal process. Load-bearing characteristics, density, dimensional and shape conformity, and ease of machining can now meet a wide range of requirements once considered available only from wrought materials.

The powdered metal industry is generally expected to continue to expand at its current rate because the competitive capability of the process is gaining wider acceptance in all sorts of uses. The largest *tonnage* consumer is and will continue to be the automotive industry, in its bearings, gears, oil pump vanes, etc. However, the largest *number* of parts, requiring a high degree of precision, are being consumed in home appliances, business machines, recreational products, and the electrical and electronics industries. It is to this latter segment of the market that Powdered Metals, Inc., has directed its efforts.

Some of the more intricate precision parts made by this segment of the industry cannot be directly compacted to exact finished dimensions and contours and thus require secondary or finishing operations, generally by machining. Powdered Metals, Inc., has a unique capability in this area, shared with only four or five other of the 90 noncaptive powdered metal parts-makers in the country. The success it has attained in becoming a primary vendor to IBM and Xerox is testimony to Powdered Metals' competence in the high value-added portion of the market. The company has the expertise to continue to penetrate premium markets where its proven competence and its highest-grade tools and equipment are demanded.

Four years ago, total industry sales of powdered metal parts was $108 million. By last year the sales had risen to $217 million, more than doubling in three years' time. About $120 million of last year's total went to the automotive industry, the balance going to the more specialized markets. And this second part of the industry grew somewhat faster than the total, almost 30 percent per year. This rate of growth may not be maintained, but industry speakers predict an average increase over the next decade of 20 to 25 percent per annum.

Powdered Metals hopes to increase the number of customers it serves; it is now somewhat vulnerable because two large firms account for over half of its business. However, because of the cost of making precision molds, reorders of specific parts are likely to be placed with the company that produces the original run. An industry rule of thumb is that, on the average, a machine part will continue to be used by a customer in making new machines for seven years. Powdered Metals has not yet had much experience with such reorders.

The company is well equipped to seek orders for complex parts. It has a very good machine shop where molds are made, its compacting presses and sintering furnaces are new, and it has equipment for secondary machining if this is required. Both Mr. Hubler and Mr. Chang, the chief engineer, are recognized for their specialized knowledge, and the company has established a reputation for high-quality output.

## Progress to Date

Mr. A. B. Hubler dropped out of engineering school, became a machinist in the Navy, and later worked at this trade while completing his engineering training at night. He was a partner in several small firms, and in one of these he hired a bright young engineer, J. K. Chang. These two men soon developed the idea of a new firm in the powdered metals field. Four years later, Mr. Hubler had assembled the initial capital and Mr. Chang had studied the latest technological developments. The new firm was launched in a suburb of Columbus, Ohio.

The early years proved to be even more difficult than anticipated. Learning how to get dependable quality from new equipment, training personnel, obtaining test orders from customers, and waiting while they evaluated the products in their own shops—all these took time and money. But now, eight years later, Powdered Metals, Inc., is a profitable business.

The plant is running on a two-shift basis. The margin between prices and costs is improving, reflecting both an ability to get more attractive orders and improved efficiency in the plant. And the company has a four-month backlog of orders. Table 1 shows the improvement in income over the last five years, from a staggering deficit to a 19 percent return on the book value of stockholders' equity.

## Present Financing

Obtaining the capital necessary to finance Powdered Metals has been a strain. During its early years the company relied on equity investments by Mr. Hubler and his friends. Equipment, especially compacting presses obtained from a Japanese manufacturer, was usually purchased at least in part with chattel mort-

**TABLE 1.**
**INCOME STATEMENT (in thousands)**

|  | Last year | 2 years ago | 3 years ago | 4 years ago | 5 years ago |
|---|---|---|---|---|---|
| Net sales . . . . . . . . . . . . . . . . . . . . . . . . | $3,732 | $3,019 | $1,778 | $ 821 | $ 316 |
| Cost of sales . . . . . . . . . . . . . . . . . . . . . . | 2,631 | 2,262 | 1,325 | 644 | 530 |
| Gross profit . . . . . . . . . . . . . . . . . . . . . | $1,101 | $ 757 | $ 453 | $ 177 | $−214 |
| Selling, general & administrative expenses . . . . . . . . . . . . . | 797 | 484 | 386 | 294 | 189 |
| Net income . . . . . . . . . . . . . . . . . . . . . . . | $ 304* | $ 273* | $ 67* | $−117 | $−403 |

*No income tax has been paid because of loss carryovers for preceding years. At the beginning of the present year the remaining loss carryover was $370,000.

gages, and other loans were secured.

About three years ago the company was successful in a significant recapitalization: (1) 50,000 shares of common stock were sold to the public at $10 per share by a local investment banker; (2) the Buckeye SBIC made a $2,000,000 mortgage loan to the company;[1] (3) debts outstanding at that time were either paid off or converted to common stock. The Buckeye SBIC loan runs for 10 years with $50,000 maturing quarterly ($200,000 per year); the interest rate is 8½ percent per annum. As part of the deal, Buckeye received warrants (rights to buy) for 50,000 shares at $8 per share, which can be exercised any time during the 10 years that the loan is outstanding.

This injection of capital, helpful though it was, has not been adequate to support expanding production. New equipment to expand capacity has been financed with chattel mortgages; $300,000 of such mortgages were outstanding a year ago, and an additional $600,000 were issued during the past year. These chattel mortgages mature at the rate of $100,000 per year and bear 10 percent interest. Incidentally, the Buckeye SBIC was willing to subordinate its claim on this new equipment because the added capacity increases the chance that its warrants will become valuable.

The present financial structure of the company, reflecting these capital inputs, is shown in Table 2.

---

[1]SBICs (Small Business Investment Corporations) are private lending organizations that are granted federal tax advantages because they concentrate on lending money to small firms that are having difficulty obtaining long-term capital.

**TABLE 2.**
**BALANCE SHEET—END OF YEAR (in thousands)**

| Assets | Last Year | | Preceding Year | |
|---|---|---|---|---|
| **Current assets:** | | | | |
| Cash............................. | $ 199 | | $ 89 | |
| Accounts receivable, net ............... | 650 | | 651 | |
| Inventories........................ | 637 | | 308 | |
| Prepaid and deferred items............. | 89 | | 61 | |
| Total current assets ................. | | $1,575 | | $1,109 |
| **Plant and equipment:** | | | | |
| Land and buildings | $ 941 | | $ 909 | |
| Machinery and equipment | 2,853 | | 2,244 | |
| Furniture and fixtures ................. | 260 | | 230 | |
| | $4,054 | | $3,383 | |
| Less depreciation reserve .............. | −747 | | −531 | |
| Net plant and equipment .............. | | 3,307 | | 2,852 |
| Research and deferred charges............ | | 74 | | 83 |
| Total assets ....................... | | $4,956 | | $4,044 |
| **Liabilities** | | | | |
| **Current Liabilities:** | | | | |
| Current portion of long-term debt ....... | $ 300 | | $ 200 | |
| Accounts payable ................... | 517 | | 345 | |
| Accrued liabilities ................... | 109 | | 73 | |
| Total current liabilities.............. | | $ 926 | | $ 618 |
| **Long-term debt:** | | | | |
| Long-term loan ...................... | $1,600 | | $1,800 | |
| Equipment mortgages ................. | 800 | | 300 | |
| Total debt due after 1 year........... | | 2,400 | | 2,100 |
| **Stockholders' equity:** | | | | |
| 200,000 shares outstanding, par value $1 . | $ 200 | | $ 200 | |
| Capital in excess of par value .......... | 1,800 | | 1,800 | |
| Retained earnings (deficit) ............. | (370) | | (674) | |
| Total equity ...................... | | 1,630 | | 1,326 |
| Total liabilities and equity ........... | | $4,956 | | $4,044 |

## Future Opportunities

"At long last," Mr. Hubler observes, "we have the opportunity to have a balance sheet look the way the bankers like it. Assuming earnings just stay steady, our cash gain from operations each year will look like this:

| | |
|---|---|
| Net Income ........... | $304,000 |
| Depreciation ........... | 216,000 |
| Available ........... | $520,000 |

"With that amount of cash, we can make our annual debt repayments of $300,000 and still increase current assets by $220,000. In two years our current ratio would be 2:1, and our long-term debt would be only 82 percent of the stockholders' equity. For anyone who has been squeezed for capital for eight years, that kind of a picture is very attractive. And maybe the equipment people would stop insisting on my personal guarantee on those mortgage notes.

"But we didn't enter the powdered metal business to stay even. We believe the industry will continue to grow rapidly, and naturally we'd like to benefit from that growth. The future is never certain, of course; too many competitors may enter the business, or some new technique may replace powdered metals. But powdered metals have grown much faster than the industries we serve—business machines, electronics, home appliances, and the like—and Powdered Metals has been growing faster than its competitors. So I feel that 20 percent increase per year for us is very conservative. We should be able to do that and at the same time be more choosy about the orders we take, which will help our profit margin. Of course, if a real recession descends on us, it's a new ball game.

"The main catch is that fast growth takes more capital—capital we do not have. With an additional $500,000 in equipment, we could produce a volume of $5,000,000 in sales. The building is big enough to handle $7,000,000—with a bit of squeezing. But as we move beyond $5,000,000, all kinds of machinery will be needed, an average of $.80 for every additional dollar of sales, or $1,600,000 of new equipment for the expansion from $5,000,000 to $7,000,000.

"In addition, more sales require more working capital. Inventory, accounts receivable, accounts payable, and accrued items all go up. My rough estimate is that the net increase in working capital would be about one-sixth of the annual sales. Where is all that money coming from? Retained earnings will help, but in any one year during the growth period the profit on the added volume (say, 9 percent) doesn't provide necessary working capital (17 percent).

"I've asked our treasurer, P. L. Jablonski, to explore all the different ways we might finance the business that I'm sure we can get during the next four years. With all these alternatives before us, we can sit down and figure out whether it is wise to go plunging ahead."

## Alternative Sources of Capital

Ms. Jablonski summarized the various potential ways Powdered Metals, Inc., might finance its growth as follows:

1. The company's commercial bank suggests no growth this year and cutting inventories $100,000. These actions will allow the company to significantly improve its working capital position. Then the bank

would make a short-term loan of $500,000 (perhaps requiring the pledging of accounts receivable if the inventory reduction was not feasible). The interest cost would be prime rate plus 1½ percent and maintenance of a bank balance of 20 percent of the bank loan.[2]

2.  The investment banker who helped sell company stock three years ago thinks that improved company performance would create an interest in an additional issue, in spite of the present depressed condition of stocks generally. However, the selling price to the public would be only $7.50 per share, and after underwriting charges and other costs the company would receive $6.70 per share. Thus, an issue of 75,000 shares would yield $502,000. Such an issue would improve debt-to-equity ratios. It would be "expensive" for present stockholders; for example, after such an issue, the people who invested $500,000 three years ago when risks were greater would hold only 18 percent of the total equity, whereas the new stockholders would have 27 percent of the total equity.

3.  An investment broker, recommended by the commercial bank, suggests a "sale and leaseback" of the company's land and buildings (for $800,000) plus the new equipment (costing $500,000). The $800,000 would be used to pay off existing chattel mortgages on equipment. The company would pay an annual rental equivalent to 9½ percent on money advanced (a total initially of $1,300,000) plus 5 percent depreciation on the buildings and equipment. The lease would run for 20 years, at which time the company would have an option to repurchase the land, buildings, and equipment at 20 percent of the total of $1,300,000 advanced.

4.  Mr. Bender, a Cleveland financier and president of Empire Investment Co., proposes a merger with another small firm that he controls. The firm, a profitable truck-leasing operation, would be merged into Powdered Metals so that the profits from the trucking operation would be offset by the tax-loss carry-forward of Powdered Metals. Empire Investment Co. owns the trucking firm and would get 75 percent of the shares of the merged companies. Mr. Bender says he can always find capital for profitable investments, and he would be able to devise some scheme to provide whatever capital the powdered metal activities can use effectively.

5.  Buckeye SBIC is willing to advance more capital if the total debt structure is improved. It proposes a combined package: (a) a $500,000 loan for the new equipment on the same terms as its present loan, plus (b) purchase of 80,000 shares of stock at $6 per share. The $480,000 from

---

[2]The minimum-balance requirement, a customary banking practice, means that the company would get only $400,000 for other uses. Assuming an 8 percent prime rate, the interest cost would be 9½ percent of $500,000, or $47,500 per year. On $400,000, this is equivalent to almost 12 percent per annum.

the stock sale, $100,000 from reduction of inventories, and current earnings are to be used to retire the equipment mortgages.

Ms. Jablonski notes, "All five of the proposals focus primarily on raising $500,000 to expand production facilities. This will enable Powdered Metals to increase its sales to $5,000,000. At the projected rise in sales, that takes care of us for only about eighteen months. Consequently, any plan adopted must also consider the ability of the company at that time to raise further growth capital."

## Questions

1. Do you recommend that Powdered Metals, Inc., buy the $500,000 worth of new equipment at this time? If so, how should the expansion be financed?
2. Assuming that your recommendation is accepted and that you have $5,000 available for investment, what price per share would you be willing to pay for Powdered Metals common stock?

# PART 3

## Corporate Strategy to Build Stronger Set of Business-Units

# CHAPTER 15

## Portfolio Strategy: Desired Mix of Business-Units

### Business-Unit Versus Corporate Strategy

Strategy for a *single business-unit* and strategy programs for its main operating departments have been our focus thus far, in both Parts 1 and 2. These single-product-line, self-contained companies are the dynamic building blocks of our economic society. Each requires individualized attention. Our prime attention on the creation of strong business-units is more than a convenient analytical approach; it reflects the cardinal importance of these units.

Nevertheless, successful business-units often outgrow their original mission. Their market may have matured; i.e., they may have strengths that can be applied to related businesses. Or, a broader base may be needed to match competition or spread risk, assurance of supplies may become critical, or perhaps an irresistible deal may present itself. For such reasons as these, many companies find themselves engaged in several different businesses.

Sooner or later the benefits of combining the collection of business-units within a corporation must be assessed. Potentially, the federation of units will be stronger than the sum of each business operating independently. But this does not happen automatically. We need a *corporate strategy* which focuses on the selection and interrelation of units that will, in fact, yield the benefits of union. In addition, the corporate strategy should identify the resources that the corporation will supply to its business-units to give them a distinctive competitive advantage.

Corporate strategy, in contrast to business-unit strategy, applies to a different level of organization, and it differs in content. It is primarily concerned with building an effective collection of business-units. This requires, first, thoughtful investment (allocation) of resources. Some units will be built up, others will be liquidated, and perhaps new units will be acquired. Because this allocation process is similar to that of a financial investment manager's changing the composition of securities in his or her portfolio, the term "portfolio problem" is widely used to identify this part of corporate strategy. (2) Then, to buttress the business-units, the corporation should provide "resource inputs" which give the businesses added strength.

Note that the addition of a corporate level does not diminish the need for well-designed strategies for each business-unit, and for department strategy programs within each unit. These continue to be essential. Although a bit of glory is lost, and some central assistance may be added, primary strategic integration takes place at the business-unit level. Unlike the organic relations of departments to their business-unit, business-units can operate without a parent corporation. That is, the corporation role, albeit beneficial, is largely an add-on.

A basic approach to formulating corporate strategy is indicated in Figure 15–1. A careful appraisal of the business-units presently owned is the first step. For each unit, the results to date, the standing relative to competitors, threats and opportunities in the environment, and projected future results based on existing plans should be studied. Moreover, the projections for all business-units should be combined into a consolidated picture of what the corporation will be and do if the status quo is maintained.

If this combined picture is not entirely satisfactory, then the second broad step is to decide what changes, executed within the projected environment, would put the corporation in the best balanced position. This then becomes the strategic ob-

**FIGURE 15–1.**
**CORPORATE STRATEGY FORMULATION**

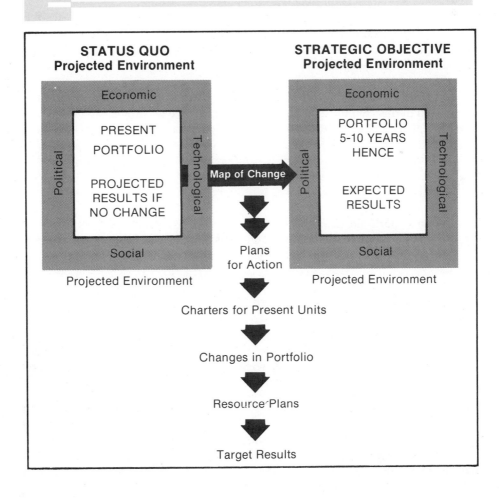

jective. It stipulates the desired portfolio of business-units 5 to 10 years hence, their relative competitive positions, the key corporate resources, the individual unit results, and the combined results for the corporation as a whole.

To move from the status quo to the strategic objective will require some supporting changes along the way. The main features of these planned changes, which become part of the corporate strategy, deal with charters for present units (domains, expectations, constraints), changes in the portfolio, resource plans including sources and allocation of capital, and target results at intervals along the course.

The main elements in corporate strategy, then, include:

1. The desired portfolio of business-units 5 to 10 years hence.
2. The distinctive corporate resources that will add power and luster to these business-units.
3. Major moves (thrusts) needed to get from the present situation to the desired holdings in the portfolio, including:
   a. charters for business-units to be retained;
   b. additions or deletions of business-units, including desired acquisitions;
   c. consolidated resource mobilization and allocation plans.
4. Target results.

The chief issues and hurdles in developing the portfolio of business-units are discussed in this chapter. The process of acquiring a new firm is explored in the next chapter, and joint ventures and inputs of corporate resources are considered in Chapter 17.

## Portfolio Design

A good portfolio has several dimensions. Four are always significant: (1) growth and profitability of the business-units considered separately, (2) synergy among the units, (3) risk and profit balance, and (4) cash-flow balance.

## First Dimension: Attractive Business-Units

The business-units within a diversified corporation will naturally vary in attractiveness. Industry growth rates change, competitors expand capacity, risks assumed turn out well or poorly, and so forth. So an initial step in reviewing portfolio strategy is to compare the relative attractiveness of the present units, especially in terms of their *future* prospects for growth and profitability. Corporation resources will be limited, especially with respect to central management time and perhaps capital. Consequently, guidance is needed on where to place the "bets."

A useful way to highlight such a comparison of business-units is on an evaluation matrix. One such matrix, adapted from layouts used by General Electric and

Royal Dutch Shell, is shown in Figure 15–2.[1] Here each business-unit is evaluated on the basis of its industry attractiveness and its competitive position in that industry.

Placing a business-unit on such a matrix involves many subjective judgments. Both the subfactors to be included and the outlook for each factor have to be de-

**FIGURE 15–2.**
**EVALUATION MATRIX**
**Area within circles indicates relative size of business-units.**

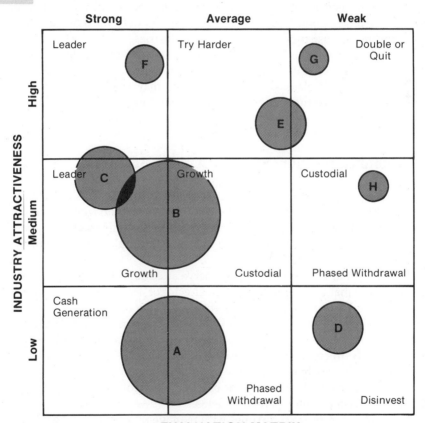

**EVALUATION MATRIX**
**Area within circles indicates relative size of business-units**

---

[1]This matrix is a significant refinement of the more familiar 2 x 2 matrix stressed by The Boston Consulting Group. The earlier B.C.G. version focused only on cash flow and simply looked at industry growth versus company market position. The resulting four boxes were designated as follows: 1:1, stars; 1:2, wildcats or problem children; 2:1, cash cows; and 2:2, dogs.

cided. Among the subfactors which determine an industry's attractiveness are market growth rate, stability of demand, availability of resources, product and process volatility, number of customers and suppliers, ease of entry, governmental support/regulation, gross and net margins, and vulnerability to inflation. A similar set of subfactors bears on the competitive position of a business-unit. These include relative market share, product and service quality and reputation, favorable access to resources, R & D strength, relative productivity and costs, and community and government relations. (See Chapters 2 and 3 for a discussion of industry and business-unit subfactors.)

The matrix is designed to provoke strategic thinking. For instance, in the example shown, business-unit D clearly should be divested, and A, the corporation's original business, has such poor prospects that it should be used to generate cash as it is phased out. In contrast, units E and G may warrant significant resource inputs because they are in attractive industries.

This sizing up of the business-units separately, of course, builds upon the thorough strategic planning done within the respective units. Each business-unit should have its own plans which, if successful, may change its location on the evaluation matrix. At the corporate level, harsher judgments about their *relative* prospects are needed as a basis for allocating scarce resources.

## Second Dimension: Synergy Among Businesses

A good portfolio is more than a collection of attractive business-units. The fact that the units are associated under a single central management should add extra value. Often, when viewed separately a unit has only medium appeal, but when combined with other holdings it may add unusual strength. Synergy and balance are both involved.

Four potential sources of synergy deserve attention. (1) Corporate executives may be able to manage (serve as "outside director of") various kinds of businesses with acumen. Historical data show that the more successful diversified companies stick to "related" businesses. For example, in its diversification, Federated Department Stores stays with retailing because its central managers understand that type of activity. In contrast, in its initial growth phase, Teledyne concentrated on new high-technology businesses. The rationale is that the experience gained and the competence needed in guiding one part of the portfolio will be especially valuable to *other business-units* in related fields.[2]

By no means rare are companies with managements that dislike decisive action. The president of a medical supply company had placed close friends in charge of branch operations and was unwilling to replace these executives in spite of submarginal performances. Nevertheless, the company was attractive for

---

[2]This argument also has negative implications. As we shall see, considerations of balance may suggest that unrelated businesses be assembled, but if this is done part of the cost will be added complexity in management.

merger because the elimination of two losing units and the change of one additional executive made the remaining activities a successful venture. Quite clearly, objective managers, introduced subsequent to the merger, were all that was needed.

(2) Synergy may be possible from the broader use of a particular strength of one of the business-units. The Campbell Soup Company provides a well-known example. Over the years this company has built up a strong national selling organization for its soups. When it acquired Pepperidge Farm, an East Coast producer of specialty breads, cookies, etc., it used its marketing strength to give Pepperidge Farm products national distribution.

In another case, the R & D capability of a production systems company helped a machine tool business develop electronic controls for its equipment. Similarly, the national repair service organization of a printing press company is a great boost to the sale of Swiss-made auxiliary equipment.

(3) Vertical integration is another potential source of synergy. For instance, Hart, Schaffner & Marx, a leading manufacturer of men's suits, has acquired retail clothing stores. This assures Hart, Schaffner & Marx that these key outlets will promote its brand of suits in a very competitive market. At the same time, the stores can build a quality reputation by featuring the Hart, Schaffner & Marx name.

(4) When business-units are relatively small, the parent may be able to provide a centralized resource more efficiently than the units could obtain that resource independently. A prime example, of course, is raising capital in major financial markets on terms which separate units could not command alone. But there are many other possibilities. For example, small commercial banks, when they are combined, find substantial economies in electronically processing checks, deposits, and billings. (The local unit is also able to make larger loans because the total capital which sets size limits is larger.) And the central room reservation service which hotel and motel chains provide is a significant advantage to local units in maintaining occupancy.

Care must be exercised, however, in seeking synergies. Some possibilities run into antitrust barriers. Also, obtaining a synergistic benefit clearly implies that two or more business-units will operate within certain constraints; and over time, that requirement may become a serious drag. Many vertical integration schemes, for instance, tend to limit flexibility, as rubber companies tied to obsolete national rubber plantations discovered.

Nevertheless, the prospect of synergistic benefits may influence decisions regarding which business-units to retain—or add—in a total portfolio. The potential impact of an executive's ability to manage, the use of special strengths, vertical integration, and central resource pools should at least be considered.

## Third Dimension: Risk and Profit Balance

A third consideration in portfolio strategy is the degree of risk and the resulting fluctuation in profits that is acceptable. The mix of businesses selected clearly affects the overall uncertainty about the stability and size of sales and profits.

An issue here is whether to reduce risk by diversifying even with some sacrifice of profits, or to support risky ventures with potentially high profits. Similarly, there may be a trade-off between liquidation with a known payout versus continuing in business with an uncertain future.

Prevailing norms provide two portfolio guides. (1) Companies in mature businesses are expected to shift investment to new lines of business in order to provide continuity even though the new businesses are more risky than the present ones. For example, Handy & Harman's traditional activity of processing silver and gold is "mature" because major new uses of these venerable metals are unlikely and rising metal prices dampen much increase in the physical volume of their present uses. So Handy & Harman has adopted a long-run objective of deriving half its future profits outside the precious metal area. It is steadily adding business-units in other high value-added industrial processes. This is an explicit strategy of reducing the risk associated with remaining in its primary field.

(2) Another indication of the importance attached to survival is the concept that a corporation should not bet its existence on a single, risky venture. No publicly owned firm relies entirely upon the success of drilling a particular off-shore oil well; rather, it gets other investors to share the risk on that well, and then it "diversifies" to part ownership in other wells, probably in other geographical areas.

*Hedging* against cyclical risks is often proposed. If you are in the construction business, the idea is to also enter a business that goes up when construction goes down. In practice, cyclical hedges are very difficult to find. A corporation supplying auto manufacturers, for example, may enter the replacement-parts market because this has a much steadier demand; but the replacement-parts industry is at most stable, not contracyclical, so the combined result is only a dampening of the auto production fluctuations. To return to the Handy & Harman example, that corporation does have a large refinery for secondary recovery of precious metals, so when metal prices rise, the refinery is busy even though the processing mill is slack.

In the shorter term, some revenue stabilization can be achieved by balancing *seasonal* products. The nostalgic "coal and ice" business is now reflected in Head's production of skis and tennis rackets, of ski clothing and shorts.

In each of these examples, one specific risk is offset (to some extent) by another with counterbalancing characteristics. The aim is greater stability of revenue and profits, even though the average result may be lower than the "expected" returns from one of the ventures alone. Carried to the extreme, this averaging of risks leads to a conglomerate where a catch-all collection of businesses is assembled with no special effort to match one against another. (Full diversification gives a corporation an average growth about the same as the GNP, a growth rate unacceptable to many managers and investors.) However, even the high-flying conglomerates rarely admit to such indiscriminate averaging. Instead, some other rationale—such as synergy—dominates portfolio selection, and risk balancing is a constraint to bring total exposure down to a level acceptable to major stockholders.

## Fourth Dimension: Cash Flow Balance

Growing businesses typically absorb cash for working capital as well as for plant and equipment, even when they are highly profitable. In fact, companies fail because their cash resources cannot support a very successful "take-off" of their product. Mature and declining businesses, in contrast, often generate cash, as assets are gradually being liquidated. Such net investment flows vary widely by kind of business, having a high early cash requirement in mining, for example, and the reverse in magazine publishing, where consumers pay in advance for subscriptions.

One additional dimension in building a portfolio, then, is balancing cash flow. *Internal* generation of needed cash is the aim. Of course, this is not the only potential source of cash: new equity and loans can be secured for profitable ventures. (Declining ventures rarely need or justify new infusions.) Nevertheless, our tax system makes internal generation of cash a significant advantage. Cash paid to stockholders as dividends is subject to personal income tax; even if the stockholders are willing to reinvest it in the corporation, they have much less—maybe only 60 percent—to so invest. However, if the corporation itself makes the reinvestment directly, the personal income tax bite is avoided. (Underwriting expenses are also avoided.) Moreover, if a new business-unit is showing a loss which can be offset against a profit of some other unit, then to that extent corporate income tax can also be avoided until the loss carry-over is used up.

Since internally generated cash is a comparatively inexpensive and convenient way to finance growing business-units, one or more "cash cows," as cash-generating units are often called, are attractive segments in a portfolio even when their long-run prospects are poor. This ability to shift cash flows from cash cows to stars and wildcats can provide a corporation with immortality—Ponce de Leon's fountain of youth!

In sum, the design of a desired portfolio considers several different factors, including the attractiveness of the business-units separately, synergy, balanced risks and profits, and cash flow. The weight attached to each factor depends upon the strengths that the corporation already possesses, environmental opportunities, and the personal values of its key executives.

## Major Moves to Attain the Desired Portfolio

### Charters for Present Business-Units

As we have just seen, the portfolio strategy for a diversified corporation blends several different considerations. Long-run strength and direction of the consolidated group is the dominant criterion. So the various business-units are assigned roles in terms of what is good for the *family as a whole*.

In this composite plan, some business-units are destined to grow rapidly; others have to modify their emphasis, overcome particular weaknesses, or demonstrate improved capability before they will be strongly supported; a few may be encouraged to take high risks because the potential gains are great; several have the role of cash cows; one or two may be retained largely for the protection or strength they give one of the "stars"; and so on.

With this overall concept in mind, it is possible to negotiate a "charter" for each business-unit. This charter will be an agreement between corporate executives and the senior management of the business-unit regarding:

1. The *domain*—the product/service/market scope—in which the business-unit will operate.
2. The *expected results*, including sales and growth, competitive position, productivity, profitability after interest and taxes, cash generation, R & D output, community leadership, and perhaps other objectives. Some of these will be numerical and sharp, others may be intangible and "soft."
3. *Constraints* regarding expected interaction with other business-units of the company, external behavior norms, required management systems, and the like. These, too, may be quantitative or qualitative.
4. *Resources* which will be made available from the corporation and those which the unit is free to acquire itself.

Such charters are the bridges, the connecting links, between corporate strategy and the strategies of the various business-units. They define the mission of each unit insofar as that mission is shaped by corporation-wide considerations. As with all strategy, the content is selective, focusing on vital issues while deliberately excluding procedural and personal relationships. For each business-unit, its charter sets the scope and broad objectives of its activities. And for the corporate office, each charter provides the major guidelines for approving or disapproving various proposals for specific actions.

Note that business-unit charters are not holy words passed down from omniscient corporate officials. Rather, they emerge from recurring give-and-take discussions between executives at the corporate and business-unit levels. Business-unit executives must be active participants because they know most about the possibilities and problems of the business and because psychologically they must accept the challenge that the charter provides. At the same time, a location within a family of business-units inherently creates needs which must be fitted into the more specific strategies of the respective units.

## Changes in the Portfolio

In addition to providing a basis for charters for existing business-units, corporate portfolio analysis flags the need for additions and deletions in the portfolio. Which of the present units are irrelevant and a drag? What gaps need to be filled with split-offs or acquisitions? And if acquisitions are called for, what characteristics should they have?

Opportunities for new synergy or improved balance may stand out during the company's careful portfolio analysis. Or proposals from internal entrepreneurs or outsiders may call attention to ways the overall portfolio could be strengthened. Once recognized, such potential additions become "opportunity gaps" for strategic planning to fill.

The next question is whether to try to fill the opportunity gaps by *internal growth* or by *acquisitions*. Sometimes there is little choice. For example, when Pan Am recognized that its international bookings were being jeopardized by lack of coordinated domestic flights, merger with an existing domestic airline was the only realistic alternative. To start its own domestic flights was neither legally feasible nor economical. So a tie-up with someone like National Airlines was the direction in which to move.

In other circumstances, gap-filling by acquisition is impractical. Procter & Gamble learned that antitrust barriers prevented it from getting a running start in the bleach business through acquisition of Clorox. For legal reasons, the bigger the parent company, the more it will have to rely on internal growth in new businesses which are closely related to its existing businesses. Moreover, in a brand-new industry, acquisition candidates may not exist. When Western Union moved into satellite communications, for example, the necessary satellites were not yet in orbit.

Between these extremes, however, a choice often exists. In many states, for example, commercial banks can increase their geographic coverage either by opening branches or by acquiring existing banks in the desired locations. Acquisitions provide faster entry and some resources (such as people, market position, trademarks, or patents) that might be difficult or time consuming to assemble. On the other hand, acquisitions often bring with them unwanted assets or traditions, they may foreclose taking other attractive steps, they may be more difficult to meld into the family, and they may be expensive.

During the late sixties and early seventies, many corporate planners fell in love with acquisitions. Corporate strategy and acquisition plans were treated as almost synonymous. Now a more balanced view prevails. A total portfolio strategy is developed, as outlined in this chapter, and acquisition criteria and opportunities grow out of this broader picture. Acquisitions often are a significant facet of corporate strategy, but they are only a part.

*Divestments* are the other side of the coin and, hence, also a part of strategy. The matrix analysis suggested at the beginning of the chapter identifies business-units which both now and in the future make little contribution to corporate goals. Further, studies of synergy, risk, and cash flow balance refine this diagnosis. In any turbulent environment, some business-units will be either a continuing drain on resources or at least a drag on energies that could be better directed elsewhere.

In practice, divestments are usually made too slowly. Even outstanding companies are reluctant to get rid of—in Boston Consulting Group language—their "dogs." RCA held on to its venture in computers until losses were in the hundreds of millions; General Foods dabbled first in gourmet delicacies, and then in the fast-food business well beyond the point of no return; and Johnson & Johnson kept TEK brushes long after that unit failed to serve the evolving corporate strategy. Such tardiness is explained partly by waiting for a propitious opportunity to sell or liquidate the unit. The primary cause, however, is personal. There is no inside champion for disposal, as there typically will be for an acquisition; some people will lose their jobs; and senior executives are reluctant to admit that they cannot make a success of everything they direct.

Without clear strategic direction, these normal pressures for inaction are likely to dominate. To avoid the high cost of inaction, both corporate strategy and effective execution are needed.

## Resource Plans and Target Results

A well-conceived corporate strategy provides several kinds of guides. It leads to coordinated charters for existing business-units, and also to plans for additions to and deletions from the present lineup, as we have just seen. In addition, two other forms of guidance should be developed.

The projected courses for various business-units will generally call for *resources* from the central corporate pool, notably capital and perhaps executives or central services. To help assure that these resources will be available when needed, a summary program of the expected flows to and from the business-units should be prepared. Such a program will alert corporate officers to any prospective need for obtaining new resources. A revision in capital structure may be involved, and, if so, groundwork for the issuance of new securities should be laid. Contingency plans reflecting shifts in capital markets may be advisable.

Also, the resource plans will show, in approximate numbers, how much will be allocated annually to each business-unit for what purposes. These allocations will probably be revised as wants unfold. Nevertheless, the strategy provides guideposts, and any major deviation in resources needed will call for a review of the continuing wisdom of the strategy. Meanwhile, the various business-units can proceed with their planning on the working assumption that the projected resource allocations will be made available to them over the next several years. We explore possibilities for strategic uses of corporate resources in Chapter 17.

A final set of guides tied in with strategy are the *target results*. Every strategy is designed to reach certain goals by given dates. These are the expected consequences of the stipulated actions. Some of these target results will be *financial*: perhaps sales, profits, return on investment, or earnings per share. Other targets may be more *qualitative*: market position in selected industries, community endorsement, product leadership, resource base, and the like. Such targets are good for keeping on course, motivation, and control, as we shall see in Part 5.

## Modifications During Execution

Portfolio strategy is a powerful tool. It pulls together the actions of the various business-units into a balanced synergistic program, it channels scarce resources, it endorses missions for operating managers, and it sets targets for results. But it is a difficult tool to use.

## The Lure of Exceptions

Cynics say that most corporate portfolio "strategy" is merely a high-sounding rationalization of acquisitions already made. Somehow, the argument runs, between risk balance, cash flows, and synergy, you can justify any combination. And it is true that many promoters who are guided by little or no consistent strategy do dress up their actions with the language of strategic management. However, the possibility of such sophistry does not reduce the strength of strategic management for those who sincerely use it as a way of harnessing their own behavior: we don't forego medical treatment just because a few quacks exist.

The real difficulties in practice are more subtle. A common problem is the temptation of "a good deal." For example, a proposed acquisition may offer attractive short-run financial benefits: one company may have a large tax loss carryover, and if a profitable unit can be merged into that company, the taxes that the profitable unit would otherwise have to pay can be avoided.

Acquisition of companies for far less than their replacement cost is also tempting, even though replacement itself would be a serious mistake.

Or, mergers may be suggested solely because of differences in price-earnings ratios. Suppose the stock of the Apple Company is selling at 20 times its earnings per share, and the stock of the less glamorous Orange Company at 10 times its earnings. Then if Apple acquires Orange and its price-earnings ratio stays at 20, the capitalized (market) value of Orange's earnings has doubled.

The acquisition of privately held businesses may be focused primarily on inheritance and estate taxes. Or, a proposal may pivot around the predilections of a few key individuals. Indeed, the resourcefulness of matchmakers is an impressive display of human ingenuity.

"Good deals" are fine *provided* that they are also compatible with corporate strategy. The danger is that managerial energies and other resources will be side-tracked into ventures that are alluring at the moment but do not contribute to a strong, balanced portfolio. In contrast, if a corporation has thought through its strategy, then it already has a screening mechanism to quickly decide which proposed deals warrant further attention. Too often, however, the strategy is fuzzy and the "good deal" is embraced as an exception.

The reverse also occurs. Actions that should be taken are postponed—as exceptions. Here the common examples are sick business-units where drastic action is unpleasant. A *Fortune* 500 corporation turned down an opportunity to sell (at a loss) one of its oldest business-units which was clearly in a declining industry; because of its long affiliation, an exception to the recognized strategy was made. Losses increased, and three years later the division was liquidated because no buyer could be found. In another corporation, an ailing division with dim prospects was nursed along for seven years, as a "special case." The serious cost in this instance was the required time and attention of senior management, which could have been much more productive if it had been spent on growing businesses.

Because exceptions to beautifully designed plans are sometimes warranted, the tough judgment to make is what special benefits are enough to justify intentionally going off course. Our observation is that exceptions too often win the day.

## Baffling Uncertainties

In designing portfolio strategy, many uncertainties must be resolved. Somehow, through some combination of facts, expert opinion, and intuition, forecasts of business conditions, industry outlooks, and business-unit success must be made. Of course, revisions and contingency plans may be included; but without agreed-upon forecasts, a full-blown strategy cannot be formulated.

Many forecasts can be made with reasonable confidence, at least within the time and tolerance limits necessary for strategic planning. Other factors, such as international political developments or finding a cure for cancer, are baffling. And when several key factors are interdependent, gross scenario forecasting is often the best we can do. For example, the attractiveness of a company planning to produce manganese from modules laying deep on the ocean floor depends upon technological advances, the world price of manganese, and international agreements on a law of the sea, to name only three related uncertainties. Forecasting in such areas is hazardous. And when a parent corporation is largely dependent upon a naturally biased business-unit for assessment data, the evaluation becomes even tougher.

Two dimensions which are increasingly frustrating for international investment are rates of inflation and foreign exchange rates. Inflation is pushing long-range planning away from profits based on conventional accounting and toward annual cash flows. Then the cash flow estimates have varying value due to shifts in exchange rates, if we assume that transfer of the money will be permitted. The cumulative uncertainty in such computations may well exceed the tolerance of practical planning.

In such circumstances, some parts of a corporate strategic plan may have to retreat to "prepared opportunism." The future is seen too dimly to lay out market positions and other expected results. Yet a conviction remains that truly attractive opportunities will develop, and those firms ready to serve such opportunities will benefit from an early start. So the corporate strategy seeks to position one or more business-units where they can move promptly as the prospects become clearer. As noted in Chapter 3, such a strategic position may involve frontier technology; local marketing and distribution systems, staffed with indigenous personnel; transportation facilities; skill and a favorable reputation in managing joint enterprises; ties to world markets; or access to raw materials.

Under prepared opportunism a particular business-unit may be encouraged to—indeed, its charter may provide that it—develop along certain lines which the unit acting alone would shun. Within the parent corporation's total portfolio may be several such business-units, each building strength on a particular front. Then, as events unfold, those strengths that prove to be valuable can be forged into a more specific plan. Rarely will all the specially directed units find a significant role in the final program, and to this extent effort and investment will have to be discarded. The hope, of course, is that the strengths actually used will be sufficiently valuable to offset losses on the others.

Such a strategy lacks the completeness, neatness, and efficiency of a fully developed plan. However, it does have the virtue of feasibility in the face of baffling uncertainties.

## Workability Test

No strategy is well conceived until its workability is weighed. If the chances of its being carried out are remote or the cost of doing so is very high, then the strategy itself should at least be reassessed.

Two implementation issues are directly created by corporate portfolio choices. Since they can be serious enough to lead to a modification of portfolio strategy, they will be noted here.

Sometimes corporate strategy makes demands of a business-unit that are inconsistent with the strategy the unit would follow if it were independent. For example, the business-unit may wish to expand whereas the corporate strategy wants it to be a cash cow. It is natural for unit executives to feel that they should be permitted to use the cash they generate to strengthen their own position, instead of denying themselves for the benefit of a small upstart activity.

In other cases, business-units are asked to incur risks (or avoid risks) because doing so helps corporate balance. Synergy may require that a business-unit refrain from developing its own raw materials. Or prepared opportunism may call for a form of expansion that is very expensive from the unit viewpoint. Such corporate demands seem especially onerous to managers of the business-unit when they arise unexpectedly because of some other activities of the corporation and the cause is therefore unrelated to their own situation.

Now, in a decentralized corporation, the commitment of local executives to their assigned role is very important for successful corporate results. If the business-unit executives think that the corporate guides "don't make sense," foot-dragging, planting misleading information, or other maneuvering is likely to occur. A conviction of unit executives that a corporate-imposed strategy "will never work" can very easily become a self-fulfilling prophecy! The basic point is that there is a practical limit to which the business-units can be "pushed around," and this limit is a constraint on what corporate strategy is workable.

Portfolio strategy may create a second kind of workability strain. Each business-unit strategy calls for a managerial system (planning, organizing, leading, and controlling) which is suited to that strategy. Thus, a large "cash-cow" unit needs a different management system than a unit experimenting with coal gasification. And the desirable management system for a commercial bank differs from that for an aircraft manufacturer. The more diverse the units within a portfolio, the more heterogeneous will be their management systems.

Few corporation managements have the capability of understanding, melding, and skillfully directing widely diverse management systems. Such diversity raises issues of temperamental and management style as well as difficulties of intellectual grasp. "We just don't know how to run that kind of business" is a frank and perceptive comment often heard.

Here again is a practical constraint on corporate portfolios. Cash flows and risk balance may appear desirable, but not beyond the point where effectively administering the diversity of units is no longer feasible.

## Summary

This chapter shifts attention from business-units, which have been the scope up to this point, to the assembly of such units by a diversified corporation.

At the corporate level, prime consideration goes to developing a strategic portfolio of business-units. Four criteria are important in this portfolio design: (1) attractive business-units, each considered separately in terms of its industry and its competitive position; (2) synergy that will arise from having a particular mix of business-units within a single corporate group; (3) the combined balance of risk and short- and long-term profitability; and (4) the prospects of internal generation of cash by some business-units that will help finance projected expansion of other business-units.

Several types of additional strategic plans should be derived from the portfolio design. (1) For each business-unit which is to be retained, a charter can be negotiated covering its domain, expected results, constraints, and resource support from the corporate pool. (2) Desirable acquisitions, spinoffs, and divestments of business-units will be indicated. (3) The total financial, critical personnel, and other corporate resource pools required can be estimated. (4) When these business-unit needs are combined with corporate resource plans—to be discussed later—consolidated results can be set for intermediate and longer range periods. Such supporting plans, coupled with the portfolio design, constitute the corporate strategy package.

Carrying out such a corporate strategy calls for unusual persistence. In addition to the array of unexpected events affecting the several business-units, alluring opportunities to make acquisitions which deviate from the portfolio design may arise. Also, the business-units cannot be treated like pawns on a chess board: the morale and responsiveness of managers within the business-units may significantly affect what can be done with those units. Consequently, compromises and adjustments in corporate strategy are likely. Nevertheless, some integrated and consistent direction is far better than mere opportunism or passive drift.

## Questions for Class Discussion

1. The recent acquisition of Hughes Aircraft by General Motors Corporation was explained in terms of electronics: an increased number of electronic controls will probably be used on automobiles, and Hughes Aircraft has considerable skill in applying electronics to aircraft and military hardware. Do you think this explanation warrants placing these two companies in the same corporate portfolio? What other considerations are involved?

2. Just a few years ago, the corporate parent of United Airlines, Allegis, acquired Hertz, the largest car rental company, and also the Hilton International Hotels. According to R.J. Ferris, Allegis' CEO, this was part of a strategy to build a diversified travel corporation. Do you think that the combination of these companies under a single corporation was a wise move?

3. The disclosure by the new president of Gulf & Western Industries, Inc. (60th in sales in *Fortune's* list of 500 industrial companies and 17th in profitability in *Forbes'* list of conglomerates), that he intended to see G&W sell off most of its $750 million stock portfolio and divest itself of some (unspecified) operating subsidiaries led to an immediate 35 percent increase in the price of its common stock. G&W announced that it would use the money from the sales and divestments to pay off its long-term debt and reduce its long-term debt-to-equity ratio far below 0.8. This move will cut off G&W's opportunities to trade on its equity and also decrease considerably the number of industries in which its subsidiaries operate. Why would the stock market suddenly revalue G&W's stock, and why would these changes win G&W many new friends?

4. For over three years corporate executives of International Chemicals, Inc., have been disturbed by the declining profits of their nitrogen-based fertilizer business-unit—a large and formerly key part of the agricultural chemicals division. Three years ago they transferred one of their able young managers to head the unit, with a broad charter to take the steps necessary to revitalize the business. Joe, the new manager, explains, "I brought in some very bright, ambitious people and moved them rapidly into key technical and managerial spots. We have been developing some imaginative, innovative, aggressive plans. Even some of the old-timers have begun to get charged up again. We'll need some money, but the incremental return on that new investment will be good."

    International Chemicals has just completed a careful review of its total portfolio. Among the conclusions are that overexpansion of the nitrogen-based fertilizer industry will persist for several years and the prospects for recovery of the industry do not justify further investment. Consequently, they have just informed Joe that while they are impressed with his efforts, in the future his unit is to be run as a net generator of cash to be used in other business-units with better industry outlooks. Do you think that this is a workable assignment for Joe? What should he do?

5. Several universities have established a "corporation" to finance and manage a variety of student enterprises. The primary purpose is to create jobs for students, but each enterprise is expected to be self-supporting. In effect, the corporation has a portfolio of small businesses. At one university, these businesses include refreshment stands at the football stadium and gym, programs for football games, student laundry services, sale and delivery of sandwiches to dormitory rooms in the evening, a secondhand bookstore, a concert series, and the daily student paper. Also, the corporation's new ventures include a literary magazine, a tutoring service, and a baby-sitting service. (a) Use the four "dimensions" discussed in this chapter to make a preliminary evaluation of this portfolio. (b) Do the basic ideas presented in the sections on "Major Moves to Attain the Desired Portfolio" and "Workability Test" have any application to this student enterprises corporation?

6. Cleartone Laboratories, a privately owned manufacturer of hearing aids, would like to be acquired by a financially strong corporation. In addition to looking for capital to finance growth, Cleartone is seeking an affiliation which can provide synergy. Cleartone is in the fastest growing segment of the market, the in-the-ear or canal device, which now accounts for about 45 percent of the one million units sold annually. The canal hearing aids are very small, with amplifiers only four-hundredths of an inch wide. That miniaturization makes quality control in production difficult, but it also permits a device which is scarcely visible when worn. Actually, only about 12 percent of the nation's 20 million hearing-impaired people wear hearing aids. Past drawbacks have included the obviousness of behind-the-ear and similar devices and a retail price ranging from $350 to $600. Cleartone is looking for an interested buyer in one of several different fields: an electronics firm with experience in producing miniaturized products; an eyeglass lens or frame distributor with a strong reputation among opticians (who often also sell hearing aids); or a distributor of medical supplies. With what kind of corporation do you think Cleartone will find the best synergistic fit?

7. Individuals vary widely in the way they balance risk and potential profit. A few endure great hardship and risk their lives for a chance to discover gold. Others take telephone operator's jobs in their home town and put their savings into government-guaranteed savings accounts. (a) Assume *you* just inherited $100,000 with the proviso that you invest it in any of the following four places in any proportion you choose: residential real estate, U.S. government short-term bonds, exploratory drilling for oil in northern Canada, and your own business. How would you allocate the $100,000? (b) Assume you inherited $1,000,000 with the same conditions; how would you allocate it? (c)

Assume a corporation has $10,000,000 in cash that is not needed for present operations; how should it decide what to do with the cash?

8. What are the chief differences in scope and content of a business-unit strategy as described in Chapter 5 and a charter described in this chapter for a business-unit which is part of a diversified corporation? What *reasons* lead to these differences?

9. Sears, Roebuck & Co. has recently bought a controlling interest in Dean Witter Reynolds, Inc., a well-known and successful U.S. stockbrokerage firm.

    *A Sears official explains,* "We do not intend to hold Dean Witter Reynolds as a passive investment. Rather, it is a major step in our move into financial services. Sears has a reputation for reliability and good values with millions of Americans, and we believe that that reputation will be helpful in financial services. We are experimenting with placing Dean Witter offices in several of our stores to give our customers an opportunity to use their services."

    *One long-term Sears customer,* when seeing such an office, said, "What are those guys doing in a Sears store? When I want to buy a good hammer, I don't go to a bank. And when I have saved a few dollars, I don't ask Sears to keep the money for me. . . . Now I'm not a betting man, but if I were I'd go to the racetrack."

    *An executive of Dean Witter Reynolds* comments, "We are pleased with the new accounts opened at our offices in the Sears stores. The typical size is o.k., about like many of our suburban branches. And most of these clients are people we've never known before. We are tapping a new market."

    Do you think Sears will find or develop a significant synergy between a Dean Witter Reynolds office and a typical Sears retail store operating in the same building? Are there any other major advantages or disadvantages for Sears in adding Dean Witter to its portfolio?

10. Thomas First, Jr., chairman and chief executive officer of Hospital Corporation of America, suddenly decided one day on a flight to Europe that his company needed "radical surgery." So it sold off 104 of its hospitals to a new company owned by employees through an employee stock ownership plan for $1.6 billion in cash, $400 million in preferred stock, and an agreement to guarantee part of the new company's debt. This left Hospital Corporation with 82 general hospitals and 50 psychiatric hospitals in the United States, 30 foreign medical properties, and management contracts to run 225 other general hospitals.

    The retrenchment was a major reversal of the company's previous strategy, which had been (a) to build and acquire hospitals and hospital management companies, (b) to attempt to acquire American Hospital Supply, the giant medical supply firm, (c) to start and to acquire health maintenance organizations, (d) to acquire insurance companies specializing in medical policies, and (e) to purchase a stake in a nursing home chain. The efforts at diversification followed the 1983 adoption by Medicare and insurance companies of a new reimbursement system that paid hospitals a predetermined amount for each illness, no matter what the actual cost of the treatment. These efforts came to little or nought, and the company had several years of flat earnings.

With all that cash, Hospital Corporation plans to build ten psychiatric and drug-abuse hospitals for $100 million. It also plans to be flexible and well positioned when a shakeout, if any, comes from the increased competition and insurers' squeeze on the expenses of psychiatric care. Mr. First said, "Ten years ago I could predict quite accurately three years out, and I had a pretty good idea where we'd be five years out. [Now] it is difficult to project three months out."

Is there a turbulent environment for medical care? Consider AIDS, drug abuse, organ transplants, and the aging population. Are the changes in strategy and positioning suitable?

# CASE
## 15 Squibb Corporation

How far to go in its retreat from diversification was the overriding issue faced by the 22-person board of directors of Squibb Corporation in January 1987. Like several other pharmaceutical companies, Squibb was cash-rich with only one hefty string remaining in its bow.

### Early History

The present Squibb Corporation was formed in 1968 when E.R. Squibb & Sons, then a division of Olin Mathieson Chemical Corporation, was spun off as a separate company and immediately merged with Beech-Nut Life Savers, Inc. Products at that time included ethical (prescribed by M.D.s) pharmaceuticals, over-the-counter drug products such as toothpaste, Life Savers, cough drops, chewing gum, baby foods, and Tetley Tea.

Within a short period Squibb Corporation acquired Charles of the Ritz, a leading perfume and cosmetics company; Dobbs House, an airline food-catering firm; and several other specialty food and pharmaceutical lines. The individual lines, and even more the total combination, were intended to be "noncyclical" in their demand.

The profit record of these businesses was varied, however, and several were sold off while others were being added. In general, the confections, specialty foods, and beverages, which contributed $259 million in sales in 1969, did not make an acceptable contribution to profits.

## The "New Squibb"

By the early 1980s health care products showed the most promise for growth and profits. Consequently, Dobbs House and the related restaurant businesses were sold to Carson, Pirie, Scott & Company in 1980, and Life Savers (this one at a capital gain) was sold in 1981.

These sales brought to a close a rather unfruitful period of diversification into over-the-counter foods and confections. Gone were all of the Beech-Nut/Life Savers products, the Squibb proprietary products, and the foods and confections acquired after the original merger. For Squibb, this type of diversification not only reduced its risk; it also resulted in lackluster profits. The Charles of the Ritz perfume and cosmetics business was the only nondrug business that survived under Squibb management.

However, while Squibb was pulling out of foods and confections, it was diversifying in the health area. During the early 1980s a "Specialty Health Products Group" was formed. Several smaller firms in this area were acquired, including Edward Weck, a company that makes surgical clips, and Convatec, a company with products used for personal care in hospitals and for sufferers of incontinence.

In addition, a Squibb Medical Systems Group was begun in 1980 with the acquisition of Advanced Technological Laboratories, Spacelabs, and several other firms dealing with equipment for diagnostic imaging and patient-monitoring.

Meanwhile, the original ethical pharmaceutical business that Squibb brought to the original merger had become the most profitable division of the Squibb Corporation.

With these changes, Squibb's CEO for many years, Richard M. Furland, reported to stockholders that 1981 "culminated a program of many years to restructure Squibb Corporation . . . 1982 is the first year of the New Squibb which focuses only on selected markets in health and personal care . . . where we can excel in what we do." Even the pharmaceutical activities, which had been spread over many fields, were cut back so that effort could be concentrated in four areas: anti-infections, anti-inflammatories, new cardiovascular medicines, and diagnostic agents. Mr. Furland continued, "We are now a science-based company . . . More centralized planning will now be possible."

A perspective on the success to date of the "New Squibb" program is provided in Table 15–1, especially in the sales and operating profits for the three continuing product groups. The dominant contributor, after inflation is recognized, is clearly ethical pharmaceuticals. The impressive gain in recent years comes from cardiovascular products, as the figures on page 440 for pharmaceutical sales, in millions of dollars, show.

**TABLE 15-1.**
**SQUIBB CORPORATION FINANCIAL HISTORY, 1978–1986**
(dollar amounts in millions except per-share figures)

| Operating Results[a] | 1986 | 1985 | 1984 | 1983 | 1982 | 1981 | 1980 | 1979 | 1978 |
|---|---|---|---|---|---|---|---|---|---|
| Net sales: | | | | | | | | | |
| Pharmaceutical products | $1521 | $1197 | $1090 | $1045 | $ 978 | $ 934 | $ 869 | $ 784 | $ 680 |
| Medical products | 264 | 412 | 396 | 377 | 340 | 264 | 178 | 85 | 44 |
| Personal care products | — | 432 | 400 | 347 | 342 | 325 | 287 | 241 | 183 |
| Total net sales | 1785 | 2042 | 1886 | 1769 | 1661 | 1524 | 1334 | 1110 | 907 |
| Profit from operations: | | | | | | | | | |
| Pharmaceutical products | 371 | 281 | 208 | 186 | 122 | 90 | 100 | 106 | 94 |
| Medical products | 40 | 23 | 37 | 28 | 52 | 33 | 28 | 13 | 9 |
| Personal care products | — | 51 | 46 | 42 | 35 | 28 | 27 | 21 | 19 |
| Total profit from operations | 411 | 355 | 291 | 256 | 210 | 151 | 156 | 141 | 122 |
| General corporate income (or expenses) | (33) | (16) | 3 | 6 | 10 | (27) | (27) | (36) | (19) |
| Income before taxes on income | 378 | 339 | 294 | 262 | 219 | 62 | 128 | 105 | 103 |
| Income from continuing businesses | 264 | 227 | 197 | 173 | 154 | 41 | 103 | 89 | 84 |
| Income from businesses sold | 13 | — | — | — | — | — | 24 | 34 | 34 |
| Gain from sales of business & restructuring | 120 | — | — | — | — | 64 | — | — | — |
| Net income | $ 396 | $ 227 | $ 197 | $ 173 | $ 154 | $ 105 | $ 127 | $ 124 | $ 117 |

**TABLE 15–1. (continued)**
**SQUIBB CORPORATION FINANCIAL HISTORY, 1978–1986**
(dollar amounts in millions except per-share figures)

| Operating Results[a] | 1986 | 1985 | 1984 | 1983 | 1982 | 1981 | 1980 | 1979 | 1978 |
|---|---|---|---|---|---|---|---|---|---|
| *Financial Position* | | | | | | | | | |
| Working capital | $ 755 | $ 760 | $ 683 | $ 617 | $ 584 | $ 598 | $ 545 | $ 398 | $ 369 |
| Property, plant & equipment (net) | 646 | 701 | 618 | 545 | 512 | 480 | 480 | 423 | 379 |
| Total assets | 2409 | 2453 | 2134 | 1946 | 1930 | 1950 | 1817 | 1717 | 1493 |
| Long-term debt | 169 | 188 | 200 | 204 | 336 | 399 | 392 | 397 | 326 |
| Shareholders' equity | 1358 | 1466 | 1328 | 1231 | 1096 | 1030 | 1002 | 918 | 836 |
| *Supplementary Data* | | | | | | | | | |
| Capital expenditures | 95 | 120 | 116 | 110 | 87 | 70 | 80 | 67 | 62 |
| Depreciation of fixed assets | 39 | 40 | 34 | 34 | 31 | 28 | 24 | 21 | 18 |
| Marketing expense | 430 | 552 | 504 | 467 | 447 | 398 | 339 | 273 | 216 |
| Advertising expenditures | 118 | 119 | 111 | 106 | 105 | 95 | 81 | 65 | 45 |
| Research & development | 163 | 166 | 151 | 142 | 123 | 95 | 74 | 65 | 59 |
| Interest income or (expense) net | 3 | 2 | 17 | 14 | 21 | (44) | (15) | (23) | (36) |
| Cash dividends | 103 | 79 | 79 | 71 | 65 | 60 | 56 | 49 | 46 |
| Average number of shares (millions) | 54 | 54 | 54 | 53 | 51 | 50 | 48 | 46 | 45 |

[a]Operating results are not strictly comparable from year to year due to sale or acquisition of specific businesses; for example, in 1986 Charles of the Ritz was dropped from Personal Care Products, and Westmark was dropped from Medical Products.

|                      | 1986  | 1985  | 1984  |
|----------------------|-------|-------|-------|
| Cardiovasculars      | 697   | 456   | 333   |
| Antibiotics          | 160   | 138   | 142   |
| Anti-inflammatories  | 123   | 116   | 125   |
| Antifungals          | 91    | 86    | 91    |
| All others           | 442   | 396   | 400   |
|                      | 1,521 | 1,192 | 1,090 |

The 1986 operating profit on one product alone, Capoten, an inhibitor of hypertension, which leads to heart failure, exceeded the operating profits from all the businesses that Squibb was in in 1978, both those continuing and those sold. Even Capoten, however, has had a roller-coaster history. By 1975 Squibb scientists had learned how to make the drug; but after experimental tests, Squibb's high hopes were dashed by a Food and Drug Administration decision in 1980 that sharply restricted use of the drug because of its side effects. Only following further tests on 12,000 patients did the FDA approve, in 1985, Capoten's use against all types of hypertension. Since then, with strong sales promotion, sales of Capoten have skyrocketed. Until Merck and other competitors market a competing product, Capoten sales will probably exceed $500 million per year.

## Sale of Charles of the Ritz

Two transactions in December 1986 further narrowed Squibb's range of businesses. The largest was the sale of the prestigious perfume and cosmetics division, Charles of the Ritz, to Yves Saint Laurent International, SA, for $631 million cash. Squibb realized an after-tax gain of $188 million. This sale effectively takes Squibb out of "personal care products," to use Squibb's designation.

In another move, Squibb spun off its medical systems group. It had combined the businesses in this group into a separate corporation, Westmark, and then distributed all the stock of Westmark to stockholders of Squibb Corporation. In March of 1987 Westmark had a market value of about $200 million. Following the Westmark transaction, Squibb's "medical products" consisted almost entirely of the "specialty health products" (Weck, Convatec, etc.) acquired in the early 1980s.

A rough indication of the magnitude of the sums involved in the sale of Charles of the Ritz and the spinoff of Westmark comes from the following published figures for the two product groups involved (in millions of dollars):

|                        | 1986 (adjusted for sale & spinoff) | 1985 (before sale & spinoff) | Difference ('86 vs. '85) |
|------------------------|------------------------------------|------------------------------|--------------------------|
| *Personal Care Products* |                                  |                              |                          |
| Net sales              | —                                  | 432                          | −432                     |
| Profits from operations | —                                 | 51                           | − 51                     |
| Assets                 | —                                  | 250                          | −250                     |

| | 1986 (adjusted for sale & spinoff) | 1985 (before sale & spinoff) | Difference ('86 vs. '85) |
|---|---|---|---|
| *Medical Products* | | | |
| Net sales | 264 | 412 | −148 |
| Profits from operations | 40 | 23 | + 17 |
| Assets | 203 | 423 | −220 |

The most conspicuous result of the sale of Charles of the Ritz is, of course, a big jump in the cash position of Squibb Corporation. At the end of 1986 Squibb's balance sheet showed cash or equivalents of $674 million.

## Current Status

The present position of Squibb Corporation can be assessed in terms of the four dimensions discussed in the present chapter. Here is the case-writer's view; yours may differ.

1. The pharmaceutical group is clearly outstanding in terms of profits and growth potential. It is *the* jewel in Squibb's crown, so sparkling that it makes Squibb a potential target for take-over. What remains of the medical products group, although much smaller, showed an attractive return on assets in 1986. So by disposing of a long line of businesses which Squibb management did not convert into stars, the corporation is now narrowed down to two very *attractive business-units*.

2. Although the two remaining product groups are both in the health field, there is limited *synergy* between them. One relies heavily on laboratory research and sells through physicians; the other makes more conventional supplies for hospital and nursing home use.

3. *Profits* have improved impressively, as noted. But *risks* have likewise jumped. The narrowing focus of Squibb, even into its research program, means that the corporation is betting on fewer horses. The typically rapid obsolescence of pharmaceuticals requires that Squibb's two or three present big winners be replaced by new research successes, and spending even $163 million on R & D does not assure winners. Moreover, the current thrust to reduce the cost of medical care may force down prices through greater use of generic drugs. And the risk of large product liability awards is real, as the bankruptcy of A.H. Robins Company shows. So Squibb's 1970s aim to reduce risk via diversification has now turned around 180 degrees.

4. *Cash flow* is now obviously not a problem. Nor has it been in recent years, at least for the programs that Squibb has undertaken. The corporation typically pays out only about 40 percent of its earnings in div-

idends, and it could easily carry more long-term debt (see balance sheets in Table 15–2). Indeed, Squibb's current problem is how to use wisely the cash it already has!

In passing, it is relevant to note that Squibb's liquidity problem is not unique in the pharmaceutical industry. At the close of 1986, Merck had liquid assets of $1.5 billion, Bristol-Myers $1.3 billion, Pfizer $1.4 billion, and Eli Lilly $0.8 billion—with more in prospect if and when it sells its Elizabeth Arden (cosmetics) division. Some pharmaceutical corporations—for instance, Syntex, Warner-Lambert, Eli Lilly, and Sterling—have been selling off their nondrug business, although not to the degree that Squibb has. Other highly successful pharmaceutical corporations, including Johnson & Johnson and Bristol-Myers, have maintained their diversification while their pharmaceutical activities flourished.

**TABLE 15–2.**
**SQUIBB CORPORATION—COMPARATIVE BALANCE SHEETS, 1978 AND 1984–86 (in millions of dollars)**

|  | 1986 | 1985 | 1984 | 1978 |
|---|---|---|---|---|
| Current assets: |  |  |  |  |
| Cash & equivalent | $ 674 | $ 368 | $ 279 | $ 58 |
| Accounts receivable (net) | 380 | 369 | 342 | 330 |
| Inventories | 315 | 292 | 255 | 369 |
| Other | 136 | 67 | 62 | 36 |
| Total current assets | 1,506 | 1,096 | 938 | 793 |
| Net assets of discontinued businesses | — | 328 | 268 | — |
| Investments & long-term receivables | 183 | 173 | 171 | 184 |
| Plant and equipment (net) | 646 | 599 | 538 | 559 |
| Other assets | 75 | 79 | 66 | 57 |
| Total assets | $2,409 | $2,276 | $1,981 | $1,593 |
| Current liabilities: |  |  |  |  |
| Current long-term debt | 6 | 2 | 100 | 3 |
| Notes payable | 54 | 216 | 59 | 86 |
| Accounts payable & accruals | 404 | 261 | 212 | 208 |
| Taxes on income | 287 | 55 | 30 | 45 |
| Total current liabilities | 751 | 533 | 402 | 343 |
| Long-term debt | 169 | 182 | 192 | 335 |
| Deferred income tax | 54 | 45 | 14 | 40 |
| Other liabilities | 77 | 50 | 45 | 30 |
| Total liabilities | 1,051 | 810 | 653 | 747 |
| Shareholders' equity | 1,358 | 1,466 | 1,328 | 846 |
| Total liabilities and equity | $2,409 | $2,276 | $1,981 | $1,593 |

## What to Do with the Cash?

Squibb's prestigious 22-person board of directors may conclude that the senior executives of the corporation are not very skilled in managing a diversified group of businesses and therefore the corporation should be shrunk. Following this course would imply that either a large cash dividend should be declared or the corporation should buy back and retire a large number of its outstanding shares of common stock.

An alternative strategy is to pursue some form of diversification. There are numerous possible directions to go. The following are only illustrative, and the specific companies are mentioned just to be more concrete—they may not be available at a reasonable price.

- Move into another growth area to diversify the risk. For example, acquire Sun Microsystems, Inc., described in Case 5 (pp. 127–134).
- Get into state-of-the-art health products outside of biochemistry. For example, see if Jack Welch, the CEO of General Electric, has become impatient with G.E.'s "medical systems" business and is ready to make a deal. See page 510 of the integrating case, "Managing RCA within G.E."
- Enter the high-potential field of manipulative biology by acquiring a company such as Bio Engineering Co., described in Case 9 on pages 254–261. Or possibly acquire Cetus Corporation, the biotechnology firm with which Squibb already has a joint research agreement.
- Integrate forward from Squibb's existing base in medical products into the expanding nursing home field. For example, acquire Care Enterprises briefly described next in Appendix A.

## Question

What strategy do you recommend that Squibb Corporation adopt now (January 1988) with respect to its portfolio of businesses?

## Appendix A: Care Enterprises

Two trends have increased the demand for long-term nursing facilities: a substantial rise in the number of people living beyond 80 years of age, and much earlier dismissal of patients from hospitals. As a significant part of the basic realignment of health care in the United States, licensed nursing homes now have an occupancy rate of 90 to 95 percent compared to about 60 percent for regular ("acute") hospitals. Medicare, which pays the fees for two-thirds of nursing home patients, has broadened eligibility requirements; and other third-party payers are providing broader coverage of nursing home expenses. So the strong demand is expected to continue.

Rapid expansion in the nursing home industry has been accompanied by the usual growing pains. Well-qualified personnel are in short supply, the large investment in facilities has burdened companies with high debt ratios, and some unscrupulous operators have created bad publicity for the industry. Well-managed companies are needed to overcome these problems.

Care Enterprises is the fourth largest chain of nursing homes in the country. Starting in California and Utah, Care Enterprises has recently expanded into Ohio, West Virginia, New Mexico, Arizona, and Montana, largely through the acquisition of existing facilities. In this way it seeks to utilize its substantial experience extending back to 1965. The growth of the company is shown in the following operating data (dollars in millions):[a]

| | 1986 | 1985 | 1984 | 1983 | 1982 |
|---|---|---|---|---|---|
| Revenues | $ 265 | $ 239 | $ 152 | $ 102 | 55 |
| Cost and expenses: | | | | | |
| Operating | 233 | 206 | 133 | 91 | 48 |
| Interest | 20 | 18 | 9 | 6 | 3 |
| Depreciation | 11 | 9 | 5 | 3 | 2 |
| Total | 264 | 233 | 147 | 100 | 52 |
| Earnings before income taxes & extraordinary items | 1 | 6 | 4 | 3 | 3 |
| Net earnings | $ (10)[b] $ | 4 | $ 3 | $ 1[b] $ | 2 |
| Number of facilities[c] | 115 | 124 | 98 | 79 | 41 |
| Number of beds | 12,025 | 13,055 | 10,376 | 8,224 | 4,294 |
| Average occupancy | 91% | 92% | 93% | 92% | 92% |
| Total assets | 260 | 263 | 137 | 100 | 38 |
| Long-term debt | 140 | 185 | 73 | 48 | 21 |
| Stockholders' equity | 36 | 33 | 28 | 25 | 3 |

[a]Columns may not add, due to rounding of figures.

[b]An extraordinary item of $1.5 million was charged against earnings in 1983 to cover a potential settlement of a legal dispute regarding a lease of facilities. In 1986 an extraordinary item of $7 million was charged against earnings as part of an overall financial restructuring.

[c]More than half of the facilities are leased. In 1985, for instance, 38 were owned, 79 leased, and 7 managed.

Three of the senior officers of Care Enterprises who own over half of the common stock are in financial difficulties with another, even larger business. Consequently, they might be interested in an offer to buy out their investment in Care Enterprises.

# CHAPTER 16

## Mergers and Acquisitions: A Tool of Strategy

Mergers are exciting. They make headlines; new thrusts into growth areas are foreshadowed; realignments of supply are imminent; the status, security, and social relationships of many people are affected; large blocks of capital are involved; and government agencies gird for action.

For managers of a specific enterprise, however, the excitement of a merger is only the tip of the iceberg: a merger with another company is a major event in the life of an enterprise and may even be the key to success or failure. And like the marriage of a man and a woman, it has deep emotional as well as economic effects. Consequently, mergers should be approached with care.

Corporate strategy, discussed in the preceding chapter, indicates the kind of new business-units desired. Now we turn to three related issues:

1. Should the new unit be developed within the corporation or be an acquisition of an existing outside company?
2. If it is to be acquired, how should the acquisition be financed?
3. What steps need to be taken to assure that the anticipated benefits will be realized after the merger takes place?

These questions apply to both mergers and acquisitions. Formerly, the term "merger" applied to the consolidation of two companies about equal in size, whereas "acquisition" implied a larger firm taking over a smaller one. Since this distinction is no longer consistently observed and is not significant to our analysis here, we use the words interchangeably.

## Acquisition Versus Internal Development

### Why Look Outside?

Every merger involves complicated financial negotiations, organizational revamping, and career adjustments. Physical moves might be necessitated as well. A central manager could avoid most of the burdens by expanding from within instead of merging with a stranger. Consequently, a merger must offer strong advantages over internal expansion. Typically, a sound merger must provide major benefits in terms of time, expense, or physical possibility.

The mergers of local banks to take advantage of new technology provide the needed volume of activity quickly; slower internal growth would postpone the use of new methods for years. Similarly, when DuPont Laboratories was successful in discovering several new drugs, a marketing organization capable of contacting doctors throughout the country was needed immediately. Building such an organization from scratch would have taken a long time, so DuPont acquired Endo Laboratories with its established marketing expertise and contacts in the ethical pharmaceutical field. Incidentally, this was the first exception in 24 years to DuPont's general policy of expansion from within rather than via mergers.

Expense as well as time is often critical. Creating a "going concern," especially in a field already keenly competitive, can be costly in terms of initial investment and losses during the buildup period. In the insurance industry, for example, finding a significant number of new policyholders requires a substantial input of time and expense. So if a corporation wishes to have an insurance division—and many do because of the cash flow advantages—acquiring an existing firm is much simpler than building one from within.

Likewise, if rare assets are needed, say a Coca-Cola franchise in Miami, or the talent of an outstanding entrepreneur, a merger may be the only feasible way to obtain the resource.

## Antitrust Restrictions

Many potential mergers that would improve productivity are illegal. So before management spends much time exploring a possible acquisition, it should "see its lawyer."

To protect the free enterprise system, the United States government has a battery of antitrust laws and regulations. Unfortunately, much uncertainty and disagreement exists regarding the application of these laws: each new U.S. Attorney General brings a different viewpoint, and court decisions provide no clear-cut guidelines.

It is helpful to recognize the basic premise of antitrust effort—broadly, that competition is best protected by having many small, viable, locally owned competitors in each industry. Of course, competitors cannot be created by the passage of a law; instead, the antitrust laws try to prevent actions that reduce the number of effective competitors.

More specifically, the Antitrust Division is likely to challenge the aquisition of a competitor (a horizontal merger) if (1) only a few companies already dominate the relevant market, (2) either of the merging companies already serves over 20 percent of the market, (3) the merger decreases the number of companies in an expanding market, or (4) the merger makes entry of other companies quite difficult. So, except for very small firms, horizontal mergers are suspect. The chief ambiguity arises in defining "industry" and "market." For instance, are skis just a small part of the sporting goods industry or an industry of their own? Is a major milk distributor in Los Angeles within or outside its market if it acquires a milk distributor in San Francisco? On such questions as these, see your lawyer.

A vertical merger (acquisition of a supplier or customer) gets into trouble when a new supplier would have difficulty entering the market or a new customer would have difficulty obtaining supplies because the merger forecloses part of the market. Here again, the bigger the company, the more likely will be the objection. Recently, further uncertainty was added when the wording of the Clayton Act was amended to cover mergers that *may* substantially lessen competition or *tend* to create monopoly. Under this revision, the effects of a merger on potential, as well as existing, competition must be considered.

Countering these guiding antitrust principles are exceptions. Recent exceptions include acquiring a failing company such as American Motors, acquisitions in a regulated industry like banking, mergers to confront severe foreign competition, and other atypical actions which "serve the public interest." Sources of competition are coming from new and unexpected directions, as pointed out in Chapter 2, so the traditional antitrust guidelines are being reinterpreted. Nevertheless, legal constraints have forced many companies to sharply alter their merger policy. Especially the larger companies are placing increasing reliance for growth on their own research and development because antitrust considerations create risks of expansion within their existing industries via mergers. Except for sharp diversification, mergers must be a highly selective aspect of corporate strategy.

## Financing the Merger

Once a potential merger is identified that seems to be the best available way to move ahead with the corporate strategy, the second major question is, What financial arrangements will be attractive to both companies?

Every merger has its unique features, and the financial arrangements must reflect these. Nevertheless, there is a common approach to the main issues that arise in most mergers. Think of a merger as a swap: the company being acquired is trading a business for cash or securities of the surviving company. Involved in this trade are two packages of assets and two sets of owners; *each* set of owners attaches its own value to the assets it is giving up and to the assets it receives. The crux of negotiating the swap is to devise an arrangement that leaves each set of owners with a new package of assets that it prefers over the assets it has parted with.

To apply this approach, we must understand (1) the value both parties attach to the business being traded and (2) the value to both parties of the payments to be made. Figure 16–1 indicates the main elements involved in a merger and the value assigned to these elements by each party.

## Value of Business Traded

In valuing the business being traded, agreement must be reached on what is to be traded and the value to be attached to it.

**FIGURE 16–1.**
**MAIN ELEMENTS IN NEGOTIATING A MERGER**

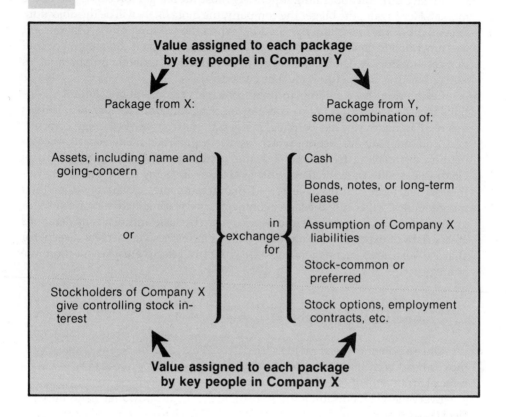

## What Is Included

A company may be acquired either by taking over ownership of the corporate stock or by purchasing the assets of the company. When stock ownership is the mechanism, the entire legal entity with its intangible assets and liabilities is acquired. Later the corporation may be dissolved and a complete melding may occur, but at the time of the merger we think in terms of the complete enterprise. (If minority blocks of stock remain outstanding, clearly only a percentage of the ownership is traded, but it is still a percentage of the total concern.)

Sometimes a corporation owns assets that the acquiring firm does not want, for example, a large tract of land or a company store. Or there may be serious disagreement over the values attached to a separable asset or liability. In such cases, most, but not all, of the tangible and intangible assets along with current liabilities and mortgages are transferred. This leaves the old corporation with the same set of stockholders, but the corporation now holds the cash or securities received in the trade instead of its former operating business, plus assets excluded from the trade.

### Basis of Evaluation

With agreement on what is to be traded, attention shifts to the subjective values each party attaches to the business. Obviously, subjective values differ. People and companies vary in their needs, opportunities, and resources. So no bookkeeping figures or simple formula can produce a value acceptable to everyone. Historical costs, book value, and market price (if the stock does have a market price) may influence the evaluation, but usually each individual feels that a particular package of assets is worth more, or less, than these conventional measures show.

A rational basis for setting a value is to estimate the incomes that the company (or its assets) will provide over a period of years, including the disposition of the assets at the end of the period; to adjust these annual estimates of income for uncertainty (for example, cut the figures in half if there is only a 50–50 chance that the estimated net income will arise in the specified year); and finally, to reduce each of the adjusted or "expected" incomes to present values by allowing for alternative uses of the resources that are being committed to the venture in question. This gives a discounted present value of future incomes.[1]

But note that present owners and the acquiring company will come out with quite different answers even if they use the same "rational" approach. The acquiring company will manage the assets differently, and it expects to obtain synergistic benefits from the consolidation; consequently, its estimated incomes, uncertainties, and alternatives are unlike those of the present owners if the merger is not consummated. In any economically sound merger, the minimum the owners will accept (their value of the property if the merger is not completed) should be well below the maximum the acquiring company will pay (the present value of all incomes, including the expected benefits arising from the merger). The spread between these two figures leaves a wide margin for bargaining. These outer limits are rarely revealed in the negotiations because both parties seek a substantial part of the margin and because they also attach different values to the payment package.

## Other Considerations

The present value of future company income, just discussed, is not a complete picture, especially to the owner of a family business. People who have devoted their lives to building an enterprise normally have deep concern about perpetuating the company name and reputation. Their interest is in the future welfare of their employees, and they want the company to continue to give support to the community in which they live. Also, in selling the company, these individuals may be sacrificing an attractive salary and a prestigious position.

---

[1] We have deliberately used more general wording here than is found in the typical "discounted cash flow" procedure because company owners usually have personal values that are broader than the strictly financial figures commonly used in cash flow analysis.

The acquiring company has no such emotional attachments to the firm being absorbed, but it does know that such considerations cannot be ignored. To a large extent, the combined company can meet the social obligations to the community; in fact, it may make substantially larger community contributions than would be made if the companies continued separate existences. Brand names and sometimes even company names are often continued because of the goodwill attached to them. Employment may actually increase, although some individuals might suffer. The acquiring company may have a more liberal pension plan (and if past-service credits are large, the final merger arrangement may be adjusted to cover them). Often key executives are given an employment contract for three to five years, and the senior executive may be elected to the board of directors of the combined company.

Unless the executives of the company to be absorbed feel that these "other considerations" will be reasonably met, serious negotiations may never start.

## Value of Payment to Be Made

The second half of a merger trade is a package of cash or securities exchanged for the acquired business. This *quid pro quo* must be attractive to the buyer and at the same time must not involve too high a sacrifice for the seller. Here, again, we must consider what is being traded and the value each party attaches to that package.

### Form of Payment

The most common type of payment in mergers is the stock of the surviving corporation. For example, Computer Associates International, a leading producer of computer software, issued over 28 million shares of its common stock as payment for Uccel Corporation. The acquisition gave Computer Associates a strong position in banking applications, where it had been weak; but since the payment was newly issued stock, existing operations were not hampered. Uccel stockholders received a 30 percent premium in the value of securities they owned, and the personnel retained are less vulnerable in a highly fragmented and competitive industry.

Payment in the form of common stock is especially likely when that stock has a high price-to-earnings ratio. Thus, Electronics Company A, with a price-to-earnings ratio of 20, would find it advantageous to use its stock to acquire Company B, having a price-to-earnings ratio of only 8. In the simplified illustration shown in Table 16–1, the market value of the shares of the combined company has increased $6 million as a result of using Company A's price-to-earnings ratio on Company B's earnings. In the example, two-thirds of this increase goes to Company A's stockholders and one-third to Company B's stockholders.

Cash is, of course, the simplest form of payment. It is used when the acquiring company is highly liquid and sellers are not confronted with high capital gains taxes.

**TABLE 16-1.**
**ILLUSTRATION OF EFFECT OF PRICE-TO-EARNINGS RATIOS**
**(Assume one share of A is exchanged for two shares of B, and A's price-to-earnings ratio remains constant)**

|  | Shares Outstanding | Total Earnings | Earnings per Share | Market Price per Share | Imputed Total Market Value |
|---|---|---|---|---|---|
|  | | | *Before Merger* | | |
| Company A | 1,000,000 | $1,000,000 | $1 | $20 | $20,000,000 |
| Company B | 500,000 | 500,000 | $1 | $ 8 | 4,000,000 |
|  | | | | | $24,000,000 |
|  | | | *After Merger* | | |
| Company A | 1,250,000 | $1,500,000 | $1.20 | $24 | $30,000,000 |
| Former Owners of Company B | — | — | — | ($24 = $12) <br> 2 | ($ 6,000,000) |

Many other forms of payment are used to meet particular circumstances. Preferred stock gives the sellers greater assurance of dividends. Debenture bonds or notes provide even greater security, but are less favorable from a tax standpoint. Bonds or preferred stock may be made more attractive by having them convertible into common stock. Or stock options (rights to purchase common stock at a fixed price) may be used to give the seller an opportunity to benefit from company growth.

Frequently, a combination of several forms of payment is used. The Ingram Company, for example, received cash for its net current assets, 20-year mortgage bonds for its fixed assets, and a large block of stock options that gave it an opportunity to share in any synergistic gains that might grow out of merged operations.

### Tax on Payment

Sellers are concerned about the income tax they will have to pay on the package of cash and/or securities they receive. If they get only voting stock in the surviving company, as in the Computer Associates example, the transaction is tax free: the stockholders are merely exchanging one form of equity for another, so that no capital gains have been realized and, hence, there is no basis for levying an income tax. (Of course, if stockholders subsequently sell their stock, any appreciation over their original cost is taxable.)

In contrast, payment in the form of cash or bonds that have a fixed value does establish a capital gain that is taxable. And some stockholders may find such a tax quite onerous. One way to avoid the tax pressure on stockholders is the sale of assets by the corporation. If a corporation exchanges its assets for cash and/or bonds, *it* will be subject to capital gains tax on any appreciation over its "cost," but the stockholders incur no tax obligation since they simply continue to hold the same stock in the same corporation.

### Market Liquidity

In addition to tax implications, the response of a seller will be influenced by liquidity. Stockholders of corporations whose stock is closely held often have difficulty selling their stock quickly. Family-held companies are the prime example, especially when cash is needed to pay inheritance tax. So in appraising any merger proposal, the stockholders will be concerned about the salability of the securities they receive. Stock in a large corporation that is actively traded on a major stock exchange is attractive because it is liquid. Of course, the significance attached to liquidity, or to a tax-free exchange, depends upon the financial position of each stockholder.

### Financial Structure of Acquiring Company

The acquiring company, likewise, evaluates the alternative forms of payment in terms of its particular situation. Cash may be readily available or extremely scarce. Long-term debt of the company may already be so high that the issuance of additional bonds would be imprudent. Of course, if the assets acquired can support more debt, then a loan from a third party may supply cash to use in partial payment to the seller. (A sale-and-leaseback of the fixed assets can be used in the same way.) But normally the acquiring company must guarantee repayment of the loan, and this becomes a contingent liability even though it does not show on the balance sheet.

Perhaps convertible preferred stock will appeal to the owners of the prospective acquisition, but a relatively small issue of an additional form of stock would interfere with larger financing by the surviving company in the future. In other words, both debt and equity payments should be appraised in terms of their effect on the total financial structure of the acquiring company.

### Loss of Control

When a common stock is used for a large acquisition, one or two of the new stockholders may become the largest owners of stock in the surviving corporation. They are then in a strategic position to gain control. This prospect may be unattractive to the executives in charge of the acquiring corporation.

### Dilution

Stockholders of an acquiring company will also be concerned about "dilution." Usually dilution refers to a reduction in earnings per share. For example, suppose that Company A with 100,000 shares of stock outstanding gives an additional 10,000 shares to acquire Company B. Then if Company A's previous earnings of $500,000 are increased to only $535,000 when A and B are combined, Company A's stockholders will see their earnings per share drop from $5.00 to $4.86. Although the management of Company A can enthusiastically report increased sales and higher total profits, the picture on a per-share basis is the reverse. Presumably such dilution is only temporary; a sound merger should help increase earnings proportionately more than the increase in shares outstanding. Nevertheless, any merger proposal that shows short-run dilution will require strong justification.

## Negotiating a "Good" Merger

Clearly, a variety of considerations enter into a good merger. We start with a potential combination of businesses that will generate productivity gains and perhaps financial benefits. Our task then turns to devising and winning acceptance of a trade that is attractive to the management and the stockholders of both the acquiring firm and the acquired firm. The following brief case illustrates the adaptation that may be necessary.

The Enid Corporation of Ohio was highly successful in manufacturing and selling indoor-outdoor acrylic carpeting in the Midwestern and Eastern United States. It had annual sales of over $50,000,000 and profits of around $3,500,000, or $1.75 per share of common stock. The stock was listed on the American Stock Exchange and had been selling in the $21–$26 range. West Coast sales, however, had declined for four years following the death of Enid's original representative in Los Angeles. To correct this situation, Enid wished to acquire Thomas & Son, an aggressive wholesale floor-covering distributor in San Francisco. This firm had been earning about $200,000 per year after taxes, and the senior Mr. Thomas was ready to retire. Executives of both Enid and Thomas thought the merger "made good sense."

Enid first suggested a simple exchange of stock, mentioning 100,000 shares of its stock, then selling at $24 per share. This would have given Thomas a price of 12 times its earnings while avoiding a dilution of Enid's earnings. Thomas felt the price was low because its earnings did not reflect two pieces of undeveloped land that Thomas believed could be sold for as much as a million dollars. Also, the debt position of Thomas & Son was complicated by the financing of this and other real estate.

The discussion then shifted to the purchase of all assets except real estate, which would remove the threat of a capital gains tax on stockholders. Thomas then said that the corporation would rather have cash than stock. Enid next proposed a package consisting of (1) $500,000 cash, (2) $1,000,000 in 10 percent notes, maturing at $100,000 per year over 10 years, (3) a "consulting" contract with Mr. Thomas, Sr., of $35,000 per year for 10 years, and (4) an employment contract with Mr. Thomas, Jr., for $60,000 per year (his present salary) for 10 years. Later, to recognize goodwill and growth potential, Enid added stock options giving Thomas & Son the option to buy 100,000 shares of Enid common stock at $27 per share any time during the next 5 years. And on these terms the deal was made.

Both sides were happy. Mr. Thomas, Sr., said, "We keep all our real estate, get a steady flow of cash into the corporation, I'm on a liberal pension, and Tom has a good job. All these incomes add up to $2,350,000, or about Enid's original offer.

Then top it off with an option that should be worth another half million in five years."

Enid's president was equally pleased. He reasoned, "Our major gain is strong distribution on the West Coast, with young Thomas committed to stay on the job. Mr. Thomas, Sr., has been drawing big bonuses, so much of his pension can come out of a reduction in executive compensation. Any way we figure it, the $300,000 in pretax earnings will more than cover the interest, capital cost, and other charges. So we expect to get an immediate improvement in net profit. True, the book value of the assets we acquired is a bit under the $1,500,000 we paid, but within a few years our profit from West Coast operations should be at least $500,000."

Note that each executive used different criteria to place a value on the business being transferred and the package of payments being received. Both packages of assets had been tailored to fit the particular situation. The swap was good. Nevertheless, the long-run soundness of the merger remains to be demonstrated in the profitable growth of Enid's West Coast business.

## Making Mergers Successful

Many mergers fail. Often the anticipated benefits do not develop, at least to the degree predicted, and unforeseen problems arise. Some of these failures are due to poorly conceived combinations—the marriages of convenience that never were thought through. Others are high-risk ventures that turn up in the losing column. Rarely can managerial skill save such ill-fated mergers.

More disturbing are the well-conceived matches that do not work out. Such results usually can be avoided by proper managerial action. Experience with successful mergers suggests a twofold approach: perceptive, careful management and special attention to communication and motivation.

### Perceptive Management

The first step in making mergers successful is a *specific program* to bring about the projected results. This requires spelling out the necessary changes and the resources—new engineering, new equipment, hiring and training people, advertising, etc.—and then setting a timetable. Probably the program will need adjustment, but this adaptation will be easier if the various moves have been delineated in advance. In addition, changes needed to reconcile the policies and the procedures of the merged companies should be identified and scheduled. Such programming demands a lot of time and thought by key people (one of the reasons it is often neglected), but it pays off because in the merger process individuals who have never worked together before are expected to do new work.

A second step is realignment of and staffing the *organization* needed to execute the program. Every merger upsets the subtle understandings of status and power in the two companies; the jockeying for new positions is inevitable. Although the situations may be too fluid to define detailed relationships, placing responsibility and providing a prompt means for resolving differences of opinion are essential for positive action. The new mixture of personalities in every merger makes this reorganizing a very delicate task.

Installing dependable *controls* is a third essential element. Cash controls and accounting reports usually are quickly adapted to a format familiar to central executives. However, meaningful cost data and information on market development, research and development efforts, management development, and other intangibles are rare. Many a merger has floundered because executives lacked a means of knowing what was really happening in their new operation.

## Communication and Motivation

Cutting across the more explicit management actions just described is a critical need for communication and motivation. A merger signals change. Just what will be changed is unknown, so anxiety builds up in many people whose jobs might be affected. Rumors substitute for facts and spread rapidly.

In such circumstances, key executives should make their plans known just as soon as possible. If some matters are unsettled, they can at least indicate how and when these will be resolved. The communication should be two-way, giving employees an opportunity to ask questions and hear frank answers. New executives have low *credibility* in the early stages of a merger, and they need to explain what will be done and then see that it happens. Suspicion of motives is apt to flare up at any time during the first year or two, and executives need to be available to make personal explanations of actions they take.

An aspect of communication is when to discuss problems and with whom. One successful pattern is to explore what changes are necessary and how merged operations will be organized *before* the agreement is final. Usually these discussions include all key executives who will have to work together. If a merger does take place after such a frank exchange, its chances of success are high. The chief drawback is that the airing of problems may cause one party to withdraw. But if these early stages cannot survive frank recognition of what working together involves, then major personnel and morale difficulties should be anticipated.

Coupled with the frankest communication possible should be positive reinforcement—tangible or intangible rewards—of desired behavior. By emphasizing the achievements of a merger and rewarding appropriate behavior, management builds a new morale. Employee attention shifts from concern with the past to interest in the future.

We shall examine programming, organizing, communicating, and controlling more fully in later parts of this book. As indicated, mergers generate some especially difficult tasks of execution. Unless these receive their full share of attention, the entire merger effort may be futile.

## Merger Via Takeover

The vast majority of mergers are "friendly," that is, they are recommended by the directors of both companies. But recently the business world has been dazzled by a rash of "takeovers" in which the acquiring company gains control of another concern without the cooperation of its existing management. Here the "raider" gets control of the majority of the stock, ousts the existing management, and then arranges a favorable merger.

## Use of Tender Offers

A raider may gain control of the desired merger partner in several ways: (1) by joining forces with key stockholders who do not support the management (for example, Hilton acquired the Statler Hotel chain in this manner); (2) by acquiring stock on the open market (for example, James Hill's classic fight for the Burlington Railroad); and (3) by soliciting proxies of stockholders (Young used this route to gain control of the New York Central Railroad). Today, these methods are becoming very expensive.

Currently, the popular path to control is a "tender offer." Here the raider makes a public offer to buy or exchange stock. The terms may be any one of the alternatives we have already discussed under friendly mergers—cash, common stock, convertible preferred stock, and so forth. However, the offer must have a value well above the prevailing price of the stock being sought, typically 25 to 30 percent higher than the market price under the present management. In other words, the raider bypasses company management and appeals directly to stockholders.

Even in the face of new laws regulating tenders, this is a cloak-and-dagger game. Surprise offers, secret deals, extra commissions to brokers, counterattacks, splitting stock, and legal injunctions are all employed in a manner reminiscent of the battles between the industrial barons of the nineteenth century.

## Wall Street Raids

Thus far, we have assumed a combined operation of the merged companies—at least as sister units within a corporate family. The aim is to secure benefits from joint activities.

Some raiders have no such intentions, however. Instead, their aim is to make a quick financial profit. The net impact on the business-units which create goods, services, and jobs is secondary to them.

There are two primary sources of quick profits from takeovers of this sort. (1) Refinancing, the more common of the two, greatly increases the debt borne by the operating units, so that the residual equity is highly leveraged. (2) Restructuring involves selling off parts of the acquired corporation to several other corporations which will pay a good price for particular pieces of the former enterprise. The parts, sold separately, are worth more than the whole.

The ingenious ways that raiders and their advisors have devised for turning a profit in these situations are neo-Machiavellian and beyond the scope of this text. Thanks to the "efficiency" of the world financial markets, billions of dollars can be quickly mobilized by the players in this game. Another part of the picture is that the senior managers of target companies often try to defend their jobs as well as the existing business-units by measures akin to the raiders' tactics: heavy debt, other financial commitments, or even restructuring. So once a corporation finds itself "in play," it has difficulty emerging unscathed.

## Who Is Vulnerable?

No company will attempt a takeover of another company unless it sees an opportunity to substantially improve the return to its stockholders by better management and/or synergistic benefits of the merger. Consequently, a firm is vulnerable to takeover (1) when it shows poor performance relative to other firms in its industry—especially when its dividends are declining more than those of its competitors; (2) when it has surplus liquid assets or large unused borrowing capacity; (3) when it holds assets that could be sold for more than their present market value; or (4) when potential synergistic benefits are being disregarded.

The best defense against a takeover is, of course, managing a company so that its assets are wisely deployed, its earnings record creates a good price for its stock, and synergistic benefits are aggressively exploited. Under these conditions, a stockholder gains little or nothing by transferring the stock to a raider.

Such a sound defense against a takeover takes time. If a company is really vulnerable and finds itself being raided before it has time to put its house in order, the management can, and often does, seek a friendly merger with some other company on terms as attractive as those of the tender. Management casualities are usually lower in a friendly merger!

## Economic Effects

The immediate effects on a company of a hostile takeover are costly: anxiety is at a peak, personal hostilities are generated, and none of the perceptive management steps discussed in the previous section can occur in advance. Indeed, debt may have increased to a level that precludes strategic flexibility (see Chapter 14); and a bankruptcy that can have serious ripple effects throughout the economy is a real possibility.

Nevertheless, a takeover does serve as one way of deposing a stodgy management. More important, the possibility of a takeover lurking in the background serves as a spur to management. No longer can executives be complacent just because company stock is dispersed among so many stockholders that no one can make a significant complaint.

From the point of view of society and of a stockholder, then, the potential threat of a takeover stimulates good management. All parties—stockholders, society, *and* management—will be better off if the company is administered so that the costly process of takeover is impractical.

## Summary

Merging with another company can be a major step in carrying out a desired strategy. The acquired company may provide a much needed resource, give access to a new market, extend company operations back into earlier stages of production, provide a scale of operation that will support improved technology, or improve company services and productivity.

Not all mergers are so well conceived. Some are opportunistic, taking advantage of short-run financial gain. Ideal, of course, is a partner that both pushes us forward on basic strategy and provides a financial advantage.

Whatever the fit, the "price" paid must also be weighed. A heavy debt burden, troublesome stock options, and exhaustion of cash reserves can result, and this unhealthy financial condition can seriously deter execution of other facets of company strategy. Or the package given to owners of the acquired company, say common stock, may create no strain. Since we know that a strong financial structure is closely related to future growth, both the *quid* and the *quo* of the merger deal require close scrutiny in terms of their impact on the master strategic plan.

Even soundly conceived mergers fail if the two institutions are not melded by good follow-up action. Numerous internal adjustments in both companies need careful planning, organizing, and controlling, and new motivations and communication flows have to be established. These are problems that we examine more fully in the next two parts of this book.

## Questions for Class Discussion

1. Suppose that you are the proprietor of a nice little business and a big company wants to acquire both you and the business. Here's the picture: While in college, you worked in and then became manager of a small restaurant located in a rundown turn-of-the-century home adjacent to the campus. Just before your graduation, the owner offered to sell you the whole business,

house and all, for $35,000. Although your career planning had never considered owning a restaurant, it was the easy thing to do and you accepted the offer.

During the three years since graduation, you have developed the restaurant's reputation as an "in" place to eat. The income has enabled you to modernize the kitchen and spruce up the dining room, as well as pay off all your loan for the purchase. The hours are long, but you take pride in what you have accomplished.

There have been two side benefits: (1) You and your spouse live upstairs in rooms that are rather dingy, but that are next on your schedule for fixing the place up. (2) Much more important, your spouse is really into health foods and runs a health food store on a large enclosed porch of the house. This separate enterprise is an outlet for a lot of missionary zeal on the part of its proprietor.

The operator of a successful chain of family-type restaurants has approached you about selling out. They want to combine your land with an adjacent property on which they have an option. All existing buildings would be torn down, and a very modern and attractive restaurant would be constructed. Moreover, they want you to be manager, although the managing and the property parts of the deal could be separated. No dollar figures have yet been discussed. The operator of a nearby drugstore remarked, "Oh, they'll give you a hundred grand because it's a good location."

Using Figure 16–1 as a framework, what "package" of compensations would you want in exchange for your present business? (For alternative career possibilities, use your actual current likes and dislikes.)

2. (a) As noted in the text, acquisition of another company—rather than inside development—is usually done to make significant gains in either time, expense, or physical possibility. A different perspective that influences what the acquiring company is seeking in a merger is the stage in the life cycle of its major product. (See Chapter 2 for a description of a product life cycle.) How might the life-cycle stage of the acquiring company affect the importance it attaches to using the acquisition to gain time? to cut expense? to get an asset not otherwise available?

   (b) Use the examples of DuPont's acquisition of Endo Laboratories and Enid Corporation's acquisition of Thomas & Son to illustrate your answer to part (a).

3. Not long ago a high-ranking monetary expert with the federal government warned board directors, lawyers, and accountants of unfortunate results from continuing emphasis on acquisitions and mergers: "Unfortunately . . . most discussions of tender offers seem to center on . . . various devices to comply with or avoid the application of the federal securities laws and the state anti-takeover requirements. . . . The most unsettling aspect . . . is the legitimacy which hostile tender offers have come to enjoy. It has become acceptable to treat corporations as the sum of their properties and to assume

that corporate control may change hands with no greater concerns of the consequences than accompanies an exchange of property deeds in a game of Monopoly." The official also took issue with the speculators, arbitragers, and lawyers who benefit from the takeovers and can then easily walk away once the transaction is completed by noting that "The corporation is more than the aggregate of its tangible assets." (a) What did the monetary expert mean by the phrase "the most unsettling aspect?" (b) What might the corporation be other than the sum of its assets? (c) Why might the lawyers and accountants be especially interested in devices to avoid the application of various laws? (d) Does the activity noted above reflect social responsibility on the part of the specialists?

4. Suppose that, in the Enid-Thomas merger described on pages 453 and 454, the following difficulties arose after the merger was completed: (a) Anxiety and communication difficulties during the first year reduced the effectiveness of Thomas's employees. (b) The Thomas product line needed trimming, and more emphasis was put on Enid products—a switch that was not readily accepted by the Thomas group. (c) Thomas, Jr., wanted to take independent action on a variety of matters and was "too rich to be motivated from Ohio," so he resigned after three years.

   What action might Enid executives have taken to minimize or forestall each of these difficulties?

5. At one stage in its defense from unfriendly takeover bids, Allegis (the corporation owning United Airlines, Hertz auto rentals, and Western and Hilton International hotels) was confronted with two offers. One came from United Airlines employees, and another was from a raider group that announced that it would sell Hertz and the hotels if it were to gain control. To discourage such offers, Allegis announced a plan to declare a special $60-per-share dividend on its common stock, or a total of $3.5 billion, while letting stockholders keep their stock. The plan would add $3 billion in debt to Allegis' balance sheet, making the total debt about $5.3 billion. The debt-to-equity ratio would then be 20 to 1.

   Most stockholders liked the plan, since they paid considerably less than the current price of $86 per share and would get most of their investment back. But doubts persist. Industry analysts said, in effect, "The only way for Allegis to raise $3 billion is to go through the airline and hock a fair number of assets." "The recapitalization plan will seriously strain United's ability to weather labor strikes and fare wars, and could crimp plans to buy new planes needed to remain competitive." "The highly leveraged position will make the airline more vulnerable in a strike which could ground the carrier and cut off its cash flow."

   Do you think the president and the board of directors of Allegis were justified in adopting this plan to fend off a takeover?

6. The reverse of a merger is a "spin-off," the separation of a single company into two or more independent concerns. In practice, relatively few spin-offs or

divestments occur, and most of these arise from antitrust activity of the federal government. (a) How do you account for the much larger number of mergers than spin-offs? Are the economic advantages predominantly in favor of increased size? What other social considerations are there? (b) Suppose that, as president, you concluded that dividing up your company made good sense. What problems do you foresee in accomplishing the split-up? (c) Do your answers to (a) and (b) apply to profit decentralization, that is, to establishing semiautonomous self-contained divisions?

7. "Vic, how would you like to be a millionaire?" Joe Javitz, the president of Roadwise Carburetor Co., asked his friend, Victor Savas. "As you know, Roadwise Carburetor is building a nationwide distribution system, and Savas Auto Parts Co. could be the northwest part of that system. So we might be persuaded to give you $1 million of Roadwise stock for your company."

"That millionaire stuff sure has a nice ring to it, Joe, but your suggestion is a bit too simple. What would I live on? You told me last month that your expansion was soaking up all the cash you have, and that dividends on your stock had to wait. Also, what about my partner, Tim Lyle? He owns 25 percent of Savas Auto Parts Co. Does he get a million, too?"

Roadwise Carburetor Co. sells *replacement* carburetors to automobile repair shops. Some are new, and some of the recent complex ones are rebuilt. Roadwise's goal is to have carburetors for any car available anywhere in the United States. To achieve this, the company needs distribution branches throughout the country, one or two plants, and four or five rebuilding shops. Savas Auto Parts has distribution branches in Washington and Oregon and does rebuilding in its Portland plant. Currently, Savas gets most (not all) of its carburetors from Roadwise. At one time Savas made replacement carburetors; but as carburetors became more complex, the firm confined production to a few older, simpler models and bought the others from companies like Roadwise. Savas is still a very strong distributor in the Northwest. Vic Savas believes that as carburetors become more sophisticated, Roadwise is likely to become one of the leading independent suppliers in the replacement field.

Two weeks after the preceding conversation, the controller for Roadwise visited Savas Auto Parts Co. and reported the following back to Javitz: (a) The Savas plant is old, but is on a valuable piece of land. Under Lyle's direction the plant is doing subcontracting, mostly aircraft parts and some "cages," which space the balls in ball bearings. The land, plant, equipment, and working capital not associated with carburetors have a book value of $150,000 and could be sold for about $250,000. (b) Lyle said that if he had the money, he would buy the plant himself. (c) Accounts payable are high, so net working capital in the carburetor business is only $300,000. (d) Last year Vic Savas paid himself a salary of $65,000. Apparently, he uses this money to live on, and he expects to continue to work.

At the next meeting of Javitz and Savas, Javitz suggested, "(a) You would work full time running our Northwest operations at least until you are 65 (in four years) at a base salary of $65,000 per year. Then, upon retirement, you would continue as director and consultant to Roadwise for life with a compensation of $30,000 per year. Assuming that your life expectancy is age 75, that adds up to $560,000. That's over half your million. (b) In exchange for all your inventory, receivables, and goodwill associated with carburetors, we will give Savas Auto Parts Co. common stock in Roadwise Carburetor Co. The book value could be low for tax purposes, but the future value would be $500,000. If you personally take that, and I hope you will, then you'll have your million. (c) Your land is indeed valuable, but frankly we are not interested in investing in land at this time. Our suggestion to you is that Lyle get all the assets not associated with carburetors. One simple way to achieve this is to spin off everything associated with carburetors into a subsidiary which you would take and then sell to us; Lyle would own the old corporation and all that would be left (with *no* taxes to pay)."

Use the factors discussed in this chapter to appraise Javitz's proposal. Is it likely to be accepted by the key parties? Do you have a better plan?

8. Corporation A offered to buy Corporation B, and when Corporation C heard about the proposal it also offered to buy B. Two directors wondered about which offer to recommend to the shareholders. The B family, including the two directors, owned a little more than 40 percent of B's common stock. The B company had no preferred stock. The common stock of both A and C was traded actively on public exchanges. The price per share offered by A and C for B's shares was almost the same, but A offered a choice of cash for half the amount and its common stock for the balance, *or* its common stock for the entire amount. The choice was left up to each person who owned B's stock. Corporation C offered a new class of its cumulative preferred stock with a dividend of 25 percent per share more than B had been paying in the recent past to its shareholders. The new preferred stock had no voting rights unless dividends were omitted for three years. Both A and C were about three times the size of B. Corporation A planned to move all central offices and staff divisions to its own headquarters in a different state, but offered to set up a subsidiary named for the B family and to keep open one plant and the B Country Club in B's former headquarters city. C planned to combine all operations in various parts of its plants in the city in which both it and B were located. It also planned to sell off all the real estate holdings of B in that city to help to increase its working capital. The two directors, like other executives in the industry and the city, respected Corporation C for its excellent products, modern plants, and first-rate human resource policies and practices. They also respected Corporation A for its excellent products, rapid growth through successful acquisitions, and high standing in the financial and investment communities.

Which offer should the two directors of Corporation B recommend to their shareholders?

9. (a) Companies that stress long-range planning often become involved in mergers. This is especially so when the long-range planning focuses on strat-

egy rather than on budgeting. How do you explain this tendency? (b) Review the key elements of strategy outlined in Chapter 5, and identify the areas where a merger is likely to be an attractive way to proceed.

10. British Printing and Communications Corporation, run as his personal fiefdom by Robert Maxwell, the flamboyant English publisher (who was also known as a wheeler-dealer and a powerful, hands-on executive), made an unsolicited bid of $44 a share for the stock of Harcourt Brace Jovanovich, the publishing, entertainment, and insurance company based in Orlando, Florida. Harcourt, Brace also owned the various Sea World and Cypress Gardens theme parks.

    Harcourt Brace's stock was then selling at $30 a share on the New York Stock Exchange. Maxwell's offer put the company in play, and other buyers pushed the price of the stock to $46 a share on the day of the offer. All told, three groups were involved: the company tried to buy back its own stock, individual speculators sought to buy, and major institutional holders held on for an expected price of $50 to $55 a share.

    Mr. Jovanovich, chairman of Harcourt, Brace, was personally insulted by the offer and said that he refused to believe that Mr. Maxwell could be allowed to preside over the largest educational publisher in the United States. ". . . a tremendous amount was at stake—including Harcourt's important role in American education and the national interest."[2] Harcourt's sales were then about $1 billion a year, and net income was $70.5 million for a price-to-earnings ratio of 16 to 1 and earnings per share of $1.91.

    British Printing soon dropped its $1.73 billion ($44 a share) offer, but left the door open for a possible future bid. Harcourt, Brace stayed in play in the financial markets, and, after an announcement by the company about a special dividend, the market price soared to close at $55.25. Then Harcourt, with Mr. Jovanovich fighting to retain control, borrowed $3 billion to pay a special dividend on its common stock of $40 a share in cash plus a newly issued preferred stock for a value of about $10 a share. This more than tripled Harcourt's long-term debt, which had already been burdensome at 56 percent of capitalization. Moody's rated the new issues of bonds at single-B-2 and single-B-3, and stated that the "enormous" debt burden taken on by Harcourt meant that it "now must perform better than in the past to make minimum capital expenditures and to meet debt requirements."[3]

    Harcourt immediately put up some of its operations for sale: its magazine unit for $400 million, some real estate for $140 million, and a television station for $11 million. To reverse an operating loss of about $98 million in six months, the company let 400 employees go and planned to drop another 400 later. Also, wages and salaries were not to be increased for at least 18 months. Interest costs rose from $21.7 million to $295 million per year. Depreciation

---

[2]*The Wall Street Journal,* August 24, 1987, p. 11.
[3]*The Wall Street Journal,* September 14, 1987, p. 30.

and other noncash charges contributed to a positive cash flow of $54 million for the year. Interest on half of the junk bonds will not come due for five years, but, by then, Harcourt will count on cost cuts and expanding operations to raise profits. Sea World of Texas should begin operations by next year. In a pinch, and with the banks' approval, Harcourt could sell off a theme park or two, or its insurance companies.

*Business Week* commented, "For Jovanovich, all of this must be a bit sobering. He has only begun to pay for his independence from Robert Maxwell. A company that grew by gobbling up others now will be busy minding its own businesses. And the fruit of its labors will be going to pay off bankers and buyers of junk bonds for decades."[4]

(a) Would the national interest of the United States have been affected by a takeover by British Printing?

(b) At $30 per share, Harcourt's price-to-earnings ratio was about 16; at $44 per share, it was 23; and at $55.25 per share, it was about 29. What justification was there for this rapid increase in the value of each share of stock?

(c) Explain the benefits of the preceding events to the various actors: Mr. Jovanovich; Mr. Maxwell; an institutional holder of Harcourt's stock; an individual stockholder; investors in bonds; Harcourt, Brace's editors and sales agents; a few large banks; stockholders in the long run; readers; and the whales.

(d) Does Harcourt, Brace still need to be wary of other unsolicited takeover offers? Explain.

(e) Who, or what group, came out on top of this whole exercise?

(f) Are these events the consequence of wise strategic planning by anyone?

# CASE
## 16  T&T Acquisition

## Background of Acquisition Proposal

Executives in Davis Data, Inc., are looking for ways to benefit from their ownership of several diverse businesses. One possibility is to develop a computerized reference service, that is, build a large data bank that can be queried via computer

---

[4]Gail DeGeorge, "How Harcourt Plans to Keep the Wolf Away," *Business Week*, No. 3016, September 14, 1987, p. 42.

to provide information on specific questions. Two existing divisions of Davis Data might sire such a service. One division designs and sells computer software programs for a variety of purposes, including library reference and catalog systems. The publishing division deals mostly in technical books, but it also has acquired several "yearbooks" for various industries. The yearbooks contain a lot of industry statistics and related matter which are updated annually.

With all the talk about having vast quantities of reference material available to people who have personal computers, Davis Data sees an opportunity to create a new service utilizing the industry data that its publishing division already compiles. Personnel in the software division could design a system for accessing this information; then subscribers could tap into the data banks quickly from any location having a personal computer and a telephone.

Since the publishing division puts out yearbooks for the hotel/motel industry and the resort industry, a computerized reference service for managers in those industries is being considered by Davis Data, Inc. Such a service would also be valuable to firms selling supplies and services to hotels, motels, and resorts. To be successful, the reference service will have to be responsive to the interests and problems of its users. And at present, Davis Data, Inc., does not have personnel "who think like a resort manager." Executives in Davis Data, Inc., believe that that kind of perspective is needed in order to be positioned to move quickly into the new service.

As Davis executives were looking for a young, imaginative person already familiar with the hotel/motel and resort industries, the name of Willis White surfaced. White is well respected for his trade association work. A follow-up check revealed, however, that White has recently become editor of two trade papers in this field. And thus the trail leads to the T&T Publishing Company, where White is now part owner and managing editor. To get White, Davis Data, Inc., may have to acquire T&T, and even then he could move to another job.

## Present Situation at T&T

T&T has been in the printing and publishing business for a long time. When Mr. Tilson died a few years ago, all the printing equipment and business went to Tilson's heirs. The building, the two monthly trade papers, and the name went to Mr. Taussig. However, most of the building is under long-term lease to the printing firm, providing Taussig with about $40,000 yearly income from that source.

Taussig wants to retire, but having recently remarried he needs an additional $20,000 per year to live on. He expects to get this sum from the trade papers. A managing editor hired three years ago to take over the running of the papers left after the first year due to a clash in personalities. Then, following extended negotiations, Taussig "sold out" to White and his wife.

The expression "sold out" overstates the arrangement. Taussig has an employment contract with T&T to remain as "publisher" for 12 years, when he will be 80, at a salary of $20,000 per year. (This salary is subordinated to the normal obligations of T&T so as not to impinge on T&T's credit standing.) Taussig sold the Whites 4,500 shares of the 10,000 shares of T&T common stock outstanding for a "nominal" $5 per share, and gave the Whites an option to buy the remaining shares at the same price when his employment at T&T ends.

This arrangement appeals to the Whites for several reasons. It gives the Whites a business of their own where they can work as a team. They now own part of the company and will eventually buy the rest at a price already fixed. Thus, they can reap the benefits of improvements they make in the business. Taussig assured them that they will have a free hand since he wishes to withdraw, and that he is retaining voting control only to safeguard his salary, which is really what he is being paid for the company.

## Acquisition Proposal

As Davis Data, Inc., enters the picture, then, either it will have to persuade White to give up the T&T venture just described, or it can try to buy the stock of both Taussig and the Whites. In fact, acquisition of T&T as a going concern might serve Davis Data's purpose very well. (1) The trade papers will probably pay all or most of White's salary. This is advantageous because the *time* when it will be wise to start the contemplated reference service is uncertain. Davis Data will probably rely on some distributor or TV channel to handle the physical transmission, and that activity in turn depends on widespread development of the whole reference service concept. It is quite possible that Davis Data could be unable to proceed for several years. (2) Mrs. White, who is 28, complements the talents of her husband, who is 32. She has a degree in operations research and would be very useful in building bridges between data bases, managers' needs, and computer programs.

The acquisition expert at Davis Data (vice-president for Corporate Planning) has been trying to design a "package" that is attractive to both Taussig and the Whites. Taussig is easy to satisfy. He'll probably sell out at $5 per share if Davis Data will take over his employment contract. Or Taussig will rent to Davis Data the space in his building that the trade papers now use at an increased rental of $20,000 per year for 12 years, an arrangement Taussig prefers because the rent would continue to flow to his young wife even if he dies during the 12-year interval.

For the Whites, the proposal is as follows: (1) Davis Data, Inc., will purchase their shares at $5 each, and the stock option on Taussig's shares will be canceled. (2) The Whites will continue to have full reign in running the trade papers—there is no one else in Davis Data who understands that kind of business. (3) At the same time, the Whites will work with other people in Davis Data on the development of a computerized reference service for the hotel/motel and resort industries. Further net income—before tax (but not losses)—from the sale of such service will be included with the income from the trade papers in the calculation of the Whites' options and bonuses. (4) For each of 12 years, starting three years hence, the Whites will receive an option to buy one share of Davis Data, Inc., stock at $20 per share for each $100 increase in the annual income before tax earned by T&T trade papers and the reference service. Such increases will be computed against last year's income before tax. (5) The Whites will be given an employment contract for five years at their present salaries (combined total of $50,000 per year) plus any cost-of-living adjustments made generally by Davis Data, Inc. Of course, the Whites may be employed by Davis Data beyond the five years by mutual agreement.

The purpose of the possible options on Davis Data, Inc., stock is to compensate the Whites for giving up their existing ownership and options on T&T stock. The reason for deferring the dates of computation is to encourage a longer run viewpoint.

The T&T trade papers are now barely breaking even financially, after paying Taussig his salary. Subscriptions have been declining, due in part to consolidations of motels; also, Taussig has become quite conservative and opinionated about the way the papers are run. Of course, it is possible that under the White's direction income from the papers could be increased $100,000 and maintained at that level for 10 years—giving the Whites options on 10,000 shares of Davis Data, Inc., stock. An improvement well below that level is more likely. The price of Davis Data stock, which is sold frequently in the over-the-counter market, will probably move up and down at about the same percentage as Standard & Poor's 500 stock index moves. Davis Data stock is now selling at $20 per share, or 10 times earnings.

The assets and liabilities of T&T are not a significant consideration in the proposed acquisition. There are virtually no fixed assets (printing and mailing are contracted out, following industry practice). The current assets are quite liquid, but this is offset by the inherently large liability for prepaid subscriptions. Because prepaid subscriptions provide most of the capital needed for growth, it is customary to distribute most of the net profits of trade papers to stockholders in the form of dividends.

## Questions

Do you recommend acceptance of the vice-president's proposals by (1) Davis Data, Inc., (2) Taussig, and (3) the Whites? If not, what changes do you think would be more likely to be acceptable to all three parties?

# CHAPTER 17

## Joint Ventures and Corporate Input Strategy

Corporate strategy has at least two important facets in addition to the portfolio and acquisition issues explored in Chapters 15 and 16. The use of joint ventures is an alternative to acquisitions, and corporate inputs are vital supplements to most portfolios. These instruments of strategy are examined in this chapter.

## Strategic Use of Joint Ventures

A company that is eager to pursue an attractive strategy may possess most of the strengths needed but lack some one crucial capability. If a different company has resources that can help jump this hurdle, but is otherwise unsuitable as an acquisition, forming a joint venture may be the course to follow. The two companies create a new third enterprise to focus on activities that will benefit each of them. By joining forces, each contributing from its strengths, they can undertake work that neither one could do alone.

Such cooperative effort might take many forms, but the kind of structures that have captured the limelight in recent years are *operating equity* joint ventures. A new corporation (the "child") is set up in which each "parent" shares the ownership, contributes resources in addition to money, and plays a role in managing the new entity.

A joint venture may, for example, combine one firm's discovery about the behavior of monoclonal antibodies with another firm's knowledge about AIDS in an effort to develop a specific treatment for this disease. Or, the marketing skills of a food distributor may be combined with a chemical company's new type of insect spray to seek national distribution of the product to home owners.

Increasing sources of competition and the rapidity of technological change put a premium on fast adjustments to new opportunities, and joint ventures are one way to become a leader in growing fields. The joint-venture concept is not new. It has long been used by companies in advanced societies to establish distribution of their services or products in developing countries. Also, joint ventures are a way to organize very large projects, such as the construction of the Alaskan pipeline for crude oil. However, in the United States especially, the use of joint ventures is spreading to a wide variety of activities.

## Joint-Venture Success Factors

Corporate managers need a way to decide when to use joint ventures. Figure 17–1 is designed for this purpose, calling attention to six variables which are critical to effectiveness.

1. *Partners' positions.* Joint ventures are rather complicated arrangements, so each partner should have a clear view of what benefits it hopes to receive and what it is prepared to contribute. This is a private assessment prior to negotiations.
2. *Attractiveness of partners.* Then there is a size-up of each partner. Can

**FIGURE 17–1.**
**MODEL FOR ANALYZING JOINT VENTURES**

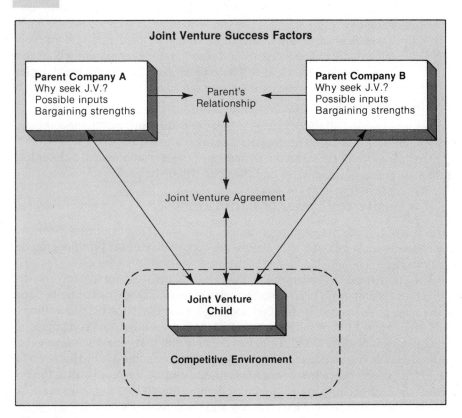

Adapted from K. R. Harrigan, *Strategies for Joint Ventures* (Lexington, MA: Lexington Books, 1985)

and will that firm provide critically scarce resources? At what cost to us? Can we work together in a fair and expeditious manner?

3. *Adequacy of joint-venture agreement.* The agreement, like a "charter" for any business-unit in a multidivision corporation, should state the objectives, scope of activities, degrees of freedom, and constraints of the new child. In addition, it should specify the inputs to be provided by each partner (know-how, services, capital, personnel, etc.) and the outputs each partner expects to receive (market position, product sales, technical knowledge, etc.).

4. *Viability of the child.* The child will have a life and character of its own. It will have its distinct competitive environment and, like any business-unit, should have a reasonable chance of achieving its assigned objectives with the resources made available and within the constraints placed upon it.

5. *Feedback loops.* A distinct feature is the need for the child to have effective communication with its *two* parents. These are important for the child to get the help from, and provide the service expected by, each parent.

6. *Capacity to adapt.* Implied, but not shown in the diagram, is an evolving structure. The interests and resources of each parent will change over time, and the child will have to adjust to *its* environment. Unless all participants in the joint venture can adapt, the venture will soon be outmoded.

Because keeping all these factors in balance is difficult, managing joint ventures requires a lot of skill. The benefits that they offer require dedicated effort by all participants. To understand the dynamics of these relationships, a closer look at the viewpoints of the parents and the child will be helpful.

## Propensity and Power of Each Parent

A search for help in executing a strategy sparks most joint ventures. But many other aspects must be dealt with before the cooperative effort produces the desired results.

The urge to build a lumber mill in the Pacific Northwest, for instance, started with a timber company's need for cash to pay taxes on a large tract of timberland. At the same time, the nearby railroad, looking for increased traffic, was willing to build a spur to a lumber millsite. Negotiations between the two companies resulted in a joint venture to build and run the new mill that would saw logs cut on the timberland. The manager of the fledgling mill faced some discord between the parents, however. The railroad sought maximum output: the more traffic, the better. But the timber company wanted to sell only enough logs to pay its taxes because the prevailing price of logs was low and the company's overall strategy was to hold the timber for several years until inflation, demand, and the tariff on Canadian lumber drove the price to at least double its present level. Fortunately for the timber company, the joint venture agreement did not permit the railroad to withdraw even if the timber company rejected the request for more volume.

## Role of Propensity and Power

The design and operation of any joint venture, including the one just described, is strongly influenced by the parents' propensities to cooperate. How vital is the agreement to each partner? For instance, will the timber company go bankrupt if it can't find a market for some of its logs?

Each parent in this lumber mill example had something to gain from forming the joint venture, and also something to give up. Its propensity, or eagerness to make an agreement, depended upon a balance of these pros and cons. But note that reaching a final agreement depended also on the propensity of the other parent. If the timber company was eager and the railroad lukewarm, the sort of agreement that could be reached would differ sharply from a venture that would emerge if the propensities were reversed.

Closely related to propensity is the question of relative power—the ability to force another person or company to do something that it would prefer not to do. Thus, in a joint venture, if one parent has power over the other (like the power of a bank to call a loan), it has a strong voice in deciding how the joint venture will work.

So to understand what is likely to occur in a joint venture, an understanding of the propensity and the power of each partner is necessary.

In a business setting, power comes mostly from an ability to withhold or stop an action that the other person wants very much. A bit of reflection shows that power and propensity are, in general, inversely related. That is, the more eager a company is to have a certain action occur, the higher is the power of another company that can prevent (or support) that action. And conversely, if the propensity is low, then ability to block the action creates very little power.

The issue of power is significant in considering the use of a joint venture because the cooperative relationships established increase the power that partners have over each other.

## Key Factors Leading to Propensity and Power

The lumber mill example suggests five key factors in assessing the propensity and power of each parent in a joint venture.

1. *What* specific *benefits does the parent want from the venture?* Among these benefits could be access to a distribution channel, use of a patent, employees with unusual knowledge and capability, an efficient manufacturing plant, the glamor of a familiar brand name, and the like. The benefit will be a resource that is difficult for the parent to develop promptly by itself.

2. *What compensating resources can be offered?* To obtain the desired benefits, each parent must offer inducements; it must "bring something to the party." These inducements will be existing strengths that the other parent and/or the child needs: a capability in marketing, production,

engineering, management, etc. Especially convenient is an underutilized capacity that can be made available quickly. The more alluring the offer, the more power the offering company will have.

3. *What are the costs of cooperating?* Most of the sacrifices made in entering a joint venture do not appear on the accounting records. They involve opportunity costs—actions that were not taken because of commitments to the joint venture, e.g., sacrificing exclusiveness, having to share a little-known technology, less friendly ties with organizations not included in the venture, and the like.

4. *Are any alternatives available?* The importance a partner attaches to forming a joint venture depends, in part, on the availability of other ways to obtain the desired resources or to employ underutilized resources. For instance, if a toy manufacturer can continue to use a California wholesaler, it will have less interest in a joint venture in a distributorship than it would have if no satisfactory wholesaler were available.

5. *How "central" are the resources involved?* The purpose of a joint venture may be crucial to the existence of one of the parents, or it may be only a desirable addition (as was the paper mill for the railroad). Or, many of the activities of the parent may depend on what happens in the joint venture, whereas in other situations operations might be able to continue with only minor disturbances.

A manager participating in a joint venture needs answers to the foregoing questions because a double issue is always involved: how far will the cooperation go, and how will the gains be divided?

## Viability of the Joint-Venture Child

A healthy child is essential if the parents are to achieve their aims in creating the joint venture. Although profitability of the venture may not be their main interest, they typically expect it to at least break even while it serves the more specific purposes of, say, entering a new market or exploring a new technology.

A joint-venture child differs from most business-units in that it (1) receives inputs and help from two (or more) active organizations, but (2) is required to focus on several very specific outputs. The manager of a joint venture is, of course, concerned whether the burden of complying with constraints will outweigh the help provided.

Consider, for example, the predicament of Telgard Products, Inc. Telgard was established by Telecom, a producer of communications equipment, and Everguard, a concern that installs and maintains security systems for offices, plants, large stores, etc.[1] Telecom knew how to make very sensitive devices that

---

[1]Names have been changed to protect proprietary knowledge.

could detect an intruder, but it had no background in the security of buildings. Everguard had long experience with security, and was glad to include Telecom's novel devices in some of its systems. A joint venture, Telgard was used to combine these two interests instead of having merely a buyer-seller relationship, because Telecom's engineers believed that with the advice and marketing effort of someone already strong in the security business, they could design a variety of unique sensing devices.

The use of Telgard's devices in Everguard's systems is working well. However, the volume of the business is not really enough to sustain Telgard. Now the big hope is a redesign fitted into a simplified system for homes. Telecom's engineers foresee no technical problems, although Telgard would have to find new suppliers for large-volume production. In contrast, Everguard keeps raising doubts. The general manager of Telgard has trouble interpreting Everguard's opinions: "Are they well-founded doubts, more a reflection of Everguard's ignorance of the home market? Or are they dislike for a very different kind of service? At least this is clear—the home system idea is stalled, and Telgard's operating deficits persist."

Three related problems face a joint venture like Telgard:

1.  *Economic soundness.* A joint venture must perform some significant functions better than competitors can do. Either the venture itself must earn a profit, or the contributions it makes to the parents must be valuable enough to justify a continuing subsidy. Alternative ways to serve the same need, i.e., competition, will win out if they have better quality or lower cost.

    Because of this requirement, joint ventures need freedom to work through outsiders as well as parents on most matters. They have to be flexible enough in outside relationships to keep up with their rivals. Not all joint ventures permit such flexibility, as Telgard is discovering.

2.  *Supportive relations with parents.* For people in the parent organizations, a joint-venture child is not really a member of the family. For instance, new technology or trade secrets are likely to become known to the other parent, via the child, and then spread like gossip. Indeed, General Motors frankly hopes this will occur at the New United Motor Manufacturing plant in California, which is a joint-production venture with Toyota. Or a parent's marketing department may be reluctant to push a child's products if there is doubt about how long that product will remain in the line. Perhaps Everguard's disinterest in the private home market stemmed from this sort of doubt.

    For such reasons, joint-venture children often receive only limited and screened support from the parent organizations. Yet without major inputs from parents, few children will survive. Realistically, support on a matter of secondary significance to a parent is much more likely to be forthcoming than a sharing of the parent's crucial competitive strength. On support issues, propensity and power make a big difference.

3.  *Adaptability to change.* Relationships among the child and both parents change over time. For each of the three participants, competition may rise, alternative opportunities will appear, technology evolves, etc. So within a year or two, the relative interests, power, and capabilities among the participants are sure to shift.

    If the child is to prosper in this dynamic setting, adjustments in the de facto joint venture have to be made. For instance, maybe the manager of Telgard should try to arrange a divorce between its parents and a replacement of Everguard with a company tied into the home security market!

    The fact that change is so likely and necessary in a three-participant arrangement does not mean that the joint-venture agreement was a mistake. For a time, it may have served all parties well. The likelihood of change does suggest, however, that the child should be organized in anticipation of an evolving set of goals.

From the preceding discussion, it is plain that a joint venture is a feasible alternative to a merger or acquisition. By creating a third entity—a child—close cooperation is possible in specific areas, providing a way to explore new possibilities and meet anticipated competition without the disruption entailed in merging two established organizations.

However, a joint venture is inherently a rather unstable arrangement. The parents have to agree on the scope of cooperative activity, what each will contribute, and how outputs will be divided. Moreover, the child has to be economically viable, either directly or indirectly. Risks and opportunity costs must be weighed, and the joint-venture participants need skill in adjusting to changing situations confronting any or all of them.

Because joint ventures are difficult to sustain, the potential benefits of cooperating must be substantial. Indeed, the recent growth in the use of joint ventures reflects the urgency and opportunity many managers sense in the turbulent state of world affairs. The gains from some joint ventures will, in fact, be substantial.

## Corporate Input Strategy

We turn now to a different part of corporate strategy. Up to this point our discussion has focused on the kinds of business-units a corporation will have through designing the portfolio, adding units via acquisitions, and perhaps entering into a joint venture. The emphasis has been on picking winners.

But active corporations do more than make investments. They provide *inputs* which strengthen their various businesses. They try to give each business-unit some differential advantage that it could not muster if it operated independently. This is called "corporate *input* strategy."

Wide variation exists in the kind of inputs diversified corporations furnish to their business-units. Familiar inputs include low-cost capital, a supply of outstanding managers, or assured access to markets. More unusual is product and process knowledge that, for example, a pharmaceutical firm can supply to its veterinary affiliate or a central room-reservation service that a motel chain furnishes to its members.

Corporate inputs are any kind of resources, tangible or intagible, that a corporation obtains or generates and provides to its business-units.

Our focus here is on *major* inputs. Every corporation provides minor services for its operating units—stockholder relations, filing consolidated reports with governmental agencies, a logo to place on the letterhead, and the like. But these minor, usually necessary, activities do not significantly affect the fate of the business-units. Even such work as central purchasing or institutional advertising is typically helpful, but does not govern, the growth or death of specific business-units. Corporate input strategy concentrates on major actions which are fundamental to success; it adds yeast, not just seasoning.

The central issues of corporate input strategy are as follows:

1. Selecting a few kinds of contributions which the corporation will make to its business-units—contributions of such quality and value that the business-units gain a significant advantage over their competitors
2. Finding ways to develop a differential advantage in the "production" or "delivery" of such services
3. Integrating these strengths into portfolio selection and the corporate mission, and into the design of charters for business-units

Note that this view supports the concept, already stressed, that business-units are the primary operating segments of a diversified corporation. To the extent that it is practical, operating activities should be placed within these business-units. We would transfer operating activities to the corporate level only when the benefits of doing so are very high. In this sense, "corporate inputs" run counter to the basic pattern of decentralization. They are exceptions. Yet experience shows that when wisely selected and carefully administered, corporate inputs can be a powerful asset.

Let us first look at the way several typical corporate inputs can serve business-units; then, later in the chapter, we will consider the management of synergies.

## Low-Cost Capital

By far the most widely recognized aid that a parent corporation gives its operating units is growth capital. As is very clear in the cable TV arena, for example, a new business-unit often incurs losses for several years before it can build a profitable niche. Obtaining a franchise, stringing cable, signing up customers, constructing distribution gear—all require capital before income even starts to flow. And even an established venture needs working capital and fixed capital to grow.

A cash-rich parent is very convenient in such situations. Growth can proceed as rapidly as technology, markets, and environmental conditions warrant. Often it is possible to get a jump on competitors.

The parent corporation need not have cash in the bank (or flowing from owned cash cows) if it can raise new funds at a favorable cost. If its capital structure permits more debt and it enjoys a favorable credit rating, the corporation can borrow additional capital.

Or, if the parent corporation enjoys a high price-to-earnings ratio on its stock, equity capital may "cost" less than the business-unit would have to pay. In this manner, the financial strategy of the corporation builds a resource that strengthens the business-units.

Many recent mergers of large corporations which create newspaper headlines actually provide no financial benefits to the merged firms. For small firms, however, the cost of capital may be significantly lowered. So the crux is whether the diversified corporation can and will give its operating units a differential advantage with respect to the supply of capital.

## Outstanding Executives

Other corporate inputs may be as invigorating. For instance, a few corporations go to great lengths to develop a pool of unusually well-qualified managers. The pompous expression, "Our greatest strength is our people," may be accurate. Selection, training, and shared expertise are designed to give managers in such corporations a competitive edge.

To cite two examples, both General Electric and IBM give high priority to executive development. General Electric's training center at Crotonville, New York, is like a college for adults. IBM devotes even more effort and money to improving the capability of its upper level as well as lower level managers. The clear aim is to have outstanding managers who can be moved into various business-units.

When a corporation develops enough "depth" of able general managers, it (1) can fill a strategic post immediately instead of searching for an outsider, (2) need not devote time and effort "socializing" a new executive to the corporate culture, (3) does not tip off plans to outsiders by searching for a particular kind of manager in the open market, and (4) reinforces the message that this corporation provides great opportunities for its own people.

This is an ambitious strategy. It deals with a soft asset, compared with capital. The people are mobile and competitors may seduce them. There is doubt about how transferable to other kinds of business some of the skills and expertise will be. Nevertheless, the potential rewards are great. If a corporation does succeed in staffing its business-units with executives who can outdistance their competitors, a whole array of other strengths may be promoted.[2]

---

[2]The problems of finding executives well suited to execute a particular business-unit strategy are explored in Chapter 20.

## Corporate R & D

Useful, creative ideas that are scientifically tested are scarce and expensive. And for most laboratories to be effective, a "critical mass" (minimum number) of such ideas is necessary. One way to seek a flow of ideas and associated specialized laboratory services without loading high costs onto each business-unit is through a centralized R & D division.

For years, Bell Laboratories served the various operating companies of the AT & T system in this manner.[3] The worldwide pharmaceutical firms also typically centralize their research work (although separate problems may be studied at separate locations). The new products can then be sold by subsidiaries throughout the world.

Such research work is inherently risky. For example, over a 15-year period Xerox poured close to $200 million into its Palo Alto Research Center with the primary hope that the output would give Xerox a decisive lead in "total office systems." This goal has not been achieved. The Center has done impressive work that has led to a variety of useful products in the computer arena, but most of their products are being produced by other companies.

The aim in each of these cases is to create a powerful research group which makes contributions to the operating divisions—contributions that the divisions acting alone would be unable to achieve or even unlikely to investigate.

Centralized R & D has its drawbacks, among which are lack of responsiveness to operating needs, the pursuit of inconsequential questions, and reluctance to piggyback on the research of competitors. The more diversified the operating divisions, the more difficult these problems become. Nevertheless, the overall success with centralized research of such corporations as DuPont indicates that this can be a viable corporate input strategy.

## Centralized Marketing

The basic concept of a business-unit places control of major functions—engineering, production, marketing, etc.—within the unit. To a large extent, the unit is self-contained and autonomous; it runs its own show. Coordination between the functions and adjustments to the environment of each particular business are decentralized.

Occasionally, however, a corporation seeks to gain strength by defying the usual pattern. One such deviation is to withdraw parts of marketing from the business-units and to perform these particular activities in a corporate marketing division. In fact, this was the original strategy of General Foods Corporation. Each of the several companies that were merged into General Foods—among them

---

[3]The future of Bell Laboratories is clouded by the split-up of AT & T. The now independent units may be unwilling to support the kind of basic research which enabled Bell Laboratories to make pioneering developments such as that of the transistor.

Post Cereals, Jell-O, and Maxwell House Coffee—continued to buy, manufacture, package, price, and ship products as they had done previously. The key contribution of the new corporation was nationwide promotion and selling for all products. By combining selling and promotion into a single division, the corporation provided the several operating companies much more complete coverage and skillful promotion than any of the companies could muster when acting separately.

The large Japanese trading companies operate in a roughly similar way for the manufacturing companies they represent, although here the manufacturers maintain a more independent existence. The scope of activities performed for a manufacturer varies; often the trading company performs all the marketing functions, both in Japan and abroad. Sometimes the trading company also buys raw materials, and it may provide financing as well. With this assistance, small companies can concentrate on making a specialized line of products.

Such centralized marketing activity creates numerous problems of coordination, adequate attention to each product, and accountability. And as the product lines grow in size and diversity, the differential benefit of the pooled service diminishes. But again we observe the corporation searching for some special input it can provide so effectively to its business-units, that they enjoy a comparative advantage over competitors.

## Caution in Choice of Strategic Inputs

The choice of corporate inputs should be highly selective. A single corporation would rarely attempt to make inputs of strategic power in all of the areas mentioned. And there are other possibilities that may suit particular situations. For instance, a corporation operating worldwide may realize a status level and develop contacts in various nations which give its subsidiary a distinct boost in introducing products and services in those nations. Similarly, corporations dealing in "big ticket" items such as automobiles or major appliances might create a financing scheme to assist dealers in carrying inventory and extending installment credit to consumers.

Note that in each of these examples—low cost capital, outstanding managers, R & D capability, and central marketing, or even a more unusual input—the corporate strategy is to focus on just a few resources. Rarely is the development of such resources justified as a distinct business; instead, the resources have value only as they are distinctive inputs to the business-units. In effect, the corporation develops a select arsenal of exceptional resources. Then, by drawing from that arsenal to supplement their own resources, the business-units gain strengths which they cannot muster alone.

Many diversified corporations, in fact, provide few, if any, strategic inputs to their business-units. This is especially true of "conglomerates"—assemblies of established firms that have little relation to each other and are merely clustered in a passive holding company. The pressure to generate short-term profits and cash flow is often so great that the parent corporation is not even a good source of capital. Moreover, the development of a truly outstanding corporate resource is difficult, time consuming, and frequently expensive. Long-term commitment to a corporate input strategy is necessary. For these reasons, corporate management must select with care any input resources in which it undertakes to excel.

## Corporate Management of Synergies

In addition to providing strategically valuable "corporate inputs," diversified corporations may seek a differential advantage from synergy among their business-units.

Building synergy is a strategy of many diversified corporations. Thus, copper firms combine mining with smelting and extend on into wire-drawing, airlines own resort hotels (often to their regret), and newspapers form ties with local TV stations. The aim is to dovetail the operations of two or more business-units in the corporation's portfolio in a way that generates extra benefits.

Of course, in selecting business for the portfolio, *potential* synergies are among the factors considered. However, the actual achievement of synergy usually requires strong guidance. The interaction between business-units has to be shaped so that the desired reinforcement does occur. Corporate strategy sets this direction.

A quick review of several possible sources of synergy among business-units will illustrate the role corporate strategy can play.

## Vertical Integration

A corporation which published several monthly trade magazines bought out a firm which did most of its printing. The chief aim of the acquisition was to assure fast, adaptable printing service for the magazines—at normal industry prices. Under the guidance of the parent corporation CEO, this service objective is working well. The manager of the printing business, however, is not entirely happy. She is expected to obtain outside business to keep her shop busy when not printing magazines, yet she is not permitted to make major investments in equipment for that purpose unless it can also be used for the magazines. Clearly, in this simple case the corporate strategy to stress vertical integration takes priority over independent operation of the printing business. Although the printing unit is constrained, the total effect on all business-units combined is a net gain.

Marshall Field & Company's history reveals attempts at both forward and backward integration. The original company started by Mr. Field became a flourishing drygoods wholesaler throughout the Midwest. The first integration was forward—a retail department store in Chicago. This venture was also very successful (and is the hub of the present Marshall Field & Company). However, the Chicago outlet quickly took on a character of its own as *the* most prestigious store in the city. Increasingly, its requirements for high quality and distinctive merchandise could not be met by the wholesale division. The retail store buyers literally traveled throughout the world searching for products that would make the store unique. With this development, the transactions between the wholesale and retail divisions became fewer and fewer until the vertical integration was of little significance.

Meanwhile, a similar upstream expansion followed by independence occurred. Several of the wholesale departments started their own production, notably textile mills in North Carolina and Virginia. As wholesale requirements changed and declined, however, the mill managers opened their own sales offices in New York. Within 10 years, the mills' managers were focusing their primary attention on the styles and service desired by their New York customers. "Fieldcrest Mills" became a kingdom of its own.

Corporate executives definitely *did not* manage these shifts in mill activities. Rather, the changes reflected the initiative of the managers of what became separate business-units. Thus, the corporate executives were slow to recognize that the synergies they sought from vertical integration of the wholesale division and the mills were disappearing. Instead, they permitted the situation to drift until heavy losses finally forced a drastic realignment.

## Full Utilization of Raw Materials

Related to vertical integration is complete use of raw materials. To paraphrase an old meat-packing quip, synergy comes from utilizing every part of the pig but the squeal. A more recent example is found in the forest products industry. Peeler logs for plywood come only from the trunks of the trees, so a lumber mill is added to use the smaller pieces. Then the pulp-and paper-making is tied to lumber operations to utilize even smaller pieces, and some of the sawdust finds its way into particle board.

Each of the products—plywood, lumber, pulp and paper, and particle board—may be managed as a separate business-unit. However, the parent corporation is also concerned that the operations dovetail in a way that minimizes raw material costs and maximizes output of the most profitable components of the mix. The corporate task is to make the combined whole more valuable than the sum of the independent parts.

## Combined Services

Offering a combination of services or of products can be a source of synergy. Thus, in a household appliance industry the volume leaders have found synergies in selling or servicing a full line (refrigerators, freezers, dishwashers, disposals, ranges, washing machines, and dryers). Each product did have its competitors— for example, Maytag in washing machines and Tappan in gas ranges—and its special design issues, but one way to compete in this mature industry is for a corporation to promote full-line service to consumers.

Such synergies are difficult to achieve. The corporate task of coordinating the actions of several business-units is burdensome, and consumers may just not care about the joint effort. Combinations of ceiling fans and furniture, for instance, are rare, and fast-food restaurants don't sell groceries. So this kind of corporate strategy must be cautiously designed.

An area currently in flux is financial services. It is far from clear that consumes want to buy their life insurance at a bank or that help on income tax fits in with selling real estate.

Normally, a set of combined services must be backed up by a series of specialized business-units, each with its own technological and institutional constraints. If these supplying organizations take the limelight or pursue strictly parochial interests, little merging of services will occur. In contrast, if the corporation manages the synchronization of the services, the strategy has a much better chance of success.

In sum, portfolio selection of compatible business-units may make synergy possible. Realization of that synergy, however, depends on a corporate strategy that requires the separate units to integrate their activities on a few selected fronts. The synergy may be possible in vertical buy-and-sell relationships, in full utilization of a common raw material, in providing a synchronized set of services, or in some other reinforcing actions. But it is the corporate strategy which sets the priority to be attached to such integrated action. A strong strategy is necessary to turn independent enterprises (e.g., states) into a "federal" organization—"a more perfect union."

## Conclusion: Beyond the Portfolio

Corporate portfolio strategy is comparable to the "domain" in a business-unit strategy. In selecting its portfolio, a diversified corporation is picking a group of domains in which to operate. In effect, the corporation is placing, and then readjusting, its bets on attractive niches in attractive industries.

The domain, however, is just one of four parts of an action-oriented business-unit strategy, as outlined in Chapter 5. Sources of differential advantage, strategic thrusts, and target results are added elements—elements that are necessary to convert business-unit strategy from the mere selection of a battleground into a more focused, action-prompting directive. Similarly, corporate strategy should push beyond the selection of a portfolio.

Effective use of mergers to rearrange the corporate portfolio, discussed in the preceding chapter, is an active facet of corporate strategy. It deals with *strategic thrusts* at the corporate level.

In this chapter, we have focused on ways corporations can help make their business-units more potent. Forming joint ventures is one approach. The development of select corporate inputs is a second approach. As a third approach, a corporation may foster particular synergies. With imagination, corporate managers can undoubtedly devise still other ways to give their business-units increased strengths.

When we think of the actions a diversified corporation should take to develop its desired portfolio and to marshal its strategic inputs, a four-part corporate strategy emerges. This four-part strategy, which parallels business-unit strategy in nature, is outlined in Figure 17-2.

Just as a good business-unit strategy includes strategic thrusts and target results, so too does a good corporate strategy. The corporate strategic thrusts deal with (1) modifying the charters of existing business-units, (2) making acquisitions and divestments of business-units, and (3) mustering corporate inputs.

The corporate target results, or expectations, should normally include both financial and nonfinancial goals. Nonfinancial targets are often suggested by a review of the corporation's standing relative to key stakeholders. Milestone targets for specific dates will help the corporation convert the strategy into operating plans.

**FIGURE 17–2.**
**SCOPE OF ACTION-ORIENTED STRATEGY**

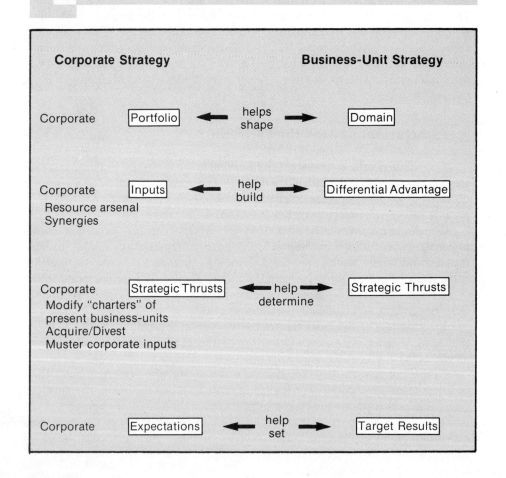

Clearly such a four-part strategy goes well beyond portfolio selection. It includes dynamic ways to strengthen the performance of the business-units that the corporation has selected.

## Questions for Class Discussion

1. A producers' co-op in Columbia (South America) ships airplane loads of cut flowers regularly to the United States—roses, carnations, orchids, and several other tropical varieties. The arrival cost per dozen is low by American standards. Federal Express has an overnight delivery system (mostly mail) to all major metropolitan areas in the continental United States. How about a joint venture? The child could accept orders for delivery of a specified kind and number of flowers to almost anyplace in the country any day. It would repack the requested flowers near the airport in specially designed cartons and turn them over to Federal Express for next-day delivery. They would arrive at the doorstep of the receiver fresher than flowers you buy at the local florist shop! For this proposed venture, discuss the propensity and power of each prospective parent, and also the viability of the child.

2. New United Motor Manufacturing's auto assembly plant in Fremont, California, is a joint venture of the General Motors and Toyota Corporations. Toyota runs the plant, which assembles subcompact cars for both parents to be sold in the U.S. While both parents want low-cost assembly of their cars, they have stated additional aims. General Motors wants to learn Toyota's labor-management techniques so that these can be spread throughout the corporation. Toyota wants to learn how to manage American workers so that these lessons can be applied to its new assembly plant in Kentucky. Does a review of the discussion of joint ventures in this chapter suggest to you that either or both parents probably have still other motives in setting up this joint venture?

3. The People's Republic of China has special laws to attract foreign joint ventures. The country wants technical know-how which can be used to raise the standard of living of its people, almost a quarter of the world's population. The legislation anticipates that a foreign parent would provide machinery and technological expertise, and would share with its Chinese counterpart the management of production. During the first 10 to 15 years of the joint venture's existence, the foreign parent will be allowed to repatriate from earnings (bring home) its investment and its share of the child's profits. At the end of the period the foreign partner's obligation and claim on profits will cease (unless new agreements have been made in the interim).

Setting aside the learning that both the Chinese and foreign parent have to do in a capitalistic/communist venture (which is substantial), do you think that joint ventures are a good mechanism for introducing Western technology into China? What are the advantages, and what problems do you foresee?

4. State University has an organization called MBA Consultants. Under its sponsorship, MBA candidates serve as volunteer consultants to small business firms that need managerial advice. Many, but not all, of these firms are minority owned and operated. Recently, a common assignment has been the introduction of a personal computer-based accounting and control system. In fact, the requests for this kind of service have grown to a level that has prompted the government's local Small Business Administration (SBA) office to suggest a joint venture. The parents would be the SBA and MBA Consultants, and the child would be a new corporation with a director and secretary plus part-time MBA candidates. Low fees to clients would cover all out-of-pocket expenses. Do you think that a joint venture is a good way to manage this activity? Would you like to have the job of director?

5. "My family has been in the health and diet food business for years," explains Sandra Lombardo. "We have a second division that sells beauty products; our angle there is skin nutrition. I believe that we should expand into related equipment. We are working on an acquisition of a firm that makes a deluxe line of personal hair dryers. Another possibility is a firm that makes sunlamps, including heat lamps. A further possibility that fits in with the current health trend is indoor exercises for the home—cycles, rowing exercisers, gym benches, and the like." Assuming that the Lombardo Corporation did acquire business-units in the three areas suggested, what major corporate input should it try to furnish to these operating divisions? What opportunities for synergy do you see?

6. At the time Joseph Flavin became president of the Singer Company, the company had the following major business-units: (a) consumer sewing machines, (b) industrial sewing machines, (c) electric power tools (e.g., drills, saws, and hedge trimmers) made for Sears Roebuck, (d) furniture, (e) control products (e.g., switches, thermostats, and valves) sold in large volume to home appliance and automobile manufacturers, (f) air conditioners, (g) residential gas meters, (h) navigation systems for aircraft and marine vessels, and (i) simulators for training aircraft pilots. Each of these separate business-units had sales of at least $100 million. However, the corporation was heavily in debt and earning low profits. What strategic corporate input, if any, do you think Singer should have provided at that time? Explain.

7. As mentioned in the text, "Fast-food restaurants don't sell groceries." Grocery stores, on the other hand, do sell fast foods. In the "convenience markets" (e.g., Circle K and 7-Eleven stores) you can buy milk, coffee, soft drinks, sandwiches (either cold or heated in a microwave oven), and pastries. In large supermarkets, such as Safeway and Giant Food stores, you can buy delicatessen items to be consumed on the premises or taken out, as is also the case in some

convenience stores. Why would grocery stores sell fast foods, but fast-food restaurants not sell groceries?

8. In the former American Telephone & Telegraph Company (AT&T), the parent corporation provided several inputs to its state and regional operating companies, including the use of product and other technical patents coming out of Bell Laboratories; a source of standardized and testing equipment manufactured by the Western Electric Company; an accounting system and array of operating ratios, along with reports comparing the performance of the several operating companies; equity capital, and often a guarantee of operating company bonds; a strong system for obtaining synergy in operations, notably compatible equipment and technology which greatly facilitated long-distance communication throughout the country; and availability of a number of consulting services dealing with human resource problems.

   The breakup of AT&T operations into fully independent, self-contained regional companies puts an end to most of these inputs. For the present, the former traditions persist, but Judge Greene, who presided over the breakup, is systematically curtailing "Ma Bell's" centralized influence. Meanwhile, managements of the newly created regional organizations are using their independence to meet rising competition from companies outside of the old system.

   From what you have read or heard about the new regional setup, do you anticipate that the operating companies will suffer a lot in the future from the withdrawal or reduction of AT&T corporate inputs?

9. (a) Use a specific example to illustrate each of the four horizontal relationships between corporate and business-unit strategy shown in Figure 17–2. For the example, use a corporation that you know, or one of the cases you have studied which involves a diversified corporation, or a university and one of its schools. (b) How well does a well-developed corporate input strategy affect the charter for one of the business-units in the entity you chose in part (a)?

10. To succeed in the highly competitive, mature major appliance industry, White Consolidated needs a long-run corporate input strategy. White grew by buying out low-profit or losing brands—Gibson, Kelvinator, Hamilton, Westinghouse, Philco, and Frigidaire. It has realized at best modest profits by consolidating plants and cutting overhead and labor costs of these brands. Competition from strong, full-line manufacturers like G.E. and Whirlpool has intensified. Should White (a) force on its divisions a continued restricted cash flow, (b) sell a full line using one or two brand names by focusing plants on a single appliance and using centralized marketing with aggressive sales promotion to reduce the overhead costs of each division, or (c) sell private-label products without any marketing costs? Each plant would then focus on low-cost, high-quality production. Note that private-label selling is common for major appliances: Whirlpool sells to Sears, and Admiral sells refrigerators and freezers to 10 other companies with their labels. What do you recommend for White?

# CASE

## 17 Trintex Joint Venture*

The Trintex Corporation—a joint venture established in 1983 by CBS, IBM, and Sears Roebuck—hopes to launch a nationwide videotex service. It is an ambitious undertaking which might significantly modify consumer business patterns.

Videotex and similar systems focus on *two-way* communication between large business concerns and individual consumers via electronic channels. The distinguishing feature of such systems is *interaction*; the person on the receiving end can talk back.

Many people believe that interactive communication systems have a great future, involving millions of users and billions of dollars. Several relatively simple systems are already in use. For example, Dow Jones & Co. has 155,000 subscribers to its "News/Retrieval" service; individuals with a personal computer and a telephone hookup can draw data from Dow Jones's bank of financial reports and news releases on many large corporations—with more general statistics and news available as a bonus. In banking, the Chemical Bank of New York has a home-banking service with 20,000 of its customers which enables them to transfer funds, make investments, and complete other transactions that normally would be done at a branch bank (or automatic teller machine).

The major uses of videotex in the near future are expected (or hoped) to be (a) business transactions such as home-banking and (b) sale of merchandise which is displayed and described, at the customer's request, on a video or computer screen in the customer's home. Other potential applications of videotex include retrieval of all sorts of information, interactive games, education courses, tax advice, "electronic mail" (including the transmission and storage of photographic images), and the like.

The Trintex joint venture is seeking a "flexible system" that utilizes telephone transmission lines connected with personal computers in subscribers' homes or offices. The three partners have equal ownership. CBS is interested in program design and marketing; IBM is developing hardware design; and Sears is a very large potential user of videotex services. The new corporation is to be staffed with employees of the partners.

In fact, the entire development of videotex is in a state of flux. So, to assess the Trintex venture, we need to look at (1) the videotex technology and system design, (2) competition, (3) the evolving interests of Trintex's partners, and (4) future prospects.

---

*Adapted from three longer cases written by Professor K.R. Harrigan (with assistance from J. G. Michel and N. T. Backaitis), Columbia University Graduate School of Business. Based largely on published materials.

## Technology and System Design

Although well-known communication, computer, and video technology makes videotex possible, a practical and dominant system has not yet emerged. The main variables are indicated in Figure 17–3.

One reason why the design of interactive systems has not yet stabilized is the variety of potential uses (see the leftmost column of the figure). Bank transaction services, for instance, do not require pictures in color, whereas merchandise sales and entertainment probably do. However, the total investment in a widespread system is so large that a single use of a system may be impractical.

**FIGURE 17–3.**
**MAJOR SYSTEM COMPONENTS OF TWO-WAY ELECTRONIC INFORMA-
TION SERVICES FOR HOMES AND SMALL BUSINESSES**

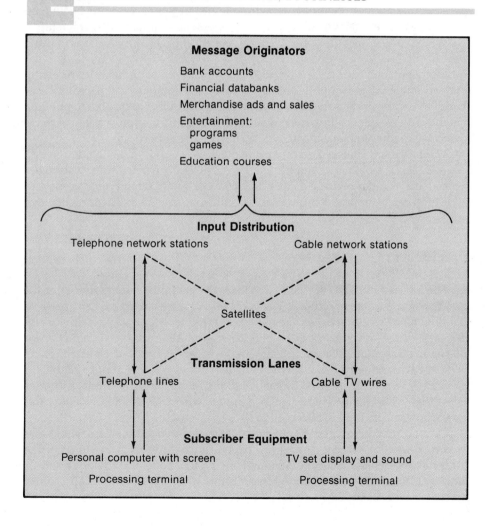

A significant distinction in services provided lies in the differences between "teletext" and "videotex." In teletext systems, subscribers can ask for various kinds of data, and receive numbers and words in response. In contrast, videotex encourages further interaction, and for the more sophisticated systems the response will be in color, include pictures (graphics), and even have movement and voice as in television broadcasts. Of course, each feature in addition to "text only" adds to the expense of creating, transmitting, and receiving the reply.

A second basic issue in system design is whether to use cable TV lines or telephone lines to transmit messages. The equipment and technology of the two modes are so different that head-end senders must select one or the other exclusively. Cable TV lines can carry a richer message, but they do not reach as many homes as do telephone lines.

Related to the transmission issue is the kind of receiving equipment which consumers (including business users) must have. Systems relying on transmission by telephone lines are being designed to tie into personal computers equipped with display panels, but not all consumers possess such equipment. Ownership of television sets is more widespread, but there are technical complications in using some of these sets for receiving.

Many potential subscribers to videotex much prefer equipment for receiving and sending that is simple and easy to use—equipment that is really "user friendly." On the other hand, some subscribers would like to be able to put data that they receive directly into their local computer for further processing, perhaps to decide whether to make changes in their investment portfolio.

The foregoing choices and other more technical issues make the design of a total videotex system very complicated. Nevertheless, great pressure exists to become an early leader because a head start with consumer familiarity, experience-curve effects on equipment and service production, and government regulations will establish substantial entry barriers for competitors.

## Videotex Competition

The forecasts for sales of electronic interactive communication services are indeed rosy. For example, Predicast, Inc., a Cleveland market research firm, predicts that one out of five homes will be equipped for videotex or teletext services by 1995, resulting in revenues of $11.5 billion per year. A more modest prediction by International Resource Development, Inc., foresees 4.5 million subscribers by 1992; at $40 per month per subscriber, the revenues would be about $2.2 billion per year, but a recently revised figure of $25 per month cuts the annual revenues to less than $1.4 billion. These figures compare with an estimated videotex and teletext revenue in 1986 of $45 million.

Even though these forecasts are generally considered optimistic, a whole succession of well-known companies has been attracted to this field. To date, the losses have been large, many companies have dropped out, and a wide variety of joint ventures have been reformed in an effort to find an economically sound system.

Warner Communications tested the first two-way cable television system, called "QUBE," in Columbus, Ohio, starting in 1977. As the venture expanded to other cities, the necessary investment became so large that Warner Communications sold a 50 percent interest in the business to American Express. By 1983, QUBE had 1,360,000 subscribers and a cumulative loss of over $100 million. Two years later both partners were seeking ways to withdraw.

The QUBE experience by no means discouraged other entrants. Here is a sample of the competitors that entered the fray: Dow Jones's "News/Retrieval" faces competition from Citicorp and Merrill Lynch's "Quotron"; from H&R Block's "CompuServe"; from IBM and Merrill Lynch's "International Market Net"; and to a lesser extent from Readers Digest's "Source." Both Time, Inc., and McGraw-Hill have also been in this teletext arena.

Several combinations of banks are experimenting with home banking, with the prospect of creating a service to compete with Bankers Trust's network. Chase Manhattan Bank set up an experiment with Cox Cable Communications in 1984, but dropped the project in 1985.

The videotex systems also have a mixed experience. Two active participants, Times Mirror Co. and Knight-Ridder Newspapers, Inc., unexpectedly withdrew in March 1986. Each of these firms offered somewhat elaborate services; for instance, the Knight-Ridder "full graphics" required a special $600 receiver. The trade press suggests that "text-only" competition stole the subscribers.[1]

On the other hand, AT&T is ready to reenter the videotex field if it can circumvent its consent decree from the Justice Department. Digital Equipment Corporation is seeking a partner in this field also, as is J.C. Penney.

The foregoing list of competitors is far from complete. There is a lot of moving in and out of the industry, usually as a partner in a joint venture. Clearly, (1) electronic interactive communication continues to attract strong, well-managed companies, and (2) an effective, synergistic combination of technology and customer service continues to be elusive.

## Evolving Interests of Trintex Partners

### CBS

When Trintex was formed, CBS was probably the most enthusiastic partner. At that time CBS was actively seeking ways to reduce its dependence on regular broadcasting. Its flagship operations were its national TV and radio networks. In

---

[1]Videotex subscriptions have languished in Japan and Germany also. However, videotex is thriving in France, where DGT, the government telecommunications authority, gives away most of the equipment and earns fees for the use of the videotex network. The French system is very simple and cheap—no high-resolution graphics, no color, no access to huge databases—because its sponsor believes that nobody really needs (or will pay for) such fancy service. Residential customers in France use videotex to chat (leave messages for other subscribers) or to get quick answers to requests like asking for telephone numbers. Commercial customers use videotex to improve the efficiency of multisite operating units.

addition, it owned five local TV stations and several radio stations. Although these are all profitable, there is some risk of erosion of network viewing. (Condensed earnings and balance sheet statements for CBS, IBM, and Sears are presented in Table 17–1.)

CBS diversification included highly successful production and marketing of music records and cassettes, motion picture films, and books. In these and related areas, CBS considered creative marketing one of its greatest strengths.

Other diversification moves have been related to *telecommunications technology*. For instance, CBS Technology Center joined with AT&T and representatives of the Canadian and French governments in establishing teletext standards. Also, beginning in 1981, CBS and AT&T made a series of tests on the commercial viability of videotex systems. (The alliance with AT&T was discontinued when CBS concluded that potential subscribers would not purchase "dedicated" terminals, i.e., terminals useful only for videotex services.) Experiments with video games and with advertiser-supported cable television programming were also carried out, but were discontinued in 1986.

**Table 17–1.**
**Condensed Earnings and Balance Sheets, 1985 (in millions)**

*CBS*

| | |
|---|---:|
| Revenues | $4,123 |
| Expenses | |
|    Cost of sales | 2,773 |
|    Selling, general & administrative | 1,055 |
|    Research & development | -0- |
|    Interest, etc. | 65 |
|       Total expenses | 3,893 |
| Operating income before tax | 230 |
| Income tax | 82 |
| Net operating income | 148 |
| Loss on disposals & minority | |
|       interests | (37) |
| Net income | $ 111 |

| Assets | | Liabilities & Equity | |
|---|---:|---|---:|
| Cash & equivalent | $ 28 | Accounts payable | $ 181 |
| Receivables (net) | 734 | Current long-term debt | 42 |
| Inventories | 306 | Unearned revenues | 199 |
| Program rights | 439 | Deferred tax | 14 |
| Prepared expenses | 172 | Accrued items | 600 |
|    Total | 1,679 |    Total | 1,036 |
| Property, plant & equipment | 626 | Long-term debt | 378 |
| Minority investments | 138 | Deferred tax | 79 |
| Intangibles | 386 | Shareholder equity | 1,336 |
|    Total | $2,829 |    Total | $2,829 |

**Table 17–1.** (*continued*)
**Condensed Earnings and Balance Sheets, 1985 (in millions)**

*IBM*

| | |
|---|---:|
| Revenues | $40,921 |
| Expenses | |
| Cost of sales | 16,395 |
| Selling, general & administrative | 10,614 |
| Research & development | 3,582 |
| Interest, etc. | 390 |
| Total expenses | 30,981 |
| Operating income before tax | 9,940 |
| Income tax | 4,455 |
| Net operating income | 5,485 |
| Loss on minority interests | 3 |
| Net income | $ 5,482 |

| Assets | | Liabilities & Equity | |
|---|---:|---|---:|
| Cash & equivalent | $ 5,536 | Accounts payable | $ 1,253 |
| Receivables (net) | 6,222 | Current long-term debt | 532 |
| Inventories | 4,381 | Unearned revenues | 382 |
| Total | 17,330 | Deferred tax | 3,220 |
| Rental assets (net) | 4,866 | Accrued items | 3,775 |
| Property, plant & equip. | 11,276 | Total | 9,162 |
| Minority investments | 3,989 | Long-term debt | 4,149 |
| | | Deferred tax | 931 |
| | | Shareholder equity | 23,219 |
| Total | $37,461 | Total | $37,461 |

Sears Roebuck & Co.

| | |
|---|---:|
| Revenues | $19,951 |
| Expenses | |
| Cost of sales | 12,456 |
| Selling, general & administrative | 5,911 |
| Interest, etc. | 1,007 |
| Total expenses | 19,374 |
| Operating income before tax | 577 |
| Income tax | 258 |
| Net operating income | 319 |
| Minority interest income | 518 |
| Net income | $ 837 |

| Assets | | Liabilities & Equity | |
|---|---:|---|---:|
| Cash | $ 321 | Accounts payable | $ 1,895 |
| Receivables (net) | 7,168 | Current long-term debt | 97 |
| Inventories | 3,092 | Unearned revenues | 483 |
| Prepaid expenses | 289 | Deferred tax | 918 |
| Total | 10,870 | Accrued items | 6,548 |
| Property, plant & equip. | | Total | 9,941 |
| (net) | 2,855 | Long-term debt | 1,903 |
| Minority investments (net) | 7,202 | Deferred tax | 271 |
| Total | $20,927 | Shareholder equity | 8,812 |
| | | Total | $20,927 |

From this background, CBS brought to Trintex considerable knowledge about what potential subscribers want in videotex services, as well as familiarity with programming and software problems.

Unlike the service CBS offered with AT&T, the planned Trintex venture's service would not require a special display terminal or a cable television connection. Instead, it would be accessible through telephone lines. Trintex intends to develop considerable software to offer with its service, but several technical and commercial difficulties still must be overcome.

All of this experimenting is expensive. Both product design and technological hurdles have delayed finding a configuration that can be promoted nationwide. Trintex was formed to overcome these obstacles. For CBS management, however, a natural question is how long to underwrite such up-front investment. With CBS net earnings coming in far below management's projections, answering this question has become a serious matter.

### IBM

IBM's perspective on Trintex is as a research project in one of many areas where its equipment might be used. IBM is not in the entertainment or banking business, where, for instance, videotex services would be an aid to its other consumer-related services.

As the world's leading producer of data processing equipment, with related software and maintenance service, IBM focused for a long time on commercial, governmental, and research applications. Its major sources of competitive strength in these areas have been the high *quality* of its products and services and persistent investment in technology to lower its production costs.

Only recently has IBM become a major factor in telecommunications—for example, with its joint venture work with Aetna Insurance and Comstat in Satellite Business Systems and its acquisition of ROLM Corporation—*and* in personal computers (PCs).

With its entry into these new arenas, IBM modified two of its previous policies. It now purchases from outside vendors significant portions of the parts for its PCs, whereas formerly it made most of its parts. Also, IBM has entered into more joint ventures so as to tap the know-how and established market positions of other firms. Trintex is an example of this willingness to pool different strengths in order to establish promptly a firm position in developing areas.

Sharing of investment risks is less important to IBM than to most other companies. IBM spends over $2 billion a year on research and development and is in strong financial condition, so it can afford to experiment in areas that show promise of high growth. For instance, in 1983 IBM acquired ROLM to quickly learn more about combining personal computing with advanced voice and data communications in a single unit. This combination is important in the development of office automation, and some of the office automation technology is related to the technical problems concerning videotex.

From IBM's perspective, Trintex is an "experiment" that may offer attractive benefits in the future. IBM houses several such experiments at its Tarrytown research facility, where over 2,000 engineers are working on technological problems related to Trintex and its sister communications ventures.

### Sears Roebuck & Co.

Sears brings to Trintex a potential user viewpoint. Indeed, Sears might use videotex in both of its primary business groups: merchandising and financial services.

Sears has been the largest nonfood retailer in the country for a long time. Starting as a mail-order house a century ago, it has added suburban retail stores, phone-order service, and over 1,400 catalog sales offices. It now has sales of around $20 billion, and more than 36 million families count on Sears for part of their merchandise needs.

A major strength of Sears is its national reputation for dependable, fairly priced products. With this reputation and an efficient distribution system already established, Sears is interested in getting its products presented to an increasing number of prospective customers. Videotex, then, is one possibility for increasing its sales exposure.

In fact, in November 1986, Sears took a new step to reach consumers through television. QVC, an organization that creates home shopping programs for broadcast over cable TV systems, began daily shows of Sears merchandise. QVC has agreements with 26 major cable systems serving more than five million subscribers. It is *not* a two-way hookup: customers who want to purchase an item displayed will have to either phone Sears or send in a mail order. Nevertheless, the response to these home shopping presentations will provide some indication of the potential for videotex programs.

A recent strategic move by Sears is major expansion in its activities in consumer financial services. For many years Sears has operated the Allstate Insurance Company, a successful nationwide automobile and casualty insurer. Then, in the early 1980s, Sears made major moves to enlarge its financial activities. It acquired Coldwell Banker, the second largest real estate broker in the country, and also Dean Witter Reynolds Organization, a leading securities brokerage firm. These three arms—insurance, real estate, and securities—provide the basis for Sears Financial Network, which will have offices in many of Sears retail stores in addition to the wide-ranging branches of Coldwell Banker and Dean Witter Reynolds.

Sears hopes that its reputation for dependability will help its Financial Network reach many new customers. Also, Sears' millions of credit cards are being converted to general credit cards to compete with Visa and MasterCards. A small bank has been acquired as a toehold in commercial banking.

Whether videotex can be adapted to help Sears Financial Network remains to be seen.

From the viewpoint of Sears, Trintex primarily offers excellent *long-term* promise for entry into an industry that will expand rapidly and revolutionize how residential consumers as well as firms do business. Yet the project is risky because the idea of videotex communications is not as well accepted as Sears had hoped it would be by 1987. By agreeing to make Trintex a telephone-line-only configuration, for example, Sears could be cutting its venture out of a lucrative portion of the market.

To date, Sears has been a passive partner in the Trintex venture: the system design has yet to reach a point where Sears personnel have much to contribute.

## Future Prospects for Trintex

Financial statements prepared by Trintex management are given in Table 17–2. These show that operating results are improving and that a break-even situ-

**Table 17–2.**
**Trintex Corporation Income Statement (in millions)**

|  | Pro Forma 1984 | 1985 | Management Estimates 1986 |
|---|---|---|---|
| Revenues: |  |  |  |
| Net sales | $ 50 | $ 138 | $240 |
| Interest & other income | 9 | 12 | 16 |
| Total revenues | 59 | 150 | 256 |
| Expenses: |  |  |  |
| Cost of sales | 75 | 91 | 118 |
| Selling, general & administrative | 41 | 53 | 78 |
| Research & development | 9 | 9 | 17 |
| Interest, etc. | 8 | 8 | 14 |
| Total expenses | 133 | 161 | 227 |
| Operating income | (74) | (11) | 29 |
| Income tax | — | — | 10 |
| Net income after tax | $(74) | $(11) | $ 19 |

**Balance Sheet**
**(in millions)**

|  |  |  |  |
|---|---|---|---|
| *Assets* |  |  |  |
| Cash & equivalents | $153 | $159 | $176 |
| Accounts & notes receivable | 17 | 25 | 32 |
| Inventories | 23 | 24 | 33 |
| Program rights & prepared expenses | 8 | 7 | 15 |
| Total current assets | 201 | 215 | 256 |
| Property, plant & equipment | 63 | 50 | 70 |
| Intangibles | 30 | 7 | 13 |
| Total assets | 294 | 272 | 339 |
| *Liabilities and Equity* |  |  |  |
| Accounts & notes payable | 3 | 4 | 9 |
| Unearned revenues | 18 | 6 | 21 |
| Short-term borrowing from parents | 8 | 2 | 6 |
| Accrued expenses | 10 | 6 | 18 |
| Total current liabilities | 39 | 18 | 54 |
| Long-term debt | 15 | 15 | 37 |
| Shareholder equity | 240 | 229 | 248 |
| Total liabilities & equity | $294 | $272 | $339 |

ation may be reached by the end of 1986. The figures are not like the customary financial reports for several reasons: (1) The important results, progress with program and equipment design, are not reported at all. Indeed, IBM advances on equipment design are highly confidential. (2) Almost all work is being performed on the partners' premises and is billed out as though it were a subcontract. (3) Trintex management has been very anxious to show a small profit and, to achieve this, has purchased and resold a substantial amount of electronic equipment and sponsored other activities that brought in immediate income. (4) Trintex has not yet marketed a regular videotex service to subscribers.

The major event affecting Trintex's future is a change in management at CBS. In some jockeying to avoid an unfriendly takeover, Loews Corporation became the dominant stockholder of CBS. Late in 1986 Mr. Laurence A. Tisch, Loew's head, also took over the reins at CBS. A resulting back-to-basics effort at CBS includes trimming out projects which will require substantial infusions of capital before they become profitable. One part of this housecleaning is a CBS announcement that it is dropping out of Trintex.

Consequently, IBM and Sears must now decide what they will do with the Trintex joint venture.

## Questions

1. If you were advising IBM, would you recommend continuing the joint venture with only Sears, assuming that CBS does withdraw?
2. Based on the data in the case, do you predict that Trintex will be an active, successful joint venture in 1990?

# INTEGRATING CASES

## Diversified Corporation Strategy

## PHILLIPS FIBRE DIVISION[1]

Lee Roberts, vice-president of The Woods Corporation and general manager of its Phillips Fibre Division, is uncertain as to just how to state his reply to a letter and telephone call from James Herbert, executive vice-president of the parent corporation in charge of all its operations. Herbert has reminded Lee Roberts of the conclusion reached at the last meeting of the parent corporation's operating committee that it probably would be beneficial to the entire firm for the Phillips Fibre Division to attempt to increase its sales revenue markedly by widening its present product line, by selling in new geographical areas, and by developing new products. Lee Roberts is not a member of The Woods Corporation's operating committee, but his boss, group vice-president Halyard, is. Halyard had acquainted Lee Roberts with the general sense of the committee meeting and had told Roberts that he would hear from James Herbert, who heads the operating committee.

Lee Roberts knows that his reply will be that he does not agree with the suggestions about his division's products, but he has held off making a reply until he has devised a positive action that he could recommend to the committee.

The Woods Corporation is a conglomerate with sales revenue last year of $800 million, post-tax profits of $20 million, and a return on stockholder equity of about 8 percent. These results can be compared with the average results for all conglomerates of a 3.6 percent return on sales and a 10 percent return on common equity. All industry composite averages were about 4.5 percent and 12 percent, respectively.

The corporation's operating organization consists of four product groups, each reporting to a group vice-president who, in turn, reports to James Herbert. The four product groups are made up of various divisions as shown in Table 1.

In general, the divisions operate as strategic, business-units, with careful attention paid to some of them by central management as their fortunes vary.

The corporation is now about 20 percent smaller than it was several years ago, and its retained earnings account has been reduced as various divisions have

---

[1]Phillips Fibre sells fiberglass reinforced panels for use in building construction as skylights and translucent panels.

**TABLE 1.**
**THE WOODS CORPORATION**

| Group | Sales Revenue (approximate) | Division |
|---|---|---|
| 1. Paints, coatings, and abrasives | $300 million | 4 paint companies, 2 specialty chemical companies, and 1 abrasive firm |
| 2. Metal buildings, siding, and outdoor furniture | $175 million | 1 metal building and siding company and 1 outdoor furniture firm |
| 3. Automotive and garden equipment | $220 million | 6 automotive parts suppliers and 1 garden and farm equipment company |
| 4. Miscellaneous products | $105 million | 1 wine division, 1 liquor division, 3 textile companies, and Phillips Fibre Division |

been sold off at a capital loss.[2] These changes have taken place subsequent to the promotion to chair of the board and chief executive officer of Thomas Roberts, who had long been the executive vice-president of the parent corporation. Thomas Roberts replaced his uncle, William Roberts, who had built the firm from a small, family-owned metalworking shop to somewhat more than its present size. William retired at age 70 and immediately set out on a three-year around-the-world trip in his 80-foot schooner. He has successfully navigated the Atlantic and Indian Oceans and, at last report, was somewhere in the South Pacific, near the Fiji Islands. Lee Roberts is his grandson and the nephew of Thomas Roberts. Lee's father, Thomas's brother, is the skipper of his father's schooner. At last count, the Roberts family owned about 12 percent of The Woods Corporation's voting stock, with the shares equally split among 10 family members. The balance of the shares are publicly owned: two mutual fund investment companies own about 9 percent each of this stock, and no other public holding amounts to more than 0.5 percent of the stock.

The financial community has generally approved the efforts undertaken on Thomas Roberts's initiative. The price-to-earnings ratio of the common stock has climbed steadily to its current reporting of 10, which can be contrasted with its level of 5 a little over two years ago.

---

[2]Including a paper tape manufacturer, a matress maker and distributor, a tableware company, and a bicycle maker.

As part of its effort to revitalize the corporation, central management is now turning its attention to the more profitable divisions in the hopes that sales and profits can be increased further. Phillips Fibre is just such a profitable division. Over the past five years its sales have increased at 2 percent per year in real terms (2 percentage points above annual inflation rates), its pretax contribution to the parent corporation's overhead and financial expense is now 25 percent of its sales, and its return on net assets has grown from 20 to 30 percent.[3] The Woods Corporation's "par" for return on net assets is 20 percent, a figure attained by only a few of its divisions.

Lee Roberts believes that his division's strategy is well known throughout the corporation. Phillips Fibre concentrates on sales to only two of the various market segments that make up the FRP (fibre–reinforced plastic) market.[4] It does this because it has well-established positions in these segments based on its contacts through the metal buildings division of The Woods Corporation and its product quality, which is especially adapted to corrosive atmospheres.

In his reply to James Herbert, Lee Roberts plans to state that the division's favorable results have come about through his constant attention to customer service problems, through minimizing the number of salespersons so that sales per individual is about 20 percent higher than that of the principal competitors, through keeping the division's overhead expense low, through dropping the cost-of-goods-sold account to 55 percent of sales (an unusually low amount for manufacturing companies), and through his spending all the time he has available on his supervisory and planning work.

Halyard told Lee Roberts that the operating committee considered the following four ideas at its meeting:

1.   Phillips Fibre's panels are suitable for the liner panel segment of the market as a result of their corrosion resistance and their potentially large size, which will be allowed by some new equipment recently installed.

2.   The high-quality polyester resins used by Phillips Fibre to coat, mesh with, and adhere to the glass mats can be made by one of the specialty chemical firms after some equipment is added. Vertical integration has proven to be profitable to The Woods Corporation, as in the case of the aluminum rolling and shaping machinery purchased by the metal siding division so that it could make its product directly from aluminum ingots and no longer buy the shapes from outside suppliers.

3.   Investment in equipment will turn some of the parent corporation's excess cash into working assets. As a result of selling off various divisions, the firm has excess cash of about $50 million.

---

[3]The return on net assets is calculated as profits after expenses, but before interest and taxes, divided by net assets. Since the net asset figure typically is a larger amount than the stockholders' equity, the return on net assets will ordinarily be reported as less than the return on stockholders' equity. Net assets equal working capital plus the book value of fixed assets.

[4]See the Alpha Pyro Glass, Inc., integrating case on pages 225–233 for an analysis of this market and its various competitors.

4.   Lee Roberts has proven his ability as a division manager and so could clearly manage a larger division.

Roberts's reaction is that the chemical company's ability to make the polyester resin of the quality that is necessary is only a dream at the moment. The firm has no experience in making a similar resin. He also likes his job just the way it is and his location in northern Indiana on the shore of Lake Michigan.

Further, if central management is interested in improving its position with the fibre–reinforced plastics panel trade, it should attempt to buy out Alpha Pyro Glass.[5] Several years ago, according to various industry sources, the large oil company which owns APG decided that it would sell off APG because the firm did not fit in with the oil company's basic strategy of finding, mining, and selling basic minerals and energy products. The oil company also wishes to decrease its position in petrochemicals and petroleum-based fibers and resins because the Saudis will soon expand the world's supply of petrochemicals greatly when their huge plant on the Red Sea comes onstream. The sale of APG has not yet taken place because it has been a consistently profitable division with steadily increasing sales.

From his knowledge of the market and competitors, Lee Roberts has concluded that APG has first-rate marketing which has overcome the disadvantage of a high-cost manufacturing process and an out-of-date production system. A new manufacturing manager has recently taken over production at APG at the insistence of the parent company. The central manager of the division is something of an enigma because the high costs and the out-of-date production system have been tolerated for many years. He is also known as something of a maverick when it comes to complying with the forecasting, planning, and budgeting requirements of the parent company. This Texas-based company also has a plant in South Carolina.

Phillips Fibre buys its polyester resins from the same firm that supplies Alpha Pyro Glass, so Lee Roberts has an indirect contact with his competitor. From his knowledge of the market, he estimates that APG's sales are somewhere in the range of $22 to $27 million. He also suspects that its operating profit before any allocation of parent company overhead is in the range of 12 to 15 percent of sales.

## Questions

1.  What is your opinion as to the wisdom of the acquisition of Alpha Pyro Glass, Inc., by The Woods Corporation? What price seems right to you? How will the acquired firm be managed and directed?
2.  What and how should Lee Roberts reply to James Herbert?
3.  As James Herbert, what would you like to see done about the Phillips Fibre Division? As group vice-president Halyard, what would you do?

---

[5]A detailed description of this company is given in the case on pages 225–233.

# Managing RCA Within G.E.

The RCA Corporation, at the time of this writing, has just agreed to be acquired by the General Electric Company for approximately $6.3 billion, or $66.50 per share of common stock. This case focuses on how General Electric will manage its new acquisition so as to get the maximum benefits from this large outlay. We first briefly describe RCA and then look at the components and the overall management structure of G.E.

## RCA

### Recent RCA History

RCA has just gone through a process of reversing its lackluster performance during the previous decade. A direct descendant of two outstanding technological successes, wireless telegraphy and home talking machines, RCA has long been a prestigious corporation.

The company's activities range from basic research in communication technology to mass media contact with the public through NBC, its nationwide TV network. The glamor of RCA research laboratories is combined with the glitter of NBC's programming. RCA is a leading brand name on both stereo records and TV receiving sets.

However, RCA products have been more impressive than its management skills, especially at the corporate level. The company's founder, General Sarnoff, was a far better promoter than manager; indeed, his indifference to sound administration set a pattern that has plagued RCA up to the present. In general, the economic performance of the company has been checkered.

Following General Sarnoff's reluctant retirement, top management problems were complicated first by a period of unwise diversification which greatly increased the company debt. Then came a siege of inept "bottom-line" consolidation moves. Senior management was weak throughout these gyrations.

To rectify these mistakes, T. F. Bradshaw, formerly president of ARCO, the well-known petroleum firm, was appointed CEO. Bradshaw had four main objectives: (1) to refocus the company on its three core businesses, viz., electronics, communications, and entertainment; (2) to strengthen the balance sheet by reducing the company's debt relative to its assets and equity; (3) to restructure top management; and (4) to provide a successor to himself (Bradshaw was close to retirement age when he took the job).

Achieving the first objective involved liquidating several small subsidiaries and selling off CIT, a billion-dollar commercial financing company, and the Hertz auto rental business. In addition, an unpleasant decision was to give up sales of video disc players and write off $175 million of related assets. This refocusing has now been completed. The continuing divisions of RCA are briefly described in Appendix A, and their financial results are shown in Table 1.

**Table 1.**
**RCA Sales and Pretax Income by Business Segments, 1985 (in millions)**

|  | Sales | Pretax Income | Assets Identified with Business Segments |
|---|---|---|---|
| Electronics: |  |  |  |
|   Consumer Products | $1,992 | $147 | $ 823 |
|   Commercial Products | 1,262 | −94 | 720 |
|   Government Systems | 1,597 | 125 | 584 |
| Entertainment: |  |  |  |
|   Broadcasting | 2,648 | 333 | 1,177 |
|   Records and Tapes | 758 | 44 | 572 |
| Communications | 425 | 57 | 1,197 |
| Other Products | 290 | 10 | 127 |
|     Totals | 8,972 | 622 | 5,200 |
| Corporate Research |  | −128 |  |
| Corporate Administration |  | −113 |  |
| Interest Expense |  | −146 | 1,505 |
| Other Adjustments |  | 135 |  |
|   Profit before Income Taxes and Total Assets |  | $370 | $6,705 |

The balance sheet has been strengthened primarily by the sale of Hertz to UAL for $587 million cash and the removal of $1 billion of debt associated with owning rental cars.

Top management restructuring involved clarifying responsibilities, making some personnel changes, and reducing the political intrigue previously associated with major decisions. Getting stable leadership in the National Broadcasting Company was a vital part of this process.

The succession problem has been resolved by hiring Robert R. Frederick, a seasoned executive and former contender for the CEO position at General Electric. A valued strength that Frederick brings to RCA is familiarity with the carefully developed management practices which have contributed so much to General Electric's success.

With these accomplishments behind him, Bradshaw has turned over the CEO job to Frederick and remains only chairman of the board of directors. There is a strong feeling both within and outside RCA that the needed restructuring has been completed and that the company is now positioned for steady growth. The financial data in Table 2 reflect this turnaround.

The acquisition of RCA by General Electric is a surprise. Although the price is impressive, RCA insiders believe that the move is unnecessary to strengthen the company. Indeed, when the offer came before the RCA board, Frederick voted against it on the grounds that within a few years RCA stockholders would be better off if the company remained independent.

**Table 2.**
**RCA Financial Results, 1981–1985 (in millions, except per-share data)**

| | Total Sales* | Net Income | Income per Share** | Price Range** per Share |
|---|---|---|---|---|
| 1985 | $8,972 | $370 | $ 3.79 | $34¾–63½ |
| 1984 | 8,671 | 341 | 3.20 | 28⅝–40 |
| 1983 | 7,605 | 227 | 1.90 | 19¾–37½ |
| 1982 | 6,682 | 216 | 1.92 | 15¾–24⅛ |
| 1981 | 6,576 | 41 | –0.36 | 16¾–32 |

*Data based on businesses owned in 1985; the effect of businesses sold off has been removed from earlier years.
**Common stock; per-share income is after dividends on preference and preferred stock.

## General Electric Company

The General Electric Company, at the time of this writing, is in transition. It is restructuring both its portfolio of investments and the way those investments will be managed.

## Portfolio Changes

During most of its history, General Electric focused on manufacturing products that generated, distributed, or used electricity. Its products ranged from huge turbines to electric clocks. In this broad range, it was a leader that no competitor dared to disregard. The company grew and prospered.

However, many of its traditional lines matured. Even with modern design and updated technology, growth in real dollars slowed down. Competition in some areas, such as vacuum cleaners, fans, and phonographs, drove profit margins so low that General Electric withdrew.

Under current management this withdrawal from mature, narrow-profit businesses has become company policy. Jack Welch, CEO, says that a modest return on investment, even though steady, is not good enough. Instead, he wants General Electric resources focused on businesses that have high growth and profit potential. Moreover, the policy is to remain in segments of industries where General Electric can be the number one or number two player in terms of sales volume.

Of course, these investment guidelines are hard to achieve, especially with a total asset base of $25 billion. General Electric has not always been successful in its growth ventures. For instance, it pushed, but finally sold off, its electronic computer line. Also, it invested $2 billion in Utah International, a worldwide mining concern, but then resold most of these properties.

The 15 major businesses that General Electric was in prior to the RCA merger are briefly described in Appendix B. Six of these lines are "core" businesses carried over from the original focus of the company; five lines are "high tech" businesses, notably aircraft engines, aerospace products, and engineered thermoplastics; and four lines are service businesses, of which financial services is by far the largest. (See Appendix B for a listing and description of each of these lines of business.)

A rough indication of the relative importance of these businesses appears in Table 3. The core businesses have been declining in their *relative* share of total company profits, currently contributing about 30 percent. (With the addition of RCA, that share will drop to about 20 percent of the total.)

## Shifts in G.E. Management Structure

General Electric's way of managing has been a major factor in its better-than-average growth rate in the last three decades. The basic design, created by Ralph

**Table 3.**
**General Electric Company Revenues, Net Earnings, and Assets by Industry Segments, 1985**

|  | Revenues ($ billions) | (percent) | Net Earnings ($ billions) | (percent) | Assets Employed ($ billions) | (percent) |
|---|---|---|---|---|---|---|
| Consumer products (mostly lighting) | 3.6 | 12% | 0.22 | 9% | 2.3 | 8% |
| Major home appliances | 3.6 | 12 | 0.22 | 9 | 1.4 | 5 |
| Industrial systems (includes motors, locomotives, industrial electronics, construction engineering) | 4.6 | 16 | 0.14 | 6 | 2.6 | 10 |
| Power systems (includes turbines and construction equipment) | 5.5 | 19 | 0.45 | 19 | 3.5 | 13 |
| Aircraft engines | 4.7 | 16 | 0.38 | 16 | 3.9 | 15 |
| Materials (mostly plastics) | 2.5 | 8 | 0.27 | 12 | 3.9 | 15 |
| Technical products (mostly aerospace and medical systems) | 5.2 | 18 | 0.26 | 11 | 2.8 | 13 |
| Financial services | 0.5 | 2 | 0.41 | 18 | 2.7 | 10 |
| Corporate items and eliminations | −0.9 | −3 | −0.01 | — | 3.3 | 11 |
| Total | 29.3 | 100% | 2.34 | 100% | 26.4 | 100% |

Net earnings per share of common stock in 1985 were $5; the market price per share ranged from $55⅝ to $73⅞ during 1985 and was around $66 when GE agreed to acquire RCA.

Cordiner, CEO, and Harold Smiddy, Vice President for Management Services, in the 1950s, set a new pattern that served the company so well. The design had four dominant features:

1. *High decentralization to strategic business units (SBUs).* Each of at least 75 SBUs was run like a single-product-line company with its own engineering, production, marketing, finance, and industrial and community relations departments. The previous large functional departments were wiped out. To assure that initiative and decision making occurred within the SBUs, group vice presidents and product division managers were prohibited from having functional staff at their higher levels.

2. *A series of "service divisions" at the corporate level provided state-of-the-art technical advice to the SBUs.* These were in-house consultants that helped each SBU be the best-run organization in its particular industry. The service divisions did *not* make operating decisions; instead, they researched and often created new management techniques and then ran training courses for managers within the SBUs. For example, they pioneered in ways of measurement and control, launched what is now the PIMS data base, created new schemes for performance evaluations, and the like. Only the accounting, legal, union relations, and government relations departments had company-wide authority—and even this was sharply constrained.

3. *Strategic planning was made the main tool for guiding the action of each SBU,* as well as guiding events at the corporate level. Indeed, General Electric created many of the strategy concepts that business uses today, and it devised new methods for formulating strategy.

4. *Systematic management development was stressed.* For instance, all managers, from vice presidents to functional managers, within SBUs took a three-month course at the new G.E. management training center in Crotonville, New York. These managers, in turn, gave shorter courses to their subordinates. Textbooks dealing with planning, organizing, integrating, and measuring were written for exclusive within-company use. In what is probably the most thorough adult education program for managers, the culture of the company was shaped.

As expected, the CEOs following Cordiner have made revisions in his design. Where coordinated effort is especially valuable—for instance, in lighting and in major home appliances—several SBUs have been combined. Also, strategic planning has been elaborated, and the review process has been changed from time to time. Nevertheless, the General Electric way of managing has become deeply ingrained.

Currently, Welch is overhauling the well-honed management system. He feels that the pattern has become too "mature"—that it has lost its excitement and is used to defend past decisions. But especially, Welch feels that overhead expense can be reduced by streamlining management.

Among the changes that Welch has made is a drastic cutback or elimination of the corporate service divisions; only small groups guiding relations with stakeholders, regional coordination, and accounting and finance seem destined to survive. Another shift is a return to more centralized functional organization for many of the basic businesses (see Appendix B), with former SBU management assigned as product coordinators in a matrix fashion. Both of these moves are intended to cut overhead substantially.

More broadly, Welch likes change for change's sake: he believes that personnel need to be shaken up a bit. With management practices well ingrained, Welch feels that the company can be leaner; it has momentum, which reduces the risks of experimenting with different structures and less supervision. For instance, fewer decentralized SBUs will indeed reduce the incentive and development of managers with overall management experience, but probably the company can get along for a while without those benefits.

In terms of basic design, the managerial heads of the 15 key businesses report to a three-person CEO office. Aside from service from the finance, accounting, legal, and external relations offices, there is now very limited "service" provided to operating divisions.

## Questions

How do you recommend that RCA be fitted into the G.E. structure? That is,
(a) What strengths should G.E. provide to RCA divisions that will improve their operations?
(b) How should the divisions of the two companies be combined, if at all?
(c) Are there other steps that will enhance the benefits of the merger?
(d) With these moves, do you think the $6.3 billion price will look low or high in three or four years?

## Appendix A
## RCA Product Segments

### Electronics: Consumer Products and Services

RCA's current consumer products are focused primarily on TV sets.

In U.S. sales of TV sets, RCA is in a very close race for leadership with Zenith. Each brand has about a 17 percent market share in color receiving sets. Next in ranking are General Electric (10 percent) and Phillips, Sears, and Sony (6 percent each), and there are at least a dozen other active competitors. Because of this competition, high quality and frequent improvements in design are essential. Industry-wide operating profits are only about 2 percent of dollar sales.

Video cassette recorders are also sold by RCA. However, these are now all manufactured abroad by other suppliers.

After 15 years of work on video disks (using a needle system), RCA recently gave up the effort. Over $400 million had been spent in this undertaking. RCA no longer sells home or auto radios, or audio systems. A premature venture into video games was abandoned in the mid-1970s.

## Electronics: Commercial Products and Services

RCA is a leader among the 10 large producers of color television picture tubes. These tubes are sold to other manufacturers of receiving sets as well as used for RCA's own purposes. The competition in this niche of the industry has resulted in sharp price-cutting, and in 1981 RCA withdrew from European joint ventures, writing off $130 million of assets at the time.

RCA also produces integrated circuits and other video components. However, competition has been so keen in this arena that RCA closed a major integrated circuit plant in 1985.

For years, RCA has made equipment for broadcasting radio and then television. It also produces equipment for cable television companies. Another venture is receiving and rebroadcasting equipment for communication satellites. This is a specialized and obviously limited market.

## Electronics: Government Systems

Government sales focus on military and space equipment for the Armed Services, NASA, and related agencies. For example, RCA made the UHF radios and closed-circuit televisions for the space shuttle Columbia and comparable equipment for the Apollo moon landing.

Military sales include the radar-based, computer-controlled weapon system, AEGIS. RCA does not design or manufacture spacecraft, but it is a prominent subcontractor for communications equipment used on such craft. Participation in this government market helps RCA keep on the technological forefront of commercial space communications. This expertise enables RCA to build the communication mechanisms—the payload—of its own satellites (see the section on communications, to follow).

As Table 1 shows, sales to the government account for only about 18 percent of RCA's total sales. Thus, while RCA plays an important role in particular niches, it has not become a major prime contractor for military hardware.

## Entertainment: Broadcasting

RCA is vertically integrated: it owns NBC and a few television and radio broadcasting stations. However, the equipment used in these operations is a necessary but minor factor in their success. The production of popular programs is the crucial variable.

NBC-TV regularly serves about 200 affiliated stations, and NBC-Radio serves 300 affiliated stations. NBC was the first broadcasting network and for years had the largest audience. During the late seventies and early eighties, however, it fell significantly behind both CBS and ABC in the audience it attracted. This drop in comparative rating had a serious adverse effect on the prices it and its affiliated stations could charge for commercial advertising interspersed with the programs. Recently, program ratings have improved, and this will help future advertising revenues.

The long-term outlook for the large national broadcasting chains such as NBC is uncertain. Cable TV enables millions of homes to get excellent reception from a much larger number of stations. And broadcasting via satellites enables local stations to economically obtain a much larger number of programs. The combined effect of these two developments could diminish the size of network audiences and, consequently, their advertising revenues.

An added unknown is the possibility of interactive links between home TVs (or computers) and broadcasting stations. Such links could be used for retail selling, banking, games, library reference, etc. To date, RCA has not been an active experimenter in this arena.

## Entertainment: Records and Tapes

RCA has been a major supplier of phonograph records for many years, and more recently of audio tapes. Annual sales of such products are about $750 million, with operating profits (before corporate expenses and taxes) under $50 million. The income from record sales, however, fluctuates from year to year, depending upon the ability to discover new talent to produce "hits." Competition is keen.

## Communications

RCA now has two subsidiaries that provide communication services: Global Communications and American Communications.

A direct descendant of Marconi wireless ventures, RCA Global Communications provides overseas voice and record communication services via radio, cable, and satellites. These services take the form of telex, telegrams, private (leased) lines, teleprinter circuits, data transmission, and variations thereof.

RCA American Communications owns and operates satellites and a number of earth stations in the United States. These are similar to a public utility and are subject to regulation by the FCC. They are used for private-line voice, television, and data services, which are sold to cable TV companies, broadcasting organizations, large business companies, and the federal government.

Satellite communication is growing and competitive. Western Union, which also owns and operates satellites, is seeking permission to enter the overseas market, while RCA-American is encroaching on Western Union's domestic turf. AT&T Long-Lines is affected both domestically and overseas, and is responding to this new competition through a joint venture with IBM, Aetna Life, and Comsat.

Other companies are entering the field, either as operators of satellites or as "re-tailers" of services to users who are not large enough to lease their own channel to a satellite.

## RCA Laboratories

Although not treated as a profit center, RCA Laboratories are a large, semi-independent part of the corporation. The bulk of RCA technical research is done in the Laboratories. The work ranges from classified research for the armed services to development of products such as Selecta Vision. The Laboratories are known primarily for their success in communications electronics; product development is sometimes too remote from the operating divisions.

This corporate service plays an important role in keeping RCA abreast of technology in electronic communications and related fields. In 1985, for example, RCA spent about $750 million on research, development, and engineering activities. Contract research for the U.S. government accounted for around two-thirds of this total. Corporate research costs (not allocated to the divisions or reimbursed by the government) were $128 million.

## Appendix B
## General Electric's "15 Major Businesses"

## Core Businesses

### Lighting Products

For many years General Electric has been the largest manufacturer of light bulbs and related products in the United States. It makes all sorts of lighting products for both household and industrial use, and has pioneered many new developments. Because of its large volume and continuing attention to production methods, it is a low-cost producer in almost all segments of this industry.

### Major Home Appliances

General Electric is a leading player in the highly competitive home appliance business. Its products include electric refrigerators, electric ranges, microwave ovens, and related equipment for the kitchen, and clothes washers and dryers for the laundry. These products are sold through a strong network of independent dealers, using both the General Electric and Hotpoint brand names. Sales are aggressively sought for new residences as well as replacements.

Within the last few years General Electric has withdrawn from several segments of the appliance industry because of the narrow profit margins that exist. It sold its small-appliance business (toasters, mixers, clocks, and the like) to Black and Decker. Room air conditioners will no longer be manufactured; instead, they will be purchased from other companies for resale through G.E. dealers.

However, having decided, after much analysis, to remain in major appliances, General Electric is spending over $1 billion to redesign and retool its plants with highly automated production, with the aim of being the lowest cost producer of such products.

### Motors

Electric motors are another core business for General Electric. As the world's leading supplier, the company makes motors ranging in size from fractional horsepower to several thousand horsepower. These motors are sold primarily to other manufacturers as original equipment, and are adapted to various end-use requirements. The motor business is price competitive, so General Electric must give close attention to updating its technology in order to be a low-cost, dependable producer.

### Turbines

Over half of the electric power in the United States is generated by General Electric equipment. Generators of various types suited to gas, coal, and water energy are made, often to an electric utility company's unique specifications. Also, General Electric makes marine steam turbines and propulsion gears for the U.S. Navy, including nuclear-powered submarines. Because of the maturity of the U.S. electric power market, General Electric is seeking to penetrate foreign markets. Meanwhile, European and Japanese companies are invading the U.S. market.

### Transportation Products

Coal-fired steam locomotives have disappeared in the United States and many other countries. The main replacements are diesel/electric engines. General Electric is a major supplier of the electric motor part of such diesel/electric combinations. In addition, electric motors are used on subways, in mines, and on electrified railroads. Related products include oil drilling drives. As with turbines, this transportation engine industry has become global in scope. For example, General Electric has recently supplied 220 diesel/electric locomotives to the People's Republic of China.

### Electrical Equipment

General Electric is a leading supplier of equipment and apparatus involved in the distribution of electricity. Such equipment—for example, circuit breakers—is purchased by electrical contractors, large industrial users, and original equipment manufacturers. Also, simpler items are bought by home owners. The sale of this kind of equipment is closely associated with building construction activity, and its distribution channels differ from other kinds of G.E. products.

## High-Technology Businesses

### Medical Systems

General Electric's involvement in medical apparatus grows out of its long experience with X-ray equipment. The company is now active in new developments in diagnostic imaging, such as "cat scans" and resonance scanners. A joint venture with IBM, Integrated Diagnostics, is devising a computer-based system for diagnosis and analysis of patient information. Imaging is a relatively small but growing technology in the medical arena.

### Aircraft Jet Engines

After a long and difficult effort to break into the jet engine business, General Electric is now the number two supplier in the United States. Company engines are sold to both the military and commercial markets, notably for jet fighter planes. Replacement part sales are an attractive follow-up.

### Aerospace

General Electric's aerospace products include ground-based radar systems, satellites, training simulators, aircraft controls, and other products used for defense, space, and aviation needs. The entire process of planning and control in this very "high-tech" business is, of course, sharply different from that needed in the core business. A large R & D input (often financed by the U.S. government) is necessary for the development of these products. General Electric is not a leading player in the aerospace arena, but its sales of over $4 billion bear witness to its competence in the particular niches that it serves.

### Materials

At General Electric, the term "materials" refers predominantly to plastics. The company is a leader in engineering thermoplastics. The characteristics of these products can be tailored to replace metals and other base materials, providing either better performance or lower processing costs. The field is rapidly growing, and General Electric is vigorously pushing both R & D efforts and production of a variety of proven applications.

In addition to engineered plastics, General Electric has a strong position in industrial diamonds, viz., production of artificial diamonds used in cutting tools.

### Industrial Electronics

The "factory of the future" is of interest to General Electric for its own use and as a potential market for sets of products that can be tied together as a production system. Included here are robots, computer-aided design (CAD), as regards both hardware and software, programmable control (instruction) devices, and a communication system that links all these components into a system suited to a specific production technology. In practice, product design, marketing, and inventory control are also involved.

Because a lot of diverse techniques are required, General Electric has entered several joint ventures in this industrial electronics field. Much development work will be necessary before the volume of sales becomes significant for a giant company like General Electric.

## Service Businesses

### Financial Services

Among the "services" which General Electric provides for a fee, financial service is by far the most important. General Electric Credit Corporation is probably the largest nonbank source of business financing in the country: including the funds it borrows from the central money markets, it has assets of $18.5 billion. These funds are used to help all sorts of firms finance the leasing of equipment and plants, leveraged buyouts, retail-credit agreements, and similar capital requirements. Unrestrained by bank regulations and traditions, the officers have been creative in devising new credit arrangements.

To supplement this innovative lending, in 1984 General Electric acquired the Employers' Reinsuring Corporation for $1 billion, a company that reinsures property and casualty policies. Then in 1986 General Electric bought 80 percent of the stock of Kidder, Peabody & Co., a prominent Wall Street stockbrokerage firm with good ties in European financial circles.

### Construction and Engineering

As an adjunct of its sale of all sorts of industrial equipment, General Electric was often involved in the design of total production systems and in "turnkey" projects for entire plants. This led the company to offer a complete construction and engineering service that embraces design, construction, and sometimes maintenance of plants. In other situations, General Electric undertakes the modernization of plants and equipment.

### Nuclear Power Plant Services

Although General Electric does not now design and sell nuclear power plants, it continues to provide expert advice on the operation of nuclear plants in the United States. In addition to plant support services, it may provide fuel assemblies and control instruments. The future of this nuclear power business is uncertain.

### Information Services

Networks for data communication and processing have intrigued General Electric. The company offers a service to a wide variety of customers for teleprocessing of sales information, inventory management, and electronic transfer of funds. Such service ties into office automation and the leasing of equipment necessary for such activities. This information service activity does not have a major impact on General Electric's overall financial matters.

## Support Operations

In addition to the fifteen "businesses" just described, General Electric also has three significant units which it calls support operations. One is a semiconductor unit that provides integrated circuits to other G.E. businesses. This unit is expected to keep up with, or even advance, the state of the art in semiconductor size, power usage, cost, etc.

A second support operation is the General Electric Trading Company. In today's world, payment for goods and services provided to foreign countries that lack foreign exchange must often be taken in products that the customer does have for export. The G.E. Trading Company finds a market for goods accepted in such barter deals.

A third support operation is Ladd Petroleum, a company involved in exploration and development of crude oil and gas reserves. The official rationale for retaining this business is to assure raw material for the plastics business. Actually, Ladd Petroleum is left over from the resale of Utah International; its success in finding new oil has been so good that General Electric officers are reluctant to sell it.

# PART 4

## Organizing to Carry Out
## Multi-Level Strategy

# CHAPTER 18

## Organizing for Strategic Action

Strategy is not a self-fulfilling prophecy. Rather, it is only a plan—an expression of intent that requires much managerial effort to execute. We turn, accordingly, to concepts that will help managers in this crucial task of making strategy happen.

The preceding parts of this book have explored strategy formulation at three levels: business-unit strategy, strategy programs of departments within business-units, and corporate strategy. Execution of such strategic plans calls for a corresponding organization and for activating steps. In this and the next part, our primary concern is with recurring active reinforcement of a selected strategy, that is, with the bridges between strategy and execution. To attempt to cover all phases of implementation of strategy is, of course, impossible in a text such as this.

We begin by examining organization design, a fundamental issue in every company.

## Organizing to Aid Strategic Behavior

The way a company is organized can expedite strategic action, or it may be a serious roadblock thereto. To cite a simple example, if the organization assigns almost everyone in a hotel to first taking care of a sales convention, a strategic thrust to attract permanent residents gets little attention. A separate group may then be necessary to provide the permanent residents the service that they expect.

Organization design—the grouping of numerous business activities into departments, sections, etc., and on into individual jobs, plus the established relationships between these organization units—strongly influences which problems receive attention first. As in television, there is always a question of who gets "prime time."

### A Basic Choice

Many company organizations are designed with the aim of achieving maximum efficiency in current activities. The work is subdivided to encourage the use of specialists, often with "professional" training, in engineering, purchasing, advertising, accounting, and other functions. Arguments for this kind of grouping include opportunities to utilize state-of-the-art techniques, low costs, and tighter control. The focus here is primarily on internal operations.

A different aim is to facilitate strategic change. Here, the dominating concern is flexibility in order to outmaneuver rivals. A close relationship with markets, with the firms that provide the company with resources and buy the output, and with competitors and legislators who may upset our plans are all critical. So the company organizes in a way that helps it respond quickly to present and predicted changes in the environment. Managers give strategic change precedence over efficiency.

Complicating this question of giving strategic change emphasis in the organization design is the necessity to deal with several diverse markets simultaneously. Part 2 highlighted a general manager's task of balancing opportunities to excel in marketing, production, finance, etc. Business-unit strategy, and especially the selected sources of differential advantage, guide this balancing act. But now, in organizing, we need to create a structure that includes a well-informed forum where such strategic choices can be made wisely and promptly.

These two basic aims of achieving efficiency and aiding integrated strategic action push toward different organization designs. Efficiency, especially in the scientific management tradition, is achieved through division of labor along functional lines; detailed planning, often with the assistance of staff experts; mechanization and automation of routine tasks; careful scheduling; and decentralized controls. This kind of organization gives us high-quality gasoline for our cars, low-cost wristwatches, electric current at the flip of a switch, dependable medicines, and videotapes by the millions; it also enables us to land a man on the moon.

In contrast, aiding integrated strategic action calls for organization units that both monitor current events and predict the future, fast face-to-face communication, decentralized authority to try new methods, versatile workers who are able and willing to take on varied tasks, less detailed planning, and more localized control. Organizations with these characteristics help companies switch from leather shoes to running shoes to walking shoes, move production into and out of countries like Sri Lanka, add new products such as genetically engineered insecticides, and move into new markets like health clubs.

Of course, most companies would like an organization design that gives them both efficiency and ability to make integrated strategic moves quickly. Indeed, while the designs do clash, it is quite possible to build in a mixture, with the proportion of emphasis on efficiency versus strategic change being determined by company strategy. These variations will become clearer as we review typical organization designs for single-line companies and for diversified corporations in the sections that follow.

One further introductory comment may be helpful. By discussing strategy first and then organization in this book, we are following A. D. Chandler's conclusion that usually strategy determines structure.[1] However, the interplay is mixed because, to some extent, the organization design that a company already has

---

[1]*Strategy and Structure* (Cambridge, MA: MIT Press, 1962).

shapes any new strategy it is likely to develop. Certainly, when a company considers the matching of its strategy and its organization design, it is concerned about *both* future strategy changes *and* the execution of present strategy.

## Efficiency Plus Strategic Integration in a Single-Line Company

In theory, achieving both efficiency and integrated strategic action in a single-line company should be easy. Because most of the day of all managers is devoted to current operations, the company is organized around specialized functions. (See Figure 18–1.) In a typical business, these functions will be manufacturing, marketing, finance, and human resources, with split-offs of purchasing, engineering, advertising, accounting, and other functions as suits the basic technology and industry of the business. Each of these departments seek functional excellence (as stressed in Part 2), which includes efficiency, timely output, quality, etc. The chief executive/general manager meets from time to time with the department managers to discuss strategy. And according to the theory, since all the key people have participated in the discussion, they will understand and feel committed to the strategic plan officially endorsed by the chief executive.

**FIGURE 18–1.**
**ORGANIZATION DESIGN CONCEPT FOR A MEDIUM-SIZED, SINGLE-LINE COMPANY**

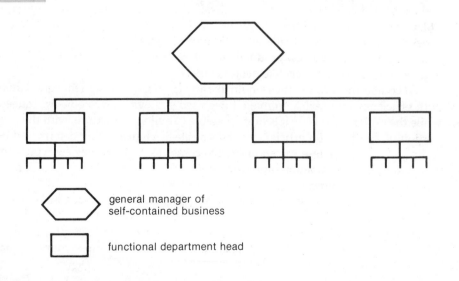

general manager of
self-contained business

functional department head

While this simplified model is basically sound, it sweeps most of the practical difficulties under the rug: there are organizational hurdles in building a coordinated team of functional specialists, in participating in strategy formulation and execution, and in dealing with increases in size.

## Building a Coordinated Team of Functional Specialists

A major shift in the activities of a general manager occurs when the company grows from a "one-man show" to groups of functional departments headed by a general manager.

The general manager has to be willing to delegate. This means no longer knowing exactly what is happening day to day and accepting decisions that are not quite the way the general manager would have made them. A cardinal purpose of creating functional departments is to give the general manager time to focus on interdepartmental coordination and on policy and strategy issues. Many executives whose success as small entrepreneurs makes possible a functional organization find this required change in their personal behavior very difficult and sometimes impossible.

Of course, by contrast, the extent of delegation can go too far, as was true of the Wardwell Vinyl Coatings company (case 6). Here, only the production manager was staying with the basic strategy of the company: serving many customers with short production runs. The chief engineer was busy designing an automated plant that would be useful only for very large customers, and the sales manager was exploring a new product that the company was unprepared to handle. The trouble arose, not from the assignment of functions to departments, but from a failure of the president to insist that all departments work toward a consistent set of goals. Delegation was out of control.

A more subtle difficulty plagued Gregg College (pseudonym), which is an ambitious outgrowth of a commercial school that had an impressive record of preparing students for bookkeeping/accounting, secretarial, and office management positions. Like many other commercial schools, Gregg has become a four-year college offering a bachelor's degree. It continues to have a strong faculty in accounting, business law, and computer programming that is dedicated to rigorous, practical training of students in these areas. A financial grant for minority students from the city in which Gregg College is located enabled Gregg to employ several behavioral scientists who believe that the college should take an active role in overcoming racial discrimination in the inner city. Meanwhile, the dean of the faculty is pushing for accreditation by the American Assembly of Collegiate Schools of Business, which puts pressure on the school to increase faculty with Ph.D.s who will do academic research and teach courses in economics and liberal arts subjects.

The president of Gregg College hesitates to put these three factions into separate departments, and without a clear mission for each group he has delegated little authority for activities outside the teaching of specific courses. According to the model for a single-line company sketched at the beginning of the chapter, the president cannot expect to get efficient, dedicated output from the faculty without narrower grouping and more delegation.

These brief examples, and even more, the discussion of department strategy programs in Part 2, indicate that efficiency within a single-line company is substantially aided by the following factors:

1. Dividing the operating work into functional departments, preferably with functions that have an established body of knowledge and recognized expertise. (Such expertise is typically related to some specific kind of market or industry, such as a product market, labor market, or financial market.)

2. Delegating enough authority to the managers of such departments so they can use their skills and build an esprit de corps within their group. (Such delegation presumes personal competence, a subject considered in Chapter 20.)

3. But, insisting that a given department's activities be coordinated with the work of other departments in the company and fulfill assigned roles in the company strategy program. Department efficiency has value only in terms of its contribution to the combined performance of the entire company.

## Participating in Strategy Formulation and Execution

The company organization just described provides people (more accurately, positions for the people) who should be the key participants in strategy formulation and execution. In a well-run single-line company, the department managers should have most of the knowledge needed to plan changes in strategy (data and forecasts about shifts in demand and supply, technology, competition, threats, opportunities, etc., in their particular areas or "industries," plus an intimate knowledge about the capabilities and commitments within their respective departments coupled with an ability to forecast the likely internal response to proposed changes). Moreover, they are the main individuals who should be committed to new strategy if it is to be well executed. The general manager (president or CEO), of course, is directly concerned with both the formulation and the execution of an *integrated* strategy.

Having this array of qualified talent at hand means that normally no additional jobs centered on integrated strategy should be located in the organization. On the contrary, the design of the strategic planning system and the assessment of threats or opportunities outside the present domain of the company are temporary needs; they do not warrant a continuing position in the organization.

Thus, instead of opening up more positions, securing integrated strategic action calls for a set of procedures and related behavior patterns—behavior patterns, that is, within existing jobs, not new jobs. Several features of this strategic management system deserve emphasis:

1.  Each department manager has a dual role: to make his or her department excellent in the performance of its functional activities, and to be part of a team that finds ways to make the total business more effective. Experience in one role makes the manager more effective in the other. However, conflicts in loyalties and in allocation of personal time frequently arise. The reward system should encourage both roles, even though conflict is present.

2.  The general manager should have recognized responsibility for final decisions about the role of each department in the strategic plan, including their relative emphases. He or she has an overall view that department managers who devote most of their time to department matters cannot be expected to have.

3.  While department managers themselves should resolve most interdepartmental coordination issues, the general manager should arbitrate major differences because these decisions play an important part in refining both the organization and the strategy.

4.  The mechanisms for resource allocation (financial budgets, key personnel assignments, the management committee agenda, etc.) should be both related and subservient to strategy plans because they significantly influence what a department actually does.

5.  The measurement, evaluation, and reward system (both formal and informal) should consistently and strongly support behavior tied to the updated company strategy.

The dependence on busy operating managers to perform key parts in strategy formulation and execution will be a safe arrangement only if the variables that shape what managers actually do are integrated into a consistent strategy direction. *With such support,* the popular statement that line managers should make the strategy is a sound organization guideline.

## Dealing with Increases in Size

Growth complicates organization. As a single-line company moves from a few hundred employees to a few thousand, the informal participation in strategy decisions just described becomes harder to achieve. The organizational adjustments that are necessary depend very much on how the growth was obtained. Diversification is one route to growth, and organizing for it will be considered in the next section. Building volume in the established line of business is a second route, but it also adds new hurdles.

Geographical expansion is a common and simple way to grow. For example, if Kentucky Fried Chicken is popular in Louisville, the manager can just duplicate the store in Lexington and Frankfort. The biological term is "clone": to make another and another just like the first. Finance companies, Redimix Cement, and chain stores, for instance, have followed this pattern.

Inevitably, as the number of operating units and distance grow, so too do centralized supervision and control. And decentralization to adapt to local needs and competition becomes an issue: maybe the unit in Boston should not be an exact duplicate of the original one in Louisville.

These size issues affect the way strategy is formulated and executed. Regional supervisors instead of functional managers are the people who have frequent face-to-face contact with the president. When they sit in on a strategy meeting, they don't have the same detailed knowledge of local threats and opportunities that the department heads in smaller, single-location firms possess, and their commitment to execute a strategy lacks a "hands-on" quality. So formal reports and perhaps market and morale surveys are added. Moreover, time is required for vertical communication from and to the "field." Of course, this linkage between headquarters and the field can be carefully built, but it is an added hurdle.

Most growth, however, is not simply cloning. Typically, additional volume leads to low cost of one or more functional activities. For example, having national, rather than local, TV advertising significantly reduces the sales promotion cost per prospect reached. Or, in another company, a large volume lowers the per unit production cost. Large companies can justify more specialized training programs and the like. To secure such economies of scale, central planning and control by a functional department is necessary. Local adaptability is sacrificed to obtain economies, and strategy options are constrained. A bureaucratic organization is created to promote the use of the newfound strength. Thus, economies are gained and interest in strategic change is reduced.

Relying on size to obtain economies leads to yet a further complication: optimum volume is not the same for each function. A men's clothing firm, for instance, found that plants with two or three hundred employees could achieve virtually all economies of scale in production, but that larger plants generated more personnel problems. However, the output of a medium-sized plant was far too small for marketing purposes. National advertising and promotion were the keys to the firm's marketing success, and the sales volume needed to support national distribution was six times the output of a single plant.

In such circumstances, the organization level best qualified to participate in strategy planning differs according to function. Personnel may be local, production regional, and marketing national, or some other mix may obtain. For problems *within* a department, decentralization or centralization can be adjusted to the most effective level, but doing so adds to difficulties of coordination between departments. And for participation in strategy planning, it is often unclear from which level the participants should come.

In large single-line companies, an organization arrangement like the one sketched on page 516 for smaller companies is common. The line managers reporting to the president/general manager participate as a group in designing and executing the company strategy. However, because of difficulties of distance, eagerness to achieve economies of scale in one or more functions, and differences among departments in the organization level at which key decision making is focused, additional organization devices are needed. Supplements such as special studies by staff assistants, formal strategy reports, and strategy planners are used to compensate for the senior managers' lack of familiarity with specific operating threats and opportunities. But these aids to vertical and horizontal communication take time to operate. Also, commitment to carry out strategy decisions is weakened when intermediaries are inserted between the doers and the decision makers. A typical consequence is that the bigger companies give more attention to economies and are less agile in strategic change.

## Organizing for Strategic Diversification

Many companies grow by diversifying. They move into new lines of business, either by building on an existing marketing or production strength or by acquiring another firm, as discussed in Part 3. When such expansion occurs, there is always a question about how to fit the enlarged activities into the organization.

Economies may suggest that each functional department be expanded to take care of the several different lines of business. Unless the new line is still very small, however, establishing a separate business-unit has distinct advantages.

## Creation of Semi-Independent Business-Units

Ordinarily, semi-independent business-units are built around product lines. Thus, that part of marketing dealing with a particular product is transferred from the marketing department to the product division. And likewise with production, engineering, and perhaps other functions. Ideally, each division has within it all the key activities necessary to run independently—i.e., it is *self-sufficient*. Moreover, the management of the newly created division is given a high degree of authority, making the division *semiautonomous*. The general manager of such a division then has virtually the same resources and freedom of action as the president of an independent company and is expected to take whatever steps are necessary to make the "little business" successful.

Examples of such units are widespread. Honda's original motorcycle division is quite separate from its automobile division. Some commuter bus-line companies also run tourist buses, but the latter activity is typically rather independent, except for maintenance. General Electric's light bulb business has virtually no ties to its refrigerator and range business, and its supplies for electricians are far removed from its electric generators.

Such business-units are not completely independent, however. Their charters—specifying their domain, constraints, resources available, and target results—are negotiated with corporate headquarters, as explained in Chapter 15. Also, they often have the benefit of "corporate inputs" described in Chapter 17, such as low-cost capital, exploratory research, and staff assistance on labor relations, law, and market research. The resulting units making up a typical corporate organization are diagrammed in Figure 18–2.

"Conglomerate" corporations are sometimes distinguished from "multi-division" corporations. In conglomerates the operating divisions have almost no business interrelationships, whereas synergy is often a possibility among units of a multi-division corporation. Conglomerates are likely to consist of acquisitions of well-established firms that were pulled together in financial wheeling and dealing rather than for operating benefits. Consequently, the divisions of conglomerates are typically even more self-sufficient than are the parts of multi-division corporations. For our purposes, the distinction between conglomerates and multi-division corporations is not important.

**FIGURE 18–2.**
**ORGANIZATION DESIGN CONCEPT FOR A MULTI-DIVISION CORPORATION**

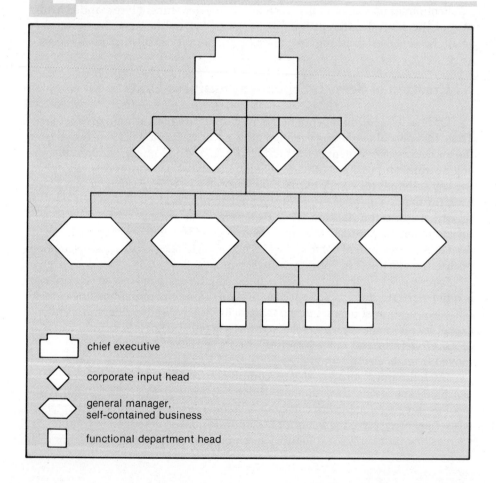

## Benefits to Strategy Management

The splitting of corporate activities into business-units will usually require some sacrifice in functional specialization. The smaller size places a limit on the division of labor, and widespread standardization of procedures and parts will no longer be consistent with the high delegation of authority to business-unit general managers. The following compensatory benefits, however, are substantial from a strategy management viewpoint:

1. The management of each business-unit can be suited to *its* strategy. Even a small portfolio of business-units will include variation in targeted growth rates, acceptable risk, customer sophistication, sensitivity to costs and inflation, technology, and other critical factors. By creating each unit with a relatively narrow focus, its total management design can be *tailored* to that particular purpose. Also, the possibility of staffing each unit with executives committed to its mission is improved.

2. The narrower focus prompts *adequate attention* to external and internal threats and opportunities. In contrast, executives with multiproduct responsibilities are likely to overlook new developments in some industries and brush some problems under the rug.

3. *Prompt, integrated response* to threats and opportunities is rendered more probable. Fewer managers have to exchange information and judgments, and they can communicate with one another swiftly and clearly. Also, bureaucratic attitudes are less likely to interfere with voluntary cooperation. As a result, the strategic programs and focused climate discussed in Chapter 15 are easier to achieve.

4. The *morale* of key people can be more easily tied to business-unit accomplishments. Executives are able to see the results of their own efforts, to take actions they believe are best, and to feel that they are playing an important role. The resulting enthusiasm and devotion to the success of their particular business-unit tend to spread to employees at all levels in the unit.

5. *Control* is more direct. The people accountable for achieving strategy targets are few and clearly defined. Although measurement of intangibles remains elusive, short-run profit results for the business-unit are available. Buck-passing, so common in large, multiproduct, functional departments, is minimized.

These benefits may not be easy to achieve. The power of the corporate staff units has to be restricted primarily to advice, and the top corporate managers have to be willing to decentralize and allow someone else to "carry the ball." Some business-units may have widely fluctuating volume—due to business cycles, rapidly shifting technology, or dependence on large government contracts—and too much effort is expended just on frequent expansion or contraction. Very small business-units may be unable to support strong departments in all functions and have to lean heavily on other units.

Because of these organizational difficulties, compromise arrangements are sometimes wise.

## Compromise Structures

Both separate business-units that can aggressively pursue a distinct strategy and strong functional departments that can muster specialized resources and cut costs are desirable. So in unusual circumstances, corporations try to have both. Following are two well-known examples.

## Excluding One Function from Strategic Business-Units

One paper corporation leaves production in a single functional department so as to achieve economies in the use of raw materials and large-scale operations. However, product engineering and marketing are divided into product-focused business-units. The managers of these business-units are expected to act like "independent businesspersons": they formulate and execute competitive business strategy. The compromise is that they must contract for their supply of products from the centralized production department.

A comparable arrangement is used by a food processor, except that in this instance it is selling rather than production that is centralized in one department. Each product business-unit does its own product design, engineering, buying, production, merchandising, and pricing, but it utilizes the sales department to contact customers. The rationale here is that a single field organization can cover the country more effectively for all business-units than the latter could do separately.

Whenever a product business-unit has to rely on an outside department for a key activity, problems of adequate attention, coordination, and control become more difficult. Occasions for bickering jump dramatically. Central management has to judge whether the harm done by restricting self-sufficiency is offset by the benefits of the larger scale activities in the functional department.

## Matrix Organization

A matrix organization is typically used to build a team effort around a major construction project (landing a person on the moon is the most dramatic example) or around the unique needs of a specific customer. Experts from functional departments are assigned to the team temporarily or on a part-time basis. Figure 18–3 illustrates the arrangement.

To pick an example far removed from physical hardware, advertising agencies regularly use a matrix setup. An agency has departments staffed with experts in market research, copywriting, art work, television shows, media selection, and other functions—all useful to various clients. Client A wants a specific advertising mission accomplished, one suited to its particular situation. The organization problem is how to draw on the outstanding capabilities of the functional departments and at the same time get an imaginative, timely, tailored program for Client A. Comparable situations in management consulting firms and in large building construction firms are easy to visualize.

The matrix organization answer to these problems is to appoint a project manager for each clear-cut mission and then to assign, from each of the functional

**FIGURE 18–3.**
**MATRIX ORGANIZATION IN A SPACECRAFT-PRODUCING CORPORATION**

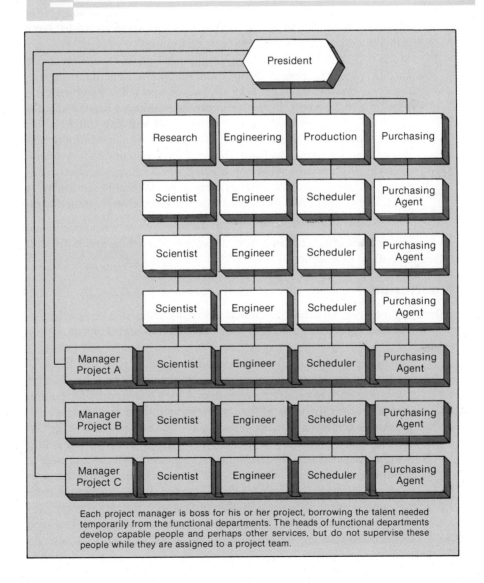

Each project manager is boss for his or her project, borrowing the talent needed temporarily from the functional departments. The heads of functional departments develop capable people and perhaps other services, but do not supervise these people while they are assigned to a project team.

departments, the talent needed to complete the mission. During the time a functional specialist is working on the project, the specialist reports to the project manager. But when the project is finished, or when he or she is no longer needed, each specialist returns to the home functional department for assignment to other duties.

The matrix concept can be adapted in various ways to promote a new strategy while retaining a basically functional organization structure. Project teams and project managers are common examples.

(a) When a new product line is still in the experimental stage, a project team can guide the pilot plant and market testing studies. The team provides the coordination of diverse specialists which is so valuable at this stage. Later, if and when the new line appears destined for large growth, a separate business-unit can be spun off.

(b) Much less ambitious is the appointment of "product managers" for specific products already being handled by the functional departments. A product manager typically has no specialists assigned even part-time to a project. Instead, the product manager follows what is happening to the product in each department and flags the need for better coordination. If the product is not making as good progress as external opportunities warrant, the product manager initiates discussions on shortcomings wherever they appear. Although limited to advising, coaxing, and occasional appealing to higher authority, a product manager often can secure cross-functional strategic action on the assigned product.

In any case, matrix organization creates delicate relationships and is difficult to manage smoothly. Consequently, it should be used sparingly.

## Conclusions

When organization structure is viewed primarily from the perspective of strategy formulation and execution, four major conclusions stand out:

1. The use of strategy cannot be assigned to separate departments, leaving the rest of the organization to run untouched by strategic considerations. Instead, to be effective, strategy has to be a dominant element that permeates the work of managers throughout the enterprise.

2. Line managers must participate personally and actively in strategy formulation and execution. They have knowledge, understanding, and insights that are valuable in forming strategy, and their commitment to the endorsed strategy is necessary for its vigorous execution. Perhaps even more important, they are the key individuals who must coordinate and dovetail their work so that *integrated* action takes place.

   The design of an organization can aid greatly in getting this kind of participation. A relatively small single-line company provides a model of an organization where integrated strategic behavior is most likely to take place. So, for strategy purposes, (a) the organization of large single-line companies should build in communication devices and decentralization arrangements which promote horizontal integration of key line managers, and (b) diversified corporations should try to divide their activities into self-contained, semiautonomous business-units, each of which can pursue an optimum strategy in its domain.

3. A significant constraint on organizing by self-contained, semiautonomous business-units is a potential reduction in the expertise and efficiency of large-scale functional departments. In many circumstances, the strategy benefits of strong business-units clearly offset the necessary loss in functional efficiency. However, when the sacrifice would be too great, compromise organizations are possible, such as one large marketing or production department serving several business-units, or an adaptation of a matrix organization.

4. In terms of multi-level strategy, the organization sketched in points 1 to 3 reinforces the emphasis on business-units as the strategy planning centers (as urged in Part 1). Within a business-unit the functional departments have distinct and important roles, but their activities are fused into the business-unit strategy via the integration linkages described in Part 2. At the corporate level, competitive strategy is decentralized to the business-units, leaving two major tasks: formulating and executing corporate portfolio strategy (including the negotiation of business-unit charters), and managing corporate inputs as services to the business-units (as discussed in Part 3).

Thus, the recommended organization design provides structural support for the multi-level strategy approach. Of course, other supportive resources and actions are also needed, such as a good board of directors, qualified executives, and an appropriate planning and control system. We turn to these subjects in the chapters that follow.

## Questions for Class Discussion

1. (a) Would a clear strategy regarding a single domain and differential advantage for Gregg College (see pages 517–518) win acceptance? increase efficiency? build morale? How would you recommend that Gregg College be organized to carry out such a strategy?

(b) Do you think that Gregg College should have two or more different strategies, reflecting the varied interests within the faculty? If so, what organization structure would you recommend?

2. Exxon USA and most other large oil corporations operating in this country have a functional organization with "departments" for exploration, crude oil (and gas) production, crude oil and product transportation, marketing, and finance and accounting. There are also corporate units for research, human resources, government relations, etc. These oil corporations are large organizations doing billions of dollars of business through thousands of employees. Of course, activities within some of the departments, such as marketing, are subdivided on a geographical basis, but the basic structure reporting to corporate headquarters is functional.

(a) What do you think explains the use of functional departments running clear to the top of the organization, and the absence of self-contained operating units?

(b) What effect do you think this tall organization has on Exxon's ability to respond quickly to environmental threats and opportunities?

3. The Metropolitan Memorial Hospital makes a clear distinction between its services for "outpatients" and those for "bed patients." The outpatients come to the hospital briefly for some sort of treatment, but do not stay overnight; the emergency room is part of this division. Bed patients, by contrast, are checked in and out, somewhat like in a hotel, and are assigned a room on a floor devoted to the sort of service they need: surgery, maternity (obstetrics), infectious diseases, etc. In many respects these two divisions are managed like separate "business-units" of a manufacturing corporation, with separate budgets, procedures, sales promotion, etc., and distinct strategies.

(a) The hospital is seriously considering the addition of a drug rehabilitation center to its services. Would you recommend that this service, if undertaken, be set up as a separate business-unit, the way the term has been used in this chapter?

(b) Do you recommend that the maternity care section be split off as a separate business-unit? Give reasons for your answer.

(c) Should a separate business-unit be established for AIDS patients? Give reasons for your answer.

4. (a) A university could be organized so that each course ran as a separate, self-contained unit (the students would sign up, use equipment, and pay for each course just as is done for private flying lessons). Several centuries ago Adam Smith, dissatisfied with the education he received at Oxford University and very unhappy about teaching there, recommended this procedure as the way to organize universities. Or each department might be so organized, or each division. What are the key factors that determine which separations, if any, of this type should be made? (b) Should any of the following be seen as self-sufficient divisions: dormitories? the book store? intercollegiate athletics? eating halls? Should they at least be expected to break even financially?

5. Several astute observers of organization design and change note that a management crisis is usually necessary before companies change from a small, single-line company to building a coordinated team of function specialists (page 516). Similar crises are necessary for a change to a line-and-staff organization for a large, single-line company or to the kind of organization necessary for a diversified major company (page 522). Now consider the following.

   Sr. Gomez, president and part-owner of Tubora, S.A., is concerned and decidedly unhappy because his company, a manufacturer of tubes and plastic bottles used to contain cosmetics, seems to be on a profit plateau. Sales are up nicely, but profits are not. He explains, "So that I could concentrate on our rapidly growing sales and on my general responsibility to hold the company together, I brought in a production manager, a chief mechanic, an accountant, and a personnel manager. But our profits show the added expense of all these managers.

   "In the meantime, I still have to walk through the plant several times a day to check on quality and on the settings of the machines. The slightest deviation can throw off the colors and the printing. I like to come in early and leave late so I can talk with the second-shift supervisor and see the results of the night's work. The personnel manager hasn't yet shown that she can get the people on the line to stop talking and work harder. I really should spend almost all of my time out of the office making sales, but troubles with machine settings and arguments between operators and mechanics seem to come to me for settlement. And the new accountant has not helped us to cut costs. What can I do with an organization like this one?"

   (a) Is Sr. Gomez's problem a crisis of the kind in question?

   (b) What would be the nature of a crisis in moving to become a diversified major corporation?

6. (a) Many executives regard acquisition of their company by a conglomerate with fear. The idea of being "taken over" comes as a great psychological blow. Along with fear goes anger at the leading individuals or groups responsible for a buy-out or acquisition. How do you account for these feelings?

   (b) Do executives have more, or less, opportunity if the company they work for becomes part of a conglomerate?

   (c) Is there any reason to presume that executives of a conglomerate will push for actions contrary to healthy growth and good service of the operating unit?

7. The Dotman Company purchased all of the cocoa powder and half of the coffee beans used in its food products from brokers in New York. It bought the other half of its coffee bean requirements in Africa and South America. The coffee beans were purchased, roasted, processed, and sold by the coffee division of this food-products company. The cocoa powder was purchased by the candy division but also used as a raw material by several other divisions, including the division of baked goods and beverages. The treasurer has put in a

strong plea to centralize the purchasing of cocoa powder and coffee beans in an "international purchasing division" for several reasons: (1) the dollar amounts of the purchases were 50 percent or more of the cost of materials of the divisions using coffee beans and cocoa powder; (2) the special skills needed to purchase these new materials had little to do with the skills needed for other activities in the coffee division and the candy division; and (3) the treasurer could then control more carefully the dollars invested in inventory, foreign exchange, and the forward-purchase commitments of the company. In fact, gains or losses in the commodity and futures markets could be as high as one-half of net profits or as much as one hundred percent of net losses.

What do you think? Should an international purchasing division be established analogous to the company's international exports division?

8. "Corporations should have their own inspectors general to monitor business ethics." So said the chief of the Securities and Exchange Commission's enforcement division. The watchdog should investigate the extent to which the corporation has been faced with demands for payoffs, kickbacks, and political contributions, and the extent to which the company has paid "greenmail" to buy out troublesome stockholders or the extent of insider trading in the corporation's stock. The inspector general should make sure that the company adheres to its code of ethical conduct. Indeed, "A senior accountant or lawyer—someone who no longer has to worry about pleasing management to further his or her career—should take up the new post."

"Current corporate audit procedures have failed in some very glaring instances to uncover questionable corporate practices," said the S.E.C. official. But the chairman of a panel considering the issue saw no need for such an officer: "The chief executive officer of the corporation should do that job. He or she should set the policy and see that subordinates understand it and carry it out."

(a) Should a chief executive officer carry out his or her responsibility by appointing such an inspector general?

(b) Would such an officer "be in an untenable position in any organization," as the chairman said?

9. Allied Manufacturing, International, recently paid $534 million (25 percent over book value) for Sunrise Electric Co., whose divisions make and sell small appliances to households and small electric products to industrial buyers. Sunrise has six product divisions, all of which save one are losing market share and are looking at a seven percent per annum post-tax return on investment. Loss in market share is attributed to out-of-date and "me-too" products, while return on investment is heavily influenced by very large inventories. One proposal for Allied is to centralize and focus manufacturing (e.g., small motors for all products made in one factory, electrical cords made in another, all consumer appliances assembled in a third plant, and industrial products in a fourth), use venture teams to design, manufacture, and test-market new or updated consumer appliances, and leave only the selling effort to what used to be the product divisions. Also, the company might regroup the product divisions into

divisions of kitchen appliances, bedroom appliances (electric blankets and sheets, specialized lighting, and electric space heaters), dining room appliances, and hobby room appliances. In your opinion, will this kind of reorganization improve the selling effort, the products' market share, and the return on investment?

# CASE
## 18 Milano Enterprises[1]

Mr. Milano is concerned about the long-run future of the group of enterprises he personally has built into a flourishing establishment. Located in a Latin American country, Milano Enterprises is recognized as a dynamic factor in the private sector of the nation's economy. In fact, the success of the business complicates its continuation.

## Scope of Activities

Mr. Milano, son of Italian immigrants, started in business forty-five years ago in a small but growing city. He anticipated a building boom and left the family grocery store to enter the building-supply business. Several of Mr. Milano's present companies are a direct outgrowth of this early start. He still owns two regional wholesale companies dealing in building supplies. A separate company imports specialty plumbing items, and another is the national representative of a worldwide electric elevator manufacturer that sells, installs, and services elevators for apartment buildings, offices, and warehouses. Currently, the largest company in the building field is a plant of his that manufactures boilers and other heating equipment. Still another plant manufactures electric fixtures.

Mr. Milano's activities in other fields followed a somewhat similar pattern. Foreseeing needs arising out of urbanization and industrialization, he sought to become the import representative for products serving these needs. Because imports were sharply restricted for economic and political reasons, he undertook the manufacture of selected items. For example, in the automotive field he has been the Ford representative for many years. One company does the importing of Ford cars, trucks, and parts. In addition, Milano Enterprises owns a controlling interest

---

[1]Newman/Summer/Warren, *The Process of Management: Concepts, Behavior and Practice,* 2nd Ed., © 1967, pp. 144–51. Reprinted by permission of Prentice-Hall, Inc., Englewood Cliffs, NJ.

in several large dealerships. It also represents the British and German Ford affiliates. Quotas and tariffs place severe restrictions on the number of vehicles that can be imported, and legislation encourages local manufacture. Consequently a separate company has been established for truck assembly and body manufacture. Also in the automotive area, Milano Enterprises owns a chain of filling stations.

In the office equipment area, Milano Enterprises has separate companies for the importation of duplicating equipment and of typewriters. In addition there is a substantial and growing unit that manufactures metal furniture for offices.

About ten years ago, a new company was established to manufacture electric refrigerators locally. Compressors are imported but the cabinets are manufactured in a plant adjacent to the furniture plant. Other Milano units include a large textile plant that weaves and finishes cotton fabrics, a prominent hotel, a soft-drink bottling company, and a small mining-exploration venture.

In total, there are twenty-five active operating companies ranging in size from twenty to five hundred employees. The textile plant and the boiler plant are the largest units in terms of employment. Milano Enterprises owns all or at least a majority of stock in each of these operating companies. In several instances, the manager of a company owns a minority interest, but he is under contract to Milano Enterprises to sell back his stock at current book value when he retires.

Obviously, a man who can put together such an array of companies in a single lifetime possesses unusual ability. Part of Mr. Milano's success arises from working in growth areas. Within these areas, Mr. Milano has been willing to invest risk capital, but he has been unusually adept in picking particular spots where growth was strong and at adjusting his operations as the economic environment shifted. Also, once an investment has been made, it has been carefully nurtured and controlled. Mr. Milano is modest in manner, eagerly seeks advice wherever he can find it, and works hard in a well-disciplined manner. His personal integrity is widely respected throughout the business community. He is a religious man and is highly devoted to his family.

## Present Organization

Each of the twenty-five companies has its manager and, with minor exceptions, each has its own offices and other facilities. As might be expected, the central organization reflects its evolutionary background and is not sharply defined. Six people, in addition to Mr. Milano, share in the general direction of Milano Enterprises.

Mr. Lopez has been closely associated with Mr. Milano during most of his business career. Both men are the same age and, like Mr. Milano, Mr. Lopez has had only elementary school education. In general, Mr. Lopez is more concerned with the operation of existing enterprises than with the starting of new ones. He acts as troubleshooter for Mr. Milano, takes care of labor problems when any arise, and represents the Enterprises at various public functions. Managers of the various companies often find that Mr. Lopez is available for consultation when Mr. Milano is concentrating on some new negotiations.

Mr. Peche has been chief accountant for Milano Enterprises for over twenty years. He has an intimate knowledge of the accounting system of each company even though great variation exists in the way records are kept. Mr. Peche keeps a close eye on profits, liquidity, expense ratios, and other key figures for each of the companies and calls Mr. Milano's attention to any significant deviations. Mr. Peche works up estimated projections for Mr. Milano's use in negotiations and in arranging financing, and he takes care of tax matters.

Mr. Gaffney has been Mr. Milano's chief associate in the automotive end of the business, although he is twelve years younger than Milano. Mr. Gaffney serves as manager of the automotive import company and exercises supervision over European imports, all distributors, and the filling stations. He spends about two-thirds of his time with this group of companies but is available for general consultation on other matters. In several new ventures, Mr. Milano has asked Mr. Gaffney to make the preliminary investigation.

Mr. Bolivar is the official representative of Milano Enterprises to the government, obtaining import licenses, which often involve protracted negotiation. Numerous changes in regulations, often without much warning, require Milano Enterprises to maintain an able representative in close contact with administrative and legislative personnel. Also involved is a certain amount of "lobbying" when new legislation is being discussed in the legislature. Mr. Bolivar devotes his full time to this government work and does not get involved in operating problems of the companies.

Mr. Juan Milano is the thirty-two-year-old son of the company's founder. He has been educated abroad. He now works with his father and with Mr. Lopez on special projects, such as several consumer studies (for the hotel, bottling company, gasoline filling stations, and electric refrigerator plant). Because of his education, he often meets with foreign visitors.

Mrs. Rodriques, who has an M.B.A. from a leading American university, serves a dual role. She is a personal assistant and interpreter for Mr. Milano, and as such she has a keen interest in learning the latest developments and management thought of companies abroad. In this capacity, she not only presents the ideas but discusses with Mr. Milano the way they might be related to the Enterprises. Mr. Rodriques' more formal assignment deals with executive and technical personnel. A few general conferences have been held, but thus far most of the work in the senior personnel field is still in the planning stage. Competent executives are scarce, and even though Milano Enterprises has an excellent reputation, executive selection and development has been more opportunistic than programmed.

All of these people are very busy and there rarely is a time when two or three of them are not working on some pressing current problem. The board of directors of Milano Enterprises is composed of Mr. Milano, his wife, Juan Milano, Mr. Lopez, and Mr. Gaffney. Because most of these people are in frequent informal contact, formal meetings of the board are held only when some official business must be transacted.

## ■ Concern for the Future

Even though Milano Enterprises has been successful and is highly regarded in business circles, Mr. Milano is concerned about the future. For one thing, Mr. Milano recognizes that the central organization lacks system and is too dependent upon him personally. He says, "I'm not proud of our organization. All I can say is that thus far it has proved to be adequate."

More pressing is what will happen after Mr. Milano's death. He is in good health, but he is already sixty-five and wishes to take steps now for the perpetuation of the Enterprises. He would like any reorganization to provide for three objectives:

1. Modern, effective management that will be flexible enough to meet changing conditions as he has done during his lifetime.
2. Continuing contribution to the economy of the country, particularly with respect to the initiative and adaptability that free enterprise can provide better than government bureaus.
3. Continuing family ownership of a controlling block of stock. This does not mean that some of the stock may not be sold publicly, as local capital markets develop, nor does it mean that members of the family will always hold top executive positions unless they are fully qualified to do so.

A banker with whom Mr. Milano has thoroughly discussed this matter urges "decentralization." He advises:

> No one can keep track of all of your companies the way you have, because only you have the background that comes from founding and working with these companies and their executives over a long period of years. Consequently, you should follow the practice of the leading United States companies by appointing able people as the chief executive of each of your operating units and then decentralizing authority to each of them. You already have this general form, but too many decisions are made in the central office. You should immediately decentralize and find out which of your managers are competent and which ones have to be replaced. The sooner you start, the better, because it will be some time before all twenty-five of the companies can stand on their own feet.

The idea of having strong managers in each operating company appeals to Mr. Milano, but he is dubious about the long-run effect of such a decentralization. He fears that Milano Enterprises will become primarily a passive holder of investments, and this certainly has not been the key to success in his personal experience. He anticipates that local managements may continue to do well what they are now doing but is not sure whether they will adapt to changing conditions, seek out new opportunities, and provide the kind of control that spots difficulties early and ensures vigorous remedial action.

Because so much is at stake, Mr. Milano decided to call in an international management consultant. On the basis of advice from companies with whom the Milano Enterprises does business and several personal interviews, Mr. Eberhardt Stempel was selected to make a thorough organization study of the Milano Enterprises. Mr. Stempel presented his recommendations orally and then wrote the following summary report.

## Recommendations of Management Consultant

### INTERNATIONAL CONSULTANTS, INC.
### New York - London - Frankfurt - Caracas

Dear Mr. Milano:

You have asked that we briefly summarize the recommendations we discussed in your office a week ago. In the original assignment you requested we focus our attention on the central management of the Milano Enterprises, and our investigation confirms your diagnosis that major problems of the future lie in this area.

No report on Milano Enterprises can be made without first recognizing past achievements. Milano Enterprises occupies a unique position in the national economy. Highly respected for its growth, financial strength, willingness to back new ventures, and alertness of management—this group of companies has become a recognized leader in the private business sector. The Milano name carries a high and well-deserved prestige throughout the business community.

The crucial question now facing Milano is not immediate. Instead, it is how to prepare for the time when you, Mr. Milano, can no longer serve as the guiding force of the combined group. Note, the problem is greater than the continuing direction of present enterprises. In addition, the future management of Milano Enterprises must have wisdom and courage to expand or contract in various lines as economic opportunities change. Any true perpetuation of your leadership must be dynamic, not static.

We believe the best way to perpetuate Milano Enterprises is to build a strong central organization. The present organization is able to cope with the problems it faces only because of long experience in the field and the exceptional talents of the senior executives. To ensure maintenance of present success and to provide for growth, a variety of high-grade specialists should be added to the central organization so that expert talent is readily available to help each of the operating companies meet their respective problems. The organization that we believe will best meet the future needs is shown in Figure 18–4. This organization is patterned after several of the most successful companies in the world and it embraces features we have found to be helpful to many of our clients.

After you have had an opportunity to study this organization carefully, we will be glad to prepare job descriptions and manpower specifications for each of the positions shown. Before doing so, however, you should be clear in your own mind that this is the direction you wish to follow. We would like to again stress the advantages of this form of organization to Milano Enterprises:

1. A strong central office is provided, including experts in marketing, production, and finance. Every company, large or small, must perform these basic functions well. Consequently, you should have the strength to deal with the problems in these areas.

2. Provision is made for current effectiveness. Subsections are provided for industrial engineering, purchasing, marketing methods, accounting, finance, legal advice, and government representation. When these sections are properly staffed, the central office will have talent to help streamline the operations of any existing and newly acquired operating company.

3. In addition, provision is made for growth. The sections on market research, new product development, financial analysis, and public relations will be primarily concerned with finding opportunities for expansion.

**FIGURE 18–4.**
**PROPOSED ORGANIZATION, MILANO ENTERPRISES**

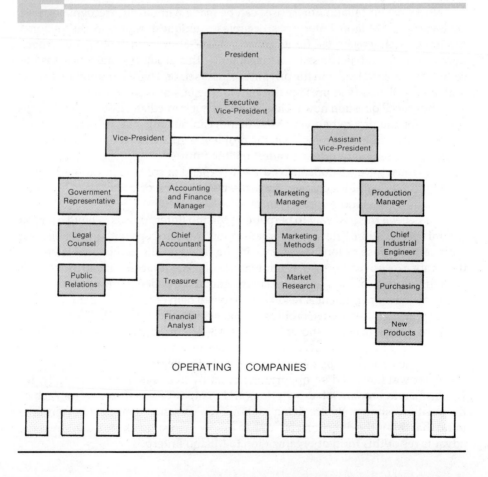

> 4. Senior executives of Milano Enterprises are given titles and recognition commensurate with the important roles they play in the group itself and in the nation.

We fully recognize that time will be required to find the proper individuals to fill these posts and to get the entire group working together effectively as a team. We believe that you can best serve Milano Enterprises by devoting most of your time toward this end. You should anticipate that it may take three or four years before the transition can be completed. It is important that the change be made while you are still able to give it your personal attention and endorsement.

It has been a pleasure to serve you and we shall be happy to be of any further assistance that we can.

Sincerely yours,

(s)Eberhardt Stempel, on behalf of

International Consultants, Inc.

Attachment

## Reactions to Mr. Stempel's Recommendations

The central management group had heard Mr. Stempel's oral report, and as soon as they had an opportunity to review the written summary, Mr. Milano called a meeting for a frank discussion of the recommendations.

Both Mr. Lopez and Mr. Peche expressed grave concern about the heavy overhead expense that the proposed organization would entail. It was far more elaborate than anything they had contemplated, and they felt the central office would be so big that personal contacts with one another would become even more difficult than they already were. Mr. Gaffney said that from the point of view of the automotive unit, he would much prefer to add staff under his immediate direction than be charged for a share of a central office staff that probably would have only superficial understanding of his particular problems. Mrs. Rodriques expressed disappointment that the report was not specifically adapted to the needs of Milano Enterprises. "Except for the special emphasis given government representation, the organization looks as if it was designed for General Electric or Unilever." Juan Milano endorsed this point of view, saying that he did not see how the particular organization would fit the hotel business or the filling station business.

To close the meeting, Mr. Milano made a general statement of his feeling:

> All of us, I'm sure, have been startled by the recommendations. I confess considerable sympathy with most points that have been made. And yet I ask myself whether I am rejecting recommendations because they are new and because they cast some reflection on the way I personally have been running the business. We asked Mr. Stempel to come here because we face a grave problem, the most serious problem of my entire life. I personally want to be sure before I reject these recommendations that it is not because

they will require a great change in my own behavior, but because I have a better plan for the future of Milano Enterprises. One of the reasons for the success of many of our companies has been a willingness to recognize a need for change and then to move in that direction aggressively. I would like to think that I am strong enough to apply that same doctrine to my behavior as the head of the Enterprises. Unless we come up with a better plan, I intend to start to put Mr. Stempel's ideas into effect because time does not permit us to stand still on this issue.

## Questions

1. Do you agree with Stempel's recommendations? If so, how would you respond to criticisms by members of central management? If not, what do you recommend and why?
2. The operating companies within Milano Enterprises vary in size. They also vary in rate of growth and change. In what way, if any, does the organization that you recommend recognize these variations?

# CHAPTER 19

## Corporate Governance: The Top Arbitrator of Strategy

Vital to the success of every enterprise is the organization for central management itself. A small group of key people decides on, or at least endorses, company strategy, policy, organization structure, and related matters. To assure positive, consistent direction, there is obviously a need for a workable understanding among this group as to "who is to do what."

More than internal organization is involved: just who wields power in modern society is also at stake. Currently the debate focuses on boards of directors, but inevitably the relation between boards and senior managers is also questioned. The primary issues from the viewpoint of strategic management include the following:

1. How can the board of directors be maintained as an independent, strong check on senior managers?
2. Should the board be composed of representatives of special interest groups, or should it be dedicated to the well-being of the enterprise?
3. How should the full-time senior managers be organized to assure that central management tasks are done well?
4. How should those in power be ousted if they are doing a poor job? (This is discussed in Chapter 20.)

## Independent Check on Senior Management

Within a company, we can trace formal authority up to the "chief executive officer." But where does the C.E.O. get power, and who checks up on his or her performance?

### Legal Theory

Stockholders of a corporation are not expected to perform management functions, and typically they are even more passive than they need be. Except for rare insurrections and tender offers, stockholders do little more than vote for directors, approve recommendations submitted by management, and, they hope, collect dividends. Normally, they simply sell their stock if they do not like the way the corporation is run.

A large stockholder may be active, to be sure, but this is almost always done as a director or perhaps as an officer of the corporation. Once in a while, when a corporation is mismanaged or has a low value on the stock market, dissident stockholders led by a raider will wrest control from the existing management. However, they too pass management responsibility to a "new" board of directors. So, the stockholders *per se* do not provide central management.

According to legal documents, the board of directors establishes objectives, sets policy, selects officers, approves major contracts, and performs many other functions. Unquestionably, the board has authority to do these things. The practical question, however, is, Can we expect the board to perform these functions well, or should most of the initiative and activity be delegated to executives of the corporation?

## An Inactive Board

The activities performed by boards of directors vary widely. Until recently, most boards left the entire administration of the firm to executives.

The rationale for such an arrangement was that operating problems can be settled best by people who have an intimate acquaintance and long years of association with the company. These people can dispose of problems in their normal daily contacts without bothering with a meeting of the directors. The directors then confine their attention to formal action on dividends; to the election of officers; to the approval of any public reports; and to decisions on various minor matters, such as the approval of a given bank to be used as depository for company funds or the granting of a power of attorney to some trusted employee. Most of these actions are taken upon recommendation of the senior executives, and consequently the meetings of the board of directors have been perfunctory affairs.

However, a sharp change is taking place. Especially for corporations whose stock is owned by many people, boards of directors are becoming much more active. Underlying this switch are (1) a restiveness about "the establishment" and a general challenge to anyone in a position of power; (2) a series of social reform movements dealing with ecology, women's rights, consumer protection, aid to developing nations, human rights, nuclear power, and the like; and (3) disclosures of illegal activities by individuals within highly respected corporations. Organizations such as the New York Stock Exchange are sensitive to these social issues, and they are insisting on reforms in the ways companies are governed.

Incidentally, this challenge to the way corporations have been run is worldwide. In Europe and many developing countries, numerous efforts are being made to enlarge participation in board activities.

Far from clear, however, is just what these reactivated boards should do. A closely related question is who should be board members.

## Inside Versus Outside Boards

### An Inside Board

In the past, a board of directors often consisted largely, if not entirely, of executives of the company. Such directors are well informed about internal operations, the success of the company is of great importance to them, and they are readily available for discussion when critical issues arise.

Unfortunately, operating executives have difficulty taking a long-run objective view of their company. They are inevitably immersed in day-to-day problems, and they are emotionally committed to making certain strategies succeed. Moreover, they cannot disassociate themselves from the social pressure of their colleagues, and particularly their bosses; they are naturally concerned with maintaining the goodwill of these persons who can make life easy or hard for them. To assume that these operating executives can change their perspective and their loyalties when they walk into an occasional board meeting is unrealistic.

Rarely can an unaided inside board develop an objective, independent, and tough-minded view of the company as a whole.

### An Outside Board

As the name implies, an outside board of directors is composed of people whose principal interest is in some other company or profession. A banker, a prominent attorney, and senior executives of companies in other industries are commonly chosen as outside directors.

The advantages and disadvantages of outside directors are just the opposite of those for inside directors. The persons coming from the outside have independence of judgment and objectivity: they can see the company from a different point of view, and they are not wrapped up in short-run problems. On the other hand, they lack an intimate knowledge of the company's operations and its relations with outside groups. More serious, they lack the time to become fully informed: having major commitments in their principal line of activity, they cannot be expected to devote large blocks of time to company problems. All too often, people accept a directorship for the prestige attached or as a friendly gesture. They are willing to give advice, but they are not prepared to take the initiative in revising corporate strategy.

Since the aim is to secure an objective appraisal and independent check on senior managers, widespread opinion now favors a *majority* of outside directors. And an increasing number of publicly owned corporations are moving toward at least two-thirds outside directors. A recent survey of about a thousand *large* corporations by the American Association of Corporate Secretaries found that almost 80 percent had at least a majority of outsiders.

These figures apply to corporations in which management and ownership are already clearly separated. In closely held corporations, however, a tight association of a few owners-directors-managers continues mostly in the traditional pattern. There is little basis for assuming that larger corporations need objective review more than smaller ones. So the contrast in board membership reflects sensitivity to external pressures rather than a need for guidance. This means that closely held corporations rarely get an outside review of their strategy.

## Extent of Board Participation

Election of outside board members only sets the stage. What are such directors expected to do? Their independence also means that they lack the knowledge and time to deal with day-to-day operations. And their interference with supervisory relationships would certainly lead to internal confusion. To cite an analogy, a U.S. senator should not try to steer a battleship.

### Who Takes the Lead?

Furthermore, it is doubtful that outside boards, acting as a group (or committee), can be expected to exercise active leadership. Again, limitations on knowledge, time, and the process of arriving at decisions stand in the way. In unusual circumstances the board may grasp the initiative. But most of the time the creative proposals and well-designed strategies will come from the full-time executives. The primary role of the board will be to make sure that senior managers do, in fact, provide the active leadership. Board members can prod, help, evaluate, occasionally veto, stimulate, or request action—all of which are aids to central management.

### Realistic Role for Board of Directors

A feasible assignment for a board of directors, then, would normally include at least the following duties:

1.  *Approve major changes in strategy, policy, organization structure, and large commitments.* This assumes that carefully prepared recommendations on such matters will flow up from the senior executives. Even if the board approves a large majority of the recommendations made, the necessity for developing a thoughtful justification of the proposals stimulates executives to think through such changes from all angles. This careful preparation of a recommendation by executives may be as valuable as the combined judgment of the board of directors.
2.  *Select top executives, approve promotions of key personnel, and set salaries for this top group of executives.* This assignment is both delicate and highly important. It requires independent and yet informed judgments. The board of directors is in a better position to perform this task than anyone else.
3.  *Share predictions of future developments, crucial factors, and responses to possible actions.* Here the board is contributing to strategy in the formulative stage. The benefits of the broad experience and the di-

verse points of view are made available to the executive group. Outside members of the board can provide this sort of counsel without unrealistic demands on their time.

4.  *Evaluate results and ask discerning questions.* The board should appraise operating results both for prudent control and to obtain background information. This evaluation process should include the asking of a variety of penetrating questions, including a review of controls to avoid illegal actions. Most of these questions will be readily answered, but a few may set off a line of thought previously overlooked. Both directors and executives should recognize that the prime purpose here is to see problems from new and useful angles.

5.  *Provide personal advice informally.* Already familiar with the company, a director may be an excellent source of advice to executives. The treasurer may call a banker-director about a recent change in the money market, or the marketing vice-president may call another company executive about a new advertising agency. Or the president may want to test out an idea before a formal recommendation is presented to the board as a whole. The informality of these contacts encourages a free exchange of tentative ideas and intuitive feelings.

A board performing the functions just described is particularly valuable because such a check and an independent viewpoint can rarely be developed within the executive group. This is a facilitating role, however: it assumes a harmony of values and objectives which, as we will see later, may not exist.

## Maintaining Independence

In the role just outlined for a board of directors, the initiative on most matters is assigned to the chief executive officer. There is danger that this full-time manager may choose to consult the board only in a perfunctory manner. This is inevitable when outside board members do not "get into the act" until after important decisions are already made.

Several devices are available to help assure that outside board members do take an active part in at least two or three areas. As one alternative, the board may appoint standing committees composed of a majority, if not all, of the outside board members. The increase in this practice in a 14-year period is indicated in Figure 19–1. Subjects most often covered by these committees are:

1.  *Audit.* With the outside auditor, this committee reviews both the auditing process and the findings. Ninety-eight percent of the large companies surveyed by Korn/Ferry International had such a committee. All of those were composed entirely of outside directors.

2.  *Senior management compensation.* Both salaries and bonuses for officers and other senior executives are approved by this committee. About 90 percent of the large companies surveyed by Korn/Ferry In-

**FIGURE 19-1.**
**INCREASE IN NUMBER OF AUDIT, COMPENSATION, AND NOMINATING**
**COMMITTEES, 1973 vs. 1986**

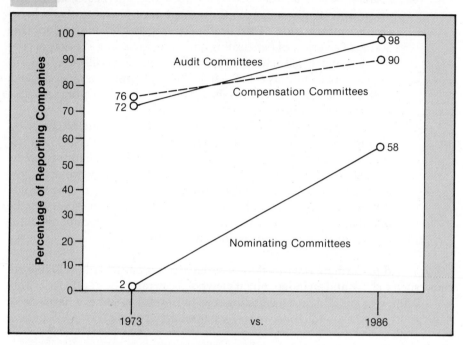

*Source:* Ferry International, *Fourteenth Annual Survey, Board of Directors.* Based on responses from 582 large U.S. industrial and financial companies.

ternational had such a committee. They were composed entirely of outside directors.

3. *Nomination of new board members and senior executives.* This committee focuses on composition of the board and on management succession; it transfers the power of picking successors from the chief executive officer to a more broadly based group. Almost 58 percent of the large companies surveyed by Korn/Ferry International had such a committee. The typical nominating committee had one inside director and four outside directors as members.

A more potent possibility, though not yet widely used, is an agenda committee. This device enables outside directors to select the subjects to which they will give the most attention. Thus, trouble is more difficult to "brush under the rug," and new opportunities can be assured of full study.

Since many smaller companies and not-for-profit enterprises are organized as corporations, they, too, face the question of just what their boards of directors should do. Managers of not-for-profit hospitals and smaller organizations often look to their boards for money-raising and wish only a minimum of interference with running the institution. Nevertheless, the issue of basic responsibility for direction of the institution is, at least legally, within the scope of the board. How it carries out this assignment is unclear.

## Dedicated Versus Watchdog Board

Who should the outside directors be? This question is closely linked with the duties assigned to the board. For instance, if a director is to help set the monthly agenda, then a resident of Saudi Arabia would be an unsatisfactory choice, no matter how much stock the person owned.

## Interest Group Representation

One proposal repeatedly heard is that various interest groups should be represented on the board. Indeed, for years it was customary to invite an investment banker or commercial banker whose firm helped finance the company to "sit on the board." Another example is the codetermination movement in Europe, which provides for labor representatives to be board members. (The Chrysler Corporation in the United States also has labor representatives on its board.)

Community representatives or a consumer representative are often proposed, but their selection and relation to their constituency has no traditional pattern. Even more ambiguous as to representational status is "a woman on the board" or "a black on the board." Nevertheless, pressure is mounting for selections based on such criteria.

The advantage of having interest group representatives as directors is also its weakness. The chances of continuing cooperation from the resource represented are improved: to some extent, the resource has been "co-opted." But the very fact that such directors are obligated to promote the interests of their particular groups undermines their loyalty and objectivity toward the company itself. A major customer, for instance, can advise regarding the market and may be inclined to buy from the company of which he or she is a director; however, inside knowledge of the company will also put him or her in an advantageous bargaining position. And when a choice has to be made, the customer's first loyalty is to the major employer.

Of course, having two or more related jobs is not unusual, and an individual may be scrupulously careful to withdraw from one or both roles when a conflict of interest arises. Most professional bankers feel that they conduct themselves in this manner. On the other hand, open and frank discussion is unlikely among persons who may find themselves on opposite sides of the table tomorrow.

If a board of directors consists largely of interest representatives—like a little United Nations—the potential usefulness of the board shifts. It might become a forum in which commitments to a program are developed. The boards of some not-for-profit institutions function in this way. For business corporations, however, much more flexible and extensive negotiations for resources are needed (as the key actor analysis described in Chapter 4 implies). Moreover, if the necessary corporations are joined together in a single board, the antitrust prosecutors would raise a storm.

Alternatively, if the board is to perform as suggested in the preceding section of this chapter, then watchdog directors are inappropriate. Instead, directors unquestionably committed to the company are required. Such directors may well have diverse backgrounds; but each is selected, like a Supreme Court Justice, for his or her capability rather than as a representative of an interest group.

## Conflicting Interests

When John Doe sells a large block of land to a company of which he is a director, we say there is a potential conflict of interest. The danger is that Doe will use his internal influence to promote a deal which is not optimum for the company but is very beneficial to him personally. There are other sorts of conflicts of interest, as with all group representatives discussed, but it is the personal gain problem that rears its ugly head most often.

The dividing line is fuzzy. A director may recommend the employment of a neighbor's son, but if that son is married to the director's daughter, the qualifications of the young man better be outstanding. The head of a very large corporation almost lost his job because by some coincidence his nephew was writing much of the company's casualty insurance. The eminent president of a large life insurance company did resign when there was public criticism about a long-term loan by his company to a firm in which the president was a significant stockholder.

It is unfair to condemn all such relationships. The normal protection is (1) to make one's connections clearly known, and (2) to insist that an objective, independent assessment be made of the benefits to the company of any such transaction. However, the mores of what is an unethical divided interest have been changing over time, and they vary from country to country.

On the borderline now is the question whether a company's investment banker or a partner in its outside legal counsel should serve on its board of directors. These have been two traditional sources of well-informed outside directors, and there has been virtually no scandal associated with the practice. Nevertheless, the presence of such individuals on the board probably does affect where the company does its banking and where it turns for legal advice.

## Obtaining Good Directors

Good directors will be increasingly hard to recruit. We have already presented a case for (1) raising the number of outside directors, and (2) significantly increasing the amount of work they will be expected to do. On the other hand, we have

(3) cautioned against using "watchdogs" and (4) raised the question about the propriety of directors who may gain personally from their part-time association. Where, then, are suitable directors to be found?

As in the past, some senior executives of leading companies will serve on each other's boards. Prestige, useful contacts, and some general knowledge comes from such posts. But as the workload gets heavier and the potential legal liability rises, this will not be an expanding source of outside directors. Professional outside directors probably will increase, though slowly. There are usually people with broad experience, either as former executives or as consultants, who devote a significant amount of time to any directorship they accept. In return, they are paid a fee—often $10,000 to $25,000 per year. University presidents and business school deans will continue to be a source.

In addition, companies will probably move down a status level to tap a larger pool of talent. Top vice-presidents of other companies are often very well qualified. They (and their main employers) probably would welcome the exposure to another corporation. Likewise, some professors may supplement administrators as an academic source. A few lawyers and financiers may find a directorship intriguing even though there is an understanding that it will not lead directly to professional engagements. Even with these additional sources, many companies will have to search to find a full complement of good directors.

Because good directors will be scarce, the development of boards as strong, independent arms of corporate government may be slow.

## "Outside Directors" within Diversified Corporations

Each business-unit within a diversified corporation needs the same kind of independent check on its activities as we have been advocating for separate companies. Someone outside the unit itself should approve major changes in strategy and organization, select top executives and set their compensation, share vital forecasts, evaluate results, insist that unpleasant problems be confronted, and provide personal counsel. This is the "outside director" role noted in Chapter 17.

A unique strength of a diversified corporation is its ability to provide people to act as "outside director" for each self-contained business. At least one corporate executive should be so designated for each business-unit; the dilemma of obtaining good outside directors is thereby avoided. The person appointed can be given the time and resources necessary to be well informed and concerned about the unit as a total undertaking. Contacts with other units and with external developments give the individual a broad perspective; at the same time, he or she is neither protecting a particular department within the business-unit nor beholden to the general manager for his or her job.

Because the parent corporation has such a large stake in each business-unit, it can afford to recruit and pay able individuals to fill this role—typically, one person will serve, say, half a dozen units. Along with finance, this "outside director" service is a primary contribution that parent corporations can make to strong operating units. Through its use, the business-unit strategy will get a frequent and thorough review.

## Organizing for Central Management

Although the board of directors has an essential role, the major burden of central management must be carried by full-time senior executives. They are the persons who must work out operational definitions of strategy based on a careful appraisal of trends, company strengths, obstacles to be overcome, impact on the rest of the company, and the like. The executives, with rare exceptions, negotiate major agreements for the company. They are the ones who represent the firm before congressional committees. A review of the annual budget with an understanding of its implications is an assignment senior executives are best able to perform.

An active outside board does not reduce the demands on the time of senior executives. Instead, preparing presentations for the board and responding to their questions adds another dimension to getting plans approved. The decisions should be wiser, but participation by an independent board complicates rather than simplifies the process.

### Legal Titles

Officers of the corporation—the president, vice-presidents, treasurer, secretary, and others—are formally elected by the board of directors in accordance with provisions of the company's bylaws. Occasionally, the bylaws also contain a realistic job description for these officers; but typically, the bylaws simply make some sweeping statements about the duties of the president and the treasurer and say little or nothing about other officers. Often a senior executive such as a general manager is not a legal officer at all, whereas an individual performing perfunctory duties in the secretary's office may be formally elected by the board. Common practice is to leave the legal authorization quite general, because this is difficult to change; instead, the actual working relationships are developed orally, by exchange of memoranda, or in a company's organization manual. Legal titles, then, give us only vague clues about how a top management actually functions.

### The Chief Executive

Normally, the chief executive officer also serves as the focal point for central management. This individual usually holds the title of president, but for diplomatic reasons may be named chairperson of the board, executive vice-president, or perhaps general manager. Ideally, the individual has vision, laying plans for 5, 10, or 20 years ahead; is a master of strategy and negotiation; has the ability to pick able personnel; stimulates and leads both immediate subordinates and employees throughout the company; is a popular and effective leader in civic and industry affairs; expects high standards of achievement by subordinates; and courageously takes remedial action when all is not well.

Again, realism forces us to admit that no single person can excel in all these respects. Even if one had the ability, that individual would not have the time to do all these things personally. Consequently, wise chief executives try to see that important activities that they cannot perform themselves are done by someone else in the company. This conclusion leads us to the question of how the chief executive's "office" can be organized.

## A "President's Office"

### Dual Executive

The most common way to relieve the central management burden on the president is to share the job with another senior executive. Various combinations of titles are used; chairperson of the board and president, president and executive vice-president, or president and general manager are examples. Whatever the titles, the two individuals have to develop their own way of splitting the total task. The division is likely to reflect the particular interests and abilities of the two individuals. One person may handle most external relations, while the other works with executives within the company. One may focus on long-range development, and the second may deal with current problems. Sometimes the division is along functional or product lines. Perhaps no continuing pattern exists: each works on whatever seems most pressing at the moment. Regardless of how the work is shared, an intimate and frequent interchange is desirable so that the two individuals function as a closely integrated partnership.

Occasionally, three people work together as peers, but the integration of their thoughts and activities into a single president's office view is difficult.

The dual executive arrangement works better in the top job than in other executive positions, probably because a higher proportion of the total work involves planning and deliberation and less time is involved in supervising daily activities. Nevertheless, it is a delicate arrangement and depends on getting the right combination of personalities.

### Group Vice-Presidents

Large diversified corporations often extend the "president's office" in another way. Group vice-presidents are added to take over relationships with clusters of business-units. These senior executives share frequently and informally in the thinking and planning for the entire corporation. However, typically they are designated as the main contact for four to eight business-units, and they keep track of these units more closely than is possible for other senior executives. These are the people who perform the "outside director" role for their assigned units.

Group vice-presidents usually have no staff of their own. Instead, they rely on staff who serve the entire "president's office." Like the dual executive, they are members of a partnership right at the peak of the executive pyramid.

## Management Committee

A further sharing device is the management committee, sometimes called a strategy committee or planning committee. Here, all top-level managers serve on a committee that deals with several central management tasks. Establishing strategy and policy, building long-range programs, appraising capital expenditures, and reviewing annual budgets are typical activities. This is where corporate strategy can best be formulated if the task is given sufficient attention.

A top management committee has all the inherent advantages and limitations of any committee. It clearly is a good coordinating mechanism; but if it is just an added assignment for executives who are already fully occupied with managing their respective departments, not much creative central management work will be accomplished. The firms with best success with a genuine central management committee have deliberately relieved their members of a significant part of their supervisory burdens, often by placing a single deputy under each member. The members are then expected to devote a quarter to half their total time to central management problems assigned to them by the president.

## Central Management Staff

Another well-recognized way to assist the chief executive with central management tasks is through the use of a staff. Special assistants to work on *strategy* are often appointed. We have stressed repeatedly that it is the line managers who should be the major architects of strategy. Nevertheless, they can use help. One role in the president's office is to help design the procedures, methods, and schedules to be followed throughout the organization for formulating and approving strategy, and to explain this common approach to numerous managers. For this purpose, an expert in the techniques (though not the substance) of strategy formulation can be used. A second role is to assemble data from outside sources that can be used by the managers as a check on their own estimates. Third, the staff person can check the internal consistency among strategic plans and their capability of being integrated into organization design, budgets, and other related management devices. If the staff help on strategy is restricted to such technical assistance, the responsibility and commitment of key managers need not be undermined.

The use of an *organization planning* staff reporting to the president is becoming more common. Such a unit assists in adapting the company organization structure to changing strategy needs. A related task sometimes combined with organization planning is *executive personnel development*. Executive development may simply be a part of the training activity of the company, but in some cases the personnel staff advisor to the president shares in the selection, development, and compensation planning for senior executives.

The role of the *business economist* is often confined to making cyclical forecasts of volume and prices in the industry; however, in a few instances the business economist has become an active participant in central management discussions. Similarly, *financial analysts* occasionally become advisers on central management issues.

These are merely illustrations of the kinds of problems the top staff might handle. Such people do more than assemble information specifically requested by the president, helpful though this may be. To be a really significant member of the team that assures that central management tasks are performed well, a staff member must be a respected, intimate adviser of the senior executive. Such staff members are hard to find, and not all chief executives know how to use staff effectively on problems involving difficult or intangible matters.

The particular combination of staff, multiple executives in the president's office, or committees obviously must be fitted to the needs of each company and to the personalities holding top positions. But whatever the design, provision for getting the central management tasks done well is crucial.

## Socially Responsible Governance

Central management of corporations can be considered from at least two viewpoints. The managerial view, which we take in this book, assumes that we are working from the inside of the enterprise trying to make it more effective. The viewpoint of society in general is different. Here, results and impact on society are all that matter. From this outside viewpoint, if corporations serve society well, they should be encouraged; if they do not, then the institution should be modified or even abolished.

As corporations become larger and more powerful, their impact comes under closer scrutiny. Also, as our society becomes more interdependent and sensitive to the health of each part, more people are deeply concerned about the behavior of each wheel in the complex machine. For these reasons, corporations are in the limelight. The very success of our business enterprises makes them the target for investigation and criticism.

With a lot of people wishing the world were different, any institution as powerful as our business enterprise system is sure to get a share of the blame. Inevitably, suggestions for altering the system will be advocated.

A popular point of attack is the board of directors. The board is presumed to have the ability to change the behavior of the corporation. Therefore, reformers propose changes in the composition of the board, or in the legal liability of board members, or in the way a board operates. The shift to more outside directors and the pressure for special interest representation on boards reflect in part this public concern. Business corporations (and powerful not-for-profit corporations) can disregard this challenge to past board practices only at their peril.

Basically, the response proposed in this chapter is that (1) corporations should indeed make sure that they strengthen their boards and use them for a continuing objective check on the direction the company goes and the results it achieves, but (2) each board should be committed to serving its company with undivided interest.

As a general scheme, we do not expect the board to be the place where agreements with various resource contributors are negotiated. If the board becomes a meeting place for special interest groups, or a device to induce cooperation, then it cannot effectively serve the function of constructive, objective "advice and consent."

Instead, each board should do its utmost to create a strong, energetic company, a company which performs its particular mission with distinction. The most potent instrument that a board of directors has to assure this result is a well-managed strategy formulation and execution system.

## Questions for Class Discussion

1. Korn/Ferry International, one of the leading executive search firms, also helps corporations find outside directors. In a recent study of boards of directors, this firm concluded the following: (a) "The responsibility of the board in determining corporate strategy will grow. The day of the 'rubber stamp' board is over."

   (b) "Renewed legal and fiduciary responsibility as well as the increased duties and time commitment will greatly reduce the population of potential qualified directors. Outside directors will find increased demands on their time limiting the number of boards on which they serve."

   What recommendations do you have for overcoming the crunch that these two trends, more demanding duties and fewer good candidates, are producing?

2. Suppose that you were hurt in an automobile accident and had to pay $6,000 in medical expenses to get patched up. As in most accidents, a variety of circumstances had to occur at the same place and time for your accident to happen. One factor was that the automobile's brakes did not hold; in fact, if they had been differently designed, you probably would not have been hurt.

   (a) Do you think that you should have the right to sue each director of the company that manufactured the automobile personally for damages? (That is, what should be the liability of a director for safety in the use of company products?)

(b) If a lawyer offered to press your claim for $6,000 in medical costs plus $34,000 for psychological suffering, with the condition that she would keep half of whatever award you received, would you turn over the case to the lawyer?

(c) Do you think that the corporation should take out an insurance policy (if it could get it) to protect its directors against such liability claims?

3. Whose company is it? A federal judge, during a heated court battle for the control of Marshall Field & Co., said, "The directors have a right to defend their company." What the directors had defended against was a tender offer to the shareholders to buy their stock at $42 a share when the market price was $16 a share. There were 10 directors and 17,000 stockholders. The directors repulsed the offer by starting a series of lawsuits against the offerer, by unrelated acquisitions that used up the cash reserves and created losses to reduce retained earnings, and by issuing press releases that stated their intention to keep the company "independent." Although their attorneys admitted that the directors would lose their positions, incomes, and status if Marshall Field & Co. were taken over, the directors asserted that they were acting in the "best interests of the company, its stockholders, employees, customers, and the community it serves." Does the company really belong to the directors, making acts such as these come within the scope of their authority? Such acts include setting up "golden parachutes" (large cash payments if the company is acquired) for the directors and chief executives, forcing "poison pills" upon the company to reduce its profits and value, paying "greenmail," and devising imaginative lawsuits to be paid for by the company.

A former chairman of a Business Task Force on Corporate Responsibility said that the shareholder "is necessary only to provide capital and is a speculator for short-term profits. Directors and chief executive officers know that the company is surrounded by a turbulent and complex environment and that they are responsible to all stakeholder groups."

When the tender offer was defeated, the price of Marshall Field stock dropped to $14 a share. In this case, whose company is it?

4. A major and thorough study of what directors of companies actually do in fact found that boards followed an unwritten set of rules. Among these were (a) keep your distance from subordinate company executives; (b) be prepared to counsel individually the chief executive officer, both at his or her request and on your own initiative; (c) don't set strategy; and (d) keep up the pretense that the board is present to act in the shareholders' interests. What is the functionality of these rules; that is, what do you think is their usefulness to the board, to the executives of the company, and to the financial community? Explain why each rule is often found in practice.

5. Look up the background and experience of the trustees (directors) of your college or university. On the basis of this information, what do you surmise are the kinds of issues each trustee is qualified to deal with? Also, make a list of

the kinds of issues that the board of trustees *should* consider. How do the qualifications of the board members match with the issues and other matters to which the board should be giving its attention?

6. Put yourself in the position of a director of Toys-B-We, Inc., a publicly held producer of electronic toys for children, and consider the following events (simplified version of an actual case):

(i) A Japanese firm that would like to enter the U.S. toy market offered to buy all the assets and liabilities of Toys-B-We for the equivalent of $38 per share of common stock, assuming that the cash would be paid out to stockholders as a liquidating dividend. (ii) The manager of Toys-B-We countered this offer with a plan for borrowing enough money to pay a special dividend of $20 per share (leaving the company with an unusually high debt-to-equity ratio) and continue its planned launch of several unique toys. The management's conservative estimate of future earnings with these new products shows a probable increase in market value of the stock from $25 (its present value) to $40 or $50 per share. (iii) You and other outside directors voted to turn down the Japanese offer and to okay the management plan.

(iv) Now, one year later, it is clear that the new toys are not winners. Because of the high interest payments, earnings per share have dropped sharply and there is even some danger that debt will have to be "restructured." The market value of the stock is $8 per share. (v) A group of shareholders is suing you personally, and also other directors, for $10 per share plus interest and costs on the grounds of negligence in studying the management's plan plus a desire to protect your position as a director.

(a) Describe the nature of the investigation that directors of Toys-B-We should have made of the management plan to have, in your opinion, a defense against the negligence charge in the stockholders' suit. Should this have been a special investigation made because of the Japanese offer, or should it have been the customary check that Toys-B-We directors make of company strategy?

(b) What are the implications of your answer to (a) on the role that you believe corporate directors should take in strategy formulation and execution? Will having directors act in this way enhance their company's ability to compete in a fast-moving market?

(c) If a company such as Toys-B-We takes out insurance to protect directors from liability in suits such as the one described, do you think the directors should—or would—behave differently than you suggested in your answer to (a)? Is this modified behavior good for the corporation? for society?

7. At the last annual stockholders meeting of the Metropole News, a question was asked about the fees paid to the paper's legal counsel, Plaistead & McCoy, and a possible conflict of interest because Mr. McCoy is a member of the board of directors of Metropole News. The president replied that, "Plaistead & McCoy have been our legal counsel for many years, and we pay them the normal legal fees for the work we ask them to do for us. The total

amount paid last year is stated in the proxy statement." At a subsequent board meeting, Mrs. Driver pursued the question. "How do we know that Plaistead & McCoy's bill is correct?" Mr. McCoy explained, "We keep track of the time each member of our firm spends on Metropole News work and bill this at our regular per diem rates." Later the president thought to himself, *Mrs. Driver, who is an officer of half a dozen women's organizations, has aggressively pushed for the employment and promotion of women. Also, "Tiny" Kelly once was president and is still an officer of the printers' union, and he sure looks out for our printers. These two both are board members, yet we make no public report about how their outside interests are served. In fact, the question has never been raised.* Are there significant differences in the potential *conflict of interest* of these three directors? What should be done to protect other stakeholders against such conflicts of interest?

8. According to the law in West Germany, a corporation with more than 2,000 employees has one-half of its board of directors elected by its employees and the other half elected by stockholders. The theory underlying this "codetermination" is that employees have as vital an interest in company operations as do stockholders. (a) What effect do you think such codetermination is likely to have on (i) the way the board functions, (ii) the decisions the board makes on strategy, policy, etc., and (iii) the long-run strength of the company? (b) Why has the codetermination concept received little support thus far in the United States?

9. Assume that you are assistant to the administrator of a nearby hospital. Nominations for the board of directors must be made soon, and the administrator asks you, "What should our directors really do? And what kind of people should we seek to do those tasks?" While thinking how to reply, you recall the problems which the administrator has confronted recently; some, but probably not all, should go to the board. His problems included union demands, federal ceilings on Medicaid payments, negotiations with Blue Cross, the public outcry about high medical costs, the use of doctors trained outside the U.S., an increase in outpatient service, the hospital's annual deficit, fund raising, a regional plan (restrictions) on specialized facilities, large liability suits against the hospital by disgruntled patients, relations with the community chest, the need to purchase a three-dimensional laser scanner, maintaining the professional ethics of the staff, and replacing the chief of the medical staff. What would you reply to the questions addressed to you by the administrator?

10. When a subsidiary company owned by Toshiba Corporation was found to have sold machine tools to the U.S.S.R. which could be used by the Russians to make the propellers of their submarines very quiet and thus hard to detect, the two top executives of the parent company resigned. The chairman and the chief executive officer of Toshiba did this "to make the highest form of apology" in the Japanese business world despite the fact that the independently

run subsidiary company responsible for the sale had a separate management. (The sale was illegal under Japanese law and also illegal according to various treaties among Japan, the United States, and the various countries which are members of NATO.) *The Wall Street Journal* commented, "Most U.S. executives probably wouldn't even *consider* resigning over an issue like that." In 1985 the president of Japan Air Lines resigned following the crash of a Boeing 747 that killed over 500 persons. He stayed in office only long enough to see that arrangements had been made to bury the dead and assist the bereaved, the latter including his personal calls on victims' families. "By contrast, never was it seriously suggested in the U.S. that top executives of Boeing Co. step down after the JAL crash, even though the accident had been linked to a faulty repair performance years earlier by Boeing mechanics." Neither have any top officials of Morton Thiokol, Inc., resigned despite their company's involvement in the space-shuttle disaster which killed its crew of astronauts and its schoolteacher volunteer.

One commentator said that by Western standards resignation would look like the act of a coward, while by Japanese standards resignation accepts the blame for subordinates' actions and is honorable.

What usefulness is there for Japanese organizations to have their chief officers resign in disgrace or as scapegoats in extreme circumstances?

One explanation of the Anglo-Saxon legal point of view is that an employee is bound by a contract rather than as a member of a corporate community. Does this explain the differing actions of the presidents of Japan Air Lines and Boeing Company?

A Japanese professor of international management at a large urban college of business on the East Coast of the United States commented, "Within Japanese corporate culture and social ethics, the whole notion is that the leader can delegate the authority to anyone he or she wishes, but *not* the responsibility. In the United States leaders delegate authority *and* responsibility." Does this accord with the facts of the cases just cited and with your understanding of management theory?

# CASE
## 19 Dorfman Corporation

The Dorfman Corporation is considering a change in its board of directors. Long merely a family holding company, the corporation needs fresh leadership.

The chief asset of the Dorfman Corporation is the Springfield Department Store, which is almost a landmark in the county-seat city of over 100,000 population. Unfortunately, the store's midtown location has lost its pulling power: two large suburban shopping centers are now the preferred locations for most of the national chain store outlets. Nevertheless, many customers continue to come to "the department store" for children's and women's clothing, houseware, gifts, luggage, etc.

Location is not the only problem, however. The store's merchandising flair has diminished, and efforts to create a chic downtown shopping mall are making slow headway. On the financial side, sales are flat and profits are down; and the present board of directors of Dorfman Corporation is having difficulty confronting the total situation.

In fact, the present board never has been active. It consists of the following individuals:

*Bernard Dorfman,* 64, president and for 20 years the dominant leader in the store. Bernard Dorfman had a serious heart attack two years ago, leaving him with much less energy and daring, yet anxious to show that his judgment continues to be keen.

*Sheila Dorfman,* 63, wife of Bernard Dorfman. Mrs. Dorfman's interests center around church and music organizations; she has never been active in department store issues.

*Karl Klemper,* 53, nephew of Bernard Dorfman, who inherited a 30 percent share of Dorfman Corporation. For ample reasons, Bernard Dorfman lacks confidence in his nephew's judgment and consults with Klemper only when necessary. Klemper believes that his children should have good jobs in the store, but they have none.

*George Atkins,* 55, vice-president of Dorfman Corporation and general manager of the Springfield department store. Atkins has risen from the ranks at the store. He is a good operating manager, but relies very heavily on Bernard Dorfman for major decisions.

*Ross Trump,* 58, a CPA and outside director for Dorfman Corporation. Trump sticks closely to reporting and interpreting the financial data he has collected, and defers all questions about how the store should be run to Dorfman and Atkins.

The ownership of stock in the Dorfman Corporation is now distributed as follows:

| | |
|---|---|
| Bernard Dorfman | 40% |
| Sheila Dorfman | 18 |
| Karl Klemper | 30 |
| George Atkins | 2 |
| Church Advancement Fund | 10 |
| | 100% |

Bernard Dorfman is taking steps to transfer his stock equally to his two children, Tim and Marion. As part of this move, he has proposed that the size of the board be increased to seven and that Tim and Marion be elected directors: "As major stockholders they should learn more about the business."

Tim Dorfman, 34, is an electrical engineer with a good job over a thousand miles away from Springfield. Having left the family nest several years ago, he has little desire now to learn more about retailing. However, his prospective share in the company has a book value of over $200,000, and he does believe that getting new leadership to replace his father is urgent.

Marion Dorfman, 28, is a schoolteacher and has no more interest in getting dunked in retailing than does Tim. Marion has recently married an MBA, and proposes that a person with such training is just what the Dorfman board needs. So both Tim and Marion are recommending that they each be represented on the board by an objective, well-trained individual: Marion's spouse and a complete outsider who would have a similar viewpoint.

## Question

Suppose that (1) Bernard Dorfman agrees, somewhat sadly, to the addition of two MBAs to the Dorfman Corporation board, and (2) you as Marion's spouse are one of them. (If you don't like this marital arrangement, assume that you are the friend who is the other new director.)

(a) List the issues that you would try to get on the board's agenda, and the sequence in which they should be resolved.

(b) For the first two issues on your list, describe how you would propose that a plan of action be developed and also how you would try to get board acceptance of such a plan. Include a tentative timetable.

# CHAPTER 20

## Management Personnel: Prime Source of Strategic Initiative

Without suitable managers in a company, sound strategy and a clear organization plan soon become unrealistic aspirations; with good management personnel, they provide the guidance and the structure for purposeful enterprise. Even more, the executives themselves are the prime source of strategic initiative.

### Developing Management Personnel

The development of a competent group of immediate subordinates is a duty that can never be fully delegated. Larger companies may have a service unit that provides assistance in dealing with human resource problems, but each manager still carries primary responsibility for having competent people in key positions under his or her direction.

The typical chief executive is concerned with only a relatively few managers and other key personnel. These are likely to be people he or she has worked with over a period of years and they may well include close friends. An executive is expected to see that they perform today's tasks effectively and also develop so that they can assume the larger responsibilities of tomorrow. This development may take years and involves habits, attitudes, and skills. Except for filling unexpected vacancies caused by death or resignation, management personnel is a long-run problem. Because of these *personal, intangible,* and *long-run* characteristics of management personnel development, general policy is inadequate to deal with specific situations.

### Wide Variation in Company Practice

Since management personnel involves personal relationships, considerable differences occur in the way selection and development are handled in various companies.

#### A President Who Evaded Responsibility

In one relatively small company with eight key managers, the president had been for many years the key figure in coordinating operations. The subordinates were given considerable latitude within their own departments, but they were expected to concentrate their attention in their own areas. These individuals were very friendly with one another, and the president had a personal interest in and a deep loyalty to each member of the group. There was a general understanding that the sales manager would probably be the next president, and beyond that the matter of executive succession was given little thought.

The cold facts of the situation were that the sales manager was an excellent salesperson but not an effective manager. As a manager, he was indecisive and preferred not to assume administrative responsibility. As long as the president was active, these traits were not a serious handicap to the company. The sales representatives were experienced individuals who were glad to accept the kindly suggestions of the sales manager and who were able to proceed with a minimum of supervision.

When the president died and was succeeded by the sales manager, the latter's lack of executive ability created an acute problem. The other managers found it difficult to get positive decisions from the new president, who, in an effort to please everyone, was likely to reverse decisions. Coordination, or lack of it, was largely a result of the voluntary contacts between the several managers. The new president could not adjust to the responsibilities of the job and suffered a nervous breakdown within three years. The person who was next appointed as president had considerably more ability, but had been given virtually no training for the job as chief executive. Six to eight years elapsed before the company really recovered from the shock of the death of the president who failed to provide adequately for a replacement.

Note also that the president made no provision for change in the scope of company activities.

Looking back on this situation, one wonders why a successful president for so many years failed to anticipate the difficulties attendant upon his withdrawal from the company. Perhaps he never faced the question squarely. More likely, he recognized the limitations of the sales manager but could not bring himself to take the drastic action that would have been involved in the selection and training of another executive to be his successor. This would have created strain and upset a personal friendship. Since no immediate action was necessary, he probably evaded the issue and hoped it would work out all right somehow. Had he taken the necessary action when he was still president, the company would certainly have been better off and the sales manager spared a nervous breakdown. Such action would have taken considerable courage, however, because there was no assurance that all the people concerned would have recognized the need for action.

## Informal Development Program

More thought is given executive development in many companies than appears on the surface. Frequently these concerns have no announced program or procedure, but do give the matter of management personnel regular attention. One company, for example, has a "little green seedbox" that contains a card for each key person who is a present or potential manager of one of the concern's principal operations. Each year the work of these people is reviewed by a senior executive along with the individual's supervisor, and when a person is assigned to a new position his or her performance is watched closely. Then, as opportunities open up, people are moved into positions of increasing importance. If it is decided, after watching a person for several years, that the individual has reached maximum potential, his or her card is removed from the file.

Wide variations exist in this type of approach. Typically, the cards or the pages of a loose-leaf notebook contain little information other than a record of the positions a person has held, the salary, and perhaps notations on any outside civic or educational work done. If the president or a senior vice-president is the one who directs the activity and makes sure that each person's performance is reviewed at least once a year (though not necessarily in a formal review session), then it is likely that considerable management development work will take place and that the selection of people for promotion will be based on a broad view of the person's experience.

Where the activity is treated more casually, or where the reviews are sponsored by an individual who lacks prestige with other executives, the attention given to management development will probably be substantially less. In any event, the kind of training that occurs on the job depends almost entirely upon the interest and the ability of the supervising manager. Given the proper company tradition, backed by the necessary inspiration and guidance of the chief executive, such informal plans for development have worked remarkably well in some companies.

These informal approaches to management development have two basic weaknesses: (1) little thought is given to preparing for growth or major changes in strategy, and (2) management development receives low priority in the plans of most executives. To overcome these limitations, formalized programs of manager appraisal and replacement schedules have been created, especially in multinational concerns where lack of qualified managers may be a major restraint on expansion.

## Essential Elements for a Sound Formal Program

Even though substantial disagreement exists on how formalized management development should be, we can identify several basic elements that every manager should keep in mind in dealing with management personnel problems. Whatever the forms and procedures used, the manager's thinking should embrace the following steps:

1. Predicting the types and number of managers the company (or department) will need for successful operations in the future

2. Reviewing or inventorying the management talent now available
3. Formulating a tentative promotion schedule, based on the two preceding steps, that provides for filling each of the positions in the anticipated organization and, insofar as possible, provides for a potential replacement for each of the key managers
4. Planning for the individual development of each person slated for promotion, so that each may be fully qualified for the responsibilities
5. Making compensation arrangements that will attract and hold the managers covered in the foregoing program and provide incentives for them to put forth their best efforts

The significance and the nature of each of these steps will be considered in the sections that follow. Even though changes in strategy may call for sharp revisions in a company's executive personnel plans, the new lineup should be based on the same sort of analysis.

## Anticipating Managers Who Will Be Needed

The basis for any long-range planning for management personnel is a prediction of the kind of people that will be needed to execute the company's present and future strategy. Surprisingly, this obvious first step is sometimes overlooked. In one company, for example, the top administrator held the view that "we always have room for good people around here" and on several occasions had hired competent people with no clear-cut idea of what they were to do. These individuals either got bored waiting for a significant assignment or created friction by interfering with the activities of other executives.

A more common failure is to assume that a title provides an adequate guide to the kind of person needed. A hard-driving, enthusiastic sales supervisor is quite a different individual from an analytical and imaginative planner of merchandising campaigns, and yet either of these persons might have the identical title of product sales manager. Before sound management development can be done, a clear understanding is needed of both the jobs to be filled and the characteristics of the persons needed for these jobs.

## Jobs to Be Filled

A study of strategy and future organization, along the lines indicated in this book, will result in a long-range organization plan with descriptions of each key position needed. These position descriptions are not necessarily put in writing, but there must be an understanding of the duties and the relationships of each executive position. If plans for the future administrative organization have not already been clarified, then organization analysis becomes a first step in the management personnel program.[1]

Position descriptions prepared to clarify organizational relationships differ in emphasis from those used in a management development program. The more ticklish aspects of organization involve defining the border lines between the various units and spelling out the interactions when activities must be closely coordinated. Such refinements of responsibility are not so important for executive development purposes. Here, interest centers on the major duties to be performed, the degree of decentralization and hence the judgment that must be exercised, the importance of initiative and enthusiasm, and similar matters. In other words, we need to sense the role the person in the management position will play. And these roles should be directly tied to future-oriented company strategy.

## Characteristics of Persons Needed for These Jobs

The second phase of the analysis of management requirements is to translate the duties into *personal specifications*, that is, the personal qualities an individual needs to fill a given position effectively. We can describe the duties of a football quarterback or a plant superintendent, but it is another matter to set up a list of qualifications that a person should have to fill such a position successfully.

These personal specifications may be stated in terms of knowledge, supervisory skill, emotional stability, judgment, dependability, ability to deal with outsiders, and social attitudes. Unfortunately, it is difficult to define requirements for positions in such terms because experience shows that people with quite different makeups may be successful in the same kind of a job.

Another way to draw up personal specifications is to list the principal things the people in question will be expected to do, such as build customer goodwill, control expenses, plan for future expansion, or stimulate and develop their subordinates. This kind of a list is easier to prepare, but its application still may require subjective judgments when an individual is being selected for work that is quite different from what he or she has been doing. Your being a crack salesperson, for instance, does not tell us how good you might be as branch manager.

One additional point should be emphasized. Much executive development work cannot be expected to show results in less than three to five years, and some of it may take longer. Consequently, the organization structure five years hence is more important than the present one. The outlook and the strategy for the company must be studied to forecast the volume and nature of future activities. These will throw light on the organization structure that will be needed and hence on the

---

[1]We clearly are recommending that organization design *precede* manager selection. Of course, in the short run a company must be managed by the talent available, and since the available managers may not fully match the ideal organization, the only practical action is to adjust the organization so that optimum results will be obtained. Management development, however, should continue to be aimed toward the best future organization we can realistically expect to achieve.

requirements for management personnel. Moreover, the existing organization may be far from ideal. A logical time to realign duties and correct organizational weaknesses is when management personnel are being shifted. If this is to be done, plans for management development should, of course, be based on the new, rather than the old, organization structure.

## Inventory of Management Talent

The second basic step in planning a management personnel program is appraising the individuals already in the organization. The organization and position analysis just discussed predicts what executive talent will be needed; the appraisal of managers, considered in this section, shows what talent is available to meet these requirements.

Generally, an inventory of management talent is taken to discover weak spots in the normal flow of managers through the promotion channel. It indicates where additional development work is needed to assure that satisfactory replacements are available when necessary.

A good inventory will also bring to light the competent managers who are not being used to their fullest capacity. For example, the president of a pharmaceutical company was shocked when her nephew resigned, along with two key salespeople, and established a competing firm. Evidence, however, clearly indicated that these people had not been assigned to challenging positions, and they considered their prospects for promotion so remote that they preferred to take the risk of establishing a new enterprise. A good plan of manager appraisal would have shown the president that these people were prepared for additional responsibilities. She should then have tried to find positions that would more fully utilize their abilities, and if this was not possible, she should at least have openly examined the situation with each individual. In other words, an executive inventory would have been useful even though there was no immediate need for replacing key personnel.

## Different Uses of Manager Appraisals

We may use manager appraisals in several different ways, and their value will be improved if we recognize these uses at the outset.

1. The primary purpose of management review may be to *select* a person for an existing or anticipated vacancy. For this purpose, an objective appraisal of the person's future potential is needed.

2. Manager appraisal may point to the need for development when abilities of managers are matched against the personal specifications for a given position. Individual *development programs* can be built to remedy deficiencies. When the emphasis is on personal development, the appraiser can identify much more closely with the individual being re-

viewed, and together they can seek out opportunities for improvement.

3.  Manager appraisal may be used to establish bonuses and to pay increases or other forms of *compensation*. Here, attention centers on past achievements rather than future potential. Objectivity is needed, as it is in considering individuals for promotion.

Be prepared to reinterpret an appraisal designed for a purpose that differs from your current interest.

## Informal Appraisal of Managers

No systematic appraisal, or inventory taking, of managerial ability is made in many companies. Nevertheless, considerable informal appraisal typically takes place. This was the method followed in a financial company, for example, that had 32 senior and junior officers and approximately 85 first-line supervisors and other key employees. The size of the company permitted each senior officer to know personally all of the executives as well as some of the outstanding operating persons.

The president and the senior vice-president made it a practice to "keep their eyes on the staff." They asked questions and otherwise followed the work of the various managers closely enough to have a clear impression of what most of the people were doing. In addition, they occasionally talked with the individual officers about the people under their supervision and what might be done to assist in their development. The officers felt that more formal ways of inventorying executive talent were unnecessary in their situation.

Informal management appraisal such as that just described is a natural and continuing process that should be used by everyone in a managerial position. The more formal appraisal techniques, discussed in succeeding paragraphs, supplement rather than substitute for this type of evaluation. The informal appraisal is done at convenient times, in connection with other work; consequently, it creates no special burden on executives.

Limitations of this method are that (1) some managers who are primarily interested in technical problems may fail to assess the complete personalities of those they come in contact with; (2) the appraisals may be incomplete, with emphasis on past performance and little attention to future potential; and (3) in larger concerns where no one executive can know personally all of the present and potential managers, it is extremely difficult to compare candidates in one department with those in another and to exercise guidance over a management development program.

## Systematic Evaluation of Managers

To overcome the limitations of informal appraisals, several companies have definite procedures for management personnel reviews. In their simplest form, these evaluations consist of only an annual memorandum written by the supervisor of each key person outlining the person's outstanding accomplishments and failures during the year, steps taken for development, and future potential.

At the other extreme are rather elaborate evaluation forms that record an overall appraisal of the person's work during the past year, a rating of personal qualities, promotion possibilities, and plans for individual development. The Armed Services use a similar technique; in fact, the file of fitness reports is the primary basis on which Navy officers are selected for promotion.

Formal evaluation plans build up a record covering each manager, which is very helpful when he or she is being considered for transfer or promotion. Usually several different people have submitted appraisals and the total record is not dominated by some single event, as may happen when sole reliance is placed upon informal appraisal. Moreover, the formal procedure tends to make the evaluation more thorough and consistent.

On the other hand, standard forms and procedures by no means ensure that appraisals will be made carefully and honestly. Unless the executives making the appraisals believe that the whole process is worth while, they may fill in the form hastily and with answers that they think will lead to the promotions and transfers they would like to see made. Also, standard forms emphasize factors that the designers of the forms think are important, and for some jobs these factors may not match the current operating requirements and, even less, the requirements of a new strategy.

Recent antidiscrimination laws have increased the importance of appraisal records. Suing someone has become a national pastime, and employers must be careful (1) not to discriminate on the basis of race, religion, sex, age, etc., and (2) to have evidence that they did not discriminate. Consequently, fair but tough evaluations should be made, regardless of their impact on individual egos.

## Plans for Filling Management Positions

Development of management personnel, as already noted, is largely a long-run problem. Individuals need time to develop the knowledge, skills, and judgment required in most executive posts.

## Planned Manager Progression

The treasurer of a medium-sized company wished to retire within a year and recently told the president. In the discussion at the next meeting of the board of directors, two facts emerged: (1) the assistant to the treasurer, specially selected two years earlier, had displayed more energy than judgment and clearly was not qualified to replace the treasurer, and (2) there was wide misunderstanding about how vital a role the new treasurer should play in overall company operations (some board members wanted a senior executive, whereas the president thought in terms of a cashier). Two years elapsed before a satisfactory, strong person could be found.

Having the right person in the right position at the right time is of supreme importance, especially when expanding or shifting into a new field. Here is an area, then, where long-range planning is of vital importance, even though human behavior is hard to measure and to predict and results may not turn out just as planned.

## Staffing-Plan Approach

Transfer and promotion of managers is a normal occurrence in a typical business concern. Deaths, retirements, firings, and resignations create vacancies. New positions, resulting from expansion, have a similar effect. If these positions are filled by promotions, additional vacancies are created in the lower ranks. In fact, one vacancy at the vice-presidential level may result in shifts of half a dozen people at lower levels. The problem is how a company can plan to meet such changes.

The staffing-plan approach rests on three ideas that have already been discussed. The first is anticipating managerial requirements in terms of positions to be filled and the personal specifications of managers needed in such positions. The second is a policy of promotion from within. The third, assuming such promotion, is the inventory of managerial talent discussed in the preceding section, which provides the personnel data needed for concrete planning. Staffing tables are simply a device for weaving this information into a tentative plan.

Staffing plans, such as the one in Table 20-1, show, for each manager position (and anticipated position), one or more persons who might be moved into that spot. The preparation of such plans requires that the personal specifications for each position be used to select the best candidate available within the company. Some companies distinguish between candidates who are already qualified and those who need a year or more of training before they would be prepared to take on the new duties. To be useful, such a chart should be realistic. Thus, if some positions contemplated are now vacant, they should be shown in this way. If there are no real candidates for a given position, this too should be frankly revealed. Of course, one individual may be considered as a candidate for two or more positions.

Such staffing plans are subject to frequent revision. Unexpected changes in company operations or in the personal lives of executives may shift requirements. Some people will develop faster and others slower than anticipated; in fact, in time, some persons will be added and others will be dropped as candidates for particular positions. Not infrequently, an understudy is moved to still another position and a new understudy must be found. Nevertheless, preparation of staffing plans serves a very useful purpose in pointing up where available replacements or candidates for new positions are lacking. Moreover, it forces a realistic review of the persons who are likely to be promoted; then, if they need further development, immediate steps may be taken to start the necessary training.

Staffing plans are, of course, confidential documents because they reflect highly tentative promotion plans that are likely to be revised later. For this reason,

**TABLE 20–1.**
**SAMPLE STAFFING PLAN**[1]

| Job Title | Job Incumbent | Age | Senior Candidate | Age | Junior Candidate | Age |
|---|---|---|---|---|---|---|
| *Management Level Group "A"* | | | | | | |
| Service Manager | K. L. Foster | 47 | | | G. E. George | 38 |
| | | | | | A. A. Day | 35 |
| Sales Engineer | B. C. Johnson | 65 | C. D. Dewey | 42 | L. M. Mason | 38 |
| Construction Manager | E. E. Bryant | 49 | No Senior | | E. F. Burnes | 37 |
| Accountant | F. G. Bray | 55 | No Senior | | No Junior | |
| *"B" Office Managers* | | | | | | |
| Arden | G. H. Miller | 63 | ) | | )E. D. Hill | 42 |
| Hightop | A. A. Day | 35 | )G. E. George | 38 | )M. N. Johns | 35 |
| Glendale | C. D. Dewey | 42 | )L. M. Mason | 38 | )W. X. Hobbs | 33 |
| *Local Service Managers "A" & "B" Offices* | | | | | | |
| "A" Office | R. R. Colby | 62 | ) | | | |
| Arden | G. E. George | 38 | )M. N. Johns | 35 | X. Y. Bell | 37 |
| Hightop | R. S. Williams | 41 | )M. X. Hobbs | 33 | E. D. Hill | 42 |
| Glendale | S. T. Fuller | 57 | ) | | | |
| Maintenance Zone | T. U. Webster | 51 | | | R. S. Williams | 41 |
| Zone Promotion | "Vacancy" | | No Senior | | T. V. Dodge | 32 |
| Zone Construction | V. W. Gary | 58 | F. E. Hyde | 39 | No Junior | |
| Zone Field Engineer | P. T. Monroe | 39 | | | T. U. Olson | 48 |
| | | | | | U. V. Larsen | 41 |

[1]Sample sheet from staffing plan of Otis Elevator Company. "Senior candidates" are qualified to take over positions without further training other than normal job indoctrination; "junior candidates" need one to five more years of training. Note that some individuals, such as Hobbs and George, are listed as candidates for more than one position.

some executives prefer never to put their ideas down in writing. For smaller companies or for a single department, this may be satisfactory *provided* that the same basic thinking takes place. The chart is merely a device to help an executive think through a very "iffy" subject; it is the systematic analysis of manager placement, rather than the particular pieces of paper, that is important.

## Methods of Selection

Planned placement of managers modifies, but by no means eliminates, the need for wise selection of individuals to fill executive positions. In a stable situation, possible candidates must first be identified; later, one of these may be designated as an understudy; and when the vacancy occurs, the final selection must be made. This sifting process should improve the selection because judgments are made at different times, often several years apart, and this provides an opportunity to reconsider earlier impressions.

When corporate or business-unit strategy changes, with corresponding shifts in organization and job requirements, executive selection is much more abrupt. There is a question of whether present executives will be effective in the new organization; and for a few new positions, there is no time for trial on similar jobs or as an understudy. For instance, a tough cost-cutter may be needed where two sales promoters were before. Or an imaginative risk-taker may be needed to head up a new business-unit. Indeed, the selection of a particular individual may really determine the nature of the job.

In such circumstances, an accumulated record about the capabilities and personal values of individuals is especially valuable because the previous staffing plans have been outmoded. To infuse the new organization with a new outlook, an outsider may have to be brought in.

In any of these situations, selection will usually be improved if *group judgment* is used. The appraisal of individuals involves so many intangibles, and personal bias is so difficult to remove, that the views of at least two or three people should be considered in making executive decisions. If there is a difference of opinion, then a warning has been raised and further observation on the points in question can be made. Probably in no other phase of business administration is group judgment more valuable than in the selection of managers.

When tentative selections of one or more candidates for a position are made several years before the actual vacancies occur, *trial on the job* may be possible. Then, a candidate may "pinch-hit" in the job when the present incumbent is off on vacation or on special assignment. A more likely arrangement is to assign the candidates to work in a department or branch where they can demonstrate ability to do certain phases of the work. Such assignments typically serve the purpose of both training and selection. If time permits, people may be tried out in several different positions. What people have done in the past is no definite assurance of what they will do in the future, but it is probably the best evidence we can obtain.

No mention has been made of psychological tests for selecting executives. When a quick selection has to be made from individuals outside the company, test data may be a useful supplement to other sources of information. However, when careful appraisals of people already in the company are possible, and group judgment and trial on a series of different jobs can be utilized, psychological tests in their present state of development rarely add much that is useful.

## Removing Ineffective Managers

Strong performances in each management position are vital to company effectiveness. More than salary expense is at stake: a weak incumbent blocks the possibility for a more capable person to do that job well.

Removing ineffective managers is always painful. As we have already noted, legal complications are increasing. A company must be wary of charges of discrimination based on race, religion, or sex; even the use of normal retirement age is now illegal. Instead, clear evidence of inadequate performance is necessary to remove a manager who wishes to stay on the job.

This need for clear evidence will force companies to maintain more elaborate, explicit (and expensive) performance evaluations—and evaluations of future usefulness. Thus, instead of merely treating old Bill kindly until he finally reaches compulsory retirement age, records which he sees will have to spell out bluntly how obsolete he has become.

These evaluations should have a future focus, covering the following, among other things:

1. Ability to contribute to projected new activities of the company—for example, willingness to move, capacity to learn new technology or language, health and energy
2. Commitment to the company versus outside interests and tendency to take jobs with competitors
3. Effectiveness in securing cooperation of people in other departments and outside the company

Unless senior managers have the courage to make unpleasant personnel decisions, and also develop the tools which enable them to act wisely, their company can become choked with mediocre performers.

More troublesome, though less ensnarled in legal red tape, is how to treat executives who could continue to perform their previous job competently but no longer fit into the organization because of a change in strategy. Again, two separate issues should be faced: (1) How do we make the new organization strong and suited to its mission? Unless this is done, many people may suffer; so, as on a baseball team, executives who no longer suit the new lineup should be removed. (2) What are our obligations due to past services? Tailor-made adjustments such as job transfers, "outplacing," early retirement, and support during the transitions are all possibilities for meeting the obligations constructively and fairly.

## Development of Management Talent

Manager training cannot be accomplished well *en masse*. As already noted, it deals with a relatively few individuals, each of whom is typically in a different stage of development and is preparing for a different job. Consequently, manager training should be approached on an individual basis.

## Plans Center on Individuals

Planning for the progression of managers points to the area where each individual needs further development. Any gap between the specifications for a position—especially for a position changed by a new strategy—and the abilities already possessed by the candidate should receive attention in the development plan. (See Figure 20–1.) Likewise, if a person's performance on the present job does not measure up to what is desired, these weaknesses should be corrected.

One company asks the following questions in designing a development program for each executive:[2]

1. WHAT IS THE PERSON? What are the candidate's executive qualifications, strengths, and weaknesses?
2. WHAT MAY THE PERSON BECOME? What are the candidate's possibilities and growth potential?
3. WHAT DOES THE PERSON NEED TO GET THERE? What experience does the candidate still need for the position aspired to?
4. WHAT PLANNED COURSE OF ACTION SHOULD BE TAKEN? What action is needed to fill the gaps in the candidate's experience?

One aspect of individual development plans deserves emphasis. Most of the initiative and the work must come from the individuals themselves. To be sure,

**FIGURE 20–1.**
**LONG-RUN PERSONNEL PLANNING**

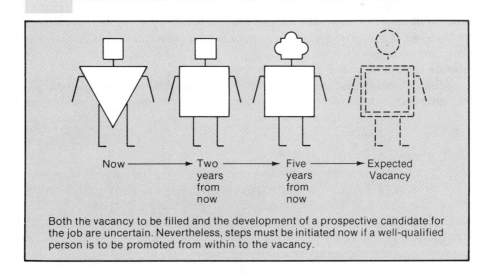

Now ⟶ Two years from now ⟶ Five years from now ⟶ Expected Vacancy

Both the vacancy to be filled and the development of a prospective candidate for the job are uncertain. Nevertheless, steps must be initiated now if a well-qualified person is to be promoted from within to the vacancy.

[2]Formulated by George B. Corless, Exxon Corporation.

the company has a vital stake in the matter and typically does a number of things to assist in the process. Nevertheless, good managers cannot be developed unless the people do a large share of the work. Since in this chapter we are concerned with company action, our discussion necessarily focuses on what managers can do to guide and aid the process.

## Training on the Job

By far the most important and lasting training a manager receives is on-the-job experience. In all types of work there is no adequate substitute for actually doing the operation, and this applies to executive planning, direction, and control fully as much as it does to selling or operating a machine.

Supervisors and other managers close to operations can make work experience much more valuable if they will *coach* the people being trained. Just as athletic coaches make suggestions, watch performance, point out weaknesses, and encourage athletes to do better, so may executives help their subordinates to learn on the job. Good coaches need to understand the emotional as well as the intellectual makeup of their proteges and to use discretion in the time and the manner in which they make suggestions. They need to cultivate mutual respect and a desire for improvement. Conceived in this manner, the combination of work experience plus coaching can become a powerful tool for executive development.

Often a manager cannot get all the needed training on a single job. For example, in preparing for the position of sales manager, the person may spend several years as a sales representative, two or three years in the sales promotion division, five years as a branch manager, and at least three or four years as an assistant sales manager. Many companies make a regular practice of such *job rotation* for purposes of manager training. The staffing plans described previously may provide for transfers that do not immediately put the best person available in each vacancy; instead, they use some of these vacancies as training spots for individuals who are thought to have high executive potentials.

Job rotation for manager development normally assumes that a person will fill a given position for a few years and show the ability to handle that job well before being moved on to the next position.

## Training off the Job

A variety of activities are useful supplements to training on the job. These are relevant for all sorts of managers, especially as rapid changes in technology, international competition, social values, and other environmental factors have made management education a never-ending process. The following list, while by no means complete, indicates some of the possibilities:

- Serving on company-wide committees or task forces
- Taking in-house company courses

- Actively participating in industry association conferences
- Attending university programs for experienced managers
- Reading professional journals regularly

## Manager Compensation

Along with careful selection and development of managers, sound compensation for managers is crucial to effective strategy execution. In fact, many observers of managers' behavior believe that a poor linking of compensation to strategy accounts for much of the foot-dragging in carrying out new strategic moves. Accordingly, in this section we will first briefly identify the kinds of incentives for managers that management has available, and then emphasize the difficult issues involved in linking these incentives to desired manager behavior.

### Base Salaries and Pensions

The level of salaries is a critical factor in attracting and holding competent managers. As with all employees, the salaries must be at least in the same general range as those offered by rival employers in order to attract good people. Other factors enter into the total compensation package, of course, but there is a base pay which is almost a social norm; it is also the sum that most managers use for current living expenses.

In many companies increases in salary, above the base just noted, are used to reward good performance. Particularly where performance is hard to measure, salary increases are used as the primary incentive. However, since cuts in a person's salary are rarely made—except when a company is in trouble and all managers get cut—the increases in salary are rarely a large percentage of pay. In other words, over the years salary becomes higher, but it does not fluctuate up and down based on short-run performance.

Money set aside for future pension payments is a typical supplement to salaries. Although in special circumstances the amount set aside for a specific individual may be relatively large, typically the pension allotment is a fixed percentage of each individual's salary say, 5 to 10 percent. The accumulation over the years may be substantial, but it is normally regarded as part of base pay, not as a special incentive. Incidentally, health plans and other fringe benefits are likewise viewed as a feature of an attractive place to work rather than as incentive pay.

### Executive Bonuses

Bonuses are by far the most common form of short-term incentives for managers. They have high symbolic value, especially when an individual receives more or less, as the case may be, than peers. They are the tangible evidence of what senior managers regard as good or weak performance.

Several factors affect the size of a manager's bonus. First is the company's policy for dividing total pay between salaries and bonuses. A common practice is to put most of the dollars into salaries, including any merit increases in salary. Then, bonuses are only an extra, say, 10 to 20 percent of the salary. Alternatively, salaries may be kept low while bonuses are anywhere up to 100 percent of the base salary. A higher bonus-to-salary ratio obviously puts strong pressure on managers to meet the targets of the incentive system, and the nature of those targets becomes especially influential. A low bonus-to-salary ratio gives more leeway to executives to do what they feel is right; this is more suitable when short-run performance is hard to evaluate.

The second basic issue in designing a bonus system is what criteria to use in deciding on the amount of payoff in a particular year. Here a wide assortment of guidelines are possible, including the following:

- Personal judgments of two or more levels of line supervisors
- A percentage of company-wide earnings before income tax
- A percentage of business-unit dollar contributions to corporate earnings
- Achievement of agreed-upon targets for the past year in areas such as sales volume, market position, per-unit costs, quality levels, ROA, and similar measurable results.
- Contributions to future strengths of the company and/or business-unit, such as innovative products, public goodwill, favorable legislation, a well-qualified work force, technological advances, and the like.

All sorts of ingenious combinations of factors can go into the calculation of a bonus. For example, one diversified corporation uses three guides. (1) Three percent of corporate profits above a six percent return on assets goes into a pool that is divided among corporate and business-unit managers on a sliding scale according to salary. (2) Each business-unit has a bonus pool consisting of 20 percent of the unit's contributions to corporate profit above the budget amount; this is divided among business-unit managers by the general manager and corporate director according to their judgment after reviewing evidence on relevant success with factors like those in the last two groups of the preceding list. (3) The compensation committee of the board of directors authorizes a few special bonuses to individuals whose outstanding work is not adequately recognized by awards coming from the bonus pools.

## Stock Options

In addition to promotions, stock options are the chief device used to give managers an incentive to help build the long-run success of their corporation. An option to buy company stock at its price when the option was issued enables managers to share in the growth of their company. This builds company loyalty, especially if the option is contingent upon continuing employment. Small firms that are unable to pay large bonuses during their struggle to get established often use stock options to attract and hold managers who could take more lucrative alternative jobs.

Personal income tax considerations add to the attractiveness of stock options. There is no tax unless and until the option is exercised. Of course, taxes are involved in all financial incentives, and ways to defer payment and taxes on bonuses are often included in sophisticated compensation systems.

## Nonfinancial Incentives

"Man doth not live by bread alone." In addition to purchasing power, which is spent off the job, managers are stimulated by recognition, the opportunity to pursue their own ideas, power, and other psychological satisfactions that are closely associated with their jobs. Unlike what can be done with bonuses and stock options, however, only to a limited extent can management vary the flow of these satisfactions separately from the job itself.

The nonfinancial satisfactions do add to the weight attached to *promotions*. In our society that was originally made up of immigrants, doing better than your parents, upward mobility, and demonstrating personal competence are widely cherished. Promotions satisfy such desires. Indeed, the prospect of promotion is commonly held out as an incentive for working hard.

Using promotions as managerial rewards has serious drawbacks, however. Earlier we stressed the importance of filling positions with individuals who have the capability to contribute to strategy execution. Past performance in another job, even though outstanding, does not mean that a person is qualified for a promotion. As we have seen, a top salesperson may make a weak sales manager. Therefore, treating promotions as rewards is fraught with danger, even though the practice fits public expectations.

## Linking Incentives to Strategy

In practice, it is difficult to make a good link between desired strategic behavior and the rewards that managers receive. Bonuses are usually based on financial results, but such payoffs are often mismatched with strategy because they emphasize the past instead of the future. In particular, the following kinds of mismatches are likely to occur:

- The most conveniently available measure of a manager's performance is profit or return on assets. But this is really only a measure of (a) *past* initiatives that (b) reflect *external luck* as much as executive action. Thus, bonuses reward these factors as much as anything else.
- The emphasis in financial reports is on *short-run* performance as defined by *accounting conventions* which were designed for purposes other than strategy. Thus, again, bonuses keyed to these elements need not reward desired strategic behavior.

Moreover, several important aspects of strategy tend to be disregarded altogether in bonus payments:

- Hard-to-measure results such as achieving employee morale, product innovation, and strategic positioning receive little or even *negative weight* in typical financial measurements.
- Strategy goals are often long run and surrounded by risk, so current measures of achievement are at best only progress reports that are often subjective in nature.
- Adjustments of evaluation standards to fast changes in strategy may be tardy and also confusing to people at lower levels in the organization.

The combined effect of bonus payments based primarily on fast, short-run financial results and promotions that reward last year's star performers sends a clear message about "what really counts around here."

Obviously, strategy action has to receive more weight in manager incentives if strategy execution is to be effective. This shifting of weights is not simple, because short-run financial results and last year's stars do deserve recognition. The necessary optimum is to encourage *both* current output and strategy thrusts. Part 5 deals with closing the strategy execution gap; and from that discussion come a variety of measurements which can and should be added to the standards for rewarding manager initiative.

## SUMMARY

An able corps of managers is crucial for the execution of any strategy. The selection and the development of manager talent often is given inadequate attention, however, because problems are not diagnosed far enough in advance and because personal relationships may make an administrator reluctant to take the necessary action.

A systematic approach to building the needed corps of managers include (1) anticipating manager requirements through advance organization planning and forecasts of the positions to be filled, along with specifications for persons needed to fill them; (2) taking an inventory of managerial talent available within a company; (3) developing tentative plans for using the available talent to fill the anticipated positions, and noting needs for further training or additions from outside the company; (4) helping individuals meet their current and planned future responsibilities through on-the-job and off-the-job training; and (5) providing compensation that will attract the quality of managers required and focus their efforts on both short-run and long-run objectives.

The crunch comes in applying this systematic approach to companies or business-units that are going through major strategy changes. For example, consider the problem faced by Joe DiMaggio, general manager of the nitrogen-based fertilizer business-unit in Intercontinental Chemicals Corporation. Joe was in the process of building a young, aggressive team of managers to reverse the lethargic performance of this unit when corporate management decided that, because of competition, the unit should stop trying to grow and adopt a strategy of being a cash cow. The news was a shock to Joe because his rapid rise in the corporation has been built on being a promoter of growth.

This strategy switch upset the unit's carefully developed organization and management development plans. The top R & D manager had to be dismissed. Two marketing managers had to switch from growth efforts to liquidating operations in foreign markets and retrenching into protected niches locally—thus scuttling training activities each had started. And the bonus plan was revised to pay off on net cash generated instead of market penetration and net profits. Even with these changes there was serious doubt whether managers, including Joe, who were selected to direct aggressive growth could psychologically adjust to being tough, parsimonious overseers of a shrinking operation.

That the company had used a systematic management development approach to build a plan for growth did provide a familiar process to follow in the replanning. On the other hand, the clear hopes and expectations created in the first round made acceptance of a less glorious role in the second round more difficult.

## Questions for Class Discussion

1. Suppose that you were general manager of the nitrogen fertilizer unit briefly described in the final paragraphs of this chapter. You predict that your salary will be as good, and bonus perhaps better, under the new strategy than under the former one. Also, your boss assures you that the corporate decision is no reflection on senior executives' confidence in your ability; instead, the different mission is an opportunity for you to demonstrate the versatility in your managerial ability. Intercontinental Chemicals is downsizing the operations in several sectors and currently has no general management job in a growth area to which they can transfer you. Would you personally dig into your new assignment, or would you start looking for another job?

2. Most executive compensation plans are based on either past performance or short-run (annual) improvements. Strategy, however, focuses on longer term moves, the results of which may not show up for five to 10 years or even longer.

How can executive incentive plans be geared, at least in part, to strategy formulation and execution?

3. An increasing number of women are embarking on lifetime careers in business with job aspirations just as high as their male counterparts. And we are seeing more and more marriages of two career-oriented people. These dual-career families complicate executive development, especially in the movement of individuals to new locations as a step in career advancement. Such a move may interfere with the career of the spouse. What can companies do to lower this strain and yet make optimum use of their executive talent? If the couple must make a choice, whose career should be interrupted or constrained?

4. When Chicago's largest commercial bank, Continental Illinois Bank and Trust Company, got into serious trouble because of poorly conceived oil loans, the directors prevailed upon one of its older members to take over as CEO. Subsequently, this individual brought in W.S. Ogden from Chase Manhattan Bank to be his deputy and, everyone expected, his successor. Two years later, however, it was announced that Mr. Ogden would not become CEO, a decision that caused surprise and a lot of uncertainty within the bank. The unannounced reason apparently was a difference in views about the geographic area that Continental Illinois should seek to cover. Mr. Ogden wanted to increase the bank's presence in the international arena, while the CEO felt that in its reduced size the bank should focus on regional banking. In other words, executive selection was treated as tantamount to a strategic decision regarding the bank's domain. Do you think it is a sound practice to treat all executive selection decisions as being equivalent to endorsing the strategy which the appointee prefers? Is changing executives a good way to change strategy?

5. The typical stock option plan is designed for companies whose stock is listed on some stock exchange; this listing helps establish a known market value and also adds to the liquidity (salability) of the stock. Small companies and not-for-profit organizations do not fit into this pattern. (a) What can a small firm do to provide its managers with an incentive something like a stock option plan? (b) Is any comparable incentive available for not-for-profit organizations?

6. Has a new faculty member been hired in your college or in your school of business? See if you can get the head of the department which the new person has joined or the chair of the recruiting committee to think about and respond to the four questions on page 571. Are these questions a regular part of the annual review of the performance of faculty members? Is there such a review? Is it informal, or is it a formal program?

7. In considering the next year's compensation package for the five top executives of Muller Tool and Hardware Company, the compensation committee of the board of directors had before it a recommendation from the company's auditors that the salary of Robert Wallace, president, be increased by 21 percent to $630,000 and that the salaries of four vice presidents be raised by 28 percent

"to bring them into line with the average salaries in comparable firms." Mr. Wallace had been chairman and chief executive officer of this once family-controlled company for the past year and was credited by the board with keeping the company's decline in sales to only 5 percent and the decline in profits to 10 percent during a year of general recession in which there had been an average drop in sales for capital-equipment suppliers of about 15 percent. Control by the Muller family had passed over to all stockholders two years before, when large primary and secondary stock offerings had been successful. Members of the compensation committee and their years of service with the board were: Herbert Muller (15 years, now retired, and former president); Jean Weber (6 months, dean of a local school of business); Marvin Fortman (4 years, legal counsel); Thomas Moses (2 years, investment banker); and William Horne (4 years, retired executive of a large nonelectrical machinery company). The auditors recommended no changes in stock-option plans, in profit-sharing bonuses, or in an insurance, health, and recreation package available to the executives. Sales of the company had shown an average yearly increase of about 4 percent for the past 20 years. The ratio of net profits to sales for the past year was 3 percent, and the return on equity was 8 percent. Mr. Muller and Mr. Horne were primarily responsible for attracting Mr. Wallace to the company and for asking the auditors to study the issue of executive compensation. Do the stockholders' interests appear primary to you in this affair? Is an accounting firm the appropriate place to seek advice on compensation of an executive for the performance of his duties? Is "the average salary in a comparable firm" a suitable norm? Are the directors mentioned suitable, by virtue of their positions, to constitute the compensation committee?

8. In an article entitled, "Business is Bungling Long-Term Compensation," *Fortune* reports that Clevepak Corporation of Purchase, New York, has gone against the conventional wisdom of executive bonuses by tying its bonuses to changes in Standard & Poor's index of 400 industrial companies. Clevepak will measure its own stock's performance against the index after three years. Thirteen top officers of Clevepak will then receive bonuses if their company's stock rises more rapidly than the index or falls more slowly than the index. Thus, it is the relative performance of the firm's stock that counts. In fact, if the stock does better than the index by 10 percent or more each of the three years on the average, the officers will receive bonuses amounting to 300 percent of their base salaries. An approach like this is anathema to most managers, who complain that the stock price often lapses into sinking spells beyond their power to control. Others say that managers should have their wages and bonuses cut during depressions, when employees lose jobs and stockholders' wealth disappears. The president of Clevepak believes that the stock market has an historical upward bias, and, therefore, his company probably will be striving more often to outpace gainers in rising markets than losers in declining markets. This way his compensation will be related to shareholders' values, in contrast to the results in almost all other corporations for which chief executives' pay has been con-

siderably fattened while the price of the companies' stock has declined in real (inflation-adjusted) terms.

Do you believe that Clevepak has acted wisely with respect to executive compensation?

# CASE
## 20 Specialty Container Company

"I just don't understand it," said John Rogers as he stood in Bill Lofton's office. "You have to get on this thing right away, Bill. I can't believe it, but Mike, vice president for operators, has given notice and he's leaving the first of next month. I tried to get him to stay, but they've just outbid us on pay. Not only that, but they're giving him four weeks of vacation his first year on the job. It really is too bad we don't have a more competitive pay and benefit program. One of these days you're just going to have to fix that problem. I'm absolutely convinced we wouldn't have lost him if we had a more competitive pay program.

"What I want you to do is to get on the phone right away and get hold of a search firm to find a replacement. I can't afford to have that spot vacant for any length of time. He was the guy that I felt could eventually take my job, but I guess I just figured wrong. He needed some additional experience, but he had the basics to do the job. This really is a disappointment to me. You know, as good as he is, I was surprised that they were willing to pay him $140,000 a year to start. We can't afford to let any time get by on this one," Rogers said.

Lofton replied, "I'll call somebody this afternoon. The search firm will need to talk with you a bit about the specifics of the job and what your expectations for candidates are. I'll make sure that they contact you directly so that there won't be any delays in the process."

## Company Background

Specialty Container Company is the largest operating division of Abba Zenith Corporation, a *Fortune 500* diverse manufacturing corporation headquartered in central Indiana. The corporation is comprised of six different operating companies, each of which is headed by a president who reports in turn to the chairman and chief executive officer of the parent corporation (see Figure 20–2). Each operating company is set up to be a freestanding entity which is given a substantial amount of autonomy by the corporation. With the exception of a legal function and a treasury function, each operating company could, in fact, be a complete freestanding organization (see Figure 20–3). Each operating company

**FIGURE 20–2.**
**ABBA ZENITH CORPORATION**

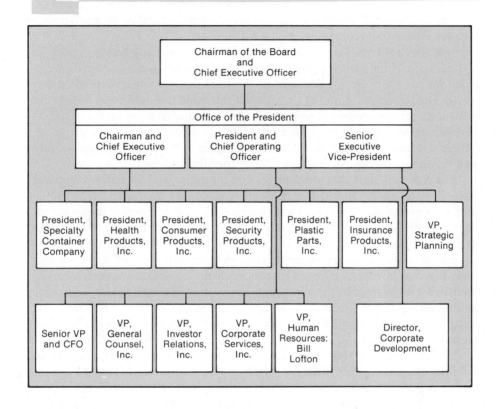

**FIGURE 20–3.**
**SPECIALTY CONTAINER COMPANY**

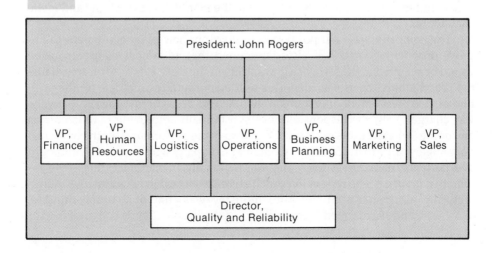

president is held accountable for the performance of his business and is provided with the economic resources for capital expenditures, working capital, and acquisition of new assets.

The Specialty Container Company was founded over 100 years ago to manufacture and distribute containers in North American markets. From its foundation as a small midwestern manufacturer, Specialty Container has grown to a position of dominance in the parts supplier industry. The company enjoys a 34 percent relevant market share of that segment of the total market which its product line serves. The Specialty Container Company is three and one-half times larger than its nearest competitor and is comprised of five manufacturing facilities and 54 customer service centers throughout the United States. Each of Specialty Containers' manufacturing facilities is located in a relatively small town in either Indiana, Kentucky, Tennessee, New Hampshire, or Mississippi.

The company started as an entrepreneurial venture, and the parent company, Abba Zenith Corporation, although publicly traded on the American Stock Exchange, is essentially a family-owned enterprise: over 65 percent of the outstanding shares are held by founding family members and their children. Throughout its history, the corporation has managed its organizations in a firm, but paternalistic fashion. People who are fortunate enough to work for any of Abba Zenith's companies assume that if they work hard and do not commit serious offenses, i.e., theft, being intoxicated at work, etc., they are assured of a well-paying, secure job for the balance of their working years. Employees also take pride in their work and recognize that Abba Zenith Corporation's companies are market leaders in the industries which they serve, and that is particularly true of Specialty Containers.

While the company has enjoyed a steadily increasing market share and an enviable level of profitability throughout its history, the chairman of the board of the parent corporation decided in 1980 that the manufacturing capability of the Specialty Container Company was not as good as it could be; and he, in conjunction with the president of the Specialty Container Company, set about to find a new vice president of operations for the company. The intention in changing the vice president of operations was to bring a new discipline to the manufacturing organization and to apply the latest technology to the manufacture of plastic and metal containers.

The company was well positioned to invest in new plant equipment to improve productivity, and had also determined that additional plant expansion would be required in the form of a new facility in the early 1980s. After an exhaustive search, John Rogers was identified as the appropriate candidate for the position of vice president of operations. When he was brought into the company, he was charged with the responsibility of substantially improving manufacturing and doing "whatever was necessary" to improve the performance of the organization. Rogers came to the Specialty Container Company with an extensive amount of experience, both domestically and internationally, in manufacturing in the automotive industry. The reputation that he had developed in his numerous manufacturing assignments in the auto industry was that of a tough-minded, autocratic, and hard-boiled executive.

Upon his joining the company in 1980, Rogers reviewed preliminary plans that had been developed for the construction of a brand-new facility to be located in central Kentucky. The plant was to be constructed in anticipation of continued market-share growth of the Specialty Container Company and as a facility in which the latest robotics technology could be applied to container manufacturing. After reviewing the current capability of the existing manufacturing facilities in the company and the plans for the new expansion, Rogers concluded that a much smaller facility should be constructed in Kentucky and that the existing facilities located in Indiana, Tennessee, and New Hampshire could be made much more productive than they had been historically by improved industrial engineering methodology and minor amounts of capital spending. Rogers's perception was that the existing management of the manufacturing organization was neither well disciplined nor particularly progressive in their thought processes or capabilities. Rogers became committed to a radical change in the entire manufacturing organization of the Specialty Container Company.

In May of 1980 labor negotiations were concluded with the labor union in Indiana. During the first two weeks of July of that same year, while all production employees were on a two-week vacation shutdown, the maintenance employees and outside contractors completely realigned the manufacturing facilities of the plant. Upon the return of the employees from their vacation shutdown, they were introduced to brand-new work methods, work assignments, and reassigned duties which resulted because of the elimination of a number of positions in the new manufacturing layout. Employees had little or no warning of the changes that were undertaken during the July shutdown, and there was a significant level of negative employee reaction to the changes that they perceived to be forced upon them without warning. The facility found itself very close to a wildcat strike on numerous occasions during July and early August of that year.

At the same time, significant changes in the work methods and management of the Tennessee operations were undertaken. An organizational attempt by the International Brotherhood of Teamsters was initiated in the facility, the fourth such organizational attempt in the 13-year history of the plant. Following the somewhat normal pattern of a union organizing campaign, the union was defeated by a margin of 17 votes out of almost 800 cast in the election. The management of the facility urged employees to give them an opportunity to rectify whatever concerns the employees had expressed, and the company was persuasive in its ability to focus attention on the somewhat unsavory background of the Teamsters as a union. At the time, many employees indicated that they would have probably voted for any other union (other than the Teamsters) if that option were available to them.

During 1981 and 1982, rigorous standards of performance were placed on each of the operations within the Specialty Container Company. Specific reporting requirements on production performance were imposed, with plant managers being required to report their production counts on an hourly basis to the vice president of operations. Also, specific standards on quality, direct and indirect labor, direct and indirect material costs, product development, standards, work methods, safety requirements, production yields, scrap, and raw material costs were set in each facility. Each plant found itself subjected to mandated standards of performance and an ever-increasing expectation of improvement.

The performance expectations on any number of measures were precisely the kinds of improvements that the chairman of the board had expected at the time Rogers was employed by the Specialty Container Company. The results of these new standards began to become evident in the operating performance of the business. At the same time, it became increasingly apparent that the requirements for improvement set by the vice president of operations were not being handled with the greatest amount of diplomacy. Each plant manager and his staff were subjected to 14 to 16 hour-long monthly operations review meetings in which every aspect of the plant's performance was reviewed in great detail. Each staff member was responsible for presenting statistical information on the performance of his or her area of responsibility, and those staff members who did not show a satisfactory level of performance were publicly declared to be stupid, incompetent, and incapable of even the simplest tasks. While recognizing the substantial performance improvements that were achieved by Rogers, manufacturing employees became very uncomfortable with the "environment" that had been established by the autocratic approach to managing employees.

Each of the manufacturing facilities was fenced in with a chain-link fence capped with barbed wire, and each employee who entered the facility was required to enter through a single gate and to open his or her lunch box, both on coming into and on leaving the plant. Managers in each of the plant facilities were told that their principal responsibility was to eliminate 10 percent of the direct or indirect positions in each of their plants each year and that they would be responsible for that level of reduction on a year-to-year basis. The positions identified for elimination were the responsibility of the industrial engineers, and each plant manager's progress against that objective was measured on a monthly basis.

There were also concerted efforts to reduce in-process inventories and finished-goods inventories throughout the operations. All of the existing manufacturing facilities were converted from single-work-station manufacturing to a unitized-flow manufacturing process, and significant levels of in-process inventories were eliminated as a result. The impact of these changes in the Specialty Container Company was significant in terms of cash-flow generation: Specialty Container Company was able to increase its cash flow during the three-year period by $21 million on about $230 million in sales without significant capital spending.

Throughout the period of these adjustments, the turnover rate began to escalate among salaried employees in the Specialty Container Company. The highest rates of turnover were among both supervisors and process and project engineers. Employees accounted for their leaving by saying that they could earn as much money and work less than the 60 hours that had become the normal requirement to meet the imposed work standards set by the Specialty Container Company.

## Current Events

As a result of a disagreement between the president of the Specialty Container Company and the chairman of the board of Abba Zenith Corporation, the president of the Specialty Container Company resigned in 1984. After much deliberation and debate among the senior executives of the corporation, a decision was made to promote John Rogers to the new position. The contributions made to the financial performance of the Specialty Container Company by the operations organization were clearly recognized by the senior executives of the corporation. At the same time, there was a clear awareness that the human resource skills displayed by the vice president of operations left much to be desired. The chairman felt that the financial performance of the organization outweighed the concerns about people that had been expressed by a number of other executives in the corporation, and as a result, Rogers was promoted to the presidency of the Specialty Container Company.

The chairman of Abba Zenith Corporation is a straightforward, no-nonsense executive who is the youngest son of the late founder of Abba Zenith Corporation. His older brothers had all worked in the Abba Zenith Corporation and had been responsible for its growth, particularly as regards Specialty Containers. The chairman had worked in the container business and for several years held a variety of positions within the Specialty Container Company, including the presidency. He is seen by most employees to be a direct, but occasionally difficut-to-read, executive. He also exhibits a high-control orientation over the entire organization, as is plain from Figure 20–2.

While his nephew, who is likewise an experienced executive, is by title the president and chief operating officer of Abba Zenith Corporation, none of the operations report directly to him. The chairman is directly responsible for identifying the need for an effective strategic planning process for the organization, and he established a very effective and sophisticated strategic planning organization in 1972. He is also responsible for having led the Abba Zenith Corporation organization through a series of acquisitions which doubled its size while also improving its profitability. Under the chairman's leadership, Abba Zenith had achieved 10-year compound annual growth rates as follows:

| | |
|---|---|
| Sales | 15.8% |
| Net Income | 12.8% |
| Net Assets | 16.6% |
| Shareholder Equity | 13.4% |

Following is a summary of the sales revenue and net income before tax for a six-year period for the Specialty Container Company:

|            | 1985  | 1984  | 1983  | 1982  | 1981  | 1980  |
|------------|-------|-------|-------|-------|-------|-------|
| Sales      | 278.5 | 252.2 | 229.3 | 207.0 | 190.4 | 169.3 |
| Operating profit | 55.9 | 47.4 | 39.5 | 37.0 | 33.0 | 34.5 |

Continuing through the period was an escalation of the rate of turnover among managers and directors in the organization. Additionally, at lower levels in the organization, union organizing efforts began in earnest.

The facility in Tennessee became organized in 1984 by the United Steelworkers of America in an election that saw the union achieve a 60 percent vote margin. Two union-organizing drives by the United Autoworkers were undertaken in 1984 and 1985 at the Kentucky facility. In the 1985 campaign, the United Autoworkers Union won the election and was certified as the bargaining agent for that facility. Also in 1985, a group of 17 mechanics in the Truck Garage operations of the Specialty Container Company was organized by the International Brotherhood of Teamsters. During the latter part of 1984, a two-week strike ensued in the facility in New Hampshire. In each of these incidents of union organizational campaigns, the overriding issue that was identified as leading to the union's certification or the cause of the union's strike was the uncaring and oppressive atmosphere that had been created in a very short period of time within the Specialty Container Company.

A number of key executives in the Specialty Container Company elected to seek positions outside the company rather than to continue in the organization. On a confidential basis, those exiting employees told Bill Lofton that they were tired of being told "do it, or you're done" or being publicly embarrassed and humiliated in front of their peers on a regular basis. But when they left the organization, the official explanations which they gave for their departures included things like they received a better job opportunity, their families could not geographically adjust to a small-town environment, or they had an opportunity to work in a completely different industry. During exit interviews, none of these individuals stated for the records the feeling that they expressed to Lofton.

In almost every case except that of the departure of Mike Wilson, John Rogers declared the departing employee to be "marginal at best" or said, "I'm sure we can do better when we find a replacement for. . . ." On numerous occasions, Lofton had approached the chairman of the board to express his concerns about the personnel problems that were becoming more acute in the Specialty Container Company. In every case in which these discussions were initiated by Lofton, he was told by the chairman of the board that he didn't want to hear anything about these petty gripes and complaints over personality issues. What was really important was the significant financial performance of the Specialty Container Company. "Look," said the chairman, "I used to run the Specialty Container Company, and while I thought I did a damn good job, I didn't do half of the things in 10 years that Rogers has done in five. We don't run our businesses to win popularity contests; we run them for the best long-term interests of our shareholders."

Lofton continued to be convinced that somehow the financial performance and operational performance improvements that had been achieved by Rogers could have been achieved without the price that was being paid, both in terms of the morale of the existing work force and the ever-increasing level of turnover within the organization. Unfortunately, a magic formula that would lead to that kind of improved environment eluded Bill Lofton.

As Lofton thumbed through his file on search firms, he jotted down some facts that he knew he would need when he got on the phone with the headhunter. These people usually wanted to know some details about the industry, the competitive environment, and the company's strengths and weaknesses. Among those details that Bill Lofton noted were the following:

1. Specialty Container has to be the cash generator for the Zenith Corporation to acquire new businesses. Therefore, projects need to have at least a 40 percent rate of return.

2. Market penetration is excellent: a lot of small regional firms exist, but very few mass-producing ones like Specialty. In the early 1980s, there were 200 manufacturers, whereas today there are only about 75.

3. Specialty is a company with a long-term commitment to quality and a high commitment to significant margins, with no desire to compete in the low-cost market.

4. There is a policy to hold prices below inflation to eliminate competition.

5. Service is extremely important. There is a significant commitment to the field sales force. These people are on strict commission and average over $100,000 per year. Frequently, salespeople bring customers into manufacturing; therefore, it is important to maintain a good image in the production facility and to have employees impress upon the salespeople the firm's commitment to quality. The company has a commitment to hire the best people and give them outstanding training. On the downside, we work people very hard and frequently get raided, a trend that is increasing.

6. Labor costs are up significantly over the last 18 months. There are now six unions in Specialty, and this is increasing manufacturing costs significantly.

As Bill looked over his list, he wondered to himself, "What kind of person do we really need to replace Mike?"

## Question

How would you answer Bill's question?

# INTEGRATING CASES

## Strategy and Corporate Design

## CRAIN COMMUNICATIONS, INC.

Crain Communications owns 25 different business publications, each serving a distinct group of readers. This array of separate "businesses" poses a tough question of what management design will encourage vigorous leadership of each publication while also achieving operating economies.

Crain's central strategy is to provide very current news, as does a newspaper, that is of particular interest to clearly focused sets of readers. This newspaper orientation, with its headline format and tight deadlines for hot news, puts Crain publications in a different niche from that of the usual trade magazine.

The typical Crain publication—for example, *Automotive News* or *Advertising Age*—provides news coverage about a single industry in more detail than appears in daily newspapers and with much more analysis and interpretation. The news covers actions of specific companies, proposed legislation, labor developments, foreign competition, new technology, and the like. Often, reading such a weekly or biweekly publication is essentially the only way a person in or dealing with the industry can keep informed on current developments. Also, Crain publishes several metropolitan area business weeklies. Of course, a similar approach can be taken for other segments of our complex society, as is suggested in the accompanying list of Crain publications.

The readers of a Crain publication are a relatively small, but highly select, set of subscribers. For advertisers, this audience permits sharply targeted sales promotion. And, as with most other news media, paid advertising to the periodicals' readers is necessary to cover the costs of assembling and communicating the primary message. Crain's success in providing a unique service to a select audience concurrently creates an advertising medium that will help support the venture.

In addition to the news and advertising that appear on the pages, there is another side to each publication: the broadside must be physically printed and distributed. This involves a whole set of activities that seem mundane to a typical journalist. Besides being prosaic, these tasks tend to be expensive for a publication with a relatively small circulation, and they come in short peaks with no activity in between. Few individuals who can either write or get others to write vibrant copy are good at watching over the details and expenses of physical production and distribution.

**FIGURE 1.**
**CRAIN COMMUNICATIONS' PERIODICALS**

*Advertising Age*

A weekly tabloid newspaper covering marketing, advertising and media developments, and related U.S. and international business news. Subscribers are primarily company marketing and advertising personnel, advertising agency personnel, media company people, and others engaged in a variety of advertising/marketing activities. The paper has a circulation of nearly 90,000.

*Automotive News*

Founded in 1925, a weekly tabloid newspaper serving all phases of the automotive market, from automobile manufacturers and related producers to automobile dealerships. It has a circulation of approximately 65,000.

*AutoWeek*

America's only weekly news of the automobile world for car enthusiasts and those especially interested in auto developments, product evaluations, and sports. Circulation is over 165,000.

*Business Insurance*

A weekly tabloid news magazine edited for corporate risk, employee benefit, and financial executives. Also widely read by insurance brokers and agents, insurance company executives, and others concerned with corporate insurance and employee benefit markets. Circulation is 45,000.

*Business Marketing*

A monthly magazine reporting on the news, the strategies, and the tactics of business-to-business advertising, sales, promotion, and planning in all industries. Circulation is more than 43,000.

*City & State*

A monthly newspaper edited for management-level executive and financial officers within state, county, and local government and government agencies, and for

those at financial institutions and business organizations serving the public sector. Launched in 1985, the paper's circulation is approximately 40,000.

*Crain's Chicago Business*

A weekly tabloid newspaper devoted to producing news and opinions of importance to business and financial executives in Chicago and surrounding areas. Circulation is approximately 50,000.

*Crain's Cleveland Business*

A weekly tabloid newspaper devoted to business and financial news, and containing opinion and feature sections. Distributed to business executives in the seven-county Cleveland SCSA. Circulation is approximately 25,000.

*Crain's Detroit Business*

Founded in February 1985, this weekly newspaper covers the Detroit nonautomotive business community with a circulation of 33,000.

*Crain's New York Business*

A weekly tabloid newspaper for business and financial executives, focusing on smaller and mid-sized companies in the greater New York tri-state metropolitan area. Circulation is approximately 85,000.

*Detroit Monthly*

Crain's first city magazine, dealing with the life-style of upscale Detroit consumers. Recently named the best city magazine in the country in its category. Circulation is 80,000.

*Electronic Media*

A weekly tabloid newspaper carrying news, news features, and information on all forms of electronic media, including broadcast and cable television, radio programming and syndication, videotex, home video, and other emerging new forms. Circulation is approximately 25,000.

**FIGURE 1.**
**(continued)**

*Florida Keys Magazine*
Published six times a year and covers the political and social highlights of the Keys. Edited for both permanent and seasonal residents, circulation is approximately 10,000.

*Humm's Guide to the Florida Keys*
Official guide to the Florida Keys and Key West. Published quarterly, each issue has a circulation of 50,000. Tourist-oriented editorial covers accommodations and restaurants, plus the full range of vacation activities.

*Modern Healthcare*
A fortnightly magazine serving executives in the hospital, nursing home, and health care market, and providing news, opinions, and features on the business problems involved in managing health care institutions. Circulation is approximately 80,000.

*Pensions & Investment Age*
A fortnightly tabloid newspaper serving financial executives and investment managers concerned with the investment of corporate, pension, and other institutional funds. Circulation is approximately 50,000.

*Rubber & Plastics News*
A weekly tabloid publication which, together with the alternate week publication called *Rubber & Plastic News II*, serves the information needs of the rubber manufacturing and plastics industries. Circulation is approximately 15,000.

*Tire Business*
A fortnightly tabloid newspaper that provides up-to-date news on the North American tire industry for independent tire dealers and wholesalers, and others involved in tire marketing. Launched in April, 1983, *Tire Business* has a circulation of 15,000.

*American Clean Car*
A fortnightly magazine going to operators and owners of car wash installations. Circulation is 18,500.

*American Coin-Op*
A monthly magazine serving the business needs of owners and operators of coin-operated washing, drying, and related services. Circulation is 19,000.

*American Drycleaner*
A monthly pocket-size magazine providing business news and features for retail dry cleaning establishments. Circulation is 26,000.

*American Laundry Digest*
A monthly pocket-size magazine which goes to retail laundry operators, bringing them news and articles designed to help them improve their business. Circulation is 13,000.

**In Europe:**

*Advertising Age's FOCUS*
A monthly magazine circulated in Europe to advertising, marketing, and other top-level executives in companies and advertising agencies in Europe. Circulation is approximately 10,500.

*European Rubber Journal*
A monthly magazine covering developments in the rubber and related industries in Great Britain and Western Europe. Circulation is 7,000.

*Media World*
A London-based monthly magazine that covers the media scene in Britain, featuring a monthly news digest and articles by the U.K.'s leading media figures. Circulation is 5,000.

Crain Communications has its answer to this uncongenial mix of activities. First, decentralize the editorial management of each publication. This means giving the editor of *each* publication freedom to carry out a distinctive editorial mission that will serve readers and thereby build a loyal circulation in the selected domain. Then, centralize the physical production and distribution of *all* Crain publications. The role of these centralized divisions is to serve the various publications by taking care of activities which the various editors typically find to be a distraction and which they usually cannot do very well.

More specifically, the organization pattern of Crain Communications consists of the following:

(1) Each publication has an editor who is responsible for preparing the news content of every issue. The editor will have a staff of reporters, writers, and assistant editors who dig out the news and write the stories. Critically important is a keen sense of what the target set(s) of readers want to know, and a flare for presenting such information in a timely and interesting form. Because each publication has its distinct target audience in its own industry, this editorial task has to be perceptively tailored to its unique setting.

(2) Each publication also has a publisher who is ultimately responsible for obtaining advertisements (selling space) that are placed in the publication as well as for overseeing the editorial operation. A separate group of advertising salespeople is assigned the task of selling ads. The rationale for placing advertising and news content under the publisher is that detailed insights into the buying and selling relationships in the specific industry are necessary for effective selling of advertising space. Also, the layout of each issue calls for sensitive placing of news and ads.

(3) The central production department is responsible for converting the soft copy (news and advertising) into printed and bound documents. All this work is subcontracted (as is common in the publishing industry), so the production department is really concerned with finding good printers. The aim, of course, is to get the work done on necessarily tight schedules, in a quality manner, and at competitive costs. Crain publications use more than a dozen printers, and the central production department is able to move the work around so as to take advantage of the technological changes that are occurring in printing and facsimile communication.

(4) A central circulation department handles the vital and tedious task of obtaining subscriptions to the various publications and then getting each copy delivered to the right address. Besides renewals, new subscriptions are crucial because some attrition among readers is inevitable. In the periodical industry, subscriptions are normally paid in advance, thus simplifying the collection of accounts receivable and also the cash flow.

(5) In addition to the four major operating functions just listed, Crain Communications has the typical corporate office activities—finance, legal, etc. Also within the corporate setup are several officers who oversee a publication or clusters of publications. These executives work with the editor of a publication in defining its editorial mission, setting subscription rates and advertising rates, and

establishing annual budgets. In addition, the corporate executives check results and assist in coordinating the four basic functions if topside mediation is necessary.

Since Crain has publications of varying size which fill different competitive positions in their respective industries, and since several of these are recently acquired magazines which have strong traditions, variations exist in the structure just outlined. Nevertheless, the basic design is clear.

To make this design work effectively, senior officers of Crain believe that four elements are crucial:

1.  A clear charter for each editor is necessary for the high degree of decentralization to work well. The charter should lay out the essentials of an astute editorial, as well as the corporation mission, to which both the publisher and the editor are committed. Related to this is a mutual understanding about the resources—the people and money—that are available to the editor.

2.  In every business publication, the degree of influence that advertisers exert on the news is a touchy subject. Crain's stand on this issue is clear: the first and primary concern should be to serve the interests of the reader (a position close to the hearts of journalists). If advertisers are unhappy with well-researched news, so be it. In the long run, readers' confidence in a publication will create a medium that most advertisers will want to use.

3.  The corporate production and circulation departments exist to serve the publications. And it is the editor and publisher who know best what the publication needs. Of course, production and circulation expenses are allocated to each publication, and it is the editor who is accountable if he or she requests costly service.

4.  There is a concept of "integrity" that Crain officials insist on. This relates to sticking to published advertising rates—i.e., making no special deals under the table. Similarly, news stories are not to be slanted to please advertisers, as already noted. Instead, the readers should expect objectivity, not currying of favors. This integrity has a moral quality of honesty—of acting as one professes to act.

Crain officials believe that all these elements are necessary for its management design to work effectively: "With these elements in operation, our mix of decentralization and centralization makes a diverse array of targeted publications both socially and economically viable."

Crain Communications, Inc., has a remarkable record of long, stable management. It has had only two chairmen and three presidents in its 70 years of existence. The founder, G. D. Crain, Jr., served as president from 1916 until 1964, when he relinquished that title to veteran employee Sidney R. Bernstein, and assumed the title of chairman of the board. His widow, Gertrude R. Crain, became chairman upon his death in 1973 and continues as an active participant in that post.

Bernstein gave up the presidency in 1973 in favor of Rance Crain, elder son of G. D. Crain, Jr., who continues in that post, with Keith Crain, his brother, serving as vice-chairman of the company. Crain Communications, Inc., has over 1,000 employees located in 13 offices in the United States, England, Germany, and Japan.

## Questions

In view of the very limited turnover of senior management, the possibility of an outmoded organization structure should be recognized. Do you think a good match exists between Crain Communications' strategy and its structure? Why not centralize advertising, as has been done for circulation? Is the structure well suited to the recent European expansion?

# INTEGRATING CASES

## Strategy and Organization Design

# QRS, INCORPORATED

### Nature of Industry

QRS[1] is among the top 20 companies producing space-age equipment. Although much of its output is airborne military equipment, QRS also produces communication equipment for commercial satellites. The work involves complex, sophisticated designs, frontier technologies, and often uncertainty about both cost and performance.

Often an order calls only for a single expensive product, perhaps a tracking missile or a communication satellite. And for military items, a first contract usually covers only the design. When the design is finally approved by the customer (for example, NASA or the Air Force), several companies will bid for the construction contract. Subcontracting for major components is also common, so if a company misses out on a prime contract it still may obtain a piece of the business as a subcontractor.

The learning curve is important in this industry, and companies develop distinct abilities to design and make particular kinds of products or to utilize particular technologies. Such expertise helps a company obtain further contracts if its strengths relate to popular technologies. The right expertise enables companies (1) to bid more wisely for new contracts and (2) to efficiently produce designs or products. Moreover, (3) customers may give preference to companies that they think will be able to fulfill contract specifications. Because of the inherent uncertainties in frontier technologies, actual results often vary from plan—so much so that renegotiation as the work proceeds is not uncommon.

Companies that wish to enter a growing area may bid low or accept considerable risk so as to learn particular techniques. They hope that their newly acquired skill will help them obtain more profitable business in the future. Millions of dollars and even company survival may be involved in such maneuvers.

---

[1]Disguised name.

## QRS Management Structure

Like other companies in the industry, QRS stresses a project form of management to deal with the business characteristics just described. Four features are crucial.

(1) Short-range planning focuses on projects. Because each new order is unique and large, it becomes a unit of planning, or a "project." Specific plans are made for the end results, the timing, the resources, and the costs for each project (like building a house). There are no continuing flows, as in a chemical plant, or regular repeating business, as in a school; annual accounting reports are merely snapshots taken to conform to conventional financial practice. Most QRS projects last from six months to four years and cost from $500,000 to $50,000,000.

(2) The work necessary to carry out a contract is also organized around the project. A temporary unit of organization is established with its own managers, engineers, and other operating personnel, and with separate offices, budget allocations, and reports and controls. This group works as a semi-independent team until the project is completed. QRS does maintain centralized production plants at Quincy, Reading, and Somerville, and other central services, but these act like subcontractors responding to the requests of various project managers.

(3) To maintain and enhance QRS's ability to take on new projects, a series of resource pools (departments) are maintained. These are the home bases for specialized personnel when they are not assigned as a member of a project team. Each such department (propulsion, electronic controls, mechanical structures, and the like) also develops and trains people in state-of-the-art concepts. Thus, QRS has a "matrix" organization, as shown in Figure 1. Along one dimension are resource and service pools; on the second dimension are projects. The resource pools (departments) have long-run continuity, serving a succession of projects. The projects, however, are the operating arm—that's where the action is.

(4) Two types of coordinating activities are necessary. One is the allocation of technical people and other resources from the pools to the projects. In QRS, when the combined needs of the active projects exceeds the size of the pool (including trained people that can be hired quickly or, say, money that can be borrowed), a management committee advises the executive vice-president about which projects should get priority. The second and more troublesome coordination is the preparation of bids for new contracts. Just as in the execution of a project, inputs from a whole team of experts are needed. In the past at QRS, if the contract sought was similar to a project currently in operation, that project team usually prepared the bid with the aid of a financial assistant. Usually, however, bids were prepared by a team of experts representing the heads of the various departments. A separate bid-preparing team was created for each bid so that the members would be qualified to assess the specific technical requirements.

QRS operates with the usual sophisticated control techniques, including accounting by projects, manpower and production scheduling, PERT networks, and monthly profit-and-loss and balance sheet estimates for the total corporation.

**FIGURE 1.**
**QRS MANAGEMENT STRUCTURE**

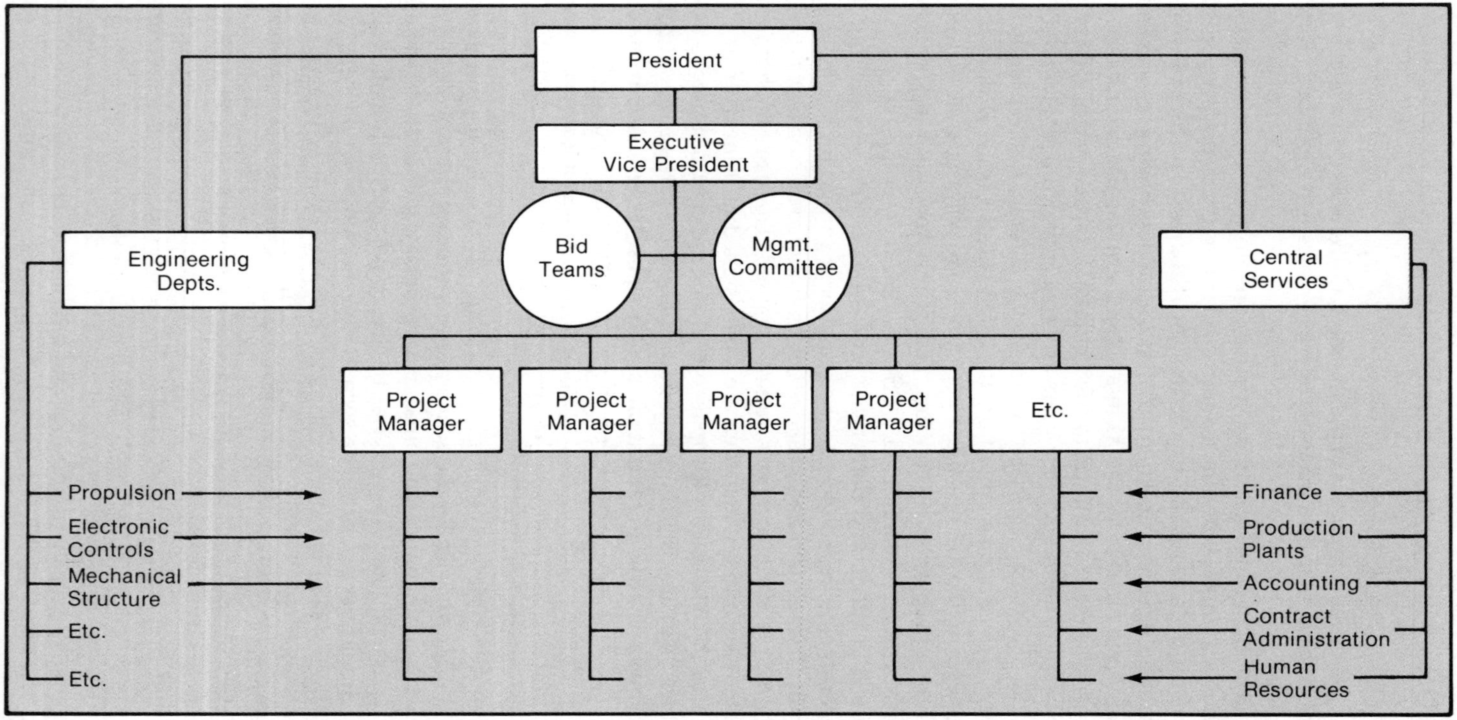

## Operating Results

During the past 10 years, QRS has been only an average performer in its industry. While it has had a few outstanding successes, in many areas it has had to accept subcontracts and try to catch up with the leaders in technology. The last three years, in particular, have yielded only mediocre financial results. The following factors have contributed to these results:

1. Project costs have often exceeded the bid price. These overruns usually occurred when engineers had to devote much more time than estimated to achieve the stipulated performance. As noted in describing QRS's form of management, many tasks are new and uncertain and the estimates proved to be overly optimistic. Less often, the bid was deliberately set low so as to win a contract in an area that QRS wished to upgrade its skills.

2. A related difficulty was failure to meet the delivery date (a common problem in this industry). Such delays often increase costs because of (a) the use of overtime to catch up, (b) interference with scheduled use of people and plants on other projects, and occasionally, (c) penalty payments in the contracts.

3. QRS appeared to have a declining number of areas where it could win large continuing contracts for further design work or actual production. These are the kinds of contracts where profit estimates are more reliable and companies have a better opportunity to recoup losses often suffered on pioneering work.

## A Shift at the Top

The board of directors finally decided that a change in top management was called for. A year ago, B. H. Spaulding was brought in from a large computer company as the new president. R. B. Zimmer, a QRS director who strongly supported the change, explains, "We concluded that the old system had to be shaken up. And we wanted someone who would take a fresh, hard look at the traditional practices in the space equipment industry. Too many industry people assume that somehow the government will bail them out. I must admit that results under Spaulding don't show much immediate improvement, but it is probably too soon to see the results of his changes in the financial figures."

After reviewing the management structure at QRS, Spaulding concluded, "The matrix organization is probably necessary in this industry. However, it has been used as an excuse for a lack of both discipline and clear responsibility. We will correct these weaknesses by adopting three simple, though basic, principles of profit accountability.

"First, we need *integrity in the bidding process*. In the past, the engineering department provided the technical estimates upon which bids were prepared, but it was the project managers—not the departments—who were responsible for fulfilling the contracts we won. As a result, the department could be optimistic while failure to perform was blamed on the project managers. To correct this in the future, we are going to have the (prospective) project manager be responsible for the cost and completion dates in each bid. The departments will continue to give their opinions of what can be done, but this will be treated as advice.

"Second, after a project manager has agreed to the provisions of a bid, we will hold him or her to it if we win the contract. The manager has taken on a *commitment* and will be held accountable to make that happen. Of course, occasionally external events may lead to an overrun or (preferably) to renegotiation; as a matter of course, we must get rid of overruns.

"Third, in addition to dubious estimates, we have been making bids which we knew in advance would hurt our earnings. The potential profit ratio to sales was very low, and that almost always meant that the *return on investment* (ROI) was also low. You can't earn a necessary profit for the stockholder unless you start out with that aim at the beginning. So following the practice of every well-run company that I know, we will set a minimum ROI hurdle rate. All bids must at least meet that standard.

"If we build a reasonable ROI into our bids, and have the project managers committed to those numbers, the basis for improved profits will be laid."

## Results of Spaulding's Changes

During the eight months since Spaulding's changes went into effect, the QRS boat has been rocking. Because of the long time-cycle of several major contracts, it is too early to measure the full impact. Nevertheless, several clues are available.

Overruns on new contracts have not yet appeared. Both the accounting office and the project managers continue to predict, on the basis of PERT feedback, that final results will be close to estimates. This is in line with Spaulding's aim.

The number of new contracts won has declined from the preceding year. This is more apparent in design contracts than in production contracts. Although many factors enter into winning a contract, in at least three important cases that QRS lost, QRS's bids were substantially higher than its competitors.

The drop in new contracts, along with some cuts which Spaulding made in overhead expenses, created a nervousness and anxiety throughout QRS. The feeling is mixed, however, partly because the space equipment industry is always volatile and people in it have learned to live with uncertainty.

More specifically, the morale of project managers is generally good. They like the opportunity to make a commitment to what they consider are realistic goals. And they say privately that the clipping of department heads' wings was long overdue. Several project managers have expressed concern about losing design contracts. For instance, one said, "I like an occasional way-out design project. In production work, there is less room for imagination and much more of just running a tight ship. Besides, design contracts are the basis of our bread-and-butter five years hence."

The mood of department heads is somber. They don't like their lower influence on bidding and think the ROI standard is unworkable. One 20-year veteran says, "Frankly, I'm looking for another job. Any project manager in his right mind will commit only to high-priced, low-risk bids. That means we will be confined to standard work. And the ROI rate will prevent us from buying our way into new developments. Spaulding ought to go back to an industry that he understands." Another department head is more patient: "I've been training engineers and project managers for a decade, and now it looks like I'll have to start training our new president."

## Question

Assume that R. B. Zimmer asks for your advice on what should be done now in QRS, Incorporated. What would you tell him?

# PART 5

## Closing the Gap Between Strategy and Actual Results

# CHAPTER 21

## Short-Range and Long-Range Programming

Establishing strategy, building organization, and developing managers are all vital to the management of any enterprise. However, there is still another group of activities that requires executive attention if the company is to achieve its goals: steps must be taken to "get things done." We can call this group of managerial duties *execution*, and the term is used here to cover:

1. *short-* and *long-range programming*—which deals with what actions are to be taken when
2. *activating*—which is concerned with direction and motivation, and
3. *controlling*—which seeks to assure that the results actually accomplished correspond with organization plans.

### Steps in Execution

A large part of the time of managers is devoted to execution, that is, detailed programming, motivating, coordinating, and controlling. No services are rendered and no profits are earned until action by first-line operators actually takes place.

A word of warning about these three steps in execution is appropriate. In practice, they are not watertight compartments that take place in just the order listed. Management is a continuing and complex activity in which the various phases are often mixed up. A program for putting a strategy change into effect may cut across policies, organization, and control procedures. Data developed in day-to-day control often are used in preparing short- and long-range programs. Nevertheless, for purposes of understanding management, the division of execution into phases is essential, and the outline puts these various parts into logical relationship and perspective.

Programming is discussed in this chapter; activating and controlling are considered in the next two chapters.

### Nature of Programming

The discussion in Part 2 of departmental strategy programs focused on a choice of moves that are the action phase of company strategy. Primarily, we considered *what* each department should do. A fully developed program, however, must also treat the logistics of strategy—the *how much, when,* and *by whom.* These quantities, dates, and individuals are additional dimensions of the instructions that go to people on the firing line.

Once an objective or "mission" has been established, a manager making the program first decides what principal steps are necessary to accomplish the objective and then sets an approximate time for each. When an entirely new activity is involved, the program may also indicate who is to undertake each of the steps.

While central management can delegate most detailed scheduling work, it should take an active part in shaping broader programs. Key issues faced in this important task will be examined in terms of short-range programming, critical path analysis, and long-range programming.

## Short-Range Programming

### Programs for Special Purposes

Numerous short-range programs are drawn up and carried out in each department of a company. These programs deal with activities ranging from launching a sales campaign to installing word processors in an insurance office. Normally, central management delegates this kind of programming to department executives. However, when several departments are involved, or a large amount of capital is committed, or delicate external relations are at stake, central management takes an active part. Often, for such situations, the program is not neat and simple, as the following examples reveal.

#### Expansion Program

The operators of the hotel facilities at the Grand Canyon wished to develop an expansion program that would enable them to give better service to the many people who want to visit this scenic spot. Investigation revealed that two types of changes were needed in the physical facilities: betterments that would improve the services in the existing plant and major expansion of room and restaurant facilities. Any significant addition to total capacity, however, would have required more water, and additional water could be secured only by investing $1,500,000 to run a pipeline to a spring several miles up the canyon. But pumping water from the bottom of the canyon to the brim would require additional electric power, and this would probably mean bringing in a new power line. Moreover, a new sewage line would have to be laid in a ditch blasted out of rock.

The investment in these new facilities would not have been justified if they were to be used only two or three months of the year. Consequently, serious attention had to be given to attracting visitors to the canyon in the spring and the fall when, in fact, the weather is more desirable than in the summer—the prime tourist season.

There were additional factors involved, but these are enough to indicate the need for some kind of a program that would divide the total problem of expansion into logical *parts* and indicate a *sequence* in which these parts should be attacked.

In this case, a schedule probably could be established only for the first two or three steps, but the program did indicate all the steps involved and a sequence for dealing with them. Thus, the program laid out a systematic approach to a very complex problem. Since the desirability of expanding facilities depended so largely on extending the tourist season and building other off-season business, changes in facilities were restricted to betterments until the practicality of the promotion program was tested.

### Tax Revision Program

The desirability of a special-purpose program also became apparent to a company that sought to reduce the federal excise tax on its products. The company quickly recognized that its chances of success would be materially improved if the industry as a whole presented its case rather than if each manufacturer operated independently. Clearly, the newly formed industry association should make contacts with all of the influential congressional representatives and senators. To be most effective, however, the pleas of the manufacturers needed to be backed up by significant pressure on the part of local constituents. This meant that the retailers and, to the extent possible, the consumers should be enlisted in the overall campaign.

If the efforts of all these people were to be most effective, there was need for a common program in which the role of each group could be clarified and some attention could be given to the timing of the several efforts. In a situation such as this, involving many independent enterprises and people, a detailed program and schedule covering an extended period probably would be of little value; but at least a general program was essential to get coordinated effort. Since the program basically concerned public opinion, there was great need for personal leadership and flexibility as the work proceeded.

Programs for special purposes, such as the two just discussed, are often difficult to project very far into the future. Forecasts of future needs and of operating conditions may be unreliable because the activity is so new and different. This unreliability in turn makes it hard to set dates and to estimate volume of work. Moreover, strategy in meeting competition or winning the support of people often plays a key part in such programs, and it is difficult to decide specific moves very long in advance.

## Basic Steps in Programming

The examples of programming given here indicate that skill is needed in fitting the general concept to specific situations. Nevertheless, six elements or steps are found in the majority of instances. Managers will do a better job of programming if they are fully aware of the nature and the importance of each of these steps.

## 1. Divide the Total Operations for Achieving the Objective into Parts

The division of a program into parts is useful for planning, organization, and control. Planning is improved because concentrated attention can be given to one part at a time. Organization is facilitated because these parts or projects can be assigned to separate individuals if this will give speedier or more efficient action. Such division also aids control because the executive can watch each part and determine whether progress is satisfactory as the work is carried on without waiting for final results.

If the division into parts or projects is to be most effective, the purpose of each step should be clearly defined. The kind of work, the quality, and the quantity should all be indicated.

Often a single part of a large program is itself again subdivided; in fact, the process of subdivision may be continued for three or four stages. For example, an anniversary program of a department store may include as one of its parts a sale of men's suits. This sale in turn may be divided into buying, advertising, displaying, selling, etc. The advertising project may be divided up into selection of merchandise to be featured, writing the copy, preparing illustrations, scheduling the days and the newspapers in which the ad will appear, and integrating the suit sale ads with other advertisements of the store. Thus, the concept of programming is applicable to situations ranging from large operations down to the work of a single individual.

## 2. Note the Necessary Sequence and the Relationship Between Each of these Parts

Usually the parts of a program are quite dependent on each other. The amount of work, the specifications, and the time of action of one step often affect the ease or the difficulty of performing the next step. Unless these relationships are recognized and watched closely, the very process of subdividing the work may cause more inefficiency than it corrects.

Any necessary sequences are particularly significant. For example, a motel chain had to complete refinancing its debt before embarking on a West Coast expansion. These necessary sequences have an important bearing upon scheduling. They tend to lengthen the overall time required for the operation, and, since a shorter cycle gives a company more flexibility, the necessity of delaying one action until another is completed should be carefully evaluated.

## 3. Decide Who Is to Be Responsible for Doing Each Part

If the operation being programmed is a normal activity for the company, the assignment of responsibility may already be covered by the existing organization. In an airline, for instance, the opening of a new route involves sales promotion, personnel, traffic, air operations, maintenance, and finance, and assignment of each of these activities is already set by the established structure. However, if the program covers a new operation, then careful attention should be given to the question of who is responsible for each part. These special assignments do not necessarily follow regular organization relationships and create only a temporary set of authorizations and obligations. In a very real sense, a special team is formed to carry out the program.

### 4. Decide How Each Part Will Be Done and What Resources Will Be Needed

The amount of attention that must be given to each step in setting up a program will depend upon the circumstances. Sometimes standing methods and procedures will cover almost all of the activities (as is true of military programming), and in other situations questions of "how" will be fully delegated to the persons responsible for each part. Nevertheless, the executive building the program must have enough understanding of how each part will be performed to appreciate the difficulties in the assignment and the obstacles that may be encountered. In particular, the executive needs some understanding of the *resources* that will be necessary to carry out each part of the program.

For realistic programming, the need for materials and supplies, facilities, and people must be recognized. Then the availability of these necessary resources should be appraised. If any of them is not available, another project to obtain the resource should be set up; this may be treated either as an additional part of the original program or as a subdivision of the project needing the resource. For example, if necessary personnel are unavailable, then plans should be made for hiring and training new employees. Many programs break down because the executive preparing them does not have a practical understanding of how each part will be carried out and of what resources will be needed.

### 5. Estimate the Time Required for Each Part

This step is, of course, closely related to steps 3 and 4 and really involves two aspects: the date or hour when the part will begin and the time required to complete the operation once it is started. The possible starting time will depend upon the availability of the necessary resources. The time when key personnel can be transferred to a new assignment, the possibility of getting delivery of materials from suppliers, and the seasons when customers are normally in the market all have a bearing on when it is possible to begin any given part of a program.

Once the activity has begun, the processing time is typically estimated on the basis of past experience. For detailed scheduling of production operations, time-study data may permit a tight scheduling of activities. For a great many activities, more time is consumed in conveying instructions and getting people to begin the work than is required for the actual work itself. Unless this "nonproductive time" can be eliminated, however, it should be included as part of the estimated time.

### 6. Assign Definite Dates (Hours) When Each Part Is to Take Place

The overall schedule is, of course, based on the sequences noted under Step 2 and the timing information assembled under Step 5. The resulting schedules should show both the starting dates and the completion dates for each part of the program.

Sometimes considerable adjusting and fitting are necessary to make the final schedule realistic. A useful procedure is to work backward and forward from some fixed date that is considered to be controlling. In promoting a new dress fabric, for example, the importance of the selling season may be so great that the retail season is taken as fixed and the schedule is extended back from these dates. In other situations, the availability of materials or facilities may be the controlling time around which the rest of the schedule is adjusted. It is, of course, necessary to dovetail any given program with other commitments the company may have.

Another important qualification is to make some allowances for delay. It is not desirable as a general practice to have such allowances all along the line, as this tends to create inefficient performance, but there should be safety allowances at various stages so that an unavoidable delay at one place will not throw off the entire schedule.

A shorthand way to label these steps is:
1.  Turn big problems into smaller ones.
    2.  Study the linkages.
        3.  Pin down accountability.
            4.  Provide the tools.
                5.  Say when.
                    6.  Integrate the schedule.

Programs may have to be revised, of course, to take account of unexpected opportunities or difficulties. If each of the six steps just outlined has been well done, however, these revisions usually can be merely adjustments of the initial planning.

## Strategic Thrusts

Thrusts are identified in Chapter 5 as one of the key parts of a company strategy. These are the clear-cut moves to be started in the near term as steps toward a longer range goal. Opening a plant in Taiwan or building a sales force to contact retailers directly instead of relying upon wholesalers are examples.

Short-range programming is an excellent device to assure that these thrusts receive adequate attention. The normal pressure of continuing day-to-day activities tends to push unusual work to "tomorrow." Also, there may be resistance to change. Consequently, if a desired thrust is merely added to a list of things to be done, it is likely to develop slowly and may be buried. In contrast, if a program including the features just outlined is prepared, action should result.

## Contingency Programs

A fire emergency plan is a classic example of a contingency program. If the event occurs, a series of predetermined actions by assigned persons is to take place, and a special set of rules guides the behavior of all other people. The event is likely to be so serious that interruption of normal operations is warranted. And the need for prompt action justifies a standard response even though the precise location and size of the fire cannot be predicted in advance.

Most contingencies, however, do not warrant such an elaborate standby program. By far the most usual way to deal with new situations is to *revise* prevailing programs. As we will outline in Chapter 23, actual (and predicted) progress is frequently compared with the program; then, whenever significant deviations are spotted, a revision of the program is at least considered. A revision has a couple of advantages over contingency planning: it avoids the costly effort of preparing many plans which are never used, and it can be fitted much more closely to the specifics of the new situation than is possible when a plan is devised far in advance.

Contingency programs may be desirable for critical events such as a labor strike, a sudden influx of orders from customers, a major break in foreign exchange rates, or the like. The factors which justify contingency programs include (1) the need for prompt action before the revision process can take place, (2) the likelihood that the contingency will occur about as predicted. In a company that has a well-developed planning and control system, not many contingencies meet these tests.

A secondary benefit of preparing contingency programs is training to deal with changes. Even though an alternative program may never be used, the managers who prepared it are more aware of where adjustments may be necessary and whom to consult. Psychologically, they are more receptive to change. Actually, most of this training benefit can also be obtained from fully exploring alternatives when the master program is adopted.[1] When planning skill is developed in decision analysis, the training benefit of contingency programs is reduced.

## Critical Path Analysis

## Development of PERT

Critical path analysis is a special technique for studying and controlling complex programs. It was developed in its more elaborate form as an aid in the design and production of Polaris missiles, and it has been used for virtually all subsequent space projects. The particular technique applied to the Polaris program was called PERT (Program Evaluation and Review Technique); many variations of the basic ideas have been used both before and since PERT received wide publicity.

---

[1]The term "contingency planning" is sometimes used in decision analysis. When the future is uncertain and two or more "states of nature" have to be considered, we may plan what we would do under each "contingency." Usually such projections are only concerned with estimating possible results, and they are not a commitment to a course of action, as in programming.

The technique is of interest to us here because the central concepts of critical path analysis can be helpful in many programming problems.

The design and production of Polaris missiles involved a staggering number of steps. Specifications for thousands of minute parts had to be prepared, the parts had to be manufactured to exact tolerances, and then the entire system had to be assembled into a successful operating weapon. And *time* was of the essence. The basic steps in programming, discussed on the preceding pages, were applicable; but the complexity of the project (and the fact that many different subcontractors were involved) called for significant elaborations in the programs.

## Major Features of Critical Path Analysis

The basic ideas involved in critical path analysis are as follows:

1.  All steps and their necessary sequences are placed on a diagram (see Figure 21–1) so that the total *network* is explicitly set forth.
2.  The estimated *time* required to complete each step after the preceding step has been finished is recorded.
3.  Then, by adding the required times for each step in any necessary sequence, or path, the path having the longest time can be identified. This is the *critical path*.
4.  If desired, the difference between the total required time of the critical path and other paths can also be computed. Such differences are *slack times*, or margins in which delays would not hold up the final completion.

Now, having identified the critical path, management can focus its attention on either reducing the time for certain steps in this path or at least watching closely for any delays. Also, management knows from slack-time data where high pressure to meet estimated process times may be unwarranted.

The calculation of the critical path should be repeated as work progresses, because some steps will be completed faster than anticipated and others will be delayed. These new data will certainly change slack-time estimates, and a different critical path may arise.

With careful thought, the network of steps and sequences can usually be assembled with reasonable reliability, at least for programs dealing with physical products. The time estimates prove to be less reliable, however, for unique activities. To deal with this uncertainty regarding time, three different estimates are often obtained from persons who will be doing the work: an optimistic, a most likely, and a pessimistic estimate. Then a weighted average of these three elapsed-time estimates is used.

In critical path analyses of complex programs, such as Polaris, the computations are sufficiently involved to make use of a computer very helpful. In simpler programming situations, such as building construction, a computer is by no means essential.

**FIGURE 21–1.**
**CRITICAL PATH ANALYSIS**

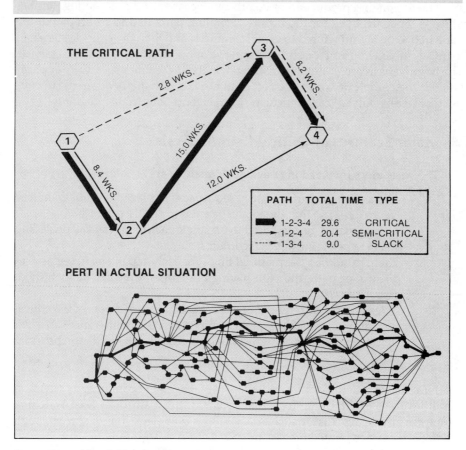

*Source:* Booz, Allen & Hamilton, Inc.

## General Applicability

The main features of critical path analysis apply to many programs that are not sufficiently complex to warrant the complete PERT treatment. Often just the preparation of a network chart of sequences of steps will clarify the interconnections between actions taken by various departments.

Moreover, the concept of a critical path can be used in many programming problems even though not an entire network is charted. In a company making nationally advertised men's shirts, for instance, the critical path runs from linebuilding through sales promotion to plant scheduling and on to order filling. Acquiring gray goods, training personnel, and similar steps have to be done, but they are not critical from a timing viewpoint because of the early leads necessary in sales promotion. Programming in other companies may be geared to filing a patent or perhaps training personnel. In all these situations, a recognition of what steps are part of the critical path will direct management efforts in "getting things done" to the crucial spots.

A word of caution is in order. Critical path analysis focuses on time, and few companies have data that enable them also to fit costs into the same framework. We would like to know how much speeding up or slowing down each step will change costs. Usually such cost estimates—even rough ones—are prepared only after critical steps are identified and a manager is trying to decide whether to make a change in plans. Similarly, critical path analysis does not deal with alternative ways of reaching a goal. The network is presumed to be settled. Of course, if the analysis identifies a serious bottleneck, then management may resort to a different method and may establish a new network.

Nevertheless, for many programming problems, timing is the major consideration. And for such programming problems, critical path analysis can be a valuable refinement.

## Long-Range Programming

### Nature of Long-Range Programming

Programming increases in difficulty as the time span covered is extended, yet such extension is well worth the trouble in some circumstances. We have been discussing program cycles ranging from a few months to perhaps two years. Long-range programming seeks to extend the period covered to, say, five to 10 years.

Underlying any long-range program should be a well-defined strategy. The strategy establishes the basic directions and the criteria for which the program is developed. The *program* introduces a time schedule—the how much and when aspects—and thereby sets the intermediate objectives (which in turn become the targets for more specific and detailed short-range programs).

### Applications

One of the classic examples of long-range programming is the conversion of the Bell System to dial telephones. Forecasts of telephone usage based on population growth, higher gross national product (GNP), and telephoning habits indicated that manual switching would not be able to handle the load. Besides, automatic dialing would improve service and perhaps cut costs. So the goal was clear, but the magnitude of the task was tremendous. Design of equipment had to be refined for recording calls, relaying long-distance calls, tying in with independent companies, and the like. Completely new exchanges had to be built, millions of dollars of switching equipment had to be manufactured, and millions of consumer units had to be produced. Before any of this physical equipment could be installed, engineers, installers, and operators had to be trained. Incidentally, company policy dictated that the transition was to be made with only seconds of interruption in service and no layoffs of regular employees. The public had to be prepared for the switch and educated to use the new equipment, and utility commissions had to be kept advised. Finally, the multimillion dollar investment had to be financed.

This incomplete list suggests the range of elements in the program. Many of the preliminary steps were taken 10 years before the conversion in that area was finished. And with new developments in technology and markets, the process is still going on.

The Bell System example is enlightening because (1) a whole series of interrelated steps were programmed years in advance, and (2) the programming was done for several elements—marketing, engineering, facilities, personnel, and finance—not just for a single element such as finance. For instance, Star Electronics, Inc., a small firm making parts for TVs and similar equipment, found its Brookline, Massachusetts, location far off from a growing number of customers in the Southwest. So a long-range plan for opening a second shop in Phoenix, Arizona, was laid out. (1) To build additional volume to justify such a shop, a sales engineer was located in Phoenix to serve customers almost as though the shop were in existence. (2) Any new equipment for Brookline was selected in anticipation of two separate manufacturing locations. (3) A year later, training of potential shop superintendents and an equipment engineer was started. (4) A cash reserve to cover startup costs was planned, and the expansion was discussed with the company banker.

These steps turned out to be especially helpful when, two and a half years after the start, an opportunity arose to buy the assets of a shop similar to Star Electronics that was on the brink of failure. Most of the equipment and related assets could be moved rapidly to Phoenix. Without the long-range planning, Star Electronics could not have seized this opportunity—it could not have developed an adequate market, a supervisory staff, or a financial plan quickly enough. Star Electronics took the plunge, earlier than it wanted and therefore in a risky fashion, but with its cash outlay cut in half.

In this example, we again see (1) a series of interrelated steps extending over a period of years and (2) a plan that embraced several different elements. The timing of the various steps was subject to adjustment, as was also true in the telephone conversion, and no attempt was made to spell out details several years in advance. But the master plan provided a definite guide for actions all along the way.

These examples may be misleading, because only a small portion of business firms actually prepare long-range programs in a clear-cut fashion. The main reason is simple: most companies cannot, or do not, forecast the nature and the volume of their activities for three, four, or five, let alone 10 years ahead. They may know the direction they would like to go (their objectives), but uncertainties about competition, technical developments, consumers' actions, political changes, economic changes and the like make timing hard to nail down.

Because of the difficulty of precise long-range forecasting, we need to examine carefully the benefits the typical company can reasonably hope to obtain from long-range programming and problems that must be overcome if it undertakes this management device.

## Major Benefits of Long-Range Programming

A central management that embarks on long-range programming usually seeks three advantages.

### 1. Long-Cycle Actions Are Started Promptly

An automated plant takes at least two or three years to design, build, and get into operation. A bright idea for a new product often requires three to five years for research, development, testing, and process engineering before it is ready to be marketed. Recruiting and training salespeople for computers takes several years, assuming they cannot be hired away from established competitors. Raising a new crop of timber for lumber may consume 25 years.

Long-term programming indicates when such actions should be started. Opportunities will be missed or crises in servicing customers may develop, unless a company takes early action. To fail to act is equivalent to a decision to postpone entry into the contemplated operation. Even though predictions of need are uncertain, there may be no feasible alternative to starting down the road.

By preparing the best program it is capable of, a company increases the probability that it will be aware of when long-cycle actions should be initiated.

### 2. Executives Are Psychologically Prepared for Change

Many actions embraced in a long-range program need not, and should not, be taken immediately. They can await a year or more of actual experience, and by then some modification in the original plan may be desirable.

Nevertheless, even though the program is changed, the process of preparing it aids adjustment to new conditions. As a result of preparing the program, the idea that some kind of change in response to shifts in the environment must take place is already accepted. And probably the nature of the adjustment will have been considered—for example, transfers of personnel, refunding a bond issue, or local production in a foreign country. Then, when conditions are ripe, executives are prepared to move quickly. Good news or bad news may arrive unexpectedly, and the company response may differ from the program; but the ability to recognize the opportunity, to appreciate the range of actions that are necessary, and to get in motion has been sharpened by the mental exercise of preparing (and revising) a program.

The pace of technological and economic change is quickening. Product life cycles are shorter, and competitors move into profitable opportunities more quickly. Consequently, the ability of a company to adjust promptly to shifts in its environment is crucial to getting ahead and staying ahead in modern competition. Accordingly, psychological preparation for change is more vital to central management today than it was a generation ago.

### 3. Actions Having Long-Term Impact Are Coordinated

Often an action taken to meet an immediate problem also significantly affects the future operations of the company. For example, to get quick coverage of the West Coast territory, one firm gave exclusive distribution rights to an agent who also sold related products. The agent was successful in establishing itself as the local representative, and the immediate problem was resolved. However, the firm soon expanded and diversified so that it needed a strong national sales organization of its own sales representatives; the successful independent distributor on the West Coast ultimately proved to be very difficult to supplant.

The selection of executives for key posts, the licensing of a company patent, and acceptance of a government subsidy are further examples where short-run solutions may prove troublesome in the future. If a company has a long-range program, central managers will be able to sense more easily whether current decisions do, or do not, fit into a consistent pattern of long-term development.

Note that in the list of benefits of long-range planning we do not include "a blueprint for future action." Only rarely are prediction and control of conditions several years hence sufficiently accurate to permit close adherence to a five-year plan. But such a program does help identify actions that should be initiated now, it lays a psychological base for prompt adjustment to opportunities in the future, and it provides a pattern so that action on today's problems can be compatible with long-range plans.

## Problems Involved in Long-Range Programming

Preparation of a long-range program requires guidance. Key problems are what topics and period to cover, how revisions will be made, and who will do the work of developing the plans.

### Topics Covered

Too often so-called long-range programs are merely financial estimates conjured up by a bright young analyst in the controller's office. Such estimates take the form of annual profit-and-loss budgets for perhaps the next five years.

For operating purposes, dollar sales estimates have little meaning unless someone has thought in terms of the products that will be sold, the customers who will buy them, the prices obtainable in the face of competition, and the selling effort necessary to obtain the orders. Similarly, the projected volume of goods must be conceived in terms of the resources necessary to produce them: plant capacity, trained workers, the flow of raw materials, engineering talent, and so on.

Therefore, long-range programs should be stated in physical terms. But it is impractical to spell out such plans in full detail; instead, management should identify the crucial factors and build the program in these terms. One of the keys to successful programming is this identifying of topics to be used; omissions of vital factors will make the program unrealistic, whereas too many factors will make it unwieldy.

The long-range program should also be translated into dollar results: revenues, costs, profits, and capital requirements. Dollars are the best common denominator we have, and the financial results are an important aspect of any program. Use constant dollars first, and then adjust for inflation. But the main point is that dollar figures alone are not enough.

### Period Covered

Five years is the most common period covered by long-range programs. There is no magic in this figure, however. Logically, long-range plans should be based on the necessary elapsed time for such important action as product development, resource development, market development, or physical facility development. Three years may be long enough; in some cases, 10 years will be needed.

In fact, the necessary time varies. Resource development may have to be started eight years before materials become available, while two years may be adequate for market development. To deal with this variation, several companies (1) plan an action *in detail* only when a start is necessary, or (2) prepare a comprehensive program for three or four years ahead and then extend the period only for those areas requiring longer lead times.

### Conflict with Current Operations

Strategy programs for change often compete with current operations for attention. In universities and automobile showrooms, this year's students and models demand attention; they should be served well. At the same time, steps in a long-range program may call for intensive preparation for a long switch two years hence to keep up with competition.

Trouble arises when the same set of people is expected to do both, often with little increase in resources. Even when managers and workers agree with the strategic objectives, their habits, measures of success, and rewards typically lead to first priority going to current operations. The longer term project gets attention only in slack time. Indeed, if effort for current tasks is transferred to a new program, the people may be penalized. So the second-priority work slips behind schedule or receives superficial treatment.

The remedy is not easy. Somehow, a realistic allocation of time and other resources must be made. Probably this allocation has to be separated from allocations for current operations, and separate measurements of progress must be made on each kind of work. Except where work is managed on a project basis, as in a laboratory, few companies have learned to keep current and long-term outputs in optimum balance.

### Revisions

As the results of the first steps become known and new information about external conditions is learned, long-range programs need revision. The typical procedure is an annual review in which near-term actions are planned in greater detail, a new year is added on the end, and adjustments are made in plans for the interim period.

Under this scheme, programs are revised several times before the period to which they apply finally arrives. This provides flexibility in long-range programming. It also entails a lot of work, and executives may become cavalier about plans for five years hence since such plans will be revised over and over again. These disadvantages of several revisions are strong reasons for restricting the period covered and making sure that the benefits listed earlier are actually being obtained.

### Treating Early Steps as Strategic Positioning

Another way to obtain flexibility in long-range programming is to think of the early steps as gaining a position, with subsequent steps to be decided after the position has been secured and a reappraisal made of opportunities then prevailing (see pages 67–68). Professor J.B. Quinn calls this "logical incrementalism."[2]

The main differences between this approach and the programming approach we have been discussing are that (1) the later steps of the program are laid out in only very broad terms and may be just one of several alternatives; (2) few, if any, resources are committed to the later steps, thereby retaining flexibility, and (3) a thorough reappraisal of what is wise after the position is secured must be made because no tentative plan has been endorsed. Perhaps the most serious drawback to the positioning viewpoint is that uncertainty prevails and enthusiastic commitment to a new mission cannot be built up. However, if the future is highly uncertain, and competitors are even more timid and slow to act, then retaining maximum flexibility may be the wise course.

### Long-Range Planning in Small Firms

Long-range planning in a small enterprise is necessarily more informal than in a large company. Managers lack the time to prepare detailed estimates, and consequently, often basic historical data will not have been recorded. Nevertheless, the basic process outlined should be followed, for the small firm has as much to gain by anticipating opportunities as a large one.

One entrepreneur with only 16 employees has a loose-leaf notebook with alternative five-year programs based on different key assumptions. Perhaps because of his engineering training, he has spelled out steps and resources for different rates of growth in any of three directions. The estimates are his personal,

---

[2]*Strategies for Change: Logical Incrementalism* (Homewood, IL: Richard D. Irwin, Inc., 1980).

subjective guesses; but when he makes a major investment or signs a long-term contract, he has a clear idea of where the action is likely to lead him.

In addition to the pressure of time, small business managers have difficulty thinking objectively about events several years away. Typically, they are so immersed in day-to-day activities that it is difficult to make a mental switch to a longer horizon. Preparing some estimates to present to a sympathetic board member can be a helpful discipline in this respect.

## SUMMARY

Through programming, a manager formulates an integrated plan covering what, how much, when, and who will be present over a range of time.

Long-range programming is part of the more inclusive process of long-range planning. So are establishing strategy and setting policy: they set directions, criteria, and limits. The *program* then introduces a time schedule—the how much and when—and breaks the broad plan into more specific steps.

Six basic steps should be taken: (1) divide into parts the program necessary to achieve the objective, (2) note the necessary sequences and relationships between each of these parts, (3) decide who is to be responsible for doing each part, (4) decide how each part will be done and the resources needed, (5) estimate the time required for each part, and (6) assign definite dates when each part will commence and end.

When faced with complex programming problems, a manager can use *critical path analysis* to identify those parts of the total activity that must be watched most closely if the final objective is to be met on time.

In practice, managers must exercise a lot of judgment in how they use long-range programming. The subjects and periods to be covered, the balancing effort devoted to current activities versus future activities, and the use of revisions to gain flexibility are recurring issues.

Multi-level issues also arise in a diversified corporation. The sort of planning stressed in this chapter requires quite specific knowledge about company capabilities, the slack time available to study future options, the likely behavior of competitors, values of key managers, and the like. This information is available only at the business-unit level. Consequently, the action-oriented commitment evoking long-range programming that we are proposing must be done by managers in the business-units. At the corporate level, both short- and long-range programming tend to degenerate into only a numbers game (except for a few corporate services).

However, the great contribution that corporate managers should make is to ensure that business-unit managers in fact utilize programming where it is appropriate. This is part of the "outside director" role described in Chapter 19.

## Questions for Class Discussion

1. Review the GAIN Software case (pages 22 to 26). Of the concepts discussed in this chapter, which one—if any—would be useful to the three owners at this stage in the company's development? What problems would the owners confront if they decided to prepare and carry out a long-range program?

2. Drilling Supplies, Inc. makes tubing used in newly drilled oil wells. Although the company has many competitors, its tubing now has special features that are distinctive, especially for offshore wells. Just prior to the break in crude oil prices, when OPEC could no longer restrain the supply of crude oil, Drilling Supplies developed a long-range program that included a new plant, plans for a worldwide marketing effort, and several added technical employees. Then came the crash. Crude oil prices dropped from around $35 per barrel to $12 per barrel or below. Drilling of new wells fell more than 80 percent. Instead of expanding, Drilling Supplies had to contract sharply. Fortunately, other markets for its tubing kept the company alive.

   Now, the president of Drilling Supplies says, "Long-range programming almost bankrupted this company. I don't want to hear about it again. We now concentrate on cash flow for a couple of months ahead; beyond that nobody knows what will happen. I'm not going to risk this company on a major war cutting off supplies from the Middle East, a new OPEC, or, even less likely, a U.S. policy of self-sufficiency in oil. Instead, we'll meet increases in demand if and when they come."

   Do you think the president's view of long-range programming is wise? Is there any sort of programming that you would recommend to him?

3. Brenda and Joe Klein are leaders of a group of citizens in Mountain View who want a community swimming pool. The village majority and council are sympathetic but say that the village cannot afford the capital costs, and they are afraid that political pressure will force them to keep admission charges so low that operating costs will not be covered. The Klein group is now considering a semiprivate swim club. A nearby village has such a club with the following provisions: Capital costs are covered by an initiation fee for the 300 family members; much of this fee will be repaid by new members who replace anyone who resigns. Operating costs are covered by annual dues and fees for guests. Any citizen in Mountain View is eligible to join on a first-come, first-served basis. The village leases the land (a good location owned by the village) to the club for twenty years at a nominal charge. At the end of the lease, the village gets the pool, dressing rooms, and so forth. The Kleins ask you to prepare a long-range program for getting a swimming pool in Mountain View as soon as possible.

4. Southwestern State University moved to prevent the cut-off of about $28,000,000 from the federal government for research contracts by preparing

a program for increasing the proportion of women in higher faculty ranks and higher administrative positions. The plan for this was accepted by the federal government. The trouble is that, although the program was accepted, in practice it has not achieved the planned results. In fact, the percentage of women faculty members has declined slightly in the past four years from 19 percent to 18 percent. An assistant academic vice president, who has been overseeing the program, said: "We have tried to hire and promote women faculty members but the deans and search committees say that the university's tenure and promotion committee turns down promotions for women because their research publication records are not adequate. And the search committees can't hire because others, especially the private universities, bid more than we are allowed to by the governor for the few available female candidates. Overall, the strong drive of the president and the provost to improve the academic quality and reputation of the university seems to go against the work we can do to meet EOOC standards."

What do you recommend to get the program back on track? (Be as concrete as you can, except that you may use "Xs" or "Ys" for specific numbers of people.) Does the concept of programming as outlined in this chapter fit this kind of situation? Explain.

5. Beckley Wardwell, to help make the decision about poromeric leather (see the Wardwell Vinyl Coatings case on pages 156–165), wants a program outlined for introducing the new product. The program will help to indicate the feasibility of taking on the poromeric leather license. Your analysis shows that the major steps will be:

| | |
|---|---|
| A. Decision to accept the license | F. Production trials completed |
| B. Engineering completed by the joint efforts of Spencer and the Belgian firm | G. Sales training completed and promotion program arranged |
| | H. Initial orders received |
| C. Financing arranged | I. Full-scale production starts |
| D. Material purchase orders placed | J. Initial orders shipped |
| E. Plant laid out and equipment in place | |

Your analysis also shows that the necessary sequences among events and the estimated time required to perform the work to advance from one event to the next are as shown in Table 1.

(a) Prepare a PERT diagram. (b) Determine the critical path. (c) Do your answers to (a) and (b) suggest any action to Mr. Wardwell?

6. Visiting the People's Republic of China has great fascination for many foreign travelers. Its vast population, ancient ruins, quaint customs, and transformation of a traditional society to a modern-day society all add interest. The major drawback is that China is not prepared to handle a large influx of foreign tourists. These tourists are accustomed to international standards of

**TABLE 1.**

| Necessary Sequence | Estimated Time | Necessary Sequence | Estimated Time |
|---|---|---|---|
| A-B | 60 days | D-E | 60 days |
| A-C | 90 days | D-I | 75 days |
| B-E | 60 days | F-I | 1 day |
| E-F | 30 days | G-H | 30 days |
| C-D | 5 days | H-I | 1 day |
| C-G | 60 days | I-J | 5 days |

quality, and China will miss an opportunity to build a significant source of foreign exchange unless it meets international standards instead of the humble provisions now provided for its own citizens. Among the shortages are fast, dependable transportation (there is no intercity highway system, most airplanes are converted Russian planes that run on an unreliable schedule, railroads are like U.S. trains of the 1920s); a network of western-style hotels; interpreters who can respond to the usual diversity of questions in several languages; a system of schedules, bookings, and confirmed reservations (now almost nonexistent). Nevertheless, building a tourist industry is one of the many goals of the government of China.

Outline a long-range program to develop China's tourist industry. Keep in mind that foreign exchange is very scarce, and that China has many other competing uses for its resources.

7. C. E. Lindblom and J. B. Quinn contend that strategy is developed and carried out, not by a comprehensive program covering events from start to finish, but instead by a succession of small steps in which the manager waits until one is finished before deciding what the next step will be. This "feeling-one's way" they call the *incremental approach,* or *incrementalism.* They report that incrementalism is used especially when uncertainty is high about the results of the present step or about future operating conditions; it also is used when agreement about the total picture is difficult to reach among key actors. (a) Which approach—incremental or fully programmed—should a manager use for (i) building an airplane? (ii) mining manganese modules from the ocean floor? (iii) opening a new drugstore? (iv) promoting a freeze on nuclear weapons? (b) How does incrementalism relate to strategic positioning as discussed in Chapter 3?

8. Chapter 4 recommends the analysis of key actors as part of the basis for formulating strategy. How can this concept of key-actor analysis be used in making a program for (a) introducing a new product into the market? (b) cutting energy costs for your university?

9. The conflict of serving current students well versus designing new courses and/or methods of instruction for future students was noted very briefly in the chapter. Assume that your school has just adopted a strategy of (a) continuing to offer its present degrees but, because of demographics and competition, to plan on smaller enrollments, and (b) looking for growth in short programs for experienced managers. Your professors have been requested to support this new strategy by designing new courses and teaching materials suited to the new type of customer. How should your professors respond? Should they minimize time they spend on present students (using old notes and cases, etc.) and focus on the new strategic thrust? Request that adjunct professors be hired to teach present students if alumni will contribute the cost of doing so? Continue serving present students as in the past, and work on the new strategy over weekends? Organize a movement to get the strategy reversed? And/or take some other kind of action that you propose?

10. Some years ago Reginald Jones, then chairman and chief executive officer of General Electric Company, decided that G.E. should add to its core businesses (aircraft engines, aerospace, plastics, medical systems, lighting, consumer electronics, household appliances, and G.E. Credit Corporation) by increasing its international operations with an emphasis on raw materials. Mr. Jones did this by agreeing to purchase Utah International, Inc. Utah's main business was mining, in Australia, coal sold to Japanese steel companies. Utah also dug up iron ore in Brazil and, as a small part of its total sales, produced crude oil and natural gas. Utah International was to be joined to General Electric's operations by making it a wholly owned subsidiary with its own management. The president of the subsidiary would report directly to G.E.'s chief executive officer. (a) Does this acquisition fit into the category of a strategic thrust as explained on page 607? (b) Is a short-range program—as explained on pages 605–607—necessary as "an excellent device to assure" that the work of acquiring Utah International and melding it with G.E. operations "receives adequate attention?" (c) Which ones of the six steps explained in this chapter would belong in such a program? (d) How might this purchase aid or increase the international operations of the core businesses?

## CASE 21    Apex Internacional

The Apex Equipment Company is embarking on its first venture in foreign manufacturing. Still unsettled is how bold Apex wants to be in this new thrust.

The company has a successful record in the automobile equipment *replacement* industry. Basically, it waits until the major manufacturers of its kind of product produce models which are incorporated into new autos. Then Apex very carefully duplicates each model and sells these in the replacement market. Auto supply jobbers sell Apex products to the thousands of shops, garages, and filling stations that repair autos and trucks.

Of course, the original equipment manufacturers (OEMs) also sell their products in the replacement market. However, with the passage of time there is a variety of models fitting various cars, and the volume of replacement sales on any one model is small relative to the production runs for new car use. Apex has designed its manufacturing activities to handle short production runs, and it is thus able to compete with OEMs in the replacement end of the industry.

Apex has decided not to seek OEM business from the big U.S. auto producers (or foreign producers in their home country). The competitors are too big and entrenched, and such a move would require Apex to do much more R & D than it does at present. But the situation in developing countries which are just getting into automobile production is quite different.

In a country such as Brazil, auto production starts primarily as assembly of imported parts. However, to save foreign exchange and to provide local employment, the governments of such countries push hard to increase the use of locally produced parts; tax benefits, tariffs, and import quotas are all used. As soon as a part is available locally, barriers to imports are likely to be imposed.

Apex sees an opportunity to be an OEM supplier in Brazil, and later in other such countries. The company has demonstrated its ability to make products that work just as well as the original equipment, and it knows how to produce in relatively small quantities. One Brazilian company is already in the business but its quality is considered to be inferior. A European producer may set up a Brazilian plant. So if Apex opens a local plant, it can promptly become a leading supplier for local OEM and replacement parts, probably with tariff protection.

### Joe Androtti, Apex Production V.P.

"The fastest way to get started, and with the least risk now, is to rent a small plant in the São Paulo area. Then when we are successful and know our way around—say, in three years—we would have to move, presumably to our own larger plant in Belo Horizonte (Brazil's third largest city, with a vigorous industrial development program). Production space can be rented in São Paulo, but at a high price. Lead time on equipment delivery in the U.S. ranges from four to nine months. Then allow three months for shipping and clearing customs, and two months to get set up. That adds up to a minimum time to get started of 14 months.

"A second alternative is to build a somewhat larger, though still small, plant in São Paulo. We would just postpone deciding what to do when we outgrow such a plant. Planning, approvals, and actual plant construction would probably take two years. But we should be able to have the equipment in and ready to go within that time. Unfortunately, São Paulo is crowded and may get worse, the smog is terrible, and the government offers no special incentives to locate there.

"In contrast, Belo is courting new industry. Maude Weaver has figures on the financial picture. It is very difficult to rent in Belo, and if we start there we would at least lay out a larger operation from the beginning. No future moves would be anticipated. The entire physical setup at Belo is more attractive than in São Paulo, but since more government approvals are involved we should figure on two and a half years to get started there."

### Maude Weaver, Apex Treasurer

"If we located in Belo, we can, in effect, get our new building at half-cost, have no real estate taxes for five years, and also receive a subsidy for training new workers. I know Brazilians have a reputation for being slow in taking official action, but two other U.S. firms told me that they had no major trouble. Their advice is to ask for your full needs while you are at it.

"My figures on our capital requirements boil down to this: renting in São Paulo gives the lowest investment, but with rent expense figured in the production, costs per unit would be at least as high as those in our owned plant in São Paulo, and we would have to move in a couple of years.

"If we go to Belo immediately, we could hold back on some of the equipment until we needed it. Of course, working capital is (or should be) a function of actual volume rather than capacity. So our capital investment when sales are running at $6,000,000 would not be much higher at Belo than at São Paulo—about $3,000,000 total. Production costs per unit should also be about the same. When volume pushes sales above $6,000,000, the advantages of the larger plant at Belo would really show up. The following table sums it up:

|  | Sales at Capacity | Investment in Plant & Equipment | Net Working Capital |
|---|---|---|---|
| Rental plant in São Paulo | $ 3,000,000 | $ 300,000 | $ 750,000 |
| Small owned plant in São Paulo | 6,000,000 | 1,200,000 | 1,500,000 |
| Full-scale plant in Belo | 12,000,000 | 1,800,000 | 3,000,000 |

"Incidentally, Brazil has high inflation, which confuses the picture a bit. But in Brazil almost everything is 'indexed,' including the amount you must repay on a loan. So we are making our estimates in constant dollars.

"Now the catch is—where do we get the $1,050,000 or the $3,000,000? Our domestic business is growing, and with inflation it soaks up most of the cash it generates. We can borrow $1,000,000 from the banks on short-term loans. Above that, and certainly for $3,000,000 (which is almost 25 percent of our present assets and 50 percent of stockholders' equity), we must negotiate a long-term loan. The negotiating should start six months before we need the cash."

### Paul Nichols, Apex President

"Key personnel will be our bottleneck in this Brazilian venture, in my opinion. Our present agent in São Paulo, Salvador Silvana, has done an excellent job of importing and selling our products. And he is promoting the expansion. However, like many Latin American businesspeople, he has several other projects and does not want to devote his full time to Apex Internacional. He does want to handle all local sales. So we will need a Brazilian general manager and a Brazilian production manager. I wish we had a Portuguese-speaking financial person to send down, but we don't.

"From a personnel angle, a modest start where we can test and train executives would be preferable. It is particularly difficult to select executives in a foreign country where you don't know the subtleties. I'd feel better about going the Belo route if I had full confidence in the general manager.

"The general manager should know the business backwards and forwards and preferably have a technical background. Maybe the general manager should work for Salvador for a while, as well as here in the U.S., and help plan and negotiate. It may be difficult to attract and hold a good person for two and a half years, however. I guess we should start looking and be ready to act. Who runs the project in the meantime? Production is a bit easier because we can send a couple of engineers to Brazil during the startup period.

"Another consideration is our organization here at headquarters. We have only an export manager who concentrates entirely on foreign sales. I'm not sure how involved our key department managers should or will get in far-off Brazil. Maybe we should be thinking in terms of an international division."

### Howard Schaller, Apex Export Manager

"It is always difficult to know how hard to push in a foreign situation. There are at least two reasons for moving fast in Brazil. First, if we are going to stake out a major position, we should get there before others do. There is room for only a couple of manufacturers in Brazil. If we move aggressively, maybe we can discourage others from entering. Second, the government attitude about foreign investments might change quickly. I don't think it will in Brazil, but other countries have had sudden shifts in governments and in economic policy. If we are already set up inside the country, our position is more secure.

"Once our production capability is established, then the more support for local production there is, the more we will benefit. Silvana believes we can develop a $12,000,000 volume in our line of business within four or five years. It may be optimistic, but the potential is there. With profit margins 50 percent higher than in the U.S., this should be a real moneymaker. Meanwhile, Silvana should do everything he can to build Apex's reputation for quality."

After some inconclusive give-and-take discussion among Apex managers, Joe Androtti decided that a Gantt chart showing one possible program would help to focus the issues. So he prepared the following chart (page 626) based on what he called "low-risk assumptions" (renting a plant in São Paulo while preparing to move to Belo Horizonte, and importing products to build up sales until this plant is in operation):

## Question

Outline a five-year program that you recommend for Apex's entry as a producer in Brazil.

626

## FIGURE 21-2.
## GANTT CHART FOR APEX INTERNACIONAL

|                                      | 1st year |   |   |   | 2nd year |   |   |   | 3rd year |   |   |   |
|--------------------------------------|---|---|---|---|---|---|---|---|---|---|---|---|
|                                      | J | A | J | O | J | A | J | O | J | A | J | O |
| Order long-lead equipment            |   |   |   |   |   |   |   |   |   |   |   |   |
| Set up local corporation             |   |   |   |   |   |   |   |   |   |   |   |   |
| Lease São Paulo plant                |   |   |   |   |   |   |   |   |   |   |   |   |
| Hire general manager                 |   |   |   |   |   |   |   |   |   |   |   |   |
| Hire production manager              |   |   |   |   |   |   |   |   |   |   |   |   |
| Plan layout of plant                 |   |   |   |   |   |   |   |   |   |   |   |   |
| Order remaining equipment            |   |   |   |   |   |   |   |   |   |   |   |   |
| Train foreman and key operators      |   |   |   |   |   |   |   |   |   |   |   |   |
| Start up plant                       |   |   |   |   |   |   |   |   |   |   |   |   |
| Develop record system                |   |   |   |   |   |   |   |   |   |   |   |   |
| Expand replacement sales organization|   |   |   |   |   |   |   |   |   |   |   |   |
| Cultivate OEM business               |   |   |   |   |   |   |   |   |   |   |   |   |
| Plan broadly Belo plant              |   |   |   |   |   |   |   |   |   |   |   |   |
| Negotiate for Belo plant             |   |   |   |   |   |   |   |   |   |   |   |   |
| Explore import protection            |   |   |   |   |   |   |   |   |   |   |   |   |
| Borrow for São Paulo operations      |   |   |   |   |   |   |   |   |   |   |   |   |
| Negotiate to finance Belo operations |   |   |   |   |   |   |   |   |   |   |   |   |

# CHAPTER 22

## Activating:
## Winning Acceptance for Strategic Action

The wisest strategy, organization, and programs are naught until they are put into action. This need to translate ideas into action has been a recurring theme throughout our discussion, but it warrants further recognition in a separate chapter. Upper level managers play an important role in activating an enterprise by (1) creating a *focused climate*, (2) *managing* strategy changes, (3) making *MBO-type evaluations* of key managers, and (4) using *incentives* in a demanding way.

Controlling is also necessary in achieving desired results. We will explore that aspect of strategy management in Chapter 23.

### Creating a Focused Climate

Every established organization has its own climate or culture. The organization embodies traditional values about customer service, spending money, accepting risks, beating competitors, dealing with communist countries, taking the initiative, and many other matters. This climate affects the ease or difficulty of carrying out a specific strategy.

### Careful Use of Executive Influence

Managers, and especially senior executives, help form the climate within their bailiwick. They cannot escape being public figures. Their behavior is closely watched for cues. The vice-president who jokingly said, "Guess I'll walk through the office in my shirt sleeves just to start a rumor," was well aware that many people would try to infer meaning from even his casual actions.

Because they are inevitably in the local spotlight, central managers should behave in a way that creates a climate favorable to the execution of company strategy. And it is actions and decisions, more than words, which convey the message. The president who is lavish with his personal expense account will have difficulty securing strong support for a cost-reduction program. Likewise, the promotion of a product manager who uncovered a new market for a product will send signals throughout the organization. Specific decisions are magnified because they help generate widespread feelings and attitudes.

The importance of climate is highlighted in a study by McKinsey and Company.[1] These management consultants carefully compared the central management practices in a set of companies with excellent performance records against a comparable set of companies whose performance has been "not outstanding." Differences in climate are closely associated with differences in results. Among their findings are the following.

## Stress Selected, Simple Goals

The excellent companies all had a few well-recognized goals or themes: "Our company is built around customer service." "Growth is essential; we expect to be the largest company in our industry within five years." "Pioneers in banking. . . ." Statements such as these illustrate an overriding goal. Usually the less successful companies did not have such clear-cut, integrating concepts of mission.

To an outsider these goals seem almost naive. However, they have taken on real meaning within the companies which use them, and, somewhat like a religious creed, they call forth emotional commitment.

Obviously, these overriding goal statements should be linked to company strategy. Strategy, of course, has more facets; but often a tersely stated mission captures its essence.

A second type of goal typically found in the successful companies is the achievement of more immediate, short-run objectives. These are the "thrusts" in our definition of strategy—for example, "a mini-size car ready to market in 1992," or "current, error-free, computerized subscription lists by the end of the year." At any one time, a successful company singles out only a few such themes for prime attention. Usually they are simple to understand, achievable, and have a strong action focus.

Of course, the thrusts and themes change as old ones are achieved and new ones are added. The more successful climate is one that avoids a complex array of themes with varying priorities. Instead, the normal pattern is to focus on a few carefully selected thrusts. The evidence suggests that the excellent companies somehow sift through a great diversity of influences and alternatives and then select a simplified set of goals for emphasis in operations. On major issues at least, a clear-cut value system replaces uncertainty and ambiguity.

## Build Acceptance Through Symbolic Behavior

The goals and thrusts become powerful values in the company climate only when they are strongly supported by the central managers. The McKinsey study shows that the chief executive can set the tone. The way the executive allocates time and attention tells what he or she considers important. But because the CEO

---

[1]T. J. Peters and R. H. Waterman. *In Search of Excellence* (New York: Harper & Row, 1982).

cannot be in many places at once and personally participate in many decisions, the more effective CEO takes actions which become symbols of the values he or she is advocating. Here are four kinds of useful symbols:

1.  *Hands-on participation* by the key executive. Calling on customers to get their reactions to products and services, attending the closing of an important sale, personally reviewing affirmative action moves, participating in new product meetings, conducting discussions, and having dinner with executive trainees are examples. Perhaps the CEO gets involved only on a sampling basis—to avoid being a bottleneck—but there is no doubt about genuine concern.

2.  *Positive reinforcement* of actions which are consistent with the overriding goal or selected thrusts. This includes making field visits to locations where positive action has occurred and praising participating workers, giving special awards for outstanding performance, and granting immediate additional assistance to people already moving in approved directions. Some executives give such reinforcement again and again over a sustained period, driving home the central message.

3.  Pointing out *role models* of desired behavior. An example of successful performance makes a goal seem real and achievable. Just as the four-minute mile is no longer a fantasy for runners, so can a pilot's on-time record or a branch manager's inventory turnover be singled out for others to follow.

4.  Support of *myths*. Every company has its stories of exceptional actions: the president who personally delivered a bicycle on Christmas Eve so as not to disappoint a customer; the power-line repairer who kept electricity flowing to a hospital during an ice storm; the president of Seagrams who dumped an entire batch of whiskey down the drain because the taste was not up to quality standards; the manager who was fired the day it was discovered that he had lied to a congressional committee. Over time, the details of the stories may get distorted, but they are part of the company lore. Such stories which support the overriding strategy can be repeated to help establish the mystique of the company.

Through such well-worn methods as these, the central managers of excellently performing companies make clear the selected company values. And by creating such a climate, people throughout the organization are more likely to execute their various assignments correctly and enthusiastically.

This repeated emphasis on a few selected themes builds focused behavior. By clarifying priorities, it improves performance. However, the analysis and testing which precedes the execution stage may be complex, prolonged, and sophisticated. Part of the skill in creating an effective, uncluttered climate is being most careful in selecting those goals and thrusts which are paramount.

## Managing Strategy Changes

Activating often involves change. The focused climate just described may become outdated by new opportunities. Or, within its general scope, a new product, new energy-saving technology, or new organization may be necessary. Central managers especially must be active in bringing these changes about.

A change in strategy always involves a difficult transition. Relations with suppliers and customers will be altered, people will have new jobs, and priorities and power will be shifted. Typically, as Figure 22–1 suggests, years, not days, are required.

During the early stage, the new strategy and the accompanying policy and programs are still being worked out. Some people will be involved in this new planning, and through this participation they will understand and probably endorse the change in direction. Other people will necessarily be "minding the store" because previous activities must be continued in order to maintain company momentum while modified activities are being planned and tested. (The 1992 model automobiles must be made and sold while the 1993 and 1994 models are being developed.) Then comes a phasing-out of the old and a building of support for the new. It is during this transition and throughout the middle stage that central managers build acceptance through symbolic behavior, as just described. Finally, pres-

**FIGURE 22–1.**
**FIVE- TO NINE-YEAR CYCLE OF STRATEGIC TRANSITION**

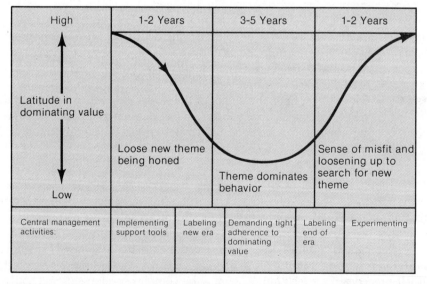

sure builds for another tack, and central managers must start preparing people psychologically for fresh leaps forward.

The transition from an old strategy to a new one creates special problems in activating. Behavior previously endorsed now has to be modified. And experience clearly demonstrates that the momentum of a going concern is not redirected merely by giving an order. Managers of the people affected can aid in the transition by (1) relieving anxiety promptly, (2) identifying areas where modifications in individual and group behavior are needed, (3) providing time to learn new behavior, and (4) giving positive reinforcement to desired behavior.

## Relieve Anxiety Promptly

Rumors about changes that might upset cherished relationships spread rapidly. Once the status quo is shattered, employees give attention to all sorts of idle speculation. For instance, just an announcement that the company has bought a new computer can generate stories about closing down an office, firing half the people in the accounting department, or transferring the engineering staff to San Diego. Anxiety builds up, each minor statement or action of central management is interpreted many ways, efficiency drops, and employees begin looking for other jobs.

Much of the anxiety comes from uncertainty—not knowing what is going to happen. To be sure, some anxiety also arises because people are unsure how well they will perform under the new circumstances. Only actual experience in the new setup can remove the latter insecurity, but anxiety about the unknown can be reduced by management.

Prompt communication is vital. Even though specific answers of precisely what will happen often cannot be given because plans have not yet been developed in full detail, full discussion of the known facts is helpful. Publicly recognizing employee concern, presenting a positive feeling about the future, and scuttling a variety of mistaken rumors all relieve uneasiness. If decisions are not yet made, then a statement of when they will be made and how they will be communicated is much better than no news at all.

An especially sensitive period is when negotiations for, say, a merger are still in the confidential stage. Then the most that can be done is to check false rumors and to assure employees that they will be informed early of any action that will affect them. Confidence in management's credibility is important at this stage.

## Identify Behavior Changes

Supplementing every formally planned organization is a host of customary though unspecified relations. Pat Lee knows whom to contact about payroll deductions, passes along advance information on big orders to the production scheduler, picks up hints on the boss's temper from her secretary, and in other ways fits into an intricate social structure. Now, when a major change in organization and activities occurs, the old social structure breaks down and for a time no one is sure (1) where to get and give bits of information, (2) who has influence in the revised power structure, and (3) whose "suggestions" to consider seriously. During this period of flux, work gets done very slowly.

By identifying the principal areas of disruption, a manager can anticipate where the trouble is likely to occur. Also, by supporting selected people in disputes, by feeding information through particular channels, and by weighing and, if possible, accepting recommendations coming from staff or line, managers help shape the new social structure.

Individual values and habits have to be modified, as well as the social interaction just discussed. For example, for years Tom Novello has worked closely with six southern wholesalers; he knows their buyers personally, and their goodwill has been a real asset. Now a decision to sell directly to customers makes these wholesalers insignificant customers. Novello has to stop giving them special attention; the priority goes elsewhere. Since, as is frequently the case, friendships are involved as well as personal skills or knowledge that give the wholesalers distinct worth, the new policy is tough to accept. Because emotions and habits are involved, the implications of a major change may lead Novello to unconsciously reject the general idea even while he gives verbal acceptance to it.

## Provide Time to Learn New Behavior

Adjustments in behavior take time. When we first do any new task, like riding a motorcycle or instructing a computer, we are clumsy and unsure how to interpret cues. The same is true of executive action. And when we *change* behavior, we may have to unlearn old habits and attitudes before picking up the new ones. Social interaction also has to be "learned"; here two or more people are involved, and they have to respond to each other as well as to their own motivations.

Managers should recognize the need for this learning period. Even when employees have no reluctance to adopt new objectives, the early operations will be hard and slow. Practice is needed, and minor adjustments often have to be made. Also, in the kind of strategy changes discussed here, some jockeying for position by energetic managers is sure to occur. Time for a "shakedown cruise" is clearly necessary; the tough question of judgment is how long to allow.

## Give Positive Reinforcement

Learning new behavior will occur faster if managers notice and strongly encourage new actions that are along the desired lines. This is the period to build acceptance through symbolic behavior, as already described. Usually the new behavior will require extra effort, and special recognition will help sustain that effort during the learning period.

Such recognition of desired behavior also helps relieve anxiety built up during the transition. People are unclear as to just what should be done in the new situation, and they will welcome reassurance when they are on the right track. Some doubt is likely to exist about the feasibility of the new direction, so every opportunity to point out where it is succeeding should be used to build confidence in the plan. Role models of desired behavior should be identified.

Activating a new strategy or reorganization, then, calls for keen perception by central managers of the modifications in customary behavior that will be necessary to make the revised plan succeed. By closely following the way people are responding, managers can spot the desired behavior and can encourage people to follow that course. Such positive management will both reduce the learning time and relieve anxiety.

## Incremental Versus Frame-Breaking Change

Most changes in strategy modify only a few dimensions of the total company operations. They build on existing customs and strengths, making readjustments in particular areas without upsetting the momentum in most of the other areas. In this respect, the changes are incremental—like the seasonal growth of a tree.

Occasionally, the strategy change will be more drastic. For instance, deregulation in the banking industry coupled with volatile interest rates has forced savings-and-loan banks to fundamentally alter their services or fold up. New technology plus foreign competition forced frame-breaking changes in the radio industry. Strategies to deal with and maybe even to promote such fundamental changes as these cannot be just incremental. Indeed, research in many industries and at corporate, business-unit, and department levels shows that a whole set of new fits must be made all at once. Usually, changes are made in strategy, organization, key managers, and technology concurrently! Because such frame-breaking change is more like a revolution than evolution, a few vigorous central managers have to conceive of a new strategic alignment with the company's environment. Then, they should promptly take the painful steps to convert to the new structure. Typically, this involves redesigning the organization, replacing several key managers, introducing new work processes, and adjusting the measurements and controls. The quicker the revised pattern is introduced, the better, for attention has to be shifted from mourning the losses to the potential benefits of the new setup. A fresh excitement about building for the future has to be cultivated.

Frame-breaking change is risky. With rare exceptions, a company winds up facing a financial crisis before the need for this sort of drastic action is accepted. That means that resources are scarce and the new alignment may be the last chance for survival. However, as soon as consensus on the basic redesign has been reached at the top of the unit involved, managers can use the measures of fostering focused climate, relieving anxiety, identifying behavioral change, learning new behavior, and giving positive management to make the situation as comfortable as possible for all concerned. Then the storm will have passed, and a new period of incremental change in strategy can build refinements on the new base.

## MBO for Key Managers

The activating methods discussed so far create a general setting or climate for actions by people throughout the company. Valuable as such a climate is, managers must do more: specific direction and motivation for each immediate subordinate are also necessary.

*Management by objectives* (MBO) is an activating technique that can be applied to specific managers. Because strategy so often calls for a variety of changes and sets ambitious targets, a normal question for most managers is what to do first—where to place emphasis. A supervising executive should provide help in answering this question, and MBO is well suited to the task.

The underlying concepts of MBO are simple, and are frequently associated with supervising first-line operators. Nevertheless, they can be easily adapted to higher level managers. The CEO of a corporation can use them with corporate vice presidents, the general manager of a business-unit can use them with department heads, and department heads can use them with their direct subordinates. To be sure, the use of MBO in the executive suite calls for both diligence and skill.

## Basic Steps

The process begins with a manager (of any rank) agreeing with his or her boss about the results that are expected during an ensuing period, say, three months, six months, or perhaps a year. Such an agreement should be based on a mutual understanding about (1) the sphere of activities the manager is concerned with, that is, the organization; (2) the desired goals for these activities, both long and short run; (3) how achievement of these goals will be measured and the level of achievement expected by the end of the period planned; (4) the help the manager may expect from executives and others; and (5) the freedom and the restraints on how the manager pursues the goal.

Then, at the end of the period the boss and the subordinate again sit down to review what actually was accomplished, to determine why deviations (both good and bad) from goals occurred, and to agree on a new set of goals for the next period. These goal-setting sessions provide an excellent opportunity to link actual behavior with strategy.

At each review there is grist for a new discussion because a new set of results is available for appraisal and a new set of targets and priorities need to be agreed upon. As the process proceeds, the executive has repeated opportunities to counsel the individual and to relate individual performance to company strategy, policy, organization, and programs. These discussions should be objective and frank. As a minimum, the manager should know what is expected and how his or her performance will be measured.

One of the advantages of this form of MBO is that it sets the stage for frequent dialogue about goals and their achievement. In fact, when people work on distinct projects, the review may occur at the close of one project and the beginning of another. In other instances the reviews and new goal-setting sessions become a part of programming discussed in the preceding chapter. So if a person's total job and total performance are covered in such a project or programming discussions, an additional period of appraisal serves little purpose. Often, however, these discussions are sharply focused on a particular end result, and an annual examination of overall performance picks up loose ends and gives balanced direction. Whatever the timing, the important thing is that open communication take place between each manager and his or her direct supervisor on the five factors previously listed.

## Benefits Sought

Several benefits should arise from such regular sessions on goal setting and reviewing results.

1. Attention is focused on *achieving results*, not just being active, and these results are promptly compared to company goals. Of course, activities will be necessary to achieve results, and much of the discussion and resource allocation will be tied to such activities. Nevertheless, if the activities are not leading to desired results—because of either internal or external events—the manager is expected to initiate revised action that will lead to the specified goals. In other words, the MBO system assumes considerable decentralization to and initiative by subordinates. And if results are not turning out as hoped, the person who has accepted the responsibility should be doing something about it.

2. *Personal commitment* to carry out the (agreed-upon) mission is rendered more likely. Having the opportunity to discuss both the assignment and the help needed to get it done usually gives junior managers a feeling that the task is achievable. Also, the goal has been endorsed by the boss as being wise and in the interests of the company. In psychological terms, the aim is to have the goal *internalized* and *legitimized*. And if the subordinate has made the stated results a personal aim, both efforts and resourcefulness are increased.

3. *Balanced goals* can be agreed upon. Especially at the upper management levels, several competing goals are almost always present. The marketing vice-president, for instance, is concerned with advertising, pricing in specific markets, new products, sales training, and branch offices, just to mention a few subjects that might arise in a single week. Some results, such as direct costs, are easily measured, while others, such as community service, are intangible. Typically, short-run results steal attention from longer run objectives even though the latter may be more significant. Senior executives are vitally concerned that goals and results be kept in optimum balance. MBO reviews provide a forum where these balancing issues can be considered in terms of concrete action.

4. *Dual accountability* can be enforced. As business operations become more complex, we often have two or more people cooperating to achieve a single result. For instance, both human resources staff and the district manager may be responsible for training recently recruited MBAs. Or, together, an engineer, plant manager, and accountant may be accountable for cutting the cost of product X by 15

percent. A good way to handle such joint projects is to hold *each* person accountable for the *total* result; this places a premium on cooperation to get the best results. The MBO process is flexible enough to use this dual accountability concept.

5. *Interrelated support* can be provided. Meeting an air pollution regulation, for example, may call for changes in product specifications, modified manufacturing processes, some new equipment, a revised cost standard, and retraining. In an MBO review, the plant manager who takes on the goal of meeting this regulation can spell out to the boss the help that will have to come from other departments. Or—as we have repeatedly stressed—strategy, programs, organization, and control are interdependent: a change in one is likely to require adjustment in others. So, for example, when expansion into Mexico is undertaken, a variety of adjustments will be necessary. Ideally, these supporting adjustments will be fitted into the expansion plans from the beginning. But MBO planning and review sessions provide another occasion when the "total package" concept can be explored.

6. The MBO process is particularly well suited for activating managers of *decentralized operating units* and of units located some distance from the central office. The greater the distance between the central office and the operating unit, the fewer the opportunities for casual contacts and informal coaching. Also, when a shift in strategy has occurred, central managers need a mechanism that gives them a chance to examine the interpretation of the new directions being made by subordinates and to reinterpret their intent. MBO reviews provide such opportunities to explore the implementation of new strategy.

The potential benefits of MBO are good reasons for activating individual managers. If for some reason the MBO procedure is not used, other methods of achieving each of these benefits should be found.

## Demanding Use of Incentives

Important as climate and individualized goals are in activating people, supervising managers still have to create a situation in which key employees get deep personal satisfaction from achieving tough company goals. These key people—managers, top staff persons, and outstanding performers in engineering, sales, etc.—are a select group: they have ability and drive, as already indicated by the positions they hold. The challenge is to keep their vigorous efforts channeled toward the strategy that the company is pursuing.

Broadly speaking, upper managers can influence this eagerness to cooperate through (1) identifying factors that motivate these persons, (2) recognizing the inherent limitations on management's capacity to use such incentives, and (3) applying the incentives wisely and courageously.

### Motivations of Managers

The influences that spur people to exert themselves are neither obvious nor clear cut. Also, individuals differ in their responses. Nevertheless, we can identify several factors that are likely to motivate the kind of persons who reach key positions.

### Financial Rewards

Overemphasized though it is, money does matter in our society. It is a crude symbol of success, but it is a means of achieving other ends such as security, living comforts, and independence.

We have already discussed the setting of managerial salary levels in Chapter 20. The desirability of keeping pay scales in line with rates being paid by other companies and in equitable internal alignment was stressed. Such a salary structure enables a company to attract and retain competent executives. But note that the base pay tends to be stable and tied to other salaries: central management is not free to jockey the pay up and down.

The variable pay elements are merit increases, bonuses, and perhaps stock options. These are the incentives that can and should be used courageously as rewards for outstanding achievement of a strategy.

### Sense of Achievement

Managers, like other people, take pride in the results of their efforts. Real satisfaction arises from knowing that telephone calls go through, homes are heated, news is timely, or test equipment improves quality. Even more rewarding is the sense of being a partner in running a business-unit that simultaneously serves economic and social needs. And there is satisfaction in being a good competitor in business just as there is in sports.

More subtle is an inner sense of achievement, of having a challenging assignment and doing it well. Here we are concerned with an important aspect of what the psychologists call "self-realization."

A sense of achievement is a personal matter; it depends on one's own aspirations and values. The boss cannot grant it. Instead, a manager tries to create conditions in which key subordinates feel that they are achieving. Toward this end, winning a strong commitment to company strategy is a primary requirement. Then, placing individuals in jobs matched to their abilities and aspirations is a second requirement. When both requisites are met, a strong drive toward company strategy can be realized.

### Social Status and Recognition

Like all of us, managers like recognition of their accomplishments. This can come only partly from their supervisors and other respected individuals who are familiar with their work. In addition, the estimation of one's friends and the community at large carries considerable weight. Since people outside the company have no direct knowledge of what the person does, they rely on titles, the nature of an office, other prerequisites, and spending patterns that presumably reflect salary. The "symbols of office," then, can provide strong motivation.

Part of our heritage is the idea that people can raise their social status. Most of our ancestors immigrated poor and uneducated; their children and the children after them improved their station in society. Success in business has been one of the major ways of improving one's social status. So central management can use the prospect of a promotion or assignment to a key job as an incentive.

### Power and Influence

History records extreme cases of lust for power, but this motivation need not be pushed that far. There is a thrill that comes with making large purchases, watching a plant operate partly as a result of one's own guidance, seeing a new product that includes one's own choice of design, or supervising a pension plan that one piloted through to final adoption. This kind of exercise in power or influence is quite legitimate—in fact, some say it is essential psychologically. We observe it especially in government and charitable enterprises where the financial rewards are low. For some individuals it is a strong motivator.

## Restraints on the Use of Motivators

Awareness of motivators is only a start; using them requires insight and skill. For example, an action intended as an incentive usually has other effects as well. Thus, W. J. McGill might respond favorably to more power, but the assignment of authority to McGill will involve an array of organization issues: scope of duties, decentralization, and the like. The same is true to a lesser extent for the use of titles to give McGill status. Perhaps maintaining a sound organization is more important than the incentive effect of a special concession to please McGill. So the use of most motivators has to be dovetailed with related considerations.

Perceived fairness poses another limitation. The feeling that any reward should be fairly won is very strong in the United States. A suspicion that favoritism or casualness has been involved in a promotion or a granting of power can cause a lot of hard feeling. Therefore, central managers try to have everyone who knows about a reward feel that it was fairly granted. This need for known reasons supporting a move cannot always be met, and managers then face a dilemma of either withholding an incentive or antagonizing a number of people who will not understand why the incentive was offered. (A misunderstood reward can have far-reaching effects. If a belief arises among employees that promotions, bonuses, and the like are made on a capricious basis, and not for supporting official strategy, then a widespread attitude of "why bother to try" may develop.)

## "Calling the Shots" Courageously

Another delicate matter is to motivate particular individuals without upsetting group cooperation and morale. Incentives frequently single out one or two persons for distinctive treatment, and this inevitably creates disappointments, if not hard feelings, among those not chosen. Clearly, when people are promoted or given more power, their status relative to their associates rises. When several individuals aspire to the same job, say vice-presidents hoping for the presidency, the disappointment of being passed by can be acute. Good people may resign, and others may lose heart and stagnate. However, such costs probably are inevitable; and the loss caused by delay or compromise might be far greater.

Going outside the organization to fill an attractive post has the same discouraging effect on those passed over. However, the message is clear: the people making the appointment will not settle for just average performance; they expect distinctive results, and are willing to make an unpopular move to get them.

Demotion or discharge of a manager is hard to do because more often than not the person has been a personal friend for several years. Procrastination is expensive, however. The main cost of a weak executive is that his or her occupancy of a key position prevents a more able person from doing that work well. By analogy, a baseball team cannot afford a right fielder who bats only .100. In addition, *if* the person's weakness is recognized by other executives, failure to clean out deadwood from an organization tends to undermine the determination of other people to exert themselves. A wise and courageous practice is to remove ineffective individuals from key posts; if the company has an obligation to them, they can be given early retirement or jobs better suited to their abilities.

The opposite kind of a move is pleasant all around. Moving a person who is widely recognized as able to a key spot motivates both the person and his or her colleagues as well. Individual justice and the good of the organization coincide.

To conclude, central managers have a never-ending task of sensing what impels their key people. Within the limits of their powers, and without undermining other aspects of administration, they seek to tie these motivations to company strategy. At the same time they must watch the impact on the group when rewards go to one person.

## SUMMARY

General managers of business-units play a dual role in activating an enterprise, that is, "putting the show on the road." They must first work with their immediate subordinates, just as all other managers must initiate and stimulate action in people assigned to them. Then, they strongly influence the activating process throughout the enterprise partly by the examples they set and partly by establishing certain practices as standard procedures that all managers are expected to observe.

Department managers have a similar dual role within their respective departments. However, they do not have as high status as general managers, and consequently are not as influential in creating a general company climate. Nevertheless, in the execution of changes in strategy these individuals are closer to actual operations, so their influence is crucial in making such changes effective.

Important elements in the activation process are (1) creating a focused climate by selecting overriding goals and major thrusts and then repeatedly stressing the importance of these key themes; (2) managing changes in strategy and in the focused climate; (3) within this general setting, carefully guiding and evaluating the performance of each subordinate, using a form of MBO adapted to high-level managers; and (4) assessing the incentives which are important to the key people in the organization and then, within constraints, courageously exercising power to encourage those incentives.

In the total management process, activating seems far removed from forecasting environmental opportunities and threats—a task highlighted in Part 1. Indeed, most academic discourses on company strategy never get around to discussing activating. Yet this final push in the execution of strategy significantly affects the degree of success any chosen strategy may have. It is a vital part of the follow-through on insightful analysis. We need not debate whether analysis is more important than activating, or vice versa: each is a necessary but insufficient part of the total process.

## Questions for Class Discussion

1. Federal Express has built a flourishing business by assuring "overnight delivery" of letters and small packages almost anywhere in the United States. Technology makes the fast delivery possible; all items received during the day are flown into Memphis during the evening, sorted by destination, and flown back out that same night. Nevertheless, more than technology is involved; the uncompromising goal of overnight delivery permeates the entire organization. (a) Explain how this focused climate affects personnel recruiting, output controls, supervision, and morale in Federal Express. (b) Do you think that the more recent introduction of "Express Mail" into the U.S. Postal Service, with similar delivery goals, has a comparable influence on activating by managers in the Post Offices? Explain your answer.

2. (a) The development of a company climate—as described in this chapter—calls for continuing, vigorous, enthusiastic effort. Do you think that the kind of personality who will do his task well is likely *also* to be a good, objective, rational planner? (b) Among your classmates, which ones do you predict will be: (i) sharp, objective, analytical planners? (ii) effective climate builders? (iii) tough makers of unpleasant decisions? Now considering yourself, do you believe that you will be good in all three of the dimensions just listed?

3. In Chapter 4 we outlined a way to analyze competitors and other key actors in a company's environment. To what extent is a comparable approach useful in activating key actors within a company?

4. Jane Sherrill, a 32-year-old ambitious MBA, was appointed president of Sci-Tech Associates when the three former owner/managers of the struggling company sold out to Cyril Electronics, Inc. The three partners, who took employment contracts with attractive bonus provisions, decided to sell primarily because they had difficulty agreeing on a clear-cut strategy for Sci-Tech and because responsibility for major decisions was shared among them as equal partners.

   Within three weeks, Sherrill set up what in effect was an MBO program with monthly progress reports. The production vice president agreed to focus on production scheduling, reducing product failures by 75 percent, and cutting $300,000 from the factory payroll. The financial vice president agreed to revise the cost accounting system so that reliable figures on profit by customer, product, and jobs could be available quickly. The research vice president agreed to propose priorities on R & D projects and estimate short-run payoffs. There were other problems, but these assignments would provide a base for future decisions on product/market targets.

   The MBO approach worked. Focused effort replaced bickering. Net profit for the first year moved up from less than 2 percent to over 5 percent return on assets, with good prospects for further improvement. How do you explain this positive effect when there was no change in key managers except the addition of an inexperienced president?

5. Why do you think successful companies like Polaroid and General Radio confined adjustments to their strategies to only incremental changes until they faced a financial crisis, and then reluctantly adopted a frame-breaking change?

6. Lesley Pond (age 53) has just been named to replace G. G. McCarthy, longtime national sales vice president of a large consumer products company, who is retiring. Pond is one of three long-service regional managers. The other regional managers are much younger, recent appointees. Pond must decide what to do with another long-service regional manager, Alvin Dart (age 61). "I don't know why McCarthy put up with Dart so long. Dart hasn't had a new idea in ten years. His volume is not even keeping up with inflation, and most of his salespeople have been in their jobs longer than Dart has been in his in Atlanta. I must admit his expense ratio is low, but there is no reason to hope Al will really push the new line. The company would go down the drain if we were all like Al. Maybe I can find him a government job or cut his salary so he will quit." What do you recommend that Pond do about leadership in Atlanta?

7. When the Chrysler Corporation took over American Motors it had already announced its intended strategy of consolidating the operations of the two companies. Put yourself in the position of the executive in charge of the con-

solidation right after the acquisition was completed. How would you proceed in dealing with American Motors personnel?

8. Most Japanese and Chinese companies do not stress bonuses and merit pay increases for *individuals;* "fast-track" promotions are also rare. Instead, the emphasis is on *group* performance, cooperative efforts, and working for the benefit of the whole enterprise. In this Eastern culture, which of the activating concepts discussed in this chapter do you think would be effective? Which one would not fit?

9. A consulting firm designed a new, computer-based information and control system to integrate all the departments of Southern Textiles, Inc., to cut information systems cost and plant overhead by 10 percent, and to bring about faster service to customers. These gains were secured largely by uniting sales-ordering with production scheduling in all of the processing departments of the mill (cotton cleaning, yarn manufacturing and weaving), and by tying gray goods production directly with fabric-dyeing and finishing in other plants. The president of Southern Textiles persuaded Tom Jones to leave his job as head of a consulting project and come to work as assistant to the president to supervise installation and operation of the new system. This work proceeded, but not without serious disagreements between Tom Swift, the mill manager, and Tom Jones. Swift stated that three months was too short a time for complete changeover from the old control system which covered the mill, but not sales-ordering and the dye plant. A year was really necessary, he believed, if the new system would work at all.

Installation of the new system led to employee turnover, in the first month, of about 75 percent in the production scheduling and production control departments. Ten percent of those persons leaving were not replaced. The rest came in new to the plant, although they were experienced with computer systems. The new system had broken down twice. Most of the old system had been retained as a backup for three months so one breakdown was covered—at the expense of double-overtime and weekend work for thirty employees. The second breakdown caused the entire plant to shut down for one day. Jones said that Swift was not utilizing the new system properly because the system itself allowed for one day's slack-time per month and, had it been "accessed" properly by Swift and his department managers, no shutdown would have been necessary. When Swift heard this, he forbade Jones to enter the plant at any time and said to the president: "Keep him in the front office. I won't have him out here second-guessing and double-crossing me." The president was very eager to gain the cost and service advantages which he believed would accrue once the new computer system was working properly because this would raise profits for the firm, put its earnings per share in the upper half of the textile industry, and probably raise the price of its common stock—all to the benefit of the managers through the stock option system and to the benefit of the stockholders.

What could the president do?

## 22 The New Manager, Tian Li-Geng

*Editor's Note:* This case was written by Yu Kai-cheng, Dean of the Management Development Center, Dalian Institute of Technology, China. Although the business structure in China is changing rapidly, the situation as described gives students an opportunity to analyze a complicated leadership problem. The original case, which is based on an actual experience in the late 1970's, has been condensed by the editor.

In the People's Republic of China, a "factory" or "plant" is a vital administrative unit where goods are actually produced. Typically, a factory has its own facilities, permanent employees, housing, health and recreation services, and other resources to make it quite self-contained. However, there is a large superstructure of planning and services. A factory usually is part of a large integrated corporation, which in turn is supervised by a national ministry of, say, mining, food processing, chemicals, or the like. Quotas are set and resources allocated by the ministries and corporations. Nevertheless, a factory may exercise considerable initiative in modifying its technology, exceeding its quotas, and diversifying its products.

As in all countries, in China there are practical limitations on what a general manager can do. In terms of culture, the Chinese have more respect for age than we Westerners do, and there is a tradition of making decisions by consensus. Politically, the Communist party designates a representative in all important organizations, such as a factory. The representative communicates Party doctrine and in a factory is also active in worker discipline and welfare decisions. Since the cultural revolution, roughly from 1966 to 1976, when all professionals including managers went through disgrace and often torture, the Party representative is not expected to interfere with technical matters.

Tian Li-geng[1] faced a knotty decision soon after his appointment as director (general manager) of the Machine Repairing Factory, a division of the Scholartree Ridge Mining & Metallurgical Corporation. The decision appears to be a technical one: whether to change the technology for making replacement wheels for mine cars. However, if Tian Li-geng decides to try one of several alternatives, his requests for capital appropriations, soon due at the corporate offices, will be affected. And, as his first major action while director, the choice will make a strong impression throughout the factory.

Since getting his mechanical engineering degree 30 years ago, Tian Li-geng has served in a variety of positions in the Mining & Metalurgical Corporation, first in maintenance work and then as head of engineering at a mine. From there, he

---

[1] In Chinese, the family name appears first and is followed by the given name.

was placed in charge of a pilot plant department at the Machine Repairing Factory, experimenting with new mining equipment. Following a five-year interruption during the cultural revolution when he was demoted to tough physical labor, he was placed in charge of construction of a new mine and later became deputy director of the mine. So his transfer at age 54 back to the Machine Repairing Factory was the return of an old acquaintance.

The Machine Repairing Factory manufactures spare parts and components for all the mines of the Mining & Metallurgical Corporation, and also nonstandard equipment. It has grown with the corporation from 100 workers in the early fifties to 1,600 today. There are 11 workshops involved in casting, forging, welding, machining, heat-treating, etc. With a fairly strong technical staff of several dozen engineers, technicians, and veteran skilled workers, this plant is considered one of the top machinery factories in the nearby area.

Tian Li-geng felt honored and pleased with his new position, and he is ready to display his talents. The Central Committee of the country is encouraging expansion of mining operations, and the newly appointed Party representative at the factory is honest, modest, and cooperative. In addition, there are a lot of old friends at the factory—former colleagues and subordinates who recall the success of Tian Li-geng's previous work there. So he enters his job with prestige and good will. And then, suddenly there is this knotty problem, a real headache.

The issue of how best to make mine-car wheels is not new, having been studied but remaining unsolved for 30 years. In the underground mines of the corporation, ore is hauled mostly in mine cars. This heavy, rough task wears out wheels frequently, creating an annual replacement demand of thousands of wheels in several sizes. The most troublesome task is machining the hubs of the newly cast iron wheels (see Figure 22–2). The hole in each end of the hub has to be machined exactly and polished to hold a roller bearing; moreover, the concentricity and par-

**FIGURE 22–2.**
**THE STRUCTURE OF A TYPICAL MINE-CAR WHEEL**

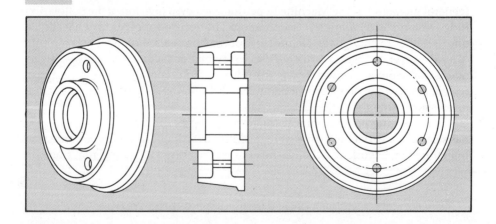

allelism of the axial lines on both ends affect the durability of the wheels. The work is complicated by the weight and relatively large outside diameter of the entire wheel, which makes holding the wheel in an exact position for machining difficult.

In the traditional process, wheels are machined on a vertical lathe one end at a time. A bar is inserted into the first machined end to attain parallelism of the machining at the other end. Difficulties encountered in this method include inadequate precision of the bar to set up the lathe for the second end; wearing of the lathe from repeated stress on a limited number of spots, thus adding to inaccuracy; and slowdowns in turning the wheels over. Due to the large volume of work on the lathes, the cranes in the shop are not able to take care of all the lathes; consequently some operators stand on the lathe, holding the wheel with both arms—sometimes even with the help of their bellies—to get it turned over when needed. This is an unsafe method which only strong, young workers can do; middle-aged operators wait for cranes, causing frequent holdups. A way to avoid these difficulties has become a long-standing, strong desire of both the operators and supervisors of the shop.

Tian Li-geng recognizes that an ideal solution would be to let the national State Planning Committee create a focused factory to make mine-car wheels of a standard size for all mines in China. With special-purpose machining, such a factory could reduce the cost of wheels and improve their quality. However, this would require a modification of mining practices by several ministries. With the many other pressures for modernization, such a change is unrealistic for many years. Consequently, Director Tian assumes that his factory will have to continue to produce wheels of its own.

The immediate questions facing Tian Li-geng are whether to continue with the traditional method of machining wheels and, if not, which alternative method to pursue. Obviously, a technological appraisal of alternatives must be made, followed by an economic assessment of costs and benefits. As Director Tian explored the problem, he discovered interpersonal and political considerations in addition, and in these areas he feels less confident about how to proceed. There are individuals favoring a change and some opposed, and perhaps because it is a long-standing issue they feel strongly about their positions.

The leading figure of the "supporting front" is Chen Nian-xin, recently appointed head of the Research & Development department. Chen worked under Tian Li-geng at the factory in the late fifties, when he was a young engineer full of vigor and vitality. His pioneering spirit and tenacity got him labeled as a "rightist" early in the "Anti-rightist Movement" in the late 1950's. Refusing to plead guilty, he was sentenced as a criminal to hard labor. However, back at the factory and now 50, Chen continues to be full of suggestions—some people say "cocky." Chen has become dedicated to finding special equipment to overcome the wheel machining problem.

Chen is supported by quite a few young technicians and workers. His most prominent supporter, however, is Huang Bi-xing, the director of the factory before Tian Li-geng. Huang became leader of the factory when he was transferred from the People's Liberation Army to civilian work in the early 1950s. Though not well educated, he has a very practical insight into machine repairing. While counseling Tian Li-geng, Huang said, "I am going to retire soon. The only thing which remains unsettled and is keeping me anxious is special tools for machining car wheels. You should consider the problem seriously and be responsible for it. It can't drag on anymore."

The "opposition front" is not well defined, but it clearly includes Wang Bao-qun, a deputy director of the Department of Propaganda of the factory Party Committee. Normally, departments of propaganda have little to do with technological improvements; however, Wang paid two successive evening visits on Tian Li-geng to advise him on how things had evolved. Director Tian is quite familiar with Wang, too. He came from poor parents and was a fitter when he first joined the factory in 1958. Always conscientious, he was adept at following superiors' instructions carefully. He joined the Party early and was often cited as an "advanced worker."

For some unclear reason, Wang seems to have a personal prejudice against Chen. Among the points emerging from Wang's account were that Chen is arrogant and conceited, that at the beginning of the cultural revolution Chen had been accused of wasting money on grandiose projects to reap personal knowledge for himself, and that perhaps Director Huang's support of Chen arose from feeling sorry for the torture he had suffered. Tian Li-geng recognizes that although Wang's conclusions may not be reliable, they do have a basis in fact. Wang cautioned Tian to "think thrice before acting; the machining project is too risky, and your prestige will suffer if by any chance it failed."

Chen also has talked at length with Director Tian, describing the evolution of his thinking about innovative ways to machine mine-car wheels (see Figure 22–3).

At first Chen considered only mechanical devices for moving a wheel casting from one vertical lathe to its partner, turning the casting over in the process. People in the shop felt this made too little improvement to warrant a change.

Next, after visiting several other factories, Chen designed a multistation machine tool with a rotary platform, wherein a separate operation was to be performed at each station. The drawback here is that wheels used in the Scholartree complex have a bearing at each end of the hub, and getting the second end aligned with the first made this solution unrealistic.

Then Chen and his students devised another multistation automatic machine, this one with stations in a straight line and lathes working on both sides of the casting simultaneously. The fixture for holding the castings was to be emptied after the last station and moved back on a conveyor to start down the line again. Calculations indicated that this elaborate piece of equipment could produce all the wheels needed by the corporation in half a month, so it would stand idle most of the year. That low utilization, combined with the high investment that was necessary, made the solution uneconomical.

Chen's most recent solution also works on both sides of the wheel simultaneously, but here the casting rotates like a wheel and cutting tools are automatically

**FIGURE 22–3.**
**ALTERNATIVE SPECIAL EQUIPMENT FOR**
**MACHINING MINE-CAR WHEELS**

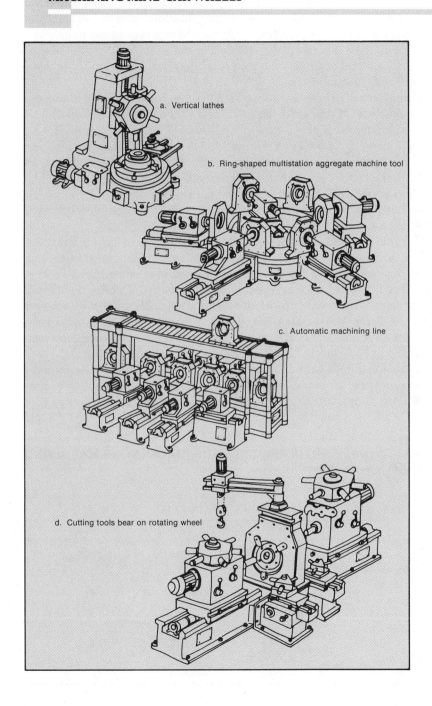

a. Vertical lathes

b. Ring-shaped multistation aggregate machine tool

c. Automatic machining line

d. Cutting tools bear on rotating wheel

changed by an automaton. This design promises greater accuracy provided that a suitable arrangement can be made for rotating the wheels so that concentricity can be automatically guaranteed. Chen's proposed solution for this is a fluid hydrostatic bearing which works well in smaller applications, and theory indicates that it will work in the larger case also. The size and accuracy of the hydrostatic bearing are beyond the capacity of the factory to make, so it would have to be purchased outside; a friend of Chen's in a factory in Shanghai has promised to make such a device at a reasonable cost.

Chen tried hard to convince Director Tian that the project is likely to succeed because it is the result of years of deliberation and is theoretically sound with a lot of relevant techniques available for reference. Professors at two technological institutes in the province, as well as a few machine designers in Shanghai, endorse the plan. Chen emphasized that if the innovation is successful, it would inspire people within the factory and enhance the reputation of all concerned. He then showed Director Tian an estimate of the investment in each alternative, which Director Tian knows from experience is only a very rough and incomplete comparison of the alternatives (see Table 22–1).

Director Tian is impressed with Chen's zeal, but, because of the importance of the decision, he decided to consult with Wei Min-xian, chief engineer of the factory. Now in his sixties, Wei is an old colleague. Because Wei worked in an airplane factory prior to liberation, he has repeatedly been a target of political criticism, and this has made Wei extremely cautious about revealing his ideas. With the new policies of the Party, Wei's status has greatly improved, and he is now vice-chairman of the People's Political Consultative Conference of the city. However, he is beginning to be senile and is no longer active in factory decisions.

Only after much reassurance from Director Tian did Wei tactfully state his misgivings about the proposed technology for machining wheels. He is concerned about the hydrostatic bearing, especially because the factory has no expe-

**TABLE 22–1.**
**ESTIMATED INVESTMENT REQUIRED FOR ALTERNATIVE MACHINING METHODS (cost in Chinese yuan)**

| SOLUTION | LABOR | MATERIAL | TOTAL |
|---|---|---|---|
| Vertical lathe | 9,519 | 15,156 | 24,675 |
| Ring-shaped multistation aggregate machine tool | 42,132 | 68,205 | 110,337 |
| Automatic machine line | 113,780 | 178,672 | 292,452 |
| Dual-boring machine tool | 20,328 | 24,836 | 45,164 |

rience with such equipment. Also, he wonders whether the automated changing of cutting tools will affect the accuracy of the machining. Because of its advanced techniques, many of the senior electricians and fitters will be tied up in maintaining the machine. And the proposal would involve many new techniques all at once, instead of going about the job little by little. Wei is unsure that such a sophisticated and expensive technique is needed for the volume of work. Nevertheless, Wei does not want to dampen the push for greater productivity, he wishes that his age permitted him to be active in this step forward for the masses, and on and on.

Wei's focus on technology and economics contrasts sharply with the ardent expression and frank requests of a group of young technicians who visited Director Tian in his home last night. They said, "You must not lose sight of the impact of your decision in getting rid of the rigidity and repressive atmosphere in the plant. We need a chance to train ourselves technically and an opportunity that challenges us ideologically. To break fresh ground is always risky, but we are confident that we can overcome difficulties. For instance, if the utilization of the equipment will be low, why can't we get orders from other mining companies? The impact of the innovation project will be far reaching, with some of its consequences defying measurement and calculation in terms of money. Everyone in the factory is looking up to you now; you should act as our powerful backing."

Tian Li-geng feels that he should get opinions from old friends in other units who have more objectivity. "Then I shall decide what to do. The decision can't be delayed anymore, indeed."

## Questions

(a) If you were one of Director Tian's old friends working in another unit, what advice would you give him? Explain your reasoning.

(b) Do you think that a manager's leadership role is more difficult in China than in the United States?

# CHAPTER 23

# Controlling: Keeping Efforts Focused on Multi-Level Strategy

Controls are commonplace; they range from thermostats to speed limits. Still, in our society, what to control and how to control are often hotly debated—one need merely witness environmental control, birth control, gun control, and diet control. For business managers, control of strategy takes a place among troublesome issues. It is important, but elusive.

Fortunately, much can be done by managers to keep company efforts focused on multi-level strategy. There are ways both to keep strategy targets up to date and to harness organized effort in support of those targets. In this chapter, after a brief review of contemporary management control concepts, we will discuss (1) steering control of business-unit and corporate strategy, and (2) controlling the execution of department strategy programs. Our focus will be on the dynamic aspects of strategy — on controlling change — rather than on the more static management of continuing operations.

## Constructive Control

Control is widespread in any well-managed effort: it seeks to ensure that the results of operations conform as closely as possible to established goals.

## Basic Control Cycle

Three elements are always involved in managerial control, whatever the subject:

1. *Control standards that represent desired performance.* These standards may be tangible or intangible, vague or specific, but until everyone concerned understands what results are desired, control will cause confusion. Note that one reason to insist on target results in a four-part strategy is to have objectives for control.
2. *Measurement of actual or predicted results against the standards.* This evaluation must be reported to someone who can do something about it.
3. *Corrective action.* Control measurements and reports serve little purpose unless corrective action is taken. People's behavior has to change because of the control.

Although accounting reports are the most commonly discussed control instruments, business firms use many other control devices, including quality controls, legal controls, timetables, personnel evaluations, market surveys, and so on. Much ingenuity is involved in deciding what to watch, where to watch it, and who does the watching.

## Three Types of Control

Much of the misunderstanding and anxiety about controls in a business situation can be avoided by recognizing three distinct types of control, based on when the control is exercised (See Figure 23–1):

**FIGURE 23–1.**
**THREE BASIC TYPES OF CONTROL**

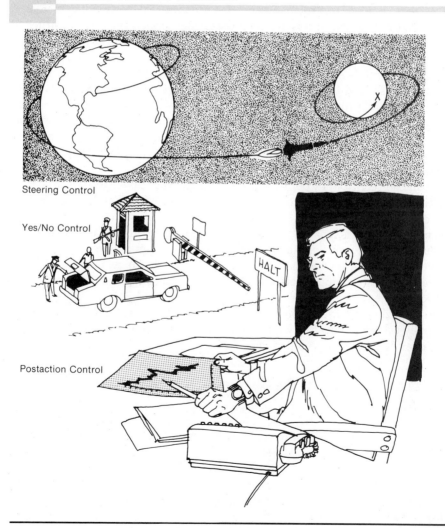

Steering Control

Yes/No Control

Postaction Control

1. *Postaction controls.* In this type of control, an action is completed, and then its results are measured and compared with a standard. The typical budgetary control and school report card illustrate this approach.

2. *Yes/no controls.* Here, work may not proceed to the next step until it passes a screening test. Approval to continue is required. Examples are legal approval of contracts, quality checks on food, and test flights of aircraft.

3. *Steering controls.* Results are predicted and corrective action is taken before the total operation is completed. For example, flight control of the spacecraft aimed for the moon began with trajectory measurements immediately after takeoff, and corrections were made days before the actual arrival.

All three types of control may be needed to control a department or major activity. But it is steering controls that offer the greatest opportunity for constructive effect. They provide a mechanism for remedial action while the actual results are still being shaped.

Yes/no controls are essentially safety devices. The consequences of a faulty parachute or spoiled food are so serious that we take extra precautions to make sure that quality is up to specifications. Avoidable expense or poor allocation of resources can also be checked by yes/no controls. If we could be confident that our steering controls were effective, yes/no controls would be unnecessary; unfortunately, steering controls may not be fully reliable, or may be too expensive, so yes/no controls are applied.

Postaction controls, by definition, would seem to be applied too late to be very effective: the work is already completed before it is measured. Actually, such controls do serve two purposes: (1) If rewards (a medal, a bonus, discharge, self-esteem) based on actual results have been promised, these results must be measured and the appropriate rewards granted. The aim is psychological reinforcement of the incentive scheme. The payoff in this reinforcement lies in future behavior. (2) Postaction controls also provide planning data if similar work is undertaken in the future.

Recognizing the distinctions between the three types of managerial control is especially valuable in dealing with strategy formulation and execution. Each type has a distinct role, as indicated in Figure 23–2.

## Steering Control of the Business-Unit and Corporate Strategy[1]

Strategy is concerned with events that have not yet occurred: it is forward looking. Moreover, it frequently deals with new businesses or with modifications

---

[1]The following section is adapted from B. Yavitz and W.H. Newman, *Strategy in Action* (New York: The Free Press, 1982), Chapter 12.

**FIGURE 23–2.**
**WAYS TO CONTROL STRATEGY DESIGN AND EXECUTION**

### CONTROL OF STRATEGY

| | *Types of Control* | | |
| --- | --- | --- | --- |
| | *Steering* | *Yes/No* | *Postaction* |
| Business-unit strategy | Monitor planning premises Progress reports MILESTONE REVIEWS | | Company comparisons |
| Corporate strategy | Monitor planning premises Progress reports MILESTONE REVIEWS | | Company comparisons |
| Department strategy programs | PROJECT CONTROLS Other progress reports | RESOURCE INPUT CONTROLS: Capital requests Operating budgets Key personnel | STRATEGIC THRUST REPORTS: Internal targets Company comparisons |

that are still to be made of existing businesses. Consequently, customary control concepts and techniques require adjustment.

Control of strategy is similar to what guided the Apollo ships to the moon. NASA officials did not wait until the space capsule either reached or missed the moon. Rather, they computed trajectories as soon as Apollo was in flight and predicted the outcome. All along the course, corrective action was based on predictions, not on final results.

Under *steering control* for strategy, in contrast to postaction control, both the target result or standard and the predicted result lie in the future, as emphasized in Figure 23–2. Corrective action is initiated before the event. Of course, each updated prediction is based on progress to date (and this part of the process relies on the customary comparison of actual achievement against the standard). To this data is added the latest information about environmental conditions, and then a new prediction about the most likely outcome is made. If the expected result is unsatisfactory, corrective action is started immediately. The whole process is completed long before any CPA sanctifies a report for the SEC.

A classic example is when the Prudential Insurance Company decided to use regional home offices as a differential advantage in its drive for top position in the life-insurance industry. This was an exercise in steering control. Experience at the first regional offices was used to project overall expenses and income. In fact, the predicted expenses were so high that the location and original schedule for converting other regions had to be modified. Conversion of corporate headquarters was sharply revised on the basis of other early feedback. Note that steering control altered the strategic thrusts long before the total plan was in place. In this example major objectives remained unchanged, but in other cases steering control may spark adjustments in these as well.

Steering control of strategic action faces four difficulties:

1. The *lead time* between starting action and attaining the desired outcome is long (and the stakes are high), so managers often start controlling on the basis of only a small parcel of experience.

2. *Predictions* of outcomes are surrounded with *uncertainty.* Managers are unsure of the favorable and unfavorable consequences of their own actions. Meanwhile, reversals in the external environment may upset their predictions.

3. The original *strategy* is likely to be *changed* because of dynamic shifts during the long lead time, before the strategy is fully executed. Thus, the control target (standard) keeps moving.

4. *Objective evaluation* during the battle is difficult. Often the managers doing the steering control are also actively committed to executing the strategy. Because of this dual involvement, it is difficult for managers to be objective about rather debatable predictions, and strong pressures are needed to provoke sharp redirection.

These inherent difficulties make the application of steering control more delicate than the basic idea suggests.

## Watch Progress on Strategic Thrusts

The action front in strategy execution is mostly located in a series of specific department programs and moves. Whenever feasible, each strategic thrust should be translated into steps and detailed programs should be developed for those steps to be taken first, as suggested in Chapter 21. In other words, by moving down the organization levels, managers convert broad strategic thrusts into quite concrete planned actions and results for individual people.

Steering control can start by watching the outcomes of these specific early actions. When the local programs are formalized and measured, data on progress can be fed to the strategy controller as well as the local manager. Similarly, when separate expense and capital budgets are set up for strategic moves, copies of the local control reports can go to the strategy controller. Strategic moves that are scrambled with current operations are harder to follow. For these, someone must identify what results related to strategy are expected by what dates, and then periodically check on progress being made.

This watching of progress at the action level serves two purposes. The first is to assure that the total program is moving ahead and that actions taken in various locations remain consistent with the overall concept. For example, a few years ago Motorola adopted a strategy to regain its position in the C.B. radio field. A check on the engineering design of a new transmitter revealed that its size and cost exceeded the assigned specifications that had been carefully tailored to a desired niche in the market. Top executives insisted that the engineers redo their work until the specifications were met. Otherwise, various parts of the strategy would have been incompatible.

The second purpose is early detection of a need to revise the strategy. A United States instrument firm did just that. Its expansion strategy called for a series of licensees in Europe who would make simpler equipment and parts and import delicate and complex parts from the United States firm. Experience during the first year cast doubt on the wisdom of the strategy. Several desirable licensees were reluctant to take up the offer: they wanted to manufacture everything or nothing. One company that did enter the agreement was having difficulty maintaining quality standards, and the United States firm lacked the power to impose its ideas on how to achieve quality. On the basis of this new data, the forecast of European business through licensees was far below hopes. Consequently, the United States firm changed its strategy from licensees to joint ventures (with much better results).

Early experience may be difficult to interpret, but it does have the great virtue of providing hard data. The practical difficulties seem to be clearly identifying and measuring early steps, and promptly reevaluating strategy in light of the early experience.

## Monitor Key External Variables

Every strategy is based on an assumed (predicted) setting. Consciously or unconsciously, assumptions are made about future demand, technology, prices, government regulation, competition, and an array of other *external* variables. These assumptions are planning premises around which company strategy is designed.

### Reliability of Planning Premises

A crucial part of steering control is checking on the continuing reliability of the planning premises. If a vital assumption is no longer valid, the strategy may have to be changed. The sooner a revised premise is recognized, the better are the chances that an acceptable shift in strategy can be devised. Therefore, each company should flag and systematically monitor its key external variables.

A small electronics firm, for example, concluded that it had to expand to maintain its lead in its market niche. A strategic plan involving technical, legal, and marketing moves was launched. The plan also included a public issue of stock after about one year of growth. Unfortunately, no provision was made to monitor financial markets. The stock issue that would have been easy when the strategy was conceived became impossible. In fact, the firm was so extended financially that it had to sell its know-how and liquidate. Whether financial monitoring would have enabled the firm to refinance before the market broke we will never know, but it undoubtedly would have led to restraining the heavy financial commitments until sources of funds were arranged.

### What to Watch

The need to monitor external variables is much clearer than knowing just which ones to focus on. Hundreds of variables might have some effect on any one company. However, to attempt to keep track of all of them would be extremely expensive, and the resulting data would swamp the analytical capacity of company managers. Accordingly, steering control must be highly selective.

Key variables are of two sorts: impersonal forces (see Chapters 2 and 3) and key actors. Impersonal forces bearing on, for instance, a steel company include new technology such as continuous casting, changes in fuel costs, shifts in government import protection or other subsidies, additional ecological restraints, reduced demand for steel in automobiles, and the like. Each company must judge for itself which of these kinds of variables to watch. Major factors bearing directly on the company's differential advantage should always be included. In general, one should monitor variables that are likely to change and that would have a major impact on the company if they did change.

A second set of variables to monitor is key actors, as the term is used in Chapter 4. Leading competitors, suppliers, unions and other powerful pressure groups, and government regulators are in this category. Their long-term behavior can have significant impact on the practicality of our strategy.

Note that identification of key external variables, both impersonal forces and key actors, is best done during the strategy-planning stage. When the analysis is being conducted, managers are more aware of the assumptions they make. Thus, part of planning should be the designation of variables that will be monitored as part of steering control. This list can, of course, be modified in subsequent milestone reviews when the total situation is reassessed and new predictions are made.

### Linking Predicted Change to Company Strategy

Monitoring of each variable that has been selected involves (1) gathering full, up-to-date information about the force or actor, (2) predicting future behavior, and (3) suggesting where in the company the predicted behavior could have significant impact.

To illustrate, suppose that the Citizens Bank of Northern New Jersey has decided to monitor federal banking laws. Then (1) the analysis of active legislative proposals might lead to (2) a prediction that "national" banks would soon be permitted to place electronic tellers in out-of-state locations, so that (3) for Citizens

Bank this would mean that large New York City banks would offer localized service, which might upset Citizens' branch setup.

Of the three components of monitoring, predicting typically receives the most discussion. Indeed, predicting is rarely easy. Nevertheless, most companies are probably weaker in the other two components—deciding what to watch and then systematically gathering data on that factor, and identifying impact linkages so that a forecast can be quickly related to specific features of company strategy. Most major external changes take time to develop and to the well-informed person do not appear as a surprise (scientific discoveries often take a generation to change technology actually in use). If you know what to look for, you often can subscribe to or purchase a suitable forecast. Recognizing the handwriting on the wall and grasping its significance are the most common troublemakers.[2]

The nature and frequency of reports from monitoring depend largely on the typical use of the reports. Sometimes, as on a fire-tower lookout, no news is good news. Only unusual threats (or opportunities) need be reported. In contrast, a report on major variables that often alters action—as in wildcat oil drilling—should go regularly and quickly to the operating division. For special circumstances in which a quick choice among a few known alternatives is necessary, a report that triggers contingency plans is appropriate. A primary use of all sorts of monitoring reports is as an input to milestone reviews, the subject of the next section.

## Full-Scale Reassessments at Milestones and Alerts

The steering concept in strategy control requires adaptability to new conditions. Dynamic adjustments are part of the very nature of strategy. Consequently, the control system must include opportunities to reappraise plans and progress in light of the latest developments. *Milestone reviews* serve this purpose.

Milestone reviews should include a searching look at the total strategy. A dramatic example was Boeing's assessment of its planned entry into the supersonic transport (SST) market. Millions of dollars and years of scarce engineering talent had gone into designing an SST. The potential market for rapid intercontinental flights was believed to be large, and European competition threatened to get a jump on the market. To continue as planned represented a billion-dollar decision for Boeing. In fact, after a thorough review, Boeing quit. The new predicted cost of an SST that would meet performance specifications became much higher than originally estimated. Also, the relatively small number of passengers expected made predicted operating expenses per passenger-mile very high. And further government subsidy was unlikely. So, in spite of its pride, patriotic pressure, and

---

[2]A sophisticated approach to these variables is SPIRE (systematic probing and identification of the relevant environment). See the article by H. Klein and W. H. Newman in *Journal of Business Strategy,* Summer 1980.

large sunk costs, Boeing withdrew. Its revised projections and its reluctance to gamble caused the abrupt change in plans. Only an objective, full-scale reassessment could have led to this unpleasant decision.

This action stands in sharp contrast to another major aircraft decision. A few years earlier, Convair chose to continue its bid for commercial jet aircraft by shifting from its 880 plane to the 990 plane *without* a full, objective reexamination. A complete milestone review at that time could have prevented a loss of hundreds of millions of dollars.

## Scope of Reassessment

A review of the kind being proposed takes another look at the total picture. Fresh data come from the two control steps already discussed.

The progress reports on strategic thrusts provide a basis for a revised projection. These new forecasts should include estimates of (1) the company's internal capability to complete the thrusts planned within acceptable time frames; (2) projected total costs based on costs to date, plus revised estimates of additional costs necessary to complete the plans; and (3) revised statements of probable outcomes, in terms of both target results and undesignated side effects. Of course, many uncertainties about outcomes will remain, but the recently acquired experience and knowledge will almost always change the probabilities and risks.

Updated forecasts on the future behavior of key actors and environmental changes, provided by monitoring reports, will flag significant shifts in opportunities and threats. Comparisons with competitors will show relative strength and often suggest ways to differentiate the strategy. Of course, external data need not be restricted to topics being monitored. A perceptive ear to the ground often turns up unexpected news. For steering, knowing how the terrain has changed is crucial.

The normal, constructive time to rebuild consistency between corporate and business-unit strategies is at milestone reviews. It is the occasion when redirection and rededication—if a change is needed—should occur.

### What Triggers Total Reassessments?

Full-scale reviews, such as those just described, consume time and energy. They also raise disconcerting questions for managers who are striving hard to carry out the existing strategy, so they should take place only when formal reassurance about the wisdom of the next actions is needed. Typically, three kinds of events trigger a full reassessment.

**Milestones in Major Programs**    Every program reaches points when large commitments of resources must be made—for example, a contract for a new plant must be signed, an issue of bonds sold, a new product placed in production, or an acquisition approved. These milestones—just ahead of the next big step—are natural times for a full-scale review. Another kind of milestone occurs when key uncertainties are resolved—at the time of an important court decision, a report of an oil gusher (or dry hole) on the continental shelf, or completion of a market test. Strategy should be reviewed in light of this vital information.

**An Alert Flashed by External Monitoring**    A political coup in the Middle East may threaten the U.S.'s fuel supply; a leading competitor probably will go bankrupt; the FDA will soon announce that salt may be injurious to health. When such news is unexpected and, if correct, would have a significant effect on strategy the company should pursue, a full reassessment may be wise. To cite a specific illustration, information about a new tie between the BBC (British Broadcasting Corporation) and Bluebird (a new pay cable network) prompted the Public Broadcasting Service to undertake a full strategy review. For years, BBC programs contributed to the Public Broadcasting Service's ability to compete with commercial networks. A reduction in this advantage, coupled with already announced competition in performing arts broadcasts, meant that the Public Broadcasting Service had to rethink its distinctive role in the television industry.

**A Maximum Period since the Last Full Review**    Note that neither of the previous two trigger points are tied to the calendar. Instead, they provide help when it can be most effective. Only rarely does strategy advance in regular annual cycles. Nevertheless, even a stable situation should be reappraised from time to time. Creeping changes do occur. So General Electric, for example, conducts a strategy review in each of its strategic business-units every two years, unless a review has already been triggered for a more pressing reason during that period.

Clearly, the recommended position is that strategy decisions, once made, are not subject to renegotiation during the annual budgeting process. Instead, once the strategy is felt to be unworkable, it should go back for full reassessment.

## Final Evaluation of a Strategy

Since a well-designed four-part strategy for business-units and corporations includes target results, a normal question is, Did the strategy succeed? Reports from departments—finance, marketing, engineering, etc.—will provide answers for targets in their respective areas. In addition, *Fortune, Forbes Magazine,* and industry trade papers love to rank companies; they respond to the public's fascination with winners and losers.

This kind of information is used by stockmarket investors, public relations writers, and sometimes in executive compensation schemes. For strategic management, however, such postaction scores have limited value as a control. There are two related reasons. (1) The strategies, including the target results, evolve and shift; typically, the targets have changed before the time for completion has arrived. Consequently, there is debate about which targets to use as control standards. The flexibility of a moving target is an inherent characteristic, and strength, of strategy.

(2) The prime use by strategic managers of this kind of postaction report is as an input to planning for the future. Clearly, actual past effectiveness relative to former goals and relative to competitors is very important data for formulating future strategy. But, as stressed in the foregoing, managers should not wait until they know that they have missed the moon before revising their trajectory. Steering controls which *anticipate* final results if the existing course is maintained avoid catastrophes and take advantage of new opportunities.

The best time to evaluate a strategy, for managerial purposes, is before it is too late to do anything about it. Perhaps the original strategy will be retained and its use extended for several more years. More likely, it will be refined. As in rearing a growing child, or in planning your own future, both the targets and the predicted results of current behavior keep moving ahead into the future.

## Controlling the Execution of Department Strategy Programs

Controlling strategy programs differs from controlling the strategy. A strategy is a *plan* for the future. It sets, on a frequently updated basis, the future direction for the enterprise. In contrast, controlling a program focuses on *execution*. Usually the aim of a strategy program remains stable until the program is completed. To ensure that action in the desired direction(s) does take place, controlling a program is more short range. The focus is on harnessing resources and achieving the program targets insofar as possible.

To a large extent, strategy programs are carried out by functional departments in a business-unit. Such programs deal with entering a new market, automating a plant, extending more liberal credit, and the like. So, to simplify the discussion, we will concentrate on controlling programs which are run by these operating departments. The reader should be aware, however, that (1) corporations may have service departments, such as centralized research or finance, and that some strategy programs are carried out by these departments; and (2) sometimes strategy programs involve primarily the coordination of several departments (as in launching a new product or a sharp reduction in the number of employees), and a special task force or other temporary organization is set up to administer them. Nevertheless, the problems and techniques of control for all these strategy programs are similar.

Three basic techniques illustrate valuable ways for managers to control strategy programs: project control, control of resource inputs, and postaction control of strategic thrusts.

## Project Control

Control of a program can be aided by dividing the program into projects. A project is narrower in scope than a program: it has a clear-cut mission and a sharp terminal point when that mission is completed. Thus, a program to launch a new product might have separate projects for preparing the engineering design, packaging the product, providing initial publicity and advertising, preparing installation manuals, and so forth.

Each project is planned as outlined at the beginning of Chapter 21. The plan shows steps, dates when each step should be completed, resources needed for each step, and who is responsible for doing each step. Then, by watching when steps are finished, a manager can tell whether the project is *on time;* and by watching the use of people, materials, and/or cash in relation to the progress of work completed, the manager can tell whether the costs are higher or lower than planned.

The value of these interim figures lies in the opportunity to take corrective action promptly before the project is completed. The early steps will have become history, but time will still be available to adjust (or even abandon) the latter steps. For instance, an airplane manufacturer set up a subassembly plant in a depressed urban center, partly to provide local employment. Controls revealed that the early training steps were much more costly than estimated, so the nature of work was modified and the timetable extended. Without step-by-step standards and measurements, the committed administrators of this project would have been reluctant to make revisions when they did.

For complex projects, PERT and critical path analysis can be used, as indicated in Chapter 21. This degree of detail usually is unnecessary, however. The critical aspects of controlling most strategy projects is actually setting down the dates and then monitoring progress against these standards.

When project control is in effect, the project manager can report progress (or lack of it) to the senior manager who has overall supervision of the strategy move. These reports become part of the grist for the milestone reviews mentioned earlier.

## Control of Resource Inputs

Not all actions necessary to achieve strategic change can be fitted into projects. The strategy may be largely concerned with just a shift in emphasis or the timing of established activities. For instance, should IBM rely more heavily on the sale of personal computers rather than large mainframe computers? Or, how fast should Bank of America use automatic teller machines to replace its very small branch offices? Especially in smaller companies, this sort of change is entwined with current operations.

The direction and degree of change are strongly influenced by the resources devoted to the task. Typically, change involves extra expense, more effort by employees, perhaps temporary hiring, often some new equipment, and always managers' attention. So, one way to control strategic change is to control such necessary inputs of resources.

Yes/no controls are widely used in companies to regulate the flow of resources to selected activities. For example, to obtain funds for low-interest financing of automobile sales, a marketing manager has to get the allocation approved at a control point. Likewise, to get personnel transferred to lobbying in the state legislature, approval at a different control point may be necessary. Clearly, a strategy program can be either stalled or supported by the quality and quantity of resources that pass through such control points.

Of course, control over resource allocation relates only to inputs; the desired resulting output may or may not be achieved. Just as the United States sending financial aid to, say, the Sudan does not assure that Sudanese children will be better nourished, similarly an advertising appropriation will not necessarily result in increased sales of a new product. That is, resources are necessary, but not sufficient. This indirect, enabling character of resource allotments adds to the fuzziness of linkages between allocations and strategy.

Ideally, control over the flow of resources (money, people, equipment, etc.) should assure that strategy programs get the resources that they need and that other activities which detract from the strategy programs do not receive support. However, this neat fit is hard to secure for at least three reasons:

1. *The people controlling allocations may use standards that do not match the strategy program.* Here are a few typical examples. (a) Financial budget allocations may be dominated by a desire to make an overall cut in expenses, and an increase for a new strategy program gets shot down in the general drive to economize. (b) ROI hurdle rates are often established by finance executives for capital investments, and a strategic move to "position" the company or block a competitor may not meet this control standard. The short-run weighting in the discounted cash flow calculation of the ROI increases the chances that the strategy proposal will be turned down. (c) Or in the human resource area, a company that is cutting back some activities may be stressing transfers of long-service employees, and the strategy program may face a Hobson's choice of taking a poorly qualified transferee or getting none at all.

2. *Internal political considerations affect resource allocations.* In any cooperative endeavor, the support of the most influential members of the group is necessary to carry out a major strategic thrust; exchange of favors is considered a part of the normal give-and-take. In the process, a strategy program may get sidetracked. For instance, in a paper company a vice president who is a member of the founding family is opposed to closing a mill in his home town. Then protecting this particular social concern is necessary to get an allocation for a new experimental pulping process, even though closing the mill is part of a related strategy program.

3. *Because of scrambled accounts, allocations of money or people may not be used for the stated purpose.* The resource needs of a strategic program may be part of the justification for, say, an enlarged research budget. The budget then passes the budget control point; however, the re-

search director and the researchers want to push to conclusion a different line of study, so the budgeted funds are "borrowed" for the latter purpose. Even more common is a squeeze on a department manager to meet short-run goals, so a strategy move that has a three-year time horizon gets postponed. Such shifting around of resources is possible, and even encouraged, by an accounting system that scrambles resources intended for several different purposes in a single account. The controls do not follow through to check how the resources are actually used.

Additional controls are not recommended to overcome these deficiencies in resource controls. Instead, refinements that tie strategy more closely to allocations are needed. Three possibilities which some companies use are the following:

1. *Set policies that bar the use of resources for activities that sidetrack.* These "thou shalt not" guides are added to the screening standards used for allocations. A West Coast electronics firm, for instance, has decided to pin its hope for fast growth on proprietary, state-of-the-art components. For this strategy, R & D is clearly the critical resource. To ensure full effort behind this commitment, a policy of no R & D support for subcontracting business has been adopted (much to the consternation of the production manager, who likes subcontracts to keep his plant busy).

2. *Withhold allocations unless support of strategy is explicit and clear.* This at least makes support of strategy one of the control standards; ROI alone is not enough. For example, a family-owned insurance company is relying on professional managers (three young MBAs) to switch company emphasis from fire to environmental hazards. Accordingly, proposals to underwrite other kinds of risks, even though probably profitable, are rejected because senior executives believe that the professional managers will have all they can do to succeed in the environmental domain.

3. *Separate allocations for old and new business.* Texas Instruments keeps one set of accounts for current business and another set for strategy programs, even though both kinds of work are done in the same office or shop. Moreover, output measurements are separated so that they have independent controls on each kind of work. To cite another example, the Sierra Shoe Company is facing reluctance on the part of its distributing organization to push its new line. Long known for its hiking, outdoor, and special working shoes, Sierra finally entered the canvas-top athletic shoe business. But the sales force clearly prefers to sell "real shoes," not "tennis shoes." By controlling the inputs and measuring the outputs for the new line separately, the company hopes to focus adequate attention on the new strategy program.

Controls such as these push employee attention into new strategy directions. They also reduce the confusion that is inevitable when a new strategy is announced and yet the controls allow efforts to support other aims.

## Postaction Control of Strategic Thrusts

Postaction controls also have a role in strategy execution. They tend to be quite specific. Strategic thrusts, the action phase of strategy, are typically executed by means of the more focused department strategy programs. And a final assessment of the results of these programs is useful. Bonuses or other rewards are often based on this assessment, and the success or failure of each program can be noted in the continuing strategy-planning process.

Although late in arriving, the postaction control report has a reliability that is not possible for the predictions used in steering controls. In effect, reliability is substituted for timeliness. If competition is not very aggressive, this may even be a good trade-off. In any event, keeping the final score lets operating managers know that they cannot be cavalier about their strategy assignments.

Two sorts of postaction assessments are useful. First, the actual results should be compared with the targets set at the start of the program (and any revised targets as well). Then, since in a strategy arena operating conditions are rarely just as predicted, comparisons can often be made with other companies in the same industry to adjust for uncontrollable variables. These comparisons, of course, reflect the starting strengths of each company, the wisdom of the program design, and the skill in its execution; nevertheless, they will often indicate where the strategic action was effective and where it was weak.

In general, until the postaction controls have been pushed down to at least the department program level, it is difficult for managers to learn much that can be safely used in future planning.

## Conclusions

Managers can control company strategy to a significant extent, even in the face of highly dynamic and uncertain conditions. But there are two quite different objectives of such control.

One objective is to keep the strategy adapted to the changing environment—to new opportunities and threats. For this, steering control is by far the most suitable form of control. Its techniques include monitoring key planning assumptions, watching progress on strategic thrusts and updating predictions of their outcomes, and using these and related inputs for full-scale milestone reviews. Such steering control results in an adaptable strategy. Based on regularly updated forecasts, the strategy seeks to anticipate what various stakeholders and rivals will do and to take corrective action while there is still time to influence the outcomes.

A second objective is to keep strategic thrusts on time and on target. Here the focus is on department strategy programs, and the techniques include strategy project control, control of resource inputs, and postaction control of department programs. Through these and similar devices, managers focus attention on selected strategy moves so that current operating problems do not crowd out longer run strategy. Moreover, such control of strategic thrusts provides valuable information that can be fed into the milestone reviews of the strategy itself.

Even though these controls are very far from exact, they help to pull together the total strategic management process. Without them, strategy formulation tends to become a sporadic, and even futile, exercise.

Control of strategy varies with organization level. The steering control of strategy formulation for a business-unit takes place at the general management level of each unit (or single-line company). This is a vital device for securing unified action in the face of an increasingly turbulent and competitive environment. Similarly, control of corporate strategy is a significant activity of central corporate executives. They can use steering controls very similar to those recommended for the general management of a business-unit. Of course, both the business-unit and corporate general managers receive control reports and advice from the managers they supervise, but the main responsibility for both strategy planning and control of that planning exists at the top level of each unit.

In contrast to strategy formulation, control of strategy execution is primarily a departmental affair. While general managers should make sure that a good control system for department strategy programs is in place, the actual exercise of these controls involves detailed knowledge which department managers know best. In emergencies central managers may step into active program control, and the senior executive performing the "outside director" role certainly expects to be kept informed about progress on strategy programs. However, if a department manager is unable (or unwilling) to control strategy programs in his or her bailiwick, the company should look for a replacement.

## Questions for Class Discussion

1. "Short-run needs tend to squeeze out longer-run strategic action. Engineers assigned to new product development, for example, are often interrupted to fix a current processing problem or to help a customer. A telephone call from the outside auditor takes priority over a study of growth trends in Brazil. Keeping Susan's even hand on labor negotiations seems more urgent than sending her to a four-week executive development program. The CEO wants a good profit to report for the third quarter. Over and over it is the strategic activities that are

deferred." Describe strategy control devices that will help prevent such under-cutting of strategy programs.

2. Every strategy involves some risk, but the degree of risk and the potential loss vary widely from one strategy to another. How—if at all—would you recommend adjusting strategy controls for a high-risk strategy compared to a low-risk strategy?

3. In most foreign countries, Pepsi-Cola Company grants a franchise to a local bottling and distributing firm. The franchised firm must use Pepsi's secret extract shipped from the United States. All other activities are performed by local nationals. The American company provides advice on production and distribution and permits use of the well-known Pepsi-Cola trademark. The company in the United States is naturally concerned about both short- and long-run profits in the foreign countries and about the worldwide reputation of Pepsi-Cola. What controls should the company establish over the strategy of a franchise dealer in a foreign country?

4. The Ascott chain of motels has a well-developed budgetary control system. In addition to monthly financial results of each motel, subdivisions of expenses for room operations and restaurant operations are budgeted. A central computer prepares comparisons of actual results versus budget for each motel within a week after the end of each month, and these reports are distributed to central executives and each motel manager. Central staff personnel promptly investigate major deviations. In contrast, Ascott has no formal controls over employee training or morale, market position of each motel in its local area, quality of maintenance, quality of service, or changes in local reputation. What do you predict will be the long-run consequence of this control structure?

5. "Steering control of a strategic thrust is difficult, partly because the entire strategy is based on a set of predictions about the external world and the reactions of key actors to our moves. [See Chapters 2, 3, and 4 for typical kinds of predictions.] If these predictions are wrong, maybe our strategy should be modified. Therefore, the steering control should include a monitoring of the continuing reliability of the main predictions." (a) Explain how this proposition would apply to control of Ford Motor Company's strategy to assemble its subcompact and compact cars in Hermosillo, Mexico, in order to reduce its costs and be able to compete against the Toyota-General Motors assembly plant in California and the Japanese cars everywhere in the Americas. (b) Explain how this proposition would apply to control of the United States Football League's strategy to schedule its games during the spring of the year.

6. (a) Will the use of steering controls for strategy, as described in this chapter, ease or complicate the determination of fair bonuses and other rewards for managers?
(b) Will the use of project control or post-action program control, as described in this chapter, ease or complicate the determination of fair bonuses and other rewards for managers?

(c) If in your answers you say that either (a) or (b) will complicate the determination of bonuses, what alternative management incentives do you suggest to keep managers motivated to support strategy change?

7. (a) The concept of a "milestone review" of a business-unit strategy was briefly described in this chapter. How might this "milestone review" concept be applied to the control of a corporate portfolio strategy (discussed in Chapter 15)? What data inputs would you want? From whom? What should determine the timing of such reviews?
(b) One of the benefits sought by many diversified corporations is synergy among the various business-units (see the last part of Chapter 17). What controls do you suggest that corporate executives use to assure that business-units do not "overlook" potential synergies among their activities?

8. Transnational, Inc., of Houston, is concerned about controlling "questionable payments" which might be made by executives of its foreign subsidiaries. "Grease" payments (payments to do promptly what the receiver is supposed to do) are involved. Either local government officials or local business executives may be receivers. Control is complicated because local custom in some but not all countries where Transnational operates condones such payments. In contrast, U.S. law prohibits payments to government officials even where local practice endorses it. What ways do you suggest Transnational use to control questionable payments?

9. The Cardiz Construction Company—builders of shopping centers, offices, schools, and churches—is concerned with its public relations. Complaints about noise, dirt, upsetting ecology, workers' disregard of community customs, and so forth are becoming increasingly troublesome. "We talk to our people over and over," Mr. Cardiz says, "and they correct the specific complaint. But two weeks later a group of mothers is picketing around 'the old oak tree' or a town clerk wants us to sweep up some dust in front of the mayor's house." Like other construction firms, Cardiz gets its business through competitive bidding for contracts that normally have a fixed price and penalty clauses for late completion. Each project manager is measured on how well actual performance stacks up against contract provisions. The project manager's job is complicated by the use of subcontractors for many parts of the work. How do you recommend that Mr. Cardiz get better control of public relations?

# CASE
## 23 Gibraltar Drug Co.

How could a large, conservative pharmaceutical company unexpectedly be confronted with over $100,000,000 in claims for product liability? More important, what might it have done to avoid the catastrophe?

The 80-year-old Gibraltar Drug Company is among the leading pharmaceutical firms in the United States.[1] Its president has served as head of the Pharmaceutical Manufacturers Association, and the company is regarded as one of the most conservatively managed firms in the industry. Never before has it faced a large product liability problem. Its success has been built on an unusually close relationship with practicing physicians and on formulations of recognized drugs for common ailments. Nevertheless, it is now in deep trouble.

We will look briefly at the way Gibraltar Drug Co. is organized, and then trace the steps that led to its present predicament.

The basic organization of the U.S. pharmaceutical activities of Gibraltar follows functional lines, thereby permitting a high degree of specialization. This structure, which is generally similar to that of competitors, is sketched in Figure 23–3. Because of sharp differences in the activities of the research, production, marketing, finance, and other divisions, the separate responsibilities of the various functions are well understood, by custom if not by written definition.

One normal consequence of this functional organization is the need to obtain ideas and judgments from several different specialists in order to arrive at a decision. People at one step in the decision process rely strongly on the data supplied by specialists in other functional areas. For instance, marketing people accept the technical judgments of the medical staff, and in turn, production people accept the sales estimates of the marketing experts. Inevitably, "uncertainty absorption" occurs at each step because the expert often passes along a boiled-down conclusion about a complex array of data. At Gibraltar Drug Co., as in any complex organization, informal procedures for such exchange of information and judgments have grown up over many years.

MILS was a new product for Gibraltar Drug Co. To pose the question of how its introduction should have been controlled, we will briefly describe five basic steps in its history at Gibraltar.

## Decision to Acquire MILS

MILS is a product that physicians prescribe for weight reduction. It had been developed, tested, approved for sale by the Food and Drug Administration (FDA), and actually marketed on a very limited scale by a small pharmaceutical research firm when Gibraltar became interested in it. The research firm was seeking a large licensee to give their new product national distribution, and Gibraltar perceived MILS as a quick way to enter a market segment where it had no other products. So Gibraltar acquired exclusive rights to produce and market MILS, giving the re-

---

[1]Because litigation is still going on, the name of the company and of the controversial drug have been changed. The problem of managerial control, which is our interest here, is not altered by avoidance of the medical technicalities involved.

**FIGURE 23–3.**
**ORGANIZATION OF GIBRALTAR DRUG CO.**

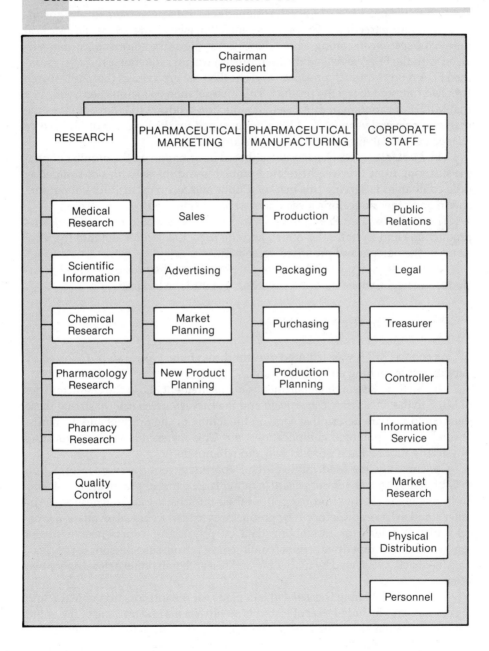

search firm a fixed sum to cover its development costs plus a royalty on all future sales.

Before the president of Gibraltar signed the licensing agreement, he got advice from four parts of the Gibraltar organization (see Figure 23–3). The *Medical Research Department*, among whose duties is serving as the company's primary liaison with the FDA, reviewed the literature on weight reduction products, examined FDA reports on such products, and checked the procedures that the research firm had followed to test the product. This investigation was simplified by the fact that MILS is a variation of other weight reduction products that have been on the market for several years. Also, Gibraltar arranged for the inventor of MILS to be its medical consultant, and he knows the area well.

The *Market Research Department* gathered information on the number of people suffering from overweight-related problems and the activities of competing drug companies in serving this market. Public and technical attitudes about saccharin and other noncaloric sweeteners were also checked.

The *Marketing Vice President* was asked how MILS would fit into Gibraltar's product line and overall sales effort, and the *Legal Counsel* looked into the legal status of the patents and proposed agreement.

All of these viewpoints were strongly positive, so the president quickly concluded the negotiations before competitors got into the bidding.

## Preparation for Marketing

As soon as MILS was acquired, it went through the typical steps followed by Gibraltar in launching any new product.

The Medical Research Department sent a statement about the characteristics of MILS to the *Advertising Department* and the *Packaging Department* so that these units could prepare descriptive copy on the nature of the product and its merits, normal dosage, potential complications, etc. This material is vital in educating physicians about what a product will and will not do.

Concurrently, the Medical Research Department sent the same information to Gibraltar's *Medical Advisory Board* (a rather large panel of practicing physicians and some medical school professors) for their information and suggestions. Another standard procedure for a new product was to start a clinical evaluation project which provides for assembling data on physicians' experiences with the product and on competitive actions, coming mostly from salespersons in the field. This feedback is reviewed by marketing and research personnel at least every two years.

The *Market Planning Department* laid plans for the introduction of MILS into the market. This included a set of test calls on physicians and training of the entire field organization about the new product, in cooperation with the *Personnel Department*. A schedule coordinating publicity, advertising, training, production, and physical distribution was also developed. All this activity was a normal way for Gibraltar to work a new product into its broad line.

## Preparation for Production

For Gibraltar, preparation for the production of MILS was simplified by the fact that it was already being produced at the time the licensing agreement was signed. The processes involved were similar to some already existing in Gibraltar plants. Consequently, the *Production Planning Department* could adapt familiar techniques.

The *Quality Control Department* laid out a set of safeguards and tests to assure that the finished product would conform to its chemical and related specifications. The *Physical Distribution Department* laid plans for building up inventories in company warehouses and wholesale drug houses so that prescriptions by physicians could be filled promptly as soon as the publicity campaign was launched.

## Product Introduction

As in the preparation for marketing and production, the actual introduction of MILS into the market followed well-established steps used by Gibraltar. The *Advertising Department* arranged publicity in professional journals and professional meetings, and letters and descriptive brochures were sent to thousands of physicians. The field representatives of the *Sales Department* stressed MILS in their calls on physicians and retail drugstores. And simultaneously, the *Production Department* started production to fill the distribution channels in accordance with schedules from the *Physical Distribution Department*.

By this stage, MILS had become another of the many products made and sold by Gibraltar. The various departments performed their customary roles. Products in the pharmaceutical industry come and go frequently as new techniques for diagnosis and treatment are developed, and MILS fit into this dynamic pattern.

## Monitoring Performance

At Gibraltar, product performance is regularly watched at five points. The Controller Department watches financial results. The Physical Distribution Department keeps track of orders being placed by drug wholesalers and uses the data to schedule further shipments to the warehouses. The data on orders received also go to the Sales Department for its guidance of the field organization. Meanwhile, the field representatives send in information on the reactions of physicians that they visit and other industry "news." This information is made available to the Market Research Department to assist it in its periodic assessment of the competitive situation.

Any information that the field representatives obtain about product performance is also sent to the secretary of the clinical evaluation project, where it is accumulated for the company's biannual reviews. Normally, this secretary is an M.D. in the Medical Research Department—the same person who responds to technical questions about the product from practicing physicians. (This establishes an M.D.-to-M.D. relationship with physicians.) Such an arrangement was followed for MILS. The secretary has a variety of such assignments and consults with other researchers in the Division when necessary, or, in the case of MILS, with the consultant (inventor) since this product did not come out of Gibraltar's own laboratories.

MILS sales grew at a very satisfactory rate; it clearly was becoming one of the leading products in its narrow niche. The first report of the clinical evaluation project at the end of 18 months dealt largely with packaging suggestions and the usual array of "crackpot" complaints that arise with most new products. One complaint, presumed to be stirred up by a direct competitor, reported that some patients apparently could not tolerate MILS over a sustained period, but there was no solid evidence to support this.

During the next six months the "tolerance" rumor turned up several times, and some physicians phoned Gibraltar to ask about it. Since overweight persons who try to lose weight often have diverse reactions, Gibraltar's response was that there was no known reason to associate MILS with the difficulties reported. But when the idea persisted, the head of the Medical Division asked Gibraltar's Medical Advisory Board to appoint a subcommittee to quietly check the experience of a sample of (friendly, objective) physicians. In a month the subcommittee reported back that, "Yes, there might be something to the rumor, but no pattern was recognized."

At this point, Gibraltar might have sent out a "Dear Doctor" letter to all practicing physicians informing them that that question had been raised about the sustained use of MILS, and while Gibraltar knew of no evidence that supported this doubt, the doctors should be alerted to such a possibility. However, no member of Gibraltar's top management committee favored such action because (a) the letter would have severely cut MILS sales, probably for no good reason, and (b) Gibraltar could not identify either conditions where difficulty was likely or a clear set of symptoms, and thus would appear not to know the effect of products it was selling.

Then the dam broke. A physician specializing in weight problems announced at a large professional meeting that he had five cases where serious injury to patients' glands was directly associated with sustained use of MILS. This led to a flurry of similar reports. Some doctors said they feared that the damage might be permanent. The evidence was unscientific, but because continued exposure for perhaps two years was presumed to be necessary to bring about the effect—and this only in some patients—Gibraltar was unable clearly to dismiss the fear.

Product liability suits immediately were filed against Gibraltar asking high damages because of gross neglect. Hungry lawyers are advertising to anyone who has ever taken MILS, and juries sympathize with people suffering from poor health; and, in some circumstances, maybe MILS does injure glands.

So, reluctantly, Gibraltar has sent out a "Dear Doctor" letter. After a few unfavorable court decisions, the company is about to withdraw MILS from the market.

## Question

(a) At what points, if any, did Gibraltar fail to exercise reasonable controls in the MILS case?
(b) What controls should Gibraltar (and other pharmaceutical companies) have for the introduction of new products?

# INTEGRATING CASES

**Execution of Strategy**

## FAMILY SERVICE OF GOTHAM[1]

Freda Maurer is regarded as a kind and considerate friend but an awesome enemy if she "really gets her dander up." And she is dangerously close to getting her dander up, according to Jim Torrent, director of casework for Family Service of Gotham.

> Mrs. Maurer has been executive director of this agency for almost 25 years [Torrent said]. I have only been here for six years, and in that time I have come to admire Mrs. Maurer as an executive as well as a humanitarian. Jan Blossom [office manager] and I have tried to persuade her to bring in a consultant to help her implement the board's request for tighter controls, but she says she doesn't need any help from consultants at this time.

### The Agency

Family Service of Gotham is a private, nonsectarian agency that provides a range of social services to the people of Gotham. The bulk of its budget of $2.7 million stems from the Gotham Community Chest. Approximately 25 percent comes from fees; direct gifts and endowments make up the balance.

> It is very frustrating to try to expand our services, Torrent said, because invariably for every extra dollar we raise through fees or gifts, the Chest reduces our annual allocation by 80 to 90 cents.

The agency is one of more than 1,000 private agencies in the United States that operate on a local, community basis. Most, like Family Service of Gotham, are members of a trade association of family-service agencies headquartered in New York City. The motto of this association, "Strength to Families Under Stress," typi-

[1]William H. Newman and E. Kirby Warren, *The Process of Management: Concepts, Behavior, and Practice*, 4th ed., © 1977, pp. 532–537. Reprinted by permission of Prentice-Hall, Inc., Englewood Cliffs, NJ.

fies the goals and frustrations of the member agencies. Their goal is to provide help, through professional social workers and volunteers, to individual family members, but primarily to strengthen the family unit. With limited resources, however, the motto highlights the dilemma. "What help, to which families, and under what kinds of stress?" is the three-part question that has been debated at length in individual agencies and at local and national priority conferences.

Family Service of Gotham (FSG) is one of three private family-service agencies serving Gotham's 200,000 population. Although each of these agencies offers several services, FSG offers the fullest range. Its services include:

1. Individual and group counseling
2. Infant day care
3. Foster-home placement
4. Drug and alcohol treatment
5. Senior-citizen services

In addition to the other two private, sectarian agencies, there are public-welfare and -assistance services and a number of other agencies offering one or more special services.

FSG has approximately 50 people on its staff, including 37 with degrees in social work. Freda Maurer, the executive director, is a youthful 60 years. She has three immediate subordinates: Jim Torrent, director of casework, supervises 30 caseworkers through four section heads. Jane Blossom, who has an MBA and CPA, manages the office and directs accounting services. Clark Whitman, the executive director's third subordinate, supervises the agency's day-care and senior-citizens programs.

Mrs. Maurer is the chief executive officer, but she is responsible to a board of directors. The board is made up of local business and professional people, clergy, and several wealthy philanthropists. Although Mrs. Maurer has great influence with the board, it selects its own members and elects a board president each year. Last month, the board selected William Garcia. A Mexican-American, Garcia has risen from poverty to prominence in his 43 years. He has been active in community affairs and is president of a large insurance and real-estate brokerage firm. He has served on the FSG board for three years and has been perhaps its most outspoken member on the need for (in his words) "running the agency in a more businesslike way."

## The Current Situation

As a result of recent inflation, recession, and pressures for reduction in government spending, agencies such as FSG are faced with more clients, who have more problems and less money. The Community Chest has indicated that it will have to reduce its allocation to FSG next year, but the amount has not been disclosed. For three of the last five years, the agency has operated at a deficit, reducing its already small endowment fund.

Garcia was elected by a six-to-four vote of the board on the promise that he would play an active role in assisting the director to set priorities for the agency and develop tighter controls and ensure greater efficiency.

## Garcia's Views

Freda Maurer is an amazing woman [said Garcia]. I respect her for what she wants to do and love her for what she tries to do. Despite our differences on how to deal with our current crisis, I think she is a good executive. Her problem is not lack of strength or the toughness to stand up to a difficult situation, but that she is too strong and refuses to believe she can't do everything she wants. She is a builder but not a planner. She has visions of how to change social evils, and they require time, patience and, unfortunately, a lot of money. When I point out that we don't have the money, she laughs and says, "Don't worry, Willie, we'll get it if we need it." Well, we can't keep spending more than we have. We must set priorities and make sure that our personnel follow them. They must be supervised more closely to keep them within the bounds of our agency priorities; and they must increase their efficiency even if the quality of their work has to drop off a bit. Agencies like ours may soon be fighting for survival; so we have to get more efficient or we won't be around to help anyone.

Once we get our basic cost studies done, we can set standards and control performance in any of the following ways. The first is very simple. For each branch of our work, select a unit of service—such as a day of care for one child, placement of a child in a new home, families counseled, senior-citizen lunches served, and number of participants in recreational activities—and then show total cost per unit of service against our original estimates. This would at least make supervisors cost/output-conscious and would give the board an idea of relative costs for the different services and of where people are working to reduce costs per unit of service.

Second, there could well be a system that got closer to individual productivity. If the service units cannot be assigned to single social workers, then keep track of the volume of the major activities they do perform: for instance, number of counseling interviews or, for placement workers, the number of home visits, number of telephone inquiries, and number of new homes investigated. A simple daily tally could easily be kept and then summarized for each two-week period to average out the variation in specific calls. Incidentally, by evaluating several caseworkers, everyone would know who was most productive. If some unusual event absorbed a lot of time, this could be noted on the summary report. Of course, the board would not be concerned with such reports, but the supervisors and Freda would. Our task would be to make sure that the system was being used conscientiously. With this sort of attention to output, even though not exact, I'm sure FSG would generate more service for its expenditures. Also, we would know where necessary cutbacks could be made with the least pain.

Third, we might use MBO. This would get each worker—or a unit of two or three people who do a job together—to participate in setting short-run goals and then reviewing output. We have well-motivated people, and if we really challenge them—and give them a chance to challenge themselves—the results will be impressive. MBO is a way to keep people thinking about getting the important aspects of their job done. And they get a real feeling of accomplishment. This system could involve everyone from caseworker to executive director.

If there are even better ways to improve productivity, let's use them. I'm not wedded to any particular forms. But it is clear to me and to a majority of the board that we now have virtually no control and yet are accountable to our supporters for spending their money. We have to do something.

## Board Sentiment

Garcia has considerable support from other members of the board, though not all feel as strongly as he does. Peter Carbonara chief of surgery at Mother Cabrini Hospital, typifies the ambivalence of several board members:

> There is no question that we have to get Freda to cut back, to set some priorities and live with them. That's as far as I go, however! I don't want to get into the details of how she does it. Bill [Garcia] wants to set up a series of cost studies on each of our major programs. Then he wants to have each program evaluated. Based on these evaluations, he envisions setting standards and controls to make certain that necessary levels of efficiency are achieved. Presumably, if the standards aren't met for a program, it will be reevaluated and perhaps even dropped.

Carbonara expressed great reluctance to try to force Mrs. Maurer to prepare such studies and develop the ensuing detailed plans and controls:

> I've seen what happens at the hospital when this starts. Within 18 months the bureaucrats take over and suffocate you with forms and control reports; and costs keep going up anyway. I say we should give Freda a flat sum, a dollar limit, for each major service and monitor her quarterly. If she goes over in one place, we can force her to shift it from another. She knows this agency better than all of us put together. We don't have the time or knowledge to try to hold her in line with detailed controls. If we try, we will waste money on the studies and controls, make people angry, and probably have Freda outfox us anyway.

Other board members, however, support Garcia's approach. Edward Nelson, president of a large pharmaceutical firm headquartered in Gotham, said:

> We have to help Freda. She's a great leader but she is not a planner. She may know where every nickel is being spent but it's mostly in her head. We don't have any real detailed information on how effectively the money is being spent. We need facts to guide us with tough priority decisions. We have to know just how much more we can get for each dollar we spend and where we get the best return. I recognize that we are dealing with tangible costs and intangible benefits, but this doesn't pose an impossible situation. Heaven knows, I have worked with enough research people in my company to know that one can set priorities and control expenses while being uncertain about the payoffs.

Nancy Morgan, another member of the board, represents a third point of view:

> To tell the truth, I'm confused by all the debate. Garcia, Nelson, and others keep talking about "cost-benefit studies," which will lead to setting "priorities," and about creating "control standards" to "monitor results" and "shift resource commitments." Frankly, it sounds like a lot of jargon to me. I don't have a lot of business experience, but I have worked with enough charities to know that most of the so-called efficiency techniques brought in from business end up lowering morale more than costs. Freda Maurer knows more about how to run this agency than any of us. I think we should listen to her. Let *her* tell *us* the minimum she needs to do the job *she* thinks should be done. Then, we should get out of her way and spend our time raising the money and squeezing more out of the Community Chest rather than creating and studying a lot of reports on agency operation.

## Freda Maurer's Thoughts

> I am very concerned about recent events. No matter how they put it, the board's support for Willie Garcia's position shows less than full confidence in me. I am certain not only that Willie's studies and reports will not help, but also that they will hurt morale and reduce the respect the people in the agency have for my position.

Mrs. Maurer went on to point out that her agency differed from business in that it had no measure equivalent to revenue or profit. The services the agency provides cannot be measured in tangible terms. Therefore, she felt that if there would be measures only for cost, they—the costs—would be unduly controlled to the detriment of long- and short-run benefits.

> I can do things that would seem to improve the "efficiency" of the agency [she said], but only because we can't measure the loss of benefits that will accompany cost-cutting. For example, my family counselors could handle twice the caseload they now have if I required it. In the short run, they

could still deal with current crises, but they would not have time to probe for the causes or develop the trust necessary to anticipate and prevent problems. Within six months they would start losing control of the situation and be giving "first aid" instead of curing and preventing family problems. Within another six months we would have *more* and *worse* problems to deal with if people still trusted us enough to come back.

Another example Mrs. Maurer gave dealt with priorities:

I'm sure Willie could show that we should give up our day-care center. If I let him, it wouldn't be hard to find figures to show that other agencies can pick up our children and service them at a lower cost per day. But where will Willie get the figures that show how much we lose in our counseling and foster-care programs when we lose the opportunity to get to know families through the day-care program?

A final example of the difference in viewpoint deals with applying efficiency techniques to foster-care programs.

The social workers in the office [Garcia said] can be more closely supervised than those in the field. They also monitor each other. If someone isn't pulling his or her share, the others know it. But the caseworkers who are out in the field seeking and checking on foster homes are hard to supervise. I am sure we could set standards for their case loads and get more out of them. They would have to spend less time drinking coffee and gabbing, but they could help a lot more kids who need foster homes if they worked harder.

Mrs. Maurer disagrees.

If I have a loafer or foot-dragger in the field, I find out. I don't need standards and reports, which make people think I don't trust them, in order to catch one sluggard. All those reports will do is force everyone to do less careful investigations on prospective foster homes and less careful review of how our kids are doing with our current foster parents.

At first, I was hurt by the board's support of Willie [she concluded]. Then I got angry and considered resigning. Now, I have calmed down. I know they want to be helpful. Things are very tough now. Money is hard to come by and everybody is nervous. But we will weather this storm like all the others. We can work harder and smarter without all these studies and reports. My concern is not survival. We will survive! My concern is how I keep Willie and his allies from making it even harder. I could fight him, and I daresay I have enough friends in town and on the board to force him to back off if it comes to a "him or me" situation. That is wrong, though. It polarizes, and it would deeply hurt Willie; and, after all, he means well.

As an alternative, I could appear to go along with Willie, it would cost us a bit in time and energy but if I can't "bury" him in useless studies and inconclusive, contradictory reports, then I should be ashamed of myself. I fought these battles years ago with the bureaucrats who were seeking to take over welfare from private agencies. I won more than I lost even then, and I'm a lot smarter now. I could probably get Willie so confused and frustrated he would go looking for another place to make more efficient. I would hate to do that, too, because Willie has helped us a lot in the past and still can help if he would just realize that many of his ideas do not fit our kind of business. Maybe if we had a heart-to-heart talk, I could convince him to slow down and let me help him help us.

## Questions

1. Suppose that Freda Maurer and the board of directors did agree to hire a consultant to help resolve the control issue, and that you are the consultant. What would you recommend?
2. Use this case to think about *integrating* the various aspects of overall management of an enterprise. For Family Service of Gotham, explain the interdependence of (a) the services provided, (b) the sources of operating funds, (c) the selection and motivation of employees, and (d) the control mechanisms used.

# MANAGEMENT OF CONVAIR[1]

## The Corporation

By 1960 General Dynamics had become one of the great corporations of the country. Its sales were around two billion dollars and it produced, profitably, some of the most complex equipment known to man. Its major operating divisions were:

- Astronautic (Atlas Missiles)
- Electric Boat (submarines)
- Forth Worth (B58 bombers)

[1]For a fuller discussion of this period in General Dynamics history, see "How a Great Corporation Got Out of Control," by Richard Austin Smith in *Fortune*, January and February, 1962. The present case is composed of excerpts from these two articles. Reprinted by special permission; © 1962, by Time, Inc. All rights reserved.

- General Atomic (nuclear development)
- Liquid Carbonic (liquified gas)
- Electrodynamics (electric motors)
- Pomona (electronics plus Terrier missiles)
- Stromberg-Carlson (telephones, electronics)
- General Aircraft (leases or sells planes traded in for jets)
- Canadair (aircraft)
- Convair

This case, reported in the January and February 1962 issues of *Fortune*, focuses on one product of one division, but the issues raised are basic to the entire scope of General Dynamics and to many other companies. The division—Convair—was by far the largest component brought into General Dynamics (in 1954); and the product—the 880 and 990 passenger jets—rolled up the largest loss ever achieved by a nongovernment enterprise on a single venture, around $425 million.

General Dynamics was founded by John Jay Hopkins. Under his inspiration net earnings, $600,000 on sales of $31 million in 1947, rose to $56 million on sales of $1.7 billion in 1957, the year of Hopkins's death. Hopkins was a man of great energy who kept posted on each division of this expanding empire largely by direct and unannounced visits. In 1953 he did bring in Frank Pace as executive vice-president "to have someone in the office to answer the phone" and especially to maintain Washington's confidence in the company. Pace had served as Director of the Budget, and during the Korean crisis as Secretary of the Army.

Aside from golf, the law, and the high order of intelligence, Pace and Hopkins were complete opposites: Pace temperate in all things, oratorical, deliberate, anxious to be liked, a product of the federal staff system, prone to rely on his second-in-command in the making of decisions; Hopkins volatile, creative, earthy, intuitive, ingrown, willing to listen but unwilling to share the making of decisions with anybody, a loner more likely to give the world the back of his hand than to extend the palm of it. In 1957 cancer caught up with Hopkins. His hand-picked board of directors decided (over Hopkins's strong objections) that Pace should be president. Hopkins died three days later.

Pace described the task of managing the enterprise he inherited in these terms: "When you have a company, employing 106,000 people, made up of eleven different divisions, each a corporation really in its own right, most of which were separate enterprises before they joined the organization, and headed by men who were presidents of corporations, with their own separate legal staffs, financial staffs, etc., all of these highly competent men—the only way to succeed is to operate on a decentralized basis. Our total central office in New York City was something like 200 people, including stenographers. This group can only lay out broad policy. Your capacity to know specifically what is happening in each division just cannot exist. If you did try to know everything that was happening and controlled your men that tightly, they would leave or would lose the initiative that made them effective."

## Convair's Move into Commercial Jets

The Convair division was headed up in 1955 by General Joseph T. McNarney with John V. Naish as executive vice-president. Tough-minded Joe McNarney, ex-chief of U.S. forces in Europe, had always been pretty much of a law unto himself, while Jack Naish wore his 15 years' experience in the airframe industry like Killarney green on St. Patrick's Day. The division had already pulled off a successful commercial-transport program; the propeller-driven 240s, 340s, and 440s were world-famous. But what prompted Convair to consider making the formidable move into jet transports was a suggestion by Howard Hughes.

Hughes wanted jets for TWA; but before Hughes and Convair could agree on a design, Boeing and Douglas came out with long-range jet transports (the 707 and the DC-8) which scooped the market. Still determined to get into jets, Convair turned to the medium-range market. For this plan, Hughes proposed to buy 30 planes. After considerable engineering work, the executive committee of General Dynamics' board, headed by Hopkins, unanimously approved McNarney's program based on the assumption it would make money after 68 planes were sold, that potential sales of 257 aircraft could be realized, and that the maximum possible loss was only $30 million to $50 million.

By this time three airlines—TWA, Delta, and KLM—had already taken options to buy the 880. Now the committee instructed Convair to go ahead and get letters of intent from them within the next fortnight. The committee laid down only three conditions in authorizing the program: first, that GE guarantee the 880's engine; second, that the ability of the airlines to pay for the jets be investigated by an *ad hoc* committee of Pace, Naish, and Financial Vice-President Lambert Gross; third, that management was not to go ahead without orders in hand for 60 percent of the estimated 68-plane break-even point.

The last provision proved to be quite flexible. The break-even point on the 880 had been understated: after closer figuring, Convair raised it to 74 planes in May, up 6 planes in two months. When KLM did not pick up its option, the executive committee indulgently dropped its 60 percent condition, allowing Convair to go ahead with only 50 percent of the break-even point assured. The new figure was made to fit the fact that by now Convair had only 40 firm orders (10 from Delta and 30 from Hughes).

## A Doubting Thomas

Both Convair assistant division manager, Allen Morgan, and B. F. Coggan, the division manager, had informed management back in 1956, at the time 30 planes were sold to Howard Hughes, that the 880 was underpriced. Their conclusions were ignored then because of the difficulty of substantiating their cost estimates at so early a date. But now a year had elapsed, the 880's design was frozen, and components had been ordered preparatory to starting up the production line. So the cost of the aircraft could be figured with precision; it was an amalgam of money that *had* been spent on research and development and money that *would* be spent on materials, fabrication, and assembly. Usually about 70 percent of the material costs of an aircraft is represented by items bought from outside suppliers—the engines, pods, stabilizers, ailerons, rudders, landing gear, autopilots, instruments, and so on—with only 30 percent of the total material costs being allocated to the airframe manufacturer himself. The 880 ratios followed this general pattern. But when an engineer in Convair's purchasing division began totaling up the various subcontracted components, he came to a startling conclusion: outlays for the vendor-supplied components of each 880 totaled more than the plane was being sold for (average price: $4,250,000). He took his figures up the line, pointing out that when research and development costs of the aircraft (they totaled some $75 million) were added in, along with the 25 to 30 percent of the material costs allocated to Convair itself, nothing could be expected of the 880 program but steadily mounting losses. He recommended that Convair abandon the whole venture, even though the loss, according to his estimates, would be about $50 million.

Whether the engineer's recommendation and his supporting data ever reached New York headquarters is something of a mystery. In any event, when the engineer persisted in his analysis, Convair decided he was a crank and fired him—he was reinstated two years later after time had confirmed the accuracy of his judgments.

## Target No. 1: United Air Lines

The sales problems that confronted Convair in 1957, however, were something that couldn't be sloughed off with the firing of a critic. At the start of the 880 program in March, 1956, the potential market had been estimated at 257 planes. By June of that year Convair had raised the figure to 342, but in September it was down to 150 after an on-the-spot appraisal had let the air out of the sales estimates for European airlines. These gyrations gave substance to an industry rumor that the division undertook a thoroughgoing market analysis only *after* commitment to the 880 program, but at least one point was clear about the "final" forecast of 150. The bulk of that number, as General Joseph McNarney, Convair's president, said at the time, had to be sold before July 1, 1957, or the 880's production line could not be economically maintained. The trouble was that an understanding with Howard Hughes had kept Convair from selling the 880 to anybody but TWA and Delta for a whole year. This had already caused the loss of customers who preferred a 707 or DC-8 in the hand to an 880 12 months down the road. So in the spring of 1957, when Convair was at last free of the commitment, it had still sold no more than the 40 880's (to TWA and Delta) that started off the program. The success of that program, with only a few months to go before McNarney's July 1 deadline, now hinged on selling the remaining airlines, American and United.

Convair's first target was United, which it had listed as a prospect for 30 aircraft. For a time things seemed to be going Convair's way in its pursuit of this critical $120-million sale. Boeing, Douglas, and Convair were all in competition for the United contract, but Convair had the edge with its 880, for it was then the only true medium-to-long-range jet aircraft being offered. All Boeing could offer was essentially the long-range 707, too big and, for its seating capacity, 50,000 pounds too heavy to suit United. The size could be reduced, of course, and some of the weight chopped out, but not 50,000 pounds unless Pratt & Whitney could substantially lighten the engines the JT3C-6s used on the 707 aircraft. With Pratt & Whitney unwilling to make this effort, United's board decided in favor of the 880 on September 27, 1957, subject to a final going-over by United's engineers.

Soon thereafter, United's President William Patterson called General Dynamics' Executive Vice-President Earl Johnson, whom Pace had put in overall charge of the jet program, out of a board meeting to tell him Convair was "in." But perhaps the most consequential call was one Pratt & Whitney's Chairman H. Mansfield "Jack" Horner then made on Patterson himself. Spurred on by Boeing, Horner had been galvanized into action, and now he wanted to know whether something couldn't be done about getting Boeing back in the competition, if Pratt & Whitney could come up with a lighter engine. Patterson referred him to United's engineers, who made very encouraging noises. They themselves had been pushing for Pratt & Whitney for just that. Both Boeing and Pratt & Whitney then went into a crash program, the former to scale down the 707.

Within a few weeks Boeing had come up with a new medium-range aircraft—the 720—45,000 pounds lighter than the 707. United then invited Boeing and Convair to cut their prices and both did, though Convair refused to cut below what Pace recently described as the "bare minimum." In November, United's chief engineer John Herlihy compared Convair's 880 and Boeing's 720 and then strongly recommended the latter. His reasoning: the commercial performance of the GE engine was an unknown quantity, while "we had the Pratt & Whitney engines in our other jets and wanted to regularize our engines if we could"; moreover, the narrower fuselage of the Convair 880 permitted only five-abreast seating, a shortcoming United had vigorously protested back in 1956 when Convair had first solicited its opinion of the 880 design; the Boeing 720, on the other hand, was wide enough for six-abreast seating, a difference of as many as 25 passengers at full load in the tourist section of a combination first-class–tourist airliner. This meant, in Herlihy's view, that the 720 with its lower operating costs per passenger-mile was a better buy than the 880 with a $200,000 cheaper price tag. On November 28, 1957, United's board approved the purchase of 11 Boeing 720s with options for 18 more.

## "Merely a Modification"

The loss of United meant a sharp reduction on the market potential of the 880, dropping it from 110 to 80 planes. Worse than this, Convair had a powerful new competitor in what had been its private preserve, the medium-range field. That competitor was now going to make it tough for Convair to sign up American Airlines just at the time when Convair expected to sell the airline 30 planes, nearly half of the 880's dwindling market potential. Discussions with American had been going on for some months, though pressure had naturally increased after United chose the Boeing 720 in November. But in January, 1958, American notified Johnson, who was in overall charge of the negotiations, that it too was going to pass up the 880 for 25 720s.

In February, however, Convair was able to reopen discussions with American on the basis of a revolutionary new engine General Electric had just developed. Called a turbo fan-jet, it required 10 to 15 percent less fuel than a conventional jet to do the same job (under flight conditions) and provided 40 percent more power on takeoff. The aircraft that Convair intended to use with these new engines, later designated the 990, was billed as "merely a modification" of the 880. It was a modification to end all modifications. The 990 had a bigger wing area than the 880 and a fuselage 10½ feet longer; weighed over 50,000 pounds more; required an enlarged empennage, a beefed-up landing gear, greater fuel capacity, and stronger structural members; and was supposed to go 20 mph faster.

Many of these changes were imposed by American's hard-bargaining C. R. Smith, whose talent for getting what he wanted out of an airframe manufacturer was already visible in the DC-7. But Smith hadn't stopped with just designing the 990; he designed the contract too, using all the leverage Convair's plight afforded him. In it he demanded that Convair guarantee a low noise level for the plane, finance the 990's inventory of spare parts until American actually used them, and accept, for American's $25-million down payment, 25 DC-7's that had been in service on American's routes. The DC-7 was then widely regarded as an uneconomical airplane, 12 percent less efficient to operate than the DC-6, and, as Convair discovered, it could not be sold for even $500,000 in the open market. When General Dynamics reluctantly accepted this down payment, worth only half its face value, American signed up for 25 990s with an option for 25 more.

## "We Had to Go Ahead"

Looking back, director Alvord recently commented on the whole affair. "Earl Johnson brought back a contract written to American specifications with an American delivery date, but the plane was not even on paper. It was designed by American and sold to them at a fixed price. There was not even any competitive pricing." What is more, Alvord says, "the 990 was signed, sealed, and delivered without board approval. It was just a *fait accompli*. An announcement was made to the board that there would be a slight modification of the 880." Pace himself believed at the time that the 990 was only a slight modification. He now says, "If we had known at the outset that major changes would be needed, deeper consideration would have been given it."

The decision to go ahead on the 990 was an important turning point in the fortunes of Convair and of General Dynamics itself. The reasoning behind it has been stated by Pace: "When the Boeing 720 took away our sale to United, we found ourselves in competition with a plane just as good as ours. This is just what we wanted to avoid. The 880 seemed doomed. We had to go ahead with the 990 or get out of the jet business. American had not bought any medium-range jets . . . . When the fan engine was developed, they told us, 'We will buy your plane if you produce a plane like the 990.' It was absolutely vital for us to follow American's wishes. We had to have another major transcontinental carrier. I thought I was taking less of a gamble than I did entering the 880 program."

But what this amounted to was that General Dynamics had now committed itself to a double-or-nothing policy, gambling that the success of the 990 (beginning with the American sale) would make up for the failures of the 880. The nature of this gamble is worth specifying, in view of the fiasco that eventuated:

The plane had been sold at a price of approximately $4,700,000. Yet nobody knew how much it would cost because its costs were figured on those of the 880, which were still on the rise and unpredictable.

The number of planes Convair must sell to put its jet-transport program in the black had gone up sharply. The break-even point on the 880 had been 68 planes at the start (March, 1956), a figure that by 1958 should have seemed impossible of fulfillment. Nothing but dribs and drabs of sales to lesser airlines could be expected of the 880, for the "majors" (TWA, United, and American) had already been sold or refused to buy. Convair's commitment to the 990, which had a break-even point of its own, meant the division must sell 200 of the 880s and 990s to keep out of the red.

The success of the 990 depended largely on its being the sole plane on the market with a fan-jet engine. When it built the plane around the GE engine, Convair was confident that Pratt & Whitney would not make a fan jet. Barred from making a *rear* fan jet—GE's licensing agreement prevented this—Pratt & Whitney simply built a *front* fan engine. Boeing used this for the 720B, which took away a good deal of the 990's potential market.

The 990 was built without a prototype, or advanced model. General Dynamics had "lucked out," to use President Earl Johnson's phrase, on the 880 without testing a prototype. So now the company was again going to gamble that it could take a plane directly from the drawing board into production without any major hitches. Said Rhoades MacBride, by way of fuller explanation: "Our time for debugging the 990 was severely compressed because we wanted to take advantage of being first with the fan-jet engine. If we had built a prototype and flown it, we would have minimized our advantage in having the fan engine before Pratt & Whitney had it. We realized that if everything went right, we would be way ahead. If the 990 didn't fly as stated, we would be in terrific trouble."

## "Our Basic Mistake"

Yet if ever a plane needed a prototype and plenty of time for testing, it was the 990. As Earl Johnson himself conceded recently: "Our basic mistake in judgment was that we did not produce a prototype to fly to virtual perfection. From a management standpoint we should have said, 'If you haven't the time to build a proto-type, then you shouldn't get into the program.'" The 990 was an extremely fast aircraft, with short-field characteristics and a brand-new engine. The decision to go it without a prototype meant that Convair had committed itself to attaining the very high speed demanded by C. R. Smith—635 mph—the first crack out of the box. As it turned out, a lag of only six minutes in the 990's flying time on a trans-continental run of 2,500 miles was to result in C. R. Smith's canceling his contract because American wouldn't be able to bill the 990 as the "fastest airliner in the world."

## "The Furnace Treatment"

Just before Convair undertook the 990 program, General McNarney retired and the division got a new president, hard-driving John Naish. Naish's succession clearly indicated that Convair was still an empire within General Dynamics' em-pire and would likely remain so. Pace had wanted the Convair job for Earl Johnson, the old Army buddy he'd made his No. 2 man. McNarney wanted Naish; McNarney got Naish. And the new Convair chief soon made plain his con-fidence he could handle anything that came along—if left strictly alone. As he said at the time: "The company has a great many people who like to solve their own problems. It believes in the furnace treatment—you throw people in the fire and you can separate the good metal from the dross very quickly."

Naish had already got a taste of the furnace treatment at Convair, for troubles were piling up on all sides. Total orders for the 990 were only 32, while those for the 880 were still stuck at 44. Overhead on the jet venture had risen as produc-tion of the Convair-made F-106 dwindled and the Atlas program, which also shared the San Diego facilities, had had to be moved to another plant on orders from the Pentagon. But these were just first-degree burns in comparison to the furnace treatment Convair's new head was about to get from Howard Hughes over the 880.

Hughes's vagaries had already caused Convair plenty of lost sales and missed opportunities. When the 880 got to the production stage, the Hughes group—TWA engineers and executives—had quietly set up shop in an abandoned lum-beryard near Convair's San Diego headquarters and for a time Hughes caused more mystification than trouble. As 1959 wore on, however, it became increas-ingly difficult to get Hughes to commit himself on the final configuration (styling and arrangements) of his 880s, making it certain that overtime would have to be used to meet the tightly scheduled delivery dates of the 990s—they'd been prom-ised to American for the spring of 1961—if their dates could be met at all. As a matter of fact, in September (1959) Sales Vice-President Zevely was already noti-fying the airlines that the 990 would be late.

Convair let more precious months slip by trying to humor Hughes before it came to a shattering conclusion: all his stalling on the final configuration of his 880s had its roots in the fact that he hadn't the money to pay for them on delivery.

Convair chose to pull his 880s off the line and put them out on the field. What made this decision so fantastic was that 13 of the planes were in different stages of completion. Now the economics of an aircraft production line are geared to "a learning curve," which simply means that labor costs go down as each production-line worker becomes familiar with his particular phase of putting the plane together. On the first 880 the learning curve was at its peak with labor costs of roughly $500,000; on the fortieth or fiftieth plane labor costs were designed to drop below $200,000. Thus removing Hughes's 13 880s from the line in *different stages* of completion meant that the learning curve for them would have to be begun again at the top—to the cost of Convair, not of Hughes.

## "It's Not a Baby Anymore"

This disastrous decision was made by Jack Naish, with an OK from Frank Pace and Earl Johnson. But even then New York was far from on top of the situation. Pace maintains that he never knew the 880 was in serious trouble until after the Hughes decision: "We knew we had problems, but there were no major difficulties as far as we knew. The information that came to us fiscally, in a routine fashion, through Naish and substantiated by Naish, would not have led us to believe the extent of the losses that were occurring." Earl Johnson is not even sure just when he himself became alarmed over the jet program. "It's difficult to answer that. It's like living with a child—when do you notice it's not a baby anymore?"

The sad truth was simply that General Dynamics was still being run as a holding company with no real control from the top. Its headquarters staff had been kept at 200, and this, in Pace's view, "automatically recognizes that it is impossible to police the operation of the divisions." But even if there had been a will, the means of policing seem slender indeed. Pace had established no reporting system that could tell him quickly when a division was in trouble; the key figures were buried in pages of divisional operating statements. General Dynamics' Financial Vice-President Richard Knight is still overhauling the system of auditing the divisional books so as to prevent any doctoring of the figures to make a divisional president look good. In short, millions of dollars of publicly owned money could be on its way down the drain at Convair before New York was aware of it.

In a letter of May 10, 1960, addressed to General Dynamics' stockholders, Pace reported jet-transport charges of $91 million (as of March 31, 1960) but added "[We] have every reason to believe [the program] will be one of our most successful ventures." By mid-August, however, Pace's springtime optimism began to show the signs of an early frost. It will be remembered that from the very beginning the 880 had been grossly underpriced in relation to its material costs; now Convair had virtually given up trying to keep those heavy costs within the budgeted amounts. For almost a year San Diego had been abuzz with rumor that losses on the 880, "the sweet bird of our economy" as local citizens called the 880, might reach $150 million. Some 880 components had overrun their original estimates by as much as 300 percent.

Four months later (January, 1961) Hughes got his financing and Convair was confronted with the problem of completing his aircraft. And some problem it was. Since no two planes were in exactly the same stage of completion, they couldn't be put back on the production line. They had to be hand-finished on the field, at costs many times those prevailing on the line. Moreover, engineering changes had to be made—some Convair's and some Hughes's.

## A $40-Million Discovery

By February of 1961, General Dynamics was beginning to reap the economic consequences of the disastrous Hughes decision. New York "discovered" that Convair had not only failed to write off all jet losses the previous September but had incurred additional ones. These, amounting to $40 million, spelled the end for Jack Naish and for August Esenwein, the executive vice-president Pace had put under Naish to try and control costs. "I felt," said Pace recently, "that if I couldn't get more accurate judgments from Naish than I had gotten, he ought to go." Then he added, "Whether these problems were passed on and not properly interpreted by Esenwein and Naish, I can't tell. There are conflicting points of view now that we go back into the problem. But we in New York didn't know the magnitude of the problem."

Regardless of whether New York knew then or not, the whole business community was shortly to learn how profound was Convair's trouble. The risky decision to build the 990 without a prototype began to bear some even more expensive fruit. Seventeen of American's 25 990s had to be delivered during 1961, the first one in March. A flight test of this particular airplane in late January, 1961, four months later than the date scheduled in a previous announcement of Pace's, disclosed wing flutter and other problems that required rebuilding the landing flaps, the leading edge of the wings, and the outboard pylons. These were not too difficult to correct from an engineering point of view, but as General Dynamics' vice-president sadly remarked, "If you get into production with a plane whose design has to be changed, the magnitude of the troubles you then encounter becomes exponential." Moreover, these corrections now had to be made on overtime because of the tight delivery schedule to American. Ultimately this was to burden General Dynamics with an additional $116-million jet write-off.

The burning question, of course, is why New York *didn't* know the magnitude of the problem. Naish maintains he leaned over backward, because of his initial opposition to the jet program, to clear important decisions with either Johnson or Pace. Last fall a member of General Dynamics' executive committee, still puzzling over why New York had been so much in the dark for so long, pressed Pace on the point. He wanted to know why, even if Naish's information had been suspect, Convair's controller hadn't told Pace of the losses, or why he hadn't learned of them from MacBride, whom Pace had sent out early in 1961 to investigate, or from Earl Johnson, whom Pace had given overall responsibility for the jet program and sent to Convair in late 1958 and early 1959 when the division was plainly in trouble. Pace, at a loss to explain, wondered whether he ought to resign.

No, said the director, and Pace needn't make any apologies. After all, he wasn't trained as a businessman. He (the director) made no apologies for not being able to walk into an operating room and perform like a surgeon. So Pace shouldn't feel badly about not being trained as a businessman.

## The Wages of Sin

Unhappily for General Dynamics, the departures of Naish and Esenwein did little to lighten the corporation's load of trouble. Nor was Rhoades MacBride, General Dynamics' No. 3 man whom Pace put in as acting president of Convair, able to bring the division under control (after 10 months he too was to be washed out of office). There had simply been too many sins of commission and omission to be cured by chopping off heads in San Diego.

General Dynamics ran into trouble with American over the 990. The gamble, mentioned earlier, that Convair's engineers could guess the jet power needed to meet the speed and fuel requirements in the American contract, had failed. In addition, the 990 was already six months late, so in September, 1961, Smith canceled his order. Now the General Dynamics board was confronted by two choices, both bleak. It could turn back the uneconomical DC-7s Smith had induced them to accept in lieu of a $25-million down payment, then with the $25-million cash reimbursement as a cushion, cut the price of the 990 and try to sell it to other carriers; or it could try to get a new contract from Smith. A few audacious directors, including Crown, were for trying choice No. 1, but the opinion of the majority, as epitomized by one member of the board was: "Now let's not get C. R. mad. Earl Johnson knows him. Let's go and appeal to him."

The upshot was that Pace, Johnson, and Henry Crown [director] paid a call on Smith. There Colonel Crown related a little story about his having let a construction company off the hook even though, legally, he had had every right to hold them to a disastrous contract. Smith made no comment but when Pace and Johnson pursued the same thought he finally said: "I understand your problem, but I have stockholders. You told me, Earl, that the plane would go a certain speed." A new contract was signed with American and it was a tough one. The airline cut its order from 25 to 15 planes, with an option to take 5 more if Convair could get the speed up to 621 mph. Upwards of $300,000 was knocked off the price of each aircraft. With wind-tunnel tests completed, chances are now good that Convair will be able to meet the 621-mph specification.

But even as this article goes to press in mid-January, the end of General Dynamics' jet travail is not in sight. Howard Hughes has just canceled his order for 13 990s, an order that, surprisingly enough, Convair had accepted during the period when Hughes couldn't even pay for his 880s. SAS and Swiss Air have cut their original order from nine 990s to seven. Moreover, the market is just about saturated insofar as additional jet sales are concerned, even for a fine plane like the 880. As for the 990, it too has missed its market. To date only 66 880s and 23 990s have been sold, which puts Convair well behind Boeing's 720 sales in the medium-range market. Small wonder that when somebody suggests selling off Convair, a General Dynamics vice-president ruefully remarks: "Would $5 be too much?"

## "This Has Hurt Us in Washington"

The failure of General Dynamics' management has had some serious collateral effects. As a member of the executive committee remarked: "The public has lost confidence in us. This has hurt us in Washington. We have to inject people of stature into the management." The company recently lost out on two of the three big defense contracts (the $400-million Apollo spacecraft contract went to North American, and Boeing got the $300-million Saturn S-1 booster system). Its executive committee has also failed to find a new chief executive officer, "a man 40 years old with 100 years of experience" as John McCone remarked in turning down the job, and this has further delayed General Dynamics' much-needed reorganization.

Though the great losses are now a matter of history, the subject of what went wrong with the company will no doubt be discussed for as long as there is a General Dynamics. "It's a grave question in my mind," said one of the company's senior vice-presidents," as to whether General Dynamics had the right to risk this kind of money belonging to the stockholders for the potential profit you could get out of it. All management has to take a certain risk for big gains. But I don't think it's right to risk so much for so small a gain."

There are, however, larger questions of management's responsibility for the well-being of the corporation. That responsibility, in the jet age, is to keep management techniques developing at the same pace as the technologies they must control.

## Question

What should Frank Pace have done to get better control at General Dynamics?

# PART 6

## Other Perspectives on Multi-Level Strategy

# CHAPTER 24

## Strategic Management of Multinational Enterprises

### The Total Task of Managing

To think sharply about a complex subject like managing, we usually divide the subject into parts for separate analysis. Thus, in this book we have shifted our focus successively from selecting strategy to formulating strategy programs, on to designing organization, and finally to guiding execution. This separate treatment helps in analysis, but also detracts from sensing the interconnections involved and the complexity of the total task of managing. Central managers necessarily give much attention to achieving a balance of the various actions they sponsor. They must build their company into an integrated whole.

In concluding, then, we want to put the parts back together again. We will do this in two ways: first, by reviewing the overall task of managing a multinational company; and second, by discussing the social role of business managers.

### Attraction of Multinational Operations

"Go abroad, young man!" is the modern paraphrase of Horace Greeley's guide to opportunity. Companies, too, seek growth possibilities in foreign markets.

For years most U.S. firms were preoccupied with the vast free-trade area within American boundaries. In terms of time and communication, Los Angeles was then much further from Chicago than Paris or Tokyo is today. But, as national markets became more competitive, exports took on added attractions. Also, oil, copper, steel, and other industries needed large supplies of raw materials from abroad. Those pressures led to substantial exports and imports.

Then, as foreign markets grew and nationalistic controls hampered trade, business moved to the next and current phase of fully integrated operations—both manufacturing and selling—in offshore locations. For example, over one-third of both the sales and net income of Ford, IBM, Colgate-Palmolive, H. J. Heinz, and Pfizer are generated outside the United States. Many other firms are also multinational in scope.

Such integrated operations abroad are growing rapidly, both for U.S. firms and for firms based in other countries. They create worldwide competition, with resources and expertise seeking opportunities in a highly adaptable fashion that is not confined to a country of origin. Most multinational companies start from a well-established domestic operation, but seek to optimize both the source and the allocation of resources on a worldwide basis. They pose new challenges to our ability to manage.

This chapter deals with the *management* of companies that conduct manufacturing, selling, and related activities in several different countries. We will focus here on the issues that are particularly significant to multinational enterprises. Effective management of local operating units is assumed.

## Elements of Multinational Strategy

Multinational operation requires careful inclusion of the international nature of the business in the overall strategy. Important issues in formulating multinational strategy are the differential advantage to be obtained, the selection of countries with the greatest long-run growth potential, the balancing of risks, and the timing of expansion.

### Differential Advantage Sought

A firm embarking on a multinational course needs synergistic advantage to offset the inherent costs of operating in more than one culture. Many of the policy, organization, and control decisions that a firm adopts tie back to the fundamental question of "why we think we can do it better" than a local national company.

Important among possible rationales for operating abroad are the following:

1. *Technical expertise.* Manufacturing companies may go abroad to make use of the research and engineering already done for domestic operations. Clearly, one of the advantages Caterpillar Tractor has in its worldwide operations is its *engineering design* of heavy earth-moving equipment. *Processing expertise* is more likely a distinctive advantage for chemical and engineering companies. In some instances, such as pharmaceuticals, either the products or the processes are protected by worldwide patents, although even here the progressive updating of technology may be fully as important as the legal protection.

2. *Access to markets.* A worldwide company itself may provide an attractive market. Thus, "Nestlé uses so much chocolate in its numerous plants that it can provide an assured market for a large supply of raw material—cocoa beans." Or the company may have a widespread marketing organization and be able to dispose of much larger quantities than could any company in the country of origin; for example, Dole has a great advantage in disposing of Philippine pineapples. Or perhaps a company has greater access to markets simply because of its superior marketing—a significant factor in Sears' success in Latin America.

3. *Capital.* Especially in developing countries, the capital resources of a multinational company contribute to its relative strength. In Taiwan, the ability to make large investments (coupled with technical expertise) has aided companies making everything from fertilizer to radios.

4. *Managerial skill.* Hard to determine and often overrated, the managerial skills provided by a multinational company often provide it with a distinctive advantage. Philips' Gloeilampenfabrieken, the giant Netherlands electronics manufacturer, obviously owes part of its success to managerial ability; and the 57 varieties of H. J. Heinz are world famous for a similar reason. Currently, business analysts are wondering whether the Japanese management style will produce unusual results in foreign settings.

If a company bases its international strategy on one or a combination of the factors just discussed, it must be sure that it does in fact have an advantage that is both relevant and continuing. For example, mass marketing techniques that are geared to suburban shopping centers can cause disaster in foreign countries. And production processes based on high labor cost are not necessarily optimum in countries with a large labor supply. Similarly, some of the "know-how" advantages are fleeting: local competitors will soon catch up. So if a long-run strategy rests upon a technological superiority, the multinational company must be reasonably confident that it can maintain its lead.

Defense rather than offense is sometimes the prime mover in multinational strategy. For years, a company making, say, radios or sewing machines may have exported to a South American or an African country. Then, local production or low-cost Japanese competition makes serious inroads. In this new environment, the company may have to choose between either establishing its own foreign plant or giving up a large segment of the market. But even if the strategy is initiated for defensive reasons, the company should have a clear advantage by which it hopes to keep a distinctive niche in each of the countries in which it operates.

## Countries Attractive for Growth

Building a strong subsidiary in a country often takes years, and to obtain a significant industry position after other companies are entrenched is costly. Consequently, the multinational company needs some strategy to identify the kinds of countries that offer the greatest long-run potential. One metal container company, for instance, is setting up plants in developing countries—even though it may merely make bottle caps initially—in order to be established when the countries' real growth occurs. Other firms operate only where the per capita purchasing power is high. Less attractive countries may be identified by strategy as well. One rubber company, for instance, will have nothing to do with countries affiliated with the Soviet bloc.

A useful approach to identifying countries that are attractive for growth is the following careful appraisal:

1. Estimate the potential demand for the major services the company expects to provide. This will be tied to industrial and economic development, living conditions, natural resources, population, education, consumption attitudes, and other social and economic influences.
2. Assess the importance in each country of the distinctive strengths of the company. These strengths will include the differential advantages the company hopes to exploit. Also, weigh the strengths of prospective competitors and the likely responses of other key actors.
3. Predict the general environment and its associated risk. Important factors to consider in this connection are prospects for:
   - controls on foreign exchange
   - inflation
   - import and export restrictions
   - legislation against foreigners
   - expropriation and nationalization
   - onerous taxation
   - political upheaval
   - war
   - deterioration of financial, utility, and other services.

Analysis of this sort led a leading manufacturer of control equipment to concentrate its expansion in Western Europe, with secondary attention to Japan. All other parts of the world are served by exports from the United States or Europe. On the other hand, a large pharmaceutical manufacturer anticipates increasing pressure to manufacture at least the leading drugs locally. Consequently, it is setting up a large number of small local plants where much of the final fabrication and packaging is done. The company hopes that this localized activity will give it an edge in the importation of new and complex drugs (which carry wide gross profit margins) from the home country.

## Building a Balanced Portfolio

A multinational firm must watch its risk and cash flow balance, as explained in Chapter 15. Some European companies, for example, are entering the U.S. market as a hedge against communist takeover of their government. At the same time, U.S. pharmaceutical firms are expanding in Europe partly because of the threats of even more U.S. government regulation of medical affairs. Large Japanese firms, which must import most of their raw materials, are clearly seeking several different sources as a protection against political disruption in any supplying country.

Similarly, the demands on scarce resources require an overall balance. A well-known advertising agency, for instance, announced that it was entering the international arena but soon ran out of experienced executives to send abroad. Consequently, it is confining its growth to northern Europe and Brazil. Capital also is a frequent constraint. Even large companies may be unable to finance vigorous growth in several countries simultaneously. Commitments already started in Australia may prevent a strong push into Japan. So the growth strategy must be kept in balance.

## Timing of Expansion

Proper timing is also critical. Five years often elapse between a decision to manufacture in a given country and the efficient operation of a new plant. Acquiring government permits and building sites, engineering design, building construction, importing specialized equipment, hiring and training workers, establishing dependable sources of materials, overcoming start-up difficulties, and shaping a viable social structure all take time. For this reason, many U.S. companies entered the European Common Market early, before trade barriers had been significantly reduced. Not all of these plants proved to be wise investments, but some companies built a strong position because they were ready to produce quality goods when the market opened up.

Multinational service organizations face a similar question of when to enter additional countries. Thus, for years all but two U.S. banks relied on "correspondents" for most of their foreign activities. Then, the growth of the Eurodollar market precipitated a great scramble for offices at least in London. In this instance, as with advertising agencies, multinational service organizations have delayed expansion until worldwide marketing and manufacturing organizations were well established. Industrial engineering and public accounting firms, on the other hand, have built strong positions by being the vanguard of economic development.

Political instability strongly affects timing strategy. Indonesia presents a classic problem of when multinational companies should enter a strife-torn area. Rich in human and natural resources, yet needing outside capital and expertise, Indonesia attracts investments of oil and other multinational companies. Nevertheless, serious losses have been incurred by companies that have entered the area under political regimes that were later overthrown. Comparable political difficulties have arisen in Central Africa. Here, companies anxious to get a foothold in the large potential market have often discovered that their early association with one political regime becomes a handicap at a later time.

In summary, recurring issues in multinational strategy include what services to perform, in which countries, with what balance, and at what time. Specific situations pose an array of additional angles, but these four issues give a sense of central management's strategy problems.

## Multicountry Versus Global Strategy

A second critical issue, after a corporation becomes committed to international expansion for the reasons just outlined, is how activities in the various countries will be fitted together. Although there are many variations, two basic designs illustrate the strategic choices. (1) A fully integrated company, similar to the parent, can be set up in each country. Thus, Hilton International has a series of comparable but self-contained hotels in most of the major countries of the world. Or, (2) the world can be considered a single arena with different functions—R & D, material supply, production, etc.—each performed in those countries which are especially suited to that function. For instance, large oil corporations are often run as such a global business-unit.

Historically, almost all multinational corporations grow through a succession of expansion steps. D.C. Shanks cites a specialty coatings manufacturer that grew from a domestic firm to a multicountry corporation in 25 years. It began exporting its products in 1955, licensed producers in Europe in 1960, developed overseas sales agency agreements in the mid-1960s, and jointly ventured with the Saudis in 1970. By 1975, the firm had established blending and packaging facilities in four South American countries, and eight years later it had several fully self-contained businesses around the world. This typical development path is shown in Figure 24–1.[1]

As a domestic firm makes thrusts into foreign countries, it soon faces the strategic choice of either building several self-contained localized businesses or running local activities as functional departments in a large global operation. Key differences in these two approaches are shown in Figure 24–2. This is such a crucial choice in today's worldwide competition that we should look more closely at how each strategy affects the resolution of sensitive international management issues. Such issues include standardization of products, regional specialization of production, transfer prices, and local participation in ownership.

## Standardization of Products

A multicountry strategy allows variation of products to suit local needs. Unilever, for example, permits its operating companies to adapt its soap and food products to the particular tastes and needs of the countries in which they are operating. This flexibility permits local units to stress, say, margarine versus cooking oils in accordance with national dietary habits.

Equipment manufacturers find standardization among countries difficult to achieve. A U.S. food machinery manufacturer, for example, had to change all its dimensions from English to metric measurement. To simplify shop operations, it also had to modify the specifications slightly. Electric motors, switches, compressors, and even bolts that were purchased had to be adjusted to what was locally available. Users of the machines wanted to be able to obtain repair parts quickly, and they preferred designs with which local workers were familiar. Consequently, the policy of this company is to have separate specifications for Europe and for South America.

---

[1]"Strategic Planning for Global Competition," *Journal of Business Strategy*, Winter 1985.

**FIGURE 24-1.**
**INCREMENTAL STEPS FROM A DOMESTIC COMPANY TO A**
**MULTICOUNTRY CORPORATION**

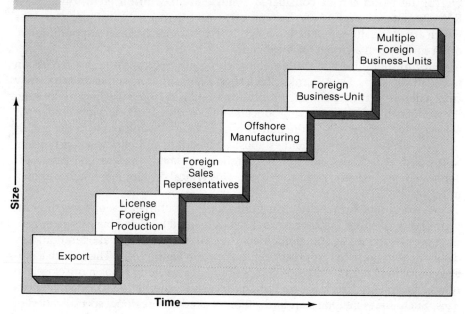

Data from "Strategic Planning for Global Competition, "*Journal of Business Strategy,* Winter 1985.

In contrast, a global strategy requires a high degree of product standardization. To assure flexibility in where products or parts are to be made, the same specifications must be used in, say, Korea, Brazil, and the United States. Thus, the parts for IBM machines are the same throughout the world. Such a policy is feasible because IBM has long stressed providing its own service to customers, which includes assuming the burden of maintaining an inventory of repair parts.

The crux of this standardization issue is whether a product can be designed so that users worldwide will like it. That day is coming, albeit slowly, for automobiles, television sets, pharmaceuticals, and even running shoes and dungarees. When such standardization is accepted, consumers will benefit from lower prices and suffer from less variety and individuality.

## Regional Specialization of Production

A global company may concentrate production of each of its products in a plant and then trade among plants. Theoretically, this permits sale of a full line in Country A, one product being made locally and the rest imported. The same situation prevails in Countries X, Y, and Z. The advantage, of course, is lower cost arising from making a large quantity of a single product in each plant instead of a variety of products only in the volume needed in the local market. In practice, the

**FIGURE 24-2.**
**TWO BASIC WAYS FOR MULTINATIONAL CORPORATIONS TO BUILD COMPETITIVE STRENGTH**

**TWO GROWTH PATTERNS FOR MULTINATIONAL CORPORATIONS**
**(Engaged in closely related lines of products or services)**

|  | *Multicountry Strategy* | *Global Strategy* |
|---|---|---|
| Corporate management structure | Federation of similar enterprises | Single integrated organization |
| Main arena of strategic action | Separate countries (and their normal trading areas) | World as a whole |
| Products | Adapted to local needs | Standardized for sale worldwide |
| Sources of products | Domestic production preferred | Any country that is attractive supplier |
| Centers of functional coordination | Semiautonomous companies in different countries | Global headquarters |

trades do not balance neatly, but the central concept of regional specialization can be utilized. The major U.S. and Japanese automobile companies, for example, are shifting toward worldwide sourcing of motors; all of a particular type of motor will be made in Mexico or Brazil for shipment to local assembly plants in many different countries.

If the parts going into products are standardized, then regional specialization of parts manufacture is possible. IBM in Europe has made considerable progress in this direction.

In practice, a regional specialization policy is difficult to apply. It relies on inexpensive and uninterrupted movement of goods across international boundaries, it assumes that product standardization and economies of scale are substantial, and it applies only when the production capabilities of the various countries are compatible. Note also that a high degree of central coordination is required.

A more subtle issue is the potential impact on producing countries. If a global corporation has the option to move its production from one country to another, its bargaining power relative to any one source is substantially increased. In a sense, national sovereignty is at stake—or so a country about to lose employment and foreign exchange will argue. Unless the global corporation is very careful in the use of its power, a backlash from potential supplying countries can develop. In contrast, a multicountry corporation that has local plants serving local needs in each country is less powerful and must be responsive to local social pressures;

however, it is in a better position to cultivate goodwill among local resource groups.

## Transfer Prices

The prices at which raw materials, parts, or finished goods are transferred from one division of a company to another is always a troublesome problem. Transfers across national boundaries create additional difficulties. For instance, a high transfer price increases the profits earned in the exporting country and decreases the profits of the importer. This in turn affects who pays more income taxes and which local managements "look good." The transfer price may also influence the choice of long-term investment, selling prices, and local allocation of effort among products.

Because a high proportion of its transactions involve imports and/or exports, a corporation with a global strategy is continually subject to local criticism. Mobil Oil Company, for instance, ships crude oil from the Middle East to a refinery in the Netherlands and then ships the refined product from the Netherlands to Sweden for sale to consumers. The managers of Mobil's affiliates in each of the three countries and the respective national governments all naturally feel that their share of the final sales income should be higher. Where the profit shows up is not a matter of indifference to them.

Virtually all companies transfer at "market price" if such a figure exists for the product at the time and the place transfer occurs. Beyond that, policies differ sharply. Some firms use a negotiated price, a figure that presumably approximates what a competitive price would be. Others use direct cost plus a markup percentage set up by headquarters. A few use total budgeted cost, including a "fair" return on local investment. In some circumstances the starting point is a budgeted selling price, from which distribution and processing costs are deducted to arrive at the value of the product received.

A guide for multinational managers among this array of possible policies is to focus on the incentive effect of transfer prices. Put the variability—the residual profits—in those units that have the greatest maneuverability to make or lose money. For divisions performing a standard function (for example, pipelines in an integrated petroleum operation), set transfer prices to cover full costs and depend on budgetary control rather than "profit margins" for incentives.

## Proportion of Local Ownership

All multinational companies are holding companies. That is, they are parent companies only, investing in local concerns that are organized in conformity with the requirements of the particular country in which they operate. A major policy question in this regard is what share, if any, of each operating company should be owned by local citizens. Billions of dollars of present and potential foreign investment are affected by this issue.

When a multicountry strategy is being pursued, the local company is predominantly concerned with domestic affairs. Its success depends on adapting to local opportunities, so sharing ownership with citizens of the country—especially if they are also managers within the company—rarely creates conflicting interests. Rather, having a minority stock position adds to a local manager's motivation. However, we believe that to preserve the parent corporation's dominant influence and power to coordinate, the corporation should hold a majority of the voting stock (or have a management contract that accomplishes the same result).

From a managerial viewpoint, an opposite conclusion holds for a corporation following a global strategy. Under a global strategy, the central managers seek to maximize profit for the total corporation, and in some circumstances this will involve cutbacks in particular countries. Or, it may seem wise not to expand in a specific country. Then, having local ownership of the unit which is being held back just complicates an already difficult decision. If the parent corporation has 100 percent ownership of the subsidiary in each country, as does IBM, then decisions can be made from a single overall perspective. Incentives for local managers can be handled as a separate problem.

The argument for sharing a minority stock ownership in local operating companies if the corporate strategy is multicountry, but urging no local ownership in local operating companies if the corporate strategy is global, needs qualification. Multinational companies face an added dimension. *National pride* and *national economic independence* enter, often with heavy emotional and political overtones. The idea that a foreigner controls even a tiny part of the national gross product or the national employment can rally popular opposition. And if a natural resource is involved and a major sector of the economy is affected—as is true of copper in Chile and Zambia and oil in Nigeria—then governments can rise and fall on the ownership issue.

Consequently, all sorts of special arrangements may be negotiated. Shares with different voting rights, options effective at a future date, long-term management contracts, and transfer of ownership at the end of a 20-year period illustrate the possibilities. A general guideline for who should eventually control each local operation, we believe, is who will make the major *continuing* contribution. "Continuing contribution" may be hard to measure, but at least it shifts the discussion from power to a constructive issue.

In conclusion, of course both corporations with a global strategy and those pursuing a multicountry strategy will need strategy programs dealing with the array of issues covered in Parts 2 and 3. The preceding discussion only adds an international flavor. It emphasizes the increased managerial complexities, as well as the potentialities, of conducting business in several different countries.

## Organizing Multinational Operations

Geographic dispersion of a multinational enterprise intensifies most of the organization problems faced by domestic firms. The variety of languages, laws, loyalties, and customs need to be adapted to; and they complicate integrated action. These complications are illustrated in three dimensions of the organization of the multinational corporations: worldwide departmentalization, decentralization versus centralization, and provision of corporate services.

## Worldwide Departmentalization

As companies increase their overseas operations, the burden of understanding the needs and opportunities in foreign countries soon exceeds the available energies of domestic managers. Also, prompt local decisions are important. Then, when marketing, production, and other activities within a single country have to be coordinated, the benefits of shifting decision making to that country become even stronger.

A common response to these pressures is to establish a separate business-unit in each country where the corporation conducts several interrelated activities. The resulting structure is sketched in Figure 24–3. This organization design is similar to the multidivision structure described in Chapter 18, except that the business-units deal with the same line of products in separate countries whereas in a multidivision corporation the business-units deal with different products in a single country.

A multicountry organization with self-contained business-units benefits from tailored strategy, adequate attention, prompt and integrated responses, improved local morale, and direct control in much the same way that decentralized business-units do in a domestic corporation. Each country's business-unit fits the local scene; and the organization supports a multicountry strategy outlined earlier.

A global strategy, however, calls for a sharply different organization. This strategy stresses managing each function on a worldwide basis so that maximum effectiveness of that function is obtained. Local adaptability is sacrificed to secure functional efficiency. An organization design suited to a global strategy is outlined in Figure 24–4.

Under the global approach, what, if anything, is done in each country is decided on functional criteria. Local coordination is downplayed, and instead there is a presumption that modern communication is sufficiently fast and reliable to permit worldwide coordination. So each global functional manager has a set of operating units located in different countries. (These units are like the "functional departments" considered in domestic business-units, except that they report to a senior functional executive instead of a general manager of a self-contained business.)

## International Decentralization vs. Centralization

Most multinational organizations are highly decentralized in some respects and centralized in others. Activities tied to consumers or operating employees—

**FIGURE 24–3.**
**ORGANIZATION DESIGN CONCEPT FOR A MULTICOUNTRY**
**CORPORATION**

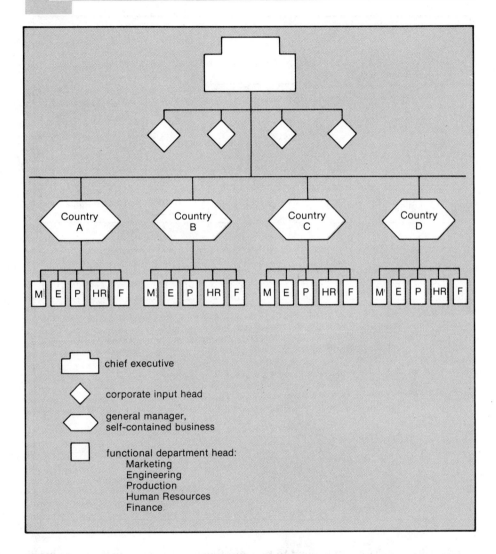

selling, granting credit, pricing, delivery, customer service, bookkeeping, warehousing, and the like—should be adapted to local conditions, and wide discretion
in such matters should be exercised by managers of national units.

The benefits of synergy, on the other hand, usually come with centralized direction. For example, process and product knowledge, a worldwide reputation for
quality, and regional specialization of production can be fully utilized when they
are centrally designed and controlled. The organizational task then is to sort out

**FIGURE 24–4.**
**ORGANIZATION DESIGN CONCEPT FOR A GLOBAL CORPORATION**

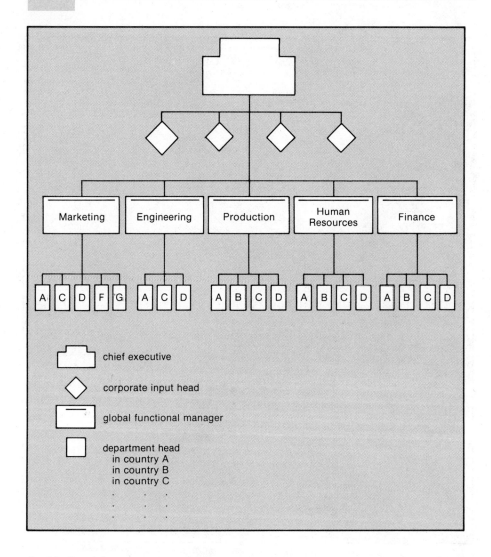

the kinds of decisions that need to be centralized from those that can be made more expeditiously in local units.

Since the aim of a multicountry strategy is to create country business-units that are adapted to local needs and opportunities, a high degree of decentralization is appropriate. In general, centralization suits only subjects on which the parent organization has expert knowledge and subjects where international synergy is strong.

In contrast, a global strategy calls for centralization of a much wider range of decisions. Here, coordination is, by design, at the top level. And the dependable performance necessary for such integration requires much more standardization. Thus, if Caterpillar Tractor Company is to make parts in Spain that will fit bulldozers assembled in Germany that will be sold in Holland, central planning is necessary. Behavioral issues may be decentralized to the respective countries, but technical matters are fitted into a centralized plan.

## Providing Corporate Services to Foreign Outposts

A perpetual problem faced by multinational management is how to obtain full advantage of the expertise that exists within the company. How can the know-how of managers in the domestic operating divisions and the wisdom of the central staff be incorporated into decisions in operating companies dispersed throughout the world?

The difficulty arises from several causes. The experts are busy with their primary assignments, and they give low priority to a request for advice from Calcutta or Copenhagen. Even when they do spare time for foreign matters, they have difficulty in communicating. Language, background, and unfamiliarity with local conditions make it hard for them to perceive the local situation and give advice that is realistic. Moreover, the local managers often lack sufficient training to sift and adapt the ideas they receive.

This difficulty is common in multicountry corporations, where the emphasis on local adaptation tends to sustain differences in cultures. Global corporations have more frequent contacts between country operating departments and central headquarters, and their centralization tends to build a lot of standardized practices. While such centralization promotes closer relationships, the need for easy communication is correspondingly greater: failures in one country affect the total system.

The most common device for overcoming this communication barrier is a *liaison staff* whose primary role is as communicator of pertinent questions to the experts and translator of answers to operating personnel. Such a staff might be attached to the chief executive of international operations or to regional managers. Unfortunately, experience with a staff of this sort is not always favorable. Both G.E. and Ford have created a large international staff, disbanded it, and then recreated it. As with all staff, there is danger that persons far removed from the scene of action will become more bureaucratic than helpful.

An alternative is to try *lowering the communications barrier* itself. This may be done by increasing opportunities for travel, personal contact, and observation. Or full-time task teams may be formed to study major problems, and cooperation may be explicitly added to the performance appraisal factors. These and other devices are intended to create a "We're all in the same family" feeling.

Few multinational companies are happy with the spotty success they have achieved in getting good advice focused on local problems. Opportunities for improvement are rife in this facet of organization. Again, multinational coordination has its particular difficulties and intensities, but it is basically the same kind of phenomenon faced by managers of domestic firms.

## Key Personnel

Operating units in each country will have their own personnel policy suited to local needs. To realize the potential benefits of their multinational affiliation, however, key technical and executive personnel must somehow acquire the best knowledge and skills available in the total system. Capturing this benefit is crucial to a successful multinational enterprise.

## Use of Nationals as Managers

IBM follows a practice of filling all management positions in the hundred countries in which it operates with local citizens. Two ends are served by this local use of nationals (that is, citizens of the country in which the IBM unit is located): managers in each country know intimately the language and customs of their market and their workers, and nationalistic demands to give jobs to local citizens rather than foreigners are fully met.

But IBM is an exception. Virtually all companies agree that *most* local managers should be nationals, for the reasons stated. Complete adherence, however, restricts promotion opportunities. Under the IBM system, the best person available *in the company as a whole* cannot be shifted into a vacancy unless that person happens to be a national of the country in which the vacancy occurs.

An alternative is to give nationals preference, but when foreigners are clearly better qualified, to place them in the positions. Still another variation used by one large oil company that wishes to "internationalize" its general managers is a clearly stated policy that no nationals will be appointed general managers in any country until they (1) serve a tour of duty in a foreign country and (2) agree to accept a transfer at a later date out of their native land. Because this guide is consistently followed, executives seek foreign assignments since they know this is the path of advancement, and local employees are less resistant to general managers who are foreigners because they are not regarded as obstacles to advancement of local people.

A final alternative is maximum use of nationals *except* in the top *financial* position; the presumption is that a nonnational in this job will be freer of local loyalties and more objective in appraising operating results.

## Developing Multinational Managers

If nationals are to fill most, if not all, of the key positions in each country, the need for manager training is obvious. In the newer countries especially, competent and dependable managers are very scarce. And a core of senior executives qualified to move from one country to another, or to top staff jobs, needs even broader training.

The special requirements for a multinational manager include (1) knowledge of the local language; (2) sensitivity and adaptability to differences in culture, especially with respect to communication and motivation; (3) a background in international trade and finance and in the economic problems of the country in question; (4) a grasp of company procedures, technology, and successful practices; and (5) an unusual degree of patience and tact combined with perseverance.

The first three of these special qualifications can be developed off-the-job; the company can assist by making time available and paying the expenses of outside courses. Knowledge about the company is normally acquired on the job in a series of assignments including working in company headquarters and in key departments. Tact and perseverance, insofar as they can be consciously developed, call for personal counseling. And so a whole array of manager development techniques should be carefully combined to foster the growth of multinational managers.

## Compensation of Managers in Foreign Assignments

Both the need to supplement local management talent and the process of manager development call for assigning people outside their home country. Such working abroad complicates pay rates in two ways.

1.  Salary scales differ from country to country. For instance, using the official exchange rate, U.S. pay is about double the British pay for a similar job. So, should a Yankee working in England be paid by U.S. or British standards? And what of a Britisher in the United States? Of course, living costs, taxes, government benefits, social requirements, and the like do differ substantially, but few executives agree on the extent to which such factors offset the differences in cash salary.
2.  People living abroad want some things that they enjoyed at home but that may be costly in a foreign country. For example, Brazilians in the United States find that domestic servants must be paid what they consider executive salaries, whereas North Americans in Brazil find that frozen vegetables are exorbitant. Few managers—and their spouses— are adaptable enough to quickly give up all of the particular living comforts they are accustomed to.

One large multinational firm meets these pay pressures as follows. (1) Executives' base salaries and their retirement accumulations are tied to what the job they hold would pay in their home country. The assumption is that the executives relate their salaries to standards in their native land and they plan to retire there. (2) In addition, they receive allowances for moving, extra living and housing cost, children's education, biennial trips home, and—if the location is unpleasant—"hardship."

This arrangement provides a consistent and "fair" pay in terms of a person's home base. However, two individuals from different countries might receive quite different total compensation for the same job, and this can become a source of irritation. (Because of this, Americans' base salaries may be paid partly in local currency and partly in dollars in the U.S., so that their local scale of living will not differ conspicuously from that of their peers.) Also, if allowances are too liberal, the managers have trouble readjusting when they return home and receive only their base pay.

Whatever the particular system of allowances, clearly a manager away from home is a high-priced person. As international assignments become recognized as valuable steps on the way to the top, instead of an inconvenient way to save a few dollars, perhaps the premium paid to our mobile managers can be reduced.

## Controlling Multinational Activities

Distance and diversity of operating conditions also create problems of control within a multinational enterprise. The following three dimensions of these control problems illustrate the special burden a multinational firm undertakes in addition to the normal control tasks in each of the operating units.

## Understanding the Concepts of Constructive Control

For cultural reasons, the control process is poorly understood in many countries. Often the significance of completing work on time and of maintaining quality is not accepted. Local life proceeds more casually; so when western control standards are imposed, the action appears to local workers as unwarranted and capricious.

Similarly, accounting records in many countries are scanty, inaccurate, and often manipulated to reduce taxes. Naturally, managers do not look to such records as aids to prompt coordination of activities.

In some cultures, business relationships are closely entwined with personal friendship, kinship, reciprocal favors, and *simpático* feelings. In such situations objective appraisal and tough corrective action are too irritating to be tolerated.

A first step, then, for a multinational manager in securing control is to win acceptance of the concept. Managers in operating units must understand that survival in world business requires realistic objectives, performance standards based on these objectives, regular measurement of performance, prompt feedback of control data to people who can undertake corrective action, overall evaluation, updating of targets, and correlation of incentives with results. Without acceptance of this process, the best-designed control systems will achieve only moderate effects.

## Operating Controls That Encourage Optimum Performance

Every multinational firm must have dependable, understandable accounting reports from each country. Due to local variations in bookkeeping practice, the establishment of a worldwide accounting system is no small task. But once in place, it does permit the introduction of annual and five-year budgets, measurement of growth in sales and profits, and other usual financial control devices.

Essential as such financial controls are, reliance on financial reports alone is especially dangerous in a multinational business. The opportunities and the difficulties in each country make necessary more complete and sensitive yardsticks.

Steering controls are especially needed, and in addition to financial reports, items such as market share, government relations, quality maintenance, customer service, cultivation of new customers, physical productivity, employee training and turnover, plant maintenance, innovation and modernization, protection of assets from inflation, and cooperation with other units of the company are all control measurements that the multinational headquarters should watch in each country.

Frequent evaluation is inappropriate. Milestone reviews plus semiannual reviews of continuing operations serve most multinational companies better than monthly reporting, which is likely to become routine.

## Periodic Product-Stream Evaluation

The controls just described help keep each operating unit "on course," but they do not check the continuing desirability of the course itself from the viewpoint of the total corporation. This broader evaluation is difficult because most multinational firms sell the same product in different countries, ship materials or parts from one country to another, and in other ways seek synergistic benefits from joint activities. Separate controls in each country do not tell whether the desired overall benefits are being obtained.

Consequently, special studies that consolidate the incomes, costs, and investment from all countries dealing with a *product line* are needed. Since several lines are typically handled, at least when all countries are considered, a lot of unscrambling of assets and joint costs may be necessary. So the analysis becomes involved, indeed too involved for routine periodic reports. Fortunately, except for global corporations facing turbulent competition, a special appraisal, say every two years, is adequate because changes in product line or production strategy can only be made in relatively long time cycles.

With an analysis of how product lines are measuring up to original plans, a reappraisal of markets, competition, technology, and other external factors is also in order. This may lead to significant shifts in company strategy, so we find ourselves completing the full management cycle of strategy, implementing plans, execution, and control—which provides the basis for a revised strategy and a new cycle.

## SUMMARY

Managers in multinational companies face a variety of issues arising from the international climate of the total operation. Balancing these issues calls for unusual skill. While company *strategy* seeks to extend strengths in one country to many other markets, it requires judicious selection of countries where these strengths will be most beneficial. Additionally, it lays out the timing of international expansion.

International business competition is changing in intensity. As communications and transportation are greatly speeding up, and Third-World countries are pushing for greater participation in international trade, competitive strategies have to be adjusted. These tensions are illustrated in the basic choice between a multicountry strategy and a global strategy. The multicountry strategy pushes for self-sufficiency and local variation in more and more locations. In contrast, a global strategy seeks to treat the entire world as a single integrated system with source and markets intermingled from a global viewpoint.

This strategic choice affects product standardization, regional specialization in production, transfer prices, and reliance on local ownership. Moreover, the corporate organization will shift from decentralization to centralization, depending on the multicountry versus global approach to world competition.

With either strategy, *staffing* with local nationals is desirable, but this creates a need for multinational training of managers. To provide such training, and in the senior levels to utilize exceptional talent, people must move across national boundaries. Whenever this is done, a prickly problem of salary and cost-of-living adjustments arises.

A multinational scope of operation increases both the need for and the difficulty of *control*. The underlying concept of constructive control has to be developed, reliable measures of tangible and intangible results must be created, and provision must be made for assessing integrated results as well as performance in each country.

Overshadowing these distinctive aspects of multinational management is the demonstration that the broad framework we have used throughout this book to analyze the central management tasks of national companies provides an equally effective means for thinking through the overall management framework of the most complex business enterprise yet conceived.

## Questions for Class Discussion

1. Does the development of satellite and other high-speed communication favor or hinder a global strategy? Explain. How about faster and cheaper transportation?

2. British banks, and to a lesser extent German and Japanese banks, are making large investments in U.S. banks—sometimes owning control. This is disturbing to some U.S. citizens. (a) Is there any more reason for us to object to foreign ownership of some of our banks than for foreign countries to object to U.S. investors (typically U.S. banks) owning control of banks in their countries? (b) Should we establish a requirement that 51 percent voting stock in each U.S. bank remain in the hands of U.S. citizens? (c) Should we establish a requirement that, say, 75 percent of the officers be U.S. citizens? (d) Would your answers to the preceding questions be the same for hotels instead of banks?

3. The Caterpillar Tractor Company of Peoria, Illinois, sells large earth-moving equipment used for construction projects worldwide. The equipment is rugged and heavy, with a variety of designs suited to different terrains and operating conditions. One factor in deciding whether to adopt a multicountry strategy *or* a global strategy is changes in foreign exchange rates—notably the value of local currencies in the world financial markets in terms of U.S. dollars. How would each of the following affect your recommendation to Caterpillar Tractor regarding a choice between multicountry or global strategy: (a) Quite stable and predictable exchange rates, rather than fluctuating rates such as we have seen in the past decade? (b) Falling and low value of the U.S. dollar relative to Swiss francs, German marks, Japanese yen, and other widely used foreign currencies?

4. Young & Rubicam, one of the leading U.S. advertising agencies, is in the process of expanding its activities worldwide. For instance, Y & R recently bought ownership control of an innovative Australian advertising agency, and it is taking steps to develop a strong presence in all countries that are economically developed. (a) Recognizing that advertising must be run in local media, use the local language, and appeal to local viewpoints, what differential advantage does a multinational advertising agency realize? (b) What kinds of policies, organization, and control will a multinational advertising agency need to provide the differential advantage you identified in your answer to (a)?

5. Explain how a matrix form of organization might be used by a multinational corporation. Consider both (a) a corporation with a multicountry strategy and (b) a corporation with a global strategy.

6. International oil companies such as Exxon, Shell, British Petroleum, and Mobil, operate crude-oil wells in many parts of the world. In these activities, they act like a global corporation. Typically, the local drilling and production of oil are run as a joint venture with either a government agency or a local company in the country involved. A common arrangement is that the parents of the joint venture each receive a percentage of the output to use or sell. While they are welcome during exploration and the early stages of development, the oil companies often face severe criticism once oil production is established. They are accused of removing the country's material wealth, affecting the local economy, and so forth. Because of such feelings, Saudi Arabia has taken over the ownership of Aramco and Nigeria has taken over foreign ownership of all crude oil production within its boundaries.

   (a) What do you recommend that oil companies (or other international companies dealing in natural resources) do to reduce or eliminate such local opposition to their activities?

   (b) Do you predict that such national fervor will become increasingly common? If so, what will happen to the world supply of raw materials?

7. One of the complications of multinational operations is the difference among countries in norms of ethical behavior and social responsibility. Both the formal standards (often expressed in law) and the strictness of their observance vary. (For example, wide differences exist with respect to bribery, tax evasion, treatment of workers, and agreements with competitors.) If you were working abroad for an England-based multinational company, which set of standards would you follow? What is the potential business impact of your ethical decisions?

8. Fieldcrest Mills, Inc., is among the better known American manufacturers of towels, blankets, sheets, and related products. Fieldcrest does excellent styling and merchandising, but the domestic market is both mature and competitive. For growth, Fieldcrest is turning to Europe. A joint venture, with a completely new $50 million towel mill, has recently been organized in Ireland; ownership is 50 percent Fieldcrest, 25 percent Bank of Ireland, and 25 percent P. J. Carroll & Company—a diversified Irish corporation. The hope for low production costs rests on modern equipment, relatively low labor rates in Ireland, and especially on Carroll Company's approach to the restless labor relations in the country. (Recently, a labor strike closed all Irish banks for nine months.) Don Carroll, board chair, states, "As a principle, we would like to see all our activities constantly raising the amount of value added, constantly increasing the real income of employees through higher productivity . . . . Our view is the *greater disclosure of information to employees* as a basis for better understanding of the subtleties of the business and of the performance which is sought from them . . . will lead to better achievement by all . . . we can build an intrinsically healthier, sounder climate and achieve a more efficient performance . . . . " Fieldcrest's distinctive input will be the application of its styling and merchandising skills to the selling of the new mill's output throughout the European

Common Market. What are the main risks for this new venture? What should Fieldcrest do to maximize its chances of success?

## CASE
### 24 Outokumpu Oy (OKO): Maintaining Finland's Position in Metals

Finland's leading metal company, Outokumpu Oy (called OKO here), must decide how it wishes to position itself in the world metal industries during the next decade. OKO has been an acknowledged leader in mining and refining technology, but currently faces severe financial constraints.

### Home Base

Finland is perhaps most widely known for its courageous fight for survival during World War II and for its ability through the diplomacy of neutrality to maintain independence ever since. Located on the Baltic Sea, with Russia on its eastern border and Norway and Sweden on its north and west, Finland serves as a buffer between the East and the West.

Geographically, Finland is larger than Great Britain or West Germany. But with a population under 5 million, it qualifies as one of the smaller of the small nations. Although about a third of Finland's length lies above the Arctic Circle, the Gulf Stream and air currents keep it warmer than other countries at the same latitude. Its major ports are open for shipping year round.

For several decades now, manufacturing has displaced the traditional forestry and agriculture industries as the leading contributor to the total economy and to employment. Incidentally, Finland's per capita GNP is higher than Japan's and Great Britain's. Companies such as OKO have played a significant role in this development.

As with many small companies, imports and exports are especially important to Finland—close to one-quarter of GNP. Raw materials are the chief imports, manufactured goods the major exports. Although the Soviet Union is the single leading country in Finland's foreign trade (20 percent of the total), at least two-thirds of exports and imports are with Western nations.

By U.S. standards, Finland has a lot of government planning and government ownership. However, compared to its immediate neighbors, it places heavy reliance on private ownership and initiative. All the leading companies are expected to be economically viable and to earn a reasonable return on invested capital.

## Synergistic Diversification

For the first 30 years of its existence, OKO was just a copper company, mining a relatively small deposit at Outokumpu. Since then, three interrelated developments have drastically changed the scope of the company.

1. OKO has greatly expanded the numbers of different metals it mines and refines. In addition to copper, its major products are zinc, nickel, cobalt, and pyrite concentrates. Other metals are often intermingled in ore bearing these major ones, with the result that OKO also produces some chrome, lead, gold, silver, cadmium, and talc. Whenever a metal ore is found in commercial quantities in Finland, OKO will mine it. Moreover, having mined this ore, OKO proceeds to refine it into base metals, with only minor exceptions.

2. For several metals, OKO has integrated forward, adding still more value to the original resource. For instance, copper is converted into tubing, bars, sheets, wire, and other forms. Much of the company's chrome now goes into its stainless steel.

3. Compared with the major ore deposits of the world, Finland's deposits are neither very large nor very rich (a high percentage of metal). Consequently, throughout its history OKO has had to give much attention to productivity. In both mining (mostly underground) and refining, the most efficient and up-to-date technology is used. Since World War II, OKO has done pioneering R & D in metal refining. So successful has this effort been that OKO is able to license some of its processes and may be hired to consult refining plants in other countries. More than anything else, OKO's "flash smelting" process has made the company world famous. Over half the world's new copper smelters are licensees of OKO. In addition, an X-ray analyzer of ore slurry is a key element in automated concentrators and is even more widely used than flash smelting. OKO's "tramp iron detector," initially designed for use on crushers, has been converted into a security device against airport hijacking.

Note that all three of these developments—different metals, forward integration, and advanced technology—have been synergistic, and they have enabled OKO to sell most of its products abroad in the face of world competition. In fact, 78 percent of OKO sales are exports.

## Recession: Impact on Financing

The diversification program just outlined enabled OKO to expand substantially in the 1960s and 1970s. In the past decade both sales and assets have grown more than fourfold. Much of this increase reflects inflation, but overall tonnage and employment did rise. The company is now divided into four operating divisions, and the relative importance of each is indicated in Table 24–1.

Unfortunately, profits have been much lower than the estimated net income that was used to justify the investment in new facilities. For example, the most recent major expansion into stainless steel is a technological success, but selling prices have dropped and this new plant is barely breaking even. During the last few years economic activity in Europe has been especially slow, and selling prices for most metals and metal products have not kept pace with rising wage and interest rates. Tables 24–2 and 24–3 show the most recent financial statements.

OKO went heavily into debt to finance its diversification. Now that profits have not risen as expected, this debt is a serious burden. In fact, the depreciation and depletion charge is less than necessary to replace capital, so the situation is even more strained than the income statement shows. (Depreciation based on replacement values would have been 220 million marks, instead of the 156 million marks used for the income statement.)

Because of this financial squeeze, the present central management has switched to a conservative investment policy during the last three years. In the OKO annual report, management says frankly, "In order to improve the financing situation, major expansion programmes will have to be shelved for the time being." Investments have been made (175 million marks last year) only to complete expansions already started and even more to improve productivity. Perhaps a clearer indication of the policy reversal is the drop in employment from a peak of over 10,000 to 9,100, a very significant action in a country where increased employment is a major social objective.

## Present Options

No one is fully satisfied with OKO's present operations. In physical terms the volume is static, profits are very small, and employment is down. So central management must weigh alternative approaches to the future. The following threefold grouping suggests several possibilities. The various thrusts can, of course, be resolved into other combinations.

### Continue the Present Strategy

This includes (a) focusing investments and R & D on improved productivity, (b) seeking to reduce the debt burden and improve the debt-to-equity ratio, (c) continuing to export products and services to the best markets currently available, and (d) deferring other expansion until metal prices and economic conditions improve and risk is reduced.

### Stress Growth from Finland's Resources

OKO's growth through diversification was based on this approach. It involves (a) finding and mining Finland's mineral resources, (b) refining these ores into

**TABLE 24-1.**
**OKO's OPERATING DIVISIONS AND MANAGEMENT**

| Division | Sales (million marks)* | Exports | Number of Employees | Management Comment on Profitability |
|---|---|---|---|---|
| Mining & Metallurgy | 615 | 85% | 5,060 | Except for cobalt (prices and profits up dramatically because of turmoil in Zaire), the profitability remains unsatisfactory due to low prices of metals. |
| Copper & Copper Alloy | 476 | 59% | 1,838 | Increased productivity has improved profitability, but a satisfactory level has not yet been reached. |
| Stainless Steel | 429 | 75% | 1,141 | Profitability remains unsatisfactory due to low price level and continuing start-up expenses. |
| Technical Export | 307 | 97% | 417 | Profitability remains favorable. However, this year was unusually high due to large deliveries of smelter equipment to Soviet Union and Republic of Korea. Preceding year sales were 175 million marks. |
| Central Management & "other" | 8 | 94% | 669 | Includes R & D, which costs 3.2 percent of sales—primarily for exploration and metallurgical research. |
| Total | 1,835 | 78% | 9,125 | |

*For quick conversion, assume that 4 Finnish marks equal 1 U.S. dollar.

**TABLE 24–2.**
**OKO INCOME STATEMENT (in million Finnish marks)\***

| | | |
|---|---:|---:|
| Gross Sales | | 1,835 |
| Adjustments | | 79 |
| Net Sales | | 1,756 |
| Expenses: | | |
| Materials and supplies | 625 | |
| Employee expense | 523 | |
| Other expenses | 321 | 1,469 |
| Operating Margin | | 287 |
| Deductions: | | |
| Depreciation | 156 | |
| Other income & expense (net) | 2 | |
| Interest | 101 | |
| Foreign exchange losses | 17 | |
| Direct taxes | 3 | 279 |
| Net Earnings for the Year | | 8 |

\*For quick conversion, assume that 4 Finnish marks equal 1 U.S. dollar.

**TABLE 24–3.**
**OKO BALANCE SHEET (in million Finnish marks)\***

| Assets | | Liabilities & Equity | | |
|---|---:|---|---:|---:|
| Cash | 52 | Current Liabilities | | 831 |
| Receivables | 533 | Long-term Debt: | | |
| Inventories | 396 | Bank loans | 634 | |
| Current assets | 981 | Loans from pension funds | 111 | |
| | | Bonds | 343 | |
| | | Other long-term debt | 231 | 1,219 |
| Fixed Assets | 1,271 | | | |
| Other assets | 178 | Reserves | | 111 |
| | | Stockholders' Equity: | | |
| | | Share capital | 283 | |
| | | Reserves | 77 | |
| | | Retained earnings | 9 | 369 |
| | 2,430 | | | 2,430 |

\*For quick conversion, assume that 4 Finnish marks equal 1 U.S. dollar.

base metals by using advanced, sophisticated technology, (c) integrating forward into metal fabrication in selected areas to increase the value added, and (d) exporting products and services to the best markets available.

The copper ore deposits now being mined will be exhausted in about 10 years, so intensive exploration will be necessary to maintain local supplies. For years local farmers and explorers have been encouraged to bring in rock samples.

The creativity of Finnish miners and engineers in taking full advantage of valuable resources has already been described. Note that under this strategy OKO's "domain" is defined by Finland's resources, not by potential world markets. Likewise, the outstanding technology has been developed primarily to improve local productivity; its salability abroad is a fortunate by-product.

### Expand Abroad

This strategy would include (a) opening sales branches (in places such as Brazil, the western U.S., South Africa, and Korea) to promote the sale of technology, (b) developing more systematically the marketing of OKO's fabricated products, perhaps through the same sales branches, (c) contracting for long-run supplies of ore or ore concentrates that can be refined in OKO's plants, and (d) looking for joint ventures with local foreign companies which can use OKO's expertise and/or products.

In exporting technologies, OKO can simply grant licenses, as it has done for its flash smelting process. Or it can *design* an entire plant. Or it can make much of the equipment in its own shops and sell that, perhaps as parts of a total plant. Of course, OKO's future ability to sell technology in any of these stages depends on its continuing development of advanced techniques suitable to conditions in users' countries.

Central management has to recognize several influences bearing on its choice of strategic thrusts. For instance, because of the country's history and strict neutrality posture, Finland is wary of becoming very dependent on materials from a single nation. Finland is so small that it does not have much power in the international arena, and it does not want to be in a position where it can be pushed around.

OKO has long been sensitive to the needs of its employees. It stresses safety and has a liberal pension plan. On several occasions it has built up inventory rather than have a layoff. In exchange, there have been relatively few work stoppages.

In such a small country the supply of engineers is naturally limited, and the number of those who speak English or other world languages is even smaller. (Finnish, like Hungarian, has Mongolian antecedents rather than Greek or Latin, and it is hard to learn. The second language in Finland is Swedish.) So there are personnel constraints, as well as financial ones, on the number of different thrusts OKO can undertake.

Relationships between OKO and the Finnish government are close. In fact, in connection with the financing of various expansion projects, different ministries have bought stock, with the result that the government now has voting control. However, government officials rely heavily on the technical judgment of company management. Thus, at present the government is going along with the conservative strategy even though it would like to see an expansion of jobs and exports. On the other hand, if company management presents a new proposal which it believes is economically viable, the government would probably make additional capital contributions.

## Question

Outline the future strategy that you recommend OKO pursue, and justify your position.

# CHAPTER 25

## Social Responsibility
## of Business Managers

Like the rising importance of global competition, the social responsibility of business managers is an irrepressible issue. Probing questions are being raised from many quarters, and as business managers become even more prominent and are seen as powerful individuals, they cannot evade public insistence that they act in a socially responsible manner. Moreover, if company strategy is the overriding guide to company action—as advocated throughout this book—then the social impact of strategy must be confronted. Accordingly, this chapter presents a concept of managers' social responsibility—a viewpoint that is both practical and constructive—followed by an application to the three levels of management: department, business-unit, and corporate.

### Acting in a Socially Responsible Manner

A business firm, like any other social institution, can endure only if it continues to contribute to the needs of society. And in our current topsy-turvy world, the actions of business firms, like all other facets of "the establishment," are being challenged. "Why should business wield so much power over the use of materials, labor, capital, and other resources?" is a typical probe. It is important, then, that both present and aspiring business managers understand how the companies they direct help meet social needs.

The concept of social responsibility is far from clear. Some idealists would like to include every reform that is socially desirable. But business executives have neither the competence nor the means to undertake improvements in prisons, churches, classrooms, and other areas remote from their normal activity. So, to give practical meaning to the idea, we need an approach to social responsibility for business managers that relates directly to actions they take in their role as managers.

A useful approach is to think of a manager as a *resource converter*. From the viewpoint of society, an enterprise justifies its existence by converting resources into desired outputs. Thus, resource inputs of labor, materials, ideas, government support, capital, and the like are converted by a firm into outputs of goods, services, employment, stimulating experiences, markets, and other things desired by those who provide the inputs. The job of managers is to design and maintain a converting mechanism that will generate continuing flows of these inputs and outputs.

An auto garage, for instance, converts labor, parts, machinery, and capital into auto repair services, jobs, rent, etc. Likewise, a poultry farmer converts chicks, feed, labor, equipment, and other resources into outputs of eggs, meat, jobs, a market for grain, and a profit on capital. Civilized society depends on a continuing flow of such conversions. And when we talk of the social responsibility of business managers, we are mainly concerned about the effectiveness and the side effects of resource conversions.

This concept of managers dealing primarily with resource conversion puts the emphasis on constructive action. Three basic elements are involved: building continuing exchange flows with resource suppliers, designing an internal conversion technology, and integrating and balancing the external and internal flows.

## Building Continuing Exchange Flows with Resource Suppliers

The relationship with each resource supplier always involves an exchange. Figure 25-1 shows these flows for five typical outside groups. For a specific company there will be a wider variety of subgroups, but the underlying concept is the same: each group of contributors provides a needed resource and receives in exchange part of the outflow of the enterprise.

Much more than money is involved. Typically, an array of conditions provides the basis for continuing cooperation. Employees, for instance, are concerned about meaningful work, stability of employment, reasonable supervision, future opportunities, and a whole array of fringe benefits in addition to their paychecks. Suppliers of materials want a continuing market, sure and prompt payment, convenient delivery times, quality standards suited to their facilities, minimum returns, and the like. Investors are concerned about uncertainty of repayment, security, negotiability of their claims, veto of major changes, and perhaps some share in management. For each resource contributor, mutual agreement about the conditions under which the exchange will continue is subject to evolution and periodic renegotiation.

Because a steady flow of resources is necessary, wise executives will

1. *predict changes* in conditions under which each resource group will be willing and able to continue its cooperation,
2. conceive and promote *revised exchange* of inputs and outputs that will be (a) attractive to the resource group and (b) viable for the enterprise,
3. start discussions of changes *early* to allow time for psychological as well as technical adjustments, and
4. assist and work with *other agencies* concerned with the changes.

Managers devote a substantial part of their efforts to negotiating, or guiding their subordinates in negotiating, these agreements covering the bases of cooperation. It is a never-ending process because in our dynamic world the needs of re-

**FIGURE 25-1.**
**ENTERPRISE = RESOURCE CONVERTER**

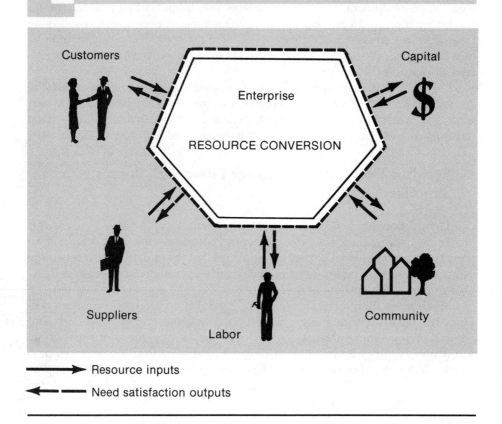

Resource inputs

Need satisfaction outputs

source suppliers shift, their power to insist on fulfilling their needs changes, and the value of their contributions to the enterprise varies. In fact, most of the widely discussed "social responsibility" issues deal with some modification of previous conditions of cooperation, such as those shown in Table 25–1.

The real core of the social responsibility of a business executive is the maintenance of resource flows on mutually acceptable terms. And this is a very difficult assignment in times of rapidly changing values and expectations, as the succession of labor disputes and energy supply crises illustrates. But note that social responsibility, at least in the view proferred here, is not something new, tacked onto an executive's job. Rather, it is reflected in the recognition of shifting social needs and the approach a manager takes in adapting to them. Thus, when we examined adjustments to environmental changes in Parts 1–3, we frequently faced questions about what is socially responsible action. The prickly issues often involved indirect "side" effects or longer run consequences, considerations that we have argued are an essential part of any wise strategic move.

> **TABLE 25-1.**
> **SOME "SOCIAL RESPONSIBILITY" ISSUES**

| Input Group | Reason Prompting a Change |
|---|---|
| Labor | "Equal opportunity" for women and minorities |
| Investors | Protection against inflation; public disclosure of information |
| Community | Environmental protection; growth in employment opportunities |
| Suppliers of materials | Predictable, long-run markets |
| Customers | "Consumerism" pressures for guarantees of quality, informative labeling |

## Designing an Internal Conversion Technology

Each enterprise, large or small, must maintain a balance between the outputs it generates and the satisfaction it has agreed to provide its suppliers of resources. For instance, promises of stable employment must be compatible with protection promised to suppliers of capital. Such ability to make ends meet depends partly on the skill of managers in devising a *conversion technology* suited to their particular company. The way the resources are converted strongly affects the outputs available. So in addition to negotiating agreements assuring the continuing availability of resources, managers must design internal systems to effectively utilize the resources.

Every enterprise has its technology for converting resources into outputs, as noted in Chapter 10. For example, a school has its teaching technology, an insurance company has its technology for policy risks, and a beauty shop has its technology for shaping unruly hair. This internal conversion technology involves much more than mechanical efficiency. The desired outputs, as already noted, include interesting jobs, low capital risks, minimum pollution of the environment, improved job opportunities for women and minorities, and a host of other features. Consequently, devising a good internal conversion technology is a very complex task.[1] This selection of an internal conversion technology is one of the key elements in each business-unit's strategy.

---

[1] In abstract symbols, the technology should meet the following conditions: With each resource contributor designated by subscripts such as $l, i, e, s, c, \ldots n$ (for labor, investors, executives, suppliers, customers, and other contributors), and

$S$  = satisfactions required by a resource contributor
$C$  = contributions by a resource contributor
$CT$ = conversion technology
$O$  = total output of satisfactions
we have

$$O = (S_1 + S_i + S_e + S_s + S_c \ldots + S_n)$$
$$O = fCT(C_1 + C_i + C_e + C_s\, C_c \ldots + C_n)$$

And as viewed by each resource contributor, $Sx > Cx$ for any x.

## Integrating and Balancing the External and Internal Flows

Important as attracting resources and designing conversion technologies may be, it is the *combination* of responding to new "needs" of resource contributors and restricting total responses to what total output permits that poses the final challenge to central management. Socially responsible managers must respond quickly enough to the ever-changing desires of resource contributors to maintain a continuing flow of needed resources, and at the same time they must keep their enterprise alive by generating the right quantity and mix of outputs to fulfill commitments. If they do not, some key resource will be withdrawn and the enterprise will collapse.

Community hospitals, to cite a not-for-profit service example, must keep their technology up to date, including both putting patient records on computers and installing sophisticated diagnostic and treatment equipment. At the same time, employees want higher wages and shorter hours. The main squeeze, however, arises from a reduction in the average number of days patients are staying in hospitals: patients want excellent service, but less of it, so hospital income is not keeping pace with improved technology and higher wages. Somehow, hospital central managers must reconcile these *combined* pressures.

Throughout this book we have explored ways in which companies can effectively cope with such a dynamic environment, partly by adjusting the exchanges of inputs and outputs with resource groups and partly by reshaping their conversion technology to generate desired outputs. A recurring theme has been anticipating pressures for change. By adjusting promptly to new conditions, a company usually increases its "output" and thereby makes a greater social contribution.

Considering a company as a resource converter uses a broad social viewpoint. We suggest that this is a better way to conceive of "the purpose of a company" than the more common cliche, "to make a profit." Obviously, every successful resource converter must make a profit in order to continue to attract capital. But this is a narrow oversimplification. To survive, a company must also provide attractive employment, be a good customer, earn the continuing support of governments and the community, and serve customers well. The task for management is to find a way to do all these things simultaneously while keeping abreast of changes in each field.

## Multi-Level Participation in Socially Responsible Action

When the social responsibility of a business is viewed as maintaining resource conversions, we quickly discover that all levels of managers are involved. Social responsibility calls for much more than lofty speeches by the CEO: department managers, business-unit managers, and corporate managers all contribute.

## Department Manager's Role

Department managers are the main actors in building ongoing relationships with resource suppliers. As explained in Part 2, most departments link a company with a specialized segment of the environment—customers, supply of labor, sources of finance, and so on. Department managers not only negotiate most of the exchange agreements, they also serve as eyes and ears for new trends, including shifts in society's values and expectations.

Some managers may be pioneers in this linkage, while others may be ultra-conservatives in adapting to social changes. Nevertheless, because they are close to company action, department managers exert a profound influence on the responsiveness of a company to shifting social needs and expectations.

Also, in forging horizontal linkages with other departments (see Figure 6–2), department managers influence the ease or difficulty that these other departments have in adjusting their respective activities to social shifts. For instance, meeting new pressures for safety features of a product typically calls for coordinated action of the engineering, production, and marketing departments, and perhaps the legal, purchasing, and human resources departments as well. In addition, if a change in the company's conversion technology will help meet social needs, probably all departments will have to modify their previous practices.

On some issues, such as moving a plant to make room for urban sprawl, inconvenience and costs are involved. Here the third linkage examined in Part 2 is involved: the department provides information and estimates to business-unit managers regarding feasibility and benefits. Company policy on social issues can be significantly shaped by departmental views and cooperation. And on matters of local interest, a department may initiate the change.

In sum, when we recognize that for a business firm social responsibility relates largely to how major activities are conducted, we see that departments become the mainsprings for constructive action. Each department works closely with one or more stakeholder groups and has a practical view of the tensions involved and what might be done to relieve them. Although a department's planning horizon is likely to be short, its opinions must be weighed because it will bear the brunt of any change.

## Role of Business-Unit Managers

In dealing with social responsibility, as in other aspects of running an effective business-unit, general managers can and should reduce their burdens by having highly competent department managers. The departments are created to interface with important segments of the environment, and they typically have more detailed knowledge of their particular segment than the general manager. The manager of the human relations department, for instance, will in general be better informed about "equal opportunity" issues than the general manager. Normally, that is where the company position on fair employment practices should originate.

It is dangerous, however, for a general manager to rely entirely on department heads. Because department heads must devote most of their energies to short-run operating problems, they have difficulty predicting long-run developments. Also, when faced with a "painful necessity" for change, they are likely to feel the pain more than the necessity. And troublesome social responsibility issues often are of this painful necessity sort: they upset the status quo. Consequently, general managers may have to set goals and priorities.

Furthermore, social pressures may come from unexpected sources; some do not even fit clearly within the purview of any department. For example, the Nestlé general manager in the United States was faced with a boycott arising from Nestlé (Europe)'s sale of a baby food product in Africa. The U.S. division neither produced nor sold the product, so none of its department managers was monitoring the controversy. Similarly, special-interest groups, like racial groups pressing U.S. banks to withdraw from South Africa, often have no other relationship with their tactical targets. So someone with a broader perspective than those assigned to departments has to foresee the shifts in social values that these protests represent.

Moreover, general managers have to deal with the thorny question of balance. Electric utility companies in the Midwest, for instance, are being pressed to reduce their prices and also to reduce discharges into the air which contribute to acid rain in the East. With present technology, these are incompatible aims, and managers of business-units must decide how much weight to give to each. We note in passing that the proponents of social reforms almost always just push for their particular cause, disregarding questions of balance with other causes and overall feasibility. Thus, the general manager of a business is thrust into the unenviable position of trying to mediate among often equally worthy aims.

Accordingly, with respect to social responsibilities, business-unit managers add an essential perspective and balance among claims competing with the views of department heads.

## Corporate Role in Social Responsibility

If business-unit managers, with the aid of their department managers, are the key people in deciding what actions are desirable to sustain the conversion of resources into desired outputs, what role in this "social responsibility" process is left for corporate managers? A quick review of Part 3 suggests three ways that corporate managers contribute to the overall result.

*First*, in allocating corporate resources, the senior managers support some units strongly and withdraw resources from other units; they (instead of a market mechanism) make quite specific decisions about who and what gets supported. Thus, within limits, they can allocate funds to business-units whose social behavior they endorse.

You or I may not agree with the way these allocations are made. For instance, a decision to close down a business or plant is rarely popular: some employees and suppliers will be hurt. But *on balance*, the gains from transferring the resources to other uses presumably more than offset these losses. To cite another example, the most serious corporate social issue in the United States currently is the balance between allocations for short-run profits and investment for long-run growth. Compared with Japan especially, the United States lacks "patient capital" and committed workers. Unfortunately, the prevailing mania for hostile takeovers sharply constrains allocations for building long-term strength. Consequently, it is unclear how far corporate managers can go in allocating funds for long-term growth even though doing so would have desirable social benefits.

These major resource allocations, then, do have significant social consequences. And it is corporate managers who are responsible for finding a workable long-run strategy for socially acceptable action.

*Second*, corporate managers help to create a climate within the various operating units that makes social consequences one of the important considerations in strategy decisions. In reviewing business-unit plans and other activating and control activities, they can, if they wish, counteract the impression that quarterly profits are all that senior management cares about. As noted in Chapter 5, corporate values, when carefully and consistently nurtured, have wide influence on actions far beyond those of immediate subordinates.

*Third*, corporate managers, especially of large corporations, can influence the external environment. They often represent their corporations before government committees. Or they may be an officer of a trade association or other industry bodies. Through these contacts, senior executives can push for legislation which promotes socially desirable action. A recent example is the packaging safety regulations following the Tylenol poisoning crisis. Industry leaders helped federal and state legislatures devise standards that significantly reduced the risk of tampering with drug products while at the same time being feasible from a manufacturing standpoint.

This sort of shaping of the industry infrastructure is complicated because most corporations most of the time seek changes which will favor their competitive position, and consequently their advice is always viewed with suspicion. However, some changes clearly have social benefits for at least some stakeholders. The challenge for corporate representatives is to develop enough credibility and respect so that their suggestions which are more than self-seeking will receive careful attention.

Broadly speaking, then, corporate managers help set the stage—create conditions—where socially responsible action by business-unit managers and their department heads will take place.

## Use of Conceptual Frameworks

The preceding observations about the roles of department heads, business-unit managers, and corporate executives illustrate the value of a multi-level framework. Department heads typically deal with the feasibility and need for specific changes; business-unit managers are concerned with overall balance, and take a longer view of potential threats and opportunities; corporate executives set the tone and make major allocations. Each is needed, but no single level is well suited to do the tasks of the other levels.

Moreover, frameworks for analyzing the tasks of each of the three levels help to cut through a lot of fuzzy thinking about social responsibility:

- The triple linkage model (Figure 6–2) for viewing departments helps us to see both the departments' external boundary relationships and their internal integrating relationships.
- The four-part strategy model for business-units stresses taking a broad, long-run perspective and then selecting a balanced plan for becoming a distinctive performer.
- The recognition of corporate inputs to business-units, in addition to a corporate portfolio or allocation tasks, provides a framework for considering how corporate executives can aid their business-units as well as move assets from one place to another.

In other words, the discussion of roles in socially responsible action presented here illustrates how to apply the frameworks set forth in this book to major strategy issues facing business firms. These frameworks aid in thinking about an issue in terms of managerial actions: What are the viewpoints and decisions that managers in various positions normally will take? And how are they interrelated? Then, after thinking through the total configuration, conclusions can be narrowed down to major points and minor considerations can be omitted, so that proper emphasis may be placed on the crux of the issue facing managers.

## Questions for Class Discussion

1. What do you think should be the obligation of an employer to protect its employees from AIDS? (a) Should all new employees be tested for AIDS prior to starting to work? (b) Should all present employees be tested for AIDS? (c) Should any indication of AIDS be the basis for immediate dismissal (with the customary termination pay)?

2. Explain *your* understanding of the phrase, "social responsibility."

3. Social standards change. We praised pioneers for clearing land and draining swamps, but now similar action may be illegal. Likewise, legislation and company practice protecting women workers was hailed as a social triumph fifty

years ago; now such practice is considered unfair discrimination. (a) Is it the responsibility of company senior managers to decide what social standards should be in their own organizations? (b) Since a new standard often affects previous jobs, markets, financial returns, and other prevailing resource conversion patterns, should management work to accept some standards, such as equal employment opportunity in hiring; keep others from the past, such as seniority in firing; and reject others, such as long, flowing hair for men working in sales?

4. The CEO of a *Fortune 500* corporation says, "My office should decide how far we go into social responsibility, not the operating people. I want each business-unit and department manager to give individual attention to meeting established strategy and operating goals; that's enough of a challenge. It is part of my job to decide when special interest groups are so strong that catering to them must be included in operating plans, and either I or my deputy will get the word to our operating people." Do you agree with the statement? Explain.

5. The vast majority of a group of about 200 managers of publicly traded stock corporations, when questioned, believe their objective (in return for suitable compensation) was to maximize the profit to the stockholders. When the managers were questioned more closely about this single-minded objective, many qualifications and doubts were added. Under difficult conditions (major recessions, substantial loss of market share, sudden new environmental demands made by the state, a tight squeeze on cash flow when prices dropped), personal and organizational survival became far more important to managers than the interest of shareholders. Explain this change.

6. (a) Foreign corporations own all or substantial blocks of the stock of several U.S. businesses. Examples include Lever Brothers, Shell Oil, A & P, Ciba-Geigy Pharmaceuticals, and BIC Pens. Do you believe that such U.S. businesses are less responsive to U.S. social problems (unemployment, inflation, consumer protection, and the like) than are locally owned companies? (b) Do you believe that businesses in Europe or developing countries which are owned by U.S. corporations are responsive to the social problems in the countries in which they are located? (c) What is your general conclusion about socially responsible behavior of multinational corporations?

7. Currently many countries, both advanced and developing, are turning away from government ownership of businesses to "privatization," that is, independently run, profit-seeking companies such as we have in the United States. Examples of the change range from aircraft building and coal mining in England to copper mining in Zambia. The aim is to increase the productivity of the companies so that they can compete effectively in world markets. (a) What does such a shift in ownership and management do to the social responsibility of a company? (b) If you were managing a recently privatized company, would you concentrate on making the company profitable in the short run?

8. Your college, along with nearby orchestras, zoos, and regional planning associations, turns to business corporations for gifts. What responsibility do you believe business firms have to aid such institutions?

## CASE
### 25 Rodo Cattle Company*

The Rodo Cattle Company is located in the metropolitan suburbs of Pleasantville, a city of over 600,000 people in a Western state. The primary business of the Rodo Company is operation of cattle feedlots for fattening cattle for slaughter. Although cattle feedlots have been used for centuries, commercial development of feedlots as a large business operation is fairly new. The Rodo Company is a specialized business of this type. Its cattle pens cover 80 acres and will feed at one time over 25,000 cattle worth several million dollars.

The entire acreage is covered by an overhead water sprinkler system that reduces the amount of manure dust in the dry afternoons. The sprinkler system also reduces the drift of dust from the feedlots to neighboring residential properties; however, the lots cannot be kept wet enough to prevent all dust, so there are many complaints from neighbors (see later). If too much water is used in dust treatment, muddy conditions develop that increase both neighborhood odor and cattle diseases.

The company regularly sprays its pens to control flies. Its monthly expenditure for insecticide exceeds $300, and both the county health officer and neighbors agree that flies are effectively controlled. Manure in the pens is mechanically handled. After it has accumulated in a pen for several months, it is scraped up by a bulldozer and mechanically loaded into trucks that take it to the edge of the property, where it is stacked in large, flat piles 30 feet high. Portions of this manure are occasionally sold to a processor who pulverizes and bags it for sale to home gardeners and farmers. The supply of manure is much greater than the demand for it, so Rodo Company has an inventory of thousands of tons, which is increasing by hundreds of tons annually. The general manager and principal owner of the company, Jesse Rodo, is not sure what to do with this growing inventory because he is running out of storage space.

The Rodo Company was established 16 years ago on 120 acres purchased especially for feedlot operation. In the beginning there were pens for only 500 cattle, but facilities expanded rapidly as the idea of custom feeding became popular with local farmers and business investors. At the time the feedlot was established

---

*Written by Keith Davis, Arizona State University.

there were three other feedlots nearby, so the property already was recognized as a stockyard area. The land is rocky and uneven, is located near a river bottom, and is unfit for residential housing. The property is six miles from downtown Pleasantville, and the nearest residential developments at the time the feedlot was opened were 1½ miles away on either side. Pleasantville is toward the west, and a suburban town is toward the southeast.

The other three feedlots in Rodo Company's area also have expanded, until this area now has pens for nearly 100,000 head of cattle. Meanwhile, the Pleasantville metropolitan area also has grown, pushing residential suburbs closer to the stockyard area. One new residential area is within 500 feet of the edge of Rodo's property, and homeowners are complaining loudly about feedlot dust and odors. In fact, the whole stockyard area is surrounded on three sides by residential and commercial developments less than ½ mile away. The municipal stadium is only one mile away, and several fine motels are on a highway about the same distance. The city auditorium, the site of operas and other gala events, is slightly over two miles away. On winter evenings when the air settles, an intense odor from the stockyard area sometimes reaches the auditorium at about the time programs begin. This one fact alone has caused strong protests from several influential Pleasantville people.

The odors and dust produced by a feedlot operation are much different from those of the common farm barnyard. Because of heavy use of the ground (several hundred cattle on one acre), the type of odor is much more putrid, and it exists in a stronger concentration than it does on the farm. The foul odor causes nausea and illness in sensitive people. And if the pens are not properly sprayed with water when the cattle are milling about in late afternoon before bedding down for the night, clouds of unpleasant dust, similar to those which arise behind an automobile moving along a dusty road at sundown, cover the neighborhood.

This combination of factors has placed a large segment of the community in conflict with feedlot operators. Residents of the suburbs southeast of the Rodo feedlot have organized a Fresh-Air Committee, whose purpose is to encourage community action to control air pollution. Committee members include many influential citizens of the suburbs. The group holds public meetings, and officers regularly attend city council meetings to offer proposals for feedlot regulation and city prosecution under nuisance laws, since three of the four feedlots are now within the city limits of the suburbs. The group is also developing proposed city ordinances for control of feedlot pollution.

The group has employed a photographer and a scientist to gather evidence of feedlot pollution, and members are outspoken against the odor and dust derived from feedlots. The committee had proposed that since the cattle feeders cannot or will not do anything about the offensive nature of the feedlots, they should move to a rural area zoned especially for long-run cattle feeding. A local journalist reported the proposal as follows:

> The hero of Western lore, the cattleman, could be headed for a reservation just like his predecessor, the Indian, if a group of unhappy citizens has its way.

The reservation proposal is the brainchild of the Fresh-Air Committee and is aimed specifically at cattle-feeding operations in urban areas.

They propose that statewide zoning be initiated by the legislature to provide a permanent area where cattle and dairy operators can work free from encroachment by residential areas. This zone would be buffered with a five-mile ring of orchards to protect against the cows, and vice versa.

The Fresh-Air Committee is only one of many groups troubled by the scent of "Corral No. 5" and the dust rising every evening from the community's cattle-feeding operations.

The list of complainants is long. It includes hotel and motel operators, airport authorities, city officials, doctors, health officials, homeowners, and tourists. The airport manager commented: "During the height of the tourist season, the airport receives the full 'benefits' of the stockyards. People get off the plane, and they want to get right back on."

In addition, a few months ago residents of some of the worst fallout areas filed lawsuits against all four cattle companies, alleging that they were maintaining a public nuisance. Some 80 citizens filed suits asking for damages totaling $859,040. The suits allege that stockyard dust settles in homes even when they are closed, requiring more frequent cleaning than in other areas of the community. They complain that use of patios and yards is denied on many evenings, that extra money must be spent for air conditioning and filters to keep odors and dust out of homes, and that home prices have depreciated more than normal. They allege that odor and dust have become worse since they moved into their homes because more cattle are being fed and larger piles of manure are accumulating. Some also allege nausea and bronchial difficulties caused by the nuisances. One of the complainants, speaking to a reporter, warned persons interested in buying a home in the area not to close the sale in the daytime. "All the people around here bought their houses during the daytime, when the dust and odor do not settle so badly," the complainant said. "The real estate people either evade the subject or ignore it when they're selling a house."

The lawyer who represented most of the complainants in their lawsuits made the following comment to a reporter: "We don't mind the stockyards, but we do mind the dust and odor. The basic legal question as I see it is the right of habitation or the right of agriculture. I believe that human habitation is superior to that of livestock."

Meanwhile, the Citizens' Council for Beautification of Pleasantville was taking an interest in the feedlot problem. The council is a civic committee appointed by the mayor to coordinate the work of all voluntary groups seeking to make the metropolitan area a more beautiful, cultured, and pleasant place to live. The council was particularly concerned because feedlots caused a large blighted area on the edge of town, several distinguished visitors had inquired about the odor when alighting at the airport, several cultural events at the city auditorium and other locations had been made unpleasant by stockyard odor, and a number of residents had complained. In fact, some businesses on the highway were so affected by the feedlots that their managers were writing letters to anyone who would heed them.

Some dispatched letters to their United States senators and representatives. They also complained to the county health officer, but at one of the council meetings he told the group that his office had investigated the feedlots and was convinced that neither their dust nor their odor constituted a health hazard to citizens.

Jesse Rodo became embroiled in the feedlot controversy in two ways. First, as owner and manager of Rodo Cattle Company, he was the object of lawsuits (which included both the corporation and its manager in each complaint), and he was under pressure to move his feedlot or take corrective action, either of which would be expensive. Second, he was at this time serving a three-year term as president of the Cattle Feeders' Association, which was the trade association of the feedlot operators. The association was working hard to offset unfavorable publicity that feedlots were receiving.

Several years ago, when complaints first started to develop, the Cattle Feeders' Association took the position that the feedlot operators were there first; hence, those who built homes or businesses in the area did so at their own peril. As one operator stated, "An age-old concept in common law is 'Let the buyer beware.' It is the buyer's legal duty to be aware of environmental conditions that might affect a home or business prior to investing in it. The feedlots should not be blamed because people insist on moving closer to them."

This argument reduced complaints and probably would have worked in the long run, except that the feedlots continued to expand their facilities and pile their refuse. The result was that people who originally built in an odor-free and dust-free neighborhood soon found that these nuisances were reaching their neighborhood also. Then, when the Fresh-Air Committee entered the controversy, its officials reported legal opinion that prior occupancy of the area did not give feedlots an easement to inflict obnoxious dust and odor on adjoining property. In other words, adjoining property owners had just as much right to use their property freely as the feedlot owners had to use theirs.

At about this time Rodo became president of the association, and he persuaded members to hire a public relations firm to improve the feedlots' public image. The firm recommended emphasis on the economic benefits of feedlots to the state. This approach gained support of operators outside the Pleasantville area because some of them were beginning to receive complaints from their neighbors also; however, nearly half the state's feedlots were in the Pleasantville area. The public relations firm prepared news releases for mailing to all papers in the state at least once a month extolling the economic virtues of feedlots. Releases reported that during the last year nearly $150 million worth of cattle were sold out of feedlots in the state. Fresh-Air Committee officials countered this argument by reporting that tourism brought $400 million to the state and that urban feedlots were driving away tourists.

Another publicity release explained that the feedlot industry provided employment for over 1,000 persons and had invested over $40 million in land and equipment. Rodo and the public relations firm also persuaded leading feedlot operators to prepare speeches and seek speaking invitations to luncheon clubs and other meetings.

The number of complaints did not diminish, so association officials persuaded a number of the worst offenders to experiment with spraying a masking agent (offsetting perfume) in their lots daily. In most cases the cattle odor and the masking odor seemed to combine to produce a third odor as obnoxious as the original one. In fact, the new odor aroused additional complaints not aroused by the original odor.

As a result of the failures mentioned, the Fresh-Air Committee continued to gain strength and worked with the city council of the suburb where Rodo Company's pens were located to develop a stringent ordinance regulating feedlots. The ordinance required operators to remove all organic refuse at least once a week and to haul it outside the city limits entirely. The feedlot operators felt that compliance with this ordinance would be expensive and unduly restrictive; therefore, they proposed a program of self-regulation to the city council. They offered to use masking agents and sprinkler systems and to remove refuse twice a year. The council "took the proposal under advisement" and continued with its plans for an ordinance.

The council's action caused feedlot operators throughout the state to become concerned that each city might set up its own special ordinance for feedlots. Differences in ordinances might cause cost variations that would upset competitive conditions. Feeding costs now were about equal throughout the state, but a local ordinance might increase costs in one city, driving a feedlot's customers to another lot and eventually driving the feedlot from the city. One influential operator proposed that the association go to the state legislature, which was then in session, and request a law requiring nuisance regulation by the state livestock sanitary board. Since the board consisted mostly of cattle feeders and ranchers, this approach would put them in the position of regulating themselves; therefore, regulations could be kept reasonable. Another operator threatened to move feeding operations from the state if the state law were passed.

Rodo decided to call a statewide meeting of the entire association membership to decide what the next move should be. He knew that a strong plea would be made for the law requiring regulation by the livestock sanitary board. He also knew that association members were looking to him for leadership, but he was not sure what to propose next. He was further confused by the situation with his own company. He owned land elsewhere in the state and was about ready to move his feedlot from the Pleasantville area; however, whenever he hinted to other operators that a move might occur, they strongly objected. They said that all feedlot operators must "stick together and not retreat at this time." They felt that if one feedlot left, it would be an "admission of guilt" and would make it necessary for the other lots to move in a short time.

## Questions

1. In the role of Jesse Rodo, president of the Cattle Feeders' Association, develop a socially responsive strategy for the feedlot operators to follow in

order to maintain their businesses along with community goodwill. Would your strategy require you to work with others? Would you consult with, or seek the help of, any government agency? Explain.

2. Comment on the strategy chosen by the Feeders' Association to emphasize economic benefits in order to reduce homeowner and other community complaints.

3. This case relates to homeowners and commercial business *moving toward* a preexisting unpleasant operation. The opposite movement is also frequent, with an unpleasant business moving near, or into, a community. Assume that you are the public affairs director of an international paper company and that the president of the company has requested you to develop a socially responsive strategy for your firm to locate an odor-emitting paper mill on a river near a city of 150,000 population. What is your strategy? As an alternative, develop a similar strategy for a firm with a noisy forging shop or a chemical plant having occasional unpleasant emissions that are thought to be safe, but whose complete safety is unproven at this time.

4. Should the city of Pleasantville be encouraged to offer compensation to Rodo to move elsewhere, such as paying a premium to purchase the land?

# PART 7

## Comprehensive Cases

# COMPREHENSIVE CASE 1

## Movie Village[1]

Dave Ringer, owner/manager of Movie Village, a video rental store, was contemplating the future of his business. "The cool, wet summer was great for video rentals and that has me worried," he thought to himself. "Everybody is talking about opening another store and the market is getting saturated. The rental market is still experiencing some growth, but there are many challenges on the horizon." Dave was particularly concerned with his reliance on video rentals for almost all of his revenue. A variety of competitive forces, including new rental outlets in the vicinity of Movie Village, chain and franchise rental store expansions, actions by some of the movie studios, and the expected growth of pay television, were threatening his business and forcing Dave to consider some changes in his strategy.

## The Video Rental Industry

The video/movie rental market developed through a marriage of the video cassette recorder (VCR) and the feature film industry. The VCR offered its owner two principal features: (1) the ability to tape television programs for playback at a more convenient time and (2) the ability to play rented or purchased movies or other prerecorded video products. A 1985 survey by the Bureau of Broadcast Measurement found that 57 percent of a typical user's VCR time was spent playing rented movies and 37 percent playing movies that had been recorded from television for playback at a different time.[2] The remaining 6 percent was used to tape television shows for later playback. The VCR, the survey declared, was essentially a movie machine.

The growth rate in VCR sales has been quite dramatic, as shown in Exhibit 1.

The VCR was expected to be in 30 percent of Canadian homes by the end of 1985. Industry observers believed that an eventual penetration of 80 percent of Canadian homes was not unreasonable to expect by 1995.[3]

---

[1]This case was prepared by Stephen Tax under the direction of Walter S. Good at the University of Manitoba and edited and rewritten by W. Harvey Hegarty at Indiana University.

[2]*Winnipeg Free Press*, October 16, 1985, p. 5.

[3]*Canadian Business*, February 1984, p. 14.

**EXHIBIT 1**
**CANADIAN VCR SALES BY YEAR**

| Year | Units Sold |
|------|------------|
| 1980 | 45,000 |
| 1981 | 200,000 |
| 1982 | 430,000 |
| 1983 | 540,000 |
| 1984 | 950,000 (estimated) |

Source: *Marketing*, August 6, 1984, p. 13.

There were two competing technologies in the VCR marketplace: VHS and Beta. The Beta system (designed by Sony) had approximately a 30 percent share, while the VHS system dominated with 70 percent. It was expected that both would continue to be available in the marketplace for many years. The two systems used different software (a VHS movie would not run on a Beta machine), which meant a movie rental retailer had to stock tapes in both formats in order to service the entire market.

Sony had recently introduced a new "hardware" system, "8mm." This new product used much smaller tapes, which provided easier portability than either Beta or VHS hardware. The movie studios were reluctant to develop prerecorded tapes until enough machines had been sold to suggest that the 8mm format would be successful. Consumers, on the other hand, were reluctant to purchase the 8mm hardware until there was an attractive selection of software on the market. This was essentially a chicken-and-egg problem. Many video retailers believed that broad acceptance of the 8mm format was still a few years away, but that it would eventually have a significant impact on the market.[4]

The movie studios' goal was to maximize their profits from film by using all possible distribution methods, including movie theaters, pay TV, network TV, and cassette sales for resale or rental. The typical sequence of events was for a movie to first be shown in theaters and then be made available to video stores in cassette form for rental purposes. Sometime after the film's release for home rental it might be shown on a pay television service such as First Choice/Superchannel or Home Box Office, and, finally, it might be shown on commercial network TV. In the home rental market the movie studios received all their revenue from the sale of cassettes to video distributors or video retailers. They did not receive a royalty or any share of the revenue received by the retailer from each rental.

Movies were rented to the public through a number of different types of outlets, including specialty video rental stores (independent and chain operations),

---

[4]*Video Business*, August 1985, pp. 1–2.

convenience stores, gas stations, food stores, drugstores, and some mass merchandisers.

## Movie Village

Movie Village, located near the southwest corner of the fashionable Osborne Village shopping district in Winnipeg, opened for business in June, 1984. Dave Ringer, a B. Comm graduate from the University of Manitoba in 1981, had spent a couple of years working, traveling, and analyzing a number of business opportunities before deciding to enter the video rental business.

The growing market and the availability of what he thought was a viable location helped make up his mind.

"Osborne Village is made up of a broad cross section of people skewed somewhat toward the elderly, singles (not necessarily elderly), and childless couples covering all points of the income spectrum," noted Dave. "In my research I found my primary trading area, within one-half mile of the store, to contain 12,000 to 14,000 people. Of course, there are also a lot of people working in the Village." Because of the abundance of video outlets in the city and the need for each customer to make two trips to his store (to rent and to return the movie), most of Dave's business was from the immediate neighborhood.

An important component of Dave's operation was his computerized information system. This system allowed Dave to keep tabs on his inventory, sales, and the frequency with which individual titles were rented. He could also take and record reservations and keep track of his membership file of 8,000 customers.[5]

## Marketing Mix

### Product

Dave rented movies and VCRs and sold blank tapes and a number of other accessories. His sales breakdown was as follows:

| | |
|---|---|
| Movie rentals | 92% |
| Blank tapes and accessories | 5% |
| VCR rentals | 3% |

When Dave first opened for business he also sold some hardware (VCRs and color TVs), but found that the profit margins were small; in addition, the equipment took up a lot of space, tied up his working capital, and required too great a selling effort.

---

[5]All renters had to be Movie Village members. This membership was free and helped Dave control his tape losses. The membership list also was used for direct mail promotions.

Dave stocked about 1,800 cassettes (total of VHS and Beta) representing approximately 1,100 different titles.[6] He purchased multiple copies of some of the new releases which were expected to be popular with the public. For example, he recently purchased 15 copies of "Ghostbusters." By having multiple copies of these popular films available, Dave felt he was providing better service to his customers.

One particular problem Dave and other video retailers faced was the increasing number of new releases. When Movie Village first opened, about 150 new releases were offered by the studios each month. A year and a half later the number had quadrupled to approximately 600. Dave felt that it was important for him to change his product assortment continually and stock new releases. Studios and distributors promoted their new products heavily, and customer demand for the newer films was very high for the first couple of months after they came out.

Dave obtained his movies from two local distributors. New releases cost him about $100 each, 60 percent of which he could get back if he returned the cassette within 40 days. The longer he kept the movie, the lower its return value was. With a movie like "Ghostbusters," Dave could buy 15 copies and return most of them within the 40 days. Older movies could be purchased for between $40 and $80 each. Their resale value was quite low (less than $30). Dave usually rotated his older stock by trading in some of his inventory. He stated, "I can take 100 movies in to my distributor and come out with 70 different ones." Dave spent about one-third of his previous month's revenue on new releases each month and, in addition, traded in some cassettes.

He used trade magazines and release lists provided by his distributors to make his purchase decisions. His computer provided him with data on the frequency with which each movie in the store was being rented. This information was useful in deciding which cassettes should be traded in.

## Price

The goal of Dave's pricing policy was to maximize his monthly revenue. This made sense, considering that most of his costs were fixed in nature.

Dave charged $1.89 per movie rental on weekdays (Monday–Thursday) and $3.99 per movie on weekends (Friday–Sunday) and holidays. Dave also offered a number of price specials designed to increase his revenue "up front" and help build customer loyalty. His price deals have included:

- a coupon providing 15 movie rentals for $25
- an offer to get one movie per week through the calendar year (non-cumulative) for $30
- a two-month summer special (July and August) whereby the customer paid $20 and could rent movies for 94¢ each during that period
- a special rental price of 94¢ for selected movies

---

[6]Dave maintained a ratio of approximately 65 percent VHS versus 35 percent Beta.

Dave felt that these price promotions had increased his overall revenue.

Movie Village did not differentiate in price between new and old movies, despite the greater popularity of new releases, except in the case of his 94¢ specials. These tended to be older films that would otherwise have been in low demand. He was concerned that too many "deals" and specials might confuse his customers and sales staff.

## Promotion

Dave used a variety of promotional tools to stimulate repeat business by his current members and to attract nonmembers to his store. He regularly sent a direct mailing to all his members informing them of new releases and current specials. He also sent a coupon for a free movie rental to the members on their birthday and on the anniversary of their becoming a member.

Bulk mailings were periodically sent to all households within the store's trading area informing potential customers of price specials, store hours, new releases, etc. Coupons for such specials as two rentals for the price of one were often included with this material to encourage the recipients to become members.

Dave had also used contests to promote his store, most notably a "guess the weight" of a huge box of popcorn, to attract the attention of pedestrian traffic in the Village. The prizes were usually video equipment (VCRs and TVs).

A changeable outdoor sign hung over the entrance to the store. Dave found this sign useful for drawing attention to monthly promotions or price specials.

Promotion had become increasingly important to Movie Village because of the growing number of locations providing movie rentals. However, the limited geographic area served by Movie Village as well as the considerable cost precluded the use of any type of mass media advertising.

## Sales and Expenses

Movie Village's sales revenue had grown slowly but steadily since its inception. "Business picks up considerably on three-day long weekends, then settles back down but to a slightly higher plateau," Dave revealed. He also indicated that the store experienced a noticeable decline in business during the Folklorama multicultural festival during the second week in August. "I had expected the whole summer to be slow," said Dave, "but the poor weather this year created what I consider to be an artificial boom."

A typical month's revenue and expenses for Movie Village is shown in Exhibit 2. The profit-and-loss statements ending December 31, 1984 and 1985 are shown in Exhibit 3. December 31, 1984 and 1985 balance sheet data are shown in Exhibit 4.

A typical weekend day provided almost three times the revenue of a typical weekday ($850 compared to $300). The nine VCR rental machines owned by the store were rented primarily on weekends.

**EXHIBIT 2**
**APPROXIMATE REVENUE AND EXPENSES FOR MOVIE VILLAGE DURING
A TYPICAL MONTH**

| Revenues | | Expenses | |
|---|---|---|---|
| Movie rentals | $14,000 | Movie purchases | $ 4,500 |
| Accessory sales | 700 | Employee wages | 2,200 |
| VCR rentals | 500 | Advertising & promotion | 1,000 |
| | | Rent | 1,000 |
| **Total Revenue** | **$15,200** | General administration | 1,400 |
| | | Purchase of accessories | 600 |
| | | Utilities | 200 |
| | | Other expenses | 300 |
| | | **Total Expenses** | **$11,200** |

## Current Video Rental Competition

Dave had identified several important bases on which stores in the video rental business competed. These included convenience, service, selection, and price.

"Convenience has several components from the viewpoint of the customer," indicated Dave. "These include store hours, parking availability, and location on the street." Movie Village was open 10:00 A.M. to 10:00 P.M. on weekdays and 10:00 A.M. to 11:00 P.M. on weekends. The store was located near the southwest corner of Osborne Avenue and River Road, a main intersection in the Village. This location had very limited available parking.

Customer service also had a number of elements. "All some people want is to come in, get their movie, and get out," volunteered Dave. "They need a 'system' that is efficient. That system includes a well-laid-out store and a fast, efficient checkout process. Other customers want help in finding and selecting a movie and may even ask for a personal review."

Movie selection was important because many customers searched for a particular film. If the store did not carry it, or it was already rented, then that customer was lost. Carrying multiple copies of popular films was essential if the store hoped to satisfy its customers.

While the rental price was important to many customers, Dave did not want to compete strictly on that basis. He felt it reduced his per-rental profit margin without a proportionate increase in volume.

Dave summarized the situation of his store in comparison to the four principal competitors in his trading area as follows:

1.  *California Connection* store was located right around the corner from Movie Village. It did not have as extensive a selection of movies, no

**EXHIBIT 3
MOVIE VILLAGE
PROFIT-AND-LOSS STATEMENT FOR THE PERIOD ENDING DECEMBER 31**

| | 1985 | 1984 |
|---|---|---|
| | | (for 9 months ending Dec. 31) |
| Revenue: | | |
| Videocassette and VCR rentals | 150,263 | 61,147 |
| Merchandise sales | 28,261* | 8,485 |
| Interest income | 820 | — |
| TOTAL REVENUE | $179,350 | $ 69,632 |
| Expenses: | | |
| Advertising and promotion | 11,953 | 5,222 |
| Automobile expenses | 2,232 | 863 |
| Bank charges | 947 | 462 |
| Business tax | 336 | 196 |
| Employee benefits | 1,731 | 397 |
| Equipment rental | 345 | — |
| Insurance | 1,662 | 474 |
| Membership cards | — | 1,450 |
| Merchandise purchases | 21,362 | 8,439 |
| Miscellaneous | 1,229 | 1,652 |
| Office & stationery | 4,090 | 2,528 |
| Professional fees | 1,883 | 1,835 |
| Property tax | 797 | 704 |
| Protection service | 185 | 185 |
| Rent | 11,900 | 4,800 |
| Repair and maintenance | 655 | 1,376 |
| Store expense | 7,041 | 2,067 |
| Videocassette purchases | 48,000 | 56,000 |
| Telephone | 1,030 | 670 |
| Travel | 1,100 | 700 |
| Utilities | 2,170 | 980 |
| Wages—store | 26,000 | 8,000 |
| Wages—management | 26,000 | 9,000 |
| TOTAL EXPENSES | $157,000 | $ 99,400 |
| Income (loss) before depreciation and amortization | 22,350 | (29,768) |
| Depreciation and amortization | 7,771 | 7,411 |
| NET INCOME (LOSS) BEFORE TAXES | 14,579 | (37,179) |
| Income Taxes | 2,287 | — |
| **NET INCOME (LOSS) FOR THE YEAR** | **$ 12,292** | **$ (37,179)** |

*Also includes an unknown volume of prepaid movie rentals.

**EXHIBIT 4**
**MOVIE VILLAGE**
**BALANCE SHEET AS OF DECEMBER 31, 1984 AND DECEMBER 31, 1985**

|  | 1985 | 1984 |
|---|---|---|
| *ASSETS* | | |
| Current assets: | | |
| Cash | $ 4,130 | $ 1,860 |
| Term deposits | 7,369 | — |
| Accounts receivable | — | 243 |
| Inventory | 3,068* | 17,932 |
| Prepaid expenses | 1,104 | 2,038 |
| TOTAL CURRENT ASSETS | $15,671 | $22,073 |
| Fixed assets: | | |
| Loan receivable | 19,700 | — |
| Other fixed assets | 31,708 | 38,353 |
| TOTAL FIXED ASSETS | $51,408 | $38,353 |
| **TOTAL ASSETS** | **$67,079** | **$60,426** |
| *LIABILITIES* | | |
| Current liabilities: | | |
| Accounts payable | $16,626 | $13,710 |
| Income taxes payable | 3,268 | — |
| Shareholder's loan payable | 8,526 | 3,954 |
| TOTAL CURRENT LIABILITIES | $28,420 | $17,664 |
| Long-term liabilities: | | |
| Notes payable | 60,000 | 60,000 |
| **TOTAL LIABILITIES** | **$88,420** | **$77,664** |
| *NET WORTH* | | |
| TOTAL NET WORTH (DEFICIT) | ( 21,341) | ( 17,238) |
| **TOTAL LIABILITIES AND NET WORTH** | **$67,079** | **$60,426** |

*Inventory value is very low, as videotapes are valued at what they might be expected to bring at liquidation prices.

Beta-format video cassettes were stocked, and it took longer to complete a transaction. Prices, however, were a bit lower.

2.   *Osborne Video* was located on the opposite side of the street, the wrong side for customers on their way home from work or shopping downtown. Otherwise, it was quite similar to Movie Village.

3.   *Shell Gas Station* had a limited selection and it took longer to rent a film. However, it was open 24 hours. Its staff was not particularly knowledgeable about the films it rented, but its prices, $1.00 on weekdays and $2.00 on weekends, were considerably lower than Movie Village's.

4.   *Mac's Store* was very comparable to the Shell gas station.

## Strategic Threats

There were a number of competitive challenges on the horizon that Dave believed seriously threatened the future viability of Movie Village if it continued on its present strategic course. Those threats included:

1. Increasing "traditional" competition from other independent video rental stores in Movie Village's trading area.
2. The growth of chain and franchised video operations throughout Winnipeg.
3. The entry of new, "nontraditional" competitors (bookstores and record stores) into the video sales and rental market.
4. Competition from other closely related entertainment vehicles (pay cable and satellite television).
5. Strategies being considered by the movie studios to increase their share of post-theater movie revenues.

## Neighborhood Competition

Dave had heard a rumor that a local Winnipeg chain specialty video store was planning to open an outlet in the vicinity of Movie Village. Historically, it had proven to be an aggressive marketer using mass media advertising and loss-leader pricing (94¢ rental price specials) to build its business, although it did not carry multiple copies of many movies. Its entry into the local market could threaten Dave's volume of business and his ability to maintain his premium pricing strategy.

## Chain Store Competition

According to the owner of the local Global Video stores, Winnipeg already had the highest number of video stores per capita in North America. Compounding this situation was the growth of national video chains and franchises.

Adventureland, a U.S.-based video franchise, was expected to have 1,000 outlets in the U.S. by the end of 1985 and 2,500 stores in the U.S. and Canada by the end of 1986. National Video, also a U.S. company, already had over 1,000 franchised stores in the U.S. and Canada and had ambitious plans for further growth as well. Local chains such as Adi's and Star Time Video had been growing at a more modest rate. Each currently had six locations in Winnipeg.

Franchise operators offered their franchisees expertise in site selection, accounting and bookkeeping systems, merchandising, staffing, and the development of their product mix (most handled hardware in addition to rentals). They also used mass media advertising and could obtain quantity discounts on movie cassettes for their franchisees through central purchasing. By having multiple store locations in one city the chains offered an added convenience to their customers, who could rent and return movies to a number of outlets.

The growth of the franchised stores added to what Dave perceived was rapidly becoming a saturated market. This concern was echoed by National Video president Ron Berger, who stated, ". . .I can tell you right now the trend on the West Coast (L.A.) is in video store closings, and it's ferocious. All those undercapitalized mom-and-pops are collapsing due to oversaturation and their inability to develop the kind of systems and support programs they need to stay competitive. Most trends in this industry start in the West and slowly move across the country."[7]

The specialty video retailer had even more rivals with the entrance of "nontraditional" competitors such as record stores and bookstores into the video market. Music/record stores were beginning to resemble home entertainment centers, and the fit, importance, and growth potential of video products in relation to their current product lines were apparent to many people in the business. According to one U.S. record store chain manager, "We are dealing with one group here. The record audience is also a video audience."[8] Record merchandisers were conceded to have larger promotion budgets and greater merchandising expertise than the small video store owner. Many of the large U.S. record chains were beginning to offer video rentals and sales, especially of music videos.

Bookstores were also venturing into the video market, although primarily as resellers of video products rather than catering to the rental market. They tended to concentrate on the low-price segment, under $25 retail. Principally three types of videos were being sold in these stores:

1. Older classic movies, drawn from the public domain.
2. Children's material, from Disney cartoons to tie-ins with current toys.
3. How-to tapes on things like exercising, cooking, fixing your car, etc.

Video studios and distributors were very interested in the potential offered by bookstores as intermediaries for the sell-through market.[9] Bookstores, however, were not expected to have much of an impact on the rental market because of the high service requirements and the space and capital needed to stock an adequate level of inventory.

## The Cable TV Challenge

On a broader basis the movie rental business competed with a number of other forms of entertainment. In the post-theater movie/video market, competition included network TV and cable television systems and satellite technologies for the reception of a wide range of specialty television services.

---

[7]*Video Business,* August 1985, p. 18.
[8]*Canadian Video Retailer,* May 1985, p. 18.
[9]Sell-through referred to the fact that the sale of movie cassettes was to individual end users.

Basic cable TV services had a very high penetration rate in Winnipeg, about 85 percent of all households. The premium pay TV service (Superchannel), however, had only a 3 percent penetration rate.[10] This premium channel cost a typical household $18 to connect plus a $16 monthly fee and offered a variety of programming, including over 20 different movies per month. Marketing efforts to encourage increased acceptance of premium pay TV services were expected to intensify.

Satellite dishes cost from $1,500 to over $5,000 and were designed to be used in rural locations where cable TV was not available. In recent years, however, they have begun to penetrate the urban residential market. They were selling in Canada at a rate of 70,000 units per year (1984) and increasing at an annual rate of 40 percent.[11] The satellite dish enabled a household to receive upwards of 30 U.S. cable and local channels with no additional monthly charge. Some specialty channels were moving toward the "scrambling" of their satellite signal so that "dish" owners would not be able to receive their service unless they acquired a decoder and paid a monthly fee.

A longer term threat posed by the cable industry was the possible implementation of pay-per-view (PPV) systems. These systems would allow basic cable subscribers to access premium channels, via addressable converters, for individual programs on a "pay-per-view" basis. The cost of "plugging" into such a system to view a movie might be in the neighborhood of $4.

## Movie Studio Actions

Another impending threat to the movie rental business came from the major movie studios (Paramount, 20th Century Fox, etc.). These studios controlled the availability of movies and were constantly looking for ways to increase their share of the post-theater revenue a movie could generate.

The studios' strategy to date had been to "manufacture" cassette copies of their films and sell them to distributors who resold them at a "high" price to the video rental stores. The price of most new releases ($100 each to the retailer) was considered too high to attract much of a "sell-through" market. The studios, however, did not receive any royalty or other revenue when retailers rented the movie to their customers. Each prerecorded cassette only cost the studios about $8 to produce. While some "through-selling" of the more popular movies had taken place even at this high price, some studios had recently begun to actively develop this market.

Some popular new releases were being sold directly to retailers for $29.95 (U.S.) with a suggested retail price of $39.95 (U.S.). Older movies were sold for somewhat less. However, the retailers the studios were using for this method of

---

[10]Videon Cable TV, Winnipeg. The basic cable included NBC, ABC, CBS, and PBS as well as Canadian commercial networks and a variety of specialty services.

[11]*Marketing*, October 28, 1985, p. 20.

distribution were principally the mass merchandisers, bookstores, record stores, gift shops, and large video chains—not the independent video rental stores. The studios believed that their movies could be more effectively merchandised by traditional gift- and sales-oriented outlets than rental stores. In addition, since the studios planned to deal directly with the retailers, it would be easier for them to sell to a few large retail chains rather than thousands of small video stores. There were also some concerns that consumers might not purchase products from rental outlets because they feared that the cassettes might have been previously used for rental purposes.

Accentuating the problem for the specialty video stores was the apparent timing the studios were using in releasing their movies to each market segment. During the first two months of release, when a movie was most popular in the rental market, it would be sold to the retail rental stores for $100. After two months it would be released for $29.95 (U.S.) to the "sell-through" outlets. Most video stores felt obliged to pay this higher price in order to have new releases available for their customers and keep up with the competition. Furthermore, it was unlikely that the resale value of new releases (60 percent within 40 days) could continue to be as high as it was presently given that the movies would be available for $29.95 (U.S.) shortly thereafter.

## Strategic Options

Consideration of all of these issues convinced Dave that he needed to reduce his reliance on video rentals for such a large portion (92 percent) of his total revenue. He was considering a number of alternatives. Among them were:

1. Developing a "sell-through" market in video cassettes.
2. Expanding his geographic trading area.
3. Increasing his accessory product sales.
4. Diversifying his rental business to include compact discs (CDs) and similar items.

## The Sell-Through Market

Dave was skeptical about his ability to sell a large number of movie cassettes at a projected price of $50 to $60.[12] However, he felt that there might be a market for "specialty videos" such as children's films and cartoons, old classic movies, "how-to" cassettes, and sports and leisure instructional tapes such as Babe Winkleman's "Guide to Fishing" and similar programs. Dave thought these kinds of products had more value for multiple viewing and could be sold for gift and

---

[12]This selling price is based on a typical retail price of $30 (U.S.) which is an exchange rate of $1.39 plus duty and a 10 percent federal tax, which resulted in a price of roughly $56.

personal use if priced at $25 or less. Since most of these tapes were produced by independent studios and not the major motion picture companies, obtaining distribution rights would not be as difficult.

Jim Kartes, an American whose company was involved in specialty video production, believed that most people were reluctant to spend more than $20 (U.S.) on a video program.[13] His company produced such films as the "Eight Minute Makeover" and "Color Me Beautiful" in 30-minute formats that wholesaled to retailers for $6.99 (U.S.). These products apparently sold very well.

Dave felt that with proper promotion, pricing, and merchandising he could sell 100 specialty cassettes per month. On average, he figured each cassette would cost him $15 and he could sell it for $25. He was also hoping that by having these specialty videos for sale it would increase the interest in his store from customers outside his current limited trading area.

## Geographic Diversification

Dave also considered opening another store which, by itself, would not reduce his dependence on the rental business but would provide him with some geographic diversification.

A similar option might be for him to acquire one or more video vending machines (VVMs). A VVM, costing approximately $35,000, could hold 500 cassettes for sale or rental purposes. The customer accessed the machine with a credit card. These VVMs could be placed inside the current Movie Village location to make better use of the store's available space. This space, however, was presently at a premium because of the room needed to display new releases and promotional materials as well as the space taken up in storing the actual cassettes. The VVM would reduce the lineup at the counter during busy rental periods.

Another option would be to place the machine outside the store to provide customers with 24-hour service. The machines could also be placed in other locations (indoor or outdoor) around the city that Dave felt offered sufficient potential and where he was able to work out a satisfactory arrangement with the owner of the space.

## Accessory Products

Accessory products, including blank tapes, cassette cases, and VCR head cleaners, presently accounted for about 5 percent of Movie Village's revenue. Dave was interested in expanding the accessory portion of his business because of the high profit margin (around 40 percent) and the diversification opportunities it offered.

---

[13]*Video Store,* July 1985, p. 90.

Success in the accessory market depended on carrying the right products at the right price points and on promoting and merchandising them well. It was also important that the product's packaging and display materials, provided by the manufacturers, took up very little space, as product display areas were at a premium in Dave's store.

With the growth of the "home entertainment center" concept, a number of accessory product manufacturers had developed specialized kits that performed one of two functions: They helped maintain the consumer's audio and video equipment, or they tied the consumer's audio and video equipment together into an integrated system. For example, the Discwasher company had developed a Video Starter Kit that showed the consumer how to tie all of his equipment together into a system that would allow him to realize all the possible benefits and utilize all the features of his VCR when used with cable TV. The company felt that their product ideally should be sold as an add-on at the time of the hardware sale, but it was also a good item for (video) specialists since new VCR owners tended to go to a video store when they had a question about hooking up the various components of their system.[14] That particular kit included a head cleaner, an A-B switch, a signal splitter, three coaxial RF cables, and an instruction manual. The suggested prices for the kit were $17.95 (U.S.) wholesale and $29.95 (U.S.) retail. There were also a number of other products, both related and unrelated to the video business, that accessory manufacturers were offering and Dave was considering carrying.

## Compact Disc Rentals

One final option being considered by Dave was building on his experience in the rental business to expand into other rental markets. Specifically, he was considering renting software for compact disc (CD) players.

The CD player, which read digital information on a doughnut-sized disc via a laser beam, had a number of distinct advantages over records and audiotape cassettes. The quality of the sound was superior due to higher fidelity, and the CD was more durable and longer lasting because it was read by a laser beam. In contrast, sound was produced on a record by a diamond needle sliding over the vinyl surface. The CDs were also smaller and easier to store.

Dave believed that, despite their current low level of market penetration (1 or 2 percent of Winnipeg homes), the CD player and software had greater potential for growth than the video market. Retail prices of CD players had dropped from about $1,500 a year ago to as low as $400 now. Software selection was also expanding very rapidly and prices were coming down as well. In addition, CD players were being heavily promoted by many retailers.

---

[14]*Video Business*, October 1985, p. 11.

Despite these trends, however, CD software was still relatively expensive ($18 to $20 per disc, retail) and limited in both the number of titles and the quantity of discs available in the stores. Dave believed that people would be reluctant to duplicate their record or cassette collection on CDs because of the cost. However, they might rent CDs to record onto audiotape cassettes (the quality of the sound would be superior to prerecorded cassettes or tapes copied from a record) or simply to listen to on their CD players. In that way they could use the compact discs to build up their collection of high-quality audiotapes or use the rental disc to help them decide whether they should purchase a disc of their own.

Dave was considering establishing a library of 500 to 600 CDs at an average wholesale cost of $14. He had a built-in customer base with his video business, but realized he would have to attract additional customers from outside his primary trading area to make the CD rentals a viable proposition. He felt that a $1.00 daily rental fee would attract customers from outside his trading area and, perhaps, encourage them to rent the discs for a couple of days. This would reduce the inconvenience of having to rent a disc one day and return it the next. Dave was also excited about the complementary effect this additional customer traffic could have on his movie rental business.

Initially at least, Dave was only considering renting CDs, because he did not have the space to properly display them for sale or the capital to invest in a large inventory. He had already discussed the possibility of starting joint promotional programs with some CD hardware retailers whereby Movie Village would give free memberships and assorted coupons for movie and CD rentals to purchasers of their players. A number of these retailers were enthusiastic about the promotion because one factor holding back their sales of CD players was the limited availability of the software.

Dave had heard of record stores that had previously tried to rent out CDs and failed. "We have an advantage over sales-oriented stores," Dave noted. "We have the necessary system in place to effectively and efficiently handle software rentals."

## Conclusion

Dave feared that a market shakeout was certain to occur in the near future, and he wanted to be a survivor. "I have to select and implement a strategy to keep my business stable in the long term," he asserted. "Otherwise I'll see my profits slowly dwindle away."

# COMPREHENSIVE CASE 2

## Crosby Home Security Company

"October 27th

"Ms. Jane Crosby
619 West 68th Street
New York, NY 10021

"Dear Jane:
"I am sorry to have to trouble you with a serious matter only two weeks after your father's unfortunate death, but my discoveries about the condition of his estate, in my capacity as executor, make it imperative that you be fully informed at once so that you can determine what course of action you may want to follow.

"As your father's personal lawyer for more than 20 years, I thought I was reasonably familiar with his financial and related matters. (You are probably aware that William Foster of Lincoln and Foster has long handled all legal matters for Crosby Home Security Company.) As executor of your father's estate, however, I have discovered that my knowledge was both incomplete and erroneous. I thought his estate would contain substantial funds and investments outside the business, where, as you know, he owned 100 percent of the common (voting) stock. I was wrong. It is now clear that in the last several years he committed substantially all his personal wealth to Crosby Home Security Company in the form of loans subordinated to other company liabilities and also in supplemental equity investment. The unpleasant fact is that there is very little of value presently in your father's estate other than the company, life insurance payable to your mother, and the family home, which is, fortunately, unencumbered by mortgage.

"What the estate tax problems may turn out to be in these circumstances is still to be determined, and I won't trouble you with these matters now. I will simply say that establishing the estate tax valuation of a privately owned going business is a complex matter and depends on judgments, often controversial, about future earnings and net worth position. I will take up this whole subject with you on another occasion.

"This brings me to the heart of the situation. While your mother's financial security is protected by the life insurance, your grandmother and the three other members of your family who share in the ownership of CHSC's preferred (nonvoting) stock are all dependent on the dividends that have been regularly paid on that stock since the company was incorporated in 1958. During the last four years, however, the business has been at best minimally profitable. Nevertheless, your father caused the company (through the board, which he controlled since the other directors were all company employees) to continue to pay the $4-per-share dividend on the preferred stock even when the dividend was not covered by earnings. One more year of this practice will put the business in an untenable working capital position. Further, I understand that minimum working capital stipulations governing outstanding bank loans would prohibit paying the preferred dividend unless working capital is strengthened. From now on, it seems clear, any dividends paid will have to be earned.

"You, as your father's only child, have inherited all the common stock. That stock will pay dividends, indeed will have any significant value, only if the company returns to the kind of prosperity it enjoyed prior to the time several years ago when your father's failing health made it difficult for him to give the close attention to daily management matters that used to be his dominant interest.

"The way the business has drifted during the years of his partial absence and what I have discovered in examining its financial statements and talking to its senior managers in recent weeks have persuaded me that there is no one presently employed by the company who is competent to take effective charge of its operation. The company is being run right now by a top management committee, but everyone, including the committee members, recognizes that this is at best a temporary device. Figure 1 shows the CHSC organization chart.

"I think there are three options for you to consider. One is to sell the business for whatever price it may bring in its present condition. The second is to recruit an experienced and competent manager from outside. The third is for you to come home and run the company yourself.

"I don't know what your attitude may be toward the idea of coming back to the town where you grew up and taking on the burden of running the family business. But I want to put the thought to you that your M.B.A. education and your management consulting experience in the past two years have gone a long way toward equipping you to handle this responsibility effectively if you should choose this option. The only further persuasion I can put before you is that the net position of the company has been so reduced that a forced sale is not likely to yield any significant sum for the holders of the preferred, and nothing at all for you as the owner of all the common, shares. I doubt that a competent outsider could be recruited to manage the company unless you are prepared to sell such a person a substantial proportion of your common stock at an extraordinarily low price, thereby creating an attractive capital gain opportunity.

"Only the third option—coming home to manage the business yourself—offers the possibility of assuring adequate continued income for your grandmother and other family holders of the preferred stock, as well as dividends and capital gain for yourself. It would also be, I know from my conversations with your father in recent years, the fulfillment of his hope that you would eventually return to succeed him as owner and manager of the business. Of course, he never

**FIGURE 1.**
**CROSBY HOME SECURITY COMPANY ORGANIZATION CHART**

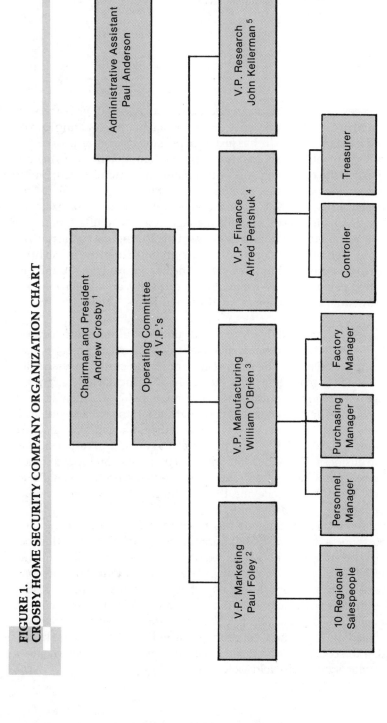

1 Deceased.
2 Age - 55; years with CHSC - 13.
3 Age - 58; years with CHSC - 17.
4 Age - 49; years with CHSC - 21.
5 Age - 31; years with CHSC - 5.

anticipated the mortal heart attack that might require making this transition so soon and with the business in as bad shape as it seems to be.

"Let me know what you think and how I can help.

"Affectionately,

/s/Lucas Elder"

## Jane Crosby

Jane Crosby received this letter two weeks ago as she was ending her second year of employment in the New York office of the management consulting firm of Hadley, Ford, and George, where she has just been promoted to the rank of senior associate. She is 28 years old. She graduated from the Columbia Business School two years ago. Earlier, she earned an A.B. with a major in economics from Smith and then worked for two years as an economic analyst in a large New York City bank. She left the bank to get an M.B.A. because she thought she was blocked in a dead-end staff position. Her post-Columbia management consulting experience has been interesting, varied, and financially rewarding. Promotion to the rank of senior associate puts her only one step away from a junior partnership in the firm, a level she hopes to reach in another three years. She has enjoyed her job and her life as an unmarried person in New York with a good salary, an attractive career line opening ahead, and a sense of independence with no family responsibilities.

Her father's heart attack and death occurred suddenly, although for several years he had been debilitated by a series of ailments which, in combination, had depressed his energy level and made it necessary for him to curtail substantially the time he devoted to the management of the business. Particularly since graduating from college, Jane enjoyed an unusually close relationship with her father. It was with his counsel and active encouragement that she left the bank to enter the Columbia Business School. She knew that he hoped the time would come when she would join him in running CHSC and ultimately take over full responsibility for managing the business. She had maintained a neutral position toward such a commitment, however, not being clear in her own mind whether she would ever want to leave New York City for Belleville, the Pittsburgh suburb where she grew up and where the family business is located.

As a result of her father's inclination not to press her for a decision, her own preference to postpone a decision she felt unprepared to make with confidence, and the family expectation that he would recover from his minor ailments, his fatal heart attack left Jane with no more than a surface acquaintance with the condition of the business. Lucas Elder's description of the situation he found in CHSC and in her father's estate was a quite disturbing revelation. With no clear sense of what should or could be done, she requested and was granted a two-month leave of absence from Hadley, Ford, and George and returned to Belleville to make her own evaluation of the condition and prospects of the business in which she now owns all the common stock and wields sole control.

## History of Crosby Home Security Company

Andrew Crosby founded Crosby Home Security Company in 1958 to manufacture and market a residential burglar alarm device which he had developed and patented. After graduating as an electrical engineer from the then Carnegie Institute of Technology in 1952, he was employed in engineering assignments by Westinghouse. His interest in developing a simple, easily installed, and effective residential burglar alarm was stimulated when his parents' home was entered and valuables taken one night while his father and mother were asleep. Working on his own time, he contrived such a device. When his employer expressed no interest in the system, he secured his own patent. Failing to persuade two electrical product companies to do anything with the product, he determined to launch his own company. He committed $100,000 inherited from his father and additional funds he borrowed from relatives, rented a factory building in his home town of Belleville, 20 miles from Pittsburgh, and opened for business as the Crosby Home Security Company.

The company prospered from the start. Andrew Crosby's design allowed simple self-installation by any home owner. "Electric Watchdog," as he called the device, was a battery-operated alarm signal consisting of a series of small remote sensors that could be readily attached to individual windows and doors and, after being switched on when a family retired at night, would ring a loud bell when an intruder raised a window or opened a door with a sensor attached. The product could be purchased with any desired number of sensors and attached lengths of wire.

CHSC marketed the burglar alarm at a suggested retail price of $99.95 (including a standard kit of six sensors, wiring, battery, and alarm) through manufacturers' agents in regional markets who in turn sold to electrical and hardware retailers. "Electric Watchdog" was promoted in small-space advertisements in national home care and news magazines, in selected metropolitan newspapers, and in spot commercials on major city FM radio stations.

Sales and profits grew rapidly. In the late 1960s, the company developed and introduced under the trademark "Fire Alert" its patented residential fire alarm device activated by chemical smoke sensors located in individual rooms and hall areas. Designed—like "Electric Watchdog"—for self-installation by home owners, the product was distributed through the same channels. "Fire Alert" sales also grew rapidly.

During the next six years, sales of the two alarm systems almost doubled, reaching $22.1 million four years ago. Competition increased sharply in this period, however, and CHSC was compelled to spend more heavily for advertising and also reduce prices in order to hold its market position. As a result, earnings have been declining sharply.

Four years ago, the company added a third product to its home security line: an ultrasonic burglar alarm system that emits inaudible sound beams that, when interrupted by an intruder, trigger an alarm. The system, trademarked "Silent Sentinel," was offered through the same distribution channels at a suggested retail price of $195.00. Sales of this product have been growing, at least partially, at the expense of "Electric Watchdog" sales. Competition developed even more rapidly than for earlier products, reflecting heightened public interest in home security products and entry into the market of several additional firms.

The drop-off in earnings during recent years and the deterioration in financial position are clearly shown in Tables 1 and 2. The performance of the three product categories is given in Table 3. Only in the past 10 months has the decline been checked, as is indicated in Table 4.

## The Home Security Market

The total home security market, including all types of intrusion and fire alarm devices, is estimated by trade sources to be in excess of $300 million annually at retail prices. This includes about $90 million in intrusion alarm systems, about $150 million in smoke alarm systems, and the balance in protective and alert devices for individual windows and doors. The market is believed to be growing at an annual rate of 20 percent. (These estimates do not include the market for comparable, but more extensive and complex, protective and alert systems for commercial and industrial applications.) At least a dozen companies, some national and others regional in scope, actively compete in the residential burglary and fire security market, in addition to a large number of local electric supply and repair retailers and individual "moonlighting" electricians who install "homemade," "amateur" alarm devices of their own fabrication.

A complex electronic security system requiring professional installation in a large suburban home can cost $3,000 or more. Simpler devices, many designed for self-installation, are available at prices ranging down to $100. Among the more elaborate systems offered by the three largest companies in the home security field (ADT, Honeywell, and Westinghouse) are combinations of perimeter devices (doors and windows) and indoor area motion "traps" (photoelectric beams, ultrasonic beams, and pressure mats under floor coverings). Critical concerns with complex systems are skilled professional installation and competent, prompt service. Critical concerns with simpler systems and unit devices are failure to perform as advertised and errors in self-installation by home owners.

Perimeter systems, as first introduced, required running wires from sensors equipped with magnetic switches, mounted on each protected door and window, to a central alarm unit. Charges for professional installation, including concealing wires for esthetic appearance, often exceed the cost of the system.

To eliminate the time or expense of extending wires through a residence, new wireless systems have been developed. In these systems each sensor or magnetic switch contains a battery-powered transmitter about the size of a pack of cigarettes. The transmitter sends a wireless signal to a central alarm unit. Installation by a home owner involves no more than attaching sensors to windows and doors and plugging the central alarm unit into the household electrical system. More sophisticated door sensors provide a time-delay setting which permits the home owner to enter and deactivate the system before the alarm sounds.

**TABLE 1.**
**CROSBY HOME SECURITY COMPANY**
**ANNUAL OPERATING STATEMENTS ($000)**

| | Last Year | 2 Years Ago | 3 Years Ago | 4 Years Ago | 5 Years Ago | 6 Years Ago | 7 Years Ago | 8 Years Ago | 9 Years Ago | 10 Years Ago |
|---|---|---|---|---|---|---|---|---|---|---|
| Net sales | $22,385 | $24,103 | $25,888 | $22,100 | $19,487 | $17,208 | $17,655 | $15,396 | $14,217 | $11,449 |
| Cost of goods sold | 20,236 | 21,428 | 22,031 | 19,072 | 16,408 | 14,099 | 14,142 | 12,055 | 10,862 | 8,884 |
| Gross profit | 2,149 | 2,675 | 3,857 | 3,028 | 3,079 | 3,109 | 3,513 | 3,341 | 3,355 | 2,565 |
| Selling, adm. and gen. exp. | 3,089 | 3,254 | 3,236 | 2,497 | 2,533 | 2,185 | 2,313 | 1,909 | 1,663 | 1,362 |
| Research and engineering | 313 | 289 | 233 | 199 | 195 | 189 | 194 | 185 | 185 | 149 |
| Pretax income | (1,253) | (868) | 388 | 332 | 351 | 735 | 1,006 | 1,247 | 1,507 | 1,054 |
| Income tax | — | — | 155 | 133 | 136 | 224 | 406 | 570 | 682 | 527 |
| Net earnings | (1,253) | (868) | 233 | 199 | 215 | 511 | 600 | 677 | 825 | 527 |
| | | | | | (Percentages) | | | | | |
| Net sales | 100.0 | 100.0 | 100.0 | 100.0 | 100.0 | 100.0 | 100.0 | 100.0 | 100.0 | 100.0 |
| Cost of goods sold | 90.4 | 88.9 | 85.1 | 86.3 | 84.2 | 82.8 | 80.1 | 78.3 | 76.4 | 77.6 |
| Gross profit | 9.6 | 11.1 | 14.9 | 13.7 | 15.8 | 17.2 | 19.9 | 21.7 | 23.6 | 22.4 |
| Selling, adm. and gen. exp. | 13.8 | 13.5 | 12.5 | 11.3 | 13.0 | 12.7 | 13.1 | 12.4 | 11.7 | 11.9 |
| Research and engineering | 1.4 | 1.2 | 0.9 | 0.9 | 1.0 | 1.1 | 1.1 | 1.2 | 1.3 | 1.3 |
| Pretax income | (5.6) | (3.6) | 1.5 | 1.5 | 1.8 | 3.4 | 5.7 | 8.1 | 10.6 | 9.2 |
| Income tax | — | — | 0.6 | 0.6 | 0.7 | 1.3 | 2.3 | 3.7 | 4.8 | 4.6 |
| Net earnings | (5.6) | (3.6) | 0.9 | 0.9 | 1.1 | 2.1 | 3.4 | 4.4 | 5.8 | 4.6 |
| Preferred dividends | $200 | $200 | $200 | $200 | $200 | $200 | $200 | $200 | $200 | $200 |
| Common dividends | — | — | 25 | 25 | 50 | 125 | 125 | 150 | 150 | 100 |

**TABLE 2.**
**CROSBY HOME SECURITY COMPANY**
**END-OF-YEAR BALANCE SHEETS ($000)**

|  | Last Year | 2 Years Ago | 3 Years Ago | 4 Years Ago | 5 Years Ago |
|---|---|---|---|---|---|
| <u>Assets</u> |  |  |  |  |  |
| Current assets |  |  |  |  |  |
| Cash | $ 125 | $ 186 | $ 277 | $ 362 | $ 315 |
| Accounts receivable (net) | 3,127 | 2,943 | 2,736 | 2,326 | 2,165 |
| Inventories (lower of cost or market) | 3,976 | 3,830 | 3,895 | 3,577 | 3,128 |
| Total current assets | 7,228 | 6,959 | 6,908 | 6,265 | 5,608 |
| Fixed assets |  |  |  |  |  |
| Land (cost) | 75 | 75 | 75 | 75 | 75 |
| Plant and equipment (net) | 1,285 | 1,360 | 1,515 | 1,427 | 1,655 |
| Total fixed assets | 1,360 | 1,435 | 1,590 | 1,502 | 1,730 |
| Total assets | 8,588 | 8,394 | 8,498 | 7,767 | 7,338 |
| <u>Liabilities and Net Worth</u> |  |  |  |  |  |
| Current liabilities |  |  |  |  |  |
| Loans payable | 2,600* | 2,030* | 1,597* | 1,367* | 1,123* |
| Accounts payable | 2,815 | 2,270 | 1,814 | 1,582 | 1,451 |
| Accrued payroll | 188 | 176 | 162 | 140 | 128 |
| Other accrued expenses | 133 | 113 | 97 | 85 | 64 |
| Accrued taxes |  |  | 155 | 133 | 136 |
| Total current liabilities | 5,736 | 4,589 | 3,825 | 3,307 | 2,902 |
| Notes payable—Andrew Crosby | 1,000 | 500 | 300 | 100 | 50 |
| Preferred stock (50,000 $1 par value shares, $4 annual dividend) | 50 | 50 | 50 | 50 | 50 |
| Common stock ($1 par value) | 10 | 10 | 10 | 5 | 5 |
| Retained earnings | 1,792 | 3,245 | 4,313 | 4,305 | 4,331 |
| Total liabilities and net worth | 8,588 | 8,394 | 8,498 | 7,767 | 7,338 |

*Bank loans secured by accounts receivable and land, plant, and equipment.

Although many protection systems are installed by professionals, a wide range of do-it-yourself kits are also available. There are many options for windows, doors, parked cars, and even personal transmitters. In addition to activating a horn or bell, devices which phone the police station are increasingly common. Smoke detectors, especially, have risen in popularity.

## Evaluations of Position of and Prospects for CHSC

During the first few days after she returned to Belleville, Jane Crosby reviewed CHSC's position and prospects with John Cunningham, senior vice-president of the company's principal commercial bank and the source of its

**TABLE 3.**
**CROSBY HOME SECURITY COMPANY**
**OPERATING STATEMENTS BY PRODUCT CATEGORY ($000)**

| | Last Year | | | 2 Years Ago | | | 3 Years Ago | | |
|---|---|---|---|---|---|---|---|---|---|
| | Electric Watchdog | Fire Alert | Silent Sentinel | Electric Watchdog | Fire Alert | Silent Sentinel | Electric Watchdog | Fire Alert | Silent Sentinel |
| Net sales | $9,562 | $9,668 | $3,155 | $11,390 | $10,936 | $1,777 | $12,822 | $12,220 | $846 |
| Cost of goods sold* | 8,128 | 9,205 | 2,903 | 9,795 | 9,624 | 2,009 | 10,770 | 10,331 | 930 |
| Gross profit | 1,434 | 463 | 252 | 1,595 | 1,312 | (232) | 2,052 | 1,889 | (84) |
| Selling, adm. and gen. exp.* | 1,879 | 648 | 562 | 2,010 | 750 | 494 | 2,075 | 861 | 300 |
| Research and engineering† | 25 | 56 | 110 | 20 | 34 | 125 | — | — | 88 |
| Pretax income | (470) | (241) | (420) | (435) | 528 | (851) | (23) | 1,028 | (472) |

*Both direct and indirect costs allocated by estimate.
†Additional research and engineering costs charged to new products still in development: Last year—$122; 2 years ago—$110; 3 years ago—$145.

**TABLE 4.**
**CROSBY HOME SECURITY COMPANY**
**OPERATING STATEMENT—TEN MONTHS ENDING OCTOBER 31ST ($000)**

|  | This Year | Last Year |
|---|---|---|
| Net sales | $20,566 | $19,587 |
| Costs of goods sold | 17,687 | 17,707 |
| Gross profit | 2,879 | 1,880 |
| Selling, adm. and gen. exp. | 2,589 | 2,703 |
| Research and engineering | 225 | 274 |
| Pretax income | 65 | (1,097) |

short-term borrowing; William Foster, legal counsel for the business for many years; the four vice-presidents, who constituted her father's top management team; and Paul Anderson, a young business school graduate, who had served as her father's assistant for the past year. With the exception of Anderson and John Kellerman, the head of research, these men had known Jane Crosby for many years and tended to treat her in a paternal style. In condensed form, here is what they told her.

### John Cunningham

"This was a growing, prosperous business until your father's health began to fail a few years ago and he had to cut back sharply on the time he devoted to it. Until then, he was totally involved in every aspect of managing CHSC, and I mean *literally every aspect.* He was a good manager, so things ran well. Unfortunately, one result of his total involvement was that the other senior managers did what he told them to do. They never had to make decisions on their own. When he became a part-time manager and they *had* to make decisions, it turned out they weren't very good at it. So costs got out of hand, profits dropped, and the company became a less effective competitor at the very time the market was becoming more competitive.

"Trouble started growing about four years ago, but the last two years were absolute disasters. I kept hoping and expecting that your father's health would improve. I think you should know that it was only for that reason that I permitted the bank to extend the credit that appears on the company's balance sheet. The bank is in a secure position because the loans are well covered by pledged receivables and fixed assets. But it is our present intent to curtail and not to increase the commitment of credit. Further, we are not willing to countenance further payment of the preferred dividend until the total bank loan is reduced below $2 million. Even with the bank's financial support in a time of weak management, the company could not have survived without your father's investment of his own funds. And you must be aware that his loans have no specific security. That's a lot of money at high risk.

"I had a tough talk with your father at the end of last year, when the company recorded a devastating loss of $1.25 million. I made it crystal clear that costs *must* be brought into line. And he talked just as tough with his vice-presidents. And they *have* improved matters—to the extent that for the first 10 months of this year they have accomplished about a break-even performance. That's not sensational, of course. But it looks pretty good compared to the previous year when they lost over a million dollars. (See Table 4.) It suggests that really capable management could restore the company to what it was when your father was in full charge.

"But now the problem is, Who is going to provide that kind of leadership? I tell you flatly that it won't and can't come from the present management group. They are good and faithful servants. They will follow a strong leader who knows what to do and how to do it. But when I've said that, I've said all the good I can say about them. I don't know, of course, how they view themselves or what political ambitions and jealousies may exist for individuals within the group.

"I understand that Lucas Elder has talked to you about *your* coming back here to run the business. Now, Jane, I've known you since you were a young girl, and I guess that my long friendship with your father entitles me to a little of the prerogative of a quasi-uncle. I know it was your father's hope that you would come into the business with him and eventually inherit and run it. But, speaking strictly as a quasi-uncle, let me warn you that breaking in with your father in learning how to manage a prosperous, growing company and starting without him to restore a very sick company to a healthy state are entirely different things. I have no reason to doubt your ability—I am familiar with your education and your consulting experience—but I wonder if you are ready for a challenge as big and complex and tough as this one. I really think you should consider selling the business. I don't know what you could get for it. But, on your instructions, I would be glad to explore the possibilities. Whatever you decide to do, I hope you will talk to me again before you take any action."

In reply to Jane Crosby's question about the company's competitive positions, the banker said, "I don't have an opinion worth respecting about that. I just don't know. I am certainly aware, as you must be, that the whole country is more conscious about and sensitive to security matters than it used to be. I've seen reports that sales of residential alarm and safety products and systems are on an uptrend. And I know that there are a number of companies, including some big ones, actively competing for the business. But whether your company has a leading or a following position, whether its products are superior or inferior, whether their distribution is well planned and aggressively executed—I don't really know much about these matters. You ought to find out, of course. What I do know is that sales are flat, costs are high, capitalization is thin, borrowings are excessive, and profits are nonexistent. Since none of these adverse conditions existed only a few years ago when your father was the full-time CEO, I suspect that weak management explains much of the unsatisfactory situation. But I don't know for sure."

## William Foster

"I'm afraid I have to tell you that you have inherited a very messy situation. It has been a sad experience for me to watch affairs deteriorate these last few years while your father was unable to give his full attention to the business. When his health began to fail, I was not optimistic about his recovering to the extent that he could resume active, full-time management of the company. This was not an easy subject to discuss with him, however, since he always insisted that his disability was temporary. I suggested more than once that he consider selling the business. That was when it was still profitable, although at a reduced rate compared to its earlier performance. But he brushed me off. Just wouldn't hear of it. He still looked forward to the time when you would join him in the business, and he wanted to keep it going for you. He was also concerned about maintaining dividends on the preferred stock, on which family members for whom he felt a deep responsibility depended. That was why he pumped his own money into the business. I advised against that, but he insisted on doing it. He was a man who took such a responsibility very seriously. I wish now I had taken a much stronger stand.

"You will want to talk with the senior managers. It may be helpful for me to make some comments about them, based on my observation of their operation of the business during recent years when your father was on the scene only half-time or even quarter-time. The first point to be absolutely clear about is that these are totally loyal people. Paul Foley, Bill O'Brien, and Al Pertshuk have worked for your father for many years. They admired him and worked hard under his direction. He liked and trusted them. I suspect he never noticed that they were not the most aggressive and imaginative managers in the world because he was really running the whole show himself, developing the products, supervising their manufacture, planning the marketing, making all the financial decisions. He was a first-class manager himself, with one blind spot—he was a one-man gang. I talked with him about this once, a couple of years before his first illness, and tried to encourage him to delegate responsibility, both to develop these associates and to find out by testing them just how capable they really were. But it just wasn't his style. He agreed with me on the desirability of doing it, but he never let go of the reins. Until he had to. And then it was too late.

"What I've observed is that each of these three gentlemen is a pretty good first mate; not one of them has the qualities of a good captain. It took great pressure from the bank to force them into cost-cutting this year. How much fat they had allowed to collect in the business is indicated by the million-dollar difference in the first 10 months now as against the same period last year. And I'd bet they still haven't come near to getting rid of all the fat there.

"Paul Foley is your typical good-fellow sales manager. He's a pal with the sales staff, plays golf, and drinks with the customers. He's worried about the failure of sales to grow when the total home security industry has been expanding at a fast clip. You should ask him about the reasons for this situation, but you shouldn't get your hopes up about hearing an analytical, documented answer.

"Bill O'Brien started as a kind of factory foreman and then rose as the business grew. He's always out in the plant in his shirt sleeves; knows all the workers by their first names and their wives' and husbands' and kids' names, too; can fix any machine that breaks down. And then I have to ask myself, 'But he is a vice-president of manufacturing?' Bear in mind that I'm a lawyer, not an M.B.A. But I do legal work for several other companies, and I have occasion to meet and talk with their managers. I have the notion that a vice-president of manufacturing needs a detailed understanding of costs and cost systems, inventory control standards and systems, policies and practices in procurement, and personnel administration. Well, Bill O'Brien gets a little shaky in those areas. On the other hand, let something go wrong on the production line and Bill will work nights and holidays to get it fixed—and *he* will fix it. There are a lot of production managers who can't do that, and some who wouldn't even if they could.

"Al Pertshuk—well. Al goes back about 20 years in the business, to a time when all your father needed to back him up in handling money was a bookkeeper. I didn't know Al then; I hadn't begun to do the legal work for the business. But I'd bet he was a perfect bookkeeper. Never made a posting error, never missed a trail balance, never was caught short in an audit. But it was your father who handled financial matters with John Cunningham at the bank, not Al Pertshuk. I don't know that Al couldn't do it. He was never given the chance to try. But he makes the wheels go round in the office every day, sees that the records are kept, kept right, and kept on time. He runs the budget and gets out the management reports when they're due, and I've never heard anyone complain about an error in them. That's a record he's likely to maintain until the day he retires.

"Then there's John Kellerman, who has the title of vice-president of research. He's relatively new. Your father was the whole research department for many years, solely responsible for product development. Five years ago, when his health began to crumble, he hired John out of an assistant professorship in electrical engineering at Carnegie-Mellon and last year gave him the vice-presidential title. I assess John as a pretty good product tester and evaluator, but surely not an inventor and maybe not even a good product developer. Now that may be doing him a great injustice. But I do know the record since John has been here, and what I have said is a fair reflection of the record. He's a nice young man, comes to work early, stays late, keeps a clean desk top. He really doesn't carry much weight in the business—not yet, at any rate. With his title, he's a member of the operating committee. But from what the other committee members tell me, he doesn't contribute much—just sits there and agrees with what is said.

"And there is also Paul Anderson. Your father hired Paul a couple of years ago out of Carnegie's Graduate School of Industrial Administration, to be a kind of administrative assistant to the president. He's an undergraduate electrical engineer with a master's degree in management, and he's bright and well educated and probably twice as smart as anyone in the company—and he sticks his nose into everything that's going on and asks questions and gets people upset and mad as hell.

"On balance, I'm sure Anderson's an asset in the business, but he is pretty hard to live with. I've seen Bill O'Brien get so furious with him that he wanted to hang one right on the button of his jaw. But Paul was right about the matter they were arguing about, and eventually got Bill to calm down and admit he was right. I think your father hoped to break Paul in gradually and train and develop him over a stretch of years into a kind of executive vice-president. And now Paul is out there at loose ends with your father gone. He's administrative assistant to a non-existent president. The vice-presidents don't know how to use him. He doesn't know how to use himself. Unless he is brought into some kind of organization structure soon, my guess is that he'll quit. And that might turn out to be a real loss to the business.

"Where does all this leave you? Well, I don't have a clear view of what you might want to do. You haven't asked me for my advice, but here it is anyhow. I think you should recruit a competent president from outside the company. To interest the right kind of person you'd have to make a stock deal—sell him or her some of the stock at a *very* attractive price, so that *if* the company gets back on the rails—healthy, growing, profitable—he or she could make a big fat capital gain by collaborating with you in selling the company when it's attractive enough to fetch a good price as a going concern. The ideal candidate would be an experienced and competent executive out of some Pittsburgh-area company, say about in the mid-fifties, who knows he or she isn't going to get the top job in the present company and wants a chance to build an estate before retirement. Allow five years or so to rebuild Crosby Home Security Company, and then put it up for sale. You'd probably have to sell the candidate half the stock you inherited—let's say 49 percent maximum so that you could be chair of the board and keep control. But it would be worth it *if* you found the right manager, *if* the recovery were accomplished. Those are big ifs, but what's the alternative?"

### Paul Foley

"Why have sales been flat for four years? Worse than flat? In the first place, total sales of the home security industry have been growing by at least 20 percent annually, so that our market share has been shrinking. And in the second place, we've been raising prices to cover rising costs. So level dollar sales have meant fewer unit sales. One other point should be made right at the start: We have one growth product, 'Silent Sentinel'; the two others have been stagnant at best and are really on the way down. What's the problem? That's a good question.

"I think it's a combination of things. First, while it's true enough that the total market has been growing, so has the competition. At least seven companies have moved into this business in a substantial way in the last five years. Three of them are a lot larger than CHSC. I'm not even counting the fly-by-nights, the little electrical shops that are designing and installing their own security systems in their local neighborhoods. Each of these units is a peanut in size, but they add up to a substantial chunk of the total market. What I'm saying is that if you could see the operating figures of all the competitors, you'd discover that many of them are in the same box we're in, taking a smaller share of a growing market and not getting rich from the experience.

"OK, that's number one. Number two: We've got a couple of aging products. Not senile, not even obsolete—although getting into that condition. But aging, getting along in years; like me, I suppose. The good one is 'Silent Sentinel,' of course, but it can't carry the whole business, and besides, we haven't got the production costs right on that one yet. So product-wise, we're not a strong competitor and we don't have an exciting story to tell to either the trade or the consumer.

"Three: A weak marketing system. I don't know how familiar you are with how we sell, but here's the picture. We distribute through manufacturers' agents, 14 of them across the country, each with an exclusive franchise to handle our line in that region. We pay them a 5 percent commission on their sales. Each agent sells to between 10 and 20 hardware and electrical supply wholesalers. The wholesaler's margin, or at least what we suggest, is about 10 percent of the selling price to the retailer. Wholesale distributors sell mostly to retail hardware and electrical supply stores. Our suggested price to consumers would give retailers a margin of about 40 percent on their selling price. What this adds up to is that our products are available to consumers in about 7,000 retail outlets across the country— theoretically available, that is: *if* every wholesale distributor of every one of our manufacturers' agents carried our line and *if* the wholesaler sold it to every one of the retail accounts. But they don't, of course. We don't have a precise sighting on our current retail dealer representation, but I'd guess it's in the neighborhood of 3,000 stores, coast-to-coast.

"Now you can probably begin to see the dimensions of our problem. If you accept the trade estimate that retail sales of home security products amount to, say, $400 million and also accept my estimate that the retail value of our line is about double our factory sales dollars, say $45 million, then right now we have a market share in the range of 11 to 15 percent. Not too bad, you might think. Except that five years ago, with the same dollar sales, we had better than a 15 percent share of a smaller total market.

"You have to recognize also that we don't represent important sales volume to anybody along our distribution channels. Divide $45 million in sales among 3,000 retailers, and you can calculate that our average dealer sells maybe $15,000 worth of CHSC products annually, not enough to get the dealers interested in promoting them. They carry them, but they don't push them. All the push has to come from our own promotion to consumers—plus the override we get from the promotion of the big boys with the fancy security systems that need professional installation. By override I mean that their advertising gets a lot of people excited about burglary and fire protection, and then some of those potential customers have the shock of discovering how much those fancy systems cost—as much as $3,000 or more for a full-sized suburban home—and they go shopping for something cheaper. Some of those shoppers read our ads about self-installation and look for a store that carries our line. And we get some business on the bounce that way.

"Our special market niche is that we still have competitive products in the do-it-yourself segment of the total market. However, serious competition is now appearing in that segment from established companies. In addition, there are the electrician-moonlighters who rig up and install their own systems. Most of these amateur systems are no good. Either they're supersensitive and go off when the family dog takes a stroll through the house at night, or they're undersensitive and respond only to a three-alarm fire or an earthquake; they just give the whole industry a bad name. So conceptually we're not in a bad position—as of right now.

"But we're not going anywhere except backwards. We need improved products to give us news to excite the consumer market and our wholesale and retail outlets. We need to get our manufacturing costs down so we can make a decent profit, so that we can increase our advertising to consumers and the trade and strengthen our sales promotion effort through the trade, so that we can build sales and become more important to our distributors and dealers and get them more interested in displaying and talking about and pushing our line. And if we can do all this, we will have a nice, healthy, growing, profitable business—the kind we had when your father was running this company. We're part of a growth industry. We still have a significant position in the industry. There's no reason we can't restore this company.

"It will take money, that's for sure. Where will it come from? Well, look at the recent record. When it became clear at the end of last year that we had to cut costs—just *had* to, to survive—we did it. We sold about a million dollars more product this year, with just about the same dollar cost of goods sold as last year. How? By laying it on the line to our factory workers and getting productivity up. That put a million dollars more on the gross profit line. Then we cut back our advertising budget by a hundred thousand, from $600,000 to $500,000—and that really hurt because, as I've explained to you, we get very little push through our distribution system. We have to *pull* our products through it by advertising and sales promotion to consumers and the trade. And we let two production engineers go. And that will hurt, too, because we need product development. But it was fish-or-cut-bait time for the whole organization, and we did these tough things.

"Can we cut more? This is where the arguments begin. I think we could get another half-million out of manufacturing costs at our present volume, but try and sell that to Bill O'Brien. We've never had a union in our plant, and he says we're begging for one, and then goodbye productivity. Or so he says. *His* idea is to take it out of selling and advertising. Well, we have 10 salespeople. They don't deal with our manufacturers' agents. That's *my* job, and I spend most of my time at it, all across the country. I've got to keep those agents feeling warm and friendly toward us, because every one of them handles other products, noncompetitive with ours, but many with bigger sales volumes that generate more commissions.

"Our salespeople work with wholesalers and retailers. They encourage wholesalers to pay attention to our line and push for more retail distribution. They do missionary work with retailers, try to get new outlets for our line, try to get displays in stores. The orders they take are funneled right back through our wholesalers. You can figure about $50,000 to $60,000 per salesperson in salary, commissions, and travel expenses. Any cut there would hurt sales. As for advertising, we ought to be spending more, not less.

"Al Pertshuk will tell you we could cut receivables by a million dollars and inventory by another million. Well, maybe we could get a little money out of inventory, but if we bear down on collections we'll lose sales. You've got to stretch payment periods and accept slow pay, too, to keep business these days. It's a shame to have to operate this way, but it's a fact of life. Al sits in his office and says it's easy to tighten collections. He doesn't know what conditions are like in the field. You've got to spend money out there to make money. We simply must be competitive, including payment terms. That's the way it is."

### William O'Brien

"The basic problem is that we let ourselves get very sloppy when your father wasn't around to watch the nickels and dimes. We did things the easy way. We oiled every squeaking wheel with money. And all this slack caught up with us. Now I've taken the slack out of manufacturing. Look at the operating statement this year for proof. A million dollars more output with no increase in cost of goods sold, and this was in a time of rising material costs, too. But every loose screw has been tightened as far as it will go. The next contribution *has* to come from marketing. We simply don't need all those salespeople—not with our distribution system through agents and wholesalers. We could save a half-million dollars right there in selling expense—and some more in advertising. And we could tighten up on collecting receivables and cut down on our finished goods inventory. I bet we could take at least half a million dollars out of each of those areas. Then we could pay down the bank loans and get some breathing room.

"But we need new products, too. In the old days your father was the source of new product ideas and product improvements. I hate to say this, but I don't think John Kellerman can do the job. He's competent enough to work on the engineering side of existing products, but he's not an inventor. I think he should be replaced, even if we have to spend more money to get the right person for the job.

"Paul and Al will argue that we can cut costs even more out in the plant. It would be very dangerous to try to do this. This is union country here in the Pittsburgh area. We've operated all these years without a union because everybody out there in the plant liked your father and trusted him. I've tried to keep it that way, and so far I've succeeded. But we're at the outer limits of tolerance right now. We've put in production incentives. We've gotten rid of some lazy people who wouldn't go along. Pushing any harder would be asking for trouble. What we *could* do, if we had the money to invest, is put in some labor-saving equipment, automate some assembly processes. But even this would have to be done very slowly and carefully, with the displacement falling to people ready to retire. Otherwise, nothing but headaches all around."

### Alfred Pertshuk

"We've made a million dollar improvement this year. With strong leadership, we could cut another million dollars. There's still fat in this organization. Look at receivables. Current dollar sales are about the same as they were four years ago, but we've got $800,000 more in receivables. You can't tell me that's necessary. Sure it's hard to go out there and press for prompt payment of bills. But our creditors beat on us, and the only way we've been able to finance those receivables is to become slow paying ourselves. I take the pressure on that. And don't think it doesn't hurt us on the prices our suppliers charge us. There are no bargains available to us anymore. Our suppliers pack that extended credit right into their prices to us.

"Look at inventories. Again, with our sales level, we've got almost half a million dollars more in inventory. It's not necessary. But when I point this out to Paul, he fights me. We sit around and discuss the situation in operating committee meetings, but we can't get agreement. The bank presses me to do something, but I don't have the authority to make it happen. We need a strong leader here, a real boss who can make a decision and stick to it."

### John Kellerman

"The weakness in this business is in sales. We've got good products, competitive products. We've got a unique market position with our self-installation feature. But our products are priced too low and are sold ineffectually through that agent-wholesaler system. What we ought to do is to get rid of the agents, increase our sales force, sell directly to wholesalers, and get our prices up to cover the added costs and make a profit. All Paul does is feed baloney to those agents, wine and dine them, and play golf with them. Our own sales force calling directly on wholesalers could do this job right, and that's what we need.

"As for R & D, the problem we have really can be traced back to the time when your father was active in the business full time. He developed our products all the way from original concept through engineering into production. He was totally responsible for our present three major products: 'Electric Watchdog,' 'Fire Alert,' and 'Silent Sentinel.'

"He brought me into the organization five years ago to take over the responsibility from him. But before his persistent illness he resisted letting go of what interested him so deeply, and after his illness all the pressure on me as head of R & D was focused on two things. One was in making minor improvements to existing products to make them more competitive in ease of installation and in sensitivity of response to any type of security invasion stimulus. The other was to redesign existing products to make them easier and cheaper to manufacture.

"As a result, the R & D function has been largely staffed with people whose competence is in engineering development, not in product innovation. Now I hope you don't misunderstand me. We have—I guess a more accurate statement would be I have—two new product concepts on the drawing board which could obsolete everything now in the self-installation section of the home security alarm business, both competitors' products and our own. They involve the incorporation of microchips in alarm, signaling, and control systems.

"But we don't have the talent in our research staff to carry this concept through design, testing, and application. I need to add people. Instead, under pressure from the bank to cut costs, this year I took over $50,000 out of our budget. It's now at a quarter-million dollar annual level. It should be double that. With the right talent and a major focus on new products, we would be in a position to revolutionize the business. And mark my words, someone in this industry will take this step. It had better be CHSC. I'd hate to be a follower when some other company takes the lead."

### Paul Anderson

"Look, Miss Crosby, I'm quitting this job, so I've got nothing to protect. I'll tell you exactly what the situation is here. There's no competent management. These people around here can't handle responsibility and don't want it. It's obvious to me that this company is loaded with unnecessary costs. But top management did nothing about the situation until the bank stepped in and told them what had to be done. So they made a first pass at the excess and knocked off a million dollars. There's at least another million that needs to go, but they won't make the effort.

"I'll tell you what you ought to do. You ought to fire your vice-presidents—all four of them. They were errand boys for your father, that's all. Then either hire some tougher people, if you're going to take charge here yourself, or hire a president who would do the recruiting. It's worth doing, too. Because under all this flab and stagnation and nonprofit operation, there's a good business in a growth industry. If I had some money, I'd offer to buy it from you myself, that's how much I think of its possibilities.

"This business needs to be taken to pieces and redesigned from the ground up. We need a first-class talent in charge of R & D who can upgrade our line and introduce new products. Then we can really distinguish CHSC products from the crap that's peddled by moonlighting electricians. We could get a premium price for our products and still be far below the systems that are sold by companies like ADT, Honeywell, and Westinghouse.

"We ought to scrap our cumbersome, ineffective distribution system through agents and wholesale distributors. They're nothing but a bunch of order-takers. Year after year we keep trying to increase the number of retail dealers who carry our line. What for? Most of them sell only a few thousand dollars worth a year. We don't mean enough to them to get the attention and promotion we need. We ought to shrink the number of dealers. Pick out just the biggest and best in each territory, give them exclusive franchises, and then require them to promote and display. We ought to contract with them for cooperative advertising, say on a 50-50 basis, dollar for dollar. We should use our own sales force to sell direct to the largest dealers. We should shrink our wholesale business the same way—pick out the best in each territory and give them exclusive rights to sell to selected dealers other than the ones we sell to directly.

"And we ought to spend more on advertising—use spot television more in major markets. Our products lend themselves to a powerful visual selling message. We ought to engage a first-class advertising agency to dramatize that message.

"Where would all the money come from? Some of it would come from the commissions we've been paying those agents who don't really work to earn them. Some of it could come out of excessive receivables and inventories. Al Pertshuk is no powerhouse of a financial manager, but he's dead right about the money tied up in those areas that just isn't working for us. His trouble is that he has no clout. He calls attention to these problems, but he lacks the force to get results. And beyond the improvement in productivity this year, under great pressure from the bank, we could get at least another half-million in factory payroll economies. Bill O'Brien is afraid of unionization. Well, we ought to have the guts to accept the risk. If we end up getting organized, so be it. That wouldn't be the end of the world. It just looks that way to O'Brien because he's never had to run a union plant. Other people do it and prosper. We could, too, if we had to.

"Maybe this all sounds pretty brash to you. But I'm certain it could be done. Hell, I could do it myself if you were willing to take the chance of putting me in charge. But I couldn't do it, nobody could do it, with those old-timers in charge of production and marketing and finance. All they know how to do is what they did in the old days. Anything new frightens them."

# COMPREHENSIVE CASE 3

## The Tulip City Ambulance Company*

In early February of 1985, Marshall (Mart) Berghorst, President and Board Chairman of Tulip City Ambulance, reviewed the recent activities of the firm to assure himself that they were appropriate at that time. He was particularly concerned whether these activities could improve the overall financial position of the company and contribute to his own long-run personal goals. The past five years were especially traumatic. Except for 1983, emergency medical service (EMS) volume, once the firm's mainstay, dropped steadily. Profits fluctuated widely. Fixed assets, which included the vehicle fleet, were almost fully depreciated, and the use of two specialty vehicles fell short of expectations. (Exhibits 6 to 9 at the end of the case contain income, balance sheet, and supplemental data for 1980 through 1984.) During 1984, morale among the work force was consistently lower than at any time in the firm's 24-year history. Further compounding these dilemmas were unfavorable competitive conditions, both locally and nationally.

Berghorst believed that the company had grown successfully during its first 20 years because of continued community acceptance of his service offerings, the spirit of cooperation that existed with Bellview General Hospital, and the absence of conflict with the city government. However, with so much turbulence beginning to show in the immediate environment, Berghorst again contemplated how the firm's direction might change. In light of these concerns, a number of recurring questions surfaced in his mind: How should Tulip City alter its basic service mix? Should the new direction be toward revitalizing emergency medical care and transport or toward the more lucrative routine transfers? What would be the most likely scenarios concerning the entry of either Bellview General Hospital or the city government into the ambulance market? If Tulip City remained in the EMS sector, what would be the personnel and equipment requirements necessary for an Advanced Life Support (ALS) state rating? Since the firm had grown beyond the limits of one-person management, what role should Karl VerBeek play in the future? In the midst of his planning, Berghorst had been contacted by James Vanlaar, Tulip City's controversial competitor. This man offered, in conjunction with St. Luke's Hospi-

---

*This case was prepared by J. Kim De Dee of the University of Wisconsin—Oshkosh and Richard C. Johnson of the University of Arkansas as the basis for class discussion rather than to illustrate either effective or ineffective handling of a managerial situation. Tulip City Ambulance is a disguised company name; however, all key relationships remain intact. The case is reprinted here by special permission of the authors and the Case Research Association.

tal, to buy the company, thus giving him almost total dominance in the regional metropolitan area.

Maintenance of Tulip City's growth pattern was particularly important to Berghorst. Although he was less than 50, he had on occasion considered leaving the firm, but only if it could stand on its own without his direct intervention. Now that his family had grown, and his wife was pressuring him to enjoy more leisure time, Mart felt a lesser need to increase his wealth. Instead, he wanted his ventures, including Tulip City, to be self-supportive with a favorable reputation within the community.

## Tulip City Company History

In 1960, following his wife's troubled pregnancy which required several emergency trips to the hospital, Mart concluded that neither of the two funeral homes nor the existing independent provider offered an acceptable degree of quality in emergency ambulance care. Soon after the baby was born, Mart solicited some friends who possessed high-speed driving skills and who enjoyed a periodic respite from home each week. Next, the 20-year-old entrepreneur combined a 500-dollar savings with other family members' capitalization to place a down payment on a low-mileage Cadillac hearse. Additional bank financing was obtained to convert the vehicle into ambulance service, build working capital, and provide initial rent on an abandoned gas station with a working hoist.

An important reason for the firm's early success came from the "gentlemen's agreement" negotiated with the Poindexter Funeral Home to handle its emergency nighttime calls. This allowed the funeral director a full night's sleep without any appreciable effect on profits.

Late in 1961, Mart left his mechanic's position at the local Ford dealership and accepted the presidency of the recently incorporated Tulip City Ambulance Company. His list of responsibilities covered the maintenance of the base, vehicle, and equipment. In addition, Berghorst surprised the industry with a promotion campaign he inaugurated that placed the firm's telephone stickers wherever there was a high probability of an emergency occurrence.

During the early growth years, Mrs. Berghorst began to handle all office and dispatching duties while Mart concentrated more earnestly on the company's transfer services. By the end of 1962 both funeral homes elected to drop out of the ambulance business. They converted their vehicles into hearses and sold their emergency telephone numbers to Tulip City. This ploy doubled the firm's emergency volume to four daily calls and cut in half the number of competitors. The fledgling enterprise, however, faced even stiffer competition from the county's only other provider, The DeYoung Ambulance Company.

With over 4,000 independent and volunteer organizations in existence, Tyson DeYoung had been able to parlay a sizable inheritance and extensive debt financing into the third largest ambulance company in the United States. He had reasoned that because most firms served relatively small local areas, economies of scale prevented them from realizing sufficient return on invested capital. By contrast, DeYoung had operations in Michigan, Illinois, and Indiana and planned to expand into Ohio and Kentucky. DeYoung ambulances were positioned at most regional sporting events, entertainment programs, and the Indianapolis Motor Speedway. This latter tactic exposed the firm's name and logo to almost 350,000 spectators who attended the various time trials and parades, as well as the Memorial Day race. Further recognition was also gained through national radio and regional television coverage of these events.

The DeYoung growth pattern in property and equipment remained consistent through the early 1970s. By 1976 he had committed a series of strategic errors, and the company's revenue and cash flow plummeted. Later that year Tyson DeYoung died of alcoholism, and his widow sold the one remaining vehicle and the accounts receivable to Tulip City for $5,000. No employees were retained.

For the rest of the decade, Tulip City held close to a monopoly position and, under the direction of Berghorst, accomplished the following results: opened and equipped a second base, doubling the firm's operating radius; acquired the assets of two bankrupt competitors; diversified into specialty emergency transport services (hospital to hospital) for premature infants and critically injured adults; vertically integrated into new ambulance construction; and introduced entry-level standards and development courses for all personnel.

## The Operating Environment

Located between two interstate highways in Michigan's lower peninsula, Manchester and its border city, Springdale, have recently experienced sizable population growth patterns. Part of this 5–6 percent annual increase was attributed to the favorable economic climate of the region, the strong religious work ethic of its inhabitants, and the community's lower-than-average age and higher-than-average income levels. Another force behind this expansion was the continuing industrialization of the tri-county metropolitan area. Because Manchester-Springdale was within close proximity to the huge automotive complexes of eastern Michigan and had a large university, industry analysts considered it ideal for the location of low-technology manufacturing plants. Prior to 1980, Tulip City's only operational constraint came from Tyson DeYoung's competitive maneuverings. Since 1980, however, the firm has faced a growing number of threatening developments.

## The Competition

Although it has gone through periods of refinement, the ambulance industry has always been intensely competitive. Tulip City has competed directly not only for consumer acceptance, but also for referrals from medical personnel concerning transfers to and from hospitals, rest homes, and related institutions. In the last five years the company has fared well in this toughening environment, demonstrating favorable user attitudes toward its services. Total ambulance requests in Manchester-Springdale exceeded industry norms, to one daily call for each 6,600 people. This, however, was only partially a reflection of Tulip City's effectiveness. While the company held a clearly dominant position, its share of the market had shown an overall steady decline in the last half-decade (see Exhibit 1).

The newest competitive threat to face Tulip City originated from a small group of missionaries organized "to provide a fully licensed and highly qualified Christian ambulance service to the people of Manchester and Springdale." Developed solely as a charitable venture, the firm relied primarily on contributions to cover its variable costs, but in 14 months was able to increase its volume load to five calls a week.

Tulip City's most significant competitive threat came from the easily recognized Van's Ambulance Service. Since its inception in early 1980, this firm's principal objective, according to founder David Vanlaar, "was to obtain market position and respect using luxury emergency vehicles. This company was created not to produce short-term profits, but to provide a viable growth-oriented activity for myself and those who follow my business philosophy."

In January of 1976 Vanlaar dropped out of college to enter the U.S. Army. While there, he worked as a heavy-equipment operator, lived frugally, and in four years was able to meet the initial payment requirements on one of the few remain-

## EXHIBIT 1
## COMPETITIVE SUMMARY OF NORMAL-DUTY AMBULANCE VOLUME FOR YEARS 1980–1984[1]

|       |             | Daily Calls | | |
|-------|-------------|-------------|-------|--------|
| Year  | Population[2] | Tulip City[3] | Van's | Total[4] |
| 1980  | 145,500     | EMS 12.0    | 0.5   | 12.5   |
|       |             | T/F 12.5    | 1.0   | 13.5   |
| 1981  | 147,525     | EMS 11.0    | 1.0   | 12.0   |
|       |             | T/F 13.5    | 1.2   | 14.7   |
| 1982  | 154,900     | EMS 10.0    | 2.0   | 12.0   |
|       |             | T/F 14.5    | 2.0   | 16.5   |
| 1983  | 162,650     | EMS 10.0    | 2.5   | 12.5   |
|       |             | T/F 14.5    | 2.5   | 17.5   |
| 1984  | 170,780     | EMS 9.5     | 3.5   | 13.5   |
|       |             | T/F 15.0    | 2.0   | 18.0   |

[1]EMS and transfers only.
[2]Manchester 85%, Springdale 15%.
[3]DeYoung calls included.
[4]Totals that don't agree reflect other competitors.

*Source:* Company records and casewriter's computations.

ing Cadillac ambulances to be produced. The firm obtained sufficient resources through loan agreements from Manchester's second largest hospital (St. Lukes, with 370 beds) to penetrate substantially into Tulip City's market position. Rather than rely on personal selling, Vanlaar's primary marketing approach was the ornate vehicle, large Yellow Page advertisements, and sales of a subscription service. The subscription service annually offered families one emergency or one transfer call at less than 35 percent of normal competitive rates. In addition, Vanlaar distributed bright green bumper stickers with the company name, logo, and phone number.

Vanlaar felt that regardless of the situation, requests for his ambulance were specific rather than general. Thus, to maintain corporate integrity, company policy stated that when the ambulance was tied up on either a transfer or emergency and a second call came in, the initial call would be completed under lights and siren status to avoid referring the later call to a competitor. Despite repeated complaints from medical personnel and patients' families, the policy was never altered.

Van's principal company strategy stressed minimizing response time to or from the trauma scene. Important to this process were the speeds attained by the high-performance vehicle. After a number of police warnings and newspaper editorials, Vanlaar was summoned with a reckless driving charge (92 mph in a 25 mph zone) and ordered to appear in court. In an effort to convince the jury and the general public of the validity of his methods, Vanlaar retained a Chicago-based law firm known for its truculence.

A motivated prosecution presented a force of expert witnesses that included a noted orthopedic surgeon who stated, "In the past 13 years I have had occasion to be familiar with more than a few emergency cases. In no instance can I recall where speed in transportation of the injured patient materially affected the patient's outcome. . . . Actually, what is necessary is appropriate methodology adequately applied at the scene and then a reasonable speed, say, 10 miles an hour over posted limits with allowed passage through red traffic lights. . . . This is required if our streets are to remain safe for all concerned." After two days of heated court debate, Vanlaar was acquitted of all charges.

After this legal victory, Vanlaar went on the offensive. To counter the growing conflict he knew was developing between his firm, the regional emergency medical industry, and the city police and fire department, he initiated a series of half-page newspaper advertisements. Each promotion began with the question "Did you know," and included at least one of the following topics:

1.  That firemen, professing to be first-aiders, have stood waiting by dying patients for professional medical help and not attempting any life-supporting techniques?

2.  That police agencies have ordered ambulance attendants away from persons needing service because the attendants were not of their particular political choice? At least one such patient died.

3. That people in need have waited 45 minutes for ambulance service because they called a police or fire agency first?

4. That the county is going to use hundreds of thousands of dollars to accomplish what is already being done "tax free" because of a lack of cooperation with available resources?

The promotional campaign, which was intended to be politically conservative, included quotes related to "progression without taxation" and "Don't waste time calling a police or fire agency first; call us directly and immediately for your medical emergencies. The Vanlaar Ambulance Company—the state's most progressive service."

## The Hospitals

In the late 1970s and early 1980s, Manchester saw a significant trend toward the provision of fuller emergency medical services being offered by both hospitals. St. Lukes seized the opportunity to increase its emergency room volume with direct and continued support of Van's Ambulance Company. In addition to providing financial assistance, St. Lukes on numerous occasions supplied materials, provided training, and shared news coverage of important events with David Vanlaar or his company.

In August of 1983, Bellview General Hospital (450 beds), the city's largest and most centrally located facility, was acquired by a national chain noted for its innovative and aggressive management style. Following a year of extensive reorganization, Jackson Baker was offered and accepted the position of Vice President of Hospital Projects and reported directly to the Executive Committee. After preparing in-depth analyses on a number of potential investments, Baker decided to promote the idea of a hospital-based ambulance service, which he felt would better position the trauma center within the organization's overall strategic objectives. Bellview was profitable and in fairly sound financial condition, but recently had experienced a reduced bed-use factor similar to the rest of the industry. To promote future growth patterns for the hospital, the following key points were stressed in his report.

A properly designed and maintained hospital-based ambulance service should:

1. Provide access to additional revenue sources from a relatively small investment base ($125,000).

2. Increase to 41–42 percent the number of patients being admitted through the trauma center, thereby utilizing more effectively the trauma center personnel.

3. Create a valuable marketing tool and generate goodwill in the community through exposure of the hospital name and logo on vehicles and uniforms.

4.  Act as an effective feeder system to more definitive and complete care, helping to alleviate the unused capacity problem.
5.  Countervail the market share gained by St. Lukes through their direct financial assistance to Van's Ambulance Service.
6.  Provide the hospital complete control over the Trauma Unit and Baby Unit vehicles and crews, and allow the hospital to absorb the 50 percent profits and cash flows now shared with the Tulip City Ambulance Company.

During September of 1984 the executive committee began deliberations on the proposal and instructed Baker to develop a management team, refine certain objectives, and begin negotiations with principal resource suppliers. Discussions continued between Baker and the Executive Committee, and by early December a tentative arrangement was reached. The project was given secondary status to allow the hospital time to evaluate any improvements in the overall EMS system, especially as it pertained to the city government's entry into the arena. Although the potential advantages of the project appeared to outweigh its shortcomings, Baker estimated the hospital's entry into the ambulance market at less than 50–50. If the city government did proceed with their EMS proposal without any corresponding improvement in the for-profit sector, that probability dropped to zero.

## Manchester's Response

The Manchester situation was much as other cities of its size. The alienation that continued to grow in the city-wide EMS sector became a political issue. After the elections, Paul Wynski, the newly elected commissioner of Manchester's Primary Services Department, set out to pursue two principal objectives. First came the desire to put his office at the forefront of the city's growth pattern, and second, he wanted to personally establish some tangible evidence that would identify his potential for higher government offices.

As commissioner, Wynski was responsible for the total operations of two separate groups, the City Protection Group (police) and the Fire Protection and Control Group. A simple breakdown of the 22 million dollar budget indicated that 76 percent covered salaries for 870 employees, while the remainder went to property, plant, and equipment. Included in this final category was the central administration building, 18 regional fire stations, 21 diesel pumpers, 7 ladder trucks, and a fleet of patrol cars.

To meet his intentions, Mr. Wynski contemplated a number of alternatives, but settled on a municipal tax-based EMS rescue and transportation system. His initial strategy was to begin strictly as an advanced emergency care treatment and extraction service, with later expansion into patient transport. Paramedic training, beyond the emergency medical technician rating that was held by many police and fire department personnel, was estimated to take one additional year. Another six months would be necessary to operationalize the total EMS process.

Wynski believed in change and innovation, but was practical enough to realize that any major variation in his department would be a formidable task. To help win approval of his proposal from the city commission, he distributed the memo shown in Exhibit 2 to all of his colleagues.

## EXHIBIT 2
## MEMORANDUM

TO:      All City Commissioners

FROM: Paul L. Wynski: Commissioner of Primary Services

RE:      Establishment of a class A emergency medical service system

DATE:   April 16, 1984

As a result of the growing unrest in the current independently operated emergency medical service (EMS) system, I would appreciate your opinions on the following project objectives. I plan to make a more formal presentation of these generalized goals at the commission meeting scheduled May 3, 1984.

Critical Objectives:

1.  Establishment of a city-wide advanced life support (ALS) emergency rescue and treatment system.
2.  Expansion into emergency transport of trauma victims.
3.  Development of billing and collection procedures, encouraging the service to become self-supporting.

Rationale for the System:

1.  No qualified paramedics operate in Manchester.
2.  Tulip City Ambulance, the city's largest provider, only offers basic life support (BLS).
3.  Manchester may set a state-recognized precedent.
4.  Alleviate the expanding turmoil in the current EMS system arising from Van's Ambulance Company's operating style.

Future Tactics Include:

1.  Additional research focusing on property, plant, equipment, and personnel costs.
2.  In-depth observation of municipal services currently operating in adjoining states.
3.  Expert judgments detailing legal complexities and antitrust laws.

Commissioner Wynski was pleasantly surprised at the outcome of the meeting. Most commissioners heartily agreed with the general intentions of the proposal and gave tacit approval to the design of his emergency medical paramedic system.

Enthusiastically returning to his office, Wynski promptly scheduled a meeting with his staff, intent on further development of the EMS model. To increase the profile of his ambulance system concept, the commissioner also called both television stations and the local paper to arrange detailed news releases. Later that year, as his plans took on a more defined focus, Commissioner Wynski commented, "There are notable differences in the design of a tax-supported EMS system from those in the for-profit sector. For example, our initial capital requirements will be high, approaching $300,000. Our operating and development costs, however, should decline rapidly in the next three years. There is an 85 percent probability that Manchester will have a government-sponsored EMS system by the middle of 1985 and, with computerized billing and collection procedures, be self-supporting by early 1988.

## The Tulip City Operations

By 1980, Tulip City and the reorganized DeYoung service had both achieved solid reputations in the private ambulance sector. Following the acquisition, the parent company and its subsidiary occupied two bases with garages at strategic points in Manchester and Springdale. The bases, both located in low-income areas, were extensively refurbished to provide living, office, and meeting space in addition to usual kitchen facilities. The Manchester location also included the central administration office and a 2,600-square-foot garage that housed a majority of the vehicles and associated maintenance and repair equipment.

In January of 1975, as a move to show support for Springdale, Tulip City enlarged its base capacity there and built a similar but smaller garage (1,800 sq. ft.). This structure covered the primary and backup vehicles and assorted rental wheelchairs, hospital beds, and ancillary devices.

All the buildings were either built or reconditioned by Berghorst and construction teams he assembled, and at the end of 1980 were in acceptable operating condition. Since 1980, however, after extensive usage and exposure, no major repairs or upgrading had been performed on any of the firm's property or facilities.

## The Human Resources

Berghorst became president of Tulip City in 1962 and board chairman in 1965 (Exhibit 3). He was regarded by various industry associations as one of the most knowledgeable experts in ambulance company management. On occasion, he had acted in this capacity to consult with various EMS agencies and private concerns. Berghorst always exercised a dynamic and personal style of management in the running of the company.

**EXHIBIT 3.**
**ORGANIZATION CHART:**
**TULIP CITY AMBULANCE COMPANY**

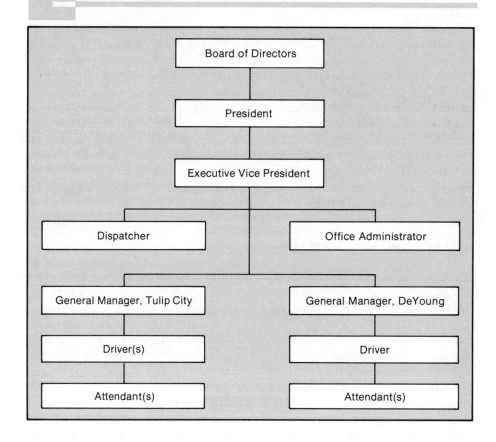

It was generally agreed, however, by the other managers that if Mart liked an idea it was implemented; if he didn't, it was dropped. Since 1980, he distanced himself somewhat from the firm when he became heavily involved with a car lot for expensive European automobiles and related foreign travel.

Karl VerBeek was hired into the position of executive vice president and general manager of Tulip City in July of 1974. He had previously been a sales manager with a large international pharmaceutical firm, a position he later gave up as too confining and without challenge in order to open a small delicatessen specializing in natural foods. Over the years he developed a close but sometimes strained friendship with Berghorst on both the professional and the social level. His initial responsibilities at Tulip City were to build a more refined technical work force, establish financial stability, and put the firm into a more effective posture with the city's political infrastructure.

Karl's manner of presenting ideas and his penchant for challenging work brought him immediate success. His 96-hour work weeks were reduced to 70 in 1983. This extra time afforded him the opportunity to continue a graduate degree in business (MBA) and put more sophistication into the daily administration of Tulip City. In anticipation of a larger organization, VerBeek began strengthening the firm's control and planning systems, showing special emphasis on reducing uncollectable accounts and formalizing equipment purchase decisions. With an eye toward eventual ownership of the firm, he has maintained his emergency medical qualifications and performed nearly every management task.

From time to time Karl received management-level offers from Bellview General and his former employer. In recent months he has become a little more than irate at the Berghorst's autocratic style and his occasional override of lower level decisions. VerBeek has made it known that he is beginning to weigh more carefully the personal costs of his moving.

Phillip Lasser joined Tulip City in 1976 as manager-driver of the newly acquired DeYoung service. Coming to the firm from a technical position in Bellview General's Emergency Department, he faced the effort of rebuilding the tarnished image of DeYoung as an exacting challenge. Lasser kept his team small, but continued to stress the state of the art in emergency ambulance technology.

Mrs. Berghorst, while continuing her role as director, has long since left the office and dispatching duties to devote more time to her family and various social obligations.

The remainder of the work force was balanced between full- and part-time people. Except for the office personnel, all were licensed emergency medical technicians, with a few pursuing paramedic-level training at the local community college.

With access to temporary help from various fire and police department emergency medical technicians, the personnel needs of the firm were usually deemed to be adequate.

## The Marketing and Operations Culture

From the beginning, Tulip City had been a market-oriented company retaining a wide view of its role in emergency health care. Rather than view itself as a provider of luxury convalescent transportation, or as an overextension of trauma center technology, the Tulip City/DeYoung organization saw itself in the business of offering high-quality cost-effective methods through the utilization of efficiently designed and maintained resources.

The total organization's philosophy normally began with the training and indoctrination of new members. Only those near completion of the 100-hour emergency medical technician course were considered for employment. Their skills and personalities were then evaluated by current team members during a two-week trial period. Once accepted, individuals were expected to cooperate fully with the team effort and to update their abilities through periodic seminars and training programs.

The Tulip City philosophy was further enhanced through the production and use of its ambulance fleet. Since 1970, the company had become almost totally integrated by producing all but one of its own heavy-duty emergency vehicles. Few firms in the industry could duplicate this achievement. To minimize production costs and allow for immediate recognition in the community, the new ambulances were specialized for two types of service.

After extensive negotiations with a number of local dealers, Berghorst settled on the Ford F-250 Econoline and F-350 chassis (driver compartment and frame/ wheels only) for the Type II and Type III units, respectively. Structurally, these trucks were purchased with the "ambulance preparation package," which, in addition to deluxe driving compartments, included extended-duty cooling, air conditioning, braking, suspension, and electrical systems. The first half of 1980 was a critical time in the upgrading of the company ambulance fleet with the purchase of three vans and two F-350 chassis.

Getting these vehicles ready for service was a temporary but central activity for Berghorst. The total process was characterized by expert craftsmanship, coordination of a host of detail work, and a deep sense of personal pride. Upon completion of each project, Berghorst often remarked, "These units are dependable, durable, good looking, and cost about 80 percent of the normal going price."

Each style of Tulip City emergency ambulance was made up of many individual parts such as cabinetry, stainless steel support and hinge devices, leather work, vacuum and pressure lines, and a labyrinth of electronic circuitry.

Toward the end of 1978 an awkward situation started to develop in the geographic area surrounding Manchester and Springdale. A number of peripheral hospitals found they could no longer cope with the increased severity of some trauma victims and the growing number of neonatal (premature) births.

At the culmination of much discussion and negotiation, Tulip City and Bellview General jointly agreed to build two vehicles capable of addressing these unique needs. The specifics of the program stated that Berghorst would design and build customized patient treatment chambers retrofitted on a Type III/ Modulance chassis for stable emergency transportation between the outlying hospitals and Bellview General.

The value of the Baby Unit was its capacity to carry a neonatologist, registered nurse, inhalation therapist, and ancillary equipment to a smaller outlying hospital and return with the crew and one to four incubators. The patient(s) could then be stabilized by the team before and during transport to Bellview's recently expanded Neonatal Intensive Care Unit (NICU).

Slightly larger in size than the Baby Unit, but with a similar internal configuration, the Trauma Unit was intended mainly for emergency transfers of adults between hospitals. Staffed by an emergency room physician and a carefully selected and trained crew, the use of this unit has been very disappointing. Revenue, maintenance, and repairs of either vehicle are shared equally by both program partners (see Exhibit 4).

**EXHIBIT 4**
**SUMMARY OF SPECIAL VEHICLE USE FOR YEARS 1980–1984**

| Year | Neonatal Unit Calls | Average Price | Trauma Unit Calls | Average Price |
|------|------|------|------|------|
| 1980* | 125 | $218.75 | 5 | $249.0 |
| 1981 | 265 | $227.50 | 12 | $257.1 |
| 1982 | 280 | $235.30 | 11 | $255.4 |
| 1983 | 300 | $249.75 | 13 | $277.8 |
| 1984 | 320 | $270.50 | 13 | $288.8 |

*Both special units were put into service 7/1/80.

*Source:*   Company records.

In addition to normal lubrication and tire replacement, every 30,000 miles the brakes, shock absorbers, batteries, and related components are upgraded or replaced, while at 100,000 miles the drive train (engine, transmission, etc.) and other major components are completely rebuilt. This final measure, which was supervised closely by Berghorst, was estimated to cost at least $5,200 and extend the life of the vehicle another 30,000 miles (see Exhibit 5).

Management rebuilt the three Ford vans according to schedule and then considered them as backup vehicles.

By contrast, the 1975 Cadillacs were purchased in poor condition and, unlike the rest of the fleet, were never upgraded. They were used essentially for long-distance transfers. The Chevrolet was purchased rather impetuously by Berghorst during a convention, but when confronted by his executive vice president on the decision, his response was "I got a deal that I couldn't pass up" and the matter was dropped.

Tulip City/DeYoung facilities and equipment were specifically designed to meet the expanding needs of Lincoln County and in a growing number of cases an even larger circle of operations. The two bases, radio network, skill level of the work force, and complexity of the vehicle fleet have given the company much flexibility to respond quickly to ever-widening consumer demands.

Management utilized a variety of promotional techniques. Supplementing the prominent positioning of the company's name and logo on vehicles and uniforms was the widespread use of Yellow Page advertisements. Since the first reaction of a person in need of an ambulance is to use the telephone or Yellow Pages, the company has tried to capitalize on the expected benefits from this medium.

In March of 1981, Tulip City introduced its first prime-time television commercial. Product awareness messages featuring the transfer, EMS, and specialty units reached approximately 300,000 people in the lower portion of the state. In addition to the single-station T.V. commercials, other advertisements were aired on three local radio stations and published in the area newspaper.

**EXHIBIT 5**
**TULIP CITY AMBULANCE VEHICLE EVALUATION SCHEDULE**
**AS OF DECEMBER 31, 1984**

| Date in Service | Vehicle | Unit Cost (000) | Average Annual Use (000 miles) | Evaluation |
|---|---|---|---|---|
| 1/76 | Van (3) | $13.9 | 5.0 | Mod/Poor Condition Life: *30,000 miles |
| 1/78 | Cadillac (5) | $12.5 | 2.0 | Very Poor Condition Life: *7,500 miles |
| 7/80** | Van | $16.9 | 20.5 | Good Condition Life: *8,000 miles |
| 7/80 | Van | $16.9 | 20.0 | Good Condition Life: *10,000 miles |
| 7/80 | Van | $16.9 | 18.0 | Good Condition Life: *19,000 miles |
| 7/80 | Modulance baby unit | $29.7 | 12.5 | Good Condition Life: *44,000 miles |
| 7/80 | Modulance trauma unit | $26.3 | 3.0 | Excellent Condition Life: *5 years |
| 1/83 | Van*** | $26.3 | 14.0 | Excellent Condition Life: *70,000 miles |

*Remaining life prior to overhaul
**All units purchased since 1980 are expected to be rebuilt or replaced at 100,000 miles.
***Chevrolet

*Source:* Company records.

Tulip City's promotional efforts in the early stages were decidedly transfer oriented. However, due to the increasing relationship between the EMS and the transfer business, the theme was later geared more specifically toward emergencies.

## Finance and Accounting

Tulip City retained a local CPA firm to draw up financial statements for management decision-making and income tax purposes. The accounting documents conformed to generally accepted reporting requirements for companies classified in this industry. Earnings not retained were taxed as personal income at both the federal and state levels. Even with the growing complexity of the business, and the resultant financial documentation, no management/accountant discussions of consequence had taken place since 1979.

**EXHIBIT 6**
**TULIP CITY AMBULANCE COMPANY**
**ESTIMATED REVENUE AND CRITICAL EXPENSES BY TYPE OF SERVICE**
**1980–1984**
**(Revenue and expenses are per trip, except maintenance and insurance, which are annual expenses per vehicle.)**

|  | 1980 | 1981 | 1982 | 1983 | 1984 |
|---|---|---|---|---|---|
| **AMBULANCE/EMS** | | | | | |
| *Revenue* | | | | | |
| Base rate | $ 60.00 | 65.00 | 65.00 | 65.00 | 65.00 |
| Mileage rate | .50 | .50 | .60 | .60 | .65 |
| Distance in miles | 8.00 | 8.00 | 8.00 | 9.00 | 10.00 |
| Misc. | 12.00 | 11.50 | 12.50 | 13.00 | 13.50 |
| Total | 76.00 | 80.50 | 82.30 | 83.40 | 85.00 |
| *Expenses* | | | | | |
| Fuel (9 mpg) | .84 | .84 | .84 | .95 | 1.05 |
| Labor | 12.00 | 12.60 | 13.20 | 14.00 | 14.60 |
| Maintenance | 310.00 | 335.00 | 350.00 | 370.00 | 390.00 |
| Insurance | 450.00 | 450.00 | 470.00 | 470.00 | 470.00 |
| **AMBULANCE/TRANSFER** | | | | | |
| *Revenue* | | | | | |
| Base rate | 60.00 | 60.00 | 65.00 | 65.00 | 65.00 |
| Mileage rate | .75 | .85 | .90 | 1.00 | 1.00 |
| Distance in miles | 17.00 | 17.00 | 17.00 | 18.00 | 18.50 |
| Total | 72.75 | 74.45 | 80.30 | 83.00 | 83.50 |
| *Expenses* | | | | | |
| Fuel (12 mpg) | 1.35 | 1.35 | 1.35 | 1.43 | 1.43 |
| Labor | 18.00 | 18.90 | 19.80 | 21.00 | 21.90 |
| **BABY VAN** | | | | | |
| *Revenue* | | | | | |
| Base rate | 125.00 | 130.00 | 130.00 | 135.00 | 140.00 |
| Mileage rate | 1.25 | 1.30 | 1.30 | 1.35 | 1.45 |
| Distance in miles | 75.00 | 75.00 | 81.00 | 85.00 | 90.00 |
| Total | 218.75 | 227.50 | 235.30 | 249.75 | 270.50 |
| *Expenses* | | | | | |
| Fuel (12 mpg) | 6.00 | 6.00 | 6.50 | 6.75 | 7.15 |
| Labor | 24.00 | 25.20 | 26.40 | 28.00 | 29.20 |
| Maintenance | 365.00 | 785.00 | 835.00 | 880.00 | 925.00 |
| Insurance | 350.00 | 725.00 | 730.00 | 740.00 | 750.00 |
| **TRAUMA UNIT** | | | | | |
| *Revenue* | | | | | |
| Base rate | 150.00 | 150.00 | 150.00 | 150.00 | 150.00 |
| Mileage rate | 1.65 | 1.70 | 1.70 | 1.75 | 1.85 |
| Distance in miles | 60.00 | 63.00 | 62.00 | 73.00 | 75.00 |
| Total | 249.00 | 257.10 | 255.40 | 277.75 | 288.95 |
| *Expenses* | | | | | |
| Fuel (11 mpg) | 5.20 | 5.50 | 5.35 | 6.30 | 6.50 |
| Labor | 24.00 | 25.20 | 26.40 | 28.00 | 29.20 |
| Maintenance | 75.00 | 150.00 | 600.00 | 175.00 | 190.00 |
| Insurance | $275.00 | 550.00 | 560.00 | 560.00 | 600.00 |

**EXHIBIT 7**
**TULIP CITY AMBULANCE COMPANY**
**COMPARATIVE INCOME STATEMENTS**
**FOR PERIODS ENDING DECEMBER 31, 1980–1984**

|  | 1980 | 1981 | 1982 | 1983 | 1984 |
|---|---|---|---|---|---|
| **OPERATING INCOME:** | | | | | |
| EMS | $332,880 | $323,207 | $300,395 | $304,410 | $294,738 |
| Transfers | 331,922 | 366,852 | 424,988 | 439,278 | 441,924 |
| Special units: | | | | | |
|    Baby unit | 13,672 | 30,143 | 32,942 | 37,462 | 43,280 |
|    Trauma unit | 623 | 1,543 | 1,405 | 1,805 | 1,877 |
| TOTAL OPER. REVENUE | 679,097 | 721,745 | 759,730 | 782,955 | 781,818 |
| **OPERATING EXPENSES:** | | | | | |
| Wages | 194,236 | 203,948 | 213,730 | 258,370 | 269,694 |
| Depreciation | 51,350 | 51,350 | 36,350 | 42,850 | 16,600 |
| Maintenance | 4,190 | 4,935 | 5,555 | 6,350 | 9,200 |
| Fuel | 13,788 | 15,253 | 15,885 | 15,678 | 17,218 |
| Uncollectable Accounts: | | | | | |
|    EMS | 126,494 | 122,818 | 114,150 | 112,632 | 109,053 |
|    Transfer | 46,469 | 51,360 | 55,248 | 57,106 | 57,450 |
|    Special units | 1,015 | 2,218 | 2,404 | 2,847 | 3,387 |
| Linen & Supplies | 1,348 | 1,482 | 1,556 | 1,635 | 1,715 |
| TOTAL OPER. EXPENSES | 438,890 | 453,364 | 444,878 | 497,468 | 484,317 |
| GROSS MARGIN | 240,207 | 268,381 | 314,852 | 285,487 | 297,502 |
| **ADMINISTRATIVE EXPENSES:** | | | | | |
| Salaries | 91,200 | 99,050 | 107,000 | 115,105 | 123,355 |
| Payroll Taxes | 20,350 | 23,816 | 24,950 | 29,056 | 31,444 |
| Employee Benefits | 52,716 | 56,055 | 59,335 | 69,093 | 72,714 |
| Telephone | 3,685 | 3,870 | 5,070 | 5,365 | 5,680 |
| Utilities | 5,460 | 6,000 | 6,550 | 6,870 | 7,220 |
| Insurance | 5,525 | 6,175 | 6,195 | 8,225 | 8,275 |
| Advertising | 0 | 800 | 900 | 1,000 | 1,100 |
| Property Taxes | 9,300 | 9,300 | 12,100 | 12,100 | 12,100 |
| Supplies | 1,208 | 1,260 | 1,330 | 1,400 | 1,460 |
| Postage | 2,480 | 2,497 | 2,800 | 2,813 | 2,933 |
| Miscellaneous | 1,606 | 1,680 | 1,815 | 1,905 | 2,000 |
| Professional Services | 3,000 | 3,300 | 3,565 | 3,750 | 3,930 |
| TOTAL ADMINISTRATIVE EXPENSES | 196,530 | 213,803 | 231,610 | 256,682 | 272,211 |
| INCOME FROM OPERATIONS | 43,677 | 54,578 | 83,242 | 28,805 | 25,291 |
| NONOPERATING INCOME/ EXPENSES | | | | | |
|    Interest Expense | 34,947 | 27,842 | 19,440 | 16,527 | 8,452 |
| INCOME BEFORE TAXES | 8,370 | 26,736 | 63,802 | 12,278 | 16,839 |
| TAXES | 2,183 | 6,684 | 21,055 | 3,069 | 4,210 |
| INCOME AFTER TAXES | 6,548 | 20,052 | 42,747 | 9,208 | 12,629 |

**EXHIBIT 8**
**TULIP CITY AMBULANCE COMPANY**
**COMPARATIVE BALANCE SHEETS**
**AS OF DECEMBER 31, 1980–1984**

|  | 1980 | 1981 | 1982 | 1983 | 1984 |
|---|---|---|---|---|---|
| **ASSETS** | | | | | |
| *Current Assets:* | | | | | |
| Cash | $ 2,500 | $ 511 | $ 2,232 | $ 1,364 | $ 1,536 |
| Accounts Receivable | 84,187 | 90,356 | 92,777 | 81,517 | 82,364 |
| Inventory | 337 | 371 | 389 | 409 | 429 |
| Prepaid Insurance | 6,175 | 6,195 | 8,225 | 8,275 | 8,690 |
| Total Current Assets | 93,199 | 97,433 | 103,623 | 91,565 | 93,019 |
| *Fixed Assets:* | | | | | |
| Land | 75,000 | 75,000 | 75,000 | 75,000 | 75,000 |
| Buildings | 128,000 | 128,000 | 128,000 | 128,000 | 128,000 |
| Less Accumulated Dep. | –73,000 | –81,000 | –89,000 | –97,000 | –105,000 |
| Vehicles | 208,275 | 208,275 | 208,275 | 234,275 | 234,275 |
| Less Accumulated Dep. | –97,100 | –138,350 | –164,600 | –197,350 | –203,850 |
| Equipment | 20,000 | 20,000 | 20,000 | 23,000 | 23,000 |
| Less Accumulated Dep. | –8,500 | –10,500 | –12,500 | –14,500 | –16,500 |
| Furniture & Fixtures, Net | 4,000 | 3,900 | 3,800 | 3,700 | 3,600 |
| TOTAL FIXED ASSETS | 256,675 | 205,325 | 168,975 | 155,125 | 138,525 |
| TOTAL ASSETS | $349,874 | $302,758 | $272,598 | $246,690 | $231,544 |
| **LIABILITIES/EQUITY** | | | | | |
| *Current Liabilities:* | | | | | |
| Current Maturity of Notes | $ 51,582 | $ 39,272 | $ 45,642 | $ 21,409 | $ 11,532 |
| Accounts Payable | 310 | 425 | 390 | 450 | 680 |
| Payroll Taxes Payable | 13,320 | 14,140 | 14,968 | 17,429 | 18,342 |
| Wages/Salaries Payable | 4,391 | 4,662 | 4,935 | 5,746 | 6,047 |
| Income Taxes Payable | 546 | 1,671 | 5,263 | 767 | 1,052 |
| Other | 245 | 380 | 589 | 325 | 430 |
| TOTAL CURRENT LIABILITIES | 70,394 | 60,550 | 71,787 | 46,126 | 38,083 |
| *Noncurrent Liabilities:* | | | | | |
| Notes Payable | 131,139 | 91,867 | 46,223 | 43,768 | 32,236 |
| TOTAL LIABILITIES | 201,533 | 152,417 | 118,010 | 89,894 | 70,319 |
| **OWNERS' EQUITY:** | | | | | |
| Common Stock ($10 PAR) | 40,000 | 40,000 | 40,000 | 40,000 | 40,000 |
| Paid in Capital | 5,000 | 5,000 | 5,000 | 5,000 | 5,000 |
| Retained Earnings | 103,341 | 105,341 | 109,588 | 111,796 | 116,225 |
| TOTAL EQUITY | 148,341 | 150,341 | 154,588 | 156,796 | 161,225 |
| TOTAL LIABILITIES/EQUITY | $349,874 | $302,758 | $272,598 | $246,690 | $231,544 |

## EXHIBIT 9
## SUMMARY OF ACCOUNTANT'S FOOTNOTES

1. Tulip City uses the accrual method of accounting for reporting and tax purposes.

2. Accounts receivable are stated at actual amounts minus an estimated sum for uncollectables based upon past trends.

   (Typically, the collection rate on receivables is about 62% for emergency medical service, 87% for transfers, 85% for neonatal calls, and 87% for trauma calls.)

3. All fixed assets are stated at cost. Depreciation for tax and reporting requirements is computed with the straight-line method with minimum salvage values. The useful lives of the assets are: buildings, 15 years; furniture and fixtures, 15 years; vehicles, 4 years; and equipment, 10 years. Full depreciation of the fixed assets are: primary base, 1984; secondary base, 1989; vehicles (Chevrolet) 1986. All other assets are fully depreciated.

4. Repairs and maintenance are generally charged to operations as they occur. When an asset is sold or removed from service, its cost and related depreciation are omitted from the accounts with the gain or loss being recognized at the time of removal.

5. The real estate mortgage is 9% on both items of property. The debt on the primary base will be released in December 1985 and the debt on the secondary base in December 1989.

---

Management was not sure whether Tulip City's billing rates were set at premium levels. This was due mainly to the uncertainty over the pricing strategies of both competitors in the greater Manchester area. While it was relatively easy to obtain reliable estimates of what Van's was charging at any one point in time, his fluctuating pricing policy made industry guidelines all but impossible to establish. Moreover, it became increasingly evident that rates patients would accept varied according to the services performed and the image of the firm within the local community.

Payroll was distributed biweekly with nonexempt personnel receiving 76 regular hours and 8 overtime hours within each of the 26 pay periods. To minimize morale and turnover problems, Berghorst advocated steady increases in pay levels (at something less than inflation) for the 12 full-time and various part-time emergency medical technicians. After the addition of the new vehicle in 1983, the number of emergency medical technicians was increased to 14.

The schedule on page 793 reflects supportive data for the calculation of total wages, salaries, and associated compensation expenses.

Initial corporate policy was to finance expansion from retained earnings, although other methods of raising funds were used when needed. Through the first 15 years of the company, the family investors continued to increase their holdings until they reached current levels.

In recent years, and for a variety of reasons, the firm often increased its debt load. Short-term requirements were met through open lines of credit with the state's two largest banks. Each note was generally secured by corporate accounts

## WAGE/SALARY SCHEDULE

| Position | 1980 | 1981 | 1982 | 1983 | 1984 |
|---|---|---|---|---|---|
| EMT/hourly | $6.00 | 6.30 | 6.60 | 7.00 | 7.30 |
| Part-time | $29,500 | 30,975 | 32,520 | 34,146 | 35,860 |
| Dispatcher | $10,200 | 10,700 | 11,235 | 11,800 | 12,390 |
| Office admin. | $11,500 | 12,100 | 12,705 | 13,340 | 14,000 |
| Office part-time | $12,000 | 12,600 | 13,230 | 13,840 | 14,585 |
| C.E.O. | $35,000 | 40,000 | 45,000 | 50,000 | 55,000 |
| Ex. V.P. | $22,500 | 23,650 | 24,883 | 26,075 | 27,380 |
| Taxes (%) | 7.13 | 7.86 | 7.78 | 7.78 | 8.00 |

receivable. Bank debt was also used to finance the vehicle fleet at prevailing interest rates, with security based on the ambulances and corporate property holdings.

Since 1978 the firm has purchased ambulances in four- or five-lot sizes, causing periodic strains to its interest and debt capacity. Also, since 1979 Berghorst has taken increased amounts of retained earnings to help finance his other business ventures.

Immediately after returning from one such trip, Berghorst called in his executive vice president for the following conversation:

> I am quite pleased with the way you have managed the operations of Tulip City and DeYoung over the past few years. I don't have your formal education, but I do have a nose for what is right or wrong concerning expenses and profits. This business seems to be doing as well as can be expected. We have talked in the past about setting up a more sophisticated planning process with budgets, objectives, goals, strategies, and a computer. I again gave your idea some thought while I was in Europe, but I still feel that this business is changing so rapidly and Vanlaar has thrown so much confusion into the local area with his severe price cutting and antagonistic operations, that we can only plan a few days at a time. Your efforts to obtain cost data on different aspects of this business have been helpful, but that is as detailed as I want to go.
>
> It has been my policy on past occasions to buy vehicles or equipment when I thought the price was right. I've made some mistakes, especially with the Cadillacs and the high interest rates we paid on them and the Fords. We've gotten fairly good use out of the truck fleet, but the luxury cars were a complete waste of money and I wish I had never bought them.

Berghorst's principal concern at this point in the discussion centered on the way his executive vice president had managed the business during periods of inflation, high interest rates, and general upheavals in the local economy. His primary reason for the meeting soon became evident:

Personally, Karl, I have struggled to reach a position in this business where I would have more time to spend on my other interests and with my family. I have been tempted to milk this venture dry and then walk away from it. Now I feel it is only fair to let you know that, much to my surprise, David Vanlaar called me about six weeks ago with an initial offer to buy the company. While at first I thought he was joking, he went on to say that St. Lukes would support his intention by providing partial financing for the acquisition.

The C.P.A. and I were to meet with Vanlaar, Dykema (Administrator of St. Lukes), and some bank officials to discuss our records, books, and financial operations. No meeting ever took place, however, and I thought the matter was dropped. Then yesterday morning Vanlaar and Dykema called from the bank and gave me an offer, which I feel is much more (but I really don't know) than the firm is worth. Even though I seriously doubt that Vanlaar could handle an operation like this one, I also think I would be foolish not to accept the offer.

As I have mentioned to you before, Karl, I will sell this company to you as well. But you know our relationship with Bellview General is becoming strained, and it is up for grabs if they will bankroll you as St. Lukes is doing for Vanlaar.

Karl VerBeek left the meeting angry and resentful, to call his wife and ponder the future.

## The View of the Future

Karl VerBeek once again considered the growing myriad of problems facing the firm through 1985. He knew that Tulip City had to clarify its direction if it were to remain a leader in the industry. Revenue from EMS operations showed almost constant decline, price battles with Vanlaar were always a threat, and volume related to the transfer business appeared headed for a plateau.

Even the specialty vehicles raised new problems, not the least of which was how these units could be used and what would happen to total revenue if Bellview General went ahead with plans to incorporate its own ambulance service.

The city government's challenge to Tulip City was also increasing; not only were plans well under way to establish municipal-based emergency aid and treatment at the scene, but it was generally assumed that once this operation was in place, a transport process for each victim would soon follow.

As the executive vice president glanced at the financial documents he had accumulated on his desk, his attention shifted to the meeting Mart had requested take place that afternoon.

In addition to the ambulance business, Mart Berghorst made frequent trips overseas to buy high-priced European automobiles. These were later converted to American pollution control standards and sold on his retail lot.

# COMPREHENSIVE CASE 4

## Sci-Tech Associates

When Jane Sherrill left the office of president Carl Thompson of Cyril Electronics, Inc., last March, she knew that she had just been handed the greatest opportunity of her life. What she didn't know was whether it would be an opportunity for a major advance in her career or an opportunity to fall on her face.

The opportunity just handed Sherrill was the presidency of Sci-Tech Associates, a small electronic components company located in El Monte, California. Cyril had recently acquired Sci-Tech from its three owner-managers in an exchange-of-stock transaction. "We bought this company," Thompson told her, "for two reasons. Number one, they supply us with two components that are critically important to our business—patented items not available from other suppliers—and they have repeatedly fouled up delivery schedules. Also, their quality control has been erratic. We need what they make, but we can't tolerate their shipping failures and their slipshod production and inspection standards. And neither can their other customers for the same components. Number two, we think they have outstanding scientific and engineering capabilities, but weak management. We think we can turn the business around and make a fine return on our investment. At the same time, we can solve the problems they've been creating for us. Your assignment is to do both of these jobs."

### Jane Sherrill

Sherrill is a confident, tough manager. She had, in effect, run away from a very conservative home to attend a large university—working and borrowing to pay expenses. This experience removed any trace of the "dependent female" syndrome. She decided that she could get ahead fastest by obtaining a master's degree from Columbia University's business school, with a major in marketing. Finding an attractive job, however, proved to be more difficult than she expected. Due to an economic slowdown the year she graduated, job offers were scarce; also, she sensed that being a female with only campus work experience did not impress recruiters with the drive that she felt.

The one company that showed a strong and persistent interest in her was Cyril Electronics. Surprised, because she had understood that this Fort Custer, Michigan, company insisted on an undergraduate engineering degree together with an M.B.A., Sherrill suspected that Cyril was out to hire at least one woman. A company visit revealed that the company had no women as managers or as engineers. Nevertheless, the recruiters stressed their need for marketing expertise, so—with some apprehension—she moved into the engineer's world.

In fact, Sherrill has been placed in challenging and varied jobs. A first assignment as a market analyst used her specialized knowledge and also gave her an opportunity to bone up—nights and weekends—on an essential technical background in electronics. Being project manager of a new computer facility and doing M.B.A. recruiting added variety. These she followed with product management, and later she became marketing manager for the Specialty Products division. By age 32, when she got the Sci-Tech assignment, she had an impressive record of successes. When asked by her friends about how marriage might fit into her life plan, she had a standard response: "I haven't missed it so far. As the politicians like to say, I'm keeping my options open."

Underneath Sherrill's assured exterior manner were two gnawing uncertainties about her own abilities for the new job: (1) She had never been a general manager and was unsure how she would act as a young boss—very young in the eyes of many of her older subordinates. (2) She had never prepared and staked her reputation on a written strategic plan. Suddenly the distinction between a staff report and a manager's report which she had to execute loomed large. How to prepare the report, how to win support of her colleagues for it, how to sell it to top management became very real questions. The following account of the *processes* that Sherrill used to meet these two challenges reveals some success, some luck, and some fumbling which showed her inexperience.

## Sci-Tech Associates

Sci-Tech Associates was organized nine years ago by three electronics engineer-scientists, two of whom were employed in middle-level staff positions in large West Coast electronics companies while the third was an associate professor in a leading California engineering school. Bernard Ash and Mark Feldstein had been classmates at California Institute of Technology, and they remained in close social contact during the next 15 years while they rose to the department-head level in their respective organizations. Conrad Woodworth had known Ash and Feldstein slightly while he was a teaching assistant at Caltech, working toward a doctorate. After joining the faculty of another California engineering school, he did consulting with the company for which Ash worked. Through this relationship he renewed his acquaintance with Ash and Feldstein, an acquaintance that developed into close friendship.

The three men often talked about cutting loose from their jobs and starting their own electronics businesses. Ash and Feldstein were increasingly frustrated by the rigidities of the formal organization structure and the procedures of their companies. Woodworth's restlessness was fueled by his mounting disinterest in teaching and his hostility to the pressure to build a publication record as a requirement for a tenured appointment. Beyond this, all three men wanted a stock-ownership position that would give them the chance to realize substantial capital gains.

Finally the three decided to launch their personal moonshot. They formed Sci-Tech Associates, Inc., with a capitalization of $700,000. Stock ownership was split evenly three ways. Ash and Feldstein each supplied $350,000, part from their own savings, part borrowed on personal notes from members of their families. Woodworth's contribution was his assignment to the company of three patents he held on electronic devices. Bernard Ash was designated president of the new firm, Mark Feldstein treasurer, and Conrad Woodworth director of research. In practice, they agreed to operate as equal partners, with all decisions made cooperatively.

The partners decided to try producing and marketing Woodworth's devices themselves. They leased a small plant in El Monte, purchased the necessary equipment, hired a small work force, produced sample units, and went out to solicit orders from California electronics companies.

They sold a few small orders for the devices and then a larger volume of repeat orders. The flow of incoming orders was erratic, however, and after six months they concluded that the business could not be profitable without a steady volume of bread-and-butter work as a basic revenue source while the market for the patented products was developing and while Woodworth was working on two other promising components. Subcontracting work for the electronic firms they were already contacting was the quickest source of such stabilizing income. It involves competitive bidding and thin margins, but it does pay for the overhead. Ever since this first grasp for stability, Sci-Tech has done subcontracting in addition to making its patented components.

Sci-Tech produces a variety of electronic components: hypersensitive unitary and interlocked-series switches, high-speed electronic-impulse transmitters, and elements for incorporation in sophisticated microvoltage regulating and measuring systems. About half of its sales have been generated by these patented products. Last year Sci-Tech sold such products to seven companies. The single largest customer, accounting for slightly more than $1 million in sales, was Cyril Electronics, which used Sci-Tech's hypersensitive switches in several of its advanced process-control systems. Among the other customers for Sci-Tech's proprietary products were Ampex, Intel, National Semiconductor, and Texas Instruments.

Customers for Sci-Tech's proprietary products, with the exception of Cyril, did not maintain a stable relationship with Sci-Tech or purchase in large quantities. They appeared to follow the strategy of using Sci-Tech as a high-technology resource for certain unique components incorporated in the early marketing stage of their own advanced products. Then, for products that developed high-volume sales, they shifted to in-house manufacture of comparable components.

The reasons for this erratic use of Sci-Tech products, according to Ash and Feldstein, were varied. They included high cost for large-volume orders, unreliable quality, and difficulties of coordinating deliveries with customer's production schedules. As already noted, Cyril Electronics also was unhappy with these matters, but Cyril preferred not to get involved with in-house design and production—at least prior to the Sci-Tech acquisition.

The subcontracting part of Sci-Tech's business generated a growing volume of sales from a diversified and constantly shifting group of customers, one of which ordinarily accounted for more than 20 percent of the total of this type of Sci-Tech's business.

The partnership mode of top management has continued at Sci-Tech. All three men—Ash, Feldstein, and Woodworth—discuss all major decisions. In daily operations, Woodworth clearly runs the research effort, whereas Ash and Feldstein often overlap. Generally, Ash spends more time on production and Feldstein on marketing and finance, although both respond to any pressing problem. The employment of a production manager—Ivar Sunderberg—facilitates this top management flexibility.

Sci-Tech's growth has been steady but not as fast as hoped, and its ability to earn a profit has been even more disappointing to the partners. The operating results for the past five years, shown in Table 1, are far below what the patterns envisaged when the company was formed, and their working relationships have begun to erode as a consequence.

The original plan was to build a record of profitable growth and then "go public," including some of their own shares together with new stock in the public offering. The mediocre profit performance prevented this step, and by the time of the acquisition the partners had become increasingly pessimistic about future prospects. Woodworth was critical of both the marketing effort for the proprietary

## TABLE 1.
### SCI-TECH ASSOCIATES: OPERATING STATEMENTS (in thousands)

|  | Last Year | 2 Years Ago | 3 Years Ago | 4 Years Ago | 5 Years Ago |
|---|---|---|---|---|---|
| **Net Sales:** |  |  |  |  |  |
| Proprietary Products | $ 4,917 | $3,543 | $2,580 | $1,760 | $1,308 |
| Subcontracts | 5,208 | 4,145 | 3,467 | 3,125 | 2,555 |
| Total Sales | 10,125 | 7,687 | 6,047 | 4,885 | 3,863 |
| Cost of Goods Sold | 8,782 | 6,667 | 5,184 | 4,287 | 3,863 |
| Operating Profit | 1,343 | 1,020 | 863 | 598 | 586 |
| R & D Expense | 600 | 450 | 450 | 300 | 300 |
| Selling & Administrative Expense | 626 | 402 | 323 | 260 | 192 |
| Net Income before Tax | 117 | 168 | 90 | 38 | 94 |
| Income Tax | 52 | 72 | 32 | 15 | 36 |
| Net Profit | $ 65 | $ 96 | $ 58 | $ 23 | $ 58 |

**SCI-TECH ASSOCIATES: BALANCE SHEET**
**END OF LAST YEAR (in thousands)**

| | | | |
|---|---|---|---|
| Cash | $    63 | Loans Payable | $   238 |
| Accounts Receivable | 1,515 | Current Installment of Long- | |
| Inventories | 925 | Term Debt | 57 |
| | | Accounts Payable | 1,056 |
| | | Accrued Items | 729 |
| Total Current Assets | 2,503 | Total Current Liabilities | 2,080 |
| Property & Equipment | | Long-Term | 720 |
| (net of depreciation) | 1,226 | Stockholders' Equity: | |
| | | Common Stock | 700 |
| | | Retained Earnings | 229 |
| | | Net Worth | 929 |
| Total Assets | $3,729 | Total Liabilities & Net Worth | $3,729 |

devices he developed and the quality of factory supervision over their production. Ash and Feldstein complained that Woodworth appeared to be more interested in the scientific novelty of his developments than in their potential for volume marketing. Ash and Feldstein were also beginning to bicker about their overlapping responsibilities for production, marketing, and finance. All three were disappointed by the continuing dependence of the business for a substantial share of its gross revenue on low-margin subcontracting activities which developed no proprietary security.

Cyril Electronic's proposal to acquire Sci-Tech Associates therefore occurred at a time when the mutual disaffection of the three owners was threatening to become a serious destabilizing factor in the business. The terms of the offer were, under the circumstances, attractive. Cyril proposed to (1) exchange its listed stock at market value (trading at 11 times per-share earnings) for Sci-Tech stock valued at net worth per share, (2) give the three owners five-year employment contracts, continuing their existing salaries and fringe benefits, (3) give them a potential for bonuses based on sales and profit increases during the employment contract period, and (4) install a new president to provide highly qualified top management direction. The three partners would have the titles of senior vice-presidents in the Cyril subsidiary. The proposal was accepted and became effective in March of this year.

## Management in Transition

Understandably, the executives of Sci-Tech were uneasy about what their new president, named by Cyril Electronics, might do. That she was more than 10 years younger than they, a nonengineer, and a woman added more uncertainty. When, after a week of getting acquainted with people and facts, Sherrill indicated that there would be no immediate rocking of the boat, tension turned to relief—even enthusiasm.

Sherrill quickly decided that a tightening up of present activities would be a necessary base for any future strategy. Consequently, she set specific targets for the rest of the year—including a 50 percent reduction in late deliveries, a 75 percent reduction in quality failures and rework requirements, a $300,000 reduction in costs, and a pretax income target of 4.1 percent of sales (compared to 1.2 percent the preceding year).

In keeping with past practice, the three partners began discussing the reasonableness of these targets. Sherrill cut them off, saying, "Look, we all know that the recent performance of this business has been no better than mediocre. It certainly hasn't achieved the goals you had in mind when you started the business. You have an opportunity now, with Cyril's backing, to achieve these goals. If this business realizes its full potential, your employment contracts will give you extraordinary bonuses during the next five years. As far as I am concerned, my neck is on the block. I've started to build a good career in Cyril and I don't intend to spoil it by failing in this assignment. All of us therefore have a powerful motivation to succeed. But we must recognize that Sci-Tech is no longer a game or an ego trip, if it ever was. You believe, and Cyril believes, that there are valuable resources in this business. So let's quit horsing around and get to work."

In addition to the specific targets for the year, Sherrill asked for written suggestions for the longer term strategy of Sci-Tech. Parts of the immediate program were assigned to each of the senior vice-presidents, while Sherrill undertook primary responsibility for drawing up a strategic plan to be submitted to the president of Cyril in December. A weekly management meeting was set up to share information on progress and problems, but she made it clear that each person was expected to proceed vigorously with his and her assignment.

## The Senior Vice-Presidents

This "immediate program" gave Sherrill further opportunities to talk with and observe her three associates. She had already received a preliminary evaluation of each of them from John Leonard, the Cyril vice-president who negotiated the acquisition. The following are highlights from the information that Sherrill picked up during her first few weeks at Sci-Tech.

### Conrad Woodworth

"He is close to the model of a pure scientist," Leonard had said, "except that he has this itch for big money. When his interest is hot, he may work straight through the night. He's independent, likely to resent direction, firmly committed to the notion that a better mousetrap will find its own market."

In Sci-Tech's laboratory, when Sherrill first met the research staff—which included four Ph.D.'s and six holders of master's degrees—Woodworth was particularly enthused about one device undergoing tests. "This little gizmo can revolutionize high-speed transmission of electronic impulses. It could transform the future of this company." Responding to Sherrill's question about when the device would be ready for demonstration to potential customers, Woodworth explained, "There are a couple of problems we haven't quite solved. But I'm sure we will—maybe next Monday, maybe six months from now." And as to problems that might arise in quantity production, "I haven't any idea. That's Bernie Ash's job. And Bernie hasn't seen this yet. If I show him something new, he wants to jump right into the factory before we've eliminated all the bugs. We've had trouble like that before. So we've learned to keep our mouths shut about something new until we know it's ready to fly. Until then, my policy is to keep it top secret. Sometimes I wish I could erect a Chinese Wall around this lab."

In response to Sherrill's further probing, Woodworth continued, "This business is off on a wrong track. We should never have gotten mixed up with that subcontracting crap. It uses our resources at their lowest level of skill and their lowest market value. In my opinion, we ought to throw the whole subcontracting nonsense out the window and concentrate our attention on building our own business."

### Bernard Ash

Of the three senior vice-presidents, Ash showed the best grasp of what has to happen in production to make the business go. But he is not really intrigued with a smoothly running shop. Instead, he—and Feldstein, too—likes to work with engineers in customer companies to discover how Sci-Tech components can radically improve the performance of customer products.

Nevertheless, it was Ash who first provided Sherrill with a thorough look at Sci-Tech's production facilities. With production manager Sunderberg, they toured the air-conditioned, immaculate, quiet shop. About 40 workers were either monitoring automated machines or operating delicate controls on other precise equipment. Another 40 workers, dressed like nurses in white smocks and caps and latex gloves, were occupied with miniaturized assembly operations observed through microscopes.

Sunderberg explained that the entire factory force was paid on a straight salary basis and rather proudly noted that management-employee relations were such that three efforts to unionize the group in recent years had been unsuccessful. The plant worked a single shift, with occasional overtime. Quality control was incorporated within production operations, with employees spot-checking their own work. Because of the irregular receipt of orders, the same group of employees worked on both proprietary products and subcontract job orders. "We could expand output 50 percent on the site. Doubling output would require moving to a new location."

In response to Sherrill's question about cost control, Ash showed her worksheets that he and Sunderberg kept on each order. "These figures are our personal estimates of what it actually cost to get each order produced. Some run smoothly, others cause headaches, overtime, and therefore expense. Of course, with a single shop producing different kinds of products, the allocation of overhead is a judgmental matter. But we do need total cost figures, especially to help us prepare bids on subcontracts.[1]

On another issue Ash explained, "Our organization is more informal than what you probably have at Cyril. Connie Woodworth runs the lab because that's where we need him and that's where he wants to be. As far as Mark Feldstein and I go, things are all mixed up. I spend quite a bit of time on sales and Mark occasionally dips into production. He is technically treasurer, but in reality we both work on that job. It has worked so far, but maybe you'll want to make some rearrangements."

### Mark Feldstein

Feldstein gave the impression of being tougher and more abrasive than his former partners—ready to shoot from the hip. His aggressiveness probably provided the push that the trio needed to launch Sci-Tech. John Leonard suspects that "he starts a lot of things going and then gets interested in something else, leaving a lot of debris behind him. But he has real talent if you can keep him focused."

"Our marketing setup is simple," Feldstein explained. "Bernie Ash and I get the orders for the proprietary products; the salespeople bring in the subcontracts. Of course, in a small organization like ours it's not quite that clean. Bernie and I am always in on the subcontracts, at least in the bidding, and the salespeople help maintain contracts with proprietary customers—our midwest rep, for example, keeps in close touch with Cyril Electronics. He damn well better, now that they own us.

"At the top level we are a mess. The three of us had the cockeyed idea that we would run this business as equal partners. It hasn't worked. It never does. We spend hours trying to reach agreements. That means the third person often yields when he is still convinced he is right, or the decision is put off, which may be worse. I've told this to Bernie and Connie repeatedly, but they like things as they are."

Responding to Sherrill's questions about budgets, Feldstein said, "We've prepared quarterly profit-and-loss budgets for years. Our banker likes them. But frankly they don't mean much. You've probably noticed that the actual figures jump around a lot. That's because of the irregular way orders come in and shipments are made. It's the orders that really count, not the budgets, so we don't pay much attention to them. By holding our inventories low we've kept Sci-Tech solvent, although I must admit our customers would be happier if we carried large stocks which they could order at the drop of a hat whenever they shuffle their own schedules around. I don't think budgets are the way to solve that problem."

---

[1]The cumulative totals on these job cost sheets indicated that subcontract job orders accounted for the following percentages of Sci-Tech's overall results: net sales, 51.4 percent; cost of goods sold, 61 percent; direct labor costs, 53.8 percent; material costs, 52.7 percent; production overhead costs, 63.4 percent. The operating loss on subcontracts last year was estimated at 2.8 percent of subcontract sales; the operating profit on proprietary products was estimated at 30.3 percent of proprietary sales.

## Short-Run Response

The response to Sherrill's "immediate program" was good. It focused effort on a series of soft spots in Sci-Tech's operations that everyone agreed should be improved. Equally important, morale picked up for several reasons. The normal early anxiety about what the new owner would do was relieved; nobody was fired and no quick-fix remedies were imposed. Rather, Sherrill was a friendly person (to people throughout the organization, not just her immediate associates), open to suggestions, and she asked probing questions that needed to be asked. At the same time, she accepted the role of final arbiter; in spite of her inexperience, a feeling of unified direction was injected.

People at the top level knew that several long-run issues remained open. But there was agreement on immediate needs, and working hard on them absorbed energy that could easily have turned into grousing. There was little time for idle hands to find mischief. And Sherrill saw decreasing evidence of irritation among the former partners.

Operating results also improved. By the end of October, Sherrill was able to prepare an estimated operating statement for the year which showed that tightening up was, indeed, paying off. (See Table 2.) There had been a few cutbacks, but primarily the organization handled a larger volume of business without a proportional increase in expenses. Also significant was an improvement in customer service. Most delivery commitments to customers, and notably to Cyril, were

**TABLE 2.**
**SCI-TECH ASSOCIATES: OPERATING STATEMENTS**
**ACTUAL LAST YEAR—ESTIMATED THIS YEAR***
**(in thousands)**

|                                   | Last Year | Estimated This Year |
|-----------------------------------|-----------|---------------------|
| Net Sales                         |           |                     |
| Proprietary Products              | $ 4,917   | $ 6,300             |
| Subcontracts                      | 5,208     | 6,100               |
| Total Sales                       | 10,125    | 12,400              |
| Cost of Goods Sold                | 8,782     | 10,600              |
| Operating Profit                  | 1,343     | 1,800               |
| R & D Expense                     | 600       | 700                 |
| Selling & Administrative Expense  | 626       | 700                 |
| Net Income before Tax             | 117       | 400                 |
| Income Tax                        | 52        | 200                 |
| Net Profit                        | $    65   | $    200            |

*Based on 10-month actual.

being met on time. The rate of quality defects had dropped dramatically. So the financial gain had not come from a sacrifice in these intangible items.

Sherrill was now confident that the first-year hurdle under the new ownership would be cleared with flying colors. Yet she was aware that the current energy level would be difficult to sustain. The "new boss" stimulation would wear off, and she had not yet been forced to make an unpopular decision. Even more worrisome were the long-run prospects for the company with its obvious management weaknesses and its dual-line operation.

## The Longer View

Most of Sherrill's time during her first six months at Sci-Tech was devoted to preparing the long-range strategy which Cyril's president wanted by the end of the year.

The written suggestions from the senior vice-presidents provided little help. They repeated personal preferences which Sherrill already knew and made "straight-line" projections with scant attention to threats, risks, and resource requirements. On her own part, Sherrill studied the company outlook in depth. She visited managers and engineers in both customer and noncustomer organizations, talked with editors of trade magazines, and spent several days with Cyril's headquarters research staff. From these and other sources she explored trends in the industry, evolving technology, the economics of make-or-buy decisions, and life cycles of proprietary products in electronics.

Within Sci-Tech she observed the scheduling and purchasing process, followed an incoming order through its entire progression, talked with employees about their work on subcontracts, and accompanied salespeople on customer and cold canvass calls. Also, she talked with Sci-Tech's banker about risks and trends in the electronics industry and why some companies succeed where others fail.

Another essential input to this study was an assessment of the long-run contributions that her three senior associates might make to Sci-Tech. Sherrill concluded that Woodworth was an extraordinarily talented scientist whose personal contributions were essential to the continuing development of the proprietary business. However, his insensitivity to market needs and production problems, as well as disinterest in research administration, disqualified Woodworth as head of R & D. A much better arrangement would be to name a new R & D director with Woodworth as chief scientist.

Feldstein, she concluded, was an able technical sales representative and an acceptable but not outstanding marketing manager. But he possessed neither the training nor objectivity of a good finance and control executive; and if Feldstein objected to turning over these functions to a more qualified person, Sherrill was willing to risk losing him. Ash, with proper direction, could serve well as production vice-president, but Sherrill doubted his ability to handle either procurement or personnel in a rapidly growing business. Here, too, another vice-president probably would be needed.

Fortunately, long-run financing was available from Cyril Electronics *if* a plan could be prepared that offered potential returns commensurate with its risks.

## Strategic Options

From this analysis and numerous "what-if" notes to capture her own thoughts, Sherrill concluded that Sci-Tech faces two basic options. One is to continue the existing dual commitment to proprietary components and to subcontracting. This is a relatively safe, slow-growth course. Because of the narrow profits on subcontracting, the returns are likely to be modest. Looking five years down the road, Sherrill projected doubling the sales volume under this strategy, with pretax income in the range of 5–7 percent of sales (compared with 3.2 percent estimated for this year).

The second option is to stop taking subcontracting orders and concentrate the full capabilities of Sci-Tech on the design, production, and sale of proprietary components. While cutbacks in factory employment would be faced next year, a vigorous building of added strength in R & D, procurement, personnel, finance, and control would be launched. With this focused strength, and the new products Woodworth was conjuring up in his laboratory, Sherrill projected a trebling of profits in three years and trebling that figure again in the succeeding three years. This is a more risky operation than the first, with a much higher growth and profit potential.

An unknown was the inclination of Cyril Electronics executives to take risks on Sci-Tech's development. President Thompson said that he wanted *both* an assured source of critical components for Cyril's other divisions *and* a rich return on the initial investment. But a tradeoff between the two objectives was not stated. Sherrill believed that she could get no clear answer on the issue until Thompson and his colleagues face spelled-out alternatives. "They don't know the answer," Sherrill quipped, "until I pose the question." Consequently, Sherrill planned to lay out both options in her forthcoming report.

Sherrill prepared a draft of her report, her first strategic plan, which she planned to send to Thompson early in December. It had to be weighed in terms of psychological impact and tactical considerations, as well as rational arguments. Before making final revisions in the document, Sherrill wanted to test the reception and obtain the advice of her senior vice-presidents. The principal elements in the draft are outlined in the following excerpts and paraphrases.

I. Strategic Choices

    A. The development of Sci-Tech can be charted along either of two strategic courses: (1) continue the existing dual commitment to proprietary products and subcontracting; (2) discontinue subcontracting (complete jobs presently under contract, but accept no new orders) and concentrate all resources on proprietary products.

B.   The first option is a low-risk strategy. It will provide satisfactory continuing fulfillment of one of Cyril's two objectives in acquiring Sci-Tech: assured supply of Sci-Tech's components, on time and meeting quality specifications. It has a high probability of earning moderate sustained profits and a moderate sustained rate of return on Cyril's investment. At this level, it will not achieve Cyril's second acquisition objective: a high rate of return on its investment in Sci-Tech. This option will require a small additional investment by Cyril three years hence (about $1 million) to assist in financing the projected steady, slow growth in sales through the next five years, but will be substantially self-financing. It will retain Sci-Tech's present senior managers and management structure, both of which are adequate to meet the administrative needs associated with this option.

C.   The second option is a high-potential but high-risk strategy. It opens the way to a rapid development of the business, with a good possibility for up to ten-fold growth in sales and a corresponding increase in profits in the next five to seven years and a high return on Cyril's initial and subsequent investment. This option will certainly involve substantial losses of sales and income in at least the first two years following its adoption. It will require large supplemental investments by Cyril because it cannot come close to being self-financing. It will also require recruiting several new senior-level executives and might result in the resignation of one or two of the three founders of Sci-Tech.

D.   There is no acceptable "middle" strategy that would preserve the low-risk feature of the first option while also developing the full potential of the second option. Successful implementation of the second option will require undivided concentration of Sci-Tech's present resources—and additional financing and organizational resources—all targeted on satisfying the demands created by the option.

## II.  Recommendation

I recommend corporate approval of the second option: rapid phasing out of all subcontracting; prompt recruiting—from Cyril if possible, from outside if necessary—of the required new top-executive resources; a corporate commitment to meet the indicated long-term financial needs for a high-growth business; and accepting operating losses for two years of the magnitude described below.

## III.  The Dual Strategy: Subcontracting Plus Proprietary Products

A.   While cost allocations between subcontracting and proprietary work have been unreliable, it is reasonably clear that subcontracting was never better than a break-even operation until this year. More important, the subcontracting business is so intensely competitive, Sci-Tech's profit-to-sales ratio on subcontracts can never be much higher than the present level. This competitive environment will not change in the foreseeable future.

B. Subcontracting uses Sci-Tech's skills at both managerial and worker levels. The same skills applied to the division's proprietary products would yield high-profit returns.

C. The presence of subcontracts in the factory work flow inevitably lowers workers' and supervisors' concern for high quality in proprietary work. The same people handle both types of assignments. It is not feasible to segregate either the two types of work or the personnel who do the work.

D. There is, of course, a positive rationale for retaining subcontracting. It absorbs overhead costs. It provides greater continuity of employment for factory personnel. It contributes to stability of annual revenues. These considerations tend to offset the risks associated with proprietary products in the volatile electronics field.

E. On balance, continuation of the dual strategy is a relatively low-risk option. Its real cost is the extent to which it will stunt the growth and profit potential of the business, which can be attained only through a total commitment of all resources on exploiting the division's present and future proprietary products.

IV. The Proprietary Concentration Strategy

A. Sci-Tech's uniquely valuable resource is its ability to invent, develop, manufacture, and market certain state-of-the-art proprietary electronic components; hypersensitive switching devices, high-speed electron-impulse transmitters, and microvoltage measurement and control elements. The central core of this resource is the inventive and developmental genius of Conrad Woodworth. His talent is irreplaceable. Of supporting, but less valuable and clearly replaceable, usefulness are the talents of Bernard Ash and Mark Feldstein. Sci-Tech's present proprietary products represent only a first step in the potential development and exploitation of the organization's capabilities.

B. The market for Sci-Tech's proprietaries includes major segments of the electronics and computer industries, with additional potential in other end-product industries in which very high-speed electronic devices will be used. These are all high-growth markets. Equally important, they are all markets in which component performance characteristics and quality are more important than price. Profit margins of component producers who stay at the leading edge of rapidly advancing technology are extraordinarily wide once high-volume semiautomated manufacture has been established.

C. Given Sci-Tech's capability and the size and growth rate of these markets, why has Sci-Tech's development to date been so slow and its profitability so low? Several factors combine to explain this mediocre performance:

1. The diversion of top management time and energy to sub-contracting, as noted above.

2. The inability of Conrad Woodworth to recruit and direct a first-quality research group and his reluctance to accept market-oriented guidance in focusing the R & D strategy. He is close to the classic case of the solo genius who is most effective when allowed to work alone.

3. The lack of first-rate managerial skills. Bernard Ash is, or with proper leadership could be, an effective manager of production. He is an amateur, to the point of being naive, in personnel administration. Mark Feldstein is, or with proper leadership could be, an effective marketing manager. He is an amateur in the finance and control area. Ash may be willing to acknowledge his limitations. Feldstein probably is not.

D. An organization plan which would overcome the managerial weaknesses and give Sci-Tech the managerial strengths it needs to take full advantage of its potential is shown in Figure 1. The success of the proprietary strategy depends on Sci-Tech's ability to maintain a strong position at the leading edge of evolving technology in the component area. This leadership, in turn, depends on the introduction of competent senior management in R & D, finance and control, and personnel administration. It further depends on the willingness of Cyril corporate to accept at least two years of operating losses while Sci-Tech backs itself out of sub-contracting and strengthens its base for exploitation of its proprietaries, and also to make substantial further investments in senior management and in manufacturing facilities. Finally, it depends on Sci-Tech's ability to absorb the shock of the breakup of the three-man founding group.

E. The projection of proprietary sales under the proprietary-only strategy (see Table 3) rests on the following assumptions:

1. Sci-Tech's presently marketed components, in existing and improved technological modes, will not be made obsolete in the next several years by new developments or lose sales because of customer's decisions to self-manufacture comparable devices. Recent discussions with customer engineering managers and other knowledgeable electronics industry sources indicate low probability of technological obsolescence for two years, with rising uncertainty thereafter. Self-manufacture is becoming less of a threat as Sci-Tech improves its quality and delivery performance.

2. The projected sales increase for proprietaries to $13 million in two years and $22 million in three years assumes completion of development and entry into production of Woodworth's multiphase triode coupling. The potential market for this revolutionary device is estimated to be as large as $100 million annually, based on discussions with

**FIGURE 1.**
**SCI-TECH ASSOCIATES:**
**PROPOSED ORGANIZATION FOR PROPRIETARY STRATEGY**

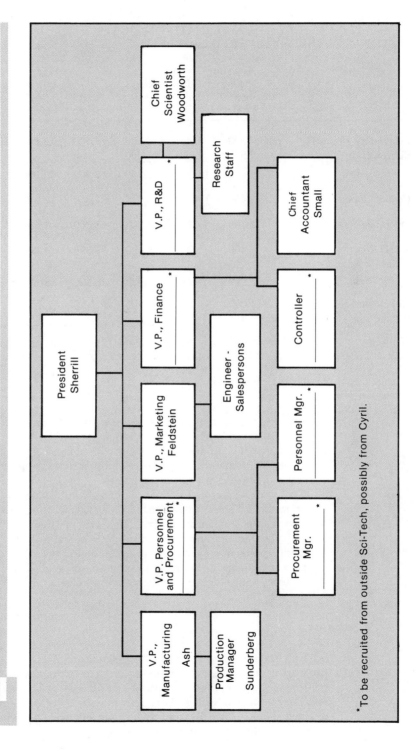

\* To be recruited from outside Sci-Tech, possibly from Cyril.

### TABLE 3.
### SCI-TECH ASSOCIATES: ALTERNATIVE BUDGETS
### FOR NEXT THREE YEARS (in thousands)

| Net Sales: | Assuming Continuance of Existing Dual-Line Strategy | | | Assuming Focus on Proprietary Products* | | |
|---|---|---|---|---|---|---|
| | Next Year | 2nd Year | 3rd Year | Next Year | 2nd Year | 3rd Year |
| Proprietary Products | $ 7,500 | $ 9,000 | $10,500 | $ 9,700 | $13,000 | $22,000 |
| Subcontracts | 7,500 | 9,000 | 11,000 | 2,600 | — | — |
| Total Sales | 15,000 | 18,000 | 21,500 | 12,300 | 13,000 | 22,000 |
| Cost of Goods Sold | 12,400 | 15,000 | 18,000 | 11,300 | 11,400 | 16,000 |
| Operating Profit | 2,600 | 3,000 | 3,500 | 1,000 | 1,600 | 6,000 |
| R & D Expense | 800 | 900 | 1,100 | 1,300 | 1,800 | 2,500 |
| Selling & Administrative Expense | 800 | 1,000 | 1,200 | 900 | 1,200 | 1,400 |
| Net Income before Tax | 1,000 | 1,100 | 1,200 | (1,200) | (1,400) | 2,100 |
| Income Tax | 460 | 510 | 550 | — | — | 100 |
| Net Profit | $ 540 | $ 590 | $ 650 | $(1,200) | $(1,400) | $ 2,000 |

*Completing presently booked subcontracts and seeking no new subcontract jobs.

customer engineers and other electronics industry sources, if it performs as anticipated and if it is susceptible to semiautomated production. I believe both of these requirements will be met within the next 12 months. If this belief is realized, the sales projection is minimal.

3. Cyril must be prepared to finance rapid growth. Under the projection in Table 3, $1 million to $1,500,000 will be needed next year to supplement mortgage financing of a new plant and office building and to cover anticipated operating losses. Equity capital to keep Sci-Tech in a position to obtain short-term bank loans at favorable rates will also be needed—probably $500,000 two years hence and perhaps $1 million the year after.

### V. Summary

A. Sci-Tech has been its own worst enemy in serving its most attractive market—the users of its proprietary products. However, correction of delivery and quality shortfalls—already well underway—coupled with prompt refinements of its existing products should enable the company to build and retain a much higher proportion of this attractive business.

B.  The potential new market for the kind of state-of-the-art components Sci-Tech already has in its laboratory is both large and profitable. Commiting balanced resources—undiluted by low-
margin subcontracting—to this attractive growth market can
convert Sci-Tech into a significant generator of profits for Cyril
Electronics.

C.  The fundamental consideration in choosing a strategy for Sci-
Tech is Cyril Electronics' objective in owning Sci-Tech. The dual
strategy at best would assure Cyril of a reliable source for certain
critical components used in other divisions, with only a moderate
long-term return on its investment. The proprietary strategy, if
successful, would represent a bold thrust into a new technological area yielding high growth and high long-term return on the
original and supplemental investments.

## Advice of the Vice-Presidents

Sherrill asked her three senior associates to meet with her at Sci-Tech's empty
office on the Saturday following Thanksgiving Day. She devoted the first hour to
reviewing orally the content of her draft report, stressing the rationale behind it,
and showing the financial estimates and proposed organization. She omitted her
assessment of the three vice-presidents. Instead, she made the case for bringing in
new senior management in terms of utilizing the special capabilities of each of the
three men in their most advantageous contribution to the long-run success of the
business.

"What I intend to do," she concluded, "unless you see strong reasons to the
contrary, is to lay both strategic options before Carl Thompson, and recommend
that he adopt the second one. If we focus all our efforts on proprietary products, I
believe Sci-Tech can become a $60 million business in five or six years, with a 20
percent pretax income. If we stick with our present strategy, I think we are unlikely
to see sales of more than $25 million, with a pretax profit-to-sales rate around 8
percent. O.K., what do *you* think?"

While what she heard in response didn't surprise her much, neither did it give
her much comfort. Mark Feldstein spoke first.

"I think you have described two basic ideas—one of them good and the other
lousy," he said. "The good idea is to get rid of subcontracting and concentrate on
our own products. When we started, we were too small to do that; we had no margin of safety, no reasonably secure income base. But we're not in that vulnerable
position now, especially with Cyril standing behind us. So I think it's the right way
to go, and I don't think the risks are all that great either.

"But your bad idea is—and I'm not going to pull my punches on this, Jane—
that you are proposing to take the management of the business away from the
three of us. I don't give a damn about all your smarmy talk about using our talents
where they'll help the business most. What you are proposing to do is obvious: demote Connie out of running R & D, demote me out of running finance, and de-

mote Bernie by taking procurement and personnel away from him. Put it all together, and what your plan amounts to is a scheme to take the management of the business away from the three of us. That is exactly what I feared would happen when we sold Sci-Tech to Cyril. But I didn't think it would happen this fast. You've been around here eight months and you're ready to get blood on your knife. I don't really blame you personally for this. You were sent here by Thompson to do this job exactly this way—and you're doing it per orders from headquarters."

Sherrill said quietly, "I wasn't sent here by Carl Thompson to do anything but help to make this business a success, Mark. And I think the four of us, working together, have made an excellent beginning this year. What I'm trying to do now is take a longer look forward and decide how to make a small success into a big success."

"Fair enough," he replied. "Then let's take your specializing strategy as it stands, and the four of us continue to manage it. I think we've shown we can do it. But let me make one thing crystal clear. If you make this recommendation to Thompson to bring in new top management, I'm not going to stay around to see if he approves it. You can count me out right from the moment you make such a proposal."

Without arguing the point with him, Sherrill said to Ash, "Bernie, what do you think?"

"The first thing I think," said Ash, "is we shouldn't get so excited until we've got something that's worth being excited about. Calm down, Mark. If Jane really has a good idea for the business, it would be stupid for us to try to kill it on the grounds of loss of personal power, status, and similar nonsense. If this business grows the way she thinks it might, and if it makes the kind of money she has projected—well, we've got employment contracts that will put a good share of those profits into our personal bank accounts. Speaking for myself at least, it wouldn't bother me a bit not to be involved in managing personnel and procurement if I was also getting rich.

"But will we get rich? As I see it, the choice Jane has laid on the table is between continuing to run a business we understand and launching ourselves into a total commitment to an extremely risky venture. The first option may not be very exciting, but the business is growing, it's starting to return to a respectable profit. And it will make more. The second option strikes me as a trip to Las Vegas—we might hit the jackpot, but we could lose our corporate shirt. I don't want to lose my share of that shirt.

"Isn't there a third option, Jane? Why can't we keep and even expand our subcontracting business and at the same time try to build a proprietary business that grows even faster than the subcontracting line? Then, if we hit a dry period in the lab, which can always happen, we would still have a reasonably secure foundation in subcontracting and our established proprietaries. Maybe we won't get as rich as we might if your second option works perfectly. But maybe also we don't get as poor as we might if it fails."

"Before I try to answer," Sherrill said, "I'd like to hear what Connie thinks."

"That's easy," he replied. "I think it's a great idea, and I think we should do it. Subcontracting isn't what we got in business to do. I'd welcome getting rid of my whole administrative job and being free to put all my attention on research. As for you, Mark, I should think you would be glad to concentrate on either finance or marketing. You can't really give both jobs the attention they'll require in a rapidly growing business. If you prefer finance to marketing, I'm sure Jane would see no difficulty in revising her proposal by putting you in the v.p.—finance position and recruiting a new marketing manager."

Without indicating her own reactions to their comments, Sherrill pushed the three to assess her proprietary strategy in greater depth, with particular emphasis on what successful execution of the strategy would require in each of the functional areas for which they were responsible. The ensuing discussion identified no substantial problems that she had not herself explored in her own analysis. At the end of the afternoon she said, "Let's call it a day. This has been very valuable to me. I want to think over what you said, and I'll let you know what I decide to do."

Early in the following week each of the men came to her office for a follow-up conference.

Mark Feldstein told her, "When I said I would quit rather than give up the finance and control function, I meant it. I endorse without qualification the proprietary strategy. Equally without qualification, I am opposed to bringing in a top management team. I'd be willing to reconsider my decision if you are willing to accept Connie's suggestion that I keep the top job in finance and control and let an outsider take over the marketing job. Otherwise, it's the end of the road as far as I am concerned."

"Mark, I don't think that would be advisable," she replied. "This is a high-risk strategy, as you recognized. I think we can lower the risk if we apply our best resources where they can make the greatest contribution. In my judgment, you can be most valuable to this business as head of marketing. If you view this as a demotion, you are totally misreading the situation. It is simply a specialization of talents to handle all of the complex needs of the business with maximum effectiveness. If you can't see it that way, I'm sorry. I don't want to lose you, but it is your decision. Think it over for a while. After all, Carl Thompson might throw the whole proposal in the wastebasket."

"Jane, I don't think you understand the full implications of what I'm telling you," he said. "When I say I'll quit if you propose your scheme, I don't mean I'll simply walk out and leave behind everything I've helped to build here. I'll take a piece of this business with me, a substantial piece, at least one and a half million dollars of annual sales, to put a figure on it. That represents our present business with two good customers for our own products. In one of those companies my brother-in-law is director of purchasing. In the other, a college classmate is chief of production engineering. I developed the business with these customers, and you better believe it goes out the door with me. I'm sorry to be this rough on you, but you're acting pretty rough with us."

"Thank you for telling me, Mark," she said. "You've given me something to think about."

Connie Woodworth said, "The more I think about what you outlined, the more I like it. I especially like the idea of being relieved of responsibility for managing the research group. As chief scientist, without the administrative burden, I'll be doing exactly what I always wanted to do."

"Suppose we lose Mark," Sherrill said. "Would that upset you? I'm not prepared to give him the finance and control position, as you suggested. I just don't think it's the best way to use his abilities for the business."

"Well, I really threw out the possibility to calm him down," he said. "I understand your point of view. If he goes, he goes."

"Suppose he goes and takes a million dollars or more of business with him?"

"Did he threaten to do that?"

"Let's not view it as a threat, but as a possibility."

"Well, I don't think it's likely to happen. We've got unique products—superior to any alternatives. He can't take that business elsewhere. It doesn't make sense to me."

"So you're prepared to accept that risk?"

"Absolutely."

Bernie Ash said, "I'm still very bothered by your either-or approach. I don't see the need to lock ourselves into this absolute choice. I don't understand why we can't set a middle course, with greater emphasis on our own products but still retaining some subcontracting as a backstop. It's probably the conservative in me."

"What bothers me about what you term a 'middle course,' " said Sherrill, "is that it really isn't a middle course. It's just continuing to do what we have been doing, dividing our attention, our resources, and our management time and energy between slow-growth, low-profit subcontracting business and what could be a high-growth, high-profit proprietary business. The record of this company demonstrates that the combination just doesn't fly very well. We've improved our performance in the last six months, but we're close to exhausting the important possibilities for improvement."

"Well, maybe so. But what I see as a middle course is a deliberate tilt toward the proprietary side of the business, without letting go of subcontracting completely."

"How strongly do you feel about this?"

"I'm very concerned. But you're the boss and I'll go along with any decision you make."

"Are you bothered about what Mark said?"

"Yes, I am. A little. Maybe more than a little. But I can live with it. I want to do what's best for the business, not what's best for any one of us, especially if what's really involved is status. I don't give a damn for status. I wish Mark didn't either, but I guess he does."

"Suppose he quits and takes a million dollars or more of the business with him?"

"I don't believe he would do that. I've known Mark Feldstein a long time. He talks tougher than he acts."

"Suppose this time he really acted?"

Ash took a deep breath. "We can live with it."

## Appendix A

## Cyril Electronics, Inc.

Cyril Electronics, Inc., is a multinational manufacturer of a broad line of electronic and related products, including data communications equipment, telephonic equipment, integrated circuits, and computer peripheral products. International business last year accounted for about 25 percent of sales and 30 percent of pretax profits. Key operating and financial data for the last five years are as follows:

|  | 5 Years Ago | 4 Years Ago | 3 Years Ago | 2 Years Ago | Last Year |
|---|---|---|---|---|---|
| Sales ($ million) | 872 | 958 | 1,098 | 1,349 | 1,621 |
| Operating Margin/Sales | 16.5% | 13.2% | 17.8% | 18.4% | 18.9% |
| Net Profit Margin/Sales | 6.0% | 3.9% | 7.1% | 7.6% | 7.8% |
| % Earned/Total Capital | 11.2% | 6.8% | 12.5% | 13.1% | 14.6% |
| % Earned/Net Worth | 12.8% | 7.3% | 13.7% | 14.8% | 16.3% |

# COMPREHENSIVE CASE 5

## Briggs and Stratton vs. Honda*

In October 1985, Briggs and Stratton President and Chief Executive Officer Frederick P. Stratton told the company's shareholders, "The most significant development in our industry in recent years has been the increased activity of Japanese manufacturers.... Their [the Japanese] stated interest in engine-powered equipment ... makes them a continuing threat."

Briggs and Stratton had long been the industry leader in manufacturing small gasoline engines for such outdoor power equipment as lawn mowers, rotary tillers, snow throwers, and lawn vacuums. Now Honda, the largest Japanese manufacturer of small engines, was in the process of challenging Briggs and Stratton's leadership position in the U.S. market.

## Company History

Briggs and Stratton (B&S) began conducting business in Milwaukee in 1908. The company's first product was a six-cylinder, two-cycle engine that Stephen F. Briggs had developed during his engineering courses at South Dakota State College. After he graduated in 1907, he was eager to produce his engine and enter the rapidly expanding automobile industry. Through a mutual friend, Stephen F. Briggs the inventor met Harold M. Stratton the successful businessman. With that introduction, the Briggs and Stratton corporation was born.

In 1920, Briggs and Stratton acquired the patents and manufacturing rights to the Smith motor wheel and the Flyer, a buckboard-like motor vehicle powered by the Smith motor wheel. The Smith motor wheel was a wheel with a small engine attached for propulsion. It could also be used on bicycles. The price for the two-passenger flyer was $150, but it still could not compete with Ford's Model T. The Model T was higher priced but was more technologically advanced.

After the war, Briggs and Stratton set out to capture a larger share of the growing lawn and garden equipment market. Recognizing the lawn mower market as a potential growth area, the company set out to make a lighter weight, low-cost engine. Briggs developed and introduced the aluminum alloy engine in

---

*This case was written by Professor Richard G. Hoffman of the School of Business Administration, College of William and Mary. It is intended to be a basis for class discussion and not to illustrate either effective or ineffective management.

1953, which achieved both a 40 percent weight and price reduction. The aluminum engine was a huge success, with initial demand outstripping supply. In response to demand, the company opened a new engine plant in Wauwatosa, Wisconsin on an 85-acre site.

In November 1975, some 56 years after the motor wheel opened the way into the small-engine business, the 100 millionth Briggs and Stratton engine came off the assembly line. In 1985, B&S ranked 379th in sales and 192nd in ROS on a list of 500 of the largest industrial U.S. corporations. Over 90 percent of the company's revenues came from the sale of small gasoline-powered engines.

## Outdoor Power Equipment Industry

In 1985 the outdoor power equipment industry (OPE) was a divergent group of various-sized manufacturers of finished goods, attachments, and components. The industry was comprised of 87 major manufacturers located in 31 states. The industry produced over 8 million pieces of equipment having an annual retail value of over $3 billion. Seven companies produced some 65 percent of the output of four key products: rotary lawn mowers, riding mowers, lawn tractors, and tillers. Six companies produced 70 percent of the walk-behind power mowers.

Approximately 75 percent of lawn mower purchases were for replacement demand, and 25 percent were first-time purchases. First-time purchases were primarily tied to new single-family housing starts. In 1985 1.77 million new single and multiple dwellings were constructed; forecasts called for new housing starts in 1986 and 1987 of 1.74 million and 1.80 million, respectively. The number of housing starts was highly dependent on interest rates. Most lawn mowers had a life of 6–8 years, making replacement demand dependent on housing starts and related demographics.

## Industry Trends

The power equipment industry had been consolidating since 1974. The number of manufacturers had declined from 145 competitors in 1974 (about half of which were power mower manufacturers) to under 90 in 1985.

In 1985, power equipment manufacturers employed about 13,000 people, with component manufacturing affiliates adding some 22,000 to 27,000 more jobs. An additional 45,000 people worked for distributors and suppliers. More than 50 percent of the industry's workers were union members. A total of 33 manufacturing plants existed nationwide. In recent years, most new plant openings had been in the South and Southwest, where unions were not as strong.

Outdoor power equipment manufacturing was not vertically integrated to any significant extent. Industry members manufactured components, attachments, or finished goods (See Exhibit 1). Component manufacturers comprised 30 percent of the industry and produced one or more of the following: engines, transmissions, gear assemblies, and other parts for use in finished outdoor power

**EXHIBIT 1**
**SELECTED U.S. OUTDOOR POWER EQUIPMENT**
**MANUFACTURERS (sales in millions of dollars)**

| Company | 1985 Sales | Main Product(s)[a] | Company | 1985 Sales | Main Product(s) |
|---|---|---|---|---|---|
| Ariens Corp. | N/A[b] | FG | Magna American Corp. | $ 9[c] | FG |
| Auburn Consolidated | | | MTD Products Co. | 400[c] | FG |
| Industries | $ 5 | A | Murray Ohio Mfg. Co. | 388 | FG |
| Bolens Corp. | 55 | FG | Roper Corporation | 307 | FG |
| Briggs & Stratton | | | Snapper (Div. of Fuqua | | |
| Corp. | 660 | E | Industry) | 245 | FG |
| Brinly-Hardy Co. | 20[c] | A | Southland Mower | | |
| Engineering Products | | | Co., Inc. | 16[c] | FG |
| Co. | 7 | A | Tecumseh Products | | |
| Excel Industries, Inc. | 19 | A | Co. | 248 | E |
| J. B. Foote Foundry Co. | 11 | FG | Teledyne Wisconsin | | |
| Jacobson/Homelite | | | Motor Co. | N/A | E |
| (Div. of Textron) | 375[c] | FG | Toro Company, | | |
| John Deere & Co. | 400[c] | FG | Inc. | 337 | FG |
| Kohler Co. | N/A | E | Wheel Horse | | |
| Lawn-Boy (Div. of | | | Products, Inc. | 80[c] | FG |
| Outdoor Marine) | 111 | FG | Yazoo Mfg. Co., Inc. | 28 | FG |

[a] A = attachments, C = components, E = Engines, FG = finished goods (mowers, tractors, tillers, etc.).
[b] N/A = Not available (usually because firm was privately held).
[c] Estimate.

equipment. Attachment manufacturers produced optional equipment that could be used with the power equipment to supplement its basic operation or to add new capabilities; these included mowers, thatchers, and plows. The finished-goods manufacturers produced final products used by the consumers, such as lawn mowers, rototillers, and tractors. Lawn-Boy was the only finished-goods manufacturer who had vertically integrated backward and manufactured its own components, including engines, in producing their outdoor power equipment. All other domestic finished-goods manufacturers had not integrated backward, and assembled their products from parts supplied by the components and attachments manufacturers. The assemblers of finished goods did do some of their own metal fabrication, such as producing the frame and housing for lawn mowers.

Largely because the power equipment manufacturers had not engaged in much backward integration, the industry was a big purchaser of materials and supplies. In 1974, supply expenses were $720 million, with raw materials amounting to $200 million, engines $360 million, and $160 million for other components. By 1984, purchases were reported to be $712 million, equal to 54 percent of finished-goods sales.

Distribution in the industry was fragmented among independent, factory-direct, and company-owned distributors. Independent distributors handled 27 percent of total manufacturing output. Sales through national department stores comprised 20 percent of total sales, whereas hardware stores, farm equipment dealers, home improvement and building suppliers, and other merchandisers accounted for 53 percent of the retail market.

In 1984, outdoor power equipment manufacturers reported annual expenditures of $60 million on advertising and promotion, $35 million on R & D, $11 million on new-product expenditures, and $67 million for new facilities and equipment. During the 1970s, sales in the industry had grown rapidly, and many companies prospered. Shipments of walk-behind rotary lawn mowers had fluctuated during the first half of the decade, peaking at 5.7 million units in 1980, dropping to 4.4 million in 1983, and rising to 5.2 million units in 1985. Much of the decline in sales was caused by the recession of the early eighties. Industry shipments are presented in Exhibit 2.

## Foreign Exports and Imports

In 1974 U.S. exports totaled $85 million, with imports amounting to a meager $2 million. By 1983 exports were $52 million, and imports into the U.S. totaled $30 million. In 1981 exports accounted for 8 percent of total shipments, but by 1985 exports accounted for only 3 percent of total shipments. Industry experts believed that exports and imports were closely tied to exchange rates. Exports went mainly to Canada, while Japan had been the largest importer to the U.S. in the past few years. Exchange rates from 1980 to 1985 are displayed in Exhibit 3.

## Industry Regulation

Prior to 1982, manufacturers of OPE were not regulated by the Consumer Products Safety Commission (CPSC); compliance was voluntary. Voluntary standards were promulgated by the American National Standards Institute and had been supported by the industry trade association since the mid-1950s. The standards were primarily concerned with improved product performance and safety. Safety standards involved both the protection from thrown objects and noise level. About 90 percent of the industry's products were in compliance with these voluntary standards. Products complying with the standards were affixed with a triangular seal.

Since 1973, the industry had been working with the CPSC for mandatory power mower safety standards. At that time, mowers ranked third on the Commission's most hazardous products list. Improvements in voluntary standards had reduced mowers to twentieth place on the hazardous products list by the end of the decade.

**EXHIBIT 2**
**SHIPMENTS OF OUTDOOR POWER EQUIPMENT,**
**1980–1985, WITH FORECASTS FOR 1986–1989**
**(in thousand units and million dollars)**

|  | Equipment | | | | | |
|---|---|---|---|---|---|---|
| Year | Walk-behind | | | Riding | | |
|  | Rotary Mowers | Rotary Tillers | Snow Throwers | Rear-Engine Mowers | Front-Engine Mowers | Garden Tractors |
| 1980 units | 5,700 | 667 | 1,577 | 314 | 494 | 220 |
| Value[a] | $701 | $159 | $397 | $185 | $345 | $351 |
| 1981 | 4,600 | 501 | 345 | 250 | 370 | 151 |
|  | $606 | $138 | $98 | $162 | $291 | $266 |
| 1982 | 4,600 | 497 | 95 | 261 | 393 | 146 |
|  | $674 | $143 | $27 | $190 | $359 | $280 |
| 1983 | 4,400 | 408 | 264 | 276 | 415 | 129 |
|  | $695 | $132 | $91 | $205 | $395 | $275 |
| 1984 | 4,950 | 399 | 348 | 354 | 502 | 152 |
|  | $742 | $197 | $122 | $278 | $482 | $311 |
| 1985 | 5193 | 362 | 421 | 355 | 548 | 147 |
|  | $792 | $181 | $144 | $287 | $535 | $303 |

EXTENDED FORECAST (Units Only)
Walk-behind

| | Mowers & Tillers | Riding Units |
|---|---|---|
| 1986 | 5,700 | 945 |
| 1987 | 5,500 | 900 |
| 1988 | 5,700 | 920 |
| 1989 | 5,900 | 1,000 |

[a]F.O.B. factory shipment value. Not available for extended forecast.

By 1982 a number of CPSC regulations went into effect. These standards called for increased safety restrictions for walk-behind power mowers, including performance and labeling requirements. The standards included the use of shields to protect people from thrown objects, deflectors and drain holes to prevent fuel ignition, and the deadman blade control system.

The most controversial regulation was the deadman blade control system. Mowers built after July 1, 1982, had to have blades that stopped within three seconds after the operator released a deadman control at the handle of the mower.

**EXHIBIT 3**
**EXCHANGE RATES FOR CANADA AND JAPAN, 1980 TO 1985**
**(units per U.S. dollar)**

|                  | 1980 | 1981 | 1982 | 1983 | 1984 | 1985 |
|------------------|------|------|------|------|------|------|
| Canadian Dollar  | 1.17 | 1.19 | 1.23 | 1.23 | 1.29 | 1.36 |
| Japanese Yen     | 227  | 221  | 249  | 237  | 237  | 238  |

*Source:* International Statistics, *Federal Reserve Bulletin*, June 1987.

Meeting this standard involved either installing a blade brake or adding a rechargeable, battery-powered electric starter. Both of these alternatives were very expensive. The CPSC estimated that the cost of compliance would be approximately $35 per unit.

By 1981, many companies, including Briggs and Stratton, had successfully developed the technology to make manual starting much easier. In that year the lawn mower industry asked Congress to amend the safety standard to allow engine stop with manual restart as a third method of compliance with the blade control requirement. President Reagan signed the amendment despite the CPSC's strong opposition.

The industry also had to comply with the Magnuson-Moss Act of 1975 requiring that all products with a written warranty and costing the consumer $15 or more come with either a statement concerning the duration of the warranty or a limited warranty. The industry from time to time also faced state and local regulations concerning noise and pollution levels of outdoor power equipment. In 1984 the industry reported annual product liability expenses for the previous year of $21 million ($18 million on warranty claims plus $3 million on insurance premiums).

## The Outdoor Power Equipment Institute (OPEI)

The trade association for outdoor power equipment was the OPEI (Outdoor Power Equipment Institute). OPEI's membership represented over 90 percent of the industry's annual volume. Founded in 1952 as a nonprofit organization, the OPEI represented the outdoor power equipment industry before governmental bodies on the state and national level. The OPEI compiled industry statistics for its members. It was active in promoting safety of equipment through voluntary industry activities and in conjunction with the federal government. The institute also monitored tariff and freight rates to reduce shipping costs for the industry's products.

In recent years, the OPEI had worked closely to help develop international safety standards for power mowers. Recently, the OPEI has had to decide whether or not foreign importers should be allowed membership. Foreign manufacturers with plants in the U.S. were automatically admitted. Several U.S. manufacturers did not want to admit foreign importers. The OPEI's executive director felt that the best way to know what the foreign competition was doing was by associating with them.

## Competition: Domestic

Competition within the industry occurred mainly within two broad strategic groups, finished-goods and components producers. The finished-goods manufacturers represented the largest group of competitors, and its members could be further subdivided by market segment. The major producers of premium-priced lawn mowers included Lawn-Boy, Toro, Snapper, Jacobson, and Deere and Co. MTD products, Murray Ohio, and Roper Corporation were the chief producers of outdoor power equipment for the medium-priced and discount markets. The latter three firms also produced equipment for the private label market.

Lawn-Boy, a subsidiary of Outboard Marine Corporation, achieved sales of $110.6 million and earnings of $5.8 million in 1985. These figures represented 12.5 and 9.5 percent of their respective corporate totals. By controlling all parts of the manufacturing process, Lawn-Boy produced a product with a distinctive integrated look (i.e., the engine didn't look bolted on). This was appealing to some consumers in the premium-priced segment. Lawn-Boy was the only leading brand-name manufacturer to produce its own engines. All of their engines were of two-cycle design (engines ran on a mixture of gasoline and oil), while the other major engine manufacturers in the industry produced four-cycle engines (engines ran on gasoline only).

The largest assembler of finished goods for the premium-priced segment was the Toro Company, Inc., headquartered in Minneapolis. Toro sold $336.8 million of OPE in 1985. Toro was also the leading manufacturer of snow-throwing equipment.

The Snapper division of Fuqua Industries was also a major producer of OPE in 1985 and competed in the premium-priced market. Snapper marketed a full line of lawn mowers, tillers, and snow blowers. The division sold $245.3 million of OPE in 1985 and accounted for 35 percent of Fuqua's total sales. Its pretax earnings of $54.5 million represented 60 percent of the corporate total.

The Jacobson/Homelite division of Textron, Inc., also produced high-quality lawn mowers, power appliances, and chain saws. In 1985 this division had sales totaling $375 million.

Finally, Deere and Company, Inc., also produced high-priced products. Their OPE sales in 1985 amounted to approximately $400 million, but a significant portion of this figure was for farm and industrial equipment. For several years, Deere, Toro, and Snapper had chosen B&S engines to power their mowers.

The finished-goods producers of lower-priced mowers included the two largest U.S. lawn mower manufacturers, MTD and Roper. MTD Products, Inc., of Valley City, Ohio, was closely held and had estimated sales of about $400 million. MTD bought its engines from Briggs and Stratton, manufactured the bodies, and assembled the units for sale. They sold their products to private label distributors and marketed nationally under the brand name Yardman. MTD was the nation's largest producer of walk-behind lawn mowers.

Roper Corporation was the nation's second largest producer of lawn mowers. Their total OPE sales in 1985 were $307 million. Seventy-three percent of Roper's 1985 output was purchased by Sears Roebuck and sold under the Sears Craftsman label. Roper was also a private label supplier to other discount chains. Roper primarily used Tecumseh engines on its equipment.

The Murray Ohio Manufacturing Co., located in Brentwood, Tennessee, was a major producer of both OPE and bicycles for the medium-priced and discount segments. Total corporate sales amounted to $387.5 million in 1985.

The major cost component of lawn mowers was the engine. The four largest producers of mower engines were Briggs and Stratton, Tecumseh Products Co., Kohler Co., and Teledyne Wisconsin Motor Co. Tecumseh posed the only real domestic competitive threat to Briggs and Stratton in their strongest product category of air-cooled aluminum alloy engines ranging from 2 to 18 horsepower.

Tecumseh Products Company was the country's largest producer of refrigerator compressors and the second largest producer of small gasoline-powered engines. The company also produced gear assemblies and related transmission parts. In 1985 Tecumseh's operating income on engine sales of $248 million (36.7 percent of total sales) was $41 million (46 percent of total income). The largest customers of Tecumseh engines were Sears and Sears' suppliers such as Roper. Exhibit 1 lists some of the key industry competitors and their sales.

## Competition: Foreign

According to industry experts, Japan was the primary importer of OPE products into the U.S. The value of Japanese imports of lawn mowers and parts had increased from less than $3 million in 1978 to $36.1 million in 1985, representing 41 percent of the total value of OPE goods imported into the U.S. that year. Most foreign imports of OPE products into the U.S. were garden tractors and rotary walk-behind lawn mowers. Garden tractors were imported as agricultural machinery and were exempted from paying U.S. tariffs. The three leading import brands of garden tractors were all Japanese: Kubota, Yanmar, and Satoh. The leading Japanese importers of riding and walk-behind lawn mowers were Honda, Kawasaki, Suzuki, and Yamaha, all of whom also produced motorcycles for the U.S. market.

In the lawn mower market, Honda was the only brand considered to be a factor by industry experts. Competition from Japan was not a new problem for the industry, but it had become much more severe since the recession of the early eighties. Japanese firms manufactured both engines and finished products. The increase in Japanese competition was attributed to the extraordinary strength of the dollar against the yen and the worldwide weakness of the motorcycle business.

Global recession in general and the softening of the motorcycle business in particular have forced Japanese motorcycle manufacturers to look to other markets in order to maintain full use of their production facilities. All four Japanese motorcycle manufacturers (Honda, Kawasaki, Suzuki, and Yamaha) had identified power products as appropriate new business opportunities. Honda had stated publicly that it intended to become a leader in the powered products field and had transferred resources from its motorcycle division to its powered products division. In many respects OPE products were a natural source of diversification for Honda, because the company was founded in 1948 to produce small internal combustion engines. Honda's production capacity for small engines was about 4 million units a year in 1985. Honda had more than doubled its capacity two years earlier. The company sold its mowers through established OPE distributors and not its own automobile or motorcycle dealers.

Although Honda sold engines, it preferred to sell finished goods. The company possessed a broad product line of power products which included pumps, generators, outboard motors, garden tillers, snow throwers, walk-behind power mowers, and lawn tractors. This product line represented approximately 9 percent of total sales in 1985. Honda and other Japanese manufacturers were also strong competitors in other parts of the world.

Honda's strategy in the OPE industry focused on the high-priced market, as a manufacturer of finished goods for the consumer market. Similarly to Lawn-Boy, it manufactured both the lawn mower engine and body, which resulted in equipment having an integrated look. Honda engines were noted for their light weight and dependability. Professional users of OPE had casually dubbed Honda's engines "Briggs-Hondas" because of their dependability. They often replaced Briggs and Stratton engines on used equipment. Honda's product strength was based on its heavy R & D expenditures. This ensured that the firm's products would remain technologically advanced. Honda marketed its products by making extensive use of advertising and promotion. They also priced their products competitively, setting prices below the competition in order to gain market share. Honda had been extremely successful in both the U.S. motorcycle and automobile markets using similar strategies and possessed extensive resources to support similar efforts in the OPE market (see Exhibit 4).

In 1983, Honda sold approximately 10,000 high-priced lawn mowers in the U.S. Honda also sold replacement engines compatible with many makes of mowers. Until 1984, Honda lawn mowers bound for the U.S. had been manufactured in Japan. Apparently satisfied that it could gain significant market share, Honda built a manufacturing plant for lawn mowers in Alamance County, North Carolina. Honda produced approximately 10,000 units in the first year and employed 80 workers. The engines were still produced at the Hamamatsu plant in Japan. Labor costs in Japan were, on average, 30 percent lower than in the U.S. and 50 percent lower than at Briggs and Stratton. Labor costs were typically around 40 percent of the total cost in outdoor power equipment.

Honda's products had been well received in the U.S., getting excellent ratings from consumer magazines. Comparisons with domestic models revealed that

**EXHIBIT 4**
**HONDA MOTOR COMPANY:**
**SELECTED FINANCIAL AND STATISTICAL DATA**
**(in millions of dollars)**

| For Years Ended February 28th | 1985 | 1984 | 1983 | 1982 |
|---|---|---|---|---|
| Sales | $10,753 | $ 9,778 | $ 8,772 | $ 8,254 |
| Net Income | 532 | 403 | 289 | 292 |
| Assets | $ 5,974 | $ 6,116 | $ 5,558 | $ 4,941 |
| Stockholders' Equity | $ 2,806 | $ 2,452 | $ 2,020 | $ 1,607 |
| Employees | 50,609 | 51,350 | 46,238 | 42,415 |

Compiled from "The International 500," *Fortune* magazine statistical service.

there were no disadvantages associated with Honda mowers themselves. The few disadvantages had to do with distribution, parts, and service. Honda mowers received high marks for convenience, performance, and safety. The starting controls were simple, easy to reach, and had an automatic choke which eliminated the need for a choke control on the throttle. The cutting performance of Honda mowers was usually rated excellent, they provided a level cut, even in tall, heavy grass, and they efficiently bagged clippings. Honda's mowers met or exceeded safety standards, including a deadman clutch that stopped the blade one second after the control was released, well within the three-second requirement. In 1985 Honda had an estimated 2 percent of the U.S. walk-behind lawn mower market, up from its 1 percent share in 1983.

Other Japanese manufacturers were actively calling on B&S's OEM customers. By 1984 Toro and John Deere switched from B&S to Suzuki and Kawasaki engines, respectively, for their consumer, walk-behind lawn mowers.

In an interview with *Business Week,* Frederick Stratton stated, "The real battle over the next five years is with the Japanese. I hate to admit it, but Japan has set a new standard for quality."

## The Briggs and Stratton Corporation

Briggs and Stratton (B&S), headquartered in Wauwatosa, Wisconsin, was the world's largest producer of small gas-powered engines used primarily for outdoor power equipment. The company operated in a mature market with growth averaging 2 percent per year. B&S had an estimated 75 percent of the small-engine market in the U.S. and over 50 percent of the worldwide market in 1985. Engines and parts accounted for 92 percent of Briggs' total revenues in 1985. The other 8 percent was from the sale of automotive lock and key sets. B&S was the largest producer of automobile ignition system locks and door and trunk locks in the U.S., with over 90 percent market share. B&S sales are summarized in Exhibit 5.

In 1985, 89 percent of Briggs' sales of $660 million were to manufacturers of lawn mowers and other OPE. Approximately 11 percent of these sales was to manufacturers of equipment used mainly in construction and agriculture; agricultural equipment purchases were tax free.

Briggs' number one customer for small engines was MTD, which bought about 10 percent of B&S's total output in 1985. Toro had also used B&S engines on its mowers. Kendrik B. Melrose, president of Toro, referred to B&S as "the General Motors of the small lawn mower engine business."

In 1980, export sales were a record 26 percent of Briggs and Stratton's engine sales; by 1985 export sales represented 14 percent of engine sales. Foreign customers received longer payment terms than domestic customers, in recognition of longer shipping times. In addition, many of B&S's domestic customers exported products powered by B&S engines. B&S estimated that 30 percent of its total engine business was derived from markets outside the United States. Frederick P. Stratton, the company's CEO observed:

> The markets for products powered by our engines is increasingly international. The flow of material around the world is truly amazing. For example, we know of cases where engines we ship to customers in Australia are mounted on equipment destined for Europe, and engines we ship to customers in Europe are mounted on equipment destined for the U.S.

**EXHIBIT 5**
**BRIGGS AND STRATTON'S**
**SALES OF OEM AND AIR-COOLED ENGINES**
**BY END USER, 1980–1985**

*Engine sales as a percentage of total revenues*

| End Uses | 1980 | 1981 | 1982 | 1983 | 1984 | 1985 |
|----------|------|------|------|------|------|------|
| Lawn & garden equipment | 84% | 83% | 85% | 88% | 89% | 89% |
| Industrial agricultural | 16 | 17 | 15 | 12 | 11 | 11 |
| All exports | 26 | 23 | 21 | 16 | 14 | 14 |
| Total Engine Sales | 94% | 93% | 94% | 93% | 92% | 92% |

*Source:* Company annual reports.

In 1981, B&S's engine sales declined 31 percent, the largest year-to-year percentage decline since 1932. Because of the slow demand and dry weather, B&S customers' inventories were at a high level. By 1985 engine sales had increased an average of 6 percent per year to return to a level close to that of four years earlier.

In March 1982, B&S made its first shipments from a new distribution center in Lambertheim, West Germany. This new facility was the stocking point for service parts and replacement engines bound for central service distributors in Europe. Later the same year, B&S opened a sales office in Manila, Philippines, to promote sales and service to lesser developed nations in the Pacific basin. These nations demanded primarily sales of larger cast-iron engines for agriculture, marine, and industrial uses. During 1983, B&S again expanded its sales network to developed countries having markets for lawn and garden equipment by opening sales offices in Oslo, Norway, and Auckland, New Zealand. B&S's international operations were coordinated by Michael Hamilton.

Economic conditions in export markets remained depressed in 1985, and the continued strength of the dollar made B&S prices less competitive in those markets. Export sales remained only 2 percent above the 1983 level, the year in which B&S exports were their lowest in 10 years.

## Current Management

The president of Briggs and Stratton, Frederick P. Stratton, Jr., was the grandson of the co-founder of Briggs and Stratton. Mr. Stratton was a Stanford M.B.A. and formerly worked for Robert W. Baird, a brokerage house. He joined B&S in 1973 and was named president in 1977. In 1985 Lawrence G. Regner retired as chairman of the Board. He had been one of Mr. Stratton's chief advisors and had spent 62 years with the firm, 51 years as an officer or director. Michael E. Batten, CEO of Twin Disc, Inc., was elected as the new chairman.

## Products

B&S possessed a wide product line of different engines. Its most popular engines were those made of aluminum alloy. These were produced in many different sizes, displacements, and horsepowers. They were all four-cycle engines that ran on straight gas (not mixed with oil). More than 95 percent of the engines sold by B&S were air-cooled, aluminum alloy gasoline engines ranging from 2 to 18 horsepower. Less than 5 percent of the engines were the air-cooled, cast-iron variety ranging from 9 to 16 horsepower. B&S also produced air- and water-cooled diesel engines ranging from 3 to 28.5 horsepower. Walk-behind power mowers generally employed a 3-to-4-hp engine. B&S engines were of high quality and had many innovative features. Some of B&S's successful innovations are listed in Exhibit 6.

**EXHIBIT 6
SMALL-ENGINE INNOVATIONS
DEVELOPED BY BRIGGS AND STRATTON**

1953: *Aluminum Alloy Gasoline Engine:* Reduced weight and cost of small engines.

1961: *Easy Spin Starting:* Engine starting effort cut in half by a simple cam-controlled, fault-proof compression release.

1962: *Oil Foam Air Cleaner:* Dirt banned from the engine for its life by an easy-to-clean polyurethane foam filter.

1966: *Synchro Balance Design:* Engine and riding equipment vibrations smoothed out by a synchronized counterweight system.

1968: *Automatic Vacuum-Controlled Choke:* Replaced manual choke, providing extra power when needed for heavy loads.

1971: *12-Volt Gear-Type Starter with Dual-Circuit Alternator:* Provided for quick starting at low temperatures. Alternator provides both D/C battery charging and A/C for lights or external loads.

1977: *Quiet Power:* The 16-hp twin-cylinder engine prompted by the noise abatement guidelines provided quiet running and low vibration levels.

1982: *Magnetron Ignition:* A self-contained transistor with no moving.parts. Provides more consistent spark for dependable starting. Can be installed on existing engines.

1983: The small electric motor was introduced for power mowers. The new 120-volt, 1,000-watt motor weighed 11 lb, had a 10-year life, and met CPSC standards for deadman blade control.

1984: MAX series of 3.5–4-hp engines featuring improved durability and appearance.

---

*Source:* Compiled from company pamphlets.

B&S continued to make product improvements. In addition to the introduction of the electronic ignition in 1982, the company had designed new features to reduce noise levels in recent years, such as better mufflers and synchro-balanced engines. In 1983 the company introduced a small electric engine for use on lawn and garden equipment. B&S introduced its MAX series of 3.5-to-4-horsepower gasoline engines in late 1984. This represented the first major redesign in the firm's small gas engines since 1967. The MAX engines offered a streamlined appearance, easier starting, and quiet, low maintenance performance. They were designed to appeal to the consumer. This engine represented the first output of a long-term product development program initiated in 1983. B&S also announced that the first radically new small gasoline engine design would be introduced in early 1987.

B&S's major form of distribution was through contractual arrangements with finished-goods manufacturers, which were generally negotiated on a yearly basis. Contracts with finished-goods manufacturers of lawn mowers accounted for approximately 75 percent of B&S's sales.

## Marketing and Promotion

Traditionally, B&S sold engines directly to finished-goods manufacturers. B&S engines were functional and did not have fancy decals or paint jobs. B&S relied heavily on its quality image and reputation to gain sales. B&S was well known among older consumers, many of whom were accustomed to seeing B&S engines on their equipment. Younger consumers, many of whom were starting to buy their first homes, were not as familiar with the Briggs and Stratton name.

B&S had put together a six-member marketing staff in the early 1980s under the direction of L. William Dewey. One of its roles was to market engines to consumers and retailers of finished goods. B&S wanted consumers to ask for their engines by name when buying a lawn mower. In 1983, the company began a television advertising campaign for the first time. The campaign slogan was "Briggs and Stratton: the power in power equipment." The commercial employed trick photography to show B&S engines floating above invisible rototillers and lawn mowers, emphasizing the fact that B&S engines were responsible for providing the power. The company quadrupled its 1982 advertising expenditures, spending $4 million in 1983 and $2 million in 1985. Company engineers had also taken steps to improve the appearance of B&S engines. Part of this effort resulted in the MAX series.

B&S assured service for its engines (even though they became components of other manufacturer's products) via a network of over 30,000 authorized service centers worldwide. To shore up relations with its OEM customers, B&S assured them that it would not enter the finished-goods market and compete with them. No customer enjoyed a special price.

## Production

Briggs and Stratton manufactured almost all of the components used in assembling its engines except for piston rings, spark plugs, and valves. All gasoline engine manufacturing facilities were located in the Milwaukee area; diesel engines were manufactured in the company-owned plant in West Germany. During 1985, 26 percent of each revenue dollar went for direct materials, 47 percent for wages and benefits, 4.4 percent for taxes, 16.8 percent for all other expenses, and 1.4 percent was reinvested; profit margin on sales was 4.7 percent. Prior to 1985 the compounded, 10-year growth rate in net plant was 13 percent; in 1985 investment in plant and equipment increased by 62 percent over the previous year. Production was highly seasonal and was heaviest from December to March. B&S manufactured engines to individual customer specifications and, as a result, did not build finished goods for its own inventory. To try to even out seasonal demand, B&S offered incentive discounts to customers who would accept delivery in the off-season; however, payment terms on these orders were very short. Growth in year-end order backlogs had averaged 13 percent over the past five years.

Labor costs represented approximately 50 percent of the total cost of a B&S mower engine in 1985. Company wages and benefits in Wisconsin averaged about $18.00 per hour, higher than that of both domestic and foreign competitors. Growth in employees had been near zero for the past 10 years. In an effort to hold down labor costs, the company proposed a three-year wage freeze and work rule concessions in return for a profit-sharing plan and an improved pension during 1983 contract negotiations with the union. Local 232 of the Allied Industrial Workers' Union (AIW) rejected the proposal, and over 7,000 employees went on a three-month-long strike. The new three-year contract which emerged did not reduce labor costs for B&S, but did reduce the rate of increase of such costs through fiscal 1986.

The ready acceptance of Japanese products by American consumers had created new production challenges for B&S. The company had committed large capital expenditures to new technologies such as robotics. Over $36 million was spent on cost-reducing machinery in 1984. This figure rose to $58.4 million in 1985. The largest single expenditure (approximately $17 million) was for a new lawn mower engine plant in Murray, Kentucky. The majority of the remaining expenditure was for more cost reduction equipment similar to the computer-aided design and manufacturing (CAD/CAM) equipment used to produce the MAX engine.

Improved production management techniques were implemented starting in 1983. This included installation of materials requirements planning (MRP), an inventory reduction program, and statistical process control. The purpose of the MRP system was to provide the correct parts in the right quantities when they were needed in the manufacturing process. This system took advantage of information stored in a computer for timely response and scheduling. The goal of the new inventory reduction program was to cut inventory in half with no loss of response to customer needs. "Quality centers" were being created to ensure a constant flow of ideas from the bottom up on how to improve inventory and other production management activities.

The statistical process control system was intended to provide detection of any trend toward making bad parts before such parts were even produced. On a regular basis, sample parts were taken from inventory and measured in terms of allowable tolerances. The average measure for each sample was plotted on a chart. Should the measures fall outside of accepted limits, corrective action would be taken immediately. Management believed that the system would produce two benefits: (1) the elimination of shipments of poorly made products, and (2) a reduction in safety stock held by the firm.

## Finance

Briggs and Stratton reported a decline in earnings despite higher sales in fiscal 1985. Growth in sales for the past five years averaged 6.5 percent annually. Sales of most types of OPE in 1985 were up slightly. However, the market for automobile locks was flat. Despite the poor earnings, the company raised the dividend rate to $1.60 from $1.58. This increase reflected a change in dividend policy for fiscal 1985. The company raised the dividend rate to make up for ending the practice of paying an extra dividend at year end. B&S tried to maintain a constant dividend pay-out ratio. The goal was to pay 50 percent of earnings to shareholders. Even in bad years, dividends paid were never reduced.

B&S was continuing its long-standing policy of financing capital expenditures entirely out of retained earnings. The company had no long-term debt. The *Value Line* survey gave B&S its highest rating of A+ for its financial strength. B&S's financial statements are presented in Exhibits 7–9.

**EXHIBIT 7**
**BRIGGS AND STRATTON'S PERFORMANCE BY BUSINESS SEGMENT, 1980–1985**
**(in millions of dollars)**

|  | Year Ended June 30 | | | | | |
|  | 1985 | 1984 | 1983 | 1982 | 1981 | 1980 |
|---|---|---|---|---|---|---|
| **SALES** | | | | | | |
| Engines and parts | $660 | $615 | $572 | $598 | $530 | $669 |
| Locks | 58 | 56 | 42 | 38 | 41 | 39 |
|  | $718 | $671 | $614 | $636 | $571 | $708 |
| **OPERATING INCOME** | | | | | | |
| Engines and parts | $ 59 | $ 59 | $ 62 | $ 67 | $ 39 | $ 85 |
| Locks | 1 | 4 | 2 | 1 | 2 | 2 |
|  | $ 60 | $ 63 | $ 64 | $ 68 | $ 41 | $ 87 |
| **ASSETS** | | | | | | |
| Engines and parts | $336 | $311 | $298 | $271 | $254 | $281 |
| Locks | 31 | 35 | 33 | 25 | 26 | 30 |
| Unallocated | 44 | 72 | 56 | 71 | 54 | 30 |
|  | $411 | $418 | $387 | $367 | $334 | $341 |
| **DEPRECIATION EXPENSE** | | | | | | |
| Engines and parts | $ 17 | $ 16 | $ 15 | $ 13 | $ 12 | $ 10 |
| Locks | 1 | 1 | 1 | 1 | 1 | 1 |
|  | $ 18 | $ 17 | $ 16 | $ 14 | $ 13 | $ 11 |
| **EXPENDITURES FOR PLANT AND EQUIPMENT** | | | | | | |
| Engines and parts | $ 55 | $ 33 | $ 31 | $ 20 | $ 26 | $ 52 |
| Locks | 3 | 3 | 1 | 1 | 2 | 3 |
|  | $ 58 | $ 36 | $ 32 | $ 21 | $ 28 | $ 55 |

*Source:* Company annual reports.

**EXHIBIT 8**
**BRIGGS AND STRATTON'S SALES, EARNINGS, AND STATISTICAL DATA, 1976–1985 (in millions of dollars except per-share data)**

| For the Years Ended June 30 | 1985 | 1984 | 1983 | 1982 | 1981 | 1980 | 1979 | 1978 | 1977 | 1976 |
|---|---|---|---|---|---|---|---|---|---|---|
| SUMMARY OF OPERATIONS | | | | | | | | | | |
| Net sales | 718 | 671 | 614 | 636 | 569 | 709 | 591 | 457 | 389 | 327 |
| Gross profit on sales[1] | 111 | 110 | 97 | 105 | 78 | 127 | 119 | 97 | 86 | 72 |
| Provision for income taxes | 29 | 31 | 27 | 34 | 19 | 42 | 45 | 37 | 32 | 27 |
| Net income[1] | 34 | 35 | 32 | 39 | 23 | 49 | 48 | 37 | 33 | 28 |
| Average number of shares of common stock outstanding[2] | 14 | 14 | 14 | 14 | 14 | 14 | 14 | 14 | 14 | 14 |
| Per share of common stock:[2] | | | | | | | | | | |
| Net income | 2.32 | 2.40 | 2.20 | 2.72 | 1.62 | 3.39 | 3.35 | 2.59 | 2.31 | 1.91 |
| Cash dividends | 1.60 | 1.58 | 1.58 | 1.54 | 1.52 | 1.46 | 1.35 | 1.22 | 1.12 | .93 |
| Shareholders' investment | 19.59 | 18.87 | 18.05 | 17.44 | 16.31 | 16.17 | 14.24 | 12.24 | 10.87 | 9.68 |

[1]Years prior to 1977 reflect the first-in, first-out (FIFO) method for pricing inventory, while 1977 and years after reflect the last-in, first-out (LIFO) method.

[2]Number of shares of common stock and per-share data have been adjusted for the 2-for-1 stock split in 1976.

*Source:* Company annual reports.

**EXHIBIT 8** (*continued*)
**BRIGGS AND STRATTON'S SALES, EARNINGS, AND STATISTICAL DATA, 1976–1985 (in millions of dollars except per-share data)**

| For the Years Ended June 30 | 1985 | 1984 | 1983 | 1982 | 1981 | 1980 | 1979 | 1978 | 1977 | 1976 |
|---|---|---|---|---|---|---|---|---|---|---|
| **OTHER DATA** | | | | | | | | | | |
| Shareholders' investment | 283 | 273 | 261 | 252 | 236 | 234 | 206 | 177 | 157 | 140 |
| Total assets | 412 | 418 | 388 | 367 | 333 | 341 | 290 | 242 | 213 | 192 |
| Plant and equipment | 391 | 340 | 310 | 283 | 266 | 240 | 190 | 168 | 151 | 138 |
| Plant and equipment net of reserves | 230 | 194 | 179 | 166 | 161 | 148 | 108 | 94 | 84 | 77 |
| Provision for depreciation | 18 | 17 | 16 | 14 | 13 | 11 | 9 | 8 | 8 | 7 |
| Expenditures for plant and equipment | 58 | 36 | 32 | 21 | 29 | 55 | 25 | 19 | 15 | 12 |
| Working capital | 93 | 110 | 109 | 111 | 95 | 102 | 111 | 94 | 82 | 69 |
| Current ratio | 2.0 to 1 | 2.0 to 1 | 2.1 to 1 | 2.2 to 1 | 2.2 to 1 | 2.1 to 1 | 2.6 to 1 | 2.7 to 1 | 2.8 to 1 | 2.5 to 1 |
| Number of employees at year end | 8,203 | 8,777 | 9,254 | 8,138 | 8,179 | 10,873 | 10,605 | 8,931 | 7,936 | 6,950 |
| Number of shareholders at year end | 8,959 | 9,310 | 10,006 | 11,140 | 11,865 | 12,893 | 13,185 | 13,388 | 12,973 | 12,634 |
| Quoted market price: | | | | | | | | | | |
| High | 31⅛ | 33¼ | 37¼ | 26⅝ | 28¼ | 29⅛ | 31¼ | 30⅜ | 33⅜ | 32¾ |
| Low | 25½ | 25½ | 23⅞ | 22 | 22 | 20¾ | 25 | 23½ | 25⅛ | 20⅞ |

**EXHIBIT 9**
**BRIGGS AND STRATTON:**
**CONSOLIDATED BALANCE SHEETS, 1981–1985 (in millions of dollars)**

| | *Fiscal Year Ending June 30* | | | | |
|---|---|---|---|---|---|
| | *1985* | *1984* | *1983* | *1982* | *1981* |
| ASSETS: | | | | | |
| CURRENT ASSETS | | | | | |
| Cash | $ 4 | $ 4 | $ 4 | $ 4 | $ 3 |
| Certificates of deposit | 21 | 57 | 41 | 52 | 35 |
| U.S. government securities | 0 | 0 | 0 | 2 | 4 |
| Receivables, net | 56 | 55 | 59 | 53 | 44 |
| Finished products | 27 | 29 | 44 | 40 | 33 |
| Work in process | 35 | 52 | 39 | 28 | 32 |
| Raw materials | 8 | 12 | 8 | 9 | 8 |
| Total inventories | 70 | 93 | 92 | 77 | 73 |
| Future income tax benefits | 0 | 7 | 6 | 8 | 8 |
| Prepaid employee health care | 16 | 0 | 0 | 0 | 0 |
| Prepaid expense | 14 | 8 | 6 | 5 | 5 |
| Total current assets | 181 | 223 | 208 | 201 | 172 |
| PLANT AND EQUIPMENT | | | | | |
| Land and land improvements | 9 | 9 | 9 | 9 | 9 |
| Buildings | 94 | 85 | 83 | 82 | 79 |
| Machinery and equipment | 250 | 219 | 193 | 176 | 159 |
| Construction in progress | 37 | 27 | 25 | 16 | 19 |
| | 390 | 340 | 310 | 283 | 266 |
| Less accumulated depreciation and unamortized investment tax credit | 160 | 145 | 131 | 117 | 105 |
| Total plant and equipment, net | 230 | 195 | 179 | 166 | 161 |
| Total assets | $411 | $418 | $387 | $367 | $333 |
| LIABILITY AND SHAREHOLDERS' EQUITY | | | | | |
| CURRENT LIABILITIES | | | | | |
| Accounts payable | 31 | 27 | 24 | 16 | 16 |
| Foreign loans | 12 | 13 | 10 | 8 | 10 |
| Accrued liabilities | | | | | |
| Wages and salaries | 14 | 15 | 14 | 15 | 13 |
| Retirement plan | 7 | 13 | 18 | 19 | 19 |
| Taxes, nonincome | 5 | 4 | 4 | 3 | 2 |
| Other | 19 | 22 | 21 | 20 | 17 |
| Total accrued liabilities | 45 | 54 | 57 | 56 | 51 |
| Federal and state income taxes | 2 | 19 | 8 | 10 | 0 |
| Total current liabilities | 89 | 113 | 100 | 90 | 77 |
| DEFERRED INCOME TAXES | 30 | 22 | 18 | 16 | 12 |

| | *Fiscal Year Ending June 30* | | | | |
| --- | --- | --- | --- | --- | --- |
| | *1985* | *1984* | *1983* | *1982* | *1981* |
| ACCRUED EMPLOYMENT BENEFITS | 10 | 9 | 9 | 8 | 8 |
| SHAREHOLDERS' EQUITY: | | | | | |
| Common Stock | | | | | |
| Authorized 15,000,000 shares, $3.00 par value, issued and outstanding. 14,463,500 shares in 1985 and 1984 | 43 | 43 | 43 | 43 | 43 |
| Retained earnings | 240 | 230 | 218 | 209 | 192 |
| Cumulative translation adjustmts | 0 | 0 | 0 | 0 | 1 |
| Total shareholders' equity | 283 | 273 | 261 | 252 | 236 |
| Total liabilities & shareholders' Equity | $412 | $418 | $388 | $367 | $333 |

*Source:* Company annual reports.

## Outlook

Frederick Stratton commented on the challenge from Honda: "We are determined to build customer awareness of our product and maintain our leadership position. We are not going to let the Japanese take this market from us." Some skeptics doubted that a component manufacturer could effectively advertise directly to a consumer. But Stratton argued that the company's advertising, combined with its clean balance sheet, modern plant, and new product commitment, would carry the day.

# COMPREHENSIVE CASE 6

## Stone Ridge Bank

Like most other U.S. banks, Stone Ridge Bank is facing one of its most crucial decisions in its long history. Instead of continued expansion, aiding, and consequently benefiting from, the economic growth of its region, Stone Ridge must sharpen its focus if it is to survive. The board of directors has asked Spencer Smythe, Jr.—an investor and part-time consultant—to help it decide how to respond to an offer to buy the branch network of Stone Ridge Bank. The following pages summarize the information that Mr. Smythe has gathered.

## The Stone Ridge Bank

For many years Stone Ridge has been one of the two leading commercial banks in the region—its history can be traced back to 1856. The stockholders and directors include members of the leading families in the area. Conservative management helped Stone Ridge survive the bank crisis of the 1930s, and astute officers achieved an attractive earnings record, especially during the 1960s and 1970s.

The bank performs all the usual commercial banking activities. (1) For its corporate customers engaged in commerce and industry, Stone Ridge accepts demand and time deposits, makes loans with various kinds of security and conditions, does lease financing, provides automated payroll services, buys and sells foreign exchange, does cash management and funds transfer functions, advises on short-term investment of excess cash, and the like. Many of these functions are also performed for local government units and other institutions. (2) For individual consumers, Stone Ridge provides checking accounts and various kinds of savings accounts, makes installment loans and real estate loans, offers travelers checks, safe deposit boxes, credit cards, and similar services.

Located over a thousand miles from the major financial centers of the U.S., Stone Ridge has long served as an intermediary between Wall Street and the little fellow in the hinterland. It shares a strong regional pride, and regards its New York and West Coast bank correspondents as convenient sources of help for regional development. In fact, especially since World War II, the region has had a significant influx of industry, and Stone Ridge has been an active participant in this development. Stone Ridge, with less emphasis on consumer and agricultural banking, has benefited more than competing banks from this industrial growth.

Affiliated with the bank is the Stone Ridge Trust Company (both are owned by a holding company). The Trust Company oversees the estates of many prominent local citizens and is the epitome of conservative respectability. Stone Ridge Bank operates under a state charter and is a member of the Federal Deposit Insurance Corporation.

Stone Ridge Bank's earnings statement for last year and the year-end balance sheet are shown in Table 1. With $2.2 billion in assets and about 2,000 employees, Stone Ridge is a big frog in a middle-sized puddle; it is proud and conservative.

**TABLE 1.**
**STONE RIDGE BANK CONDENSED INCOME STATEMENT**
**(in millions)**

| Operating Revenues: | |
|---|---:|
| Interest and fees on loans | $171 |
| Interest and dividends on securities | 29 |
| Other | 42 |
| Total operating revenues | 242 |
| | |
| Expenses: | |
| Salaries and other personnel expenses | 34 |
| Interest on deposits | 110 |
| Other interest expense | 42 |
| All other expenses | 36 |
| Total operating expenses | 222 |
| Income tax | 3 |
| Total expenses and tax | 225 |
| | |
| Net income from operations | $ 17 |

**Condensed Balance Sheet, at Year End (in millions)**

| Assets | | Liabilities and Equity | |
|---|---:|---|---:|
| Cash and due from banks | $391 | Deposits: | |
| Federal government securities | 121 | Demand | $618 |
| State and local obligations | 125 | Savings and other time | 936 |
| Federal funds sold | 310 | Federal funds purchased | 406 |
| Mortgages and loans | 1,123 | Other borrowed funds | 51 |
| Direct lease financing | 92 | Other liabilities & accruals | 64 |
| Land, buildings, and equipment | 39 | Total liabilities | $2,075 |
| | | Common Stock | 38 |
| | | Retained earnings | 88 |
| | | Total equity | 126 |
| Total assets | $2,201 | Total liabilities & equity | $2,201 |

# A New Ball Game

In a few short years the setting in which Stone Ridge Bank succeeded so well has changed drastically. The old order passeth—for banking everywhere.

## Disrupting Forces

*New technology* has altered bank services and internal operations. Computerized bookkeeping has lowered operating costs significantly when large volumes are processed; this changes optimum bank size. Electronic-communication links across the nation make feasible centralized credit files, plastic credit cards, automated transfers of funds, and new forms of cash management. Automatic teller machines lower deposit and withdrawal costs and, more important, make cash available 24 hours a day in many locations. A further possibility is the use of interactive TV for home banking. Such changes as these are modifying the role of branch offices of banks and are moving us toward a checkless society. And with satellite communication, some of the techniques can be applied nationwide and even worldwide.

*Deregulation* has dramatically changed who competes with whom. For example, savings banks now are permitted to engage in activities previously confined to commercial banks; they can offer checking accounts and make commercial loans. The commercial banks are now permitted, through affiliates or other ties, to offer securities brokerage services, real estate brokerage services, life insurance and casualty insurance, and so on. In turn, the brokerage houses such as Merrill Lynch and the insurance companies such as Prudential are invading commercial banking turf. They provide personal checking accounts, auto loans, credit cards, and an array of related services.

In addition, deregulation has extended the geographical reach of commercial banks. For years, each bank was restricted to a single state, and often by local legislation to a single county or city. These barriers are breaking down. Bank holding companies are buying up banks in several states. Big New York and California commercial banks are buying chains of out-of-state savings banks with the clear intention of converting these into branches of a nationwide system. Already the big banks have regional offices which ferret out industrial and commercial loan opportunities—as do the large life insurance companies. With competing brokerage firms and insurance firms well established on a national basis, and deregulation in vogue, most people in the financial industry believe that nationwide banks will soon be here.

The combination of *deregulation plus new technology* is especially disruptive to traditional banking. New, cheap communications, for instance, make the management and control of far-flung branch offices much easier. Similarly, tying automated teller machines located thousands of miles apart into centralized accounts for individual customers is now possible; your friendly banker may even follow you abroad.

Double-digit *inflation* forced interest rates up (so that lenders could recover at least as much purchasing power when the loan was paid off as they gave up when the loan was made). This pressure, plus deregulation and an associated change in Federal Reserve policy, led to a crumbling of traditional interest rate ceilings.

The resulting wide *interest rate fluctuations* have led to massive flows of capital in and out of banks—notably the savings banks. Also, banks and other institutions with fixed interest assets but varying interest costs often have gyrating profit or loss. Both these forces affect a bank's capacity to make loans. In addition, high interest rates have attracted nonbank lenders into the arena; General Electric Company, for instance, has billions of dollars for leasing and business loans of many kinds. The high and fluctuating interest rates likewise make corporate treasurers more vigorous in watching their bank balances, government security investments, and financing fees. The days of large inactive balances kept with the banks are gone.

## Changing Competition

The inflexibility of the former regulated banking system, mixed with a good measure of conservative inertia, opened the way for more venturesome invaders. "Financial services" became a fashionable target for strategic planners in nonbank companies.

American Express Company, a well-known example, expanded its international travelers check and booking agency business into credit cards and insurance, and its has acquired small commercial banks and is poised to enter nationwide banking when legislation permits. Merrill Lynch converted its stockbrokerage business into an array of financial services including investment banking, insurance, and the equivalent of a checking account. Prudential Insurance Company acquired a brokerage firm, and now Prudential Bache claims to give individuals "complete financial service." Sears, Roebuck & Company, with its millions of credit card holders and long experience in automobile insurance, acquired a major stockbrokerage firm and a nationwide real estate company; it clearly seeks to use its reputation for reliability to move into a wide range of consumer financial services. As noted, G.E. has moved into industrial loans and leasing.

These examples indicate that much of the competition which banks will face in the future will come from nonbank companies.

Within the banking industry itself, many consolidations are taking place. To gain lending power and to obtain economies in operations, formerly independent local banks are merging into statewide chains. And to operate in several states, bank holding companies are acquiring commercial (or savings) banks in other states. These mergers do require approval of federal regulating boards, but in the current deregulation climate restraints are being relaxed.

The merger movement is going so fast that some analysts are predicting that before long U.S. banking will be dominated by only a few very large and powerful megabanks. Commercial banking in England and Canada has such a structure. Such a development would run counter to a well-established tradition in the United States. In 1837, President Andrew Jackson abolished the second Bank of the United States in a Populist move against the money centers of the northeast coast. This feeling was strong well before our antitrust doctrines and legislation were formulated. A deep-seated fear of the size and the concentration of power in only a few sources of funds has fostered the thousands of independent banks we now have.

The current mood, however, is that (1) electronic communication and processing have made large-scale financial organizations so efficient that concentration is irresistible, and (2) aggressive competition among a few giants will force modernization of services, a search for available markets, and narrow profit margins. Indeed, the argument runs, the mobility of both borrower and lender now greatly increases competition compared with the horse-and-buggy days when one or two local banks enjoyed a local monopoly.

Much of the current merging of banks and other financial institutions is an effort to be positioned, defensively or offensively, to survive in the new realignment. The specific form of future competition is uncertain. So there is a lot of jockeying and getting ready to jump. The number of banking and nonbanking organizations laying plans to seize a big piece of the pie is so great that severe competition with a future shakeout is inevitable.

## Plight of Regional Banks

Regional banks such as Stone Ridge Bank must decide where and how they wish to fit into the future banking structure. Among the broad options each bank has are these four:

1. *Expect to become a part of a megabank organization.* With this aim, the regional bank should develop assets that will be attractive to merger partners—such as a large customer base in a growing area, or unusual skills, or preferred locations. Since the bank will become only a part of a larger organization, overall balance is not so important as outstanding strength in one or more activities that will be vital in the new setup.

2. *Become an aggressor.* Typically this involves identifying a niche—for instance, a particular service like credit data or a special industry—and then seeking to become the dominant supplier in that niche. Probably some acquisitions will be necessary, and in the process the bank shifts its identity from being associated with a region to having a more specialized domain.

3. *Defend a special piece of turf.* Here the assumption is that in some activities regional firms can be more effective than national (or local) organizations. So the regional bank develops topflight capability in

those activities and tries to erect some entry barriers to forestall incoming competition.

4. *Build a cooperative processing organization.* To offset the economies large banks enjoy, several local and regional banks can form a central processing company to do computer work, purchasing, and the like for the entire group. Such associations already exist in several parts of the country. By becoming a part of one or more coalitions, the independent units counter the power of large competitors.

Each of these options involves uncertainties. The environment may not change as predicted; the bank may not build the strengths it wants; the timing may be wrong. Perhaps more than one option could be pursued at the same time. And, of course, the bank could assume that the wave of national centralization will pass and that the wise strategy is to hold tight until legislation and loyalties again favor regional banking.

## Declaration of Independence

In considering its strategic options, Stone Ridge Bank made an early decision to maintain its independence. The chair of the board of directors (a former president) explains: "We enjoy a unique position in our region. We are the oldest bank, the strongest financially, number two in assets, and number one in earnings. We have always been active in regional development. Our people come from the region and know its history and traditions. We are proud of the region and our share in its growth.

"Because of this strong position, our board decided when all this merging started that we would follow an independent course. We don't need a lot of help from big organizations. Of course, we work through our correspondent banks to provide top service to our customers, but we don't need them to tell us what to do. So we have discouraged the feelers about merger and other forms of affiliation. At the same time, we don't assume that we can tell other established banks like ourselves how to run their businesses. That means we are not out on the prowl looking for a bank which we might take over.

"There is also the matter of integrity. Stone Ridge is more than a fair-weather friend. The east coast capitalists are eager to support a venture where the economy is strong, but then disappear whenever they estimate that they can earn a quarter of a percent more someplace else. Their commitment to the region is not genuine and continuing. Local people have learned that they can't trust outsiders in the sense that outsiders do not provide dependable help. In comparison, Stone Ridge is committed. We've been here over a century and we intend to be here for the next hundred years."

Other directors share the chair's feeling that Stone Ridge Bank can serve its region best by maintaining its independence. That view, however, leaves open the question of how much Stone Ridge should adjust to current changes in banking technology and competition.

# ▧ Financial Counselor Concept

Mr. Bruce Wallender, president and CEO of Stone Ridge Bank for the past year, wrote a memorandum outlining the "financial counselor concept" when he was still senior vice-president in charge of loans. This plan deals directly with the issue of the bank's distinctive service in the face of increasing competition. The following is a digest of the points Mr. Wallender made at that time.

A. In the industrial and commercial area, Stone Ridge should concentrate on the "middle market"—that is, companies with sales of $5 million to $100 million. The advantages of this concentration are:

1. Typically these companies cannot afford to employ specialists in the various branches of finance. Consequently, they need the kind of technical advice and assistance which we can provide. In contrast, the large *Fortune* 1,000 firms have in-house specialists who deal directly with money center organizations.
2. A significant number of companies of this size have headquarters in, or close to, our region. Many already do business with us.
3. Several big New York and California banks are already trying to make loans and provide special services to this "middle market"—operating through small regional offices. However, the personnel turnover in such offices is high and they have difficulty developing the personal relationships which we enjoy.

B. We should seek to provide these customers with a full range of banking services—including short- and long-term loans, lease financing, collection services, short-term investments, cash management, direct payroll transfers, letters of credit, and foreign exchange. The advantages of providing a variety of services are:

1. Fees for services can be an even greater source of bank income than net interest on loans—especially because outside competitors, noted in A3, use low rates as a primary wedge in securing business.
2. By providing good services at competitive prices, we will forestall nonbank competitors from getting a "foot in the door" of our legitimate customers.

C. We should go even further and become "financial counselors" to this set of customers. Financial counseling includes:

1. Studying the total financial needs of each company and advising its officers on such matters as capital structure, risk protection, ways to finance expansion, options in restructuring the sources of capital, credit management, cash management, financial controls, and the like.

2. Interpreting and explaining the significance to the company of new legislation and regulations in the financial field and summarizing national and international forecasts of economic conditions.
3. When a company can benefit from a financial service that Stone Ridge does not itself provide (e.g., public sale of securities, a foreign banking connection, Eurodolloar loans), using our contacts to obtain that service for the company.

Mr. Wallender summarized: the advantages of financial counseling are in providing our customers with a service they will have difficulty obtaining elsewhere and creating an entry barrier for our get-rich-quick competitors.

This financial counseling concept was presented to the board and warmly endorsed. Perhaps even more significant was the selection of Mr. Wallender as the new president of the bank. In making this choice, the board in effect adopted the strategy which Mr. Wallender advocated. Loan officers of the bank have been redesignated financial counselors, but no other explicit moves have been made in this direction.

## Pressure on Retail Business

Since taking over the top spot at Stone Ridge Bank, Mr. Wallender has faced a more pressing issue of what to do about the dwindling profit on the bank's retail business (transactions with individual consumers and small businesses). The vice-president in charge of Stone Ridge's 60 branches explains: "First we were hit with unprecedented interest costs. Balances in checking accounts, a good source of funds, have been shifted to NOW accounts on which we pay high interest, and depositors will shift onto money market accounts when those rates are even higher. With the deregulation of interest rates on savings accounts, the cost of these funds is creeping up, too. So the days are gone when the retail part of the bank generated low-cost funds which the industrial loan officers could lend, often at a percent or two above the prime rate.

"It is true that we now collect some fees for small balances, checks, and the like. But the catch is that our operating expenses are rising faster than the fee income. Personnel costs and rental expenses at each branch are going up and up, and competition is forcing us to keep open longer hours. We have automated some, but it will take several years to recover the installation costs.

"I have finally come to the conclusion that the only way we can keep our expenses even close to those of the banks with many branches all over the state is to join—or perhaps create—a co-op servicing company. If all of us who want to stay independent can pool our overhead, we could lower processing costs considerably. Stone Ridge could be a leader among a group of other financially strong local banks in such a venture. By picking our associates carefully, we could avoid any appearance of weakness.

"The installment loan business has so many competitors that the margins have gone out of that, too. Again expense reduction is essential. Thank God for Visa. Local people like to have a card with the Stone Ridge name on it, and we make some money on their slow pay balances.

"Our leading competitor has bought up small banks or opened new branches all over the state. That puts it ahead of Stone Ridge in deposits. It has enough volume to help on overhead expenses. It is anybody's guess, however, just how it'll make out in the long run. A co-op service organization would help us meet that competition, and at the same time we could maintain our independence."

## Opportunity to Exit

What to do with the retail end of the bank has suddenly become a pressing question. Stone Ridge has received an informal offer to buy all its branches and the business connected with them. The offer comes from First National Bank, which is strong in the opposite end of the state. First National has recently acquired several savings banks and wishes to build a network of branches that will blanket the entire state. Acquisition of Stone Ridge branches would be a major step in this plan; they would give First National real strength in an area where it now is unrepresented, and the association with Stone Ridge's image would lend prestige to the entire expansion program. The combined network would make First National the main rival of the state's largest bank in retail banking.

Although the specific details have not been examined, the basic proposal is clear. Stone Ridge would sell its retail banking business to First National for $40 million net gain. More specifically, First National would take over all the *deposit liabilities* at the branches—that is, the checking and savings accounts of individual depositors. It would also *buy* the equipment, buildings, and other physical assets of the branches, the automobile and other installment loans arranged at the branches, the home mortgages that were arranged at the branches, and in general other banking services provided by the branches to individuals. The *net* differences between (1) the liabilities that First National assumes and (2) the book value of the assets transferred, plus the purchase price of $40 million, would be settled in cash.

Furthermore, the proposal provides that all Stone Ridge personnel engaged in retail banking would be transferred (with the pension reserves) to First National. Stone Ridge would agree not to solicit retail banking business during the next five years, and its name would be removed from the branches. First National would not solicit during the next five years industrial or commercial deposit accounts in the territories presently served by Stone Ridge branches.

A few qualifications and exceptions have been noted. Business and industrial customers now served through Stone Ridge branches would be given the option of banking with the main office of Stone Ridge, and officers of such customers could transfer their personal accounts to the main office if they so wished.

Mr. Wallender says, "The immediate effect of such a transaction would be a $40 million (less tax) increase in our equity. Also we would have the income earned on that sum to add to our operating profit. Last year we earned only $1 million on our retail operations, so you might say that we aren't sacrificing a lot.

"However, the proposal would have a more profound impact on Stone Ridge than would show up in the financial statements of the first year. We must think about the long-run prospects for our piece of the retail banking business. That industry is mature and highly competitive, with narrowing profit margins. According to Professor K. R. Harrigan, we have three options: (1) Become a large-volume, low-cost operator—and hold on through the period when weaker competitors drop out. (2) Find a protected niche that we can dominate. (3) Sell out quickly while someone else is still interested in such assets as we possess.[1] Stone Ridge is not big enough to try the first option on a national basis, and we have not discovered a protected niche. That leaves only the third option—sell soon.

"The trouble with that reasoning is the impact of selling on the rest of the bank. We are talking about giving up over one-third of our deposits—shrinking the bank personnel and physical presence in the region even more. A contraction of that size *could* have a devastating effect on our remaining personnel and on our public image. Some people would view us as losers.

"There is a personal angle, too. I hate to go down in history as the president of Stone Ridge who started to retreat almost as soon as he got into office—in fact, gave up a very large part of the business that others before me worked so hard to create. Statues are not built for people who draw back so that they lose less money than they otherwise might."

The chair of the board is also concerned. He says, "Cutting the size of the bank is a serious matter. You lose your status as a leader. Stone Ridge has helped to set a progressive business climate for the region. We've preached confidence, hard work, venturesomeness, and growth; in our own actions, we followed what we preached. Now, if we give up on retail banking, throw in the towel for the most conspicuous part of our business, what sort of respect will our opinions deserve and get?

"It is true that combining operations with another bank within the state is not like selling out to a large national organization of some sort. Our branches would continue to be staffed by local people serving local needs. In this respect, it is just that Stone Ridge's role would be smaller. If at some future time First National gets swallowed up by an east coast megabank, the onus will not be on us. But we would escape criticism because we no longer would be considered important."

A shareholder's opinion is expressed by the president of Stone Ridge Trust Company, a personal trustee of several estates owning large blocks of the holding company stock and a respected director of the bank. "First National's proposal gives Stone Ridge Bank an opportunity to concentrate on what it can do best. The 'financial counselor' concept fits the primary strength of the bank and also reinforces the Trust Company. That will build Stone Ridge in circles which really count.

---

[1]*Strategies for Declining Businesses.* Lexington, MA: D.C. Heath & Company, 1980.

"I realize that selling the branches to First National would make us smaller and less prominent. However, the sale would remove us from an area which is likely to become a dogfight, and the purchase price—although too small—would be a cushion to earnings that the bank will need to retool and redirect its resources on the industrial and commercial markets. I don't see another attractive bidder on the horizon, and we should not pass up this chance."

## Tooling Up for Financial Counseling

Mr. Charles Farnum was promoted to take Mr. Wallender's position when Mr. Wallender became president of the bank. Mr. Farnum, a long-service employee of Stone Ridge, is enthusiastic about the financial counseling concept and has prepared a private list of steps to carry it out:

1. Appoint a New York representative of Stone Ridge Bank, probably an economist who would keep the bank informed on the latest economic and financial forecasts, and would inform the bank of any new kinds of services being offered by large banks or nonbank companies that will compete with Stone Ridge financial counseling.

.2 Employ and train future counselors, preferably M.B.A.'s with good connections in the region. Include present loan officers in training to ensure breadth of service.

3. Consider appointment of lawyer or tax specialist as in-house expert to advise counselors.

4. When ready, launch P.R. campaign, focused on the business community, about Stone Ridge service.

5. Have systematic and comprehensive plan for market development. Target all potential accounts and assign to specific counselors. Develop form for systematic recording and annual review of status of each existing and potential account.

6. Develop method of income and cost analysis for each account.

Mr. Farnum explains that this program is still in the planning stage. Mr. Wallender has indicated that he wants to be sure that he understands the total bank and is recognized as a total bank person before he pushes his own pet project. Also, because of the squeeze in interest rates, Mr. Wallender has urged all officers to keep expenses in line with income, and several of the preceding steps will involve additional expense.

A note just received by Mr. Smythe from Mr. Wallender says, "Am concerned about a leak or rumor of the First National offer. This would create problems with both customers and employees. So would like to have your recommendation as soon as possible."

# COMPREHENSIVE CASE 7

## Goodwill Industries of the Midwest

Bill Watts, President of Goodwill Industries of the Midwest, Inc., wondered what to do next with the organization he had led for the past 12 years. After almost uninterrupted growth during the 1970s, Goodwill had stalled. Growth had slowed since 1981, and revenues in 1985 were actually less than in 1984 (see Exhibit A). The new year was not off to a good start financially, and there were some signs that more shrinking of the organization might be necessary to get expenses back in line with revenues.

### Background: 1930–1974

Goodwill of the Midwest, one of 175 locally autonomous Goodwill organizations in North America, began in 1930. Emory Daniels, a minister with an entrepreneurial makeup, took over the fledgling organization in 1934 and during the next 35 years built it into one of the largest and finest organizations of its type in the country. Daniels and his Midwest Goodwill had nationwide reputations as innovators and had begun numerous programs to help further the organization's mission of helping disabled and handicapped people develop their abilities so that they could live and work at the highest level they are capable of (see Exhibit B for current mission statement).

In the early days, Goodwill accomplished its mission primarily by providing jobs for people who were disabled so severely that they could not find work in the normal labor market. Disabled people were employed to collect, sort, repair, clean, price, and sell donated merchandise. Later, Goodwill began helping some of the employees who had progressed find jobs with other firms, thus opening slots so that Goodwill could bring in more disabled persons. Eventually, Goodwill added formal vocational evaluation, training, and job placement services so that still more people could be assisted. These structured services were (and still are) paid for by units of government which refer persons to Goodwill for needed services.

From the beginning, Goodwill operated on what could be viewed as an impossible formula. The organization took people no one else would hire and goods no one else wanted, and put them together to provide on-the-job training, temporary employment, and long-term employment opportunities. When workers progressed enough, Goodwill would find them jobs with other firms and start over again with others who had serious vocational limitations. Nationally, this system

**EXHIBIT A**
**GOODWILL INDUSTRIES OPERATING REVENUES**
**1977–1985**

| | 1977 | 1978 | 1979 | 1980 | 1981 | 1982 | 1983 | 1984 | 1985 |
|---|---|---|---|---|---|---|---|---|---|
| Retail Sales | $1,780,959 | $1,869,945 | $2,028,304 | $2,157,511 | $2,322,786 | $2,351,096 | $2,671,837 | $2,855,742 | $2,790,894 |
| Salvage Sales | 212,018 | 278,274 | 388,785 | 442,172 | 390,822 | 264,277 | 258,546 | 268,744 | 279,162 |
| Rehab & Training Fees & Grants | 718,193 | 695,879 | 881,692 | 1,448,742 | 1,971,912 | 1,982,588 | 2,138,017 | 1,839,543 | 1,675,282 |
| Industrial Contract Sales | 639,172 | 672,889 | 709,153 | 625,191 | 895,534 | 633,367 | 615,218 | 616,252 | 446,700 |
| Wood Product Sales | 270,676 | 364,781 | 259,624 | 305,186 | 450,750 | 511,064 | 356,246 | 445,911 | 478,067 |
| Industrial Sewing Sales | — | — | — | — | — | — | 8,019 | 105,910 | 124,506 |
| Furniture Restoration Sales | — | — | — | — | — | — | — | — | 72,669 |
| Print Shop Sales | 32,014 | 36,355 | 43,865 | 35,249 | 27,597 | 41,360 | 101,642 | 120,827 | 125,170 |
| Cafeteria Sales | 73,156 | 78,803 | 93,055 | 109,295 | 177,067 | 216,513 | 267,134 | 259,090 | 208,571 |
| Greenhouse Sales | — | — | — | — | — | 32,984 | 61,631 | 97,240 | 118,375 |
| The Home Cleaning Service | — | — | — | — | — | — | 21,808 | 174,065 | 201,317 |
| United Way | 283,708 | 283,708 | 310,000 | 306,599 | 343,172 | 354,369 | 345,162 | 385,137 | 414,152 |
| Other Contributions | N.A. | 40,458 | 52,520 | N.A. | 67,992 | 103,845 | 94,406 | 101,736 | 93,572 |
| Other Revenue | 57,618 | 17,543 | — | 72,828 | 13,170 | 25,787 | 10,545 | 26,289 | 21,406 |
| Total | $4,067,514 | $4,338,635 | $4,766,998 | $5,502,773 | $6,660,802 | $6,571,317 | $6,972,072 | $7,304,701 | $7,065,164 |

**EXHIBIT A (Cont.)**
**GOODWILL INDUSTRIES OF THE MIDWEST, INC.**
**BALANCE SHEET**
**FEBRUARY 28, 1986**

| *Current Assets* | | *Current Liabilities* | |
|---|---|---|---|
| Cash | $(43,200) | Accounts Payable | $  142,484 |
| Accounts Receivable | 559,570 | Wages Payable | 253,396 |
| Inventory | 408,477 | Taxes Payable | 67,290 |
| Other | 97,055 | Notes Payable | 572,000* |
| Total Current Assets | $1,021,902 | Accrued Operating Expense | 40,418 |
| | | Deferred Revenue | 110,108 |
| | | Total Current Liabilities | $1,185,696 |
| *Fixed Assets* | | | |
| Land, Bldgs., Equip. | $7,342,488 | Long-Term Liabilities | |
| Less Accum. Deprec. | (3,860,468) | Notes and Contracts | |
| | | Payable | $  233,176 |
| Total Fixed Assets | $3,482,020 | | |
| | | Total Liabilities | $1,418,872 |
| Fund Balances | 3,085,050 | | |
| | | Total Liabilities | |
| Total Assets | $4,503,922 | and Fund Balances | $4,503,922 |

**GOODWILL INDUSTRIES FOUNDATION OF THE MIDWEST, INC.**
**BALANCE SHEET**
**MARCH 31, 1986**

| *Current Assets* | | *Current Liabilities* | |
|---|---|---|---|
| Cash | $    12,784 | Accounts Payable | $    11,608 |
| Accounts Receivable | 16,162 | Total Liabilities | $11,608 |
| Note Receivable | 300,000* | | |
| Investments | 1,098,890 | | |
| Total Current Assets | $1,427,836 | Fund Balances | $1,469,808 |
| Fixed Assets | 80,145 | | |
| Less Accum. Depreciation | (26,565) | | |
| Total Assets | $1,481,416 | Total Liabilities and | |
| | | Fund Balances | $1,481,416 |

*The Foundation has loaned Goodwill $300,000 for operating purposes.

**EXHIBIT A (Cont.)**
**GOODWILL INDUSTRIES OF THE MIDWEST, INC. INCOME STATEMENT**
**1-1-86 through 2-28-86**

|  | 1986 YTD | BUDGET | 1985 YTD |
|---|---|---|---|
| *Revenues* | | | |
| Store Sales | $ 385,536 | $ 444,456 | $ 402,946 |
| Salvage Sales | 55,279 | 49,026 | 51,220 |
| Cafeteria | 28,849 | 31,439 | 39,582 |
| Rehabilitation | 289,735 | 305,087 | 276,005 |
| Industrial Operations | 228,148 | 249,178 | 218,661 |
| Home cleaning | 29,648 | 30,500 | 29,544 |
| Greenhouse | 13,748 | 11,500 | 5,289 |
| Miscellaneous | 3,974 | 3,150 | 7,240 |
|  | $1,034,917 | $1,124,336 | $1,030,487 |
| *Expenses* | | | |
| Retail Ops. | 427,655 | 458,497 | 411,047 |
| Cafeteria | 20,257 | 27,445 | 30,159 |
| Rehabilitation Ops. | 252,332 | 252,179 | 251,588 |
| Industrial Ops. | 200,169 | 213,680 | 180,190 |
| Home cleaning | 34,493 | 29,434 | 27,106 |
| Greenhouse | 22,080 | 24,125 | 25,719 |
| Admin. Overhead | 138,155 | 133,036 | 157,997 |
| Occupancy | 93,165 | 94,685 | 84,925 |
|  | $1,188,306 | $1,233,081 | $1,168,731 |
| OPERATING INCOME | ($ 153,389) | ($ 108,745) | ($ 138,244) |
| Subsidies: | | | |
| United Way | $ 74,168 | $ 74,168 | $ 69,025 |
| Contributions | 6,032 | 8,900 | 8,651 |
| Net Operating Income | ($ 73,189) | ($ 25,677) | ($ 60,568) |

had been working for more than 80 years and was still thriving in some parts of the country.

In the 1950s, Goodwill's work base was expanded with the addition of a subcontracting department to provide labor-intensive small assembly and packaging services for business and industrial firms. In addition to broadening revenue sources and providing a greater number of in-house job opportunities, this and subsequent diversification moves provided Goodwill with a wider variety of types of jobs on which disabled people could be trained or employed. This helped increase referrals to Goodwill for evaluation and training services. By the time Daniels retired, Goodwill consisted of three well-established divisions: donated goods, industrial services, and vocational rehabilitation services. All were major revenue generators, with the result that Goodwill required an operating subsidy

**EXHIBIT B.**
**GOODWILL INDUSTRIES**
**OF THE MIDWEST, INC.**
**MISSION STATEMENT**

> Goodwill Industries will actively strive
> to achieve the full participation in society
> of disabled people and other individuals
> with special needs by expanding their
> opportunities and occupational capabilities.

The principal emphasis of Goodwill Industries of the Midwest,
Inc., should be focused toward providing opportunities for
and assisting persons who, because of some physical, mental,
emotional, or social limitation, have difficulty succeeding
in other, more traditional, educational, vocational training,
or employment settings. Many of the persons for whom Goodwill
is best suited have little work experience, inadequate self-
image, inadequate concept of what it takes to hold a job,
and/or no vocational skills.

Goodwill should provide individually tailored services as
needed to build skills and confidence, develop abilities, and
reduce or eliminate characteristics which may render the individual less employable.

Goodwill should make every effort to assist trainees in finding
and keeping employment in which they might work and develop as
fully as possible.

All of Goodwill's activities should, by providing training or
employment opportunities or by generating revenue to make such
opportunities possible, contribute toward fulfilling this basic
mission. This includes the operation of business enterprises
which provide opportunities for on-the-job training, trans-
itional work experience, or extended employment.

of only 6 to 7 percent of its total operating revenue. Other organizations providing similar services required significantly larger subsidies.

When Daniels retired in 1969 he was succeeded by Greg Gordon, a brilliant young CPA with a strong desire to help the less fortunate. Gordon's style was vastly different from Daniels's, and he brought to the organization skills which had been lacking. He instituted financial controls and a formal planning process, and moved at a deliberate pace with all actions well thought through.

One of the brightest Goodwill executives in the country, Gordon died of cancer in 1974 at the age of 36. Watts, an industrial engineering graduate of the University of Illinois, had joined Gordon's staff seven months earlier as vice president of operations. He was named acting director upon Gordon's death, and two months later the Board of Directors named him the organization's new president. He was 30 years old at the time.

## The Current President's Background

Watts reminisced at how green and ill-prepared he had been, although he didn't realize it at the time. He had climbed faster than anyone in the modern history of Goodwill. Basically because of religious motives, he had sought an opportunity to use his engineering background in a service organization, and in September 1970 he had accepted a position as an executive intern at a Goodwill in Texas. He spent 15 months working in Texas under Sam Newman, a dynamic leader who was a master at public relations and fund raising and who worked at a furious pace. Watts had been strongly influenced by Newman, who was very action oriented and had little patience for time-consuming processes. Newman would remind others that while people sit around discussing what should be done, disabled people are growing old and dying, and no one is doing anything to help them.

In January 1972 Watts was put in charge of a Goodwill branch in Texas and proceeded to strengthen it enough in nine months that it became an autonomous unit. He stayed on another year before accepting an invitation to join Gordon's staff.

When Watts became president of the Midwest Goodwill, the organization was sound financially. It had a strong board of directors, a lot of community support, and a reputation for effective programs. Many of the key staff were older people who had retired from one career and then come on with Goodwill. Others had been with the organization for many years. For most of these people, Goodwill was a comfortable place to work. And while it may have been one of the most solid Goodwills in the country, Watts thought it was slow moving, bureaucratic, and dull. The contrast with the flashy, fast-moving Texas organization was dramatic, and there was no doubt in Watts's mind which of the two was more fun to work in. He felt that the Midwest organization was more professionally managed than the one in Texas, but it needed more dynamism.

## Years of Growth: 1974–1981

Over the next several years, building on its reputation and strong community support, Goodwill expanded in size and scope. Key moves included the following:

- In 1974 Goodwill began manufacturing high-quality wooden boxes for the federal government under a profitable contract which is still in force. Volume in units has generally been 40,000–50,000 boxes per year.

- In 1975 Goodwill purchased some property and opened an independent-living training program for people who were being released from state mental institutions.
- In 1976 a retail store was opened in a nearby town. Also, Goodwill began cutting up salvage material and retailing wiping cloths.
- In 1977 Goodwill opened a retail outlet in a city 60 miles away.
- In 1978 Goodwill established a branch in a neighboring city to provide basic vocational rehabilitation services and operate as a hub for the collection, processing, and distribution of donated goods.
- In 1979 Watts replaced the long-time vice president of rehabilitation with an individual who greatly expanded Goodwill's vocational training programs. Included was an innovative project in which Goodwill trainees made up the entire direct labor force in a commercial bakery.
- Also in 1979, specialized services for deaf persons were established.
- In 1980 a greenhouse was built.
- In 1981 more skills training programs were added, as were small retail outlets in three other neighboring cities.

Goodwill's operating revenues doubled between 1974 and 1981. Midwest Goodwill was the seventh largest of 175 Goodwills in North America and was widely recognized as being among the two or three best Goodwills in the world. For several years this Goodwill provided services for more people than any other Goodwill in the world.

In addition to being successful in accomplishing its service objectives, Goodwill was also quite successful financially in 1979, 1980, and 1981. The Goodwill Industries Foundation, a separate entity, had also grown tremendously. The Foundation's endowment fund, which then stood at over $1,000,000, provided seed money for new programs and matching funds for other grants the organization would receive. It also provided funds for some capital improvements and equipment.

## The Recession

Then came the recession. The world market for textile salvage materials collapsed, resulting in a net loss to Goodwill of over $200,000 a year. Retail sales sagged as Goodwill's supply of donated goods declined. Industrial contract sales, always cyclical, dropped 29 percent from 1981 to 1982. (This segment continued to weaken through 1985 with the gradual closing of operations of a major manufacturer in the area. In the 1970s this company had consistently accounted for 40–50 percent of Goodwill's industrial contract revenue, and the work was very profitable for Goodwill.)

As a result of all of these factors, Goodwill incurred heavy financial losses during the first half of 1982, while the demand for its services—especially employment for disabled people—increased tremendously. The only part of the organization that continued to grow was rehabilitation and training (partly a function of the scarcity of jobs in the community), but Watts knew that that wouldn't last long if Goodwill couldn't find jobs for the people who were completing training.

With the donated goods and industrial services operations suffering from the effects of a deep recession, Goodwill searched for some new business ventures which could replace lost revenue and provide additional employment opportunities for the people the organization was training. These efforts led to the purchase of equipment and securing of a contract for Goodwill to manufacture hospital garments for a consortium of area hospitals. Then, in 1983, Goodwill became the first organization of its type in the country to purchase and operate a franchised business by purchasing franchises in a home cleaning business.

In 1984 Goodwill laid plans for a furniture restoration business which would seek work from commercial and institutional accounts. Such an operation had been very successful in a sheltered workshop in upstate New York, grossing 1.2 million dollars annually and providing employment for 35 mentally retarded persons.

## Personnel Problems and Reorganization

In late 1983, one of Goodwill's vice presidents was in ill health. During his absences in late 1983 and early 1984, it became increasingly apparent that he had been running essentially a one-man show and had not let any of his 45 staff make any significant decisions. Complaints about the quality of services became more and more frequent, and revenues began dropping. Morale was very poor, and relationships between his department's staff and other parts of Goodwill worsened.

Watts realized that for 10 years he had almost totally delegated Goodwill's rehabilitation and training functions to the professionals on the staff. As long as the numbers (financial and service statistics) looked good, he had overlooked the occasional comments made about some of the department's weaknesses. In 1984, however, he forced some changes, and the vice president in charge of the area resigned. Watts gave considerable attention to selecting a successor who would build depth, improve quality, and work well with other parts of the organization. Watts knew later, however, that his choice of a successor was one of the worst choices he had ever made. Things began to deteriorate within three months after the new VP arrived, and nine months later Watts forced him to leave. This was in May 1985.

As Goodwill was again losing money, Watts began a reorganization effort to reduce overhead and create a structure that would enhance interdepartmental cooperation. Most of Goodwill's enterprises were operating semiautonomously, and opportunities for synergy were not being fully realized. The reorganization was completed in September 1985 and changed Goodwill from having basically a divisional structure to basically a functional organizational structure. (See Exhibit C).

# EXHIBIT C.
# ORGANIZATIONAL STRUCTURE

**In Early 1985**

President (Watts)

- VP Rehabilitation
  - All rehab and training functions and ancillary services
- VP Industrial Operations (Smith)
  - Industrial sales
  - Industrial contracts operations
  - Manufacturing
- VP Merchandise Operations (Jones)
  - Fleet operations
  - Donated goods collection and processing
  - Retail of salvage materials
  - Maintenance
- VP Human Resources
  - All personnel functions, training, safety
- Controller (Cunningham)
  - Accounting
  - EDP
- VP Public Relations & Marketing (Marshall)
  - PR
  - Greenhouse
  - Home cleaning business
- Director Remote Division
  - All rehabilitation and donated goods operations in outlying towns
- Director of Development (Knight)
  - All fund raising

**After 1986 Reorganization**

President (Watts)

- VP Human Services (Davis)
  - All rehab and training functions and ancillary services
  - All personnel functions, training, and safety
- VP Sales (Jones)
  - All retail sales
  - Wiping cloth and industrial sales
- VP Operations (Smith)
  - Fleet operations
  - All donated goods collections and processing
  - Manufacturing
  - Industrial contract operations
  - Maintenance
- VP Public Relations and Marketing (Marshall)
  - PR
  - Greenhouse
  - Home cleaning business
- Controller (Cunningham)
  - Accounting
  - EDP
- Director of Development (Knight)
  - All fund raising

Rehabilitation, related services, and the personnel functions were put under Joan Davis, who has the title of Vice President of Human Services. Mrs. Davis, who came to Goodwill in 1983, had a personnel background and had also run her own wood products business. Watts considered her a very capable manager and a good judge of people. She was one of the people on whom he depended the most, and the improvements she had made in less than one year in Goodwill's human services departments were impressive.

All industrial operations at Goodwill had been consolidated under Joe Smith, who had also come to Goodwill in 1983. Smith had been a plant manager with a large jewelry manufacturer, following which he had run his own home decorating products business. He had made significant improvements in his areas of responsibility and was another person Watts considered to be crucial in his structure.

In the reorganization Watts put industrial and retail sales under David Jones, a retired military officer who had come to Goodwill in 1982. Jones, a good-humored person, had for the past three years been responsible for all of Goodwill's donated goods operations and sales. While he was well liked by nearly everyone, he was very turf oriented and had little enthusiasm for working with other Goodwill departments. He didn't like to take any initiatives or risks, and didn't like to rock the boat. When Watts heard a definition of an "abdicative" manager, he felt it was written for Jones. Watts felt that Jones's position could probably be eliminated. However, Jones had recently encountered some serious health problems, and Watts didn't feel he could take any action affecting his employment at this time.

Also reporting to Watts were Judy Marshall, the VP of public relations and marketing; Charles Cunningham, the Controller; and Ann Knight, a part-time director of development. The persons holding these positions had been with Goodwill four or five years and were performing their functions capably. All three had improved steadily, and there was on the whole a high level of commitment from them.

Watts was pleased with the improvement in his top staff. For several years he had gone after more capable people and had upgraded salaries to enhance recruitment and retention efforts. Davis, Smith, Marshall, and Cunningham worked well together and were committed to the organization. Marshall, in addition to her "staff" responsibilities for public relations, also had "line" responsibilities for the greenhouse and the home cleaning business. Both of these were small enterprises which didn't fit well into any other part of the organization.

## The Situation Today: 1986

The steps taken during the summer of 1985 had reduced expenses enough to reverse the early-year losses. Goodwill operated in the black in each of the last five months of the year, but still had a loss of $94,000 on total revenues, which declined $239,000 from 1984. Watts felt a good job had been done in identifying critical success factors for 1986 (Exhibit D), and clear performance expectations

**EXHIBIT D**
**CRITICAL SUCCESS FACTORS FOR 1986**

1. Add at least six well-located, attended donation centers by April 1.
2. Increase inventory levels and inventory turns in Goodwill stores.
3. Increase referrals from units of government.
4. Increase industrial contract and furniture restoration business.
5. Develop improved information systems related to the preceding.

had been established for key managers (Exhibit E). Information systems were being improved, and no new ventures were planned for 1986. Morale had improved substantially during the past several months. Watts felt, though, that there was still a lot of room to improve internal processes and procedures and that the entire organization needed a breather from the frenetic activity and sometimes traumatic changes of the past several years. He had been optimistic about 1986.

Unfortunately, the financial losses in January and February were considerably worse than budgeted, largely because of sagging revenues in nearly every area, and in March 1986 Goodwill's various enterprises were faced with the following situations:

- Retail sales were sluggish, as there was not nearly enough donated merchandise to adequately stock all of Goodwill's stores. Although Goodwill was getting a 45 percent share of the used goods in the metropolitan area, aggressive action was under way to add more collection centers and increase promotional activity for donated goods.
- Industrial contract sales had increased in January and February. March had been sluggish, but the outlook for April and May was encouraging.
- Orders for wooden boxes had dropped by half in January and February as a result of federal budget-cutting moves. Orders received in March, however, were back to budgeted levels. The outlook for future orders was uncertain.
- Furniture restoration business was increasing gradually.
- Rehabilitation caseloads were still at low levels. Watts felt that the improved economy was a major factor, as more jobs were available in the community for low-skilled people. Also, fewer people were entering the labor force. Watts had developed a theory that the demand for Goodwill's services was directly related to the unemployment rate. If this were true, Goodwill should try to be involved in countercyclical businesses, since the demand for Goodwill to provide jobs as well as training would be greatest during recessionary times.
- The greenhouse was no longer a significant cash drain. Neither, however, would it contribute much financially to Goodwill. Its chief value to the organization was in the good public relations opportunities which developed from it.

## EXHIBIT E
## PRIMARY PERFORMANCE MEASURES FOR EXECUTIVE STAFF FOR 1986

### JOAN DAVIS VP, HUMAN SERVICES

Bottom line of human service departments compared with budget.
Program effectiveness compared with goals.
Satisfaction level of referring counselors and employers of clients.
Human Services staff morale and turnover.

### JOE SMITH VP, OPERATIONS

Contribution margin compared with budget for industrial contract and
    manufacturing departments.
Materials collection cost/revenue generated.
Donated goods cost/revenue generated.
Customer and contributor satisfaction (donors of materials, customers of industrial
    services and manufactured products).
Morale of hourly and salaried employees.
Physical appearance and ongoing maintenance of physical facilities and equipment.

### DAVID JONES VP, SALES

Bottom line of retail stores compared with budget.
Sales of industrial services, furniture restoration services, manufactured products,
    and wiping cloths compared with budget.
Number of new locations secured for attended collection centers.
Physical appearance of retail stores.
Morale of store employees.

### JUDY MARSHALL VP, PUBLIC RELATIONS AND MARKETING

Bottom line of home cleaning service and greenhouse compared with budget.
Increase in share of donated goods received as measured by survey in September.
Development and implementation of customer, contributor, and user satisfaction
    survey system to be applied for all Goodwill departments.
Satisfaction level of users of services of Public Relations Department.
Department expenses compared with budget.

### CHARLES CUNNINGHAM CONTROLLER

Development and implementation of useful information systems for critical success
    factors of all Goodwill departments.
Satisfaction level of users of services of Accounting Department.
Department expenses compared with budget.

### ANN KNIGHT DIRECTOR OF DEVELOPMENT

Number of planned giving contacts made.
Net from all nondeferred giving fund-raising activities.
Increase in number of contributors.
Use of information processing equipment to do more segmentation of donors and
    prospects.

**EXHIBIT F**
**PRIMARY CUSTOMERS OF GOODWILL'S ENTERPRISES**

*Retail Operations.* General Public

*Rehabilitation and Training Services.* Units of government (primarily state government).

*Industrial Contracts.* Large industrial firms.

*Wood Products.* Federal government.

*Furniture Restoration Services.* Colleges and universities, hospitals, churches, restaurants, and retirement homes.

*Print Shop.* Small businesses and not-for-profit corporations.

*Cafeteria.* Goodwill employees.

*Greenhouse.* Employees of large firms which permit Goodwill to conduct sales on their property.

*Home Cleaning Service.* Households with incomes above $50,000/year.

---

- The home cleaning service had a new manager, and the outlook was encouraging. It had become obvious, however, that it would not likely ever be as large as Goodwill thought possible when the franchises were purchased.

- The industrial sewing operation had been shut down in January. It had become a cash drain, and the employees in the department were transferred to other positions.

Watts knew that the organization was still too diversified to be able to operate all its enterprises well (see Exhibit F), but any reduction in scope would mean the loss of jobs for disabled people at Goodwill (Exhibit G). While this might not be a major problem right now since there seemed to be plenty of jobs available elsewhere, it would reduce the organization's ability to provide employment for low-skilled people during any future recession. On the other hand, Goodwill had within the past few years developed some excellent relationships in which other firms provided on-the-job training or permanent employment for individuals trained at Goodwill.

If any divestiture was desirable, the home cleaning service would probably have the greatest marketability of any of Goodwill's small enterprises. There might also be a possibility of selling the group home the organization owned. This would not reduce employment opportunities for disabled people, but would reduce the scope of Goodwill's human services area and would provide some badly needed cash. Discussions were under way with an interested potential buyer.

**EXHIBIT G**
**SELECTED DATA**
**1985**

| UNITS | Operating Revenue | Percent of Total Revenue | Contri-bution Margin | Margin as Pct. of Sales | Hourly Employees | Salaried Employees | Disabled* Employees | No. of** Trainees |
|---|---|---|---|---|---|---|---|---|
| Collection and Sale of Merchandise | 3,076,056 | 44% | 422,691 | 14% | 178 | 21 | 99 | 15 |
| Rehabilitation and Training Services | 1,675,282 | 24 | 185,496 | 11 | 13 | 51 | 18 | 120 |
| Industrial Contracts | 446,700 | 6 | 101,736 | 23 | 73 | 3 | 71 | 10 |
| Wood Products | 478,067 | 7 | 114,539 | 24 | 17 | 1 | 17 | 2 |
| Industrial Sewing | 124,506 | 2 | 2,962 | 2 | 9 | 1 | 8 | 1 |
| Furniture Restoration | 72,669 | 1 | 25,372 | 34 | 7 | 1 | 4 | 5 |
| Print Shop | 125,170 | 2 | 11,413 | 9 | 1 | 1 | 0 | 6 |
| Cafeteria | 208,571 | 3 | 44,145 | 21 | 2 | 2 | 1 | 12 |
| Greenhouse | 118,375 | 2 | (29,298) | (25) | 4 | 2 | 4 | 6 |
| Home Cleaning Service | 201,317 | 3 | 7,381 | 4 | 21 | 2 | 13 | 1 |

*These numbers are also included in the hourly and salaried employee columns.

**Indicates the number of disabled trainees who can be accommodated at any given time in addition to the employees assigned to the unit.

From his contacts with others around the country, Watts knew there were some financially thriving Goodwills in other cities. They tended to be (1) in much larger metropolitan areas where recently improved management was effecting "catch-up" growth, (2) in areas where the population was increasing, or (3) in states with high tax structures which spent a lot more money on social services than this state. Many small Goodwills which were thriving financially did little other than collect and sell used goods and employ some disabled people.

Goodwill's board of directors had always felt that the organization's services to people (especially training, placement, and employment of disabled people) were more important than financial gains. While they did not want to see a lot of red ink, they were willing to make tradeoffs between service objectives and financial needs, and they were completely supportive of Watts. Watts felt, however, that Goodwill very much needed two or three years of significant operating profits to be able to reduce an operating debt that had risen substantially during the past four years.

Watts knew that there were many unanswered questions about the strategy Goodwill should take during the next few years. Given Goodwill's financial condition, the local economy (an area with essentially no population growth and a declining industrial base), and Goodwill's restriction to operating only within a 30-county territory, Watts wondered whether his Goodwill may have reached its potential and should perhaps not even be trying to continue growing beyond inflationary levels.

While it was difficult to know where future growth might come from (or, indeed, whether it was even desirable), Watts realized there was still a lot of room for internal improvements. He realized that until recently he had not paid much attention to internal morale and the development of his staff. He had been a results-oriented person who had paid little attention to processes and didn't like to focus much of his attention inward. Only recently had he begun to appreciate the importance of the process in accomplishing the aims of an organization. In the fall of 1985 he had made improving morale a 1986 objective for several key managers. In addition, he had gotten some money from the Goodwill Foundation to provide additional staff training. Training was a function that always seemed to get cut when the organization was losing money, and that had been most of the time for the past four years.

Watts felt he had the best staff he had ever had. He was bewildered, however, at the inability of the organization to regain its positive momentum. He had never until recently blamed external factors for Goodwill's problems, but he was convinced that the organization was still suffering from several of the significant external changes which had occurred during the previous four years.

Watts and his staff had tried a lot of things in response to the changing conditions—maybe too many, he thought. His staff was stretched very thin, and he wondered if in their fast-paced efforts to respond whether they had implemented any of the internal changes very well. Watts was used to juggling a lot of balls at the same time, and he knew he had had a tendency (since reduced) to throw too many ideas at his staff in too short a period of time. Perhaps it would be desirable to embark on some type of structured organizational development effort that might enhance future performance and staff morale. But he wasn't sure where to begin. He also wasn't sure if it was a good idea to begin a major structured effort at organizational development until the organization was stable financially and had answered some major questions about future strategy. He wondered at times, though, if this might be a "chicken or egg" situation.

# COMPREHENSIVE CASE 8

## Crown Cork—The Tough Maverick (Revised)

For a quarter of a century, from the mid-1950s to 1980, Crown Cork & Seal Company, Inc., increased its sales and its earnings every year without interruption. In fact, during most of this period the earnings each three months exceeded those of the corresponding period a year earlier. The company moved from the verge of bankruptcy to sales of one and a half billion dollars.

This record is remarkable because (a) the company is substantially smaller than its leading competitors, (b) it operates in the very competitive, mature container industry, where profit margins are narrow and precarious, and (c) the packaging revolution and technological changes have led to frequent shifts between metal, glass, paper, and plastic containers. By pursuing a strategy of not following the leaders, Crown Cork has found a way of obtaining the widest profit margin in its industry.

Uninterrupted growth cannot go on forever. Fierce competition and especially devaluations in third-world countries finally slowed down Crown Cork. In 1981 and 1982 both sales and earnings turned down, and sales slipped a bit more in 1983. By 1986 Crown Cork was back on a growth pattern.

Two questions naturally arise: What accounts for Crown Cork's success in a basically hostile environment? and, Are the strategy and policies that worked so well in the past good for the future?

### Strategy Leading to Success

Survival in a mature field such as the "tin can" business is never easy; growth and profitability are even more elusive. Four basic guidelines account for much, though not all, of Crown Cork's impressive showings.

### 1. Concentration Versus Diversification

The two leading producers of metal containers have actively diversified. Both American Can Company and Continental Can Company expanded into a wide variety of packaging materials with an aim of being able to provide customers with most, if not all, of their packaging requirements. Indeed, both companies are now divisions of conglomerate corporations. Both companies have substantial research operations studying new forms of flexible materials, plastic containers, and printing and finishing techniques. The "business we are in" has expanded from traditional cans to active participation in the packaging revolution.

Moreover, Continental's interest in paper has led to major vertical integration back into forest industries. American Can has diversified into chemicals and an array of consumer products such as paper towels and tissues, paper cups, dress patterns, and food service products used in fast-food chains and elsewhere. Both companies are earning a higher rate of return from these "outside" activities than from their packaging business (including cans). Even National Can Corporation, a firm close to Crown Cork in size, moved into glass and plastic containers and has experimented with diversification outside of the packaging field.

In contrast, Crown Cork has stuck closely to its traditional lines of business. In fact, it has narrowed its focus to predominant emphasis on one part of the metal can industry—cans for "hard-to-hold products." These are notably aerosols, beer, and carbonated beverages, all of which must be held under pressure. This means that with minor exceptions, Crown Cork has no interest in packer cans for fruits and vegetables, cans for oil, and many other types of containers. (See Table 1.)

Crown Cork's concentration on hard-to-hold products started at its founding in 1891. A shop foreman invented what we know as a soda bottle cap—a flanged disk of tinplate with a cork insert to make a tight seal. To the present day, the company has been a leader in what is now called the "closures" segment of the packaging industry. Many competitors have entered the field, and twist-top, tear-tops,

**TABLE 1.**
**U.S. CONTAINER AND PACKAGING INDUSTRY**

|  |  | Shipment Value in billions of dollars 1982 |
|---|---|---|
| Paper and Paperboard |  | 24.8 |
| Corrugated & Solid Fiber Boxes | 10.9 |  |
| Folding Paperboard Boxes | 3.6 |  |
| Bags | 3.0 |  |
| Sanitary Food Containers | 5.3 |  |
| Fiber Cans, Tubes, Containers | 1.5 |  |
| Set-up Paperboard Boxes | 0.5 |  |
| Glass Containers |  | 5.3 |
| Metal Cans, Barrels, and Drums |  | 10.7 |
| Plastic Packaging |  | 9.2 |
| Flexible Packages | 4.4 |  |
| Packaging and Shipping | 4.8 |  |
| Total |  | 50.0 |

and an ingenious variety of plastic lids vie for consumer preference. But in this niche (50 billion closures per year) Crown Cork has remained an innovator and a low-cost producer.

A related facet of the business is the manufacture of filling machinery for use in customers' plants. In this highly automated operation, the containers and closures must be precisely integrated with the process of filling and sealing. And Crown Cork is a leading manufacturer of high-speed equipment used for this purpose. The volume of machinery sales and profits is cyclical, ranging from 6 to 12 percent of the total; but filling equipment helps keep the company abreast of the shifting needs of customers.

Nevertheless, in recent years metal cans have been the major product, as the estimates in Table 2 show. That is the area which accounts for most of Crown Cork's growth, and it is the area where present company management has chosen to bet its future.

The product-line strategy of Crown Cork is clear. It has elected to be a specialist rather than to diversify. In its particular niche, which has been the core of its business throughout its history, it seeks to outsmart its larger competitors by being expert and low cost. It meets threats from other types of containers by fighting them, not joining them. Fortunately for Crown Cork, the segment of its concentration has been growing, although uncertainties continue to appear—as will be discussed later.

## 2. Selective Service

A second facet of Crown Cork's strategy relates to the importance of containers to its customers. For all beer and soft-drink producers, the container costs more than its contents. Next to payroll, containers are their biggest expense item. Moreover, the appearance of the container plays a significant role in selling, especially in the supermarkets. Of course, reliable quality is vital for repeat sales, and this

**TABLE 2.**
**CROWN CORK: ESTIMATED SOURCES OF SALES AND OPERATING PROFIT**

|  | Total Company | Sales U.S. | International | Operating Profit Total Company |
|---|---|---|---|---|
| Cans | 68% | 90% | 34% | 65% |
| Closures | 27 | 6 | 60 | 27 |
| Machinery | 5 | 4 | 6 | 8 |
|  | 100% | 100% | 100% | 100% |

quality must be maintained on filling machines running at speeds of up to 1,200 cans per minute. Because of their bulk, inventories of empty cans are typically kept low; this means that reliability of delivery is crucial to keeping a plant in operation—thousands of cans week after week.

Crown Cork seeks to be an attractive supplier by responding promptly and personally to these customer needs. John Connelly, chair of the board, takes calls from any customer and follows up immediately. Other executives as well as salespeople do likewise, spending a large portion of their time traveling to customer plants whenever problems arise. Since there is little difference in the physical quality of cans from major producers, and pricing is so competitive that there is virtually no margin for "deals," this personalized top-brass service becomes more important. Crown Cork tries to build its plant capacity somewhat ahead of customers' requirements so that it has capacity available to meet customers' peak requirements.

Soon after the two-piece aluminum can won customer acceptance, Crown Cork pioneered in the development of a two-piece steel can. This type of can is "drawn and ironed" so that the entire can except for the top is a single piece of metal. It is lightweight, economical because of the reduction in material required, and has no side seams or bottom joints that some health researchers think might contribute to lead poisoning. Crown Cork promoted and assisted in the development of production technology; and it invested millions of dollars between 1971 and 1977 in 27 new production lines to serve its customers. Then, when the low price of aluminum versus steel made aluminum the preferred raw material, Crown Cork modified these production lines to make aluminum cans.

Limits on service do exist, however. As already noted, Crown Cork does not offer a "full line" of cans, let alone other packaging materials. The presumption is that the products Crown Cork does offer are so important to customers that they will seek out separate suppliers for these items alone. At first, the new two-piece can was offered only in steel and not in aluminum even though many large customers buy both. Reynolds and Kaiser aluminum companies produce large quantities of two-piece aluminum cans (they originated the product), and Crown Cork preferred not to be in a position where its metal suppliers could squeeze fabricating margins while making a profit in the base metal. Only in the last few years (when aluminum became plentiful) has Crown Cork switched almost entirely to aluminum.

Moreover, Crown Cork has been unwilling to build a can manufacturing facility at a customer's plant. The issue here is defense against the "self-manufacturer." Large customers, especially in the beer industry, may decide that they can make their own cans more cheaply than they can buy them. A compromise arrangement adopted by Crown Cork's competitors is to build a plant at the site of customer production and share with the customer the resulting savings from high-capacity utilization and the transportation expense. Crown Cork has rejected such arrangements, which may involve an investment of $20,000,000, because it doesn't want to be dependent on a single customer for the efficient operation of a plant.

Crown Cork cherishes flexibility. It will go to great lengths to help customers by adjusting its schedules to meet their needs. But it is leery of being boxed in. It is selective about the areas where it participates and wants to play from relative strength.

## 3. No-Frills Expenses

Crown Cork has a simple approach to low-cost production; it spends money only to the extent that it has to. When John Connelly became president of the ailing firm over 30 years ago, he cut the payroll 24 percent, and the company has run on lean expense ratios ever since. Spartan offices, few secretaries, and direct personal communication are symptomatic. The executive organization is simple, and senior executives spend much of their time in the plant or with customers. Staff units are small and close to the action they serve; the number of salespeople in a territory is trimmed to the number of active accounts.

Crown's approach to research and development is typical. Most of the attention of the small R & D staff is devoted to customers' problems—how to pack a new lacquer in an aerosol container, for example. In many packaging areas, the company prefers to be a quick follower rather than a pioneer. It has no think tank in sylvan surroundings. Moreover, when confronted with the two-piece aluminum can competition, Crown Cork called on U.S. Steel (not its own personnel) to develop a sheet steel that could be processed in a similar fashion. Since the steel industry was threatened with losing much of its attractive tinplate business, it did most of the development work.

In its closures and machinery lines, Crown Cork operates at the forefront of technology. But development work is down within those divisions and is charged to their operating expenses. They are not expected to make big leaps into new fields.

A person working for Crown Cork has to like the work—because the hours will probably be long—and has to do it well. Saturday morning staff meetings are normal. The rewards are good for those who fit into this kind of regime; those who don't fit don't stay around.

Data on orders, prices, outputs, costs, and the like are known promptly, and problems are confronted on a factual and objective basis. The deadly parallel is often used in comparing plant performances. *Both* production and salespeople are "responsible for profits," and both are expected to initiate corrective action when profits earned by a plant fall below target.

The net effect of this no-frills approach to expenses is a drop in selling and administrative expenses from 6.3 to 3.3 percent, as indicated in Table 3. Crown Cork's more diversified competitors have comparable ratios ranging from 4.5 to over 10 percent. Although part of this drop reflects a change in product mix toward cans for large customers, the ratio is strikingly low. In one area, however,

**TABLE 3.**
**SELECTED CROWN CORK OPERATING STATEMENTS**

| | 1986 | | 1982 | | 1977 | | 1972 | | 1967 | |
|---|---|---|---|---|---|---|---|---|---|---|
| | *millions* | *%* | *millions* | *%* | *millions* | *%* | *millions* | *%* | *millions* | *%* |
| Net Sales | $1,619 | 100.0 | 1,352 | 100.0 | 1,049 | 100.0 | 489 | 100.0 | 301 | 100.0 |
| Cost of Goods Sold | 1,370 | 54.6 | 1,215 | 89.8 | 906 | 86.4 | 407 | 83.2 | 242 | 80.3 |
| Selling & Administrative Expense | 47 | 2.9 | 44 | 3.3 | 35 | 3.3 | 21 | 4.3 | 19 | 6.3 |
| Operating Profit before Interest & Income Tax | $ 153 | 9.5 | $ 93 | 6.9 | $ 108 | 10.3 | $ 61 | 12.5 | $ 40 | 13.3 |

there is no holding back; the equipment in company plants is both modern and fast.

## 4. Foreign Spinoffs

A fourth pillar in Crown Cork's strategy is early entry into foreign markets. Cans and closures cannot be exported economically. Instead, Crown Cork has provided machinery (including rebuilt U.S. equipment) and production expertise to locally organized firms. Many of these companies are in developing countries, where the demand is primarily in bottle caps.[1] Crown Cork had established these companies long before its U.S. competitors considered such locations worthy of attention.

These foreign subsidiaries are managed by local citizens in a highly decentralized manner. Having created a technological beachhead, each outpost must run its own show. There is no international vice-president at headquarters (which is consistent with the low-overhead philosophy of the company), although the presidents of the Canadian and European group serve on the Crown Cork board of directors. And to a large extent, each foreign unit generates its own capital. In terms of people, markets, and capital, each becomes part of the local scene—even more than the local Coca-Cola bottler. It is, of course, on the spot if and when a local demand for cans develops. There is little attempt or need for mutlinational coordination.

With a relatively small amount of U.S. management attention, the foreign operations have grown over the years along with the total company. Income from foreign sales have ranged between 27 and 48 percent of the total over the last decade, and assets abroad account for almost half of the total. The trends are shown in Tables 4 and 5.

## "The Pause That Refreshes"?

For a quarter of a century Crown Cork achieved an unusually steady growth in sales and profits. Up to 1981, under John Connelly's guidance each year was better than the preceding one. During this era Crown Cork's profit margin on sales, though narrow, was significantly better than its competitors. The company appeared to be doing the right thing in the right place. But then a combination of forces reversed the direction of results—if not the company strategy—for a couple of years. A closer look at this period may reveal vulnerabilities that could rise again in the future.

---

[1]Crown Cork has subsidiaries in the following regions: Canada, Mexico, Puerto Rico, West Indies, Argentina, Brazil, Chile, Colombia, Costa Rica, Ecuador, Guatemala, Peru, Venezuela; Austria, Belgium, Denmark, France, Italy, Holland, Germany, Switzerland, Ireland, Portugal, Spain, Great Britain; Ethiopia, Kenya, Nigeria, Zimbabwe, Zaire, Morocco, Mozambique, Zambia; Indonesia, Malaysia, Thailand, Singapore.

**TABLE 4.**
**CROWN CORK & SEAL COMPANY, INC., OPERATING DATA**
**(in millions of dollars, except where otherwise indicated)**

| | 1986 | 1985 | 1984 | 1982 | 1980 | 1976 | 1972 |
|---|---|---|---|---|---|---|---|
| Net Sales | 1,619 | 1,487 | 1,370 | 1,352 | 1,460 | 910 | 489 |
| Cost of Goods Sold | 1,370 | 1,260 | 1,172 | 1,215 | 1,271 | 784 | 407 |
| Selling & Administrative Expenses | 47 | 43 | 42 | 44 | 45 | 32 | 21 |
| Interest Expense | 6 | 12 | 9 | 9 | 15 | 4 | 4 |
| Tax on Income | 69 | 56 | 46 | 38 | 55 | 44 | 25 |
| Net Income (excluding minority interests) | 79 | 72 | 60 | 45 | 73 | 46 | 31 |
| Shares of Common Stock (average in millions) | 11 | 11 | 12 | 14 | 15 | 16 | 20 |
| Earnings per share (dollars) | 7.46 | 6.52 | 4.78 | 3.15 | 4.98 | 2.84 | 1.58 |
| Net Income from Foreign Subsidiaries | 27 | 24 | 23 | 12 | 35 | 15 | 13 |
| Net Income from U.S. Operations | 53 | 48 | 37 | 33 | 38 | 31 | 18 |
| Number of Employees (1000s) | 12 | 13 | 13 | 13 | 15 | 16 | 14 |
| Plant & Equipment Expenditures | 94 | 51 | 54 | 50 | 50 | 22 | 28 |
| Ratio Net Income/Total Assets (percent) | | | | | | | |
| Foreign Subsidiaries | 6.7 | 6.6 | 6.8 | 3.0 | 8.3 | 5.4 | 7.3 |
| U.S. Operations | 9.9 | 9.6 | 7.9 | 7.5 | 8.3 | 11.2 | 8.1 |
| Common Stock Price (dollars/share) | | | | | | | |
| High | 114¼ | 89⅝ | 45¼ | 32 | 31⅜ | 22⅓ | 27½ |
| Low | 77¼ | 44⅛ | 34¼ | 22¾ | 27⅞ | 16⅞ | 18½ |

In his annual letter to stockholders for 1982, Crown Cork's chairman said, in part:

> We sold, produced and delivered more cans, crowns, machinery, and other products than during any previous year in our history, yet the dollar sales are down . . . .
>
> In the United States economic conditions plus the effect of our industry's excess capacity has created bitter competition which has reduced our prices.
>
> Overseas every company has performed well . . . but when the results are restated in United States dollars, profits sometimes are converted into losses. We have absolutely no control over the world's currency fluctuations.

## TABLE 5.
## CROWN CORK & SEAL COMPANY, INC.
## COMPARATIVE BALANCE SHEET
### (in millions of dollars)[a]

| | 1986 | 1985 | 1984 | 1982 | 1980 | 1976 | 1972 |
|---|---|---|---|---|---|---|---|
| | *Total Company—Consolidated* | | | | | | |
| Current Assets | 477 | 466 | 419 | 457 | 496 | 281 | 175 |
| Plant & Equipment (net) | 404 | 347 | 348 | 358 | 355 | 249 | 211 |
| Investments & Goodwill | 58 | 53 | 39 | 25 | 22 | 17 | 14 |
| Total Assets | 939 | 866 | 806 | 841 | 873 | 547 | 400 |
| Current Liabilities | 249 | 225 | 226 | 192 | 264 | 158 | 105 |
| Deferred Income Tax | 79 | 71 | 61 | 58 | 52 | 39 | 26 |
| Long-Term Debt | 31 | 33 | 18 | 24 | 10 | 26 | 31 |
| Minority Equity in Subsidiaries | 4 | 5 | 4 | 7 | 8 | 7 | 8 |
| Common Stock | 50 | 53 | 57 | 70 | 73 | 78 | 97 |
| Retained Earnings | 526[b] | 479[b] | 440[b] | 490[b] | 466 | 238 | 133 |
| Total Liabilities & Equity | 939 | 866 | 806 | 841 | 873 | 547 | 400 |
| | *Foreign Subsidiaries* | | | | | | |
| Current Assets | 249 | 230 | 209 | 253 | 297 | 170 | 82 |
| Plant & Equipment (net) | 155 | 136 | 131 | 147 | 118 | 99 | 96 |
| Total Assets | 404 | 336 | 340 | 400 | 415 | 269 | 178 |
| Current Liabilities | 107 | 99 | 93 | 104 | 133 | 77 | 37 |
| Deferred Income Tax | 21 | 15 | 11 | 8 | 11 | 10 | 6 |
| Long-Term Debt | 16 | 19 | 4 | 9 | 0 | 1 | 9 |
| Minority Equity in Subsidiaries | 4 | 5 | 4 | 7 | 8 | 7 | 8 |
| CC&S Equity | 256 | 228 | 228 | 272 | 263 | 174 | 118 |
| Total Liabilities & Equity | 404 | 366 | 340 | 400 | 415 | 269 | 178 |
| | *United States Operations[c]* | | | | | | |
| Current Assets | 228 | 236 | 210 | 204 | 199 | 111 | 94 |
| Plant & Equipment (net) | 249 | 211 | 217 | 211 | 237 | 150 | 115 |
| Investments & Goodwill | 58 | 53 | 39 | 25 | 22 | 17 | 14 |
| Total Assets | 535 | 500 | 466 | 441 | 458 | 278 | 223 |
| Current Liabilities | 142 | 126 | 133 | 88 | 131 | 81 | 68 |
| Deferred Income Tax | 58 | 56 | 50 | 50 | 41 | 30 | 20 |
| Long-Term Debt | 15 | 14 | 14 | 15 | 10 | 25 | 22 |
| CC&S Equity | 320[b] | 304[b] | 269[b] | 288[b] | 276 | 141 | 113 |
| Total Liabilities & Equity | 535 | 500 | 466 | 441 | 458 | 278 | 223 |

[a]Columns may not add exactly, due to rounding.

[b]Net after deduction for foreign currency translation of $74 million in 1982, $151 million in 1984, $138 million in 1985, and $111 million in 1986. These adjustments relate to the valuation of assets on the balance sheets, not to operating income.

[c]Assets and liabilities assigned to U.S. operations are total company figures minus those of foreign subsidiaries.

These two forces, bitter competition and adverse currency fluctuations, are the primary villains—at least on the surface.

Increased competition was caused by several factors:

1.  Crown Cork's growth and relative profitability has attracted additional capacity to serve the beer and soft drink markets. All three competitors moved in: American Can, Continental, and National Can each installed new, efficient two-piece can manufacturing machinery to serve this market.

2.  The rapid rise in popularity of two-piece aluminum cans forced all competitors to replace old can-manufacturing equipment. Delay was no longer a realistic alternative. And when building new plants, each competitor was overly optimistic about the share of the market it would obtain.

3.  Meanwhile, self-manufacture of cans by large brewers expanded. Between 1978 and 1981 self-manufacture of cans grew from 30 to 33 percent of total can shipments. This actually reduced the number of cans sold by independent producers from 63 billion to 60 billion. And most of this contraction occurred in the markets served by Crown Cork.

4.  Crown Cork's move to establish a differential advantage by making steel rather than aluminum cans did not turn out to be effective. As will be seen, the cost of aluminum relative to steel declined, instead of increasing as expected. The result was that Crown Cork did not have a differentiated product.

In effect then, Crown Cork now found itself in a commodity-like market within the United States. Excess capacity of expensive, modern equipment in the plants of financially strong competitors led to the "bitter competition" noted by Connelly.

Even more devastating to Crown Cork's 1982 profits were sharp fluctuations in foreign currency values. In Crown Cork's strategy, international operations were expected to complement U.S. operations and to benefit from U.S. expertise. And within the various foreign subsidiaries this scheme worked reasonably well. Trouble occurred, however, in the consolidation of these foreign results back into U.S. dollars.

The magnitude of the profit write-downs due to currency adjustments is shown in the first three columns of Table 6 (income and losses stated in millions).

Substantially all of these losses reflect a drop in the value of local currencies relative to the U.S. dollar in the hyperinflation-plagued countries of Argentina, Brazil, Costa Rica, and, beginning in 1982, Mexico. The increase in 1982 over 1981 is due exclusively to Mexico.

So foreign operations did indeed buttress Crown Cork's position, but at the same time they subjected this narrow-margin business to severe risk.

**TABLE 6.**
**EFFECT OF CURRENCY ADJUSTMENTS ON NET INCOME**

|  | 1980 | 1981 | 1982 | 1985 | 1986 |
|---|---|---|---|---|---|
| *Foreign operations* | | | | | |
| Reported net income | $35 | $29 | $12 | $24 | $27 |
| Devaluation losses | 3 | 11 | 30 | 13 | 10 |
| Net before devaluation losses | $38 | $40 | $42 | $37 | $37 |
| Return on foreign assets before devaluation losses | 9.2% | 9.4% | 10.5% | 10.1% | 9.2% |
| *Consolidated results* | | | | | |
| Reported net income | $73 | $65 | $45 | $72 | $79 |
| Devaluation losses | 3 | 11 | 30 | 13 | 10 |
| Net before devaluation losses | $76 | $76 | $75 | $85 | $89 |
| Earnings per share before devaluation losses | $5.17 | $5.22 | $5.28 | $7.70 | $8.40 |

## Future Prospects

During the last few years Crown Cork has made an impressive recovery from the troublesome period in the early 1980s, as shown in Table 4. Both sales and net earnings have reached new peaks. This recovery is due primarily to a reversal of prior difficulties. Devaluation losses taken into cost of goods sold dropped from $30 million in 1982 to $10 million in 1986; this made a sharp improvement in the dollar earnings from foreign operations. Several of the beer companies decided that their investment in can operation could be better utilized elsewhere, and they withdrew from self-manufacture of cans; this permitted a small but significant rise in the selling price of cans. Meanwhile, Crown Cork kept selling and adminis-trative expenses from rising as fast as total sales, so these overhead outlays dropped from 3.3 percent of sales to 2.9 percent.

While these changes are indeed very helpful, Crown Cork will have to work hard to maintain them. The industry continues to be highly competitive, and the wisdom of continuing the past strategy is debatable. For Crown Cork, the outlook for pressure-resistant cans is crucial.

Crown Cork has been in the midst of a packaging revolution. Many products formerly sold in bulk are now further processed (trimmed, frozen, polished, pre-cooked, glued, precut, and the like), placed in convenient-to-use containers, and labeled with enticing instructions. Usually such products are swathed in clear plastic and cradled in an attractive paper box. The change includes products rang-ing from soap to piston rings to pocket calculators. Nevertheless, Crown Cork per-sists in making cans and closures.

Moreover, in its own domain the can has been and continues to be threatened by substitutes. Environmentalists would like to legislate it out of existence. So Crown Cork's future is far from assured.

## Growth of Underlying Demand

The U.S. consumption of both beer and soft drinks has been growing, as is shown in Table 7.

On a per-capita basis, the demand for beer is level or perhaps dropping slightly. So any increase here is probably limited to population growth and is slow at most.

In contrast, the consumption of soft drinks continues to rise. Soft drinks have clearly replaced coffee as the leading national drink. The growth rate may be dampened as the proportion of teenagers in the population drops, but no one can be sure what the present young guzzlers will prefer years hence. The sponsors of leading brands have launched the "Great Cola War of the 80s," which is expected to affect relative market position much more than total demand. Most forecasts project an annual increase in the total demand of about 3.5 percent.

Aerosol cans, Crown Cork's third market segment (about 15 percent of its total), experienced rapid growth from their introduction in the 50s to 1974. Then demand took a sharp dip, partly because aerosol packaging is relatively expensive and partly in response to a threatened ban for ecological reasons on the use of fluorocarbons as a propellant. Although demand has picked up again, substantial further growth is unlikely unless the ecological issues are resolved favorably.

Overall, for beer, soft drinks, and aerosol products, the U.S. growth rate is estimated at about 3 percent per annum, barring shifts due to new ecological legislation. It is a mature market.

## Battle of Materials

Not long ago every individual-size container for beer or soda was a glass bottle, and the bottle was returned to be refilled many times. There was no alternative. Then the metal can entered the picture. It saved the mess and labor of

**TABLE 7.**
**PER-CAPITA CONSUMPTION PER YEAR**

| Year | Beer (gallons) | Soft Drinks (gallons) |
|------|------|------|
| 1967 | 16.8 | 19.9 |
| 1972 | 19.5 | 23.7 |
| 1977 | 22.6 | 30.8 |
| 1981 | 24.6 | 35.2 |
| 1986 | 23.9 | 42.1 |

returning empty bottles, was lighter to handle, packed more closely, and didn't chip or shatter. The can companies and steel companies had to undertake a major educational campaign to persuade the consumer that a can did not affect the flavor of the product, but finally the tradition of the glass bottle was broken.

This switch to nonreturnable cans involved billions of containers and millions of dollars, as the data already presented indicate. But about the time it seemed likely that the soda bottle would follow the milk bottle into oblivion, the glass industry created the lighter weight, cheaper, nonreturnable glass bottle. With a competitive product and a potential market many times the size of that of the old returnable bottle, the fight was on. Broadly speaking, the glass industry has been able to retain about one-fourth of the beer container business (with 96 percent nonreturnable bottles). In the soft drink field, the division between glass and cans is about the same.

Actually, glass bottles are cheaper than cans. However, they weigh more, take more space, are slower to fill and break occasionally. For the bottler, the difference in total cost is so narrow that it usually will use the container which consumers like and that fits best into its market program. Several years ago Owens-Illinois introduced a plastic-shielded glass bottle. The shield helps to keep beverages cooler longer than a metal can does, and the bottle can be resealed. This improved package has been a major factor in checking the decline of glass containers.

A second conflict has been between steel and aluminum. When cans invaded the beverage field they were the traditional three-piece steel cans (a few conical tops never won an enduring position). Then around 1960, Reynolds and Kaiser aluminum companies moved in with their two-piece aluminum can. This can— now manufactured by all major can companies—has made rapid progress.

At first aluminum cans were more expensive than steel cans. And when Crown Cork and U.S. Steel succeeded in using steel for a two-piece can, there was a good chance that aluminum would be priced out of the market. This did not occur because (1) the base price of aluminum fell, instead of rising as expected, thus narrowing the spread in raw material costs; (2) improved technology permitted the use of lighter sheets of aluminum, so that by 1986 only 27.5 pounds of aluminum were needed to make 1,000 cans compared with 51.6 pounds in 1965; and (3) many aluminum cans are recycled. Aluminum can makers have established about 6,000 recycling centers in the U.S. which handle a billion pounds of scrap aluminum annually. By 1986 more than half of the aluminum cans produced were made from recycled material. The net result of these three forces has been a 40 percent reduction in the price of aluminum cans during the last six years.

Aluminum makes a somewhat better looking can than steel, and it is lighter in weight. Its exceptional ductility simplifies the drawing and ironing process for production of two-piece cans.[2]

---

[2]Crown Cork's machinery for making two-piece steel cans is easily converted to aluminum. Conversion of machinery designed for aluminum to steel would be much more difficult.

For all these reasons, in 1982 aluminum accounted for 95 percent of all beer cans, 75 percent of all soft drink cans, and 55 percent of the total number of cans produced. Unless the world price of base aluminum increases sharply, steel has lost the beverage can market.

A serious threat on the materials horizon is the prospect of plastic bottles. Compared with glass, plastic bottles are lightweight, durable, and almost unbreakable, and they can be formed into special shapes that have distinctive merchandising advantages.

In fact, Du Pont's PET (polyethylene tirepthalate) bottle has virtually taken over the large-size (two-liter) soft drink market. Experiments are under way to design a satisfactory single-service (eight-ounce) PET bottle, and some are in use. However, the smaller size has a short shelf life and may affect the taste of the contents. (The difference in performance between the large and small sizes is primarily a function of the ratio of contents to surface exposure.) If these difficulties can be overcome, plastic will be a sharp competitor of regular-size glass bottles and probably would take some business from cans.

Several major firms are committing large research efforts toward producing plastic bottles for this 60-billion-unit beer and soft drink market. In addition to the Du Pont and Monsanto efforts, Dow Chemical is working with Owens-Illinois and Anchor Hocking has teamed with Coca-Cola on a plastic-coated glass bottle (returnable) that has a low breakage rate and is lightweight. Mitsubishi Chemical already has a bottle of the latter type. Imperial Chemical of England is also active.

## Strength of Contestants

The way these future competitive forces will develop is strongly affected by the power and concerns of the major contestants—or actors. We have already noted that Crown Cork's traditional U.S. competitors in can production— American Can, Continental, and National Can—are larger and more diversified.[3] This is a capital-intensive industry. The number of direct competitors is small because large investments are required and profit margins are unattractive.

Moreover, the metal can industry has had chronic overcapacity. New capacity installed by self-manufacturers plus new capacity of aluminum can producers left excess machinery for the traditional three-piece steel can. During the early seventies, American Can and Continental each dismantled old plants to reduce this depressing overhang. This is a tough climate for firms with limited capital.

Actually the competitors are more numerous. Two large aluminum companies, Reynolds and Kaiser, have obtained significant positions in the beer and soft drink markets. The leading brewers still make some of their own cans, as do several food companies. And companies making glass bottles, such as Corning and Owens-Illinois, aggressively compete for the same end use. These are all powerful, sharp contestants.

---

[3]Continental changed its name to KMI Continental, Inc., in 1984. National Can was acquired by Triangle Industries in 1985. American Can changed its name to Primerica Corporation in 1987.

Customers include large and relatively small firms. Bottlers of beer tend to be large, and the industry is becoming more concentrated. In soft drinks the prevailing pattern of local franchises makes the number of customers much larger than might be inferred from brand concentration; the five largest firms get over 75 percent of the business, but they have several hundred distributors who actually purchase containers. Producers of aerosol products may be even smaller because they use aerosol cans for quite special markets. Nevertheless, containers represent a major expense for all these customers, and the buyers usually are very sophisticated in their purchasing.

Material suppliers are another set of actors. Materials account for roughly two-thirds of the cost of a can, so the dollar volume of materials consumed is very large. The big steel firms as well as the aluminum companies are vitally interested in this market. And as noted in the preceding section, at least five of the powerful chemical concerns are vying for advantage in a growing plastic bottle market.

By most standards Crown Cork is itself a large company. But compared with many of the firms whose actions impinge on its destiny, it is "just one of the boys."

In foreign countries the competitive picture varies widely. Because the market for cans and bottles is inherently local, each country has its own characteristics. Developing countries with low consumption in each locality, low purchasing power, and low labor costs typically use returnable bottles; this creates a demand for closures. In Europe the consumption of beverages is growing and there is a shift toward disposable containers; nevertheless, the size of individual purchasers of cans and closures is much smaller there than in the United States. Because of this diversity, a strategy for profitable growth varies from country to country.

Superimposed on this cast of actors are government regulatory agencies. The ones whose actions will have profound effect on the container industry deal with environmental issues.

## Environmental Protection

Containers for beer and soft drinks represent well over half of durable highway litter. The chief remedy proposed is a mandatory deposit to be repaid when the can or bottle is returned to the retailer.

Effective July 1983, New York became the ninth state to enact such regulations. Earlier action had been taken by Maine, Vermont, Massachusetts, Connecticut, Delaware, Michigan, Iowa, and Oregon. The New York law calls for a $.05 deposit on beer and soft drink containers, a $.01 retailer handling fee, and bans on detachable pull-tabs and plastic loops on six packs.

Experience in Oregon and Vermont, which have had such laws longest, indicates that (1) litter is substantially reduced, (2) total sales decline slightly, (3) consumers and especially retailers find the system something of a nuisance, and (4) prices have risen a bit to cover the additional cost of handling returned bottles. The impact on the type of container used is less clear. Originally it was assumed that the beverage industry would return to refillable glass bottles, virtually eliminating the use of cans. To some extent this happens. However, the recycling of aluminum cans is simpler for both consumers and retailers. The expectation now is that cans will win out, with single-use glass bottles the chief loser.

Opposition to these so-called "bottle bills" is also strong. Shortly after New York passed its mandatory deposit law, the voters in four other states (California, Colorado, Arizona, and Washington) defeated referendums calling for such legislation. Environmentalists are confronted by labor unions which might lose jobs and manufacturers who might lose sales. Emotions run high and lobbying pressures are intense. Probably the final outcome will be determined by the way politically active consumers balance a somewhat cleaner environment against the nuisance of returning cans and bottles.

## Crown Cork's Distinctive Resources

The future for Crown Cork is filled with uncertainties, as the preceding discussion indicates. The consumer industries it serves are basically mature, and a whole series of questions must be answered about the kind of containers which will carry products to those consumers. Moreover, the actions of powerful companies and political groups will profoundly affect Crown Cork; the extent and manner of Crown Cork's attempt to influence these actors will have to be decided.

As a further basis for assessing Crown Cork's future strategy, we should review several of its distinctive strengths.

1.  Crown Cork is in a strong cash position. Its long-term debt is a mere five percent of equity, leaving large unused borrowing capacity. For the past three years, its net income plus depreciation has averaged $114 million per year. Moreover, the company has a clear policy of paying no dividends to stockholders. So the cash flow is available for management's use.

    The no-dividend (on common stock) policy—which runs back for more than two decades—is interesting, because in several years more cash was generated than was needed in the business. Instead of paying dividends, management elected to buy back common stock. The repurchase price has been around book value per share. From 1972 to 1986 the number of shares outstanding was cut almost in half. Of course, this reduction has an effect on earnings per share: if the money used to buy back stock had instead been paid out as dividends, the earnings per share in 1986 would have been only about $4.00 compared with the actual earnings of $7.46.

2.  The strong cash position has permitted the company to invest heavily in new equipment. During the past four years $255 million went into capital outlays. As a result, Crown Cork's plants are at least as efficient as those of its competitors.

3.  The company's expense ratios are low, and it has a tradition of lean operation. At the same time, there is a tremendous morale built up around John Connelly, for many years president and now chair.

Connelly is a Vince Lombardi-type of leader—demanding of himself and of others, generous to subordinates in need, and inspiring subordinates through recognized success. Now 80, he continues to be the architect of company strategy.

4.  The machinery division of the company, in addition to being profitable, provides valuable insight into customer problems. When it sells and services high-speed filling equipment, it must keep tabs on where expansion is planned and what competitors are offering. This helps Crown Cork keep on its toes.

5.  The foreign subsidiaries provide Crown Cork with a widespread base for using its technological expertise. To date, the benefits have been predominantly on the sale of closures. However, if and when foreign subsidiaries can market, say, two-piece cans, Crown Cork will already be an established local vendor.

**TABLE 8.**
**U.S. VERSUS FOREIGN OPERATIONS**
**(in millions)**

|  | U.S. | Europe | All Other | Intracompany Sales, or Corporate Assets | Total |
|---|---|---|---|---|---|
| Sales to Customers | 1,010 | 366 | 269 | −26 | 1,619 |
| Operating Profit | 93 | 22 | 40 | − 2 | 153 |
| Assets (excluding cash, etc.) | 497 | 208 | 194 | 38 | 939 |
| Capital Expenditures | 68 | 15 | 11 | — | 94 |
| Depreciation Expense | 28 | 9 | 10 | — | 47 |

# COMPREHENSIVE CASE 9

## Citicorp–British National Life Assurance[1]

Ira Rimerman, Group Executive, Consumer Services Group, International, Citicorp, was in his third-floor office at Citicorp's headquarters in New York City on January 16, 1986, when he received notice from the Board of Citicorp that his MEP (major expenditure proposal) to acquire the British National Life Assurance Company, Ltd. (BNLA), in England had been approved. For a total investment of $33.3 million, Citicorp was now in the life underwriting business.[2]

Although pleased with the Board's approval, there were several issues on Mr. Rimerman's mind as he thought back over the last few months when his staff analyzed and developed suggestions for a business strategy for BNLA, including key policies, tactics, and organizational changes.

## Citicorp's Strategy

Citicorp's corporate history spanned 175 years, from its early inception as a small commercial bank in New York City in 1812 through its growth into one of the world's largest financial services intermediaries. A recurring historical theme seemed to be the firm's ability to correctly identify the developing trends in the marketplace and to devise appropriate strategies for taking advantage of them. Exhibits 1 and 2 provide a summary of the firm's recent financial profile.

The firm's strategic plan called for three separate kinds of world-class banks, all of which could leverage off an unrivaled global network. By the mid-1980s the Investment Bank, also known as the Capital Markets Group, enabled the firm to fully intermediate the capital flows of the world, with over $6 billion in transactions in the swap market. The Institutional Bank was the principal supplier of financial service mechanisms to corporations and governments worldwide. Finally, the Individual Bank served the individual consumer on a worldwide basis.

The holding company structure was used to overcome the geographic constraints of the domestic businesses. It also allowed for a few acquisitions and for the creation of *de novo* units to build a global network which, among other things, featured a unique competitive franchise for bank cards within the Individual Bank.

---

[1]This case was prepared by Professors John M. Gwin, Per V. Jenster, and William K. Carter at the University of Virginia.

[2]All financial information related to BNLA has been changed for proprietary reasons.

**EXHIBIT 1**
**CONSOLIDATED BALANCE SHEET**
**CITICORP AND SUBSIDIARIES**
**(in billions of dollars)**

|  | 12/31/85 | 12/31/84 |
|---|---|---|
| *Assets:* | | |
| Cash, deposits with banks, and securities | $ 40 | $ 31 |
| Commercial loans | $58 | $59 |
| Consumer loans | 55 | 43 |
| Lease financing | 3 | 2 |
| Allowance for credit losses | 1 | 1 |
| Net | $115 | $103 |
| Premises and other assets | 18 | 17 |
| Total | $173 | $151 |
| | | |
| *Liabilities* | | |
| Deposits | $105 | $ 90 |
| Borrowings and other liabilities | 42 | 39 |
| Long-term debt | 16 | 13 |
| Capital notes and redeemable preferred | 2 | 2 |
| | $165 | $144 |
| | | |
| *Stockholders' Equity* | | |
| Preferred stock | 1 | 1 |
| Common stock | 1 | 1 |
| Additional paid-in capital | 1 | 1 |
| Retained earnings | 5 | 4 |
| | $ 8 | $ 7 |
| Total | $173 | $151 |

*Source:* Citicorp 1985 Annual Report.

The worldwide orientation was further encouraged as cross-border lending started to slow down. Citicorp predicted that individual countries would be forced to develop their own indigenous capital markets. Thus, there was an opportunity to develop a "multidomestic" strategy which would enable Citicorp to offer full financial services in 60–80 countries before 1990.

## The Five I's

In the early 1980s Citicorp added two more "I's" to the strategic thrust which had initially included development of the Investment Bank, the Individual Bank, and the Institutional Bank. The two embryonic "I's" were the Information and Insurance businesses.

**EXHIBIT 2**
**CONSOLIDATED INCOME STATEMENT**
**CITICORP AND SUBSIDIARIES**
**(in billions of dollars, except per-share amounts)**

|                              | 1985   | 1984   | 1983   |
|------------------------------|--------|--------|--------|
| Interest revenue             | $19.5  | $18.2  | $15.2  |
| Less: Interest expense       | 14.0   | 13.9   | 11.2   |
| Provision for credit losses  | 1.3    | 0.6    | 0.5    |
| Net                          | $4.2   | $3.7   | $3.5   |
| Other revenues               | 3.0    | 2.3    | 1.8    |
|                              | $7.2   | $6.0   | $5.3   |
| Operating expenses           | 5.5    | 4.5    | 3.7    |
| Income before income taxes   | $1.7   | $1.5   | $1.6   |
| Income taxes                 | 0.7    | 0.6    | 0.7    |
| Net income                   | $ 1.0  | $ 0.9  | $ 0.9  |
| Earnings per share:          |        |        |        |
| Common and equivalent        | $7.12  | $6.45  | $6.48  |
| Fully diluted                | 7.11   | 6.36   | 6.15   |

*Source:* Citicorp 1985 Annual Report.

The rationale for entering the insurance business was simple: insurance services accounted for fully 40 percent of all financial services in 1985. Citicorp would therefore not be a truly effective financial services enterprise without offering these products. Insurance was also a natural adjunct to the consumer business, considering the outmoded and expensive agency method of distribution that dominated the industry. Moreover, the firm was already a major factor in credit insurance. For example, one-third of its second-mortgage customers bought credit life insurance.

The Banking Holding Company Act of 1956, and specifically Regulation Y, Section 4(c)–8 for the Board of Governors of the Federal Reserve System, prohibited banks from engaging in life insurance underwriting (with certain exceptions). Thus, the firm's insurance strategy was primarily aimed at overseas expansion. This expansion was made possible by the Federal Reserve Board's ruling, requested by Citicorp, which enabled the firm to establish a fully competitive insurance operation in the United Kingdom.

This shift in the Board's attitude enabled Citicorp to consider expansion into insurance, to identify the U.K. as a potential country in which to do so, and ultimately to pursue BNLA for acquisition.

Citicorp's goals for the five I's as of 1986 are summarized as follows:[3]

---

[3]Citicorp and *Business Week*, December 8, 1986.

## INSTITUTIONAL

- Trim work force from 20,000 to 17,000.
- Pull back from middle markets overseas.
- Push investment banking products more.
- Clean up loan portfolio, reduce write-offs.

## INVESTMENT

- Build a credible corporate finance group, especially by mergers and acquisitions.
- Hold on to investment banking talent.
- Wire 90 trading rooms around the globe.
- Improve coordination between London, Tokyo, and New York.

## INDIVIDUAL

- Continue to grow fast in retail banking.
- Make all acquired S&Ls profitable.
- Push international consumer business.

## INFORMATION

- Leave Quotron alone to calm customers.
- Develop new products.

## INSURANCE

- Push for easing limits on banks.
- Grow overseas.
- Cross-sell more insurance products through customer base.

## Citicorp's Structure and Objectives

The Investment Bank, the Institutional Bank, and the Individual Bank were each organized into a sector and headed by a sector executive. Activities related to insurance and information were under the auspices of group executives within the three sectors, until such time as they justified the creation of their own sectors.

Each of the three sectors was composed of several groups, divisions, and business families, headed by a group executive, with business managers reporting to him or her. The organization of the Individual Bank, which is of particular interest in this case, was somewhat different from the other banks. As dictated in John S. Reed's (chairman of Citicorp since 1985) memorandum of March 9, 1976 (internally known as the "Memo from the Beach"), the business manager was responsible for the day-to-day operation, whereas a division executive's responsibility was strategic in nature.

This meant that a branch manager in, say Hong Kong would report to an area manager, then a country manager, a division manager, a group executive, a vice-chairman or sector executive, and finally the chairman. In effect, the flat structure placed only three layers of management between the most junior branch manager and the Policy Committee (30 senior executives) of Citicorp.

## The International Opportunity

In the 1985 Annual Report,[4] the board stated:

> We recognize that, ultimately, our success will be directly attributable to our ability to offer our consumers worldwide preeminent service for each of their relationships with us. Our view is that by pursuing service excellence across all of our efforts, we enhance our standing with our customers and thereby the likelihood that they will choose us for a growing share of their financial needs.

Internationally, Citicorp expanded its presence in a number of markets during 1985, while maintaining returns well in excess of corporate standards. In that year, Citicorp completed significant acquisitions in Italy (Banca Centro Sud), Belgium (Banque Sud Belge), and Chile (Corporación Financiera Atlas), as well as consumer businesses in Colombia, Guam, and India.

Richard S. Braddock, sector executive of the Individual Bank and director of Citicorp and Citibank, explained:

> We view our opportunities in the international marketplace as substantial, not only because our share tends to be relatively small in most places, but also because we have the opportunity to apply lessons learned from market to market and to expand attractive and proven product packages . . . .[5]

## The Consumer Service Group, International (CSGI)

The Consumer Service Group, International, within the Individual Bank, was organized in separate divisions: the Asia-Pacific division had its headquarters in Tokyo; the Europe–Middle east–Africa (EMEA) division in London; the Western division in Rio de Janeiro; the Payment Products Division (Diners Club) in Chicago; and the Systems Division in New York. The group employed 26,000 people in 70 businesses located in 40 countries.

John Liu, Senior Human Resource Officer, Consumer Services Group, International, summarized how Citicorp's culture was reflected by the Group:

> We want to be part of the largest low-cost provider of financial service in the world. As such, we don't focus only on banks such as Chase Manhattan. Rather, we look also at Sears, AMEX, and others who provide financial services. This is the stretch we hold in front of us.

---

[4]Citicorp 1985 Annual Report, p. 11.
[5]Ibid., p. 13.

In order to help achieve this, we have to find new ways of doing things. Taking insurance as an example, Citicorp practices its decentralized operational mode, sometimes referred to as the "thousand flowers" approach.

In insurance, to use a metaphor, we want to have a thousand flowers bloom. Over time, we'll put the flowers together in a bouquet, and if we don't like the shape of it, we'll take this or that flower away. However, today we just started our picking, and that is why you'll find insurance activities in the Institutional Bank (commercial insurance), the Investment Bank (brokerage insurance activities), and with us in the Individual Bank (life underwriting, mortgage insurance, etc.). It's all emerging slowly out of our philosophy, and the BNLA acquisition is the first major life underwriting acquisition we have ever had.

As part of this stretch, the corporation applies certain hurdle rates to guide this vision. We have a stated hurdle rate, internally, such as an ROE of no less than 20 percent. Additionally, we have an ROA hurdle rate of 90 basis points. In our group, we use our own internal hurdle rates as a way of managing our businesses. One such hurdle rate which comes to mind is to target a ratio of 1.5 between consumer net revenue and delivery expenses.

Within the Group, we want to more than double our earnings over the next five years. We want to do this partly through acquisitions, of which we must have done at least 10 over the past three years and added more than 6,000 people. Although we still will make acquisitions, we clearly must slow down and develop these new businesses.

The acquisitions have not been hostile and for the most part have been either "hospitalized" or unprofitable businesses. This has given us certain advantages, but also created challenges when it comes to integrating a new business into our organization.[6]

## The Search for an Acquisition

Liu further explained how the BNLA acquisition came about:

About three years ago, we started a drive to get into insurance and encouraged our people in the U.K., Australia, Germany, and Belgium to start to look into insurance. As you know, there are three ways you can get into a new business: either (a) acquire, (b) start a *de novo* unit, or (c) do a joint venture.

In England, which was one of the largest and most profitable markets (relatively) for life insurance, we initially identified Excelsior Life Assurance[7] as a possibility in early 1984. As an insurance company of substantial size in the U.K., Excelsior would immediately bring us into this market on a

---

[6]Interview with John Liu.
[7]The name has been changed to protect confidentiality.

large scale. However, the more we analyzed the numbers, the more concerned we got. This was a significant investment, and we had little knowledge about life insurance. So when our joint-venture partner (a large U.S. insurance company) withdrew, we reconsidered our options.

Then Citicorp's U.K. Country Manager and the European Division Manager of the United Kingdom sponsored (i.e., identified) BNLA as a potential candidate for our move into life underwriting insurance. After the identification of the candidate, an acquisition team was put together. The team consisted of people from across our U.K. businesses as well as outside consultants, and they were all selected for their specific skills as they related to this opportunity.

One of the important issues for us now is to decide how to integrate the business: should we fully integrate, keep it at an arm's-length distance, or keep it somewhere in between, and how should we do it? With this decision also comes the question of what type of person to put into the driver's seat.

## The U.K. Life Assurance Market

The U.K. economy is the sixth largest in the world and is in transition, as is the U.S. economy, from an industrial to a service orientation. By 1985, the U.K. had the lowest level of legal/regulatory control for domestic and international financial activity of any developed country. However, U.K. regulation of life insurance underwriting, particularly with regard to reserves, was among the most stringent in the world. The government was considered politically stable, and the conservatives in power were committed to controlling inflation and government spending to provide a platform for economic growth. Even though 12 percent of the work force was unemployed, there was little social unrest.

The U.K. was expected to remain self-sufficient in oil for the remainder of the century. Inflation was expected to be controlled in the 5–7 percent range, and there were expected to be no major changes in either the political system or the regulatory environment. Expected growth figures for U.K. GNP for 1986 and 1987 were 1.5 and 2.6 percent, respectively. Inflation was expected to be around 5.0 percent for the same two periods.

The U.K. life assurance market was considered large and growing. Growth in new premiums went from $1.9 BN in 1980 to $4.7 BN in 1983. During the same period average growth of premium income rose from $7.8 BN to $13.2 BN, and total sums insured grew an average of 17 percent to $295 BN. There were 289 licensed underwriters in the U.K.

Analyses showed that life assurance in the U.K was seen as both a protection instrument and a consumer investment. The policies accumulate cash value and also yield dividends to policyholders. There were basically three types of underwriters in the marketplace: industrial, orthodox, and linked life.

The industrial companies offered small-value policies which were targeted at the lower socioeconomic groups. The premiums were collected in person, usually monthly, by employed agents, who did little actual "selling." The policies carried high administrative overheads and were, therefore, relatively poor values for the consumer. This sector of the market was dominated by Prudential, which wrote 65 percent of the new policies issued each year. This type of insurance had a vast customer base, with over 70 million policies in existence. At the same time, the policies had a declining market share, and smaller companies were retrenching because of overhead inefficiencies.

The orthodox life companies offered larger value policies which catered to the more affluent customer. This type of policy was distributed through "independent" professionals who usually had some other relationship with the customer. These independent agents could be insurance brokers, solicitors (attorneys), accountants, banks, or estate agents. It was fairly common in the U.K. for all of these groups to offer insurance as a part of their service portfolio to their clients. These independent agents typically offered policies from three to six different underwriters. The firms which offered orthodox policies had traditionally not "marketed" to their consumer base for fear of offending the professional intermediary. There were different "classes" of agents who covered specific market segments.

The linked-life policy was relatively new, having been introduced in the 1960s as an alternative to the orthodox life policy. It targeted the same consumer as the orthodox policy, but was sold normally by a commission-paid, self-employed sales force, much like insurance representatives in the U.S. Policyholders of linked-life insurance did not "participate" in the profits of the underwriter through dividends, but their investments were placed in a number of funds (similar to mutual funds) managed by the underwriter. Thus, the linked-life policyholder took investment risk/return, and the underwriter provided a death guarantee.

Trends in the U.K market indicated that the role of single-premium life assurance was expanding. This type of policy was one in which a single payment was made to the underwriter at the beginning of the policy life and no further premiums were due. Before the creation of the single-premium policy, most life policy premiums were paid yearly over the life of the policy. Logically, there was no single-premium industrial underwriting, given the socioeconomic status of most policyholders. The target for the single-premium policies was the "banked homeowner"—a person who had a relationship with a bank and who owned his or her home.

In addition to the expansion of the single-premium policy, there had been a decline in share of the industrial policy from 13 percent of total insurance in 1980 to 6 percent in 1983. The growth sectors of the market were linked-life assurance and personal pensions (which were similar to the Individual Retirement Account in the U.S.).

Premium income had generally become increasingly volatile, because single-premium income had grown from 12 percent of total premium income in 1980 to 22 percent in 1983. Since 1968, the growth segments for premium income were linked life, personal pensions, and mortgage endowment.

In their attempt to expand their share of the market, traditional companies had begun moving into the linked-life segment. Major growth was expected in pension-related policies as the most efficient savings medium from a tax perspective.

For the future, the desire of the government to increase the "portability" of pensions could open a major new market. At this time, personal pensions were sold by law only by life assurance companies. The removal of this restriction was under consideration and would bring new banks into the market. There was some concern that the government policy of "fiscal neutrality" between savings mediums could cause further amendment to tax laws, but this was not expected in the short term.

In the future marketplace, it would be possible for banks to exploit their customer bases and "sell" insurance, instead of being passive providers. Building Societies (very similar to U.S. savings and loan institutions, and responsible for writing most home mortgages in the U.K.) did not currently have legislative permission to function as insurance brokers, as did the banks. It was expected that the Societies would request that power in 1986–87, which would bring more new players into the market. There would be an increase in the pensions business to reach the large self-employed group in the U.K.

In summary, the U.K. life underwriting market was the seventh largest in the world and was growing. Life assurance in the U.K. filled a dual role for the consumer: protection and savings/investment. The market was led by large and well-established players, but there were major market opportunities for other well-managed companies. The market was differentiated by distribution methods, and the long-term profit stream generated by most firms led to high investor confidence and high share prices. U.K. premium income in 1982 totaled $28 billion, of which $12 billion was in life assurance underwriting. The market was predominantly U.K.-owned, as were the major players, although a company did not need to be a general insurance firm to compete successfully in either market. Each market involved different legislative bases, different distribution channels, and different skills. U.K. firms were significant in world markets, particularly nonlife, where they received over 50 percent of the premium income.

## The U.K. Financial Services Market

There were five major categories of financial services in the U.K.: transaction accounts, savings, shelter (home) financing, lending, and protection. The total savings market had grown from $124 billion in 1980 to $193.6 billion in 1983. Shelter finance had grown from $62.8 billion to $108.8 billion in the same period.

Banks were leading the expansion into the related areas of mortgage financing, estate agency (trust), stockbroking, and life assurance underwriting. Building Societies now offered checkbook access to savings and ATM networks. Legislation intended to equalize competitive roles in the market had been passed. Technological advancements were expected at this point, but were not yet in place. The market would continue to change rapidly due to continuing deregulation and increasing technological sophistication. Traditional barriers were falling, and banks were leading the way into other sectors of the economy to satisfy consumer demand. Insurance was an integral part of the market and was supported by past and present government and fiscal policy.

## Citicorp in the U.K.

The Consumer Services Group (U.K.) was dominated by Citibank Savings, a mature business operating in four specific markets:

| | |
|---|---|
| Finance House: | Indirect financing for autos and home improvement. |
| Mortgage Banking: | Consumer mortgages through association with Insurance firm partners. |
| Retail Cards: | Private label card operation for London's High Street retailers, as well as the European Banking Centre, Travellers Checks, and Diners Club. |
| Consumer Banking: | Cross-selling a portfolio of products to consumers, such as personal loans, checking (transaction) accounts, mortgages, and insurance. |

Citibank Savings had 39 branches in the U.K., 19 of which were recognized as direct branches within the consumer bank.

## U.K. Life Assurance Consumers

U.K. life assurance consumers were underinsured relative to those of other developed nations. The total life coverage as a percent of yearly average wage as compared with seven industrialized nations was as follows:

| | |
|---|---|
| U.K. | 88% |
| France | 147% |
| Sweden | 148% |
| Australia | 178% |
| U.S.A. | 183% |
| Canada | 184% |
| Japan | 325% |

The product was seen by U.K. consumers as intangible and offering no present benefit. The contracts were viewed as a "mass of small print" and were inflexible once purchased. The purchase pattern was characterized as infrequent and having a high unit cost, and the consumer had a "low knowledge base" about the product. The benefits perceived were "peace of mind," a response to issues of social responsibility, and investment/tax avoidance. Seventy-four percent of U.K. households, including 45 percent of all adults (predominantly men), had life coverage. The major reasons for purchase were "protection" and "house purchase." In general, no major alternatives were considered, and the decision to buy insurance coverage was a joint one in the family. The amount of coverage was generally based on affordability rather than need, and shopping among companies was minimal.

The life assurance market was not as mature as its size might indicate. Most consumers were underinsured, and over half the adult population had no coverage at all. There was a key role to be played for protection products (as distinct from investment products). Linked-life companies concentrated on "investment policies," and the benefits to the policyholder were neither fixed nor guaranteed by the company but were invested in a separate range of funds (at the risk/return of the consumer). In this sense, linked-life firms worked very much like mutual fund companies in the U.S. Their sources of income were profits from insurance underwriting, a 5 percent bid/offer differential on investments in the funds, and a ¾ percent fund management fee. The products were sold through a direct sales force, which was normally paid only by commission.

In the U.K. market, 15 percent of adults had a linked-life policy (33 percent with life assurance coverage). The policies were most popular in the under-55 age range, and in London and the southeast of England.

## The British National Life Assurance

In January of 1986 BNLA employed 351 people, 101 at its headquarters and 250 comprising the sales force from 22 branches. Each branch had a branch manager and an administrative assistant.

There were 47,600 policyholders and $305 million dollars in life insurance in force. However, BNLA policy lapses and salesperson turnover were twice the industry average. The commission-only sales force was the major distribution method for BNLA products, and productivity was some 75 percent below average. The sales force was inappropriately trained, and the commission structure resulted in low pay relative to the competition.

BNLA spent considerable sums of money training a sales force that was paid poorly relative to industry averages. The management subscribed to the philosophy that a high-quality product would essentially sell itself and that, therefore, high commissions were unnecessary. Their view was that sales goals would be achieved in the long run as a result of high training levels and high-quality products. This philosophy constrained promotional activities to direct selling only. The marketing department was therefore mostly engaged in arranging flashy conventions and gimmicks for the sales force.

Communication between top management and the organization was generally considered poor or nonexistent. Bad news, such as the lack of profits, the low sales force performance, and information about the negative cash flows, was never passed along to the management team. Although annual budgets were compiled, their content was never shared with departments. Conversely, no formal system existed for monthly reporting on departmental activities.

It was believed that financial reporting should be kept to a minimum, although all required disclosures were always filed on time. The financial officer had a small minicomputer at his disposal. Moreover, the firm had taken steps to automate the office environment at its headquarters by establishing a word-processing pool.

Toward the end of 1984, the holding company of BNLA decided that it was not going to make a go of BNLA (or of financial services generally) and put the company up for sale. The company knew that it was "on the block," and employee morale took a nose dive.

## BNLA Product/Market Posture

At the time of the Citicorp acquisition, BNLA was a linked-life firm which offered six basic products to the market:

1. Plan-for-Life—a highly flexible policy that offered the consumer control over the content of his or her plan. The consumer decided what proportion of the premium to devote to savings and what proportion to protection, and this could be changed as needs and circumstances warranted.

2. Plan-for-Capital—a regular savings plan with high investment content and minimum life coverage. It was ideal for someone who wanted to save dynamically for 8 to 10 years. The proceeds were free from basic-rate income tax (the "off the top" rate in the U.K.), from personal capital gains tax, and, after 10 years, from higher rate tax as well. This product was quite similar to the Individual Retirement Account in its tax treatment. It differed in its small insurance coverage.

3. Plan-for-Investment—a lump-sum plan to invest in the company's different funds. The capital invested was allocated a set number of units, depending on the current value of the fund. At any time, the plan had a value equivalent to the bid (selling) value of the price of units multiplied by the number of units held. This fund was very similar to the mutual funds offered through brokerage houses in the U.S., except there were certain tax advantages not offered in U.S. mutual funds.

4. Plan-for-Retirement—a retirement annuity policy which was suitable for the self-employed and those who had no private pension scheme—a unit-linked plan with outstanding tax advantages. This plan was similar to the Keogh plans in the U.S., but was free of investment limits.

5. Plan-for-Executive—an individual pension plan suitable for senior members of a trading company (brokerage house) who wished to add to their retirement benefits. This was a very specialized policy and was, once again, similar to the IRA, except that both the executive and his or her employer could contribute.

6. Plan-for-Pension Preservation—a specialized plan conforming to legislation passed in 1970 which allowed the transfer of vested pension funds from a previous employer into this plan without tax penalties.

In addition to these plans, a brokerage provided access to general insurance such as motor, house contents (home owners), and building insurance. (U.K. insurance companies are not permitted to act as insurance brokers.) The BNLA product line was generally complete and well rounded, and fulfilled the all-around needs of the consumer, from protection and investment to retirement planning.

## BNLA—A Financial Perspective

Accounting standards in the U.S. required earnings on a life insurance policy to be recognized evenly over the years of premium payments. U.K. life insurance regulations, by contrast, required maintenance of prudent reserves that resulted in a new life assurance company's generating losses or very low profits during its early years. The function of the regulations was to severely restrict dividend payments and thereby protect policyholders. U.S. accounting was significantly less conservative; when the balance sheet of a U.K. life firm was recast to comply with U.S. accounting, the reported equity generally increased considerably.

Citicorp's customary financial goals and targets were designed for traditional banking businesses and did not lend themselves to evaluating an investment in a life insurance company. For that reason, Citicorp measured BNLA performance against a hurdle rate of 20 percent on BNLA's recorded equity. Based on Citicorp's projections at the time of the acquisition, BNLA was expected to produce negative ROEs in 1985 and 1986 and to achieve the 20 percent hurdle rate for the first time in 1991. To comply with U.S. accounting, BNLA's recorded equity at the time of the acquisition was adjusted as follows (in millions; note that all BNLA financial data have been changed for proprietary reasons):

| | |
|---|---|
| Book value of assets | $77.1 |
| Book amount of liabilities | 66.9 |
| Book value of equity | $10.2 |
| Adjustments to comply with U.S. accounting: | |
| Write-down of assets | −3.5 |
| | $ 6.7 |
| Reduction of reserves | +6.5 |
| Adjusted equity | $13.2 |
| Portion acquired | 100% |
| Purchased equity | $13.2 |
| Purchase price | 13.7 |
| Goodwill | $ 0.5 |
| Additional capital infusion | 19.6 |
| Total investment[8] | $33.3 |

---

[8]Investment was made in pounds sterling and was fully hedged via the forward market.

Exhibit 3 presents summary financial data on BNLA, including forecasts. For 1985, production of new life policies was 40 percent below forecast. Operating expenses were 50 percent higher than forecast and about 50 percent higher than the industry norms for a firm at this stage of development. This is fairly consistent with expense levels of previous years.

## The Acquisition

During the time when Citicorp U.K. was actively seeking an insurance company to acquire, Bob Selander was the new country manager of Citicorp's U.K.

**EXHIBIT 3**
**BNLA OPERATING FORECAST, INCLUDING REQUIRED SYNERGIES RESTATED ACCORDING TO U.S. ACCOUNTING PRINCIPLES**
**(in millions)**

|  | 1985 | 1986 | 1987 | 1988 | 1989 |
|---|---|---|---|---|---|
| Premiums, net | $19.9 | $47.0 | $74.5 | $109.9 | $153.1 |
| Reinsurance | 0 | 2.7 | 8.5 | 12.5 | 15.0 |
| Investment income | 3.2 | 8.4 | 12.9 | 19.8 | 30.4 |
| Total revenues | $23.1 | $58.1 | $95.9 | $142.2 | $198.5 |
| Benefits paid | $ 3.1 | $ 4.2 | $ 7.2 | $ 13.3 | $ 34.1 |
| Increase in reserves | 12.0 | 40.5 | 66.4 | 96.4 | 119.3 |
| Commissions | 2.9 | 6.7 | 11.6 | 17.2 | 23.4 |
| Operating expenses | 5.5 | 7.8 | 7.4 | 9.1 | 12.5 |
| Total expenses | $23.5 | $59.2 | $92.6 | $136.0 | $189.3 |
| Income before taxes* | $(0.4) | $(1.1) | $3.3 | $6.2 | $9.2 |
| Income taxes | 0 | 0 | 0.8 | 2.8 | 4.3 |
| Net income | $(0.4) | $(1.1) | $ 2.5 | $ 3.4 | $ 4.9 |
| ROE: |  |  |  |  |  |
| On BNLA equity | (7%) | (5%) | 7% | 9% | 12% |
| By Citicorp formulas | (30%) | (40%) | 6% | 11% | 16% |

*Reconciled with BNLA's stand-alone forecast, under U. K. accounting principles, as follows:

|  | 1985 | 1986 | 1987 | 1988 | 1989 |
|---|---|---|---|---|---|
| U.K. pretax income, without synergies | $(0.7) | $(3.9) | $(2.4) | $(0.6) | $ 1.5 |
| Adjustment for U.S. accounting rules |  | (0.1) | (0.1) | (0.1) | (0.1) |
| Impact of synergies |  | 1.1 | 4.0 | 4.9 | 5.6 |
| Impact of capital infusion | 0.3 | 1.8 | 1.8 | 2.0 | 2.2 |
| Income before taxes, as reported above | $(0.4) | $(1.1) | $ 3.3 | $ 6.2 | $ 9.2 |

*Source:* Citicorp MEP; the data have been altered for proprietary reasons.

**EXHIBIT 4**
**BNLA FORECAST BALANCE SHEETS, INCLUDING REQUIRED**
**SYNERGIES RESTATED ACCORDING TO U.S. ACCOUNTING PRINCIPLES**
**(in millions, as of December 31 of each year)**

|                        | 1985  | 1986   | 1987  | 1988  | 1989  |
|------------------------|-------|--------|-------|-------|-------|
| Securities             | $91   | $126   | $177  | $257  | $363  |
| Reinsurance receivable | 0     | 1      | 7     | 13    | 15    |
| Other assets           | 4     | 8      | 21    | 38    | 59    |
| Total assets           | $95   | $135   | $205  | $308  | $436  |
| Insurance reserves     | $62   | $103   | $169  | $266  | $385  |
| Other liabilities      | 1     | 1      | 3     | 6     | 10    |
| Common stock           | 32    | 32     | 32    | 32    | 32    |
| Retained earnings      | 0     | $ (1)  | 1     | 4     | 10    |
| Total                  | $95   | $137   | $205  | $308  | $437  |

*Source:* Citicorp MEP; the data have been altered for proprietary reasons.

**EXHIBIT 5**
**BNLA HISTORICAL BALANCE SHEETS**
**ACCORDING TO U. K. ACCOUNTING PRINCIPLES**
**(in millions, as of December 31 of each year; all balances restated at an exchange**
**rate of 1 pound sterling = $1.4)**

|                    | 1984  | 1983  |
|--------------------|-------|-------|
| Securities         | $56   | $38   |
| Other assets       | 4     | 1     |
| Total assets       | $60   | $39   |
| Insurance reserves | $56   | $31   |
| Other liabilities  | 1     | 5     |
| Capital            | 3     | 3     |
| Total              | $60   | $39   |

*Source:* Citicorp MEP; the data have been altered for proprietary reasons.

**EXHIBIT 6**
**BNLA HISTORICAL INCOME STATEMENTS**
**ACCORDING TO U. K. ACCOUNTING PRINCIPLES**
(in millions; all balances restated at an exchange rate of 1 pound sterling = $1.4)

|                        | 1984    | 1983    |
|------------------------|---------|---------|
| Premiums, net          | $31     | $ 5     |
| Investment income      | 4       | 3       |
| Total revenues         | $35     | $ 8     |
| Benefits paid          | $ 3     | $ 3     |
| Increase in reserves   | 25      | 7       |
| Commissions            | 1       | 1       |
| Operating expenses     | 9       | 1       |
| Total expenses         | $38     | $12     |
| Income before taxes    | ($ 3)   | ($ 4)   |
| Income taxes           | 0       | 0       |
| Net income             | ($ 3)   | ($ 4)   |

*Source:* Citicorp MEP; the data have been altered for proprietary reasons.

*Note:* Caution should be exercised in comparing BNLA financial data with that of Citicorp, or even with that of other U.K. life assurance companies. This is because, first, there were some significant differences between traditional banking businesses and a U.K. life insurance operation, especially in rules governing the accounting recognition of earnings and in U.K. tax and regulatory requirements. Second, these differences were exaggerated in the case of a relatively new, rapidly growing U.K. life assurance company, where the reported amount of equity may have been as much as 60 percent of reported assets because of the conservatism inherent in regulatory requirements. Third, it was also difficult to make meaningful financial comparisons among different U.K. life companies. An immature firm had a financial picture bearing little resemblance to that of an older, established competitor, which may have reported equity as low as 2 percent of total assets.

business. The acquisition of an insurance company was a part of the strategic plan he inherited from his predecessor, Sir William Baltimore, who had previously developed a list of potential acquisitions for consideration.

The first possibility which came to light was Excelsior Life Assurance, one of the largest life assurance firms in the U.K. Sir William Baltimore had been a director of Excelsior Life Assurance and knew its inner workings very well. Upon his recommendations, and with the joint-venture participation of another life assurance firm, an acquisition plan was put together. Late in the process the joint-venture partner withdrew from the deal, and Citicorp decided that Excelsior Life Assurance was too large to acquire alone. The search was reopened.

After considering several moderately sized firms, it was decided that the goodwill portion of the purchase price for a moderately sized firm would never allow such an acquisition to make Citicorp's internal hurdle rates. The search was moved to smaller firms. From a list of 12 life assurance firms, BNLA emerged as the most desirable candidate. Not only was BNLA of a size that permitted the acquisition to be managed, but there was fairly little to be paid for the goodwill of the company. Because Citicorp believed that the price was right and the potential was there, it purchased BNLA.

# BIBLIOGRAPHY

## CHAPTER 1: Strategy—Unified Guidance of a Whole Enterprise

Ansoff, H. I. "The Emerging Paradigm of Strategic Behavior." *Strategic Management Journal* (November, 1987).

Day, G. S. "Tough Question for Developing Strategies." *Journal of Business Strategy* (Winter, 1986).

Hayden, C. *The Handbook of Strategic Expertise: Over 450 Key Concepts Defined, Illustrated, and Evaluated for the Strategist.* New York: The Free Press, 1986.

Mintzberg, H. "Another Look at Why Organizations Need Strategies," *California Management Review* (Fall, 1987).

Whitney, J. O. *Taking Charge: Management Guide to Troubled Companies and Turnarounds.* Homewood, IL: Dow Jones-Irwin, 1987.

Yavitz, B. and W. H. Newman. *Strategy in Action: The Execution, Politics, and Payoff of Business Planning.* New York: The Free Press, 1982.

## CHAPTER 2: Forecasting Attractiveness of an Industry

Ascher, W. and W. H. Overhold. *Strategic Planning and Forecasting Political Risk and Economic Opportunity.* New York: John Wiley & Sons, 1983.

Lenz, R. T. and J. L. Engledow. "Environmental Analysis: The Applicability of Current Theory." *Strategic Management Journal* (July, 1986).

Porter, M. E. *Competitive Strategy: Techniques for Analyzing Industries and Companies.* New York: The Free Press, 1980.

Wheelwright, S. C. and S. Makridakis. *Forecasting Methods for Management,* 4th ed. New York: John Wiley & Sons, 1985.

## CHAPTER 3: Assessing a Company's Competitive Strengths

Bogue, M. C. and E. S. Buffa. *Corporate Strategic Analysis.* New York: The Free Press, 1986.

Porter, M. E. *Competitive Advantage: Creating and Sustaining Superior Performance.* New York: The Free Press, 1985, Parts I and II.

Rothschild, W. E. "Evaluating a Competitor's Product Strategy." *Strategic Planning Management* (June, 1986).

Shrivastrava, P. "Integrating Strategy Formulation with Organizational Culture." *Journal of Business Strategy* (Winter, 1985).

## CHAPTER 4: Predicting Interplay Among Competitors and Other Key Actors

Allison, G. T. *Essence of Decision: Explaining the Cuban Missile Crisis.* Boston: Little, Brown, 1971.

Freehill, M. "Customer Intelligence for Industrial Product Firms." *Strategic Planning Management* (May, 1986).

Freeman, R. E. *Strategic Management: A Stakeholder Approach.* Boston: Pitman Publishing, Inc., 1984.

Fuld, L. M. *Competitor Intelligence: How to Get It—How to Use It.* New York: John Wiley & Sons, 1985.

MacMillan, I. C. "Seizing Competitive Initiative." *Journal of Business Strategy* (Spring, 1982).

Rothschild, W. E. "Competitive Analysis: Understanding Winners and Losers." *Strategic Planning Management* (May, 1984).


## CHAPTER 5: Forming Four-Part Business-Unit Strategy

Gilbert, X. and P. Strebel. "Strategies to Outpace the Competition." *Journal of Business Strategy* (Summer, 1987).

Gluck, F. W. "A Fresh Look at Strategic Management." *Journal of Business Strategy* (Fall, 1985).

Hofer, C. W. *Strategy Formulation: Issues and Concepts.* St. Paul, MN: West Publishing Company, 1986.

Porter, M. E. *Competitive Advantage: Creating and Sustaining Superior Performance.* New York: The Free Press, 1985, Part IV.


## CHAPTER 6: Department Programs: Channeling Functional Excellence into Integrated Strategic Action

Brodwin, D. K. and L. J. Bourgeois. "Five Steps to Strategic Action." *California Management Review* (Spring, 1984).

Gladstein, D. L. and D. Caldwell. "Beyond the Boundary: Managing External Relationships in New Product Teams." Sloan School of Management, *MIT Working Paper* (1986).

Guth, W. D. and I. C. MacMillan. "Strategy Implementation vs. Middle Management Self-Interest." *Strategic Management Journal* (July, 1986).


## CHAPTER 7: Strategy Programs in Marketing: Product Line and Customers

Bart, C. K. "Implementing 'Growth' and 'Harvest' Product Strategies." *California Management Review* (Summer, 1987).

Feldman, L. P. and A. L. Page. "Harvesting: The Misunderstood Market Exit Strategy." *Journal of Business Strategy* (Spring, 1985).

Heany, D. F. "Degrees of Production Innovation." *Journal of Business Strategy* (Spring, 1983).

O'Shaughnessy, J. *Competitive Marketing: A Strategic Approach.* Boston: George Allen & Unwin, 1984, Part II.

Reeder, R. R., E. G. Brierty, and B. H. Reeder. *Industrial Marketing: Analysis, Planning, and Control.* Englewood Cliffs, NJ: Prentice-Hall, 1987, Chapters 6–11.

## CHAPTER 8: Strategy Programs in Marketing: Pricing and Marketing Mix

Kottler, P. *Marketing Management: Analysis, Planning, and Control,* 5th ed. Englewood Cliffs, NJ: Prentice-Hall, 1984, Chapters 15–22.

O'Shaughnessy, J. *Competitive Marketing: A Strategic Approach.* Boston: George Allen & Unwin, 1984, Part IV.

Reeder, R. R., E. G. Brierty, and B. H. Reeder. *Industrial Marketing: Analysis, Planning, and Control.* Englewood Cliffs, NJ: Prentice-Hall, 1987, Chapters 12–17.

Stern, A. A. "The Strategic Value of Price Structure." *Journal of Business Strategy* (Fall, 1986).

Thomas, H. and D. Gardner (eds.). *Strategic Marketing and Management.* New York: John Wiley & Sons, 1985.

Webster, F. E. "Marketing Strategy in a Slow Growth Economy." *California Management Review* (Spring, 1986).

## CHAPTER 9: Strategy Programs in Research and Development

Burgelman, R. A. "Managing the Internal Corporate Venturing Process." *Sloan Management Review* (Winter, 1984).

Frohman, A. L. "Putting Technology into Strategic Planning." *California Management Review* (Winter, 1985).

Ruekert, R. W. and O. C. Walker. "Interactions Between Marketing and R&D Departments in Implementing Different Business Strategies." *Strategic Management Journal* (May, 1987).

Ruggles, R. L. "How to Integrate R&D and Corporate Goals." *Management Review* (September, 1982).

## CHAPTER 10: Strategy Programs in Production

Hayes, R. H. and S. C. Wheelwright: *Restoring Our Competitive Edge: Competing Through Manufacturing.* New York: John Wiley & Sons, 1984.

Meredith, J. R. "The Strategic Advantages of the Factory of the Future." *California Management Review* (Spring, 1987).

Meredith, J. R. "The Strategic Advantages of New Manufacturing Techniques for Small Firms." *Strategic Management Journal* (May, 1987).

Schonberger, R. J. *World Class Manufacturing: The Lessons of Simplicity Applied.* New York: The Free Press, 1986.

Skinner, W. *Manufacturing: The Formidable Competitive Weapon*, 2nd ed. New York: John Wiley & Sons, 1985.

Wheelwright, S. C. "Manufacturing Strategy: Defining the Missing Link." *Strategic Management Journal* (January, 1984).

## CHAPTER 11: Strategy Programs in Procurement

Chase, R. B. and N. J. Aquilano. *Production and Operations Management: A Life Cycle Approach*, 4th ed. Homewood, IL: Richard D. Irwin, 1985, Chapters 13 and 14.

Harrigan, K. R. *Strategies for Vertical Integration.* Lexington, MA: D. C. Heath & Company, 1983.

Schonberger, R. J. and J. P. Gilbert. "Just-in-Time Purchasing: A Challenge for U.S. Industry." *California Management Review* (Fall, 1983).

## CHAPTER 12: Strategy Programs in Human Resources

Flamholtz, E. G. *How to Make the Transition from an Entrepreneurship to a Professionally Managed Firm.* San Francisco: Jossey-Bass, 1986.

Fombrun, C., N. M. Tichy, and M. A. Devanna. *Strategic Human Resource Management.* New York: John Wiley & Sons, 1984.

Hagedorn, H. J. "The Factory of the Future: What About the People?" *Journal of Business Strategy* (Summer, 1984).

Hall, D. T. and J. G. Goodale. *Human Resource Management.* Glenview, IL: Scott, Foresman and Company, 1986.

London, M. *Developing Managers: A Guide to Motivating and Preparing People for Successful Managerial Careers.* San Francisco: Jossey-Bass, 1985.

Schuler, R. S. and S. E. Jackson. "Linking Competitive Strategies with Human Resource Management Practices." *Academy of Management Executive* (August, 1987).

## CHAPTER 13: Strategy Programs in Finance: Allocating Capital

Govindarajan, V. and J. K. Shank. "Cash Sufficiency: The Missing Link in Strategic Planning." *Journal of Business Strategy* (Summer, 1986).

Hambrick, D. C. and I. C. MacMillan. "Asset Parsimony—Managing Assets to Manage Profits." *Sloan Management Review* (Winter, 1984).

Helfert, E. A. *Techniques of Financial Analysis*, 6th ed. Homewood, IL: Richard D. Irwin, 1986.

Seid, A. H. "New Approaches to Asset Management." *Journal of Business Strategy* (Winter, 1983).

Van Horne, J. C. *Financial Management and Policy*, 7th ed. Englewood Cliffs, NJ: Prentice-Hall, 1986, Chapters 5–8.

## CHAPTER 14: Strategy Programs in Finance: Sources of Capital

Helfert, E. A. *Techniques of Financial Analysis,* 6th ed. Homewood, IL: Richard D. Irwin, 1986.

Piper, T. R. and W. A. Weinhold. "How Much Debt Is Right for Your Company?" *Harvard Business Review* (July, 1982).

Van Horne, J. C. *Financial Management and Policy,* 7th ed. Englewood Cliffs, NJ: Prentice-Hall, 1986, Chapters 16–22.

Worthy, F. S. "Trying Times for Junk Bonds," *Fortune,* December 7, 1987.


## CHAPTER 15: Portfolio Strategy—Desired Mix of Business-Units

Duhaime, I. M. and J. H. Grant. "Factors Influencing Divestment Decision-Making: Evidence from a Field Study." *Strategic Management Journal* (October 1984).

Hamermesh, R. G. *Making Strategy Work: How Senior Managers Produce Results.* New York: John Wiley & Sons, 1986.

Harrigan, K. R. *Strategies for Vertical Integration.* Lexington, MA: Lexington Books, 1983.

Heany, D. F. and G. Weiss. "Integrating Strategies for Clusters of Business." *Journal of Business Strategy* (Summer, 1983).

Peker, P. "A Strategic Approach to Diversification." *Journal of Business Strategy* (Spring, 1985).


## CHAPTER 16: Mergers and Acquisitions—A Tool of Strategy

Bogue, M. C. and E. S. Buffa. *Corporate Strategic Analysis.* New York: The Free Press, 1986.

Davidson, K. M. *Megamergers: Corporate America's Billion Dollar Takeovers.* Cambridge, MA: Ballinger, 1985. See also review of this book by D. Votaw in *California Management Review* (Winter, 1986).

Ebeling, H. W. and T. L. Doorley. "A Strategic Approach to Acquisitions." *Journal of Business Strategy* (Winter, 1983).

Hopkins, H. D. "Acquisition Strategy and the Market Position of Acquiring Firms." *Strategic Management Journal* (November, 1987).

Hunker, J. A. *Integrating Acquisitions.* New York: Praeger Publishers, 1983.

Salter, M. and W. A. Weinhold. *Diversification Through Acquisition: Strategies for Maximizing Economic Value.* New York: The Free Press, 1979.


## CHAPTER 17: Joint Ventures and Corporate Input Strategy

Contractor, F. and P. Lorange (eds.). *Cooperative Strategies in International Business.* Lexington, MA: Lexington Books, 1987.

Harrigan, K. R. *Strategies for Joint Ventures*. Lexington, MA: Lexington Books, 1985.

Killing, J. P. *Strategies for Joint Venture Success*. New York: Praeger Publishers, 1983.

Porter, M. E. *Competitive Advantage: Creating and Sustaining Superior Performance*. New York: The Free Press, 1985, Part III.

Porter, M. E. "From Competitive Advantage to Corporate Strategy." *Harvard Business Review* (May, 1987).

## CHAPTER 18: Organizing for Strategic Action

Galbraith, J. R. and R. K. Kazanjian. *Strategy Implementation: Structure and Systems*, 2nd ed. St. Paul, MN: West Publishing Company, 1986.

Hax, A. C. and N. S. Majluf. "Organization Design: A Case Study on Matching Strategy and Structure." *Journal of Business Strategy* (Fall, 1983).

Horovitz, J. H. and R. A. Thietart. "Strategy, Management Design and Firm Performance." *Strategic Management Journal* (January, 1982).

Janger, A. R. *Matrix Organization of Complex Business*. New York: Elsevier North-Holland, 1983.

Jelinek, M. and M. Burstein. "The Production Administrative Structure: A Paradigm for Strategic Fit." *Academy of Management Review* (April, 1982).

MacMillan, I. C. and P. E. Jones. "Designing Organizations to Compete." *Journal of Business Strategy* (Spring, 1984).

## CHAPTER 19: Corporate Governance—The Top Arbitrator of Strategy

Boulton, W. R. "Effective Board Development: Five Areas for Concern." *Journal of Business Strategy* (Spring, 1983).

Henke, J. W. "Involving the Board of Directors in Strategic Planning." *Journal of Business Strategy* (Fall, 1986).

Molz, R. "The Role of the Board of Directors: Typologies of Interaction." *Journal of Business Strategy* (Spring, 1985).

Patton, A. and J. C. Baker. "Why Won't Directors Rock the Boat?" *Harvard Business Review* (November, 1987).

Vance, S. C. *Corporate Governance*. New York: McGraw-Hill Book Co., 1983.

Weidenbaum, M. L. "Updating the Corporate Board." *Journal of Business Strategy* (Summer, 1986).

## CHAPTER 20: Management Personnel: Prime Source of Strategic Initiative

Cox, C. and J. Beck. *Management Development: Advances in Practice and Theory*. New York: John Wiley & Sons, 1984.

Hall, D. T. and associates. *Career Development in Organizations*. San Francisco: Jossey-Bass, 1986.

Hambrick, D. C. and C. C. Snow. "Strategic Reward Systems." In C. C. Snow (ed.), *Strategy, Organization Design, and Human Resource Management*. Greenwich, CT: J.A.I. Press, 1988.

Kotter, J. P. *The General Managers*. New York: The Free Press, 1986.

MacMillan, I. C. and W. D. Guth. "Strategic Implementation and Middle Management Coalitions." In R. Lamb (ed.), *Advances in Strategic Management*, Volume 3. Greenwich, CT: J.A.I. Press, 1985.

## CHAPTER 21: Short-Range and Long-Range Programming

Camillus, J. C. and J. H. Grant. "Operational Planning: The Integration of Programming and Budgeting." *Academy of Management Review* (July, 1980).

Dean, B. V. (ed.). *Project Management: Methods and Studies*. New York: Elsevier North-Holland, 1985.

Roman, D. D. *Managing Projects: A Systems Approach*. New York: Elsevier Science Publishing Co., 1985.

Stonich, P. J. "How to Use Strategic Funds Programming." *Journal of Business Strategy* (Fall, 1980).

Yavitz, B. and W. H. Newman. *Strategy in Action: The Execution, Politics, and Payoff of Business Planning*. New York: The Free Press, 1982, Chapters 7 and 11.

## CHAPTER 22: Activating—Winning Acceptance for Strategic Action

Bass, B. M. *Leadership and Performance Beyond Expectations*. New York: The Free Press, 1985.

Block, P. *The Empowered Manager: Positive Political Skills at Work*. San Francisco: Jossey-Bass, 1986.

Kantor, R. M. *The Change Masters: Innovation for Productivity in the American Corporation*. New York: Simon & Schuster, 1983.

Schein, E. H. *Organizational Culture and Leadership*. San Francisco: Jossey-Bass, 1985.

Tichy, N. M. and M. A. Devanna. *The Transformational Leader*. New York: John Wiley & Sons, 1986.

## CHAPTER 23: Controlling—Keeping Efforts Focused on Multi-Level Strategy

Hurst, E. G. "Controlling Strategic Plans." In P. Lorange (ed.), *Implementation of Strategic Planning*. Englewood Cliffs, NJ: Prentice-Hall, 1982.

Lorange, P., M. F. Scott-Morton, and S. Ghoshal. *Strategic Control*. St. Paul, MN: West Publishing Company, 1986.

Merchant, K. A. *Control in Business Organizations.* Cambridge, MA: Ballinger, 1985.

Newman, W. H. *Constructive Control: Design and Use of Control Systems.* Englewood Cliffs, NJ: Prentice-Hall, 1975. See also *Managerial Control.* Chicago, IL: Science Research Associates, 1984.

Schreyogg, G. and H. Steinmann. "Strategic Control: A New Perspective." *Academy of Management Review* (January, 1987).

Yavitz, B. and W. H. Newman. *Strategy in Action: The Execution, Politics, and Payoff of Business Planning.* New York: The Free Press, 1982, Chapters 12–14.

## CHAPTER 24: Strategic Management of Multinational Enterprises

Contractor, F. and P. Lorange (eds.). *Cooperative Strategies in International Business.* Lexington, MA: Lexington Books, 1987.

Chakravarthy, B. S. and H. V. Perlmutter. "Strategic Planning for a Global Business." *Columbia Journal of World Business* (Summer, 1985).

Dyment, J. J. "Strategies and Management Controls for Global Corporations." *Journal of Business Strategies* (Spring, 1987).

Porter, M. E. (ed.). *Competition in Global Industries.* Cambridge, MA: Harvard Business School Press, 1987.

Prahalad, C. K. and Y. L. Doz. *The Multinational Mission: Balancing Local Demands and Global Vision.* New York: The Free Press, 1987.

Shanks, D. C. "Strategic Planning for Global Competition." *Journal of Business Strategy* (Winter, 1985).

## CHAPTER 25: Social Responsibility of Business Managers

Anshen, M. *Corporate Strategies for Social Performance.* New York: MacMillan, 1980.

Chrisman, J. J. and J. B. Carroll. "Corporate Responsibility: Reconciling Economics and Social Goals." *Sloan Management Review* (Winter, 1984).

Drucker, P. F. "The New Meaning of Corporate Social Responsibility." *California Management Review* (Winter, 1984).

Mintzberg, H. "The Case for Corporate Social Responsibility." *Journal of Business Strategy* (Fall, 1983).

Sturdivant, F. D. *The Corporate Social Challenge,* 3rd ed. Homewood, IL: Richard D. Irwin, 1985.

# · I N D E X

# T